Paul's First Epistle
to the Corinthians

Other books in the BYU New Testament Commentary series:

The Testimony of Luke by S. Kent Brown

The Revelation of John the Apostle
  by Richard D. Draper and Michael D. Rhodes

Paul's First Epistle
to the Corinthians

BRIGHAM YOUNG UNIVERSITY
NEW TESTAMENT COMMENTARY

Richard D. Draper
and
Michael D. Rhodes

BYU Studies
Provo, Utah

BYU New Testament Commentary Series Board of Editors

This Commentary Series is made possible by a generous gift from John S. and Unita W. Welch.

Significant support from the John A. Widtsoe Foundation in Los Angeles, California, as the Publication Sponsor for this Commentary Series is gratefully acknowledged.
http://www.widtsoefoundation.org/

JOHN A. WIDTSOE

FOUNDATION

Published by BYU Studies. To contact any member of the board of editors or BYU Studies, write to 1063 JFSB, Brigham Young University, Provo, Utah, 84602, or visit http://byustudies.byu.edu or http://www.byunewtestamentcommentary.com.

Cover images courtesy John W. Welch

Scripture quotations marked SBLGNT are from the SBL Greek New Testament. Copyright © 2010 Society of Biblical Literature http://www.sbl-site.org and Logos Bible Software http://www.logos.com.

First time in print. Substantive corrections, additions, questions, or comments may be sent to byu_studies@byu.edu.

Library of Congress Cataloging-in-Publication Data

Names: Draper, Richard D., author.
Title: Paul's First Epistle to the Corinthians / Richard D. Draper and Michael D. Rhodes.
Description: Provo, Utah : BYU Studies, 2017. | Series: Brigham Young University New Testament commentary series | Includes bibliographical references and index.
Identifiers: LCCN 2017026046| ISBN 9781942161325 (hardcover : alk. paper) | ISBN 9781942161110 (ebook : alk. paper)
Subjects: LCSH: Bible. Corinthians, 1st--Commentaries. | Church of Jesus Christ of Latter-day Saints--Doctrines. | Mormon Church--Doctrines.
Classification: LCC BS2675.53 .D73 2017 | DDC 227/.2077--dc23
LC record available at https://lccn.loc.gov/2017026046

Printed in the United States of America
10 9 8 7 6 5 4 3 2 1

About the Brigham Young University New Testament Commentary Series

Welcome to the BYU New Testament Commentary, a project by a group of Latter-day Saint specialists offering to readers a careful, new look at the biblical records that witness the life and ministry of Jesus Christ and the first generation of his church. The commentary series seeks to make the New Testament more accessible to Latter-day Saint general readers and scholars by employing much of current biblical scholarship while reflecting important LDS insights. At the same time, this effort may also be helpful to interested readers of other faiths who want to learn how a group of Latter-day Saint scholars understands the Bible. A fundamental article of faith for Latter-day Saints (Mormons) affirms the Bible "to be the word of God" while adding, understandably, that it needs to be "translated correctly" in order for it to be accurately comprehendible to modern language speakers.

These objectives have helped shape the purposes and parameters of this commentary series. Serious LDS readers of the Bible search the scriptures, looking for depth and breadth in passages whose meanings and mandates may ultimately be plain but not shallow. Such readers and interpreters are served by treatments that unite faith and research, reason and revelation, in prayerfully confronting profound and difficult issues that arise in the texts and affect one's path of progression. The New Testament has served as an influential guide to western civilization for centuries. As such, its records have long been studied by lay people and scholars alike, resulting in a rich reservoir of information that illuminates the New Testament era culturally, historically, and linguistically. Selectively, the BYUNTC builds upon this vast body of knowledge, resting on the Greek texts of the New Testament and connecting helpful elements of linguistic, literary, historical, and cultural research and traditional scholarship together with LDS scriptures and doctrinal perspectives. The combination of all these features distinguishes the BYUNTC from other commentaries, which are readily available elsewhere and which readers may also want to consult for more encyclopedic or specialized discussions.

The tone of the BYUNTC aims to be informative rather than hortatory, and suggestive rather than definitive in its interpretation. The opinions expressed in this series are the views of its contributors and should not necessarily be attributed to The Church of Jesus Christ of Latter-day Saints; Brigham Young University, where many of those involved here are headquartered; or anyone else, though these works have benefitted from input and guidance from a number of colleagues, advisors, editors, and peer reviewers.

Each volume in this series sets in two parallel columns the King James Version (KJV) and a new working translation of the New Testament. Calling this a new "rendition" clarifies that it does not seek to replace the authorized KJV adopted by the LDS Church as its official English text. Rather, it aims to enhance readers' understanding conceptually and spiritually by rendering the Greek texts into modern English with LDS sensitivities in mind. Comparing and explaining the New Rendition in light of the KJV then serves as one important purpose for each volume's notes, comments, analyses, and summaries. This effort responds in modest ways to the desire President J. Reuben Clark Jr. expressed in his diary in 1956, that someday "qualified scholars [would provide] . . . a translation of the New Testament that will give us an accurate translation that shall be pregnant with the great principles of the Restored Gospel."

Depending on their personal skills and interests, the authors of these volumes approach their scholarly sources and LDS materials differently, but always with careful exposition and engaging perspectives. In several ways, they employ various interpretive tools, including semantic considerations of Greek vocabulary; cultural, historical, critical, literary, and structural analyses; and intertextual comparisons with other biblical passages, the Book of Mormon, and other scriptural works including the Joseph Smith Translation of the Bible. Observations are also proffered about the doctrinal and spiritual reception of New Testament teachings and practices in the broad LDS religious tradition.

The format also varies moderately from volume to volume regarding introductory materials and the style of commentary. Throughout, Greek and Hebrew terms appear in transliterated form in conformity with standards adopted by the Society of Biblical Literature. In some cases, a volume reproduces the Greek New Testament text, based on the Greek text published by the Society of Biblical Literature (2010) or draws upon the twenty-eighth edition of the Nestle-Aland text in *Novum Testamentum Graece* (2012).

Contents

Abbreviations

For ancient works, the footnotes follow the style of Patrick H. Alexander and others, *The SBL Handbook of Style for Ancient Near Eastern Biblical and Early Christian Studies* (Peabody Mass.: Hendrickson Publishers, 1999).

ABD   David Noel Freedman, ed. *Anchor Bible Dictionary.* 6 vols. New York: Doubleday, 1992.

BAGD   Walter Bauer. *A Greek-English Lexicon of the New Testament and Other Early Christian Literature.* Trans. William F. Arndt and F. Wilbur Gingrich. 2d ed. rev. and ed. F. Wilbur Gingrich and Frederick W. Danker from Bauer's 5th ed., 1958. Chicago: University of Chicago Press, 1979.

BDAG   Walter Bauer. *A Greek-English Lexicon of the New Testament and Other Early Christian Literature.* Ed. F. W. Danker. 3d English ed. Chicago: University of Chicago Press, 2000.

BDB   Frances Brown, Samuel R. Driver, and Charles A. Briggs. *A Hebrew and English Lexicon of the Old Testament.* 1952. Rpt., Oxford: Clarendon Press, 1987.

CR   Conference Report of The Church of Jesus Christ of Latter-day Saints. Salt Lake City: The Church of Jesus Christ of Latter-day Saints, 1897–1970.

DNTC   Bruce R. McConkie. *Doctrinal New Testament Commentary.* 3 vols. Salt Lake City: Bookcraft, 1965–73.

D&C   Doctrine and Covenants. Salt Lake City: Church of Jesus Christ of Latter-day Saints, 1981.

EM   Daniel H. Ludlow, ed. *Encyclopedia of Mormonism.* 4 vols. New York: Macmillan, 1992.

HAL   L. Koehler, W. Baumgartner, and J. J. Stamm. *The Hebrew and Aramaic Lexicon of the Old Testament*. Trans. and ed. M. E. J. Richardson. 5 vols. Leiden: E. J. Brill, 1994–2000.

JD   *Journal of Discourses*. 26 vols. London: Latter-day Saints Book Depot, 1854–86.

JSNT   *Journal for the Study of the New Testament*.

JSOT   *Journal for the Study of the Old Testament*.

JS–H   Joseph Smith—History. In the Pearl of Great Price, 47–59. Salt Lake City: The Church of Jesus Christ of Latter-day Saints, 1981.

JS–M   Joseph Smith—Matthew. In the Pearl of Great Price, 43–46. Salt Lake City: The Church of Jesus Christ of Latter-day Saints, 1981.

JST   Joseph Smith Translation of the Bible.

KJV   King James Version of the Bible.

LSJ   Henry G. Liddell and others, eds. *Greek English Lexicon*. Oxford: Clarendon Press, 1968.

LXX   Septuagint, Greek Old Testament.

MT   Masoretic Text of the Hebrew Bible.

NRSV   New Revised Standard Version of the Bible.

NIV   New International Version of the Bible.

NJB   New Jerusalem Bible.

REB   Revised English Bible.

RSV   Revised Standard Version of the Bible.

SBLGNT   Michael Holmes, ed. *The Greek New Testament: SBL Edition*. Atlanta: Society of Biblical Literature; Bellingham, Wash.: Logos Bible Software, 2010.

SCI   LDS Scripture Citation Index. http://scriptures.byu.edu.

TDOT   G. Johannes Botterweck and Helmer Ringgren, eds. *Theological Dictionary of the Old Testament*. Trans. John T. Willis. 15 vols. Grand Rapids, Mich.: Eerdmans, 1976–2004.

TDNT   Gerhard Kittel and Gerhard Freidrich, eds. *Theological Dictionary of the New Testament*. Trans. Geoffery W. Bromiley. 10 vols. Grand Rapids, Mich.: Wm. B. Eerdmans, 1964–76.

Preface

"Now when I myself came to you, brothers and sisters, I did not come with eloquent speech or wisdom as I proclaimed to you the mystery of God. For I resolved to know nothing among you except Jesus Christ and him crucified. And I appeared before you in weakness and fear and with considerable trepidation, and my speaking and my preaching was not with the persuasiveness of wisdom, but with the convincing proof of the Spirit and of power, so that your faith would not be based on human wisdom but on the power of God" (2:1–5, Rendition).

These words of Paul to the Corinthian Saints clearly set before them what he considered to be the foundational doctrine of the gospel he had been called to preach—"Christ, and him crucified." His words also reveal the humility he felt in fulfilling that responsibility and also his absolute faith in the power of the Spirit to bring "convincing proof" to all who would exercise faith in his preaching.

Though Paul's imagery focuses on the horror of crucifixion, his witness is centered on the Atonement of Christ and what grew out of it: grace, love, justification, transformation, resurrection, and eternal life. The divided and bickering congregations of the Church in Corinth needed to understand that message for it would be, in large part, the cure for their problems. Indeed, it was a misunderstanding or rejection of this key doctrine and its ramifications that energized the factionalism that abounded in that Christian community and led to unconventional and even potentially disastrous practices and opinions. Paul reached out to them, showing the breadth, depth, and application of this and related doctrines as the means of bringing them into oneness, partnership, and wholeness.

Though many feel that Paul's most important epistle is the one addressed to the Romans, it is 1 Corinthians that addresses more of the issues faced by the modern disciple than those found in any other New Testament epistle. This is because many of the conditions and concerns faced by the Corinthian branches have proved universal to Christians across time and culture. The breadth of the epistle's doctrinal sweep has greatly contributed to the restoration of the fullness of the gospel in these latter days. It has done this not only by preserving the many key doctrines it articulates but also by acting as a window through which additional light and truth flow.[1]

Much of modern religious scholarship, however, has not given this or the other writings of the New Testament their proper due. Too often scholars have treated these texts, and especially the writings of Paul, not so much as historical documents but as curiosities revealing the trajectory of the history of ideas. Paul's work is also often seen as little more than "abstract collections of theological and ethical ideas" and thus some scholars have divorced them from their historical roots and context.[2] In doing so, they hamstring these texts so far as having meaning in and direction for the postmodern era. This has resulted in a great disservice, especially given the relevance of these works to current problems and conditions.

Because of its relevance and contribution to the Restoration, and especially the epistle's applicability to the situations in which the Saints find themselves today, a detailed commentary on this wonderful epistle—written from a Restoration perspective—seems not only appropriate but necessary. It allows for an emphasis on the work's historical position as a foundational document of the early Christian movement—an actual record of historical situations—and, more importantly, as a witness and declaration of the doctrines laid down by the Lord and his early Apostles.

The commentary, based on the ancient Greek language in which Paul's work has been preserved, provides a clear rendering of that text into modern English. The introduction offers background information on the epistle as well as setting forth the guiding principles that form the foundation for the volume. The commentary provides a detailed look at every verse in 1 Corinthians. It makes clear the ancient issues and their resolution both then and now. Its central witness is to the importance of the Atonement of

---

1. Examples would be the material in D&C 128, dealing with baptism for the dead, and Joseph Smith's instructions to the "Female Relief Society," dealing with love and service. See "A Record of the Organization and Proceedings of the Female Relief Society of Nauvoo," holograph, Archives of the Family and Church History Department, The Church of Jesus Christ of Latter-day Saints, Salt Lake City, 34, 37, 40.

2. Ben Worthington III, *Conflict and Community in Corinth: A Social-Rhetorical Commentary on 1 and 2 Corinthians* (Grand Rapids, Mich.: Eerdmans Publishing, 1995), x.

the Lord, allowing as it does the transforming power of the Spirit to flow, bringing eternal life.

As with any undertaking of this size, many hands and minds have contributed to the outcome. To those sincere and talented Christian scholars of the past and present who have spent their lives studying and writing about aspects of the New Testament we owe much. To those LDS scholars who have blazed the trails opened by the Restoration we feel a deep debt of gratitude. To the host of Brigham Young University students who have spent hours doing research, source checking, and style editing we are most grateful. Special thanks must go to Anne Burt, whose careful reading, editing, and suggestions have made the work much more readable. Especially helpful were comments and observations by Neylan McBaine, who read chapter 11 focusing on gender issues.

We are also indebted to our reviewers: Craig Blomberg, Kevin Barney, S. Kent Brown, and Melissa Howland. Further, we wish to thank the participants in the BYU New Testament Seminar held in June and July 2015 for their very helpful suggestions and comments: Jacob Renneker, Stephen Betts, Alan Farnes, Christopher Morey, David Larson, Ben Spackman, and Avram Shannon.

Finally, we give thanks to our wives, whose enthusiasm and support for our work has been most gratifying and encouraging.

Throughout this study, we have sought to faithfully interpret the Greek into English, to be in harmony with the doctrines of The Church of Jesus Christ of Latter-day Saints, to follow teachings found in the standard works of the Restoration, and to accurately represent to all readers the powerful testimony of the Apostle Paul as captured in 1 Corinthians. Even so, the assertions, conclusions, and the overall work represent our own thinking and not that of the Church, the publisher, the University, or any of those associated with this work.

Richard D. Draper
Michael D. Rhodes

Introduction

THE RELEVANCE OF PAUL'S WRITING FOR THE MODERN DISCIPLE

"I am reminding you, brothers and sisters, of the gospel which I preached to you, which you also accepted, on which you also stand firm, 2 and by which you are also saved, if you hold fast to the message that I preached to you. Otherwise, you have believed in vain" (15:1–2, Rendition). With these words, Paul virtually wrote his own introduction not only to this epistle but the other he would write to the Corinthian Saints.[1] In that bustling city, the word of God had spread, bringing many—Jew, Gentile, slave, freeman, rich, and poor—into the gospel framework and under the saving power of the Messiah. Not long thereafter, however, troubles developed. Divisions formed with members separating into distinct groups. These wrangled one with another and tried to bolster their position by claiming loyalty to one or more of the Church's leaders. Debate raged over various theological and doctrinal questions as well as practical issues, including how to translate the gospel into daily life. Feelings became raw and widened the gap separating the parties. Dissension became so great that it threatened to destroy the Church.

This situation, with others, prompted Paul to write at least three, and possibly four letters to the Corinthian Saints.[2] Only two of these have been

---

1. Richard Lloyd Anderson, *Understanding Paul* (Salt Lake City: Deseret Book, 1983), 91.

2. Besides 1 and 2 Corinthians, in 5:9 Paul refers to a previously written letter which we do not have. Also in 2 Cor 2:3–4 and 7:8, Paul talks about the so-called Severe Letter or Letter of Tears, which he wrote to the Corninthians. There are three possible identifications for this Severe Letter. (1) 1 Corinthians, (2) a letter incorporating 2 Cor. 10–13, and (3) a lost letter sent between 1 and 2 Corinthians. For a good discussion of the pros and cons for each option, see M. J. Harris, *The Second Epistle to the Corinthians: A Commentary on the Greek Text* (Grand Rapids, Mich.: Eerdmans, 2005), 3–8.

preserved. First Corinthians, as the epistle is known today, is the second longest of the Pauline corpus of letters. Only his letter to the Romans is longer. If, however, we add the size of his second Corinthian letter to the first, it constitutes more than a quarter of the content of all of Paul's epistles taken together. In them, the Apostle answered questions and objections from friends, skeptics, critics, and outright enemies. In doing so, he left a treasure of doctrinal insights and practical advice on a range of topics. But we must never forget that 1 Corinthians is, first and foremost, a re-conversion letter. Paul's purpose was to unite, under Christ and his gospel, all the disparate factions. His intent was to bring them together in oneness and love.[3] In short, his major purpose in writing was to re-convert them to the gospel.

Many of the issues Paul addressed have not gone away; the conditions and attitudes found in ancient Corinth have reemerged in the modern western world. Just like the Corinthians, many have placed their values on gaining wealth, ease, success, fame, and power. The Corinthian microcosm, like that today, was a pluralistic, immoral society whose standards were strictly contrary to those of the Christian community. As one scholar has so aptly put it:

> With today's "postmodern" mood we may compare *the self-sufficient, self-congratulatory culture of Corinth coupled with an obsession about peer-group prestige, success in competition, their devaluing of tradition and universals, and near contempt for those without standing in some chosen value system. All this provides an embarrassingly close model of a postmodern context for the gospel in our own times, even given the huge historical differences and distances in so many other respects.* Quite apart from its rich theology of grace, the cross, the Holy Spirit, the ministry, love, and the resurrection, as an example of communicative action between the gospel and the world of given time, 1 Corinthians stands in a *distinctive position of relevance to our own times.*[4]

President Howard W. Hunter put it this way: "This was the witness of Paul to the saints at Corinth, and the message applies to us in this day, living as we do in a world that can be compared in many ways to Corinth of old. In a society of turmoil, immorality, freethinking, and questioning of the reality of God, we reach out for the simplicity of the gospel of Jesus Christ."[5]

---

3. Anderson, *Understanding Paul,* 91.

4. Anthony C. Thiselton, *The First Epistle to the Corinthians: A Commentary on the Greek Text* (Grand Rapids, Mich.: William B. Eerdmans Publishing; Carlisle, U.K.: Paternoster Press, 2000), 16–17; italics in the original.

5. Howard W. Hunter, in CR, April 1969, 138.

Paul was compelled to address the issues that such a society had and, as a result, the Corinthian letters, perhaps more than those of any other New Testament epistles, are highly germane to the Saints living in these last days.[6] Elder Bruce R. McConkie emphasized this idea:

> The document, as we now have it, is an inspired and inspiring recitation of some of the most glorious aspects of the doctrines of salvation. In it we read profound explanations of spiritual gifts, of the resurrection, and of the degrees of glory in the world to come. We learn of baptism for the dead, are reminded that Christ is the God of Israel, and that there are gods many and lords many. We read of charity, unity, moral cleanliness, personal revelation, the sacrament, the spiritual powers of the saints, and much, much more. Truly the Lord's hand has been in the preservation of this storehouse of gospel knowledge, so needed for our edification and guidance.[7]

THE AUTHENTICITY OF THE WORK

In both the eastern and western branches of the proto-orthodox church (by proto-orthodox, we mean that large Christian movement that would eventually result in the self-proclaimed orthodox community including such denominations as the Eastern Orthodox and Roman Catholic), 1 Corinthians, along with twelve of the other thirteen epistles attributed to the Apostle Paul, was considered authentic. Debate centered only on Hebrews. 1 Corinthians was never left out of any known ancient list of works and no one ever challenged its Pauline authorship.[8] Modern scholars likewise overwhelmingly concur that Paul is the author.

Though it is doubtful that Paul considered that his writings were scripture, he knew he was speaking, for the most part, by inspired apostolic authority. Because certain Christians collected and preserved his writings, it is clear they saw the inspiration and authority behind them as well.

---

6. See Mary Jane Woodger, "The 'I's' of Corinth: Modern Problems not New," in *Go Ye into All the World: Messages of the New Testament Apostles* (Salt Lake City: Deseret Book, 2002), 41–46; Thiselton, *First Epistle*, 15–17.

7. Bruce R. McConkie, *Doctrinal New Testament Commentary*, 3 vols. (Salt Lake City: Bookcraft, 1970), 2:310 (hereafter cited as *DNTC*).

8. This ranges from the earliest list known—Chester Beatty manuscript $\mathfrak{P}^{46}$ composed about AD 200—through Athanasius' 39th festal letter written in 365 to the fifth-century Augustine (*On Christian Learning* 2.13) and beyond.

Within at most fifty years after his death, many Christians felt his writings ranked as scripture. For example, the Gnostic leader Basilides, in referring to Paul's words in 1 Corinthians, did not hesitate to call them scripture.[9] Because the Christian community by and large agreed with this assessment, it was almost inevitable that when the New Testament canon was finally formalized, this work would enter its ranks. Many of the Christian parties viewed it as part of the official word of God as spoken through Paul. Copies flourished over the decades and centuries that followed. Given that errors have entered into the text due to various copying mistakes or deliberate changes, the question remains: how closely does it resemble the original work Paul wrote? The material below addresses that question.[10]

THE INTEGRITY OF THE WORK

For Latter-day Saints, the above question is particularly relevant since we believe in the authenticity of any portion of the Bible only insofar as it is transmitted and then translated correctly. Some modern scholars, after carefully studying the epistle, believe the original was much different. Based on the current document's length and certain places where the tone changes or the flow of ideas jumps,[11] they have concluded that it is more likely a composite of several letters, perhaps as many as five, all redacted into this single work before the mid-second century. It was this redacted work that has been passed down through time.[12]

Though these scholars have acted in good faith in trying to identify which verses constituted which letters, they have had a tendency for overkill and,

---

9. He referred to 2:13 as quoted by Hippolytus, *Refutations* 7.26.3.

10. See the section on "Important Manuscripts and Variants" in this introduction, p. 33.

11. For example, Paul discusses the problems related to fornication in 5:1–13 and 6:12–20. The flow is interrupted, however, by a digression into petty lawsuits in 6:1–11. He forbids participating in cultic meals in 10:1–22 but in 8:1–13 and 10:23–11:1 his stance is softer, being concerned only with offending those with weak testimonies. In 11:2–16 he addresses the issue of head coverings for women but admits the sisters have place to teach and prophesy in the meetings while in 14:34–35, he says they should remain silent in church.

12. H. Hagge, in 1876, was the first to raise the question for a list of authors and their theories. See Thiselton, *First Epistle,* 36–37; and more especially Anthony C. Thiselton, "Luther and Barth on 1 Cor. 15: Six Theses for Theology in Relation to Recent Interpretation," in *The Bible, the Reformation, and the Church: Essays in Honour of James Atkinson,* ed. W. P. Stephens (Sheffield: Sheffield Academic Press, 1995), 275–78.

as a result, see more seams than are actually there. Nearly all the arguments they put forth as evidence that the current epistle is a composite can be explained through very exacting exegesis.[13] For example, as one carefully reads Paul's words, there is no doubt that a change in tone occurs, but this change does not necessarily mark a transition from one epistle to another. There is a better explanation. For example, we know that, by and large, Paul dictated his epistles and then signed them himself (for example, see 16:21).[14] It is unlikely that the Apostle, due to the epistles' size and content, dictated it in just one sitting. If some time elapsed between dictations, conditions could have changed that would have influenced Paul's tone. Taking everything together, the epistle presents a carefully reasoned and organized whole.

STRUCTURE AND ORGANIZATION

Other modern scholars who accept the integrity of the epistle have felt that it gives every mark of being written "on the fly" with Paul responding in order to both oral reports (chapters 1–6) and written questions (chapters 7–16). This approach, they insist, has resulted in arguments that are, by any standard, both labored and convoluted.[15] Others have effectively argued that such is not the case.[16] Once one sees the impediments to understanding Paul and overcomes them, they insist, his message is clear and powerful. After a careful study of the text, we, the present authors, find that we agree with this conclusion.

One contributing factor to the problem is the way modern Bibles are laid out with verses and chapters. These have a tendency to dictate what the reader sees and understands by suggesting that there is a straight line

---

13. Jerome Murphy-O'Connor, *Paul: A Critical Life* (Oxford: Oxford University Press, 1998), 253.

14. Evidence for Paul's habit of dictating his letters can be clearly seen in 16:21; Col. 4:18; Gal. 6:11; 2 Thes. 3:17, which show he dictated and then signed each; and Rom. 16:22, where the scribe, in this case, Tertius, actually identifies himself as the one who took the dictation.

15. Richard B. Hays, *First Corinthians* i*nterpretation: A Bible Commentary for Teaching and Preaching* (Lewisville, Ky.: John Knox Press, 1997), 183; C. K. Barrett, *The First Epistle to the Corinthians* (Peabody, Mass.: Hendrickson Publishers, 1993), 15–17.

16. Chief among these is Kenneth E. Bailey, *Paul through Mediterranean Eyes: Cultural Studies in 1 Corinthians* (Downers Grove, Ill.: InterVarsity Press, 2011).

sequence of ideas and arguments. Unfortunately, this breakdown into chapters and verses in many instances obscures the original author's intents. Rather, it is better to allow Paul's scheme to drive the reader's understanding. For example, Paul's treatise on the cross begins in 1:17 but it does not end until 2:2. Thus, the modern chapter division is in the wrong place. Paul's intended organization can be seen in this pericope as he refers to Christ crucified in its beginning (1:17), middle (1:23), and end (2:2). The point is this: as one observes Paul's thoughtful, sophisticated, and artfully composed pieces, an appreciation of his skill as a writer escalates, making him on par with the poetic and inspired prophets who preceded him.[17] By allowing Paul's structure to inform his modern readers, they can best see and understand his message.

Another challenge arises because English translations often work to put Paul's words into flowing and idiomatic English, thus, inadvertently obscuring his organization. As a result, the Apostle's point can be missed. For example, it may be that a key word ties two pieces of Paul's prose together, but the same Greek word is translated by two different English words in the modern version. Or, conversely, two different Greek words are both translated by a single English word, thus suggesting a tie where one does not exist. In either case, Paul's thoughtful organization is concealed.

It is very important to keep in mind that Paul was using a style that was very familiar and comfortable to him and his Jewish readers, but one not fully recognized by many modern students of the New Testament. This was the parallelistic style used in Hebrew prose and poetry. It is found throughout the prophetic writings of the Old Testament. Unlike English, this style rhymed thoughts rather than words or sounds. The most common formula was parallelism where "a thought, idea, grammar pattern, or key word" was paired with a similar one that followed.[18] As with English, various patterns were used such as A, A, B, B; or A, B, A, B, etc. What makes seeing this hard, as one scholar noted, is that, "English readers are often unfamiliar with the forms of speech and symbolism used by the biblical authors." Further, "The cultural settings differ so much between ancient and modern times that the context and original application of the messages are sometimes unclear to contemporary readers." Finally, "Whenever a message is delivered in highly structured patterns, (such as in chiastic parallelism) it may lose its

---

17. Bailey, *Mediterranean Eyes,* 52.

18. Victor L. Ludlow, *Isaiah: Prophet, Seer, and Poet* (Salt Lake City: Deseret Book, 1982), 33–39.

clarity and power as concepts and words are stretched and forced by the author to fit the pattern. Thus, the message may be stilted or awkward even though it is presented in an organized and polished poetic form."[19]

Though Paul used a number of these patterns in this epistle (the Commentary will point these out), one he often used was chiasmus. The format of this rhyme scheme is A, B, C, D, C', B', A', with the punch of the poem usually in the middle. An example of this scheme can be seen in the last half of his epistle.

A The proper form of worship for men and women (11:2–16).

    B Disorder in church services (problems with the sacrament) (11:17–34).

        C The proper use of spiritual gifts (theoretical use) (12:1–31).

            D Love as the greatest and most necessary the spiritual gift (13:1–13).

        C' The proper use of spiritual gifts (practical use) (14:1–15).

    B' Disorder in church services (the misuse of tongues) (14:16–33a).

A' The proper form of worship for men and women (14:33b–40).[20]

Once one recognizes Paul's deliberate and carefully worked out format, the unity and cohesion of the whole epistle become apparent, as do the points he wants to emphasize. As a result, it is necessary to use the Greek text to dictate the structure of Paul's thoughts. Doing so also helps us to better bring out the power and accuracy of those thoughts.[21] Throughout the Commentary, we have been careful to follow Paul's structure and thus allow the reader to better follow Paul's arguments.

In sum, there is nothing convoluted or haphazard about Paul's writings. Though it is true that he does repeat himself (as this kind of poetic form demands), the reality is that he put this epistle together in such a way as to forcefully teach the points he wanted to make. The epistle breaks nicely into two unequal but related parts. The last half focuses on the need for the spiritual power of love to overcome the problems faced by the Corinthian branches of the Church addressed in the first half of the epistle.

Seen in the above light, it appears that it was Paul, not the Corinthians, who dictated the content of this letter. He was in charge, he set the agenda, and he deliberately and carefully stitched the various parts together into a powerful and beautiful whole. It is not surprising that Paul, a Pharisee

---

19. Ludlow, *Isaiah*, 38.
20. Bailey, *Mediterranean Eyes*, 15.
21. Bailey, *Mediterranean Eyes*, 53.

trained in Jewish law, would reach to the rich forms of biblical poetry found in the prophetic writings of the Old Testament and with which he and many of his readers were very familiar. These forms helped give his writings the weight and gravitas he needed them to carry.

Paul's Understanding and Use of the Old Testament

To bolster his arguments, Paul often appealed to scripture.[22] The text that he used, however, was not that preserved in Hebrew but in Greek. Known today as the Septuagint (often denoted by the roman number LXX), this work was a translation of Old Testament documents completed sometime between 300 and 100 BC. Many of the Jews living outside of Palestine, in what is called the "Diaspora," would have preferred this version since it was written in the language they spoke. Being from Tarsus, a city in the province of Cilicia (today a portion of southeast Turkey), Paul was one of these. His knowledge and use of this work may have helped him during his ministry since Jews, proselytes (converts to Judaism), and God-fearers (Gentile men drawn to Judaism but who did not go through the ordeal of circumcision) primarily spoke and read Greek. All of these would have seen the Old Testament writings as both authentic and binding. Thus, Paul often appealed to them in his teachings and directions.

Paul was trained within the rabbinic circle (Acts 23:6; 26:5) and was thus very familiar with their way of understanding and interpreting the biblical texts. His commitment to the scriptures clearly parallels theirs. To both, the Old Testament books preserved the word and will of Jehovah. Both showed their deep reverence by quoting specific verses as accurately as possible. They also saw a coherence of the whole to the parts as demonstrated by their combining various passages to make a single point. Their reverence for the scripture, however, did not prevent them from using passages in a new context. Nonetheless, both show that they had an understanding of the larger context in which the various scriptures were found.[23]

But there was a point at which Paul broke with the rabbinic circle. Through the stunning incident that triggered his conversion, he realized

---

22. To give just a few examples, 1:19 references Isa. 29:14; 1:31 references Jer. 9:23–24; 9:9 references Deut. 25:4; 10:7 references Ex. 32:6; and 15:45 references Gen. 2:7.

23. Garth Lee Cockerill, *The Epistle to the Hebrews* (Grand Rapids, Mich.: Eerdmans, 2012), 54–56.

the Old Testament was more than a catalogue of divinely inspired performances, ordinances, laws, statutes, and commandments. It was a primary source that revealed the nature, work, and ministry of Jesus Christ. He came to understand what the Book of Mormon makes very clear: God gave the Mosaic law to Israel "from day to day, to keep them in remembrance of God" (Mosiah 13:30). But he designed the law to do more. Through its "many signs, and wonders, and types, and shadows," it showed to them "concerning [the Savior's] coming." In addition, the "holy prophets [also] spake unto [Israel] concerning his coming" (Mosiah 3:14–15). Though the law was full of performances and ordinances, the Book of Mormon notes, "all these things were types of things to come" (Mosiah 13:30–31). Paul's writings show he understood the Old Testament in much the say way (see for example, 10:6; Rom. 4:23–24).[24] His use and interpretation of these texts clearly reveal his ever deepening understanding of the revelation of Christ that he found there.

Paul had made it clear that much of his understanding of Gospel truths came not from human sources. He told his readers that "the gospel which was preached of me is not after man. For I neither received it of man, neither was I taught it, but by the revelation of Jesus Christ" (Gal. 1:11–12). That portion of his understanding, however, seems limited to the mission and Atonement of the Lord. But this was not his only contact with the divine that brought him understanding. He notes that "he was caught up into paradise, and heard unspeakable words, which it is not lawful for a man to utter" (2 Cor. 12:4). These experiences would certainly have established a divine basis for his doctrines. He told the Corinthians he had "delivered unto you first of all that which I also received, how that Christ died for our sins according to the scriptures; And that he was buried, and that he rose again the third day according to the scriptures" (15:3–4). This witness could describe in part what came from his theophany. But he goes on to say that Jesus "was seen of Cephas, then of the twelve: After that, he was seen of above five hundred brethren at once; of whom the greater part remain unto this present, but some are fallen asleep. After that, he was seen of James; then of all the apostles. And last of all he was seen of me also, as of one born out of due time" (15:3–8). His words suggest that he is passing down material he received from others. It would seem, therefore, that only part of Paul's gospel understanding came via revelation. Other sources include

---

24. Moises Silva, *New International Dictionary of New Testament Theology and Exegesis* (Grand Rapids, Mich.: Zondervan, 2014), 507.

the scriptures, Church conventions and practices as taught and preserved by his follow Apostles and other Church leaders, and also Jewish traditions.[25]

Nonetheless, there was tension because, as broad as these sources were, none covered all the situations the Church was encountering. Jesus had clearly stated that though he had fulfilled some of the law, "Till heaven and earth pass, one jot or one title shall in no wise pass from the law, till all be fulfilled" (Matt. 5:18). These words suggest the need for continued adherence to some aspects of the teachings of the Old Testament, but which ones? The Apostle clearly understood and taught that there was no salvific power in the law. Nonetheless, its moral teachings and admonitions as well as its guidelines for social behavior, whenever they applied to conditions met by the expanding Church, seemed in order.

The decision made by the Jerusalem Council in AD 49 was helpful with a few of the major problems, but it dealt mostly with issues concerning pagan cultic practices and immorality (Acts 15:23–29). As a result, even that official declaration left much to be resolved. We see in Paul's writings a man who cherished the word of God and used it to the best of his ability as a guide to determine doctrine and establish practices within the congregations of the Church for which he was responsible.

CONCLUSION

Given the above, there is little doubt that the epistle as it stands today is almost identical to the one Paul originally dictated.[26] In spite of its change in tone and the many themes it addresses, the epistle proceeds from a specific point and loops back to that point—namely the Atonement and Resurrection of Christ—and in the process holds all the disparate pieces together. The ground of the whole epistle is based on the crucifixion of the Lord and the transformative grace that results from it (see 2:2; 11:23–26; 15:3–6, 55–57). That grace, Paul shows, strengthens and converts souls and brings them into the unity of Christ, his Apostles, and the household of faith (see 2:9; 3:22–23; 10:16–17; 12:12–13; compare 1 John 1:3–4; 3:2).[27]

---

25. Peter J. Tomson, *Paul and the Jewish Law: Halakha in the Letters of the Apostle to the Gentiles* (Minneapolis: Fortress Press, 1990), 82–85.

26. J. C. Hurd, *The Origin of I Corinthians* (London: SPCK, 1965), 61–211.

27. Karl Barth, *The Resurrection of the Dead,* trans. Henry J. Stenning (London: Hodder and Stoughton 1933), 113–15.

The Historical, Geographical, and Cultural Background to the Epistle

The Geographical, Political, Social, and Economic Setting of Corinth

The area in which Corinth was located had excellent soil for farming and bounteous clay deposits for making ceramic items, roofing tiles, and other terra cotta objects. Also available were large deposits of hard limestone, ideal for paving roads and streets as well as supplying material for monumental buildings. It also boasted an abundant water supply—the Peirene Springs—that yielded nearly twenty cubic yards of water per hour, more than enough for the needs of this large and growing city.[28] Further, the Acrocorinth, the high, steep hill to the northeast, provided excellent security.

The city sat at the head of an isthmus and thereby at the crossroads of the peninsula. This gave it easy access to and dominance over two harbors— Chencherea, which was just over five miles away and opened into the Sardonic Gulf and the way to Asia Minor, and Lechaeum, which was just over one mile away and opened to the Corinthian Gulf and the way to Italy. Thus, the city was referred to by some Latin writers as *bimaris Corinthus,* "Corinth of the two seas."[29] Concerning its excellent position, the ancient geographer Strabo stated, "Corinth is called 'wealthy' because of its commerce, since it is situated on the Isthmus and is master of two harbours, of which the one leads straight to Asia, and the other to Italy; and it makes easy the exchange of merchandise from both countries."[30]

Another key factor was the δίολκος (*diolkos,* "hauling across"), the paved roadway built across the narrowest part of the isthmus (about three miles long) in the sixth century BC and maintained over the years by Corinth.[31] To save time and assure safe passage, cargo and even light ships were hauled across it. By going across land, ships avoided a six-day trip

---

28. See Donald W. Engels, *Roman Corinth: An Alternative Model for the Classical City* (Chicago: University of Chicago Press, 1990), 10–11.

29. Horace, *Carmina* 1.7.2; Ovid, *Heroides* 12.72.

30. Strabo, *Geog.* 8.6.20. See also Pausanias, *Descriptions of Greece* 2.1.5–7. For a modern work, see Jerome Murphy-O'Connor, *St. Paul's Corinth: Texts and Archaeology* (Wilmington, Del.: Michael Glazier, 1983), 6–10, 51–54.

31. For description and details, see James Wiseman, "Corinth and Rome I: 228 B.C.– A.D. 267," in *Aufstieg und Niedergang der römischen Welt*, part 2, *Principat*, vol. 7, *Politische Geschichte (Provinzen und Randvölker: Griechischer Balkanraum; Kleinasien)* (Berlin: de Gruyter, 1979), 1:439–47. The map on page 440 is very informative.

around the Peloponnesus with its unpredictable and often fierce winds and bad currents so common in the area of Maleae. Reflecting on this, Strabo quotes the sailor's maxim: "When you double Maleae, forget your home."[32] The winter winds were especially bad, capsizing and sinking many ships (including at least one, if not more, on which Paul sailed).[33] The city's location, tying as it did the east-west route, provided great economic gain, but the north-south axis added strategic and political strength. It not only tied Attica to the Peloponnesus but also provided a central meeting point.

In 146 BC, Rome destroyed Corinth due to rebellion, but in 44 BC, Julius Caesar saw that the place had strategic value for eventual Roman expansion to the east. More importantly, he saw that it had immediate commercial value which could benefit his veterans as well as Roman freedmen and merchants. He therefore established the city as a Roman Colony (πολίτευμα, *politeuma*). Julius named it *Colonia Laus Julia Corinthiensis* ("Colony of Corinth in honor of Julius") and put it on the road to expansion and fame.[34] The result was it enjoyed all the benefits of a free city, including liberty from Roman taxation. Its magistrates also had more broad commercial, civil, and criminal powers than those found in other Greek cities. Due to Roman influence, its government was therefore based on Roman, not Greek, models, and its citizens were highly Latinized. That the primary language of this major Hellenic city was Latin and not Greek shows how closely it was bound to Rome.[35]

Putting both the manmade and natural elements together, it is not surprising that Corinth became the largest city in ancient Greece. By Paul's day, this very cosmopolitan metropolis ranked as the fourth greatest city in the Roman Empire being surpassed only by Rome, Syrian Antioch, and Egyptian Alexandria.[36] It drew citizens not only from the west but also

---

32. Strabo, *Geog.* 8.6.20. The Roman emperors Julius Caesar, Caligula, and Nero all contemplated digging a canal across the strait, but the feat had to wait until 1893 when the French succeeded in the operation.

33. See Engels, *Roman Corinth*, 51.

34. Dio Cassius, *Rom. Hist.* 43.50.3–5; see also D. W. J. Gill, "Corinth: A Roman Colony in Achaea," *Biblische Zeitschrift* 37 (1993): 259–64.

35. This conclusion is based in part on the fact that of the 104 official inscriptions found in Roman Corinth, only three are in Greek; the rest are Latin. See J. H. Kent, *Corinth: Results of Excavations Conducted by the American School of Classical Studies at Athens*, vol. 8, part 3, *The Inscriptions, 1926–1950* (Princeton: American School of Classical Studies at Athens, 1996), 19.

36. Joseph A. Fitzmyer, *First Corinthians: A New Translation with Introduction and Commentary* (New Haven, Conn.: Yale University Press, 2008), 21.

Introduction 13

from the east, including people from Syria and Judea. Thus the Jewish community got its start there, providing a base for Paul's work. The city also held a strong contingent of "resident aliens" (μέτοικοι, *metoikoi*), making it very diverse in population and culture. Evidencing this was the number of deities who had temples and shrines there. Though Poseidon, god of the sea, was the chief deity, temples could be found dedicated to Zeus, Hera, Athena, Asclepius, the Ephesian Artemis, and the Egyptian Isis and Sarapis, among others. Tyche, goddess of fortune, also had her followers. But, as will be shown more fully later in this section, none of these gods and goddesses surpassed the worship of Aphrodite.[37]

The city bustled with enterprises that outstripped even Athens for the amount of goods and people who flowed through it. Employment was high and, for the most part, paid well enough though the difference between rich and poor was marked. Still, if one was willing to work, the jobs were there and all profited.

The city also hosted the biannual "Isthmian Games," which was one of the four great festivals of Greece that brought in a good deal of income to the host cities. One Isthmian Game was held in AD 51, the very time Paul was present in the city. His writing suggests he was enthused about and delighted in watching the games.[38]

On the downside, due to the illnesses people passing through brought with them, the place was afflicted with a good deal of sickness, resulting in an unusually high mortality rate. The statistic is saddening, but it kept the demand for good workers high and unemployment very low.[39] Another downside to Corinth's success was that the city's population surpassed the ability of the surrounding area to produce enough food for its consumption. As a result, the specter of famine ever hung over the city, casting an uncomfortable pall that rested more especially over the poor.[40]

There was another downside, which was, to put it bluntly, the great immorality of the city. Predatory bankers were a scourge over the whole of the Roman Empire, but, according to Plutarch, none surpassed those at Corinth.[41] Cheating was also rampant and greed was everywhere. One

---

37. Fitzmyer, *First Corinthians*, 33.
38. See Oscar Broneer, "The Apostle Paul and the Isthmian Games," *Biblical Archaeologist* 25, no. 1 (1962): 2–31.
39. Engles, *Roman Corinth*, 51–52.
40. Bruce W. Winter, *Seek the Welfare of the City: Christians as Benefactors and Citizens* (Grand Rapids, Mich.: Eerdmans; Carlisle, U.K.: Paternoster, 1994), 53–57.
41. Plutarch, *Mor.* 3.883–885.

Greek poet decried Corinth as a city to be pitied and went so far as to say Greece would have been better off if the city had never been restored since it was given over to good-for-nothing slaves and profane souls.[42]

As with many large cities, Corinth had its seamy side. Promoting this was the city's devotion to Aphrodite, goddess of lust, whose temple dominated the Acrocorinth, the citadel of the ancient city. Strabo reports that a thousand prostitutes served in her temple.[43] Though this is likely an exaggeration reflecting more the second century BC city than that of the bustling Roman colony,[44] Aphrodite still had many devotees and priestesses most willing to serve any and all patrons. The city's reputation for immorality went back for centuries. For example, the poet Aristophanes (450–347 BC) coined the verb κορινθιάζομαι (*korinthiazomai*), "to act like a Corinthian," to denote the deeds of the debauchee,[45] while Plato (429–347 BC) used the phrase κορίνθια κόρη (*korinthia korē*), "a Corinthian maid," to designate a prostitute.[46]

The widespread decadence left its mark on the soul of the city. Wealth and ease did not bring comfort and security but rather a continual and unremitting restlessness. Beneath the façade of comfort and security was an uneasiness that contributed to self-promotion, glory seeking, and one-upmanship. Success and applause took on disproportional importance.[47] The whole also put pressure on people to get ahead and some, especially among the less scrupulous, as noted, slipped into shady if not outright dishonest dealings. Appearance was all-important. It was a society in which shame and honor were of high importance. To bring shame upon oneself or upon one's house was considered a grievous offense, one that extended to one's fraternal, social, and civil relations. Honor (but not honesty) meant everything, and many used whatever means they could to capture as much as possible.[48]

---

42. Crinagoras, *Anthologia Gracea* 9.294.

43. Strabo, *Geog.* 8.6.20.

44. Murphy-O'Connor, *St. Paul's Corinth,* 56, notes that no temple has been found that could accommodate that number of priestess-prostitutes. Still, the city, no doubt, had many women working as harlots. Even so, it may not have been any worse than many large Greek or Roman cities. See Richard Neitzel Holzapfel and Thomas A. Wayment, *Making Sense of the New Testament: Timely Insights and Timeless Messages* (Salt Lake City: Deseret Book, 2010), 345.

45. Aristophanes, *Fragm.* 354.

46. Plato, *Resp.* 3.404d.

47. See Quintilian, *Inst.* 2.2.9–12; Seneca, *Dec.: Cont.* 9.1.

48. For a short study, see Halvor Moxnes, "Honor, Shame, and the Outside World in Paul's letter to the Romans," in *The Social World of Formative Christianity and Judaism:*

Unfortunately, members of the Church got caught up in this social climbing. Paul's humble attitude and lack of self-promotion would have been contrary to all that was popular in the city and would have stood out in glaring contrast to it, exemplifying what it meant to be a Christian.[49]

Some found the restless ferment unsettling and looked for a better way. Little wonder Paul found the area rich for missionary work as well as job opportunities. A number of Paul's converts were people who had made good and had risen in both wealth and prestige. For example, the remains of first-century Corinth have a number of monuments with their dedications. One is of particular importance to the New Testament. Just north of the city proper is a dedicatory paving, the inscription of which was once filled with bronze. It states, in Latin, *Erastus pro aedilit[at]e s[ua] p[ecunia] stravit:* "Erastus in return for his aedileship laid [this pavement] at his own expense."[50] Most scholars feel that this is the very Erastus who Paul notes in Romans 16:23 was the "treasurer of the city" (ὁ οἰκονόμος τῆς πόλεως, *ho oikonomos tēs poleōs*) and who assisted him in his missionary labors (see Acts 19:22).[51]

Corinthian Environmental Factors' Influence on Paul's Writings

The factors noted above greatly influence Paul's writings in three distinct ways. First, *"the city community and city culture of Corinth were formed after the Roman model,* not a Greek one, even if many immigrants came from Achaea, Maceadonia, and the East to constitute an equally cosmopolitan superstructure."* Second, *"the city community and the city culture felt themselves to be prosperous and self-sufficient,* even if there were many 'have nots' who were socially

---

Essays in Tribute to Howard Clarke Kee, ed. Jacob Neusner and Peder Borgan (Philadelphia: Fortress Press, 1988), 207–18. For an extended study, see Ramsay MacMullen, *Roman Social Relations, 50 BC to AD 284* (New Haven, Conn.: Yale University Press, 1974), 62–106.

49. Thiselton, *First Epistle,* 12–14.

50. The position included the supervision of public works, markets, grain supply, games, and the water works.

51. Murphy-O'Connor, *Paul,* 268–70; Raymond F. Collins, *First Corinthians* (Collegeville, Minn.: Glazier/Liturgical Press, 1999), 168. The major point against this view is that a magistrate would have to swear an oath of loyalty to Rome and her gods which no worthy Christian would do. See David W. J. Gill, "Erastus the Aedile," *Tyndale Bulletin* 40, no. 2 (1989): 293–301. But based on Rom. 13:3; 1 Pet. 2:14, Christians seem to have been involved in city politics, and Gallio's treatment of Paul in Acts 18 suggests the authorities saw Christianity as a *religio Licita* along with Judaism and, therefore, did not demand all its members obey all civil constraints. See Bruce W. Winter, "Gallio's Ruling on the Legal Status of Earliest Christianity (Acts 18:14–15)," *Tyndale Bulletin* 50, no. 2 (1999): 213–24.

vulnerable or dependent on others." And third, *"the core community and core tradition of the city culture were those of trade, business, and entrepreneurial pragmatism in the pursuit of success,* even if some paid a heavy price for business failures or for the lack of the right contacts or the right opportunities."[52] As a result, a large number of citizens had a keen and pragmatic business sense that promoted a very successful exchange of goods and services.[53] All these were colored by Latin values. The whole dictated much of the attitude of Paul's audience and structured his counsel to the Saints.

The Christian Community in Corinth

Advantages of Corinth to the Spread of the Gospel

Given the well-deserved but bad reputation Corinth had, it might seem surprising that Paul would pick it as the best place to begin his work in taking the gospel to Europe. It must be noted, however, that though many of the citizens were less than honorable, quite a number were very moral. Further, many yearned for a better life—a life that had purpose and meaning beyond the immediate and superficial. These made ready converts to the message Paul brought.

There were other factors in its favor as well. Due to Corinth's unique situation, it was a logical place to do missionary work. As a trading hub, it had superb communications that opened the door to whole populations both east and west. Thus, it had the potential of being a great center for the spread of the gospel with traders, merchants, and thousands of tourists coming in from all areas, especially during the Isthmian Games. Contributing to the appeal of the area for a mission center was the wealth of the city that allowed people some leisure to pursue activities outside that of making a living. The large Jewish population at least initially helped Paul by providing a place to push forward the Christian agenda. The cosmopolitan nature of the city also allowed, if not encouraged, a wide variety of opinions and large-scale diversity of thought, thus opening the door to new ideas. All these conditions opened the way for the establishment of a strong Christian base there.[54]

---

52. Thiselton, *First Epistle,* 3–4; italics in original.
53. Engels, *Roman Corinth,* 1–7, 22–65.
54. Wiseman, "Corinth and Rome," 504; Engles, *Roman Corinth,* 20.

Of further importance is that Paul, having no benefactor or sponsor and not wanting to be a financial burden on or obligated to any of the Saints, had to work for a living. His skill as a "tentmaker" (σκηνοποιός, *skēnopoios;* see Acts 18:3), that is, one who worked in fabrics and leathers, would have been in high demand since there was need for awnings and tents, especially during the Isthmian Games, as well as sails for the many ships that came into the area.[55]

Challenges These Conditions Made for the Church

As attractive as these conditions made Corinth, the city also provided a definite downside. For instance, though many pagans joined the Church, many did not give up their attitudes and mores but rather tried to fit them into the gospel context. One-upmanship played out on many levels as members sought for status or power in their newly found community.[56] They also misinterpreted the freedom that the gospel brought, turning it into license to ignore social conventions. We see this especially in Paul's concern with women who went into public areas without wearing hoods or head coverings. Because such behavior suggested sexual availability, or at the very least a total lack of concern for respectability, Paul came down hard on those who did this.[57] Further, the architecture of the Roman villas with their atrium and the adjoining *triclinium,* along with Latin dining conventions, greatly contributed to improper sacramental meetings and practices which, as the Apostle noted, "are not beneficial, but rather the opposite" (11:17, Rendition).[58] Archaeologists have found a number of residences large enough to have easily served as "house churches." Both the atrium and *triclinium* could be set up for quite a number of guests, but the layout could have contributed to a "first class" and "second class" division among the people. Another problem was that some sought to prove themselves spiritually superior to others either by speaking in tongues, which neither they nor any others really understood (14:6–17), or by claiming revelations, or by dominating the meetings and not allowing others to speak (14:29–33).

---

55. Engles, *Roman Corinth,* 112.

56. Bart D. Ehrman, *The New Testament: A Historical Introduction to the Early Christian Writings* (Oxford: Oxford University Press, 1997), 272.

57. See Aline Rousselle, "Body Politics in Ancient Rome," in *A History of Women in the West, Volume 1: From Ancient Goddess to Christian Saints,* ed. Pauline Schmitt Pantel (Cambridge, Mass.: Harvard University Press, 1994), 296–337.

58. Murphy-O'Connor, *St. Paul's Corinth,* 154–55.

Driving some of the Saints to obtain spiritual and community status was their mistaken belief that the Lord's Second Coming and the triumph of the Church over the world was very near. These people were jockeying for position in the expected new order of things. Paul's task was to counter this hyper- and misspent activity and its resultant competitiveness by establishing a correct value system based on the grace of God, the importance of the cross, the universal brother- and sisterhood of humankind, and the promise made by the resurrection.[59]

How Paul Came to Corinth

During the year AD 50, Paul and his companion Silas (Σιλουανός, *Silouanos*) revisited the cities where he had proselyted during his first mission. He then decided to push further into Asia Minor. The Spirit prompted him not to head north, so he headed west instead. At Troas, the Lord opened a vision to Paul. In it, "there stood a man of Macedonia, and prayed him, saying, Come over into Macedonia, and help us" (Acts 16:9). Paul immediately made arrangements to pass over to Greece and began his work there. Within a year, he had established branches in Philippi, Thessalonica, and Berea. He then headed south to Athens.

If he thought the old capital of Achaia would produce a rich harvest, he was wrong. Athens had become a counterculture to Corinth. The once-vibrant community had stagnated. Indeed, it had become an old, decrepit, even sick city, no longer sustaining a productive and creative citizenry. Though once a bustling university town, its academic acumen had fallen, and such places as Paul's home town of Tarsus and the up-and-coming Corinth had eclipsed it. Too staid and conservative to open its doors to new ideas, it was not a place where the Church could get any root. Little wonder Paul looked to Corinth as a more strategic center for the preaching of the gospel and as a European base for the new Church.[60] An added value was that success in this city could give the Church a good deal of cachet. As one scholar has noted, "The bustling emporium was no place for the gullible or timid; only the tough survived. What better advertisement for the power of the gospel could there be than to make converts of the pre-occupied and skeptical inhabitants of such a materialistic environment."[61]

Here he was joined by his two companions, Silas and Timothy, and began his work.

---

59. Thiselton, *First Epistle,* 40.
60. Murphy-O'Connor, *Paul,* 108–9.
61. Murphy-O'Connor, *Paul,* 109.

Paul's Strategy

The Apostle had already determined he would not use his skill as a rhetorician, though that would likely have appealed to the Corinthian mindset and may have given him a good hearing. But, as he said, he came, "not with excellency of speech or of wisdom, declaring unto you the testimony of God. For I determined not to know any thing among you save Jesus Christ, and him crucified" (2:1–2). Paul fully understood that it would not do to "market the gospel as a consumer commodity designed to please the hearers and to win their approval," one authority noted. "Whether such a strategy would have been successful, the nature of the gospel of Jesus Christ excluded its being treated as a market commodity tailored to the tastes and desires of market consumers."[62] To have made it common or even popular would have exposed it to the will and capriciousness of the people. The result would have emptied it of its essence and stripped it of its power, a power manifest in the transforming of the human soul through the grace of Christ Jesus. No, no alteration of the message or compromise of the doctrine would do for popularity's sake.

Though the message was repugnant to many among both Jews and Gentiles, Paul stood by his word to preach "Christ, and him crucified." That was a bold move since death by crucifixion brought such a stigma with it that most Greeks would have found it impossible to take seriously anyone who died by that means and more especially one who claimed to be divine.[63] Even so, Paul did not back away but made the cross the centerpiece of his message. He knew well that, for some, it was a σκάνδαλον (*skandalon,* translated as "stumblingblock" in the KJV), something that caused offense, revulsion, even hostility.[64] Metaphorically, a *skandalon* was a kind of trap that led one to sin. The Jews saw Christianity as such a trap because it took people away from the saving law of Moses. The Greeks, on the other hand, felt that such an idea was μωρία (*mōria,* 1:23) "foolishness." The English word "moron" is derived from the cognate adjective μωρός (*mōros*) "foolish." Their prejudice did not stop the Apostle. He declared, "we preach Christ crucified, unto the Jews a stumblingblock, and unto the Greeks foolishness" (1:23). What Paul did in essence was adopt a strategy completely

---

62. Thiselton, *First Epistle,* 21.

63. Raymond Pickett, *The Cross in Corinth: The Social Significance of the Death of Jesus* (Sheffield, Eng.: Sheffield Academic Press, 1997), 58–84.

64. Walter Bauer, *A Greek-English Lexicon of the New Testament and Other Early Christian Literature,* ed. F. W. Danker, 3d English ed. (Chicago: University of Chicago Press, 2000), 926 (hereafter cited as BDAG).

at odds with the sophisticated and self-promoting Corinthians. He moved away from using clever words, enticing phrases, or popular ideas to promote his message.[65] Instead he provided a new beginning by proclaiming a new way of looking at God and salvation.

This epistle fully reveals the Apostle's approach. Though he had to prove his points, he was ever careful not to follow the ways of the professional rhetoricians so popular in the area. There was good reason. From the time of Aristotle through Cicero to Quintilian, a number of well-educated men had encouraged "the science of speaking well," and taught "methods of articulation and rational argument and expression," but it was almost always with the view of promoting truth.[66] Not so at Corinth and other like places. There truth took second to appeal, approval, and applause. In this extra-linguistic world, "truth" lost its moorings and became relativistic, yielding to an ever-popular "situational ethics" as we call it today.[67]

As one LDS scholar has so ably noted, "The declining years of ancient civilization were beset by a feverish preoccupation with rhetoric which suggests nothing so much as a hopeless alcoholic's devotion to the bottle. Everywhere the ancients give us to understand that rhetoric is their poison, that it is ruining their capacity to work and think, that it disgusts and wearies them, and that they cannot let it alone, because it pays too well."[68] One of the very strong wellsprings for this later addiction was the Corinth of Paul's day.

So instead of engaging in rhetorical games, Paul carefully built up his arguments based on tradition, scripture, reason, and shared premises.[69] It should be noted, however, that most of these were part of the rhetorician's arsenal. Therefore, Paul did not avoid entirely this tool. Indeed, if one defines rhetoric as the art of influencing "thinking and behavior through the strategic use of symbols,"[70] then it was a means the Apostle

---

65. Thiselton, *First Epistle,* 22.

66. Note particularly Quintilian, *Instituo Oratoria* 2.14.5, and compare 2.15.34, 38. An excellent study can be found in George A. Kennedy, *The Art of Rhetoric in the Roman World* (Princeton: Princeton University Press: 1972).

67. Thiselton, *First Epistle,* 42.

68. Hugh Nibley, *The Ancient State: The Rulers and the Ruled,* ed. Donald W. Parry and Stephen D. Ricks (Salt Lake City: Deseret Book; Provo, Utah: Foundation for Ancient Research and Mormon Studies, 1991), 243.

69. Anders Eriksson, *Traditions as Rhetorical Proof: Pauline Argumentation in 1 Corinthians* (Stockholm: Almqvist and Wiksell, 1988), 7.

70. Douglas Ehninger, *Contemporary Rhetoric: A Reader's Coursebook* (Glenview, Ill: Scott, Foresman, 1972), 3. Though many studies on Paul spend time on his use of rhetoric, none does so with the concentration and skill of Kenneth Bailey's work, *Paul through Mediterranean Eyes.*

used to good advantage. It must be stressed, however, that he refused to play the games.[71]

In order to make his points, he successfully used eight premises upon which most of his Christian readers were agreed. These were: there is but one God and one Savior (8:6); Christ died to save souls (8:11b); the sacrament celebrates the Atonement (10:16); the wine and bread represent the body and blood of the Lord that he shed for all (11:23–25); one can witness that Jesus is the Christ only via the Spirit (12:3); only through the power of the Spirit do all become one with Christ (12:13); having died for sins, Jesus was buried and resurrected (15:3–5); and, finally, those who do not love the Lord should be accursed (16:22). By staying firm on these points, Paul did not let his audience define the message but kept it grounded in the remarkable Atonement of Christ and its results.[72]

Even though Paul was careful to avoid rhetorical tricks and gimmicks, he was acutely aware that, for the most part, his message would be heard rather than read, and therefore he wrote in such a way that his words would be memorable. As a result, he did employ vividness, even hyperbole, in choosing his images and examples. Tone was also important, so he let his feelings show. In short, he did not mince words but made them as impressive as possible.[73] That is not to say that he let his enthusiasm get away from him. His responses were measured and careful. He did not want to undermine his previous efforts, "therefore, he was careful in his epistle to instruct as well as correct, not wanting to become overbearing to the newly formed branch leadership."[74]

At the same time, he was careful to direct his message to the peculiar psyche of the people he was addressing. In his earlier epistles to the

---

71. Gary Layne Hatch, "Paul among the Rhetoricians: A Model for Proclaiming Christ," in *The Apostle Paul, His Life and His Testimony: The 1994 Sperry Symposium on the New Testament,* ed. Paul Y. Hoskisson (Salt Lake City: Deseret Book, 1994), 62–78.

72. John D. Moores, *Wrestling with Rationality in Paul* (Cambridge: Cambridge University Press, 1995), 1–32, 132–60.

73. Many studies have been done that look for rhetorical aspects in Paul's writing. For a bibliography, see Stanley E. Porter, "The Theoretical Justification for Application of Rhetorical Categories to Pauline Epistolary Literature," in *Rhetoric and the New Testament: Essays from the 1992 Heidelberg Conference,* ed. S. E. Porter and T. H. Olbricht (Sheffield, Eng.: Sheffield Academic Press, 1993), 100–122. Our purpose here is not to enter into the debate as to how much or little Paul applied the rules of this "science." Paul, himself, states that he rejected the forms and means of the rhetorician (2:1–5) and we take him at his word.

74. Thomas A. Wayment, *From Persecutor to Apostle: A Biography of St. Paul* (Salt Lake City: Deseret Book, 2006), 162.

Thessalonians, Paul tied the Christian message to its Jewish background, but nowhere did he actually quote the Old Testament, likely because the majority of his readers would have been unfamiliar with it. At Corinth, however, conditions were quite different. A number of Jews had joined the faith as well as a number of well-educated pagans who were familiar with Jewish matters. Based on evidence from 1 Corinthians itself, it appears that Paul had frequently used the Old Testament during his lengthy stay among them to show that the scriptures anticipated Jesus' death and resurrection. Therefore, it is not surprising that in his letter he continually cites or alludes to the Old Testament to affirm his position (see, for example, 9:9–10; 10:1–13). Further, he insisted that the scriptures were not written exclusively or even primarily for the Jews in past ages but to the Christians of his time.[75] His emphasis was God's concern for his children and what he was willing to do for them as summed up in the gift of Christ including the Atonement and what grew out of these, namely, the universal resurrection. He also used the scriptures to stress that God's demand for his followers was to live a modest life devoted to service and love.

Through this emphasis, Paul tried to militate against the infiltration into the Church of the seductive Corinthian culture with its dangerous attitudes. Concerns with self-promotion, status seeking, material advantage, station, or office had no place in Christ's kingdom. These Paul replaced with a new criterion that rested firmly on the cross of Christ. The cross provided a new framework consisting of love, respect, self-sacrifice, and caring. It left no room for status or competition.

Paul's Social and Economic Status

Paul's eighteen-month stay in Corinth began about March AD 50 and lasted until late September or early October AD 51.[76] The length of his stay suggests that the work went very well. Of great assistance was the hospitality of Aquila and Priscilla, two Jews already converted to Christianity. They had been forced from their home in Rome by the edict of Claudius Caesar in AD 49 that banished all Jews from the city due to contentions between

---

75. Ehrman, *Historical Introduction,* 274–75.

76. The dating of Paul's mission was greatly assisted by the discoveries of the Delphic letter of Claudius in relation to Lucius Junius Gallio, the proconsul of Achaia during Paul's time at Corinth (see 18:12–17). The letter puts Gallio in Corinth not earlier than AD 51 or later than AD 53 with the earlier date being the better. See Murphy-O'Connor, *Paul,* 16–21.

them and the Christians.[77] It makes sense that these two would find their way to the Roman colony of Corinth where they once more set up shop. Though the KJV calls them "tentmakers," the Greek word (σκηνοποιός, *skēnopoios,* Acts 18:3) denotes much more than tent making. It included labors dealing with animal hides and weaving hair and wool, but more particularly making leather products. Their goods could also include items for theaters and temples.[78] Thus, there was an ever-ready market for products that people with such skills could produce, and these two Jews seem to have had no trouble setting up shop and hiring laborers. Being good at the trade and a fellow Christian, Paul was readily hired.

The job helped Paul promote missionary work. As people came into the shop to purchase items or have odd jobs done, the Apostle could readily engage them in conversation and turn the topic to religion. But there was a downside to his employment. Many of the prestige-conscious Corinthians would not have been drawn to one engaged in such a menial trade. Indeed, Paul condemned some Christians for feeling smugly superior to him. He complained that they felt honorable while despising Paul and others who "labour, working with our own hands." He was quick to note the true Christian's proper if humble response: "being reviled, we bless; being persecuted, we suffer it: Being defamed, we entreat: we are made as filth of the world, and are the offscouring of all things unto this day" (4:12–13).[79]

Some among the Christians would likely have preferred that Paul use his considerable skills as an orator to join the ranks of the ever-popular and highly respected sophists who generated a good deal of money and acclaim due to their speaking skills.[80] Instead, he chose to be a day laborer and

---

77. Suetonius, *Life of Claudius* 25.4, notes that the edict led to the expulsion of the Jews *impulsore chresto,* "on account of Chresto," likely contentions between Jews and Christians over a person Suetonius identified as *Chresto.* Most scholars believe the word refers to Jesus since due to iotacism, Χρηστός (*Chrēstos*) and Χριστός (*Christos*) would have been pronounced the same, *Christos.* Fitzmyer, *First Corinthians,* 37. See also F. F. Bruce, *Paul: Apostle of the Free Spirit* (Exeter: Paternoster, 1977), 250–51, 381.

78. BDAG, 928–29. Tents were made of *cilicium* (woven goat hair), the name coming from the province in which Tarsus, Paul's home town, was found. Patristic writers used the word interchangeably with σκυτοτόμοι (*scytotomoi*), "leather workers." See Fitzmyer, *First Corinthians,* 40.

79. See Ronald F. Hock, *The Social Context of Paul's Ministry: Tentmaking and Apostleship* (Philadelphia: Fortress Press, 1980); and especially Ronald F. Hock, "The Workshop as a Social Setting for Paul's Missionary Preaching," *Catholic Biblical Quarterly* 41 (1979): 438–50.

80. See Michael A. Bullmore, *St. Paul's Theology of Rhetorical Style: An Examination of 1 Cor. 2:1–5 in Light of First-Century Greco-Roman Rhetorical Culture* (San Francisco: International Scholars Publication, 1995), 212–13.

for good reason. He could not afford to cheapen the word of God for self-aggrandizement even if it meant that he would not draw as many hearers from the pagans or find more acceptance from the socially conscious Christians. He adopted instead "a communicative strategy entirely at odds with the confident self-promotion of the sophist or pragmatic rhetoricism who played to the gallery."[81] This may have forced him to spend more time making a living than he would have liked,[82] but it served to foster the correct attitude about the gospel and its message. His hope in Christ, and, ideally, that of all other Christians, should not be in gaining status in the world but pleasing God. The gospel was not about fame or power but self-sacrifice and service. It was not about finding place in this transitory, capricious, and short-lived world but finding place with God in the eternal world to come. It was not about competition leading to self-accrued glory but assisting others to a higher quality of life both in this world and the next. Pride, or as Paul calls it, being "puffed up" (4:18–19), had no place in Christ's kingdom. Rather, the Saint needed to generate that humility that looked after and cared for others as much as self.

As a result, the gospel did not attract many of the upper class. It would be wrong, however, to view the early Corinthian Church as entirely made up of peasants and slaves.[83] Indeed, there seem to have been a number of men and women of means who were attracted to the gospel. Among these would have been Aquila, Priscilla, Erastus, Phoebe, Gaius, Stephanas, Crispus, and Quartus, all friends of Paul. Thus, the socioeconomic station of the Saints seems to have been rather mixed and produced some stratification between the "haves" and "have nots."[84] The wealthy and well-born would have had a disproportionate influence. Paul had to fight against this by reminding the Saints that "the body is not one member but many," and, therefore, the foot is as valuable as the hand and the ear as valuable as the eye. Indeed, "by one Spirit are we all baptized into one body, . . . and

---

81. Thiselton, *First Epistle*, 22.

82. Paul speaks of his hard work as a laborer (4:11–12; 9:6; 1 Thes. 2:9; 2 Thes. 3:7–8; 2 Cor. 11:27). There is little doubt that he did not live high but the idea put forth by Justin J. Meggitt, *Paul, Poverty and Survival* (Edinburgh: T and T Clark, 1998), 75–97, that Paul frequently labored under extreme and harsh conditions, destitute perhaps to near starvation, seems too strong. His life was not easy, but he had good skills and many friends who supported him in his work. See Murphy-O'Connor, *Paul*, 117–18, 261–67, for counterbalance.

83. This is the picture developed by Adolf Deissmann, *Light from the Ancient East*, trans. Lionel Strachan, rev. ed. (London: Hodder and Stoughton, 1927), 144.

84. Gerd Theissen, *The Social Setting of Pauline Christianity: Essays on Corinth*, trans. John H. Schütz (Philadelphia: Fortress Press, 1982), 69–75.

have been all made to drink into one Spirit" (12:13–16). He further admonished them to remember that they "are the temple of God, and that the Spirit of God dwelleth in you" (3:16).

Paul left Corinth having had much success. Indeed, the branches there were thriving and vibrant at the time, and the work was moving apace among all socioeconomic classes. The Apostle's choice of Corinth as the strategic center of his missionary efforts to the west had proved well founded. Even so, the Church was young and still trying to find its way as it moved into pagan lands. Its primary task was to determine what it could accept and what it had to reject among the various societies in which it was growing. As a result, Paul continually kept track of happenings there and gave the Saints instructions through a series of letters. The one covered in this volume is the earlier of the two that have been preserved.

BACKGROUND TO THE EPISTLE

Why Paul Wrote the Epistle

After his lengthy stay at Corinth, Paul returned to Jerusalem, making a stop at Ephesus, where he found that many Jews were most willing to hear the gospel message. His dear friends Aquila and Priscilla accompanied him this far and may have decided to stay because the area was ripe for missionary work. Promising to return after he reported to the authorities at Jerusalem, Paul went his way. He did not stay at Jerusalem very long but returned to Syrian Antioch, where he spent some time with Church members. Restless to see how the branches were faring, he departed, visiting all the Galatian branches and some in the province of Asia before eventually arriving at Ephesus some time in AD 54.[85] In the meantime, Aquila and Priscilla had made a number of converts, including one of special importance. His name was Apollos, an Alexandrian Jew who was well educated, eloquent, and fluent with the scriptures. He was also a disciple of John the Baptist. Picking up on this, Aquila and Priscilla began teaching him the gospel in full. He readily accepted their teachings and joined the Church, using his considerable skills to convince all who would listen that Jesus was, indeed, the Jewish Messiah and the Savior of all humankind. After his conversion, he left for Achaia, where he continued his missionary efforts among the Corinthians (see Acts 18:24–28).

---

85. Wayment, *Persecutor to Apostle,* ix.

It was some time after Apollos's departure that Paul arrived in Ephesus, where he stayed for the next two years. For the first three months, Paul and the other Christians continued to attend synagogue with Paul using the time to show from the scriptures that Jesus was the Messiah. Eventually, friction developed, most likely because some of the Jews began to see the ramifications of Paul's teachings—Christianity was not a subset of Judaism. Indeed, it had left the Mosaic law, the very foundation of Judaism, far behind. Paul was ever bold to declare that forgiveness of sins came not via the law but through Christ alone. "All that believe" in Christ, he declared, "are justified from all things, from which [they] could not be justified by the law of Moses" (Acts 13:38–39).[86] Those who could see that the law was designed to bring them to Christ held to Paul. Those who believed the law was *the* means of salvation became adamant in its defense. As a result, they "became hardened and believed not." Filled with anger and fear, they began speaking evil of the gospel to all who would hear. As a result, Paul "departed from them, and separated the disciples" so that the Jews and Christians no longer met together (Acts 19:9).

Losing the Jewish base for his teaching did not stop Paul. He was able to find place in the "school of one Tyrannus" where he lectured daily to all who would listen (Acts 19:9). What followed was a season of tranquility and success for the Apostle.[87]

Some time in AD 57, Apollos returned to Ephesus, reporting on conditions among the Corinthian Saints. It is likely that this sparked a fast trip by Paul back to Corinth. The evidence for this is scant but strong. In 2 Corinthians 12:14 and 13:1–2, Paul twice mentions that he is prepared to return to Corinth a "third time." Acts, however, only tells of two visits. It may be that Luke was unaware that Paul had made a quick trip to see how things were going. According to manuscript evidence, it appears the problem was not initially too bad and Paul was hoping he could solve it quickly.[88] Such hope, however, proved to be overly optimistic. Reports soon came to Ephesus

---

86. Luke preserves three discourses of Paul: one to the Jews (Acts 13:14–41); one to the Gentiles (Acts 17:22–31); and one to the Saints (Acts 20:17–35). In this way, the honorable physician gives the reader a model of how Paul addressed each group and by doing so did not have to spend precious time retelling Paul's methods and subject matter.

87. Wayment, *Persecutor to Apostle*, 158.

88. Though the KJV mentions "divisions" at 1:10, the oldest complete codex of Paul's writing uses the singular "division" (σχίσμα, *schisma*) here suggesting that problems were in their infant state and Paul was hoping he could quickly correct it.

that the troubles did not go away but rather had become worse. Either a Christian visitor or a local leader began to attack Paul and his teachings and was successful in leading a number of members away from the truth.[89]

Paul had already faced opposition. By and large this came from the Judaizers, those rigorist Christians, mostly former Pharisees, who continued to insist that Christianity was a subset of Judaism and that the Saints had to obey the Mosaic law, albeit as interpreted by Messiah Jesus. The new attack, however, did not come from that source. It was grounded in a perversion of certain doctrines, chief among them the resurrection of the dead, but followed closely behind by spiritual gifts and the propriety of eating food stuffs once offered as sacraments to idols.[90]

This sparked a response from Paul, who wrote a letter which has now become lost.[91] In this epistle, it seems that Paul addressed specific concerns of the Saints and hoped his instruction would have settled these matters once and for all. Unfortunately, it did not, for there came another report to him "by them which are of the house Chloe" that the branches were further fracturing (1:11). Sometime in AD 55, the Apostle wrote his next epistle, now preserved as 1 Corinthians.[92]

Paul is clear that a major cause of his writing was the report of "Chloe's people" (ὑπὸ τῶν Χλόης, *hypo tōn Chloēs*), that is, her business agents or managerial slaves who oversaw her affairs at Ephesus and other ports. These brought word that conditions had worsened to the point that there was "quarrels" (ἔρις, *eris*), among the Saints (1:11, Rendition).[93] But there was another impetus, namely that of at least one letter he had received from branch members (see 7:1). It is likely that chapters 1–6 are a response to problems mentioned by Chloe's people while chapters 7–16 respond to items in the letter.[94] Given the organization of the letter, one thing seems sure: Paul organized his thoughts to meet all the concerns with memorable force.

---

89. Wayment, *Persecutor to Apostle*, 163.

90. Wayment, *Persecutor to Apostle*, 163–64.

91. The letter is clearly referred to in 5:9. See Murphy-O'Connor, *Paul*, 184, 252–53, 276–77.

92. Dating is always problematic, but given that Paul left Corinth about September AD 51, then a period of around two years had passed before he arrived at Ephesus, placing him there in 54. Sometime between then and his departure in 57, he wrote the epistle. A good date, given all that went on, would be around AD 55. See Thiselton, *First Epistle*, 31–32.

93. BDAG, 392.

94. Wayment, *Persecutor to Apostle*, 161.

All the information he received pointed to the same problem—discord. Paul initially attacked this problem with some fire but, toward the end of the epistle, he softened his tone. This softening may have resulted from personal and favorable reports from Stephanas, Fortunatus, and Achaicus, who had arrived at Ephesus (16:17–18) before Paul finished dictating his letter. Their combined witness likely suggested conditions were not as bad as they looked and mollified Paul, as reflected in his softened tone.

Still, the various problems did have to be addressed and the Apostle apparently felt his earlier tone was okay, so Paul sent his letter. To give it as much weight as possible, Paul wanted Apollos, his fellow missionary with whom he shared a deep and abiding trust (3:4–9), to take it. However, the disciple declined (16:12), likely because he felt disenchanted with the Saints because some had been using his name, style, and manner to push forward their own divisive agenda. Paul did commission Timothy, however, to take the letter and, thus, added some gravity to it.

Paul's Greater Audience

There is no doubt that the impetus of Paul's writings was an array of reports about events in Corinth. However, it was not these Saints' needs alone that were driving him. Rather, it included those of the broader Church. Reinforcing this idea is his statement that there were other issues he would "set in order when I come" (11:34), likely because these specific problems had less application to the Church as a whole and other branches would not need to concern themselves about them.[95]

Paul seems to have built his letter around five carefully executed essays. Though the following outline reduces these to their simplest forms and focuses only on their dominant themes, it does show the careful and interrelated way they fit together:

I. The Cross and Christian Unity 1:5–4:16

II. Men and Women in the Human Family 4:17–7:40

III. Food Offered to Idols (Christians and Pagans) 8:1–11:1

IV. Men and Women in Worship 11:2–14:40

V. The Resurrection 15[96]

---

95. Bailey, *Mediterranean Eyes,* 26–27.

96. Bailey, *Mediterranean Eyes,* 26. Bailey picks up and refines the work of two nineteenth-century scholars, G. G. Findlay, "St. Paul's First Epistle to the Corinthians," in *The Expositor's Greek Testament,* ed. W. Robertson Nicoll, vol. 2 ([1901]; rpt., Grand

The outline also makes clear Paul's three major concerns: The importance of the cross and the resurrection as the beginning and ending of the Christian message; the Christian community, both men and women, following proper forms of worship; and, finally, the proper Christian response to the pagan environment in which they lived.[97]

Paul's Solution to the Corinthian Problems

There is little doubt that the Corinthian Saints, and the Church as a whole for that matter, were facing a wide range of complex problems that Paul systematically addressed in his letter.[98] The seat of the problem, however, came from just one problem—a number of the Saints continued to hold to some of the attitudes of the secular, immoral, materialistic, status-loving culture in which they lived. Because they did not give these up, they caused a devaluation of the universalism, including key truths and growing traditions, that the Church was promoting.

Exacerbating the problem was the lack of chapels where the Saints could meet together as a whole. At this period of time, they met, as noted above, in the more spacious homes of the wealthy.[99] These homes, however, could not accommodate more than a couple dozen families. Therefore, a number of homes had to be used. When troubles developed, it was easy for the members to congregate with those who believed as they did while ostracizing those who did not. This condition allowed the fissures to widen, threatening the very foundation of the Church.

Rapids, Mich.: Wm B. Eerdmans, 1980), 754; and Frédéric Louis Godet, *Commentary on First Corinthians* (1893; rpt., Grand Rapids, Mich.: Kregel Publications, 1979), 27–31.

97. Bailey, *Mediterranean Eyes*, 26.

98. For discussion of the epistle that systematically answers the questions and arguments presented by the Corinthian Saints, see Hurd, *Origin*, 61–211. There are a number of quotations the author takes to be lifted directly from the Corinthian letter to Paul (they are found at 6:12, 13; 7:1; 8:1, 4, 5, 6; 10:23; 11:2) and also uses Paul's phrase "now concerning" (περὶ δέ, *peri de,* found at 7:1, 25; 8:1; 12:1; 16:1, 12) as a marker for items in the letters. From these he reconstructs the letter Paul received. Though his work is dated, much of it is still valid, though others have softened his thesis by noting that Paul's rhetorical and diatribe style explains much of what is in the letter without him having to move along point by point. See, for example, Margaret M. Mitchell, *Paul and the Rhetoric of Reconciliation: An Exegetical Investigation of the Language and Composition of 1 Corinthians* (Tübingen: Mohr; Louisville, Ky.: Westminster/John Knox Press, 1992), 20–64.

99. See Richard Neitztel Holzapfel, "From Temple and Synagogue to House-Church," in *The Life and Teachings of the New Testament Apostles: From the Day of Pentecost through the Apocalypse,* ed. Richard Neitzel Holzapfel and Thomas A. Wayment (Salt Lake City: Deseret Book, 2010), 117–33.

Paul had to act. It must be emphasized, however, that the Apostle did much more than address specific problems. This point is important because if a modern reader focuses strictly on the problems, he or she could miss the real message of the epistle. There is a single but beautiful thread that runs through the complex tapestry of this commanding letter which binds it together. Indeed, one doctrine solves all the individual problems Paul addressed and gives the epistle coherence and unity. Paul's remedy was not to correct the misappropriated value system by reformulating church organization and policy but rather to place the whole of the Christian community under one standard as defined by the Atonement of Christ and symbolized by the cross. In doing so, he created a reversal of the Corinthian value system and attempted to get all to realize the wonder of divine love and its gift of grace that God had given in the life, death, and resurrection of his Son. In short, taking the epistle as a whole, Paul's real push was not to bring unity out of discord, though that is important, but to proclaim clearly the love-inspired grace of Christ confirmed by the cross and how the Saints should respond to it. This doctrine, he insisted, all must accept. Thus, 1 Corinthians stands with Romans in placing the Messiah's death and resurrection as the centerpiece of salvation. Indeed, Paul stressed, the Lord's saving grace that these acts made possible will exalt all who will receive him.[100] Therefore, the Lord's loving and selfless act sets the standard for all Christian behavior. All should continually live in a state in which they extend grace to one another through love and service (compare D&C 93:12–20). Where love dominates behavior, there is no place for contention and division.

Paul's Methodology

In addressing the major issues the Corinthian Church faced, Paul did not simply identify each problem and then give the solution. Instead, he first laid down the doctrine or tradition that he had formerly taught them. Only when he had made that clear did he point out the problem. Next he established the theological base from which his readers could glean the solution to the problem. He then had them reexamine the problem in this theological light. Finally, he admonished his readers to follow him as one having both authority and the Spirit.[101] In this way, he kept the doctrine pure and continually brought his readers to the theological foundations of the gospel. In doing so, he showed them a way by which they could and should handle all situations that might arise in the future.

---

100. See Thiselton, *First Epistle,* 33–34.
101. Bailey, *Mediterranean Eyes,* 28.

The State of the Early Church

A point that must be clearly made is that we can understand only approximately what was going on in Paul's day. The reason can be understood by looking at the beginnings of the Restoration. The first few decades were marked by a great deal of fluidity as doctrines and practices were firmed up. To this day, though greatly reduced, fluidity still exists. The Lord has chosen to reveal his truths "line upon line" (Isa. 28:10; 2 Ne. 28:30; D&C 98:12). This will continue until at least the Second Coming when the Lord has promised that "he shall reveal all things—Things which have passed, and hidden things which no man knew, things of the earth, by which it was made, and the purpose and the end thereof—Things most precious, things that are above, and things that are beneath, things that are in the earth, and upon the earth, and in heaven" (D&C 101:32–35).

Knowing how dynamic the Lord's means of instruction made the early period of this Church's history, it would be dangerous to be too dogmatic in stating precisely what was going on in Paul's day, for the same line-by-line process of revelation seems to have been operating. President Brigham Young taught, "If we have eyes to see, we can understand at once, the difficulties that the Apostles had to encounter. . . . There can be no doubt but they were mistaken with regard to the time of the winding up scene, thinking it was much nearer than it really was, and they might have made mistakes in other respects. Many of the difficulties they had to encounter, we are not troubled with. We have not only the sure word of prophecy delivered in the days of the Apostles, but we actually have that surer word of prophecy delivered to us through the Prophet Joseph."[102] Based on President Young's insights, the meridian Church had more to learn more than even our own, suggesting that there may have been even more fluidity and experimentation then than now. The Lord's Apostles seem to have been working together to clarify doctrine, establish procedures, and determine how best to fulfill their charge to take the new religion into the world (see Matt. 28:19–20).[103] We must keep in mind that Paul began his ministry only two decades after the Lord's ministry. This was yet a period, as the New Testament record shows, in which a great deal of flux was still going on.

---

102. Brigham Young, in *Journal of Discourses,* 26 vols. (London: Latter-day Saints Book Depot, 1854–86), 12:65 (hereafter cited as *JD*).

103. Working out doctrine and procedure did not always go smoothly even among the leaders as evidenced by the tension that rose between Peter and Paul (Gal. 2:11–14) and Barnabas and Paul (Acts 15:36–40).

Because Paul himself was part of this milieu, we should expect inconsistencies within and among his epistles. He was learning and growing along with everyone else. The Apostle to the Gentiles was, therefore, no systematic theologian who had worked out and set in place all the pieces of the gospel puzzle. As a scholar noted, "Paul's epistles displayed a logic which seems homiletical and pastoral rather than systematic, and they read most naturally as *ad hoc* letters written to various communities in different situations. Obviously these situations involve not only theological issues, but all kinds of practical questions reflecting the vicissitudes of daily life. In view of Paul's Jewish background we may even suspect that his concern with such practical questions was at least as important as his theological expositions."[104]

In noting that his was an era of fluidity, we are not suggesting that Paul was ignorant of key doctrines known since the ministry of the Lord. The bright threads of core gospel principles illuminate the whole tapestry of Paul's writings. He preached faith, repentance, and baptism. He understood, among other doctrines, the nature and importance of the Atonement and the grace and mercy that flowed therefrom, bringing justification and sanctification. He knew of vicarious work for the dead, the Second Coming, the final judgment, and the universal resurrection. Some of these teachings were established to a degree that he could designate them as παραδόσεις (*paradoseis*), "traditions" (11:2, Rendition)—that is, teaching that had been carefully preserved and handed down (παραδίδομι, *paradidomi*) from the time of the Lord (11:23; 15:2–3)—and admonish his readers to "hold the traditions which ye have been taught" (2 Thes. 2:15).[105] Even so, much still remained that had to be clarified and worked out. That this process was, indeed, going on is clearly revealed in Paul's epistles.

---

104. Tomson, *Paul and the Jewish Law,* 56.

105. Paul's use of both the noun παράδοσις (*paradosis*) and the cognate verb παραδίδομι (*paradidomi*) follows that of Jewish usage and, therefore, carries a nuance associated with the "mysteries," that is, teachings of a highly sacred nature that are revealed only to the faithful and are to be kept from the world. See Gerhard Kittel and Gerhard Freidrich, eds., *Theological Dictionary of the New Testament.,* trans. Geoffery W. Bromiley, 10 vols. (Grand Rapids, Mich.: Wm. B. Eerdmans, 1964–76), 2:172–3 (hereafter cited as *TDNT*); BDAG, 763. Evidence that Paul was well aware of and followed the apostolic tradition can be found at 2:1; 7:10; 9:14; 11:23; and 14:37.

A Note on the Greek Manuscripts and Translation Methods

Important Manuscripts and Variants

The earliest-known text containing 1 Corinthians is the papyrus codex $\mathfrak{P}^{46}$, with a most probable date between AD 175 and 225,[106] which places it from 120 to 180 years after Paul wrote the letter. The codex contains virtually all of 1 Corinthians as well as most of the other Pauline epistles. The Greek text of the codex is representative of the Alexandrian text-type.[107] There are a number of variant readings in the various manuscripts of 1 Corinthians, but few of them are of any theological importance. Those variants that are of theological importance are discussed in this commentary where necessary. The KJV is based on the Textus Receptus, the first printed Greek New Testament, published in 1516 by the Catholic scholar Erasmus using late Byzantine text-type manuscripts.

The Nature of Paul's Greek

Paul used standard Koine Greek in his epistles, but in a way that revealed his education and skill as a writer. He was completely fluent and comfortable in Greek and was, therefore, able to utilize the full capacity of that remarkably flexible language to clarify and explain his messages to his audience. It also allowed him to see and understand the implications and nuances of the Septuagint, his primary Old Testament text, which he skillfully put to full use.

Translation Philosophy

In our translation, we have attempted to present, as faithfully and clearly as possible, the true sense of Paul's writings in modern English. We have constantly felt the need to balance the esoteric details of a text with the importance of communicating the breadth of its meaning as clearly as possible

---

106. Bruce W. Griffin, "The Paleographical Dating of P-46," paper delivered at the Society of Biblical Literature conference, New Orleans, November 1996, available onlline at http://biblical-data.org/P-46%20Oct%201997.pdf.

107. Kurt Aland and Barbara Aland, *The Text of the New Testament: An Introduction to the Critical Editions and to the Theory and Practice of Modern Textual Criticism,* trans. Erroll F. Rhodes (Grand Rapids, Mich.: Eerdmans; Leiden, Neth.: E. J. Brill, 1995), 99.

to English readers. Fortunately, because this is a commentary and not a standalone translation, the Notes and Comments section has allowed us to further elucidate and expand the range of meanings of a word or phrase and, thereby, render it to a greater extent.

We were ever aware that individual words have both denotations and connotations and are best understood within their semantic fields. Further, meaning does not reside in individual words alone but in collections of words found in clauses, phrases, sentences, and ultimately in whole discourses. Our task was to first determine the meaning of any given cluster of words in the biblical text and then convey that meaning as accurately as possible into *natural* English. Sometimes grammatical and syntactical forms that make good sense in Greek or Hebrew seem stilted, odd, and even weird when translated word for word into English. Our purpose has been to render the Greek in such a way that an educated reader could readily understand its meaning. And so, because of the marked difference between English and Greek grammar and syntax, we have especially tried to avoid an overly "literal" translation, which we feel could often obscure Paul's intent. We have, therefore, followed Bruce Metzger's dictum to be "as literal as possible, but as free as necessary" in order to communicate to the educated reader the meaning of the text.[108]

Still, individual words do count and, therefore, we have labored carefully to determine how each word contributes to the clause, phrase, or sentence in which it is found. Our intent has been to convey, to the best of our ability, the meaning of the whole. Therefore, our Rendition should not be seen as prescriptive but as descriptive. It is in no way intended to be the ultimate LDS translation but, rather, a rendering of the Greek to assist the modern reader in understanding the power and beauty of Paul's message.

Where textual variants in the ancient manuscripts have significant impact on the meaning of the text, we have tried to select the one that is the most likely to have been the original, but when the variants do not affect the understanding of the text, we have ignored them.

There are times when the words in our Rendition will be exactly the same as those in other translations. This is because that is the best, and in some cases, the only way a Greek text can be brought into English.

---

108. The dictum is found in the NRSV introduction, "To the Reader." For discussion on the challenges of translation, see Douglas J. Moo, *We Still Don't Get It: Evangelicals and Biblical Translation Fifty Years after James Barr* (Grand Rapids, Mich.: Zondervan, 2014).

GUIDELINES IN THIS VOLUME ON THE USE OF MATERIAL FROM SCHOLARS AND GENERAL AUTHORITIES

With all due respect to those scholars, both within and without the Church, whose works have contributed so heavily to this volume, we have chosen not to refer to them by name in the body of the text. The major reason is to give greater emphasis to a teaching or thought rather than to the person who said it. The exception are quotes from General Authorities of the Church. Since this is a work that focuses on how Latter-day Saints view Paul's teachings, we thought it helpful to note which Church authorities said what. We have been very careful, however, to recognize and give credit to all the contributors in the footnotes.

The criteria that determined which statements of both scholars and Church authorities to use—either to emphasize or to expand on various teachings—is their harmony with the Standard Works. Early in this dispensation, the Lord revealed the means by which his doctrine would be established. To Oliver Cowdery he said, "And now, behold, I give unto you, and also unto my servant Joseph, the keys of this gift [of translation], which shall bring to light this ministry; and in the mouth of two or three witnesses shall every word be established" (D&C 6:28; see also D&C 128:3).[109] It is this principle we have tried to constantly apply. Because any number of line segments can be drawn through a single point but only one can be drawn between two points, at least two anchors are needed. With the scriptures, we have four, the Bible, the Book of Mormon, the Doctrine and Covenants, and the Pearl of Great Price.

The reason we have adopted this criteria is based on a statement by President Harold B. Lee. He said that if a Church authority "says something that contradicts what is found in the standard works (I think that is why we call them 'standard'—it is the standard measure of all that men teach), you may know by that same token that it is false; regardless of the position of the man who says it."[110] President Joseph Fielding Smith confirmed this position, writing that "you cannot accept the books written by the authorities of the Church as standards of doctrine, only in so far as they accord with

---

109. On the divine law of witnesses, see Joseph Fielding Smith, *Answers to Gospel Questions*, 5 vols. (Salt Lake City: Deseret Book, 1976), 1:205.

110. Harold B. Lee, "The Place of the Living Prophet, Seer, and Revelator," address to seminary and Institutes of Religion Faculty, BYU, July 8, 1964, L. Tom Perry Special Collections, Harold B. Lee Library, Brigham Young University, Provo, Utah.

the revealed word in the standard works. Every man who writes is responsible, not the Church, for what he writes." He went on to say that if anyone
"writes something which is out of harmony with the revelations, then every
member of the Church is duty bound to reject it. If he writes that which is
in perfect harmony with the revealed word of the Lord, then it should be
accepted."[111] In this volume, we have tried to follow this dictum for quotes
from both LDS and non-LDS scholars and authorities, including within
the section "LDS Leaders' Use of 1 Corinthians." There we have not quoted
everyone who has spoken on a specific scripture, but rather we have chosen
a few statements that are good examples of what others have said.

LDS Leaders' Use of 1 Corinthians

Joseph Smith's Instructions to the Female Relief Society of Nauvoo

Joseph Smith recognized the power of Paul's words and used them to good
effect. One of the most telling places was in his instructions to the "Female
Relief Society of Nauvoo" which he organized on March 17, 1842. Thereafter, he attended a number of its meetings. At the one on April 28, he
addressed the Society stating that the purpose of "his being present on
the occasion was, to make observations respecting the Priesthood, and
give instructions for the benefit of the Society." He further stated, "he was
going to instruct the Society and point out the way for them to conduct
[themselves], that they might act according to the will of God." He went on
to note that "this society is to get instruction thro' the order which God has
established—thro' the medium of those appointed to lead."[112] By so stating,
the Prophet made it clear that the Relief Society was not an independent
organization but subject to priesthood leadership. Even so, the sisters were
given a certain amount of autonomy. "Those ordain'd to lead the Society,"
Joseph Smith instructed, "are authoriz'd to appoint to different offices as
the circumstances shall require."[113]

---

111. Joseph Fielding Smith, quoted in *Doctrines of Salvation: Sermons and Writings
of Joseph Fielding Smith,* ed. Bruce R. McConkie, 3 vols. in one (1954–56; rpt., Salt Lake
City: Bookcraft, 1999), 3:203–4.

112. "A Record of the Organization and Proceedings of the Female Relief Society of Nauvoo," holograph, 34, 37, 40, Church History Library, The Church of Jesus Christ of Latter-
day Saints, Salt Lake City.

113. "A Record," 39.

For the purpose of emphasizing and guiding the points he wanted to make, so the Relief Society could conduct itself according to the will of God, the Prophet used as his text chapters 12 and 13 of 1 Corinthians.

He began his instructions by noting that, in 12:3, the phrase "no man can say that Jesus is the Lord but by the Holy Ghost," should read, "no man can know" that Jesus is Lord but by the Holy Ghost.[114] The change emphasized the need for divine witness in order for a person to be in a position to bear true testimony of the Savior.

As he continued to read the chapter, he gave "instructions of the various offices, and the necessity of every individual acting in the sphere allotted to him or her; and filling the several offices to which they were appointed." Taking his text from 12:22–25, he noted that it is "the disposition of man, to consider the lower offices in the church dishonorable and to look with jealous eyes upon the standing of others." Correcting that idea he said, "It was better for individuals to magnify their respective callings, and wait patiently till God shall say to them come up higher."[115]

An issue that had arisen focused on women laying hands on the sick for the purpose of giving healing blessings. Taking his cue from 12:9, he responded that, within the confines of their ordination, "it is the privilege of those set apart to administer in that authority which was confer'd upon them—if the sisters should have faith to heal the sick, let all hold their tongues, and let every thing roll on."[116] His point made it clear that men did not have a monopoly on the gifts of the Spirit but that these blessings belonged to all the faithful Saints that all might profit thereby (12:7).

Taking his lead from 12:10, he addressed the sisters on another issue. Though he did not forbid it, he warned them about "indulging too much in the gift of tongues." It was alright, he said, "to speak in tongues for your comfort but I lay this down for a rule that if anything is taught by the gift of tongues, it is not to be received for doctrine."[117] His counsel put a needed delimitation on this ecstatic gift without forbidding it.[118]

Turning to chapter 13:1, he stressed that the sisters were to form "the charitable society." Moving on to 13:2, he warned them that "though one

---

114. "A Record," 34.

115. "A Record," 33–34.

116. "A Record," 34–35.

117. "A Record," 39–40.

118. Joseph Smith had already seen what happened when ecstatic gifts went uncontrolled and was not about to let that happen again. See Richard Lyman Bushman, *Joseph Smith: Rough Stone Rolling* (New York: Alfred A. Knopf: 2005), 146–52.

should become mighty—do great things, . . . [but] should then turn to eat and drink with the drunken; all former deeds would not save them—but he would go to destruction."[119]

By right of membership, he stated, "you are now plac'd in a situation where you can act according to those sympathies which God has planted in your bosoms." He admonished them not to be "limited in your views with regard to your neighbors' virtues, but be limited towards your own virtues, and not think yourselves more righteous than others." He stressed, based on 13:4, the need to "be longsuff'ring and bear with faults and errors of mankind."[120]

He promised them that "this Society shall have power to command Queens in their midst—I now deliver a prophecy," he pronounced, "that before ten years shall roll around, the queens of the earth shall come and pay respects to this Society—they shall come with millions and shall contribute of their abundance for the relief of the poor—if you will be pure, nothing can hinder."[121] Joseph Smith's words reveal his enthusiasm about the Society and what it could accomplish and the power he wished it to have and exercise.

Other General Authorities

Other General Authorities have also appealed to Paul's witness but only one, Elder Bruce R. McConkie, has commented systematically on this epistle. He did this in his three-volume work *Doctrinal New Testament Commentary.*[122] In talks and writings, other leaders have cited specific verses in various chapters. Looking at citations and allusions in conference talks, it becomes clear that Paul's first epistle to the Corinthians has supplied a good deal of doctrinal content for the LDS Church. Three chapters in particular have been used by the Church's General Authorities as proof texts and authoritative statements on key doctrines.[123] The most popular chapters are 2 and 12 with over three hundred references or allusions each in conference talks. Eclipsing these, however, is chapter 15 with over six

---

119. "A Record," 38.

120. "A Record," 35–40.

121. "A Record," 38.

122. See *DNTC*, 2:309–406.

123. This is based on those talks referenced in the LDS Scripture Citation Index, http://scriptures.byu.edu (hereafter cited as SCI).

hundred citations. The next closest to these three is chapter 13 with about two hundred references. All other chapters fall well behind these.[124]

Chapter 15

It is little wonder that chapter 15 is the most popular for the LDS leaders. It bears Paul's strong witness of the reality of the Lord's corporeal Resurrection. The verses the General Authorities refer to most often are 15:6, 19–20, 22, 29, and 55. These are used as proof texts for a literal corporeal Resurrection. After citing various verses in this chapter, Elder McConkie explained their significance by stating,

> in a way incomprehensible to us, he [Jesus] took up that body which had not yet seen corruption and arose in that glorious immortality which made him like his resurrected Father. He then received all power in heaven and on earth, obtained eternal exaltation, appeared unto Mary Magdalene and many others, and ascended into heaven, there to sit down on the right hand of God the Father Almighty and to reign forever in eternal glory. His rising from death on the third day crowned the Atonement. Again, in some way incomprehensible to us, the effects of his resurrection pass upon all men so that all shall rise from the grave.[125]

This statement expresses well the universal assent of this doctrine by the General Authorities since the founding of the Church. Their combined witness is that all men and women who have or will occupy a mortal body shall rise in the Resurrection with a perfect body just as Christ has done.

From the LDS leaders' point of view, this chapter clearly refutes those who do not accept a literal Resurrection. As Elder Dallin H. Oaks explained, "Despite these biblical witnesses, many who call themselves Christians reject or confess serious doubts about the reality of the resurrection. As if to anticipate and counter such doubts, the Bible records many appearances of the risen Christ. In some of these He appeared to a single individual, such as to Mary Magdalene at the sepulcher. In others He appeared to large or small groups, such as when 'he was seen of [about] five hundred brethren at once' (1 Cor. 15:6)."[126]

---

124. The breakdown is as follows: chap. 1 = 119; chap. 2 = 390; chap. 3 = 153; chap. 4 = 25; chap. 5 = 34; chap. 6 = 102: chap. 7 = 12; chap. 8 = 30; chap. 9 = 67; chap. 10 = 76; chap. 11 = 150; chap. 12 = 361; chap. 13 = 209; chap. 14 = 92; chap. 15 = 609; chap. 16 = 10.

125. Bruce R. McConkie, "The Purifying Power of Gethsemane," *Ensign* 15 (May 1985): 10.

126. Dallin H. Oaks, "Resurrection," *Ensign* 30 (May 2000): 14.

Even so, there are many modern Christians for whom the idea of a corporeal Resurrection is just too much to believe. Acknowledging this, Elder Oaks taught,

> The possibility that a mortal who has died will be brought forth and live again in a resurrected body has awakened hope and stirred controversy through much of recorded history. Relying on clear scriptural teachings, Latter-day Saints join in affirming that Christ has "broken the bands of death" (Mosiah 16:7) and that "death is swallowed up in victory" (1 Cor. 15:54). . . . Because we believe the Bible and Book of Mormon descriptions of the literal Resurrection of Jesus Christ, we also readily accept the numerous scriptural teachings that a similar resurrection will come to all mortals who have ever lived upon this earth. . . . As Jesus taught, "Because I live, ye shall live also" (John 14:19).[127]

Thus, the leaders have used 1 Corinthians 15 to illustrate that death is not the end of life for anyone but merely a reentrance into eternity.

They have used 15:20, which states that Jesus is "the first fruits of them that slept," to show that the Savior's Resurrection was but the beginning of the process. For example, President Gordon B. Hinckley stated, "Only a God could do what He did. He broke the bonds of death. He too had to die, but on the third day, following His burial, He rose from the grave, 'the firstfruits of them that slept' (1 Cor. 15:20), and in so doing brought the blessing of the Resurrection to every one of us."[128] The reason a physical resurrection is necessary, according to President Hinckley, is that man is a "dual being of spiritual entity and physical entity." Both are to be redeemed, Christ being the source of power to overcome physical death.[129]

Paul noted that because of one man's act, physical death entered the world, but, as a corollary, because of another man's act, it shall forever be banished (15:22). Elder Russell M. Nelson stated, "The Atonement of Jesus Christ became the *immortal creation.* He volunteered to answer the ends of a law previously transgressed. And by the shedding of His blood, His and our physical bodies could become perfected. They could again function without blood, just as Adam's and Eve's did in their *paradisiacal* form. Paul taught that 'flesh and blood cannot inherit the kingdom of God; . . . [therefore] this mortal must put on immortality'" (15:50–53).[130]

---

127. Oaks, "Resurrection," 14–15; compare Albert E. Bowen, "The Son of God," in CR, April 1947, 104–10.

128. Gordon B. Hinckley, "He Is Not Here, but Is Risen," *Ensign* 29 (May 1999): 70–71.

129. Gordon B. Hinckley, "The Father, Son, and Holy Ghost," *Ensign* 16 (November 1986): 49.

130. Russell M. Nelson, "The Atonement," *Ensign* 26 (Noember 1996): 34.

The relationship of the fall of humankind through Adam and the rise of humankind through Christ is one of the central doctrines of the LDS faith. President Wilford Woodruff, having quoted parts of 1 Corinthians 15, taught:

> I wish to say a few words on one of the verses I have read, the 22nd: "For as in Adam all die, even so in Christ shall all be made alive." The world, more or less, has found a great deal of fault with Mother Eve and with Father Adam, because of the fall of man. . . . Adam fell that man might be, and men are, that they might have joy [2 Ne. 2:25]; and some have found fault with that. It has been said that God commanded Adam to multiply and replenish the earth; and it has been said that Adam was not under the necessity of falling in order to multiply and replenish the earth, but you will understand that the woman was deceived and not the man; and according to the justice of God she would have been cast out into the lowly and dreary world alone, and thus the first great command could not have been complied with unless Adam had partaken of the forbidden fruit. We acknowledge that through Adam all have died, that death through the fall must pass upon the whole human family, also upon the beasts of the field, the fishes of the sea and the fowl of the air and all the works of God, as far as this earth is concerned. It is a law that is unchangeable and irrevocable. . . . The Savior himself tasted of death; He died to redeem the world; His body was laid in the tomb, but it did not see corruption; and after three days it arose from the grave and put on immortality. He was the first fruit of the resurrection. There was no prophet, no saint or sinner, from the days of Father Adam to the days of Jesus that ever rose from the dead through the keys and power of the resurrection.[131]

All must be given a chance to prepare for that day. As a result, God instituted the ordinance of proxy baptism. As Paul asked, "Else what shall they do which are baptized for the dead, if the dead rise not at all? why are they then baptized for the dead?" (15:29). In all of Paul's writings, no verse is more popular among LDS leaders than this one.[132] Joseph Smith taught, "In regard to the law of the priesthood, there should be a place where all nations shall come up from time to time to receive their endowments; and the Lord has said this shall be the place for the baptisms for the dead. Every man that has been baptized and belongs to the kingdom has a right to be

---

131. Wilford Woodruff, in *JD*, 23:125–26.

132. The verse has been cited more than seventy times in various talks. For instances, see SCI, 1 Cor. 15:29.

baptized for those who have gone before."[133] Not only does each Latter-day Saint have the right but also a responsibility. As Joseph Smith taught, "Let me assure you that these are principles in relation to the dead and the living that cannot be lightly passed over, as pertaining to our salvation. For their salvation is necessary and essential to our salvation, as Paul says concerning the fathers—that they without us cannot be made perfect—neither can we without our dead be made perfect" (D&C 128:15).

The practice of proxy baptisms is peculiar to the Latter-day Saints and some of the Church's offshoots. Its aim is to allow all people the chance to be prepared and enter into eternal life. President Hinckley stated, "The word of Jesus to Nicodemus [that to enter heaven a person must be baptized (see John 3:5)] did not allow for exemption. In each of the temples of The Church of Jesus Christ of Latter-day Saints is a font wherein living proxies may be baptized in behalf of the dead. I do not like to speak of them as 'the dead.' I believe that under the great plan of our Eternal Father and through the atonement of Christ, they are living. Though they have died as to their mortal bodies, they have retained their identity as individuals. They are personalities as much so as are we, and as entitled to the blessings that pertain to eternal life."[134]

The brethren continually preach to the Church that this ordinance must be continued. The Prophet Joseph Smith declared,

> And now as the great purposes of God are hastening to their accomplishment, and the things spoken of in the prophets are fulfilling, as the kingdom of God is established on the earth, and the ancient order of things restored, the Lord has manifest to us this duty and privilege, and we are commanded to be baptized for our dead, thus fulfilling the words of Obadiah, when speaking of the glory of the Latter Day: "And saviors shall come upon Mount Zion to judge the remnant of Esau, and the kingdom shall be the Lord's." A view of these things reconciles the scriptures of truth, justifies the ways of God to man; places the human family upon an equal footing, and harmonizes with every principle of righteousness, justice and truth. We will conclude with the words of Peter: "For the time past of our life may suffice us to have wrought the will of the Gentiles." . . . "For, for this cause was the Gospel preached also to them that are dead,

---

133. Joseph Smith Jr., *History of the Church of Jesus Christ of Latter-day Saints,* ed. B. H. Roberts, 7 vols. (Salt Lake City: The Church of Jesus Christ of Latter-day Saints, 1973), 6:365.

134. Gordon B. Hinckley, "Rejoice in This Great Era of Temple Building," *Ensign* 15 (November 1985): 59.

that they might be judged according to men in the flesh, but live according to God in the Spirit." [1 Pet. 4:6][135]

The Lord has given the task of proxy baptisms to his people. It is their responsibility to make available this ordinance to their ancestors who may not have had the opportunity to receive it. Thus, the leaders show that through the resurrection of Christ (15:4), all people can have hope for salvation (15:19–20) that comes through the merciful act of the Savior (15:22). In this way, the great plan of salvation can reach those beyond the grave (15:29). Therefore, with Paul, many can ask, "O death, where is thy sting? O grave, where is thy victory?" (15:55). "There is nothing more universal than death," taught President Hinkley,

> and nothing brighter with hope and faith than the assurance of immortality. The abject sorrow that comes with death, the bereavement that follows the passing of a loved one are mitigated only by the certainty of the Resurrection of the Son of God that first Easter morning. What meaning would life have without the reality of immortality? Otherwise life would become only a dismal journey of "getting and spending," only to end in utter and hopeless oblivion. . . . The pain of death is swallowed up in the peace of eternal life. Of all the events of the chronicles of humanity, none is of such consequence as this.[136]

"There is no victory in the grave," President Spencer W. Kimball assured the Saints, "for death is replaced with life. Immortality is a free gift for all men through the atoning ransom paid by the Son of God."[137]

When this doctrine is properly understood and believed, death is put in its proper perspective. It is but a passage into the next phase of existence. The core belief of the Latter-day Saints was declared by President Lorenzo Snow who said, "As man now is, God once was: As God now is, man may be."[138] Thus, the brethren place emphasis on the idea that God designed this mortal experience to be a temporary but necessary step into eternity and godhood.

---

135. "History, 1838–1856, Volume C-1 [2 November 1838–31 July 1842]," 1324, Church History Library, available online at Church Historian's Press, *The Joseph Smith Papers,* http://www.josephsmithpapers.org/paper-summary/history-1838-1856-volume-c-1 -2-november-1838-31-july-1842/498.

136. Gordon B. Hinckley, "This Glorious Easter Morn," *Ensign* 26 (May 1996): 67.

137. Spencer W. Kimball, "An Eternal Hope in Christ," *Ensign* 8 (November 1978): 72.

138. Eliza R. Snow Smith, *Biography and Family Record of Lorenzo Snow* (Salt Lake City: Deseret News, 1884), 46; see also "The Grand Destiny of Man," *Deseret Evening News,* July 20, 1901, 22. Elder Snow did not begin teaching this doctrine until Joseph Smith taught it. See Smith, *Biography,* 45–47.

Chapter 2

The number of times LDS leaders refer or allude to verses in chapter 2 makes it the second most quoted in Paul's work. Due to the central place that revelation plays in the Church, Paul's discourse on the necessity of the Holy Spirit in order to understand the "deep things of God" (2:10) has great appeal. Of particular interest are 2:9, 11, and 14, where Paul distinguishes the difference between the spiritual man and the natural man.[139]

Speaking on 2:9, Elder Orson Pratt declared, "it has not entered into the heart of man to conceive the things which God has laid up for them that love Him, unless he is filled with the Holy Ghost."[140] The Apostle's words stress the idea that no person, no matter how bright or well educated, is able to even *conceive* the things that God plans to give righteous people. That information comes to them only via the Spirit. Elder McConkie declared, "Now the truths about God and salvation are not gained by the wisdom of men. They are not to be found by the research of the world."[141] Both brethren, though ministering in differing centuries,[142] place emphasis on the idea that no one can know the things of God without assistance from the Holy Spirit.

In 2:11, Paul noted that humans know "the things of . . . man" because of the "spirit of man which is in him." The things of God, however, cannot be known "but [by] the Spirit of God." President Kimball stated, "Desirable as is secular knowledge, one is not truly educated unless he has the spiritual with the secular. The secular knowledge is to be desired; the spiritual knowledge is an absolute necessity."[143]

In 2:14, Paul mentioned that the "natural man receiveth not the things of the Spirit of God" because "they are spiritually discerned." Elder Charles W. Penrose, referring to this verse, taught that "we see natural things by the light of the sun. We see spiritual things by spiritual light, and he that is spiritual discerneth all things and judgeth all things, and he that is not spiritual cannot comprehend spiritual things."[144]

---

139. For references, see SCI for each verse.

140. Orson Pratt, in *JD*, 1:294.

141. Bruce R. McConkie, "The Holy Ghost—a Revelator," in CR, April 1953, 75.

142. Orson Pratt died in 1881 and McConkie died in 1985.

143. Spencer W. Kimball, "Wisdom and Great Treasures of Knowledge, Even Hidden Treasures," in CR, October 1968, 127–31.

144. Charles W. Penrose, in *JD*, 26:23.

Chapter 12

The number of citations or allusions by LDS leaders in their conference talks to specific verses in chapter 12 makes it the third most quoted from Corinthians. Given the importance of unity in the Church, it is little wonder that Paul's treatment of this subject would have appeal. The leaders have concentrated mostly on 12:3, 7, 10, 13, 21, and 28.[145] It is of note, however, that 12:7, 10, and 13, which deal with the gifts of the Spirit, are quoted far more frequently by Church leaders in the nineteenth century than in the twentieth.[146] That these verses have received so little attention in the past seventy years while those dealing with the necessity of the Spirit to receive revelation suggests that the emphasis of the leadership has shifted from the importance of spiritual gifts to that of revelation.

The following quotes are representative of the teachings of the leaders on the material in chapter 12. "The gifts of the Gospel are given to strengthen the faith of the believer," said President Brigham Young.[147] The particular faith those gifts boost is, of course, in the Lord. Paul taught in 12:3 that "no man can say that Jesus is the Lord, but by the Holy Ghost," and that "no man speaking by the Spirit of God calleth Jesus accursed." The leaders have used Paul's ideas to teach the necessity of the Holy Spirit in order to have a testimony of Christ and, even more so, to sincerely and fully witness his reality. The Prophet Joseph Smith stated, "We believe in the gift of the Holy Ghost being enjoyed now, as much as it was in the Apostles' days. . . . We believe in its being a comforter and a witness bearer. . . . We believe that 'no man can know that Jesus is the Christ, but by the Holy Ghost.'"[148] A number of leaders tie this verse to Matthew 16:15–17, where Peter bears his witness that Jesus is "the Son of the living God" to show that the Apostle received the witness of the Spirit and this allowed him to bear a powerful testimony.

The higher powers of the Holy Ghost, according to Church leadership, come only after one has received confirmation by those having authority. Elder Charles W. Penrose explained,

---

145. For specific talks, see SCI for each given verse.

146. Notice the dates of the discourses citing these verses in the SCI.

147. Brigham Young, in *JD*, 10:324.

148. "History, 1838–1856, Volume C-1 Addenda," 65, available online at Church Historian's Press, *The Joseph Smith Papers*, http://josephsmithpapers.org/paper-summary/history-1838-1856-volume-c-1-addenda/65.

Now, our testimony to the world is that God has restored [the] ancient priest-hoods—that is, the power to administer in the name of the Lord by authority, and that the power of God accompanies that authority. Here are men who profess to have . . . the authority to lay hands upon the people for the gift of the Holy Ghost. Now, an impostor might profess to have this power. Having read about it in the New Testament, and seeing that the ancient servants of God possessed such power, a man might profess to have authority to lay hands upon people for the bestowal of the Holy Ghost. But an impostor cannot really confer the Holy Ghost. That comes from God. No man can bestow the gift of the Holy Ghost upon anyone; that is the gift of God.[149]

As the latter half of the twentieth century began, the focus of spiritual gifts shifted to the diversity of talents among the members of the Church. One evidence of this shift is Elder LeGrand Richards teaching that "the Lord has not left any without some gift and as you look about you, you will find that where one is strong in one way he may be weak in another. The Lord never did give all His gifts to any one individual. Even in the great work the Prophet Joseph accomplished, the Lord told him that his gifts were limited in some respects (D&C 46:11)."[150] The leaders have stressed that the Spirit is needed within the Church for the further development of the various talents that each member might obtain or already have. Using 12:21 as their text, "the eye cannot say to the hand I have no need of thee: nor again the hand to the feet, I have no need of you," certain leaders have also taught the importance of each person using his or her talents in order for the Church to function properly.[151] As Joseph Smith taught:

The cause of God is one common cause, in which all the Saints are alike interested; we are all members of the one common body, and all partake of the same spirit, and are baptized into one baptism and possess alike the same glorious hope. The advancement of the cause of God and the building up of Zion is as much one man's business as another. The only difference is, that one is called to fulfill one duty, and another, another duty; "but if one member suffers, all the members suffer with it, and if one member is honored all the rest rejoice with it, and the eye cannot say to the ear, I have no need of thee, nor the head to the foot, I have no need of thee;" party feelings, separate interests, exclusive designs should be lost sight of in the one common cause, in the interest of the whole.[152]

---

149. Charles W. Penrose, in *JD*, 21:142–43.
150. LeGrand Richards, "Shepherds of the Flock," in CR, April 1943, 46–50.
151. See SCI for 12:21 for references.
152. "History, 1838–1856, Volume C-1," 1327; punctuation standardized.

The need for each person's talents necessitates concord. "Within this Church there is a constant need for unity," declared President Howard W. Hunter, "for if we are not one, we are not his. (See D&C 38:27.) We are truly dependent on each other, 'and the eye cannot say unto the hand, I have no need of thee: nor again the head to the feet, I have no need of you.' (1 Cor. 12:21.) Nor can the North Americans say to the Asians, nor the Europeans to the islanders of the sea, 'I have no need of thee.' No, in this church we have need of every member, and we pray, as did Paul when he wrote to the church in Corinth, that there should be no schism in the body; but that the members should have the same care one for another."[153]

Of real importance to Church leadership is Paul's teaching in 12:28 that "God had set some in the church, first apostles, secondarily prophets, and thirdly teachers." Though this verse bolsters the superior position of the Apostles, it is of note that other officers are also of importance. For instance, "The Apostle Paul placed the priority of teachers in the Church next only to the Apostles and the prophets," M. Russell Ballard stated.[154] President George Q. Cannon explained, "The Church of Christ is not perfect without Apostles. Apostles were as necessary as Teachers; they were as necessary as Evangelists; they were as necessary as Pastors."[155] From this statement, the brethren agree with Paul's theme that all people and all talents are essential to the proper working of the kingdom and no one part can work the whole, all parts must work together.

Chapter 13

The appeal of certain verses in chapter 13 has made it the third most-quoted chapter by LDS leaders. The most popular verses by far are 13:1, 8, and 12–13. Though Paul's discussion of love is cited a good deal by twentieth-century leaders, they have left little by way of commentary. It is the nineteenth-century leaders who more extensively examined the doctrine. For example, the Prophet Joseph Smith stated, after quoting 13:1, "Don't be limited in your views with regard to your neighbor's virtues, but beware of self-righteousness, and be limited in the estimate of your own virtues and do not think yourselves more righteous than others; you must enlarge your souls towards each other, if you would do like Jesus and carry your fellow-creatures to Abraham's bosom. He said he had manifested long-suffering,

---

153. Howard W. Hunter, "That We May Be One," *Ensign* 6 (May 1976): 105–6.
154. M. Russel Ballard, "Teaching—No Greater Call," *Ensign* 13 (May 1983): 69.
155. George Q. Cannon, in *JD,* 22:265.

forbearance, and patience towards the Church and also to his enemies; and we must bear with each other's failings, as an indulgent parent bears with the foibles of his children."[156]

President Brigham Young taught, "The Apostle Paul says we are nothing without charity, whatever else we may possess. Using my own language I should say, without the pure principle of the love of God in the heart to subdue, control, overrule, and utterly consume every vestige of the consequences of the fall, the fire that is kindled within the nature of every person by the fall will consume the whole in an utter and irretrievable destruction."[157] One of the few twenty-first-century leaders who expanded on this verse was President Dieter F. Uchtdorf, who said, "True love requires action. We can speak of love all day long—we can write notes or poems that proclaim it, sing songs that praise it, and preach sermons that encourage it—but until we manifest that love in action, our words are nothing but 'sounding brass, or a tinkling cymbal.'"[158]

Leaders frequently use this chapter to stress the need for speakers to have the Spirit as a witness to the truthfulness of what they say. "The countenance of a holy angel would tell more than all the language in the world," taught President Young. "If men who are called to speak before a congregation rise full of the Holy Spirit and power of God, their countenances are sermons to the people. But if their affections, feelings, and desires are like the fool's eye . . . and the kingdom of God is far from them . . . they may rise [before a congregation] and talk what they please, and it is like sounding brass or a tinkling cymbal—mere empty, unmeaning sounds to the ears of the people."[159] From the inception of the Church, the leaders have focused on this idea because they recognized a person's inability to share the message of God affectively without it. "In confusion of today's beliefs, philosophies, sophistries, changing standards of personal behavior, and the bold voice of unorthodox extremists," stated Elder Delbert L. Stapley, "man's need for spiritual guidance to choose the right and forsake the wrong is of paramount importance to his assurance of hope for peace and happiness. Without the light of the spirit, people see through a glass, darkly (1 Cor. 13:12). Their judgments and decisions are so often faulty. They bog down in confusion, frustration, and utter bewilderment."[160] The condition of seeing

---

156. "History, 1838–1856, Volume C-1 Addenda," 41; punctuation standardized.
157. Brigham Young, in *JD*, 9:267–68.
158. Dieter F. Uchtdorf, "You Are My Hands," *Ensign* 40 (May 2010): 70.
159. Brigham Young, in *JD*, 8:142.
160. Delbert L Stapley, in CR, October 1966, 111–14.

"through a glass, darkly," however, will not outlive mortality. Again from Elder Pratt, there will come a time "when the Church has become perfect in the eternal world. After we pass through this state of existence and are exalted, we shall no longer see through a glass darkly."[161]

It is of note that these and other leaders do not appeal to love, as Paul did, as the key to seeing "through a glass, darkly," but to the Spirit. In fact, in all the general sermons from the Nauvoo period on, the emphasis has been on the need of the Spirit as the key to proper spiritual understanding.[162]

The Brethren have often appealed to Paul's statement in 13:8 that "charity never faileth: but whether there be prophecies, they shall fail: whether there bs tongues, they shall cease; whether there be knowledge, it shall vanish away." Many of the talks recorded in the *Journal of Discourses* note that the gifts of the Spirit will fail because they will not be needed in the Celestial realm. Elder Pratt articulated this idea:

> Here, then, it is clearly foretold that when there will be no more need of prophecy, healing, speaking in tongues, etc., the day of perfection will have arrived; in other words, when the Church of God shall have overcome and be perfected, when the Church of God shall need no more Prophets, when it shall have no more sick, (for if all its members become immortal, there will be no sick to be healed, hence healing will be done away, when the Church of God all speak one language—the pure language, the language spoken by angels, restored to the earth by the Lord), there will be no need of speaking with tongues. But until that day of perfection comes, all these gifts will be necessary.[163]

His words showcase what we find in the emphasis of most leaders, that the emphasis in 13:8 is not on the eternal nature of love but on the perishability of many spiritual gifts. That is not to say that faith, hope, and charity have been totally ignored. As Elder Joseph B. Wirthlin noted, "These divine attributes should become fixed in our hearts and minds to guide us in all of our actions."[164] Even though these are the most enduring of all the gifts of God, few leaders have seen a need to explore or expand on that fact. Among the few who have, Elder Vaughn J. Featherstone testified,

---

161. Orson Pratt, in *JD,* 16:295.

162. For example, see David O. McKay, in CR, April 1943, 20; Harold B. Lee, in CR, April 1955, 18; in CR, October 1956, 96; ElRay L. Christiansen, in CR, October 1991, 10; Mark E. Petersen, in CR, October 1966, 74.

163. Orson Pratt, in *JD,* 16:137.

164. Joseph B. Wirthlin, "Cultivating Divine Attributes," *Ensign* 28 (November 1998): 26.

Only those who are true possessors of charity can measure up to the full stature of this new commandment [to love one another (John 13:34)]. This is the commandment that lifts us to the more noble and virtuous life. We cannot nor ever will love one another as He has loved us until we exercise in our own lives the full dimensions of charity. Those who practice charity may not always receive the promised benefits and ultimate successes. Ours is a different time schedule, but by and by we will all learn and know that "charity never faileth" (1 Cor. 13:8). The pure love of Christ will triumph over all the evils, including power, pride, boasting, worldly acclaim, cruelty, wars, perversion, sadness, and heartache. The Lord through His servants has promised that charity will never fail. One day charity, the pure love of Christ, will triumph over all the world. Those who are possessors of charity will triumph over all evil and will dwell with the author of this "new commandment" forever and forever.[165]

Chapters 3 and 6

LDS leaders have used three verses in chapter 3, namely 3:6, 16, and 17, to teach specific lessons. Verse 3:6, "I have planted, Apollos watered; but God gave the increase," is often used in a missionary setting. The focus, however, is not on the work of the servants but on the readiness of the hearer to accept the word. Typical is the sentiment of President Young, who stated that:

> We can say to the Latter-day Saints, it is the mind and will of God that we organize according to the best plans and patterns and system that we can get for the present. We can do this, and thus far give to the Latter-day Saints the mind and will of the Lord; but we cannot make a man or a woman yield to the will of God unless they are disposed to. I can plant, I can water, but I cannot give the increase; I cannot cause the wheat and corn to grow. It is true I can break up and prepare the ground and cast the seed therein, but I cannot cause it to grow, that can only be done by the people having willing hearts, ready minds, and a disposition to go forth with a firm determination and a willing hand to build up the kingdom.[166]

Other leaders have emphasized the same point. "Our understanding of the scriptures and our conversion to the truth today," taught President Henry D. Moyle, "must follow the same pattern as was set for Paul's conversion and followed by Paul in his ministry in the conversion of others. . . . Where there is no increase given, of such as Paul spoke, there is no conversion. Job's declaration is all-enlightening. 'But there is a spirit in man: and

---

165. Vaughn J. Featherstone, *The Incomparable Christ: Our Master and Model* (Salt Lake City: Deseret Book, 1995), 79.
166. Brigham Young, in *JD*, 17:155.

the inspiration of the Almighty giveth them understanding' (Job 32:8). Therefore, when we come to fulfil all righteousness by delivering the message of the gospel as it has been revealed to us, to our fellow men, we must teach by the Spirit. The Spirit must bear witness of the truthfulness of our message to the world. No one need fear to hear our message. If we speak of ourselves, our work will come to naught."[167]

Verses 3:16–17, which contains Paul's statement that the community of the Saints is "the temple of God" and his warning against defiling that temple, have also been used by Church leaders to stress the importance of each person keeping his or her body pure. In this same connection they use 6:19–20. Both sets of verses are used most often in connection with either the Word of Wisdom or the law of chastity. The following statement by President John Taylor is typical: "The apostle said, 'Grieve not the Spirit of God, by which you are sealed to the day of redemption;' do not grieve it, do not sin against God, do not violate his laws, do not corrupt yourselves; do not corrupt your bodies, for are they not, as one has said, 'the temples of the living God?' Do not allow your spirits to be contaminated and led astray from correct principles, but cleave unto God in all humility, fidelity, faithfulness; observing his laws and keeping his commandments."[168] In referring to 6:19–20, President Young taught, "I would to God that every soul who professes to be a Latter-day Saint was of that character, a holy temple for the indwelling of the Father, the Son, and the Holy Ghost."[169]

Though these verses are referenced or alluded to more than one hundred times in conference addresses, none of the leaders use them in the same sense that Paul did, that is, as referring to the corporate Church not to individuals.[170] Since the Church is made up of individuals, however, the leaders' points are well made for the cleanliness of the whole is dependent largely on that of each member. On the other hand, Paul's emphasis that it is the corporate Church in which the Spirit dwells is a very important doctrine that has been largely ignored.

Chapter 11

Only 11:11 has received significant attention by LDS leaders. There Paul states that "neither is the man without the woman, neither the woman without the man, in the Lord." The leaders have used this verse specifically

167. Henry D. Moyle, in CR, April 1966, 99.
168. John Taylor, in *JD*, 21:346.
169. Brigham Young, in *JD*, 1:3.
170. See SCI for 1 Cor. 3:16 and 16–17.

to stress the importance and sanctity of marriage between a man and a woman. Elder Russell M. Nelson declared, "Marriage is not only an exalting principle of the gospel; it is a divine commandment."[171] Adam and Eve were commanded in the garden to "be fruitful and multiply and replenish the earth" (Gen. 1:28). With that commandment, God instituted the family order. Elder Nelson noted, "Marriage is the foundry for social order, the fountain of virtue, and the foundation for eternal exaltation. Marriage has been divinely designated as an eternal and everlasting covenant. Marriage is sanctified when it is cherished and honored in holiness. That union is not merely between husband and wife; it embraces a partnership with God. . . . Marriage is but the beginning bud of family life; parenthood is its flower. . . . Families may become as eternal as the kingdom of God itself."[172]

Paul's words suggest the importance of each spouse to the other. According to President Hugh B. Brown, "God instituted marriage in the very beginning. He made man, male and female, in his own image and likeness (Gen. 1:26–27) and designed that they should be united together in sacred bonds of marriage and declared that one is not perfect without the other (1 Cor. 11:11). Marriage, the family, and the home are among the most important subjects of our whole theological doctrine, and as the family is the basic and fundamental unit of the Church and of society, its preservation and its righteous needs should take precedence over all other interests."[173]

Leaders also use the scripture to show that women are invaluable in the Lord's program. "From the beginning God has made it clear that woman is very special," taught President N. Eldon Tanner, "and he has also very clearly defined her position, her duties, and her destiny in the divine plan. Paul said that man is the image and glory of God, and that woman is the glory of the man; also that the man is not without the woman, neither the woman without the man in the Lord. (See 1 Cor. 11:7, 11.) You will note that significantly God is mentioned in connection with this great partnership, and we must never forget that one of woman's greatest privileges, blessings, and opportunities is to be a co-partner with God in bringing his spirit children into the world."[174]

---

171. Russell M. Nelson, "Celestial Marriage," *Ensign* 38 (November 2008): 93.

172. Russell M. Nelson, "Nurturing Marriage," *Ensign* 36 (May 2006): 36–37.

173. Hugh B. Brown, in CR, October 1966, 101.

174. N. Eldon Tanner, "No Greater Honor: The Woman's Role," *Ensign* 3 (November 1973): 123.

Chapter 1

Only two verses in chapter 1 have, to any degree, caught the attention of the General Authorities. These are 1:21 and 27, which are often linked to make a single point. Paul told the Corinthians that "the world by wisdom knew not God, [but] it pleased God by the foolishness of preaching to save them that believe" (1:21). He went on to say that "God hath chosen the foolish things of the world to confound the wise; and God hath chosen the weak things of the world to confound the things which are mighty" (1:27). It is of little wonder these two verses are quite popular given that the LDS Church has both a lay clergy and young missionary force.

Paul's idea that the wisdom of the world has not brought people to know God has been stressed by LDS leaders. One of the big forces that created the Apostasy was the loss of the knowledge of the true character of the Godhead. As a result, as the Lord declared, many "have strayed from mine ordinances, and have broken mine everlasting covenant; they seek not the Lord to establish his righteousness, but every man walketh in his own way, and after the image of his own god, whose image is in the likeness of the world, and whose substance is that of an idol, which waxeth old and shall perish in Babylon, even Babylon the great which shall fall" (D&C 1:15–16). To counter this, the Lord "gave commandments to others, that they should proclaim these things unto the world; and all this that it might be fulfilled, which was written by the prophets—The weak things of the world shall come forth and break down the mighty and strong ones, that man should not counsel his fellow man, neither trust in the arm of flesh—But that every man might speak in the name of God the Lord; even the Savior of the world" (D&C 1:18–20). The leaders have used 1:21, 27 to bolster this point.

History has shown that the wisdom of men has failed to bring people to a united understanding of God. "The fact is," stated President George Albert Smith, "the world through their wisdom know not God, and have lost sight of and forgotten the simplicity of our fathers, and the plainness of the Gospel of Jesus Christ."[175] The truth is that it does not take a great intellect or deep training to understand either the Godhead or the Gospel. Therefore, the "weak things" are very capable of understanding and explaining both.

In every dispensation the "strong and mighty" have, by and large, regarded the Saints as lowly and simple. President Woodruff noted that "one thing is

---

175. George Albert Smith, in *JD,* 3:25.

evident to everybody who reflects at all upon the things of the kingdom of God—whenever the Lord chooses a people out of the world, they are hated by the world, and are unpopular in the world. This has been the case in every age. . . . Christ came as the babe of Bethlehem, the lowest almost of the human family, and remained so up to the day of his death. A poorer man never lived, that I know of, in Judea and Jerusalem, than Jesus Christ."[176]

Why is it that the "weak things of the world" really can break "down the mighty and strong"? Elder Neal A. Maxwell comments that the reason possibly is "their meekness and larger capacity for spiritual contentment may be one reason why God uses the weak of the world to accomplish His work (see D&C 1:19, 23; D&C 35:13; D&C 133:58–59; 1 Cor. 1:27). The worldly are usually not very interested in doing what they regard as the Lord's lowly work anyway."[177]

Chapter 14

Though the subject matter of this chapter deals with spiritual gifts, somewhat surprisingly the more popular verses referred to by LDS leaders, 14:8 and 33, are used to warn against either teaching or accepting false doctrine.[178]

Paul stressed the need to be clear when explaining one's ideas for "if the trumpet give an uncertain sound, who shall prepare himself for battle?" (14:8). President Marion G. Romney noted that:

> For want of a knowledge of the true and living God, this world is today dying. And please do not be deceived. Such a knowledge is not widespread. It is true that, in their great concern about world conditions, men are almost frantically proclaiming from the pulpit, the platform, over the air, and through the press that a return to God is the only way out of our difficulties. The tragedy is their cries, like Paul's trumpet of uncertain sound (1 Cor. 14:8), are unheeded. Now the obvious reason is that neither the trumpeters nor the hearers know the God to whom we must return. They use the familiar term with which we are all so well acquainted. But when they attempt to define the God to whom they would have us return, they reveal a woeful lack of knowledge concerning the living and true God. Frequently they actually deny him.[179]

---

176. Wilford Woodruff, in *JD*, 18:188.

177. Neal A. Maxwell, "Content with the Things Allotted unto Us," *Ensign* 30 (May 2000): 74.

178. SCI for 1 Cor. 14.

179. Marion G. Romney, in CR, October 1964, 50.

President Joseph F. Smith, keying off 14:8, identified the source of false doctrine among the Saints. He stated:

> Among the Latter-day Saints the preaching of false doctrine disguised as truths of the gospel may be expected from people of two classes and practically from these only; they are: First, the hopelessly ignorant, whose lack of intelligence is due to their indolence and sloth, who make but feeble effort, if indeed any at all, to better themselves, by reading and study; those who are afflicted with a dread disease that may develop into an incurable malady—laziness.
>
> Second, the proud and self-vaunting ones, who read by the lamp of their own conceit; who interpret by rules of their own contriving; who have become a law unto themselves, and so pose as the sole judges of their own doings, more dangerously ignorant than the first. Beware of the lazy and the proud; their infection in each case is contagious; better for them and for all when they are compelled to display the yellow flag of warning, that the clean and uninfected may be protected.[180]

The Brethren often compliment their explanations of 14:8 with 14:33, where Paul declares that "God is not the author of confusion." General Authorities, since the Church's founding, have assured its members that there is but one true Church upon the face of the earth having the fullness of the gospel. President Taylor stated:

> Were I among the Christians, I would think if the Baptists are right the Presbyterians are not; if the Presbyterians are right then the Baptists are not; if the Church of England is right then the others are wrong; if the Roman Catholics are right then others are wrong; and if any of the others are right the Roman Catholics are wrong. I cannot conceive of two ways to go to Heaven and both be right. I cannot think of a God of intelligence, who has created the whole human family, and who has organized every living thing, and adapted them to the varied positions which they occupy, being the author of the confusion that exists in the world in relation to the forms of worship. But if God is not the author of it, who is? Where did it come from? I know that men generally are not inclined to investigate these subjects.[181]

President Taylor's statement nicely summarizes how the General Authorities have used these verses. As President Hugh B. Brown noted, "Personally, I wish to bear my testimony with those that have already been borne that

---

180. Joseph F. Smith, as quoted by Harold B. Lee, in CR, April 1949, 47.
181. John Taylor, in *JD*, 13:14.

the Church today, the kingdom of God, is being led by revelation. God is not the author of confusion (1 Cor. 14:33). He does not work in dark places. He makes it known to the world when he appoints a prophet, and I testify that I know as I know I live, that this Church today is guided by prophecy and by revelation, and that these men whom we honor are prophets of God."[182]

Chapter 10

In chapter 10, LDS leaders have focused only on 10:13. There Paul teaches that God "will not suffer you to be tempted above that ye are able; but will with the temptation also make a way to escape, that ye may be able to bear it." The General Authorities have continually preached that the Lord is with his people and will not try them above their ability to resist. Many in the modern Church have experienced such trials and looked to this scripture for comfort and solace. It is little wonder, then, that the Brethren have focused on it. Indicative of these are Elder Wirthlin, who, using the example of a marathon race, stated:

> I suppose some of you, at one time or another, feel that you are "hitting the wall," feeling an almost compelling urge to quit, give up, or give in to temptation. You will meet challenges, adversities, and temptations that seem to be more than you can bear. In times of sickness, death, financial need, and other hardships, you may wonder whether you have the strength, courage, or ability to continue.
>
> You young people face the same temptations that have been common throughout history, plus many others that were unknown to earlier generations. However, be sure you understand that God will not allow you to be tempted beyond your ability to resist. (See 1 Cor. 10:13.) He does not give you challenges that you cannot surmount. He will not ask more than you can do, but may ask right up to your limits so you can prove yourselves. The Lord will never forsake or abandon anyone. You may abandon him, but he will not abandon you. You never need to feel that you are alone.[183]

Chapter 9

Like chapter 10, LDS leaders have focused on but one verse in this chapter, namely 9:16, where Paul teaches that "though I preach the gospel, I have nothing to glory of; for necessity is laid upon me." General Authorities have used this verse in connection with the evangelizing efforts of the Church to stress the obligation its members have to preach the gospel.

---

182. Hugh B. Brown, in CR, October 1958, 63.
183. Joseph B. Wirthlin, "Running Your Marathon," *Ensign* 19 (November 1989): 75.

"Any people into whose hands is committed a dispensation of the Gospel," stated President Woodruff, "has a great responsibility. And Joseph Smith, Brigham Young, and the Twelve Apostles would have been under condemnation and would have rendered themselves liable to the curse of God if they had not gone forth into the world and borne record of this work."[184] The leadership has also stressed that to refuse a call to preach the gospel will bring condemnation upon those who refuse. Representative of this view is the counsel of President Taylor. He stated, "The Gospel that we preach is not for ourselves only. . . . I have traveled a great many thousands of miles to preach this Gospel without purse and without scrip, and I see many men around and before me who have done the same thing. . . . God had revealed certain principles to us pertaining to the salvation of the world in which we live; he had committed a dispensation of the Gospel to us, and it was woe unto us if we preached not that Gospel. . . . We went forth in the name of Israel's God, and God went with us and sanctioned our testimony by his Spirit, and by the gift of the Holy Ghost. We could not have done these things . . . unless God had been with us."[185]

Chapter 8

The leaders' focus in chapter 8 has been on 8:5–6, where Paul notes that "there be gods many and lords many," but for the Saints there is "but one God, the Father, of whom are all things, and we in him; and one Lord Jesus Christ, by whom are all things, and we by him." The Prophet Joseph Smith, in his comments on these verses focused on the idea of a plurality of Gods:

> "Some say I do not interpret the Scripture the same as they do. They say it means the heathen's gods. Paul says there are Gods many and Lords many; and that makes a plurality of Gods, in spite of the whims of all men. Without a revelation, I am not going to give them the knowledge of the God of heaven. You know and I testify that Paul had no allusion to the heathen gods. . . . I have a witness of the Holy Ghost, and a testimony that Paul had no allusion to the heathen gods in the text. . . .
>
> "In the very beginning the Bible shows there is a plurality of Gods beyond the power of refutation. . . . The word *Eloheim* ought to be in the plural all the way through—Gods. The heads of the Gods appointed one God for us; and when you take [that] view of the subject, its sets one free to see all the beauty, holiness and perfection of the Gods."[186]

---

184. Wilford Woodruff, in *JD*, 23:80.
185. John Taylor, in *JD*, 17:210.
186. Smith, *History of the Church*, 6:475, 476.

In making this bold assertion, the Prophet went against the more popular and also scholarly views in his day (and ours[187]). However, many of the Church's leaders have followed Joseph Smith's path. Elder Orson Pratt taught:

> In one sense of the word, there are more Gods than one; and in another sense there is but one God. The Scriptures speak of more Gods than one. Moses was called a God to Aaron, in plain terms; and our Savior, when speaking upon this subject, says, "If the Scriptures called them Gods unto whom the word of God came, why is it that you should seek to persecute me, and kill me, because I testify that I am the Son of God?" This in substance was the word of our Savior; those to whom the word of God came, are called Gods, according to his testimony.
>
> All these beings of course are one, the same as the Father and the Son are one. The Son is called God, and so is the Father, and in some places the Holy Ghost is called God. They are one in power, in wisdom, in knowledge, and in the inheritance of celestial glory; they are one in their works; they possess all things, and all things are subject to them; they act in unison; and if one has power to become the Father of spirits, so has another; if one God can propagate his species, and raise up spirits after his own image and likeness, and call them his sons and daughters, so can all other Gods that become like him, do the same thing; consequently, there will be many Fathers, and there will be many families, and many sons and daughters; and they will be the children of those glorified, celestial beings that are counted worthy to be Gods.[188]

Making a different point from these verses, President Harold B. Lee said to the members, "I would have you note particularly the use of the preposition 'of,' in reference to the Father, and the preposition 'by,' in reference to our Lord, Jesus Christ. In this statement is clearly defined the role of each, the Lord to do the bidding of the Father, in the execution of the whole plan of salvation for all mankind. (Abr. 4:1–31)."[189]

Chapter 5

Though this chapter centers on immorality and contains Paul's admonition for members to not associate with flagrant and unrepentant sinners, the focal point of the General Authorities has been on but two of the points Paul made.

---

187. For a more full discussion, see Gordon D. Fee, *The First Epistle to the Corinthians* (Grand Rapids, Mich.: Eerdmans, 1983), 371–73l; Thiselton, *First Epistle*, 631–33.

188. Orson Pratt, in *JD*, 1:56.

189. Harold B. Lee, "Time to Prepare to Meet God," CR, October 1970, 115.

The first is that "a little leaven leaveneth the whole lump" (5:6). Those who have used the phrase have ignored Paul's point that condoning sin among the members can greatly damage the Church. Instead, some leaders have used the phrase to show the influence of the Church upon the world.[190] Typical of those following this use is President George Q. Cannon, who stated: "The Gospel of Christ was to produce union, its mission was to produce love, to destroy strife, to make men and women live together as brethren and sisters, and it has done so for us and it is doing so and it will do so more and more, and it will build up a system such as cannot be found on the face of the earth. And it is growing and increasing. It is like a little leaven, and by and by it will leaven the whole lump, and the influence and the power that will go forth from this people will be felt throughout the whole earth."[191] Also, John A. Widstoe stated, "Truth is always the winner, truth is never defeated. In the words of the old poet: 'Truth crushed to earth will rise again.' He left on that occasion the message to me and to others that we must cleanse our hearts. . . . We must gather up our courage, and we must set forth to battle for righteousness in the world. Then, just as a leaven leavens the lump (1 Cor. 5:6), so we shall leaven the whole world."[192]

The second is on Paul's counsel that with grievous sins local leaders should "deliver such an one unto Satan for the destruction of the flesh, that the spirit may be saved in the day of the Lord Jesus" (5:5). Typical of how this verse is interpreted are Joseph Smith's words that certain "sins will be visited with judgment in the flesh, and the spirit being delivered to the buffetings of Satan until the day of the Lord Jesus."[193] Any physical punishment, however, must be left up to the state.

Chapter 4

The intriguing aspect of chapter 4 is that hardly a single LDS leader has referred to any part of it after 1940. During the nineteenth century, a number of leaders did look to 4:13, "being defamed, we instruct, we are made as the filth of the world, and are offscouring of all things unto this day." Given the early history of the Mormon faith, it is easy to see why the early leaders identified with this verse. The words of President Taylor reflect well the general view:

---

190. See SCI for 1 Cor. 5:5–6.
191. George Q. Cannon, in *JD*, 22:324.
192. John A. Widstoe, in CR, April 1951, 99–100.
193. Smith, *History of the Church*, 5:391; compare John Taylor, in *JD*, vol:162.

Man, assisted by the Lord, is the founder of his own destiny. We do not always see this principle developed at once. Sometimes the hand of God is withheld, and he suffers his people to be chastened. At present this appears hard, and to some it seems urgent; yet it is for their good. . . . Good men have had to endure affliction, privations, trials, and sorrow, it is true. Abraham had to pass through afflictions that were harrowing to his feelings. Men of God have had to wander about in sheepskins and goat-skins, and been considered the scum and offscourings of society, by men who understood not their relationship to God. They appeared destitute, but were, in reality, not. They had a hope that was buoyant, and looked for a city that had foundations, whose builder and maker is God.[194]

With less persecution and broader acceptance, the sentiment in this scripture has lost its institutional relevance for the time being.

LDS SCHOLARS' WORK ON 1 CORINTHIANS

Though 1 Corinthians has not been neglected by LDS scholars, neither has any, before the present, sought to do a commentary on just that book. The epistle, therefore, has received, at best, coverage that is limited and generally targeted to a popular audience.[195] Some scholars have analyzed specific issues in this epistle in various symposia proceedings, but again, none of these have focused exclusively and comprehensively on the epistle as a whole.[196]

---

194. John Taylor, in *JD*, 8:97.

195. For example, see Sidney B. Sperry, *Paul's Life and Letters* (Salt Lake City: Bookcraft, 1955), 118–36; Anderson, *Understanding Paul*, 91–129; D. Kelly Ogden and Andrew C. Skinner, *Verse by Verse: Acts through Revelation* (Salt Lake City: Deseret Book, 1998), 128–58; Wayment, *Persecutor to Apostle*, 161–74; Holzapfel and Wayment, *Making Sense*, 344–67.

196. See, for example, Robert C. Freeman, "Paul's Earnest Pursuit of Spiritual Gifts," in *The Apostle Paul: His Life and His Testimony*, ed. Paul Y. Hoskisson (Salt Lake City: Deseret Book, 1994), 34–46; Hatch, "Paul among the Rhetoricians," 65–79; Woodger, "'I's' of Corinth," 41–56; and Kent R. Brooks, "Paul's Inspired Teaching on Marriage," in *Go Ye into All the World*, 75–97.

Chapter 1

Dissensions in the Corinthian Church

INTRODUCTION

Though Paul had been away from Corinth for four to five years, he never lost interest in what was happening there. No wonder, this city—due to its excellent geographical location—was the headquarters for proselyting of the whole of Europe. Paul's letter reveals how acutely aware he was of all that had happened there and of his concerns for their spiritual health. After all, he was the founder of those branches of the Church and felt a keen paternal interest in them. Over the years, however, reciprocal feelings seem to have lessened. The Apostle, therefore, felt it necessary to remind them of his relationship to them as one who sacrificed much as he worked hard in their behalf. His detractors seem to have questioned his right to direct affairs there. Likely they inferred that he was interfering where he should not. In his greeting, therefore, he stressed his own God-given authority as well as his role as an Apostle. With that authority, and because of his great concern for them, he also pronounced a blessing upon them.

Though he does not say so in the introductory verses, Paul is quite clear in his purpose for writing them: "I am not writing these things to make you feel ashamed, but to admonish you as my own dear children" (4:14, Rendition). Paul's use of the word νουθετέω (*noutheteō*), "I admonish," places his epistle in "the ancient letter-type known as τύπος νουθέτικος (*typos nouthetikos*), an admonition intended to instill proper action in the person(s) so counseled."[1] This idea gives light to the blessing Paul pronounces upon these Saints in his salutation; it will be through the divine power of grace that the people will hear, accept, and implement his counsel. The result will be heavenly peace, something the divisive congregations desperately needed.

---

1. Fitzmyer, *First Corinthians*, 55–56.

SALUTATION
(1:1–3)

Greek Text

1 Παῦλος κλητὸς ἀπόστολος Χριστοῦ Ἰησοῦ διὰ θελήματος θεοῦ καὶ Σωσθένης ὁ ἀδελφὸς 2 τῇ ἐκκλησίᾳ τοῦ θεοῦ, ἡγιασμένοις ἐν Χριστῷ Ἰησοῦ, τῇ οὔσῃ ἐν Κορίνθῳ, κλητοῖς ἁγίοις, σὺν πᾶσιν τοῖς ἐπικαλουμένοις τὸ ὄνομα τοῦ κυρίου ἡμῶν Ἰησοῦ Χριστοῦ ἐν παντὶ τόπῳ αὐτῶν καὶ ἡμῶν· 3 χάρις ὑμῖν καὶ εἰρήνη ἀπὸ θεοῦ πατρὸς ἡμῶν καὶ κυρίου Ἰησοῦ Χριστοῦ. [SBLGNT]

King James Version

1 Paul, called to be an apostle of Jesus Christ through the will of God, and Sosthenes our brother, 2 Unto the church of God which is at Corinth, to them that are sanctified in Christ Jesus, called to be saints, with all that in every place call upon the name of Jesus Christ our Lord, both theirs and ours: 3 Grace be unto you, and peace, from God our Father, and from the Lord Jesus Christ.

New Rendition

1 Paul, called as an apostle of Christ Jesus through the will of God, and Brother Sosthenes, 2 to the Church of God that is in Corinth, to those who have been sanctified in Christ Jesus, who are called as Saints, together with all those who call upon the name of our Lord, Jesus Christ, in every place, their Lord as well as ours. 3 Grace to you and peace from our Father and our Lord Jesus Christ.

Translation Notes and Comments

1:1 *Paul, called to be an apostle of Jesus Christ / Paul, called as an apostle of Christ Jesus:* The JST reads, "Paul, an apostle, called of Jesus Christ." In doing so, that text emphasizes the source of the calling. This follows Paul's pattern in each of his epistles where he emphasizes that his apostolic calling is from God, making him a special witness of Jesus Christ, with the same authority and privileges as the other members of the Twelve. The title ἀπόστολος (*apostolos*), "apostle," was chosen by the Lord to designate those he selected as his leaders (Luke 6:13; John 15:16). The term denoted persons set apart with extraordinary power to carry out specific responsibilities.[2] The Twelve were God's messengers specifically ordained to bear witness of him and to carry out his ministry (see Matt. 28:19–20; D&C 107:23–24). It is in this sense that Jesus is given this designation in Hebrews 3:1–2.

---

2. BDAG, 122.

Paul's call is the basis of his authority and position over the Christian community in Corinth.[3] His words stress the idea that "Neither apostles nor any church officers call themselves," states Elder McConkie. "Either they are called of God or they are not, and if they are not their teachings and performances have no saving virtue and are not binding in heaven."[4]

Jesus Christ / Christ Jesus: The better reading is "Christ Jesus."[5] Paul often uses this word order to stress the messianic quality of the Lord, the word Χριστός (*Christos*), being the Greek translation of the Hebrew מָשִׁיחַ (*māšîaḥ*) *messiah,* or "anointed one."[6] The Jews used the word to designate one who was anointed under the direction of God to be king or priest. In an eschatological sense, the Jews used the word specifically to identify the king who would deliver them from their enemies and bring in the Golden Age.[7] The Christians accepted Jesus as this figure. He is, first and foremost, the Messiah, that is, "the Anointed One," or the one whom God had called and anointed to save his people. The title pulled Paul's reader/hearer toward a Jewish understanding of what the Savior was and links Paul's witness to its Old Testament roots.

Apostle . . . through the will of God: The genitive phrase δία . . . θεοῦ (*dia . . . theou*) stresses that the agent of the act is God and, thus, he is the immediate agent behind Paul's call.[8] The words make it perfectly clear that the Apostle's call and standing is divine. He is, therefore, on the Lord's errand and working under his authority.

and Sosthenes our brother / and Brother Sosthenes: Since Paul uses "I" instead of "we" through most of the letter, some argue that Sosthenes

---

3. Fitzmyer, *First Corinthians,* 123.

4. *DNTC,* 2:311. In a few of the early manuscripts the word "called" is missing. It is impossible to tell if the word was left out by scribes who wished to challenge Paul's authority or was added to support it. See Holzapfel and Wayment, *Making Sense,* 345.

5. Bruce M. Metzger, *A Textual Commentary on the Greek New Testament,* 2d ed. (New York: United Bible Society, 1994), 478.

6. Paul uses this word order in 1:2, 30; 4:15; 15:31; 16:24.

7. *Megillah* 17b–18a, *Ta'anit* 8b; *Soṭah* 9a.

8. Though the preposition δία (*dia*) is translated as "by" in the NRSV, NIV, and REB, the translation as "through" better catches the nuance of the Greek because it shows agent, mode, means, and efficient cause. See Walter Bauer, *A Greek-English Lexicon of the New Testament and Other Early Christian Literature,* trans. William F. Arndt and F. Wilbur Gingrich, 2d ed. rev. and ed. F. Wilbur Gingrich and Frederick W. Danker from Bauer's 5th ed., 1958 (Chicago: University of Chicago Press, 1979), 179–81 (hereafter cited as BAGD).

is not a coauthor of the epistle.[9] Though that is correct, he still may have been Paul's advisor or editor and Paul felt to recognize him. We do not know who Sosthenes is partly because the name was quite common in the first century.[10] It may be that he was the same Sosthenes (also called Crispus) mentioned in Acts 18:8, 17, who was the ruler of the synagogue in Corinth who brought charges against Paul before the Roman governor Gallio.[11] It seems certain that this Sosthenes was well known and trusted by many of the Corinthians, and Paul was using Sosthenes's reputation to strengthen the points in his letter.[12]

Throughout his epistles, Paul regularly uses the term ἀδελφός (*adelphos*) to designate a member of the Church, and when used in the plural, it refers to both male and female members and thus the word can be translated as "brothers and sisters" as in our Rendition.[13]

1:2 *Unto the church of God / to the Church of God:* The phrase τοῦ θεοῦ (*tou theou*), "of God," is a genitive of possession and by using it Paul stresses that the Church belongs neither to any certain one (no matter how rich or well positioned) nor to some inner circle of elite (no matter how spiritual or holy), but to God alone. It is of note that Paul is well aware of the social stratification that existed in the branches where freedmen and slaves, rich and poor all met together. He in no way tries to change this social condition, but he does believe that such stratification should not stand in the way of spiritual equality and oneness.[14]

The word ἐκκλησία (*ekklēsia*), translated "church" in the KJV, did not have an exclusively religious connotation in Paul's day. Rather, it denoted any assembly to which the townspeople were "called" by herald's trumpet or cry.[15] On this basis, it is easy to see why the Saints referred to their meetings as *ekklēsia,* for they were called of God to meet regularly and do his will. Identifying the *ekklēsia* with God did give it a spiritual dignity and authority.[16]

---

9. Paul Ellingworth and Howard A. Hatton, *A Handbook on Paul's First Letter to the Corinthians,* 2d ed., UBS Handbook Series Helps for Translators (New York: United Bible Societies, 1995), 4–5.

10. Anthony C. Thiselton, *The First Epistle to the Corinthian: A Commentary on the Greek Text* (Grand Rapids, Mich.: W. B. Eerdmans, 2002), 70.

11. Holzapfel and Wayment, *Making Sense,* 344.

12. Fitzmyer, *First Corinthians,* 121.

13. BDAG, 18.

14. Fitzmyer, *First Corinthians,* 125.

15. Thiselton, *First Epistle,* 75.

16. Findlay, "St. Paul's First Epistle," 758.

Which is at Corinth / that is in Corinth: Some manuscripts put the phrase τῇ οὔσῃ ἐν Κορίνθῳ (*tē ousē en korinthō*), "that is in Corinth," after "to those who have been sanctified in Christ Jesus" rather than before it. The SBL Greek New Testament prefers this reading, whereas Nestle-Aland Greek New Testament, 28th ed., prefers placing it before. Both the KJV and our Rendition have followed the latter.

Paul understands that there is only one Church but that it has different branches or congregations. Paul's words remind the Corinthians that the congregations are not self-contained democracies that can choose their own way, but they belong to the whole and are governed by the rules and officers of the whole.[17]

called to be saints / called as Saints: Just as Paul had received a calling from God to be an Apostle, so too had the members of the Church at Corinth to be "Saints" entering into a common fellowship.[18] As Elder McConkie stated, they have been "called out of the world and into the Church, called by the election of grace, which includes being foreordained to be members of the Church (See Rom. 8:28–34a; 9:1–33)."[19]

The English word "saints" is the translation for the Greek ἁγίοις (*hagiois*). The singular ἅγιος (*hagios*) connoted either objects created with such care and workmanship or people of such high moral quality and purity that they could stand in the presence of the divine. It denoted that quality which was peculiar to God but which people could attain (Lev. 11:44; 20:7). On the mortal plane, it denoted particularly people or objects dedicated to the service of a deity. Synonyms are holy, devout, pious, or dedicated.[20] But there was a Jewish nuance that should not be overlooked. Among them it denoted someone who had a share in the coming messianic kingdom.[21]

In applying the title to the Christians at Corinth, Paul was reminding them that they had been called to the service of God and should dedicate themselves to his service at all times. The title does not imply that these people were sanctified or had received that characteristic of God known as holiness (see Moses 7:35). Indeed, they were often admonished to become

---

17. Thiselton, *First Epistle,* 70.

18. Findlay, "St. Paul's First Epistle," 757.

19. *DNTC,* 2:312.

20. BDAG, 10–11; Johannes P. Louw and Eugene A. Nida, *Greek-English Lexicon of the New Testament Based on Semantic Domains,* 2 vols. (New York: United Bible Societies, 1988), §§88.24; 53.46 (hereafter cited as Louw-Nida).

21. See Owen E. Evans, "New Wine in Old Skins: XII. The Saints," *Expository Times* 86 (1975): 196–200.

sanctified or holy (see, for example, 1 Pet. 1:15–16). The title did emphasize that they had been called to separate themselves from the world and
that, through baptism, they had entered into a special relationship with the
Divine.[22] As Paul would say, they had been called to "walk in newness of life"
(Rom. 6:4), a life patterned after the celestial order (compare D&C 105:3–5).

*that are sanctified in Christ Jesus / those who have been sanctified in
Christ Jesus:* A Greek perfect passive participle denotes a past event, the
effects of which remain in the present and continue into the future. Here
Paul uses that form with the verb ἁγιάζομαι (*hagiazomai*), "to be made holy,
to be sanctified," to show that the Savior, because of their covenant with
him at baptism, has separated them from the world and made them his
people. Paul's words remind them, therefore, that they, as sanctified people,
should not use worldly ways or objectives but reach for higher ideals.[23]

But what does it mean to be "sanctified in Christ"? Does the Greek preposition ἐν (*en*) mean "by" or does it mean "in"? Here it precedes a noun in
the dative case which can indicate instrumentality or agent. Since the sanctifying power does come through the Savior, a person is, indeed, sanctified
"by" him. In that case the phrase carries the idea that at some point early
on, Christ had separated these people out from the world and they were
yet in that state. Paul, however, often uses the phrase "being-in-Christ" to
denote the theological idea of corporate status, that is, being in union with
the Lord, a close union that both triggers the sanctification process and
provides the foundation of the Christian life (see, for example, 4:15; 15:31;
Rom. 1:1–2; 8:1–2; 16:3; Gal. 2:4; 3:28; 6:15; Eph. 1:1; 2:6, 10, 13; 3:11).[24] Our
Rendition follows this idea.

*with all that in every place call upon the name of Jesus Christ our Lord
/ with all those who call upon the name of our Lord, Jesus Christ:*[25] The
verb ἐπικαλέω (*epikaleō*), "to call," describes an act in which an appeal or
request is made to the Lord. Behind it stands an abiding trust and simulta-
neous commitment to him on the part of the person praying.[26] The phrase
would have resonated with the Jewish members of the Church because of

---

22. Louw-Nida, §11.27; Fitzmyer, *First Corinthians*, 122.

23. Findlay, "St. Paul's First Epistle," 758.

24. Thiselton, *First Epistle*, 76. The pronoun *en* with a dative of person expresses a
relationship broader than instrumentality or agent. It can connote, at least, a personal
presence if not a very close personal relationship. See BAGD, 326–30.

25. The phrase parallels that found in LXX Joel 3:5. Compare Rom. 10:13, where Paul
quotes it verbatim. The context gives the scripture an eschatological nuance.

26. Thiselton, *First Epistle*, 78–79.

an Old Testament echo where it denoted recognition of Jehovah as Israel's God and its attendant praise (compare Ps. 116:13, 17; Zeph. 3:9).[27]

Paul's choice of words reveals his desire to unite himself with the Corinthian Saints. The topic is "our Lord," the common bond between Apostle and Saint. Further, in using the title κύριος (*kyrios*), "Lord," Paul acknowledges with all the Christians that the risen Christ is equivalent to the Old Testament Jehovah and is the ever-abiding power in his life and should be that of the Christians everywhere.[28]

both theirs and ours / their Lord as well as ours: Paul's words again stress that unity of faith in Christ should prevail among the various congregations. His words were specifically meant to remind those who were causing dissent that the Church did not belong to them, but to all members equally.[29] These self-absorbed and selfish souls believed somehow that they had a monopoly on faith and spiritual gifts. They were sure the spiritual world revolved around them, and only they correctly understood how to interpret it. Paul's words forcefully remind them that neither the Lord nor the Spirit belongs to any one group, but rather both, with the Father standing as the head of the whole.[30]

1:3 ***Grace be unto you, and peace, from God our Father, and from the Lord Jesus Christ / Grace to you and peace from our Father and our Lord Jesus Christ:*** Though a greeting, the words also serve as an apostolic prayer in behalf of these people. The Greek noun χάρις (*charis*), "grace, favor, mercy, kindness, good will," carries the idea of generously and graciously giving some beneficence to another. The bestowal, however, does imply some kind of obligation on the part of the receiver.[31] Therefore, the word "grace," as opposed to "mercy, kindness, or goodwill," is the better translation here because the word does imply that the beneficiary of God's grace is under obligation to carry out his will.[32]

---

27. Fitzmyer, *First Corinthians,* 127.

28. Fitzmyer, *First Corinthians,* 127.

29. Findlay, "St. Paul's First Epistle," 759.

30. Thiselton, *First Epistle,* 77–78.

31. Louw-Nida, §57.103.

32. For a full study of grace, see the forthcoming discussion on Galatians 3 and Romans 3, 8 in this commentary series. For a careful study of the ancient meaning of χάρις (*charis*), "grace," see Brent J. Schmidt, *Relational Grace: The Reciprocal and Binding Covenant of Charis* (Provo, Utah: BYU Studies, 2015), who concludes that "The meaning commonly understood by a broad range of cultures up until the fifth century was that grace was the essence of a two-way, unequal, reciprocal, binding agreement between two parties in which both were obligated to each other" (201).

Paul's emphasis, however, is not so much on grace itself but on its source and its result. It is God whose loving kindness is expressed in his giving to his Saints such things as the gospel, the Spirit, its witness of the truth, and ultimately, his Son. But grace comes not from God alone. Indeed, the Savior has also given much for the Saints, including his whole mortal life. It is, in fact, by this means—this supernal act of grace—that eternal life, as well as all the powers, blessings, and gifts of the gospel, were made possible. But it also opened up the reception of another dimension of grace, that of transforming power. Indeed, all the perfecting attributes are ultimately "'bestowed upon all who are true followers of . . . Jesus Christ' (Moro. 7:48) by grace through his atonement."[33] As one LDS scholar concluded, it is through the grace of God "that individuals, through faith in the atonement of Jesus Christ and repentance of their sins, receive strength and assistance to do good works that they otherwise would not be able to maintain if left to their own means. This grace is an enabling power that allows men and women to lay hold on eternal life and exaltation after they have expended their own best efforts."[34]

Grace, however, is not the only condition bestowed by God and Christ. They also give peace. Though often interpreted in the modern sense of tranquility, rest, and harmony, which does conform partially to its meaning in Koine Greek, the noun, in a religious sense, referred to a state of harmony between a god and his followers. For Christians, peace was "nearly synonymous with messianic salvation."[35] Paul understood that peace comes through the justification which brings harmony between God and the Saint (see Rom. 5:1).

Analysis and Summary

The opening lines follow the standard format of a Greek letter during New Testament times—"Sender(s) to receiver(s), greeting." Verse 1:1 says who the senders are, Paul and Sosthenes. Verse 1:2 identifies the recipients, the members of the Church in Corinth. Verse 1:3 contains the greeting.

Paul's greeting here follows that of the typical letter form of his day with two exceptions. First, he includes another writer, Sosthenes,[36] and second,

---

33. Bruce C. Hafen, "Grace," in *Encyclopedia of Mormonism*, ed. Daniel H. Ludlow, 4 vols. (New York: Macmillan, 1992), 2:562 (hereafter cited as *EM*).

34. Robert L. Millet, *What Happened to the Cross?* (Salt Lake City: Deseret Book, 2005), 120.

35. BDAG, 288.

36. Though very rare in letters of the time, Paul does it frequently. See 2 Cor. 1:1; Philip. 1:1; Col. 1:1; 1 Thes. 1:1; 2 Thes. 1:1; Philem. 1:1.

he uses not only the usual Greek valediction "grace" but also adds εἰρήνη (*eirēnē*), "peace." The latter was the common greeting of the Jews in his day (שָׁלוֹם, *šālôm*). By using it, Paul connected his God to that of the Jews and the Old Testament. This connection is an important point. Paul was often accused by his Jewish contemporaries of attempting to destroy their faith, but this one word shows that he was actually reaching out to them.[37]

That he departs little from the epistolary conventions of his day suggests that Paul does not set up Christianity as a counterculture to all things Greek or Roman. At times he does this, but it is only when it is theologically and doctrinally important for him.[38] Paul shows us that the gospel message does not stand apart from this world, but is a part of it and, therefore, can take in all that is good, true, and wholesome. Only that which is soul destroying need be left behind.

With his very first words, Paul reminds his readers of his rank, that of Apostle. By the modern definition of that word, there can be no question that Paul held that office. He was in very deed one of the "special witnesses of the name of Christ in all the world" who differed "from other officers in the church in the duties of their calling" (D&C 107:23). But was he a member of the Quorum of the Twelve Apostles? Because individuals have been called to that office without also being members of the high Quorum in this dispensation,[39] it is possible the same occurred in the meridian of time. Further, the Greek word ἀπόστολος (*apostolos*) had the basic sense of "envoy or delegate." Even so, within the New Testament, it is used as "predominately . . . a group of highly honored believers w[ith] a special function as God's envoys."[40] These made up the one Quorum. Paul was likely one of them. He begins each of his epistles with "Paul, an apostle" thus, consistently showing claim to the office. His statement in 1:1–7 shows that he had no doubt he held full apostolic authority. He insists that he had the same rights and privileges as Peter, James (the brother of the Lord), and the other apostles. In Galatians 2:7–9, he convincingly shows that he was directly called by Christ to preside over the work of taking the gospel to the gentile world. In Galatians 1:17, he refers to the other apostles as "οἱ πρὸ ἐμοῦ ἀπόστολοι" (*hoi pro emou apostoloi*), those "who were called

---

37. Tertullian, *Adv. Marc.* 5.5.1.

38. Thiselton, *First Epistle,* 62.

39. These include Joseph Smith, Oliver Cowdery, Joseph F. Smith (Apostle for a year before being added to the Quorum), Joseph Angell Young (never added to the Quorum), Brigham Young Jr., Sylvester Q. Cannon, and Alvin R. Dyer, who was ordained an Apostle and served in the First Presidency from 1968 to 1970.

40. BDAG, 122.

before me," which suggests he was now one of them.[41] In sum, there is no evidence in the New Testament that ἀπόστολος (*apostolos*) was used for anyone other than a "special witness of Christ," that is, an apostle and member of the Quorum as we understand the term in this dispensation (see D&C 27:12; 107:23).

It is very likely that Paul's purpose in emphasizing his office was an effort to make his readers take his words seriously. Indeed, he brings their attention to the fact that the call was extended by God himself. In short, Paul did not speak on his own authority but that of the Father. In giving credit to God, rather than putting himself forward as the authority, Paul humbly steps back and puts God in the foreground. Paul's emphasis was not on his word. Rather it was on Christ's shown by the Apostle invoking the name of the Lord nine times in the invocation.[42] Though he is, indeed, an "Apostle of Christ Jesus" and functions under that authority, he puts Jesus center stage. By doing so, Paul demonstrates that he is unwilling to play the Corinthian game of one-upmanship, probably to the disappointment of some. As noted in the introduction of this volume, some objected to Paul because they wanted him to act like the Sophists who dazzled people with their show of verbal excellence and intellectual wit and sagacity.[43] When Paul humbly refused, they turned against him likely because they felt he was letting the cause down. But Paul's humility reflected that of the Lord himself and marked what the gospel was really all about—not ascendancy over others, but service under Christ Jesus.[44] In his role as an Apostle, he stressed not his own agenda but rather that of the Lord. Through the words of the epistle, he makes the word and the will of the Lord known.[45]

---

41. The only other men in the New Testament besides the original Twelve who are called Apostles are: Matthaias (Acts 1:25–26)—who was definitely a member of the Twelve—Barnabas (Acts 14:14, 15:2), and James, the Lord's brother (Gal. 1:19). Based on Rom. 16:7, some want to include Andronicus and Junia/Junias (possibly a woman's name), because it states οἵτινές εἰσιν ἐπίσημοι ἐν τοῖς ἀποστόλοις (*hoitines eisin episēmoi en tois apostolois*) "who are well-known among the apostles." However, the Greek is ambiguous and could also be understood to mean they were well-known *to* the apostles rather than known to *be* apostles. The NET translates this phrase as "They are well-known to the apostles."

42. Chrysostom, *Ep. Com. Hom.* 1.1; 2.2.

43. Plato characterized the Sophists working in his day as pompous educators whose primary aim was fame and money who inflamed the students to the same ends. See his works *Gorgias* and *The Apology*.

44. Ben Witherington III, *Conflict and Community in Corinth* (Grand Rapids, Mich.: Eerdmans; Carlisle, U.K.: Paternoster, 1995), 123–24.

45. Thiselton, *First Epistle*, 65–66.

But another point must be stressed. Paul is "an Apostle of Christ Jesus *through the will of God*" (italics added). The phrase reveals Paul's care to always put God in the center. As important as Jesus is in the salvation process, Paul never lets his reader forget that all the Saints work according to God's, not Jesus', will. Nothing can eclipse the importance of the Father in all that the Church does. Even the Savior's life and ministry was summed up in his words "thy will be done" (Matt. 26:42), and Paul would not let his readers forget that.[46]

In 1:2, Paul stresses that the Church belongs to God. The principle defect of the Corinthian Saints was twofold: first, they did not understand the real God because they replaced him with one of their own understanding, and second, they were willing to go with the interpretations and teachings of the particular leader they followed.[47] Paul stresses the point to show them that the Church is not some human institution that they can use as a means of gaining prestige, fame, or power. The Church is God's assembly and he is in charge. He has, however, delegated the responsibility to his Son. In 1838, when the Lord revealed the name of the Church, he stated, "For thus shall my church be called in the last days, even The Church of Jesus Christ of Latter-day Saints" (D&C 115:4). The first phrase is a genitive of possession showing that the Church belongs to the Savior. The second is a genitive of composition showing that it consists of the Saints.[48] The Savior stands as the sole possessor of the Church and he alone directs its affairs, not any one member or any set of members.

Paul addresses the people as "Saints." Of the significance of this title, Elder Mark E. Petersen stated: "The members of the true church anciently did not call themselves Christians, for that was but a nickname applied to them in derision by those who hated Christ. The members of the Church called themselves *saints,* as may be seen from various New Testament references (see 1:2; Rom. 16:2), which are confirmed by Webster's dictionary and by the Bible scholars. This, then, is one of the identification marks of the true Church. The members are called *saints.*"[49]

The title "saints" is a nominal use of the Greek adjective ἅγιος (*hagios*), "sacred, holy," which is related to ἁγιωσύνη (*hagiōsynē*), "holiness," an

---

46. James Moffatt, *First Epistle of Paul to the Corinthians* (London: Hodder and Stroughton, 1938), 250–51.

47. Barth, *Resurrection of the Dead,* 17.

48. Hyrum M. Smith and Janne M. Sjodahl, *Doctrine and Covenants Commentary,* rev. ed. (Salt Lake City: Deseret Book, 1978), 740.

49. Mark E. Petersen, "Signs of the True Church," *Ensign* 9 (May 1979): 22. See also Ogden and Skinner, *Verse by Verse,* 130.

attribute that is the very essence of God. When applied to mortals, it expresses the idea of being "sanctified," that is, entering into a new state where one receives the qualities and characteristics of the divine.[50] Paul notes that these people have been "sanctified in Christ Jesus." The phrase carries the idea that the Savior used his power to separate them from the world and make them his people. The application of the word does not, however, describe what they are (for in some instances, like some members in Corinth whose divisive attitude suggests they stood in need of more saintliness), but stood as a reminder of what they were chosen to become. Baptism, the first step in a long development leading to full saintliness, began a transformation process by cleansing and, thus, sanctifying them, but only to a degree.[51] The process goes well beyond being sin free. Through the power of the Redeemer, the person slowly and eventually changes such that he or she becomes a new creature, even a son or daughter of Christ. Along the path they eventually lose every desire for sin and become "submissive, meek, humble, patient, full of love, willing to submit to all things which the Lord seeth fit to inflict upon him, even as a child doth submit to his father" (Mosiah 3:19; see also D&C 20:31; 2 Cor. 5:17; Gal. 6:15; Mosiah 5:2, 7; 27:25–27; Ether 3:14).

By leaving Christ or disobeying his commandments, the Corinthian Saints would lose this status that only deep repentance would restore. Paul's greeting suggests that, even though some of the Saints were having problems, most were, as yet, still in their initial sanctified state, and Paul wanted to keep them there. The danger was that through divisiveness, they could lose that union and thereby that sanctified state.[52]

Paul reminds the Corinthian Saints that they are a part of a whole by tying them to "all [those] who call on the name of the Lord" (a paraphrase from LXX Joel 3:5 [KJV Joel 2:32]). To understand the nuance of this act, we must turn to the Old Testament. There Jehovah revealed his name as "I am that I am" (Ex. 3:14). Israel came to understand what the name meant through the miraculous and saving acts Jehovah performed, acts he designed to show the Hebrews that they could put their full trust in him. Therefore, his name carried the idea of the one who could be trusted, trusted because he was there—immediate, cognizant, omnipotent, and caring. Therefore, to call on the name of the Lord was not an act of calling on some shadowy, ethereal

---

50. Otto Procksch, "ἅγιος: E. ἅγιος in the NT," in *TDNT*, 1:100–110.
51. See C. Eric Ott, "Sanctification," in *EM*, 4:1259–60.
52. See Translation Notes on 6:11 and the Analysis that follows.

being, but a faith-filled invocation to a known and personal deity whose character and nature were such that his people could put their complete trust in him.[53] In this, Paul had a second witness in the "Lectures on Faith." There we find the declaration that:

> An acquaintance with these attributes in the divine character is essential so the faith of any rational being can center in him for life and salvation. For if, in the first instance, he did not believe him to be God, that is, the creator and upholder of all things, he could not *center* his faith in him for life and salvation, for fear there should be a greater one than he who would thwart all his plans, and he, like the gods of the heathen, would be unable to fulfil his promises. But seeing he is God over all, from everlasting to everlasting, the creator and upholder of all things, no such fear can exist in the minds of those who put their trust in him, so that in this respect their faith can be unwavering.
>
> But secondly, unless God was merciful and gracious, slow to anger, long-suffering and full of goodness, such is the weakness of human nature and so great the frailties and imperfections of men that unless they believed that these excellencies existed in the divine character, they could not have the faith necessary to salvation. For doubt would take the place of faith, and those who know their weakness and liability to sin would be in constant doubt of salvation if it were not for the idea which they have of the excellency of the character of God, that he is slow to anger, long-suffering, and of a forgiving disposition, and does forgive iniquity, transgression, and sin. having an idea of these facts does away with doubt and makes faith exceedingly strong.[54]

Paul's words emphasize that the uniting core of the Christian faith is their trust in the Father and the Son and obedience to their will. To call on the name of the Lord was a vote of confidence that the Savior would continue to act in accordance with his character as disclosed in the Old Testament. The prayer also meant that the invocator guaranteed his or her desires and acts would conform to the nature, will, and disposition of Deity.

---

53. Thiselton, *First Epistle,* 79.

54. "Lecture 3," in *The Lectures on Faith in Historical Perspective,* ed. Larry E. Dahl and Charles D. Tate Jr. (Provo, Utah: Religious Studies Center, Brigham Young University, 1990), 68.

EXCURSUS ON GRACE

Introduction

Paul was very clear on what was central to his doctrine: "I determined not to know any thing among you," he declared, "save Jesus Christ, and him crucified" (2:2). That knowledge, however, included much that the Atonement entailed. To communicate a key motivation behind the Savior's act and one of the greatest benefits that grew out of it, the Apostle chose the Greek word *charis,* generally translated as "grace."

Because some Christian churches' interpretation and application of the word "grace" does not square with LDS beliefs on how the Atonement works, Latter-day Saints have commonly ignored the doctrine of grace. Even today, some wonder if believing in grace might carry a hint of heresy.[55] That reaction is sad but understandable given the lack of clear articulation in the Church's past. When dealing with the teachings of the Apostle Paul, however, the doctrine is so central that it cannot be dismissed or overlooked but must be carefully examined.

The question is whether the Jewish or Greco-Roman social and religious viewpoint is the best tool to extract the earliest Christian understanding of the doctrine of grace. Before the 1980s, most scholarship tended to concentrate on the Classics as the best means of understanding; then a shift in emphasis occured where many scholars began to see Second Temple Judaism as the key.[56] However, since Paul grew up as a diaspora Jew under Hellenistic pressures and Judaism itself was influenced by Hellenistic strands of thought, the best course is to combine the two.[57]

We must keep in mind Paul's own witness to the source of his understanding of the gospel, however: "But I certify you, brethren, that the gospel which was preached of me is not after man. For I neither received

---

55. For example, see the attitudes exposed by Robert L. Millet, *Grace Works* (Salt Lake City: Deseret Book, 2003), 6–7; Robert Millet, "The Perils of Grace," *BYU Studies Quarterly* 53, no. 2 (2014): 7–19.

56. Though scholars like C. G. Montefiore, *Judaism and St. Paul* (London, 1914); and S. Sandmel, *A Jewish Understanding of the New Testament* (New York, 1956), had insisted that the key to properly interpreting Paul was Second Temple Judaism, most looked to the classics. With the work of W. D. Davies, *Paul and Rabbinic Judaism: Some Rabbinic Elements in Pauline Theology,* 4th ed. (Philadelphia: Fortress Press, 1980), and others, many scholars pivoted more toward Judaism.

57. More recent scholarship has shown that a sharp separation between the two is no longer tenable. Davies, *Rabbinic Judaism,* viii–ix.

it of man, neither was I taught it, but by the revelation of Jesus Christ"
(Gal. 1:11–12). Part of his divine education came from his own conversion experience. Zealously persecuting God's children was no small sin.[58]
Indeed, the Lord took it personally, asking Paul, "Why persecutest thou
me?" (Acts 9:4).[59] Certainly such a deed deserved exacting punishments,
but none came. Instead, the Lord redirected Paul's enthusiasm, cleansed
him through baptism, filled him with the Holy Ghost, and called him to
the ministry (Acts 9:15–18). Not one whit of such kindness and forgiveness did Paul earn or merit. All grew out of Christ's loving grace, and Paul
knew it (Gal. 1:15). To some extent, the ramifications and implications of
this experience and what it taught about Christ and the gospel dawned on
Paul almost immediately, for Luke states that "straightway [Paul] preached
Christ in the synagogues, that he is the Son of God" (Acts 9:20). Even so,
shortly thereafter, the Apostle did take some time to sort everything out,
noting that he did not confer "with flesh and blood: neither went I up to
Jerusalem" (Gal. 1:16–17) but to the desert for reflection, meditation, and
learning. The result was, among other things, Paul's understanding of grace
and its role in the salvation process. Thus the ultimate source of his understanding, as he emphasized, was divine.

The noun *charis,* "grace," carried enough of a nuance for the Apostle
to use it for his purposes. However, it did require some tweaking to get it
exactly right, which the modern reader must pick up. Helpful in this quest
is that the very Jewish Paul was also a converted Christian and also "the
apostle of the Gentiles" (Rom. 11:13). He therefore tailored his message in
such a way as to be understandable to both Gentiles and Jews.

Paul was not a bit hesitant in adopting the word and making it the linchpin of his testimony. By incorporating the concept into his theology, he
made it a central element in Christian doctrine and a key to understanding
a major result of the Atonement of the Redeemer. In doing so, he relied
on elements from the cultural matrices in which he lived, but he modified
them to conform to inspiration. By taking the general meaning of the term
and noting how Paul tweaked it for his purposes, the modern reader can
come to an understanding of this important doctrine.

The difficulty in precisely understanding Paul's message is due to the fact
that *charis* carries many denotations, connotations, and nuances. It is not

---

58. According to Acts 9:1, Paul was "breathing out threatenings and slaughter against
the disciples of the Lord." Thus, his zeal was so intense that he sought execution.

59. Through a parable, the Lord made it very clear that "inasmuch as ye have done it
unto one of the least of these my brethren, ye have done it unto me" (Matt. 25:40, 45).

so much that the word cannot be translated as that it is hard to stop translating it.[60] Fortunately, in most instances, context helps.

Charis in the New Testament

Of the 184 times that χάρις (*charis*) is used in the New Testament, the overwhelming majority occurs in Paul's writings—109 times. The word is only found 31 times in the gospels: 24 times in the writings of Luke and 7 times in the writings of John.[61] It is also found in the epistles of James, Peter, and Jude.[62] In the actual sayings of Christ, *charis* is used only 5 times (all in Luke), and *never* in the technical sense sometimes used by Paul.[63]

Etymologically, it carried a rather wide range of denotations and connotations throughout the New Testament. In an objective sense, it referred to a graceful, favorable, or beautiful appearance—anything that brought delight to a person, including a work of art, a scenic view, or a well-written piece of prose or poetry (for example, see Luke 4:22; Col. 4:6). In the subjective sense, it denoted the favor, delight, or pleasure that either a giver or receiver felt for another beloved person (for example, see Luke 2:40; Acts 11:23).[64] On the giver's part, it denoted the goodwill, favor, and kindness that moved him or her to act in behalf of the receiver (for example, see Acts 7:9–10; 2 Cor. 1:15). On the receiver's part, it referred to his or her sense of gratitude and thankfulness toward the giver (for example, see Rom. 6:17; 1 Tim. 1:12; and 3 John 1:4 [translated as "joy"]).[65] It is not surprising that the term was often equated with the noun χαρά (*chara*), "joy," for this emotion exactly described the reaction of the one who came under grace.[66]

---

60. In 2 Cor. 8 and 9, χάρις (*charis*) occurs ten times with a remarkable number of different meanings including "offerings" (8:19), an increase in goods (9:8), the disposition of the givers (8:6), the power of God that provides that disposition (8:1; 9:14), the Savior's condescension (8:9), and Paul's thanksgiving (8:16; 9:15).

61. The word is found in Luke 2:40; 6:32–34; 7:47; 17:9; Acts 2:47; 4:33; 6:8; 7:10, 46; 11:23; 13:43; 14:3, 26; 15:11, 40; 18:27; 20:24, 32; 24:27; 25:3, 9; where it refers almost exclusively to an attribute of God or Christ. It is found in John 1:14, 16–17 (as an attribute of Jesus that can be shared with others); 2 John 3; 3 John 4; and Rev. 1:4; 22:21.

62. It is found in James 4:6; 1 Pet. 1:2, 10, 13; 2:19, 20; 3:7; 4:10; 5:5, 10, 12; 2 Pet. 1:2; 3:18; and Jude 1:4.

63. In Luke 6:32–34, where it is used three times, the word carries the sense of "what credit is that to you?" In Luke 7:47, it means "on account of" or "for which reason." In Luke 17:9, it means "to thank."

64. Henry G. Liddell and others, eds., *Greek English Lexicon* (Oxford: Clarendon Press, 1968), 1978 (hereafter cited as LSJ); BDAG, 1079–81.

65. LSJ, 1978; BDAG, 1079–81.

66. In Greek poetry, especially, there was little differentiation between *chara* and *charis*. Apolodorus, 244, fragment, 90; BDAG, 1079.

In the New Testament, the word continued to connote, in its broadest sense, anything that was gratifying, pleasing, brought favor, or engendered joy (for example, see Acts 2:47; 4:33; 24:27; 25:3, 9). In its religious sense, it both identified the attractive power within the gospel and that which characterized the beautiful message of salvation (Luke 4:22; Acts 14:3; 15:11; 20:24, 32; Col. 4:6) as well as denoting the pleasing force that attended gospel teachings (Luke 4:22; Acts 18:27).

In "the reciprocity-oriented world dominated by Hellenic influence . . . as well as the Semitic sense of social obligation expressed in the [Hebrew] term [חֶסֶד] *hesed*," it took on a near technical quality, denoting "that which one grants to another, the action of one who volunteers to do someth[ing] not otherwise obligatory."[67] Specifically, it denoted a generous gift that was given freely and graciously, but with emphasis on "freely."[68]

This nuance is the basis of the word's spiritual context. It referred to God's positive predisposition as expressed in his acts of kindness, good will, and his empowerment of his children (Rom. 3:24; 5:15, 20–21; 11:5; Gal. 2:16; Eph. 1:6; 2:5, 7–8; 2 Thes. 2:16; Titus 2:11; 3:7; Heb. 2:9; 4:16). In this connection, God's grace predates their goodness or righteousness. Indeed, it depended on neither. No one earns, deserves, or merits God's grace. He loves his children even when they are yet in their sins (1 John 4:19) and, therefore, reaches out to them with the plan of redemption and the help of spiritual power and the attendant gifts.[69]

The heart of the word, then, pointed to the beneficial acts of the Father and the Son to realize their objectives for humankind, the greatest of which is eternal life (John 3:16; Moses 1:39). To bring about this end, both bestowed free gifts (Rom. 5:15; 2 Cor. 1:12; 2 Thes. 1:12). Some of these gifts came in recognition of the gracious actions of certain persons, which brought them into favor with others (for example, see Acts 7:10; 14:26) and, thereby, with the divine (Matt. 5:3–11; Luke 1:30; Acts 13:43; Rom. 5:2; 1 Pet. 5:12; 2 Pet. 3:18).[70] Being in such favor, they received God's grace (2 Cor. 8:6, 19), which gave them the power and skills necessary for the ministry (3:10; Rom. 1:5; 12:6–8; 15:15; Gal. 2:9; Eph. 3:2, 7).[71]

---

67. BDAG, 1079.

68. Louw-Nida, §57.103.

69. Robinson, *Believing Christ*, 61. The most important gift was his Son, John 3:16–17.

70. The word translated as "blessed" in Matt. 5:3–11 is *makarios*. The adjective describes the state of one who is happy due to the favorable circumstances in which he finds himself. Louw-Nida, §25.119.

71. Hans Conzelmann and Walther Zimmerli, "χάρις, χαρίζομαι, χαριτόω, ἀχάριστος," in *TDNT*, 9:372–402; BDAG, 1079–81.

Because the New Testament sets grace in contrast to a debt (Rom. 4:4), works (Rom. 11:6; 2 Tim. 1:9), and the law (John 1:17), it stressed grace's free and spontaneous character as a response of God's redemptive mercy and compassion (Rom. 6:14).[72] Paul recognized and expanded on these themes and used them as the central concept that explained how salvation was possible.

In its passive sense, *charis* described the feelings of thanksgiving and gratitude on the part of the recipient for the wonderful gifts and associated blessings God bestowed upon him or her (15:57; Rom. 6:17; 7:25; 2 Cor. 8:16; 9:15).[73] Thus, the word's use at the beginning and closing of most of the New Testament epistles carried the author's wish for divine favor to be with his audience.[74]

In summary, two components come out of the etymology of the word that must continually play in the background to fully appreciate the doctrine of grace and its role in the salvation process. The first is that grace expresses itself as unearned and unmerited divine favor that is often expressed with a gift that makes way for other valued gifts. For example, "God so loved the world, that he gave his only begotten Son, that whosoever believeth in him should not perish, but have everlasting life" (John 3:16). The Father's giving of the Son was an act of sheer grace. That valuable gift opened the way for another gift. Jesus identified it when he said, "Greater love hath no man than this, that a man lay down his life for his friends" (John 15:13). The Savior's submission to the cross gave humankind the gift of universal, immortal, and physical life as well as the potential for exaltation, another act of sheer grace. These two acts of grace opened the door to yet other divine gifts, the greatest being godhood, for of those who keep their covenants: "it is written, they are gods. . . . Wherefore, all things are theirs, whether life or death, or things present, or things to come, all are theirs" (D&C 76:58–59; compare D&C 132:20, 37).

The second component is the close relationship of *charis* to χαρά (*chara*), "joy." The use of *charis* implies that *chara* accompanies the giving or the receiving of the gift or favor. The two should, therefore, not be separated. It must be noted, however, that *chara*, "joy," does not necessarily equate

---

72. John R. Kohlenberger III, contributor, *Hebrew and Aramaic Dictionary* accompanying James Strong, *The New Strong's Expanded Exhaustive Concordance of the Bible* (Nashville: Thomas Nelson Publishers, 2001), §2587.

73. Conzelmann and Zimmerli, "χάρις, χαρίζομαι, χαριτόω, ἀχάριστος," in *TDNT*, 9:372–402; BDAG, 1079–81.

74. BDAG, 1079.

with happiness. Indeed, it stands apart from either ἱλαρότης (*hilarotēs*) or μακαρισμός (*makarismos*), both nouns denoting aspects of "happiness."[75] When Lehi explained the reason for God's creation of humankind, he stated that "men are, that they might have joy" (2 Ne. 2:25). He did not say "happiness." As one LDS scholar noted, this noun "describes the feeling associated with a state of well-being. When that state is unachieved, threatened, or disrupted, we are not happy. Joy [on the other hand] is the agreeable emotion which accompanies the possession, acquisition, or expectation of something good or very desirable. Joy can, but does not necessarily, arise out of present circumstances. We can also feel joy over something we anticipate." A person can also feel joy in anticipating or in actually giving a gift or favor. This scholar went on to note that "happiness relies heavily on the present; joy much less so. Joy adds the dimension of acquisition and continuance to happiness."[76] "Those who have died in Jesus Christ," Joseph Smith taught, "may expect to enter into all that fruition of joy when they come forth [in the resurrection], which they possessed here."[77] Thus, the future will bequeath a fulness of the joy that was either won or anticipated in the present. "The Savior himself endured all things, including the cross, 'for the joy that was set before him' (Heb. 12:2). . . . What we must understand is that sometimes we have to forsake *happiness* for the moment so we can experience lasting *joy* in the future."[78] Nonetheless, joy awaits. It can be both expressed and experienced in the present through acts of grace.

Charis in the Epistles of Paul

Paul uses the word *charis* ten times in 1 Corinthians, where it is translated in the KJV as "thanks" (15:57), "liberality" (16:3), and "grace" (1:3; 10:30), but mostly, it describes the selfless, giving attribute of the Father or the Son (1:4; 3:10; 15:10; 16:23).

Among those influenced by Hellenistic thought, it also denoted a favor done in order to put another in one's debt—the greater the favor the more obliged the receiver was (Luke 17:9; Acts 24:27).[79] Being, as Paul says, "an

---

75. Louw-Nida, §25.116, 118.

76. Richard D. Draper, *A Fulness of Joy* (American Fork, Utah: Covenant Communications, 2002), 6–7.

77. Smith, *History of the Church*, 5:362.

78. Draper, *Fulness of Joy*, 7; italics added.

79. LSJ, 1979; Louw-Nida, §57.103.

Hebrew of the Hebrews" (Philip. 3:5), however, he would have been more influenced in his understanding of the word by the Old Testament.[80] There it means, first and foremost, God's deep and abiding favor toward his children that causes him to act to their benefit.

Jewish Influence

Looking at the Septuagint, where the word *charis* is found over 150 times, three Hebrew words gave color to its meaning. These were רַחוּם (*raḥûm*), חַנּוּן (*ḥannûn*), and חֶסֶד (*ḥesed*) with their related forms. The adjective *raḥûm* denoted a positive inclination toward someone based on feelings of compassion and love.[81] The adjective *ḥannûn* was used exclusively to describe divine graciousness.[82] The related word חֵן (*ḥēn*) described all that was agreeable or pleasant and included such things as the way a person, especially a woman, looked or spoke (Prov. 11:16; 22:11; compare Ps. 45:2), but more specifically the favor given by one to another. That favor, however, was sustained only so long as the giver desired. Thus, it could be withdrawn unilaterally at any time.[83] This aspect served to round out the idea of divine grace and served as a warning to God's people not to take it for granted.

Of the three defining words, the noun *ḥesed* carried the greater weight. Its connotations included mercy, devotion, and especially loving kindness.[84] It presumed (1) a lasting relationship, (2) the demands of rights and obligations on the part of all parties in the relationship, and (3) the sincerity and

---

80. This would have been most likely the Septuagint, but with heavy Aramaic and Hebrew influence.

81. Frances Brown, Samuel R. Driver, and Charles A. Briggs, *A Hebrew and English Lexicon of the Old Testament* (1952; rpt., Oxford: Clarendon Press, 1987), 933 (hereafter cited as BDB).

82. BDB, 337.

83. BDB, 336; G. Johannes Botterweck and Helmer Ringgren, ed., *Theological Dictionary of the Old Testament,* trans. David E. Green, 15 vols. (Grand Rapids, Mich.: Eerdmans, 1986), 5:22–36.

84. BDB, 338. L. Koehler, W. Baumgartner, and J. J. Stamm, *The Hebrew and Aramaic Lexicon of the Old Testament,* trans. and ed. M. E. J. Richardson, 5 vols. (Leiden: E. J. Brill, 1994–2000), 336–37 (hereafter cited as *HAL*), defines it as a " joint obligation between relatives, friends, host and guest, master and servant." It means "closeness, solidarity, loyalty," especially "lasting loyalty" and "faithfulness." With God it expresses his "relationship with the people or an individual" and means "faithfulness, goodness," and "graciousness" but includes "godly action" and "achievements." Specifically it is God's "proofs of mercy."

devotion that all participants should have in maintaining the relationship.[85] Between humans, it pointed to a very willing show of favor and kindness. It made it possible for a weaker party to seek protection or favor from a stronger to which it had no claim. Through *ḥesed,* the stronger party remained "committed to his promise, but retains his freedom, especially in regard to the manner in which he [would] implement its promises."[86]

The one receiving *ḥesed,* however, was expected to respond with similar *ḥesed* (for example, see Gen. 21:23; Josh. 2:12, 14; 1 Sam. 20:8, 14–16). This suggests that in cases where the mutuality was not specifically mentioned, it still operated behind the scenes. Though the giver gave freely without obligation, the receiver was expected to return the favor either toward the giver or to others.[87]

This aspect was the seat of God's covenant making with his people. By this means they became his people and came under his protection, but more importantly, keeping the covenant was an assurance that they would be engaged in his work. Motivated by loving kindness, Jehovah set down the rights, duties, and obligations of both parties and stressed the reciprocal nature of the agreed upon relationship. In short, *ḥesed* undergirded the rules within which all were to operate. Through the covenant, each party clearly understood its obligations, responsibilities, and expectations. On Jehovah's part, he would be the people's God (Lev. 26:12; Ex. 19:5), watching over them and sharing with them his power (Gen. 17:1–8; Abr. 2:8–11). His people were to obey his commandments, including pushing forward his work (Gen. 28:14; Deut. 28:2; Isa. 49:6; Abr. 2:11). It was also the force that assured his people that he would keep his word.[88]

When describing the divine, the word connoted Jehovah's central characteristic.[89] Loving kindness was a permanent part of his nature (Deut. 7:9; Ps. 136:1–26; compare Deut. 5:10; Ex. 20:6). It had three main components: strength,[90] steadfastness, and love. It was his omnipotence, his

---

85. Botterweck, *Theological Dictionary,* 5:44–64.

86. Kohlenberger, *Hebrew and Aramaic Dictionary* §2617.

87. Kohlenberger, *Hebrew and Aramaic Dictionary,* §2617.

88. Kohlenberger, *Hebrew and Aramaic Dictionary,* §2617; Botterweck, *Theological Dictionary,* 5:44–64.

89. In this sense the aspect of love dominates. See Deut. 4:37; Isa. 63:7; Jer. 31:3; John 3:16; 16:27; Rom. 5:8; 2 Cor. 13:11; 1 John 3:1; 4:7; 1 Ne. 11:22.

90. A primitive nuance of the word connoted strength or permanence. This is its force in Isa. 40:6, "All flesh is grass, and all the goodliness [*ḥesed*] thereof is as the flower of the field."

constancy, and his abundant "loving kindness" through which redemption came from troubles, enemies, and especially sin (for example, see Ex. 34:6; Neh. 9:17; Ps. 103:8; Jonah 4:2).

However, the word also implied a personal involvement in that relationship that went beyond—indeed, transcended—the rules. That is to say, rules were not the binding factors, God's love was. Because Jehovah's *ḥesed* went beyond the covenant, he would not necessarily have abandoned it even if the covenant people proved unfaithful and must, therefore, come under his censure (Isa. 54:8, 10).[91]

Its association with covenant making shows that *ḥesed* was something more than God's general love for all his creatures. It was, rather, his specific and focused positive feeling he had toward those who entered into and kept covenant with him. It was through his concrete acts of faithfulness and of extending mercy (generally expressed in the plural; for example, see Isa. 55:3) that Jehovah fulfilled his covenant promise of redemption.[92] Because its "final triumph and implementation is eschatological, the word nuances the goal and end of all salvation-history (Ps. 85:7, 10–11; 130:7; Mic. 7:20)."[93]

The word also denoted, on the part of those under the covenant, the deep feeling of respect and care they were to have toward their Maker. Those who possessed it strove to keep the ethical and moral requirements asked by Jehovah. The word was, therefore, used in the sense of covenantal love. In the Old Testament, it expressed itself most forcefully in an individual's commitment to the divine covenant (for example, see Hosea 6:6; Micah 6:8).

In a related sense, it was Jehovah who brought about the feeling of *ḥesed* in others in behalf of his favored ones.[94] Therefore, even though this was a divine quality, humans could feel and even possess it as an impartation from God. They expressed it, in turn, in reciprocal acts of kindness and loyalty to God (for example, see Jer. 2:2) and to other humans (for example, see 2 Sam. 9:7). All this stands in the background of Paul's use of the word *charis*.

---

91. Kohlenberger, *Hebrew and Aramaic Dictionary,* §2617.

92. Kohlenberger, *Hebrew and Aramaic Dictionary,* §2617.

93. Kohlenberger, *Hebrew and Aramaic Dictionary,* §2617; Botterweck, *Theological Dictionary,* 44–64.

94. For example see Gen. 39:21; Ezra 7:28; Esth. 2:8–10, 17; Dan. 1:9; where each describes a situation in which the favor shown to the subject is not ascribed to their own actions, but tacitly to Jehovah.

The Pauline Setting of Grace

The Apostle (and others) set grace in contrast to a debt (Rom. 4:4), works (Rom. 11:6; 2 Tim. 1:9), and the law (John 1:17), stressing its free and spontaneous character as a reflection of God's redemptive mercy and compassion (Rom. 6:14). Paul recognized and expanded on these. For the Apostle, *charis* was the central concept that explained how salvation was possible. It undergirded the new or restored covenant established by Christ (11:25; 2 Cor. 3:6; Heb. 8:8; 9:15). In his writings, Paul shows this understanding of the term. It is, first, God's divine loving kindness and its objective demonstration for all men, specifically in giving his Son and in the Son's submission to the cross (1:23; Rom. 4:25; 2:2). It is, second, the special proof of that loving kindness as imparted to Christians, bringing justification and the gifts of the Spirit (12:4–7; Rom. 3:20–28; 5:9, 18). It is, third, the personal possession of an enabling power (2 Cor. 8:1; 9:8, 14; compare 1 Cor. 4:1; 15:10); and, fourth, it is, in the Christian, his service as empowered by divine grace (2 Cor. 8:4, 6, 7, 10; compare 1 Cor. 16:3).

For Paul, in its deepest theological sense, *charis* refers to God's positive predisposition to favor and bless his children. But, because God's actions are motivated by grace, they are freely given (Rom. 4:4; 11:6). The core meaning of *charis* as "a gift" should always be remembered. Indeed, grace is expressed through a gift, gesture, or benefit that is neither merited nor earned. Therefore, since God calls a person to grace—that is, God gives it to him (Gal. 1:6, 15)—the individual has no claim on it nor is it given because he deserves it. Rather, it predates the individual's goodness or righteousness and is extended to him even as a sinner (Rom. 3:23–25; 5:10; 1 John 4:19; compare Rom. 11:32; Gal. 2:17–21). Its power, however, is displayed in the overcoming of sin (Rom. 5:20–21). It is important to understand that grace is *unilateral and independent of the receiver.* In every case, God makes the first move. It is this that makes it possible for the individual to *respond* graciously and so move "from grace to grace" (D&C 93, heading). But the absolutely essential element of that transaction is that God moves *first* in each instance, giving the person gracious gifts and then additional gifts, rather than the person first exercising his or her goodness and then being rewarded with earned blessings.[95]

Grace expressed itself most clearly in the justification of the sinner—that is, in God's forgiving the sin and then imputing righteousness to the

---

95. Robinson, *Believing Christ*, 61.

forgiven one (Rom. 4:6, 11, 21–25; compare Ps. 32:2). The result was that the person not only stood innocent before the law but also stood fully righteous. Grace was, therefore, both the basis of justification and its manifestation. Justification, however, was not the object of grace—the salvation of the sinner was. Justification was but one part of the salvation process. Paramount was faith in Jesus Christ. It was that faith, expressed even though the person was yet weak and in his sins, which brought the grace that resulted in justification (Rom. 3:22–31; 4:11–20; 5:1–2).

The idea of "salvation by faith" excludes, therefore, the works of the Law as a means of salvation because the Law stands opposed to it. Indeed, it is the antithesis of *pistis kai charis*, "faith and grace" (Rom. 6:14–16; Gal. 2:21; 5:4). The doctrine of grace, therefore, does not support man's striving for good on his own as the means of gaining eternal life. Instead, it evidences that any attempt to stand on one's own is futile. In Romans 3:24, Paul makes it clear that a person is "justified *freely* [*dōrean*] by [God's] grace through the redemption that is in Christ Jesus." The adverb δωρεάν (*dōrean*) refers "to being freely given, *as a gift, without payment, gratis.*"[96] The JST replaces "freely" with "only" in this verse and thereby emphasizes the central and exclusive role grace plays in the salvation process.

The Apostle understood, however, that grace included a person doing his part. Paul did not attempt to move his readers from the law of works to a state of lawlessness. Rather, he gave them the alternative of living by a new law, the "law of faith" (Rom. 3:27). This law centered on faith in Christ and doing his will. The Lord himself insisted that those who follow him must live the commandments (see Matt. 7:21; Luke 9:23; John 14:15). He stated very clearly, "He that hath my commandments, and keepeth them, he it is that loveth me: and he that loveth me shall be loved of my father, and I will love him" (John 14:21). The Apostle was very specific in saying that a person must work out his own salvation "with fear and trembling" (Philip. 2:12). In the very next verse, however, he says that "it is God which worketh in you both to will and to do of his good pleasure" (Philip. 2:13). According to Paul, each person must not fight against the grace that God extends to him or her. All must choose to be changed. For that reason, each person plays the central and critical role in his or her personal salvation by accepting the extended grace with all the solemnity and seriousness it deserves.

---

96. BDAG, 266; LSJ, 464, "as a free gift, freely."

In sum, Paul specifically used the term to describe how God made salvation possible. At its base, *charis* carried the sense of making one glad through a gift that betokened an expression of free unmerited favor. It was the freedom in the giving that constituted the gift's essence. There was no compulsion, obligation, sense of duty, or even merit behind the act (Rom. 3:24–25; 4:1–3; 5:10, 15, 17; compare Rom. 3:23; Gal. 2:17–21; 1 John 4:10). In God's case, it was a pure expression of divine love. That love took its final and ultimate form in the Atonement of the Savior. Thus, on the cross, grace was actualized (Gal. 2:15–21) because the Savior gave, as a gift, his life that all may live and, for those who kept the covenants, be exalted. Further, God's favor was also actualized in the gift of his Son. The Atonement is, then, an actual demonstration of what grace is and how it was ultimately expressed by the divine.

Grace in a Latter-day Saint Context

Before discussing the idea of grace in its LDS context, it is paramount to note that the Savior's Atonement is central, fundamental, and foundational in LDS theology. "It provides meaning and purpose of every other doctrine and every covenant and ordinance."[97] The Atonement was the supernal act of grace and, indeed, through it grace became actualized. By the grace of God and Christ, a person can be forgiven of sin (2 Ne. 2:6, 26; Mosiah 27:24–26; Alma 5:21; 11:40; Hel. 5:10), reconciled to God (Rom. 5:10; 2 Cor. 5:18; Jacob 4:11), resurrected (15:21; Rom. 6:5; 2 Cor. 1:9; Philip. 3:21; Alma 11:44; 40:23), redeemed from death and hell (Mosiah 15:22–24; Hel. 14:15–17; Morm. 9:2–13), and brought back into God's presence (Hel. 14:15; Morm. 9:13; Ether 3:13; D&C 76:62, 94, 118; 121:32).

For centuries, among some Christian adherents, a misunderstanding of Paul's teachings has introduced the idea of an "easy grace," which guarantees salvation with nothing more than a personal confession of Christ as one's Savior. Though fully accepting the Atonement, the early Latter-day Saints rejected the idea of an "easy grace" with its accompanying threat of antinomianism. Their stance bequeathed to the generations that followed an emphasis on "works righteousness" as the necessary means of salvation.[98]

---

97. Millet, *Grace Works*, 2.

98. This was the term used by Martin Luther. He did not believe that "works righteousness" assisted in salvation. See Martin Luther, "Two Kinds of Righteousness," in *Martin Luther: Selections from His Writings,* ed. John Dillenberger (New York: Anchor Books, 1961), 87.

Such a stance, however, did not contradict the New Testament. Indeed, it reflected Paul's own teaching as revealed in his question, "What shall we say then? Shall we continue in sin, that grace may abound? God forbid" (Rom. 6:1–2).[99] Neither in Paul nor in LDS theology does deliberate sin invoke grace. But neither in Paul nor in LDS theology does "works righteousness" preclude grace. Nonetheless, the stress among many of the Saints continues to be that righteous works are the main ingredient in exaltation.

Over the last few decades, a number of Latter-day Saint authorities and scholars have begun addressing the idea of grace and the role it plays in an individual's salvation. Some of other faiths, taking note of what is happening in the Church, have expressed delight that it is, at last, taking seriously the idea of God's mercy and grace.[100] Critics, on the other hand, have insisted that the LDS position is but "a convenient eclecticism." That, however, is not the case. It is, rather, "a repossession [through the Restoration] of a New Testament understanding that reconciles Paul and James."[101] Even so, some confusion yet exists allowing for differences in understanding as to just what grace is and how it operates.

Saved by Grace after All We Can Do

The major misunderstanding concerning grace comes from a misinterpretation of 2 Nephi 25:23, "it is by grace that we are saved, after all we can do." Usually, this phrase is interpreted to mean that grace becomes active only after a person has done absolutely everything he or she can, and even then grace functions only to make up the difference between effort and success. There are a number of problems with this view. First, since, theoretically, we can always do more than we are doing, we could never qualify for such grace. Second, God has already acted. For example, he did not wait until we had done all we could before he provided the basis and means of salvation, or executed the plan of salvation and revealed it to humankind, or gave the gift of his Son. Third, Christ has already acted. He did not wait until we had done all we could before atoning for all sin, or making reconciliation and redemption possible. Further, he has not waited until we have done all we can before bequeathing the gifts of the Spirit with their

99. Millet, "Perils of Grace," 7–19.

100. Millet, *Grace Works*, v.

101. John Dillenberger, "Grace and Works in Martin Luther and Joseph Smith," in *Reflections on Mormonism: Judaeo-Christian Parallels,* ed. Truman G. Madsen (Provo, Utah: Religious Studies Center, 1978), 175.

enabling powers—powers that invest us with the ability to do whatever is necessary. Indeed, the Lord often gives the Spirit to help a soul overcome weakness and grow spiritually. He does not wait until they are strong and then give it.

Some mistakenly believe that they really can do all that is required and thereby either earn or merit exaltation, but the truth is no one can. According to the scriptures, all are unprofitable servants and will be as long as they are in mortality (Luke 17:10; Mosiah 2:21; Hel. 12:7–8; compare Rom. 3:23). But no one is asked to be profitable; simply to be loving and faithful. God is easy to please and impossible to satisfy (at least until we reach his stage of perfection and holiness). Pleasing God, for now, is enough, and his grace will attend us.

To earn or even merit salvation, a person would have to put God in his or her debt. This is impossible, as King Benjamin emphasized to his subjects. "If ye do keep his commandments he doth bless you and prosper you," he said. "And now, in the first place, he hath created you, and granted unto you your lives, for which ye are indebted unto him. And secondly, he doth require that ye should do as he hath commanded you; for which if ye do, he doth immediately bless you; and therefore he hath paid you. And ye are still indebted unto him, and are, and will be, forever" (Mosiah 2:22–24).

Because all are continually indebted to God, salvation cannot be earned and, therefore, must be free (2 Ne. 2:4). As Nephi testified, Jesus "hath given it free for all men . . . and none are forbidden" (2 Ne. 26:27–28). It is God's gift and all a person has to do is accept it and enter into a covenant with the Lord and strive to keep his or her promises.[102] Though "the Lord cannot look upon sin with the least degree of allowance" (D&C 1:31), he exercises his grace by accepting a person's striving for fully keeping the law.

Humility allows the Saint to recognize this and gain a proper attitude. As one LDS scholar noted, "It is necessary to live in a state of divine indebtedness, in a condition of always acknowledging the goodness and greatness of God as well as our utter helplessness without him. Inextricably linked to this truth is the need to love and serve others, particularly those in need. That is how we 'remain guiltless' before God (Mosiah 4:25)."[103]

The point is, God's grace operates all the time. It does not activate only when a person has done all he or she can. As one LDS scholar noted, God "can and does help us all along the way. Nephi seems to be emphasizing

---

102. Millet, *Grace Works*, 13.
103. Millet, *Grace Works*, 81.

that no matter how much we do, it simply will not be enough to guarantee salvation without Christ's intervention [2 Ne. 25:23]. To paraphrase Nephi, above and beyond all we can do, it is by the grace of Christ that we are saved. And what is true of our ultimate salvation is true of our daily walk and talk, of our personality and our passions. Above and beyond all our efforts at self-control, behavior modification, or reducing our sins to manageable categories, 'everything which really needs to be done on our souls can be done only by God.'"[104] Alma 24:10–12 suggests that all we can really do anyway is "come before the Lord in reverent humility, confess our weakness, and plead for his forgiveness, for his mercy and grace."[105]

Joseph Smith on Grace

The doctrine of grace was not something Joseph Smith paid much attention to. He addressed the concept only four times in his recorded sermons. The impetus for his first foray into the subject likely came from an extended piece written by Brigham Young and Willard Richards and published in the *Millennial Star,* titled "Election and Reprobation." The Prophet noted it was "one of the sweetest pieces that has been written in these last days" and had it copied verbatim into his history.[106] One of the reasons these two Apostles wrote it was to "prevent the necessity of repeating a thousand times" the answer to the question, "Do you believe in election and reprobation?"[107]

During Joseph Smith's day, the subject generated a lot of attention in both England and the United States. Interest was largely due to debates that raged between Methodists and Presbyterians. The latter (along with the Calvinists and Dutch Reformed) championed a strong monergism. According to this view, the Holy Spirit produced God's effective work in bringing about the salvation of an individual enacting an instantaneous

---

104. Millet, *Grace Works,* 131, quoting C. S. Lewis, *Mere Christianity: An Anniversary Edition of the Three Books The Case for Christianity, Christian Behavior, and Beyond Personality* (New York; Macmillan, 1981), 164.

105. Millet, *Grace Works,* 132. Robinson, *Believing Christ,* 90–91, puts it this way: The preposition "after" acts as "a preposition of separation rather than a preposition of time. It denotes logical separateness rather than temporal sequence. We are saved by grace 'apart from all we can do,' or 'all we can do notwithstanding.' Another acceptable paraphrase of the sense of the verse might read, 'We are still saved by grace after all is said and done.'"

106. Smith, *History of the Church,* 4:256–66.

107. Smith, *History of the Church,* 4:256.

and unilateral spiritual regeneration in the person without that person's cooperation. Grace was undeniable, irresistible, and free to the extent that it worked even if a person did not seek or even want it. Further, once a person was in this state of grace, he or she could never fall.

Conversely, the Methodists insisted on a strong synergism. In this view, in its simplest form, the individual had to yield to the call of God and cooperate with his grace. Regeneration was a process that began with a person's response to God's gracious outreach and required faith, repentance, and loving service to the Father and his mortal children. This state of grace could be easily lost through sin, but also easily regained through repentance. Unfortunately, it was difficult to know whether one was in or out of grace. As a result, it was possible for a person to be saved in ignorance of his condition.

It was in February 1841 (a month after Joseph Smith read the article by the Apostles Young and Richards) when the Prophet first addressed the subject of grace. He did so in connection with a point concerning the doctrine of the Fall. He noted that the Lord appointed humankind not only to fall but also to be redeemed. To explain how redemption took place, the Prophet quoted Paul, "Where sin abounded [due to the fall], grace did much more abound" due to the Atonement (Rom. 5:20). He quoted Paul further to make the point that "when we were enemies, we were reconciled to God by the death of his Son, much more, being reconciled, we shall be saved by his life" (Rom. 5:10).[108] From this statement, it is clear that the Prophet saw that redemption centered on the Lord's Atonement. It was through the grace that it activated that sinners could repent and be reconciled to God. Grace preceded any action on the part of the recipient.

His second foray into the subject took place just three months later, in May 1841. In a revelation he received in September 1832, he learned that there would be a future redemption of Israel "according to the election of grace, which was brought to pass by the faith and covenant of the fathers" (D&C 84:99). He now expounded on the subject. Using Romans 9 as his text, he explained that election by grace pertained to the flesh and specifically to Abraham's seed. It consisted of having the keys of "adoption, and the covenants" by which future Israel would become "the 'ministers of our

---

108. McIntire Minute Book, entry for February 9, 1841, as quoted in Andrew F. Ehat and Lyndon W. Cook, comps. and eds., *The Words of Joseph Smith: The Contemporary Accounts of the Nauvoo Discourses of the Prophet Joseph,* Religious Studies Monograph Series, no. 6 (Provo, Utah: Religious Studies Center, Brigham Young University, 1980), 63.

God.'" However, the Prophet stressed, the promise was corporate, not individual. It pertained to the house of Israel as a whole and to the priesthood in general. Therefore, Joseph Smith concluded, the idea taught by some sectarians of a personal and unconditional election to eternal life was not a doctrine taught by the early Apostles.[109]

His third foray into the subject did not take place for another three years. He raised it again to counter some sectarians who were justifying sin on the basis that grace would then abound. He categorically denied any truth to this antinomian heresy. Deliberate and unrepentant sin, he insisted, did not invoke divine grace.[110]

Calvinist ideas continued to stir through the area and, therefore, a few months later he again returned to the subject for the fourth and final time. Because this sermon was recorded in some detail, it clearly shows his understanding of grace and where it fit in the greater theological context.

The Prophet introduced the subject by noting the conflict that existed between the Methodists and Presbyterians concerning grace. Joseph Smith objected to the position of both, insisting that they were too extreme and that "truth takes the road between them." The truth, he taught, came from understanding the power and function of the sealing keys revealed by Elijah the prophet.[111] Through these, what was sealed on earth was also sealed in heaven. By this means the faithful could be sealed into eternal life, thus making their calling and election sure. On the other hand, the unfaithful could "be sealed by the spirit of Elijah unto the damnation of hell until the day of the Lord."[112] The Prophet turned to Hebrews 6:4–8 to confirm his point: If those who "have tasted the good word of God, and the powers of the world to come" should fall away, they could not be redeemed. The Prophet summarized this point stating that it was totally possible for a person, once under grace, to lose that grace and fall away, "for the power of Elijah cannot seal against this sin [that is, betraying the Lord], for this is a reservation made in the seals and power of the priesthood."[113]

---

109. *Times and Seasons* 2 (June 1, 1841): 430. The Calvinists and Presbyterians championed this view.

110. The entry is made in Smith, *History of the Church,* 4:494, for January 16, 1844. The original statement is likely from the "Book of the Law of the Lord."

111. For the context, see D&C 110 and 131:5–6.

112. Smith, *History of the Church,* 6:252. Spelling has been standardized in this quote.

113. Wilford Woodruff Diary, entry March 10, 1844, as quoted in Ehat and Cook, *Words of Joseph Smith,* 331. Spelling and grammar have been standardized.

In the Prophet's context, to be under grace constituted having one's calling and election assured by receiving the more sure word of prophecy, which, he said, "means a man's knowing that he is sealed up unto eternal life, by revelation and the spirit of prophecy, through the power of the Holy Priesthood." Then, taking a swipe at the Methodists, he noted that "it is impossible for a man to be saved in ignorance" (D&C 131:5–6). But being under grace did not mean one could never lose it. Rebellion would forfeit heaven.

Two Aspects of Grace

The Universal Aspect

This aspect of grace is unconditional and unilateral with the recipients playing no part in the gift. It applies to all whether they ask for or even want it. In no way will they have earned, merited, or deserved this gift, nor are they the impetus or controlling force behind God's action. The following are eight examples of this aspect of grace: birth as a child of God, the gift of God's Son, Christ's atoning for Adam's transgression, the saving of children who die before they are accountable, the revealing of the gospel and plan of salvation, the restoration of priesthood power with its attendant keys, the establishment of covenants and ordinances, and the universal, physical resurrection.[114]

God's greatest universal gift was the gift of his Son. "Justice did not require that the Father provide a Savior, nor did justice require that Jesus Christ offer to be that Savior and suffer in our place to redeem us. When he saw our weakness, our peril, and our need, his love and compassion for us moved him to offer his intervention—to volunteer."[115] No one forced Jesus to make an atonement. He was in no one's debt. Indeed, as Paul stated, when we were yet enemies to God (that is, natural men and women, see Mosiah 3:19), "we were reconciled to God by the death of his Son" (Rom. 5:10). Or, as John put it, "Herein is love, not that we loved God, but that he loved us, and sent his Son to be the propitiation for our sins" (1 John 4:10).

One is saved "because of the righteousness of [the] Redeemer" (2 Ne. 2:3), for "there is no flesh that can dwell in the presence of God, save it be through the merits, and mercy, and grace of the Holy Messiah" (2 Ne. 2:8). Indeed, God can take away "the guilt from our hearts, through the merits of

---

114. Robinson, *Believing Christ,* 63–64.
115. Robinson, *Believing Christ,* 66; italics in original removed.

his Son" (Alma 24:10). Therefore, "if ye believe on his name ye will repent of all your sins, that thereby ye may have a remission of them through his merits" (Hel. 14:13; compare D&C 3:20).

The point is that reconciliation does not come from some merit on humankind's part. A person cannot "merit anything of himself; but the sufferings and death of Christ atone for their sins" (Alma 22:14). As one LDS scholar noted, "It is, in fact, the sufferings and death and resurrection of Christ that make possible true spiritual progress."[116] All must, therefore, rely "alone upon the merits of Christ, who was the author and the finisher of [our] faith" (Moro. 6:4). The Restoration gives people access to the gospel and, thereby, to be able to "rely upon the merits of Jesus Christ, and be glorified through faith in his name" (D&C 3:20).

The Nonuniversal Aspect

This aspect is reactive, responsive, and conditional on human behavior. It applies only to those who want it and exercise the works of faith (Rom. 3:27). The following are five examples of nonuniversal grace: payment for personal sin, the gift of the Holy Ghost, the gifts of the Spirit, the gift of enabling power, and finally, exaltation.

Through this aspect of grace, individuals "receive strength and assistance to do good works that they otherwise would not be able to maintain if left to their own means. This grace is an enabling power that allows men and women to lay hold on eternal life."[117] We participate in the process of salvation because it does have its conditions. Grace is neither random nor irresistible nor predestined. God clears the path, but he will not force us to walk down it. And why? "What doth it profit a man if a gift is bestowed upon him, and he receive not the gift? Behold, he rejoices not in that which is given unto him, neither rejoices in him who is the giver of the gift" (D&C 88:33). We must consent to exaltation. That means, though God makes the first move, by providing the gospel covenant on the basis of his grace, we must accept it. All have their own free will to choose whether to enter into it (2 Ne. 2:27). It is each person's free choice.[118] Thus, it can be sought after (D&C 46:8; 1 Ne. 10:19; Matt. 7:7–8), increased (Luke 2:52; 1 Pet. 5:5; John 1:16; D&C 93:12–13, 19–20), and even lost (Gal. 1:6; 5:4), but it is always there.[119]

---

116. Millet, *Grace Works*, 43.
117. LDS Bible Dictionary, 697.
118. Robinson, *Believing Christ*, 68.
119. Millet, *Grace Works*, 65.

This is the aspect in which both God and the Saint must play their parts, and this is where the debate comes. Whose part is the most important? C. S. Lewis, on the debate between the importance of grace or works in the salvation process, observed sagely that it "does seem to me like asking which blade in a pair of scissors is most necessary."[120] The Church's emphasis on personal responsibility and the need for self-disciplined obedience has given many of the Saints the feeling that the individual does most of the work. The truth is that exaltation is a team effort, but the greater portion is the Lord's.

On the Relationship between Works and Grace

The scriptures are replete with the insistence that good works are absolutely necessary for eternal life.[121] They are equally clear that works, as necessary as they are, are still insufficient. What are good works for, then, if they are insufficient to save? As an LDS scholar noted, "They are necessary because they evidence our desire to keep our covenant, to be true to our promise to follow the Lord and keep his commandments."[122] He went on to say, "We will be judged according to our works, not according to the merits of our works, but to the extent that our works manifest to God who and what we have *become.*"[123] That is what our works are all about. They reveal not just what we want, but what we want to be. Elder Dallin H. Oaks taught that "the Final Judgment is not just an evaluation of the sum total of good and evil acts—what we have *done.* It is an acknowledgment of the final effect of our acts and thoughts—what we have *become.*"[124] In short, even when the Saints fail to do the requirements perfectly, their consistent determination to try demonstrates two things: first, their willingness to do as the Father wishes, and second, what they really want to become.

Though the works of faith are necessary in the salvation process, "to insist that salvation comes by works alone, that we can earn it ourselves

---

120. Lewis, *Mere Christianity,* 125.

121. The combined witness of the following scriptures overwhelmingly show the necessity of good works in order to achieve exaltation: Ps. 62:11–12; Prov. 24:12; Jer. 17:10; Matt. 7:21; 16:27; Rom. 2:6, 13; 2 Cor. 5:10; Tit. 3:8; James 1:19–22, 26; 1 Pet. 1:17; 1 John 3:18; Rev. 20:12; 1 Ne. 15:32; 2 Ne. 28:23; Mosiah 3:23–24; 16:10; Alma 5:15; 11:41; 12:12; 33:22; 36:5; 41:3; 3 Ne. 26; D&C 20:11.

122. Millet, *Grace Works,* 118.

123. Millet, *Grace Works,* 122; italics in original.

124. Dallin H. Oaks, "The Challenge to Become," *Ensign* 30 (November 2000): 32; italics in original.

without needing the grace of God, insults the mercy of God and mocks the sacrifice of Jesus Christ in our behalf. On the other hand, to insist that salvation comes by belief alone and that God places no other obligations upon the believer insults the justice of God and makes Christ the 'minister of sin' [Gal. 2:17]."[125]

A major premise of the Book of Mormon is that without grace there is no salvation: "It is only in and through the grace of God that ye are saved" (2 Ne. 10:24).[126] The source of this grace is God's favorable predisposition toward his children actualized in the atoning sacrifice of Jesus Christ: "mercy cometh because of the atonement" (Alma 42:23). Accepting the offer of salvation, which God extends though his grace, does not suggest that somehow we either earn or merit it. It ever remains the Lord's free gift to us, whether we partake of it or not. When we do, his "grace is sufficient for" our salvation (Ether 12:27; Moro. 10:32–33). In sum, all must rely *"wholly* upon the merits of him who is mighty to save" (2 Ne. 31:19; italics added) and *"alone* upon the merits of Christ" to be saved (Moro. 6:4; italics added). Thus, as an LDS scholar noted, salvation "is not a matter of self-confidence; it is a matter of confidence in Christ. I have a role in my own salvation, but peace and assurance and hope come because of what Jesus the Redeemer has done and will do to qualify me for life with him one day."[127]

Very often in the Church, the feeling is that grace expresses God's gracious enabling of the Saint to merit or earn what was otherwise out of his or her reach. God sometimes simply gives a gift to the Saint just because he or she needs it, wants it, and asks for it. God, in essence, bridges the gap between what each Saint can do and what is necessary. The problem with this idea is that it is only partially correct. The real problem with it is that no one can earn salvation. Further, it puts the emphasis in the wrong place. Its focus is on the person's works and righteousness rather than of the transforming power that comes from God as the key to gaining eternal life. The point is that if grace isn't free, it's not grace—it's a wage—and those who ascribe to the idea that they can earn grace make salvation something earned by works. Paul ardently fought against this idea.

---

125. Robinson, *Believing Christ,* 70.

126. Compare JST Rom. 3:24, 28, "Being justified only by [God's] grace . . . we conclude that a man is justified by faith alone without the deeds of the law."

127. Millet, *Grace Works,* 128.

It must be emphasized that works do count and greatly so, but God's free gift not only comes first but continually operates, making way for his children to both progress and become new creatures, "changed from their carnal and fallen state, to a state of righteousness, being redeemed of God, becoming his sons and daughters; And thus they are new creatures; and unless they do this, they can in nowise inherit the kingdom of God" (Mosiah 27:25–26). Note that God does not just give each person the opportunity to change, he actually changes them. The change, expressed in both justification and sanctification, comes through the grace of Christ "to all those who love and serve God with all their mights, minds, and strength" (D&C 20:31). Elder B. H. Roberts wrote: "There is an absolute necessity for some additional sanctifying grace that will strengthen poor human nature, not only to enable it to resist temptation, but also to root out from the heart concupiscence—the blind tendency or inclination to evil. . . . Man's natural powers are unequal to the task; . . . Mankind stand in some need of a strength superior to any they possess of themselves, to accomplish this work of rendering pure our fallen nature."[128]

Though it is true that striving to keep the commandments takes practice and that practice does make one ever better at doing a task, practice alone does not suffice. In the parable of the vineyard (Matt. 20:1–16), the emphasis of the story is that, at the end of the day, no matter how long the harvesters worked, each received the same wage. When some complained that their extended efforts had not been taken into account, the good man of the house responded, "Is it not lawful for me to do what I will with mine own? Is thine eye evil, because I am good?" (Matt. 20:15). The parable stresses two very important points: First, and vitally important to the point, only those who worked got the wage. Second, with the exception of the first group (who agreed to the wage), the pay for the rest of the workers was based neither on the length of their efforts nor on the skills brought to the task, nor on what they gained in the process. The pay was based on the grace of the good man of the house.

Likewise, in the parable of the talents (Matt. 25:14–30), the servant who turned five talents into ten and the one who turned two talents into four were both greeted in the same way by the Lord, "Well done, thou good and faithful servant: thou hast been faithful over a few things, I will make thee ruler over many things: enter thou into the joy of thy lord" (Matt. 25:21,

---

128. B. H. Roberts, *The Gospel and Man's Relationship to Deity* (Salt Lake City: Deseret News, 1901), 170.

23). Again, the commendation was based not on the amount of work each had done nor the skills gained in the process. It was based on the grace of their lord.

The point is this: in the process of sanctification, no amount of desire, practice, or work actually brings about the change. What these do is demonstrate to God that the desire and determination is there. "A person's works, then, are the token, always incomplete and imperfect, that join him or her to Christ. But it is Christ who exalts us."[129] "The Atonement does more than fix the mistakes. It does more than balance the scales. It even does more than forgive our sins. It rehabilitates, regenerates, renews, and transforms human nature."[130]

The end of salvation is theosis, the transformation of the human soul into a divine being. This transformation comes through the Divine as an additional endowment of grace, a divine gift that boosts us to a higher level of spirituality and capacity. This enables us to serve ever more freely and lovingly through which we bestow our own grace by freely lifting the Father's other children. The Savior's promise is that, for those who constantly strive to do his will, they "shall receive of his fullness, and be glorified in me as I am in the Father; therefore, I say unto you, you shall receive grace for grace" (D&C 93:20). Thus, the prophet Nephi prayed that God would grant "in his great fulness, that men might be brought unto repentance and good works, that they might be restored unto grace for grace, *according to their works*" (Hel. 12:24, italics added). John bore record that "of his fulness have all we received, and grace for grace. For the law was given by Moses, but grace and truth came by Jesus Christ" (John 1:16–17).

No "Easy" or "Cheap Grace" among the Latter-day Saints

Faith is ever at play in the salvation process, but not as a good deed through which one gets grace as a reward. Rather, it is the faith in Christ that motivates a person to enter into a covenant with him and receive of his grace. The point is, as an LDS scholar noted, "Faith always manifests itself in faithfulness. Salvation may come by grace alone, but grace is never alone."[131] Thus, the Saints reject the idea of "easy" or "cheap grace." They are not alone. As one non-LDS theologian observed:

---

129. Stephen E. Robinson to Richard D. Draper, email, May 12, 2014.
130. Millet, *Grace Works,* 95.
131. Millet, "Perils of Grace," 10.

The more I have examined Jesus' public ministry and His dealings with inquirers, the more apprehensive I have become about the methods and content of contemporary evangelism. On a disturbing number of fronts, the message being proclaimed today is not the gospel according to Jesus.

The gospel in vogue today holds forth a false hope to sinners. It promises them they can have eternal life yet continue to live in rebellion against God. Indeed, it encourages people to claim Jesus as Savior yet defer until later the commitment to obey Him as Lord. It promises salvation from hell but not necessarily freedom from iniquity. It offers false security to people who revel in the sins of the flesh and spurn the way of holiness. By separating faith from faithfulness, it leaves the impression that intellectual ascent is as valid as wholehearted obedience to the truth. Thus the good news of Christ has given way to the bad news of an insidious easy-believism that makes no moral demands on the lives of sinners. It is not the same message Jesus proclaimed.[132]

Supporting the view, Elder Jeffrey R. Holland observed that

The road leading to the promised land "flowing with milk and honey" of necessity runs by way of Mount Sinai, flowing with "thou shalts" and "thou shalt nots." Unfortunately, messengers of divinely mandated commandments are often no more popular today than they were anciently. . . .

[I]t is a characteristic of our age that if people want any gods at all, they want them to be gods who do not demand much, comfortable gods, smooth gods who not only don't rock the boat but don't even row it, gods who pat us on the head, make us giggle, then tell us to run along and pick marigolds. . . .

[T]hese folks invoke the name of Jesus as one who was this kind of "comfortable" God. Really? He who said not only should we not break commandments, but we should not even *think* about breaking them. And if we do think about breaking them, we must have already broken them in our heart. Does that sound like "comfortable" doctrine, easy on the ear and popular at the village love-in?[133]

The law of faith insists on obedience. There certainly is no "cheap grace" for Paul. There is only "costly grace." "Such grace is *costly*," observed one theologian, "because it calls us to follow, and it is *grace* because it calls us to follow *Jesus Christ*. It is costly because it cost a man his life, and it is

---

132. John MacArthur, *The Gospel According to Jesus: What Is Authentic Faith?* (Grand Rapids, Mich.: Zondervan, 1988), 15–16.

133. Jeffrey R. Holland, "The Cost and Blessings of Discipleship," *Ensign* 44 (May 2014): 7; italics in original.

grace because it gives a man the only true life. It is costly because it condemns sin, and grace because it justifies the sinner. Above all, it is *costly* because it cost God the life of his Son: 'ye were bought at a price,' and what has cost God much cannot be cheap for us."[134] Obedience is the key to showing that one recognizes that cost and expresses gratitude for it. But obedience is not a kind of work that one does to either earn or merit grace. It is what a person does out of love, and, even if it is imperfectly done, it is acceptable to God.

Some may feel that asking only that the Saint strive to keep covenants may not be "easy grace" but it certainly looks like "easy salvation." They need to remember an important lesson taught in the Book of Mormon. Looking at the time when God sent fiery serpents among rebellious Israel to make them repent (Num. 21:7–9), Nephi notes that Jehovah "prepared a way that they might be healed; and that labor which they had to perform was to look; and because of the simpleness of the way, or the easiness of it, there were many who perished" (1 Ne. 17:41). The point is, God does demand that we do our part, and he accepts no shirking, malingering, or laziness.

As with everything else, the Savior is the model. As he went from "grace to grace" by "giving grace for grace," so must we. The implications of this idea should be most sobering. The ultimate act of grace was Christ's giving of his life. So, too, it will be with all. In the "Lectures on Faith," we find the following: "Let us here observe that a religion that does not require the sacrifice of all things never has power sufficient to produce the faith necessary unto life and salvation. For from the first existence of man, the faith necessary unto the enjoyment of life and salvation never could be obtained without the sacrifice of all earthly things. It is through this sacrifice, and this only, that God has ordained that men should enjoy eternal life." Grace

---

134. Dietrich Bonhoeffer, *The Cost of Discipleship* (New York: Touchstone, 1995), 45; italics in original. Hafen, "Grace," in *EM*, 2:561, states that "in recent years, some Protestant theologians have questioned the way an exclusive emphasis on unmerited grace negates a sense of personal responsibility." John MacArthur expressed concern that contemporary evangelism promises sinners that they "can have eternal life yet continue to live in rebellion against God." See MacArthur, *Gospel According to Jesus*, 15–16. And Paul Holmer, "Law and Gospel Re-examined," *Theology Today* 10 (1953–54): 474, insisted that stressing the dangers of works is "inappropriate if the listeners are not even trying! Most Church listeners are not in much danger of working their way into heaven."

is the free giving to others of all that a person has—his time, talents, and material things. Each of these is a part of his life, and by giving them, he gives himself.[135]

And what comes from exercising grace by sacrificing all things? Again from the "Lectures on Faith": "It is through the medium of the sacrifice of all earthly things that men do actually know that they are doing the things that are well pleasing in the sight of God. When a man has offered in sacrifice all that he has for the truth's sake, not even withholding his life, and believing before God that he has been called to make this sacrifice because he seeks to do His will, he does know, most assuredly, that God does and will accept his sacrifice and offering and that he has not sought nor will he seek His face in vain. Under these circumstances, then, he can obtain the faith necessary for him to lay hold on eternal life."[136]

The vehicle that makes such sacrifice possible, as Paul well knew, is love.[137] Indeed, χάρις (*charis*), "grace," and ἀγάπη (*agapē*), "love," are simply two aspects of God's divine character which he insists that we obtain, for "love never fails" (13:8, Rendition). It was Moroni who stated that "except ye have charity ye can in nowise be saved in the kingdom of God" (Moro. 10:21; compare Ether 12:34). There is good reason, for without this power, we cannot give what is required. The Savior made it clear that "greater love hath no man than this, that a man lay down his life for his friends" (John 15:13). In these latter days, that life-giving occurs one day at a time with one selfless act following another.

Though this requirement could be intimidating or disheartening or discouraging, remember that we do not arrive at such a noble station in a moment. While we are striving to get there, God is not holding back his grace. It is coming, little by little and bringing with it the necessary spiritual powers and gifts. Love may come gradually, but it will come as we love on whatever level we are on. The Apostle John promised, "If we love one another, God dwelleth in us, and his love is perfected in us" (1 John 4:12). When we finally receive a fullness of that gift, we will be as God and have eternal life, "for God is love" (1 John 4:8).

---

135. "Lecture 6," in Dahl and Tate, *Lectures on Faith in Historical Perspective*, 92–93.
136. "Lecture 6," in Dahl and Tate, *Lectures on Faith in Historical Perspective*, 93.
137. See the extended study of this subject in chapter 13 of this volume.

Summary

Because of his great love for us, the Father willingly provides everything we need to grow and progress towards our full potential as his children. Through his grace, God provides, as it were, a one-way elevator to heaven. As with all elevators, the ride up is free. No one will force us onto the elevator. The Godhead will, however, make sure that we know it is there and waiting. We can freely enter at any time. We are also free to exit at any floor along the way. Unfortunately, some of the floors can be very alluring. If we get off, we must get back on or miss getting to heaven. Eternal life requires riding the elevator all the way to the top. By choosing to ride, however, we do not make the elevator go up. It is Christ who does that. Our progress upward is all his doing. Even so, we are the ones who choose and, thereby, play the critical role in our personal salvation. But God is ever with us. As John stated: "Behold, what manner of love the Father hath bestowed upon us, that we should be called the sons [and daughters] of God. . . . Beloved, now are we the sons [and daughters] of God, and it doth not yet appear what we shall be: but we know that, when he shall appear, we shall be like him; for we shall see him as he is" (1 John 3:1–2).

THANKSGIVING
(1:4–9)

In his salutation, Paul includes an expression of thanksgiving to God for all he has done for the Saints.[138] In doing so, Paul also touches on themes he will develop in the epistle: grace through Christ; testimony; spiritual gifts; revelation; the day of the Lord; and fellowship with Jesus. One of Paul's objectives is to put the Savior center stage. He does this by using the Lord's name in every verse of this prayer.[139] In each instance, he teaches something about the Messiah: He is the source of grace (1:4) and the one who enriches the Saints in testimony and knowledge (1:5). They know this to be true because his testimony has been confirmed in them (1:6). Further, he is the one who is coming (1:7) and will confirm the Saints such that they are blameless at the time of judgment (1:8).

Verse 1:5 contains the theme of the first four chapters of Paul's letter, namely, that the Saints have been enriched by the Lord in all their proclamations and understanding. This enrichment has come to them through their testimony of the Lord, which has been greatly confirmed among them through the powers of the Spirit.[140]

Greek Text

4 Εὐχαριστῶ τῷ θεῷ μου πάντοτε περὶ ὑμῶν ἐπὶ τῇ χάριτι τοῦ θεοῦ τῇ δοθείσῃ ὑμῖν ἐν Χριστῷ Ἰησοῦ, 5 ὅτι ἐν παντὶ ἐπλουτίσθητε ἐν αὐτῷ, ἐν παντὶ λόγῳ καὶ πάσῃ γνώσει, 6 καθὼς τὸ μαρτύριον τοῦ Χριστοῦ ἐβεβαιώθη ἐν ὑμῖν, 7 ὥστε ὑμᾶς μὴ ὑστερεῖσθαι ἐν μηδενὶ χαρίσματι, ἀπεκδεχομένους τὴν ἀποκάλυψιν τοῦ κυρίου ἡμῶν Ἰησοῦ Χριστοῦ· 8 ὃς καὶ βεβαιώσει ὑμᾶς ἕως τέλους ἀνεγκλήτους ἐν τῇ ἡμέρᾳ τοῦ κυρίου ἡμῶν Ἰησοῦ Χριστοῦ. 9 πιστὸς ὁ θεὸς δι' οὗ ἐκλήθητε εἰς κοινωνίαν τοῦ υἱοῦ αὐτοῦ Ἰησοῦ Χριστοῦ τοῦ κυρίου ἡμῶν. [SBLGNT]

King James Version

4 I thank my God always on your behalf, for the grace of God which is given you by Jesus Christ; 5 That in every thing ye are enriched by him, in all utterance,

New Rendition

4 I am continually expressing gratitude to my God for you because of the grace of God which has been given to you in Christ Jesus, 5 that you have been

---

138. He will do so in other letters as well. See Rom. 1:8–9; 1 Thes. 1:2–5; Philip. 1:3–8; Philem. 1:4–7.

139. Fitzmyer, *First Corinthians*, 130.

140. Fitzmyer, *First Corinthians*, 132.

and in all knowledge; 6 Even as the testimony of Christ was confirmed in you: 7 So that ye come behind in no gift; waiting for the coming of our Lord Jesus Christ: 8 Who shall also confirm you unto the end, that ye may be blameless in the day of our Lord Jesus Christ. 9 God is faithful, by whom ye were called unto the fellowship of his Son Jesus Christ our Lord.

enriched in everything through him, in all your speech and understanding, 6 in the same way that the testimony of Christ has been confirmed among you, 7 so that you do not fall short in any spiritual gift as you look forward to the revealing of our Lord, Jesus Christ, 8 who will also strengthen you until the end, so that you will be found blameless in the day of our Lord, Jesus Christ. 9 God is faithful, who has called you to fellowship with his Son, Jesus Christ, our Lord.

Translation Notes and Comments

1:4 *I thank my God always on your behalf / I am continually expressing gratitude to my God for you:* The adverb πάντοτε (*pantote*), "at every opportunity," "as a regular habit" (compare 15:58), combined with present tense εὐχαριστῶ (*eucharistō*), "to thank," carried the idea that Paul habitually prayed for these people.[141]

for the grace of God which is given you / because of the grace of God which has been given to you: The dative preposition ἐπί (*epi*), "for," denotes the cause or basis of an action.[142] In this case, Paul rejoices because of the grace of God that the Corinthian branch has received, which grace is evidenced in the gifts of the Spirit they enjoy. Those gifts manifest God's acceptance of them, as of yet, and show it is not too late for repentance on the part of those who need it.

1:5 *in every thing ye are enriched by him / you have been enriched in everything through him:* The passive form of the verb πλουτίζω (*ploutizo*), "to cause to abound in something, make rich, to cause to be relatively high on a scale of opulence,"[143] hides the outstretched hand of God who has greatly enhanced them in specific areas of their life and work though the power of the Spirit.

in all utterance, and in all knowledge / in all your speech and understanding: Paul cites here two particular areas in which they have been blessed. The Greek noun λόγος (*logos*), often translated as "word," in this

---

141. Thiselton, *First Epistle*, 89.
142. Findlay, "St. Paul's First Epistle," 759.
143. BDAG, 831.

context means "speech" or "utterance," denoting specifically that which one says. In this context, it connotes the spiritual power that stands behind their preaching of the gospel. But the power of the Spirit did not end there. They were also enhanced in γνῶσις (*gnōsis*), "knowledge," which denotes "comprehension" or "the intellectual grasp" of specific material.[144] It is translated as "understanding" in our Rendition. By the Spirit, these people could understand the things of God. They had access to deep spiritual insights that those without the Spirit could not comprehend (see 2:14).

1:6 *Even as the testimony of Christ was confirmed in you / in the same way that the testimony of Christ has been confirmed among you:* The subordinating conjunction καθώς (*kathōs*), "as," in this context denotes just how they have been enriched, that is, by the confirmed testimony they have. The word carries the nuance of "in the same way as."

The verb βεβαιόω (*bebaioō*) denotes putting something beyond doubt, thus, "to confirm, to establish, to strengthen."[145] What has been placed beyond doubt is the testimony these people have received. In short, the power of the Spirit has established beyond doubt the truthfulness of the apostolic witness that Jesus is the Christ. But was that witness individual and, therefore, confirmed *in* each member, or was it communal and, therefore, confirmed *among* them? Since the witness resulted in the stabilizing of the corporate identity of the Christian community, the phrase ἐν ὑμῖν (*en hymin*) is translated as "among you" in our Rendition.[146]

1:7 *So that ye come behind in no gift / so that you do not fall short in any spiritual gift:* Because the infinitive ὑστερεῖσθαι (*hystereisthai*) precedes the preposition ἐν (*en*), the phrase does not mean "to suffer some kind of lack," but rather "to come behind in or fall short of" something.[147] What Paul is saying is that the display of the Spirit has assured them that they have not fallen short in any of the spiritual gifts had by other Christian communities.

The noun *charisma*, properly translated as "gift" in the KJV, denotes simply "that which is freely given."[148] In the Christian context, however, it connotes that which comes from God as generated by his grace and, there-

---

144. BDAG, 203.

145. BDAG, 172.

146. The word can relate to the establishment and further development of a specific community. See Hans Conzelmann, *1 Corinthians: A Commentary on the First Epistle to the Corinthians* (Minneapolis: Fortress Press, 1975), 27.

147. Fee, *First Epistle*, 41; Conzelmann, *1 Corinthians*, 27.

148. BDAG, 1081.

fore, manifests itself as a "spiritual endowment."[149] Thus, even though the adjective "spiritual" cannot be found in any Greek manuscripts, our Rendition translates the word as "spiritual gift."

waiting for the coming of our Lord Jesus Christ / as you look forward to the revealing of our Lord, Jesus Christ: The noun ἀποκάλυψις (*apokalypsis*), literally "uncovering," translated as "coming" in the KJV and "revealing" in our Rendition, carries the idea of making something fully known and, often in the Christian context, "of the disclosure of secrets belonging to the last days."[150] In this verse, Paul tacitly refers to one important revelation that will occur at the time of the Second Coming—that of the Christians' status as the children of God and the glorious position which that revelation will bring them.[151] The reminder is also an admonition for his readers to continue faithful. The war is not yet over and the fight is real.

1:8 ***Who shall also confirm you unto the end / who will also strengthen you until the end:*** As noted above, the Greek verb βεβαιόω (*bebaioō*) means to put beyond doubt. Here it carries the idea of being kept or guarded by the Divine. Specifically, it denotes spiritual assistance by which faithful individuals will be given strength that will assure them vindication at the coming judgment.[152]

that ye may be blameless in the day of our Lord Jesus Christ / so that you will be found blameless in the day of our Lord, Jesus Christ: The adjective ἀνέγκλητος (*anengklētos*) means to be beyond reproach, thus, free from any charge that might be leveled against a person—"to be blameless" in a judicial sense.[153] Those strengthened by the Lord will have nothing to fear from the final judgment.

1:9 ***God is faithful:*** The word πίστος (*pistos*) carries the idea of being true to one's word, reliable, a person who can be counted on. Such a one cannot lie or go back on a promise. Faithfulness is a primary attribute of God, and his fidelity is the ground for Paul's hope for his readers.[154]

---

149. The Moffet translation uses the word as "spiritual endowment," and the NRSV and NIV translate it as "spiritual gift."

150. BDAG, 112.

151. BDAG, 112. Paul uses the words with various meanings: the revelation of truth (Rom. 16:25) and revelation through a specific means (Gal. 2:2), also the revelation of Jesus Christ at the Second Coming (Rom. 8:19).

152. BDAG, 172–73.

153. BDAG, 76; Findlay, "St. Paul's First Epistle," 761.

154. In the LXX, the Hebrew נֶאֱמָן (*nĕ'emān*), "trustworthy, faithful, true," is translated as πίστος (*pistos*). See BDB, 52–53.

by whom ye were called unto the fellowship of his Son / who has called you to fellowship with his Son: The preposition διά (*dia*), "through," does not denote the mediation but rather the source of the Saints' assurance that they have been called to fellowship with the Lord.[155] They have been called by none other than God himself. Paul reminds his readers of the Father's faithfulness to stress the point that he has confirmed them, that is, assured them beyond doubt that they have been called to one purpose, that of full fellowship with the Savior. The noun κοινωνία (*koinōnia*), "fellowship," connotes the deepest and most intimate relationship a community of people can have one with another—only that of husband and wife is more intimate.[156] The word does not carry the idea of merely being in one another's company or even enjoying close association (albeit, that is part of what it entails) but rather of being "a shareholder" (κοινωνός, *koinōnos*) with Christ in all that the Father has. Those in the fellowship share fully in all the blessings of the community. In this case, it is to share in the community of the Divine, that is, to receive eternal life.

Analysis and Summary

The Corinthians, in general, highly prized the ability to speak convincingly and to show superior knowledge. The problem was that these people honored performance rather than the promotion and defense of truth. Some in the Church did not see the danger in this and, therefore, held these skills in too high a regard, believing them to evidence superior holiness or virtue (see 12:8; 13:1, 2; 2 Cor. 8:7). Unfortunately, some used their exquisite teaching abilities or debate skills (translated in the KJV as "all utterance and knowledge") to promote status and self-importance. The misuse of these abilities and skills caused Paul to censure them in this epistle. In this verse, however, we see that Paul actually prized these gifts. It was their abuse he castigated.[157]

In speaking of the gifts of the Spirit, Paul also emphasizes the point that these gifts are no longer the provenance of the small, somewhat homogeneous Jewish people with their given mind-set and culture. Rather, he notes, the Spirit has now manifested itself in the urban, multicultural, pluralist Corinthian way of life. In this widening and continually diversifying community, the work of the Spirit has been openly displayed. The Apostle reassures

---

155. Fitzmyer, *First Corinthians,* 134.

156. BDAG, 552–53, which notes that a following noun in the genitive case can express the sense of "with." Louw-Nida, §§34.5; 57.98.

157. Thiselton, *First Epistle,* 91.

his readers that each revelation, each miracle, each witness, each demonstration of a spiritual gift has confirmed beyond doubt the truth of Jesus.[158]

Even though they are enjoying an outpouring of the Spirit, Paul reminds them that the war is not yet over. They must yet wait for "the revealing of our Lord Jesus Christ" (1:7). Though it is true that the decisive battle has been won by Christ, thus assuring future victory, the war still goes on and the Christian cannot let up his intense fight until the enemy has been fully vanquished. Paul's words, then, point his readers to the time when Christ will be fully revealed and all enemies subdued or destroyed.[159] Only then can they relax.

The noun "revealing" is the translation for the Greek ἀποκάλυψις (*apokalypsis*). This word is full of meaning. On the simplest level, it refers to uncovering something, that is, to make something visible. Then, in the more abstract sense, "revealing" denotes making something known. In its theological context, it refers first and foremost to a revelation of Deity; note here that the preposition is "of" not "from" Jesus Christ. Certainly, revelations do come *from* God, but the *apokalypsis* translation looks to divine disclosure, that is, *of* a divine being revealing himself fully, including his character, attributes, and work. Thus, it differs from other forms of revelation in which only God's will is made known. One of the primary places where *apokalypsis* occurs is in temples.[160] In these sacred edifices, God makes himself more fully known to his people.[161] Finally, the word can be taken in an eschatological sense where it carries the meaning of "to appear." For Paul, it especially referred to the Second Coming of Jesus with all that will happen at that time, most specifically the disclosure and vindication of the Christians as the true people of God.[162]

Paul assures his readers that continued faithfulness leads to two blessings: first, faithfulness opens the way for the Lord to strengthen the Saints so that each one can endure in righteousness until judgment day and, second, God will make sure they will be found blameless of any charges.

---

158. Thiselton, *First Epistle*, 95.

159. Oscar Cullmann, *Christ and Time: The Primitive Christian Concept of Time and History*, 2d ed., rev. (Louisville, Ky.: Westminster Press, 1964), 75.

160. Albrecht Oepke, "ἀποκαλύπτω, ἀποκάλυψις," in *TDNT*, 3:563–92.

161. In the LXX, ἀποκαλύπτω (*apokalyptō*) translates the Hebrew גִּלָּה (*gillāh*), which carries the idea of "uncovering" (see Lev. 18:6–9). Note that Ex. 20:26 has a niphal form (that is, passive), not a piel.

162. BDAG, 112. Paul's expression comes from the LXX, ἡμέρα (τοῦ) κυρίου (*hēmera [tou] kyriou*), which is the translation of the Hebrew יוֹם־יְהוָה (*yōm Yhwh*), denoting the future day when Jehovah will judge his people. Here, Paul notes that the Christians will be judged by their Messiah and none else. See Fitzmyer, *First Corinthians*, 133–34.

Finally, Paul reminds his readers that God is faithful and true and, there-fore, can never go back on his word. This divine being has called them into the same "fellowship" (κοινωνία, *koinōnia*) he has with his Son. Thus, they are "shareholders" (κοινονός, *koinōnos*) with Christ in all that the Father has. In short, Paul's words are a tacit reminder that God has called the Christians into the intimate circle of the Divine.[163] Drawing a lesson from God's faithfulness, the Prophet Joseph Smith admonished the Saints saying: "If God should speak from heaven, he would command you not to steal, not to commit adultery, not to covet, nor deceive, but be faithful over a few things. As far as we degenerate from God, we descend to the devil and lose knowledge, and without knowledge we cannot be saved, and while our hearts are filled with evil, and we are studying evil, there is no room in our hearts for good, or studying good. Is not God good? Then you be good; if He is faithful, then you be faithful."[164]

DIVISIONS AND FACTIONS IN THE CHURCH (1:10–17)

Having greeted the Christian community, Paul turns to the major issues that prompted him to dictate this epistle, namely, the growing factional-ism that threatens the very existence of the Church. Paul feared and hated divisions.[165] Chapters 1:10 through 4:21 make up the second unit of the epistle and sets the theme for the whole.[166] The issue that Chloe's people have brought to Paul's attention is that of "splits" or "divisions" (σχίσματα, *schismata*), that is, rigid differences in opinion and understanding among the members that have led to infighting and bitterness. Paul's choice of very political words in this section suggests that the problem actually orig-inated in a power struggle that has now divided the congregation into definite factions. Even as Paul writes, certain members seem to be doing a good deal of campaigning to win recruits either to maintain their position or to gain status.[167]

---

163. Thiselton, *First Epistle*, 103–5.

164. Smith, *History of the Church*, 4:588.

165. Wayment, *Persecutor to Apostle*, 152.

166. Mitchell, *Paul and the Rhetoric of Reconciliation*, 65–111.

167. Mitchell, *Paul and the Rhetoric of Reconciliation,* 65–111. Paul does not actu-ally name anyone who is a factional head. He may be doing this out of tact, but it may also mean there were no hardened parties. Thus, rather than there being three or four

Paul makes the solution to the problem very clear: first, they need to realize that they all share jointly in being one with Christ who has no favorites and, second, they need better understanding of the gospel as centered in the Atonement or, as Paul puts it, "the cross of Christ" (1:17–31; 2:1–5). He stresses that no single element in the Church has a monopoly on the Lord (μεμέρισται ὁ Χριστός, *memeristai ho Christos*, "Is Christ divided?" [1:13]). All share not only in the community of believers but also in a deep and abiding fellowship with the Savior made possible by his wondrous and exemplifying self-sacrifice.

Paul then shows how these two fundamental doctrines have become obscured. First, the Saints simply have not understood the message of "the preaching of the cross" (1:18). This message was never designed to compete with the rhetoric of the world or to bring fame to the preacher or to win souls through tricks of persuasion. Rather, the message was meant to magnify God through Christ and bring people to him through the quiet voice of the Spirit. There was no room for power, position, prestige, or any kind of self-promotion in the community of Christians. Christ set the example by continually pointing beyond himself to the Father and to the service of others (see 1:31; 2:1–5). Second, they have not understood the true work of Church ministers and, more especially, the Apostles. Here Paul calls for balance. Too high a view of a leader's role has caused some to place too much emphasis on the person holding the position and caused undue loyalty to that person. Too low a view of the role of the minister has caused some to feel they could go it alone and ignore any direction or supervision. Both produce a kind of self-centeredness either in the leader or the individual that is foreign to the Spirit and breeds division.[168] To counterbalance this, Paul sets up the example of the Apostles who labor daily, toiling to live out the Christian life as a public spectacle as if in the ignominious arena (4:1–11) thus devoid of any self-aggrandizement.[169]

---

clear-cut groups, he may be referring to people's hardened preferences. See Fitzmyer, *First Corinthians*, 139.

168. Paul's teaching can be summarized as, "Do not have too high a view of the ministry, supposing the minister is the one who makes the Church. On the other hand, do not have too low a view of the ministry feeling ministers are little more than part time leaders, for they are God's agents. But never forget that it is God who sets the direction." See Rupert E. Davies, *Studies in 1 Corinthians* (London: Epworth Press, 1962), 42–43.

169. Thiselton, *First Epistle*, 107–8.

Greek Text

10 Παρακαλῶ δὲ ὑμᾶς, ἀδελφοί, διὰ τοῦ ὀνόματος τοῦ κυρίου ἡμῶν Ἰησοῦ Χριστοῦ ἵνα τὸ αὐτὸ λέγητε πάντες, καὶ μὴ ᾖ ἐν ὑμῖν σχίσματα, ἦτε δὲ κατηρτισμένοι ἐν τῷ αὐτῷ νοΐ καὶ ἐν τῇ αὐτῇ γνώμῃ. 11 ἐδηλώθη γάρ μοι περὶ ὑμῶν, ἀδελφοί μου, ὑπὸ τῶν Χλόης ὅτι ἔριδες ἐν ὑμῖν εἰσιν. 12 λέγω δὲ τοῦτο ὅτι ἕκαστος ὑμῶν λέγει· Ἐγὼ μέν εἰμι Παύλου, Ἐγὼ δὲ Ἀπολλῶ, Ἐγὼ δὲ Κηφᾶ, Ἐγὼ δὲ Χριστοῦ. 13 μεμέρισται ὁ Χριστός; μὴ Παῦλος ἐσταυρώθη ὑπὲρ ὑμῶν, ἢ εἰς τὸ ὄνομα Παύλου ἐβαπτίσθητε; 14 εὐχαριστῶ ὅτι οὐδένα ὑμῶν ἐβάπτισα εἰ μὴ Κρίσπον καὶ Γάϊον, 15 ἵνα μή τις εἴπῃ ὅτι εἰς τὸ ἐμὸν ὄνομα ἐβαπτίσθητε· 16 ἐβάπτισα δὲ καὶ τὸν Στεφανᾶ οἶκον· λοιπὸν οὐκ οἶδα εἴ τινα ἄλλον ἐβάπτισα 17 οὐ γὰρ ἀπέστειλέν με Χριστὸς βαπτίζειν ἀλλὰ εὐαγγελίζεσθαι, οὐκ ἐν σοφίᾳ λόγου, ἵνα μὴ κενωθῇ ὁ σταυρὸς τοῦ Χριστοῦ. [SBLGNT]

King James Version

10 Now I beseech you, brethren, by the name of our Lord Jesus Christ, that ye all speak the same thing, and that there be no divisions among you; but that ye be perfectly joined together in the same mind and in the same judgment. 11 For it hath been declared unto me of you, my brethren, by them which are of the house of Chloe, that there are contentions among you. 12 Now this I say, that every one of you saith, I am of Paul; and I of Apollos; and I of Cephas; and I of Christ. 13 Is Christ divided? was Paul crucified for you? or were ye baptized in the name of Paul? 14 I thank God that I baptized none of you, but Crispus and Gaius; 15 Lest any should say that I had baptized in mine own name. 16 And I baptized also the household of Stephanas: besides, I know not whether I baptized any other. 17 For Christ sent me not to baptize, but to preach the gospel: not with wisdom of words, lest the cross of Christ should be made of none effect.

New Rendition

10 I urge you, brothers and sisters, in the name of our Lord, Jesus Christ, to all speak with a united voice, and not allow any divisions to be among you, but to be completely unified in your thoughts and intentions. 11 For it has been brought to my attention by Chloe's people that there are quarrels among you. 12 This is what I mean: some of you say, "I follow Paul," others say "I follow Apollos," or "I follow Cephas," or "I follow Christ." 13 Christ is certainly not divided! Surely Paul was not crucified for you, nor were you baptized in Paul's name! 14 I thank God that I did not baptize any of you except Crispus and Gaius, 15 so that none of you can say that you were baptized in my name. 16 Now I also baptized the household of Stephanas. Beyond that I do not recall if I baptized anyone else. 17 Because Christ did not send me to baptize, but to preach the gospel, without clever speaking, so that the cross of Christ would not be made ineffective.

Translation Notes and Comments

1:10 *Now I beseech you, brethren / I urge you, brothers and sisters:* As Paul turns to the purpose of his epistle, he uses the word παρακαλέω (*parakaleō*), "to beseech, plead, appeal to," which carries the idea of asking for something not only with earnestness, but also with propriety.[170] In other words, Paul is not asking them for anything that is unreasonable but, rather, only that which is expected of Christians.

Ἀδελφοί (*adelphoi*) is literally "brothers," but, as mentioned earlier, it is used generically for members of the Church both male and female, and even in nonbiblical Greek it can mean "brothers and sisters."[171]

by the name of our Lord Jesus Christ / in the name of our Lord, Jesus Christ: Paul does not appeal to rhetorical persuasion in trying to bring unity to the house churches at Corinth, but directly to the Lord, thus giving a divine sanction to his appeal and reinforcing its seriousness.[172]

all speak the same thing / speak with a united voice: The words ἵνα τὸ αὐτὸ λέγητε πάντες (*hina to auto legēte pantes*) translate literally to "that you all might say the same thing," but this makes a very wooden translation and also misses the nuance of the Greek. In that language the words have a very political overtone. They are the language of classical politics.[173] Their purpose is to ask the hearers to make up their differences and become united behind one authority. Thus, the Moffet Bible translates the phrase as "drop these party cries." In short, Paul's request is that they "all be in agreement in what you profess" (NJB).

that there be no divisions among you / not allow any divisions to be among you: The noun σχίσμα (*schisma*), "tear, division, dissension, schism," describes "the tearing of a group apart through differences in aims or objectives."[174] The word denotes such bitter discord that the opposing factions can become enemies.[175]

Paul's words (1:12) suggest that the divisions came due to strong personalities who pitted themselves one against the other and sought devotees to their

---

170. Louw-Nida, §33.167.

171. BDAG, 18.

172. Findlay, "St. Paul's First Epistle," 762.

173. This point is not new. J. B. Lightfoot, *Notes on the Epistles of St Paul from Unpublished Commentaries* (London: Macmillan, 1895), 151, noted this more than a hundred years ago.

174. BDAG, 981.

175. Louw-Nida, §39.13.

position. Taking the epistle as a whole, however, suggests that differences on key doctrinal issues also played a major part in driving people apart.[176]

be perfectly joined together in the same mind and in the same judgment / be completely unified in your thoughts and intentions: The verb καταρτίζω (*katartizō*) has the basic meaning "to put into proper condition, adjust, make complete, fix up any deficiencies."[177] Disciples of Jesus Christ must all be as Christ prayed, "one; as thou, Father, are in me, and I in thee, that they also may be one in us" (John 17:21). The noun νοῦς (*nous*), "mind," denotes "the faculty of intellectual perception" and, therefore, connotes "understanding, attitudes, thoughts, and opinions."[178] The noun γνώμη (*gnōmē*) also means "mind," but in this case denotes "that which is proposed or intended," and, thus, connotes "purpose or intention."[179] The two purposed are very close in meaning, but *nous* looks more to the idea of observing and thinking while *gnōmē* focuses on planning and judging.[180] Thus, Paul's words suggest that he is concerned not only with what they say but also with what they think and how they plan.[181]

1:11 *the house of Chloe / Chloe's people:* The Greek τῶν Χλόης (*tōn chloēs*), which translates literally to "of those of Chloe," is ambiguous. It could refer to members of her family or, more broadly, to other dependents, such as slaves or former slaves.[182] In our Rendition, we have used the translation "Chloe's people" to preserve that ambiguity. It is likely, however, that these were trusted slaves responsible to oversee Chloe's business ventures outside of Corinth.

there are contentions among you / there are quarrels among you: The Greek word ἔρις (*eris*), "strife, discord, contention," in the plural is best rendered as "quarrels"[183] as it is in our Rendition. The heart of *eris* is rivalry,

---

176. See Wayment, *Persecutor to Apostle*, 163–64. Before 1960, most theologians saw doctrinal differences as the major cause of the splits. Since then, some have seen personality cliques as being a driving force. See Nils Alstrup Dahl, *Studies in Paul: Theology for the Early Christian Mission* (Minneapolis: Augsburg Press, 1977), 40–61. The two positions are not exclusive, and it is likely that both doctrinal issues and strong personalities played a part.

177. BDAG, 526

178. BDAG, 680.

179. BDAG, 202.

180. Rudolf Bultmann, "γνώμη," in *TDNT*, 1:717–18.

181. Fitzmyer, *First Corinthians*, 141.

182. The households (οἶκος, *oikos*) of the very wealthy could include hundreds of workers and slaves. These houses were very powerful and very competitive. Otto Michel, "οἶκος, οἰκία," in *TDNT*, 5:119–34.

183. BDAG, 392.

one side trying to best the other. The Greek members of the Church would likely have connected the word to the goddess Eris who was responsible for discord and even war. So skilled was she at the craft that she even caused suffering and chaos among the gods.[184] The English word "quarrel" very accurately catches the nuance of the Greek because it suggests discord, even anger, sown by people stubbornly standing at opposite sides of an issue. The word also carries the idea of undignified, heated verbal contention leading to stressed or even broken relationships with ill will persisting even after the verbal discord has ceased.[185]

1:12 *every one of you saith / some of you say . . . others say:* The Greek ἕκαστος ὑμῶν λέγει (*hekastos hymōn legei*) translates literally to "each one of you says." The genitive form of the proper nouns in this verse (Paul, Apollos, Cephas, and Christ) are likely genitives of relationship, like "child of . . ." or "husband of . . . ."[186] If that is the case, then these nouns give a more broad association with the objects ("some of you") and are enhanced by Paul's use of the constructive particles μέν (*men*) and δέ (*de*) (often translated, "on the one hand, . . . on the other hand . . .").

The Apostle's use of the Greek particles μέν (*men*) and δέ (*de*) emphasizes the issue of competition that so abounds in Corinth. Therefore, though the Greek phrase is exactly the same for each element, a better sense can be given by rendering the text as "I, for one, am one of Paul's people; I, for my part, am for Apollos; I am a Peter person; As for me, I belong to Christ."[187] It is very likely that these strong factions were a manifestation of aspects of patronage that was so prevalent in the Greco-Roman world. Those of lower order often received prestige, stature, and even prominence from their patrons while the latter received support and service from those below.[188]

1:13 *Is Christ divided?/ Christ is certainly not divided!:* This verse contains an important variant. Though the majority of ancient manuscripts read μεμέρισται ὁ Χριστός (*memeristai ho Christos*), some of the earliest

---

184. Homer, *Il.* 4.441–45; 5.518; 11.3; 20.48; Hesiod, *Theog.* 225. She conforms to the Latin goddess Discordia. Virgil, *Aen.* 8.702.

185. *Merriam Webster's Dictionary of Synonyms* (Springfield, Mass.: Merriam-Webster, 1984), 656, s.v. "quarrel."

186. Mitchell, *Paul and the Rhetoric of Reconciliation,* 85.

187. Thiselton, *First Epistle,* 122.

188. For studies, see Andrew Wallace-Hadrill, *Patronage in Ancient Society* (London: Routledge, 1989); and, more specifically for the New Testament, John E. Stambaugh and David L. Blach, *The New Testament in Its Social Environment* (Philadelphia: Westminster Press, 1986).

insert μή (*mē*), "not," at the beginning. Many feel this variant reflects the original because the *mē* indicates a question where a negative response is expected ("Certainly Christ is not divided?"), and it becomes parallel in construction with the rest of the sentence.[189] Our Rendition follows this. The verb μερίζω (*merizō*) means "to separate into parts." Thus, Paul's question and presumed answer can be rendered, "Can Christ be divided? Of course not!"

1:14 *I thank God that I baptized none of you, but Crispus and Gaius / I thank God that I did not baptize any of you except Crispus and Gaius:* Several early manuscripts omit τῷ θεῷ (*tō theō*) "God." SBLGNT also omits it, but Nestle-Aland Greek New Testament, 28th ed., includes it since it better reflects Paul's normal usage.[190] Thus, it is retained in our Rendition.

Though Paul's words could be taken to mean he did not feel baptism was important, such is not the case. The fact that he personally took the time to baptize Crispus, Gaius, and all those dwelling with Stephanas shows he neither belittled nor refused baptism to converts. The point Paul is making here is that he is grateful that no one can claim he did everything by himself. Rather, he shared in the ministry with many others.[191] Further, the purpose of this shared ministry was to bring all not to the ministers but to Christ.[192]

Not unlike modern Apostles and other General Authorities, for the most part, Paul left baptizing to others so he could concentrate on what he did best, preach the gospel. That Gaius and Crispus were exceptions is very likely because they were two of the earliest converts, and there were few if any who had authority as yet to baptize. Crispus, before his conversion, is likely the rabbi that headed the local Jewish synagogue (see Acts 18:8),[193] while Gaius seems to have used his home and means to support the fledgling branch (see Rom. 16:23).

1:15 *Lest any should say that I had baptized in mine own name / so that none of you can say that you were baptized in my name:* Paul uses sarcasm here to make the point that no one can claim he felt he had all power to do all things. His work was not to bring glory to himself but to bring others to Christ.

---

189. See Metzgar, *Textual Commentary*, 479, where it is noted that μὴ μεμέρισται (*mē memeristai*) is the best reading.
190. See Metzgar, *Textual Commentary*, 479.
191. On this, see Tertullian, *Bapt.* xiv.
192. Thiselton, *First Epistle*, 140.
193. Ogden and Skinner, *Verse by Verse*, 130.

1:16 *The household of Stephanas / the household of Stephanas:* The noun οἶκος (*oikos*) denoted a residence ranging from a peasant's hut to a king's palace. Figuratively, it designated a specific family or clan.[194] In the Greco-Roman world, it often designated every one associated with a particular home, including family members, servants, slaves, and even lodgers.[195] In the Christian context, it could also mean "house church"—the full congregation of those meeting at one location.[196] If that is the case, Paul actually baptized quite a few people, but likely, as noted above, all these were possibly very early converts and associates of Stephanas.

1:17 *For Christ sent me not to baptize, but to preach the gospel / Because Christ did not send me to baptize, but to preach the gospel:* Paul's statement should not be taken to undercut the importance of baptism or other ordinances. Here Paul explains why he did not spend time performing baptisms. Any with authority could do that and, therefore, it was not Paul's specific calling. What he could do, and what the Lord specifically called him to do that many could not, was effectively proclaim the gospel in the very difficult environment of Corinth.[197]

not with wisdom of words / without clever speaking: Translating the phrase οὐκ ἐν σοφίᾳ λόγου (*ouk en sophia logou*) presents a number of problems. For example, translations of the word λόγος, (*logos*), "word," can be but are not limited to: word, statement, report, proverb, speaking, proclamation, instruction, message, matter, thing, computation, reckoning, account, respect, regard, reason, ground, and motive.[198] It was also used by John to refer to Christ in the well-known beginning of his gospel, "In the beginning was the Word" (John 1:1). No less than six columns of the *Greek-English Lexicon* of Liddell and Scott are devoted to the various possible nuances of the word.[199] Only context can give the correct nuance. Here the word's attachment to *sophia*, "wisdom," is helpful in understanding how Paul wanted his readers to understand the word. Generally, the word *sophia* carried a very positive meaning denoting the capacity to understand and,

---

194. BDAG, 698–99.

195. See Theissen, *Social Setting*, 83–87.

196. Fitzmyer, *First Corinthians*, 147.

197. Fitzmyer, *First Corinthians*, 147.

198. BDAG, 598–601

199. Louw-Nida, §2.153 includes ten semantic fields in its treatment of the word, and definitions fill six columns in BDAG, 598–601.

thereby, act wisely.[200] It also denoted "knowledge which makes possible skillful activity or performance,"[201] and the "accumulated philosophic, scientific, and experiential learning that includes an ability to discern essential relationships of people and things."[202] It connoted a profound understanding of such human endeavors as philosophy, literature, and art. Though generally positive in meaning, it also connoted that which was bound to the mortal plane. Of greater concern for Paul was that it promoted worldly values. This is the sense in which Paul took it. Therefore, Paul's phrase *sophia logou* could be translated "cleverness in speaking,"[203] but carrying the nuance of "manipulative rhetoric" or "tricks of speech" as used by the Sophists to beguile and catch hearers.[204]

lest the cross of Christ should be made of none effect / so that the cross of Christ would not be made ineffective: Paul chose the verb κενόω (*kenoō*), "to make empty," which also carries the idea of causing an act "to be without result or effect." Thus, words like "destroy, render void, or of no effect" work well. That which empties an act divests it of the prestige or the importance it deserves.[205] Paul's point is that he chose a preaching method that deliberately stayed clear of the persuasive but ill-used, if popular, ways of the Sophist and orator. To use verbal tricks to convert people would bring attention and renown to the speaker but, in doing so, would take away from Christ and his Atonement—where the real power lay.

Analysis and Summary

"Unity within the Church and among the saints is the goal of the gospel," states Elder McConkie, "There is no place in the Church of God for division, for disagreement on doctrine, for cults and cliques, for liberal views as contrasted with the conservative concepts. Among the faithful saints there is only one mind and one judgment and these are the Lord's."[206] The Lord's injunction "Be one; and if ye are not one ye are not mine" (D&C 38:27) holds true for all periods of time. Again from Elder McConkie, "there is and can be only one true Church on earth. (D. & C. 1:30.) To imagine that

---

200. Louw-Nida, §32.32, 37.
201. Louw-Nida, §28.8.
202. Fitzmyer, *First Corinthians*, 148.
203. BDAG, 934.
204. Thiselton, *First Epistle*, 143.
205. BDAG, 539.
206. *DNTC*, 2:313.

two organizations teaching different systems of salvation can both be true is a philosophical absurdity. . . . Two conflicting religions can both be false but only one can be true. . . . Christ is not divided."[207]

Elder Mark E. Petersen noted that: "Paul named four subdivisions or separate denominations already existing in Corinth, a thing which he firmly condemned (see 1 Cor. 1:12–15). His former converts in that city actually began to alter the doctrines of Christ, even denying his resurrection (see 1 Cor. 15:12). But this was not all. Division continued to develop throughout Christianity in that first century after Christ. Most of the epistles of the New Testament were written to combat it."[208]

Perpetrating disunity is no small matter. Indeed, those who do so are on the road that leads initially to hell and ultimately to telestial glory if not perdition.[209] According to the Lord, "These are they who are of Paul, and of Apollos, and of Cephas. These are they who say they are some of one and some of another—some of Christ and some of John, and some of Moses, and some of Elias, and some of Esaias, and some of Isaiah, and some of Enoch; But received not the gospel, neither the testimony of Jesus, neither the prophets, neither the everlasting covenant" (D&C 76:99–101).

Paul bases his appeal for unity on trifold authority: first, as a member of the family of Saints (his "brothers and sisters"), second, as an Apostle, and third, in the name of Jesus Christ. All three bolster his plea but from different directions and thus give it the weight and the seriousness it deserves.

Paul's request that they all speak with a united voice shows that a power struggle was going on. Corinth, as a microcosm of the Greco-Roman world, was a model of the competitive, social climbing, status-obsessed culture that prevailed in the big cities. Some of the early converts to Christ brought these traits with them, which resulted in the divisions that so concerned Paul. Further, some of these belonged to the great houses where honor and face were of primary importance. That condition exacerbated the problem by making the people less inclined to back down from a position. The Apostle was begging them to release their pride and "to all take the same side."[210]

---

207. *DNTC*, 2:314.
208. Petersen, "Signs of the True Church," 21.
209. Ogden and Skinner, *Verse by Verse*, 130; *DNTC*, 2:313.
210. Thus, the translation in Thiselton, *First Epistle*, 118 emphasizes, "the contemporary hellenistic Greek idiom of being political co-partisans," and, at the same time, suggests holding to shared theological conceptions of the larger Christian community.

Paul's concern with the σχίσματα (*schismata*), "divisions," seems to have been based not only on personal rivalries and arguments but also on the Corinthians' perceived levels of spirituality. The Church was plagued with a "holier than thou" attitude with various groups or individuals insisting on a greater degree of spirituality either by tracing their conversion to a supposed more holy leader or possessing a seemingly greater gift of the Spirit.[211]

Quarrels erupted as each side tried to best the other. Unwittingly, elements of the Christian community in Corinth provided a body in which the deadly cancer of pride took hold. That disease threatened to destroy the Church. What made pride so dangerous was that at its heart stood competition, the striving to be above the rest. Pride will abide no equal and, therefore, cannot admit to wrong or weakness. As President Ezra Taft Benson stated:

> Pride does not look up to God and care about what is right. It looks sideways to man and argues who is right. Pride is manifest in the spirit of contention. Was it not through pride that the devil became the devil? Christ wanted to serve. The devil wanted to rule. Christ wanted to bring men to where he was. The devil wanted to be above men. Christ removed self as the force in His perfect life. It was not *my* will, but *thine* be done. Pride is characterized by "What do I want out of life?" rather than by "What would God have me do with my life?" It is self-will as opposed to God's will. It is the fear of man over the fear of God. Humility responds to God's will—to the fear of His judgments and to the needs of those around us. To the proud, the applause of the world rings in their ears; to the humble, the applause of heaven warms their hearts. Someone has said, "Pride gets no pleasure out of having something, only out of having more of it than the next man." Of one brother, the Lord said, "I, the Lord, am not well pleased with him, for he seeketh to excel, and he is not sufficiently meek before me" (D&C 58:41).[212]

The Saints "seeking to excel" describes exactly what the major problem was at Corinth. Paul attacked this pattern by showing his readers the absurdity of such a proposition. He does so by formulating the series of rhetorical questions found in 1:13. Essentially, they force Paul's readers to consider three questions: Can the spirit of Christ be apportioned out such that only one group can enjoy it? Did anyone die for you and thereby bring salvation,

---

211. Holzapfel and Wayment, *Making Sense,* 345–46; Wayment, *Persecutor to Apostle,* 163–65.

212. Ezra Taft Benson, *A Witness and a Warning* (Salt Lake City: Deseret Book, 1988), 78.

other than Christ? Are saving ordinances performed in any other name but that of the Lord? Paul's intent is to show these people that no single congregation can claim exclusive right to Christ's spirit, doctrine, and power. Indeed, the Spirit of Christ, as the Apostle will demonstrate in chapter 3, belongs to the body of the Church as a whole. No single congregation is more important than another.

In 1:17, Paul carefully distances himself from the Sophists, whose major aim was to gain popularity and wealth through the sophistication, skill, and sometimes tricks of their arguments. The Sophists' aim was to impress their audience by winning arguments rather than expounding truths. Paul was intent on fulfilling God's assignment, that is, to preach. And, as one scholar noted, "what he has to preach is not a philosophy to be discussed, but a message of God to be believed."[213] Therefore, he carefully went opposite the Sophists and philosophers choosing a most appalling symbol on which to make his case—the cross. That imagery connoted a most gruesome, ignoble, even ignominious, death.

Paul stated that he refused to follow the ways of the Sophist because it would make the cross of the Lord ineffective. But how could using skilled speech do that? Such speech was meant to impress and bring to the speaker praise and wealth. We see the same phenomenon in the Book of Mormon. Its pages describe the various antagonists to the gospel. Sherem, the first mentioned, "was learned that he had a perfect knowledge of the language of the people; wherefore, he could use much flattery, and much power of speech, according to the power of the devil" (Jacob 7:4). He was followed by Nehor (Alma 1:2–6) then Korihor (Alma 30:12–16), and, finally, Gadianton, all educated, articulate, and persuasive—and each driven by pride and want for wealth, fame, and power.[214] Their abilities would have caused but a ripple in Corinth.

The status-hungry Corinthians enjoyed cleverness and were ever ready to give a skilled person high reward. But Paul understood that if one used the gospel message for self-adulation and aggrandizement, it would take the hearer away from Christ and to the speaker and, thus, would make the Atonement ineffective. As one scholar noted, "if everything rests on human cleverness, sophistication, or achievement, the cross of Christ no longer functions

---

213. Findlay, "St. Paul's First Epistle," 767.

214. For an excellent study see Hugh Nibley, *An Approach to the Book of Mormon* (Salt Lake City: Deseret Book, 1964), 302–16.

as that which subverts and cuts across all human distinctions of race, class, gender, and status to make room for divine grace alone as a sheer unconditional gift."[215] Paul would have none of that and, therefore, refused to use tricks to make adherents for himself. He wanted all conversions to be to his Lord. But what we must get clear is that Paul did have the skills to run with the best of the Sophists. Some of the Corinthian Saints seem to have recognized this and criticized Paul for not using them. He, however, steadfastly refused to take this course. He would not bring the spotlight upon himself, for to do so was to stand between the convert and Christ. Such a thing Paul would not allow for himself or others.

Opposition against Paul was very widespread and seems to have arisen after he left the community and, therefore, was promoted largely by people who did not actually know him. Its existence suggests that many of these early converts did not comprehend the real message of the gospel that he had preached during his mission there, namely, "Christ, and him crucified" (2:2).[216] Early in his letter (1:13), Paul introduced the imagery of the cross, his graphic way of referring to the Atonement of Jesus, and later spoke of the "preaching of the cross" (1:18), which he saw as the heart of the gospel and that which stood opposite σοφίᾳ λογοῦ (*sophia logou*), "cunning speeches," that is, the world's wisdom that only served to blind people to the eternal matters.[217]

The problem with alternative voices is not peculiar to Paul's day. What he taught the Corinthians has value today. As pointed out by Elder Dallin H. Oaks:

> In the five years since I was called as a General Authority, I have seen many instances where Church leaders and members have been troubled by things said by these alternate voices. I am convinced that some members are confused about the Church's relationship to the alternate voices. As a result, members can be misled in their personal choices, and the work of the Lord can suffer.
>
> Some alternate voices are those of well-motivated men and women who are merely trying to serve their brothers and sisters and further the cause of Zion. Their efforts fit within the Lord's teaching that his servants should not have to be commanded in all things, but "should be anxiously

---

215. Thiselton, *First Epistle*, 145, his italics removed.
216. Fitzmyer, *First Corinthians*, 139.
217. Fitzmyer, *First Corinthians*, 148.

engaged in a good cause, and do many things of their own free will, and bring to pass much righteousness" (D&C 58:27).

Other alternate voices are pursuing selfish personal interests, such as property, pride, prominence, or power. Other voices are the bleatings of lost souls who cannot hear the voice of the Shepherd and trot about trying to find their way without his guidance. Some of these voices call out guidance for others—the lost leading the lost.

Some alternate voices are of those whose avowed or secret object is to deceive and devour the flock. The Good Shepherd warned, "Beware of false prophets, which come to you in sheep's clothing, but inwardly they are ravening wolves" (Matt. 7:15; see also 3 Ne. 14:15). In both the Bible and the Book of Mormon the Savior charged his shepherds to watch over and protect the flock from such wolves. (See Acts 20:28–29; Alma 5:59.)

There have always been alternate voices whose purpose or effect is to deceive. Their existence is part of the Plan. The prophet Lehi taught that there "must needs be . . . an opposition in *all* things" (2 Ne. 2:11; italics added). And there have always been other alternate voices whose purpose or effect is unselfish and wholesome.

In most instances, alternate voices are heard in the same kinds of communications the Church uses to perform its mission. The Church has magazines and other official publications, a newspaper supplement, letters from Church leaders, general conferences, and regular meetings and conferences in local units. Similarly, alternate voices are heard in magazines, journals, and newspapers and at lectures, symposia, and conferences.

The Church of Jesus Christ of Latter-day Saints does not attempt to isolate its members from alternate voices. Its approach, as counseled by the Prophet Joseph Smith, is to teach correct principles and then leave its members to govern themselves by personal choices.[218]

Both in his introduction and throughout his epistle, Paul continually pointed to what would cure the Corinthian problem, and by application, safeguard the Church today, namely, living the gospel of Christ—the real gospel—not someone's interpretation of it. To emphasize that he was speaking for the Savior, he invoked the name of the Lord in his request for a blessing of grace and truth upon them. Once that was done, he set forth the Savior's true doctrine, which Paul learned not from "flesh and blood" (Gal. 1:16), but directly from the Lord and his Spirit.

---

218. Dallin H. Oaks, "Alternate Voices," *Ensign* 18 (April 1989): 27.

The Foolish Wisdom of the Cross (1:18–25)

From 1:18 to 2:5, Paul explores the meaning of the preaching of the Atonement, or, to use his imagery, the foolishness of the cross (compare 1:18). In doing so, he shows how true Christianity stands opposed to the fallen, temporal, and sinful world with its deep-seated, yet misplaced, values. And, it is important to note, he supplies the antidote to the social climbing, self-centered attitudes that have resulted in the factionalism that threatened to destroy the Corinthian branches of the Church. Paul expands on the idea of human wisdom and shows it to have no relationship to the gospel of Christ. He does so by setting up a contrast between the two to show the effect each has on humankind, whether Jew or Gentile.[219] In doing so, the Apostle showed that the preaching of the cross opens up a new way of life by which one can escape the allure of the world and find joy and life.[220]

However, Paul shows that such an escape is not without its dangers. Indeed, those yet in the world see the preaching of the cross as nothing short of folly if not madness. Indeed, some in the Church, who initially embraced the idea of the cross, have now come to see it as foolishness and, therefore, also deny the corporeal resurrection. The members had begun to interpret the Christian message through the use of σοφία (*sophia*) (which Paul describes as "man's wisdom"), that is, by the use of philosophy. In doing so, these Christians rejected the real meaning of the cross.[221] In this portion of his epistle, Paul sets the record straight, showing that "man's wisdom" is far inferior to the understanding brought by the Spirit, more especially because it cannot bring one to happiness and salvation. Indeed, it is only though Christ Jesus that one can understand the real meaning of the cross and partake of the transforming power that grows out of it.

In this section Paul argues that the gospel should not be confused with *sophia* for three reasons: first, the gospel centers on the crucifixion of the Lord, an idea philosophers find untenable—even repulsive (1:18–25); second, the Christians themselves are not philosophers or "wise" because,

---

219. Fitzmyer, *First Corinthians*, 151–52.

220. Thiselton, *First Epistle*, 147.

221. Paul's emphasis on the folly of "human wisdom"—*vis-à-vis* the wisdom of God—suggests that the Greek converts were the primary source of the Corinthian problem. Holzapfel and Wayment, *Making Sense*, 346.

unlike many philosophers, they have little influence in the world (1:26–31); and finally, Paul's own preaching did not use the cleverness or tricks of missused and abused rhetoric or any other philosophical means to prove the gospel true (2:1–5).

Greek Text

18 Ὁ λόγος γὰρ ὁ τοῦ σταυροῦ τοῖς μὲν ἀπολλυμένοις μωρία ἐστίν, τοῖς δὲ σῳζομένοις ἡμῖν δύναμις θεοῦ ἐστιν. 19 γέγραπται γάρ· Ἀπολῶ τὴν σοφίαν τῶν σοφῶν, καὶ τὴν σύνεσιν τῶν συνετῶν ἀθετήσω. 20 ποῦ σοφός; ποῦ γραμματεύς; ποῦ συζητητὴς τοῦ αἰῶνος τούτου; οὐχὶ ἐμώρανεν ὁ θεὸς τὴν σοφίαν τοῦ κόσμου; 21 ἐπειδὴ γὰρ ἐν τῇ σοφίᾳ τοῦ θεοῦ οὐκ ἔγνω ὁ κόσμος διὰ τῆς σοφίας τὸν θεόν, εὐδόκησεν ὁ θεὸς διὰ τῆς μωρίας τοῦ κηρύγματος σῶσαι τοὺς πιστεύοντας. 22 ἐπειδὴ καὶ Ἰουδαῖοι σημεῖα αἰτοῦσιν καὶ Ἕλληνες σοφίαν ζητοῦσιν· 23 ἡμεῖς δὲ κηρύσσομεν Χριστὸν ἐσταυρωμένον, Ἰουδαίοις μὲν σκάνδαλον ἔθνεσιν δὲ μωρίαν, 24 αὐτοῖς δὲ τοῖς κλητοῖς, Ἰουδαίοις τε καὶ Ἕλλησιν, Χριστὸν θεοῦ δύναμιν καὶ θεοῦ σοφίαν. 25 ὅτι τὸ μωρὸν τοῦ θεοῦ σοφώτερον τῶν ἀνθρώπων ἐστίν, καὶ τὸ ἀσθενὲς τοῦ θεοῦ ἰσχυρότερον τῶν ἀνθρώπων. [SBLGNT]

King James Version

18 For the preaching of the cross is to them that perish foolishness; but unto us which are saved it is the power of God. 19 For it is written, I will destroy the wisdom of the wise, and will bring to nothing the understanding of the prudent. 20 Where *is* the wise? where *is* the scribe? where *is* the disputer of this world? hath not God made foolish the wisdom of this world? 21 For after that in the wisdom of God the world by wisdom knew not God, it pleased God by the foolishness of preaching to save them that believe. 22 For the Jews require a sign, and the Greeks seek after wisdom: 23 But we preach Christ crucified, unto the Jews a stumblingblock, and unto the Greeks foolishness; 24 But unto them which are called, both Jews and Greeks, Christ the power of God, and the wisdom of God. 25 Because the foolishness of God is wiser than men; and the weakness of God is stronger than men.

New Rendition

18 For the message about the cross is foolishness to those who are on their way to spiritual ruin, but to those of us who are on our way to salvation, it is the very power of God. 19 For it is written: "I will destroy the wisdom of the wise and the intelligence of the intelligent I will reject." 20 Where is the sage? Where is the scriptural scholar? Where is one skilled in the philosophy of this world? Has not God shown the wisdom of the world to be foolishness? 21 For since, in the wisdom of God, the world, by its wisdom, did not understand God, God resolved to save those who believe through the foolishness of preaching. 22 For Jews demand signs, and Greeks seek for wisdom, 23 but we preach Christ crucified, an affront to the Jews, and foolishness to the Gentiles. 24 But to those who are called, both Jews and Greeks, Christ is the power of God and the wisdom of God. 25 Because the

foolishness of God is wiser than men and the weakness of God is stronger than men.

Translation Notes and Comments

1:18 *For the preaching of the cross is to them that perish foolishness / for the message about the cross is foolishness to those who are on their way to spiritual ruin:* Again, Paul uses the noun λόγος (*logos*) and the translator's challenge is to determine which nuance Paul intended it to have. The KJV translation, "preaching of the cross," does not quite work because, though it carries the idea of earnest advocation, it is not in the act of preaching where the power lies. Rather, it is in the underlying theme that the cross symbolizes. Thus, "the message about the cross" seems to be the better translation and is used in our Rendition.

The present passive participle ἀπολλυμένοις (*apollymenois*) indicates one who is, in the present, on his way to destruction or ruin. The word "spiritual" does not appear in the Greek text, but our Rendition adds the adjective to clarify the kind of ruin Paul has in mind.

Paul's use of the word μωρία (*mōria*), "foolishness," gets right to the heart of the matter. It describes an unacceptable position because it is ridiculous by going beyond what is considered reasonable or commonly accepted.[222] This message of the cross is considered foolishness because those on their way to spiritual ruin judge by the standards of the world and not by the standards of God.

but unto us which are saved it is the power of God / but to those of us who are on our way to salvation, it is the very power of God: The phrase δύναμις θεοῦ (*dynamis theou*), "power of God," does not have a definite article, but the definite article has been added for flow. Even so, Paul is talking about "a power" that is both an attribute of the divine being and that which "designates what God has done for those whom he calls (1:24)."[223]

The message about the cross is how salvation works—how God uses his divine power to bring souls to him. The message can be summed up in two passages: "For God so loved the world, that he gave his only begotten Son, that whosoever believeth in him should not perish, but have everlasting life" (John 3:16) and "Greater love hath no man than this, that a man lay down his life for his friends" (John 15:13). Those who are saved, that is, those with spiritual eyes, can see that what happened on the cross opened

---

222. BDAG, 663.
223. Fitzmyer, *First Corinthians*, 155.

the way for salvation for all. It did this by permitting God's transformative grace to flow to all who would accept his Son, making them sons and daughters of God (see John 1:12).

1:19 *I will destroy the wisdom of the wise, and will bring to nothing the understanding of the prudent / "I will destroy the wisdom of the wise and the intelligence of the intelligent I will reject":* The quote is from LXX Isaiah 29:14. The Septuagint text, quoted by Paul, differs from the Hebrew text, which reads: "and the wisdom of the wise will perish, and the intelligence of those who are intelligent will be hidden." Our Rendition brings out the text's use of cognate nouns—τὴν σοφίαν τῶν σοφῶν καὶ τὴν σύνεσιν τῶν συνετῶν (*tēn sophian tōn sophōn kai tēn synesin tōn synetōn*) "the *wisdom* of the *wise* and the *intelligence* of the *intelligent*."[224]

Paul's words serve as a revelation and a warning: God has set up conditions that will destroy the wisdom and intelligence of the world and, therefore, we should not buy into them.

1:20 *Where is the wise? where is the scribe? where is the disputer of this world? / Where is the sage? Where is the scriptual scholar? Where is one skilled in the philosophy of this world?:* The phrase "of this world" is not found in the most ancient manuscripts.[225] Likely, a scribe added it to show that Paul was not attacking rationality per se but rather the ideas of those who cannot see beyond the present world.

Paul's questions point to three branches of human expertise: First is the σοφός (*sophos*), "wise man," the word denoting one who is skilled, clever, sagacious and thus a sage.[226] The second is the γραμματεύς (*grammateus*), "scribe, or expert in the law," one who advises on items of Jewish law, thus, a scriptual scholar.[227] The third is the συζητητής (*syzētētēs*), "debater or disputer," one who debates issues of philosophy, thus, a philosopher.[228] Paul's list includes the most wise of both the Jews and the Gentiles, thus, leaving none out who despise the word of God.[229] "The three rhetorical questions"

---

224. Paul's quote exactly follows the LXX with the exception of the last word. Where the LXX has κρύψω (*krypsō*), "I will hide," Paul has ἀθετήσω (*athetēthō*), "I will nullify." The difference may be attributed to Paul quoting from memory.

225. See Metzgar, *Textual Commentary*, 479–80.

226. Ulrich Wilckens and Georg Fohrer, "σοφία, σοφός," in *TDNT*, 7:465–526.

227. BDAG, 206. Though the Gospels distinguish between the γραμματεύς (*grammateus*), "scribe," and the νομικός (*nomikos*), "lawyer," it is likely Paul is using the word *grammateus* to denote one who is expert in the law and advises others on such matters.

228. BDAG, 954.The word is found nowhere else in the NT. See Johannes Schneider, "συζητέω, συζήτησις, συζητητής," in *TDNT*, 7:747–48.

229. Findlay, "St. Paul's First Epistle," 768.

notes one scholar, "emphasize with irony the futility of such learning in view of 'the message of the cross,' which makes known 'the power of God,' who is implementing the threat announced in v. 19."[230]

hath not God made foolish the wisdom of this world? / Has not God shown the wisdom of the world to be foolishness?: Paul uses the aorist active indicative form of the verb μωραίνω (*mōrainō*), "to make foolish, show to be foolish,"[231] emphatically. By using the cross as the means of salvation, God caused the rational, logic, and reasoning of the world to be foolish.

1:21 For after that in the wisdom of God the world by wisdom knew not God / For since, in the wisdom of God, the world, by its wisdom, did not understand God: Because the Greek word order in this phrase does not flow well in English, a literal translation does not communicate. Our Rendition, therefore, presents the idea Paul put forth.

Paul's use of the conjunction ἐπειδή (*epeidē*), "for, because," is causal, stressing the idea that God deliberately designed his work such that human wisdom would fail in recognizing either it or him. He knew what he was doing. To come to an understanding of God and his ways through human reason and self-sufficiency would undercut faith and reliance on him and promote the very situation Paul was fighting.

Paul uses the aorist active form of the verb γινώσκω (*ginōskō*) "come to know or to comprehend," with telling effect.[232] The verb form stresses the effect of a single action of the Divine. In this case, it was that God made it impossible for the world to comprehend him or his ways through human logic.

it pleased God by the foolishness of preaching to save them that believe / God resolved to save those who believe through the foolishness of preaching: Though the verb εὐδοκέω (*eudokeō*), "to please," carries the idea of being glad or delighted with something, it came to mean the consideration of something as good or pleasing and, therefore, worthy of one's choice. The word "resolve," denoting that God resolutely chose to do his saving work in a particular way, works well and is used in our Rendition.[233]

Given what Paul wrote in 1:22–24, the nuance of the noun κήρυγμα (*kerygma*), "preaching," does not center on the act itself but on its content. In other words, the phrase "the foolishness of preaching" (1:21) is not

---

230. Fitzmyer, *First Corinthians*, 156.
231. BDAG, 663.
232. BDAG, 200.
233. BDAG, 404; *Dictionary of Synonyms*, 215, "decide."

focusing on the method God chose to get the word out, namely, public discourse. What the world considered foolishness was the subject matter of that teaching, that is, Christ crucified.[234]

1:22 *For the Jews require a sign / For Jews demand signs:* The verb αἰτέω (*aiteō*) means to ask or request—but with urgency or force. Therefore, "demand" is used in our Rendition.[235] The noun σημεῖον (*sēmeion*), "sign," denotes a divine confirmative proof of something and, therefore, can be interpreted as "miracle."[236] Paul uses the plural here, indicating that the Jews found what the Christians were saying was so absurd that only multiple acts of confirmation would authenticate it. The Jews may have felt they had good reason. According to Deuteronomy 21:23, anyone "hanged on a tree" was accursed of God. In Paul's day, the Jews saw that as a reference to crucifixion and, therefore, the Lord's death signified that he could be nothing short of accursed in God's sight.[237] That made his being the Messiah impossible. Thus, one little "sign" was not going to convince them he was divine. They demanded multiple proofs.

the Greeks seek after wisdom / Greeks seek for wisdom: The noun σοφία (*sophia*) here denotes the knowledge or those activities or skills that will bring success, fame, or wealth to the individual.[238]

1:23 *But we preach Christ crucified, unto the Jews a stumblingblock / but we preach Christ crucified, an affront to the Jews:* The noun σκάνδαλον (*skandalon*) is hard to translate. The translation "stumbling block"—in the sense of something that blocks progress—is too weak. The Greek word literally denotes either the trigger or the actual trap used to catch animals alive, thus, "a snare." Metaphorically, it denoted "an action or circumstance that leads one to act contrary to a proper course of action or set of beliefs," thus "temptation or enticement."[239] But the word connoted any action or belief in one person that caused another person to take offense to the point of anger.[240] The English word "affront," in the sense of deliberately doing something that annoys, humiliates, or vexes another person, carries

---

234. Fee, *First Epistle,* 73; Barrett, *First Epistle,* 53.

235. Louw-Nida, §33.163; BDAG, 30.

236. BDAG, 920.

237. 4QpNah 3–4 I 4–9; 11QTemplea 64:6–13 in light of Josephus, *Ant.* 13.14.2 §380 and *J.W.* 1.4.5 §93–98.

238. Stephen M. Pogoloff, *Logos and Sophia: The Rhetorical Situation of I Corinthians* (Atlanta: Scholars Press, 1992), 108–27.

239. BDAG, 926.

240. Louw-Nida, §25.181.

that idea.[241] Thus, the Jews were affronted by the Christian preaching of a crucified Messiah.[242]

unto the Greeks foolishness / foolishness to the Gentiles: The best manuscripts read ἔθνεσιν (*ethnesin*), "Gentiles," rather than Ἕλλησιν (*hellēsin*), "Greeks."[243] For the Gentiles, to accept the idea of a common criminal, which Jesus' execution demonstrated he was, as being the Son of God was the epitome of absurdity, if not insanity.

1:24 ***But unto them which are called, both Jews and Greeks / But to those who are called, both Jews and Greeks:*** Paul's mentioning both Jews and Greeks suggests that one of the dividing lines in the Corinthian branches could have been along ethnic lines.[244] There were, however, among both groups those who were friendly toward Paul and who accepted Jesus as Savior and Messiah. These constituted a special class that Paul refers to as τοῖς κλήτος (*tois klētois*), "the called ones." In secular Greek, the term *klētos* referred to anyone who received an invitation to some event. For Paul, however, it meant those who actually responded to it. Based on D&C 29:7, "mine elect hear my voice and harden not their hearts," Paul's idea is best caught by the noun "elect."

Christ the power of God, and the wisdom of God / Christ is the power of God and the wisdom of God: The word δύναμις (*dynamis*), "power"—as it applies here, refers to the transformative power enabled by the Atonement that changes people into new creatures (2 Cor. 5:17; Gal. 6:15). The word σοφία (*sophia*), "wisdom"—as used here, refers to the teachings of Christ that disclose God's will and direction (John 3:34; 7:17; 14:10; Col. 1:9; 2:3; 3:16).[245] By linking "power" and "wisdom" with God, Paul is showing that true wisdom is not some kind of speculation, theory, or intellectual position, but rather the manifestation of God's dynamic power as expressed in the salvation of his children through the work of Jesus.[246]

---

241. Thiselton, *First Epistle*, 171.

242. This was not the only thing about Jesus that offended them. See George Q. Cannon, "The Blessings Enjoyed through Possessing the Ancient Records, Etc." in *JD*, 22:262; Wilford Woodruff, in *JD*, 18:188.

243. A scribe likely made the change so that this verse was parallel to 1:22 and 24. See Metzger, *Textual Commentary*, 480.

244. Holzapfel and Wayment, *Making Sense*, 346.

245. The Jews viewed the Torah, the law of Moses, as the wisdom from God, indeed, as "a breath of the power of God." See Sir. 6:37; 24:23–25; Bar. 4:1; and especially Wis. 7:25. Paul seems to be playing on this typology, allowing him to reveal Jesus as the new Torah.

246. Fitzmyer, *First Corinthians*, 160.

1:25 *Because the foolishness of God is wiser than men; and the weakness of God is stronger than men:* The subordinate conjunction ὅτι (*hoti*) is causal and explains how it is (or why it is) that Christ is the power and wisdom of God. In the phrase τὸ μωρὸν τοῦ θεοῦ (*to mōron theou*), the neuter definite article modifies the neuter adjective *mōron* and actually refers to "the foolish *thing* of God," but is translated as "foolishness of God" to keep the reading parallel. The "foolish thing" seems to relate to the death of Jesus on the cross, which has prevented both Jew and Gentile from taking Christ seriously.[247] But Paul will not back away from the importance of the cross, insisting that—despite what "wise" men think—God knows what he is doing. Though an action cannot be wise, it can express wisdom. In this case, the crucifixion of the Lord expresses the height of God's wisdom. Thus, that which the wise of the world considered God's weakness, namely salvation through sacrifice, is actually God's strength, sacrifice being the key to salvation. It is this point that Paul is trying to get the Corinthian Saints to see.

Analysis and Summary

The imagery of the cross was extremely important to Paul though it was most repellent to both the Jews and the Greeks.[248] Justin Martyr noted that many Roman citizens called the idea of the Christian worship of a crucified person "madness" (μανία, *mania*).[249] Pliny the Younger confirmed this view, calling the whole Christian movement "madness" (*amentia*) and "a perverse and outlandish superstition" (*superstitio prava et immodica*).[250] The feeling that anyone who believed in Jesus must be mad shows how radically different "the message of the cross" was. Indeed, it differentiated the Christians from all the mythology, legends, and traditions of the ancient world.[251] Therefore, it is not surprising that, despite crucifixion's awful repute, Paul kept it forefront to his readers. He understood the full breadth of the Savior's act: first, it made atonement for past sins, thus allowing them to be forgiven; second, it provided the remedy against those very human weaknesses that caused the sins in the first place through

---

247. Tertullian, *Adv. Marc.,* 5:5 spent a lot of ink on this.
248. The Roman Orator Cicero called it, "a most cruel and disgusting punishment," (*Verr.* 2.5.65) and a death *"unworthy* of a Roman citizen" (*Rab. Post.* 5.16).
249. Justin Martyr, *Apology I,* 13.4.
250. Pliny the Younger, *Ep.* 10.96.4, 8.
251. Fitzmyer, *First Corinthians,* 154.

the enabling power of his grace; and third, that grace went further—even reshaping the Christian soul and bringing about a new kind of existence in the present world as well as in the future heavenly one.[252] The cross was, for Paul, the symbol for this triple effect. Those who partook of the power of the Atonement by accepting Christ through making and keeping covenants with him would have the antidote against the allure of the world. The antidote would work by enabling them to look beyond themselves to serve others. Paul understood that if he could get the Corinthian Saints to partake of the power of the Spirit released by the Lord's selfless act on the cross, it would inoculate them against the pride so affecting the body of the Church. This pride was a major reason why Paul had to attack the mindset of those Christians who were denying the soteriological significance of the Lord's crucifixion.[253]

If some Christians were having a hard time with the cross, it is little wonder that the spiritually unregenerated populous of Corinth simply could not accept as God a person who suffered the ignominious death of a slave. For those whose spiritual eyes suffered from acute myopia, thus disallowing them to see beyond the mortal sphere, attaining station, fame, glory, power, or wealth was what life was all about. Thus, the message of the cross—self-sacrifice and service that demanded seeing others as equals— seemed nothing short of folly (μωρία, *mōria*) if not downright madness (μανία, *mania*). As a result, they would not accept Christian ideals and, thus, were on the path to spiritual ruin.

What they could not believe, as Elder McConkie has noted, is that "God is known only by revelation. All the wisdom of all the world combined cannot search him out. He stands revealed or remains forever unknown. Religion is a thing of the Spirit; it is made known by revelation; hence, it is foolishness to the carnal mind."[254]

For those, however, who had spiritual eyes to see, the message about the cross was the seat of salvation. The contrast between those on their way to spiritual ruin and those on their way to celestial glory, as one scholar has noted, "does not correspond to the antithesis between human folly and human wisdom; it reflects the contrast between *human* folly (*moria*) and *divine* power (*dynamis theou*)."[255] Therefore, the issue is not who is wiser as to the things of

---

252. Thiselton, *First Epistle,* 147.
253. Fitzmyer, *First Corinthians,* 157.
254. *DNTC,* 2:315.
255. Thiselton, *First Epistle,* 154.

the world with the Christians mounting some kind of superior but still mortal ethic. Paul leaves the mortal plane altogether, thus refusing to play the game of one-upmanship. The contrast Paul makes is "that between what is humanly self-defeating, stultifying, and foolish on one side and what becomes effective, operative, powerful, and transformative by divine agency" on the other.[256]

In 1:19, Paul uses a passage from LXX Isaiah 29:14 to prove his point: God will not bow to human reason or understanding but, rather, will destroy both as a means to bring his people to spiritual understanding. Here again, we see Paul's dependence on the Old Testament as the seat for understanding the work of both God and Messiah. In this case, the passage fits precisely. Isaiah had to stand against King Hezekiah's chief advisors who wanted to make a treaty with Assyria. The Lord, against all that was reasonable, advised against any treaty with that nation, promising that, through his own intervention, the Assyrian army would not take Jerusalem (see 2 Kgs. 19).[257] Such proved to be the case and the "wisdom of the wise" failed. Paul says that such is happening again and, therefore, the Christians should not listen to their detractors.

It is important to note that Paul's argument is against neither reasonable thinking nor in wisdom itself.[258] It is rather the manipulative, self-serving, status-seeking, and otherwise flawed thinking that diverts a person from accepting and serving the Lord. Paul's use of the aorist active verb μωραίνω (*mōrainō*), "to make foolish, show to be foolish," is emphatic; God has shown this earth-bound thinking and effort to be foolish through his Son's power to transform souls into new creatures. Paul contrasts the wisdom of the world with that of God, showing their antithetical nature. The former is temporary, short termed, fallible, and self-absorbed while the latter is eternal, infallible, and other-seeking. In short, God has made fools of these self-important persons by showing that their assumed status or achievements are, at best, illusory and, at worst, damning.[259]

Paul's quote from Isaiah shows that he was convinced that the warning found there still had relevance and value for the believer. What he wants them to see is that God will not only reject human wisdom—so highly

---

256. Thiselton, *First Epistle*, 154; italics in original removed.

257. R. E. Clements, *Isaiah 1–39* (Grand Rapids, Mich.: Eerdmans, 1980), 239.

258. For an excellent treatment, see Stanley K. Stowers, "Paul on the Use and Abuse of Wisdom," in *Greeks, Romans, and Christians: Essays in Honor of Abraham J. Malherbe*, ed. David Balch (Minneapolis: Fortress Press, 1991), 253–86.

259. Thiselton, *First Epistle*, 165.

esteemed by those who believe the message of the cross to be foolishness—but he will destroy it, thus proving the folly to be theirs.[260]

The point Paul is pushing is that God constructed his saving means in such a way that it forced people to exercise faith and trust in him, not in themselves. He did this by making it understandable only through revelation.[261]

Paul mentions two ways people want him to prove the gospel true. He notes that the Jews demand signs (the Greek here is plural)—that is, a series of extraordinary and heavenly generated events—in order to prove Jesus really is the Messiah. On the other hand, the Gentiles want well-reasoned and convincing arguments as their proof. Paul will give them neither.

Paul states clearly the reaction of the Jews and the Gentiles to preaching of a crucified Messiah. For both Jew and Gentile, the Corinthian lifestyle demanded gaining status, honor, success, or power by whatever means possible. Those obsessively and blindly caught up in these pursuits would find the idea of a crucified Messiah either totally foolish or a stumbling block. Both Jew and Gentile viewed Jesus as a person of the lowest possible social status, namely, a crucified criminal.[262] For the Jews, to be asked to accept as a heavenly sign of God's saving power the humiliating and disgraceful execution of a Jewish teacher by a foreign power was an affront. They wanted a victorious Messiah heralded by a display of divine power. For the Gentiles, to be asked to accept as a God one whose suffering and death shouted dishonor, shame, and especially failure was nothing short of foolishness.[263] They wanted a philosopher king whose wisdom and intellect none could challenge. In these ways, both Greeks and Jews became adversaries of the crucified Messiah.[264] But, as Paul insisted, the real Messiah was neither a conquering hero nor a worldly sophist. As a result, neither side would readily accept him.[265] Elder Bruce R. McConkie noted the following: "Like many devout people today they had inherited from their fathers lies, vanity, and things in which there was no profit (Jer. 16:19).

---

260. Fitzmyer, *First Corinthians,* 155.

261. Conzelmann, *1 Corinthians,* 46.

262. Pogoloff, *Logos and Sophia,* 156.

263. Thiselton, *First Epistle,* 170.

264. Fitzmyer, *First Corinthians,* 160.

265. Archibald T. Robertson and Alfred Plummer, *A Critical and Exegetical Commentary on the First Epistle of Paul to the Corinthians,* 2d ed. (Edinburgh: T and T Clark, 1958), 22.

They did not know that God the Eternal Father was the Father of Christ, and that Christ was of the seed of David through Mary, his mother. People in that day needed, just as did the people in Joseph Smith's day, a new revelation of God and of the plan of salvation."[266]

There were, however, those who did accept Paul's witness. The Apostle calls these "the called ones." The word κλητός (*klētos*) is a verbal adjective referring to anyone who receives an invitation to some event. Paul's use of the term as a noun, however, gives it a technical cast that refers specifically to those who actually accept the call and, in this case, actually entered into the kingdom of the Son—therefore, in LDS parlance—the idea is best caught in the word "elect."[267] Jesus noted that the call was extended to many, but few become chosen, that is, actually accept the call (see Matt. 22:14). In modern revelation, he has explained why: "Because their hearts are set so much upon the things of this world, and aspire to the honors of men, that they do not learn this one lesson—That the rights of the priesthood are inseparably connected with the powers of heaven, and that the powers of heaven cannot be controlled nor handled only upon the principles of righteousness" (D&C 121:35–36). Only those with a deeply spiritual nature receive the call and gain the title of "called ones."

Those who enter the kingdom come to understand who and what Christ really is. First, he is the power of God, that is, he holds the full power of Elohim for the salvation of humankind through the divine investiture of authority.[268] Through that authorization, the Son can transform those who will yield to him into sons and daughters of God (see John 1:12; 1 John 3:2; Moro. 7:48), thus, directly assisting the Father in his work "to bring to pass the immortality and eternal life of man" (Moses 1:39).

Second, the Savior is the "wisdom of God," that is, he is the one who "makes possible [the] correct understanding" of God, his nature, and work.[269] He is the full revelation of the Divine to humankind. As Elder B. H. Roberts noted: "Henceforth when men shall dispute about the 'being' and 'nature'

---

266. Bruce R. McConkie, in CR, October 1948, 23.

267. Karl Ludwig Schmidt, "κλητός," in *TDNT,* 3:494–96. Matthew 22:14 makes a distinction between the *klētoi,* those who are called, and the *eklektoi,* those who are chosen or elected. However, in other instances the two are equated. See Rev. 17:14 (where "the called, the elect, and the faithful" are one and the same) and Jude 1 (where the called are those beloved of God and preserved by Jesus).

268. For a full treatment, see "The Father and the Son: A Doctrinal Exposition by the First Presidency and the Twelve," in James E. Talmage, *The Articles of Faith* (Salt Lake City: The Church of Jesus Christ of Latter-day Saints,1968), appendix 2.

269. Louw-Nida, §28.8.

of God, it shall be a perfect answer to uphold Jesus Christ as the complete and perfect revelation and manifestation of God; and through all the ages it shall be so—eternally so. For there shall be no excuse for men saying that they know not God, for all may know Him from the least to the greatest, so tangible, so real a revelation has God given of himself in the person, character, and attributes of Jesus Christ."[270]

Speaking of the result of "the wisdom of this world," Joseph Smith stated:

> The great and wise of ancient days have failed in all their attempts to promote eternal power, peace and happiness. Their nations have crumbled to pieces; their thrones have been cast down in their turn, and their cities, and their mightiest works of art have been annihilated; or their dilapidated towers, or time-worn monuments have left us but feeble traces of their former magnificence and ancient grandeur. They proclaim as with a voice of thunder, those imperishable truths—that man's strength is weakness, his wisdom is folly, his glory is his shame.
>
> Monarchial, aristocratical, and republican governments of their various kinds and grades, have, in their turn, been raised to dignity, and prostrated in the dust. The plans of the greatest politicians, the wisest senators, and most profound statesmen have been exploded; and the proceedings of the greatest chieftains, the bravest generals, and the wisest kings have fallen to the ground. Nation has succeeded nation, and we have inherited nothing but their folly. History records their puerile plans, their short-lived glory, their feeble intellect and their ignoble deeds.[271]

In 1:25, Paul concludes his first of three arguments by making two points: First, that which the wise of the world consider God's foolish thing—namely, the Savior's self-sacrifice—is the seat of true wisdom because the Savior's act shows the true way to success and happiness. And second, that which the wise see as God's weakness—that is, giving Christ his power—is where his real strength lies. With the cross, God revealed what he expects of his followers. It was the idea of giving of one's self for the good of others that most Corinthians just did not get. As a result, they were suffering from the cancer of pride that manifested itself in self-aggrandizement and competition. Consequently, they sought for happiness and fulfillment where they could not be found. Unfortunately, this vile sickness had found its way into the Church and could destroy it if it were not cured. Understanding and applying the message of the cross was the cure.

---

270. Truman G. Madsen, "The Meaning of Christ—The Truth, the Way, the Life: An Analysis of B. H. Roberts's Unpublished Master Work," in *BYU Studies* 15, no. 3 (1975): 273.

271. Smith, *History of the Church,* 5:62.

GOD'S CHOICE OF THE FOOLISH (1:26–31)

Paul now begins his second argument, showing the folly of human wisdom and the astuteness of divine wisdom by turning to the condition in which the Corinthian Saints find themselves.[272] Because of their acceptance of Christ, they have been marginalized by the majority of the Corinthians, whether Jew or Greek. They have found themselves without influence or power. Paul shows them that the wisdom of men, which has led to this condition, is itself folly, for it will fail. The reason for the failure is the coming judgment of God, which will vindicate the Christians' faith and damn the faithlessness of the "wise." Paul, as one scholar noted, pushes his readers to see "the risks of human wisdom when it is exalted disproportionately to the detriment of the meaning of Christ and his cross. Wisdom, eloquence, and rhetoric may have their place in human life, but there is further consideration for Christians, whether they come from a Jewish or Gentile background, namely, the gospel or the message of the cross. Paul insists that all Christians must draw strength for human life and its endeavors from 'Christ crucified.'"[273] The reason, as Paul clearly concludes, is that the Savior is the single source of our wisdom, our righteousness, our sanctification, and, ultimately, our redemption.

Greek Text

26 Βλέπετε γὰρ τὴν κλῆσιν ὑμῶν, ἀδελφοί, ὅτι οὐ πολλοὶ σοφοὶ κατὰ σάρκα, οὐ πολλοὶ δυνατοί, οὐ πολλοὶ εὐγενεῖς· 27 ἀλλὰ τὰ μωρὰ τοῦ κόσμου ἐξελέξατο ὁ θεός, ἵνα καταισχύνῃ τοὺς σοφούς, καὶ τὰ ἀσθενῆ τοῦ κόσμου ἐξελέξατο ὁ θεός, ἵνα καταισχύνῃ τὰ ἰσχυρά, 28 καὶ τὰ ἀγενῆ τοῦ κόσμου καὶ τὰ ἐξουθενημένα ἐξελέξατο ὁ θεός, τὰ μὴ ὄντα, ἵνα τὰ ὄντα καταργήσῃ, 29 ὅπως μὴ καυχήσηται πᾶσα σὰρξ ἐνώπιον τοῦ θεοῦ. 30 ἐξ αὐτοῦ δὲ ὑμεῖς ἐστε ἐν Χριστῷ Ἰησοῦ, ὃς ἐγενήθη σοφία ἡμῖν ἀπὸ θεοῦ, δικαιοσύνη τε καὶ ἁγιασμὸς καὶ ἀπολύτρωσις, 31 ἵνα καθὼς γέγραπται· Ὁ καυχώμενος ἐν κυρίῳ καυχάσθω. [SBLGNT]

King James Version

26 For ye see your calling, brethren, how that not many wise men after the flesh, not many mighty, not many noble,

New Rendition

26 Consider your own calling, brothers and sisters. Not many of you are clever by human standards, not many are

---

272. Fitzmyer, *First Corinthians*, 161.
273. Fitzmyer, *First Corinthians*, 153–54.

are called: 27 But God hath chosen the foolish things of the world to confound the wise; and God hath chosen the weak things of the world to confound the things which are mighty; 28 And base things of the world, and things which are despised, hath God chosen, yea, and things which are not, to bring to nought things that are: 29 That no flesh should glory in his presence. 30 But of him are ye in Christ Jesus, who of God is made unto us wisdom, and righteousness, and sanctification, and redemption: 31 That, according as it is written, He that glorieth, let him glory in the Lord.

people of importance, not many are of high status. 27 But God chose the foolish things of the world to put the wise to shame, and God chose the weak things of the world so that he might put the powerful things to shame. 28 God chose the insignificant things of the world, and the things that are despised, things that are regarded as nothing, to nullify the things that are regarded as being something, 29 so that no one can boast in God's presence. 30 It is because of him that you have a personal relationship with Christ Jesus, who has become for us wisdom from God, as well as righteousness, and sanctification, and redemption, 31 so that, as it is written, "Let him who boasts, boast in the Lord."

Translation Notes and Comments

1:26 *For ye see your calling / Consider your own calling:* The verb βλέπω (*blepō*), "see," means "to perceive with the eye," but it carries the nuance of mental activity expressed by the word "consider." The word κλῆσις (*klēsis*), "calling," denotes the position one holds or the condition in which one finds himself. In this case, Paul is referring to their conversion.[274] Thus, Paul is saying, "Consider your own conversion." The point the Apostle is making is that the membership of the Church, for the most part, consisted in men and women that the world considered to be insignificant and of little worth. What he wants them to realize is that if the gospel were a new and grand philosophy, God would not have addressed it to weaklings, base-born, even those considered fools. Yet, God reached out to these with the gift of his gospel and the blessing of deep spiritual endowment because the gospel is not philosophy.[275] God's call suggested that, in spite of what the wise believed, these converts were actually of great value. In essence, they were the proof that God does not use human wisdom or strength to successfully accomplish his tasks.[276]

---

274. BDAG, 549.
275. Findlay, "St. Paul's First Epistle," 771.
276. Fitzmyer, *First Corinthians,* 161.

not many wise men after the flesh, not many mighty, not many noble are called / Not many of you are clever by human standards, not many are people of importance, not many are of high status: Paul uses the Greek word σοφοί (*sophoi*), "wise persons," with a pejorative spin that the idea of "clever people" catches. They are very mentally quick and adroit at contrivances and schemes and, thus, clever at what they do.[277]

The phrase κατὰ σάρκα (*kata sarka*), literally, "according to the flesh," carries the idea of being measured according to human standards and is translated that way in our Rendition. Because Paul connects the idea with οἱ σοφοί (*hoi sophoi*), "the wise or clever," he is pointing out, "Not many of you are clever as the world counts cleverness."[278]

The noun δυνατοί (*dynatoi*), "important people," denotes people of high standing because of their ability to influence others,[279] while the noun εὐγενεῖς (*eugeneis*), "noble" (literally "well born"), also refers to "important people," but it looks to their rank or birth. Since, however, it also includes those outside of the nobility, our Rendition uses "high status."[280]

The JST changes the word "called" to "chosen." In doing so, it shows that the call is not exclusive. People are called from all stations but, among the stubbornly self-sufficient, few accept that call and, therefore, deny themselves the blessing of becoming the chosen of God.

1:27 *But God hath chosen the foolish things of the world to confound the wise / But God chose the foolish things of the world to put the wise to shame:* Paul uses the noun τὰ μῶρα (*ta mōra*), "foolish things," ironically since he is referring to the Saints. From the world's perspective, what they believe is foolish. However, God will prove the world's view wrong. Paul uses the verb καταισχύνω (*kataischynō*), "to cause someone to be much ashamed—to humiliate, to disgrace,"[281] to show the depth of humiliation the world will feel when it realizes God successfully used the humble Saints as his tools to bring about his marvelous work. The world powers would not only be robbed of their glory and power but, more importantly, of their actual being.[282]

God hath chosen the weak things of the world to confound the things which are mighty / and God chose the weak things of the world so that

---

277. BDAG, 935; *Dictionary of Synonyms*, 152, s.v. "clever."
278. See Thiselton, *First Epistle*, 183.
279. Louw-Nida, §87.43.
280. BDAG, 404; Louw-Nida, §87.27.
281. Louw-Nida, §25.194.
282. Findlay, "St. Paul's First Epistle," 772.

he might put the powerful things to shame: Paul uses the term τὰ ἀσθενῆ (*ta asthenē*), "the weak things," ironically, since he is again referring to the Saints. The Apostle again uses the word καταισχύνω (*kataischynō*) to show the depth of humiliation God will bring upon τὰ ἰσχυρά (*ta ischyra*), "the strong things," a term denoting those of power and might.[283]

1:28 *And base things of the world, and things which are despised / God chose the insignificant things of the world, and the things that are despised:* Continuing his parallel structure, Paul continues with irony, now referring to the Saints as τὰ ἀγενῆ (*ta agene*), literally, "things not of noble birth," but meaning here that which is base, obscure, or insignificant.[284] The latter definition, carrying the nuance of "inconsequential," works well as it stands in contrast to the wise, the mighty, and those of station. But Paul really pushes his point by referring to the Saints as τὰ ἐξουθενημένα (*ta exouthenēmena*), "the despised things." The word describes that which is seen as having no merit or value. It carries, however, the strong negative connotation of something despised and, therefore, rejected.[285]

things which are not, to bring to nought things that are / things that are regarded as nothing, to nullify the things that are regarded as being something: The phrase τὰ μὴ ὄντα, ἵνα τὰ ὄντα καταργήσῃ (*ta mē onta, hina ta onta katargēsē*) translates literally as "the things that do not exist, so that the things that exist might be nullified." Paul has been describing the Saints with very pejorative words, going from bad to worse. Here he hits bottom. He calls them τὰ μὴ ὄντα (*ta mē onta*), "the nonexisting things." Again, using irony, Paul shows the world as viewing the Saints of such little significance and influence so as to be nonexistent. But the real irony is that, through them, God will bring to nothing the powerful, the significant, and the influential. In short, the Christians will remain while the Greco-Roman world will not.

Paul is emphasizing the vast difference between how God views things and the world views them. Those things that the world values most are of little or no worth from a divine, eternal perspective, and the things the world considers worthless are of immense, eternal worth.

The JST reads "to bring to naught the things that are mighty." The change focuses particular attention on those in high position in the various

---

283. BDAG, 483.
284. BDAG, 9; Louw-Nida, §87.59. Ogden and Skinner, *Verse by Verse*, 130, notes that "in the early 1600s, *base* meant lowly or humble."
285. BDAG, 352.

fields—the very ones whose power, authority, or ideas are least likely to sink into oblivion. But the power of the gospel makes a shame out of them.

1:29 *That no flesh should glory in his presence / so that no one can boast in God's presence:* Paul now expresses the reason God does what he does. The verb καυχάομαι (*kauchaomai*), "to boast," carries the idea of bragging to bring upon one's self glory or honor.[286] The phrase πᾶσα σάρξ (*pasa sarx*), literally, "any flesh," refers to mortals. Paul's point is that because God did things the way he did, none will be able to take credit. The foolish, weak, despised, and inconsequential see themselves as tools of the Lord and, therefore, will not take credit, while the wise, strong, and influential will see their folly and be unable to brag.

1:30 *But of him are ye in Christ Jesus / It is because of him that you have a personal relationship with Christ Jesus:* In the writings of both Paul and John, the preposition ἐν (*en*) is used to designate a close personal relationship, so that sense of the phrase ὑμεῖς ἐστε ἐν Χριστῷ ᾽Ιησοῦ (*hymeis este en Christō Iēsou*), literally "you are in Christ Jesus" is best rendered in English "you have a personal relationship with Christ Jesus,"[287] as in our Rendition. Paul's point is clear: their new life was derived from God and remained ever grounded in the Savior.[288] The Christians cannot even take credit for their coming into relationship with the Lord, for even this is God's handiwork. He was the one who gave the Lord to all as Savior; he was the one who sent missionaries; he is the one who, through the power of the Holy Ghost, witnessed that Jesus was the Messiah; he was the one who restored the Melchizedek priesthood; he is the one who prepared the way for entrance in the kingdom; he is the one who made spiritual rebirth possible; he is the one who gave the powers of the Spirit to each soul as a *gift*. Therefore, none can boast.

who of God is made unto us wisdom, and righteousness, and sanctification, and redemption / who has become for us wisdom from God, as well as righteousness, and sanctification, and redemption: Paul now shows where the real strength of the Saints lies; it is with Christ. He is God's wisdom, meaning that he is the one who both reveals and executes the Father's will.[289] By accepting that idea, the Saints themselves become wise. He is

---

286. BDAG, 536.

287. BDAG, 327.

288. Findlay, "St. Paul's First Epistle," 773.

289. Though Paul describes Jesus as "the wisdom of God," he is not identifying the Lord with the figure of wisdom that the Gnostics will later develop. Neither Paul nor the Corinthians at this time see "wisdom as a pre-existent divine hypostasis or person." For discussion,

also the source of the Saints' righteousness.[290] Here the word δικαιοσύνη (*dikaiosynē*) denotes a declaration by the Lord that a person is acquitted from all guilt. Further, the Lord imputes righteousness to him.[291] Thus, the person receives not only divine acquittal but also moral virtue. This station opens up the way for sanctification. The noun ἁγιασμός (*hagiasmos*) comes from the same root as "holy" and "Saint." The word is cultic in that it is most closely associated with the temple and denotes something consecrated or dedicated to God. Over time the connotation broadened to include the resultant moral behavior that comes from close association with Deity. Even so, the emphasis is not so much on morality as it is on that kind of religious activity that evidences dedication to God and his will.[292] The result is redemption.[293] The noun ἀπολύτρωσις (*apolytrōsis*), "redemption," is most closely related to the slave market where a slave was traded from one master to another when the latter paid the required price. A slave could be liberated if his owner paid a redemption price at the temple. At that point, the former slave came under the protection of the god.[294] Redemption had three components: (1) liberation from some kind of bondage; (2) liberation by some costly act, and (3) liberation to a new station of service, freed from the old master but indebted to the new. For the Christian, however, there was real freedom in the process.[295] The model works well in 1 Corinthians

---

see James D. G. Dunn, *Christology in the Making: An Inquiry into the Origins of the Doctrine of the Incarnation,* 2d ed. (Grand Rapids, Mich.: Eerdmans, 1996), 176–87, 194–95. Jesus is, rather, the word of God (see John 1:1–3) and, following the idea of "wisdom" as found in Judaism (see especially Prov. 1:1–6; 8:1–14; 9:1–10; 14:1–8; 24:1–7), he is the one who not only expounds the will of God but also brings about his purposes.

290. The noun δικαιοσυνη (*dikaiosynē*) occurs only here in this epistle though the cognate verb δικαιόω (*dikaioō*) is found in 4:4; 6:11. In each instance the word is declarative in judging something as righteous.

291. For discussion, see Translation Notes for Rom. 4:13; 5:15 and James 2:23 in this commentary series.

292. See Louw-Nida, §53.44.

293. Slaves could become free by manumission (Latin *manumissio censu*) and by buying their way out (Latin *peculium*). For a study on Greek and Roman slave practices, see K. R. Bradley, *Slaves and Masters in the Roman Empire: A Study in Social Control* (Oxford: Oxford University Press, 1987). Paul's model does not include these means of becoming free likely because they have no counterpart in the plan of salvation.

294. Deissmann, *Light from the Ancient East,* 318–32.

295. The imagery is not dependent solely on Greco-Roman society. Israel itself was in slavery in Egypt, and God brought them out at a price of the firstborn of the Egyptians. Further, the firstborn of the Hebrews were redeemed from God's service through the temple donation made in their behalf.

in that these people lived in the lowly condition of being "nothings," but through the costly death of the Savior, they gained status and freedom from sin and death. All this came solely through Christ's Atonement and, thus, they could glory only "in the Lord."

1:31 *He that glorieth, let him glory in the Lord /* "*Let him who boasts, boast in the Lord*": The quote is from Jeremiah 9:24.[296] Paul began this pericope by quoting scripture; he ends the same way, thus giving his argument divine force. His point is that all boasting should be in the Lord who opened the way of salvation. This verse, strengthened by its scriptural source, puts into sharp focus Paul's point—not only for the first chapter but also for the whole epistle.[297]

Analysis and Summary

At this point, Paul begins his second of three arguments showing the superiority of God's wisdom over that of humankind by using the nature, composition, and social status of the Christian community either as it stands or as it is perceived. Some have taken Paul's words to suggest that the early Christian movement was among the poorest class of the Greco-Roman world.[298] The latest studies, however, have modified this view somewhat, showing that quite a number of influential people were drawn through the Church's doors.[299] Thus, Paul was addressing a community experiencing "status inconsistency,"[300] with high and low born, rich and poor, free and bond, all meeting together. Thus, the branches evidenced a cross section of Corinthian society.

Unfortunately, this diversity did not protect the Church from problems but exacerbated them. Many Christians from all classes and levels of society were infected with the Corinthian disease of pride and, thus, competed with one another for status and position. Paul likely chose his words in 1:26 as a reminder to many of them of their humble origins.[301] The Apostle's argument accomplishes two tasks: "it lowers the conceit of the readers,"

---

296. The quote is not exact, for Paul replaces τούτῳ (*toutō*), "this," with κύριῳ (*kyriō*), "Lord," but the meaning is the same.

297. Barth, *Resurrection of the Dead*, 17–18.

298. See, for example, Deissmann, *Light from the Ancient East*, 144.

299. See, for example, E. A. Judge, *The Social Pattern of the Christian Groups in the First Century* (London: Tyndale Press, 1960), 60.

300. Wayne A. Meeks, *The First Urban Christians: The Social World of the Apostle Paul* (New Haven, Conn.: Yale University Press, 1983), 54, 68–73.

301. Witherington, *Conflict and Community*, 23–24.

as one authority notes, "while it discloses the true mission of the Gospel."[302] Paul's point is that the gospel plan is not a mere self-improvement program. It is rather a radical rescue brought about through the transforming power found in the grace of Christ. Thus, as one scholar noted, "Grace is not only the great unifier but also the great leveler."[303] The Corinthian branches needed to understand that point—all were equally dependent on Christ and his Atonement, therefore, none could take credit for any degree of spiritual superiority or righteousness.

Paul's concern is giving credit where it is due. Many of the Corinthians, being heavily involved in self-reliance and self-promotion, bragged about all they did. Self-glory was a large part of the game they played. In this portion of his argument, Paul redirects this καύχασθαι (*kauchasthai*), "glorying, boasting," to God and Christ. He shows that God has used the Christians to put down the wise, the influential, and the powerful and, in the process, made them wise, influential, and powerful in the eternal scheme.[304] In 1:29, Paul makes his point, showing that "glorying is inappropriate in God's presence because whatever provides grounds for such glorying [station, gifts of the spirit, rebirth, etc.] has come from God as his gift."[305] Thus, the Apostle begins 1:30 with ἐξ αὐτοῦ (*ex autou*), "It is from him that," the phrase forcing Paul's readers to remember that God alone made their relationship with Jesus possible. Therefore, they have no right to brag about anything. But the idea goes a step further; in Christ they have not only access to salvation but also to the perfect model of leadership.[306] That model does away with any self-glorying and puts a stop to all boasting.

Paul is trying to get his readers to see that the message of the cross brings a complete reversal to how the Greco-Roman world assesses success. It is not wealth, education, birth, or position that gives one status before God, but obedience, humility, and—above all—self-sacrifice displayed in loving service. Paul builds his thesis using two triads: the foolish things, the weak things, and the insignificant stand in contrast to the wise, the strong, and the influential.[307] Using both irony and hyperbole, Paul refers to the Saints

---

302. Findlay, "St. Paul's First Epistle," 771.

303. Witherington, *Conflict and Community*, 118.

304. Thiselton, *First Epistle*, 180–81.

305. Thiselton, *First Epistle*, 188.

306. Dale B. Martin, *The Corinthian Body* (New Haven, Conn.: Yale University Press, 1995), 59.

307. Τὰ ἀγενῆ (*ta agenē*), "the insignificant," (see BDAG, 8) is contrasted with the τὰ ὄντα (*ta onta*), "those with station," not the εὐγενεῖς (*eugeneis*), "noble born."

as τὰ μὴ ὄντα (*ta mē onta*), literally "things that are not," because, by their society's standards, the Christians are "nothings." The reality is, however, that in God's eyes they are not only "somethings" but also the force by which he will bring to nothing the works, policies, and philosophies of their society's assessed wise, strong, and influential.[308]

Paul's argument finds force in Isaiah 55:8–9 wherein the Lord states, "For my thoughts are not your thoughts, neither are your ways my ways, saith the Lord. For as the heavens are higher than the earth, so are my ways higher than your ways, and my thoughts than your thoughts." Thus, Jehovah made clear that his ways are not human ways. One fact that emphasizes this point is the nature of those whom he calls into his kingdom. He feels free to call those whom the world sees as weak, untrained, even naïve, but the Lord is proving a point: that he can give understanding and insight to any, both learned and unlearned, who are willing to humble themselves and follow his ways. The Lord has made it clear that "I call upon the weak things of the world, those who are unlearned and despised, to thresh the nations by the power of my Spirit" (D&C 35:13). He assured Joseph Smith that "for unto this end have I raised you up, that I might show forth my wisdom through the weak things of the earth" (D&C 124:1; compare D&C 1:19; 35:13; 133:59).

There is a reason for this. It is the humble who can master spiritual things. This ability is "in large measure a matter of pre-existent preparation," notes Elder McConkie. "Some people developed in the pre-mortal life the talents to recognize truth, to comprehend spiritual things, to receive revelation from the Spirit; others did not. Those so endowed spiritually were foreordained and sent to the earth to serve at God's command as his ministers."[309]

In all his response to human wisdom, God had his purpose. It was to stop all boasting. For Paul, boasting exhibits the fundamental mindset he is trying to change. It shows that people are putting trust in their own cleverness, strength, ability, and even righteousness to save themselves. God found fault with ancient Israel for this very attitude, noting that he treated that people the way he did "lest Israel vaunt themselves against me, saying, Mine own hand hath saved me" (Judg. 7:2). It was this same mindset that separated many Jews from Jesus (see Rom. 1:16–32). Paul is trying to get the Corinthians to understand that human beings cannot bring about their own salvation no matter how wise, clever, or strong they are. Paul

---

308. Thiselton, *First Epistle*, 185.
309. *DNTC*, 2:317.

ends his second argument by making this very point. Indeed, he insists that all are dependent on God and Christ for quality of life in this world and in the world to come. Therefore, there is no room to brag of one's deeds or the positions one has held, for none of these count. What counts is Christ whose teachings hold real wisdom for they are from God, whose righteousness is the model, whose grace brings sanctification, and finally, whose Atonement brings redemption. All these he bestows on the Saints so that they become wise, righteous, sanctified, and redeemed. Therefore, all glorying should be in praise of Christ and all he has done. The idea is confirmed in a commandment found in D&C 76:61, "let no man glory in man, but rather let him glory in God."

Chapter 2

The Contrast between Human Wisdom and God's Wisdom

INTRODUCTION

In chapter 1, Paul reminded the Corinthians of the lesson they should have learned concerning the valueless nature of human wisdom with which they had become so enamored. Using every means possible to him, Paul has attempted to prove the folly of such wisdom (particularly interpreting the gospel through the lens of philosophy) and to undermine their fascination with and dependence upon it. His particular concern was with the spiritually dangerous self-congratulation and the self-sufficiency it promoted.[1]

Another lesson they should have learned, based on their own new status as God's people, was the way the Holy Spirit operates in the conversion process. Their conversion had been brought about by their very personal experience with the Spirit. Paul now shows how his method of preaching while at Corinth confirms the same lesson. As Elder Bruce R. McConkie has pointed out, "there was of old, there is now, and . . . there shall be only one approved and proper way to preach the gospel—Preach by the power of the Spirit. Anything short of this is not of God and has neither converting nor saving power."[2]

Paul's point is that the Spirit works through humble, noncontentious means—independent of human ways and methods. He has already shown them the truth of this position based on "the gospel's obvious independence of human intelligence" (see 1:18–25) and "the lowly calibre of those called" (see 1:26–31). He now emphasizes that lesson by stressing "the

---

1. Fee, *First Epistle*, 89–90.
2. *DNTC*, 2:318.

manner in which he had consistently introduced the gospel at Corinth" (see 2:1–5).[3]

To push his point, Paul goes on to note that the Christians "speak the wisdom of God in a mystery" that even the elite of the world cannot fathom because they do not have access to the Spirit, which is necessary for understanding (2:6–14). He ends by assuring the Saints that those who have the Spirit can judge all things while the world is completely incapable of judging them (2:15–16).

PAUL'S PREACHING OF CHRIST TO THE CORINTHIANS (2:1–5)

Greek Text

1 Κἀγὼ ἐλθὼν πρὸς ὑμᾶς, ἀδελφοί, ἦλθον οὐ καθ᾽ ὑπεροχὴν λόγου ἢ σοφίας καταγγέλλων ὑμῖν τὸ μαρτύριον τοῦ θεοῦ. 2 οὐ γὰρ ἔκρινά τι εἰδέναι ἐν ὑμῖν εἰ μὴ Ἰησοῦν Χριστὸν καὶ τοῦτον ἐσταυρωμένον· 3 κἀγὼ ἐν ἀσθενείᾳ καὶ ἐν φόβῳ καὶ ἐν τρόμῳ πολλῷ ἐγενόμην πρὸς ὑμᾶς, 4 καὶ ὁ λόγος μου καὶ τὸ κήρυγμά μου οὐκ ἐν πειθοῖ σοφίας ἀλλ᾽ ἐν ἀποδείξει πνεύματος καὶ δυνάμεως, 5 ἵνα ἡ πίστις ὑμῶν μὴ ᾖ ἐν σοφίᾳ ἀνθρώπων ἀλλ᾽ ἐν δυνάμει θεοῦ. [SBLGNT]

King James Version

1 And I, brethren, when I came to you, came not with excellency of speech or of wisdom, declaring unto you the testimony of God. 2 For I determined not to know any thing among you, save Jesus Christ, and him crucified. 3 And I was with you in weakness, and in fear, and in much trembling. 4 And my speech and my preaching was not with enticing words of man's wisdom, but in demonstration of the Spirit and of power: 5 That your faith should not stand in the wisdom of men, but in the power of God.

New Rendition

1 Now when I myself came to you, brothers and sisters, I did not come with eloquent speech or wisdom as I proclaimed to you the mystery of God. 2 For I resolved to know nothing among you except Jesus Christ and him crucified. 3 And I appeared before you in weakness and fear and with considerable trepidation, 4 and my speaking and my preaching was not with the persuasiveness of wisdom, but with the convincing proof of the Spirit and of power, 5 so that your faith would not be based on human wisdom but on the power of God.

---

3. C. Clare Oke, "Paul's Method Not a Demonstration but an Exhibition of the Spirit," *Expository Times* 67 (1955): 35–36.

Translation Notes and Comments

2:1 *And I, brethren, when I came to you / Now when I myself came to you,*
brothers and sisters: Paul here continues his theme of the previous chapter
that God has chosen the weak things of the world to accomplish his purposes (1:28). He uses the emphatic pronoun ἐγώ (*egō*), "I myself," to stress
that, like the Saints at Corinth, he, too, is weak and one that the world considers of little consequence. As already noted above, Paul regularly uses
ἀδελφοί (*adelphoi*), literally "brothers," to refer to both male and female
members of the Church. Hence our Rendition translates it as "brothers
and sisters."

came not with excellency of speech or of wisdom / I did not come with
eloquent speech or wisdom: In the phrase καθ᾽ ὑπεροχὴν λόγου ἢ σοφίας
(*kath hyperochēn logou ē sophias*), the noun *hyperochē* literally meant
"a natural formation that protrudes," thus "a projection, or prominence,"
but in New Testament Greek it was used figuratively as "a state of excel-
ling, superiority, preeminence."[4] Thus the phrase could be translated "with
excellence of speech or wisdom." But the idea behind the phrase is that of
excess, going beyond what is required, in other words, showing off.[5]

A hallmark of Greco-Roman teaching and oratory was the use of rhetoric: eloquent, polished, well-reasoned argumentation designed to persuade. Paul emphasizes that he did not follow this practice. Indeed, he
deliberately set himself, as a preacher, against those others who made a
practice of the art of persuasion.[6] He would be no part of the competitive
showmanship so prevalent in that area that was all about self-promotion.

the testimony of God / the mystery of God: A number of manuscripts
have μαρτύριον (*martyrion*), "testimony," which the KJV follows. Earlier
manuscripts, however, suggest that the correct word should be μυστήριον
(*mystērion*), "mystery," and our Rendition follows these.[7] In 2:7, Paul clarifies what he means by the word "mystery." The word denoted knowledge
unknown before, which God reveals only to a select group of people who
were not to share it.[8] The emphasis is on its property as something revealed,

---

4. BDAG, 1034.

5. See *hyper* in BDAG, 1031.

6. On the abundance of the rhetoricians and Sophists competing for attention during
the Isthmian Games, see Plutarch, *Quaest. Conv.* 8.4.1; Dio Chrysostom, *Virt.* (Or. 8), 8:9.

7. See Metzger, *Textual Commentary*, 480. For a careful analysis, see Collins, *First*
Corinthians, 118.

8. BDAG, 661. In apocalyptic literature of the Jews, *mystery* was associated with the
outpouring of revealed knowledge of those salvific events associated with the age to

something too profound to be arrived at through human reason or intellect. Paul's use of the word emphasizes that the Christian gospel comes strictly through revelation from God.[9]

The word *mystērion* also had a strong cultic connotation referring as it did to sacred ceremonies and rites that were part of temple worship among certain Greco-Roman religions. Those initiated into these rites became possessors of special divine knowledge which was to be kept from the uninitiated.[10]

2:2 *For I determined not to know any thing among you, save Jesus Christ, and him crucified / For I resolved to know nothing among you except Jesus Christ and him crucified:* The phrase οὐ γὰρ ἔκρινα τι εἰδέναι ἐν ὑμῖν (*ou gar ekrina ti eidenai en hymin*) presents some grammatical difficulties in translation. Taken literally it seems to say, "For I did not resolve to know anything among you." This, however, is an example of the privative use of the negative particle οὐ (*ou*), in which "οὐ with the principal verb may be equivalent in sense to μή with a dependent infinitive."[11] Thus the correct translation is "I resolved to know nothing among you," as in our Rendition.

The coordinating conjunction γάρ (*gar*), "for," with which Paul introduced his thought, is explanatory. The Greek text makes it clear that Paul very deliberately chose his method of preaching. Unlike many of the philosophers and teachers in the Greco-Roman world who claimed to have great knowledge of many things to pass on to their students, Paul committed himself only to that which concerned "Christ, and him crucified." Paul's settled policy was to focus exclusively on Jesus Christ and the salvation he brought.[12]

2:3 *in weakness, and in fear, and in much trembling / in weakness and fear and with considerable trepidation:* The noun ἀσθένεια (*astheneia*), "weakness," usually denotes a state of illness but can refer to limitation. Here it expresses Paul's feeling of inadequacy given his great responsibility

---

come. Among the Christians, it pointed to God's dealings with his people in preparation for his millennial reign. See Collins, *First Corinthians*, 115.

9. BDAG, 662; Louw-Nida, §28.77, compare 53.15.

10. G. Bornkamm, "μυστήριον," in *TDNT*, 4:802–27.

11. Herbert Weir Smyth, *Greek Grammar* (Cambridge, Mass.: Harvard University Press, 1956), §691.

12. Thiselton, *First Epistle*, 211. President J. Reuben Clark Jr. declared, "The great mission of this Church is to proclaim Christ and him crucified and his Gospel (1 Cor. 2:2). This should be the message that all Christendom declares." CR, April 1954, 18.

of not only proclaiming the word but also in doing it the correct way.[13] Therefore, the word should be construed with πρὸς ὑμᾶς (*pros hymas*), meaning "as I was with you," showing that he expressed this "weakness" as he ministered among them.[14] He further expresses the distress he was under when he arrived by noting the depth of his fear that both he and his message would be rejected.

With these words, Paul contrasts himself with the self-promoting and egotistical Sophists who dominated the rhetorical stage. His words stress the idea that he did not see himself as one of them—crowd pleasing, arrogant show-offs who came and went as the tide. Paul's words also suggest the humble attitude of one who bore great responsibility before God and men to adequately and properly proclaim the word of God to all who would hear.[15]

2:4 *my speech and my preaching / my speaking and my preaching:* Paul's words here denoted the two methods by which he proclaimed God's word. The first was through λόγος (*logos*), "word, speech," which here likely means private conversations and teachings. The second was through κήρυγμα (*kerygma*), "public declaration."[16] His words suggest the consistency of his message and his method. His method never varied in public or in private. Though it is true that his words may have lacked the elegance of some orators because he chose not to follow their ways—and this is his point—he did not lack knowledge, and it was his knowledge that counted.[17]

enticing words of man's wisdom / the persuasiveness of wisdom: Ancient manuscripts give eleven different readings of this verse. Of the variants, the ones that include the adjective ἀνθρωπίνης (*anthrōpinēs*), "human," are almost certainly an added gloss. The two variants most likely to be the original are ἐν πειθοῖ σοφίας (*en peithoi sophias*), "by persuasion of wisdom," and ἐν πειθοῖς σοφίας λόγοις (*en peithois sophias logois*), "by

---

13. BDAG, 142.

14. There are two reasons to take this meaning: (1) It follows precisely 16:10, showing Timothy was coming and should not fear while he is "with you," and (2) 2:1–2 shows what Paul resolved to do on the way, and 2:3 shows how he did during his ongoing visit. See Fee, *First Epistle,* 92.

15. Thiselton, *First Epistle,* 213.

16. BDAG, 543. Robertson and Plummer, *Critical and Exegetical Commentary,* 32; and Conzelmann, *1 Corinthians,* 54, both suggest that the words simply reflect a hendiadys of terms. It seemed to us that Paul was stressing the idea that his public and private methods and message were the same.

17. Fitzmyer, *First Corinthians,* 172–73.

persuasive words of wisdom."[18] Because the adjective πειθός (*peithos,* "persuasive") appears nowhere else in all of extant Greek literature, the former reading seems to be the best, and is the one chosen by the editors of the SBLGNT. Therefore, our Rendition follows the same reasoning.

Also, the noun πειθώ (*peithō*) does not carry the negative feel that the KJV translation "enticing" suggests. The word simply means "persuasiveness," and we have so translated it in our Rendition.[19]

Again, Paul emphasizes the uniqueness of the method by which he delivered his message. He did not use the rhetorical tricks and cunning devices of the Sophists. It was not through the persuasive or compelling words of the missionary that the message grabbed the people, but by the right of its own power.

but in demonstration of the Spirit and of power / with the convincing proof of the Spirit and of power: The noun ἀπόδειξις (*apodeixis*), "demonstration, proof," carries the idea of the verification or proof that a statement or position is true, thus the word is translated "convincing proof" in our Rendition.[20] We have translated the phrase πνεύματος καὶ δυνάμεως (*pneumatos kai dynameōs*), "of the Spirit and of power," as a subjective genitive, thus showing that through the power of the Spirit (as opposed to the preaching of Paul) truth was revealed. Further, in Paul's writings, he uses the words "Spirit" and "power" almost interchangeably. Therefore, we could have here a hendiadys ("the use of two words . . . to express a single complex idea"[21]), suggesting that Paul's convincing proof was "the Spirit," that is, "power," even the power of God.[22] Paul's point is that what sold his message was not "persuasive words." Skillful reasoning and argument were not the basis of its success. Rather, the Spirit was the powerful Rhetor with the Apostle being but its spokesman. These people should have known, through their own conversion experience, that the full assurance of what he said came only through the "convincing proof" of the Spirit.[23]

2:5 *That your faith should not stand in the wisdom of men, but in the power of God / so that your faith would not be based on human wisdom but on the power of God:* In the phrase ἐν σοφίᾳ ἀνθρώπων (*en sophia*

---

18. See Metzger, *Textual Commentary,* 481. Though the verse presents some difficulty in translation, the thrust of Paul's thought is not in doubt.

19. Louw-Nida, §33.304.

20. Louw-Nida, §28.52.

21. Smyth, *Greek Grammar,* §3025.

22. Fee, *First Epistle,* 95.

23. Collins, *First Corinthians,* 120.

anthrōpōn), literally "in the wisdom of men," we have translated the preposition ἐν (*en*) as "based on" to best convey the sense of the passage.

In this sentence, Paul explained why he chose the manner in which he proclaimed the gospel message. The Apostle knew that conversion based on intellectual arguments and clever phrases could neither endure persecution and tribulation nor bring salvation. He wanted his converts to have a firm foundation sustained by the revelatory power of the Spirit of God.

Paul shows his readers that God uses the witness of the Spirit to his own ends. It is through that power that Paul makes it possible for the spiritually sensitive to get beyond reason and logic, opinion and belief, argument and rebuttal—those methods used by the uninspired—to find eternal truths. Using the power of the Spirit meant that people came to know that the source of their testimony was not man-made manipulation or emotionalism, but divine confirmation.

Analysis and Summary

Paul begins this chapter by noting that he came to Corinth proclaiming the "mystery of God" (2:1, Rendition). Many of his readers, coming from a pagan background, would have, as Paul intended, tied the word to the rites practiced by certain religions whose initiates were given secret knowledge that pertained to the gods and their work with humankind. Those who received such knowledge were known as οἱ τέλειοι (*hoi teleioi*) "the perfected,"[24] and their esoteric knowledge was not to be shared by those outside the religious order.[25] Here, in contrast to members of those religions, Paul shows that he presented the Christian mystery openly to all who would hear.

Paul's method of presentation was very deliberate. In no way was he, through clever words and high-sounding phrases, going to overshadow the message. He understood that the Sophists were more anxious to please their hearers than to present the truth. Not so with Paul. The message was all-important, not the one who delivered it.

Further, he stressed that what some of the Saints found so impressive ("the persuasiveness of wisdom" used by certain men [2:4]), he deliberately avoided. Nonetheless, his method was not without persuasion as their own conversions testified. What it deliberately omitted was the personal appeal and self-aggrandizement of which the methods of the Sophists and

---

24. BDAG, 995–96.
25. G. Bornkamm, "μυστήριον," in *TDNT*, 4:802–27.

rhetoricians were so full. Its strength was that it brought understanding for and faith in the Messiah and his Atonement.[26]

Some scholars have suggested that Paul's less-than-successful experience at Athens, where he had used a more philosophical approach, lent itself to his resolve to back away from that method. Such, however, does not seem to be the case. A careful study of Acts 17:19–34 suggests Paul was moving his message toward his core teaching—"Christ, and him crucified" (2:2)—when he was interrupted over the idea of the Resurrection and conditions inhibited him from returning to his subject. Luke's account gives not the slightest hint that Paul felt disenchanted with his experience at the Areopagus.[27] Paul's resolve at Corinth, then, was based not on past experience but on the new condition he faced—men preaching for self-glory and mammon.[28]

Nonetheless, his approach did bring reproach. As one scholar has noted, certain branch members seemed to have "felt they had the right to judge Paul and his message and were evaluating him by the same criteria by which popular orators and teachers were judged. Paul disputed this right."[29] Paul refused to adopt the cajoling and wheedling methods used by most and, particularly, the more aggressive verbal bullying and demagogic tactics used by many.[30] His objective was to let truth speak for itself, not to manipulate his audience through clever rhetorical speech or an intimidating display of oratorical power.[31] Paul's method was grounded in his Jewish background and understanding. Power came from God through seeming weakness (compare Ex. 4:10; Isa. 6:5; Jer. 1:6; see especially Isa. 53). Paul's words made it plain to the Corinthian Saints that the clear and demonstrative "proof" (ἀπόδειξις, *apodeixis*) of the gospel came not in external manifestations of verbal eloquence but only by the power of the Spirit.[32] It

---

26. Fee, *First Epistle,* 94.

27. James Moffatt, *The First Epistle of Paul to the Corinthians* (London: Hodder and Stoughton, 1938), 22.

28. Fee, *First Epistle,* 92.

29. Witherington, *Conflict and Community,* 47.

30. Timothy B. Savage, *Power through Weakness: Paul's Understanding of the Christian Ministry in 2 Corinthians* (Cambridge: Cambridge University Press, 2004), 73.

31. Paul, likely unknowingly, was following the advice of Aristotle, who taught the importance of clear proofs over mere opinions convincingly dressed up as fact. See *Top.* 1.1; 1.4; 1.8; 1.11; *Rhet.* 1.1–3; 1.1.11.

32. James A. Davis, *Wisdom and Spirit* (Lanham, Md.: University Press of America, 1984), 78–81.

was on this that their initial faith was born and on this which they must continue to rely.

Though Paul often equates faith with obedience to God's will (see, for example, Rom. 1:5; 16:19), here his use suggests a fervent and heartfelt belief coupled with an intellectual certitude in the salvific powers of the Atonement. In doing so, Paul was not denigrating the total use of persuasion and argument. These do play an important part in getting the message heard (compare 1 Pet. 3:15), but Paul was insisting that there is a higher spiritual means that speaks to both the mind and the heart and, in doing so, creates in the believer a new and more sure reality (compare 1:18; D&C 8:2–3).[33]

Part of Paul's willingness to use such humble means was based on his sure sense of his own authority. That authority undergirded his message and gave him that inner confidence that allowed him to proceed as he initially determined. He knew, as one scholar noted, that his authority did not lie in "smooth, competent, impressive, powers of elocution, but in the faithful and sensitive proclaiming rendered operative not by the applause of the audience, but by the activity of God."[34] Paul's ways fit comfortably with the Lord's latter-day instruction to his missionaries, "Ye are not sent forth to be taught, but to teach the children of men the things which I have put into your hands by the power of my Spirit; And ye are to be taught from on high" (D&C 43:15–16) and, "if ye receive not the Spirit ye shall not teach" (D&C 42:14). Paul seems to have understood that it was "the Comforter which was sent forth to teach the truth" (D&C 50:14). Indeed, the Comforter "shall teach them all things that are expedient for them" (D&C 75:10).[35] But Paul also seems to have known, too, that "No power or influence can or ought to be maintained by virtue of the priesthood, only by persuasion, by long-suffering, by gentleness and meekness, and by love unfeigned; By kindness, and pure knowledge, which shall greatly enlarge the soul without hypocrisy, and without guile" (D&C 121:41–42). Therefore, he relied on his authority but did not use it to bully the people into submission. Instead, he carefully explained himself.

Paul's concluding clause, "that your faith should not stand in the wisdom of men, but in the power of God" (2:5), states clearly his purpose in both the form his message took and how he delivered it. In modern times, the

---

33. Thiselton, *First Epistle,* 223.

34. Thiselton, *First Epistle,* 214, the italics and bold from the original have been removed.

35. See *DNTC,* 2:318–19.

Lord has confirmed the same means, "you shall have power to declare my word in the demonstration of my Holy Spirit" (D&C 99:2). Paul's methods were meant to disarm the effective force of the worldly wise and influential and bring his listeners to trust in God and Christ alone and completely. That trust, however, was based neither on his words or personality nor on those of anyone else. It was based on the power of the Spirit that came upon them when they heard and exercised faith in the message. Though Paul's words, "in demonstration of the Spirit and of power" (2:4), could suggest that he was here referring to signs and, therefore, suggesting that faith rests upon that kind of evidence, such is not that case. For Paul the paradigm is always the same: "Christ, and him crucified," and the power that comes from that act, namely the transforming of the human soul that brings spiritual insight and conversion (compare Alma 32:21–43).[36]

THE TRUE WISDOM OF GOD (2:6–8)

Greek Text

6 Σοφίαν δὲ λαλοῦμεν ἐν τοῖς τελείοις, σοφίαν δὲ οὐ τοῦ αἰῶνος τούτου οὐδὲ τῶν ἀρχόντων τοῦ αἰῶνος τούτου τῶν καταργουμένων· 7 ἀλλὰ λαλοῦμεν θεοῦ σοφίαν ἐν μυστηρίῳ, τὴν ἀποκεκρυμμένην, ἣν προώρισεν ὁ θεὸς πρὸ τῶν αἰώνων εἰς δόξαν ἡμῶν· 8 ἣν οὐδεὶς τῶν ἀρχόντων τοῦ αἰῶνος τούτου ἔγνωκεν, εἰ γὰρ ἔγνωσαν, οὐκ ἂν τὸν ͺ ύριον τῆς δόξης ἐσταύρωσαν· [SBLGNT]

King James Version

6 Howbeit we speak wisdom among them that are perfect: yet not the wisdom of this world, nor of the princes of this world, that come to nought: 7 But we speak the wisdom of God in a mystery, even the hidden wisdom, which God ordained before the world unto our glory: 8 Which none of the princes of this world knew: for had they known it, they would not have crucified the Lord of glory.

New Rendition

6 However, we do speak wisdom among the spiritually mature, but not the wisdom of this world or of the leaders of this present age who are doomed to perish. 7 But we speak God's wisdom which is hidden in a mystery, which God foreordained for our glory before the world was, 8 which none of the leaders of this present age has understood, for if they had understood, they would not have crucified the Lord of glory.

---

36. Fee, *First Epistle*, 96.

Translation Notes and Comments

2:6 *Howbeit we speak wisdom among them that are perfect / However, we do speak wisdom among the spiritually mature:* The δέ (*de*) here is clearly adversative and so is translated as "however" in our Rendition. The adjective τέλειος (*teleios*) means literally "perfect, complete, or finished." It was also a technical term used to describe one who had been initiated into one of the mystery religions of classical antiquity by which they were made complete or fully finished in their religion.[37] Among the Christians, it could describe one who had been brought into full fellowship within the community, which may have included temple blessings.

In addition, the word referred to a mature adult. For Paul, it contrasted those who were spiritually immature (mere spiritual "babes," see 3:1) with those who were spiritually mature and could, therefore, understand the wisdom of God.

Paul admits that he does, indeed, speak a specific kind of wisdom (again note the adversative δέ [*de*], "but," at the beginning of 2:7), but his is radically different from the one with which some of the Corinthian Saints had become enamored.[38] His words, however, show us that there is nothing inherently evil about wisdom and using the intellect, but, to be proper or correct, it must be guided and informed by the Spirit of God, which the world in general has not prepared itself to receive.[39]

not the wisdom of this world, nor of the princes of this world, that come to nought / not the wisdom of this world or of the leaders of this present age who are doomed to perish: The noun ἄρχων (*archōn*) describes broadly anyone of eminence or administrative authority.[40] Paul seems to use it to include all those who shaped the world order of his day. Thus, our Rendition translates the word as "leader," giving it its broadest meaning. The noun αἰών (*aiōn*) had the basic sense of "a long period of time," but it was also used to refer to "a segment of time as a particular unit of history, [such as an] age."[41] Paul is clearly using it in this sense as reflected in our Rendition.

---

37. LSJ, 1769–70; BDAG, 995–96. Those initiated into the temple rites were called τέλεις (*teleios*), that is, "perfected ones." See G. Bornkamm, "μυστήριον," in *TDNT*, 4:802–27.

38. The word here does not have the definite article, "a wisdom," and contrasts with τὴν σοφίαν (*tēn sophian*), "the wisdom" the world knows.

39. Elder McConkie notes that "there is much reasoning and intellectuality in the world which prepares men for that preaching which carries conviction and brings conversion." *DNTC*, 2:319.

40. BDAG, 140.

41. BDAG, 32.

In this verse, Paul assures his readers that the wisdom he proclaims is associated neither with this nor any other age nor with the very sophisticated wisdom of those who shaped Greco-Roman society.[42] Because such wisdom is both self-regarding and self-serving, it can lead neither to truth nor salvation,[43] but rather to spiritual death. Paul's use of the present passive participle here, τῶν καταργουμένων (*tōn katargoumenōn*), "which are coming to an end," shows that the present age, along with all those who created it, are doomed to destruction.[44]

2:7 *But we speak the wisdom of God in a mystery, even the hidden wisdom / But we speak God's wisdom which is hidden in a mystery:* The prepositional phrase ἐν μυστηρίῳ (*en mystēriō*) is ambiguous. Does it modify the verb "speak" (that is, "we speak . . . in a mystery"), or does it modify the noun "wisdom" (that is, "wisdom . . . hidden in a mystery")? The KJV chooses the former translation. In our Rendition we have chosen the latter as the more likely because the words "wisdom" and "hidden" are both in the accusative with "hidden" working as an appositive to "mystery" to show where the "wisdom" was hidden.

Paul regularly used the word "mystery" to describe the spiritual knowledge that can only come from God and which mere mortal intellect, without divine help, cannot grasp. In doing so, he stressed the importance of ongoing revelation. In this case, the mystery is God's means of salvation, namely, strength through weakness referring specifically to the crucifixion of Jesus, an act that caused such a scandal among both Jews and Greeks.

which God ordained before the world unto our glory / which God foreordained for our glory before the world was: The verb προορίζω (*prohorizō*) means "to decide or plan beforehand," and it is translated as "ordained" in the KJV and "foreordained" in our Rendition. The word carries no implication of predeterminism, but it accords with the Latter-day Saint concept of that which God has planned beforehand. His planning includes not only the operation of historical processes and movements but also when and where he will place each of his children. At its center is the means through which he will save his children. None of this preplanning, however, takes away his children's freedom to choose for themselves. The word does, however, show that God left nothing in the salvation process to chance. According to the Prophet Joseph Smith,

---

42. Thiselton, *First Epistle*, 236.
43. C. K. Barrett, *Essays on Paul* (Louisville, Ky.: Westminster John Knox Press, 1982), 10.
44. BDAG, 525.

The great Jehovah contemplated the whole of the events connected with the earth, pertaining to the plan of salvation, before it rolled into existence, or ever "the morning stars sang together" for joy; the past, the present, and the future were and are, with Him, one eternal "now;" He knew of the fall of Adam, the iniquities of the antediluvians, of the depth of iniquity that would be connected with the human family, their weakness and strength, . . . He was acquainted with the situation of all nations and with their destiny; He ordered all things according to the council of His own will; He knows the situation of both the living and the dead, and has made ample provision for their redemption, according to their several circumstances, and the laws of the kingdom of God, whether in this world, or in the world to come.[45]

Paul notes that what God foreordained was, at its heart, for "our glory." The word δόξα (*doxa*), "glory," denotes, in this case, the state of divine approbation and affirmation with its accompanying endowment of power, splendor, and intelligence that awaits all those who accept the Lord and follow his way (see Rom. 8:18, 21; Philip. 3:21; 1 Pet. 5:1, 10; Rev. 21:11; D&C 76:50–57; 93:36).[46]

2:8 *Which none of the princes of this world knew: for had they known it, they would not have crucified the Lord of glory / which none of the leaders of this present age has understood, for if they had understood, they would not have crucified the Lord of glory:* The KJV translates the verb ἔγνωκεν (*egnōken*) as "knew." But it is not an aorist, which expresses a simple past tense, but a perfect tense of γινώσκω (*ginōskō*), "to know, understand." The most common usage of the perfect tense in Greek is "to *emphasize* the completed action of a past action or process from which a present state emerges,"[47] and is best translated by an English present perfect tense as we have done in our Rendition—"none of the leaders of this present age has understood" (and in fact *still* do not understand).

Next follows a past contrary to fact condition,[48] which explains that if the leaders had understood, they would not have crucified Christ.

---

45. Smith, *History of the Church*, 4:597.

46. The glory that comes to the believer is the goal and fulfillment of the divine call to service. See Gerhard Kittel and Gerhard von Rad, "δόξα," in *TDNT*, 2:233–53. For discussion, see Fitzmyer, *First Corinthians*, 176.

47. Daniel B. Wallace, *Greek Grammar beyond the Basics: An Exegetical Syntax of the New Testament* (Grand Rapids, Mich.: Zondervan, 1996), 577; italics in original; Smyth, *Greek Grammar*, §1945, explains, "The perfect denotes a completed action the effects of which still continue in the present."

48. Wallace, *Greek Grammar*, 694–96; Smyth, *Greek Grammar*, §2302.

Grammatically this presents no problems, but interpreting the reason why the leaders would not have crucified Christ does. Some commentators take it to mean that "if they [the leaders of this present age] had had access to God's wisdom which decreed the effects of the cross, or indeed could have known that the cross formed a central place in God's wise purposes, they would not have lent their aid unwittingly to furthering these purposes."[49] But this contradicts the clear statements of Jacob, the brother of Nephi:

> Wherefore, as I said unto you, it must needs be expedient that Christ—for in the last night the angel spake unto me that this should be his name—should come among the Jews, among those who are the more wicked part of the world; and they shall crucify him—for thus it behooveth our God, and there is none other nation on earth that would crucify their God. For should the mighty miracles be wrought among other nations they would repent, and know that he be their God. But because of priestcrafts and iniquities, they at Jerusalem will stiffen their necks against him, that he be crucified. (2 Ne. 10:3–5)

According to Jacob, had Christ come to Rome, Greece, Parthia, Egypt, or any other of the nations of that time period, they would have recognized his divinity and not crucified him. It was only the Jewish leaders of that time, who, because of their priestcrafts and unparalleled wickedness, would crucify Christ in the face of the overwhelming evidence of his divinity. And yet, in spite of their wickedness, they unwittingly assisted God in his eternal plan of redemption. It was necessary that Christ be crucified, but as Christ told his disciples, "It is impossible but that offences will come: but woe unto him, through whom they come!" (Luke 17:1).[50]

Another irony this verse holds is that the Jewish leaders, whose aim was glory and fame, killed the very source of ultimate glory. Indeed, as Paul's witness testifies, Jesus possessed all glory (compare Col. 1:19; 2:9; D&C 93:11–17) and, therefore, was the source of all glory (see Matt. 16:27; John 17:5, 20–23; Jacob 4:4; D&C 29:12), which, by killing him, the Jewish leaders had eternally denied themselves.

Analysis and Summary

Paul is very forthright in telling his readers his message is not for all. Indeed, only the spiritually mature (τοῖς τελείοις, *tois teleiois*) are in a position to

---

49. Thiselton, *First Epistle*, 248.

50. Similarly, Christ referring to Judas Iscariot said, "The Son of man goeth as it is written of him: but woe unto that man by whom the Son of man is betrayed! it had been good for that man if he had not been born" (Matt. 26:24).

really understand and embrace it. Since Paul's term *teleios* (given its technical nuance) applied to those initiated into the mystery religions, it hints to a Christian mystery that centered on sacred rites not shared with the world through which the Christian came into full fellowship and maturity with other Christians.[51] By this means they come to know, at least in part, "the deep things of God" (see 2:10). These deep things include the means God had ordained for the salvation of his children (see Translation Notes on 2:10 below).

The nuance of the Greek word translated "this world" (τοῦ αἰῶνος τούτου, *tou aiōnos toutou*) is of an age and, therefore, Paul was not referring to the earth but to the present world order. This period, he knew, was going to come to an abrupt end.[52] The reason for its demise was that this order was not self-sustaining and, therefore, could not endure. Giving the verse this apocalyptic nuance suggests that Paul knew that, in God's own time, the present order would be replaced with one that was eternal. Therefore, the Christian must not anchor himself or herself to it.

Up to this point, Paul's use of the term σοφία (*sophia*), "wisdom," was deliberately pejorative, and he was doubly justified in not using the ways of the Sophist: first, because of the true nature of the gospel and, second, because of the nature of the community of the Saints in Corinth. The gospel was not philosophy and, further, they were not philosophers.[53] He now, however, adopts it, but only after redefining and, in the process, lifting it from a philosophical, rhetorical, and mundane plane to a historical, soteriological, and eternal one. In the process, he reveals that his argument is not based on the *form* of wisdom, to which he does not object, but on its *content* and *means of expression*. He has already shown that the central core of true or divine wisdom is "Christ, and him crucified" (2:2). Only by accepting that fact does one have the ground on which to build true wisdom and, thereby, come to realize what true fame and glory are and how they are acquired. The whole is based on an understanding of how God saves his children and what the reward of that salvation is.[54]

51. On the early Christian mystery, see Donald W. Parry and Stephen D. Ricks, eds., *The Temple in Time and Eternity* (Provo, Utah: Foundation for Ancient Research and Mormon Studies at Brigham Young University, 1999), 88, 214–17, 247; Hugh Nibley, *Temple and Cosmos: Beyond This Ignorant Present,* ed. Don E. Norton, vol. 12 of The Collected Works of Hugh Nibley (Salt Lake City: Deseret Book; Provo, Utah: Foundation for Ancient Research and Mormon Studies at Brigham Young University, 1992), 28, 56, 65, 71, 213–14.

52. Thiselton, *First Epistle,* 232.

53. Findlay, "St. Paul's First Epistle," 774.

54. Fee, *First Epistle,* 101–2.

Paul's writings reveal that there were some Christians who were developing a Christian philosophy that did not include the Atonement or, at the least, greatly distorted it. They viewed Jesus as a great teacher and moralist, a person with superior ethics and one to be revered and followed. Some Church members may have, in their devotion to Jesus, argued that his ways and thoughts were superior to Socrates, Plato, or any of the great philosophers.[55] But that view denied the very nature of the Lord, stripped out the central aspect of his mission, and gutted the real message of the gospel. He did not come merely to make earth life easier, though his gospel certainly does that, but to open the way to salvation. He did that through his power as God and out of self-sacrificing love expressed in his death on the dreaded cross. But the cross, as noted in the introduction of this volume, was the sticking point for Paul's detractors. It was a scandal of such magnitude that for some, even among the Christians, it simply could not be accepted.

There was another aspect of human wisdom that gave getting rid of the Atonement great appeal. It opened the door to "works of righteousness" as the means of salvation. Many of those converted from Judaism were already well exposed to this idea. At its heart, this school of thought insisted that the base of justification and salvation was not the Savior and the grace that was his but in following the gospel law.[56] In short, one could save one's self. The idea had great appeal to those inured with self-importance and self-promotion, for it allowed them to be in charge of their own salvation, owing no one or anything for their success. This was heady stuff indeed and appealed to quite a number of Church members. Thus, they had an impetus for denying any need for the grace coming out of the cross.

But this belief also stopped them from seeing Jesus for what he really was. Oh, they were willing to accept him as their master, their leader, and their guide. He was, after all, in Jewish terms the Messiah, the divine "anointed one," who brought God's message to earth. But only secondarily was he a savior. Paul could not abide such an idea. Jesus was *the* Savior and the only source of salvation. In order to allow people to understand the proper place of Jesus, the Apostle had to remind them of the very core of

---

55. Jewish writers such as Aristobulus (c. 170–150 BC) and Philo Judaeus (c. 20 BC– 50 AD) had already made this claim about Moses who, they insisted, was the inspiration behind much Greek philosophy. For details, see Edwin Hatch, *The Influence of Greek Ideas on Christianity* (Gloucester, Mass.: Peter Smith, 1970), 66–69, 183–88. These were the Hibbert lectures given in 1888.

56. For a full discussion, see the Translation Notes on Gal. 3:10–13, 24–26 and Rom. 3:23–28 in this commentary series.

the gospel, that is, the beauty, power, and, most importantly, the absolute necessity of the Atonement.

Paul admitted that the gospel, referencing as it did the wisdom of God, could only be described as mysterious. The Greek term μυστήριον (*mystērion*), unlike the English word "mystery," did not denote that which was impenetrable because it was inherently unintelligible or incoherent. Rather, it pointed to that which was too profound for human ingenuity and could not be obtained by unassisted human logic or reasoning.[57] It could be gained only by the Spirit.[58] Once disclosed, however, it made perfect sense to the spiritually mature. For those living in the last days, the Lord has promised that as his prophets abide in him; he will give them "the keys of the mystery of those things which have been sealed, even things which were from the foundation of the world, and the things which shall come from this time until the time of my coming" (D&C 35:18).

But there is an echo in Paul's use of the word *mystērion* that should not be overlooked. As noted above, Paul's use of the words τοῖς τελείοις (*tois teleiois*), "the mature," referred not only to an adult person but also to initiates in certain religious systems. The word *mystērion* was also connected with those same religions whose rites were kept from the uninitiated. Some aspects of the Christian meetings "were indeed associated with 'secret rites' known only to initiates, as in the mystery religions."[59] Paul's use of the word indicates he was not telling all he knew. Instead, he was selecting out that material from the mystery that could be made public.

His detractors insisted that they were the spiritually elite who understood the things of God better than he. They complained, therefore, that his doctrine was but milk compared to the meat they had. (In chapter 3, Paul will address this attitude directly.) The problem with Paul's detractors was that, in their self-reliant claim to special wisdom, higher spirituality, and superior spiritual gifts, they had become blind to the fact that they had been seduced by a false wisdom, one anchored in the present world order which actually put them in deadly spiritual peril.[60]

Using acute irony, Paul demolished both their false boasting and imprecations. He showed his readers that these people were not as spiritual as they claimed. Indeed, they had missed the point in not seeing the cross for

---

57. Findlay, "St. Paul's First Epistle," 778.
58. BAGD, 661–62; Thiselton, *First Epistle*, 240–41.
59. Thiselton, *First Epistle*, 241.
60. Thiselton, *First Epistle*, 247.

what it was, namely, an expression and revelation of the superior wisdom of God. This oversight had made them incapable of making proper judgments. As a result they were, like those in the world, pursuing wisdom but of the wrong kind. Ironically, their supposed spirituality was, in reality, not spiritual at all.[61]

Paul developed his argument against them in three stages. First, the nature of God's wisdom he set forth by contrasting it between those who receive it with those who do not. Though God's wisdom was foreordained to bring glory to all who would realize it, it was held "in a mystery"—that is, it could only be fathomed by revelation—and thus hidden from all levels of spiritually immature society (2:6–10a). Second, he explained how some were let in on the mystery while others are not. Those who had the spirit of revelation, the spiritually mature, knew the mind of God and, thus, understood how the salvation process worked (2:10b–13). Finally, he divided all into "natural" and "spiritual" people, confirming that the former simply could not know the things of God because they refused to seek them through the proper process. Therefore, they saw the cross as foolishness and, in doing so, made themselves incapable of proper judgments. In contrast, those with the Spirit were the only ones capable of making such judgments (2:14–16).[62]

For Paul, the Spirit is the key that opens up proper understanding and makes it possible to judge the truthfulness or falseness of all things. Therefore, one must have the Spirit to understand God's wisdom. The comfort in the message is that understanding is not just for the leadership. Paul's point fits well with Joseph Smith's teaching that "God hath not revealed anything to Joseph [Smith], but what He will make known unto the Twelve, and even the least Saint may know all things as fast as he is able to bear them."[63] There is a caveat, however. "We never can comprehend the things of God and of heaven," the Prophet taught, except "by revelation."[64] In this vein, Elder McConkie pointed out that "until men receive personal revelation they are without God in the world, they are not on the course leading to salvation, and they cannot go where God and Christ are. . . . Men may study about religion, about God, and about his laws, but they cannot receive that knowledge of them whom to know is eternal life except by revelation from the Spirit of God."[65]

---

61. Fee, *First Epistle*, 98–99.
62. Fee, *First Epistle*, 99–100.
63. Smith, *History of the Church*, 3:380.
64. Smith, *History of the Church*, 5:342.
65. *DNTC*, 2:321.

Paul identified three aspects of God's wisdom that he wanted his readers to understand: first, it was wisdom hidden in mystery and, therefore, dependent on revelation for understanding (2:7); second, even before the world began, God foreordained it to bring glory to those who would receive it (2:7); and third, it was of such a nature that, even with all their sophisticated learning, none of the leaders of the world could figure it out (2:8). The irony of it all was that some of the Corinthian Saints were enamored with a philosophy that was, at that very moment, passing away and in the process taking its greatest supporters, the impressive leaders of that age, with it (2:6).[66]

One more critical point needs to be made. Some scholars, critical of the traditional understanding, have taught for years that the divine Jesus was an invention of late first- and second-century Christians who, being decades away from their Lord, were able to explain for themselves and to others who and what Jesus really was and the enigma and ignominy of his death.[67] But, as one scholar has boldly noted, Paul, writing as he did in the mid-first century, belies this idea: *"There can scarcely be a clearer statement in Scripture that the cross was no unfortunate historical accident; a mere act of bravery* or political martyrdom *later* turned to good account."[68] The true followers of the Lord knew from the beginning his true and divine nature and the role that played both in the Atonement and the plan of salvation.

Intellectual versus Spiritual Understanding (2:9–16)

Greek Text

9 ἀλλὰ καθὼς γέγραπται· Ἃ ὀφθαλμὸς οὐκ εἶδεν καὶ οὖς οὐκ ἤκουσεν καὶ ἐπὶ καρδίαν ἀνθρώπου οὐκ ἀνέβη, ὅσα ἡτοίμασεν ὁ θεὸς τοῖς ἀγαπῶσιν αὐτόν. 10 ἡμῖν γὰρ ἀπεκάλυψεν ὁ θεὸς διὰ τοῦ πνεύματος, τὸ γὰρ πνεῦμα πάντα ἐραυνᾷ, καὶ τὰ βάθη τοῦ θεοῦ. 11 τίς γὰρ οἶδεν ἀνθρώπων τὰ τοῦ ἀνθρώπου εἰ μὴ τὸ πνεῦμα τοῦ ἀνθρώπου τὸ ἐν αὐτῷ; οὕτως καὶ τὰ τοῦ θεοῦ οὐδεὶς ἔγνωκεν εἰ μὴ τὸ πνεῦμα τοῦ θεοῦ. 12 ἡμεῖς δὲ οὐ τὸ πνεῦμα τοῦ κόσμου ἐλάβομεν ἀλλὰ τὸ πνεῦμα τὸ ἐκ τοῦ θεοῦ, ἵνα εἰδῶμεν τὰ ὑπὸ τοῦ θεοῦ χαρισθέντα ἡμῖν· 13 ἃ καὶ λαλοῦμεν οὐκ ἐν διδακτοῖς

---

66. Fee, *First Epistle*, 106–7.

67. See, for example, James D. G. Dunn, *Jesus Remembered*, vol. 1 of Christianity in the Making (Grand Rapids, Mich.: Eerdmans Publishing, 2003), 25–127; and Ehrman, *Historical Introduction*, chapters 13, 15.

68. Thiselton, *First Epistle,* 248; italics in original.

ἀνθρωπίνης σοφίας λόγοις, ἀλλ' ἐν διδακτοῖς πνεύματος, πνευματικοῖς πνευματικὰ συγκρίνοντες.

14 Ψυχικὸς δὲ ἄνθρωπος οὐ δέχεται τὰ τοῦ πνεύματος τοῦ θεοῦ, μωρία γὰρ αὐτῷ ἐστίν, καὶ οὐ δύναται γνῶναι, ὅτι πνευματικῶς ἀνακρίνεται· 15 ὁ δὲ πνευματικὸς ἀνακρίνει τὰ πάντα, αὐτὸς δὲ ὑπ' οὐδενὸς ἀνακρίνεται. 16 τίς γὰρ ἔγνω νοῦν κυρίου, ὃς συμβιβάσει αὐτόν; ἡμεῖς δὲ νοῦν Χριστοῦ ἔχομεν. [SBLGNT]

King James Version

9 But as it is written, Eye hath not seen, nor ear heard, neither have entered into the heart of man, the things which God hath prepared for them that love him. 10 But God hath revealed them unto us by his Spirit: for the Spirit searcheth all things, yea, the deep things of God. 11 For what man knoweth the things of a man, save the spirit of man which is in him? even so the things of God knoweth no man, but the Spirit of God. 12 Now we have received, not the spirit of the world, but the spirit which is of God; that we might know the things that are freely given to us of God. 13 Which things also we speak, not in the words which man's wisdom teacheth, but which the Holy Ghost teacheth; comparing spiritual things with spiritual. 14 But the natural man receiveth not the things of the Spirit of God: for they are foolishness unto him: neither can he know them, because they are spiritually discerned. 15 But he that is spiritual judgeth all things, yet he himself is judged of no man. 16 For who hath known the mind of the Lord, that he may instruct him? But we have the mind of Christ.

New Rendition

9 But as it is written: "That which neither eye has seen, nor ear heard, nor entered into a person's heart—all these things God has prepared for those who love him." 10 But to us God has revealed them by the Spirit, for the Spirit fathoms all things, even the deep things of God. 11 For what human being understands human things except the human spirit that is in him? So too, no one understands the things of God except the Spirit of God. 12 Now we have not received the spirit of the world, but the Spirit which comes from God, so that we can understand the things which God has generously given to us; 13 which we also speak, not with words taught by human wisdom but those taught by the Spirit, interpreting spiritual things by means of spiritual things. 14 But the natural man does not accept the things of the Spirit of God, because they are foolishness to him and he cannot understand them, because they are spiritually discerned. 15 But one who is spiritual discerns all things, but is himself discerned by no one. 16 For who knows the mind of the Lord so that he can advise him? But we have the mind of Christ.

Translation Notes and Comments

2:9 *But as it is written:* Paul's introductory words seem to indicate he is quoting scripture, but if so, it is not in any single verse in the Old Testament as it stands today.[69] It is not clear what the antecedent is of the contrastive conjunction ἀλλά (*alla*), "but," that begins the verse.[70]

Eye hath not seen, nor ear heard, neither have entered into the heart of man, the things which God hath prepared for them that love him / That which neither eye has seen, nor ear heard, nor entered into a person's heart—all these things God has prepared for those who love him: The phrase "entered into a person's heart" reflects the biblical לֵב עַל עָלָה (*'ālāh 'al lēb*), literally "to go up into the heart," but the idiom means "to enter into the most deep and profound areas of human thought." The phrase emphasizes the complete inability of human senses or the power of the human mind to even imagine what God intends for the faithful.

Our Rendition treats the neuter plural relative pronoun ἅ (*ha*) as the object of the three verbal phrases: οὐκ εἶδεν (*ouk eiden*), "did not see," and οὐκ ἤκουσεν (*ouk ēkousen*), "did not hear," and οὐκ ἀνέβη (*ouk anebē*), "did not enter in." This relative pronoun is then clarified by the correlative neuter plural pronoun ὅσα (*hosa*) in the sense "all these things."[71]

This verse contains one of only three examples, in the writings of Paul, where God is the object of ἀγαπάω (*agapaō*), "to love," that is, where the love flows to God (for the other two, see 8:3; Rom. 8:28). Usually he speaks of God's love as it flows to the Saint (see, for example, Rom. 5:5, 8; 2 Cor. 13:14; Titus 3:4). In God, ἀγάπη (*agapē*), "love," flows "spontaneous, unmotivated by anything outside himself, creative, elective, and free."[72] Whereas in humans, *agapē* is neither spontaneous nor unmotivated and, therefore, rests on an unstable foundation. Paul overcame this human limitation by appealing to the need for faith and trust in the Father that results in a more mature love that is directed fully and freely toward God. When, however, love does gain these more divine qualities, and thereby becomes stable, it is through the Spirit as its highest gift (see Analysis on 13:1–3). Being able to give love freely, then, comes when one is profoundly touched by the Spirit of God. When the Saint reciprocates God's love

---

69. Possible sources for various parts of the quotation include Isa. 64:4 for lines 1 and 2, and the Septuagint version of Isa. 65:16 for line 3. Other possible sources are the *Apocalypse of Elijah,* the *Testament of Jacob,* and the *Gospel of Thomas* 17. For discussion, see Fitzmyer, *First Corinthians,* 177–78.

70. See B. Frid, "The Enigmatic ἀλλά in 1 Cor. 2:9," *New Testament Studies* 31 (1985): 603–11.

71. BDAG, 729.

72. For discussion, see Anders Nygren, *Agape and Eros,* two volumes in one (London: SPCK, 1953), 123–33.

back to him, the door to "God's wisdom" opens and this child can understand the mind of God, which the world cannot. Again, the central point of "God's wisdom" is "Christ, and him crucified" (2:2) and what comes out of it: namely, the salvation of God's children. God's wisdom includes, therefore, all that he and Jesus have done for humankind as well as those principles and ordinances humankind must obey to achieve exaltation (see Rom. 8:28).[73]

2:10 But God hath revealed them unto us by his Spirit / But to us God has revealed them by the Spirit: The early papyrus 𝔓[46] (c. 200) and the codex Vaticanus (c. 400) have γάρ (*gar*), "for," but all other early manuscripts have δέ (*de*), "but," and both the KJV and our Rendition follow these.[74]

Paul's word ἡμῖν (*hēmin*), "to us," refers back to 2:9, meaning those who love God. His witness is that human love, directed fully and freely to the Father, opens up avenues of spiritual insight (compare 8:3; 13:2; 1 John 4:7).[75] His words point to a specific inner circle—those who are truly spiritually mature expressed by their possession of divine-like love—who have exclusive right to the "deep things of God" (2:10).

the Spirit searcheth all things, yea, the deep things of God / the Spirit fathoms all things, even the deep things of God: The present active verb ἐραυνάω (*eraunaō*) means "to search, examine, investigate."[76] In our Rendition, we have chosen to translate it as "fathom" because the Spirit is presented here as being able, as it were, to penetrate even into the depths of the sea to perceive what is there. Paul's point is that all things—"even the inscrutable judgments and untraceable ways of God"[77]—are known to the Spirit and, therefore, can be revealed to those who love the Father. Indeed, love is the key that unlocks the depths of God and brings his ways more fully into focus. As John, Paul's fellow Apostle, taught, "God is love" (1 John 4:8) and those who love understand him, for, in this way, they are like him (1 John 4:7, 16–17). Thus, to them the Spirit can reveal the Father's innermost heart—"the deep things of God" (2:10) and of Christ—allowing them to understand his ways and his means. Here, Paul moves his readers one step closer toward the Christological understanding that he will arrive

---

73. Fitzmyer, *First Corinthians*, 179.

74. Metzger, *Textual Commentary*, 481.

75. Findlay, "St. Paul's First Epistle," 781.

76. BDAG, 389.

77. Fitzmyer, *First Corinthians*, 180.

at in 2:16.[78] Paul's point is that it is only through the Spirit that the Saint can really fathom the message of the cross and its results.[79]

2:11 *For what man knoweth the things of a man, save the spirit of man which is in him? even so the things of God knoweth no man, but the Spirit of God / For what human being understands human things except the human spirit that is in him? So too, no one understands the things of God except the Spirit of God:* The Apostle's thought here aligns with a Greek proverb, "Like is known only by like."[80] Therefore, Paul's statement should not be construed as addressing the issue of human duality—the tension between body and spirit and where the seat of thought or mind are—but rather to express, as one scholar put it, "our common experience of personal reality. At the human level, I alone know what I am thinking, and no one else, unless I choose to reveal my thoughts in the form of words. So also only God knows what God is about."[81] Humans left to their own devices can never know God's mind and will. The Spirit, however, being one with God and being able to fathom the mind of God, can reveal "the things of God" to the loving, righteous soul. Again, Paul's words underscore the need for continuous revelation.

2:12 *Now we have received, not the spirit of the world, but the spirit which is of God; / Now we have not received the spirit of the world, but the Spirit which comes from God:* Paul here, after a digression in 2:10–11, returns to the central point of the entire paragraph and applies it to the issue at hand, namely the wisdom of the world verses the wisdom of God.[82] The conjunction δέ (*de*), usually translated as "and" or "but," becomes a connecting link and is, therefore, translated with "now" in both the KJV and Rendition.

He speaks of the τὸ πνεῦμα τοῦ κόσμου (*to pneuma tou kosmou*), "the spirit of the world," a pejorative phrase denoting that which is at odds with God and his realm. The phrase points to all that makes earthly conditions secular. It also looks to that which promotes a condition of spiritual blindness that allows people to spend so much of their time on the transitory and inconsequential.[83]

---

78. Thiselton, *First Epistle*, 181.

79. On the various designations of the term "spirit," see R. B. Hoyle, *The Holy Spirit in St. Paul* (London: Hodder and Stoughton, 1927).

80. Plato, *Leg.* 4.716c. Compare Philo *Gig*, 2 §9; Homer, *Odys*, 17.218.

81. Fee, *First Epistle*, 112.

82. Fee, *First Epistle*, 112 and n. 60.

83. Fitzmyer, *First Corinthians*, 181.

Standing in contrast to the "spirit of the world" is "the spirit which comes from God." The preposition ἐκ (*ek*) in the phrase τὸ πνεῦμα τὸ ἐκ τοῦ θεοῦ (*to pneuma to ek tou theou*) carries the idea of coming or issuing forth from something.[84] The preposition ties the spirit directly to the Father. As such, God's spirit is an enabling power that flows from him as a gift to those willing to receive it (see John 15:26–27; 16:27; and concerning Christ, compare John 1:14; 6:46; 7:29; 17:8). It should not be confused with the gift of the Holy Ghost, but rather points to what that gift brings.[85] That is, as President Joseph F. Smith stated, "the influence of Deity, the light of Christ, or of Truth, which proceeds forth from the presence of God to fill the immensity of space, and to quicken the understanding of men"[86] (see also D&C 88:6–13).

that we might know the things that are freely given to us of God / so that we can understand the things which God has generously given to us: Here Paul expresses God's purpose in sharing his spirit with the Saints. The verb εἴδωμεν (*eidōmen*) is the subjunctive of οἶδα (*oida*) and translated as "know" in the KJV. The word connotes more than mere intellectual knowledge. It is "to grasp the meaning of something, *understand, recognize, come to know, experience.*"[87] Hence, our Rendition translates it as "understand."

Paul's words emphasize an important point—that the Father has no intention of keeping his "deep things" from his children. The word Paul uses, χαρίζομαι (*charizomai*), means "to give graciously or generously, with the implication of good will on the part of the giver."[88] Paul's use underscores God's gracious and generous willingness to bestow wonders of understanding from the eternal realm.[89] Indeed, the Lord has promised that "he will give unto the faithful line upon line, precept upon precept; and I will try you and prove you herewith" (D&C 98:12). To them, he has promised he will eventually reveal "all things—Things which have passed, and hidden things which no man knew, things of the earth, by which it was

---

84. BDAG, 296. It would have been but a short step for some of the philosophy-bound Christians to see the spirit in Stoic terms as a quasi-agent all-pervasive substance. See Hoyle, *Holy Spirit*, 219.

85. Fitzmyer, *First Corinthians*, 181.

86. Joseph F. Smith, *Gospel Doctrine* (Salt Lake City: Deseret Book, 1939), 60.

87. BDAG, 694.

88. Louw-Nida, §57.102. The form of the word here is an aorist passive participle *charisthentai*.

89. BDAG, 1078.

made, and the purpose and the end thereof—Things most precious, things that are above, and things that are beneath, things that are in the earth, and upon the earth, and in heaven" (D&C 101:32–34). Only by this means can one attain to true wisdom, meaning the proper understanding of the salvation that the crucified Christ opened for all who would believe.

2:13 *comparing spiritual things with spiritual / interpreting spiritual things by means of spiritual things:* The phrase πνευματικοῖς πνευματικὰ συγκρίνοντες (*pneumatikois pneumatika syngkrinontes*) is ambiguous. It could mean "comparing spiritual things with spiritual [things]," as in the KJV, or "interpreting spiritual things for spiritual [people]," or "interpreting spiritual things by means of spiritual things."[90] To us, the third alternative seems to best fit the context and is, therefore, found in our Rendition.

The present active participle συγκρίνοντες (*synkrinontes*) denotes the act of comparing.[91] Though it is the usual definition, it does not exactly fit this context. There is a strong possibility that the Septuagint, Paul's favorite translation of the Old Testament, influenced his use of the word for there it takes on more of the meaning of "to interpret" or "explain."[92] Taking into account the anterior force of the temporal participle, Paul's thought is that the Saints must *always* explain "the things of the Spirit [as described in 2:12] by means of the words taught by the Spirit" and not those of the world that showcase cleverness, adroitness, and especially artifice.[93]

2:14 *the natural man:* The Greek phrase is ψυχικὸς ἄνθρωπος (*psychikos anthrōpos*). The adjective *psychikos* in Koine Greek refers to "the life of the natural world and whatever belongs to it, in contrast to the realm of experience whose central characteristic is πνεῦμα, *natural, unspiritual, worldly.*"[94] The phrase corresponds exactly with King Benjamin's characterization of "the natural man" as found in Mosiah 3:19. The natural man, at his best, is one whose choices and actions are motivated by the natural desires of the flesh in contrast to a spiritual man, whose choices and actions are inspired by the Spirit of God.[95] The term "natural man," then, designates that class of people whose acute spiritual myopia prevents them from seeing beyond the limits of the temporal horizon.

---

90. See Thiselton, *First Epistle,* 264–65; Fee, *First Epistle,* 115 and n. 76.
91. Paul is the only person to use this word in the NT—here and in 2 Cor. 10:12.
92. BDAG, 953.
93. Fee, *First Epistle,* 115.
94. BDAG, 1100.
95. Findlay, "St. Paul's First Epistle," 783.

they are foolishness unto him / they are foolishness to him: On foolishness, see Translation Notes on 1:18. The natural man, uninspired by the Spirit of God, simply cannot understand the things of God, and so he dismisses them as complete nonsense.[96]

neither can he know them / and he cannot understand them: The force of this phrase is the absolute inability of the natural man to understand spiritual things. It is not because God has precluded him, but, tragically, because the natural man has incarcerated himself in a realm (the present world order [see Comment on 3:18]) where spiritual things cannot, no matter how hard he or others may try, be understood. The simple truth is that no one who is carnal or natural can understand, let alone see, God (see D&C 67:10).

because they are spiritually discerned: In this phrase, Paul explains why the natural man "cannot" understand spiritual things. The Greek verb used here, ἀνακρίνω (*anakrinō*), means "to carefully study a question, to examine, discern."[97] It was also used in a legal context with the sense of "to conduct a judicial hearing."[98] The word "discern" works well because it carries the idea of being able to "make appropriate 'judgments' about what God is doing in the world."[99] The things of God, therefore, can only be judged—that is, examined or discerned—by those who possess the Spirit of God.

2:15 *But he that is spiritual judgeth all things, yet he himself is judged of no man / But one who is spiritual discerns all things, but is himself discerned by no one:* Paul uses the same Greek verb, ἀνακρίνω (*anakrinō*), here as he did in the previous verse. The sense is that one who has the Spirit of God can examine all things and discern between truth and error, but no one lacking the Spirit can properly discern and, therefore, judge him. These words are not only a jab at the uselessness of listening to those of the world but also to those in the Church who profess higher spirituality and, by that claim, pass judgment on Paul and those who follow him.[100]

---

96. Ogden and Skinner, *Verse by Verse,* 131.

97. BDAG, 66.

98. BDAG, 66.

99. Fee, *First Epistle,* 117; see also Thiselton, *First Epistle,* 273; compare Ogden and Skinner, *Verse by Verse,* 131.

100. The post history of this verse evidences the importance of not taking scriptures out of context. By the fifteenth century, there were those who appealed to "the spiritual" as an excuse for not having to follow conventions of good judgment and reasoning, while certain ecclesiastical regimes appealed to it to justify their power. Thus, it has been used, as Robertson and Plummer have stated (*Critical and Exegetical Commentary,* 50), as a

2:16 *who hath known the mind of the Lord, that he may instruct him? / who knows the mind of the Lord so that he can advise him?:* This is a quote from LXX Isaiah 40:13. Paul uses the scripture as a proof text to show that a person who lacks inspiration cannot understand God's thoughts and purposes. Such a person is, therefore, in no position to give counsel or advise on spiritual matters to those who do.

But we have the mind of Christ: With these few words, Paul arrives at his point: those who are inspired by the Spirit of God can know what God and Christ are thinking and, in fact, become like them. Here he presents his deep Christological understanding: the Saint can share in the mind of God though Christ. "Christ acts and speaks by the power of the Spirit," states Elder McConkie. "Those saints who walk in the light as he is in the light, who keep his commandments, who actually enjoy the presentment or gift given them following baptism, thereby have his mind. They think what he thinks, know what he knows, say what he would say, and do what he would do in every situation—all by revelation from the Spirit."[101]

Analysis and Summary

Paul's words in this section appear to address the claims of his detractors who boasted that they lived on a higher spiritual plane than Paul and other Saints. The Apostle, therefore, spends some time giving a clear and forthright corrective redefinition of the true nature of spirituality.[102] First, it does not come from the world but is centered in and is a gift from God (2:12); second, it is based on revelation through which one comes to "have the mind of Christ" (2:16); and third, it consists of being "mature" (τέλειος, *teleios*), which reveals itself in terms of unity and deference (3:1–3).

And Paul does more. He also sets up his framework about the nature and work of the Spirit upon which he will later expand (see chapters 12–14). In the present paragraph, he shows that the term "spirit" (πνεῦμα, *pneuma*) has no relationship with the Greek notion of the spiritual "inner self" of platonic dualism, but, in contrast with all that is human, it is an exhibition of divine power that acts upon the righteous person. It is at all times "inseparable from the work of God as revealed in Christ."[103] Indeed, it is the

---

recipe for "either anarchy or tyranny." When Paul is properly read, however, both positions will be found baseless.

101. *DNTC*, 2:322.
102. Thiselton, *First Epistle*, 252.
103. Thiselton, *First Epistle*, 256.

major source of revelation and, therefore, indispensable in understanding all things spiritual.[104]

To bolster his point, Paul quotes a scripture (2:9) that is not found in our Old Testament. It states that so supernal are God's rewards for those who truly love him that even the most expansive imaginations have failed to comprehend them (compare D&C 133:45). Speaking of this, Elder Orson Pratt said, "It has not entered into the heart of man to conceive the things which God has laid up for them that love Him, unless he is filled with the Holy Ghost, and by vision gazes upon the thrones and the dominions, the principalities and powers, that are placed under His control and dominion; and He shall sway a righteous scepter over the whole."[105] Speaking of those "things God hath prepared for those who love him" (2:9), Elder Wilford Woodruff stated that those who will be exalted will have to submit to all that "God may decree. But for all this they will receive their reward—they will become Gods, they will inherit thrones, kingdoms, principalities and powers through the endless ages of eternity, and to their increase there will be no end, and the heart of man has never conceived of the glory that is in store for the sons and daughters of God who keep the celestial law."[106] Even so, as Paul notes, there are some things—indeed, the most important things—the faithful can know because "God hath revealed them unto us by his Spirit" (2:10).

As noted in the paragraph above, the very essence of spirituality and the key that unlocks the door to understanding the things of God is love, especially love directed toward him (2:9). To those who fully love, the Father is willing to reveal the mysteries of his kingdom (see D&C 6:7, 11; 42:61–65), or as Paul describes them, "the deep things of God" (2:10).

Speaking of these "deep things," Elder Alvin R. Dyer stated that "the 'deep things of God,' also referred to scripturally as 'the mysteries of the kingdom' and the 'mystery of his will,' pertain to laws, principles, and conditions of man's eternal existence. The whole vast and intricate system of life is a mysterious challenge unto man unless he is truthfully informed."[107] Elder Neal A. Maxwell noted that "God's purposes, His patience, His power, and His profound love . . . and other truths are among what Paul called 'the deep things of God' (1 Corinthians 2:10)."[108]

---

104. Collins, *First Corinthians*, 132.

105. Orson Pratt, in *JD*, 1:294.

106. Wilford Woodruff, in *JD*, 18:39.

107. Alvin R. Dyer, *Who Am I*, 4th ed. (Salt Lake City: Deseret Book, 1973), 333.

108. Neal A. Maxwell, *A Wonderful Flood of Light* (Salt Lake City: Bookcraft, 1990), 58.

Only to those who are spiritually mature does God grant an understanding of these high blessings. "I testify to you," stated Elder David E. Sorensen, "that the key to spiritual maturity is the endowment. As we come here [to the temple] regularly with open minds, in humility and prayer, contemplating the things of the Spirit and 'the deep things of God,' we will become better and stronger. We will be equipped to withstand the challenges, temptations and problems of our world. Temples are the great garners of the Lord."[109]

In contrast, Paul stresses that the spiritually immature cannot know these things, for to them the mysteries of God seem foolish (2:14). As Joseph F. Smith explained, "It behooves the Latter-day Saints, and all men, to make themselves acquainted with 'the only true God, and Jesus Christ whom he has sent.' But can we through our own wisdom find out God? Can we by our unaided ingenuity and learning fathom his purposes and comprehend his will? We have, I think, witnessed examples enough of such efforts on the part of the intelligent world, to convince us that it is impossible. The ways and wisdom of God are not as the ways and wisdom of man. How then can we know 'the only true and living God, and Jesus Christ whom he has sent?'—for to obtain this knowledge would be to obtain the secret or key to eternal life."[110] A statement from President Spencer W. Kimball answers the question, "How can we know?" He states, "Desirable as is secular knowledge, one is not truly educated unless he has the spiritual with the secular. The secular knowledge is to be desired; the spiritual knowledge is an absolute necessity. We shall need all of the accumulated secular knowledge in order to create worlds and to furnish them, but only through the 'mysteries of God' (D&C 6:7) and these hidden treasures of knowledge (D&C 89:19) may we arrive at the place and condition where we may use that knowledge in creation and exaltation."[111] And only by being taught by the Spirit can we come to really know God and Christ.

In 2:12, Paul speaks of the "spirit which is of God." Since this "spirit" stands in contrast to the "spirit of the world," the term is not, as in other cases, referring to the Holy Spirit, or, more precisely, the Holy Ghost.

109. David E. Sorensen, in "San Diego Temple Dedication: Temples—Linking Heaven and Earth," *Church News,* May 8, 1993, available online at http://www.ldschurchnews archive.com/articles/23260/San-Diego-Temple-dedication-Temples---linking-heaven -and-earth.html (accessed March 26, 2015).

110. Smith, *Gospel Doctrine,* 59.

111. Spencer W. Kimball, "Wisdom and Great Treasures of Knowledge, Even Hidden Treasures," in CR, October 1968, 127–31.

Rather, it denotes the more abstract power and influence that centers in God and emanates from him. The scriptures define it as "the light which shineth, which giveth you light," which is "through him who enlighteneth your eyes, which is the same light that quickeneth your understandings; Which light proceedeth forth from the presence of God to fill the immensity of space—The light which is in all things, . . . which is the law by which all things are governed, even the power of God who sitteth upon his throne, . . . who is in the midst of all things" (D&C 88:11–13). Elder Charles W. Penrose, expounding on this, said, "God is not everywhere present personally, but He is omnipresent in the power of that spirit—the Holy Spirit— which animates all created things; that which is the light of the sun, and of the soul as well as the light of the eye, that which enables the inhabitants of the earth to understand and perceive the things of God. As the light of the sun reveals natural objects to our eyes, so the spirit that comes from God, with a fitting place to occupy and conditions to operate in, reveals the things of God."[112]

Paul was anxious that the Christian Saints partake of this spirit and not be filled with that of the transitory world. Indeed, if they were to be saved, he knew it was critical that they desist from thinking in worldly terms.[113] In 2:12 he explains why. Only through this wondrous spirit can they understand God's ways. Paul's words testify that God has already, through his graciousness (χαρίζομαι, *charizomai*), given certain of the Saints an understanding of these things. The word "graciousness" points to God's deep desire for the Saints to have a share in the knowledge of his ways and shows how anxious he is to make that knowledge available to his people. The central message, of which the spirit bears record and the ground for the "deep things of God" (2:10), is the revelation of the plan of salvation in which the Atonement of Christ plays such a central role. Such an understanding includes the loving ways of God and how far he is willing to go to save his children. As Paul's fellow Apostle John testified, "God so loved the world, that he gave his only begotten Son, that whosoever believeth in him should not perish, but have everlasting life" (John 3:16). This is the major point Paul's detractors needed to more clearly understand.

Paul next turned to an explanation of how he came to use his particular teaching method. In 2:13 he states he did not follow the ways of the rhetoricians and sophists, but rather the revelations of the Holy Ghost, "comparing

---

112. Charles W. Penrose, in *JD*, 26:23.
113. Fee, *First Epistle*, 113.

spiritual things with spiritual." His point is that the things of the spirit (see 2:12) must be explained in terms taught through the inspired words given by the Spirit and not in terms used by those clever at selling worldly ideas.

In 2:14 Paul picks up the negative side of the equation and, in doing so, sets the stage for the polemic he will deliver in 3:1–4.[114] His juxtaposition acts as a foil to the points he has made in 2:10–13. Here the Apostle explains the limitations of being a "natural man." To such persons, because they are unenlightened, the things of God seem ridiculous, contrary to reason, even foolishness (μωρία, *mōria*). They have locked themselves in the temporal box and refuse to see beyond its limits. As a result, they are completely incapable of understanding the things of the Spirit. As Elder Charles W. Penrose stated: "We see natural things by the light of the sun. We see spiritual things by spiritual light, and he that is spiritual discerneth all things and judgeth all things, and he that is not spiritual cannot comprehend spiritual things. They are foolishness to him. And while the Saints of God, quickened by the spirit which they have obtained through obedience to the Gospel, can comprehend these things of which I am speaking and discern their meaning and signification, those that are wicked and corrupt and obey not the ordinances of God, cannot see these things nor comprehend them as they are, but they are foolishness to them."[115]

Finally, in 2:15–16, Paul brings to a conclusion his entire line of thought that he began developing in 1:17. This contains four parts that can be outlined thus:

A. But the spiritual person discerns or correctly judges all things:

   B. But he or she, in turn, can be correctly discerned or judged by no one.

   B'. "For who has known the mind of the Lord that he may instruct him?"

A'. "But we have the mind of Christ" and can, therefore, make proper judgments.[116]

The adversative δέ (*de*), "but," in the first line of 2:15 emphasizes the contrast he is going to make with the "natural man" mentioned in the first line of 2:14. The natural man is, by his self-imposed limitations, unable to discern and, therefore, judge (ἀνακρίνω, *anakrinō*) the things of God and his people because they can be understood only by the Spirit. The spiritual person, on the other hand, not binding himself to the transitory and

114. Fee, *First Epistle,* 115.
115. Charles W. Penrose, in *JD,* 26:23.
116. Fee, *First Epistle,* 117.

temporal, can discern (*anakrinō*) godly things. It is important to understand, however, that it is the Spirit who "searcheth all things, yea, the deep things of God" (2:10), not the Saints. No mortal, no matter how righteous, can know all the ways of God. Some things simply remain outside of the Saints' purview.[117] The righteous, however, can know much. According to the Prophet Alma, "It is given unto many to know the mysteries of God; nevertheless they are laid under a strict command that they shall not impart only according to the portion of his word which he doth grant unto the children of men, according to the heed and diligence which they give unto him" (Alma 12:9). There is one part of the mystery, however, that all the Saints have access to, and this is Paul's point: they can understand the plan of salvation and the central role of Christ therein. For the natural man, however, these things are foolishness.

The second line stands in contrast with the first and reverses the image in the fore line. Paul plays on the same word used in the first line, ἀνακρίνω (*anakrinō*), "to discern, judge." The natural man cannot discern or judge correctly the spiritual man while the spiritual man, who can fully understand the profane and temporal world order, can discern and properly judge those therein.[118]

The third line gives scriptural support to Paul's point in the second line. To get his point across, the Apostle reworks Isaiah 40:13, turning it into a rhetorical question: "Who can know God's mind and counsel Him?" The implied answer is "no one!" Paul's point is that no sensible person would want to match wits with God. The jab is pointed at his Corinthian detractors who are so taken with the wisdom of the world that they have denounced the cross and with it the Resurrection. Paul's reproach skillfully shows them that rejecting the cross and saying that God would not work in that way are tantamount to telling God what he can and cannot do. That is real foolishness.[119]

With the final line, Paul returns to the point of the first one. He explains exactly why he, and those who follow him, can properly discern and judge: "We have the mind of Christ." Here the nuance of the word "mind" (νοῦς,

---

117. An example is the Lord's refusal to tell Joseph Smith when the Second Coming would occur. See D&C 130:14–17.

118. This is another scripture that needs to be kept in context. The reason is that, as one scholar notes, "there are always some who consider themselves full of the Spirit in such a way as to be beyond discipline or the counsel of others." In Corinth, Paul faced a group of these. Fee, *First Epistle*, 118.

119. Fee, *First Epistle*, 119.

nous) appears to refer to the Savior's thoughts as revealed to the righteous by the Holy Spirit.[120] The word "mind," therefore, does not look to the instrument of thought but at the mode of thought. It encompasses the whole range of inspired ideas and beliefs that provide the basis for proper judgment and action.[121] The Prophet Nephi admonished his people to "receive the Holy Ghost, [for] it will show unto you all things what ye should do. Behold, this is the doctrine of Christ" (2 Ne. 32:5–6). King Benjamin told his people to open their "minds that the mysteries of God may be unfolded to your view" (Mosiah 2:9). The Lord has assured the Saints of this day that all that is declared "by the Holy Ghost shall be scripture, shall be the will of the Lord, shall be the mind of the Lord, shall be the word of the Lord, shall be the voice of the Lord, and the power of God unto salvation" (D&C 68:4). Indeed, the Lord has promised, "I will tell you [the things of God] in your mind and in your heart, by the Holy Ghost, which shall come upon you and which shall dwell in your heart" (D&C 8:2). The Lord has also instructed his leaders that "in case of difficulty respecting doctrine or principle, if there is not a sufficiency written to make the case clear to the minds of the council, the president may inquire and obtain the mind of the Lord by revelation" (D&C 102:23).

In the "Lectures on Faith," we learn that "the Father and the Son possess the same mind, the same wisdom, glory, power, and fullness." Further, "all those who keep his commandments shall grow from grace to grace, and become heirs of the heavenly kingdom, and joint-heirs with Jesus Christ. They will possess the same mind, being transformed into the same image or likeness, even the express image of him who fills all in all, being filled with the fulness of his glory, and become one in him, even as the Father, Son, and Holy Spirit are one."[122] These exalted souls, then, have the "mind of Christ" fully. But, Paul's words teach that one need not wait until then to know in part the Savior's mind.

The point of the Apostle's message can be understood in light of what he wrote in another of his epistles. There he quotes an early Christian hymn that begins, "Let this mind be in you, which was also in Christ Jesus" and goes on to say that the Savior, though being the greatest, took upon himself the "form of a servant" and humbled himself, submitting fully to the

---

120. In Paul's Bible, the Septuagint, the Greek word *nous* translates the Hebrew *ruach*, "spirit," often referring to the spirit that emanates from God.

121. Thiselton, *First Epistle*, 275.

122. "Lecture 5," in Dahl and Tate, *Lectures on Faith in Historical Perspective*, 84.

will of the Father even to death on the ignominious cross (Philip. 2:5–11). This is the message that the sophisticated and prideful Corinthian Saints, those who felt they were so spiritually superior, needed to hear.[123] Humble submission, as evidenced by the Lord's willingness to follow the will of the Father, opens the way to true spirituality and brings understanding through which they, indeed, anyone, can discern the things of God and make proper judgments.

According to Elder Dallin H. Oaks, "The Apostle Paul said that persons who have received the Spirit of God 'have the mind of Christ' (1 Cor. 2:16). I understand this to mean that persons who are proceeding toward the needed conversion are beginning to see things as our Heavenly Father and His Son, Jesus Christ, see them. They are hearing His voice instead of the voice of the world, and they are doing things in His way instead of by the ways of the world."[124]

Having now carefully developed his argument, Paul, in the next chapter, explicitly addresses his detractors and shows them the higher way.

123. Fitzmyer, *First Corinthians,* 185–86.
124. Dallin H. Oaks, "The Challenge to Beocme," *Ensign* 30 (November 2000): 34.

Chapter 3

The Wisdom of God and the Wisdom of Men

INTRODUCTION

In the last chapter, Paul brought his discussion full circle. He began by pointing out that his message was, like his critics', based on wisdom, albeit his was based on the wisdom of God, not of man. This type of wisdom, he insisted, was so far superior to human wisdom that the "natural man" (2:14), having no access to the Spirit of God, could not comprehend let alone originate it. On the other hand, the truly spiritual person, having the Spirit, actually had access to the mind of Christ and, therefore, had the ability to discern and judge all things, both temporal and spiritual. Having this mind constituted true spirituality and was the basis to come to trustworthy wisdom.[1]

The rub was, as he will now show, that although all the Corinthian Saints had access to this same mind and therefore had the Spirit, they were not allowing it to make a difference. Indeed, they were acting and thinking otherwise. Their attitudes and practices betrayed an absence of true spirituality. They had become enamored with the wisdom of the world and it had led them to spiritual blindness and was propelling them toward spiritual death. But that was not the worst of it. Their contentions had erupted into quarrels, divisions, and outright factions within the Christian community, which threatened to destroy the Church of God. Paul's efforts from this point on were twofold: (1) to bring them to acknowledge the foolishness of their position and admit to the folly of human wisdom, and (2) to bring them to a unity in the faith through which they could gain deep spirituality and true wisdom, and therewith save the Church.[2]

---

1. Fee, *First Epistle*, 120.
2. Fee, *First Epistle*, 120.

DIVISIONS IN THE CORINTHIAN CHURCH (3:1–9)

Greek Text

1 Κἀγώ, ἀδελφοί, οὐκ ἠδυνήθην λαλῆσαι ὑμῖν ὡς πνευματικοῖς ἀλλ' ὡς σαρκίνοις, ὡς νηπίοις ἐν Χριστῷ. 2 γάλα ὑμᾶς ἐπότισα, οὐ βρῶμα, οὔπω γὰρ ἐδύνασθε. ἀλλ' οὐδὲ ἔτι νῦν δύνασθε, 3 ἔτι γὰρ σαρκικοί ἐστε. ὅπου γὰρ ἐν ὑμῖν ζῆλος καὶ ἔρις, οὐχὶ σαρκικοί ἐστε καὶ κατὰ ἄνθρωπον περιπατεῖτε; 4 ὅταν γὰρ λέγῃ τις· Ἐγὼ μέν εἰμι Παύλου, ἕτερος δέ· Ἐγὼ Ἀπολλῶ, οὐκ ἄνθρωποί ἐστε;

5 Τί οὖν ἐστιν Ἀπολλῶς; τί δέ ἐστιν Παῦλος; διάκονοι δι' ὧν ἐπιστεύσατε, καὶ ἑκάστῳ ὡς ὁ κύριος ἔδωκεν. 6 ἐγὼ ἐφύτευσα, Ἀπολλῶς ἐπότισεν, ἀλλὰ ὁ θεὸς ηὔξανεν· 7 ὥστε οὔτε ὁ φυτεύων ἐστίν τι οὔτε ὁ ποτίζων, ἀλλ' ὁ αὐξάνων θεός. 8 ὁ φυτεύων δὲ καὶ ὁ ποτίζων ἕν εἰσιν, ἕκαστος δὲ τὸν ἴδιον μισθὸν λήμψεται κατὰ τὸν ἴδιον κόπον, 9 θεοῦ γάρ ἐσμεν συνεργοί· θεοῦ γεώργιον, θεοῦ οἰκοδομή ἐστε. [SBLGNT]

King James Version

1 And I, brethren, could not speak unto you as unto spiritual, but as unto carnal, even as unto babes in Christ. 2 I have fed you with milk, and not with meat: for hitherto ye were not able to bear it, neither yet now are ye able. 3 For ye are yet carnal: for whereas there is among you envying, and strife, and divisions, are ye not carnal, and walk as men? 4 For while one saith, I am of Paul; and another, I am of Apollos; are ye not carnal? 5 Who then is Paul, and who is Apollos, but ministers by whom ye believed, even as the Lord gave to every man? 6 I have planted, Apollos watered; but God gave the increase. 7 So then neither is he that planteth any thing, neither he that watereth; but God that giveth the increase. 8 Now he that planteth and he that watereth are one: and every man shall receive his own reward according to his own labour. 9 For we are labourers together with God: ye are God's husbandry, ye are God's building.

New Rendition

1 And yet, brothers and sisters, I could not speak to you as spiritual people, but as fleshly people, as infants in Christ. 2 I gave you milk to drink, not solid food, because you were not yet ready for it. But even now you are still not ready, 3 because you are still under the influence of things of the flesh. For as long as there is jealousy and dissension among you, are you not under the influence of things of the flesh, and are you not behaving in a fleshly manner? 4 For whenever someone says, "I follow Paul," and another says, "I follow Apollos," are you not merely human? 5 Now what is Apollos? Or what is Paul? We are servants through whom you came to believe, even as the Lord assigned to each of us. 6 I did the planting, Apollos watered, but God caused the growth. 7 So then neither the one who does the planting nor the one who does the watering matters, but rather God who causes the growth. 8 But he who does the planting and he who does

the watering are united, and each will receive his own reward according to his own work. 9 For we are God's coworkers, you are God's field, God's building.

Translation Notes and Comments

3:1 *And I, brethren, could not speak / And yet, brothers and sisters, I could not speak:* See Translation Notes on 1:10. Up to this point Paul has been using the first person plural "we." Here his first word, κἀγώ *(kagō)*, "and yet I," returns the subject to himself.

carnal / fleshly people: The pronominal adjective σαρκίνοις *(sarkinois)* means, literally, "composed of the flesh"—thus, "fleshly" or "carnal." The nuance also points to those who are earthbound in vision and attitude. In many of Paul's writings, he makes a stark contrast between πνεῦμα *(pneuma)*, "spirit," and σάρξ *(sarx)*, "flesh" (see, for example, Rom. 8:4–6, 9, 13; 2 Cor. 7:1; Gal. 3:3; 4:29; 5:17). Indeed, *sarx* denotes "all that keeps a human being tied to earthly, worldly, or selfish tendencies and makes him or her unresponsive to God's Spirit."[3] Paul is addressing people who had been influenced by Greek philosophy to the point that they even denigrated present physical existence and, therefore, were denying the future bodily resurrection, and so his choice of words contained biting irony.[4] The word *sarkinois* emphasizes the present human, fleshly existence and thus points to a future one. It describes a condition of those who live according to the flesh.[5] To reflect this nuance, our Rendition translates the word as "fleshly people."[6] Paul contrasts these with the πνευματικοῖς *(pneumatikois)*, "spiritual people"—that is, those who are bound to God.[7] In keeping with conditions at Corinth, Paul could be pointing to those Christians who were being "moved by entirely human drives" and thus were looking to their own self-sufficiency and importance.[8]

---

3. Fitzmyer, *First Corinthians,* 186.

4. Three of the major philosophical schools—Epicureanism, Cynicism, and Stoicism—rejected the idea of an afterlife and, therefore, denied the resurrection. See Simon Hornblower and Antony Spawforth, ed., *The Oxford Classical Dictionary,* 3d rev. ed. (Oxford: Oxford University Press, 2003), 418–19, 532–35, 1446. A number of educated Christians would have been influenced by one or more of these schools.

5. BDAG, 914.

6. Louw-Nida, §79.4.

7. Ogden and Skinner, *Verse by Verse,* 131.

8. Thiselton, *First Epistle,* 288–89.

even as unto babes / as infants: Paul uses the plural noun νηπίοις (*nēpiois*) in a pejorative sense carrying the nuance of "mere infants," denoting a condition that is infantile and unfitting for adults.[9] Thus, the image here is not that of children who need to mature, but of adults acting in childish ways.[10]

3:2 ***I have fed you with milk, and not with meat: for hitherto ye were not able to bear it / I gave you milk to drink, not solid food, because you were not yet ready for it:*** The noun βρῶμα (*brōma*) denotes food in general.[11] In the KJV "meat" was not restricted in its meaning to "flesh" but referred to any solid food. The verb δύναμαι (*dynamai*), "to be able," can be used without a following infinitive if that infinitive can be easily deduced from context.[12] The KJV added "to bear it," and in our Rendition we supply "ready for it."

The JST replaces the KJV "bear it" with "receive it" and, in doing so, highlights the real problem the Corinthian Saints had created for themselves. Their worldly preoccupation with Greek wisdom had created a barrier that precluded them for receiving the meat of the gospel, or what Paul called "the deep things" of God (2:10), most notably the Atonement of the Savior with its attendant Resurrection. Paul, therefore, has been forced, like a good mother, to give them only what they could digest (compare Isa. 28:9).

neither yet now are ye able / But even now you are still not ready: Paul's wording emphasizes the Corinthians' lack of readiness that has continued right into the present. Of course, Paul fed them baby food when they were spiritual babies; that is only appropriate. The problem with them was that three or four years later, they are still insisting on spiritual baby food.

3:3 ***For ye are yet carnal / because you are still under the influence of things of the flesh:*** With this phrase, Paul shows the people why they cannot receive the things of the Spirit. The Apostle here uses the adjective

---

9. Though it is true that Paul addresses his converts by the affectionate term "children," the word he uses is τέκνον (*teknon*), not νήπιος (*nēpios*), the use suggesting people who are acting childish. See, for example, 2 Cor. 6:13; Gal. 4:19; Eph. 5:1; 1 Thes. 2:11. He uses the term *nēpios* again 13:12 and softens the pejorative nuance but only a bit. From that verse we see that Paul feels that infants behaving like infants is perfectly alright, but such behavior is not acceptable for grown-ups.

10. The word generally carried the idea of one moving from a simple or elementary grasp of something to a more advanced and deep understanding of that thing. See, for example, Philo, *Agr.* 9; compare *Congr.* 19; *Prob.* 160. Paul, however, did not use it that way. See Thiselton, *First Epistle,* 289–90.

11. BDAG, 184.

12. BDAG, 262.

σαρκικός (*sarkikos*), literally "fleshly." In 3:1 he used the closely related adjective σάρκινος (*sarkinos*) "fleshly," and in 2:14 he used the adjective ψυχικός (*psyichos*) "natural." Though the word *sarkikos* denotes that which is "fleshly" and "physical," it carries the negative connotation of that which is human but on "a disappointing level of behavior or characteristic."[13] All three adjectives share the same semantic field, which stands opposite the πνευματικός (*pneumatikos*), "spiritual." Therefore, the word here carries the idea of the "unspiritual," and, therefore, that which is solely under the influence of the flesh.[14] Paul's words show that these people, centered as they are on their own selves, promoted self-sufficiency—that which precludes humility—and pursued their own ends, which precluded building God's kingdom.[15] Thus, they were locking out the Spirit.

for whereas there is among you envying, and strife, and divisions, are ye not carnal, and walk as men? / For as long as there is jealousy and dissension among you, are you not under the influence of things of the flesh, and are you not behaving in a fleshly manner?: In the phrase ζῆλος καὶ ἔρις καὶ διχοστασίαι (*zēlos kai eris kai dichostasiai*), the words *kai dichostasiai*, "and divisions," is missing from the earliest and best manuscripts. The word is most likely a gloss some early copyist added trying to make the passage parallel with Galatians 5:20.[16] In doing so, he may have been wanting to impose on the original text the reality of dissentions and apostasy they were experiencing. Because of its doubtful origin, it is not included in our Rendition. The absence of the word, however, does not dilute Paul's message. The noun *zēlos,* "jealousy, envy," carries the negative connotation of intense resentment, interestingly, "over another's achievements or successes."[17] Here it suggests the rivalry that erupts when a person zealously defends his position against all comers no matter what the consequences are. The evidence that these people were under the influence of the world and were behaving in a worldly manner was their uncompromising promotion of their causes and positions. The verb περιπατέω (*peripateō*) means literally "to walk around," but Paul uses it in its secondary sense denoting a behavior that reflects the ways of the world,[18] indeed, that of the present age with its pseudosophistication and attention to things worldly and mundane.

---

13. BDAG, 914.
14. Louw-Nida, §79.1; Thiselton, *First Epistle*, 292–93.
15. Thiselton, *First Epistle*, 293.
16. Metzger, *Textual Commentary*, 482–83.
17. BDAG, 427.
18. BDAG, 803.

Paul designed his rephrase of the question, "are you not under the influence of the flesh?" with "are you not behaving in a worldly manner?" to heighten his rebuke by pointing out that these people, who claimed to be on such a high spiritual plain, were, in reality, behaving on the base human level of the worldly.

3:4 *For while one saith, I am of Paul; and another, I am of Apollos; are ye not carnal? / For whenever someone says, "I follow Paul," and another says, "I follow Apollos," are you not merely human?:* Though usually the subjunctive mood suggests lack of facts, here Paul pairs the subjunctive λέγῃ (*legē*), "says," with ὅταν (*hotan*), "when," expressing a "recurring contingency" that our Rendition translates as "whenever someone says."[19]

In the Greek phrase Ἐγὼ μέν εἰμι Παύλου (*egō men eimi Paulou*), literally, "I am of Paul," the verb εἰμι (*eimi*), "to be, exist," can denote a close affiliation or bond such as that which binds disciple and master.[20] Thus, the word is translated as "follow" in our Rendition.

Again, Paul proved his point with an example that ties his argument back to 1:11–12. As both Greeks and Jews fortified or defended their position by claiming allegiance to a well-known philosopher or rabbi, so too did these Christians. Their action proved that they were not, as they boasted, highly spiritual people but were acting, like the Greeks and the Jews, "all too human."[21]

It is of note that Paul included in this circle of "mere humans" not only those who followed Apollos but also those who cohered, or thought they cohered, to Paul. The problem was that none of these factions, including those who claimed to follow Peter and even the Lord (1:12), could see the great incongruity between their behavior and what the gospel demanded. And that is where the trouble lay. They should have seen it—they not only had access to the Spirit but actually enjoyed its power from time to time and yet they did not let its fruits ripen in them. The Spirit's gentleness, kindness, and loving unifying power were missing from their lives. In their stead was quarreling, backbiting, up-staging, even bullying. There was a great disconnect that these people simply were not seeing. The Savior, backed by the power of the Spirit, should have been the major determinant of their beliefs and actions but instead they were following the short-sighted, even

---

19. Findlay, "St. Paul's First Epistle," 787.
20. BDAG, 285.
21. The Revised English Bible (REB) translates Paul's question as, "are you not all too human."

destructive, ways of the worldly. Paul simply could not let this condition continue and, therefore, had to disabuse these people of the idea that their stand was correct. No matter how much they wanted to believe that somehow the gospel led to worldly esteem and prestige, it simply was not true.[22] Paul had to forcefully teach them that following any idea or any person not confirmed by the Spirit led, at best, away from the gospel and, at worst, into destruction.

Paul had another point he needed to make. Though these people enjoyed access to the Spirit, at least for the time being, the Apostle's rebuke shows that they still needed to repent. Paul makes it very clear that remaining worldly is not one of the options available to the true follower of Christ.[23]

3:5 Who then is Paul, and who is Apollos, but ministers by whom ye believed / Now what is Apollos? Or what is Paul? We are servants through whom you came to believe: The late Textus Receptus, followed by the KJV, has τίς (*tis*) "who" rather than τί (*ti*) "what," and it also reverses the order, putting Paul first. Our Rendition follows the earlier manuscripts because "what" is the better question. "Who" looks to background while "what" looks to use, office, and calling. Paul's question with its answer makes a very important point: the officer does not make the Church. Paul emphasizes this point when he refers to both Apollos and himself as διάκονοι (*diakonoi*), that is, persons who are empowered to act as intermediaries between two or more parties.[24] Church officers, both men and women, are but assistants or intermediaries, albeit authorized and, therefore, indispensable ones, in the Lord's Church, but it is Christ who stands ever at its head.

Paul defines the specific work both he and Apollos did. The Apostle's grammar is instructive. The aorist active verb looks to the inception of an event. In this case, the event is ἐπιστεύσατε (*episteusate*), "you came to believe," that is, to have faith in Christ. The preposition διά (*dia*) with the genitive case indicates the channel or means by which an event happens but not its source.[25] Paul states that faith came *dia*, "through," the work of Apollos and him, but they were not its source. The source was the Holy Spirit.

even as the Lord gave to every man / even as the Lord assigned to each of us: With this phrase, Paul makes his point. The challenge of this verse is how to translate the dative pronoun ἑκάστῳ (*ekastō*), "to each." Does it

---

22. Thiselton, *First Epistle*, 295.

23. Fee, *First Epistle*, 128.

24. BDAG, 230.

25. Thiselton, *First Epistle*, 300.

refer to the witness that God gave to the Corinthian Saints or to the assignments given to the ministers? Taking Paul's argument as a whole, it seems to point to the work of the leaders. Thus, our Rendition translates the word as "to each of us," referring to Paul and the other ministers.

Paul's words show that the active agent is the Lord. It is he who appoints the workers and assigns them to their tasks. God's kingdom moves forward not on the back of one man or woman, no matter how high the station, but through the cooperative effort of all its members doing their assigned tasks.[26]

3:6 I have planted, Apollos watered / I did the planting, Apollos watered: Paul's use of the aorist verb ἐφύτευσα (*ephyteusa*), "I planted," refers back to his work as the one who initiated missionary work in Corinth. His use of the aorist verb ἐπότισεν (*epotisen*), "he watered," refers to the work of Apollos, who came after Paul arrived but continued the work after Paul left. The point is that each did God's assignment, not his own.

Another important point is that the seed did not originate with Paul, and the water did not originate with Apollos. Admittedly, both worked with these items, but it was God who bestowed them. The imagery, once again, underscores the idea that God is the one who orchestrates his work.[27]

but God gave the increase / but God caused the growth: Here Paul switches from the aorist to imperfect tense with telling effect. The imperfect form of the verb αὐξάνω (*auxanō*), "to cause to grow, increase,"[28] emphasizes the idea that God's work is ongoing. Indeed, it never stops (compare Moses 1:37–38). Though ministers may come and go, God's work ever continues. For this reason, people should not become attached to certain leaders but to the Lord.

3:7 So then neither is he that planteth any thing, neither he that watereth / So then neither the one who does the planting nor the one who does the watering matters: The phrase ἐστίν τι (*estin ti*) means "to be or amount to something."[29] Used together with the negative particles οὔτε . . . οὔτε (*oute . . . oute*), "neither, nor," it emphasizes that it really doesn't matter who does the preaching or baptizing—it is God who is the source of the actual spiritual growth.

In this verse, Paul reiterates and, thus, emphasizes the thought in 3:6. To push his point, he begins the sentence with the strong inferential conjunction

---

26. Thiselton, *First Epistle*, 302.

27. Jews were very familiar with the imagery of God as a farmer. See, for example, Isa. 41:19; 44:3–4; 60:21; 61:3.

28. BDAG, 151.

29. BDAG, 1008.

ὥστε (*hōste*), "so then." The words that follow act as a crushing rejoinder to those who sought advantage, prestige, and honor by following the general society's practice of patronage. The practice entailed aligning oneself with someone of importance for personal advantage. Paul strongly defuses that notion by pointing out that Church authorities are but "servants" (διάκονοι, *diakonoi*) who deserve respect but neither adoration nor allegiance. Patronage was to have no place in the Church because all loyalty must go to God and Christ.

God that giveth the increase / rather God who causes the growth: The present active participle αὐξάνων (*auxanōn*), "causing to grow," emphasizes Paul's point. All the efforts that he and the other missionaries had put into their service would have amounted to nothing if God's power had not preceded and continued with them. Indeed, it was that power, not the work of the missionaries, that enlivened the work and allowed it to grow. Therefore, all glory and honor should go to God alone.

3:8 *Now he that planteth and he that watereth are one* / *But he who does the planting and he who does the watering are united:* The phrase ἕν εἰσιν (*hen eisin*), literally "are one," does not mean that the two mentioned parts constituted a single organism but, rather, that both independent entities are united in a single cause.[30] We have not taken the word "one" to denote status or equality, though that is certainly a possibility, but to mean unity in accomplishing a common task or goal. Thus, our Rendition translates the idea as "united," that is, being "one in the work."[31]

With this sentence, Paul returns to the point made in 3:5, "even as the Lord assigned to each of us" (as in our Rendition). The Apostle never lets his readers forget that God is central. Even so, his emphasis here is on the unity of the workers. None saw his work as superior to that of the others for, properly seen, every role was indispensable. The result was total unity. This attitude stood in contrast to the divisions among the members of the Church at Corinth. Paul here emphasizes how he and Apollos both acted in a unified way to carry out the work of the ministry. As the Lord stated in this dispensation, "I say unto you, be one; and if ye are not one ye are not mine" (D&C 38:27).

every man shall receive his own reward according to his own labour / each will receive his own reward according to his own work: As the

---

30. This also applies to the relationship between God and Christ. "To be one" does not mean they constitute two parts of the same entity.

31. For discussion, see Thiselton, *First Epistle*, 303. Given the factionalism that divided the Romans for centuries leading from one civil war to another, for the Church to be united would have indeed set the Saints apart from the world they lived in.

first part of the sentence emphasized the unity of the workers, the latter part emphasized their diversity. In this case, this forepart looked to the individual reward each will receive. In doing so, it placed neither greater nor lesser value on the task each did but on the effort each put into it. Paul here foreshadows the point he will make in 3:13, that fire will test the value of each person's work. His words should have served as a warning to those in the ministry at Corinth. It was not the position that they held but the effort each put into it that would bring true reward.[32] Believing that one's position was more important than that of another fed the fires of discord and destruction. Doing one's duty with full purpose of heart brought community oneness and individual reward.

3:9 *we are labourers together with God / we are God's coworkers:* The Greek noun συνεργοί (*synergoi*), "coworkers," emphasizes the privilege each person can have in participating in God's work and glory "to bring to pass the immortality and eternal life of man" (Moses 1:39). Each can contribute something. The English word "synergy," which comes from the same root, is used to describe how several people or things working together can accomplish that which they could not accomplish individually.

The challenge in translating this phrase is how to understand the genitive θεοῦ (*theou*), "of God." Does it mean that Paul, Apollos, and God all work to the same purpose, thus making all coworkers? Or is the force a possessive genitive which would define Paul and Apollos as belonging to God? It may be that the ambiguity of the genitive implies that both ways of interpreting the phrase are correct. Paul and Apollos (and indeed all who labor in the Gospel) do belong to God and are *his* helpers. But each is also a *coworker* with God, working together with him to accomplish his eternal purposes. Indeed, this is part of the learning process that we, as his children are going through, so that someday we can provide salvation and exaltation to our own spirit children.

ye are God's husbandry / you are God's field: Paul continues his agricultural metaphor by noting that the people are "God's field." Construing the θεοῦ (*theou*), "of God," as a possessive genitive, the words indicate a field that belongs to God. The field symbolizes the Church. That being the case, the Corinthian Saints should understand that it is neither the members nor the leaders but God alone who dictates what happens to it, what direction it takes, and who should play what role.

---

32. Fee, *First Epistle,* 133.

ye are God's building / God's building: With this image, Paul introduces another metaphor that he will use through 3:17: that of a building or, most notably, a temple.[33] The metaphor assists him in two ways. First, it helps Paul make a very important point: a building represents a unified whole, a single object with a specific function. Since it symbolizes the Church, the imagery excludes individualism and emphasizes the unity that is so necessary in God's kingdom. Second, it allows him to introduce the foundation, the essential base that supports and gives stability to the rest of the structure, an image he will play on in 3:10.

Analysis and Summary

In 3:1, Paul transitioned back to the theme he had begun to develop in 1:10–13 dealing with divisions. His long digression on wisdom, however, had been necessary to show the seat of the divisions and their cure, a cure necessary to save not only the branch but also the gospel. His purpose was to show that the people could not be both spiritual and divided. The two conditions were mutually exclusive. His reproof consists of a frontal attack focusing on the very heart of the matter.

The Apostle forcefully reminds them that they are behaving as carnal or worldly people. Speaking of those who are in this condition, Elder McConkie has stated,

> Since the fall, all men have become carnal, sensual and devilish by nature. (Moses 5:13; 6:49; Alma 42:10; Mosiah 16:1–4; D. & C. 20:20.) In this fallen state they are subject to the lusts, passions, and appetites of the flesh. They are spiritually dead, having been cast out of the presence of the Lord; and thus "they are without God in the world, and they have gone contrary to the nature of God." They are in a "carnal state" (Alma 41:10–11); they are of the world. *Carnality* connotes worldliness, sensuality, and inclination to gratify the flesh.
>
> To be saved men must forsake carnality and turn to the things of the spirit. They "must be born again; yea, born of God, changed from their carnal and fallen state, to a state of righteousness, being redeemed of God, becoming his sons and daughters," (Mosiah 27:25.) All accountable persons who have not received the truth and the spiritual re-birth that

---

33. J. Massyngberde Ford suggests the imagery plays on the booths that the Jews erected during the feast of tabernacles. See "You Are God's 'Sukkah' (I Cor. III. 10–17)," *New Testament Studies* 21 (October 1974): 139–42. Though that may be the case, Paul's point does not rest on it.

attends such reception are yet in a carnal state. (Mosiah 4:2; 16:1–4; 26:4; Alma 22:13; 4:10–15.)

Even members of the Church who have not forsaken the world, and who have not bridled their passions (Alma 38:12), are yet in a carnal state. "Ye are yet carnal," Paul said to the Corinthian Saints, "for whereas there is among you envying, and strife, and divisions, are ye not carnal, and walk as men?" (1 Cor. 3:3; Mosiah 3:19.) "To be carnally minded is death; but to be spiritually minded is life and peace. Because the carnal mind is enmity against God." (Rom. 8:6–7; 2 Ne. 9:39.)[34]

Such a condition must be avoided by any who would call themselves the Saints of God.

Where these Corinthian Saints felt themselves to be more spiritually mature than others, Paul shows that they are not at all. Indeed, he calls them νηπίοις (*nēpiois*), "infants." In doing so, he partially explains why he approached them the way he did. They were acting childishly, which forced him to concentrate on the "milk" of the gospel rather than the solid food they believed they deserved. His purpose in so addressing them was to shame them into seeing how spiritually immature they really were.[35]

Thus, Paul's call is not so much a request that these people grow up as it is for them to quit acting infantile. His warning, and a lesson that all Saints should learn, is that the narcissistic and self-centered competitiveness that often characterizes young children and precludes them from seriously respecting the interest of others leads through spiritual myopia to spiritual blindness and eventually spiritual death. On the way, it precludes them from making proper judgments about what the Lord's message is, how he operates in bringing it to the world, and how he intends it to be taught.[36]

When certain of the Corinthian Saints aligned themselves with one or more of the Church leaders, they may have thought they were complimenting and boosting the prestige of their supposed patrons. The all-pervasive Roman environment would have greatly contributed to their willingness to do so. The patron-client relationship, so distinctive to Roman culture, was one of the ways both parties used to climb the social ladder. The more those on the lower rungs supported those above them, the more prestige all enjoyed. This led to supporting one's house above all else.[37] Paul crushes

---

34. Bruce R. McConkie, *Mormon Doctrine,* 2d ed. (Salt Lake City: Bookcraft, 1979), 113.

35. Fee, *First Epistle,* 123–25.

36. Thiselton, *First Epistle,* 291.

37. Matthew Dillon and Lynda Garland, *Ancient Rome: From the Early Republic to the Assassination of Julius Caesar* (Florence, Ky.: Routledge Press, 2005), 87–88.

that notion. Essentially he says, "By creating these divisions you are saying nothing about us—you are *talking about yourselves,* and what you are saying is not flattering! Do not imagine that we are pleased! Your fights are *all about you*—not *about us*!"[38]

The Apostle had already made it abundantly clear that "God hath chosen the foolish things of the world to confound the wise; and God hath chosen the weak things of the world to confound the things which are mighty" (1:27), and that included Cephas, Apollos, and Paul.

The Lord has confirmed Paul's position for the modern Church, noting that "the weak things of the world shall come forth and break down the mighty and strong ones, that man should not counsel his fellow man, neither trust in the arm of flesh" (D&C 1:19; compare D&C 133:59). "Wherefore," the Lord continues, "I call upon the weak things of the world, those who are unlearned and despised, to thresh the nations by the power of my Spirit" (D&C 35:13). The point is that the Lord knows what he is doing and, as foolish as it might seem to others, those who are mature in the spirit can see the wisdom behind it.

With the phrase "I gave you milk to drink" (3:2, Rendition), Paul begins to answer the charge leveled by his detractors that he fed them only pabulum and not the real substance they felt they were getting by interpreting the gospel through the lens of Greek philosophy. Paul used this somewhat polemical metaphor to show them that he acted as a mother giving to these children only what they could handle.[39] What must not be overlooked in Paul's metaphor, however, is that he is not talking about two completely different diets. Both the meat and the milk represent gospel truths that he has shared with them. He is speaking only of different degrees of it. Both are true and nourishing spiritual foods. In our day, the Lord has instructed his missionaries that if their investigators "cannot bear meat now," then "milk they must receive" (D&C 19:22). Even so, what they get is pure, sweet nourishment that will prepare them for the meat later on.

Some Corinthian Saints, in their self-deluded feeling of advanced spirituality, had sought for deeper understanding through Greek philosophical speculations with its often accompanying rhetorical eloquence and, in so

---

38. Bailey, *Mediterranean Eyes,* 123; italics in the original.

39. The Savior often used parables to conceal deep truths from the innocent or unprepared, thus mercifully precluding them from judgment until such time as they were ready for more understanding. See Robert J. Matthews, *The Parables of Jesus* (Provo, Utah: Brigham Young University Press, 1969), 7.

doing, had actually partaken of a synthetic, non-nourishing food that could prove deadly because it allowed them to reject the solid food of the gospel, namely the Atonement of Jesus Christ, and put in its place the poisonous philosophies of men.[40]

For example, the Cynic philosophers believed that mortality was all there was. Because there was no afterlife, this life was all the more important. The goal was to live according to nature as understood by human reason. Life was to be lived simply without unnecessary detractions and accouterments. They, therefore, rejected owning property, seeking for wealth, fame, or power. Their ascetic lifestyle appealed to some Christians.[41] On the other end of the spectrum were the Epicureans. The objective of this philosophical system was to attain the greatest good by avoiding fear and pain and living in pleasure. That condition was achieved by limiting one's desires, living modestly, and in gaining knowledge of how the world worked. Though the gods existed, they took no thought of humankind and made no arrangements for their salvation. When a person died, that was the end.[42] Such philosophies went counter to many of the doctrines of the kingdom and led to incorrect understandings of God, Christ, and their purposes.

Paul insisted the Saints had to reject the wisdom of the world and in its place accept the true wisdom from God. Many Gentiles resisted such wisdom. There is little wonder, for the message of the cross was wisdom turned upside down, specifically the giving of self for a higher cause and gaining strength through seeming weakness. It was critical, however, that the Saints accept this idea, for only in this way could they add meat to the milk of the gospel. Thus, the Corinthian Saints needed less a change of diet and more a change of perspective.[43]

Paul insisted they were carnal, acting as did those bound down by the flesh. In 3:3 he supplied his evidence. In short, it was because they promoted envyings and jealousies. Members of each faction zealously advanced their point of view and doctrinal stance. For example, there were those who, like the Greeks, rejected the idea of a corporeal resurrection (15:12, 35). There were others who promoted self-indulgent license by misreading the power of the Atonement (5:1–6). These and others endlessly battled for

40. Morna Dorothy Hooker, "Hard Sayings: 1 Cor. 3:2," *Theology* 69 (1966): 19–22; Fitzmyer, *First Corinthians,* 187.

41. A. A. Long, "The Socratic Tradition: Diogenes, Crates, and Hellenistic Ethics," in *The Cynics: The Cynic Movement in Antiquity and Its Legacy,* ed. R. Bracht Branham and Marie-Odile Goulet-Cazé (Berkeley: University of California Press, 2000), 28–46.

42. Howard Jones, *The Epicurean Tradition* (New York: Routledge Press, 1989).

43. Fee, *First Epistle,* 125.

dominance. But the allure on all sides was the same—a carnal attitude that seduced them into mistaking their ideas and their will for those of God. In other words, because of their obstinacy and self-righteousness, these Corinthian Saints ascribed their own doctrines and causes to the Lord and, because of the aura of holiness and legitimacy that gave, they jealously defend them at all costs.[44] In the process, they were tearing the Church apart. Their dedication to their false ideas blinded them from seeing that the power of the Spirit promoted harmony, unity, and peace.

Paul insisted on setting the record straight, noting that he and Apollos were in one accord though each did his own task—one planted while the other watered (3:6). Giving insight, Brigham Young taught,

> We can say to the Latter-day Saints, it is the mind and will of God that we organize according to the best plans and patterns and system that we can get for the present. We can do this, and thus far give to the Latter-day Saints the mind and will of the Lord; but we cannot make a man or a woman yield to the will of God unless they are disposed to. I can plant, I can water, but I cannot give the increase; I cannot cause the wheat and corn to grow. It is true I can break up and prepare the ground and cast the seed therein, but I cannot cause it to grow, that can only be done by the people having willing hearts, ready minds, and a disposition to go forth with a firm determination and a willing hand to build up the kingdom.[45]

Paul emphasized that though both Apollos and he had essential tasks to perform each had no independent importance. Indeed, the real power was God who caused their efforts to bloom, evidenced by the faith of the Corinthian converts. His point, like the insight shared by Brigham Young, was that, despite their efforts, without God there would have been no success at all. The Church owed its very existence to the work of the Father. Thus, and here is the thrust of Paul's argument, these silly and all too human Saints should quit quarrelling over which leader was best or greatest or whose doctrine they should follow. (After all, these men are but servants who are nothing compared to Christ.) Instead they should concentrate their efforts on God and try to follow the inspiration of his Spirit.[46]

The last point Paul made in this section was of critical importance. Each person will receive his own unique reward (3:8). The reward would not be based on the task that God assigned but on the effort the person put into

---

44. C. K. Barrett, *A Commentary on the First Epistle to the Corinthians,* 2d ed. (London: Black, 1968), 81.

45. Brigham Young, in *JD,* 17:155.

46. Fee, *First Epistle,* 132.

magnifying it. It is the magnification, not the job, that is all important. As President Thomas S. Monson has said, "What does it mean to magnify a calling? It means to build it up in dignity and importance, to make it honorable and commendable in the eyes of all mankind, to enlarge and strengthen it, to let the light of heaven shine through it to the view of other men. And how does one magnify a calling? Simply by performing the service that pertains to it. In short, we magnify our callings by learning what our duties are and then by performing them."[47] Doing so brings great reward. As the Lord has promised, "he who doeth the works of righteousness shall receive his reward, even peace in this world, and eternal life in the world to come" (D&C 59:23). Note that the blessings of doing one's calling have both a temporal and an eternal aspect. The Lord promised his disciples that "peace I leave with you, my peace I give unto you: not as the world giveth, give I unto you" (John 14:27). We can best comprehend what Jesus meant when we understand just what the term "peace" meant to the ruling powers in his day.[48] Many in the Greco-Roman world understood peace as an absence of hostile feelings between parties large or small, but it seldom included the idea of kindly feelings between individuals. In short, the word essentially described an external condition. For the Christians, however, the emphasis was on concord between individuals and particularly on friendship between the Saint and God. Though the word always carried the idea of the state of mind in the celestial realm, for mortals it meant the total lack of inner turmoil coupled with knowing one was reconciled to God.[49] For Jesus, then, the emphasis was on the internal not the external environment.

Paul concludes his thought in 3:9 by stating that they are "God's field," even "God's building"[50] (as in our Rendition), the point being that the Church belongs to God and him alone. Therefore, its members should not follow some leader or forceful personality. All should give their total allegiance to God exclusively.

---

47. Thomas S. Monson, *Be Your Best Self* (Salt Lake City: Deseret Book, 1979), 147.

48. Neither the Greeks nor the Romans really knew about peace. Both histories reveal one bloody conflict after another. The doors of the temple of the Roman god of war, Janus, were closed during times of peace. From the founding of Rome in 743 BC, those doors were closed only a couple of times. See Plutarch, *Num.* 20.1–2.

49. Gerhard von Rad and Werner Foerster, "εἰρήνη," in *TDNT*, 2:400–17.

50. Jewish scripture tied the images of field and building together. See Jer. 1:10; Isa. 61:4–7. The imagery is also found in the Dead Sea scrolls where the "council of the community" was referred to as both an everlasting plantation and a precious corner-stone. See Geza Vermes, "The Community Rule," in *The Complete Dead Sea Scrolls in English* (Baltimore: Penguin Books, 1973), 85.

BUILDING THE CHURCH OF GOD (3:10–15)

Greek Text

10 Κατὰ τὴν χάριν τοῦ θεοῦ τὴν δοθεῖσάν μοι ὡς σοφὸς ἀρχιτέκτων θεμέλιον ἔθηκα, ἄλλος δὲ ἐποικοδομεῖ. ἕκαστος δὲ βλεπέτω πῶς ἐποικοδομεῖ· 11 θεμέλιον γὰρ ἄλλον οὐδεὶς δύναται θεῖναι παρὰ τὸν κείμενον, ὅς ἐστιν Ἰησοῦς Χριστός· 12 εἰ δέ τις ἐποικοδομεῖ ἐπὶ τὸν θεμέλιον χρυσόν, ἄργυρον, λίθους τιμίους, ξύλα, χόρτον, καλάμην, 13 ἑκάστου τὸ ἔργον φανερὸν γενήσεται, ἡ γὰρ ἡμέρα δηλώσει· ὅτι ἐν πυρὶ ἀποκαλύπτεται, καὶ ἑκάστου τὸ ἔργον ὁποῖόν ἐστιν τὸ πῦρ αὐτὸ δοκιμάσει. 14 εἴ τινος τὸ ἔργον μενεῖ ὃ ἐποικοδόμησεν, μισθὸν λήμψεται· 15 εἴ τινος τὸ ἔργον κατακαήσεται, ζημιωθήσεται, αὐτὸς δὲ σωθήσεται, οὕτως δὲ ὡς διὰ πυρός. [SBLGNT]

King James Version

10 According to the grace of God which is given unto me, as a wise masterbuilder, I have laid the foundation, and another buildeth thereon. But let every man take heed how he buildeth thereupon. 11 For other foundation can no man lay than that is laid, which is Jesus Christ. 12 Now if any man build upon this foundation gold, silver, precious stones, wood, hay, stubble; 13 Every man's work shall be made manifest: for the day shall declare it, because it shall be revealed by fire; and the fire shall try every man's work of what sort it is. 14 If any man's work abide which he hath built thereupon, he shall receive a reward. 15 If any man's work shall be burned, he shall suffer loss: but he himself shall be saved; yet so as by fire.

New Rendition

10 According to the grace that God has given me, like a skilled master-builder I have laid a foundation. Another is building upon it. But let each one pay close attention to how he builds. 11 For no one can lay any other foundation than the one that has been laid, which is Jesus Christ. 12 And if anyone builds on the foundation with gold, silver, precious stones, wood, hay, or straw, 13 each builder's work will be plainly seen, for the Day will make it clearly known, because it will be revealed by fire, and that very fire will test the kind of work each has done. 14 If anyone's work which he has built upon the foundation survives the test, he will receive his reward. 15 If anyone's work is consumed by the fire, he will suffer loss, but will himself be saved, but only as by fire.

Translation Notes and Comments

3:10 *According to the grace of God which is given unto me / According to the grace that God has given me:* Though the aorist passive participle δοθεῖσαν (*dotheisan*, "given") acts as an adjective modifying χάριν (*charin*, "grace"), in keeping with modern English, it is translated as a relative clause in the active voice in our Rendition.

Paul's purpose, as he built his case, was to emphasize the authority upon which he fulfilled his calling. In this case, it was derived from the grace of God. Though he could have been alluding to his original call (see Acts 9:1–9), it was more likely he was referring to his apostolic assignment to preach the gospel to the Gentiles and to open the work in Europe (see Rom. 11:13; Acts 13:2–3; 16:9–10; 18:5–6).[51]

as a wise masterbuilder / like a skilled master-builder: Paul calls himself a σοφὸς ἀρχιτέκτων (*sophos architektōn*), "a skilled master-builder."[52] This title helped him make his point. First, he played on the word *sophos.* The adjective denotes one who is experienced and skillful at a task, but it also describes one who is wise.[53] The wordplay reached back to his argument that he possessed the true wisdom of God (2:7). Second, he was the *architektōn,* master-builder. The noun pointed to persons whose skills were very rare and who, therefore, could demand very high wages.[54] By giving himself this title, Paul emphasized both his uniqueness and just how well he had laid the foundation.

I have laid the foundation, and another buildeth thereon / I have laid a foundation. Another is building upon it: These words stress that though Paul laid the foundation, he did not stay to finish the building. That task had to be entrusted to others.

But let every man take heed how he buildeth thereupon / But let each one pay close attention to how he builds: The word βλεπω (*blepō*) meant "to see," but Paul used the third-person imperative form, βλεπέτω (*blepetō*), as a warning to those now doing the building to pay very close attention to how they proceeded.[55] Just because the foundation was correct and strong did not mean the superstructure would be as well, unless its materials matched the quality and its construction the excellence of that foundation.

3:11 *For other foundation can no man lay than that is laid, which is Jesus Christ / For no one can lay any other foundation than the one that has been laid, which is Jesus Christ:* The aorist infinitive θεῖναι (*theinai*), "to lay down," denotes the single act of laying something down while the present passive participle κείμενον (*keimenon*), which was regularly used

---

51. Fitzmyer, *First Corinthians,* 196–97; Fee, *First Epistle,* 137.

52. Paul's title is found in LXX Isa. 3:3.

53. BDAG, 935.

54. For example, a person could buy the labor of a simple carpenter for six *minas* (a small bronze coin used in Asia Minor and Greece), while that of a master builder would cost one hundred thousand *minas.* BDAG, 139.

55. BDAG, 179.

for the perfect passive of τίθημι (*tithēmi*), "place,"[56] denotes the permanence of that which has already been done.[57] Indeed, no one can properly lay any foundation other than (παρά, *para,* in the comparative sense[58]) the one Paul laid without slipping off the gospel footings.

3:12 *Now if any man build upon this foundation gold, silver, precious stones, wood, hay, stubble / And if anyone builds on the foundation with gold, silver, precious stones, wood, hay, or straw:* The best manuscripts support the reading without τοῦτον (*touton*), "this," which appears to be a later addition to clearly identify which "foundation" Paul is referring to. Thus, our Rendition omits it.

Paul's words here are a warning. He gives this warning by using the analogy of two very different kinds of materials. The contrast is not only between precious and common but also between noncombustible and combustible. The symbol points to each individual Saint's acts, or better, the motives that drive those acts. Deeds done in love and with full purpose of heart are precious and eternally endure while those done for self-aggrandizement, popular acclaim, or personal advancement are worthless and end in ashes. Unfortunately, myopic mortal eyes, often made dimmer by the world's seductions, are often incapable of telling the difference. That condition, Paul noted next, will all too soon come to an end when every person's works are made fully known.

3:13 *Every man's work shall be made manifest: for the day shall declare it, because it shall be revealed by fire / each builder's work will be plainly seen, for the Day will make it clearly known, because it will be revealed by fire:* Four terms are important in understanding Paul's point here. The neuter adjective φανερὸν (*phaneron*), "open, plain, evident," with the verb γίνομαι (*ginomai*), "to become," means that something that was obscure becomes visible in a very public way.[59] The future active verb δηλώσει (*dēlōsei*), "will reveal, show," denotes making something known that has not been known previously.[60] The noun with definite article ἡ ἡμέρα (*hē hēmera*), "the Day," as used by Paul, nearly always referred to the Final Judgment (see Rom. 13:12; 1 Thes. 5:4; compare 1:8; 5:5; Rom. 2:16; 2 Cor. 1:14; Philip. 1:6, 10; 2:16; 1 Thes. 5:2; 2 Thes. 2:2). For this reason, our Rendition

---

56. Smyth, *Greek Grammar,* §791.
57. Thiselton, *First Epistle,* 310.
58. BDAG, 757.
59. Louw-Nida, §28.28.
60. BDAG, 222; Louw-Nida, §28.42.

capitalizes the word "Day." Finally, the word πῦρ (*pyr*), "fire," can refer to the product of combustion, but it more often means a power that is of heavenly origin.[61] Fire has three qualities: it can reveal, destroy, or refine.

Paul's point is that "the Day" will make each person's work publicly known (*phaneron*) through the instrument of fire. Note that here, fire is not a punitive agent but one used for disclosure and testing.[62] By holding a torch next to an object, it is revealed. Hold it closer and the object can be destroyed. Turn up the heat and the object can be refined. At the Second Coming, the glory of God will make all things visible and disclose their value by either refining or destroying them. In this way, everything—even that which has been hidden, secret, or not fully disclosed—will be made public, wrenchingly known, and tried (see Morm. 5:8; Matt. 10:26; Luke 12:3; 2 Ne. 27:11; D&C 1:3; 88:108). "Fire" symbolizes the light that exposes not only the deeds but also what stood behind them to the joy and praise of some and to the shame and embarrassment of others. The fire will reveal that which lasts and that which does not. Judgment Day, therefore, discloses the kind of material with which each Saint built, whether it was transitory or eternal. It is noteworthy that in Paul's context, the emphasis is not on the deeds of those in the world—natural men and women—but on the activities of the individual Saint. Paul is asking each of his readers to look inside themselves and judge their own motives.

and the fire shall try every man's work of what sort it is / and that very fire will test the kind of work each has done: The verb δοκιμάζω (*dokimazō*) means to examine an object very critically to determine its genuineness.[63] In the phrase τὸ πῦρ αὐτὸ (*to pyr auto*), the ancient manuscripts are almost equally divided on the presence of the pronoun *auto* that follows *pyr,* but it is more likely to have been mistakenly omitted by a copyist than added, so our Rendition translates the phrase as "that very fire." The work that the fire tests is of two types only: that which stands unharmed and that which burns down. Again, the test looks to one thing—the motivation that stands behind the deed.

Paul has already shown that everyone's work stands on but one foundation, "Christ, and him crucified" (2:2). The whole of the superstructure rests on this, but the foundation itself must be made of enduring materials.

---

61. BDAG, 898.

62. Fitzmyer, *First Corinthians,* 199. *T. Ab.* 13:18–20 tells how the angel Pyruel uses fire to test people's deeds.

63. Louw-Nida, §27.45; BDAG, 255.

Anything that takes away from the true knowledge of the Lord's character, attributes, nature, mission, and gospel is not solid building material and will cause the edifice, despite the solid foundation, to burn to ashes.

What proves the worth of the building material is fire. At the time of judgment, whether that is the Final Judgment or partial judgment at the time of death (Alma 40:11–14), each person's work will be tried as by fire, that is, it will be put to the test to show its quality. That quality is determined largely by the motivation that stood behind it. If its purpose was for pride, self-promotion, fame, or power, it will fail the test. If it was to promote the ends of the kingdom, bring people to Christ Jesus, or for the glory of God, it will pass.

3:14 *If any man's work abide which he hath built thereupon, he shall receive a reward / If anyone's work which he has built upon the foundation survives the test, he will receive his reward:* The verb ἐποικοδομέω (*epoikodomeō*) means "to build something on something already built,"[64] and so it is translated as "has built upon the foundation" in our Rendition. Paul here announces the positive result of the test. Each person receives a μισθός (*misthos*), "reward, wage." The word denotes "remuneration for work done," but it also denotes, on a more celestial level, the recompense God gives to the faithful.[65] Quality work brings eternal reward.

3:15 *If any man's work shall be burned, he shall suffer loss / If anyone's work is consumed by the fire, he will suffer loss:* The verb κατακαίω (*katakaiō*), "to burn," carries the nuance of the total destruction of the object. Therefore, the fire brings a loss so great that nothing can be salvaged.

These words reveal the negative result of the test. It is of note that Paul does not say the foolish person will be burned. Instead, he will suffer great loss, for the verb ζημιόω (*zēmioō*) implies a loss sufficient to produce suffering and hardship. Interestingly, his punishment is not direct, that is, it is not imposed externally, but rather it results naturally from the consequence of his own actions.

but he himself shall be saved; yet so as by fire / but will himself be saved, but only as by fire: JST changes "shall be saved" to "may be saved." The force of the change moves salvation from surety to possibility. Paul's words are a warning meant to get these self-serving Corinthian Saints to see their folly and immediately stop what they are doing. Paul's warning, "saved, but only as by fire," could also be rendered "saved as if plucked from the fire," meaning saved at the very last moment. The phrase reflects an axiom

---

64. BDAG, 387.
65. BDAG, 653.

popular at the time that carried the same nuance as the English idiom, "saved by the skin of one's teeth."[66] These Corinthian Saints were pushing their luck and had better stop doing so right now or they will find their luck has run out, for the Day of Judgment will be upon them in which no turning back is possible (see Alma 34:33).

Analysis and Summary

Paul abruptly changed his metaphor in 3:9 from field to building.[67] However, three particulars remain the same with both figures: first the focus on the branch at Corinth as a whole, not on individual members; second, God as the owner and, therefore, master of all; and third, Paul as the initiator of the work.[68] These three elements help Paul keep his argument on a consistent path.

For instance, Paul never backs away from the fact that he was the one who founded the Church at Corinth. He uses two particulars to show he did it properly and with authority. First, he acted under "the grace of God" (3:10). The word "grace," as used here, suggests heavenly empowerment. He was, by divine assignment, the "apostle of the Gentiles" (Rom. 11:13) and the first to bring the glad tidings to Corinth, a point he returns to often (see 4:15–17; 9:1–2; 2 Cor. 3:1–3; 10:12–16). Therefore, their whole Church sprang from his authority and rested upon it.[69]

Second, Paul emphasized that he was a skilled builder. The title he gave himself, ἀρχιτέκτων (*architektōn*), pointed to a craftsman of wide-ranging experience and expertise such that he often acted as the overseer or foreman in building projects.[70] Paul's words suggest that he not only had all the expertise necessary but also used it precisely. As a result, he had laid down a proper and strong foundation. Further, because of his position as the *architektōn*, he could determine how others built on the foundation he laid.

---

66. BDAG, 898. For examples, see Jude 1:23; Livy, 20.35; Euripides, *And.* 487; *Elec.* 1182. For discussion, see Friedrich Lang, "πῦρ," in *TDNT*, 6:928–48; Witherington, *Conflict and Community*, 134.

67. It is the Christian community, as the building *of God*, whose purpose is the common good, that is central to Paul's argument here. See Mitchell, *Paul and the Rhetoric of Reconciliation*, 98–111.

68. Fee, *First Epistle*, 137.

69. One could correctly argue that priesthood power was the authority upon which the Church was grounded. Paul would likely agree, but his point is that he was the one who used his authority to bring the gospel to them and, therefore, that authority still held, and it made no sense to question his authority now.

70. Thiselton, *First Epistle*, 308.

It is important to note that Paul never identifies himself as the foundation. The foundation is Jesus Christ.[71] He is the base of the Church, not Paul. But there is more. The foundation also consists of a doctrinal component, namely, "Christ, and him crucified" (2:2), that is, the Atonement and all that grows out of that horrific yet sacred act. Though Paul does not claim to be the foundation, nevertheless, he bases his authority on it, and that authority gives him the right to instruct the community.[72]

The Apostle at this point expands on the new imagery focusing on the foundation. His first sentence forms a chiasmus:

A. Paul laid the foundation for the church;

   B. Someone else is now building on it;

     B'. But let that someone take care how he/she builds;

A'. The foundation Paul laid is Jesus Christ.[73]

His words show that he was continuing his focus on the Church and its leadership, but he was changing his emphasis in order to give a warning to his readers in the strongest terms possible to build upon the foundation with the greatest of care. Because he does not mention Apollos who followed him in the ministry but had since left, Paul's focus was on what was currently happening in the branch, not on what had happened. His specific targets were those who were, at that time, active. However, with the use of the indirect pronouns, with which the paragraph (3:10–15) is laced,[74] Paul was careful not to point any fingers.

Nonetheless, the Apostle's concerns are clear. His words, "For no one can lay any other foundation than the one that has been laid" (3:11, Rendition), identify his first concern. They suggest that some of the more liberal elements in the Christian community were trying to replace the very foundation of the Church by instituting another one composed of the wisdom of men. This simply could not happen and still have the Church be Christ's Church.

---

71. In Eph. 2:20, Paul used a different analogy, stating that the Church was built upon a foundation of Apostles and Prophets with the Savior "being the chief corner stone" (compare 1 Pet. 2:6–8; Matt. 21:42). That metaphor would not work at Corinth, however, because its factions boasted of following one Apostle or another. Paul had to push the idea that there was only one basis of authority and doctrine and that was the Lord.

72. Fitzmyer, *First Corinthians*, 197.

73. Fee, *First Epistle*, 137.

74. Paul uses ἄλλος (*allos*) once (3:10), οὐδείς (*oudeis*) once (3:11), ἕκαστος (*hecastos*) three times (3:10, 13), and τις (*tis*) three times (3:12, 14, 15).

Paul's second concern was with both the material and the skill that some were using to build the superstructure. Even if the basic foundation was not replaced, that did not mean the edifice would be strong unless the same skill and quality of building materials was used. Indeed, the wrong theology would cause the doctrinal structure to fail and the spiritual building to be set ablaze. He, therefore, stressed the necessity of building with the most enduring and flame-resistant material as possible and with the greatest skill because every kind would be tested by fire and only that which was properly set and imperishable would withstand the heat of the Day.[75] Little wonder, then, that Paul urged them to pay very close attention to what they were doing. As Elder McConkie has clearly pointed out,

> If the building (and the saints "are God's building"!) conforms to God's blueprint, it will become a stable structure which will withstand the fiery tests; otherwise it will be burned and destroyed. And the same is true of all men, if their works are good, they shall abide the day and not be cast into the fire; otherwise when He who "is like a refiner's fire" (Mal. 3:2), sits in judgment, they "shall be stubble: and the day that cometh shall burn them up." (Mal. 4:1.)
>
> "If it so be that the church is built upon my gospel," the Lord Jesus proclaimed to the Nephites, "then will the Father show forth his own works in it. But if it be not built upon my gospel, and is built upon the works of men, or upon the works of the devil, verily I say unto you they have joy in their works for a season, and by and by the end cometh, and they are hewn down and cast into the fire, from whence there is no return. For their works do follow them, for it is because of their works that they are hewn down" (3 Ne. 27:10–12). And as to false churches—churches built upon ". . . wood, hay, stubble" [3:12]—all such shall be burned. "And the great and abominable church, which is the whore of all the earth, shall be cast down by devouring fire." (D. & C. 29:21.)[76]

Note that fire will be the final judge, not only of all people's work but also of the people themselves. When the angel Moroni appeared to Joseph Smith, he addressed this very situation (see JS–H 1:30–42). He quoted Malachi 3:2, which asks a question: who shall abide the day of the Lord's coming? The question is a good one because the Lord would be "like a refiner's fire, and like fullers' soap" (Mal. 3:2). The first image refers to purifying and the last to cleansing. The Lord's purpose in this coming would be to purify and make clean those who are his. His primary instrument would

---

75. Fee, *First Epistle*, 136.
76. *DNTC*, 2:325–26.

be fire. He would, however, come again with fire, but this fire would destroy all that would not be purified or cleansed. Both comings would bring judgment, but of very different kinds.

Often, judgment is categorized wrongly as two distinct events: either as proscribing penalty and reward or as the result of testing. The two are actually inseparable. Until the Final Judgment, all human evaluations must remain limited and tentative because unknown factors and missing information, especially that of motive, remains somewhat hidden. Therefore, human judgment is ever incomplete and, therefore, often inaccurate (see Mosiah 29:12). At the Final Judgment, however, God will make his pronouncements taking into account the total context of all actions, motives, influences, reasons, hopes, and desires. What he will not take into account are self-justifications and self-rationalizations. The fire of judgment tests, that is, discloses each and every deed in its full context.[77] Therefore, God's judgment is fully correct with the perfect balance of justice and mercy (see Rev. 19:2; 20:12–13; Mosiah 3:18; 16:1; 29:12; Alma 12:15). Thus, the test is the basis of proscribing either reward or penalty, making both inseparable.

The aggregate of all choices and what stood behind them determines what the person will be forever. The Lord has made it clear that "they who are not sanctified through the law which I have given unto you, even the law of Christ, must inherit another kingdom [than the celestial], even that of a terrestrial kingdom, or that of a telestial kingdom. For he who is not able to abide the law of a celestial kingdom cannot abide a celestial glory. And he who cannot abide the law of a terrestrial kingdom cannot abide a terrestrial glory. And he who cannot abide the law of a telestial kingdom cannot abide a telestial glory; therefore he is not meet for a kingdom of glory. Therefore he must abide a kingdom which is not a kingdom of glory" (D&C 88:21–24). Indeed, "that which is governed by law is also preserved by law and perfected and sanctified by the same. That which breaketh a law, and abideth not by law, but seeketh to become a law unto itself, and willeth to abide in sin, and altogether abideth in sin, cannot be sanctified by law, neither by mercy, justice, nor judgment. Therefore, they must remain filthy still" (D&C 88:34–35). All deeds are put to the test—that is, fully disclosed—and the result is a proper and full self-judgment, for nothing is hidden—not even from one's self (Alma 41:7; 11:43). It is here that testing (or disclosure) joins with punishment and reward, making a whole. Earthly reward in the shape of blessings or eternal recompense in the form of eternal glory are

---

77. Thiselton, *First Epistle*, 313–14.

the consequences for proper motives behind one's deeds (see Heb. 11:6; Alma 3:26–27). Conversely, undue mortal misery and loss of glory are the consequences of improper motivation behind one's deeds.

Paul's final words in this section serve as a warning and admonition. The Apostle states that his readers may yet be saved, as if plucked from the fire (3:15), but it will take immediate action on their part to be so. Any delay could prove their spiritual death.

GOD'S TEMPLE (3:16–17)

Greek Text

16 Οὐκ οἴδατε ὅτι ναὸς θεοῦ ἐστε καὶ τὸ πνεῦμα τοῦ θεοῦ οἰκεῖ ἐν ὑμῖν; 17 εἴ τις τὸν ναὸν τοῦ θεοῦ φθείρει, φθερεῖ τοῦτον ὁ θεός· ὁ γὰρ ναὸς τοῦ θεοῦ ἅγιός ἐστιν, οἵτινές ἐστε ὑμεῖς. [SBLGNT]

King James Version

16 Know ye not that ye are the temple of God, and that the Spirit of God dwelleth in you? 17 If any man defile the temple of God, him shall God destroy; for the temple of God is holy, which temple ye are.

New Rendition

16 Don't you understand that you are a temple of God and that God's Spirit dwells within you? 17 If anyone tries to destroy God's temple, God will destroy that person, for God's temple is holy, and you are that temple!

Translation Notes and Comments

3:16 *Know ye not that ye are the temple of God / Don't you understand that you are a temple of God:* Paul uses the phrase οὐκ οἴδατε ὅτι (*ouk oidate hoti*), which carries the nuance, "Surely you didn't miss this!" ten times in this epistle, each time to show the intensity of his feelings (5:6; 6:2, 3, 9, 15, 16, 19; 9:13, 24). His words emphasize that these Saints should not have overlooked or missed these doctrines for each was a core principle upon which every Saint should agree.[78]

In moving to the point Paul makes here, he cleverly transitions from a building that belongs to God (3:9) to the most sacred of all buildings, the

---

78. Thiselton, *First Epistle*, 316.

one in which the Lord resides.[79] Temples were so prevalent in both Jewish and Gentile cultures that all of Paul's readers would have resonated with his imagery one way or another.[80] Though both the Greeks and Romans built many temples, the more orthodox Jews recognized but one, that in Jerusalem.[81] Temple defilement was a common concern among all those responsible for the upkeep of the various temples, whether Jew or Gentile. Many believed that such an act would bring, at best, the withdrawal of the god's spirit and, at worst, divine wrath, not only upon the perpetrator but also upon the people who let it happen. Paul was drawing on this idea as he made his next point.

In the Greek text, the noun ναός (*naos*), "temple," lacks the definite article; hence, our Rendition translate the word as "a temple" rather than "the temple." Greek makes a distinction between ναός (*naos*), which referred to the temple building proper and often to the most holy area that contained the image of the god or goddess, and ἱερόν (*hieron*), which referred to the whole temple complex.[82] The *naos,* the word used by Paul, was the actual place where people thought the spirit of the various gods resided.[83] For Paul, such was indeed the case, for it was "the temple of the living God" (2 Cor. 6:16). The Jews of the Diaspora defined the word even more narrowly, focusing on the heightened sanctity associated with the innermost rooms of the temple. Paul's fellow Apostle John illustrated the severe sacredness of those rooms through the imagery of the rays and currents that flowed through and from them manifesting the presence and glory of God (Rev. 4:3, 5; 7:15; 11:19; 14:17; 21:10). Paul used the imagery of the temple to remind the people that, when all was said and done, they were the living temple of God. At issue was the Father's very holiness, for a violation

79. Fitzmyer, *First Corinthians,* 203.

80. It is likely that at the time of Paul's writing there were no Christian temples. Though he does allude to baptisms for the dead, an ordinance Latter-day Saints associate exclusively with the temple, it must be remembered that between 1840 and 1844, the Saints practiced this sacred ordinance outside of temples. See H. David Burton, "Baptism for the Dead," in *EM,* 1:95.

81. Less orthodox Jews had built two temples in Egypt, one on the Elephantine Island and another at Leontopolis. See Jonathan Kantrowitz, "Jewish Temples of Onias and Elephantine in Egypt," *Archaeology News Report,* September 6, 2008, http://archaeology newsreport.blogspot.com/2008/09/jewish-temples-of-onias-elephantine-in.html.

82. LSJ, 1160.

83. BDAG, 470, 665.

of his sanctuary was to show contempt for his very nature.[84] For anyone to do harm to the Church, therefore, was tantamount to blaspheming against God himself and would bring severe consequences.

The image of the temple assisted Paul in showing the Corinthian Saints the relationship between the Church and its mission. Both were inextricably woven together. The Church was an institution made up of officers and members, but it existed for specific purposes. Though Paul does not say so here, he knew the Church's mission full well, as evidenced in his letter to the Ephesians. To them he stated that the Church existed to build testimonies concerning the nature and mission of the Savior, to edify the congregations, to help the Saints move toward perfection, and to carry out missionary work (Eph. 4:12–13). As the Church accomplished these tasks, it grew in holiness and strength. Thus, the Church perpetuated the mission and the mission contributed to the Church. Because of improper focus, however, some Saints were, at best, diluting the Church's mission and, at worst, pushing it off course. Of even graver concern for Paul, however, was that service motivated by self-interest, status-seeking, or financial gain could severely damage if not destroy the Church.[85] It was a form of idolatry, the idolatry of self, and any association with idols, no matter how small, defiled the temple (2 Thes. 2:4; 2 Cor. 6:16). The grave sin of idolatry would leave the temple vulnerable to destruction.

Paul's use of the plural verb ἐστέ (*este*), "all of you are," makes it clear that Paul saw the Church as a whole, not any given member, as the place where God's Spirit resided. His word suggests he was trying to get his readers to see that the Holy Spirit dwells in the Christian community. As long as the bulk of the community was sufficiently pure, the Spirit of God would continue to dwell there (compare D&C 1:30–31). When it was not, the Spirit would withdraw.

the Spirit of God dwelleth in you / God's Spirit dwells within you: By the use of the articular phrase ὁ πνεῦμα τοῦ θεοῦ (*to pneuma tou theou*), literally, "the Spirit of the God," Paul emphasized that he was referring to the spirit of a specific God, indeed, the only true and living one. It was God's

---

84. In John's writings, God and the temple are ultimately one (Rev. 21:22). For discussion of God as a temple, see Jay A. Parry and Donald W. Parry, "The Temple in Heaven: Its Description and Significance," in *Temples of the Ancient World: Ritual and Symbolism,* ed. Donald W. Parry (Salt Lake City: Deseret Book; Provo, Utah: Foundation for Ancient Research and Mormon Studies, 1994), 515–32.

85. Thiselton, *First Epistle,* 315.

Spirit, and his alone, that dwelt within the Church. By making that distinction, Paul underscored the importance, exclusiveness, and sacredness of the wonderful privilege that the members of Church shared. Paul's point squares with that found in D&C 130:22, where it states that the Holy Ghost "has not a body of flesh and bones, but is a personage of Spirit," otherwise, he "could not dwell in us."

3:17 *If any man defile the temple of God, him shall God destroy / If anyone tries to destroy God's temple, God will destroy that person:* Paul uses the same Greek verb φθείρω (*phtheirō*) in both parts of this conditional clause. *Phtheirō* has a broad range of meanings, including "to cause harm to in a physical manner or in outward circumstances, to destroy, ruin, corrupt, spoil"; "to cause deterioration of the inner life, ruin, corrupt"; "to inflict punishment, destroy in the sense 'punish with eternal destruction'"; and "to break rules of a contest, violate rules."[86] Since no single English verb covers these various meanings, the KJV chose to use two different English verbs. In our Rendition, we use "destroy" in both cases to preserve the parallelism of Paul's statement. Also, in the first half of the conditional clause, the present tense has a conative sense, as it sometimes does in Greek,[87] and so our Rendition translates it as "tries to destroy."

Paul's point is that God is not going to let anyone get away with trying to destroy the Church. That includes any perversion of its organization, doctrines, or mission. It is of note that Paul's words do not suggest the impossibility of the destruction of the Church, for he knew well it could be and, indeed, was happening (see, for example, Gal. 1:6–8; 2 Cor. 11:4). His words do show that those who participated in that destruction would pay a very heavy price. That price would be divine punishment with its eternal consequences, even the damnation of the soul (see, for example, 5:1–7; 2 Thes. 1:9; compare Heb. 6:4–8; 2 Pet. 2:20; Jude 1:7).

Analysis and Summary

In Paul's day, the city of Corinth boasted no less than six temples in the downtown area.[88] One of these temples, now called "the temple of Venus Fortuna," celebrated the age-old patron deity of the city, Aphrodite. Her

---

86. BDAG, 1054.

87. Wallace, *Greek Grammar*, 534–35; Smyth, *Greek Grammar*, §1878.

88. The temple district had edifices to Herakles, Poseidon, Apollo, and Hermes, among others.

original temple sat atop the Acrocorinth—the high, steep hill that served as the fortress for the city from its beginning.[89] Both fortress and temple were destroyed by the Romans in 146 BC and, though the fortress was rebuilt, the temple was not. A much smaller temple sat at the west end of the Agora and served the goddess and her patrons. There, ritual prostitution continued to be practiced, which sanctioned immorality within the culture itself. It was believed that such practices warded off the much-feared "evil eye" that brought distress and even death.[90] Paul countered this and other pagan beliefs by teaching how real happiness and salvation were achieved.

Though unholy by Christian standards, even Venus's temple carried an aura of sanctity in the eyes of its devotees. Its priests and hierodules were ever on guard against defilement. It was the aspect of sacredness that Paul appealed to as he used the imagery of the temple. The Church was God's temple at Corinth, and it was to act as a counterpoint to Aphrodite's temple and those of all the other gods.

Though Paul often referred to the temple in his writings, it was mostly as a metaphor.[91] As one LDS scholar noted,

> Occasionally the body is a temple for God's Spirit, but usually the Church is the temple of God. The members ("ye," older plural English for the plural Greek) are "God's building" (1 Cor. 3:9), with Christ its foundation (1 Cor. 3:11), or, in summary, "the temple of God" (1 Cor. 3:16). Elsewhere, Paul taught about Christ as cornerstone, apostles as foundation, and members fitting into their places as a "holy temple in the Lord" (Eph. 2:21). And in one of his last letters, Paul still spoke of "the house of God, which is the church of the living God" (1 Tim. 3:15). Paul must define Paul [where possible], and his own words show that he was here referring to the Church.[92]

---

89. The Acrocorinth rose about 1,800 feet above the plain. Due to its imposing height and steepness, it continued to serve as a fortress until AD 1821, when it was finally abandoned.

90. Miroslav Marcovich, "From Ishtar to Aphrodite," *Journal of Aesthetic Education* 30, no. 2, Special Issue: Distinguished Humanities Lectures II (Summer 1996): 49, tells of ritual prostitution practiced in Aphrodite's temples. The Greek *hierodoule,* literally, "sacred slave" was a euphemism for the prostitute priestesses of the goddess of lust.

91. Richard L. Anderson, *Guide to Acts and the Apostles' Letters,* 3d ed. (Provo, Utah: Brigham Young University, 1999), 33. Generally, LDS leaders interpret this verse as pertaining to individuals and often with the focus of moral cleanliness or obedience to the word of wisdom. For two typical examples of many that could be given, see Heber C. Kimball, in *JD,* 7:17; Bruce R. McConkie, "Upon This Rock," *Ensign* 11 (May 1981): 75–77.

92. Anderson, *Understanding Paul,* 86.

The imagery of the temple allowed Paul to stress the holiness of the Church of Christ and set up the warning against anyone who would defile it. For the Christian, there was only one God, and he could have but one temple in Corinth and they were it.[93] The Apostle assured his readers that "the Spirit of God dwelleth *among* or *within* you [plural]," but warned, "If any man defile the temple of God"—meaning the apostate who distorts the doctrine and draws away disciples after him—"him shall God destroy" (3:16–17). His statement seems a bit jarring since in 3:15 the Apostle noted that though a person's work might be destroyed, he could be saved, albeit barely. The answer may be that Paul was looking in this verse not at those who made up the factions and inadvertently promoted their doctrine but at those who were leaders and creators of the destructive teachings.[94]

President Thomas S. Monson stated:

> In a revelation given through the Prophet Joseph Smith at Kirtland, Ohio, December 27, 1832, the Master counseled: "Organize yourselves; prepare every needful thing; and establish a house, even a house of prayer, a house of fasting, a house of faith, a house of learning, a house of glory, a house of order, a house of God." (D&C 88:119.) Where could any of us locate a more suitable blueprint whereby he could wisely and properly build a house to personally occupy throughout eternity? Such a house would meet the building code outlined in Matthew—even a house built "upon a rock" [Matt. 7:24]; a house capable of withstanding the rain of adversity, the floods of opposition, and the winds of doubt everywhere present in our challenging world.[95]

President Monson later said, "Some might question: 'But that revelation was to provide guidance for the construction of a temple. Is it relevant today?' I would respond: 'Did not the Apostle Paul declare, "Know ye not that ye are the temple of God, and that the Spirit of God dwelleth in you?"' (1 Cor. 3:16.) Perhaps if we consider these architectural guidelines on an individual basis, we can more readily appreciate this divine counsel from the Master Builder, the Creator of the world, our Lord and Savior, Jesus Christ."[96]

---

93. Fee, *First Epistle*, 147.

94. Fee, *First Epistle*, 148–49 and especially n. 19.

95. Thomas S. Monson, *Pathways to Perfection* (Salt Lake City: Deseret Book, 1973), 243–44.

96. Thomas S. Monson, "Building Your Eternal Home," *Ensign* 29 (October 1999): 2.

A WARNING AGAINST SELF-DECEPTION (3:18–20)

Greek Text

18 Μηδεὶς ἑαυτὸν ἐξαπατάτω· εἴ τις δοκεῖ σοφὸς εἶναι ἐν ὑμῖν ἐν τῷ αἰῶνι τούτῳ, μωρὸς γενέσθω, ἵνα γένηται σοφός, 19 ἡ γὰρ σοφία τοῦ κόσμου τούτου μωρία παρὰ τῷ θεῷ ἐστιν· γέγραπται γάρ· Ὁ δρασσόμενος τοὺς σοφοὺς ἐν τῇ πανουργίᾳ αὐτῶν· 20 καὶ πάλιν· Κύριος γινώσκει τοὺς διαλογισμοὺς τῶν σοφῶν ὅτι εἰσὶν μάταιοι. [SBLGNT]

King James Version

18 Let no man deceive himself. If any man among you seemeth to be wise in this world, let him become a fool, that he may be wise. 19 For the wisdom of this world is foolishness with God. For it is written, He taketh the wise in their own craftiness. 20 And again, The Lord knoweth the thoughts of the wise, that they are vain.

New Rendition

18 Let no one deceive himself. If any one of you thinks he is wise in the ways of this world, let him become a fool, so that he might become truly wise. 19 For the wisdom of this world is foolishness from God's point of view, for it is written, "He traps the wise in their own trickery," 20 and further, "The Lord knows that the reasoning of the wise is futile."

Translation Notes and Comments

3:18 *Let no man deceive himself* / *Let no one deceive himself:* That Paul uses the third person singular pronoun in this warning shows that he is no longer addressing the Church as a whole or even just the factional leaders, but each individual member.[97] The issue here is self-deception. The third person singular imperative ἐξαπατάτω (*exapatatō*), "let him deceive, cheat," denotes an act that causes another to accept a false idea and therefore connotes leading someone away from the truth.[98] In this case, it was the ego that was the culprit. It gave rise to a prideful quest for σοφία (*sophia*), "wisdom," to be considered wise by those in the Church, and this quest resulted in some of the Corinthian Saints deceiving themselves and then leading others astray.

---

97. Fitzmyer, *First Corinthians*, 206.

98. Louw-Nida, §31.12. Rather than produce a very awkward translation of the third person singular imperative in gender-neutral, "politically correct" English, we have chosen to translate the Greek literally.

seemeth to be wise / thinks he is wise: The Greek verb δοκέω (*dokeō*) can be used both personally and impersonally. The KJV takes it as impersonal whereas our Rendition treats it as personal, which is the more likely case because it is self-deception that makes people "think" they are wise when they are not.[99] It was the affectation of Greek philosophy, what Paul calls "the wisdom of the world," on the gospel that was at the heart of the Corinthian problems.[100] What Paul is doing for his readers is subtly critiquing the many problems of Greek philosophy to show that it really does not contain real wisdom. This is every bit as applicable for us in today's modern world, which focuses on science and logical thinking as the only way to find truth and rejects inspiration and revelation.

in this world / in the ways of this world: The Greek word translated "world" is αἰών (*aiōn*). In its root sense it refers to a long period of time, and the English word "eon" is derived from this sense. But here it takes on the sense of "this present age or time period," and, by extension, the present world order.[101] To emphasize this sense, our Rendition has translated this as "the ways of this world."

let him become a fool, that he may be wise / let him become a fool, so that he might become truly wise: The word "wise" is translated from the Greek adjective σοφός (*sophos*). Wisdom was one of the great virtues that the Greeks sought after. The word philosopher (φιλόσοφος, *philosophos*) means "one who loves wisdom." The aorist subjunctive verb γενέσθω (*genesthō*), "become," with the conjunction ἵνα (*hina*) expresses purpose and carries the sense of "in order to become wise."[102] The adverb "truly" is not found in the Greek text, but it is added in our Rendition to catch the full thrust of the thought Paul is conveying—"if you truly want to be *sophos,* then you need first of all to recognize that you really know nothing; then, with God's help, you can truly become *sophos.*"[103]

Harkening back to the imagery he created in 1:20, 27, Paul again refers to the fool. The adjective μωρός (*mōros*) describes a person who is at the extreme opposite on the intellectual scale from the wise. Paul is, of course, using hyperbole here to get across his point. The only way to be truly wise

---

99. Thiselton, *First Epistle,* 321.

100. Findlay, "St. Paul's First Epistle," 793.

101. BDAG, 32.

102. Thiselton, *First Epistle,* 321.

103. The more educated among Paul's readers would have picked up an echo to Socrates, whom the oracle at Delphi proclaimed to be the wisest of all men because he knew he knew nothing and was ready to learn from the gods. See Plato, *Apol.* 20–21.

is to appear to be a fool in the eyes of the world: to believe ideas that are so preposterous, nonsensical, ridiculous, silly, or absurd that no truly sensible person would even consider them. In this case, it is "Christ, and him crucified" (2:2).

3:19 *For the wisdom of this world is foolishness with God / For the wisdom of this world is foolishness from God's point of view:* The noun "world" is translated from the Greek κόσμος (*kosmos*), which has the basic sense of "order," and it was used to describe the ordered world or universe in which we live (English "cosmos").[104] Paul uses it to describe the all-pervasive thinking of "the natural man" that dominates the world (see Translation Notes on 2:14). The preposition παρά (*para*) with the dative, literally "at, by," or "near,"[105] here has the sense of "in the sight of or judgment of someone." Thus we have translated it as "from God's point of view" in our Rendition.

For it is written, He taketh the wise in their own craftiness / for it is written, "He traps the wise in their own trickery": As a proof text, Paul quotes Job 5:13 but translates directly from the Hebrew text of Job rather than using the LXX.[106] The noun πανουργία (*panourgia*) carries the idea of "trickery involving evil cunning."[107] Paul's choice of words suggests how devious the world's ways are, but that they are no match for God's wisdom. Indeed, he "traps" them (δράσσομαι, *drassomai*) by turning their own evil plans against them[108] (see, for example, Ps. 7:15; Prov. 26:27; 28:10; Isa. 60:12; Zech. 12:9; Rev. 17:16–17; 1 Ne. 14:3; 22:14; 2 Ne. 28:7–10; D&C 109:25).[109]

3:20 *And again, The Lord knoweth the thoughts of the wise, that they are vain / and further, "The Lord knows that the reasoning of the wise is futile":* To push his point, Paul uses another proof text.[110] The quote is from Psalm 94:11 (LXX 93:11). Unlike the previous Old Testament quote, Paul follows the LXX. The quote allows Paul to show the weakness of

---

104. BDAG, 561.

105. BDAG, 757.

106. The evidence for this is that he uses δράσσομαι rather than καταλαμβάνω to translate קָמַץ (*qāmaṣ*) and πανουργία (*panourgia*), "craftiness," rather than φρόνησις (*phronēsis*), "understanding," for עׇרְמׇה (*'ormāh*). This seems to be the only quote from Job in the New Testament.

107. Louw-Nida, §88.270.

108. Louw-Nida, §27.32.

109. For two good studies of Paul's use of the scriptures, see E. Earle Ellis, *Paul's Use of the Old Testament* (rpt., Grand Rapids, Mich.: Baker Book, 1981); Richard B. Hays, *Echoes of the Scriptures in the Letters of Paul* (New Haven, Conn.: Yale University Press, 1989).

110. Paul often uses the phrase καὶ πάλιν (*kai palin*), "and again," to introduce a second or third scriptural quote. See, for example, Rom. 15:10–12; Heb. 1:5; 2:13; 4:5; 10:30.

human reasoning. The word he chose, μάταιος (*mataios*), means "valueless, empty," and, particularly, "impotent"—that which is in every way useless and therefore utterly futile.[111]

Analysis and Summary

In this section, Paul disarms those Christians who think they are wise. He warns against self-deception that originates in a kind of thinking that seems wise but is actually foolish. He shows them that by following the reasoning of the world, they have transformed the gospel of Christ into some impotent and worthless hybrid. As a result, they have left its saving principles for the damning philosophies of the world. Since it is wisdom they are after, he shows them the proper way to achieve it.

His statement in 3:18, that one need become a fool in order to gain true wisdom, would have appealed to some of his more educated gentile converts. They would have heard echoes of Socrates's maxim that no one is truly wise until he recognizes his own ignorance. Paul was, however, using hyperbole to make his point. To be a fool, as understood among such philosophers as the Cynics and Stoics, was to show such a lack of sophisticated thinking that the word "asinine" would have been a compliment.[112]

With 3:19–20, Paul picks up the theme he started in 1:18–25, contrasting the wisdom of the world with that of God, but he more fully develops it. In this instance, however, he makes a contrasting point. In the earlier passage he stated that the world saw God's wisdom as foolishness. Here he shows that it is the world's wisdom that, from God's perspective, is foolishness.[113] The reason is that the best thinking of those in the world is flawed by shortsightedness, self-interest, and secularism. It is, therefore, flawed from the top down.[114] The adjective Paul used to describe the world's wisdom, μάταιος (*mataios*), stresses its impotency. The best efforts of the wise of the world, so far as achieving any kind of lasting salvation is concerned, are utterly futile for they had no power.

---

111. BDAG, 621. See also Collins, *First Corinthians,* 164–65, who notes that these peoples' self-deception was due to their willingness to follow certain factional leaders whose acts were destroying the "temple of God."

112. Thiselton, *First Epistle,* 321, n. 105. As Witherington, *Conflict and Community,* 135, notes, Paul's position simply turned all philosophical reasoning upside down and, therefore, met with tremendous resistance even among the more self-sophisticated members of the Church.

113. Fee, *First Epistle,* 152.

114. Thiselton, *First Epistle,* 323.

Addressing this theme, Elder McConkie asked, "What is the relative value of intellectuality and spirituality?" He answered,

> In this life, those who are learned, who have intellectual capacity, who gain scholastic degrees, are held up to dignity and renown; their views are sought; their opinions are valued. But from the Lord's eternal perspective, there is almost no language sufficient to depreciate the importance of intellectuality standing alone and to magnify the eternal worth of spirituality.
>
> There is no salvation in intellectuality standing alone. "The wisdom of this world is foolishness with God." But through spirituality the door is open to the saints to progress until they inherit all things—literally, all things—including all the intellectuality known in the world and more. Those who seek the Lord, who find him, who keep his commandments, who grow in the things of the Spirit, shall gain the fulness of the kingdom of the Father. They gain exaltation; they become gods. They inherit all things—literally.
>
> Why then, Paul contends, should the saints glory in intellectuality, in the wisdom of the world? And the Lord, in latter-day revelation, makes the same presentation. Speaking of those who gain exaltation, he says: "All things are theirs, whether life or death, or things present, or things to come, all are theirs and they are Christ's, and Christ is God's. And they shall overcome all things. Wherefore, let no man glory in man, but rather let him glory in God, who shall subdue all enemies under his feet." (D. & C. 76:59–61.)[115]

All Things Belong to the Saints (3:21–23)

Greek Text

21 ὥστε μηδεὶς καυχάσθω ἐν ἀνθρώποις· πάντα γὰρ ὑμῶν ἐστιν, 22 εἴτε Παῦλος εἴτε Ἀπολλῶς εἴτε Κηφᾶς εἴτε κόσμος εἴτε ζωὴ εἴτε θάνατος εἴτε ἐνεστῶτα εἴτε μέλλοντα, πάντα ὑμῶν, 23 ὑμεῖς δὲ Χριστοῦ, Χριστὸς δὲ θεοῦ. [SBLGNT]

King James Version

21 Therefore let no man glory in men. For all things are yours; 22 Whether Paul, or Apollos, or Cephas, or the world, or life, or death, or things present, or things to come; all are yours; 23 And ye are Christ's; and Christ *is* God's.

New Rendition

21 Therefore, let no one boast in mankind, for everything belongs to you, 22 whether Paul or Apollos or Cephas or the world or life or death, or the present or the future, everything belongs to you, 23 and you belong to Christ, and Christ belongs to God.

---

115. *DNTC*, 2:327–28.

Translation Notes and Comments

3:21 *let no man glory in men / let no one boast in mankind:* The verb καυχάομαι (*kauchaomai*) means "to take pride in something, boast, glory, pride oneself, brag."[116] Paul's phrase forbids the self-conceit coupled with the vaunted allegiance to one faction or another that so afflicted the Corinthian branch (compare 1:29). It should be noted that Paul was not opposed to the acts of glorying or boasting, but they must be in the right person. To glory in someone means to give them praise, honor, or distinction above others. Indeed, the word suggests a worshipful attitude toward them. To boast in them moves these feelings from the private to the public arena by openly proclaiming a leader's virtues and affirming the followers' allegiance to them.[117] The problem was that allegiance to any mortal deprived God of glory that was his due (compare 1:29–31; Rom. 3:23–27; Jer. 9:22–23).[118] Thus, as Paul had already stated, if the Saints insist on glorying, let them glory in the Lord alone (1:31).

3:22 *Cephas:* that is, Peter. Πέτρος (*petros*) "rock" is the Greek translation of the Aramaic כֵּיפָא (*kēpā*), "the Rock," the surname Christ gave to Simon when he called him to be one of his disciples (Matt. 16:18).

all are yours / everything belongs to you:[119] Paul's use of the second person plural genitive pronoun ὑμῶν (*hymōn*), "yours," shows that he has turned his attention once more to the entire branch; no one was excluded from the point he was making. Paul's words effectively turned the thinking of many of the Corinthian Saints end for end. Where certain Church members made hay of being a devotee of one prominent figure or another, whom they supported as the person with power and authority—whether Paul, Apollos, or Cephas—the Apostle showed them that all these were actually *their* servants. And more—everything else, for that matter, actually belonged to them as well.[120]

---

116. BDAG, 536.

117. See Louw-Nida, §33.368, 371, 372.

118. Fitzmyer, *First Corinthians*, 207.

119. Paul could have here adopted a Stoic maxim for his purposes. It states, "All things belong to the wise man" (see Diogenes Laertius, *Vitae* 6.37; and Cicero, *De finibus* 3.22.75). This view is supported by Collins, *First Corinthians*, 66; and Conzelmann, *1 Corinthians*, 80. If Paul did use it, he redefined it and gave it a Christian context by showing that "all things" did not come to the wise man due to his wisdom but due to the Atonement of the Lord.

120. These were the figureheads of the Church who were used by factional leaders to support their positions. Paul does not include Christ here, likely because he is listing human agents. Findlay, "St. Paul's First Epistle," 795.

3:23 *ye are Christ's; and Christ is God's / you belong to Christ, and Christ belongs to God:* With these pointed words, Paul explained exactly how all things belong to the Christian. The phrase ὑμεῖς δὲ Χριστοῦ (*hymeis de Xristou*), literally, "but you are of Christ," is possessive and shows that the Saints do not own themselves but they belong to Christ (compare Rom. 14:8; Gal. 3:29), indeed, they bore the very name of Christ, Χριστιανοί (*Christianoi*).[121] Further, Paul points out that there were great benefits to this relationship. They possess or will possess all that he possesses, albeit in some things they must wait for a season. And what does he possess? Because he belongs to God, he is heir to all that God has, for, as Paul has already noted, Jesus is "the power of God, and the wisdom of God" (1:24). Paul's point was that the Saints are the ones to whom all things belong because they are Christ's and Christ is God's and God owns everything.[122] In other places, Paul will say it another way: they are joint heirs with Christ and heirs of all that God has (see Rom. 8:17; Gal. 3:29; compare Heb. 1:14; 6:17; 11:9).

Analysis and Summary

With his emphatic coordinating conjunction ὥστε (*hoste*), "and so, therefore, and further," in 3:21, Paul signals to his readers that he is now concluding his argument. That conclusion, found in 3:21–23, holds a quiet but powerful grandeur that beautifully summarizes the points he has made. He begins with an exhortation—let no one boast in humankind—then supplies its theological basis: that the individual Saint can achieve total unity with the Father and the Son.[123] These words succinctly solved the Corinthian problem by undercutting both its factionalism with its devotion to certain leaders and the pride-based self-sufficiency that it supported.

The problem of the factional leaders was that they were following false gods, ones of their own creation. Because of this, they had developed and promoted false doctrines derived from the wisdom of the world. As a result, they were leading themselves and others away from the truth.

The sin of these leaders was no small matter. The impulse of the Divine is toward unity while that of the adversary is toward division. In Corinth, the wicked impulse divided the people, causing them to accept some Church leaders and reject others, accept some doctrines while rejecting others, all

---

121. Fitzmyer, *First Corinthians*, 209.

122. Fee, *First Epistle*, 151.

123. Fee, *First Epistle*, 153.

the while pursuing their own agendas.[124] The Doctrine and Covenants notes that the telestial kingdom is composed, in part, of those "who are of Paul, and of Apollos, and of Cephas. These are they who say they are some of one and some of another—some of Christ and some of John, and some of Moses, and some of Elias, and some of Esaias, and some of Isaiah, and some of Enoch; But received not the gospel, neither the testimony of Jesus, neither the prophets, neither the everlasting covenant" (D&C 76:99–101). These verses clearly identify the twofold consequence of their sin: first, they rejected the spirit-born testimony of Jesus and his Apostles, and second, as a result, they did not enter into the everlasting covenant. Therefore, they will be "thrust down to hell" and "shall not be redeemed from the devil until the last resurrection" (D&C 76:84–85). Their penalty is serious but so is the depth of their sin. They had access to the truth but rejected it in favor of their own agendas. The fires of hell await such sinners.

The exhortation "let no one boast in mankind" (as in our Rendition) is the logical extension of Paul's insistence on the futility of human wisdom. That insistence included belonging to a faction even if it claimed to derive its prestige and doctrine from Paul, Apollos, or even Cephas. Even in deference to the important position these leaders held, they were still mere mortals. Further, neither the Church nor its members were their property. The Church was the exclusive property of God, and the members were not slaves but fellow workers. Reversing the perceived order, Paul insisted that, properly seen, it was the leaders who were the servants of all.[125] Full trust must only be placed in God and Christ. Only in them should the Saints glory. We are reminded of Ammon in the Book of Mormon who, when glorying of his success, was rebuked by his brother Aaron. He defended his actions by saying, "I do not boast in my own strength, nor in my own wisdom; . . . I will rejoice in my God. Yea, I know that I am nothing; as to my strength I am weak; therefore I will not boast of myself, but I will boast of my God, for in his strength I can do all things" (Alma 26:11–12).

Paul next explained why they should not follow mortals in their effort to gain acceptance, prestige, and security. What they simply did not get was that all of these things were already theirs. In his analogy of the field (3:5–9), he already showed them that they were not *of* Apollos or *of* Cephas. They were, however, *of* God. That meant that they had become members

---

124. Stephen E. Robinson and H. Dean Garrett, *A Commentary on the Doctrine and Covenants* (Salt Lake City: Deseret Book, 2000), 2:324.

125. Robertson and Plummer, *Critical and Exegetical Commentary,* 72.

of his family (Rom. 8:15; Eph. 1:5; Gal. 4:5) and were heirs of all that he had (Rom. 8:17; Gal. 3:29; Titus 3:7). It also meant that each individual could, while in mortality, have a personal and deeply spiritual relationship with God. The fact that a person could establish such a personal relationship with the Father and Son (see John 14:23) placed heavy responsibility upon Paul's readers, for it meant that they must reach in faith beyond men, the world, and the immediate. It meant that, as hard as it might be, they had to give up philosophy and anchor themselves to God and his revealed truths. Such was necessary even when that truth went counter to logic and reason, demanding belief in "Christ, and him crucified" (2:2), that is, in the Atonement with its attendant Resurrection.

Paul's insistence that "everything belongs to you" (3:21, Rendition) showed the silliness of factionalism. That the pronoun he used, "you," was plural showed he had the whole community of faithful believers in mind. His point was that the Saints were heirs of everything because of the work of Christ. Indeed, because of Christ, each Saint inherited a new birthright by which they received everything that was important. Paul wanted them to see that in God they were freed from self-enslavement to mere mortals. But there was more. They were freed from worry and bondage to the world and even from life, death, the present, and the future: items with which many, even in our day, become obsessed. Each of these, if one does not have the proper perspective, can act as a tyrant, debilitating each person in its demands for attention and resources.[126] But the Savior's death freed people from concern for any of these.

And how? Taking each in turn, first, the Savior freed people from the world, meaning those systems, practices, and goods associated with secular society.[127] Because of the example of Christ, the Christians knew how to put all these to their use. He gave them the proper standards, which allows them to enjoy the fruits of the world without being enslaved by them (compare D&C 59:16–23). Further, according to LDS theology, the earth itself will someday become a celestial sphere on which they will have an inheritance (see D&C 38:20; 45:58; 77:1; 88:25–26).

Second, the Savior freed people from "life and death" with their cognates "the present and the future." Either set summarizes mortal existence. Again, because the Savior showed his disciples how to see these things in

---

126. Fee, *First Epistle*, 154.

127. Paul's word *kosmos* pointed to conditions devoid of any requirements or obligations to God. Louw-Nida, §41.38.

their proper perspective, he taught them how to be masters of all. Even death, the king of fears for the unrighteous (Rom. 5:17, 21; Heb. 2:15), loses its sting (15:55). Though speaking of the second death—the only death really to be feared (Rev. 2:11; 20:6; Alma 12:16, 32; D&C 76:37)—the Savior promised, "If a man keep my saying, he shall never see death" (John 8:51). Because the Savior overmasters life and death (Rom. 14:9; Eph. 4:9–10), he can and will give his heirs mastership over them.[128]

Third, the Savior freed people from "the present and the future." The Savior was very explicit in how to control these. Gospel obedience in the present brings blessing now and creates a positive future (Matt. 6:25–29, 34). And yet, there is another dimension to overmastering the present and the future—knowing the fullness of both. According to LDS theology, the Lord will eventually make all things known to the Saints: "Things which have passed, and hidden things which no man knew, things of the earth, by which it was made, and the purpose and the end thereof—Things most precious, things that are above, and things that are beneath, things that are in the earth, and upon the earth, and in heaven" (D&C 101:33–34). Indeed,

> nothing shall be withheld, whether there be one God or many gods, they shall be manifest. All thrones and dominions, principalities and powers, shall be revealed and set forth upon all who have endured valiantly for the gospel of Jesus Christ. And also, if there be bounds set to the heavens or to the seas, or to the dry land, or to the sun, moon, or stars—All the times of their revolutions, all the appointed days, months, and years, and all the days of their days, months, and years, and all their glories, laws, and set times, shall be revealed in the days of the dispensation of the fulness of times—According to that which was ordained in the midst of the Council of the Eternal God of all other gods before this world was, that should be reserved unto the finishing and the end thereof, when every man shall enter into his eternal presence and into his immortal rest. (D&C 121:28–32)

In summary, all things belong to the Saints—all that are material, societal, spatial, temporal, and celestial.[129] Seen in this light, which Paul did, to be bound to one person or even a group of people imposed too narrow a view upon the Christian.[130] Each had to see the eternal reality. And

---

128. Findlay, "St. Paul's First Epistle," 795.

129. The Lord stated that "all things unto me are spiritual, and not at any time have I given unto you a law which was temporal" (D&C 29:34). In so saying, Jesus shows nothing that is good, neither material nor spiritual, falls outside his realm and, therefore, the realm of the Saints.

130. Fee, *First Epistle*, 154.

what was that? As Paul said, "Ye are Christ's; and Christ is God's" (3:23). Because they belonged to the family of Christ, they were his fellow heirs and Christ was God's and, therefore, his eternal heir. According to modern scripture, those who obtain exaltation in the celestial kingdom inherit all that the Father has. The Savior explained why: "He that receiveth my servants receiveth me; and he that receiveth me receiveth my Father; and he that receiveth my Father receiveth my Father's kingdom; therefore all that my Father hath shall be given unto him" (D&C 84:36–38). "Wherefore, all things are theirs, whether life or death, or things present, or things to come, all are theirs and they are Christ's, and Christ is God's" (D&C 76:59).

Another point in Paul's writings that must not be overlooked is a doctrine that is admittedly subtle but nonetheless clear: Paul believed in apotheosis, that the righteous really could become as the Gods. Only if they held this rank could all things become subject unto them. Paul would fully agree with the doctrine that all those who received the testimony of Jesus and were baptized in his name and kept the commandments, who overcame by faith and were sealed by the Holy Spirit of Promise would become "gods, even the sons [and daughters] of God" (D&C 76:58; Ps. 82:1, 6; compare John 10:34–36). These "shall pass by the angels, and the gods, which are set there, to their exaltation and glory in all things, as hath been sealed upon their heads, which glory shall be a fullness and a continuation of the seeds forever and ever. Then shall they be gods, because they have no end" (D&C 132:19–20).

Chapter 4

Servants of Christ

INTRODUCTION

In the last chapter, Paul concluded his response regarding some of the Corinthian Saints' pride in the "wisdom of man" with its accompanying factionalism. That was not, however, the worst of their problems that the Apostle also had to address. But accepting his counsel and correction on these weightier problems depended on their accepting the authority of the Apostle himself.[1] This was his major challenge, for under the declaration that some members were *for* Cephas and *for* Apollos was the very firm, if tacit, acknowledgement that these members were very much *against* Paul. These parties denied his authority and rejected much of his doctrine. The Apostle, therefore, had to unite them to him if his correction was to have any effect.[2] He wrote this section of his epistle in an attempt to bring about that acceptance.

However, he faced a dilemma and, interestingly, one of his own making. He had already stressed the idea that the Corinthian Saints should not put their trust in men (including Church leaders who were, in reality, but the servants of all). All trust must be in God and Christ alone. Nevertheless, he had to get them to accept his authority above that of any of the local leaders and factional heads if they were to come to a unity of the faith. He knew his way out of the dilemma. All he had to do was prove to them that he was not representing himself but the Father and the Son and that he preached

---

1. The apologetic thrust of this section works against those who see the epistle as made up of segments derived from other epistles. Some authors divide the first few chapters into three parallel sections: 1:18–2:5; 2:6–3:4; finally 3:5–4:5. Paul's development mitigates against this view. For discussion, see Benjamin Fiore, "'Covert Allusion' in 1 Corinthians 1–4," *Catholic Biblical Quarterly* 47 (1985): 85–102.

2. Fee, *First Epistle*, 155–56.

not his own doctrine but theirs.[3] In doing this, he also reenforced his relationship with this branch of the Church.[4] But he was doing more—and this is important: he was also making very clear the apostolic authority over all the Churches.

In the first paragraph (4:1–5), he introduced his argument. He explained that the da were but stewards who indeed rule but are ruled in turn. Though they possessed a great deal of authority, it was not theirs but their Lord's.[5] And he had given them the model of the perfect servant—one who was both trustworthy and faithful—and Paul showed the Corinthian Saints how he had fulfilled that role and then related it to their misjudgment of him and his methods. He stressed that he was beyond reproach (judgment) in this matter and ended by cautioning them about making harsh judgments in light of the future judgment all must face.

In the next paragraph (4:6–13), using both irony and sarcasm, he directly hit his detractors and he hit them hard.[6] He contrasted, in bold relief, his authority and work with theirs. He pitted his supposed "shame" against their self-proclaimed "high station." He showed that his doctrine alone was consistent with "Christ, and him crucified" (2:2).

In the final paragraph (4:14–21), with consummate skill, he reasserted his God-given authority with its attendant right to correct both their false doctrine and bad behavior. He did this with the warm and appealing metaphor of a father's care for a child. There was, however, a downside to this relationship, for if the child would not respond to gentleness and love then he must face the prospect of the rod. Paul gives them the choice.[7]

This portion of his epistle shows us Paul at his best. It does this largely by giving us a glimpse into the soul of the man, revealing what drives him. He is thoroughly tied to the Savior. There is no doubt that he is *for* Christ, indeed, he is "in Christ" (4:17), the phrase suggesting the close and deeply spiritual relationship between him and his Lord. That connection, he knew, was made possible by the cross and the grace that flowed out of it. As the Lord's grace touched and transformed him, so too it would do the same for others.

Paul and the other Apostles were acutely aware of the coming apostasy and were highly motivated to do what they could to postpone it. For a

---

3. Bailey, *Mediterranean Eyes,* 142.

4. Fitzmyer, *First Corinthians,* 210.

5. Findlay, "St. Paul's First Epistle," 796.

6. Sperry, *Paul's Life and Letters,* 120.

7. Fee, *First Epistle,* 156–57.

time, they also believed that the Restoration and Second Coming would not be long behind it. The Apostles' energy was greatly enhanced by these expectations. They had especially high hopes concerning the Second Coming and its outcome. That outcome had already been predetermined by the Atonement, for out of it would come a full, accurate, and complete judgment. Indeed, as he had already noted, each person's work would be tested by fire. He knew full well that the outcome of that judgment would turn worldly wisdom and ranking upside down. Paul's challenge was to get his audience to see the situation as it really was and to respond appropriately. At issue was their very souls.[8]

FAITHFULNESS (4:1–5)

Greek Text

1 Οὕτως ἡμᾶς λογιζέσθω ἄνθρωπος ὡς ὑπηρέτας Χριστοῦ καὶ οἰκονόμους μυστηρίων θεοῦ. 2 ὧδε λοιπὸν ζητεῖται ἐν τοῖς οἰκονόμοις ἵνα πιστός τις εὑρεθῇ. 3 ἐμοὶ δὲ εἰς ἐλάχιστόν ἐστιν, ἵνα ὑφ᾽ ὑμῶν ἀνακριθῶ ἢ ὑπὸ ἀνθρωπίνης ἡμέρας· ἀλλ᾽ οὐδὲ ἐμαυτὸν ἀνακρίνω· 4 οὐδὲν γὰρ ἐμαυτῷ σύνοιδα, ἀλλ᾽ οὐκ ἐν τούτῳ δεδικαίωμαι, ὁ δὲ ἀνακρίνων με κύριός ἐστιν. 5 ὥστε μὴ πρὸ καιροῦ τι κρίνετε, ἕως ἂν ἔλθῃ ὁ κύριος, ὃς καὶ φωτίσει τὰ κρυπτὰ τοῦ σκότους καὶ φανερώσει τὰς βουλὰς τῶν καρδιῶν, καὶ τότε ὁ ἔπαινος γενήσεται ἑκάστῳ ἀπὸ τοῦ θεοῦ. [SBLGNT]

King James Version

1 Let a man so account of us, as of the ministers of Christ, and stewards of the mysteries of God. 2 Moreover it is required in stewards, that a man be found faithful. 3 But with me it is a very small thing that I should be judged of you, or of man's judgment: yea, I judge not mine own self. 4 For I know nothing by myself; yet am I not hereby justified: but he that judgeth me is the Lord. 5 Therefore judge nothing before the time, until the Lord come, who both

New Rendition

1 So people should consider us as assistants of Christ and stewards of God's mysteries. 2 In this case, moreover, what one looks for in a steward is that he is trustworthy. 3 But it is to me of little or no importance that I am judged by you or by any human tribunal, indeed, I do not even judge myself. 4 For I am not conscious of any wrongdoing, but I have not been acquitted on account of that; it is the Lord who judges me. 5 So do not pass any judgment before the

---

8. Fee, *First Epistle,* 157.

will bring to light the hidden things of darkness, and will make manifest the counsels of the hearts: and then shall every man have praise of God.

proper time, until the Lord comes, who will both bring to light things hidden in darkness and will disclose the motives of our hearts. Then each person will receive recognition from God.

Translation Notes and Comments

4:1 *Let a man so account of us, as of the ministers of Christ / So people should consider us as assistants of Christ:* The verb λογίζομαι (*logizomai*), "to reckon, to account, to consider," carried with it the idea of giving a reasonable estimation of a person or thing. It also designated the positive attitude one should have toward another person holding a definite assignment within the context of a specific institution. Paul was directing his readers to consider the Apostles as assistants within the Church.[9] The noun translated "ministers" in the KJV and "assistants" in our Rendition is ὑπηρέτης (*hypēretēs*). This noun was commonly used to describe a governmental or other official who acted in a subordinate position, such as an aide or assistant, but with attendant authority or power.[10] Paul's application of the term, so far as the Church was concerned, insisted that the Apostles should be viewed as legitimate and duly set apart teachers who had been given sacred stewardship over all the affairs of God's kingdom. His words did stress, however, that the role and power of Apostle was secondary; they acted under authority of another, namely, the Savior. Even so, the Apostles played an indispensable role in that they were the presiding officers of the Church with the commensurate authority to guide and direct the spreading of the Gospel of Jesus Christ throughout the world.[11]

stewards of the mysteries of God / stewards of God's mysteries: An οἰκόνομος (*oikonomos*), "steward," was a manager of a household or estate and, in a more general sense, an administrator in both societal and political affairs.[12] Though the position was sometimes held by a slave, it was one of responsibility, prestige, and authority. Those who held it had specific assignments that they either carried out themselves or supervised others in so doing. Often these men acted directly under the head of the house or

---

9. Findlay, "St. Paul's First Epistle," 796; BDAG, 597–98.
10. BDAG, 1035. Collins, *First Corinthians*, 167, 172, translates the word as *assistants*.
11. Matt. 28:18–20.
12. BDAG, 698.

government official and always carried their authority.[13] By applying the term to the Apostles, Paul emphasized that the Apostles had divine authority and responsibility.

Paul identified the particular stewardship carried by the Apostles—that of overseeing the "mysteries" of God. For a more full treatment on this subject, see the Translation Notes on 2:7 with the associated Analysis. As used here, the term described the teachings of "the highest stage of Christian knowledge, revealed only to the τέλειοι [*teleioi*]."[14] Paul's use of the term worked well for the gospel message because the Greek word denoted knowledge that could not be obtained through human reason or logic, but only through direct revelation. Tacitly, Paul implied that the only way the members could receive these sacred truths was through the Apostles.[15]

4:2 *Moreover it is required in stewards, that a man be found faithful / In this case, moreover, what one looks for in a steward is that he is trustworthy:* The adverb ὧδε (*hōde*), literally "here," but in this case it is used in the sense of "in this case," with λοιπόν (*loipon*), an accusative of reference used in the sense of "in addition, moreover."[16]

The adjective Paul used to describe the primary virtue that God demanded of his stewards was πιστός (*pistos*), the word carrying the idea of something in which people could put their total faith and trust.[17] The Apostle was teaching the people that a primary attribute of a steward, as it pertained to the Church, was one of total trustworthiness.

This verse builds on what Paul had already taught. It was neither the depth of wisdom one possessed nor the eloquence with which he could persuade others that counted. It was, rather, the total fidelity that he gave to the one from whom he received his authority.[18]

4:3 *But with me it is a very small thing that I should be judged of you, or of man's judgment / But it is to me of little or no importance that I am judged*

---

13. Otto Michel, "οἰκονόμος," in *TDNT,* 5:149–51; Findlay, "St. Paul's First Epistle," 796–97.

14. BDAG, 662. The adjective τέλειος (*teleioi*) described someone who was "fully developed in a moral sense" as well as being a technical term of one who had been initiated into mystic rites. See BDAG, 995–96.

15. Findlay, "St. Paul's First Epistle," 797. For a more full discussion on the term *mystery,* see Translation Notes on 2:10–16.

16. BDAG, 602–3, 1101; Thiselton, *First Epistle,* 337.

17. Rudolf Bultmann and Artur Weiser, "πιστεύω, πίστις, πιστός, πιστόω, ἄπιστος, ἀπιστέω, ἀπιστία, ὀλιγόπιστος, ὀλιγοπιστία," in *TDNT,* 6:174–228; BDAG, 820–21.

18. Fitzmyer, *First Corinthians,* 213.

by you or by any human tribunal: With these words, Paul turned to the heart of the matter. Pointing directly at his detractors, he made his point. He used the contrastive conjunction δέ (*de*), "but," to show that he felt no concern whether they judge him or not. Emphasizing this idea was his use of the superlative ἐλάχιστον (*elachiston*), "very small, very little," to mean "of little or no importance."[19] The verb ἀνακρίνω (*anakrinō*) in its technical aspect referred to the careful inquiry made by a civil tribunal and our Rendition carries that idea.[20] Paul's use showed that he did not care at all if the judgment came from within or without the Church, for neither had any validity.[21]

yea, I judge not mine own self / indeed, I do not even judge myself: Paul's point was that he felt completely justified in his actions and, therefore, had a completely clear conscience so far as his activities with the Corinthian Saints were concerned.[22] His repetition of the verb ἀνακρίνω (*anakrinō*), "judge," showed he was not even willing to be a tribunal of one against himself. There was good reason. It was because he, like the rest of the Corinthian Saints, was mortal, and, therefore, his judgment might not be any better than theirs. Only the Final Judgment, conducted by an omniscient God, counted.

4:4 *For I know nothing by myself; yet am I not hereby justified / For I am not conscious of any wrongdoing, but I have not been acquitted on account of that:* The phrase οὐδὲν γὰρ ἐμαυτῷ σύνοιδα (*ouden gar emautō synoida*) reads literally, "For I am not conscious of anything against me."[23] He admitted, however, that a clear conscience did not necessarily mean that he was justified in all he had done. The JST backs up this idea: "For *though* I know nothing *against* myself; yet I am not hereby justified." Only God could determine whether the Apostle had acted as he should have.

---

19. O. Michel, "μικρός (ἐλάττων, ἐλάχιστος)," in *TDNT,* 4:648–59; BDAG, 314.

20. BDAG, 66; Friedrich Büchsel, "ἀνακρίνω, ἀνάκρισις," in *TDNT,* 3:943–44.

21. The phrase reads ἢ ὑπὸ ἀνθρωπίνης ἡμέρας (*hē hypo anthrōpinēs hēmeras*), literally "or by human day." The idea is similar to the English idiom, "having one's day in court," but the contrast here is with the "Day of the Lord," or the Final Judgment. Paul sees two kinds of judgment, one mortal and the other divine. Each one will have its "day," but for him, the only one that counts is the final one. Robertson and Plummer, *Critical and Exegetical Commentary,* 76.

22. On Paul's feelings of rightness with the law vis-à-vis forgiveness for sin the context of his clear conscience, see Krister Stendahl, *Paul among the Jews and Gentiles* (Philadelphia: Fortress Press, 1976), 78–96.

23. Some have argued that the idea behind σύνοιδα (*synoida*) is that of self-awareness; thus, Paul is saying he is not aware of any transgression on his part. See P. W. Gooch, "'Conscience' in I Cor 8 and 10," *New Testament Studies* 33 (1987): 244–54. The context of this verse, however, suggests the better understanding is "consciousness."

yet am I not hereby justified / but I have not been acquitted on account of that: δεδικαίωμαι (*dedikaiōmai*) is the perfect passive form of δικαίοω (*dikaioō*) which is often, in the passive, translated as "justified." It is a legal term that indicates that one has been found innocent in a court of law and, therefore, is acquitted of all charges. Paul's point is that even though he is not aware of any wrongdoing on his part, that alone does not make him innocent and, therefore, he has not yet been acquitted.

but he that judgeth me is the Lord / it is the Lord who judges me: Paul's point is that the members of the opposition party had no right to judge him because he stood before a higher tribunal, namely, the Lord himself.[24] Both men and women in the early Church were appointed to their various positions by divine authority of which apostleship was of the highest order. Even so, all—and that included Paul—were responsible only to the one who appointed them. The Apostle was, therefore, perfectly willing to leave the matter in God's hands. What he had done, he had done, and only God could disclose its worth.[25] Therefore, no one should judge him or others.[26]

4:5 *Therefore judge nothing before the time, until the Lord come / So do not pass any judgment before the proper time, until the Lord comes:* With these words, Paul summed up his argument. The JST reads, "Therefore *I* judge nothing before the time," showing that he was setting the example that others should follow.

The Greek text gives an important nuance that should not be overlooked. Paul did not use the normal word for time, χρόνος (*chronos*), which denoted time in general, but rather καιρός (*kairos*). This noun carried the sense of "the right, appropriate, or proper time,"[27] which is used in our Rendition. But this noun was sometimes used in the sense of "the last time, the end of time," that is, the period just before the Second Coming,[28] which also fits in this context. In either case, Paul was admonishing the Saints at Corinth not to pass judgment until the time was proper. Ultimately, that would be at the Second Coming of Christ.

bring to light the hidden things of darkness, and will make manifest the counsels of the hearts / bring to light things hidden in darkness and will disclose the motives of our hearts: Paul explained why the Lord's coming would allow all to make proper judgments. The Lord would reveal not

---

24. Anderson, *Understanding Paul*, 101.
25. Thiselton, *First Epistle*, 341–42.
26. Anderson, *Understanding Paul*, 101.
27. BDAG, 497.
28. BDAG, 498.

just what happened but also what lay behind it. The phrase τὰς βουλὰς τῶν καρδιῶν (*tas boulas tōn kardiōn*), "the motives of the hearts," denoted that which was at the very center of one's being, that is, what one cared for more than anything else. It was this that determined his objectives.[29] Paul's point was that all objectives and motives would be fully revealed at the Second Coming. One could do the right thing for the wrong reason, and if so, "it is not counted unto him for righteousness" (Moro. 7:7).

then shall every man have praise of God / Then each person will receive recognition from God: The noun ἔπαινος (*epainos*) generally means "praise, commendation," but Paul was hardly disposed to say all would be praised.[30] Therefore, his use of ἑκάστῳ (*ekastō*) "each person," must refer to those who take his counsel to postpone judgment until the Day of the Lord. Every right, decent, and kind thing that a person had done would receive recognition from God; every petty, mean, and wicked thing he or she had done, and not repented of, would also be recognized. The Book of Mormon points out, however, that it shall not just be God who knows, but all shall know for "all things which are hid must be revealed upon the house-tops" (Morm. 5:8).

Analysis and Summary

As noted in the introduction, Paul's task was to convince the Corinthian Saints that they should follow the Lord's Apostles and, since he was the one at hand, more particularly him. In chapter 3, however, he had insisted that the Apostles, as well as all other Church leaders, were but servants and one's loyalty should not be set on any of them, but on the Father and Son. His task now was to show them why they should accept him and his authority in context of what he had already taught.

With remarkably clear insight, one philosopher/theologian identified precisely what an Apostle is and why those called to this holy office should be followed. He stated: "An apostle is not born [as in, say, someone with very high intelligence or a superb gift for music]; an Apostle is a man called and appointed by God, receiving a mission from him." He went on to say that "as a result of this call he does not become more intelligent, does not receive more imagination, a greater acuteness of mind and so on; on the contrary, he remains himself and by that paradoxical fact he is sent on a particular mission by God. By this paradoxical fact the Apostle is made

---

29. BDAG, 181.
30. BDAG, 357.

paradoxically different from all other men." As to the Apostle's responsibility, the philosopher noted,

> The man who is called by a revelation and to whom a doctrine is entrusted, argues from the fact that it is a revelation. . . . I have not got to listen to St. Paul because he is clever, or even brilliantly clever; I am to bow before St. Paul because he has divine authority; and in any case it remains St. Paul's responsibility to see that he produces that impression, whether anyone bows before his authority or not. St. Paul must not appeal to his cleverness, for in that case he is a fool; he must not enter into a purely aesthetic or philosophical discussion of the content of the doctrine, for in that case he is side-tracked. No, he must appeal to his divine authority and, while willing to lay down his life and everything, by that very means *prevent* any aesthetic impertinence and any direct philosophic approach to the form and content of the doctrine.[31]

These words nicely summarize Paul's position and explain the task he had to accomplish.

Note that, in his attempt to bring the Saints to his side, Paul began by defining the role of an Apostle. They were "assistants," but the word he used, ὑπηρέτης (*hypēretēs*), though describing one having a subordinate role, stressed the legitimacy of that person to act.[32] In addition, they were the οἰκόνομος (*oikonomos*), that is, stewards—persons of trust and authority.[33] Often such persons had specific responsibilities. Paul defined the Apostles; they were stewards of the Lord's mysteries. Among the Greeks, the word *mystery* carried a very heavy religious nuance being associated with specific religions whose sacred rites were guarded with secrecy and only shared with a select group of persons who had proven themselves true to the order.[34] For Paul, however, it also defined that sacred knowledge unknown until God revealed it, namely, the fullness of the gospel with all the saving ordinances that went with it.

---

31. Søren Kierkegaard, *The Present Age* and *Of the Difference between a Genius and an Apostle,* trans. Alexander Dru (London: Fantana Library, 1962), 107–9.

32. Paul often refers to himself as the "servant" of Christ, but he uses the word δοῦλος (*doulos*), "slave" (for example, see Rom. 1:1; Gal. 1:10; Titus 1:1), the word stressing the idea that he belongs to Christ as a slave does to a master. See Louw-Nida, §§87.76; 87.81. By applying the term ὑπηρέτης (*hypēretēs*) to himself and others, he stresses a different relationship, that of assistant or helper, but one having authority. Louw-Nida, §35.2; Karl Heinrich Rengstorf, "ὑπηρέτης, ὑπηρετέω," in *TDNT,* 8:530–44.

33. The word applied to household stewards as well as executives of estates and of those with civil responsibilities. See Louw-Nida, §37.39; Otto Michel, "οἰκονόμος," in *TDNT,* 5:149–51.

34. BDAG, 530; G. Bornkamm, "μυστήριον," in *TDNT,* 4:802–27.

In this regard, the position of the Apostles was indispensable and two-fold: first, they were the recipients of God's saving word for all the Church; and second, they were responsible to keep the doctrine pure. Highlighting the first idea, Joseph Smith declared, "Salvation cannot come without revelation; it is in vain for anyone to minister without it. No man is a minister of Jesus Christ without being a Prophet. No man can be a minister of Jesus Christ except he has the testimony of Jesus; and this is the spirit of prophecy. Whenever salvation has been administered, it has been by testimony. Men of the present time testify of heaven and hell, and have never seen either; and I will say that no man knows these things without this."[35]

Obtaining personal knowledge of the mysteries of godliness was never meant for a select few, but for all those who would prove faithful to the Lord (D&C 63:23; 76:7). He promised that "unto him that keepeth my commandments, I will give the mysteries of my kingdom, and the same shall be in him a well of living water, springing up unto everlasting life" (D&C 63:23). Indeed, the Lord's admonition was to seek his wisdom, then "the mysteries of God shall be unfolded unto you" (D&C 6:7), and he promised that "if thou wilt inquire, thou shalt know mysteries which are great and marvelous" (D&C 6:11; 8:11; 42:61).[36]

Even so, as it was in Paul's day, it is the leadership of the Church that has stewardship over the mysteries for the whole Church. Indeed, the leaders hold the fulness of the Melchizedek Priesthood and thereby "hold the keys of all the spiritual blessings of the church," including "the privilege of receiving the mysteries of the kingdom of heaven" (D&C 107:18–19; compare D&C 84:19) and revealing them to the Church as a whole. One of Joseph Smith's stewardships was holding these very keys (D&C 28:7; 35:18; 64:5). On these modern stewards the Lord has laid heavy responsibility, for he will require "an account of this stewardship . . . of them in the day of judgment" (D&C 70:4). Further, they are forbidden to delegate this authority to anyone else (D&C 70:3–6). In this way, the purity and force of the doctrines remains under God's control through his chosen leaders.

---

35. "History, 1838–1856, Volume C-1," 12 [addenda at end of volume]; punctuation and spelling have been standardized. See also *DNTC,* 2:330.

36. The term "mystery" also has a negative connotation in LDS circles. In that sense it means "information unnecessary for our salvation or for our personal progress, information the Lord has chosen, for whatever reason, to withhold from us. A preoccupation with such things can distract us from the really important truth that *has* been revealed and often leads to a loss of spiritual balance, then to contention, doubt, and apostasy." Robinson and Garrett, *Commentary on the Doctrine and Covenants,* 1:65.

Paul next defined the most important quality of a steward—trustworthiness (4:2). It was not the steward's managerial or organizational skills or his ability to handle finances and command people that counted most. It was, rather, his total dedication and trustworthiness in carrying out his responsibilities.[37] Paul's point was that he had fulfilled that trust in proclaiming, in its purity, the gospel message and organizing the branches. Therefore, no Corinthian tribunal, whether ecclesiastical or civil, had any right to judge him (4:3).[38] There was only one who had the authority to judge his stewardship and that was the one who assigned it, namely, his Master. Therefore, all human judgment, because it could not take fully into account his motives and objectives, was invalid, and that included his own. As Elder Jedediah M. Grant noted, "While people are in the dark, they do not see the light; their deeds are not made manifest, for it is the light that maketh manifest. If a room be dark, the objects in that room are not discernible, but when light breaks into the room, the objects therein can be plainly seen."[39] The key is having the light. Judgment, Paul insisted, must therefore wait for the coming of the Lord. Only with the judgment would all things be brought to light and understood in their proper context. Since, however, both he and the Corinthian Saints believed that this event was not far off, he was not asking for undue patience.

ADMONITION AGAINST PRIDE (4:6–8)

Greek Text

6 Ταῦτα δέ, ἀδελφοί, μετεσχημάτισα εἰς ἐμαυτὸν καὶ Ἀπολλῶν δι' ὑμᾶς, ἵνα ἐν ἡμῖν μάθητε τό· Μὴ ὑπὲρ ἃ γέγραπται, ἵνα μὴ εἷς ὑπὲρ τοῦ ἑνὸς φυσιοῦσθε κατὰ τοῦ ἑτέρου. 7 τίς γάρ σε διακρίνει; τί δὲ ἔχεις ὃ οὐκ ἔλαβες; εἰ δὲ καὶ ἔλαβες, τί καυχᾶσαι ὡς μὴ λαβών; 8 Ἤδη κεκορεσμένοι ἐστέ, ἤδη ἐπλουτήσατε, χωρὶς ἡμῶν ἐβασιλεύ-σατε· καὶ ὄφελόν γε ἐβασιλεύσατε, ἵνα καὶ ἡμεῖς ὑμῖν συμβασιλεύσωμεν.

---

37. As was known by Paul's readers, during this period, a number of former slaves had amassed great wealth and such power and position that they were actually running most of the civil concerns and many religious affairs of the Roman Empire. Highly trusted, they reported only to the Emperor himself. See Suetonius, *Claud.* 25. It is of note that Paul was using the contemporary political milieu of his day as a means of explaining his relationship to the Savior and the Church.

38. Fee, *First Epistle,* 160.

39. Jedediah M. Grant, in *JD,* 4:123.

King James Version

6 And these things, brethren, I have in a figure transferred to myself and to Apollos for your sakes; that ye might learn in us not to think of men above that which is written, that no one of you be puffed up for one against another. 7 For who maketh thee to differ from another? and what hast thou that thou didst not receive? now if thou didst receive it, why dost thou glory, as if thou hadst not received it? 8 Now ye are full, now ye are rich, ye have reigned as kings without us: and I would to God ye did reign, that we also might reign with you.

New Rendition

6 Brothers and sisters, I have applied these things to myself and Apollos for your benefit, so that by our example you might learn "not to go beyond what is written," so that you will stop your prideful favoring of one person over another. 7 For who considers you superior? What do you have that you have not received? And if you have received it, why do you boast as if you had not received it? 8 You already have enough! You are already rich! You have become kings without us! Indeed, I wish that you had become kings so that we might rule with you.

Translation Notes and Comments

4:6 *brethren / Brothers and sisters:* See Translation Notes on 1:10.

And these things . . . I have in a figure transferred to myself and to Apollos for your sakes / I have applied these things to myself and Apollos for your benefit: The verb μετασχηματίζω (*metaschēmatizō*) means literally "to change the form of."[40] Paul, however, used it here in the sense of teaching something by comparison.[41] This word made clear to Paul's readers that he was using secular figures—that of servant and steward—to help the Saints better understand the spiritual role of the Apostles.

that ye might learn in us not to think of men above that which is written / that by our example you might learn "not to go beyond what is written": With the use of the first of two purpose clauses (both introduced by ἵνα [*hina*], "that, in order that"), Paul explained his first reason for using the metaphor. It identified the example that he and Apollos had set, namely ἵνα ἐν ἡμῖν μάθητε (*hina en hēmin mathēte*). This text is translated literally,

---

40. BDAG, 641.

41. Just what Paul meant by use of this word has caused a lot of discussion over time. For a summary, see Thiselton, *First Epistle*, 348–51. It seems most likely that the Apostle used the word to maintain a certain degree of anonymity of his detractors so as not to further antagonize them while applying an excellent metaphor to get his teachings across. See F. N. Colson, "Μετεσχημάτισα in I Cor iv 6," *Journal of New Theological Studies* 17 (July 1916): 380–83; Fitzmyer, *First Corinthians*, 214–15; Barrett, *First Epistle*, 106.

as in the KJV, "that ye might learn in us," but is better expressed in English and in our Rendition as "that by our example you might learn."[42] And what example had they set? The answer was "not to go beyond what is written." Since ancient Greek did not have quotation marks, writers often indicated a quote by placing the neuter, singular, definite article τό (*to*) before the cited phrase, as Paul did here.[43] Though Paul is quoting, just what writing he had in mind is unknown.[44] He could have been referring to something as broad as the Torah (the works of Moses) or as narrow as some written instructions previously given by Church authorities. He may have even been referring to his own letters. Whatever the case, the Apostle seems to be appealing to a written standard he felt all should agree on and adhere to.

that no one of you be puffed up for one against another / so that you will stop your prideful favoring of one person over another: With the use of his second purpose clause, Paul explained his second reason for using the metaphor. It emphasized the example that he and Apollos had set in viewing one another as equals. The Apostle desperately wanted his readers to quit yielding to that arrogance that had caused the schisms in the branch. The verb Paul used, φυσιοῦσθε (*physiousthe*), though passive in form, was used in an active sense: "Having an exaggerated self-perception."[45] The basis of the word meant to be puffed up but metaphorically it meant to have an inflated ego. This condition was a direct result from the sin of pride.[46] (For a discussion on pride, see Translation Notes on 1:10–17 with the associated Analysis.) The force of the passive suggests that these people

---

42. Thiselton, *First Epistle,* 351.

43. Wallace, *Greek Grammar,* 237–38; Friedrich Blass and Albert Debrunner, *Greek Grammar of the New Testament,* trans. Robert W. Funk (Chicago: University of Chicago Press, 1961), §267.

44. For discussion, see Fitzmyer, *First Corinthians,* 214–15.

45. BDAG, 1069; Anderson, *Understanding Paul,* 101.

46. The verb φυσιόω (*physioō*) is never translated as "to be proud" in the KJV though it is very closely related conceptually to the three words that are translated by "pride" or "to be proud," namely: ἀλαζονεί (*alazoneía*) that describes the actions of one who is an imposter or quack and denotes an arrogance displayed through empty boasting (1 John 2:12; Gerhard Delling, "ἀλαζών, ἀλαζονεία," in *TDNT,* 1:226–36); τυφόω (*typhoō*) that means literally "to be wrapped in smoke" but metaphorically denotes the actions of one with an inflated ego and who is, thereby, lifted up in pride (1 Tim. 3:6; Wolfgang Schrage, "τυφλός, τυφλόω," in *TDNT,* 8:270–94); and ὑπερηφανία (*hyperēphania*), that means "arrogance" and points to a person who is full of himself and looks down on others with contempt and insolence (Mark 7:22; *TNDT,* 8:525). It would be hard for a person afflicted with one of these not to be touched by all the others. Such persons continually betray an arrogant conceit that manifests itself in a superior attitude. All four Greek words show

had been infected by this spiritual cancer for quite some time, and they were still suffering from it.

As can be seen by the difference between the translations given in the KJV and our Rendition, this phrase is difficult to render precisely. Nonetheless, it is clear that Paul was concerned about the pride-driven competing factions within the Christian community that caused certain members to favor one person over another. In their zeal, they ridiculed and belittled those in the other parties, and thus contributed to the growing antagonisms that were fracturing the Church. By showing such respect for persons, they were committing grievous sin (James 2:9) and clearly not following the example of the Lord (Acts 10:34; Rom. 2:11; Eph. 6:9; Col. 3:25; D&C 1:35; 38:16).

4:7 *For who maketh thee to differ from another? / For who considers you superior?:* The verb διακρίνω (*diakrinō*), "to consider, differentiate; evaluate, judge," also denoted the act of making a distinction between items to determine which was inferior or superior.[47] Paul's question asked his readers just exactly who it was that gave some the authority to determine the superiority or inferiority of others. His intent was to show that the "puffed up" were way out of place in believing and promoting the idea that they somehow possessed some superior virtue or holiness that allowed them this right. Such an attitude could only come from somebody who lacked gratitude and perspective.[48] Such persons had entirely missed the importance that God's grace had played in their lives, and thereby overlooked what he had done for them in bringing them the gospel with its attendant priesthood and spiritual gifts.

and what hast thou that thou didst not receive? now if thou didst receive it, why dost thou glory, as if thou hadst not received it? / What do you have that you have not received? And if you have received it, why do you boast as if you had not received it?: The Apostle's next set of questions was designed to undercut any feeling of superiority. The bite of his remark was found in the word λαμβάνω (*lambanō*), "to get, receive," which emphasized the idea of receiving—not possessing—something. The word had particular force because the stress was that "the initiative rests with the giver."[49] In short, the receiver had little or nothing to do with generating the gift. So Paul was

---

that the basis of the proud person's sense of self-importance is false. Because that basis has no actual substance, these persons are, in reality and ironically, fools.

47. BDAG, 231; Louw-Nida, §30.99.
48. Fee, *First Epistle,* 170.
49. Louw-Nida, §57.125; BDAG, 584; Thiselton, *First Epistle,* 356.

asking these people—who had received God's authority and the Spirit's gifts from another—how they could possibly boast in their acquisition as if these blessings had been somehow self-generated. What made matters even worse was that they drew some kind of distinction from their possession. What these people needed to realize was that, like the Apostles, they were but stewards over what God had given them.[50]

4:8 *Now ye are full, now ye are rich / You already have enough! You are already rich!*: With biting irony, Paul described the result of the presumptuous pride of these Corinthian Saints. The adverb ἤδη (*ēdē*), "now, already," along with the perfect passive participle, κεκορεσμένοι (*kekoresmenoi*), "to be satiated, have enough," highlighted their attitude. These people had come to believe that they had all the spiritual food they needed, indeed, they were sated with it.[51] They saw themselves as rich in the sense of having received the Spirit with its accompanying gifts. Unfortunately, their perverted view kept them from humility and gratefulness. Instead, it generated feelings of superiority. They felt that they had arrived at near perfection and needed nothing more. Salvation was theirs.[52]

***ye have reigned as kings without us / You have become kings without us!*:** Continuing his biting sarcasm, Paul noted that these people felt that they had realized the highest of exalted stations, that of spiritual royalty.[53] And they had accomplished this, they thought, χωρὶς ἡμῶν (*chōris hēmōn*), "without our help."[54] Therefore, they falsely believed that they had achieved all and were not dependent on anyone or anything for their salvation. Paul's use of the aorist verb, ἐβασιλεύσατε (*ebasileusate*), is inceptive and,

---

50. The idea had been around for a while. In the *Ep. Aristeas,* 196 (c. second century BC), readers are admonished not to be struck by fortune or fame because all good things come from God. Though they have preeminence over these things, they must keep in mind that they are but caretakers. Compare D&C 104:14–17.

51. BDAG, 559.

52. Fee, *First Epistle,* 172. It is of note that the Stoics used the phrases "to be rich" and "to reign" as catchwords to show the result of accepting and applying their philosophy. It made one self-sufficient and free of the cares of the world. See Collins, *First Corinthians,* 183–88.

53. The *basileus* denoted the highest station a person could arrive at. BDAG, 169. Paul's statement may be reflecting a well-known philosophical motif that the sage or sophist is both rich and kingly due to his wisdom. See Horace, *Ep.* 1.1.16–7; Philo, *Sobr.* 11 §57. Paul's words could betray a satirical nod to the Platonic motif of the king-philosopher so praised by Plato. See specifically his *Rep.* 473 c–d, but generally his discussions in books V–VII.

54. Findlay, "St. Paul's First Epistle," 801.

therefore, does not mean "to reign" as in the KJV, but rather to "become kings" as in our Rendition.[55]

I would to God ye did reign, that we also might reign with you / Indeed, I wish that you had become kings so that we might rule with you: The verbal particle ὄφελόν (*ophelon*), "would that, I wish," expressed an unfulfilled desire.[56] Paul's words undercut his antagonist's whole position. His statement showed that he did not, for a second, buy into their false claims. They had not arrived! If they had (and Paul sarcastically stated he wishes they had), that would mean that the Millennium had arrived and God's kingdom had been set up. If that were the case, Apostles and Saints would be reigning. Though that was a nice thought, it was entirely false.

Analysis and Summary

Paul attacked these factional leaders and their followers for unjustifiable glorying, bordering on gloating, with an abruptness that evidenced his deep repugnance for their attitude. To think that they had been "so well fed by Paul's successors, so furnished in talent and grace, that they desired nothing more" was arrogance beyond belief.[57] To get them to see the ridiculousness of their attitude, Paul used questions dripping with sarcasm. The force of these questions betrays his desperate attempt to move his readers away from their complacent and dangerous situation. He had to bring them back to the Atonement and the obligating grace that grew out of it. Their misguided and damaging efforts to use "wisdom" as the means of interpreting the cross had caused them to lose sight of its value and to believe that they were saved without it. They had created a kind of cheap grace resulting in "forgiveness without repentance" and "baptism without church discipline" with the result that they were living not like Christians but like the rest of the world.[58] Their smugness over their perceived holiness and superior knowledge showed just how far afield they were. But more seriously, it prevented them from much needed repentance.

What greatly contributed to their error was believing that they had somehow already entered God's promised kingdom and were enjoying its rewards. They had an over-realized eschatology in which "already and not yet" were held in tension. Paul, along with the other New Testament

---

55. Findlay, "St. Paul's First Epistle," 801.
56. Louw-Nida, §71.28.
57. Findlay, "St. Paul's First Epistle," 800.
58. Thiselton, *First Epistle,* 356.

writers, knew that some aspects of the kingdom had now been realized, but they were waiting for others to come. The problem with the Corinthian Saints was that they had accepted the "already" to the point that they missed the "not yet." They had come to believe that, having received the Spirit, they had been transported into a new and higher sphere in which they were above all things earthly and fleshly. Thus, they had entered a condition in which they felt they had all they needed and more.[59] They certainly did not need anything from God's stewards, the Apostles. As one scholar noted, "These Corinthians are lucky. *Already* they enjoy favours that the apostles dare only hope for. They no longer 'hunger and thirst after righteousness'; for they are *filled;* in theory of the Spirit, they have eaten to satiety. . . . In short, the Messianic kingdom seems to have come to Corinth and these people have been given their thrones, while the apostles . . . are placed with the servants."[60] In view of their misplaced belief that they had arrived, Paul's sarcastic rejoinder was essentially, "I only wish you had!" (see 4:8).

There was no doubt in Paul's mind that their belief came from going beyond what they had been taught. The Apostle's use of himself and Apollos as persons who did not "go beyond what is written" set the standard (4:6, Rendition). His words also suggest that there was a reliable source he felt all should accept, one that vindicated his position. What he needed to show was that it was his detractors, not him, who were introducing teachings into the Church that had no authoritative support.

One of the reasons his detractors had such an elevated view of themselves was that they had come to believe that they themselves were the source of their perceived high spiritual state. They had forgotten that the powers of the Spirit that they so enjoyed resulted not from their efforts but from the Atonement of the Savior and the door it opened. Those who were "puffed up" segregated the Christian community between those who were supposedly spiritually elite and those who were not. Paul challenged them on this, demanding from them to identify where they got that right (4:7). Tacitly, he was also asking other members just why they bought into these people's ideas.[61]

---

59. Fee, *First Epistle,* 172.

60. Gaston Deluz, *A Companion to I Corinthians* (London: Darton, Longman and Todd, 1963), 46–47.

61. Paul was not addressing the issue of individual talents and abilities, but of by whose authority or by what authentic criteria these people felt they could judge. It must be recognized that there really are individual differences. According to Elder McConkie, many of these are due to pre-mortal training and choice. See *DNTC,* 2:330.

THE WORLD'S TREATMENT OF THE APOSTLES (4:9–13)

Greek Text

9 δοκῶ γάρ, ὁ θεὸς ἡμᾶς τοὺς ἀποστόλους ἐσχάτους ἀπέδειξεν ὡς ἐπιθανατίους, ὅτι θέατρον ἐγενήθημεν τῷ κόσμῳ καὶ ἀγγέλοις καὶ ἀνθρώποις. 10 ἡμεῖς μωροὶ διὰ Χριστόν, ὑμεῖς δὲ φρόνιμοι ἐν Χριστῷ· ἡμεῖς ἀσθενεῖς, ὑμεῖς δὲ ἰσχυροί· ὑμεῖς ἔνδοξοι, ἡμεῖς δὲ ἄτιμοι. 11 ἄχρι τῆς ἄρτι ὥρας καὶ πεινῶμεν καὶ διψῶμεν καὶ γυμνιτεύομεν καὶ κολαφιζόμεθα καὶ ἀστατοῦμεν 12 καὶ κοπιῶμεν ἐργαζόμενοι ταῖς ἰδίαις χερσίν· λοιδορούμενοι εὐλογοῦμεν, διωκόμενοι ἀνεχόμεθα, 13 δυσφημούμενοι παρακαλοῦμεν· ὡς περικαθάρματα τοῦ κόσμου ἐγενήθημεν, πάντων περίψημα ἕως ἄρτι. [SBLGNT]

King James Version

9 For I think that God hath set forth us the apostles last, as it were appointed to death: for we are made a spectacle unto the world, and to angels, and to men. 10 We are fools for Christ's sake, but ye are wise in Christ; we are weak, but ye are strong; ye are honourable, but we are despised. 11 Even unto this present hour we both hunger, and thirst, and are naked, and are buffeted, and have no certain dwelling place; 12 And labour, working with our own hands: being reviled, we bless; being persecuted, we suffer it: 13 Being defamed, we entreat: we are made as the filth of the world, and are the offscouring of all things unto this day.

New Rendition

9 For it seems to me that God has put us apostles on display as the most insignificant of mortals, like men condemned to die, because we have become a universal spectacle, both to angels and to mortals. 10 We are fools on account of Christ, but you are wise in Christ; we are weak, but you are strong; you are honored, we are despised. 11 Even until this present time we are hungry and thirsty, poorly clothed, beaten and homeless. 12 We are worn out from working with our own hands. When we are insulted, we respond with kind words; when we are persecuted, we endure it patiently; 13 when we are defamed, we seek to reconcile. We have become the scum of the earth, the refuse of all people, even until this present time.

Translation Notes and Comments

4:9 *For I think that God hath set forth us the apostles last, as it were appointed to death / For it seems to me that God has put us apostles on display as the most insignificant of mortals, like men condemned to die:* Paul's words show that he considers (δοκῶ, *dokō*) the situation in which the Apostles found themselves as under divine decree. The adjective ἔσχατος (*eschatos*) has the basic meaning of "farthest" or "last," but in this context it expressed the idea of "least, most insignificant" in rank.[62] In the eyes of the world, the Apostles were considered of little or no worth.[63] The verb ἀποδείκνυμι (*apodeiknymi*) carried the idea of showing or pointing out something to another and, by extension, to exhibit or put something on display.[64] Paul's phrase suggests that the position of the Apostles was determined by God. The imposition he put on the Apostles contributed to the world's view of them as not just weak, but worthy of death. Supporting this idea was Paul's use of the adjective ἐπιθανάτιος (*epithanatios*), which meant "sentenced to death."[65] Their role was analogous to that of Jesus, who was also marked for death.[66]

for we are made a spectacle unto the world, and to angels, and to men / because we have become a universal spectacle, both to angels and to mortals: The phrase θέατρον (*theatron*), denotes "a theater, play, or spectacle."[67] Paul says that he and the other apostles ἐγενήθημεν (*egenēthēmen*), "have become," a public spectacle.

Paul's words may have stirred his readers' memory of the grand Roman triumph with the victors marching in the lead followed by wagons of war booty, with captives coming next, usually those to be sold in the slave markets, and finally, those who were condemned to death.[68] Paul's point was that the Apostles were but spectacles used as sport for others.

The noun κόσμος (*kosmos*), "world," could be used independently, making Paul say the Apostles were spectacles before the world, angels, and mortals. However, because he introduced angels (here depicted not as messengers but transcendent and holy beings) with mortals, he was giving the view a cosmic or universal dimension, thus making the Apostles "a universal spectacle" as in our Rendition.[69]

---

62. Louw-Nida, §87.66.

63. Elder McConkie believes that Apollos and Paul were members of the quorum albeit he admits that sometimes the term applies to witnesses in general because Paul calls them "the ministers of Christ" who have been "appointed unto death." *DNTC,* 2:332.

64. BDAG, 108.

65. BDAG, 371.

66. Fitzmyer, *First Corinthians,* 218–19.

67. BDAG, 446.

68. Thiselton, *First Epistle,* 359–60. Ancient sources describe these spectacular events in detail. For example, see Dio Cassius, *Roman History,* 6; Josephus, *J.W.* 7.132–57; H. S. Versnel, *Triumphs: An Inquiry into the Origin, Development, and Meaning of the Roman Triumph* (Leiden: Brill, 1970).

69. Fitzmyer, *First Corinthians,* 218–19.

4:10 *We are fools for Christ's sake, but ye are wise in Christ / We are fools on account of Christ, but you are wise in Christ:* For a study of the word "fools," see Translation Notes on 1:26–30. Here, the noun μωρός (*mōros*) denoted one who was unwise to the point of being devoid of understanding or incapable of proper thinking.[70] With the accusative, the preposition διά (*dia*) acts as a marker of cause,[71] thus showing that the Apostles were fools, not for the good of Christ or even in behalf of him but "because of" or "on account of" him. In other words, the restrictions Christ placed upon them, including strict adherence to him and his teachings, contributed to the world's view of them as both fools and worthy of death.

Paul's irony reaches back to what he had taught them in verses 1:18–25 and 3:18–19, showing that God's wisdom was often considered foolishness by the world. That is where the bite of his point lay, for some of the Corinthian Saints, accepting the standards of the world, had placed themselves in the seats of the scorners (compare 1 Ne. 8:24–28). Paul blasted them because they thought that they were so wise in Christ.[72] He described their condition with the adjective φρόνιμος (*phronimos*), though similar in meaning to σοφός (*sophos*), "wise," it added the dimension of the sensible character of the one possessing it.[73] Paul, however, was using the word in a pejorative sense, heightening his sarcasm to their shame. Their problem, as Paul had noted in 2:6–16, was that they were following a wrong Christ, one of their own making, and thereby, they were way off the mark in their judgment of Paul or any other Apostle.

we are weak, but ye are strong / we are weak, but you are strong: These words betray Paul's continued stinging sarcasm. The adjective ἀσθενής (*asthenēs*), "weak," could refer to illness or bodily weakness, but Paul used it in the sense of inadequacy or timidity.[74] The adjective ἰσχυρός (*ischyros*), "strong," usually referred to bodily strength, but Paul used it in the sense of high or mighty.[75] Though few of the Saints would have actually been of influence in Corinthian society, through their brazen judgment of Paul, they placed themselves in the position of acting high or mighty in the Church.[76]

---

70. Louw-Nida, §33.56, 58.
71. BDAG, 225.
72. Fee, *First Epistle*, 176–77.
73. Louw-Nida, §32.31.
74. BDAG, 142.
75. BDAG, 483.
76. Fee, *First Epistle*, 176.

ye are honourable, but we are despised / you are honored, we are despised: The adjective ἔνδοξος (*endoxos*), "honored," denoted the high degree and respect with which one was viewed in society.[77] Conversely, ἄτιμος (*atimos*), "despised," looked to those having society's least respect. Where the opinions of the former carried weight, that of the latter had none.[78] Even worse, the *atimos* were viewed not simply with disfavor but also with loathing.

4:11 *Even unto this present hour / Even until this present time:* Paul brought the Apostles' plight up to date with the adverb ἄρτι (*arti*), "right up to the present moment."[79] In other words, the past condition in which the Apostles had found themselves continued right into the present. Nothing had changed.

we both hunger, and thirst, and are naked, and are buffeted, and have no certain dwelling place / we are hungry and thirsty, poorly clothed, beaten and homeless: Hunger and thirst followed those whom others would not employ or assist. They also found themselves γυμνιτεύω (*gymniteuō*), not "naked" but "poorly clothed," often going about in rags.[80] Worse, they were κολαφίζομαι (*kolaphizomai*), "to be struck with the fists,"[81] a term often used for general mistreatment. However, since it also carried the idea of torment, the word suggested that people went out of their way to harass or hurt the Apostles.[82] Finally, they were ἀστατέω (*astateō*), "homeless." Such a condition highlighted the total lack of security they experienced.[83] In short, they were adrift and defenseless.

4:12 *labour, working with our own hands / We are worn out from working with our own hands:* The verb κοπιάω (*kopiaō*) denoted hard physical labor to the point of weariness, if not exhaustion.[84] Paul's phrase ταῖς ἰδίαις χερσίν (*tais idiais chersin*), "with our own hands," stressed the manual nature of the labor they perform, the kind of labor that was looked down upon by the Greco-Roman gentry because it was often viewed as the work of slaves.[85]

---

77. Louw-Nida, §87.6.

78. Louw-Nida, §87.72.

79. BDAG, 136.

80. BDAG, 208.

81. Louw-Nida, §19.7.

82. BDAG, 555. We are reminded of Joseph Smith's experience as a teenager. See JS–M 1:22–23.

83. BDAG, 145; Albrecht Oepke, "ἀστατέω," in *TDNT*, 1:503.

84. Louw-Nida, §42.47.

85. Hock, *Social Context*, 35–36, 67.

being reviled, we bless; being persecuted, we suffer it / When we are insulted, we respond with kind words; when we are persecuted, we endure it patiently: Paul's use of the present passive participle of the verb λοιδορέω (*loidoreō*), "reviled, insulted," suggested that people went out of their way to make life difficult for the faithful.[86] The verb εὐλογέω (*eulogeō*), literally "to speak well of,"[87] is often translated "bless," as in the KJV (for example, Matt. 14:19; 21:9; 23:39; Mark 6:41; 14:22; Luke 1:28; 9:16; John 12:13). However, given Paul's context, it seems better, in this instance, to take it in its more secular nuance, to "respond with kind words," as in our Rendition.[88] The verb διώκω (*diōkō*), "persecute, revile," also carried the nuance "to run after" and therefore carried the idea of actively going after someone often because of their beliefs.[89] The verb ἀνέχομαι (*anechomai*), "tolerate, endure, bear with," included the virtue of patience.[90] Thus, the leaders did not simply put up with persecution but consistently endured it with persistence and lack of complaint.

4:13 *Being defamed, we entreat / when we are defamed, we seek to reconcile:* The verb δυσφημέω (*dysphēmeō*), "slander, defame," denoted the attempted destruction of another's good reputation.[91] The verb παρακαλέω (*parakaleō*) meant literally "to call to one's side," but the word had quite a number of nuances, such as "to encourage," "to entreat," and "to give comfort to another."[92] However, since Paul was using it to differentiate between the acts of those who despise the Apostles and the Apostle's lack of reciprocation, the idea of placating, appeasing, or reconciling works best.[93] The Apostles were very willing to reach out to their detractors in an attempt to make things right.[94]

we are made as the filth of the world, and are the offscouring of all things unto this day / We have become the scum of the earth, the refuse

---

86. Louw-Nida, §33.393.

87. BDAG, 408.

88. Thiselton, *First Epistle*, 363.

89. Louw-Nida, §§15.158; 39.45.

90. BDAG, 78; Louw-Nida, §25.171.

91. Louw-Nida, §33.398. Some ancient manuscripts replace the participle δυσφημούμενοι (*dysphēmoumenoi*) with βλασφημούμενοι (*blasphēmoumenio*). Both carry the idea of slandering but the latter carries a bit more of a religious nuance because it is associated with disrespect to the divine, and the copyist may have wanted such an echo when it came to disparaging the Lord's servants.

92. BDAG, 764–65.

93. BDAG, 765.

94. Thiselton, *First Epistle*, 354.

of all people, even until this present time: The noun περικάθαρμα (*peri-katharma*) referred to the material removed when a floor was swept, thus, dirt or garbage. It also referred to persons of unsavory reputation.[95] The noun περίψημα (*peripsēma*) referred to the offscouring or scum that came with the cleansing of a pot.[96] The genitive plural nominal adjective πάντων (*pantōn*), "of all," is ambiguous. It could be neuter, meaning "all things," or it could be masculine, meaning "all people." Since it is parallel with κόσμος (*kosmos*), "world," we have translated it as "all people" in our Rendition. Using this very forceful language, Paul showed the depth of disrespect the world had for the Christian leaders. His phrase ἕως ἄρτι (*heōs arti*), "even till now," showed that the world's view of the Apostles and other leaders remained the same, even to the present moment.

Analysis and Summary

With the final sentence of the last paragraph (4:8), Paul set up the contrast he wished to develop in this new sentence. The contrast was not only between his authority and that of his detractors but also between their view and his concerning the Christian situation in the world. He boldly pointed out to them that the Apostles had not entered into any kind of era of rest and peace and, by implication, neither had they. He carefully laid out his reasoning throughout this pericope, but his main point was that the Apostles were not in a comfortable box seat watching all that was going on. In reality they were made a spectacle not unlike those condemned to the gladiatorial arena. They were like common criminals condemned to die as sport for others (compare 15:22).

Paul used the imagery of being made a spectacle (4:9) ironically, as a means of illustrating that those in the world consider the Apostles as little more than wretched beings destined for mere entertainment until their death. The reality was that God saw them as his stewards carrying forward his work.[97] Paul's description of the lowly state of the Apostles was

---

95. Josephus, *J.W.* 4.241; BDAG, 801.

96. BDAG, 808. The words περικάθαρμα (*perikatharma*) and περίψημα (*peripsēma*) were also used to describe the lowest of criminals, those who were bound over as sacrifices to the Greek or Roman gods in cases of disaster. The words, therefore, carried the idea of expiation or ransoming, that is, buying off the wrath of a god. In a Jewish context, the idea of a "scapegoat" would work. Though some scholars see Paul alluding to this nuance, the context suggests otherwise. For discussion, see Thiselton, *First Epistle*, 364.

97. Since the Stoics felt themselves "spectacles" in the world because of the courage they showed before the gods, some feel Paul was mimicking their point. See Gerhard

admittedly exaggerated, but it helped him make his case and likely gave the Corinthian Saints pause about how they viewed the current situation in light of what was happening to the leadership of the Church. It may also have forced them to consider, by comparison, their own prideful state when viewed against the humble state of the Apostles.[98]

The condition in which the Apostles found themselves proved that the day of God's power had certainly not arrived. In this world, they were like their Lord, always under the shadow of the cross. Like master, like servant (see Matt. 10:25), they were not there to please the world, but rather they were bound over for death (Luke 21:12; John 16:2; compare Rom. 8:17; Philip. 3:10). In each dispensation, the righteous had their cross to bear: Noah had the flood; Abraham faced God's requirement to sacrifice his son Isaac. In the meridian of time, the particular cross the righteous had to bear was persecution and death. Indeed, during that time, the persecution of the Christians became severe.[99] Whatever the consequences, the Apostles would do God's will. In Paul's words we find a tacit rebuke to the prideful attitude of his detractors who had ignored the Lord's will and had shown embarrassment because of Paul's ways and his message.[100]

With 4:10, Paul continues his contrast between his detractors' perceived view of the Apostles in comparison to themselves. To sharpen his point, he continued to use rather severe sarcasm. He employed three antitheses— foolish versus wise in connection to their education, weak versus strong in connection with their demeanor, and despised versus honored in connection with their position in society.[101]

The key in determining what Paul was doing here is to understand that the senior Church leaders' (or general authorities', to use Latter-day Saint terminology) position was due to their calling by and work for Jesus. They were fools—weak and despised *by the world*—because that is how the Savior wanted it. Indeed, that is how the world viewed *him*. The problem Paul was

---

Kittel, "θέατρον, θεατρίζομαι," in *TDNT*, 3:42–43; J. N. Sevenster, *Paul and Seneca* (Leiden: Brill, 1961), 115–16. However, this does not seem to be the case given that Paul is not exalting in some kind of victory but rather stressing the tragedy of the way the Apostles are viewed and treated. Rather, he reflects the views of tragedy. See Sallust, *Jug.* 14:23; Pliny, *Pan.* 33.3.

98. Thiselton, *First Epistle*, 359–60.

99. *DNTC*, 2:333. See Translation Notes on Rev. 6:9–11 in this commentary series.

100. Fee, *First Epistle*, 174–75. Just why Paul introduces angels here is problematic, though some feel they may be fallen angels like those met in Job who gloat over personal disaster. See Gerhard Kittel, "θέατρον, θεατρίζομαι," in *TDNT*, 3:43.

101. Robertson and Plummer, *Critical and Exegetical Commentary*, 86.

trying to correct was generated by certain Christians who adopted the world's views and, as a result, had their perspective of reality turned upside down. Paul admitted that they were "in Christ" (ἐν Χριστῷ, *en Christō*) in that they had joined the Church and received its blessings. On the other hand, he noted that the Apostles were "through Christ" (δια Χριστόν, *dia Christon*), that is, empowered by him to carry on his mission, but in the way *he* determined. That meant giving up station in and the respect of the world. This is what the Saints needed to understand: first, to fully comprehend why the Apostles acted the way they did, and second, to accept them as their leaders.

In 4:11, Paul finally dropped his irony to put the record straight. The Apostles, he noted, found themselves hungry, cold, poorly clothed, persecuted, homeless, and working themselves to exhaustion. It is likely that he was exaggerating for effect, but his words do reflect the tension and general conditions in which the Apostles and other ministers of Christ lived. The image he paints encapsulated the consequences of being ἄτιμος (*atimos*), "despised." Each element he listed was the result of the world's contempt for those who insisted on following the Lord and doing his will.[102] The word *atimos* also revealed the impossibility that the Christian leaders faced in ever achieving rank or respect from the world. It simply dismissed them without a hearing.[103]

Paul stressed the hard work he and others had to do (4:12). To what degree Paul's description of having to labor to the point of exhaustion was true of all the Apostles and Church leaders is unknown, but it certainly fit Paul's condition. As one engaged as a leather worker (σκηνοποιός, *skēnopoios*),[104] Paul's profession certainly brought him no prestige but did demand very hard labor and arduous hours of work. Shops in which the artisans plied their trade were often noisy, dirty, and even dangerous. These were places avoided by the wealthy whenever possible. This may have been why some of the Corinthian Saints were upset when Paul refused their patronage. Had he accepted it, he would have had the ease and status of a professional rhetorician.[105] Paul knew, however, that was not the way the Lord wanted it and therefore refused their largess.

---

102. Paul's list reflects the condition of the poor and despised in the Greco-Roman world. See Josephus, *J.W.* 2.151–53; 2 *En.* 66:6. See Robert Hodgson, "Paul the Apostle and First Century Tribulation Lists," *Zeitschrift für die neutestameltliche Wissenschaft* 74 (1983): 59–80.

103. Findlay, "St. Paul's First Epistle," 802.

104. Wilhelm Michaelis, "σκηνοποιός," in *TDNT*, 7:393–94; BDAG, 928.

105. Hock, *Social Context*, 50–62.

In 4:12–13, Paul gave the Apostles' response to ill-treatment: "When we are insulted, we respond with kind words; when we are persecuted, we endure it patiently; when we are defamed, we seek to reconcile" (Rendition). In putting over his point, Paul used a series of present active participles. Their use highlights an action not "when" it occurs but "while" it is actually taking place.[106] In other words, the Apostles constantly acted, not reacted, to the various forms of abuse they suffered. In this way they ceded no power to their enemies but rejected the worldly and typical patron-client relationship so prevalent at the time. Their stance allowed them to express the difference between themselves and both Gentiles and Jews (Matt. 5:43–44; Luke 6:28; 1 Pet. 2:23; 3:9).

Nonretaliation and patience in affliction would not have been viewed with respect, however, in the Roman world. On the contrary, such persons would have been seen as weak or unmanly and, therefore, despised.[107] The standards of the world, however, were not those of the Church. The Lord had set the standard, and he expected his disciples to follow it (Matt. 5:48). Paul's examples showed that the leaders did.

One reason the world despised the Apostles was that by and large, they did not represent the upper class. As Elder George G. Bywater taught:

> The Apostles he [Jesus] was pleased to select from among the unlettered, the uncultivated and the undistinguished among His fellow men, were called to be ministers of his word, to be ambassadors of the message of salvation, to be His heralds of peace—peace on earth and good will to all men. It is true He selected them from among the humble fishermen that were following their occupation of fishing on the Sea of Galilee. It is true He did not select them from the learned doctors of the law. It is also true that they were men that had not attained to any high repute, or had been elevated to any dignified or scholastic position in the land, either ecclesiastical or political. They were graded as the offscourings and dregs of the human race. They were, so to speak, the dregs of human society. . . . [These servants] bore in their possession the principles of life and salvation unto all the world, and these men were in their day bold to make affirmations such as fell very unwelcomely, very unacceptably upon the ears of the *elite,* of the educated, of the refined, of the professional classes of Jewish and of Roman society, and also upon those who were cultivated in Greek

---

106. This is what grammarians would call the "internal" or "progressive" aspect. See Wallace, *Greek Grammar,* 500–501.

107. Thiselton, *First Epistle,* 363.

literature, and constituted the most refined element of human society. Yet they were bold to declare, "We know that we are of God, and the whole world lieth in wickedness [1 John 5:19]."[108]

Because of their knowledge, these apostolic leaders were not willing to make compromises. Paul demanded the same of his Corinthian brothers and sisters. His words, "even until this present time" (4:13, Rendition) once again mitigated against some of the Saints' belief that the time of peace had come and their salvation had been realized. No, now was the time of battle, not rest.

ADMONITION (4:14–17)

Greek Text

14 Οὐκ ἐντρέπων ὑμᾶς γράφω ταῦτα, ἀλλ᾽ ὡς τέκνα μου ἀγαπητὰ νουθετῶν· 15 ἐὰν γὰρ μυρίους παιδαγωγοὺς ἔχητε ἐν Χριστῷ, ἀλλ᾽ οὐ πολλοὺς πατέρας, ἐν γὰρ Χριστῷ Ἰησοῦ διὰ τοῦ εὐαγγελίου ἐγὼ ὑμᾶς ἐγέννησα. 16 παρακαλῶ οὖν ὑμᾶς, μιμηταί μου γίνεσθε. 17 διὰ τοῦτο ἔπεμψα ὑμῖν Τιμόθεον, ὅς ἐστίν μου τέκνον ἀγαπητὸν καὶ πιστὸν ἐν κυρίῳ, ὃς ὑμᾶς ἀναμνήσει τὰς ὁδούς μου τὰς ἐν Χριστῷ Ἰησοῦ, καθὼς πανταχοῦ ἐν πάσῃ ἐκκλησίᾳ διδάσκω. [SBLGNT]

King James Version

14 I write not these things to shame you, but as my beloved sons I warn you. 15 For though ye have ten thousand instructors in Christ, yet have ye not many fathers: for in Christ Jesus I have begotten you through the gospel. 16 Wherefore I beseech you, be ye followers of me. 17 For this cause have I sent unto you Timotheus, who is my beloved son, and faithful in the Lord, who shall bring you into remembrance of my ways which be in Christ, as I teach every where in every church.

New Rendition

14 I am not writing these things to make you feel ashamed, but to admonish you as my own dear children. 15 For though you may have countless guardians in Christ, you do not have many fathers, because I became your father in Christ Jesus through the gospel. 16 Therefore I encourage you to imitate me. 17 For this reason I sent Timothy to you, who is my beloved and faithful son in the Lord, and he will help you remember the ways I conduct my life in Christ Jesus, as I teach them everywhere in every church.

---

108. George G. Bywater, in *JD*, 26:288–89.

Translation Notes and Comments

4:14 *I write not these things to shame you, but as my beloved sons I warn you / I am not writing these things to make you feel ashamed, but to admonish you as my own dear children:* The verb ἐντρέπω (*entrepō*) meant "to turn," but metaphorically it meant to bring shame or disgrace upon someone.[109] The verb νουθετέω (*nytheteō*), "to admonish, warn, counsel," denoted counsel extended to change or stop improper behavior.[110] Since nowhere does Paul give a clear warning, the better translation is "to admonish," as in our Rendition. The noun τέκνον (*teknon*), "child," often denoted a close genetic relationship, but Paul used it as a means of showing his care for his readers. Indeed, with the phrase ὡς τέκνα μου ἀγαπητά (*hōs tekna mou agapēta*), "as my beloved children," Paul identified, in the most tender way possible, what has motivated him to write. All he had and would say was generated by love.

4:15 *For though ye have ten thousand instructors in Christ, yet have ye not many fathers / For though you may have countless guardians in Christ, you do not have many fathers:* The Greek here is a little difficult.[111] Fortunately, Paul's meaning is clear, but it takes a little restructuring to make it flow in English. The Apostle used the particle ἐάν (*ean*) followed by a present subjective as the protasis of a conditional sentence of what may be possible.[112] The tentative nature of his statement is picked up by translating *ean* as "though you may." The apodosis lacks a verb, but "have" is understood.

The adjective μύριος (*myrios*)[113] denoted an incalculable number while the noun παιδαγωγός (*paidagōgos*), literally "boy leader," denoted a slave of rank responsible for teaching etiquette and good manners to the children

---

109. BDAG, 341.

110. BDAG, 679.

111. One reason is that the force of ἐάν (*ean*) "with the subjunctive cannot usually be expressed in English." Smyth, *Greek Grammar,* §1768b.

112. This is a third-class condition, which consists of a protasis with ἔαν (*ean*) followed by the subjunctive in any tense, and an apodosis in any mood-tense combination. This class of condition covers a broad semantic range in Koine Greek, and can express what is likely to occur in the future (the primary sense in Classical Greek), what could possibly occur, or what is only hypothetical and will not occur. The latter two cases being the result of the subjunctive mood encroaching on the domain of the optative in the Hellenistic era (Wallace, *Greek Grammar,* 696–97). As Wallace notes, "The context will always be of the greatest help in determining an author's use of the third class condition." Wallace, *Greek Grammar,* 470. In this passage, context best favors the sense of what could possibly occur.

113. The word designated the number ten thousand, but because that was the largest number in the Greek language, it could also connote a countless amount. LSJ, 1154.

of the rich, somewhat akin to a British nanny. They also shepherded these children to and from their formal places of instruction and, therefore, performed the service of guardians and guides. The title came to denote a person "to whom respect is due, beside the father."[114] When a male became of age, he left the discipline of his guardian, having established his ability to take care of himself and act, ideally, with all the deportment his station demanded.

Paul used *myrios* as an exaggeration to make the point that, whereas there can be any given number of guardians and guides, there are few fathers and, therefore, the guardians may deserve some respect, but they do not replace the authority of the father.[115]

for in Christ Jesus I have begotten you through the gospel / because I became your father in Christ Jesus through the gospel: The preposition ἐν (*en*) can be translated two ways. It can be construed as "in," thus making it a marker of close association. In that context, it would denote the closeness the Saints could have with the Savior such that his spirit filled their souls and directed their lives.[116] It can also be translated as "with," in which case it would be a marker of immediate instrument showing that the Savior was the instrument through which Paul became their father.[117]

Paul's words were no mere metaphor but spoke reality, of a literal rebirth and renewal such that people walked in a "newness of life"—one dictated by the Holy Spirit (see Rom. 6:3–6; 8:1). How was it done? Initially through the preaching of the gospel by the missionaries and the accepting of that gospel by the investigators.[118] Later on came fatherly admonition, instruction, and, when necessary, rebuke (Deut. 8:5; Prov. 13:24; 19:18; 2 Tim. 4:2; Heb. 12:6; D&C 121:43). And who first preached that gospel in Corinth? It was Paul. Indeed, he was the one who brought the message and the power to all of Greece. In that way he was their spiritual father. He used the verb γεννάω (*gennaō*), "to father," in the metaphorical sense of "to bring into

---

114. BDAG, 748.

115. Some Roman households had hundreds of slaves who could serve as these guardians and guides but not as fathers. Sometimes these slaves corrupted the youth. Cato the Elder, a distinguished Roman Senator, insisted that fathers and mothers educate and raise their own children to prevent corruption by slaves. He even undertook his son's education himself rather than entrust it to a slave. See Plutarch, *cat. maj.* 20.3–5.

116. BDAG, 327.

117. Louw-Nida, §90.10.

118. A pattern of conversion wrought by the preaching of the gospel is laid out in Alma 32:16–33:23, and its results are noted in Mosiah 5:2, 7; Alma 5:7, 12–15; 7:22–24; 26:22.

being." The word also carried the idea of causing a radical change in someone that involved their total personality.[119]

4:16 *Wherefore I beseech you, be ye followers of me / Therefore I encourage you to imitate me:* The noun μιμητής (*mimētēs*) means "an imitator," and when used with the verb "to be," it had the sense of "to use another as a model."[120] It does not mean "to follow," in the sense of being loyal or devoted to a specific person. Paul continually put the Father and Son center stage. They were the ones who must be followed. Paul, however, was a prime example of one who followed them and his desire was that the Saints follow his example. Jesus said, "Be as I am" (see 3 Ne. 27:27), and Paul said, in essence, "Follow my example in following the Lord."[121]

4:17 *For this cause have I sent unto you Timotheus, who is my beloved son, and faithful in the Lord / For this reason I sent Timothy to you, who is my beloved and faithful son in the Lord:* The preposition διά (*dia*) with the accusative expressed purpose, that is, the reason for an action. Timothy was the executor of what Paul needed done. Paul's use of the aorist verb ἔπεμψα (*epempsa*), "I sent," suggests that Timothy was already on his way.[122]

Paul first met Timothy years before in Lystra (central Turkey today) and had deep respect for him and his family. Timothy was his mission companion for a while (see Acts 16:1–3; 2 Tim. 1:1–5) and eventually became Paul's beloved and most trusted disciple (see 1 Tim. 1:2, 18; 2 Tim. 1:2).[123] In Paul's letter, he acknowledges his love for Timothy but also added a note on his faithfulness. Both of these enhanced Timothy's position as spokesperson for Paul.

who shall bring you into remembrance of my ways which be in Christ, as I teach every where in every church / he will help you remember the ways I conduct my life in Christ Jesus, as I teach them everywhere in every church: Using the verb ἀναμιμνήσκω (*anamimnēskō*), "to remind, cause to remember,"

---

119. Louw-Nida, §13.56; BDAG, 194.

120. BDAG, 652.

121. *DNTC*, 2:333; Ogden and Skinner, *Verse by Verse*, 132. The issue is one of obedience to which Paul has set an example in doing what the Lord wants done. Now he asks the Corinthian Saints to obey him, for he has obeyed the Lord and has, therefore, received his authority to reveal God's will. See Wilhem Michaelis, "μιμέομαι, μιμητής, συμμιμητής," in *TDNT*, 4:659–74.

122. By deleting "Though," the sentence becomes complete. It is possible the verb could be translated as an epistolary aorist, in which case it would read, "I am sending Timothy," as in the NRSV mg and NIV. The context, however, suggests that Timothy is already on his way, and that nuance is followed in the NJB and REB. Conzelmann, *1 Corinthians*, 92, n. 19.

123. Sperry, *Paul's Life*, 49.

Paul explained the reason for sending Timothy on this errand. Timothy's task was to remind the Saints of what they already knew about Paul's lifestyle and teachings. Since Paul had lived among them for months, many of these Saints would have had time for very close inspection of his actions as a Christian Apostle. Remembering, however, was not an end in itself; it was to give ground for Paul's admonition that the Saints follow his example.

Paul wanted them to remember τὰς ὁδούς μου τὰς ἐν Χριστῷ Ἰησοῦ (*tas hodous mou tas en Christō Iēsou*), "my ways in Christ Jesus."[124] The word ὁδός (*hodos*), "way," could also be used to describe one's way of life and, in the broadest sense, the very ground on which that way of life sat.[125] For the Christians, the term ἡ ὁδός (*hē hodos*), "the way," encapsulated the entire gospel of Christ, which included the spiritual road they were to follow to achieve eternal life (see Acts 9:2; 19:9, 23; 24:22).[126] In this passage, Paul uses the plural "ways" rather than the singular to describe the total conduct of his life.[127]

The phrase πανταχοῦ ἐν πάσῃ ἐκκλησίᾳ (*pantachou en pasē ekklēsia*), "everywhere in all the congregations," stressed the consistency and universality of Paul's teachings.

Analysis and Summary

In 4:13–14, Paul softened his criticism of the Corinthian Saints by explaining what it was that motivated him to write to them. He assured them that, despite appearances, he was not writing to shame them but, because they were his beloved children in Christ, to admonish them. His remarks may sound self-defensive, but in reality, he felt pressure neither to justify himself nor to refute any claim by others. His remarks had but one goal: to get the Saints to understand the real role of the Apostles as the ministers of Christ and stewards of his mysteries so that the Saints would heed their admonitions. His stern tone reflected the seriousness of the situation and the importance of the Saints to respond appropriately.[128]

Paul's softer tone was meant to conciliate his readers to him, but given the strength of his words and his heavy handed use of irony, it is hard to

---

124. There are three variants to this verse with "Christ Jesus" having the best support.
125. BDAG, 691–92; *TDNT*, 5:42.
126. This context would reflect the Jewish background of the Apostle who understood the Torah's הֲלָכָה (*hălākāh*), literally "way of walking," as the metaphorical road to God.
127. BDAG, 691–92.
128. Fitzmyer, *First Corinthians*, 211.

see how he could claim his intent was not to shame them, at least to a small degree. Paul's objective, however, was not to generate low self-esteem but to promote realism.[129] His derisive words, exaggerated images, and biting sarcasm were meant to forcefully correct myopic vision and misplaced loyalties, not to humiliate his readers. He dearly loved these people (he called them ἀγαπητά [*agapēta*], "beloved") and was anxious for their salvation and, therefore, wanted to provide a warning in such a way that it could not easily be dismissed.

Having referred to his readers as his "dear children," Paul then expanded on the metaphor in two ways. First, in 4:15, he called himself their "father." This relationship was, of course, in a spiritual sense, but worked because he was the one who initially brought the gospel into the area.

Second, his status as father also came with some accompanying rights and obligations. Most of all, it gave him a unique authority over his Corinthian "family." Among other powers, it allowed him to demand that they conform to his example as their "father."[130] As noted already, many Gentile Corinthians were highly conscious of status, living as they did in a shame-honor culture.[131] That status-consciousness produced the major sore point with Paul and his methods among them. Paul's objective here, however, was not to do away with status but to place it on a sure, spiritual foundation, one that focused on Christ's atoning sacrifice, "the cross," and its meaning. This kind of status turned Corinthian social mores on their heads. But the posture the Saints were to take had already been defined by the Lord. "Ye know," he taught, "that the princes of the Gentiles exercise dominion over them [their subjects], and they that are great exercise authority upon them. But it shall not be so among you: but whosoever will be great among you, let him be your minister; And whosoever will be chief among you, let him be your servant: Even as the Son of man came not to be ministered unto, but to minister, and to give his life a ransom for many" (Matt. 20:25–28). Paul's arguments from chapters 2 through 4 gave the Saints all the material they needed to reappraise and redefine the nature of true wisdom and status. He provided them with a correction to their ways of evaluating others, more particularly him, Apollos, Peter, and—most likely—the other Apostles.[132]

---

129. Thiselton, *First Epistle*, 368.
130. Fee, *First Epistle*, 185.
131. Witherington, *Conflict and Community*, 8, 24; Pogoloff, *Logos and Sophia*, 203.
132. Thiselton, *First Epistle*, 369; Fitzmyer, *First Corinthians*, 220–21.

Paul's phrase "my dear children" also revealed what really motivated him to write. All he did was based on a deep and parental-like love. That love, however, did not mean that he was unwilling to rebuke them as needed. Some may see a contradiction between Paul's stinging words and loving feelings. There was none. As Elder Neal A. Maxwell has pointed out, "Perhaps our difficulties with receiving justified reproof stem from our thinking of love as being all sweetness. Love surely includes sweetness. But love must sometimes be tough love, sinew as well as sweetness."[133] He further stated:

> When we see someone striding towards a cliff or the unpleasant consequences of his actions, what are we to do? Joseph [Smith] said it—move early as the first challenge appears; do early on what is right, without worrying unduly. And what is the manner of reproof, if such is needed?
>
> "Reproving betimes with sharpness, when moved upon by the Holy Ghost; and then showing forth afterwards an increase of love toward him whom thou hast reproved, lest he esteem thee to be his enemy; That he may know that thy faithfulness is stronger than the cords of death" (D&C 121:43–44).
>
> Tough love is doing all one can, risking being misunderstood in the process, yet finally accepting that others are meant to be "free to choose." Tough love never quits; it is unconditional. But neither is it unaware of Lehi's "trembling parent" (2 Nephi 1:14). We are to write off neither individuals nor Ninevehs. Yet we are to engage in "speaking the truth in love" (Ephesians 4:15).[134]

It was because he felt true love for these people that Paul could write the words he did. That love could not allow him to lose any of these beloved souls without a fight. If that meant using harsh words—words that could not easily be ignored and did sting—so be it. As one noted LDS scholar said, Paul

> refused to be rejected by those he was called to lead. Although he criticized them, they were literally "his children" (*tekna*); he was their father in the gospel (1 Cor. 4:14–15). Parents are often hurt by rebelliousness and lack of appreciation by their children, but in that role Paul did not complain. He listed inconvenience, strain, and danger constantly suffered to bring the gospel to new souls. If they rejected him, he would speak plainly

---

133. Neal A. Maxwell, *All These Things Shall Give Thee Experience* (Salt Lake City: Deseret Book, 1976), 80.

134. Neal A. Maxwell, *But for a Small Moment* (Salt Lake City: Bookcraft, 1986), 131.

but not cease to love. He personifies the role of the priesthood (and by implication motherhood) repeatedly outlined by Jesus—the higher the office, the more generous the sacrifice of time and concern (Luke 22:26).[135]

The image of the father helped Paul in another way. He could contrast it with others who exercised authority over children, namely those whom he refers to as "guardians" (παιδαγωγός, *paidagōgos*). Just who Paul was referring to is unknown, but his exaggeration suggests he could have in mind his self-appointed detractors, those men and women who had not been properly building on the foundation he had laid. These would be people who were very willing to act as self-appointed guides and guardians over the Church and delighted in directing the lives of others. By promoting their own perceived holiness and deep spiritual understanding, they felt free to expound their teachings. They induced the more gullible and easily persuaded them to follow them. In all these ways, they effortlessly led many in the Church astray.[136]

Paul understood that the purpose of the gospel was to bring people not only *to* the Lord, but also to establish a spiritual bond *between* them. They were to be ἐν Χριστῷ Ἰησοῦ (*en Christō Iēsou*), "in Christ Jesus." To be *in* him meant to have that close spiritual tie that brought oneness, a oneness the Savior earnestly prayed for (John 17:20–23). Such a oneness was developed through a love of the Lord such that one was willing to keep his commandments (John 14:15, 21). The Savior explained the results, "If ye keep my commandments, ye shall abide in my love; even as I have kept my Father's commandments, and abide in his love" (John 15:10). Thus, he promised, "Abide in me, and I [will] in you," (John 15:4) and further, "If ye abide in me, and my words abide in you, ye shall ask what ye will, and it shall be done unto you" (John 15:7). The Savior knew whereof he spoke for, as he taught Philip, "The words that I speak unto you I speak not of myself: but the Father that dwelleth in me, he doeth the works." He went on to say, "Believe me that I am in the Father, and the Father in me: or else believe for the very works' sake" (John 14:11). Thus, the Father and Son shared an "indwelling relationship" by which they were one. Paul understood that through gospel living, the Saints could develop that same relationship with the Lord by which they would be *en Christō Iēsou*.

Paul admonished his readers to imitate him in his obedience to the Lord (4:16). He was asking them to prove by their conduct that they truly had

---

135. Anderson, *Understanding Paul*, 102.
136. Fee, *First Epistle*, 185.

been born anew through the regenerating power of the Spirit brought by accepting the gospel in faith. He was forcing them to look at their conduct to see if it exhibited divine parentage.[137] Paul was saying that the lifestyle of the Corinthian Saints should be fully apostolic. His admonition was not a case of "do as I say," but of "do as I do." The doing, however, was not to be in some wooden, unthinking way.[138] Paul did not want a bunch of automatons automatically following some preset program. He wanted people in whose lives the Spirit breathed and whose actions flowed from that power.

Since Paul was not yet free to come himself, he sent his excellent representative, Timothy. The young man had a two-fold task: first, to help the people remember the mode of Paul's apostolic life revealed by his devotion to the gospel, and second, to reinforce Paul's consistency in his teachings (4:17). The Apostle's words stressed the fact that what he taught and was teaching the Corinthian Saints was that which he taught to all branches of the Church. There was but one standard for all Churches everywhere.

Both of these tasks, however, were but to effect one purpose—to get the people to follow his example as one living a Christian life. The Apostle's words, τὰς ὁδούς μου τὰς ἐν Χριστῷ (*tas hodous mou tas en Xristō*), "my ways in Christ," echoed the words used by Christians, ἡ ὁδός (*hē hodos*), "the way," to express succinctly the gospel with its attendant lifestyle. Paul's "ways," then, were bound to the Savior and his plan of salvation anchored in the reality of the Atonement.

Paul's example had two components: first, that of living the Christian lifestyle, and second, that of accepting true doctrine. Though both are linked, they do not go hand in glove. Many have high ethical values without following the doctrine of the Lord. However, such can be a slippery slope. Ethics, in and of themselves, often being tied to present circumstances and current mores, can be shaped by political or social agendas and follow fads and fashions. Even Christian ethics can actually cause mistranslations of the Lord's will. Pure doctrine, being based on eternal principles, defines the foundation of the gospel and assures that all that is built thereon is correct and proper. Keeping the doctrine pure, therefore, is essential because, as President Gordon B. Hinckley emphasized, "Small aberrations in doctrinal teaching can lead to large and evil falsehoods."[139]

---

137. Robertson and Plummer, *Critical and Exegetical Commentary*, 90.
138. Thiselton, *First Epistle*, 371.
139. Gordon B. Hinckley, *Teachings of Gordon B. Hinckley* (Salt Lake City: Deseret Book, 1997), 620.

Paul was faced with that very problem. Some of the Saints had reinterpreted Christ and, as a result, were promoting beliefs, behaviors, and causes, as will be shown in the next chapters, not in accordance with the gospel. The Savior was no longer the center of their religion because they had left the doctrine of "Christ, and him crucified" (2:2). "This truth is the very root of Christian doctrine," stated President Boyd K. Packer. "You may know much about the gospel as it branches out from there, but if you only know the branches and those branches do not touch that root, if they have been cut free from that truth, there will be no life nor substance nor redemption in them."[140] Some of the Corinthian Saints, perhaps unwittingly, had left the Atonement and, as a consequence, were leaving the gospel. All that could save them was to return to their doctrinal base. Again from President Packer, "True doctrine, understood, changes attitudes and behavior." He goes on to say, "The study of the doctrines of the gospel will improve behavior quicker than a study of behavior will improve behavior. . . . That is why we stress so forcefully the study of the doctrines of the gospel."[141] Elder Maxwell, backing up this idea, stated that "doctrines believed and practiced do change and improve us, while insuring our vital access to the Spirit. Both outcomes are crucial."[142] Paul, therefore, had to bring the Saints back to a pure religion undefiled by the philosophies of men.

APPROACHING VISIT (4:18–21)

Greek Text

18 ὡς μὴ ἐρχομένου δέ μου πρὸς ὑμᾶς ἐφυσιώθησάν τινες· 19 ἐλεύσομαι δὲ ταχέως πρὸς ὑμᾶς, ἐὰν ὁ κύριος θελήσῃ, καὶ γνώσομαι οὐ τὸν λόγον τῶν πεφυσιωμένων ἀλλὰ τὴν δύναμιν, 20 οὐ γὰρ ἐν λόγῳ ἡ τθβασιλεία τοῦ θεοῦ ἀλλ' ἐν δυνάμει. 21 τί θέλετε; ἐν ῥάβδῳ ἔλθω πρὸς ὑμᾶς, ἢ ἐν ἀγάπῃ πνεύματί τε πραΰτητος; [SBLGNT]

---

140. Boyd K. Packer, "The Mediator," *Ensign* 7 (May 1977): 80.

141. Boyd K. Packer, "Little Children," *Ensign* 16 (November) 1986): 20.

142. Neal A. Maxwell, *One More Strain of Praise* (Salt Lake City: Deseret Book, 2002), x. See also Robert L. Millet, "What Is Our Doctrine?" in *Getting at the Truth* (Salt Lake City: Deseret Book, 2004).

King James Version

18 Now some are puffed up, as though I would not come to you. 19 But I will come to you shortly, if the Lord will, and will know, not the speech of them which are puffed up, but the power. 20 For the kingdom of God is not in word, but in power. 21 What will ye? shall I come unto you with a rod, or in love, and in the spirit of meekness?

New Rendition

18 Some of you have become arrogant, as if I were not going to come to you. 19 But I will come to you soon, if the Lord is willing, and I will find out not what these arrogant people have been saying, but what they can actually do. 20 For the kingdom of God is not demonstrated by mere words, but by power. 21 What do you prefer? Should I come to you with a rod, or with love and in a spirit of gentleness?

Translation Notes and Comments

4:18 *Now some are puffed up, as though I would not come to you / Some of you have become arrogant, as if I were not going to come to you:* Paul again hits the heart of the matter. There were those who had "become arrogant" (ἐφυσιώθησαν, *ephysiōthēsan*)[143] because of their disdainful belief that he would be too timid to come and face them.[144]

4:19 *I will come to you shortly, if the Lord will / I will come to you soon, if the Lord is willing:* With these words, Paul undercut their self-assurance and false belief. The word ταχέως (*tacheōs*), "quickly, soon," points more to the assurance of the event than to its immediateness.[145] Just how long it would take Paul to get to Corinth, he did not know because some of it depended on circumstance only known to God, but the point was, as quickly as he could, he was most definitely going to come.

I . . . will know, not the speech of them which are puffed up, but the power / I will find out not what these arrogant people have been saying, but what they can actually do: The Greek here is very compressed, γνώσομαι οὐ τὸν λόγον τῶν πεφυσιωμένων ἀλλὰ τὴν δύναμιν (*gnōsomai ou ton logon tōn pephysiōmenōn alla tēn dynamin*), literally "I will find out not the word of those who are puffed up, but the capability." Our Rendition gives the sense of the passage in modern English. These arrogant members of the Church have a lot to say, but Paul's goal was to actually put them to the test to see if their teachings had any real power.[146]

---

143. BDAG, 1069.
144. Fitzmyer, *First Corinthians,* 224.
145. BDAG, 992.
146. Thiselton, *First Epistle,* 376–77.

4:20 ***For the kingdom of God is not in word, but in power / For the kingdom of God is not demonstrated by mere words, but by power:*** In this verse, Paul explained the reasoning behind his challenge. Though the phrase ἡ βασιλεία τοῦ θεοῦ (*hē basileia tou theou*), "the kingdom of God," as used by Paul, often referred to the political condition that would be ushered in at the time of the Lord's coming, in this instance it referred to the Church in Paul's day with its attendant powers that evidence God's endorsement of the Church (compare D&C 1:30).[147] Its truthfulness was not proved in mere words—even showy, impressive, convincing words—but in the demonstration of the power of the Spirit.

4:21 ***What will ye? shall I come unto you with a rod, or in love, and in the spirit of meekness? / What do you prefer? Should I come to you with a rod, or with love and in a spirit of gentleness?:*** Paul asks his detractors to determine how they wish him to greet them. The verb θέλω (*thelō*) means "wish, desire," but when two options are possible, as in this case, it is best translated as "prefer" rather than "wish."[148] The noun ῥάβδος (*rhabdos*) denotes a stick used for a special purpose, such as a scepter or cane. It could also refer to a cudgel or rod used to punish those who broke the law, which is the case here since Paul's detractors were guilty of offense against the gospel law.[149] The noun πραΰτης (*prautēs*) denoted the qualities of those who were not overly proud of their state or station, thus, "humbleness, gentleness, meekness."[150] Because Paul was giving the Saints a choice, the best antonym for the treatment associated with a "rod" would be "gentleness."

Analysis and Summary

Paul's actions in sending Timothy ahead could well have played into the hands of the Apostle's detractors who could have interpreted it as evidence of Paul's reluctance to face them. He therefore assured them not to read Timothy's visit as some sign that he was not planning to show up. Indeed, he planned to come as quickly as possible, and they could count on that.

Paul's words to the Saints revealed two points: First, the phrase "some of you" (4:18, Rendition) indicated that the contention was coming from within, not without the Church, by persons who were very opposed to

---

147. Paul does not use the phrase very often, but when he does, it is usually in terms of the kingdom to come. See 6:9–10; 15:24; Rom. 14:17; Gal. 5:21; Eph. 5:5; 2 Thes. 1:5; Col. 1:13; 4:11; 2 Tim. 4:18. Thiselton, *First Epistle,* 377; George W. Pace, "Kingdom of God," in *EM,* 2:790.

148. Thiselton, *First Epistle,* 378.

149. BDAG, 902.

150. BDAG, 861.

Paul. Second, though these self-important malcontents did not represent the majority, they did exercise quite an influence over many and had swayed quite a number to accept their false doctrines.[151]

Up to this point, Paul had not directly acknowledged them, but he did so now. Because he had not been around for quite some time, they had come to believe he never would and, therefore, felt that they could disregard him with impunity.[152] His words gave a clear and pointed warning that their belief that he would not dare show up was utterly false. Because they were "puffed up" (πεφυσιωμένος, *pephysiōmenos*, "inflated, filled with air"), he was going to put them to the test to see if these windbags could actually muster any real power.

The real bite in Paul's challenge was in his use of the word λόγος (*logos*), "word, speech," in juxtaposition with δύναμις (*dynamis*), "power, might." Paul was using the word *logos* to express an idea that was much broader than the usual meaning of talk or preachment. He was defining the term as that rhetorical ability to persuade with which his detractors had become so enamored. It was because Paul, who had the ability, would not use these means that they rejected him.

Paul understood, however, that clever, persuasive words were not good enough even when those words came from an authentic source. Jews had the word in the Torah and all the Christian factions had it in the gospel, but that was not where authority lay. Though the "word" was necessary, it was not enough. It must be authenticated and witnessed by divine power. Two expressions of this power were the priesthood and the gift of Holy Ghost. "Where God's power is manifest," testified Elder McConkie, "there is the Church and kingdom of God on the earth, and where his power is not found, there the Church and kingdom is not."[153]

On Paul's part, he had taught the truth, and it had been authenticated by the power of the Spirit (2:4–5). Upon his return, he would see if the words of his detractors had had the same results. They must prove that their *logos*, with all its sophisticated worldly wisdom, was also filled with spiritual affluence. Their challenge was specifically to emulate the Apostle in producing the powerful dynamic of the Spirit that converted, sanctified, and saved. Of course, Paul knew full well that he had nothing to fear from

---

151. Fee, *First Epistle*, 190.

152. Nils A. Dahl, "Paul and the Church at Corinth according to 1 Corinthians 1:10–4:21," in *Christian History and Interpretation: Studies Presneted to John Knox*, ed. W. R. Farmer, C. F. D. Moule, and R. R. Niebuhr (Cambridge: University Press, 1967), 325–29.

153. *DNTC*, 2:333.

these men, for, as he pointed out in 4:20, the real proof of one's authority was not in persuasive words and clever arguments but in the power of the Spirit that transforms the natural man into a child of God.[154]

In this section of the epistle, we see Paul fully exercising his apostolic responsibilities. As an Apostle, he was responsible ultimately to God for the use of his authority. One of his responsibilities was to set the Church in order. No amount of defaming, challenging, or rejecting could or would diminish his right to set the Church's affairs in order. The question he posed to his detractors was not whether he would do it, but which method he would use. He left that choice up to them.[155]

Due to cultural customs, his threat had weight. Because Corinth was a Roman colony, it did not have the same level of democratic spirit as most Greek cities. As a result, the people there were more used to being subject to a ruler figure. Whether emperor or father, these men were to be given allegiance. In turn, they were expected to keep their children in line. Many of the Saints, therefore, would have understood that Paul, as the "father" of the Corinthian branch, was not only within his rights but also obligations to correct his erring children.[156]

One last point seems important. That Paul asked his detractors to choose between the harshness of the rod or the gentleness of love should not be taken to mean that punishment could not be administered without love. As noted above, real love means sweetness balanced with sinew and that brings with it attention and action to both good and bad behavior. So the question Paul asked did not force his readers to choose between love and hate, but between which actions love would bring.[157]

---

154. Fee, *First Epistle*, 191–92.

155. Anderson, *Understanding Paul*, 101; Sperry, *Paul's Life*, 120–21.

156. Eva M. Lassen, "The Use of the Father Image in Imperial Propaganda in 1 Cor. 4:14–21," *Tyndale Bulletin* 42, no. 1 (May 1991): 127–39.

157. Barrett, *First Epistle*, 119.

Chapter 5

Church Discipline for Immorality

INTRODUCTION

Though Paul introduced a new topic in this part of his epistle, he tied it directly to what he had said before. His concern with the effects of pride— or being "puffed up," especially as it contributed to schisms within the community—continued unabated. Further, the actions he demanded toward an immoral member, which covers a major portion of this chapter, was also related to its contribution toward schisms. At issue, however, was more than the unity of the branch; Paul was establishing the breadth of apostolic authority. In this chapter are the first of two test cases concerning that apostolic authority which the Corinthian situation provided.[1]

In chapters 5 and 6, Paul directly confronts clear-cut moral issues. Later on (chapters 7–11) he will confront those that were less clear and needed to be acted upon in their context. The issue faced in chapter 5, however, demanded direct, speedy, and unequivocal action on the part of the Church at Corinth. The Apostle attacked two distinct but separate challenges: first, the grossly immoral act of a branch member and, second, the grossly immoral act of the community in not only tolerating but also condoning the member's actions. There was a thread, however, that ran though both of these and tied them to a greater issue—the purity of the community as a whole. Paul wanted to emphasize the idea of corporate responsibility—that what a member did was not a mere individual matter but reflected on the community as a whole and, therefore, had to be addressed by that community. Paul had already pointed out (3:16–17) that only if all were pure could the Church be rightly considered the temple of God and maintain

---

1. Thiselton, *First Epistle,* 381; Fee, *First Epistle,* 212–13.

the holiness that was required, a holiness that allowed the sanctifying Holy Spirit to dwell within it.[2]

The chapter breaks down into two main sections. Verses 5:1–8 deal first with the need to discipline a certain member of an appalling breach of moral law and, second, was the need for certain members of the Christian community to repent of their laissez-faire attitude toward that deed. Verses 5:9–13 deal with the need for the Christians to purge out any others whose deeds were a gross violation of gospel living.

THE INCESTUOUS RELATIONSHIP (5:1–8)

Greek Text

1 Ὅλως ἀκούεται ἐν ὑμῖν πορνεία, καὶ τοιαύτη πορνεία ἥτις οὐδὲ ἐν τοῖς ἔθνεσιν, ὥστε γυναῖκά τινα τοῦ πατρὸς ἔχειν. 2 καὶ ὑμεῖς πεφυσιωμένοι ἐστέ, καὶ οὐχὶ μᾶλλον ἐπενθήσατε, ἵνα ἀρθῇ ἐκ μέσου ὑμῶν ὁ τὸ ἔργον τοῦτο ποιήσας; 3 Ἐγὼ μὲν γάρ, ἀπὼν τῷ σώματι παρὼν δὲ τῷ πνεύματι, ἤδη κέκρικα ὡς παρὼν τὸν οὕτως τοῦτο κατεργασάμενον 4 ἐν τῷ ὀνόματι τοῦ κυρίου ἡμῶν Ἰησοῦ, συναχθέντων ὑμῶν καὶ τοῦ ἐμοῦ πνεύματος σὺν τῇ δυνάμει τοῦ κυρίου ἡμῶν Ἰησοῦ, 5 παραδοῦναι τὸν τοιοῦτον τῷ Σατανᾷ εἰς ὄλεθρον τῆς σαρκός, ἵνα τὸ πνεῦμα σωθῇ ἐν τῇ ἡμέρᾳ τοῦ κυρίου.

6 Οὐ καλὸν τὸ καύχημα ὑμῶν. οὐκ οἴδατε ὅτι μικρὰ ζύμη ὅλον τὸ φύραμα ζυμοῖ; 7 ἐκκαθάρατε τὴν παλαιὰν ζύμην, ἵνα ἦτε νέον φύραμα, καθώς ἐστε ἄζυμοι. καὶ γὰρ τὸ πάσχα ἡμῶν ἐτύθη Χριστός· 8 ὥστε ἑορτάζωμεν, μὴ ἐν ζύμῃ παλαιᾷ μηδὲ ἐν ζύμῃ κακίας καὶ πονηρίας, ἀλλ' ἐν ἀζύμοις εἰλικρινείας καὶ ἀληθείας. [SBLGNT]

King James Version

1 It is reported commonly that there is fornication among you, and such fornication as is not so much as named among the Gentiles, that one should have his father's wife. 2 And ye are puffed up, and have not rather mourned, that he that hath done this deed might be taken away from among you. 3 For I verily, as absent in body, but

New Rendition

1 Now it is common knowledge that there is an illicit sexual relationship occurring among you, and such immorality is not even tolerated among the Gentiles—a man is having sexual relations with his stepmother. 2 And you are proud of yourselves! Shouldn't you rather have been saddened and had the one who committed this act expelled from your

---

2. Thiselton, *First Epistle*, 390.

present in spirit, have judged already, as though I were present, concerning him that hath so done this deed, 4 In the name of our Lord Jesus Christ, when ye are gathered together, and my spirit, with the power of our Lord Jesus Christ, 5 To deliver such an one unto Satan for the destruction of the flesh, that the spirit may be saved in the day of the Lord Jesus. 6 Your glorying is not good. Know ye not that a little leaven leaveneth the whole lump? 7 Purge out therefore the old leaven, that ye may be a new lump, as ye are unleavened. For even Christ our passover is sacrificed for us: 8 Therefore let us keep the feast, not with old leaven, neither with the leaven of malice and wickedness; but with the unleavened bread of sincerity and truth.

midst? 3 For although I am physically absent, I am present in spirit, and as if I were present, I have already passed judgment 4 in the name of our Lord Jesus on the one who has perpetrated such a thing. When you have met together, and my spirit is present, then with the power of our Lord Jesus, 5 hand over this man to Satan for the destruction of his flesh, so that his spirit might be saved in the day of the Lord. 6 Your pride is not a good thing. Don't you understand that a little yeast can leaven a whole batch of dough? 7 Purge out the old yeast so you can become a new batch of dough, as indeed you are unleavened. For even Christ, our Passover Lamb, has been sacrificed for us. 8 And so let us celebrate the festival, not with the old yeast, the yeast of evil and wickedness, but with the unleavened bread of pure intent and truth.

Translation Notes and Comments

5:1 *It is reported commonly that there is fornication among you / Now it is common knowledge that there is an illicit sexual relationship occurring among you:* The phrase Paul used, ὅλως ἀκούεται (*holōs akouetai*), literally "it is heard everywhere," showed that the scandalous sexual impropriety of a member of the Christian community had not been discreet—everyone knew about it.

The Greek noun πορνεία (*porneia*) was a general term that referred to any type of unlawful sexual activity.[3] As noted in the introduction to this volume, Corinth was notorious anciently for its immoral practices—the verb κορινθιάζομαι (*korinthiazomai*), literally "to Corinthize" meant "to fornicate."[4] But the type of sexual intercourse that Paul was here condemning was one that even the more liberal of Gentiles looked upon as abhorrent.

not so much as named among the Gentiles / and such immorality is not even tolerated among the Gentiles: There is no verb with ἐν τοῖς ἔθνεσιν

---

3. BDAG, 854.
4. *LSJ*, 981.

(*en tois ethnesin*), "among the gentiles." The KJV supplies "as named" and
the NIV uses "tolerate," but neither gets at the sense of Paul's feelings. Sexual immorality (at least among males—women were expected to be chaste)
was generally tolerated in Greco-Roman society,[5] but even among those
people, having sexual relations with one's step-mother was not acceptable.
Therefore, our Rendition supplies the phrase, "not even tolerated."

**that one should have his father's wife / a man is having sexual relations
with his stepmother:** The Greek verb ἔχω (*echō*) meant literally "to have,"
but it was often used as an oblique reference to sexual relations.[6] That
Paul used the present active infinitive ἔχειν (*echein*) suggests that, shock-
ingly, the illicit relationship was still going on. The phrase γυναῖκά τινα τοῦ
πατρός (*gynaika tina tou patros*), literally "a wife of the [his] father," designated a stepmother. If it were a person's own mother, Paul would have
used the noun μήτηρ (*mētēr*), "mother." This also parallels the wording of
the Mosaic prohibition in Deuteronomy 27:20, "Cursed be he that lieth
with his father's wife"—μετὰ γυναικὸς τοῦ πατρὸς αὐτοῦ (*meta gynaikos
tou patros autou*) in the Septuagint. Under the Mosaic law, both the man
and the woman who committed such an act were condemned to death (see
Lev. 18:18).

That the Apostle identified the transgressor with neither a name nor definite masculine article, but only with the indefinite accusative pronominal
τινα (*tina*), "someone, a certain one," suggests his personal disgust.[7]

Because of the resistance of both Jews and Gentiles to such an act, it is
mind-boggling that any Christians would commit it. It is also astonishing
that members of the Christian community would not only condone but
support it. Their decision to uphold the act, however, revealed the degree
of misunderstanding this group had about the Atonement. They somehow
felt that the Savior's merciful act freed people from all constraints of law,
both religious and civil. They rationalized, therefore, that such behavior
was acceptable. For further discussion, see Translation Notes on 6:12.[8]

---

5. Under the Julian laws of 18–17 BC, attempts were made to elevate the morals of the
upper class and to increase the population by encouraging marriage and having children
(*lex Julia de maritandis ordinibus*). Laws were also laid down to make adultery both a
private and public crime (*lex Julia de adulteriis*).

6. BDAG, 420.

7. BDAG, 1007.

8. This is likely a case of incipient antinomianism which holds that "under the gospel
dispensation of grace the moral law is of no use or obligation because faith alone is necessary for salvation." *Merriam-Webster's Collegiate Dictionary*, 11th ed. (2008), 55. Though

5:2 *And ye are puffed up, and have not rather mourned / And you are proud of yourselves! Shouldn't you rather have been saddened?:* On "puffed up," see Translation Notes on 4:6.

The condition of their being "puffed up" explained how certain members rationalized the man's behavior. Their pride prevented them from believing they could be wrong. The perfect passive participle πεφυσιωμένοι (*pephysiōmenoi*), "puffed up, arrogant, proud," denoted continuous effect[9] and revealed that they remained continually complacent to this deed.

Our Rendition takes the aorist passive verb ἐπενθήσατε (*epenthēsate*), "to be sad, grieve, mourn," as an empiric aorist, which is often best translated with an English perfect.[10] Paul's phrase showed that there was never a moment when these pride-filled people even considered that their view might be wrong. Their spiritual malady blinded them to reality.

that he that hath done this deed might be taken away from among you / and had the one who committed this act expelled from your midst: The verb αἴρω (*airō*), "take away, remove, expel," designated a very firm action including forcefully casting something away. In extreme cases, it connoted destroying or executing someone for a severe breach of the law.[11] Since Paul used the term in an ecclesiastical sense, it should not be construed as "execute" but rather as "excommunicate," with the idea of expelling the evil doer from the congregation.

There is a significant manuscript variant in this verse. A number of ancient texts have the aorist participle ποιήσας (*poiēsas*), which is derived from ποιέω (*poieō*), "to do a deed,"[12] while others have πράξας (*praxas*), which is derived from πράσσω (*prassō*), "to follow a course of action." Because the latter word in certain contexts could carry the nuance of committing an evil or disgraceful deed, it is more likely the word Paul used.[13] The force of Paul's meaning is, therefore, a bit stronger than that conveyed by the KJV phrase "he that hath done this deed" but rather "the one who committed this act" as given in our Rendition.

---

the controversy over this idea would not become full blown until the sixteenth century, its roots reached back into the first century.

9. Thiselton, *First Epistle*, 387.

10. Smyth, *Greek Grammar*, §1940.

11. BDAG, 28; Louw-Nida,, §20.43, 65; Joachim Jeremias, "αἴρω, ἐπαίρω," in *TDNT*, 1:185–86.

12. BDAG, 839.

13. BDAG, 860. For discussion, see Metzger, *Textual Commentary*, 484.

5:3 *For I verily, as absent in body, but present in spirit, / For although I am physically absent, I am present in spirit:* By using the personal pronoun ἐγώ (*egō*), "I," Paul contrasted himself with that segment of the Christian branch (referred to with the plural pronoun ὑμεῖς (*hymeis*), "all of you" in 5:2, who refused to see the grievousness of the situation. The Apostle clearly did, even though he was not there. And how so? Because of the Holy Spirit that gave him the power to discern. Being "present in spirit" empowered him to make as accurate an assessment of what was going on as if he were physically present.[14]

have judged already . . . concerning him that hath so done this deed / I have already passed judgment in the name of our Lord Jesus on the one who has perpetrated such a thing:[15] The KJV takes "in the name of our Lord Jesus" in 5:4 as going with the phrase following it, "when ye are gathered together." However, it is better taken with 5:3, as in our Rendition. In this way the phrase emphasizes that Paul based his judgment of this man on his apostolic authority as derived from Jesus Christ.[16] By using the perfect indicative active κέκρικα (*kekrika*), "I have pronounced judgment," along with ἤδη (*ēdē*), "already," Paul indicated that he had come to a firm decision about this man from which there would be no negotiation, and because of which, he was now ready to make a public declaration.

The verb κατεργάζομαι (*katergazomai*), "to bring about, accomplish,"[17] with the intensive prefix κατ- (*kat-*), intensify the charge against the man. The English word "perpetrate" gets at the meaning, and it is so translated in our Rendition. The Apostle's words, therefore, reveal his revulsion toward the one who perpetrated such a heinous deed.[18] Further revealing his indignation was his use of the adverb οὕτως (*houtōs*), "in this way" or "under such circumstances."[19] The phrase then shows that Paul had judged

---

14. Based on the mind-body dualism of Plato and Descartes, some commentators see the reference to being "present in spirit" to mean little more than, "my thoughts are with you." In Paul's writings, however, τῷ πνεύματι (*tō pneumati*), "in the spirit," links to the Holy Spirit and its attendant powers (for examples, see 7:34; 12:3; 14:15; Rom. 1:9; 2:29; 8:13, 16; 12:11; 2 Cor. 6:6; Eph. 1:13; Col. 2:5). For discussion, see Thiselton, *First Epistle*, 391.

15. The JST reads "*I have judged already him who hath so done this deed, as though I were present,*" italics added to highlight the changes. Though the JST changes the word order, it adds nothing doctrinally insightful.

16. The passage is difficult to translate and a number of opinions have been offered. See Thiselton, *First Epistle*, 393–94, for discussion.

17. BDAG, 531.

18. Lightfoot, *Notes*, 204.

19. Thiselton, *First Epistle*, 392.

the man who had "perpetrated this act under such circumstances,"[20] likely meaning when the perpetrator knew better.

5:4 ***when ye are gathered together / When you have met together:*** In this phrase, Paul was telling the leaders to convene what we call today a Church disciplinary council to judge the man. As one LDS scholar noted, "Such provisions and disciplinary procedures are especially pertinent to a community of covenanters, as the evidence that Manfred Weise and others have marshaled regarding rules of discipline at Qumran and in the earliest Christian communities tend to show."[21]

and my spirit, with the power of our Lord Jesus Christ / and my spirit is present, then with the power of our Lord Jesus:[22] The JST reads, "When ye are met together, and have the Spirit with the power of the Lord Jesus Christ," thus showing that the meeting was not to be directed by Paul's spirit but by that of the Lord. The sense of the whole passage revealed the need for the effective power of Christ (taking δύναμις [*dynamis*], "power" in the sense of putting into effect the Lord's authority) to give competency to the council so that it could act in the Lord's name.[23]

5:5 ***To deliver such an one unto Satan for the destruction of the flesh, that the spirit may be saved in the day of the Lord Jesus / hand over this man to Satan for the destruction of his flesh, so that his spirit might be saved in the day of the Lord:*** Paul again did not dignify the individual with a name but simply referred to him with τὸν τοιοῦτον (*ton toiouton*), literally "such a one." The colloquial English "that so-and-so" catches the flavor of it. Paul thus left the reader to supply any adjective he wished. Our Rendition supplies "man" rather than the less charitable "moron" or "idiot."[24]

---

20. Thiselton, *First Epistle,* 384.

21. John W. Welch, *Illuminating the Sermon at the Temple and Sermon on the Mount: An Approach to 3 Nephi 11–18 and Matthew 5–7* (Provo, Utah: Foundation of Ancient Research and Mormon Studies, 1999), 65. For the work of Manfred Weise referred to, see "Mt 5:21f—ein Zeugnis sakraler Rechtsprechung in der Urgemeinde," *Zeitschrift der neutestamentliche Wissenschaft* 49 (1958): 116–23. Such scriptures as Matt. 5:21–22; 18:15–17; and 1 Tim. 1:20 support the idea that disciplinary councils were used from the earliest period of the Church. See also Eduard Lohse, "συνέδριον," in *TDNT,* 7:860–71.

22. The earliest manuscripts lack Χριστοῦ (*Christou*), "Christ," and so the Rendition omits it. Metzger, *Textual Commentary,* 484–85.

23. See Robertson and Plummer, *Critical and Exegetical Commentary,* 98–99; Collins, *First Corinthians,* 207.

24. "When Paul writes, 'surrender this . . . to Satan,' the readers can add whatever adjective they want. It can be 'this *idiot*' or 'this *fool*' or something stronger." Bailey, *Mediterranean Eyes,* 164.

In this phrase, the Greek reads τῆς σαρκός (*tēs sarkos*), "of *the* flesh," and τὸ πνεῦμα (*to pneuma*), "*the* spirit." However, the definite article often takes the place of an unemphatic possessive pronoun when there is no doubt as to the possessor.[25] Hence, our Rendition translates both definite articles as "his."

The council was to consign the man "such as he is," τοιοῦτον (*toiouton*)—alluding to his present spiritual state—to Satan for a specific purpose. Paul's exact instructions were εἰς ὄλεθρον τῆς σαρκός, ἵνα τὸ πνεῦμα σωθῇ (*eis olethron tēs sarkos, hina to pneuma sōthē*), "for the purpose of destroying the flesh that the spirit might be saved." To understand Paul's intent, we must carefully examine the crucial elements in this phrase. The first is the preposition εἰς (*eis*). Though this word can be a marker of intent, "in order to, for the purpose of," it can also denote an anticipated result, "with the result that."[26] Since the qualifying verb is παραδίδωμι (*paradidōmi*), "to hand over, deliver," the expressed purpose was that the man's spirit might be saved. Therefore, εἰς (*eis*) should not be construed as purposeful but as anticipatory; it anticipates that the action of Satan will result in the salvation of the man's spirit.[27]

The second critical word was σάρξ (*sarx*), which meant primarily the "flesh," or "human body."[28] In a secondary sense, however, the noun denoted "human nature," that is, "the psychological aspect of human nature which contrasts with the spiritual nature; in other words, that aspect of human nature which is characterized by or reflects typical human reasoning and desires in contrast with other aspects of human thought and behavior which relates to God and the spiritual life."[29] The term did not necessarily point to a lower, corrupt, or depraved nature (an axiom of Greek philosophy), but it did not preclude those factors in humans that allowed them to become willing instruments of sin and Satan.[30]

The third critical word was πνεῦμα (*pneuma*), which most often denoted the immortal spirit within a person.[31] In a secondary sense, however, it

---

25. Smyth, *Greek Grammar*, §1121; Wallace, *Greek Grammar*, 215.

26. BDAG, 290.

27. Fee, *First Epistle*, 209.

28. BDAG, 914; Eduard Schweizer, Friedrich Baumgärtel, Rudolf Meyer, "σάρξ, σαρκικός, σάρκινος," in *TDNT*, 7:98–151.

29. Louw-Nida, §26.7.

30. Louw-Nida, §26.7, 368.

31. BDAG, 833.

referred to the inner soul of a person that determined what he really was and defined what drove his thinking.[32]

Taking all these together, Paul's reference to the "destruction of the flesh" may not have been to capital punishment. It is more likely that he was thinking of allowing the powers of Satan, both in mortality and in the afterlife, to work on the man such that he would repent and, thereby, receive some degree of glory (D&C 76:81–88, 103–6). This idea is reflected in the 1980 NIV where this phrase reads, "that his sinful nature may be destroyed."[33] However, the 2011 NIV changed this back to "the destruction of the flesh."

be saved in the day of the Lord Jesus / might be saved in the day of the Lord: Paul's words suggest that one of the purposes of Church discipline was to help the sinner become saved. The man's salvation, however, was neither assured nor immediate. His deed was so outrageous that it would take much for his soul to be changed and repentance to be achieved, and the buffetings of Satan[34] over time would do that.[35] Still, Paul held out hope that in "the day of the Lord" the sin could be forgiven and the soul saved from the second death (Rev. 2:11; 21:8; Jacob 3:11; Alma 12:16; Hel. 14:18–19; D&C 63:17; 76:37).

5:6 ***Your glorying is not good. / Your pride is not a good thing:*** The phrase οὐ καλόν (*ou kalon*), "not good," taken at face value, softens Paul's intent. His words, as shown by what he has previously said, actually expressed his deep shock at the depth of certain members' arrogance and misunderstanding.[36] The noun καύχημα (*kauchēma*), "boasting, glorying, pride in one's self," expressed the idea of placing very high value in something or someone.[37] Therefore, the idea is that their pride in themselves was ill-founded.[38]

---

32. Louw-Nida, §§26.9; 30.6; Hermann Kleinknecht, Friedrich Baumgärtel, Werner Bieder, Erik Sjöberg, and Eduard Schweizer, "πνεῦμα, πνευματικός, πνέω, ἐκπνέω, θεόπνευστος," in *TDNT*, 6:332–451.

33. James T. South, *Disciplinary Practices in Pauline Texts* (Lewiston, N.Y.: Mellen Biblical Press, 1992), 43, but compare 44–71. For an exhaustive discussion of various views of this verse, see Thiselton, *First Epistle*, 392–400.

34. See D&C 78:12; 82:21; 104:9–10; 132:26.

35. For the idea in Paul that affliction can be a benefit to the soul, see 9:27; 11:30–33; 2 Cor. 4:16–17; 12:7.

36. Thiselton, *First Epistle*, 400.

37. Louw-Nida, §33; BDAG, 536.

38. Thus, the translation in the NJB.

***Know ye not that a little leaven leaveneth the whole lump? / Don't you
understand that a little yeast can leaven a whole batch of dough?:*** The
phrase οὐκ οἴδατε ὅτι (*ouk oidate hoti*), "do you not know that," occurs
ten times in this epistle (3:16; 5:6; 6:2, 3, 9, 15, 17; 9:13, 24) and only once
outside it (Rom. 6:16). That is understandable given that it served a good,
if biting, purpose explicitly for the problems at hand. These pride-filled
people claimed to have superior "wisdom." The Apostle's questions were
designed to highlight what such wise persons were supposed to know if,
indeed, their theology were correct. What the questions actually did was
expose the falseness of these members' position and the wrongness of their
actions.[39] The Apostle's questions pointed to maxims, proverbs, or metaphors commonly accepted in the Church, whether based on scripture or
custom that should have been well-known to all members.

The noun ζύμη (*zymē*) referred to fermented dough, not yeast; that
product was unknown to the New Testament world.[40] The metaphor of
"leaven" emphasized the penetrating and influential effects of something
that seemed small, perhaps even irrelevant, but which should not—indeed,
could not—be ignored for fear of deadly contamination.[41]

**5:7 *Purge out therefore the old leaven, that ye may be a new lump, as ye
are unleavened / Purge out the old yeast so you can become a new batch
of dough, as indeed you are unleavened:*** The verb ἐκκαθαίρω (*ekkathairō*),
"purge, clean out," denoted getting rid of that which was unclean in both a
cultic and physical sense, but the verb also carried the idea of a thorough
cleansing.[42] The noun φύρημα (*phyrēma*), "batch, loaf," denoted anything
that was kneaded or mixed together, including potters clay and bread
dough.[43] Here Paul had reference to dough.

Bread was leavened by taking a bit of one batch and letting it ferment
and then adding it to the next batch. The practice did have a downside in
that the fermented piece could become tainted over time with unfortunate results. The Israelite practice at Passover of purging their homes of
all leavened materials militated against this concern by forcing the whole

---

39. Hurd, *Origin*, 77.

40. BDAG, 429.

41. The Lord used the metaphor in this way. See Mark 8:15; Luke 12:1. He did use the
metaphor in a positive way in Matt. 13:13. Fee, *First Epistle*, 216.

42. BDAG, 303; Findlay, "St. Paul's First Epistle," 810; Friedrich Hauck, "ἐκκαθαίρω,"
in *TDNT*, 3:430.

43. BDAG, 1069.

congregation to begin bread making anew.[44] Thus, the new dough was totally uncontaminated and fresh.

The phrase καθώς ἐστε ἄζυμοι (*kathōs este azymoi*) and the adverb *kathōs* could be translated at least two ways: "just as" (comparison) or "since" (causal). Our Rendition has "as indeed you are unleavened" since "as" in English can have a comparative or causal sense. What Paul is saying is that through the Atonement of Christ, they are already leaven free, but to retain that condition, they must purge out the leaven, which is the man guilty of sexual immorality. If they do not, they are in danger of becoming contaminated by him.

For even Christ our passover is sacrificed for us / For even Christ, our Passover Lamb, has been sacrificed for us: Continuing with the Passover symbolism, Paul explained that Christ was the Passover Lamb that had been sacrificed for all. The noun πάσχα (*pascha*) comes from the Aramaic פַּסְחָא (*pashā'*), "the Passover," which in turn derives from the original Hebrew פֶּסַח (*pesah*). It designated either the Passover feast itself or the lamb sacrificed to observe the Passover.[45] Here Paul's word clearly referred to the lamb and is so translated in our Rendition. With these words, Paul bore witness to the reality of the Savior's Atonement.

5:8 ***Therefore let us keep the feast / And so let us celebrate the festival:*** Paul's words suggest the Passover feast, which was also known as "the feast of unleavened bread" (Lev. 23:6), was near at hand. If not, he was certainly taking inferences from it. Before that holiday began, all leavened bread and dough were removed from the household, and only unleavened bread was eaten for the duration of the festival.

The conjunction ὥστε (*hōste*), "therefore, so," provided Paul's moral corollary. Coupled with the hortatory subjunctive ἑορτάζωμεν (*heortazōmen*), "let us celebrate a festival," he was telling his readers that, because Christ died for them, they were obliged to celebrate the old holiday, but—and this is the point—in a new way.[46]

not with old leaven, neither with the leaven of malice and wickedness; but with the unleavened bread of sincerity and truth / not with the old yeast, the yeast of evil and wickedness, but with the unleavened bread of pure intent and truth: Paul's readers were not to be concerned with real leaven as were their Jewish brothers, but with what these symbolized,

44. Fee, *First Epistle,* 216.
45. BDAG, 784.
46. Fitzmyer, *First Corinthians,* 242.

namely, κακία (*kakia*) and πονηρία (*ponēria*). The former denoted a state of sin of such depth that it was harmful, depraved, and, therefore, disastrous. Because the noun also connoted a willful contravention of moral laws, it is translated as "evil" in our Rendition.[47] The latter term referred to the nature of individuals who lacked all social and moral values but it added the sense of an active opposition to that which was proper and good.[48] Thus, it is translated as "wickedness" in our Rendition.

It is interesting that Paul did not want old leaven replaced with new. Rather, he wanted the body of the Church to remain leaven-free. Any idea, teaching, or attitude that would ferment immorality or evil was to have no place.[49] Only in that way could the Church guard against recontamination. In place of the old tainted loaf, Paul wanted leaven-free bread composed of εἰλικρίνεια (*eilikrineia*) and ἀλήθεια (*alētheia*). The former denoted the state of purity of motive free from all dissimulation and self-serving and is, thus, translated as "pure intent" in our Rendition.[50] The latter referred to a state of being in accord with all that is true. Such synonyms as "dependable, upright, truthful" work, but since it connotes "the avoidance of error, misrepresentation, or falsehood," the simple but powerful word "truth" is used in our Rendition.[51]

Analysis and Summary

Paul's writings in this section show how he responded when an absolute standard was at play. Later in this epistle we will see how he responded to circumstances of a more situational nature. His position on immoral practices stood on eternal absolutes that reached beyond situational circumstances and variables. On these rules, Paul was not willing to even consider dialogue. That was not the case on situational issues. We see his response to these in chapters 7–11, where he showed the legitimate nature of some "situational ethic" that must take into account the circumstances being met at that moment. There he was willing to negotiate, dialogue, and even explore "What if . . . ?" questions. His willingness to combine a situational ethic with an absolutist stand reveals his skill when making pastoral

---

47. BDAG, 500; Louw-Nida, §88.105; Walter Grundmann, "ἄκακος," in *TDNT*, 3:482–84; *Dictionary of Synonyms*, 82, s.v. "bad."

48. BDAG, 851; Louw-Nida, §88.109; Günther Harder, "πονηρία," in *TDNT*, 6:562–66; *Dictionary of Synonyms*, 416–17, s.v. "immoral."

49. Thiselton, *First Epistle*, 406.

50. BDAG, 282; Friedrich Büchsel, "εἰλικρινής, εἰλικρίνεια," in *TDNT*, 2:397–98.

51. BDAG, 42; *Dictionary of Synonyms*, 837, s.v. "truth."

judgments, showing his sensitivity to issues at hand that involve different kinds of cases.[52] A point that should not be missed, however, is that the response the Saints were to take on both absolute and situational cases was determined and put into perspective by one having divine authority.

There is no doubt that some in the Christian community at Corinth exhibited a flagrant disregard for both civil and religious law. This may have been generated by their belief that they lived on a new and higher plane that put them beyond the law because they were "kings" and ruled in their own right (4:8). Paul's concern, therefore, was with both the moral sin and the arrogance that condoned it. As one scholar noted, "A significant body of opinion in Corinth (compare 6:12ff.) thought that this was rather a fine assertion of Christian liberty, of emancipation from Jewish Law and Gentile convention alike."[53] These Saints seem to have thought that they possessed an enlightened tolerance. Unfortunately, their attitude encouraged feelings of smugness and superiority that worked against any sense that they were wrong.[54]

So concerned was Paul with this situation that he used his full apostolic powers to judge a man guilty of committing an immoral act of such odious nature that even the very liberal gentile inhabitants of Corinth found disgusting. Paul's phrase κέκρικα ὡς παρών (*kekrika hōs parōn*), "I have judged as being present" (5:3), is very telling. Paul was not saying that he was judging as though he *were* present in a fictive sense. He was saying that, through the power of the Holy Ghost, he *is* present with them in a very real but spiritual way.[55] His words confirm the fact of a temporal reality in which he really was with them and, thus, could make a fair and accurate judgment.

In 5:4, Paul demanded that a disciplinary council be held, but under clear conditions. Because it was going to deal with a man's spiritual life, it was to function "with the Spirit" and through the "power of our Lord Jesus Christ" (JST 5:4). Under those conditions, both the Church and the individual would be fairly treated. Further, meeting these conditions assured that God's will would be done and the necessary discipline be administered. So it is today. In this connection, one LDS scholar asked and answered these pointed questions:

---

52. Thiselton, *First Epistle*, 381–82.

53. F. F. Bruce, *1 and 2 Corinthians* (London: Oliphants, 1971), 54.

54. Robertson and Plummer, *Critical and Exegetical Commentary*, 97.

55. Fee, *First Epistle*, 204.

Which churches today have a court system for serious transgressions? Which churches by their actions teach cheap forgiveness and repeated sin? In a half-dozen major places, Paul lists the sins that will keep one out of God's kingdom if unrepented, whether before or after conversion. Included are the major sins of dishonesty and physically or verbally harming one's fellowmen. And such lists never fail to include sexual relations outside of marriage. If God will really exclude the unrepentant on that basis, how honest is a church with its members if it will not? The false prophet is one who teaches a false expectation. The integrity of the Early Church and the restored Church is shown in their discipline of immorality in wise but firm court decisions on membership.[56]

Paul made it absolutely clear what the decision of the council would be: delivery of the man "unto Satan for the destruction of the flesh" (5:5). Elder Joseph Fielding Smith once addressed the principle behind Paul's demand. He stated,

> Man may commit certain grievous sins—according to his light and knowledge—that will place him beyond the reach of the atoning blood of Christ. If then he would be saved, he must make sacrifice of his own life to atone—so far as in his power lies—for that sin, for the blood of Christ alone under certain circumstances will not avail. . . . Joseph Smith taught that there were certain sins so grievous that man may commit, that they will place the transgressors beyond the power of the atonement of Christ. If these offenses are committed, then the blood of Christ will not cleanse them from their sins even though they repent. Therefore their only hope is to have their own blood shed to atone, as far as possible, in their behalf.[57]

He went on to say that "to be 'destroyed in the flesh' means exactly that. We cannot destroy men in the flesh, because we do not control the lives of men and do not have power to pass sentences upon them which involve capital punishment. In the days when there was a theocracy on the earth, then this decree was enforced [Gen. 9:4–6; Lev. 20:10]. What the Lord will do in lieu of this because we cannot destroy in the flesh, I am unable to say, but it will have to be made up in some other way."[58]

Some of the Corinthian leaders, due to their arrogance and misunderstanding of the doctrine, as noted above, were willing to give the man a

---

56. Anderson, *Understanding Paul,* 103.

57. Joseph Fielding Smith, quoted in McConkie, *Doctrines of Salvation,* 1:134–35.

58. Joseph Fielding Smith, quoted in McConkie, *Doctrines of Salvation,* 2:96–97; brackets in original. Compare *HC,* 5:391–92.

pass. That stand, however, was dangerously wrong, not only for the Church but for the man himself. According to Elder Orson Pratt,

> The apostle, knowing the great magnitude of the crime, decided by the spirit of inspiration quite otherwise; therefore he commanded them, saying, "In the name of our Lord Jesus Christ, when ye are gathered together, and my spirit with the power of our Lord Jesus Christ to deliver such an one unto Satan for the destruction of the flesh that the spirit may be saved in the day of the Lord, Jesus." (Verses 4, 5.) Here, then, we perceive the penalty to be inflicted for this particular transgression: first, a deliverance unto Satan; second, a destruction of the flesh; and third, no salvation for the spirit until the day of the Lord Jesus. The wisdom of man would have been entirely at a loss how to have rendered a correct judgment concerning this matter therefore it required the wisdom of God by revelation. The Corinthians themselves seem to have been ignorant of their duty on this subject; for Paul says to them, "Ye are puffed up and have not rather mourned, that he that hath done this deed might be taken away from among you." (Verse 2.) Oh! How different are the decisions of the Spirit from the decisions of fallible man![59]

The problem still remains concerning exactly what Paul had in mind when he demanded "the destruction of the flesh" since the Church in his day had no more power to execute someone than the Church today. It is very unlikely that he was demanding that the elders break civil law to punish a man who had broken civil as well as religious law. The answer may lie in how Paul visualized the work of Satan in this instance. This may also answer the question of how the Lord can make up for the inability to the Church to exercise capital punishment.

As Paul's words read, the devil was to be the executor in destroying the man's flesh. The adversary had been given power to bruise man's heel (Gen. 3:15); however, he does not have power to destroy bodies. On the other hand, he does have power to torment human beings both in this world and the world to come. Therefore, the destruction of the flesh likely referred to a change in a person's mortal nature that would result from the devil's incessant and excruciating torment. Through this means, ideally, stubbornness and rebelliousness, a result from being far away from God, would be purged from the soul and the door to a sincere and complete repentance opened. We are reminded of the conversion of Alma the Younger, who

---

59. Orson Pratt, *Divine Authenticity of the Book of Mormon,* pamphlets 1–6 (Liverpool: printed by R. James, 1850–51), 28–29.

because of sin was "racked, even with the pains of a damned soul." His torment went on for three days until he finally cried to the Lord, begging that the Savior would "have mercy on me, who am in the gall of bitterness, and am encircled about by the everlasting chains of death" (Alma 36:16–18). Only then did pain cease and forgiveness come. For some particularly hardened souls, such humility and repentance may require being turned over to the "buffetings of Satan" for a substantial period (see D&C 78:12; 82:21; 104:9–10; 132:26).

Concerning the "buffetings of Satan," one LDS scholar noted, "To the Prophet Joseph Smith the Lord revealed the situation of some who had broken the covenants by which they had entered the United Order. That revelation reads, 'The soul that sins against this covenant, and hardeneth his heart against it, shall be dealt with according to the laws of my church, and shall be delivered over to the buffetings of Satan until the day of redemption (D&C 82:20–21).'" He went on to say that "an individual who receives extensive spiritual knowledge, enters into sacred covenants, and then turns away from those promises to the Lord may be left to the buffetings of Satan until complete repentance has occurred."[60] That is an important point. The buffetings are not an end in themselves, but the means of saving an otherwise sinful and hardened soul. Persons can be changed, but for some, the conditions require an unimaginable severity. Elder McConkie, explained that to be "turned over to the buffetings of Satan is to be given into [Satan's] hands; it is to be turned over to him with all the protective power of the priesthood, of righteousness, and of godliness removed, so that Lucifer is free to torment, persecute, and afflict such a person without let or hindrance. When the bars are down, the cuffs and curses of Satan, both in this world and in the world to come, bring indescribable anguish typified by burning fire and brimstone. The damned in hell so suffer."[61] When, however, the spirit of rebellion and sin have been beaten out of these souls and have been replaced by humility and an acceptance of the grace of Christ, then, "in the day of the Lord," the door to Telestial glory will open.

Paul's reprimand in 5:6, that in which they prided themselves was ill-founded, points to the false but seductive belief promoted by some Corinthian Saints that Jesus' death had freed them from the constraints of all law. As a result, they wrongly believed that nothing was forbidden them.[62]

---

60. Dennis D. Flake, "Buffetings of Satan," in *EM*, 1:236.

61. McConkie, *Mormon Doctrine*, 108.

62. This idea will be developed more fully at 6:12.

Their arrogance and pride forced them to maintain their belief system even though it meant defending the incestuous actions of the immoral man. Paul blasted their doctrine not only for being false but also as ill-founded, meaning that its basis was evil or malevolent.

His use of the metaphor of leaven in 5:7 emphasized that what might seem insignificant to certain Corinthian Saints was actually deadly on at least two levels. First, the idea itself was so virulent that it had the potential of corrupting the whole body of Church doctrine. Second, harboring the man tainted the reputation of the Church community as a whole and could bring not only disgrace upon it but also disastrous consequences, including its corporate destruction.[63] Therefore, immediate action had to be taken.[64]

To save the Church, the infected leaven had to be completely purged for, as Paul's symbol shows, it could infuse and poison the whole. Paul's list of inappropriate behaviors in 6:9–11 suggests that the symbol of leaven did not refer to the man, but to the false beliefs that upheld the man's behavior.[65] Paul's push was, therefore, threefold; first, excommunicate the man, thus freeing the Church from any suspicion by those "outside" that it condoned such behavior; second, get rid of the false and pernicious doctrine that supported it; and third, destroy the prideful arrogance that upheld it. In this way, the old leaven would be purged. Further, no new leaven was to be introduced. The Church was to be kept from anything that could contaminate and corrupt its doctrine.

In place of the old leavened bread, Paul wanted a new leaven-free loaf composed of purity of motive and absolute conformity to doctrinal truths. These characteristics nicely summarized the obligations necessitated by being a Christian.[66] The Saints' motives were to be pure, not driven by pride, arrogance, or profit, and they were to adhere to truth and avoid the self-deception that had led some to accept gross and dangerous ideas. All pride and arrogance were to be purged out. In this way, the vice that fed so many of the Church's problems would be destroyed.

---

63. Findlay, "St. Paul's First Epistle," 809; Thiselton, *First Epistle*, 401.

64. Gerald Harris, "The Beginnings of Church Discipline: 1 Cor. 5," *New Testament Studies* 37 (1991): 3–9; Hildagard Himmelweit, "Deviant Behavior," in *A Dictionary of Social Sciences*, ed. Julius Gould and William L. Kolb (New York: Free Press, 1964), 196–97.

65. Bruce R. McConkie, *The Mortal Messiah*, 4 vols. (Salt Lake City: Deseret Book, 1979), 1:164, notes that these people had partaken too much of the spirit of the world and it affected their conduct and how they viewed the gospel.

66. Thiselton, *First Epistle*, 406–7.

At the heart of Paul's admonition was the need to adhere to the pure doctrine of the kingdom again centered on the implications and ramifications of "Christ, and him crucified" (2:2). Indeed, as Paul noted, "Christ, our Passover Lamb, has been sacrificed for us" (5:7, Rendition). The noble purpose of that sacrifice, keeping with Paul's imagery, was to make the Saints an unleavened loaf, that is, one free of false doctrines and false practices. The end result was the salvation of both the Church and the individual. By that means, the Church would not fear destruction and the member, death. As President Boyd K. Packer taught, "It is not from mortal death that we shall be spared in such a passover if we walk in obedience to these commandments, for each of us in time shall die. But there is spiritual death which you need not suffer. If you are obedient, that spiritual death will pass over you, for 'Christ our passover is sacrificed for us,' the revelation teaches (1 Cor. 5:7)."[67]

DEALING WITH GENERAL IMMORALITY (5:9–13)

Greek Text

9 Ἔγραψα ὑμῖν ἐν τῇ ἐπιστολῇ μὴ συναναμίγνυσθαι πόρνοις, 10 οὐ πάντως τοῖς πόρνοις τοῦ κόσμου τούτου ἢ τοῖς πλεονέκταις καὶ ἅρπαξιν ἢ εἰδωλολάτραις, ἐπεὶ ὠφείλετε ἄρα ἐκ τοῦ κόσμου ἐξελθεῖν. 11 νῦν δὲ ἔγραψα ὑμῖν μὴ συναναμίγνυσθαι ἐάν τις ἀδελφὸς ὀνομαζόμενος ᾖ πόρνος ἢ πλεονέκτης ἢ εἰδωλολάτρης ἢ λοίδορος ἢ μέθυσος ἢ ἅρπαξ, τῷ τοιούτῳ μηδὲ συνεσθίειν. 12 τί γάρ μοι τοὺς ἔξω κρίνειν; οὐχὶ τοὺς ἔσω ὑμεῖς κρίνετε, 13 τοὺς δὲ ἔξω ὁ θεὸς κρίνει; ἐξάρατε τὸν πονηρὸν ἐξ ὑμῶν αὐτῶν. [SBLGNT]

King James Version

9 I wrote unto you in an epistle not to company with fornicators: 10 Yet not altogether with the fornicators of this world, or with the covetous, or extortioners, or with idolaters; for then must ye needs go out of the world. 11 But now I have written unto you not to keep company, if any man that is called a

New Rendition

9 I wrote to you in my (previous) letter not to associate with sexually immoral people. 10 By no means did I mean the immoral people of this world or the greedy or swindlers or idolaters, since you would then need to depart this world. 11 But I am now writing to you not to associate with anyone who is a

---

67. Boyd K. Packer, "The Word of Wisdom: The Principle and the Promises," *Ensign* 26 (May 1996): 19.

brother be a fornicator, or covetous, or an idolater, or a railer, or a drunkard, or an extortioner; with such an one no not to eat. 12 For what have I to do to judge them also that are without? do not ye judge them that are within? 13 But them that are without God judgeth. Therefore put away from among yourselves that wicked person.

member, who is sexually immoral or greedy or idolatrous or verbally abusive or a drunkard or a swindler. Don't even eat with such a person. 12 For what business of mine is it to judge people outside the church? Isn't it those within the church that you are supposed to judge? 13 Doesn't God judge those outside the church? Drive out the wicked person from among you.

Translation Notes and Comments

5:9 *I wrote unto you in an epistle / I wrote to you in my (previous) letter:* Paul here referred to a previous letter he had written to the Saints at Corinth, which, unfortunately, has not been preserved. It is of note that "Paul wrote letters, in addition to those we have in our Bible, and speaks of them. He wrote a third letter to the Corinthians (1 Cor. 5:9) and at least another one to the Ephesians (Eph. 3:3). Where are they? He also wrote an Epistle to the Laodiceans (Col. 4:16), but it is not in our possession. Is the Bible then complete? Does it contain all of God's word?" The obvious answer is no.[68]

not to company with fornicators / not to associate with sexually immoral people: The verb συναναμίγνυσθαι (*synanamignysthai*) meant "to mingle, accompany, or associate with" and implied some kind "of reciprocal relationship or involvement."[69] As noted above, the noun πόρνος (*pornos*) referred to sexually immoral people. Paul's words show that he was very upset with these people because he had already made the Church's position clear—the Saints were to have no camaraderie whatsoever with "a brother," (that is, a member of the Church) who refused to live the moral law. In short, any *close* association was to be avoided. On the other hand, such people were not to be treated as enemies either.[70] The Church's posture was to be one of cautious distance but not ostracism, unless the offender, refusing to repent, continued in his salacious ways.

---

68. Mark E. Petersen, in CR, April 1964, 18.

69. BDAG, 965; Louw-Nida, §34.1; Heinrich Greeven, "συναναμείγνυμι," in *TDNT*, 7:852–55; Paul also used the term in 2 Thes. 3:14, where it carries the idea of inclusion. Thus, here it would mean to exclude. See *LSJ*, 1, 474.

70. Fee, *First Epistle*, 222. Some translators see the negation as qualifying the adverb only. For example, see REB 1 Cor. 5:10; and Fee, *First Epistle*, 223. But the sense seems to be that Paul was referring to more than those in the Church.

5:10 Yet not altogether with the fornicators of this world, or with the covetous, or extortioners, or with idolaters / By no means did I mean the immoral people of this world or the greedy or swindlers or idolaters: Paul's opening phrase οὐ πάντως (*ou pantōs*), "not wholly" or "not entirely," qualified his former injunction. Because the negative οὐ (*ou*), "not," negates "the whole concept expressed in the clause," the whole phrase is translated in our Rendition as "By no means did I mean."[71] His words clarified for his readers that his prohibition referred only to those within the Church.

In this phrase, Paul added three more kinds of people Church members needed to be wary of: πλεονέκτης (*pleonektēs*), ἅρπαξ (*harpax*), and εἰδωλολάτρης (*eidōlolatrēs*). The first were those who desired more than their due, that is, "greedy and grasping" people.[72] The second were those who had a rapacious desire for other people's goods, that is, "swindlers and extortionists."[73] The final were those who worshiped false gods, that is, idolaters.[74]

for then must ye needs go out of the world / since you would then need to depart this world: Here Paul used hyperbole, if not sarcasm, to make his point: in a world of such wickedness as Corinth, the only way to avoid association with bad people was to leave, likely by dying. There were, of course, less drastic ways to achieve that. One was to follow those like the Qumran community, who more or less walled themselves off from the outside world. Paul's words, however, militated against any action of physical separation. The Christians were not to follow such a monastic practice. Christians were to work out their salvation within the context of and challenges presented by the world, not by withdrawing from it but by overcoming it.

5:11 But now I have written unto you not to keep company, if any man that is called a brother / But I am now writing to you not to associate with anyone who is a member: The Greek noun ἀδελφός (*adelphos*), "brother," generally referred to a male sibling, but it also denoted a member of a community and, therefore, the terms "fellow member" or "associate" work.[75] Since Paul was referring to those in the Christian community at large, our Rendition translates the word as "member." While of necessity Christians must have contact with wicked people in this world, Paul was instructing

---

71. Thiselton, *First Epistle*, 410.

72. BDAG, 824.

73. BDAG, 134. These stand in contrast to the λῃστής (*lēstēs*), that is, the robber—meaning one who uses force or the threat of force to commit his crimes.

74. BDAG, 280.

75. BDAG, 18; Hans Freiherr von Soden, "ἀδελφός, ἀδελφή, ἀδελφότης, φιλάδελφος, φιλαδελφία, ψευδάδελφος," in *TDNT*, 1:144–46.

the Saints to avoid close association with those people who were members of Christ's Church but, nevertheless, continued in serious, even blatant sin.

a fornicator, or covetous, or an idolater, or a railer, or a drunkard, or an extortioner / sexually immoral or greedy or idolatrous or verbally abusive or a drunkard or a swindler: To the list of those to avoid, Paul adds two more: the λοίδορος (*loidoros*) and the μέθυσος (*methysos*). The former described abusive persons who slandered others,[76] while the latter described those who were drunkards.[77]

with such an one no not to eat / Don't even eat with such a person: Paul's prohibition here likely reflected the practice of the early Church of having a dinner as part of the sacrament service. His instructions forbade anyone from having the incestuous man attend these meetings.

5:12 *For what have I to do to judge them also that are without? / For what business of mine is it to judge people outside the church?:* The highly idiomatic phrase τί γάρ μοι (*ti gar moi*), literally "for what [is it] to me," is best translated with the English idiom, "For what business is it of mine"[78] as in our Rendition. Paul's stewardship and responsibility to judge were restricted to members of the Church—those who have received and understood the gospel message. This may be why he made no mention of the woman involved in this sordid affair. She, likely, was not a member of the Church. Therefore, any action brought against her would have to come by civil, not ecclesiastical, authority.

The verb κρίνω (*krinō*), "to judge," also carried the nuance of bringing a verdict against another.[79] Paul's point was that the Church's responsibility was to take care of itself and maintain its own order and to judge only those within its specific domain. Because, however, the Church did act within the larger context of society, self-protection against the encroachment of the world into the religious sphere was to be maintained.

do not ye judge them that are within? / Isn't it those within the church that you are supposed to judge?: The presiding officials of the Church in Corinth had the responsibility of passing judgment on the members of their congregation and taking care of the internal affairs of the kingdom. Paul's question defined the limits of ecclesiastical authority. That authority did not extend beyond the steps of the Church.

---

76. BDAG, 602; Louw-Nida, §33.395.
77. BDAG, 626.
78. Thiselton, *First Epistle*, 416.
79. Louw-Nida, §56.30.

The JST adds an interesting insight here. It reads "do not *they* judge them that are within?" The question suggests that, though the Christians were careful not to judge those outside, that courtesy was not being reciprocated, and the Church found itself having to defend itself against detractors. This condition may have arisen because of those defending the incestuous man.

5:13 *But them that are without God judgeth / Doesn't God judge those outside the church?:* Paul's point was that all will be judged. Just because there were those who were "outside" the jurisdiction of the Church did not mean they got a free pass when it came to being judged for their actions. It was, however, God who would pronounce judgment on these. All must account for their lifestyles, but it was not the responsibility of the Church to impose its house rules upon them. The Lord would judge them upon the standard of light and truth that they had and how they responded thereto (2 Ne. 9:15; Alma 12:27; D&C 42:32; 101:78).

Therefore put away from among yourselves that wicked person / Drive out the wicked person from among you: The force of the imperative ἐξάρατε (*exarate*), "exclude," is enhanced by Paul's use of the prefix ἐξ- (*ex-*), "out of, from," and, therefore, carried the idea of "rooting out, banishing," or "driving out."[80] Our Rendition, to catch the force of Paul's command, uses the latter verb. Paul's words reflect several passages in Deuteronomy where the Lord commands that evil people be removed from the community of Israel (Deut. 17:7; 19:19; 22:21, 24; 24:7). Members of the Church who committed serious sin were to be dealt with in a disciplinary council and, if unrepentant, were to be excommunicated.

Analysis and Summary

Despite the abrupt reference to the command he had given in a former letter in which he told the Saints not to associate with immoral people (5:9), Paul was not introducing different subject matter in this new paragraph. He was still concerned about these people's pride and their sustaining the incestuous man. He used the quote from his former letter, therefore, to reinforce his present position by showing that it was not new. Indeed, branch members should have known his stance already and followed it. His words show that he remained insistent that the fornicator be "driven out" of the company of Saints. "Verse 11 appears to preserve a specific reference

---

80. BDAG, 344; Thiselton, *First Epistle,* 417.

to eating with the Saints at sacrament meeting with instruction that the man in question was to be excluded from doing so."[81]

President N. Eldon Tanner made Paul's counsel current by teaching that Latter-day Saints, especially the youth, should never associate with those whose standards are low. He quoted President Spencer W. Kimball, who admonished the youth to "always keep good company, to never be found with those who tend to lower their standards! We must repeat what we have said many times: Fornication with all its accompanying sins, great and small, was evil and wholly condemned by the Lord in Adam's day, in Moses' day, in Paul's day, and [today]. The Church has no tolerance for any kind of perversions."[82]

The Greek term πορνεία (*porneia*) is probably derived from πόρνημι (*pornēmi*), "to sell."[83] Thus, a πόρνη (*pornē*) was a woman for hire, that is, a prostitute. In the classical world, the word-group referred only to harlots and prostitution.[84] This was not the case, however, among Jews and later among Christians. The Diaspora Jews, who translated the Hebrew Bible into Greek, adopted the words cognate with πόρνη (*pornē*) to translate זָנָה (*zānāh*) and its cognates. This set of words denoted all kinds of immorality, including adultery, but emphasized prostitution. By the second century BC, however, the Jews had diminished the particular emphasis on prostitution and broadened πορνεία (*porneia*) to include all forms of extramarital sexual relations. The Christians took over this meaning and, in the New Testament, we find a hard and unconditional repudiation of all extramarital and unnatural immoral acts.[85]

---

81. Holzapfel and Wayment, *Making Sense,* 350.

82. N. Eldon Tanner, "The Purpose of Conferences," *Ensign* 6 (November 1976): 82.

83. LSJ, 1450.

84. Cultic prostitution (widespread in Asia Minor) carried no stigma since this debased religion required that most girls give their virginity to the gods. The same is true of hierodules, or temple prostitutes, whose wages went to the gods. But this did not carry over into Judaism. See Friedrich Hauck and Siegfried Schulz, "πόρνη, πόρνος, πορνεία, πορνεύω, εκπορνευω," in *TDNT,* 6:579–95.

85. Friedrich Hauck and Siegfried Schulz, "πόρνη, πόρνος, πορνεία, πορνεύω, εκπορνευω," in *TDNT,* 6:579–95. The word πορνεία (*porneia*) differs from adultery in some uses. Note that Matt. 15:19 lists both fornication and adultery as offenses against God (see also Mark 7:21). Though 6:15–16 and Rom. 1:29; 9:21 include all sexual sins, the word generally denoted lewdness, illicit sex between unmarried partners, and whoredom. Verses 6:13, 19 look specifically at prostitution. Gal. 5:19, 21 show it companies with adultery, uncleanness, and licentiousness. Eph. 5:3 states that, like uncleanness and covetousness, it should not exist among the Saints. Col. 3:5 lists it with uncleanness and insists that it, with other gross vices, must be put to death. All these show the meaning of the word

The Lord warned that the evil "which cometh out of a man, that defileth the man." He specified particularly adultery, fornication, and lasciviousness. The reason they were so defiling, he said, was because "these evil things come from within" (Mark 7:20–23). They exposed the heart and soul of the doer. Therefore, Paul admonished his readers to "flee fornication" (6:18).

The Apostle stressed the incompatibility of *porneia* with the kingdom of God. For him such acts unmasked a person who has apostatized from the Savior. No πόρνος (*pornos*), therefore, could have any part in God's kingdom (see 6:9; Eph. 5:5). Church leaders, Paul instructed, were duty bound to keep the Church free from such sins by cutting off the unrepentant person (see 5:1; Heb. 12:14–16). Members themselves were to have nothing to do with those who refused to repent from *porneia* (see 5:13). The Church had to excommunicate such people because a man not only shamed his own body but also brought blame upon the Church—the very temple of God (see 6:19). Unrepentant fornicators also jeopardized the operation of the Spirit of God within the Church (see 3:16–17) because licentiousness expressed the unbridled passions of the flesh (Gal. 5:19) and, therefore, was opposed to the work of the Holy Spirit (Gal. 5:22).

Some have suggested that the New Testament shows a softening attitude toward *porneia*. Such is not the case. It is true that the Lord invited publicans and sinners into his fold, and those included harlots. However, he did this—and this is the point that is often overlooked—only on condition of repentance. The *porneia* must be over, for it was at heart an anti-God state of mind that excluded the person from fellowship (see Matt. 15:18–19).

In sum, as with adultery, the New Testament heightened the Old Testament prohibition on fornication, making the sin not only a physical act but also a state of heart. Those whose lives and hearts were set on *porneia* polluted the body of Christ and had to be cut off for the sake of the holiness of the Church. Nothing less would do, for to compromise was to destroy the communal body of the Saints.

Again, Restoration scripture follows the New Testament lead. The Book of Mormon prohibits fornication outright (see Jacob 3:12) with God insisting that "whoredoms are an abomination before me" (Jacob 2:28). In this

---

is very broad and (though it can include uncleanness, licentiousness, adultery) it can also stand apart from them to include sexual sins they do not, for example, incest, pederasty, and homosexuality. See Rousas John Rushdoony, *Institutes of Biblical Law* (Phillipsburg, N.J.: P and R Publishing, 1980), 407.

connection, Mormon ascribes the destruction of many Nephites to the murders and fornications that were so rampant among them (Hel. 8:26). No Book of Mormon prophet was more clear on the depth of the sin than was Alma. To his prodigal son, Corianton, Alma asked, "Know ye not my son, that these things are an abomination in the sight of the Lord; yea, most abominable above all sins save it be the shedding of innocent blood or denying the Holy Ghost?" (Alma 39:5). As the Lord's prophet, Alma clearly viewed fornication as among the worst of sins.

The Doctrine and Covenants contains little on the sin. Even so, it prohibits admitting anyone guilty of fornication into the Church unless "they shall repent of all their sins" (D&C 42:77); that is, they must change not only their actions but their hearts as well.

Paul did have to refine his instructions concerning avoiding association with the *pornois* to those who belonged to the Church. So flagrant was immorality in Corinth that the only way one could avoid not associating with the immoral in daily interactions was to either move or die. As Elder McConkie notes: "Here he qualifies his previous command. What he intended to forbid was the fellowshipping of such persons in the Church. They should be handled for their membership, unless of course they repent. Now also he extends his instructions to include members of the Church who are covetous, idolaters, railers, drunkards, or extortioners. Manifestly, he explains, to avoid all such who are in the world, would require us to 'go out of the world' itself."[86]

Paul drew upon his beloved Old Testament, especially Deuteronomy, and his Jewish background to set the moral standard for the Christians. These standards allowed the Church to offset conditions the Saints faced daily in Corinth. Paul's instructions in 5:10 provide a window into the members' challenges. They were confronted by grasping people who wanted more than they had—more wealth, more power, more prestige, more social status. There were also those willing to practice extortion, that is, the use of illicit means, in the form of either commodities or services, "in such a way to gain speedy and disproportionate wealth at the expense of others."[87] The general aim of this misplaced and malicious entrepreneurial spirit was likely social status and influence. Finally, there were the idolaters, which included nearly everyone in the city. A major problem with idolatry was its total lack of a moral base. It offered nothing to mollify the propensities of

---

86. *DNTC*, 2:336.
87. Thiselton, *First Epistle*, 411; italics in original removed.

"the natural man" (2:14), which drove the spiritually debilitating conditions in the Roman city. In 5:11, Paul added to the list slanderers, those willing to gossip, lie, or use any other verbal means to cut others down that they might advance. He also added drunkards. The nuance of the word points more to the abusive and shameful behavior of a person under the influence of alcohol than to the state of inebriation itself.[88]

In a society where these vices dominated, righteousness, service, and self-sacrifice were not only foreign but also despised values. Those Christians who were "puffed up" found it hard to resist the prevailing attitudes and goals concerning status and prestige. This weakness expressed itself in two ways. On the one hand, some were willing to let certain standards slip to gain acceptance while on the other hand some supported outrageous breaches of custom and law to show their superiority. It was, however, the avoidance of all vices that separated the Christian from his worldly counterparts and, therefore, members who refused to repent and conform to Church standards were not to be fellowshipped.[89]

Though this act may seem to contradict the actions of the Lord who freely ate and drank with sinners, there was a difference. He told those who complained of his actions that he did it as a means of calling "sinners to repentance" (Mark 2:15–17). His was a missionary effort and he accepted all who would hear him. In Paul's case, however, the focus was not on those investigating the gospel but on those already in the Church, that is, those who had been baptized and were under covenant to obey the Lord. To find fellowship in the Church, the Christians had to adhere to a very high standard.[90]

In 5:12, Paul asked two rhetorical questions designed to give his reasoning for the stand he championed in 5:9–11. These questions made it clear that the Apostle did not promote a physical separatism wherein the Saints would cloister themselves in their own communities. There was to be free association with those outside the Church. This free association, however, did not mean an abandonment of standards. Church administrators were fully free to judge those within the Church. The Apostle's point was that the Christian leadership had a strict responsibility to oversee Church matters but not those belonging to the Gentile community. For that reason, he

---

88. Fee, *First Epistle*, 225–26.

89. In his admonitions, Paul was following the Old Testament injunctions in dealing with such people. See Deut. 19:15–19; 21:20–21.

90. Fitzmyer, *First Corinthians*, 244.

refused to "judge" those outside the Church.[91] As two LDS scholars summarized, "Paul is saying that we should not do what gross sinners do, nor be influenced by them, nor spend time going to the places they frequent. We should admonish sinners and love them but stay away from their evil ways (see also 2 Thes. 3:14–15). Paul also says it is not his or the Church's business to judge and regulate the world but rather to keep the Church pure and leave the world to God."[92] It should be noted, however, that the Gentiles would face a judgment day, but that belonged to God alone.

In 5:13, Paul returned to the major point of this part of his epistle: what the branch should do about the incestuous man. To give his instruction some real punch, Paul used a wordplay. Up to this point he had referred to the immoral as πόρνοι (*pornoi*), "fornicators" (5:9–11), but here he referred to the incestuous man as πονηρός (*ponēros*), "an evil one." His words tied directly to those found in LXX Deuteronomy 17:7, wherein Israel was commanded to drive out the evil from among them. As it was in ancient Israel, so, too, it was to be in the meridian Church. The Christian community was to maintain its purity and spiritual separation from the world while still functioning within it by excommunicating all members who refused to live its standards.[93] As one LDS scholar noted, "Some politicians frequently place popularity over principle, disguising their compromises with noble words. So do some religious leaders who ignore, explain away, or dispense with the commandment of chastity as given through Moses and repeated by Christ and Paul and Joseph Smith in modern revelation. Another form of religious avoidance is teaching a standard of morality but looking the other way. The Early Church countered serious sexual transgression with action."[94]

This section of the epistle carries important implications for the Church today. First, it shows us that the Church has a right to impose its rules and standards of conduct upon its people. Militating against the attitude of many in today's "laissez-faire, consumerist culture," Paul's words confirm that being a part of the Christian community means that the Saints place themselves under the discipline of the Church and the standards it upholds.[95] Second, the right to impose rules stops at the Church's own front door. It

91. Fee, *First Epistle,* 227; Eldin Ricks, "A Short Glossary of Obsolete Words in the King James New Testament," *New Era* 7 (April 1977): 7.
92. Ogden and Skinner, *Verse by Verse,* 133.
93. Fitzmyer, *First Corinthians,* 244–45.
94. Anderson, *Understanding Paul,* 102.
95. Thiselton, *First Epistle,* 417.

does not have the right to force its standards on those outside. There is, however, a caveat: the Church does have a right to protect itself against incursions into its territory by the world. Because it operates in the world, it must maintain a voice in the public square. Whenever those "outside" seek to impose their will on those "inside," the Church is obligated to take a stand against them. That includes fighting against those who would try to silence its voice concerning moral issues that affect societal standards. The Church stands in the world and, therefore, has interest in and an obligation to that world. Though it cannot impose its will or standards on others, it is morally obligated to offer counterpoint and direction and to use its influence to promote and maintain a moral and spiritually healthy society.

One last point needs to be made. That Paul placed demands in which he invoked the name of the Lord on the Church leadership reinforced the reality of apostolic authority as superior to that of local authority. Later in this epistle, he will articulate that fact by stating that Christ had set some over the Church, "first apostles, secondarily prophets," with other officers following (12:28). Understanding this fact and knowing the importance of Church order, Paul did not hesitate to exercise his full authority and, in doing so, prevented a dilution of apostolic power.

Chapter 6

"Ye Are Bought with a Price"

INTRODUCTION

Paul, with absolute clarity, having articulated the principle that the Church was not to judge those "outside" but only those "inside" (specifically in the case of an incestuous man) now expands on it. The overarching theme in this section of his epistle continues to be that of Church order and discipline. He also continues to deal with institutional boundaries.[1] Though he had not finished with his explicit counsel against sexual matters (he will resume these later in this chapter in 6:12–20 and again in chapter 7), he turns to certain issues that deal with everyday life within the Christian community. The first major issue, and one that was apparently reported to him by the representatives of Chloe, was that some members of the Church, having grievances against others, were taking them to civil court (6:1–6). Just what the issue was is unstated, but given that chapters 5–7 deal with immoral practices by some members, it could be that the court case dealt with adultery.[2]

The action of these Christians was in direct violation to Church order and revealed a gross misunderstanding of Church procedure. Because of this, as one scholar noted, "Everything in this church, [was] in reverse order. If the church does not 'judge' those outside, neither does it go outside with inside affairs."[3] The result of such an action was a defeat for both sides of the controversy and for the Church at large, for it hurt the image of the institution and made the members look petty, avaricious, or vindictive.

---

1. Thiselton, *First Epistle*, 419.
2. See Peter Richardson, "Judgment in Sexual Matters in 1 Corinthians 6:1–11," *Novum Testamentum* 25 (1983): 37–58.
3. Fee, *First Epistle*, 228.

The Apostle insisted that the Church should be settling its own cases (6:3–5) but, more importantly, that the members should not be suing each other at all (6:7).[4]

Once again, the Apostle's indignation is clearly evident as he again blasts the whole community for its flippant attitude toward items that should be of greatest concern for all. With a series of very pointed questions (6:2–9), he levels his charges. His animus is fully revealed through his use of some of the most biting sarcasm in the whole epistle (6:5).[5]

Though this section bristles with a show of apostolic authority, it is less evident than in the previous chapters. Nonetheless, Paul's pointed counsel came backed by that authority as he identifies the major sources of his aggravation: first, with the Saints total lack of understanding of who they are and what it meant to be a Christian (6:2–4), and second, how their actions could undermine the force for good the Christian community is to have in the world (6:6).[6] It is this last point that is the central theme of the rest of this section. In it Paul identifies many of those sins that deprive one of a heavenly reward (6:8–11); the importance of propriety (6:12–14); and the need to escape from all sins, most especially sexual immorality (6:15–18). He concludes with a witness of each Saint's dependence upon Christ (6:19–20).

LAWSUITS AMONG BELIEVERS (6:1–8)

Greek Text

1 Τολμᾷ τις ὑμῶν πρᾶγμα ἔχων πρὸς τὸν ἕτερον κρίνεσθαι ἐπὶ τῶν ἀδίκων, καὶ οὐχὶ ἐπὶ τῶν ἁγίων; 2 ἢ οὐκ οἴδατε ὅτι οἱ ἅγιοι τὸν κόσμον κρινοῦσιν; καὶ εἰ ἐν ὑμῖν κρίνεται ὁ κόσμος, ἀνάξιοί ἐστε κριτηρίων ἐλαχίστων; 3 οὐκ οἴδατε ὅτι ἀγγέλους κρινοῦμεν, μήτιγε βιωτικά; 4 βιωτικὰ μὲν οὖν κριτήρια ἐὰν ἔχητε, τοὺς ἐξουθενη-μένους ἐν τῇ ἐκκλησίᾳ, τούτους καθίζετε; 5 πρὸς ἐντροπὴν ὑμῖν λέγω. οὕτως οὐκ ἔνι ἐν ὑμῖν οὐδεὶς σοφὸς ὃς δυνήσεται διακρῖναι ἀνὰ μέσον τοῦ ἀδελφοῦ αὐτοῦ, 6 ἀλλὰ ἀδελφὸς μετὰ ἀδελφοῦ κρίνεται, καὶ τοῦτο ἐπὶ ἀπίστων; 7 ἤδη μὲν οὖν ὅλως ἥττημα ὑμῖν ἐστιν ὅτι κρίματα ἔχετε μεθ᾽ ἑαυτῶν· διὰ τί οὐχὶ μᾶλλον ἀδικεῖ-σθε; διὰ τί οὐχὶ μᾶλλον ἀποστερεῖσθε; 8 ἀλλὰ ὑμεῖς ἀδικεῖτε καὶ ἀποστερεῖτε, καὶ τοῦτο ἀδελφούς. [SBLGNT]

---

4. Fitzmyer, *First Corinthians*, 248.

5. Fee, *First Epistle*, 229.

6. Fee, *First Epistle*, 229.

King James Version

1 Dare any of you, having a matter against another, go to law before the unjust, and not before the saints? 2 Do ye not know that the saints shall judge the world? and if the world shall be judged by you, are ye unworthy to judge the smallest matters? 3 Know ye not that we shall judge angels? how much more things that pertain to this life? 4 If then ye have judgments of things pertaining to this life, set them to judge who are least esteemed in the church. 5 I speak to your shame. Is it so, that there is not a wise man among you? no, not one that shall be able to judge between his brethren? 6 But brother goeth to law with brother, and that before the unbelievers. 7 Now therefore there is utterly a fault among you, because ye go to law one with another. Why do ye not rather take wrong? why do ye not rather suffer yourselves to be defrauded? 8 Nay, ye do wrong, and defraud, and that your brethren.

New Rendition

1 If any of you have a legal dispute with another, how do you have the effrontery to bring yourselves to take the matter to court before unbelievers rather than before the saints? 2 Don't you understand that the saints will judge the world? Now if the world is to be judged by you, are you not competent to judge trivial cases? 3 Don't you understand that we will judge angels, to say nothing of things pertaining to daily life? 4 So if you have legal cases dealing with ordinary matters, should you bring it before judges who have no standing in the church? 5 I am saying this to your shame. Isn't there a single person among you wise enough to settle a dispute between members? 6 Instead, one member sues another before an unbeliever! 7 Legal disputes against each other demonstrate that you have already lost from a moral perspective. Why not rather be wronged? Why not rather be cheated? 8 But instead you yourselves wrong and cheat—and you do it to fellow members at that.

Translation Notes and Comments

6:1 *Dare any of you . . . go to law / how do you have the effrontery to bring yourselves to take the matter to court:* The verb τολμάω (*tolmaō*) had the root sense of "to dare," but Paul used it here in the negative sense of "to presume" or "have the effrontery" to do something.[7] Paul's opening words then, revealed his outrage over the fact that Christians were suing Christians in civil courts. The verb, taken in the context of Paul's question, expressed deep censure for their actions. His purpose seems to have been to create a further sense of shame among these Saints for their actions.[8]

---

7. BDAG, 1010; Collins, *First Corinthians,* 224, 227.

8. Reginald H. Fuller, "First Corinthians 6:1–11: An Exegetical Paper," *Ex Auditu* 2 (1986): 98, translates it as, "Has any of you the gall to . . ."

having a matter against another / have a legal dispute with another:
The noun πρᾶγμα (*pragma*), "matter, occurrence," in the legal sense, meant "dispute" or "lawsuit."[9] The context of ἕτερον (*heteron*), "another," pointed to another member of the branch. The middle/passive infinitive κρίνεσθαι (*krinesthai*), "to judge," was used in the forensic context of seeking judgment at court.[10] Paul's question was aimed at forcing his readers to look at the propriety of members suing other members using Gentile courts. One factor that made this action so inexcusable was that local civil courts were, in many instances, tarnished for their biased decisions and lack of integrity.[11]

Before the unjust, and not before the saints / before unbelievers rather than before the saints: The nominally used adjective ἄδικος (*adikos*) had the basic meaning of "unjust, dishonest," but could also refer to the "ungodly." Here it is best understood in a less pejorative sense of "unbeliever" not unlike Latter-day Saints use "Gentile" to describe non-Latter-day Saints.[12] Paul seems to have been using it to refer to those who were, from the supposed spiritually advanced Christians' point of view, impious unbelievers.[13] Given the context, it likely reflected less on any single individual and more on the Gentile legal practice as a whole where the rightness of judgments was often questionable. Thus, taking the word in this broader generic sense, Paul was referring to pagan law courts and legal practices.[14] If that is the case, his use of the plural noun ἁγίων (*hagiōn*), "saints, holy ones,"[15] referred to the Christian council system headed by righteous men through which matters could be fairly and justly arbitrated.

6:2 *Do ye not know that the saints shall judge the world? / Don't you understand that the saints will judge the world?:* Once again Paul referred his readers to a teaching that all the Saints should have known and adhered to. The tacit message behind the question was that if any were ignorant of this point, any idea that they promulgated or deed that they performed should be highly suspect.

---

9. BDAG, 859; Louw-Nida, §56.2.

10. Louw-Nida, §56.23; Friedrich Büchsel and Volkmar Herntrich, "κρίνω," in *TDNT*, 3:921–41; Thiselton, *First Epistle*, 424.

11. Thiselton, *First Epistle*, 419.

12. Fee, *First Epistle*, 232.

13. BDAG, 21.

14. Thus, the REB's rendering of the passage as "before a pagan court." Thiselton, *First Epistle*, 424. Compare Holzapfel and Wayment, *Making Sense*, 350.

15. BDAG, 11.

The noun κόσμος (*kosmos*) denoted the ordered affairs of systems ranging from a household to the universe.[16] It primarily denoted the world and its inhabitants. It is likely this more restricted nuance was what Paul intended.

The verb κρίνω (*krinō*), "to judge," was generally used in a forensic sense and, therefore, connoted the power to pass judgment upon another.[17] In a broader sense, it carried the idea of making and administering rules for others, that is, of governing them. It was in this sense that Jesus promised the Twelve that they would sit on thrones and "judge" Israel (Luke 18:28–30; 22:28–30). The power of the Twelve would greatly exceed that of merely deciding legal cases, but would run to actually governing nations.[18] The implication suggests that the power Paul referred to went beyond that of merely settling disputes to actually making laws and governing people. The power to adjudicate cases, however, always remained behind the word. This is in stark competition to the Roman world's legal system which was the first to make laws and govern "uncivilized" people.

and if the world shall be judged by you, are ye unworthy to judge the smallest matters? / Now if the world is to be judged by you, are you not competent to judge trivial cases?: The adjective ἀνάξιος (*anaxios*) meant "unworthy," "not good enough," or "incompetent,"[19] while the superlative ἐλάχιστος (*elaksistos*) denoted "smallest, insignificant" or "trivial."[20] The noun κριτήριον (*kritērion*) referred to both a judgment and to the place where the judgment took place, that is, the tribunal.[21] The context of this question suggests that Paul was making a case for the power of judgment itself.[22] In other words, he was making the point that the Saints were perfectly capable of holding tribunals for small claim items.[23] Paul's question could be interpreted this way: "If you think that you will be called to judge the *great issues of the world,* why do you act as if to imply that you are

---

16. BDAG, 561–63; Louw-Nida, §§1.1, 39; 6.188; 9.23; 41.38; 59.55; 79.12.

17. BDAG, 567.

18. Louw-Nida, §37.49. Paul's Jewish background would have allowed him to nuance the word in this way. The LXX used κρίνω (*krinō*) to translate the Hebrew שָׁפַט (*šāpaṭ*). That word carried the double meaning of ruling and judging.

19. BDAG, 69.

20. BDAG, 314.

21. Louw-Nida, §56.1.

22. Fee, *First Epistle,* 234.

23. Robertson and Plummer, *Critical and Exegetical Commentary,* 112. Findlay, "St. Paul's First Epistle," 814.

not qualified to adjudicate matters of *very little* (ἐλαχίστων) importance?"[24] Roman law usually requires a person to represent himself so it would be rare, unless one were very powerful or angry, to bring someone to court for an insignificant or trivial case or later try to enforce one. It is more surprising, then, that these kinds of cases were not decided by Saints because these cases were typically and easily decided—even among Gentiles.

    6:3 *Know ye not that we shall judge angels? / Don't you understand that we will judge angels:* Again, Paul introduced his point with a statement of belief, hidden within the question, that all should have known and agreed to. To this day, there is some debate as to the identity of the angels the Apostle referred to. Many see them as fallen beings who have or will come under divine censure.[25] For Latter-day Saints, they seem to be righteous beings who are yet on the road of eternal progression. See Analysis below.

    How much more things that pertain to this life? / to say nothing of things pertaining to daily life?: The adverb μήτιγε (*mētige*) anticipated an emphatic negative answer to a question. Here it gave force to Paul's rhetorical question and carried the force of, "to say nothing of . . ."[26] as in our Rendition. The nominal adjective βιωτικά (*biōtika*) referred to those matters that were necessary in carrying out daily activities including business transactions.[27] Thus, Paul's question pointed out the entire range of affairs in which the Saints could make competent judgments. These included not just small claims items but about every condition one met in life.

    6:4 *If then ye have judgments of things pertaining to this life, set them to judge who are least esteemed in the church / So if you have legal cases dealing with ordinary matters, should you bring it before judges who have no standing in the church?:* This verse is difficult to translate because much depends on how one reads the punctuation. The original manuscripts had none; it was only later that copyists inserted it. Our Rendition treats the sentence as a question.[28] Thus, it takes καθίζετε (*kathezete*) as a second person plural active indicative of καθίζω (*kathizō*) "you set," or "you bring." That being the case, τοὺς ἐξουθενημένους (*tous exouthenēmenous*), "the despised,"[29] either referred to the Roman juries or to the magistrates who

---

24. Thiselton, *First Epistle,* 426; italics in the original.
25. For details, see Thiselton, *First Epistle,* 430–31.
26. Conzelmann, *1 Corinthians,* 105.
27. BDAG, 177. On the basis that the NEB translates the phrase as "matters of business."
28. This follows the USB 4th ed. that takes the phrase as a question.
29. See Translation Notes on 1:28 for a more full definition of this term.

presided over the courts. These were of very low esteem among many Christians because they did not belong to the community of the Saints.[30]

The point that Paul is probably making is that those Christians who were of the lowest standing were almost certainly not citizens and, therefore, had no rights in these courts. In Roman law, *rei vindicatio* was a legal action by which the plaintiff demanded that the defendant return a thing that belonged to the plaintiff. It could be used only when the plaintiff owned the thing and the defendant was somehow impeding the plaintiff's possession of it. The plaintiff could also institute an *actio furti* (a personal action) to punish the defendant. If the thing could not be recovered, the plaintiff could claim damages from the defendant with the aid of the *condictio furtiva* (a personal action). The rub was that the *Rei vindicatio,* derived from the *ius civile,* was available only to Roman citizens.[31] In short, if a Christian defendant was not a citizen, then he had no chance against a Christian who was a citizen. To protect these, Church members should be the judges of such cases. Thus, to create equality among the Saints, the least esteemed should be included in any judgments.

6:5 *I speak to your shame / I am saying this to your shame:* The noun ἐντροπή (*entropē*) referred to the act of deliberately embarrassing or humiliating someone for the purpose of causing them shame.[32] Paul was very blunt in expressing his purpose. He did not back away from the deed because it was for their own good. If he could make them feel ashamed of themselves, they might overcome their pride and be more willing to change. Therefore, this seems to be an act of tough love, a form of charity, which was in the Corinthians' best interest or for their own good.

Is it so, that there is not a wise man among you? no, not one that shall be able to judge between his brethren? / Isn't there a single person among you wise enough to settle a dispute between members?: Since the noun ἀδελφός (*adelphos*), literally "brother," as shown above, also includes all members of an association, both male and female, it is translated as "member" in our Rendition. The future indicative middle deponent verb

---

30. If the passage is not construed as a question, then "despised" refers to members whom others of the Church consider the least esteemed. On this matter, Bruce, *1 and 2 Corinthians,* 60, has concluded that the evidence is too close to make a definitive call. Even so, the balance seems to be tipped a bit to the interrogative side. See Thiselton, *First Epistle,* 433; Fee, *First Epistle,* 235–36.

31. See H. Galsterer, "The Administration of Justice," in *The Cambridge Ancient History: The Augustan Empire, 43 B.C.–A.D. 69* (Cambridge University Press, 1996), 400–404.

32. Louw-Nida, §25.196.

δυνήσεται (*dynēsetai*) denoted that one would at some point have "power" or "ability,"[33] while the aorist infinitive διακρῖναι (*diakrinai*) meant "to judge, discern."[34] Compounded together, they contain immense irony which was magnified by Paul's main barb in the adjective σοφός (*sophos*), "wise." This was a branch with quite a number of self-proclaimed wise members. Therefore, it should have been overflowing with those capable of arbitrating cases. Cutting through Paul's sarcasm, his question suggested that there should be people now as well as in the future who were totally capable of deciding cases. Why, then, were Saints going to the non-Christians? The Apostle's question was designed to bring this non sequitur to their attention so forcefully that they had to address it.

6:6 *But brother goeth to law with brother, and that before the unbelievers / Instead, one member sues another before an unbeliever!:* Though this sentence can be construed as an interrogative, based on the constructive force of ἀλλά (*alla*), "but, instead," our Rendition treats it as an exclamation, answering the question Paul asked in 6:5.[35] Taking it this way, the sentence highlights Paul's affront and amazement at the absurdity of the actions of these people.

6:7 *Now therefore there is utterly a fault among you, because ye go to law one with another / Legal disputes against each other demonstrates that you have already lost from a moral perspective:* The plural noun κρίματα (*krimata*), "judgments," also referred to lawsuits and is translated as "legal disputes" in our Rendition.[36] The rare noun ἥττημα (*hēttēma*) carried the nuance of falling short or failing, albeit in moral matters. Coupled with the adverb ὅλως (*holōs*), "completely, utterly or generally," it highlighted the depth of the Corinthian Saints' moral failure.[37] Paul's phrase, ἤδη μὲν οὖν ὅλως ἥττημα ὑμῖν ἐστιν (*ēdē men oun holōs ēttēma hymin estin*), literally "now, therefore, it's a total defeat for you," emphasized that even should they win the lawsuit, from a moral perspective they had lost. This was because a true Christian did not seek revenge but would rather be wronged than wrong someone else (see Matt. 5:38–42; Luke 6:27–31).

---

33. BDAG, 262–63.

34. BDAG, 231–32.

35. Findlay, "St. Paul's First Epistle," 861; T. C. Edwards, *A Commentary on the First Epistle to the Corinthians*, 2d ed. [Greek Text] (London: Hodder and Stoughton, 1885), 149–51.

36. Louw-Nida, §§30.110; 56.2, 20.

37. J. Héring, *The First Epistle of St. Paul to the Corinthians* (London: Epworth Press, 1962), 41. This translation is implied in Barrett, *First Epistle*, 138; see also Louw-Nida, §13.22.

Why do ye not rather take wrong? why do ye not rather suffer your-
selves to be defrauded? / Why not rather be wronged? Why not rather
be cheated?: The verb ἀδικεῖσθε (*adikeisthe*) is translated as a causative-
reflexive passive or "permissive" in the middle voice in our Rendition carrying the meaning "to let oneself be deprived of one's rights,"[38] that is, "to
suffer a wrong." The verb ἀποστερεῖσθε (*apostereisthe*) is also translated
as a "permissive" in the middle voice denoting the condition of allowing
oneself "to be defrauded" or "to be cheated."[39]

Paul's teaching may have especially stung Gentile and Jewish converts
who knew that, according to Plato, Socrates advocated that to be good and
become just, one was expected to suffer a wrong rather than to do a wrong.[40]
Certainly the Lord's teachings were much higher than Socrates', so why
couldn't these converts live up to even Gentile standards?

Paul's two questions focus on how the Christian was to respond when
his "rights" were violated. This was a new concept that was still developing
in Roman law at this time. Such rights were not available to everyone, only
Roman citizens (and that accounted for about three percent of the population of the whole empire). To be "good" according to the Gentile standard
and more importantly as a follower of Christ, a person must not become
preoccupied with a notion of rights for the sake of keeping unity with a
brother (see Matt. 18:15).

6:8 *Nay, ye do wrong, and defraud, and that your brethren / But instead*
you yourselves wrong and cheat—and you do it to fellow members at that:
The verb ἀποστερέω (*apostereō*) meant to "cause another to suffer loss by taking away through illicit means," thus, "to defraud" or "to cheat."[41] Construing
the adversative ἀλλά (*alla*), "but," with ὑμεῖς (*hymeis*), "you yourselves," the
sense is "but instead, you yourselves are cheating others of the justice they
deserve." The scandal involved more than the matter of the lawsuits but of
a deeper sin. Some of the Saints were actually defrauding or cheating other
members of their rights and goods.[42] Paul used the demonstrative adjective
τοῦτο (*touto*), "this," with telling effect. Since ἀδελφούς (*adelphous*), "brothers
and sisters" ("fellow members" in our Rendition), is the direct object of "cheat,"
the *touto* is best construed as "at that," making his disgust clearly visible.[43]

---

38. Thiselton, *First Epistle,* 437. This interpretation is based on Paul's theology that the
Christian has a moral obligation to sacrifice his rights for the peace of the community.

39. Thiselton, *First Epistle,* 437.

40. This phrase can be found in Plato's *Gorgias* and in many of his other works.

41. BDAG, 121.

42. BDAG, 121.

43. Conzelmann, *1 Corinthians,* 106, n. 29.

Analysis and Summary

In 6:1–8, Paul addressed the issue of Saints going to court.[44] He never identified the issue or issues over which the Saints were contending. Given that the major theme of chapters 5–7 dealt with matters of morality and sexual propriety, it is likely, but not certain, that issues growing out of adultery were causing the fuss. To bring this type of litigation before Gentile judges, whose views on matters of morality would have been at odds with those of the Church, would certainly have caused concern for Paul.[45] Certainly the lack of legal status of most Christians would have prevented them from receiving any kind of Roman justice.

The question naturally arises, just who was suing whom? The nature of civil legislation at the time supplies a probable answer. Though high Roman criminal courts could be trusted to take seriously the charges brought before them, that was less so with the local civil courts. Local judges and juries were open to influences of patronage, vested interest, station, and outright bribery as well as other factors. The clever, the prominent, the wealthy, or the skilled could easily manipulate the system.[46] When later codified under Justinian, Roman law was created to protect the interests of society. The judiciary was, therefore, greatly tilted toward the wealthy and powerful while the weak and powerless could find little justice there. It is likely, therefore, that those Saints who were bringing the lawsuits were the more wealthy in the branch since only they could afford good assistants and expect the law to act in their favor. When rich went against rich, there could be some balance, but when the rich sued the poor, the rich won.[47]

---

44. Since Paul did not state his rationale for his position on litigation, exegetes and scholars have proposed a number of possibilities. For discussion, see Robert D. Taylor, "Toward a Biblical Theology of Litigation: A Law Professor Looks at 1 Cor. 6:1–11," *Ex Auditu* 2 (1986): 105–16. Of these, the two most convincing are the "Christological scheme" and the "ecclesial-eschatological scheme" and they are followed here.

45. Richardson, "Judgment in Sexual Matters," 53–55.

46. Alan C. Mitchell, "Rich and Poor in the Courts of Corinth: Litigiousness and Status in 1 Cor. 6:1–11," *New Testament Studies* 39 (1993): 562–63; Bruce W. Winter, "Civil Litigation in Secular Corinth and the Church: Forensic Background to 1 Cor. 6:1–8," *New Testament Studies* 37 (1991): 559–72. For studies on the broad issues involving justice under Roman law, see John A. Crook, *Law and Life of Rome* (Ithaca, N.Y.: Cornell University Press, 1967); and Peter Garnsey, *Social Status and Legal Privilege in the Roman Empire* (Oxford: Oxford University Press, 1970). Both show that prestige, patronage, and wealth greatly influenced the courts.

47. Theissen, *Social Setting,* 97.

This system that gave rich Christians, as well as their Gentile equals, unfair advantage also put the Church in jeopardy. First, the litigation furthered the schisms that were destroying the unity of the Church by (a) causing resentment and anger between poor and rich and (b) separating the wealthier and, likely, the better educated and more administratively savvy into opposing factions. Second, because those with the most prestige would likely have been the ones with the most influence in Gentile society, their actions threatened the Church's reputation and, therefore, any influence it could have on the community at large. One aspect of the Christian message stressed reconciliation and forgiveness. Through their actions, these members were, perhaps inadvertently, invalidating that message. The result was significant damage to the mission of the Church. As one scholar put it, "A united community in which love dominates is the existential affirmation of the gospel. A community which contains within itself divisions which characterize the 'world' has no power to transform its environment because of the contradiction between theory and practice."[48] And, according to another scholar, the Church community "could be put at risk either by practicing manipulative strategies in full view of Gentile patrons or clever legal advocates, whom wealthy Christians might hire, and the Gentile world be exposed to the sight of believers obsessed with acquisition of property or of their 'rights,' as against the sacrificial service of others which truly identifies what it is to be 'of Christ.'"[49] In short, they brought shame upon the Church.

Making that shame even greater was that the Christians had another recourse they could have used. It would appear that at this time the Christians shared the privilege the Romans extended to the Jews of conducting their own courts of law.[50] Having this ability, Paul was outraged that the members had the effrontery of putting trust in pagan courts to settle personal disputes. Elder McConkie has noted that:

> Judges and courts are and always have been part of the kingdom of God on earth. Whenever that kingdom has been set up in its fulness, glory, and power, the church court system has been empowered to handle both civil

---

48. Jerome Murphy-O'Connor, *1 Corinthians* (Wilmington, Del.: Michael Glazier Books, 1979), 47.

49. Thiselton, *First Epistle*, 419.

50. Rabbis argued, based on Ex. 21:1, the illegal nature of Jews suing at Gentiles courts. Texts supporting the idea can be found in the Dead Sea scrolls 1QS 5:1–4, 13–18; 9:7; 1QSa 1:13–14. See also B. S. Rosner, "Moses Appointing Judges: An Antecedent to 1 Cor. 1–6?" *Zeitschrift für die neutestamentliche Wissenschaft* 82 (1990): 275–78.

and ecclesiastical matters. All such cases rested in the hands of the Lord's judges from the day of Adam to the time Saul was chosen to rule in Israel. Since then the perfect law has been modified to fit into world conditions.

In Paul's day there were both church courts and civil courts, as there are today. If the saints go to law with each other, they may choose to do so under either state or church jurisdiction. Paul is here counseling them to handle their own affairs in their own courts, and his counsel is good and might well be followed by church members today. Manifestly where grievances involve non-members of the Church, redress must be sought before civil tribunals. (D. & C. 134:11.)[51]

Before Utah became a state, President John Taylor taught the Saints that Paul's admonition still applied and stake presidents were to hold disciplinary councils on any member who sued another at the law.[52] That will likely become the course in the future when Zion is established. As one LDS scholar noted, "When in full operation under a theocratic system, Church disciplinary councils will handle both ecclesiastical and civil matters. For now the Lord has said that those who keep the laws of God will have no need to break the laws of the land"[53] (see D&C 58:21–22).

Paul enhanced his point on the competency of the Saints to judge earthly matters by noting that the day would come when they would actually judge both the peoples of the earth and the angels of heaven. Speaking on this matter, Elder Joseph F. Smith taught:

> The man who passes through this probation, and is faithful, being redeemed from sin by the blood of Christ, through the ordinances of the Gospel, and attains to exaltation in the kingdom of God, is not less but greater than the angels, and if you doubt it read your Bible, for there it is written that the Saints shall "judge angels," and also they shall "judge the world." And why? Because the resurrected, righteous man has progressed beyond the pre-existent or disembodied spirits, and has risen above them, having both spirit and body as Christ has, having gained the victory over death and the grave, and having power over sin and Satan, in fact having passed from the condition of the angel to that of a God. He possesses keys of power, dominion and glory that the angel does not possess—and cannot possess without gaining them in the same way that

---

51. *DNTC*, 2:336–37.
52. John Taylor, in *JD*, 20:106.
53. Ogden and Skinner, *Verse by Verse*, 133.

he gained them, which will be by passing through the same ordeals and proving equally faithful.[54]

The idea that the righteous would "judge" the world is found in both Jewish and Christian apocalyptic materials.[55] Though final and ultimate justice rests with the Savior, others will assist. For example, the Twelve Apostles will judge the righteous among the twelve tribes of Israel (D&C 29:12; Matt. 19:28; 1 Ne. 12:9–10), and the twelve Nephite disciples will judge the Nephites (3 Ne. 27:27). These are not the only ones, for other prophets and righteous Saints will be appointed to help judge the works and deeds of those for whom they have had responsibility (6:2; Morm. 3:18–20; D&C 20:13; 75:21). Thus, "there will be a whole hierarchy of judges who, under Christ, shall judge the righteous. He alone shall issue the decrees of damnation for the wicked."[56]

Since it is likely that it was the well positioned and better educated who were bringing suits against other members, Paul's argument was irrefutable. In essence he was asking, "If there are those in the church who think highly of themselves, how is it that their 'wisdom' to arbitrate between fellow Christians remains inferior to that of Gentiles who do not have the gifts of 'wisdom,' 'the Spirit,' 'revelation,' or 'knowledge,' and who 'reign as kings'? On the other hand, if being initiated as 'persons of the Spirit' makes them superior to the Gentile world around them (4:8–11), might not the very lowliest low-status Christian be better equipped 'to sit as judges' than high-status pagans?"[57] The point was that "the addressees really [could not] have it both ways."[58]

The Apostle, as very clearly stated in 6:5, desired in this part of his epistle to shame those who had the effrontery to do such an act. He emphasized his point using biting sarcasm in the question, "Is it so with you that there is nobody among you who is sophos [σοφός] ('wise'), so that he [or she] might render a decision between the brothers?"[59] Paul's question was designed to force the Saints to see their true condition in light

---

54. Joseph F. Smith, in *JD*, 23:173, see also Brigham Young, in *JD*, 19:7; Orson Pratt, in *JD*, 3:98.

55. For example, 1Qp–Hab 5:4; Dan. 7:22; Matt. 19:28; Rev. 2:26; 20:4.

56. Bruce R. McConkie, *The Millennial Messiah: The Second Coming of the Son of Man* (Salt Lake City: Deseret Book, 1982), 520.

57. Thiselton, *First Epistle*, 434.

58. Thiselton, *First Epistle*, 434.

59. Fee, *First Epistle*, 237.

of their perceived one. Bringing suits against one another was no small matter, but it was a sign of the depth of their spiritual flaws.[60] Indeed, the lawsuits were merely an aggravation to a condition that was already out of hand. In 6:7, the Apostle pinpointed the area where they suffered their total moral failure. His opening phrase in this verse, ἤδη μὲν οὖν (*ēdē men oun*) "Now [at this very moment] therefore," pointed to the period before any litigation even began. Right then, before they ever went to a Gentile court, they had already suffered a complete moral breakdown.[61] Indeed, even the Christian court of arbitration was a concession and a spiritual step down. The Lord taught the law each true Christian should follow when he admonished his disciples, saying, "But I say unto you which hear, Love your enemies, do good to them which hate you, Bless them that curse you, and pray for them which despitefully use you. And unto him that smiteth thee on the one cheek offer also the other; and him that taketh away thy cloak forbid not to take thy coat also. Give to every man that asketh of thee; and of him that taketh away thy goods ask them not again. And as ye would that men should do to you, do ye also to them likewise" (Luke 6:27–31; compare Matt. 5:38–42).

The Lord established the way contention should be handled. He instructed:

> Moreover if thy brother shall trespass against thee, go and tell him his fault between thee and him alone: if he shall hear thee, thou hast gained thy brother. But if he will not hear thee, then take with thee one or two more, that in the mouth of two or three witnesses every word may be established. And if he shall neglect to hear them, tell it unto the church: but if he neglect to hear the church, let him be unto thee as an heathen man and a publican. Verily I say unto you, Whatsoever ye shall bind on earth shall be bound in heaven: and whatsoever ye shall loose on earth shall be loosed in heaven. Again I say unto you, That if two of you shall agree on earth as touching any thing that they shall ask, it shall be done for them of my Father which is in heaven. (Matt. 18:15–19)

It was only when the person-to-person discourse failed that the circle of those involved was to be enlarged and that in two additional stages. It was that there were those who did not even attempt the first stage that revealed

---

60. Fee, *First Epistle*, 237.
61. Findlay, "St. Paul's First Epistle," 816.

their total moral failure. That the branch either supported or did not stand in their way made the whole community culpable.[62]

Paul's questions in the second part of 6:7 reached the heart of the matter. With them, he demanded that his readers examine the seat of their actions. One's first desire should be to defuse any situation before it gets out of hand. The Christian was morally obligated, despite the urgings of pride and a desire toward self-preservation, to meet his antagonist face-to-face and try to work things out. Even when this move did not work, he was not yet free to make matters public, but must ask for the arbitration by people of trust. Only when these failed, was he free to bring in the weight of the community. "Hence," as one scholar noted, "[Paul] turns the issue upside down, just as justice, penalty, and 'rights' of the self are turned upside down in the theology of the *cross* (1:18–31) and in the mind of *Christ* (2:16–3:4)."[63]

Paul's position has never been rescinded. It is still up to the Saints of God to forgive. As President Spencer W. Kimball taught, "We Must Forgive Regardless. It would have been easy for Paul, Stephen and Jesus to be revengeful—that is, if they had not assiduously cultivated the forgiving spirit. Revenge is a response of the carnal man, not the spiritual one. It enters into one's life when he allows it to through misunderstandings and injuries." He went on to say that "a common error is the idea that the offender must apologize and humble himself to the dust before forgiveness is required. Certainly, the one who does the injury should totally make his adjustment, but as for the offended one, he must forgive the offender regardless of the attitude of the other. Sometimes men get satisfactions from seeing the other party on his knees and groveling in the dust, but that is not the gospel way."[64]

In 6:8, Paul made it very clear exactly why these people should feel shame. They were guilty of greed and the fraudulent acts it produced. That being the case, they were no better than the pagans over whom they felt so superior. In fact, his words insinuate that many pagans were more righteous than these Saints. Thus the Corinthians had serious need to repent. Once again Paul's words forced his readers to take a close audit of their spiritual strength. They were rapidly slipping off the way and they desperately needed a course correction.

---

62. Conzelmann, *1 Corinthians*, 105; Thiselton, *First Epistle*, 436.
63. Thiselton, *First Epistle*, 436.
64. Spencer W. Kimball, *The Miracle of Forgiveness* (Salt Lake City: Bookcraft, 1969), 280, 282.

THE WICKED WILL NOT INHERIT THE KINGDOM OF GOD (6:9–11)

Greek Text

9 ᾿Η οὐκ οἴδατε ὅτι ἄδικοι θεοῦ βασιλείαν οὐ κληρονομήσουσιν; μὴ πλανᾶσθε· οὔτε πόρνοι οὔτε εἰδωλολάτραι οὔτε μοιχοὶ οὔτε μαλακοὶ οὔτε ἀρσενοκοῖται 10 οὔτε κλέπται οὔτε πλεονέκται, οὐ μέθυσοι, οὐ λοίδοροι, οὐχ ἅρπαγες βασιλείαν θεοῦ κληρονομήσουσιν. 11 καὶ ταῦτά τινες ἦτε· ἀλλὰ ἀπελούσασθε, ἀλλὰ ἡγιά-σθητε, ἀλλὰ ἐδικαιώθητε ἐν τῷ ὀνόματι τοῦ κυρίου ᾿Ιησοῦ καὶ ἐν τῷ πνεύματι τοῦ θεοῦ ἡμῶν. [SBLGNT]

King James Version

9 Know ye not that the unrighteous shall not inherit the kingdom of God? Be not deceived: neither fornicators, nor idolaters, nor adulterers, nor effeminate, nor abusers of themselves with mankind, 10 Nor thieves, nor covetous, nor drunkards, nor revilers, nor extortioners, shall inherit the kingdom of God. 11 And such were some of you: but ye are washed, but ye are sanctified, but ye are justified in the name of the Lord Jesus, and by the Spirit of our God.

New Rendition

9 Or don't you understand that the unrighteous will not inherit the kingdom of God? Don't deceive yourselves; neither the sexually immoral, nor idolaters, nor adulterers, nor those who engage in homosexual acts, 10 nor thieves, nor the greedy, nor drunkards, nor the verbally abusive, nor swindlers will inherit the kingdom of God. 11 And some of you used to be those sorts of sinners, but you have been washed and purified and made innocent in the name of the Lord Jesus and through the Spirit of our God.

Translation Notes and Comments

6:9 *Know ye not that the unrighteous shall not inherit the kingdom of God? / Or don't you understand that the unrighteous will not inherit the kingdom of God?:* For the fourth time, Paul opened his argument with a question that housed a doctrinal statement all should have known. Through his repetitious use of the question "Don't you understand," Paul's words began to take on a damning quality as they continued to expose either the Saints' ignorance or rebellion.

The opening coordinating conjunction ἤ (*ē*), "or," ties this verse to the one before and follows up Paul's accusation in 6:8.

Be not deceived / Don't deceive yourselves: The second person plural middle/passive imperative verb πλανᾶσθε (*planasthe*), "to deceive,"[65] is

---

65. BDAG, 821–22.

here best understood in the middle voice sense of "deceive yourself." Often in the New Testament, the middle voice is used to emphasize spiritual benefits for the subject. Paul was not warning the Corinthian Saints to beware of someone else deceiving them. It was in their own self-deception where danger lay. He wanted them to understand that being a member of the Church, even having a witness that Jesus was the Messiah, did not assure them a place in God's kingdom. That the Apostle had already warned them against self-deception (3:18), and did so again here, emphasized its danger.[66] His warning was clear: "Don't think for a minute that if you engage in acts like the wicked, you will not be judged like the wicked."[67]

fornicators / the sexually immoral: See Translation Notes on 5:11.

The noun πόρνος (*pornos*) was a general term that referred to a person, married or unmarried, who practiced sexual immorality,[68] that is, one who had sexual intercourse with anyone who was not his or her lawful spouse.

adulterers: The noun μοιχός (*moichos*) referred specifically to an adulterer, that is, a married person who has sexual intercourse with someone other than his or her spouse.[69]

effeminate, nor abusers of themselves with mankind / those who engage in homosexual acts: Two Greek nouns are used here to describe homosexual activity. The first, μαλακός (*malakos*) was an adjective used nominally, and literally meant "soft." In this context it referred to the passive partner in homosexual relations.[70] This was in contrast to ἀρσενοκοίτης (*arsenokoitēs*), the noun denoting the active partner in homosexual relations.[71] Since English does not make such a distinction, our Rendition translates the two terms as "those who engage in homosexual acts." The key point was that homosexual activity of any kind, as with all forms of sexual immorality, was sinful in the eyes of God.

6:10 *Nor thieves, nor covetous, nor drunkards, nor revilers, nor extortioners, shall inherit the kingdom of God / nor thieves, nor the greedy, nor drunkards, nor the verbally abusive, nor swindlers will inherit the kingdom of God:* For the covetous, drunkards, revilers, and extortionists, see Translation Notes as well as Analysis on 5:11.

---

66. In 3:18, Paul used the verb ἐξαπατάω (*exapatatō*), "to delude," but the intent is the same. He will warn them again 15:33.

67. Fee, *First Epistle*, 242.

68. BDAG, 855.

69. BDAG, 657.

70. Louw-Nida, §88.281.

71. Louw-Nida, §88.280.

To his previous list Paul added κλέπται (*kleptai*), "thieves": those who use deception as a means of gaining the goods of another.[72]

6:11 *And such were some of you / And some of you used to be those sorts of sinners:* With the phrase καὶ ταῦτά τινες ἦτε (*kai tauta tines ēte*), literally "and these things some of you used to be," Paul reminded the Corinthian Saints that before their conversion some of them had been guilty of the aforementioned sins. His use of the neuter plural adjective *tauta*, "these things," revealed his sense of loathing for their former lifestyle, for some of them "were these things." His words brought together both their former state of being and the actions this had led to.[73] The implication of his use of the imperfect verb ἦτε (*ēte*), "used to be," should not be overlooked. It denoted a "continuous habituation."[74] The Apostle's point was that some of his readers were heavily invested in some very serious sins and, therefore, at that time, stood in jeopardy of losing their souls.

but ye are washed, but ye are sanctified, but ye are justified, / but you have been washed and purified and made innocent: The middle aorist verb ἀπελούσασθε (*apelousasthe*), means "to wash something away from one's self" or "to cause a state of moral purity."[75] The force of the middle voice in the present context, however, likely acted as one of self-interest and, therefore, did not imply that the Saints had washed themselves, but that they had let themselves be cleansed by Christ for their own spiritual benefit.[76] Though the imagery of being washed tied to baptism, the words that follow suggest that what Paul had in mind included much more than that single act. He likely meant all that went into the conversion and transformation process. In short, to be washed meant becoming pure and therewith transitioning into a newness of life (Acts 22:16; Rom. 6:3–4).[77]

Paul described the Corinthian Saints as being in two additional states. The aorist passive verb ἡγιάσθητε (*hēgiasthēte*) meant "to be made holy," thus, "to be sanctified" or "purified."[78] An important nuance of this verb

---

72. As opposed to the λῃστής (*lēstēs*), the robber or plundered. Louw-Nida, §57.433; Herbert Preisker, "κλέπτω, κλέπτης," in *TDNT,* 3:754–56.

73. Thiselton, *First Epistle,* 453.

74. Wallace, *Greek Grammar,* 548.

75. BDAG, 117; Louw-Nida, §88.30.

76. Thiselton, *First Epistle,* 453.

77. James D. G. Dunn, *Baptism in the Holy Spirit: A Re-examination of the New Testament Teaching on the Gift of the Spirit in Relation to Pentecostalism Today* (London: SCM, 1970) 120–23.

78. Louw-Nida, §88.26; BDAG, 10; Otto Procksch, "ἁγιάζω," in *TDNT,* 1:111–12.

connoted that which was set apart for God's purposes and, therefore, possessed, at least to a degree, the same qualities he did. The aorist passive verb ἠδικώθητε (edikōthēte, from δικαιόω, dikaioō), in the strictest sense, meant "to be declared innocent or right," but its range of meanings was much broader. Indeed, it was a word rich in significance and implication. Its breadth could better be understood by comparing its related adjective δίκαιος (dikaios) with its antonym, κοινός (koinos), which described that which was "common, ordinary," but also that which was "worthless, defiled," or "profane."[79] Therefore, dikaios connoted such ideas as "uncommon, clean, sacred, and pure." When used in association with the mystery religions, dikaios connoted "a radical inner change which the initiate experiences" such that it brings him or her closer to God and his character. Therefore, the religious nuance of the verb approached the sense "to become deified."[80]

The telling importance of the aorist tense of each of these verbs must not be overlooked. The reading in the KJV, being in the present tense, could be construed to mean that all of Paul's readers yet remained in their pure state. The aorist tense, however, showed this to be a past condition, and though it was likely true that many of Paul's readers remained in this state, those who were flagrantly sinning certainly were not. Paul fully recognized the evidence of weakness, sin, and moral shortcomings that existed among the branch members (see 3:3), but he also knew that if the people would stay true, sooner or later, even among the weakest, the converting power of Christ would overcome the natural man and the child of God would stand supreme.[81]

in the name of the Lord Jesus, and by the Spirit of our God / in the name of the Lord Jesus and through the Spirit of our God: It is only in the name of Christ, who mediates all transitions between God and man, that all things redemptive are accomplished. "Ye must not perform any thing unto the Lord," taught Nephi, "save in the first place ye shall pray unto the Father in the name of Christ, that he will consecrate thy performance unto thee" (2 Ne. 32:9; compare Hel. 3:27–28; 3 Ne. 4:30; D&C 133:6, 37–40; Moses 5:8). In other words, one does not perform any ecclesiastical or spiritual act without prayer in the name of the Son.

---

79. BDAG, 552; Louw-Nida, §§53.39, 65.15.
80. BDAG, 249.
81. Thiselton, *First Epistle,* 454.

The tremendous spiritual blessings the Corinthian Saints had experienced had God behind them. The preposition ἐν (*en*), used here as a marker of agency, "with the help of" or "through," emphasized that it is through God's Spirit that their transformation, either realized or in potential, took place. Without this spiritual endowment, self-improvement was just that, the improving of what the person was. The gospel purpose, however, was much higher: to transform the individual into a new creature filled with godly power and holiness.

Analysis and Summary

In 6:9, Paul continued the list of grievous sins (5:10–11) that kill the Spirit and cause one to lose his or her inheritance in the kingdom of God. To the six sins he previously mentioned—fornication, greed, idolatry, verbal abuse, drunkenness, and swindling—he added two more: adultery and homosexual relations.

Though all were bad, μοιχός (*moichos*), an "adulterer," committed a particularly heinous sin. It was a sin against the marriage covenant. To protect marriage and its sacred purposes, God put strong safeguards around it.[82] These included his laws against sexual immorality. Fidelity to partner—that is, cleaving to him or her *alone*—rested at the center of the whole. Therefore, adultery was specifically forbidden. The Lord could not have been more clear when he said, "Thou shalt not commit adultery" (Ex. 20:14). So important was this commandment that the Lord has repeated it in every standard work, often multiple times (see, for example, Deut. 5:18; Matt. 19:18; Mosiah 13:22; D&C 59:6).

Adultery is here defined as sexual relations between a married person and any other person except his or her spouse.[83] The Proverbs particularly brought adultery under fire insisting that "whoso committeth adultery with a woman lacketh understanding: he that doeth it destroyeth his own soul" (6:32; see also Prov. 6:20–35; 7:1–27).[84]

---

82. "*The covenant family* is central to the Kingdom of God and hence marriage was at its inception hedged about with safeguards in order to establish the precedent of responsibility." Rushdoony, *Institutes*, 342.

83. The Hebrew verb נָאַף (*nā'af*) and Greek verb μοιχεύω (*moicheuō*) which translated it, did, in some instances, include other kinds of immorality. See, for example, Jer. 3:9; Ezek. 23:37; Luke 16:18; Rom. 2:22; and D. N. Freedman and B. E. Willoughby, "*nā'ap*," in *Theological Dictionary of the Old Testament* ed. G. Johannes Botterweck and Helmer Ringgren, trans. John T. Willis, 15 vols. (Grand Rapids, Mich.: Eerdmans, 1976–2004), 9:113–18 (hereafter cited as *TDOT*).

84. The adulterer or adulteress is worse than the prostitute, for the latter takes mere payment while the former, in his or her lust, devours the partner with fatal consequences.

The Lord was very clear on the punishment for those who broke this law. According to Deuteronomy 22:22, "If a man be found lying with a woman married to an husband, then they shall both of them die, both the man that lay with the woman, and the woman: so shalt thou put away evil from Israel." The severity of the punishment emphasized how abhorrent the sin was to God. There is good reason. God designed biblical law to sustain a family-centered society, and the central social offense to his intent was adultery. He placed it on the same level as murder in that both require the same penalty—the forfeiture of life.[85]

God's commandments against adultery did not diminish in New Testament times. In fact, that book sharply broadens and intensifies the concept of adultery. No longer was it a matter of physical intercourse. It now included desire and lust: both, the Savior said, broke the law of fidelity that he demanded of his disciples (see Matt. 5:27–30). He parted sharply from the scribes and lawyers who attempted to relativize the divine command by modifying it to meet cultural demands.[86] Jesus insisted on how absolute the divne requirement was.[87]

The Lord further sharpened the concept of adultery in another way. He said, "It hath been said, Whosoever shall put away his wife, let him give her a writing of divorcement: But I say unto you, That whosoever shall put away his wife, saving for the cause of fornication, causeth her to commit adultery: and whosoever shall marry her that is divorced committeth adultery" (Matt. 5:31–32). He assured his hearers that "Moses because of the hardness of your hearts suffered you to put away your wives: but from the beginning it was not so" (Matt. 19:8). With these words we see that Jesus rejected the permissive attitude some Pharisees held toward divorce. He

---

85. Rushdoony, *Institutes*, 395.

86. F. Hauck, "μοιχεύω, μοιχάω, μοιχεία, μοῖχος, μοιχαλίς," in *TDNT*, 4:729–35.

87. Hauck, "μοιχεύω, μοιχάω, μοιχεία, μοῖχος, μοιχαλίς," 4:734. The story of the woman taken in adultery (see John 8:1–8) is often used to suggest that the Lord softened his views on the act. The context, however, shows us that the Lord was only rejecting the purely legal view of the law (see 6:4–5). He took this same stand in connection with the contested estate (Luke 12:13–14). In the case of the woman taken in adultery, he did not say the woman should not be stoned. What he did demand was that all requirements of the law be met, namely the judges must be free from sin as well. She no doubt came under the death penalty, but he maintained a religious and moral position *vis à vis* the law. He appealed to a judgment of conscience. Only he who himself was without sin should cast the stone. Jesus did grant the woman pardon, but this only on condition of repentance. He preserved the unconditional demand of God by adding his stiff warning that the woman must "sin no more" (John 8:11). Thus, his was not a civil judgment but rather a religious one. He in no way interfered with whatever action her husband might take against her.

proved that divorce was "in conflict with the will of God (Mt 19:6 ff.). For this reason the remarriage of a man after divorcing his wife, or the remarrying of the divorced woman is tantamount to adultery."[88]

As we have seen, Paul's preaching showed that he took very seriously the Lord's assessment of adultery. Nowhere did he budge on the importance of marital fidelity as an unconditional and ongoing divine commandment (see 5:1–5; 6:9). Adultery was more than a matter of civil law (see Rom. 7:3); its prohibition was based on the holy will of God (see 6:18; 1 Thes. 4:3). By breaking the command, a person forfeited his right to a place in the kingdom of God (6:9). This included both males and females, for women were fellow heirs of the glory of God and thus worthy of the same honor *and* responsibility as men (see 1 Pet. 3:7).

Paul particularly stressed that the marital covenant must be maintained at all times, even if there was no human witness (see Heb. 13:4).[89] Just because no one found out about an affair did not make it right. The omniscient God, he assured his readers, would be the judge of the adulterer (compare Heb. 10:30–31).

In summary, the New Testament no longer confined the Old Testament prohibition of adultery to the mere avoidance of the sinful act. The commandment, in the gospel sense, found its true fulfillment only in the love of spouses who were joined together by God (see Matt. 19:5–6; Rom. 13:9). Under the new law, the uncontrolled, even impulsive, lustful glance was sinful (see 2 Pet. 2:14).[90] In sharpening his position vis à vis the Old Testament, the Lord gave a higher standard for those who would be his.

---

88. Hauck, "μοιχεύω, μοιχάω, μοιχεία, μοῖχος, μοιχαλίς," 4:733. In this regard, see Matt. 5:32; 19:9; Mark 10:11–13; Luke 16:18. For a more detailed look at this, see the "Excursus on Marriage and Divorce" in chapter 7.

89. In this passage, Paul admonishes the reader to "let the marriage be held in honor among all" (τίμιος ὁ γάμος ἐν πᾶσιν, *timios ho gamos en pasin*). In so doing, he places the responsibility upon the whole community to safeguard marriage. He further exhorts his audience to "let the marriage-bed remain pure" (ἡ κοίτη ἀμίαντος, *hē koitē amiantos:* here *koitē*, literally "bed," is a euphemism for marital sex.). Again, it is the responsibility of the Christian community to protect the sacred character of intimacy. Those who do not, Paul assures his readers, will find God to be their judge.

90. Hauck, "μοιχεύω, μοιχάω, μοιχεία, μοῖχος, μοιχαλίς," 4:734. Peter warns the Church against those who have "eyes full of adultery" and thereby "cannot cease from sin" (ἀκαταπαύστους ἁμαρτίας, *akatapaustous hamaritias*) (2 Pe. 2:14). The idea is that once one falls so deeply into sin, there is no restraint.

Nothing has changed today.[91] In both the Book of Mormon and the Doctrine and Covenants, the Lord commanded, "Thou shalt not commit adultery; and he that commiteth adultery, and repenteth not, shall be cast out" (D&C 42:24; see also Mosiah 13:22).[92] With those words, the Old Testament prohibition became part of the Restoration. But what of the New Testament position? In the Doctrine and Covenants, the Lord says, "he that looketh upon a woman to lust after her shall deny the faith, and shall not have the Spirit; and if he repents not he shall be cast out" (D&C 42:23; see also D&C 63:16). Even the unrepentant, lustful look evidences spiritual bankruptcy and is cause for excommunication. From these verses we can see that the Lord's attitude has not softened toward this sin.

In addition to the πόρνος (*pornos*) and the μοιχός (*moichos*), the Apostle also castigated the μαλακός (*malakos*) and ἀρσενοκοίτης (*arsenokoitēs*). *Malakos* means "soft" and, when applied to persons, designated the effeminate man or boy who played the passive role during homosexual activities. The *arsenokoitēs* was the active homosexual partner.[93]

The position of those who insist that Paul did not have general homosexual practices in mind but spoke within a specific Greco-Roman context does not stand up to close scrutiny.[94] Paul's attitude toward homosexuality is clear. In no way does he see it as an alternative lifestyle acceptable to God. To interpret him otherwise is to ignore his context and setting. Paul condemned the sin primarily on theological, not moral, grounds. Moreover, although Paul stood with Judaism, which strictly condemned homosexuality, he was writing to a primarily Gentile audience which held vastly different attitudes towards homosexuality, some insisting that it was natural.[95] Paul's teaching actually pushed against the moral current of many in Corinth and elsewhere. He was not, therefore, as some claim, simply

---

91. For further discussion, see "Excursus on Marriage and Divorce" in chapter 7.

92. In the Book of Mormon, see 3 Nephi 12:27–32.

93. The word is a combination of ἄρσην (*arsēn*), male, and κοιτή (*koitē*), literally "bed" but often used as a euphemism for sexual intercourse, thus the English word "coitus." The word, apparently coined by Paul, clearly designated sexual activities between males. See Fee, *First Epistle*, 244, where he notes that the word, used in the context of sexual sins, "does seem to refer to male homosexuality, especially to the active partner."

94. For a more extended study on this issue, see Translation Notes and associated Analysis for Rom. 1:25–27 in this commentary series.

95. Fee, *First Epistle*, 261, notes that Paul was fighting against a number of "Corinthian slogans," that is, ideas that passed into the Church without critical examination and were used by the defiant party against Paul. One of these could have been that homosexuality

reflecting the attitude of the time. He saw homosexuality as a "wandering from the truth" of God's purpose for sexuality.[96]

In summary, Paul condemned homosexual acts as a sin against God's created order. In doing so, he reaffirmed the Old Testament prohibition against the act as found in the Leviticus holiness code (Lev. 18:22; 20:13). Paul's stand clearly showed that the practice cannot be seen as part of an ethical backwater of archaic Hebrew purity laws, as some insist.[97] Certainly Christians adopted the spirit of these purity laws from the law of Moses in defining appropriate sexual relationships. For him, the law consisted of relevant standards protecting God's order—commandments that remain an important part of the new covenant. In Romans and Corinthians, Paul definitely ties the *arsenokoitai* to those who break up the divine order and the natural law that God set up. In so doing, Paul followed Old Testament Jewish and Platonic traditions, not hedonistic, epicurean ones.[98]

Deadly sin, however, reaches well beyond those pertaining to sexual matters. Paul had already listed several, but he now included κλέπται (*kleptai*), "thieves." This sin was part of a larger range of sins forbidden in the eighth commandment, "Thou shalt not steal." The commandment forbade taking another person's property "by coercion, fraud, or without his uncoerced consent. Cheating, harming property, or destroying its value is also theft."[99] The verb Paul used focused on that aspect of stealing done by stealth and cunning, most notably taking advantage, embezzling, cheating,

---

was not against nature. Paul refutes the idea by tying the discussion to the created order that God ordained.

96. This is the literal meaning of πλάνη (*planē*), translated "perversion." BDAG, 822. See James R. Edwards, *Romans,* vol. 6 of *New International Biblical Commentary* (Peabody, Mass.: Hendrickson Publishers, 1992), 55–56.

97. For a discussion, see Margaret Davies, "New Testament Ethics and Ours: Homosexuality and Sexuality in Romans 1:26–27," *Biblical Interpretation* 3, no. 3 (1995): 315–31.

98. Philo, in his denunciation of homosexuality, uses the same terms Paul uses describing it as παρὰ φύσιν (*para physin*) "against nature," (*Change of Names* 111–12; *Special Laws* 4.79; *Dec.* 142, 150). See also Josephus, *Against Apion,* 2.273, who describes homosexuality in the same terms. Joseph A. Fitzmyer argues convincingly that Paul followed his religious traditions and the Old Testament throughout Romans 1–3 in *The Jerome Biblical Commentary,* ed. Raymond E. Brown and others (Englewood Cliffs, N.J.: Prentice-Hall, 1968). Since all three condemn homosexuality, Paul cannot be construed as being ambivalent about it. Paul clearly condemns homosexual activity, using it as his best example of how far people can fall from God. See Douglas Moo, *The Epistle to the Romans,* New International Commentary on the New Testament (Grand Rapids, Mich.: Eerdmanns, 1996), 112–17.

99. Rushdoony, *Institutes,* 452.

or various forms of legal trickery (though something may be lawful, that does not make it morally right). An often overlooked aspect of any kind of theft is that it is "a violation of God's fundamental order."[100] He has given people the right to have what they work for and expects others to respect that. The thief, however, seeks a short-cut path to wealth by avoiding the work necessary for its proper attainment and, in doing so, violates God's system.[101] Such an act among the Christians, who were preparing the spiritually legal and moral superstructure for God's kingdom, simply could not be tolerated.

Paul did not let his desire to shame his readers stand in the way of giving them hope. As noted above, one of his objectives was to force them to see the reality of their situation as opposed to how they perceived it. Though many had fallen to grievous transgressions before their conversion, these sins were now in the past. Ideally, no longer were they like the wicked. The kingdom of God still stood open before them. Through the grace of God they had found forgiveness, their former sins had been removed, and a change of character initiated. Through the power of God's Spirit and in the name of the Lord, they had come under his transforming power and, therefore, were expected to live up to their new condition.[102] If they did not do so, all the cleansing, purification, and empowering would come to naught and they would be, just like the wicked, shut out forever. Their lot, indeed, might even be worse, for having had access to the Spirit and having turned away, they would suffer the full wrath of God (see Heb. 6:4–6; 2 Pet. 2:20–22; D&C 42:25–26).

Paul used his words to remind them of the state they once enjoyed (and many still did) and, more particularly, how they got there. The path began with *the* supernal act of grace on Christ's part, namely, his atoning sacrifice. Having received of that grace through their willingness to be baptized by water and fire, they were now obligated to live the Christian life. Though right behavior neither preceded nor led to grace, such behavior was evidence that grace had been received, acknowledged, appreciated, and acted upon. Thus, Paul tied proper behavior and grace together in the ancient context of the covenant of Christ's Atonement. Once grace had come, one could not continue to enjoy its benefits without proper behavior. To believe that proper behavior was unnecessary was to see the gospel as nothing

---

100. Rushdoony, *Institutes,* 452.
101. Rushdoony, *Institutes,* 453–55.
102. Fee, *First Epistle,* 254.

more than a simple whitewashing of the sinner. Nothing internal changed. Without any regeneration or transformation, belief was nothing and stood outside Paul's theology. "The Corinthian problem was not with their experience of the Spirit," one scholar noted, "but with their misunderstanding of what it meant to be Spirit people."[103] That misunderstanding was leading them out from under Christ's grace and away from God's kingdom.

In 6:11, Paul told the Corinthian Saints that they had been purified "in the name of the Lord." His words show that there was an official, authorized act behind the spiritual endowments that they now enjoy. Insight to what the phrase meant comes from Moses 5:6–8 in which an angel appears to Adam and asks why he has been offering sacrifices. After Adam confessed he had no idea but to obey God's command, the angel revealed the symbolism behind the act, stating, "This thing is a similitude of the sacrifice of the Only Begotten of the Father, which is full of grace and truth. Wherefore, thou shalt do all that thou doest in the name of he Son, and thou shalt repent and call upon God in the name of the Son forevermore." The word "wherefore," as used here, is telling because it gave the reason why he was to do "all that thou doest" in the Lord's name. It was because of the Atonement. The word "all," however, is restrictive. It related to all spiritual and institutional matters of the kingdom. It meant that everything in that context was to be done in accordance to revealed rule and order as set down by the Son to bring about the ends of his sacrifice. To speak properly in the name of Jesus, then, was to have his authority to act in a given matter, but it also imposed abiding by the limits that order demanded. The person, then, became the Lord's agent and did all to the Savior's credit and benefit. Since prayer was central to finding out God's will and, thus, acting in his behalf, it too was to be done in his name.

FLEE SEXUAL IMMORALITY
(6:12–20)

Greek Text

12 Πάντα μοι ἔξεστιν· ἀλλ᾽ οὐ πάντα συμφέρει. πάντα μοι ἔξεστιν· ἀλλ᾽ οὐκ ἐγὼ ἐξουσιασθήσομαι ὑπό τινος. 13 τὰ βρώματα τῇ κοιλίᾳ, καὶ ἡ κοιλία τοῖς βρώμασιν· ὁ δὲ θεὸς καὶ ταύτην καὶ ταῦτα καταργήσει. τὸ δὲ σῶμα οὐ τῇ πορνείᾳ ἀλλὰ τῷ

---

103. Fee, *First Epistle,* 248.

κυρίῳ, καὶ ὁ κύριος τῷ σώματι· 14 ὁ δὲ θεὸς καὶ τὸν κύριον ἤγειρεν καὶ ἡμᾶς ἐξεγερεῖ διὰ τῆς δυνάμεως αὐτοῦ. 15 οὐκ οἴδατε ὅτι τὰ σώματα ὑμῶν μέλη Χριστοῦ
ἐστιν; ἄρας οὖν τὰ μέλη τοῦ Χριστοῦ ποιήσω πόρνης μέλη; μὴ γένοιτο. 16 ἢ οὐκ
οἴδατε ὅτι ὁ κολλώμενος τῇ πόρνῃ ἓν σῶμά ἐστιν; Ἔσονται γάρ, φησίν, οἱ δύο
εἰς σάρκα μίαν. 17 ὁ δὲ κολλώμενος τῷ κυρίῳ ἓν πνεῦμά ἐστιν. 18 φεύγετε τὴν
πορνείαν· πᾶν ἁμάρτημα ὃ ἐὰν ποιήσῃ ἄνθρωπος ἐκτὸς τοῦ σώματός ἐστιν, ὁ δὲ
πορνεύων εἰς τὸ ἴδιον σῶμα ἁμαρτάνει. 19 ἢ οὐκ οἴδατε ὅτι τὸ σῶμα ὑμῶν ναὸς τοῦ
ἐν ὑμῖν ἁγίου πνεύματός ἐστιν, οὗ ἔχετε ἀπὸ θεοῦ; καὶ οὐκ ἐστὲ ἑαυτῶν, 20 ἠγοράσθητε γὰρ τιμῆς· δοξάσατε δὴ τὸν θεὸν ἐν τῷ σώματι ὑμῶν. [SBLGNT]

King James Version

12 All things are lawful unto me, but all things are not expedient: all things are lawful for me, but I will not be brought under the power of any. 13 Meats for the belly, and the belly for meats: but God shall destroy both it and them. Now the body is not for fornication, but for the Lord; and the Lord for the body. 14 And God hath both raised up the Lord, and will also raise up us by his own power. 15 Know ye not that your bodies are the members of Christ? shall I then take the members of Christ, and make them the members of an harlot? God forbid. 16 What? know ye not that he which is joined to an harlot is one body? for two, saith he, shall be one flesh. 17 But he that is joined unto the Lord is one spirit. 18 Flee fornication. Every sin that a man doeth is without the body; but he that committeth fornication sinneth against his own body. 19 What? know ye not that your body is the temple of the Holy Ghost which is in you, which ye have of God, and ye are not your own? 20 For ye are bought with a price: therefore glorify God in your body, and in your spirit, which are God's.

New Rendition

12 It is said, "I can do anything," but not all things are beneficial. "I can do anything," but I will not be controlled by anything. 13 "Food is for the stomach and the stomach is for food. But God will do away with them both." The body is not meant for sexual immorality but for the Lord, and the Lord for the body. 14 Now God both raised the Lord and will raise us through his power. 15 Don't you understand that your bodies are members of Christ? Should I take the members of Christ and make them the members of a whore? Certainly not! 16 Don't you understand the one who is joined together with a prostitute becomes one body, for it is said, "They shall become one flesh." 17 But one who is joined with the Lord becomes one spirit with him. 18 Flee from sexual immorality! Any other sin that a person can commit is external to his body. But one who practices sexual immorality sins against his own body. 19 Or don't you understand that your body is a temple for the Holy Spirit that is within you, which body you have received from God? Indeed, you are not your own, 20 for you were bought for a price. So glorify God with your own body.

Translation Notes and Comments

6:12 *All things are lawful unto me / It is said, "I can do anything"*: The phase πάντα μοι ἔξεστιν (*panta moi exestin*) meant literally "all things are lawful / possible for me." The phrase appears to be a slogan bandied about by one or more of the Church factions to justify their indiscriminant and morally wrong behavior.[104] The present active verb ἔξεστιν (*exestin*) meant either that which was "lawful," that is, "permitted," or that which was "possible."[105] The context makes it clear that Paul was using it in the last sense and, therefore, showed that this group felt that they could do anything they wanted to because it was possible to do so. Their position seems to have derived from a gross misunderstanding of the Atonement that led them to believe that they were beholden to no law.

The JST changes this verse to read, "All these things are not lawful unto me, and all these things are not expedient. All things are not lawful for me, therefore I will not be brought under the power of any." The changes emphasized that Paul understood that all things were neither lawful nor expedient for him and because they were not lawful, he would not give them power over him by yielding to them. Though the JST does not reflect the nuance of the Greek text, it accurately shows Paul's mindset. Our Rendition updates the KJV and captures the sense of the JST expressing Paul's mindset.

but all things are not expedient . . . but I will not be brought under the power of any / but not all things are beneficial . . . but I will not be controlled by anything: The present active verb συμφέρει (*sympherei*) denoted the act of bringing things together for one's advantage and defined what was "beneficial, useful," or "helpful,"[106] while ἐξουσιάζω (*exousiazō*) meant "to have authority over, exercise power over" or "to control."[107] Having authority over is the most common use.

Paul admitted that his audience could, indeed, do anything they wished, but that did not necessarily make their actions right. Their position fell apart for two reasons. First, just because something could be done did not mean it was beneficial to the Christian or to his community. That reason

---

104. Its derivation is unknown. It may have been generated from the Stoic philosophy concerning freedom (ἐλευθερία, *eleutheria*) and the right of self-determination (ἐξουσία αὐτοπραγίας, *exousia autopragias*). See Diogenes Laërtius 7.121; Epictetus, *Diss.* 1.1.21. However, the idea was not unknown to the Jews. See Philo, *Prob.* 9 §59.

105. Collins, *First Corinthians*, 243.

106. Louw-Nida, §15.125.

107. BDAG, 353–54.

alone should have acted as a break on their activities. Second, just because they could do something did not mean they would be free of its consequences. Indeed, some choices could lead to a loss of control and, therefore, to the loss of the very freedom they boasted in having.

Giving his point real thrust was a wordplay Paul used that cannot be translated into English. His phrase πάντα μοι ἔξεστιν· ἀλλ᾽ οὐκ ἐγὼ ἐξουσιασθήσομαι ὑπό τινος (*panta moi exestin all' ouk egō exousiasthēsomai hypo tinos*) played on two word forms derived from ἐκ (*ek*) + εἰμί (*eimi*): first, the impersonal verb ἔξεστιν (*exestin*), "it is possible, lawful," or "permitted," connoting that which was proper,[108] and second, ἐξουσιάζω (*exousiazō*) "to have authority or control over," connoting a person's right to act based on "freedom of choice." In the passive voice, it meant to be mastered by a thing.[109] Paul's use of that voice here emphasized that he would not put himself under the control of anything that would limit his ability to carry out God's will. God's commandments provided the framework within which anyone could safely exercise their God-given agency by not infringing on the rights of others and avoiding being trapped by addiction or habituation.

6:13 *Meats for the belly, and the belly for meats: but God shall destroy both it and them / "Food is for the stomach and the stomach is for food. But God will do away with them both":* This phrase appears to be another slogan used by the licentious element among the Christians to justify their untoward behavior. The noun βρῶμα (*brōma*) meant "food," especially solid food as opposed to drink.[110] Here it is in the plural with the sense of food in general. In King James English "meat" did not have the more restricted sense of "flesh" that it does in modern English, but it was a general term for solid food. Following the sense of the Greek, the word βρῶμα is translated as "food" in our Rendition.

The noun κοιλία (*koilia*), "stomach," also denoted the entire digestive track.[111] The verb καταργέω (*katargeō*), "destroy," also denoted making something ineffective or powerless as well as abolishing or doing away with it.[112]

The punctuation in the KJV suggests that the slogan ended with the word "meats." It is more likely that the slogan included the idea that in the divine

---

108. BDAG, 348.

109. Thiselton, *First Epistle*, 461; Fitzmyer, *First Corinthians*, 264; BDAG, 354.

110. BDAG, 184.

111. Johannes Behm, "κοιλία," in *TDNT*, 3:786–89.

112. BDAG, 525.

end, God would do away with both food and the digestive tract. The reason, these people seem to have felt, was that nothing physical was to survive mortality.[113] Therefore, the implication of the slogan was that as food was digested and the remains cast off, the same was true of all other things physical. These were to be left behind. Since God was concerned only with eternal things, what was done with, to, or for the body simply did not matter to him. Only the spiritual did. Βρῶμα (*brōma*), by extension, represented all passions and appetites and, therefore, inferred the idea that the body was for sex and sex for the body. Since there was nothing immoral about eating food, there was also nothing immoral about satisfying any other of the body's cravings.[114] Taking the verse this way, it is easy to see how it flows into Paul's denouncing fornication.

Now the body is not for fornication, but for the Lord; and the Lord for the body / The body is not meant for sexual immorality but for the Lord; and the Lord for the body: The noun πορνεία (*porneia*) is the general term for any kind of sexual immorality. In the context here (6:15–16), however, it appears to refer to sexual relations with a prostitute.[115] Paul denied the truthfulness of the slogan. The body did indeed have a purpose but that purpose was not for self-gratification but for service to God within the parameters of the principle of chastity.

Just what Paul meant by saying that "the Lord [was] for the body" is unclear. It is likely that he was simply using a stylistic device mimicking the rhythm and force of the slogan matching "the body is for food and food for the body" with "the body is for the Lord and the Lord for the body." Whatever the case, his point is clear: the Lord had high interest in any and all things the body did.[116]

6:14 *And God hath both raised up the Lord, and will also raise up us by his own power / Now God both raised the Lord and will raise us through his power:* Taking the coordinating conjunction *de* as marking a narrative segment and thus translating it as "now,"[117] the word showed

---

113. Fee, *First Epistle*, 254–55 and n. 28.

114. Fee, *First Epistle*, 255; C. T. Craig, "The First Epistle to the Corinthians," *Interpreter's Bible*, 12 vols. (New York: Abingdon Press, 1953), 10:73–74.

115. Fitzmyer, *First Corinthians*, 265.

116. Fee, *First Epistle*, 256; Fitzmyer, *First Corinthians*, 265. There is little wonder the Lord is interested in what the body does since one of his objectives for mortality was to give his children a physical body that could be celestialized. One of the punishments of the devil is being deprived of a body. See Ehat and Cook, *Words of Joseph Smith*, 60.

117. BDAG, 213.

that Paul was, at this point, going to explain the theological underpinning of what he had just said. That underpinning was that the body was not, as the antiresurrection faction believed, transitory. The aorist verb ἤγειρεν (*ēgeiren*), "raised up," also denoted being raised to a newness of life and Paul used it here to refer to the resurrection of the Lord.[118] The future verb ἐξεγερεῖ (*exegerei*), "will raise up" also denoted God raising us from the dead,[119] and Paul used it to describe the future resurrection of the Saints. His point was this: as surely as God raised Jesus from the grave, so, too, he would raise the Saints. Emphasizing the majesty of the resurrection, Paul noted that behind it stood the power of God himself. Therefore, future and eternal corporeality was of divine intent. The body would not be left behind and, therefore, its deeds—here and now—mattered.

6:15 *Know ye not that your bodies are the members of Christ? / Don't you understand that your bodies are members of Christ?:* This verse contained the sixth use of Paul's phrase, "Don't you understand," and, again, appealed to a doctrinal principle all should have known and agreed to. The noun μέλος (*melos*), "member" denoted a human body part such as a limb or organ.[120] Paul's analogy emphasized that each person played an important and life-sustaining role in the kingdom. Each person was, as it were, the Lord's hands or his feet by which he accomplished his will. Therefore, the close degree of unity that was to exist between the Lord and his disciple demanded a high degree of holiness on the Saint's part.

shall I then take the members of Christ, and make them the members of an harlot? / Should I take the members of Christ and make them the members of a whore?: The present aorist participle ἄρας (*aras*), "taking, taking away," also carried the force of snatching, wrenching, or carrying something off by force.[121] The verb ποιήσω (*poiēsō*) is an aorist subjunctive used in a deliberative question, "should I take?" The answer is a definitive μὴ γένοιτο (*mē genoito*) "certainly not!"[122] The noun πόρνη (*pornē*) denoted

---

118. BDAG, 271; Louw-Nida, §23.94.

119. BDAG, 346; Louw-Nida, §23.94. There are manuscript variations on the tense of this verb, but the context gives the future tense the priority. Metzger, *Textual Commentary*, 486–87.

120. BDAG, 628.

121. Louw-Nida, §15.203; Thiselton, *First Epistle*, 465.

122. Wallace, *Greek Grammar*, 467. Paul uses the same construction in Rom. 6:1–2, ἐπιμένωμεν τῇ ἁμαρτίᾳ, ἵνα ἡ χάρις πλεονάσῃ; μὴ γένοιτο (*epimenōmen tē hamartia hina hē charis pleonasē mē genoito*) "Should we continue in sin, so that grace may abound? Certainly not!"

a prostitute.[123] To pick up Paul's disgust, our Rendition translates the word by the more coarse word, "whore."

Though Paul framed his point in the form of a question, it was actually a statement of fact designed to force his readers to see the incongruity of taking something that was holy and wrenching it away to make it part of something that was very unholy.

God forbid / Certainly not!: The optative phrase μὴ γένοιτο (*mē genoito*), literally "may it not happen," was very emphatic. The KJV phrase "God forbid" was used during a much less secular era when the name of the divine was highly respected and carefully used. At that time, the idiom denoted very strong negation. Today the thought can be rendered by such phrases as, "Never!" or "Unthinkable!" or, as in our Rendition, "Certainly not!"[124]

6:16 *What? know ye not that he which is joined to an harlot is one body? for two, saith he, shall be one flesh / Don't you understand the one who is joined together with a prostitute becomes one body, for it is said, "They shall become one flesh":* Once again, Paul asked his damning question: "Do you not know?" The present passive participle κολλώμενος (*kollōmenos*), "bound together, joined closely,"[125] carried no sexual connotation per se. The emphasis was on the tightness of the bond, thus it carried the idea of cleaving, clinging to, and even being glued or welded to something.[126] The only way to undo such a bond was to wrench, rip, or tear it apart.

Using LXX Genesis 2:24, Paul, however, gave the word a sexual spin by appealing to the phrase ἔσονται γάρ . . . οἱ δύο εἰς σάρκα μίαν (*esontai gar . . . hoi dyo eis sarka mian*), "and they two shall be one body." Admittedly the phrase nuanced the whole relationship between wife and husband, but Paul's focus was strictly on the physical aspect. His point was that during sexual activity with a prostitute, there was a literal and illicit joining of

---

123. BDAG, 854. Miroslav Marcovich, "From Ishtar to Aphrodite," *Journal of Aesthetic Education* 30, no. 2, Special Issue: Distinguished Humanities Lectures II (Summer 1996): 49, focuses on ritual prostitution practiced in her temples. The Greek ἱροδούλη (*hierodoulē*), "sacred slave," was a euphemism for a ritual prostitute, but Paul did not use this term. Though Corinth had been renowned for its temple prostitution and Paul turned to the imagery of the temple in this section, it is unlikely he had ritual sexual intercourse in mind. See Murphy-O'Connor, *1 Corinthians*, 55–57; Fee, *First Epistle*, 258 n. 39.

124. Thiselton, *First Epistle*, 466.

125. BDAG, 555–56.

126. Louw-Nida, §18.21. The *LSJ*, 825, notes the word's use to describe the joining and welding of metals and the gluing the pieces of pottery. The word found in the LXX is *proskollasthai*, "to cleave to, to be faithfully devoted to," nuances the ideal bond between husband and wife. Karl Ludwig Schmidt, "κολλάω, προσκολλάω," in *TDNT*, 3:822–23.

two bodies.[127] This illicit action is in stark contrast with how a disciple of Christ should be joined to Christ through his Atonement and likewise joined to his/her lawful spouse.

6:17 *But he that is joined unto the Lord is one spirit / But one who is joined with the Lord becomes one spirit with him:* Paul was quick to point out that the joining (κολλάω, *kollaō*) between disciple and Lord, though close, strong, and intimate as implied by the verb, was strictly spiritual. In our Rendition we have added "with him," which is not in the Greek, to clarify that this is a spiritual union with the Lord.

6:18 *Flee fornication / Flee from sexual immorality!:* The verb φεύγω (*pheugō*) had the basic meaning, "to seek safety in flight," or "to flee" to avoid danger.[128] Sexual sin, if indulged in, would bring spiritual death and loss of eternal life in the celestial kingdom. A disciple of Christ could only find safety by fleeing from sexual immorality.

Every sin that a man doeth is without the body[129] */ Any other sin that a person can commit is external to his body:* Paul did not mean for πᾶν ἁμάρτημα (*pan hamartēma*) literally "every/any sin," to be all-inclusive— he was clearly dividing sin into two distinct categories: sexual sin, which is committed against one's own body, and any other type of sin. In our Rendition, we have added "other" to clarify this contrast. The preposition ἐκτός (*ektos*) meant "outside of" or "external to" something.[130] Though this phrase could be one of the slogans popular among the libertine element of the Christian community,[131] the context suggests otherwise. The phrase showed that Paul gave sexual sin a depth all of its own. Unlike all others, he pointed out, it was an internal sin, one that was generated by yielding to the passions of the flesh. As a result, this deep-seated carnality and sensuality wrenched the body away from Christ and joined it profanely to another.

---

127. Fee, *First Epistle*, 259.
128. BDAG, 1052. The wording brings to mind Joseph's fleeing Potiphar's wife in Gen. 39.
129. What Paul meant by this phrase remains so ambiguous that over twenty different theories have been posed. See Ernest-Benard Allo, *Saint Paul: Première Épitre aux Corinthiens* (Paris: Gabalda, 1934), 148; and C. Senft, *La Première Épitre de Saint Paul aux Corinthiens,* Commentaire du Nouveau Testament, 2d ed. (Geneva: Labor et Fides, 1990), 84–85.
130. BDAG, 311.
131. Upholding this view are Conzelmann, *1 Corinthians*, 112; Collins, *First Corinthians*, 249; Jerome Murphy-O'Connor, "Corinthian Slogans in 1 Cor. 6:12–20," *Catholic Biblical Quarterly* 40 (1978): 391–96; Roger L. Omanson, "Acknowledging Paul's Quotations," *Bible Translator* 43 (April 1992): 201–13.

but he that committeth fornication sinneth against his own body / But one who practices sexual immorality sins against his own body: In the phrase εἰς τὸ ἴδιον σῶμα (*eis to idion sōma*), the preposition *eis,* which has the root meaning "into, in, toward,"[132] is used here in a hostile sense[133] and is thus translated "against" in both the KJV and our Rendition. With this phrase Paul explained just why sexual sin was so bad. It has, as one scholar noted, "a destructive quality with metaphysical repercussions." Indeed, "other sins do not necessarily take the believer by force away from the body of Christ and join him or her to a new body. In Paul's view fornication does," and, therefore, it stands among the most spiritually deadly of sins.[134]

6:19 *What? know ye not that / Or don't you understand that:* This was the eighth time Paul used this damning phrase to point out either the depth of these members' ignorance or their blatant disregard for established doctrine.

your body is the temple of the Holy Ghost which is in you / your body is a temple for the Holy Spirit that is within you: Instead of ἱερόν (*hieron*), which generally referred to "the temple at Jerusalem, including the whole temple precinct with its buildings, courts, etc.,"[135] Paul used the noun ναός (*naos*), which usually referred to "a place or structure specifically associated with or set apart for a deity, who is frequently perceived to be using it as a dwelling."[136] In doing so, he stressed the extreme holiness of the pure body.

Though Paul used the plural pronoun ὑμῶν (*hymōn*), "your," his point was that the Holy Spirit dwelt in each individual Saint. Each person's body was, then, the holy habitation of the Spirit.[137] Since both Jews and Gentiles understood and believed in the need for temple purity, the analogy had real force.[138] To defile such a holy place was unthinkable. The same applied to the human body.

---

132. BDAG, 288.

133. BDAG, 290; Wallace, *Greek Grammar,* 369.

134. Bailey, *Mediterranean Eyes,* 192. Thiselton, *First Epistle,* 47–72.

135. BDAG, 470.

136. BDAG, 665.

137. Note that D&C 130:22 states the Holy Ghost is a spirit, "were it not so, [he] could not dwell in us."

138. Youlin Liu, *Temple Purity in 1–2 Corinthians* (Tübingen: Mohr Siebeck, 2013), 165–73, states that prostitution was analogous to "image-mutilation," an act that rendered the temple impure and stripped sovereignty and power from the god. In the case of Christians, the immoral act stripped them of Godly power and protection.

which ye have of God / which body you have received from God: Compounding his view of the sanctity and holiness of the body, Paul noted that it was God given.

6:19–20 ye are not your own? For ye are bought with a price / you are not your own, for you were bought for a price: With this statement Paul underscored the reality of their situation. The passive verb ἠγοράσθητε (*ēgorasthēte*), "you were bought" spoke volumes. It felled the view of those who felt they were self-made men and, therefore, were free to do anything they wanted. "No," Paul said, "they had been bought for a price." The noun τιμῆς (*timēs*) in the genitive denoted the amount at which something was valued, thus, "price, value."[139] The price each one of them cost was the Savior's agony on the cross. In the ancient world, receiving a gift implies obligations to keep his commandments. In this case, it is essential that disciples keep the law of chastity.

therefore glorify God in your body, and in your spirit, which are God's / So glorify God with your own body: The phrase "and your spirit, which are God's" is not found in any of the early manuscripts.[140] Because it appears to be a later addition, it is not found in our Rendition.

To emphasize his point, Paul began his last sentence with the particle δή (*dē*), "thus, therefore, so," which denoted that an argument had been so clearly and irrefutably made that a point could now be drawn from it.[141] Paul's point was that the Saints were to use their bodies for the purpose for which they were given them for which we came to earth. The proper use of the procreative powers allows us to be happy and participate in the plan of salvation as legitimate earthly parents to spirit children of our Father and Mother in Heaven.[142]

Analysis and Summary

Paul turned to the next area of improper conduct perpetrated by some members of the Corinthian branch. The problems here derived from the influence of idolatry with its sexually immoral overtones which acted to compromise the Saints' exclusive faithfulness to God and Christ. It

---

139. BDAG, 1005.

140. Metzger, *Textual Commentary,* 487–88.

141. BDAG, 222.

142. The First Presidency and Council of the Twelve Apostles of The Church of Jesus Christ of Latter-day Saints, "The Family: A Proclamation to the World," *Ensign* 25 (November 1995): 102, available online at https://www.lds.org/ensign/1995/11/the-family-a-proclamation-to-the-world?lang=eng.

expressed itself in advocating the misuse of the body in two ways: self-gratification and inappropriate sexual activity, in this case going to a brothel. Paul's major point here was that the believer's body was "for the Lord" and not *for* the purpose of self-gratification (6:13). There was no dualism in early Christianity as there was in Platonic philosophy between the body and the spirit/mind. Indeed, the body was the physical temple that the Holy Spirit sanctified and then inhabited (6:19) and the means by which the Saints brought glory to God (6:20). The major point Paul was making in this section was the inseparability of "Christian identity and Christian lifestyle, or of theology and ethics."[143]

In putting this view across, Paul distanced himself from two theological slogans popular among a segment of the Church that they used to justify their illicit behavior. The first was "all things are lawful unto me," that is, "I can do anything."

So far as the first was concerned, Paul did not attack their view directly but rather raised the point of debate to a higher plane by appealing to the theology that provided the ground for proper behavior. This allowed him to qualify their view so sharply that it essentially negated it. No longer was the concern with what they could or could not do, but with what was beneficial and helpful to the community, both civil and religious. He forced his readers to consider their freedom in the context of what it meant to be a Christian. The verb he used, συμφέρω (*sympherō*), meant "to bring together" and hinted at that unity that was so vital to the harmony required for full enjoyment of the Spirit. Just because they were free to act did not free them from the obligation of acting for the greater good because of Christ's Atonement. That which was beneficial had to be the guide to determine how they were to express their moral agency. Just because something was "lawful" or "right" or even "all right" in the world at large did not mean it was moral to God. The Christian must act on the basis of what was proper, good, harmonic, and spirit inducing—in short, what was in keeping with God's will.[144]

There was, however, another area in which their theological position was false. They bragged of having the authority, that is, the right or liberty (ἐξουσία, *exousia*) to do anything they wanted. Their view was likely grounded on the false belief that they lived on such a high spiritual plane that they were beyond all laws, religious or civil. What they did not seem to

---

143. Thiselton, *First Epistle*, 458–59.
144. Thiselton, *First Epistle*, 458–59; Fee, *First Epistle*, 251–52.

realize was that they were walking into a paradox, for if everyone acted as though they had "unqualified autonomy, no one [could] be free, for everyone [would be] threatened by the freedoms of the other."[145]

Further, their feeling that they had the liberty to do anything they wanted opened the door through which they could become the servants of sin (John 8:34; Rom. 6:16; Alma 3:26–27). Using a forceful wordplay revolving around the idea of "authority, liberty" (*exousia*), Paul drove his point home: though he could express his moral agency any way he wished and therefore had liberty to do all things, he would not let any of these take liberties with him. It was as if he were saying, "I will never by the abuse of my liberty forfeit that liberty" by allowing sin to control him.[146] In essence, what Paul did was redefine freedom. Because of the Christians' concern for the physical and spiritual welfare of their brothers and sisters, they must be willing to forego the full range of their liberty. Morality, ethics, and lifestyle had to be one.[147]

The other slogan some Saints adopted was that "'food is for the stomach and the stomach is for food.' But God will do away with them both" (6:13, Rendition). They used this to justify their giving in to sexual passion and lust. The implication of the slogan was that there was nothing wrong or sinful about satisfying natural bodily appetites.[148] The slogan, influenced as it likely was by epicurean and cynic ideas, allowed them to separate the "low" physical plane from the "higher" spiritual one and to believe that the lower had no impact on the higher. Because the physical body would not be regenerated, it did not count and, therefore, anything done to satisfy its temporal wants, even if they were carnal and sensual, did not hurt anyone.

Paul's response set the record straight. He did not address the issue of the permanence of either βρῶμα (*brōma*) "food" or the κοιλία (*koilia*) "stomach." Instead he focused on the σῶμα (*sōma*), "the body." Though he would address the issue more fully in chapter 15, the reality of the resurrection lay at the heart of his point here. Whatever may be said for food or digestion, the *sōma* was not transient and, therefore, should not to be equated with the *koilia*. Though the present body would be transformed in the resurrection, the indisputable fact was that corporality still remained. Therefore, what one did to, for, or with his or her body counted on the

---

145. Thiselton, *First Epistle*, 461.

146. Findlay, "St. Paul's First Epistle," 818; Thiselton, *First Epistle*, 461.

147. Thiselton, *First Epistle*, 462.

148. Conzelmann, *1 Corinthians*, 110; Murphy-O'Connor, "Corinthian Slogans," 391–96.

eternal scale of things.[149] Hence the purpose of the body was not for gratification, especially not in sexual areas, but for service to the Lord.

The point was that while the physical body has sexual desires, these desires must be controlled and kept within the bounds set by God. Sexual intercourse outside of marriage was strictly forbidden. And from an LDS perspective, a major purpose of mortality is to raise families that will continue into the eternities. The requirement to do this can only be met through the proper use of the power of procreation in the context of celestial marriage. The proper use of procreative powers combined with the authority to use them, then, opens the door to the joy of "eternal lives" whereby couples have the right to have children in the eternities.[150]

Paul next addressed a major concern generated by the belief by some of the libertine elements among the Saints, that it was perfectly alright to frequent the local brothels. Through the force of a rhetorical question (6:15), Paul attempted to get the Corinthian Saints to see the asininity of their insistence that physical acts do not harm spiritual standing. It was their belief that, because the body dies and stays dead, it is morally irrelevant. In other words, what the body did in no way affected personality.[151] Of the many items they did not understand, a very important one was that the Saints, having made covenants with the Lord, became one with him in a very profound, deeply spiritual, and intimate way (6:15). This close bonding, using Paul's analogy, made one a "member" (μέλος, *melos,* a limb or organ) of Christ. The Saints, body and soul, were, therefore, metaphorically part of the Lord's body and shared in his holiness. Each person was to be one exclusively with the Lord.

In Paul's thought, the whole person—body and spirit—belonged to the Savior. His Atonement redeemed both and, therefore, he had claim on both. Therefore, sexual relation with a whore was much more than a "mere" physical act. It broke the physical bond between Saint and Savior.[152] To join with a prostitute, therefore, violated both the holiness and oneness so essential to the spiritual life. Using LXX Genesis 2:24, the Apostle showed that intercourse with a prostitute constituted becoming "one" with her, thus violating and destroying the Saint's oneness with Christ (6:16–17).

---

149. Craig, "First Corinthians," 10:73–74. The Savior's Atonement made it possible for the disciple to "be one, as we [God and Christ] are" (John 17:11), that is to say, to be united through the Holy Spirit in love, purpose, and ministry.

150. For more, see Shirley S. Ricks, "Eternal Lives, Eternal Increase," in *EM*, 2:465.

151. C. F. D. Moule, *Idiom Book of New Testament Greek,* 2d ed. (Cambridge: Cambridge University Press, 1956), 196–97, Murphy-O'Connor, "Corinthian Slogans," 391–96.

152. R. H. Gundry, *Sōma in Biblical Theology with Emphasis on Pauline Anthropology* (Cambridge: Cambridge University Press, 1976), 69.

Paul's argument revealed his deep respect for the body and the importance of keeping it holy (separated from the lusts and passions of the world)
in order for it to be a fit tabernacle, not just temporally but eternally, for the
individual's spirit and that of the Lord in the plan of happiness.

In addition, Paul's position in no way devalued martial intimacy. In fact,
his stand did just the opposite. He reached beyond the myopic perspective of his time and revealed the physical relationship as one ordained by
God that imposed a self-commitment between the marital partners that
involved the whole person, body and soul.[153] In marriage each partner was
fully giving himself or herself to the person to whom he or she belonged. It
was this self-giving and self-commitment that made intimacy in the marital
context holy (7:14). Since both of these were totally lacking in any relationship with a prostitute, that sexual act was most reprobate and unholy. It
was the aspect of self-giving and self-commitment that linked the relationship between husband and wife to that of disciples and Lord. In both, the
covenantal relationship made the participants "one."[154]

From Paul's point of view, all sin but one happened external to the body.
The phrase emphasized the outrageous nature of illicit sex. Indeed, it was
"most abominable above all sins save it be the shedding of innocent blood
or denying the Holy Ghost" (Alma 39:5). Though it is true that other sins,
such as drunkenness, gluttony, or drug abuse, do indeed come from yielding to appetites within the body, yielding to sexual passion is particularly
damning because it involves the debasing of not just one soul but two and
sometimes unborn children or immediate family members, the family unit,
and even society as a whole. From the Old Testament perspective, it is
generated by a selfishness known to no other sin and one that was the most
destructive to the self (Prov. 6:22–33).

Paul's view of sexual sin came, in part, due to his respect of the physical
body and the fact that it constituted a part of the whole self that, through
covenant, was joined to Christ. The problem with sexual sin was that it
wrenched (αἴρω, *airō*) the soul away from the body of Christ (both spiritually and communally) and joined it to another. No other sin did that.[155]

---

153. Derrick S. Bailey, *The Man-Woman Relation in Christian Thought* (London: Long-
mans, 1959), 9–10. See also Brendan Byrne, "Sinning against One's Own Body: Paul's
Understanding of Sexual Relationships in 1 Cor. 6:18," *Catholic Biblical Quarterly* 45
(October 1983): 608–16.

154. Bailey, *Man-Woman Relation*, 9–10.

155. Bailey, *Mediterranean Eyes*, 192.

Showing Paul's extreme regard for the holy nature of the pure body was his comparing it to the temple (ναός, *naos*) of God. Unlike the imagery he used in 3:16, where the temple represented the community of the Saints, here it referred to each individual. Not only does the Spirit of God dwell in the Church as a whole, it also dwells in each individual member. It was, in large measure, to achieve this relationship—a higher endowment than had been possible before—that the Savior faced the terrible weight of the cross.[156] Indeed, he prayed that his disciples "may be one, as we [the Father and Son] are" (John 17:11). As one LDS scholar noted,

> This union implies an indwelling relationship like that which exists in the relationship that Christ has with his Father. When the Holy Spirit is developed in those who truly accept Christ, so that they become his sons and his daughters and mature in the divine attributes and powers of Christ, the full and complete union is produced for which Jesus prayed. . . . Of how this indwelling union was to be achieved, Jesus then explained: "And the glory which thou gavest me I have given them; that they may be one, even as we are one: I in them, and thou in me, that they may be made perfect in one." (John 17:21–23.) Thus we see that it is when men [and women] receive the glory of the Father through Christ that they are made one in the indwelling relationship of celestial life.[157]

As two LDS scholars have noted, in Paul's writings, there is a "precise allusion to the individual body-as-temple. . . . Jesus, his disciples, and the authors of the New Testament were concerned about the defilement of the temple-body. The temple at Jerusalem and its place in early Christian scripture (our present-day Old Testament) became a vehicle to help the early Saints understand their own divine potential as temples of the Holy Spirit."[158] God takes this relationship seriously and therefore has warned that "whatsoever temple is defiled, God shall destroy that temple" (D&C 93:35).

Paul's position concerning the holiness and importance of the body cut across the grain of Greco-Roman thinking influenced by Cynics and Epicureans concerning the spirit and body. Indeed he reversed the supposed hierarchy between spiritual and bodily states in which "lower things" (food,

---

156. In John 14:17, he promised his disciples that the Holy Ghost which had been "with you" shall now "be in you."

157. Hyrum L. Andrus, *Joseph Smith—a Modern Witness for Christ* (Provo, Utah: Brigham Young University, BYU Extension Publications, 1963), 28–29.

158. Richard Neitzel Holzapfel and David Rolph Seely, *My Father's House: Temple Worship and Symbolism in the New Testament* (Salt Lake City: Bookcraft, 1995), 197.

drink, and intimacy) did not relate to "higher things" (intellect, spiritual station). The Apostle insisted that each Saint revealed what he or she really was in what they did *in the body* in the daily acts of life. It was, indeed, in this way that emerged what it meant to be "in Christ."[159]

Paul made his point very clear. To interpret his words: "Each of you is God's holy temple and, therefore, you possess a degree of holiness. Beware lest your pride in possessing the Holy Spirit turn to your ruin. Since your body has been sanctified, put it to the use for which it was intended, the glorification of God through self-mastery and acts of kindness."[160]

The Saints' bodies, he assured them, were not their own, but gifts from God (6:19–20) and the salvation of the body was purchased by the precious blood of Jesus Christ. That blood bought them from the slave block of sin (Rom. 6:17–22). The act did not, however, make them free men and women. Indeed, they now belonged to a new master, Jesus, and were under obligation to do his bidding. That did not, however, make their position lowly. Indeed, being the slave of one of high rank, and especially being a member of his court, brought the individual a great deal of prestige. Indeed, some slaves had greater prestige than did most freemen,[161] thus, the importance of being ὁ δοῦλος ᾽Ιησοῦ Χριστοῦ (*ho doulos Iēsou Christou*), "the slave of Jesus Christ" (Rom. 1:1; Gal. 1:10; Titus 1:1), a station that brought with it high status.

To summarize, by the blood spilled in the Garden of Gethsemane and on the cross of Calvary, Christ bought them both body and soul. Thus, both spirit and body were obliged to unite in service to him. Both were essential and by the everyday righteous deeds the Christians did they not only proved that Christ dwelt in them but also brought him glory.

---

159. Martin, *Corinthian Body,* 178.

160. Henry B. Seete, *The Holy Spirit in the New Testament* (London: Macmillan, 1909, 1921), 181.

161. Dale B. Martin, *Slavery as Salvation: The Metaphor of Slavery in Pauline Christianity* (New Haven, Conn.: Yale University Press, 1990), 1–49; Marleen B. Flory, "Family and *Familia:* Kinship and Community in Slavery," *American Journal of Ancient History* 3 (1978): 78–95.

Chapter 7

On Marriage, Divorce, and Missionary Service

INTRODUCTION

At this point in his epistle, the Apostle began to answer questions that were posed in a letter written to him. From the nature of his remarks, it would appear that not all of these were requested by faithful Saints asking a recognized spiritual leader for advice. Some of the letters reflected rejoinders to his initial letter (5:9). From the way Paul answered some of the questions, it appears he was responding to demands that he give his proofs for the positions he had taken. He responded to all the questions answering them point by point, each one introduced with the phrase περὶ δέ (*peri de*), "now concerning" (7:1, 25; 8:1; 12:1; 16:1, 12).[1] The exception seems to be 11:17–34, where he inserted a comment on an item that came to his attention from a different context. Given, however, the close organization and flow of this epistle, it would seem that Paul chose the order in which he made his responses.[2] It is of note, though, that his tone was that of a shepherd trying to guide his flock through a morass of problems generated by the societal issues that they faced, as opposed to a verbal pugilist trying to knock out his foes.

Because some of these issues had no black or white answers, Paul could do no more than give his opinion. Each, however, was based on solid gospel principles or inspiration. Even so, some concerns admitted to no hard

---

1. Some scholars see περὶ δέ (*peri de*) only as a marker denoting a change of subject rather than pointing to a response to a letter. For example, see Mitchell, *Paul and the Rhetoric of Reconciliation*, 190–91. But even among these there is agreement that Paul was addressing questions that had been posed to him by the Corinthians. For arguments see Hurd, *Origin*, 61–71.

2. Fee, *First Epistle*, 266–67.

answers. On the other hand, for those concerns that did, Paul spoke from the position of doctrine and authority and made that clear.

Because he was responding to a letter we do not have, Paul's answers are highly contextualized. The result is like listening to only half of a telephone conversation; the other half can only be guessed at.[3] As a result of the indeterminate nature of the text and due to biases, misinterpretations, and mistranslations, this chapter has lent itself to a good deal of misunderstanding and misapplication.[4] Concerning certain verses one scholar noted, "the literature is voluminous and unrewarding."[5]

The problem of misinterpreting Paul's intent is not new. From the second century on, some Christians felt that Paul advocated an ascetic lifestyle as a higher and more spiritual way to live than that of wedlock. They based their interpretation on a misunderstanding of the Fall of Adam and Eve, which they saw as the seat for sexual desire. Indeed, some of these sectarian interpretations went so far as to believe that true holiness could be achieved only by avoiding all sexual contact whether in or out of marriage. We can trace a root of this idea into first century Corinth where some insisted that "it is good for a man not to have sexual relations with a woman" (7:1, Rendition). Exactly where this idea came from is unknown, but it certainly did not come from Paul. When all of his statements on marriage are taken together, and in context, they provide the Apostle's clear and unmistakable endorsement of marriage. In this chapter, properly read, Paul not only sanctioned marriage but also the mutual sexual responsibility that it demands.[6]

The theme that runs throughout this section is the need for the Saints to act as Christians in whatever social condition they found themselves. Paul's counsel, over and over, was that they should abide and flourish in their particular circumstance. In this chapter, as in those before, he fought against Christians getting caught up in the desperate Corinthian disease of social climbing and status gathering. The Saints' concern, he counseled, was to cultivate their fellowship with God and remain ever as a member of his household.

---

3. Sperry, *Paul's Life*, 121; Holzapfel and Wayment, *Making Sense*, 351; *DNTC*, 2:343.

4. For a discussion of the many views used to interpret Paul, see Will Deming, *Paul on Marriage and Celibacy: The Hellenistic Background of 1 Corinthians 7* (Cambridge; Cambridge University Press, 1995), 5–49; and Thiselton, *First Epistle*, 487–93.

5. Bailey, *Mediterranean Eyes*, 225.

6. Ogden and Skinner, *Verse by Verse*, 134.

Latter-day Saints are fortunate because Joseph Smith's inspired version and other insights coming from the Restoration provide important pieces of context so needed in understanding Paul's intent and, thereby, interpreting him correctly. Even so, there are some passages that remain unsettled.

The layout of this chapter suggests the specific set of questions Paul was answering. They dealt with intimacy in marriage (7:1–6), whether widows and widowers should remarry (7:7–9), under what conditions Christians should divorce (7:10–11), what believers married to unbelievers should do (7:12–16), what slaves should do (7:17–24), what those called to the ministry should do (7:25–34); what engaged couples should do (7:35–38), and if widows should remarry (7:39–40).

THE MUTUAL OBLIGATIONS OF HUSBAND AND WIFE (7:1–9)

Greek Text

1 Περὶ δὲ ὧν ἐγράψατε, καλὸν ἀνθρώπῳ γυναικὸς μὴ ἅπτεσθαι· 2 διὰ δὲ τὰς πορνείας ἕκαστος τὴν ἑαυτοῦ γυναῖκα ἐχέτω, καὶ ἑκάστη τὸν ἴδιον ἄνδρα ἐχέτω. 3 τῇ γυναικὶ ὁ ἀνὴρ τὴν ὀφειλὴν ἀποδιδότω, ὁμοίως δὲ καὶ ἡ γυνὴ τῷ ἀνδρί. 4 ἡ γυνὴ τοῦ ἰδίου σώματος οὐκ ἐξουσιάζει ἀλλὰ ὁ ἀνήρ· ὁμοίως δὲ καὶ ὁ ἀνὴρ τοῦ ἰδίου σώματος οὐκ ἐξουσιάζει ἀλλὰ ἡ γυνή. 5 μὴ ἀποστερεῖτε ἀλλήλους, εἰ μήτι ἂν ἐκ συμφώνου πρὸς καιρὸν ἵνα σχολάσητε τῇ προσευχῇ καὶ πάλιν ἐπὶ τὸ αὐτὸ ἦτε, ἵνα μὴ πειράζῃ ὑμᾶς ὁ Σατανᾶς διὰ τὴν ἀκρασίαν ὑμῶν. 6 τοῦτο δὲ λέγω κατὰ συγγνώμην, οὐ κατ᾽ ἐπιταγήν. 7 θέλω δὲ πάντας ἀνθρώπους εἶναι ὡς καὶ ἐμαυτόν· ἀλλὰ ἕκαστος ἴδιον ἔχει χάρισμα ἐκ θεοῦ, ὁ μὲν οὕτως, ὁ δὲ οὕτως. 8 Λέγω δὲ τοῖς ἀγάμοις καὶ ταῖς χήραις, καλὸν αὐτοῖς ἐὰν μείνωσιν ὡς κἀγώ· 9 εἰ δὲ οὐκ ἐγκρατεύονται, γαμησάτωσαν, κρεῖττον γάρ ἐστιν γαμῆσαι ἢ πυροῦσθαι. [SBLGNT]

King James Version

1 Now concerning the things whereof ye wrote unto me: It is good for a man not to touch a woman. 2 Nevertheless, to avoid fornication, let every man have his own wife, and let every woman have her own husband. 3 Let the husband render unto the wife due benevolence: and likewise also the wife unto the husband. 4 The wife hath not power

New Rendition

1 Now regarding that which you wrote saying: "It is good for a man not to have sexual relations with a woman." 2 On the contrary, because of the numerous enticements for sexual misconduct, let each man have his own wife, and each woman have her own husband. 3 Let the husband grant conjugal rights to his wife, and likewise the wife conjugal

of her own body, but the husband: and likewise also the husband hath not power of his own body, but the wife. 5 Defraud ye not one the other, except it be with consent for a time, that ye may give yourselves to fasting and prayer; and come together again, that Satan tempt you not for your incontinency. 6 But I speak this by permission, and not of commandment. 7 For I would that all men were even as I myself. But every man hath his proper gift of God, one after this manner, and another after that. 8 I say therefore to the unmarried and widows, It is good for them if they abide even as I. 9 But if they cannot contain, let them marry: for it is better to marry than to burn.

rights to her husband. 4 A wife does not hold exclusive rights over her own body—her husband also has rights; neither does a husband hold exclusive rights over his own body—his wife also has rights. 5 Do not deprive each other of intimate relations, except perhaps by mutual agreement for a specified time, so that you can devote yourselves to prayer, and then come together again, so that Satan will not tempt you because of your lack of self-control. 6 I'm telling you this as a concession, not as a command. 7 Now I wish everyone was like me, but each person has his own gift from God, one having one kind, another a different kind. 8 To the widowers and widows, I say it is good for them to remain even as I am. 9 However, if their desires become too strong, then they should get married, for it is better to get married than to be consumed by those desires.

Translation Notes and Comments

7:1 *Now concerning the things whereof ye wrote unto me: It is good for a man not to touch a woman / Now regarding that which you wrote saying: "It is good for a man not to have sexual relations with a woman"*: The KJV suggests that Paul taught it was not good for a man to touch a woman. That was not the case. As the introduction notes, it was a quote from a letter that the Corinthians wrote to Paul. The JST supports this by adding "saying" after "ye wrote unto me."

The verb ἅπτομαι (*haptomai*) in the middle voice with a genitive object meant "to touch" or "take hold of." However, it was widely used in Greek literature as a euphemism for having sexual relations, and that is certainly the sense it has here.[7] The noun γυνή (*gynē*) denoted "a woman," but most often referred to a wife.[8] Though it is likely that the Corinthians' question dealt with intimacy within context of a marriage, that is uncertain and so

7. BDAG, 126.
8. BDAG, 208–9; Louw-Nida, §10.54.

our Rendition translates the word as "woman."[9] Even so, it would appear that there was an element within the Church that believed that a higher state of spirituality could be obtained if sexual abstinence was practiced even in marriage.

7:2 *Nevertheless, to avoid fornication, let every man have his own wife, and let every woman have her own husband / On the contrary, because of the numerous enticements for sexual misconduct, let each man have his own wife, and each woman have her own husband:* Traditionally this has been interpreted to mean that Paul believed that the general and major reason for marriage was to safeguard against immorality.[10] Because the Corinthians' statement was one with which Paul disagreed, the adversative δέ (*de*), "but, nevertheless," needs more force and, therefore, is translated as "on the contrary," in our Rendition. JST reads "Nevertheless, I say, . . ." making it clear that Paul was responding to the statement in the Corinthians' letter to him. The prepositional phrase διὰ . . . τὰς πορνείας (*dia . . . tas porneias*), literally "because of the fornications," presents some difficulty in translation since Paul used the plural rather than the singular. His use of the plural suggests that he was referring to the various factors that could tempt a person to engage in sexually immoral acts.[11] Hence our Rendition translates this as "because of the numerous enticements for sexual misconduct." Paul was therefore saying that, especially for those who were already married, they should not abstain from normal sexual relations with their spouses.

7:3 *Let the husband render unto the wife due benevolence: and likewise also the wife unto the husband / Let the husband grant conjugal rights to his wife, and likewise the wife conjugal rights to her husband:* The KJV follows the Textus Receptus which has ὀφειλομένην εὔνοιαν (*opheilomenēn eunoian*), "due benevolence" which denoted "the favor that is owed." The phrase was a softened version of ὀφειλή (*opheilē*), literally "obligation," which is supported by all the earliest and best manuscripts in contrast to Textus Receptus.[12] Paul was referring, not to something that was a favor or benevolence, but to the sexual obligations that husbands and wives owe to their spouses. To catch this nuance the word is translated "conjugal rights" in our Rendition.

---

9. Holzapfel and Wayment contend that the question concerned married couples and whether or not they should live a celibate lifestyle. See Holzapfel and Wayment, *Making Sense,* 351.

10. Fee, *First Epistle,* 277; Thiselton, *First Epistle,* 501.

11. BDAG, 854.

12. Metzger, *Textual Commentary,* 488.

7:4 *The wife hath not power of her own body, but the husband: and likewise also the husband hath not power of his own body, but the wife / A wife does not hold exclusive rights over her own body—her husband also has rights; neither does a husband hold exclusive rights over his own body—his wife also has rights:* In this verse, Paul explained why each partner should not deny the other. Paul's intent turns on his use of the present active verb ἐξουσιάζω (*exousiazō*), "to have the right of control."[13] The point is that, in marriage, there is a "mutual giving of the self" to the other party. As a result, "the husband cannot abuse the wife, for his body is no longer his own to use as he wills without her consent; the wife cannot opt out of intimacy permanently, for her body [is], *similarly*," or "likewise" (ὁμοίως, *homoiōs*), "not [exclusively] hers."[14] The point is that there is an equality that should exist between partners. Under the Christian ideal of marriage, both should take into consideration the needs of the other.

7:5 *Defraud ye not one the other, except it be with consent for a time, that ye may give yourselves to fasting and prayer / Do not deprive each other of intimate relations, except perhaps by mutual agreement for a specified time, so that you can devote yourselves to prayer:* The JST reads, "Depart ye not one from the other, except it be with consent for a time." The inspired translation emphasizes the need for a couple to remain closely and emotionally linked partners. Separation was to be brief when necessary so that the couple could give themselves time for uninterrupted meditation and prayer. The Textus Receptus and some earlier documents add "fasting," but all the earliest and best texts support the shorter text.[15]

In pushing his point, Paul used the present imperative, ἀποστερεῖτε (*apostereite*), "to cause another loss by taking away by illicit means," thus, "to rob, steal," or "defraud." The word connoted depriving someone of something that was their due.[16] This was the very word the Apostle used with force in 6:7 when he told his readers not to "steal." His choice of the word here betrayed how strongly he felt sexual duty was, since continence amounted to theft.[17]

Paul used the negated μή (*mē*) with the present (as opposed to an aorist) tense, ἀποστερεῖτε (*apostereite*), "do not defraud," which can also be translated, "Stop defrauding." He was, therefore, likely addressing a present

---

13. BDAG, 353–54.
14. Thiselton, *First Epistle*, 505.
15. Metzger, *Textual Commentary*, 489.
16. BDAG, 121; Louw-Nida, §57.47.
17. Fee, *First Epistle*, 281.

occurrence.[18] It may be that some had already determined that a more spiritual Christian life required ascetic living, principally by overmastering the body, including renouncing physical intimacy, and began practicing it.[19] Since, however, the text of the letter stated that "it is good for a man not to touch a woman," it is likely that some men had adopted that position.

Paul did allow for separation for the purpose of uninterrupted prayer and meditation. He put two caveats on the practice, however. The first was that it was to be ἐκ συμφώνου (*ek symphōnou*), "to agree upon," implying a joint decision,[20] and, thus, translated as "mutual agreement" in our Rendition. His second was that it was to be πρὸς καιρόν (*pros kairon*), "for a set time." The action precluded debate as to when the time was over.

and come together again, that Satan tempt you not for your inconti-nency / and then come together again, so that Satan will not tempt you because of your lack of self-control: The noun ἀκρασία (*akrasia*) denoted a "lack of self-control" or giving over to "self-indulgence."[21] For these weak ones, a goal of marriage was to nullify Satan's effect and this would not hap-pen if the time for prayer were over long.[22] There is a bit of a barb in Paul's words here.

7:6 But I speak this by permission, and not of commandment / I'm telling you this as a concession, not as a command: The JST reads, "And now what I speak is by permission." The phrase κατὰ συγγνώμην (*kata syngnōmēn*), "as a concession," denoted an agreement based on a compro-mise.[23] In translating the text, the problem is identifying the antecedent to τοῦτο (*touto*), "this." The context suggests that Paul's concession referred not to marriage (as some suggest), but to the married couple's mutual agreement to cease intimacy for a season.[24] If that is the case, then Paul's point was that he would not normally agree that sexual relations should be suspended even for extended periods of prayer, but, given these members' disposition, he was willing to meet them halfway.

---

18. Robertson and Plummer, *Critical and Exegetical Commentary,* 134; Fee, *First Epis-tle,* 281.

19. Antoinette Clark Wire, *The Corinthian Women Prophets* (Minneapolis: Fortress Press, 1990), 82–90.

20. Louw-Nida, §31.15.

21. BDAG, 38.

22. Thiselton, *First Epistle,* 508.

23. BDAG, 950.

24. Fee, *First Epistle,* 284; Thiselton, *First Epistle,* 495, and 510–11 for the full range of possible antecedents for the word τοῦτο (*touto*).

7:7 ***For I would that all men were even as I myself / Now I wish everyone*** ***was like me:*** The verb θέλω (*thelō*), "wish, desire," expressed strong desire for something or someone.[25] The noun ἄνθρώπος (*anthrōpos*) "human being," referred to a person of either sex, and is translated as "everyone" in our Rendition.[26] Paul's wish was that everyone were like him in some respect. Unfortunately, he does not identify just what that was, and that has led to much speculation. Those who insist that Paul was referring to an unmarried state, however, are reading into the text.[27] See Analysis below.

But every man hath his proper gift of God, one after this manner, and ***another after that / but each person has his own gift from God, one hav-*** ***ing one kind, another a different kind:*** The pronominal adjective ἕκαστος (*hekastos*), "each man" is masculine, but keeping Paul's audience in mind, it is translated generically, "each person," in our Rendition. The adjective ἴδιον (*idion*), "one's own," pertained to an exclusive or unique relationship of the person to the object (in this case a gift from God) and suggested how unique, special, and proper it was to that person.[28] The noun χάρισμα (*charisma*), "gift," denoted a favor, deed, or object that was freely and graciously bestowed.[29]

Whatever Paul's circumstance was, he recognized that it was a special and specific gift from God granted to him in light of his ministry. It is of note that Paul did not fall into the trap of advocating that all could or should do as he did. What was best for him, he tacitly admitted, was not necessarily that which was best for everyone else.[30] He fully recognized that others received their gifts from the same divine source he did and so one gift was not superior to another. His gift, therefore, was not somehow better, higher, or more holy than theirs. It was only "better" given the circumstances in which the Church found itself at the moment.

7:8 ***I say therefore to the unmarried and widows, It is good for them*** ***if they abide even as I / To the widowers and widows, I say it is good for*** ***them to remain even as I am:*** The adjective ἄγαμος (*agamos*), denoted an

---

25. BDAG, 447.

26. BDAG, 81.

27. Some authors who see Paul referring to a state of celibacy are Findlay, "St. Paul's First Epistle," 823–24; Fee, *First Epistle,* 284–85; Fitzmyer, *First Corinthians,* 282; Collins, *First Corinthians,* 260. Some translations of the Bible also take liberties with this passage. For example, the RSV reads, "remain single as I am;" the NIV reads, "stay unmarried as I am," and the Phillips translation reads, "remain unattached as I am."

28. Louw-Nida, §57.4; BDAG, 466–67.

29. BDAG, 1081.

30. Murphy-O'Connor, *1 Corinthians,* 59; Fee, *First Epistle,* 285.

unmarried person, male or female.[31] In the case of a man, it could mean either a bachelor or a widower.[32] Because the plural noun has a masculine definite article and is juxtaposed with ταῖς χήραις (*tais chērais*), "the widows," some have suggested it denoted "widowers."[33] Others, however, have felt that that particular translation was too exclusive, and prefer "unmarried men," a class in which widowers would belong.[34] Because Paul addressed people who were married (7:10–17), never married (7:25–28), serving missions (7:29–34), engaged (7:35–38), and recently widowed (7:39–40), our Rendition follows the former view, translating the word as "widowers."

The adjective καλόν (*kalon*), "good, useful," should not be construed to mean "preferable, better, or best."[35] Paul was saying that, given the present circumstances, what he had chosen to do was something he recommended to others as "a good thing." This state was "good" only for the time being. He explained his reasoning in 7:26, 28, and 32–35.[36] He does not feel, however, it was a "good thing" for everyone or for all times.

Again, Paul referred to his unique circumstance without explicitly identifying it. He may not have had to since he had lived among the Corinthians for months and they knew, first hand, of his situation. He did feel strongly enough about the propriety of his lifestyle that he did not hesitate to denote it as "good thing."

7:9 *But if they cannot contain, let them marry / However, if their desires become too strong, then they should get married:* The present middle/passive deponent verb ἐγκρατεύομαι (*engkrateuomai*), "be self-controlled," means to keep one's passions in check.[37] The conditional clause with a present indicative indicates the assumption of truth for the sake of argument, but it does not necessarily imply that the speaker believes it to be true.[38] Paul is counseling widows and widowers to remain single, but he is leaving them the option to remarry if they find their sexual desires become too strong for them to handle.

---

31. BDAG, 5.

32. LSJ, 5.

33. For example, see William F. Orr and James A. Walther, *1 Corinthians* (Garden City, N.Y.: Doubleday, 1976), 210; Fee, *First Epistle*, 228, 287–88; Thiselton, *First Epistle*, 515–16.

34. For example, see Robertson and Plummer, *Critical and Exegetical Commentary*, 138; Bruce, *1 and 2 Corinthians*, 68; Barrett, *First Epistle*, 160.

35. BDAG, 504–5.

36. Fitzmyer, *First Corinthians*, 283.

37. BDAG, 274.

38. Wallace, *Greek Grammar*, 450–51.

for it is better to marry than to burn / for it is better to get married than to be consumed by those desires: The passive of πυρόω (*pyroō*), literally "to be burned," could also mean "to burn with sexual desire."[39] The JST reads, "But if they cannot abide, let them marry; for it is better to marry than that any should commit sin." The translation certainly highlights the danger these persons were in.

Taken in context, Paul was not recommending marriage as a remedy against sexual passion in general, as the verse is usually understood.[40] Paul appears to have been talking specifically to widows and widowers who "do not have power over their passions" such that they could devote proper time to God and gospel living.[41] His point was that those whose sexual passions kept them from total devotion to the gospel should marry or they would lose their souls.[42]

Analysis and Summary

With this section, Paul began to respond to questions he had received in one or more letters from the Corinthian branch. President Howard W. Hunter taught, "The communications revealed that there were factions forming in the branch with different views regarding moral conduct and doctrine. ... Some were defending loose sexual standards that were rampant in the notorious city."[43] On the other extreme were some who advocated an abandonment of intimacy even in the context of marriage. Having previously addressed the attitudes of the libertines who felt that "anything goes," he now addressed those of the ascetics who felt that "nothing goes."

His first topic was that of the sexual relationship in marriage. This subject followed naturally from his discussion of sexual immorality treated in chapters 5 and 6.

Writing in 1983, one LDS scholar wrote, "Most translations have Paul begin with the grim generalization, 'It is good for a man not to touch a woman' (1 Cor. 7:1). This is a strange statement for a scripturalist who elsewhere relies on Genesis, which commands man to leave parents and be 'one flesh' with his wife (Gen. 2:24), a passage cited by Christ himself

39. BDAG, 899.

40. Note the KJV translation, "if they cannot contain," and the NIV, "if they cannot control themselves."

41. Thiselton, *First Epistle*, 518–19.

42. Fitzmyer, *First Corinthians*, 284.

43. Howard W. Hunter, "The Reality of the Resurrection," *Improvement Era* 72 (June 1969): 106.

(Matt. 19:5). But Joseph Smith's translation makes 'not to touch a woman' part of the Corinthian's letter of inquiry and not Paul's answer. . . . In this case Paul's refutation [was] the tender picture of married love . . . , exactly reversing the mood of 'not to touch a woman.'"[44]

Paul was quite direct in addressing those members who felt that a higher mode of spirituality could be achieved by celibacy even within marriage and were advocating this idea. This ascetic portion of the Christian community likely picked up the idea that was growing among certain followers of neo-Platonic philosophy that austere abstinence was a good thing.[45] Indeed, some advocated that intimacy should be strictly reserved exclusively for procreation.[46] Paul's counsel was that abstinence could be practiced, but only for a specific reason, a short period, and with mutual agreement (7:5).

Paul's response to the position of the ascetics that one should not "touch a woman," was "On the contrary!" It is of note that his views were not generated by a kind of high idealism, but rather as a response to a positive and realistic view of human nature.[47] There were certain cases of sexual misconduct (τὰς πορνείας, *tas porneias*) that had come to his attention.[48] These intensified the need for the expression of conjugal rights in marriage with its obligatory fidelity.

Paul's view of love within the marriage relationship actually went against the general view of much of Gentile and Jewish society at the time. Although Corinthian society was rather libertine in its views of chastity, the popular view in much of the Greco-Roman world was that marriage was primarily for "the procreation of legitimate heirs who would inherit and continue the name, property and sacred rites of the family."[49] In saying that, we do not want infer that marriages lacked commitment and affection. Though it

---

44. Anderson, *Understanding Paul,* 104.

45. Origen commented on this in his analysis of 1 Cor. 7. See Claude Jenkins, "Origen on I Corinthians. III," *Journal of Theological Studies,* o.s., 9 (July 1908): 500–501.

46. Musonius, a first century stoic philosopher, popularized this view. See Musonius, *Is Marriage a Handicap?* 85.5–6.

47. Fitzmyer, *First Corinthians,* 274.

48. Given Paul's polemic against patronizing prostitutes in chapter 6, it may be that the cases of immorality (*tas porneias*) he mentions sprang from women not being willing to fulfill their obligation and men seeking illicit relief. Fee, *First Epistle,* 278.

49. R. B. Ward, "Musonius and Paul on Marriage," *New Testament Studies* 36 (1990): 286–87. The erotic poet Ovid, in *Ars Amatoriae* 2.585–86, taught that sexual pleasure could never be fully enjoyed in marriage because intimacy was a matter of duty. Among the Jews, equality in sexual matters was unknown. Women were penalized much more than men when they withheld conjugal rights. See *Midrash Rabbah* on Gen. 20:8–18; Bailey, *Mediterranean Eyes,* 202–3.

is true that nearly all marriages among the nobility free-born classes were arranged, many reached the ideal of becoming warm and congenial.[50]

The Apostle, in effect, redefined the purpose of marriage putting it in the context of a mutually satisfying sexual relationship. Indeed, Paul did not even mention procreation as the primary and dutiful purpose of marriage.[51] Instead, he lifted intimacy to its rightful place as the binding and holy self-commitment and self-giving of one lover to another. His high and enlightened view of the role sexual relations had in marriage gave fire to his hatred of sexual immorality that he castigated so severely in chapters 5 and 6.[52] To find such an enlightened view, as one scholar noted, "is truly amazing to discover in a first-century document!"[53] Verses 7:2 and 7 do present a more negative view for reasons to marry, namely as a stopgap measure for immorality, a crutch for those with low self-control, and as a means of resisting Satan. Even so, it showed Paul's realism.

On the other hand, 7:3 and 6 present a very positive view. As one scholar noted, "the marital relationship is now presented as a positive 'right' that each partner is expected to *give as a gift* to the other. The husband and the wife are equal in this regard. Neither partner is to demand those rights, rather each is to *give gifts* to the other. Gifts given in love are always seen by the giver as valuable, otherwise they would not be given. Furthermore, by definition, a gift is always offered as a result of free choice. If it is coerced, it is not a gift."[54] Even so, giving a gift, many felt, obligated the receiver in some way. This scholar went on to say that "equality between the wife and the husband in Christian marriage is here presented in unforgettable terms. Each partner in a marriage has authority over the body of the other. No sexual games are possible in this kind of marriage. There can be no power plays such as, 'Give me what I want, and I will sleep with you.' No form of abuse is even thinkable. *Each* partner can say to the other, 'I have gifts, and I have rights . . . over your body.'"[55]

In this light, Elder Boyd K. Packer taught: "You should be attracted to one another and to marry. Then, and only then, may you worthily respond to the strong and good and constant desire to express that love through

---

50. Carolyn Osiek and David L. Blach, *Families in the New Testament Times: Household and House Churches* (Louisville, Ky.: Westminster John Knox Press, 1997), 60–62.

51. Ward, "Paul on Marriage," 285.

52. Bailey, *Mediterranean Eyes,* 200.

53. Bailey, *Mediterranean Eyes,* 202.

54. Bailey, *Mediterranean Eyes,* 201–2.

55. Bailey, *Mediterranean Eyes,* 202.

which children will bless your lives. By commandment of God our Father, that must happen only between husband and wife—man and woman—committed to one another in the covenant of marriage (see 1 Cor. 7:2; D&C 42:22). To do otherwise is forbidden and will bring sorrow."[56]

Being a realist, Paul recognized that temptation occurs both before and after marriage. Paul counseled couples: "Do not deprive each other of intimate relations, except perhaps by mutual agreement for a specified time" (7:5, Rendition). President Spencer W. Kimball said: "There are many aspects to love in marriage, and sex is an important one. Just as married partners are not for others, they *are* for each other."[57] An LDS scholar noted, "Paul's counsel to married couples [was] that they [were to] not depart nor abstain from sexual intimacy except by mutual consent . . . and then only for brief periods of time lest they be tempted for their *incontinency*."[58]

"Incontinency," Elder McConkie noted, "is lack of restraint and failure to bridle one's passions (particularly where sex desires are concerned)."[59] Paul's use of the noun ἀκρασία (*akrasia*), "lack of self-control" is telling for even in marriage there must be discipline. Elder Packer noted: "A married couple may be tempted to introduce things into their relationship that are unworthy. . . . If you do, the tempter will drive a wedge between you. If something unworthy has become part of your relationship, be wise and don't ever do it again."[60] President Kimball concluded: "Sexual relations in marriage are not unrestrained. Even marriage does not make proper certain extremes in sexual indulgence. . . . If it is unnatural, you just don't do it. That is all. . . . There are some people who have said that behind the bedroom doors anything goes. That is not true and the Lord would not condone it."[61]

Taking a different tack, one LDS scholar noted:

But while prophets have counseled married couples to keep their sexual passions and behaviors within appropriate boundaries, the context of 1 Corinthians 7 suggests that Paul is referring to something else. More likely Paul's concern here has to do with a husband or wife who rejects or

---

56. Boyd K. Packer, "Ye Are the Temple of God," *Ensign* 30 (November 2000): 73.

57. Kimball, *Miracle of Forgiveness*, 73.

58. Brooks, "Paul's Inspired Teachings on Marriage," 78–81.

59. McConkie, *Mormon Doctrine*, 556.

60. Boyd K. Packer, *The Things of the Soul* (Salt Lake City: Bookcraft, 1996), 113.

61. Spencer W. Kimball, *The Teachings of Spencer W. Kimball*, ed. Edward L. Kimball (Salt Lake City: Bookcraft, 1982), 311–12.

withholds sexual intimacy from the spouse for long periods of time in an attempt to hurt, manipulate, control, or seek revenge. Abstinence in marriage can cause unnecessary temptations and tensions. Temptations often occur during times of abstinence, particularly vengefully imposed abstinence. The mind of the spouse begins to wander and the heart begins to stray, thereby allowing Satan to gain greater power to tempt and destroy the marriage.[62]

Verse 7:5, like 7:2, taken at face value, presents a somewhat negative reason for marriage—as a counter to temptation. The same appears to be true for 7:9. However, the Greek text suggests that Paul was directing his remarks to widows and widowers, suggesting that they should remain unmarried unless their sexual passions were so strong that these distracted them from full devotion to the gospel. In that case, it was better for them to remarry. In such cases, marriage would be a real boon in preserving chastity.

To counter the problem, the Apostle was quick to set himself up as an example, saying, "It is good for them to remain even as I am" (7:8, Rendition). Unfortunately he did not specify exactly what he meant, likely because many of his readers had known him while he labored among them for months and, therefore, clearly understood his ways. Whatever the breadth of his remark, we can say with confidence that he was moral, dedicated, and exhibited strong self-control.

It would be helpful if we knew his marital status at the time he wrote. Unfortunately we do not, but it seems very likely that he was a widower who determined not to remarry in order to give himself fully to the ministry during this time of crises.

---

62. Brooks, "Paul's Inspired Teachings on Marriage," 80–81.

EXCURSUS ON THE MARITAL STATE OF PAUL

Discussion on whether Paul was married has spanned the centuries. A major cause is that Paul's writings never directly address this issue. Paul's statement that "I wish everyone were like me" could refer to any one of five conditions: he was a life-long celibate, he was once married but widowed, he was once married but divorced, he was married but separated from his wife due to the rigors of missionary work, or he was married and had his wife with him.

It is very unlikely, after marital age, that Paul was always celibate and advocated it. The major proof texts that some have used to show that he condoned if not advocated celibacy are his supposed statements that it was "good for a man not to touch a woman" (7:1) and that he stated he had always been "unmarried" (7:8). As shown in the Translation Notes above, this view comes only from misreading the text. He did not advocate celibacy in 7:1, but rather was quoting the statement only to refute it. Paul's refutation constituted the tender picture of married love he developed in 7:2–5, which completely "revers[ed] the mood of 'not to touch a woman.'"[63] Further, Paul did not say he was never married. He did align himself with the ἄγαμοι (*agamoi*), but that word referred to widowers. The point is that the Apostle was not advocating celibacy as the way of life. Among the earliest Christians the idea of perpetual virginity was, indeed, foreign. Patristic studies have shown that none of the early Christian writers viewed Paul's counsel as advocating such a lifestyle. The use of 7:7, "I would that all men were even as I," as a proof text for celibacy came only after the ascetic life became an official vocation among the Christians about the mid-third century.[64]

---

63. Anderson, *Understanding Paul*, 104.

64. This was very likely a later development in Christianity brought in by those highly influenced by middle-Platonic philosophy and who were trying to seek a high tension discipleship outside of martyrdom. See the studies by J. Massingberd Ford, "St. Paul, the Philogamist (I Cor. vii in Early Patristic Exegesis)," *New Testament Studies* 11 (July 1965): 326–48; J. Massyngberde Ford, "Levirate Marriage in St. Paul (I Cor. vii)," *New Testament Studies* 10 (April 1964): 361–65. Ariel E. Bybee, "From Vestal Virgin to Bride of Christ: Elements of a Roman Cult in Early Christian Asceticism," *Studia Antiqua* 1 (Fall 2001): 3–19, traced the influence of Vestal virgins on Roman attitudes. Though that society promoted family and fecundity, thus stressing the woman's roles as wife and mother, the sacredness of the Vestals gave rise to respect for virginity as a way of life. Some brought these feelings into the Church and that opened the door, over time, to asceticism.

The circumstantial evidence that Paul was or had been married at one time is quite strong. As a Jew, and one who lived "after the most straitest sect" of its religion, that is, as a Pharisee (Acts 26:5), he would have followed the ideal of marriage as a religious duty.[65] Indeed, as one who, as he says of himself, excelled in obeying all aspects of the Law (Gal. 1:14), he would have viewed marriage as mandatory. Further, he was a member of Jewish councils wherein the members were married and had at least one child.[66] That he was married, at least as a young man, and that his wife died, fits with his aligning himself with the ἄγαμοι (*agamoi*), "widowers."[67] It also fits well with the scenario that he was alone when he wrote Corinthians. In that case, Paul's counsel to the Corinthian Saints meant simply "that widows and widowers should remain unmarried as he (a widower) had done."[68]

On the other hand, he could have been divorced. If Paul's wife refused to convert to Christianity and remained loyal to her Jewish heritage, she would have had very good grounds to divorce him. Pharisees particularly would have viewed him as an apostate imposing on his wife the need to divorce him.[69] It is also possible that, because she would not convert, he divorced her. Taking 7:2–4 coupled with 7:11–14 at face value, he would not have felt it ethical to leave a wife to whom he owed support and responsibility. That suggests she divorced him. On the other hand, if he divorced her, he must have later regretted it.[70]

Paul could have been married at the time he wrote. As one LDS scholar noted,

> The apostles as a group were examples of both marriage and companionship in the ministry, for Paul said that he had "power to lead about a sister, a wife, as well as other apostles, and as the brethren of the Lord, and Cephas" (1 Cor. 9:5). That whole chapter argues that Paul could have required the Corinthians to support him but didn't. But Paul stresses his literal "authority" to ask for support for self and for wife. Would he

65. *Kiddushin* 4:13; *Aboth* 5:21; both in Herbert Danby, *The Mishnah* (Oxford: Oxford University Press, 1977).

66. Anderson, *Understanding Paul*, 24; Brooks, "Paul's Inspired Teachings on Marriage," 77.

67. Sperry, *Paul's Life*, 131.

68. Sperry, *Paul's Life*, 131; compare Ogden and Skinner, *Verse by Verse*, 135.

69. American-Israeli Cooperative Enterprise, *Jewish Virtual Library*, s.v. "apostasy," http://www.jewishvirtuallibrary.org/jsource/judaica/ejud_0002_0002_0_01188.html; Fitzmyer, *First Corinthians*, 283–84, Osiek and Blach, *Families in the New Testament Times*, 62–63.

70. Thiselton, *First Epistle*, 512–13.

renounce a right of support that was never a possibility? That passage really takes for granted Paul's marriage and the Corinthians' knowledge of it.[71]

Some feel that a statement by Clement of Alexandria, who wrote about AD 200 and likely worked from earlier sources, supports this idea. "He claimed knowledge of Paul's marriage, indemnifying his wife with the 'yokefellow' of Philippians 4:3: 'Paul himself does not hesitate in one of his letters to address his yokefellow, whom he did not take about with him in order to facilitate his mission.'"[72] Clement treated the noun σύζυγος (*syzygos*), "yokefellow," which could be either masculine or feminine, as clearly denoting a wife.

There is a problem with Clement's appeal to Philippians as a proof text for Paul's marriage. The phrase in Philippians is γνήσιε σύζυγε (*gynēsie syzyge*), "beloved yokefellow." As noted above, *syzygos* can be either masculine or feminine, its gender being defined by an accompanying definite article or adjective. The modifying adjective, γνήσιος (*gnēsios*), always has three endings, masculine, feminine, and neuter, and, in this case uses the masculine form of the vocative singular, indicating that the noun is masculine. As such, the word would not refer to Paul's wife but to some dear male friend and fellow missionary. In Clement's writing, as noted, the noun is feminine, showing that Clement felt the word referred to Paul's wife. Unfortunately, he does not explain why the word in Philippians was masculine.[73] Another problem is that, even if the masculine form could reference a female, the word still did not necessarily mean "wife" but could mean simply "female companion," and, therefore, a fellow missionary.[74] Thus, it is uncertain from the Greek text just what Paul meant.

One point is very clear, however: Clement was refuting those who were promoting celibacy, and he was definitely using his sources to prove that Paul was married. Also, the word *syzygos* in the LXX and Church Fathers almost always refers to a spouse, not a companion, either male or female.[75]

---

71. Anderson, *Understanding Paul,* 105.

72. *Stromata* 3.6.74–76, quoted in Eusebius, *Hist. Ecc.* 3:30.

73. In *Com. Rom,* 1.1, Origen noted that there were some Christians who believed that Philip. 4:3 referred to Paul's wife. His words suggest that Clement was not the only one who held this view. Origen, an aesthetic, however, did not believe it.

74. Thomas A. Wayment and John Gee, "Did Paul Address His Wife in Philippi?" *Studies in the Bible and Antiquity* 4 (2012): 76–77.

75. Wayment, "Did Paul Address His Wife," 80–84.

Another point that is clear is that Paul held a very high view of marriage. Paul's writings reveal an acute understanding of the relationship between men and women. His insights suggest he was married. As one LDS scholar noted, according to the Apostle,

> the parties are free to choose to be married (1 Cor. 7:36), and marriage is righteous (1 Cor. 7:28). These verses add that duties of marriage may compete with serving the Lord, conflicting somewhat with the positive views of the family in Ephesians. The skepticism on widows remarrying (1 Cor. 7:39–40) is directly contradicted by the young widow's duty to marry and raise a family noted in 1 Tim. 5:14. So 1 Corinthians 7 seems to relate to special circumstances. Following Christ, Paul warns against easy divorce (1 Cor. 7:10–11). Throughout the chapter [there] is a steady theme of loyalty to a married partner once that relationship is made.[76]

As another LDS scholar summarized, "Was he married? In our opinion, the answer . . . [is] an emphatic Yes."[77]

From an LDS point of view, marriage is critical for entrance into God's kingdom (D&C 131:1–4; 132:19–21). It is true that circumstances can place a hold on marriage for a season,[78] but that is always temporary. As an Apostle, Paul would have lived according to gospel standards. The evidence seems to support the idea that Paul was, at one time, married. That he was still so when he wrote the Corinthian letters is possible but not certain. So far as Clement's remarks are concerned, they do not prove Paul was married when he wrote to the Corinthian Saints from Ephesus. It is possible that he could have married or remarried after leaving that assignment and, therefore, had a wife when he wrote to the Philippians.

What seems relatively certain is that, while Paul was in Ephesus, he did not have a wife with him. If that is the case, then it opens the possibility of understanding the "proper gift" (7:7) he said he enjoyed. He was, as one LDS scholar stated, "using himself as an example of sexual self-control (1 Cor. 7:7). 'With consent for a time' (1 Cor. 7:5)," the scholar asked, "did

---

76. Anderson, *Understanding Paul*, 104. Lowell L. Bennion, *Teachings of the New Testament* (Salt Lake City: Deseret Book, 1956), 276–77, notes that taking Paul's writing together, he confirmed the state of marriage.

77. Sperry, *Paul's Life*, 9, 131. See also Ogden and Skinner, *Verse by Verse*, 135–36; Brooks, "Paul's Inspired Teachings on Marriage," 76–78.

78. The prophet Jeremiah was forbidden to marry due to the circumstances in which he labored. See Jer. 16:2–4.

he leave his wife to pursue a dangerous mission at Ephesus?"[79] We do not know. One thing we do know, however, is that he exercised ἴδιον χάρισμα (*idion charisma*), "his own special gift." The word suggests a gift freely bestowed for a specific purpose or task. It would appear that, according to another scholar, Paul's gift "lay in his capacity to sublimate his sexual drives (rather than in one direction merely suppressing them, or in the other direction gratifying them) with the result that his creative energy is poured forth into the work of the gospel at every level of consciousness to great effect, and with no desire for something further (compare Philipp. 4:11)."[80]

We must keep in mind that the issue Paul addressed was not marriage versus celibacy, but a positive attitude that ran two ways. First, it "makes the most of the freedoms of celibacy without frustration,"[81] and second, it "caringly provides the responsibilities, intimacies, love, and 'dues' of marriage while equally living out the gospel."[82] It would seem, therefore, that Paul's gift was one of divinely added self-control, and it is this condition he recommended to others.

---

79. Anderson, *Understanding Paul*, 105; see also Ogden and Skinner, *Verse by Verse*, 135.
80. Thiselton, *First Epistle*, 513.
81. Thiselton, *First Epistle*, 513.
82. Thiselton, *First Epistle*, 513–14.

COUNSEL ON HUSBAND AND WIFE RELATIONSHIPS (7:10–16)

Greek Text

10 Τοῖς δὲ γεγαμηκόσιν παραγγέλλω, οὐκ ἐγὼ ἀλλὰ ὁ κύριος, γυναῖκα ἀπὸ ἀνδρὸς μὴ χωρισθῆναι— 11 ἐὰν δὲ καὶ χωρισθῇ, μενέτω ἄγαμος ἢ τῷ ἀνδρὶ καταλλαγήτω—καὶ ἄνδρα γυναῖκα μὴ ἀφιέναι. 12 Τοῖς δὲ λοιποῖς λέγω ἐγώ, οὐχ ὁ κύριος· εἴ τις ἀδελφὸς γυναῖκα ἔχει ἄπιστον, καὶ αὕτη συνευδοκεῖ οἰκεῖν μετ’ αὐτοῦ, μὴ ἀφιέτω αὐτήν· 13 καὶ γυνὴ εἴ τις ἔχει ἄνδρα ἄπιστον, καὶ οὗτος συνευδοκεῖ οἰκεῖν μετ’ αὐτῆς, μὴ ἀφιέτω τὸν ἄνδρα. 14 ἡγίασται γὰρ ὁ ἀνὴρ ὁ ἄπιστος ἐν τῇ γυναικί, καὶ ἡγίασται ἡ γυνὴ ἡ ἄπιστος ἐν τῷ ἀδελφῷ· ἐπεὶ ἄρα τὰ τέκνα ὑμῶν ἀκάθαρτά ἐστιν, νῦν δὲ ἅγιά ἐστιν. 15 εἰ δὲ ὁ ἄπιστος χωρίζεται, χωριζέσθω· οὐ δεδούλωται ὁ ἀδελφὸς ἢ ἡ ἀδελφὴ ἐν τοῖς τοιούτοις, ἐν δὲ εἰρήνῃ κέκληκεν ἡμᾶς ὁ θεός. 16 τί γὰρ οἶδας, γύναι, εἰ τὸν ἄνδρα σώσεις; ἢ τί οἶδας, ἄνερ, εἰ τὴν γυναῖκα σώσεις; [SBLGNT]

King James Version

10 And unto the married I command, yet not I, but the Lord, Let not the wife depart from her husband: 11 But and if she depart, let her remain unmarried, or be reconciled to her husband: and let not the husband put away his wife. 12 But to the rest speak I, not the Lord: If any brother hath a wife that believeth not, and she be pleased to dwell with him, let him not put her away. 13 And the woman which hath an husband that believeth not, and if he be pleased to dwell with her, let her not leave him. 14 For the unbelieving husband is sanctified by the wife, and the unbelieving wife is sanctified by the husband: else were your children unclean; but now are they holy. 15 But if the unbelieving depart, let him depart. A brother or a sister is not under bondage in such cases: but God hath called us to peace. 16 For what knowest thou, O wife,

New Rendition

10 To those who are married, I give this command—not I but the Lord—that a wife should not divorce her husband. 11 But if she does, she should remain single or become reconciled to her husband. Likewise, a husband should not divorce his wife. 12 To the rest I say—I, not the Lord—if any brother has a wife who is not a believer, and she is willing to live with him, he should not divorce her. 13 Also, if any woman has a husband who is not a believer, and he is willing to live with her, she should not divorce him. 14 For a man who is not a believer is sanctified by his believing wife, and a wife who is not a believer is sanctified by her believing husband, otherwise your children would be unclean, but as it is, they are holy. 15 But if the unbelieving spouse wants a divorce, then let the divorce take place. The believing husband or wife is not under bondage

whether thou shalt save thy husband? or how knowest thou, O man, whether thou shalt save thy wife?

in such circumstances—God has called us to live in peace. 16 Wife, how do you know whether you might save your husband, and husband, how do you know whether you might save your wife?

Translation Notes and Comments

7:10 *And unto the married I command, yet not I, but the Lord / To those who are married, I give this command—not I but the Lord:* The verb παραγγέλλω (*parangellō*) meant to announce something that must be done and, therefore, "to order, instruct, command" or "to give a charge to."[83] Paul chose his word knowing that the Lord's teachings stood behind it. By its use, none of his readers should have failed to understand that he was speaking by divine authority and that his words were not to be ignored or even trivialized.

Let not the wife depart from her husband / that a wife should not divorce her husband: The infinitive χωρισθῆναι (*chōristhēnai*), though passive in form, had an active force and meant "to separate oneself" from another, and was used in the legal sense of "divorce."[84]

Though we do not know where Paul got his information, the synoptic gospels have preserved some of the Lord's strong views on the practice of divorce (see Matt. 5:31–32; 19:3–9; Mark 10:2–12).

7:11 *But and if she depart, let her remain unmarried, or be reconciled to her husband / But if she does, she should remain single or become reconciled to her husband:* This phrase follows exactly Jesus' teachings on the subject (for a study, see "Excursus on Marriage and Divorce" below). As such it was not, as some say,[85] an interjection by Paul stated to meet the unusual conditions affecting either the Church as a whole or the branch in Corinth at the time.[86]

---

83. BDAG, 760. James A. Fischer, "1 Corinthians 7:8–24—Marriage and Divorce," *Biblical Research* 23 (1978): 26–30, argues that in this sentence the Greek falls "somewhere between gnomic exhortation and administrative decision," and on that basis Thiselton argues for the translation of παραγγέλλω (*parangellō*) as "give a charge to."

84. BDAG, 1095.

85. It seems unlikely Paul would quote Jesus just to refute him, therefore, something is going on beneath the text that is hidden from the modern reader. See David L. Dungan, *The Sayings of Jesus in the Churches of Paul* (Oxford: Blackwell Press, 1971), 82.

86. Paul's prohibition echoes one found in Deut. 24:1–4 that forbids a divorced woman from remarrying her former husband. In effect, it guarded against her going after a paramour and then, if things did not work out, returning to her spouse.

let not the husband put away his wife / Likewise, a husband should not divorce his wife: The verb ἀφίημι (*aphiēmi*) means "to send away," but as a legal term, it denoted "to divorce."[87] The charge not to divorce goes equally for the husband, but in his case, Paul gave no caveat. For discussion on the background and theological bases of Paul's position, see "Excursus on Marriage and Divorce" below.

7:12 *But to the rest speak I, not the Lord / To the rest I say—I, not the Lord:* The phrase τοῖς δὲ λοιποῖς (*tois de loipois*), "to the rest," referred to other married couples. Once again, Paul makes a clear distinction between Church doctrine and his counsel.

The reason he was cautious was that he had no precedent for the situation he was now turning to. The Savior never addressed the issue of what should happen if tension arose in a marriage when one spouse converted to Christianity and the other did not. That is not to say that the Savior viewed his teachings as a universal source of peace and joy. Indeed, he declared, "Think not that I am come to send peace on earth: I came not to send peace, but a sword. For I am come to set a man at variance against his father, and the daughter against her mother, and the daughter in law against her mother in law. And a man's foes shall be they of his own household" (Matt. 10:34–36). Note, however, that his statement does not include couples dividing over the issue. Therefore, Paul was left on his own.

If any brother hath a wife that believeth not, and she be pleased to dwell with him, let him not put her away / if any brother has a wife who is not a believer, and she is willing to live with him, he should not divorce her: The adjective ἄπιστος (*apistos*), "unfaithful, nonbeliever," in Paul's context, referred to a non-Christian.[88] As noted above, the verb ἀφίημι (*aphiēmi*), "to send away," when referring to a married couple, meant "to divorce."[89] Note that the decision was left with the unbelieving spouse.

7:13 *And the woman which hath an husband that believeth not, and if he be pleased to dwell with her, let her not leave him / Also, if any woman has a husband who is not a believer, and he is willing to live with her, she should not divorce him:* Though Paul used the word γυνή (*gynē*), "woman, wife," because it is parallel to ἀδελφός (*adelphos*), "brother," in the preceding verse, the context shows the reference is to a *Christian* woman.

---

87. BDAG, 156–57.
88. Louw-Nida, §11.19.
89. BDAG, 156–57.

Again the decision whether to keep the marriage intact is left up to the non-Christian.[90]

7:14 *For the unbelieving husband is sanctified by the wife, and the unbelieving wife is sanctified by the husband / For a man who is not a believer is sanctified by his believing wife, and a wife who is not a believer is sanctified by her believing husband:* Paul here explained why he recommended that the partners stay together. The verb ἡγίασται (*hēgiastai*) is the perfect passive of ἁγιάζω (*hagiazō*), "to consecrate, sanctify."[91] In Greek, the perfect tense emphasized the result or present state of a past action,[92] so the sense here is that an unbelieving husband or wife is sanctified by the past righteousness of their spouse.[93]

The strongest variant manuscripts replace the word *andri*, "husband" with the word *adelphō*, "brother."[94] The change is significant in that it shows that the early Christians used the terms *adelphō*, "brother," and *adelphē*, "sister," to refer to fellow Christians.

else were your children unclean; but now are they holy / otherwise your children would be unclean, but as it is, they are holy: The adjective ἀκάθαρτος (*akathartos*), "impure, unclean," denoted any object or person so religiously defiled that such was banned from association with the divine.[95] Some Jews believed children were unholy and, therefore, were banned from Jehovah's presence unless they were circumcised. This belief caused tension in part-member families since the Christian, believing the law of Moses was fulfilled, did not want the child operated on. So to keep the marriage solvent, the belief that little children were unholy had to be done away by the nonmember as evidenced by not having the child circumcised (D&C 74:1–7).

7:15 *But if the unbelieving depart, let him depart / But if the unbelieving spouse wants a divorce, then let the divorce take place:* The middle

---

90. Liu, *Temple Purity*, 190–91 suggests that the major concern of the believing partner was with the purity of the temple-community that he or she did not want profaned. Divorce was seen as a way to keep the "temple" pure.

91. BDAG, 9–10.

92. Wallace, *Greek Grammar*, 574.

93. On the word "sanctified" and "holy," see Translation Notes on 1:2.

94. Though the noun *andri*, "man," correlates better with *gunē*, "woman," in the passage, the better manuscripts have *adelphō*. The KJV follows the inferior witnesses while the Rendition and the Greek text from which it draws follows the stronger. See Metzger, *Textual Commentary*, 489.

95. BDAG, 34; Louw-Nida, §53.39.

voice of the verb χωρίζω (*chōrizō*), "to separate, depart," has the force of separating oneself from another and, therefore, to be divorced.[96] Again, it was the unbelieving spouse who had to take the step to divorce.

A brother or a sister is not under bondage in such cases / The believing husband or wife is not under bondage in such circumstances: The perfect passive verb δεδούλωται (*dedoulōtai*) meant "to have been enslaved" or "been under bondage."[97] Unfortunately, the phrase "not under bondage," due to the vagueness of the text, can be interpreted two ways and the interpretation one chooses has important theological implications. The question is, to what was the person no longer enslaved? Was it to the spouse or to the marriage tie? Christ taught that a divorced person could not remarry (Mark 10:7–12). If, therefore, one takes Paul's words as referring to the spouse, the Saint was freed from the slavery of the person they were married to, but he or she could not remarry. If, however, it is the marriage, then the person was no longer under slavery to that law and, therefore, free to remarry (see "Excursus on Marriage and Divorce" below).[98]

The latter interpretation of this phrase has resulted in what scholars call "the Pauline privilege," which essentially states that, contrary to the early Church's understanding of Christ's teaching on marriage, as found in Mark 10:7–12, Paul believed that, under certain circumstance, a Christian could and ought to divorce and was also free to remarry.

It is true that the general thrust of the chapter is against remarriage, supporting the idea that Paul was referring to being freed from the unbelieving mate.[99] The general thrust, however, is, as the adjective states, only general. There is a certain element of "It all depends . . ." that runs through the whole as well.[100] We must remember that Paul was expressing here his own views as he addressed specific situations that the church was encountering for the first time. His words show that he was taking the contingencies he faced very seriously and was trying to solve them within the context of the revealed gospel. Therefore, Paul was concerned with adaptation. This opened the door to a certain degree for situational ethics, but, we must stress, only to a certain degree. There was no compromise when situations were clear and involved that which was right or moral as evidenced in

---

96. BDAG, 1095.
97. BDAG, 260; Louw-Nida, §37.24.
98. For full discussion, see Thiselton, *First Epistle,* 534–37.
99. Fee, *First Epistle,* 303.
100. Thiselton, *First Epistle,* 536.

chapters 5 and 6. But when they were not, Paul was willing to look at the present conditions and give advice on the basis of what he knew. Even so, he always played within the context of "Christ, and him crucified" (2:2) and the doctrines that stood upon it. Therefore, it would appear that Paul felt that, if an unbelieving spouse divorces his or her believing mate, the Saint was perfectly free to remarry.[101] Paul's decision may have been based on the fact that Jesus allowed for divorce under certain very strict circumstances (Matt. 5:32; 19:9). Whichever way the argument goes, one point is certain, as an LDS scholar has noted, "If the spouse refuses to live with the Church member, the Church member is forced to choose the Lord."[102]

but God hath called us to peace / God has called us to live in peace: The ancient manuscripts are almost equally divided between ἡμᾶς (*hēmas*) "us" and ὑμᾶς (*hymas*) "you" in this passage. SBLGNT has *hēmas,* whereas NA28 prefers *hymas.* In the Greek of the New Testament period, the two words had very similar pronunciation. We have followed the NA28 in our Rendition, feeling "us" as the more likely.

The phrase marks Paul's conclusion to his answer on a very tough issue. Essentially, his view on divorce and remarriage was based on a gospel principle, namely that the Lord ἐν δὲ εἰρήνη κέκληκεν ἡμᾶς (*en de eirēnē keklēken hēmas*), "called us to live in peace." The noun εἰρήνη (*eirēnē*), "peace, harmony," denoted not only a feeling of tranquility, but also of an absence of worry.[103] It connoted both an internal and external quality of life. In addition, and more importantly, it connoted a life of harmony or reconciliation and hope, a life "in which peace holds sway."[104]

7:16 ***For what knowest thou, O wife, whether thou shalt save thy husband? or how knowest thou, O man, whether thou shalt save thy wife? / Wife, how do you know whether you might save your husband, and husband, how do you know whether you might save your wife:*** The nuance of Paul's thought in this verse is hard to tell. The phrase τί γὰρ οἶδας (*ti gar oidas*), literally "what/how do you know," can be taken two ways.[105] One is optimistic and sees Paul as saying in essence, "Don't divorce because you

---

101. Thiselton, *First Epistle,* 536–37.

102. Ogden and Skinner, *Verse by Verse,* 136.

103. BDAG, 287–88; Louw-Nida, §§22.42; 25.248.

104. Thiselton, *First Epistle,* 537.

105. Sakae Kubo, "I Corinthians vii. 16: Optimistic or Pessimistic?" *New Testament Studies* 24 (July 1978): 539–44.

just may save your spouse."[106] The other is pessimistic and sees Paul as asking, "How do you know that you will even save your spouse?" The implication is that one should divorce because the chance of the mate converting is not worth the anxiety of taking the chance.[107] Though grammatically either interpretation is possible, statements of LDS prophets and apostles favor the optimistic view. President David O. McKay stated:

> In the light of scripture, ancient and modern, we are justified in concluding that Christ's ideal pertaining to marriage is the unbroken home, and conditions that cause divorce are violations of his divine teachings. . . . Unfaithfulness on the part of either [husband or wife], or both, habitual drunkenness, physical violence, long imprisonment that disgraces the wife and family, the union of an innocent girl to a reprobate—in these and perhaps other cases there may be circumstances which make the continuance of the marriage state a greater evil than divorce. But these are extreme cases—they are the mistakes, the calamities in the realm of marriage.[108]

Analysis and Summary

Paul next turned to questions the Saints had concerning divorce and also interfaith marriages. He first addressed the issue of divorce. Paul seemed well aware of the Lord's very positive and supportive view of the importance of marriage and adopted it himself (see "Excursus on Marriage and Divorce" below). Adhering to that view, however, did not seem to have attracted certain members of the Church.[109] Given the attitude concerning divorce among the Gentile Corinthians as well as that of the Greco-

---

106. Among the proponents of this view are the following: Findlay, "St. Paul's First Epistle," 827–28; Fee, *First Epistle,* 305–6; Bruce, *1 and 2 Corinthians,* 70; Barrett, *First Epistle,* 1266–67.

107. Among the proponents of this view are the following: Bailey, *Mediterranean Eyes,* 210; Robertson and Plummer, *Critical and Exegetical Commentary,* 144; Conzelmann, *1 Corinthians,* 124 and nn. 47–48; Kubo, "I Corinthians," 542–43; Thiselton, *First Epistle,* 539–40. Translations are split on how to render the phrase. RSV, NAB, and NIV translate it as "how do you know," while the MJB has "how can you know," and the NRSV has "for all you know."

108. *The Teachings of David O. McKay* (Salt Lake City: Deseret Book, 2004), 389–90.

109. It may have arisen as a reaction to the newly found freedom the gospel gave women. Late in this study, we will see that some women, misunderstanding the gospel, began to take excesses. Some may have determined that the freedom extended to separating from their husbands. On this issue see Findlay, "St. Paul's First Epistle," 825; Wire, *Corinthian Women,* 82–97.

Roman world in general, it is not surprising that some of the members would have questioned the Church's position.[110] It seems that some men divorced women and some women divorced men at every whim. Divorce occurred with so much ease in the Roman world that one ancient authority complained in satirical tones that men "leave home in order to marry and marry in order to divorce."[111] The Jews were also affected with the disease albeit with them it was more lopsided, with males mostly initiating the action.[112]

There were a number of factors that contributed to the high divorce rate. First, among all elements of the society, it was relatively easy for either gender to initiate a divorce for any number of reasons.[113] Second, marriages were mostly arranged, often for reasons of social advancement without consideration of the couple's compatibility. Further, females married young, many as early as twelve, allowing immaturity to exacerbate conditions in a poor marriage.[114]

Also contributing to the instability of marriages was the high mortality rate, especially among younger women. Most did not live beyond thirty years with the death rate due to childbirth being particularly high.[115]

As a result, as one scholar noted, "the notion of a partner for life seemed almost an innovative concept." He went on to say that Paul's counsel for

---

110. Osiek and Blach, *Families in the New Testament Times,* 62–63.

111. Juvenal, *Sat. 6,* but see also Seneca, *de Beneficiis* 3.16.2. See also his work *Helvia* 16.3; Musonius, *Fragment* 14.94.2–19; and Tacitus, *Agricola* 6.1. See also Witherington, *Conflict and Community,* 171; Eva Cantarella, *Pandora's Daughters: The Role and Status of Women in Greek and Roman Antiquity* (Baltimore: Johns Hopkins University Press, 1987), 36–37.

112. Jeremy Moiser, "A Reassessment of Paul's View of Marriage with Reference to 1 Corinthians 7," *Journal of the Study of the New Testament* 18 (1983): 109; H. J. Boecker, *Law and the Administration of Justice in the Old Testament and Ancient Near East* (London: SPCK, 1980), 110–11.

113. There appears to have been a bit of a double standard, but not much. See Conzelmann, *1 Corinthians,* 120–21; Rousselle, "Body Politics in Ancient Rome," 302–10.

114. In classical Greece, it was common for women to marry when they were between fourteen and eighteen years old while men married between twenty-five and thirty. See Osiek and Blach, *Families in the New Testament Times,* 62. For the Jews, the rabbis set the minimum age for marriage of girls at twelve and that of boys at thirteen. Most seem to have married a bit later than this, but they married as teenagers nonetheless. See J. A. Thompson, *Handbook of Life in Bible Times* (Downers Grove, Ill.: InterVarsity Press, 1987), 85.

115. Rousselle, "Body Politics in Ancient Rome," 302–18.

married couples to stay together was "no conservative 'status quo' ethic, but a radical and high evaluation of Christian marriage."[116] Another declared that Paul's position "swam against the stream of Greco-Roman readiness to change everything to suit personal desire" that had resulted in the relativization of "the importance of all worldly conditions and relationships." He went on to say that what Paul did was "place 'the things of the Lord' first in a complex variety of real situations."[117] Christianity was coming onto the stage of history, and its leaders were very willing to go against social ethics and standards in an effort not to dilute or compromise the Savior's doctrines and practices.

Verses 7:10 and 11 must be explored together because they highlight one aspect of Paul's teachings, that of mutuality. Paul would have agreed with the old adage, "What is good for the goose is good for the gander." He insisted that the command from the Lord was against divorce between Christians. Paul did include a caveat that if a woman should divorce her husband, she should remain single. He did not explain why at that point, but would later on (see Translation Notes on 7:26 below).

These verses make one point very clear, Paul generally counseled against divorce. As one scholar noted:

> In [our modern] culture [where] divorce has become the norm, this text [7:10–11] has become a bone of contention. Some find Paul and Jesus too harsh and try to find ways around the plain sense of the text. Others turn the text into law and make divorce the worst of all sins in the church. Neither of these seems an appropriate response. On the one hand, there is little question that both Paul and Jesus disallowed divorce between two believers, especially when it served as grounds for remarriage. . . . On the other hand, Paul does not raise this norm to law. Divorce may happen, and such a person is not ostracized from the community. . . . What [was] not allowed is remarriage, both because for him [that is, Paul] that presupposes the teaching of Jesus that such is adultery and because in the Christian community reconciliation is the norm. If the Christian husband and wife cannot be reconciled to one another, then how can they expect to become models of reconciliation before a fractured and broken world?[118]

---

116. Thiselton, *First Epistle*, 523; italics in the original removed.

117. Vincent L. Wimbush, *Paul, the Worldly Ascetic: Response to the World and Self-Understanding According to 1 Corinthians 7* (Macon, Ga.: Mercer University Press, 1987), 16–17.

118. Fee, *First Epistle*, 296.

In 7:12–16, Paul turned to the issue of interfaith marriages. In this section, the Apostle sought to allay the anxiety that had arisen because one mate had not accepted the gospel. A new convert who had abandoned a former pagan lifestyle might wonder if living with an unrepentant and unbelieving spouse might pollute the atmosphere of the home and corrode the Saint's sanctity. Paul's answer was a surprise saying in essence, "No. In fact, just the opposite is true."[119] As he saw it, the unbelieving spouse was actually made holy, at least to a degree, by the believing mate. Paul may have had the Old Testament principle of holiness by association in mind.[120] In that case, holiness was not a static but a dynamic quality that could be passed from one source to another. His view opened the door to future possibilities for the unbelieving spouse, especially that of becoming fully holy by example of the mate. Holiness could be attached to the unbeliever because of his or her willingness to make the necessary compromises needed to keep the marriage intact. Those compromises would have included decisive changes in behavior, belief, and attitude. The willingness to make these changes brought the Spirit not only upon the spouse but also upon the home and the children.[121]

Joseph Smith was so troubled by these verses that he made inquiry of the Lord. In response he received the following revelation:

> Now, in the days of the apostles the law of circumcision was had among all the Jews who believed not the gospel of Jesus Christ. And it came to pass that there arose a great contention among the people concerning the law of circumcision, for the unbelieving husband was desirous that his children should be circumcised and become subject to the law of Moses, which law was fulfilled. And it came to pass that the children, being brought up in subjection to the law of Moses, gave heed to the traditions of their fathers and believed not the gospel of Christ, wherein they became unholy. Wherefore, for this cause the apostle wrote unto the church, giving unto them a commandment, not of the Lord, but of himself, that a believer should not be united to an unbeliever; except the law of Moses should be done away among them, that their children might

---

119. Thiselton, *First Epistle,* 528.

120. Fee, *First Epistle,* 300–302; see also Barrett, *First Epistle,* 165; Bruce, *1 and 2 Corinthians,* 69; Collins, *First Corinthians,* 271.

121. On the whole idea of holiness being a dynamic principle and a condition that can be shared by association see Jerome Murphy-O'Connor, "Works without Faith in 1 Corinthians VII:14," *Revue biblique* 84 (1977): 350–58; L. J. Kuyper, "Exegetical Study on 1 Corinthians 7:14," *Reformed Review* 31 (1977): 62–64.

remain without circumcision; and that the tradition might be done away, which saith that little children are unholy; for it was had among the Jews; But little children are holy, being sanctified through the atonement of Jesus Christ; and this is what the scriptures mean. (D&C 74:2–7)

Notice, once again, that reconciliation between spouses played a key role here. There was to be no reconciliation that diluted either ethics or morals. The believing spouse continued to stay true to the gospel but allowed the other a choice. Though the mate may not be willing to come fully into the kingdom, his or her decision to compromise on certain issues and support the spouse on his or her stand brought a degree of holiness upon the whole family.

If, however, the unbelieving spouse insisted on divorce, Paul felt the Christian partner should not stand in the way. For the Apostle, such a divorce left the partner in the same position as if the spouse had died; the Saint was free to marry again, but within the confines of the Church (7:39). His reasoning was based on the Lord's injunction that his disciples should live in peace. Since the believer could never be sure that the spouse would ever convert, it was best to yield to the unbelieving spouse's wish and avoid the pain of fighting a divorce.

Once again, it is important to keep in mind that Paul was expressing his view and that view was based on conditions as he saw them.

EXCURSUS ON MARRIAGE AND DIVORCE

The Lord told his Galilean disciples that "it hath been said Whosoever shall put away his wife, let him give her a writing of divorcement," a position well-known to his hearers. But the Lord did not stop there. He went on to say something that, given the custom of the day, was quite shocking.[122] "Verily, verily, I say to you, that whosoever shall put away his wife, saving for the cause of fornication, causeth her to commit adultery; and whosoever shall marry her that is divorced, committeth adultery" (JST Matt. 5:32; compare 3 Ne. 12:31–32).[123] What exactly was, and is, the Savior's stand on divorce, under what conditions does God condone it, and how does a man cause his ex-wife and her new husband to commit adultery? Answering these questions will give us a better understanding of the purpose and importance of the marriage covenant.

A number of months after the Lord made this shocking position on divorce clear, in an attempt to trap him,[124] the Pharisees asked him, "Is it lawful for a man to put away his wife for every cause?" (Matt. 19:3). Among the Jewish scholars and religious leaders of Jesus' day and earlier, viable reasons for divorce had been hotly debated. In the end, they could not reach a consensus. The scriptures yielded but three texts that the rabbis could dissect concerning the subject. The first text was Genesis 2:22–24, which states, "And the rib, which the Lord God had taken from man, made he a

---

122. Divorce was a given among all classes and sects of the Jews. Few questioned its rightness. What they did question was its grounds and most opted for a very liberal application. See Louise M. Epstein, *Marriage Law in the Bible and in the Talmud* (Cambridge, Mass.: Harvard University Press, 1942). Therefore, the Lord's bold statement would have been quite shocking to many. For a solid if brief overview of the subject, see Robert W. Wall, "Divorce," in *The Anchor Bible Dictionary,* ed. David Noel Freedman, 6 vols. (New York: Doubleday, 1992), 2:217–19 (hereafter cited as *ABD*).

123. The Joseph Smith Translation makes minor but very important changes to these verses. In 5:31, it replaces "said" with "written" and in 5:32 it removes the word "but" and inserts the words "Verily, verily." The changes bring the Lord's words in line with those recorded in 3 Ne. 12:31–32. The changes also emphasize the importance the Lord placed on His words as having precedence over the written text.

124. The Greek word translated "tempting" (πειράζω, *peirazō*) carried the idea of testing but usually with the intent of putting one in a bad light. The gospel writer does not include the actual nature of the test. The Pharisees may have expected the Lord to call the law into question. Another possibility is that they hoped to get the Lord in trouble with the political authorities. John the Baptist had been arrested because of his stand on the issue of Herod's marriage to Herodius. The Pharisees may have hoped to get Jesus in the same trap.

woman, and brought her unto the man. And Adam said, This is now bone of my bones, and flesh of my flesh: she shall be called Woman, because she was taken out of Man. Therefore shall a man leave his father and his mother, and shall cleave unto his wife: and they shall be one flesh." The second text was Deuteronomy 24:1–4:

> When a man hath taken a wife, and married her, and it come to pass that she find no favour in his eyes, because he hath found some uncleanness in her: then let him write her a bill of divorcement, and give it in her hand, and send her out of his house. And when she is departed out of his house, she may go and be another man's wife. And if the latter husband hate her, and write her a bill of divorcement, and giveth it in her hand, and sendeth her out of his house; or if the latter husband die, which took her to be his wife; Her former husband, which sent her away, may not take her again to be his wife, after that she is defiled; for that is abomination before the Lord: and thou shalt not cause the land to sin, which the Lord thy God giveth thee for an inheritance.

The final text came from Malachi 2:16: "For the Lord, the God of Israel, saith that he hateth putting away," that is, divorce.

The difficulty in determining a justifiable claim for divorce was the strength of Genesis in championing marriage and the clear statement in Malachi that God was against divorce juxtaposed to the ambiguous position in Deuteronomy. Jewish religious leaders seemed to have agreed that, according to Genesis, God created marriage and it was thus a holy state. They also agreed that in accordance with Deuteronomy, certain inappropriate behaviors annulled God's holy union, thus allowing for divorce. Unfortunately, the text was not clear as to what that inappropriate behavior was.[125] Malachi's prophetic writing revealing God's strong intolerance for divorce heightened the need to be sure divorce was done for the proper reasons.

The extreme positions taken by two popular rabbis illustrate the range of views. The school of Shammai insisted that only unlawful sexual transgressions annulled the marriage. Unfortunately, surviving records do not tell us what those unlawful sexual transgressions were, but they must have fallen somewhat short of outright adultery since the law clearly marked such infidelity as punishable by death. The school of Hillel, on the other hand,

---

125. The problem arose from an inability to agree on the meaning of the phrase עֶרְוַת דָּבָר (*'erwat dābār*), usually translated as "some uncleanliness," but meaning literally, "the nakedness of the thing." The Septuagint translated the phrase as ἄσχημον πρᾶγμα (*aschēmon pragma*), "some unseemly thing" or "some shameless deed."

argued that such things as childlessness, argumentativeness, or even failure to properly keep house were grounds for divorce.[126] Some of the Lord's detractors sought to entangle Him in the morass of disagreement in hopes of discrediting him. It did not work.

In the New Testament, there are four accounts where the Lord defined his position on the subject of marriage and divorce (Matt. 5:31–32; 19:3–9; Mark 10:2–12; Luke 16:18; the scriptures of the Restoration give us 3 Ne. 12:31–32; D&C 42:22, 74–76), and in them lies no ambiguity. The earliest place where Christ revealed his stance was during his Sermon on the Mount. The Lord introduced his position by prohibiting sensual thoughts, warning that "whosoever looketh on a woman to lust after her hath committed adultery (μοιχεία, moicheia) with her already in his heart" (Matt. 5:28). Jesus emphasizes that the thought fosters the deed, and, therefore, the thought alone was enough to defile (see also Matt. 15:18–20).

It is in this connection that the Lord, then, made his case against divorce, saying, "Whosoever shall put away his wife, saving for the cause of fornication [πορνεία, porneia], causeth her to commit adultery [μοιχεία, moicheia]: and whosoever shall marry her that is divorced committeth adultery" (Matt. 5:32). The purpose of the writing of divorcement was to allow the former wife remarriage. Jesus objected to this procedure except on the grounds of porneia (often translated "fornication" but nuances a wide range of sexual sins) because it forced the wife into an adulterous relationship when she remarried. The language of the scriptures is important to get a clear understanding of the Lord's teachings.

The Greek word used in Matthew, porneia, holds at its core the idea of apostasy from God, which the immoral act simply confirmed.[127] Note that, for the Lord, both the thought and deed were evidence of disbelief in the true God.[128] Unlike Shammai, the Lord insisted that immorality includes not only the physical act but also the condition of the heart (that is, apostasy) out of which the act grew. Adultery (μοιχεία, moicheia) was the technical term for copulating with a married person to whom one was not married. Though the law condemned porneia, it made moicheia punishable

---

126. Wall, "Divorce," in *ABD*, 2:218. The Hebrew phrase with which the schools wrestled was עֶרְוַת דָּבָר (*'erwat dābār*). The school of Shammai emphasized עֶרְוַת (*'erwat*), seeing in it reference to things morally objectionable, while the school of Hillel stressed דָּבָר (*dābār*), translating it as "any cause."

127. The JST of Luke, as pointed out below, confirms the point.

128. Friedrich Hauck and Siegfried Schulz, "πόρνη, πόρνος, πορνεία, πορνεύω, ἐκπορνεύω," in *TDNT*, 6:591.

by death. Therefore, a writing of divorcement, if not done for the proper cause, put the former wife and her new husband in a frightful position before the law.

The Lord's insistence on *porneia* as the only proper cause for divorce clearly reveals that he stood opposite Hillel's position. The Savior's stance underscores the serious and important nature of marriage which could be properly annulled only in the most severe and specific of circumstances, namely *porneia.* The Lord's position not only rejected the arbitrary practice that allowed a Jewish husband to divorce a wife simply by giving her a bill of divorcement[129] but also emphasized that, excluding the exception, according to the will of God, marriage was meant to establish a permanent relationship.

On the surface it may seem that the Savior's position may have been more lenient than that of Shammai. However, such a view does not hold up when one considers it against three other accounts found in Luke 16 and Matthew 19 with its parallel Mark 10, where Jesus more fully justified his position.

The Joseph Smith Translation of Luke's account puts the Lord's teachings on divorce in an interesting context that sheds a bright light on his understanding of it. While Jesus was teaching his disciples, the Pharisees began to deride him, saying they refused to "receive him to be [their] ruler; for he maketh himself to be a judge over [them]" (JST Luke 16:16). The Lord shot back, insisting that they perverted "the right way; and the kingdom of heaven suffereth violence of you; and you persecute the meek; and in your violence you seek to destroy the kingdom." He ended his rebuke with a strong warning, "Woe unto you, ye adulterers!" (JST Luke 16:21). His hearers did not take the slam sitting down. "And they reviled him again, being angry for the saying, that they were adulterers. But he continued, saying, Whosoever putteth away his wife, and marrieth another, committeth adultery; and whosoever marrieth her who is put away from her husband, committeth adultery" (JST Luke 16:22–23). Here the Lord attacked one of their cherished assumptions: that divorce was not only condoned but proper. In his rebuke, he left no grounds whatsoever for divorce and thus

---

129. If the practice as defined in the second century AD is an indication of the position taken by the Pharisees in the early first century, then the position toward an adulterous wife had hardened. In the days of the prophets, a husband could forgive an unfaithful wife (as in the case of Hosea with Gomer). Not so later when the interpretation of the law forbade the wife to have any sexual relations with her husband or the adulterer. Thus, the husband was forced to divorce her. See *Soṭah* 5.1.

exposed their assumption as being opposite to reality. They were, therefore, adulterers for there was no proper grounds for divorce, and giving a writing of divorcement did not, in God's eyes, disannul their marriages. Further, they contributed to the corruption of the age through their false assumption by opening the way for others to commit adultery as well.

Some months later, the Pharisees asked the Lord directly where he stood on the divorce issue. The Pharisees framed their question ("Is it lawful for a man to put away his wife *for every cause*" [Matt. 19:3; emphasis added]) in a manner they thought would force the Lord to take a position in relation to the popular schools of thought.

According to Mark, Jesus put his tempters on the hot seat by asking them to cite exactly what the law had to say on the subject (Mark 10:3). If their intent was to see if Jesus came down on the side of Shammai or Hillel, they failed. The Savior appealed to the law itself and thus freed himself from the narrow confines of the rabbinic debate. The Savior's question forced the Pharisees to admit that no such commandment existed, only that "Moses suffered to write a bill of divorcement" (Mark 10:4).[130] They had to confess that they were not dealing with a commandment of God but a practice that Moses reluctantly allowed because of the hardness of Israel's heart.

The Lord then showed them that, though the law had nothing to reveal about divorce, it did say something very strong about marriage. God created male and female for the cause of making "one flesh" (Gen. 2:24).

There is a world of meaning in that little phrase "one flesh." To understand it, we must move to a Genesis text a bit earlier than the one Jesus cited. In Genesis 2:18, God decreed that it was not good for man to be alone and declared that he would make "an help meet for him." The English word "meet," as it was understood in the fifteenth and sixteenth centuries, carried the right idea of being "fit" or "perfectly suited for" a given task. The Hebrew phrase עֵזֶר כְּנֶגְדּוֹ (*ʿēzer kĕnegdō*) would be, literally, "a help of his like." God made Eve עֵזֶר (*ʿēzer*). The word denotes "help, assistance."[131] She could be *ʿēzer* because she was כְּנֶגְדּוֹ (*kĕnegdo*), "of his like." To say it in other words, Eve was of the same *genus* as Adam. That genus, in Hebrew, was אָדָם (*ʾādām*), "Adam," "a human being." Genesis stresses that point. Before Eve's

---

130. In Matt. 19:7, the Pharisees say that Moses "commanded" (ἐνετείλατο, *eneteilato*) the writing of a divorce, but the Savior corrected them saying that Moses "suffered" (ἐπέτρεψεν, *epetrepsen*, "permitted") the writing of divorcement.

131. HAL, 811.

introduction, God had Adam name all the animals and concluded that "for Adam there was not found an help meet for him" (Gen. 2:20). None of the animals were fit, suited, or "of his like" and, therefore, not of the right genus. Thus, they could not help him fulfill his God-given tasks.

Eve, on the other hand, was of such a nature that she made it possible for him to do what he could not do alone. God had given the man a commandment to do two things: multiply and fill up the earth and to have dominion over it. But 'ādām was yet incomplete and, therefore, was incapable of doing either alone. It was only with his companion, Eve, as his indispensable helper, that 'ādām became whole and was able to fill God's designs.

Genesis uses the method of Eve's creation to underscore the point that she was not only of Adam's like but also his partner and equal. Of her origin Genesis states that "the rib, which the Lord God had taken from man, made he a woman" (Gen. 2:22). Note, Eve was not made *from* the rib of Adam as Adam was made *from* the dust of the earth. Eve *is* Adam's rib, for God made the rib into a woman. Though the account is allegorical, it reveals God's intended relationship between husband and wife. "There is a perfect unity between these two mortals; they are 'one flesh.' The word *rib* expresses the ultimate in proximity, intimacy, and identity. When Jeremiah speaks of 'keepers of my *tsela* rib' [שֹׁמְרֵי צַלְעִי (*šōmrē ṣalʿi*)] (Jeremiah 20:10), he means bosom friends, inseparable companions."[132] That is the cause of marriage, to make inseparable companions.

When he first meets Eve, Adam exclaims, "This is now bone of my bones, and flesh of my flesh:[133] she shall be called Woman, because she was taken out of Man" (Gen. 2:23). Adam instantly saw the design of God in creating woman. The phrase "This is now" (זֹאת הַפַּעַם, *zōʾt happaʿam*), literally "this time," or "this at last," expressed Adam's astonishment at his perfect match, which he instantly recognized in Eve. This created being unlike any other was, at last, bone of his bone. The name he gave her emphasized his recognition. She was "woman." In Hebrew the male principle is אִישׁ ('*īš*); the female principle is אִשָּׁה ('*iššāh*) designating the female component of the genus 'ādām or mankind.

Genesis concludes the account with the words quoted by Jesus, "Therefore shall a man leave his father and his mother, and shall cleave unto his

---

132. Hugh Nibley, *Old Testament and Related Studies,* ed. John W Welch, Gary P Gillum, and Don E Norton, vol. 1 of The Collected Works of Hugh Nibley (Salt Lake City: Deseret Book; Provo, Utah: Foundation for ancient Research and Mormon Studies, 1986), 87.

133. The imagery of bone and flesh symbolized blood relationship. See, for example, 2 Sam. 5:1; 19:12–13. For discussion, see BDB, 782c.

wife: and they shall be one flesh" (Gen. 2:24). These words embody the divinely appointed result of marriage. God intended it to have the deepest corporeal and spiritual unity of any relationship and, therefore, transcend the demands of any other relationship, including that of parents upon a child. The vital oneness of the husband and the wife includes a spiritual union of both the body and the heart.

Adam was to "cleave unto" Eve. The Hebrew verb (דָּבַק, *dābaq*) means "to stick to, cling to, adhere to."[134] The Greek word used by Matthew (κολλάω, *kollaō*), derived from κόλλα (*kolla*), "glue,"[135] nicely expresses the idea of the Hebrew. The word means to join together, bind, weld, and stresses the idea of making two things into one.[136] The man and woman are to be regarded as one entity—no longer considered two persons but one body.[137] The Savior emphasized that God created males and females to be re-created in an inviolable union through marriage. In doing so, God creates a new spiritual and physical relationship marked by the words "one flesh" (σάρξ μία, *sarx mia*). Underscoring the point, Genesis 5:2 declared that God created male and female "and blessed them, and called *their name Adam*" (emphasis added). God no longer regarded them as two beings but rather as one unit, *'ādām*. Paul understood this, stating, "So ought men to love their wives as their own bodies. He that loveth his wife loveth himself" (Eph. 5:28). He verified that "they two shall be one flesh" (Eph. 5:31) but admitted that the latter statement "is a great mystery" (Eph. 5:32).

It is of importance that Paul juxtaposes marriage and mystery. The Greek understanding of the word "mystery" (μυστήριον, *mysterion*) does not denote something that cannot be understood, but rather something that should not be spoken of commonly.[138] The Greeks used the word "mystery" to describe the sacred rites associated with some kinds of temple worship. As a technical term, it denoted those sacred doctrines that could only be known to the initiates who were sworn never to reveal them to outsiders. For Paul, and other early Christians, it denoted God's work of salvation that was to be disclosed to the Christian community but not to the world (see 2:7–10).[139]

---

134. HAL, 209.

135. LSJ, 972.

136. Karl Ludwig Schmidt, "κολλάω, προσκολλάω," in *TDNT*, 3:822–23.

137. C. S. Mann, *Mark: A New Translation with Introduction and Commentary*, vol. 27 of The Anchor Bible (New York: Doubleday, 1986), 391.

138. BDAG, 661.

139. James H. Moulton and George Milligan, *The Vocabulary of the Greek Testament: Illustrations from the Papyri and Other Non-literary Sources* (1930; rpt., Grand Rapids, Mich.: Eerdmans, 1985), 420.

C. S. Lewis caught the significance of the Savior's teachings. He taught that single humans are but half beings whom God designed to be combined in pairs.[140] The combination, as noted above, is designated as "one flesh" in the scriptures. Lewis nicely illustrated the meaning of the word "one flesh" by comparing a man and a woman to a violin and its bow which makes but one musical instrument, just as a lock with its key are but one mechanism.[141] Only when the two work together do we have a whole. So it is with 'ādām.

The cause or purpose of marriage, then, is to make that whole. To understand the full implications of this union, we must see the relationship in its eternal context. God's work is to exalt us and make us divine, that is, to make us like Deity. But what is Deity like? Genesis tells us that God made 'ādām after God's likeness and image. It then goes on to show that that image was a male and a female sealed together in eternal marriage. The text of Genesis insists that Adam and Eve, as 'ādām, were made in the image and likeness of the divine, therefore, the image of the divine is a married male and female. Erastus Snow, an early Apostle of the Church, said that

> the being we call man, but which in the language of these Scriptures was called Adam—male and female created he them, and called their name Adam, which in the original, in which these Scriptures were written by Moses, signifies "the first man." There was no effort at distinguishing between the one half and the other, and calling one man and the other woman. This was an after distinction, but the explanation of it is—one man, one being, and he called their name Adam. But he created them male and female, for they were one, and he says not unto the woman multiply, and to the man multiply, but he says unto them, multiply and reproduce your species, and replenish the earth. He speaks unto them as belonging together, as constituting one being, and as organized in his image and after his likeness. ... That which we see before our eyes, and which we are experiencing from time to time, day to day, and year to year, is an exemplification of Deity.
>
> "What," says one, "do you mean we should understand that deity consists of man and woman?" Most certainly I do. If I believe anything that God has ever said about himself, and anything pertaining to the creation and organization of man upon the earth, I must believe that Deity consists of man and woman.[142]

140. Plato, *Symp.* 189c–189d; 193d–193e, also allegorically teaches that men and women combine together as halves to make one soul. Thus, the idea was not confined to the Jewish culture but explored in the Gentile culture as well.

141. Lewis, *Mere Christianity*, 88.

142. Erastus Snow, in *JD*, 19:269.

God's work and glory is to exalt us. That means to make us everything Deity is. Since the office of Deity is composed of eternally married couples, marriage is key to God's work. Therefore, the cause of marriage and the work and glory of God are one. The Father will not long abide anyone who tries to thwart his efforts.

Jesus told the Pharisees that "what therefore God hath joined together, let not man put asunder" (Matt. 19:6). Marriage was of God. He joined (συνέζευξεν, *sunezeuksen*, "yoked") male and female together. It was brazen for anyone to pull them apart (Matt. 19:6). The point is that marriage is held together by an indissoluble covenant and, therefore, neither the male (Mark 10:11) nor the female (Mark 10:12) should ever consider divorce.

Marriage creates what God intended to be an eternal kinship ("one flesh"). Divorce, except for *porneia,* cannot void that relationship. Therefore, when one divorces and then remarries, he enters into an adulterous relationship because the original union that made "one flesh" remains intact.[143] Indeed, as Mark 10:10–12 notes, any man who remarries after divorcing his wife commits adultery *against his former wife.* The position taken by the Lord thus goes beyond that of the Mosaic law that recognized a man could commit adultery against another married man. Jesus insists that the man can do it against his former wife because their kinship remained intact.[144]

Therefore, the only way to avoid adultery after one divorced his mate was to remain single. The Lord's disciples recognized the strictness of his teaching and concluded that "If the case of the man be so with his wife, it is not good to marry" (Matt. 19:10). The Lord admitted that his position was hard for "all men cannot receive this saying" (Matt. 19:11). He then stated that some "have made themselves eunuchs for the kingdom of heaven's sake" (Matt. 19:12). In this way, the Lord here endorsed celibacy for those who could not live the higher law of marriage.

There is no doubt that we are dealing with a hard saying of Jesus, one of those teachings that pulls at the heart of the believer. Some disciples may find it a bit tough to accept the ideal laid down by the Lord that a person gets one chance at marriage and if he or she botches it, celibacy must follow.

---

143. It is on this ground that Deut. 24:1–4 should be understood, where Moses forbade a divorced woman to return to her first husband. The command is a logical extension of the Levitical prohibition (Lev. 18:6–18) against marrying close relatives. Wall, "Divorce," in *ABD,* 2:217–18.

144. Mann, *Mark,* 392.

We could view the Lord's appeal to Genesis 19:4–6 as supporting the position of Shammai or, at least, admitting the lawfulness of divorce if the necessary condition is met. But

> a close look shows that Jesus attacked the very foundation of both the schools of Shammai and Hillel. He showed that their preconceived notion that God allowed for divorce was wrong. The Lord clearly insisted that God never made provision for divorce. . . . The disciples, whose lives were to be more righteous than those of the Pharisees and Sadducees, could not have the hardness of heart that made the Mosaic legislation necessary, nor could they yield to the lusts of the flesh described as *porneia*. Thus the Lord effectively forbade any divorce at all to anyone who would have eternal life. Divorce fights against the heart of the work and glory of God. The Savior noted, "By this law [of eternal marriage] is the continuation of the works of my Father, wherein he glorifieth himself" (D&C 132:31). God said he instituted marriage "for the fulness of my glory; and he that receiveth a fulness thereof must and shall abide the law, or he shall be damned" (D&C 132:6).[145]

All the scriptures combine to make one point: the Lord deliberately created an intolerance for divorce that he intended his disciples to fully adopt. His new covenant invited his disciples into the higher ideal demanded by the perfect will of God. The new covenant made "no provision for, or concession to, the weakness of the flesh" and thereby outlawed divorce.[146] In doing so, the Lord emphasized the importance and eternal nature of marriage and the purpose for which God instituted it on the earth—for the eternal life, even deification, of his children.

Having said that, it is important to note that the Father never intended for one of his children to live in an abusive relationship. Abuse consists of "behavior that deliberately threatens or injures another person. It may be physical, emotional, or sexual. Some forms of physical and emotional abuse include beatings, neglect, and threats of abandonment. While it also may take varied forms, sexual abuse of another adult usually involves the use of force or intimidation to coerce sexual activity."[147] Thus, "The Church

---

145. Richard D. Draper, "What Therefore God Hath Joined Together, Let No Man Put Asunder," in *The Sermon on the Mount in Latter-day Scripture,* ed. Gaye Strathearn, Thomas A. Wayment, and Daniel L. Belnap (Salt Lake City: Deseret Book, 2010), 119.

146. Donald A. Hagner, *Matthew 14–28,* vol. 33B of Word Biblical Commentary (Dallas: Word Books, 1995), 549.

147. Jeanne B. Inouye and Robert K. Thomas, "Abuse, Spouse and Child," in *EM,* 1:11.

of Jesus Christ of Latter-day Saints officially disapproves of divorce but does permit both divorce (the legal dissolution of a marriage bond) and annulment (a decree that a marriage was illegal or invalid) in civil marriages and 'cancellation of sealing' in temple marriages."[148]

Those guilty of abuse such that divorce is necessitated have reason for deep repentance. The victims, however, should not feel they carry any stigma. President Gordon B. Hinckley, addressing these, assured them that "we do not look down upon you as failures because a marriage failed. In many, perhaps in most cases you were not responsible for that failure. Furthermore, ours is the obligation not to condemn, but to forgive and forget, to lift and to help. In your hours of desolation, turn to the Lord, who said: 'Come unto me, all ye that labour and are heavy laden, and I will give you rest. . . . For my yoke is easy, and my burden is light' (Matt. 11:28, 30)."[149]

148. Kristen L. Goodman, "Divorce," in *EM,* 1:391.

149. Gordon B. Hinkley, Single Adult Fireside Satellite Broadcast, February 26, 1989, as quoted in *Teachings of Gordon B. Hinckley,* 161.

FULFILLING YOUR CALLING IN THE CHURCH (7:17–24)

Greek Text

17 Εἰ μὴ ἑκάστῳ ὡς ἐμέρισεν ὁ κύριος, ἕκαστον ὡς κέκληκεν ὁ θεός, οὕτως περιπατείτω· καὶ οὕτως ἐν ταῖς ἐκκλησίαις πάσαις διατάσσομαι. 18 περιτετμημένος τις ἐκλήθη; μὴ ἐπισπάσθω· ἐν ἀκροβυστίᾳ κέκληταί τις; μὴ περιτεμνέσθω. 19 ἡ περιτομὴ οὐδέν ἐστιν, καὶ ἡ ἀκροβυστία οὐδέν ἐστιν, ἀλλὰ τήρησις ἐντολῶν θεοῦ. 20 ἕκαστος ἐν τῇ κλήσει ᾗ ἐκλήθη ἐν ταύτῃ μενέτω. 21 Δοῦλος ἐκλήθης; μή σοι μελέτω· ἀλλ' εἰ καὶ δύνασαι ἐλεύθερος γενέσθαι, μᾶλλον χρῆσαι. 22 ὁ γὰρ ἐν κυρίῳ κληθεὶς δοῦλος ἀπελεύθερος κυρίου ἐστίν· ὁμοίως ὁ ἐλεύθερος κληθεὶς δοῦλός ἐστιν Χριστοῦ. 23 τιμῆς ἠγοράσθητε· μὴ γίνεσθε δοῦλοι ἀνθρώπων. 24 ἕκαστος ἐν ᾧ ἐκλήθη, ἀδελφοί, ἐν τούτῳ μενέτω παρὰ θεῷ. [SBLGNT]

King James Version

17 But as God hath distributed to every man, as the Lord hath called every one, so let him walk. And so ordain I in all churches. 18 Is any man called being circumcised? let him not become uncircumcised. Is any called in uncircumcision? let him not be circumcised. 19 Circumcision is nothing, and uncircumcision is nothing, but the keeping of the commandments of God. 20 Let every man abide in the same calling wherein he was called. 21 Art thou called being a servant? care not for it: but if thou mayest be made free, use it rather. 22 For he that is called in the Lord, being a servant, is the Lord's freeman: likewise also he that is called, being free, is Christ's servant. 23 Ye are bought with a price; be not ye the servants of men. 24 Brethren, let every man, wherein he is called, therein abide with God.

New Rendition

17 Nevertheless, let each person live as the Lord has assigned him and as God has called him. And I give this same instruction in all the churches. 18 If a man was circumcised when he was converted, he should not have that surgically altered to an uncircumcised state. Likewise, if a man was uncircumcised at his conversion, he should not get circumcised. 19 Circumcision is unimportant and uncircumcision is unimportant. What matters is keeping the commandments of God. 20 Let each person continue in the calling to which he or she was called. 21 If you were a slave when you were converted, don't let that worry you. But if you can indeed obtain your freedom, then do so. 22 For whoever was a slave when converted is the Lord's freedman, likewise whoever was free when converted is Christ's slave. 23 You were all bought with a price. Don't become slaves of human masters. 24 Brothers and sisters, in whatever situation you found

yourself when you were converted, there you should continue with God at your side.

Translation Notes and Comments

7:17 *But as God hath distributed to every man, as the Lord hath called every one, so let him walk / Nevertheless, let each person live as the Lord has assigned him and as God has called him:* The verb καλέω (*kaleō*), "to call," denoted such things as an invitation to a social event, a summons to appear before a counsel, or an assignment to perform a task. In the latter case, it also referenced the authority the calling agent had to make the assignment.[150] In a religious sense, it denoted the whole course of salvation to which God called a person and included that person's assignment in the process.[151] In this verse, Paul used the perfect active form κέκληκεν (*keklēken*), the tense showing that his referent had been called and the calling was still in effect. His use of the aorist verb ἐμέρισεν (*emerisen*) carried the meaning of dividing or apportioning out, thus, "to distribute" or "assign."[152] The imperative περιπατείτω (*peripateitō*), literally "let each one walk," also connoted proper deportment.[153] As such it stressed the Christian's responsibility to live according to gospel standards and carry out his calling.

Paul's use of these verbs is telling. Each Christian was called to live the religion and carry the specific assignment God apportioned to him or her. The excepting conjunctional phrase εἰ μή (*ei mē*), "nevertheless,"[154] tied this verse to what Paul had said in 7:15. Though there were certain cases in which a Saint could change a relationship or social situation, *nevertheless,* such was not to be the rule. Each person should exemplify the Christian life and serve in whatever station he or she was when they received the call. Paul was in no way implying, however, that retaining their present social standing was necessary, but that they recognize that they could fully serve the Lord in it or any other.[155]

Paul's view cut across the social current in which so many Corinthians lived. Status was everything, and many were willing to sacrifice much for

---

150. BDAG, 502–4.

151. Karl Ludwig Schmidt, "καλέω," in *TDNT,* 3:487–91: Louw-Nida, §33.312.

152. BDAG, 631–32.

153. BDAG, 803; Heinrich Seesemann and Georg Bertram, "πατέω, καταπατέω, περιπατέω, ἐμπεριπατέω," in *TDNT,* 5:940–45.

154. For this translation, see Fee, *First Epistle,* 309 n. 12.

155. Fee, *First Epistle,* 309; Thiselton, *First Epistle,* 544–45.

upward mobility. The gospel gave men and women a spiritual, and there-fore an eternal, status and freedom in whatever social condition they lived, thus making social climbing both unnecessary and irrelevant.[156]

And so ordain I in all churches / And I give this same instruction in all the churches: The middle voice of the verb διατάσσομαι (*diatassomai*) meant "to give detailed instructions for what must be done."[157] Paul's point was that the instructions he was giving were not only for the Corinthian Saints but also for the Church in general.

7:18 *Is any man called being circumcised? let him not become uncircum-cised. Is any called in uncircumcision? let him not be circumcised / If a man was circumcised when he was converted, he should not have that surgi-cally altered to an uncircumcised state. Likewise, if a man was uncircum-cised at his conversion, he should not get circumcised:* The verb ἐπισπάω (*epispaō*) denoted the operation that reversed circumcision.[158] The earliest Greek texts did not include punctuation. The later texts included question marks with these two phrases. In our Rendition, we have treated them as conditions, which we thought better conveyed Paul's meaning. Influencing us was that περιτετημένος (*peritetēmenos*), literally "having been circum-cised," is a circumstantial participle used to indicate a condition.

Paul's point was that, from the viewpoint of salvation, being a Jew or Gentile was irrelevant. The only condition that was relevant was the Chris-tian's acceptance of his call and remaining faithful to it.

7:19 *Circumcision is nothing, and uncircumcision is nothing, but the keeping of the commandments of God / Circumcision is unimportant and uncircumcision is unimportant. What matters is keeping the command-ments of God:* Paul's very succinct οὐδέν ἐστιν (*ouden estin*), "is nothing," reflected his strong feelings about the valuelessness of previous religious distinctions. Because the usual translation of ἀλλα (*alla*) "but," does not fully carry the force of the Apostle's point, it is translated as "what matters" in our Rendition. The noun τήρησις (*tērēsis*), "keeping," connoted persis-tence and constancy in doing a task.[159] Paul's use of the word stressed the

---

156. Deming, *Paul on Marriage and Celibacy*, 159.

157. BDAG, 273–74.

158. BDAG, 380. The middle imperative Paul used, ἐπισπάσθω (*epispasthō*), was derived from the very rare ἐπισπάομαι (*epispaomai*), which equates to the Hebrew מָשַׁךְ (*māshak*), a term denoting the surgery some Hellenistic Jews underwent to hide their identity when participating in the Greek gymnasium. 1 Macc. 1:15; Josephus, *A.J.* 12.5.1.

159. BDAG, 1002.

need for each Christian to continue in following God no matter what his or her former religious affiliation was.[160]

7:20 *Let every man abide in the same calling wherein he was called / Let each person continue in the calling to which he or she was called:* The imperative μενέτω (*menetō*), "let each stay, remain," denoted the need for a person to continue in a specific sphere or area.[161] In this verse, Paul focused on the sphere of God's call to salvation in Christ.

This verse acts as the connector between two separate but related tensions existing in the branch: that between Jewish and Gentile members as noted in the verses above and between slave and free members as noted in the verses below.[162] To both sets, the answer is the same: remain true to your calling. Paul's focus was not on socioeconomic position but on one's loyalty to the position and assignment God had given to him or her. Though there is a subtle hint of an admonition not to leave the Church,[163] the main thrust of Paul's appeal was for his readers to remain content where they were and to fulfill their Christian duty in that sphere.

7:21 *Art thou called being a servant? care not for it / If you were a slave when you were converted, don't let that worry you:* The aorist passive verb ἐκλήθης (*eklēthēs*), "were called" implied that God was the originator of the call. The impersonal verb μέλει (*melei*) plus the dative meant "to care for" or "have concern for" something.[164] Coupled with the negative μή (*mē*) the connotation is "don't let that worry you," as in our Rendition. Paul assured those members of the slave class that they could fulfill their callings in the Church even as slaves and, therefore, should not be overly concerned about their state.

but if thou mayest be made free, use it rather / But if you can indeed obtain your freedom, then do so: This phrase is very difficult to translate. Determining what Paul meant turns largely on the interpretation of two words. The first is μᾶλλον (*mallon*), "rather," which denoted "a greater or higher degree," but the word was also used as a marker to indicate an alternative to something else.[165] It is difficult to determine which force it should take here. The second is χρῆσαι (*chrēsai*), the aorist middle imperative of χράομαι (*chraomai*) which meant "to make use of, employ." The two words

---

160. Louw-Nida, §36.19.
161. BDAG, 630–31.
162. Bailey, *Mediterranean Eyes*, 214.
163. Bailey, *Mediterranean Eyes*, 215–16.
164. BDAG, 626–27.
165. BDAG, 613–14.

taken together expressed something like "rather (or by all means) take advantage of (it)."[166] Unfortunately, Paul leaves the object of the verb unexpressed, and as a result, we do not know for certain what Paul wanted his readers to take advantage of.[167] Grammatically the most obvious object is "freedom" since we have the conditional clause, "If you can indeed obtain your freedom, by all means do so."[168] However, some commentators and translators prefer to take "slavery" as the unstated object. In that case, the sense of the passage is that if the chance for freedom came, the slave should choose to stay as a slave.[169] This second option, however, requires skipping over the closer adjective ἐλεύθερος (*eleutheros*) "free" and moving back to the noun δοῦλος (*doulos*) "slave" at the beginning of the verse. We consider the first option to be the more reasonable, and in our Rendition, we have taken the unexpressed object to be "freedom."

Whichever view one takes, Paul's major point is clear: the gospel can be lived under any circumstance in which a person lives. Slaves, freedmen, and free men and women can all live a Christian life, be transformed by its powers, and fulfill their callings therein.

7:22 *For he that is called in the Lord, being a servant, is the Lord's freeman: likewise also he that is called, being free, is Christ's servant / For whoever was a slave when converted is the Lord's freedman, likewise whoever was free when converted is Christ's slave:* The noun δοῦλος (*doulos*), as noted above, referred to a slave while the nominally used adjective ἀπελεύθερος (*apeleutheros*), "freedman," referred to one freed from slavery.

With this verse, Paul asked his readers to take a look at their social condition through the lens of Christianity. God's call to those who were in slavery gave them a kind of freedom from the concerns of this world and of any need for higher station. Being the slaves of Christ but heirs of his kingdom gave them very high status. From Paul's point of view, and within

---

166. BDAG, 1087–88; Louw-Nida, §41.5.

167. For a full discussion of the problem, see Thiselton, *First Epistle,* 553–59.

168. Among biblical translations that adopt this view are the KJV, NIV, and RSV. Some of the major authorities who support this view are the following: BDAG, 1087; Karl Heinrich Rengstorf, "δοῦλος, σύνδουλος, δούλη, δουλεύω, δουλεία," in *TDNT,* 2:261–79; Fee, *First Epistle,* 315–18; Wire, *Women Prophets,* 86 and n. 10; Bruce, *1 and 2 Corinthians* 72; Findlay, "St. Paul's First Epistle," 880; and Fitzmyer, *First Corinthians,* 309.

169. Some of the major authorities who support this view are the following: Robertson and Plummer, *Critical and Exegetical Commentary,* 147–48; Barrett, *First Epistle,* 170–71; Deming, *Paul on Marriage and Celibacy,* 158–59; Collins, *First Corinthians,* 285–86; Mitchell, *Paul and the Rhetoric of Reconciliation,* 124; Conzelmann, *1 Corinthians,* 127; and Thiselton, *First Epistle,* 544, 553–59.

the context of the status-conscious Greco-Roman world, to be a slave in the household of Christ outranked both that of being a slave in any other house and the status of most freedmen.

On the other hand, Christ freed all from the slave block of sin and in this way made them free men and women. In the Greco-Roman world, to receive manumission from a person of rank brought status. Therefore, within the Christian community, all had high station being the freedman *of* Christ. Being the Lord's freed person, the Saint shared in both the benefits and status but also—and this is important—in the obligations and responsibilities which that relationship demanded.[170]

7:23 ***Ye are bought with a price; be not ye the servants of men / You were all bought with a price. Don't become slaves of human masters:*** On the phrase "bought with a price," see Translation Notes on 6:20. The noun ἄνθρωπος (*anthrōpos*) denoted a "human being,"[171] but since Paul used it in connection with slavery, the plural noun is translated as "human masters" in our Rendition.

Paul's use of the phrase μὴ γίνεσθε (*mē ginesthe*), an imperative middle/passive deponent of γίνομαι (*ginomai*), "do not be, become,"[172] stressed his point: being the Lord's slaves, with all the high status, rights, and obligations that it brought, the Saints were not to cheapen or forfeit their position by selling themselves as slaves to mere mortals. No matter what the prestige of the potential master, or the rank promised, or the wealth to be gained, none could surpass that of being in God's household.

7:24 ***Brethren, let every man, wherein he is called, therein abide with God / Brothers and sisters, in whatever situation you found yourself when you were converted, there you should continue with God at your side:*** For "brothers and sisters" see Translation Notes on 1:10. In the phrase ἐν ᾧ ἐκλήθη (*en hō eklēthē*), literally "in which he was called," the relative pronoun ᾧ (*hō*) referred to that condition in which the individuals found themselves at the time of their call and is, therefore, translated as "whatever situation" in our Rendition. As noted above (7:20), the imperative μενέτω (*menetō*) referred to continuing in a certain sphere or condition. The preposition παρά (*para*) with the dative was a marker for nearness in space.[173] As such it could mean "near, close" or "with." In our Rendition, we

---

170. Martin, *Slavery as Salvation*, 64.
171. BDAG, 81–82.
172. BDAG, 196–99.
173. BDAG, 756–57.

have translated the phrase as "with God at your side," which best catches the sense of the preposition in this context.

Again, Paul concluded that a Saint's social or economic status did not dictate his or her standing with God. Therefore, the Saints should be content in whatever station they found themselves. Instead of being overly concerned with their social status, they should concentrate on keeping their spiritual tie with God very strong.

Analysis and Summary

Having addressed the issue of marriage between member and nonmember, Paul next turned to the topic of social standing. His counsel was to remain in whatever station one was when converted. The Saints' call to live on a higher spiritual plane did not mean that they were to fight against the current social order. The depth of their spirituality was not contingent on their social or ethnic condition but on how they fulfilled their call. "The call *to* Christ," as one scholar noted, "has created such a change in one's essential relationship (with God) that one does not need to seek change in other relationships (with people). These latter are transformed and given new meaning by the former."[174]

Due to the unrelated nature to the general topic he was treating in this chapter (marriage and divorce), it is likely that the Apostle's comments in this section were not a response to a question but rather a continuation of thoughts produced as he wrestled with the former issue, that is, the growing tension of Christian married to non-Christian. That tension may have triggered his sensitivity toward two others areas of strain that existed in the branch, namely, that between Jewish members and Gentile members and between free members and slave members.[175] Though he will more succinctly state his position in his letter to the Galatians—"There is neither Jew nor Greek, there is neither bond nor free, there is neither male nor female: for ye are all one in Christ Jesus" (Gal. 3:28)—the point he made here is clear enough.

The reason social status should not have been a major concern was because of the nature of "the call." In the meaning of the verb καλέω (*kaleō*), "to call" (which he repeated eight times in just six verses), we find the central doctrine on which Paul placed his counsel. The verb denoted an urgent

---

174. Fee, *First Epistle*, 307.
175. Bailey, *Mediterranean Eyes,* 213.

invitation for the person called "to accept responsibility for a particular task, implying a new relationship to the one who [did] the calling."[176] As noted previously (1:2), God called people to be "in Christ," the preposition suggesting the spiritual bond developed between Savior and disciple during conversion. The phrase also connoted the individual's commitment to Christ such that he or she was willing to do as the Lord commanded.[177]

God's call to come into his kingdom came to individuals within their various social and ethnic settings, thus, making those settings irrelevant. This fact meant that change of station was unnecessary because the Saints could live fully Christian lives under whatever conditions they found themselves. It also meant that should changes take place, they, too, were irrelevant. No Saint, therefore, needed to seek change on the grounds that it had some kind of spiritual significance, for there was none. Real spiritual significance lay first, in the call itself and, second, in how each individual responded to it in whatever situation they found themselves. In sum, Paul was not advocating a status quo but that the Saints should see that they could serve in whatever situation or condition they found themselves and should do so. Thus, social setting or standing had no religious significance. To reinforce that idea, he next turned to the one mark of social distinction with which the Church was most familiar, that of circumcision.[178]

In 7:18–19, the Apostle made the point that, within the kingdom, all were one and, therefore, there should be no higher sacred culture, no higher sacred language, no higher sacred heritage. All were brothers and sisters and children of one culture, that of the divine. God's call was tailored to each individual and the Saint did not need to become socially or culturally someone or something else to fulfill it. They could remain as they were when God called them. Whatever the personal shaping that occurred by the Saint's cultural identity, it in no way detracted from his or her value to the kingdom.[179] The Church accepted what was good in all cultures. The caveat, however, was "what was good." That which was not good—that is, did not adhere to gospel principles and practices—had to be abandoned. What really mattered for all was constancy in keeping God's commandments.

---

176. Louw-Nida, §33.312.

177. Fee, *First Epistle*, 309.

178. Fee, *First Epistle*, 309–11.

179. Bailey, *Mediterranean Eyes*, 217–18.

In 7:22–23, Paul was not attempting to reduce the psychological and physical hardship of slavery by telling his readers that they were all slaves of Christ and, therefore, to some degree, shared the same condition. Nor was he saying that, paradoxically, because of Christ, all were in some sense free, concluding that the external status of each person really did not matter.[180] What Paul was stressing was the benefit that befell to one who had a relationship with Christ. To be the slave *of* Christ, as we have noted above, carried a certain cachet, but to be his freedman carried even more. Paul used the metaphor of slavery not as a sign for a servile and lowly status, but as a very positive symbol of the promise of salvation through spiritual progression.[181]

We see this same idea expressed by the Lord to his disciples when he said, "Greater love hath no man than this, that a man lay down his life for his friends. Ye are my friends, if ye do whatsoever I command you. Henceforth I call you not servants; for the servant knoweth not what his lord doeth: but I have called you friends; for all things that I have heard of my Father I have made known unto you" (John 15:13–15). The word translated "servant" δοῦλος (*doulos*), denoted a slave, which station his disciples held because he had purchased them from the slave block of sin.[182] And that cost him dearly. As a result they—like any slave to master—belonged to him. He next moved them, due to his power of spiritual manumission, to the station of freedmen. Not content therewith, he made them φίλοι (*philoi*), "friends," that is, those with whom he shared loving and intimate association. Here the noun "friends" referred to those who belonged to his inner circle and, therefore, were more than associates but dear and trusted confidantes who shared equal rank.[183] In addition, Paul is also teaching that Jesus grants freedom from the worries of both physical and spiritual death.

Even though that was the case, Paul never let the Christian forget that they were deeply indebted to their Savior. They had been bought at the price of his blood (7:23) and, as a result, he now owned them until such time as he freed them. Being the Lord's own, however, had great benefits. It became his responsibility, which he took on gladly, to care for and keep them. His care, however, put them in even deeper debt. Thus, they even

---

180. Martin, *Slavery as Salvation*, 63–68.
181. Martin, *Slavery as Salvation*, 65, and see also 117–35.
182. Slaves were frequently purchased from slave blocks found in markets throughout the Roman world.
183. Louw-Nida, §34.11.

more fully belonged to him.[184] Nonetheless, they shared in his status and honor. Even so, they bore the responsibility of fully representing him at all times and in all places. The relationship also brought them great freedom from the cares and concerns of the world, for the Saints were the Lord's responsibility and had him to care for and direct, inspire, and assist them.[185]

Paul's unease was with Christian slaves who were overly restless about gaining freedom and Christian freedmen who were overly concerned with status and prestige. The position of the latter was particularly perilous because of the temptation to sell themselves for financial and social benefit.[186] The Apostle's words were directed to all who were preoccupied with "status-betterment," whether it was in gaining freedom or social climbing among the merchants, bankers, power brokers, politicians, or patrons. Paul's position, as noted before, cut across the grain of the achievement-oriented, status-conscious, ever grasping, ambitious society of Corinth.[187] The Christian position, as Paul articulated it, was to be content with and make the most of one's station. There were at least three reasons. First, God did not see it as the most important issue of life as so many others did.[188] He called to his service men and women of all ranks and conditions: bond and free, Jew and Gentile, rich and poor. Therefore, station neither impeded nor advanced one's association with God. Second, a Christian could live his or her religion in any station. One could be an honest councilman or an honest slave. Third, the result of being a Christian, from the perspective of the divine, gave each Saint a position in Christ's household, which brought the highest form of spiritual status and prestige. Properly seen, that fact alone should have cheapened and dulled anything the world could possibly offer and assisted the Saints in being content where they were. Therefore, the Saints should not concentrate on social status but on keeping the Spirit close and active in their lives.

---

184. Compare King Benjamin's analogy in Mosiah 2:20–25.

185. Thiselton, *First Epistle*, 561.

186. Winter, *Seek the Welfare of the City*, 146, but compare 145–77.

187. Thiselton, *First Epistle*, 561–62.

188. This statement should not be taken to mean that God condoned slavery. That condition was a fact of life in the era in which the Church operated and against which it did not fight, existing as it did in the mores of the larger society. Since God's Spirit was available to all, both bond and free, the Church could carry out its mission despite sad social conditions.

To the Unmarried
(7:25–28)

Greek Text

25 Περὶ δὲ τῶν παρθένων ἐπιταγὴν κυρίου οὐκ ἔχω, γνώμην δὲ δίδωμι ὡς ἠλεημένος ὑπὸ κυρίου πιστὸς εἶναι. 26 νομίζω οὖν τοῦτο καλὸν ὑπάρχειν διὰ τὴν ἐνεστῶσαν ἀνάγκην, ὅτι καλὸν ἀνθρώπῳ τὸ οὕτως εἶναι. 27 δέδεσαι γυναικί; μὴ ζήτει
λύσιν· λέλυσαι ἀπὸ γυναικός; μὴ ζήτει γυναῖκα· 28 ἐὰν δὲ καὶ γαμήσῃς, οὐχ ἥμαρ-
τες. καὶ ἐὰν γήμῃ ἡ παρθένος, οὐχ ἥμαρτεν. θλῖψιν δὲ τῇ σαρκὶ ἕξουσιν οἱ τοιοῦτοι,
ἐγὼ δὲ ὑμῶν φείδομαι. [SBLGNT]

King James Version

25 Now concerning virgins I have no commandment of the Lord: yet I give my judgment, as one that hath obtained mercy of the Lord to be faithful. 26 I suppose therefore that this is good for the present distress, I say, that it is good for a man so to be. 27 Art thou bound unto a wife? seek not to be loosed. Art thou loosed from a wife? seek not a wife. 28 But and if thou marry, thou hast not sinned; and if a virgin marry, she hath not sinned. Nevertheless such shall have trouble in the flesh: but I spare you.

New Rendition

25 Now concerning those who have not yet married, I do not have any commandment from the Lord, but I do give my opinion as one shown mercy by the Lord to be trustworthy. 26 Therefore, in view of the impending crisis, I think it is best for a person to remain as he is. 27 Are you engaged? Don't consider breaking the engagement. Has your engagement been broken? Don't go looking for a wife. 28 But if you should marry, you are not committing a sin. And if an engaged woman marries, she is not committing a sin. But those who do marry will experience difficulties in this life, and I would like to spare you from those.

Translation Notes and Comments

7:25 *Now concerning virgins I have no commandment of the Lord: yet I give my judgment, as one that hath obtained mercy of the Lord to be faithful / Now concerning those who have not yet married, I do not have any commandment from the Lord, but I do give my opinion as one shown mercy by the Lord to be trustworthy:* With this verse, Paul picks up his next subject, that of unmarried persons. The plural noun τῶν παρθένων (*tōn parthenōn*), "the virgins," offers no hint of gender and can refer equally to males, females, or both.[189] The Apostle could have been addressing engaged couples, but it seems more likely that, here, the Apostle addressed males and, following his pattern of mutuality, addressed females in 7:28.[190] At any rate, he was definitely addressing those who were single.

Paul was once again clear that he was aware of nothing in what Jesus taught that covered the current situation and, therefore, was stepping out on his own. The noun γνωμη (*gnōmē*), "opinion, judgment," reflected Paul's attitude about his opinion: it was just that, his opinion, although he does end the chapter by saying, "I think that I have the Spirit of God" (7:40, Rendition). It was based on the circumstances that Corinthian Saints, if not the whole Church, were facing. Even so, he did give his reason for why his readers should take his advice seriously. He described his state with two important words. The perfect passive participle ἠλεημένος (*eleēmenos*), "having received mercy, having been graciously favored,"[191] highlighted Paul's standing with the Lord. The adjective πιστος (*pistos*), "faithful, trustworthy"[192] indicated the consequence of that standing: Paul was trustworthy.

7:26 *I suppose therefore that this is good for the present distress / Therefore, in view of the impending crisis:* The noun ἀνάγκην (*anankēn*) had the basic meaning of "force, constraint, necessity."[193] Paul, however, was using it in the more abstract sense of "calamity" or "crisis."[194] The verb ἐνίστημι (*enistēmi*) referred to a current event, but the force of the perfect active participle, ἐνεστῶσαν (*enestōsan*) used by Paul, coupled with the idea of a threat, connoted something that was about to occur, thus, "impending."[195]

---

189. Fee, *First Epistle*, 326.

190. Matthew Black, *The Scrolls and Christian Origins: Studies in the Jewish Background of the New Testament* (New York: Charles Scribner's Sons, 1961), 85; J. F. Bound, "Who Are the 'Virgins' Discussed in 1 Corinthians 7:25–38," *Evangelical Journal* 2 (1984): 3–15. Both of these writers argue that this whole section deals with unmarried males, but in 7:28, Paul definitely addressed *hē parthenos,* that is, "the female." Even so, 7:25–27 do seem to be directed to unmarried men. See Thiselton, *First Epistle*, 569–71; Fee, *First Epistle*, 326–27.

191. BDAG, 315.

192. On πιστός (*pistos*), see Translation Notes on 2:4. On the weight of Paul's counsel, see R. A. Ramsaran, "More Than an Opinion: Paul's Rhetorical Maxim in First Corinthians 7:25–26," *Catholic Biblical Quarterly* 57 (1995): 532–41.

193. LSJ, 101.

194. BDAG, 60–61.

195. BDAG, 337.

One event that influenced much of Paul's thinking paralleled the general belief held among the Christians that the Second Advent would not be long in coming.[196] Given the catastrophic events associated with it, many would have viewed it as an impending crisis.[197] There was, however, a more immediate occurrence that the Corinthian Saints, as well as all Christians, were facing. This was the impending Apostasy. Paul was greatly distressed over the nearness of this event (Acts 20:29–30; 2 Thes. 2:3; 2 Tim. 1:15; 3:1–7).[198] Both concerns were likely at play and combined to give force, urgency, and direction to Paul's counsel.

it is good for a man so to be / it is best for a person to remain as he is: The Greek phrase καλὸν ἀνθρώπῳ τὸ οὕτως εἶναι (*kalon anthrōpō to houtōs einai*) is translated literally in KJV, but that does not quite catch the Greek nuance. Paul used the neuter definite article τό (*to*) with the present infinitive of the verb "to be." The present infinitive expressed continuing action.[199] Since English lacks this grammatical nuance, our Rendition catches it with, "to remain as he [or she] is."

Paul once again articulated his running theme: "stay as you are," with the caveat that this counsel was only necessary until the impending crisis was over. The JST provides a reason why Paul felt the status quo was okay. It was so that the Saints "may do greater good" (JST 7:26). The imminent distress demanded that one postpone any change in either station or relationship in order to accomplish something more important. Although Paul did not identify, at this point, what that "greater good" was, he did a few verses later (see JST 7:29).

7:27 *Art thou bound unto a wife? seek not to be loosed. Art thou loosed from a wife? seek not a wife / Are you engaged? Don't consider breaking the engagement. Has your engagement been broken? Don't go looking for*

---

196. For discussion, see Thiselton, *First Epistle,* 580–86.

197. For example, see Holzapfel and Wayment, *Making Sense,* 352; Collins, *First Corinthians,* 293. For analysis of the coming apostasy, see "Excursus on the State of Apostasy at the End of the First Century," in Richard D. Draper and Michael Rhodes, *The Revelation of John the Apostle* (Provo, Utah: BYU Studies, 2016), 196–99.

198. Because the term does not necessarily carry an eschatological nuance, some scholars feel that it referenced a dislocation and crisis caused by the severe famines that hit the Mediterranean area during the sixth decade. See Bruce W. Winter, "A Secular and Christian Response to Corinthian Famines," *Tyndell Bulletin* 48 (1997): 57–65; and Thiselton, *First Epistle,* 492–93.

199. As opposed to the aorist infinitive which expressed simple occurrence. Smyth, *Greek Grammar,* §1865b.

a wife: In this verse, Paul gave concrete examples of what he meant by his counsel that people should "remain as you are."

There are two different ways to interpret this verse. The KJV gives an older one, namely that Paul was talking about married men. But the beginning of 7:26 seems to argue against that view since Paul said he was giving advice to those who had not yet married, that is, to engaged men. Supporting this idea is Paul's phrase δέδεσαι γυναικί (*dedesai gynaiki*), "bound to a woman." The perfect passive infinitive *dedesai*, "to be bound" or "tied,"[200] carried the idea of being constrained by duty, custom, or law, but that did not refer to marriage as much as to engagement.[201] Though the word γυνή (*gynē*) could be used in the Greek world to designate a wife, it primarily referred to an adult woman.[202] Paul also counseled, μὴ ζήτει λύσιν (*mē zētei lysin*), "do not be loosed." The noun *lysis* meant "release" or "separation,"[203] but it could also mean "release, discharge" from bonds or obligations.[204] Though the word could pertain to marriage, most commentators feel it fits better with betrothal.[205] Our Rendition follows this interpretation since Paul appears to have been talking to certain unmarried men, advising them about their engagements. His counsel was, if engaged they should continue therein, but if the engagement had been previously broken off, they should not be looking for a potential wife.

7:28 But and if thou marry, thou hast not sinned; and if a virgin marry, she hath not sinned / But if you should marry, you are not committing a sin. And if an engaged woman marries, she is not committing a sin: The second person singular aorist subjunctive γαμήσῃς (*gamnēsēs*), "marry," inferred the pronoun "you," meaning the engaged man. Paul was careful to make sure his readers understood that even with the impending crisis, to ignore his counsel did not constitute sin of any kind. In no way and under no conditions was marriage to be considered sinful. However, Paul felt the current situation demanded that marriage be postponed for those in a position to do so. For those who could or would not, marriage was fine.

Nevertheless such shall have trouble in the flesh: but I spare you / But those who do marry will experience difficulties in this life, and I would like to spare you from those: The noun θλῖψις (*thlipsis*), "trouble, difficulties"

---

200. Louw-Nida, §18.13.

201. BDAG, 221–22

202. BDAG, 208–9.

203. BDAG, 605.

204. LSJ, 1066.

205. Thiselton, *First Epistle*, 576–77. See also Fee, *First Epistle*, 331–32.

denoted "trouble involving direct suffering," and also carried the idea of that suffering coming from "tribulation" and "oppression."[206] The phrase τῇ σαρκὶ (*tē sarki*), literally "in the flesh," connoted mortal life and is translated with that tone in our Rendition.[207]

Paul explained why, under the current situation, he was recommending that a certain segment of his readership stay single. It was because they would have *thlipsis,* "tribulation, affliction," in this life. The noun he chose expressed well why he was concerned. Unfortunately, he did not explain what would cause those trials. Likely they were tied to "the impending crisis." The context suggests that distress would come particularly on married couples. It is unlikely he had in mind the usual pressures that come with married life since such would hardly discourage marriage and, therefore, need no warning. Paul saw something on the horizon, but he did not articulate what it was.

The way the Greek text reads, the Apostle's counsel was based on his desire to save his readers from more pain and suffering than necessary (φείδομαι, *pheidomai*). The JST puts a different spin on Paul's attitude. There, after Paul gives his counsel not to seek marriage because of the coming troubles, it reads, "For I spare you not" (JST 7:28), meaning that, as unpopular as his counsel might be, he was not going to soft pedal it. His readers needed to understand what marriage under the coming conditions meant and he would not back away from telling them.

Analysis and Summary

In this section, Paul addressed the question as to what unmarried men should do given the conditions the Church faced. In the preserved teachings of Jesus, there was nothing that addressed Paul's concerns and the Apostle was quick to admit that. Indeed, there was no precedent for his position. He validated his counsel, however, on two facts: first, through the grace of the Lord, he had been placed in a position of trust, and second, there was an impending crisis coming that informed his decisions. That crisis was, most immediately, the Apostasy (for discussion see Analysis for the next section).

Due to what was coming, his continual counsel was "stay as you are" so that you may do the "greater good" (JST 7:26). Right then was not the time to worry about changing either marital state or social status. Indeed,

---

206. Louw-Nida, §22.2; BDAG, 457.
207. BDAG, 914–16.

time was pressing (7:29) and, therefore, all who could must devote themselves to the Lord's ministry. Their task was to save as many people as possible and accomplish other Church objectives before it was too late.

Therefore, he counseled those men who were married or engaged not to change their state. For those who were either divorced, widowed, or now had their engagements broken, he asked them not to worry about romance for the time being. He did make it perfectly clear, however, that if any of these, along with any engaged sisters, chose to marry, even in light of the unusual and very stressful situation in which the Church found itself, they would in no way sin. He gave, however, a clear warning: the immediate period would be marked by unusual trials and difficulties for married couples and, therefore, he felt that it would be best if, for its duration, they remained single.

To Those in the Ministry (7:29–35)

Greek Text

29 τοῦτο δέ φημι, ἀδελφοί, ὁ καιρὸς συνεσταλμένος ἐστίν· τὸ λοιπὸν ἵνα καὶ οἱ ἔχοντες γυναῖκας ὡς μὴ ἔχοντες ὦσιν, 30 καὶ οἱ κλαίοντες ὡς μὴ κλαίοντες, καὶ οἱ χαίροντες ὡς μὴ χαίροντες, καὶ οἱ ἀγοράζοντες ὡς μὴ κατέχοντες, 31 καὶ οἱ χρώμενοι τὸν κόσμον ὡς μὴ καταχρώμενοι· παράγει γὰρ τὸ σχῆμα τοῦ κόσμου τούτου. 32 Θέλω δὲ ὑμᾶς ἀμερίμνους εἶναι. ὁ ἄγαμος μεριμνᾷ τὰ τοῦ κυρίου, πῶς ἀρέσῃ τῷ κυρίῳ· 33 ὁ δὲ γαμήσας μεριμνᾷ τὰ τοῦ κόσμου, πῶς ἀρέσῃ τῇ γυναικί, 34 καὶ μεμέρισται. καὶ ἡ γυνὴ ἡ ἄγαμος καὶ ἡ παρθένος μεριμνᾷ τὰ τοῦ κυρίου, ἵνα ᾖ ἁγία καὶ τῷ σώματι καὶ τῷ πνεύματι· ἡ δὲ γαμήσασα μεριμνᾷ τὰ τοῦ κόσμου, πῶς ἀρέσῃ τῷ ἀνδρί. 35 τοῦτο δὲ πρὸς τὸ ὑμῶν αὐτῶν σύμφορον λέγω, οὐχ ἵνα βρόχον ὑμῖν ἐπιβάλω, ἀλλὰ πρὸς τὸ εὔσχημον καὶ εὐπάρεδρον τῷ κυρίῳ ἀπερισπάστως. [SBLGNT]

King James Version

29 But this I say, brethren, the time is short: it remaineth, that both they that have wives be as though they had none; 30 And they that weep, as though they wept not; and they that rejoice, as though they rejoiced not; and they that buy, as though they possessed not;

New Rendition

29 But let me tell you, brethren, the time is short. So from now on, even those who have wives should be as though they had none. 30 Those who weep, should be as those who do not weep, those who rejoice should be as those who do not rejoice, those who buy should be as

31 And they that use this world, as not abusing it: for the fashion of this world passeth away. 32 But I would have you without carefulness. He that is unmarried careth for the things that belong to the Lord, how he may please the Lord: 33 But he that is married careth for the things that are of the world, how he may please his wife. 34 There is difference also between a wife and a virgin. The unmarried woman careth for the things of the Lord, that she may be holy both in body and in spirit: but she that is married careth for the things of the world, how she may please her husband. 35 And this I speak for your own profit; not that I may cast a snare upon you, but for that which is comely, and that ye may attend upon the Lord without distraction.

those who have no possessions, 31 and those who must deal with the world should not be completely occupied with it, for the way of life in this world is passing away. 32 But I would have you to be free from care. An unmarried man is concerned with the things of the Lord and how he might please him. 33 But a married man is concerned about the things of the world and how to please his wife, 34 and he is pulled in two directions. An unmarried woman, old or young, is concerned with the things of the Lord so that she might be holy both in body and spirit. But a married woman is concerned with the things of the world and how to please her husband. 35 Now I am telling you these things for your own benefit, not to hamper you, but to promote good order and undistracted service to the Lord.

Translation Notes and Comments

7:29 *But this I say, brethren, the time is short / But let me tell you, brethren, the time is short:* Paul's opening phrase τοῦτο δέ φημι, ἀδελφοί (*touto de phēmi, adelphoi*), signaled a new development in his argument and underscored its importance. The KJV translation "I say" is simply too weak, describing more the verb λέγω (*legō*), "to say, speak,"[208] than the verb φημί (*phēmi*), which is the verb that is actually used here. In this context it connotes "saying something that provides a more full explanation of a statement."[209] Paul used the phrase to stress the seriousness with which he wanted his readers to take his counsel. To pick up that nuance, our Rendition translates the phrase as "But let me tell you."

Paul gave reason for his counsel. The basic sense of the verb συστέλλω (*systellō*) is "to limit, shorten."[210] Here Paul uses the perfect middle/passive, which is grammatically ambiguous. If taken as a passive, the sense would

---

208. BDAG, 588–90.
209. BDAG, 1053.
210. BDAG, 978.

be "the time has been shortened," with the idea that God has intervened to shorten the time. On the other hand, if it is taken as a middle, the sense is simply, "the time is short."[211] In either case, Paul is referring to the "impending crisis," that is, the Apostasy,[212] which he mentioned in 7:26. This coming Apostasy was certainly not caused by the Lord, but rather it was brought about by the wickedness of men. We have followed the KJV and translated the phrase as "time is short." Paul is warning the Saints at Corinth that conditions were moving more rapidly than he had at first anticipated, thus, forcing his counsel, a counsel that broke from the norm. It is also of note that Paul used the word καιρός (*kairos*), "time," rather than χρόνος (*chronos*), "time." The latter denoted chronological order while the former stressed the idea of a critical moment in time, a time during which much was at stake.[213] Such periods demand action but also present opportunity.[214] Though the word carried the idea of a limited period, and the context of Paul's words suggests he viewed it this way, that limitation also increased the seriousness of the moment and heightened the need to act. Now there was opportunity; later it would be lost. Therefore, all who could should work.

it remaineth, that both they that have wives be as though they had none / So from now on, even those who have wives should be as though they had none: The adjectival phrase τὸ λοιπόν (*to loipon*), literally "the remaining," referred to that which had not previously been included and, thus, "in the future," or, in the context here, "from now on."[215]

The JST makes significant changes to this verse and helps put this whole section into context. It reads: "But *I speak unto you who are called unto the ministry. For* this I say, brethren, the time that remaineth is but short, *that ye shall be sent forth unto the ministry.* Even they who have wives, shall be as though they had none; *for ye are called and chosen to do the Lord's work*" (JST 7:29; italics added to highlight changes). The Prophet's change made it clear that Paul was not giving counsel to the Church in general, but to those who had been called to missionary service. Thus, Paul initiated a policy change in this area. From that time on, for those so called, family concerns must be put aside so they could devote full time to the ministry.

---

211. BDAG, 978.

212. Ogden and Skinner, *Verse by Verse*, 136.

213. BDAG, 1092; 497–98.

214. Louw-Nida, §22.45.

215. BDAG, 602–3.

7:30 *And they that weep, as though they wept not; and they that rejoice, as though they rejoiced not; and they that buy, as though they possessed not / Those who weep, should be as those who do not weep, those who rejoice should be as those who do not rejoice, those who buy should be as those who have no possessions:* The JST reads, "And it shall be with them who weep, as though they wept not." The change makes it clear that, due to missionary service, certain restrictions would be laid upon those serving that were not required for the rest of the Christian community.

7:31 *And they that use this world, as not abusing it: for the fashion of this world passeth away / and those who must deal with the world should not be completely occupied with it, for the way of life in this world is passing away:* Paul here contrasts two verbs: χράομαι (*chraomai*) and καταχράομαι (*katachraomai*). The first had the basic meaning "make use of," but here it is used in the sense of "have dealings with."[216] The second is the same verb with the prefix κατα- (*kata-*) which added an intensive sense to the simple form of the verb, i.e. "completely, thoroughly use."[217] So Paul is telling the missionaries that, although it is necessary to have dealings with the world (obtaining food and clothing, paying rent, etc.), nevertheless, their focus should be on the things of God.

The noun σχῆμα (*schēma*) meant "form, shape" and also, "way of life."[218] Though the word referred to outward appearance, it did not refer to the physical nature of the earth, but to the lifestyle of those who inhabited it. Paul was emphasizing, from the perspective of missionary service, the transitory nature of the lifestyle of those around them. He recognized, however, that some could not break away totally and so admonished them to put in as little time and resources into worldly matters as possible. His desire was for them to live a different lifestyle, one of moderation and discipline.[219] They were not to grieve, rejoice, or enter into unnecessary business transactions for the duration of their mission.

7:32 *But I would have you without carefulness / But I would have you to be free from care:* The JST makes a significant change to this phrase, reading, "But I would, brethren, that ye magnify your calling. I would have you without carefulness." The change makes it clear, once again, that Paul was directing his admonition to missionaries. With the use of the adjective

---

216. LSJ, 2001–2.
217. Smyth, *Greek Grammar*, §1690, 3.
218. BDAG, 981; Louw-Nida, §58.7.
219. Thiselton, *First Epistle*, 584.

ἀμέριμνος (*amerimnos*), "free from care," Paul explained the reasoning behind his counsel. He wanted them to avoid the anxieties and stresses of the world as much as possible. In this he was following Jesus who warned his disciples against the cares of the world (Matt. 13:22; Mark 4:19; compare Matt. 6:34). The Apostle's solution to worldly cares was simple: break off or suspend all associations and be fully and completely dedicated to the ministry.

He that is unmarried careth for the things that belong to the Lord, how he may please the Lord / An unmarried man is concerned with the things of the Lord and how he might please him: The verb μεριμνάω (*merimnaō*), "to care for,"[220] carried the nuance of being anxious about something. Paul, however, had just stated that he wanted the Saints to be free from care. Likely he was using a play on words. He seems to be saying that the Saints should not care for worldly matters but for the things of the Lord.

The JST adds an insight. It has Paul saying that when a person devotes himself fully to the Lord, "therefore he prevaileth." Successful missionaries are focused on doing what the Lord wants and, therefore, can overcome what opposition may arise.

7:33 *But he that is married careth for the things that are of the world, how he may please his wife / But a married man is concerned about the things of the world and how to please his wife:* The JST adds the following to the end of this verse: "therefore there is a difference, for he is hindered." The change emphasizes the inability of people to serve two masters (Matt. 6:24) and, in this case, to give full service to the Lord.

7:34 *There is difference also between a wife and a virgin / and he is pulled in two directions:* This phrase, as is underscored by comparing the KJV interpretation with that of our Rendition, contains one of the biggest textual problems in all of 1 Corinthians.[221] Because the early manuscripts did not use punctuation, the phrase καὶ μεμέρισται (*kai memeristai*), "and be divided," could be read two ways. The phrase could point back to the previous verse, thus referencing the men, or forward to the next one, thus referencing the women. The KJV chooses the last option while our Rendition follows the first. The main reasons we did so are that the perfect passive

---

220. BDAG, 632.

221. There are at least nine variant readings showing that the problem developed very early. These break down almost evenly between those that look back to what Paul said about married men or forward to what he will say about the difference between married and unmarried women. On this see Metzger, *Textual Commentary*, 490.

verb μεμέρισται (*memeristai*) is singular in number and, therefore, would not easily modify the plural "married and unmarried women," and the verb is hard to translate as "there is a difference." The word denoted "divisions into different tendencies, views, [and] party positions" but not people.[222] Our Rendition, therefore, translates the phrase as pointing back to the men who, due to marriage, were divided, that is, pulled in two directions.

The unmarried woman careth for the things of the Lord, that she may be holy both in body and in spirit: but she that is married careth for the things of the world, how she may please her husband / An unmarried woman, old or young, is concerned with the things of the Lord so that she might be holy both in body and spirit. But a married woman is concerned with the things of the world and how to please her husband: The textual tradition is mixed here with some leaving out the phrase "and a virgin."[223] The KJV follows these. The motivation for this omission may have been to align the subject with the singular verb μεριμνᾷ (*merimna*), "to care for, about." The stronger evidence is that the phrase ἡ παρθένος (*hē parthenos*), "virgin, young girl" was in the original. To make the nouns agree with the singular verb, our Rendition translates the phrase ἡ γυνὴ ἡ ἄγαμος καὶ ἡ παρθένος (*hē gynē hē agamos kai hē parthenos*) as "the unmarried woman, old or young."

Paul noted that the unmarried woman cares for the things of the Lord in order to be holy in body and spirit. The nouns σώματι (*sōmati*), "body," and πνεύματι (*pneumati*), "spirit," should not be taken in opposition here, but rather as referring to the whole person. These Saints took their stance to remain holy not only inwardly but outwardly as well, thus maintaining both a high spiritual state and chaste body.[224]

Paul's point was that married people are pulled in two directions and, therefore, cannot fully put in the energy the impending crisis demanded if the Church were going to be successful in carrying out its mission.

7:35 *And this I speak for your own profit; not that I may cast a snare upon you, but for that which is comely, and that ye may attend upon the*

---

222. Heinrich A. W. Meyer, *Critical and Exegetical Commentary on the New Testament*, trans. and ed. William P. Dickson and Frederick Combie, 2 vols. (Edinburgh: T and T Clark, 1892), 1:225–26; see also Thiselton, *First Epistle*, 589; Fee, *First Epistle*, 345–46. Most translators and Biblical translations follow this view. For example, see RSV, NRSV, ASV, NIV, REB, NJB, and Conzelmann, *1 Corinthians*, 134 n. 1; Barrett, *First Epistle*, 180; Fee, *First Epistle*, 334; Collins, *First Corinthians*, 296.

223. See Metzger, *Textual Commentary*, 490.

224. Fitzmyer, *First Corinthians*, 319–20.

Lord without distraction / Now I am telling you these things for your own benefit, not to hamper you, but to promote good order and undistracted service to the Lord: The adjective σύμφορον (*symphoron*) denoted that which was "advantageous, beneficial." The phrase οὐχ ἵνα βρόχον ὑμῖν ἐπιβάλω (*ouch hina brochon hymin epibalō*), literally "not that I cast a noose over you," connoted the idea of "restricting someone's behavior" or "hampering their desires."[225] The adjective εὔσχημον (*euschēmon*) referred to that which was "appropriate for display."[226] Here it is nominalized by the definite article and has the sense of "good order," and is so translated in our Rendition.

Paul's stance was very rigorous and, therefore, he wanted to assure his readers that his intent was not to control them or tell them what to do, but to show them the most beneficial way they could serve the Lord.[227] In this respect, he held himself up as the model having no extraneous encumbrances or distractions.

Analysis and Summary

Properly interpreting this section demands an understanding of conditions, both immediate and future, that the Church faced. Paul's phrase ὁ καιρὸς συνεσταλμένος ἐστίν (*ho kairos synestalmenos estin*), "the time is short," meant that "the impending crisis" he referred to in 7:26 will shortly occur. That nearness dictated that the tempo of the Church's mission had to be stepped up. Everything he did was in response to this "impending crisis." His use of the noun καιρός (*kairos*), "time," is telling. It shows that he recognized that the Saints were living in a critical, if limited, period. Therefore, much was at stake.[228] Opportunity as well as necessity dominated his agenda and structured his counsel. Paul's directions to the Saints were, therefore, temporary, that is, restricted to the immediate condition at hand and directed to a specific body of Saints, namely those called to missionary work (JST 7:29). Though temporary, as 7:29–35 show, the moment had to be taken with such seriousness as to push all other activities into the background. And why? Because "the way of life in this world [was] passing away" (7:31, Rendition).

---

225. Louw-Nida, §37.2.
226. BDAG, 414.
227. Mitchell, *Paul and the Rhetoric of Reconciliation*, 25–39 treats Paul's desire to that which was beneficial (*symphoros*) for his readers.
228. Cullmann, *Christ and Time*, 39–45.

Imminence was driving everything, but the imminence of what? Was world history about to come to an end with the ushering in of God's kingdom? Or was the Saints' condition going to change resulting in severe pressure? Paul was aware of prophecies that dealt with both.

Much of the scholarly world has focused upon only one of these, the ἔσχατον (*eschaton*), or Second Coming of the Lord. Many insist that Paul felt it would take place in his lifetime.[229] However, there is much that argues against this idea. For example, nowhere does Paul hint at how the Saints should prepare for the end of the world. Instead, he recommended marriage and normal activities except for those called to missionary service or those who were willing to do so. In short, it was not the expectation of the *eschaton* that drove him and, therefore, he did not advocate that the Saints abandon the world. Their primary task was to keep the commandments (7:19) and fulfill their callings in the world (7:17) "in view of the impending crisis" (7:26, Rendition). He knew that conditions were rapidly changing. These changes straitened his expectations for those called to missionary service.[230] For them, social, civic, and economic concerns had to take their proper place. Paul did not say these were not worth doing, but for those "called and chosen to do the Lord's work" (JST 7:29), he recommended limited attachment.

Some have argued that Paul's offhand comment in 1 Thessalonians 4:15 (where he mentioned that "we which are alive and remain" at the Second Coming will be caught up with Jesus) testifies to his belief that he would experience the Second Coming. Too much weight has been placed on this comment. Given his statement in 2 Thessalonians 2:2–5, it is obvious that he knew the *eschaton* was distant. In 1 Thessalonians, he was using "descriptive logic" rather than "participation logic" to make a point. That rhetorical device demanded that he use the first person plural "we" rather than the second person plural "you" to make his view more vivid and weighty.[231] No, it was not the *eschaton* that was his immediate concern.

In saying that, we do not mean to imply that the promise of the Lord's coming played no role in Paul's theology and counsel. We are simply noting that he never mentioned the subject specifically in these verses. Therefore,

---

229. Holzapfel and Wayment, *Making Sense,* 352; compare Anderson, *Understanding Paul,* 106.

230. Richard D. Draper, "New Light on Paul's Teachings," *Ensign* 29 (September 1999): 25–26.

231. See Anthony C. Thiselton, "The Logical Role of the Liar Paradox in Titus 1:12, 13: A Dissent from the Commentaries," *Biblical Interpretation* 2 (1994): 207–23.

we see the idea of the *eschaton* as pushing Paul's thinking but only as an undercurrent. Paul knew that it would take place, but he did not know when. Even so, reading his letters suggests he felt it was distant.[232]

His major concern was with another catastrophic event, one about which he warned the Saints continually, namely the ἀποστασία (*apostasia*), that is, "the Apostasy."[233] During his second mission, he warned the Thessalonians that it was coming (2 Thes. 2:5), and during his third mission, it was a major teaching to all the Saints in Asia Minor (Acts 20:31). Therefore, he knew that the the the fullness of the gospel and apostolic authority would be short-lived. His concern, as one LDS scholar noted, was not so much with apostasy *from* the Church as it was the apostasy *of* the Church.[234] The fact that the Apostasy would leave the Church without divine leadership, priesthood authority, and revelation made the period during which these were still available all the more important.

Whatever Paul thought about the timing of the *eschaton,* he knew the Apostasy was imminent and, therefore, the more urgent event to prepare for. It seems that, by AD 57, when he wrote to the Corinthians, he was surprised to see how rapidly conditions were moving that would allow the Apostasy to happen. As a result, he seems to have felt a particularly keen interest in having all the Saints who could devote their fulltime efforts to accomplishing the Church's objectives to do so. Clearly, the missionaries did not have a moment to lose. Time was pressing if the Church was to accomplish the mission for which Christ had set it up, namely, the preaching of the gospel to "all the world" (Matt. 24:14; 28:19–20; Acts 1:8; JS–M 1:31).

The Apostles were perfectly aware that their work was not to set up the Church permanently upon the earth. The Apostasy was expected. Their commission from the Lord worked within that parameter. Their task was to secure the gospel onto the stage of history (Acts 1:6–7). That work had

---

232. Two works are particularly helpful when dealing with the how the New Testament writers understood the Second Coming. These works treat the theology of eschatological eminence *vis à vis* the chronology of theological imminence and show that the idea of a Second Coming was used to help the Saints know how to stand in relation to the world, even though the event was a ways off. See George B. Caird, *The Language and Imagery in the Bible* (London: Duckworth Publishing, 1988), 243–71; and Wimbush, *Paul, the Worldly Ascetic,* 1–93, especially 23–48. For a summary, see Thiselton, *First Epistle,* 578–83.

233. Anderson, *Understanding Paul,* 85–87; Ogden and Skinner, *Verse by Verse,* 136.

234. James E. Talmage, *The Great Apostasy* (Salt Lake City: The Church of Jesus Christ of Latter-day Saints, 1968), 23.

to be done so well and fully that when the Apostasy occurred, the gospel message—salvation in and through Christ alone—could not be lost.

For those who chose to marry, Paul's warning was clear: they would feel the distress of the age (7:28). He did not say what special problems married people, in comparison to young single people, would have. Part of their suffering may have been that, when the priesthood was removed, their children would not have the fullness of the precious gospel or share in the priesthood's sealing keys.

Paul taught his readers that the key to missionary success was single-mindedness. The Savior had already stressed the same thing (Matt. 6:25, 28; 10:19; Luke 12:22; compare 3 Ne. 13:22; D&C 4:5; 82:19). "No man, having put his hand to the plough," he taught, "and looking back, is fit for the kingdom of God" (Luke 9:62). Paul applied the teaching as he explained why those in the ministry must act as if they were single, emotionally secure, and free of earthly entanglements. To be otherwise, the missionary would be pulled in two directions and, therefore, unable to prevail against cares and anxieties of neither his wife nor the world. Only when these distractions were missing could the minister put his or her full energy into carrying out the Lord's mission. And considering the imminent crisis the Church was facing and the little time they had to prepare for it, it is little wonder Paul called on his fellow missionaries to devote full time to that service.[235]

CONCERNING ENGAGED COUPLES (7:36–38)

Greek Text

36 Εἰ δέ τις ἀσχημονεῖν ἐπὶ τὴν παρθένον αὐτοῦ νομίζει ἐὰν ᾖ ὑπέρακμος, καὶ οὕτως ὀφείλει γίνεσθαι, ὃ θέλει ποιείτω· οὐχ ἁμαρτάνει· γαμείτωσαν. 37 ὃς δὲ ἕστηκεν ἐν τῇ καρδίᾳ αὐτοῦ ἑδραῖος μὴ ἔχων ἀνάγκην, ἐξουσίαν δὲ ἔχει περὶ τοῦ ἰδίου θελήματος, καὶ τοῦτο κέκρικεν ἐν τῇ ἰδίᾳ καρδίᾳ, τηρεῖν τὴν ἑαυτοῦ παρθένον, καλῶς ποιήσει· 38 ὥστε καὶ ὁ γαμίζων τὴν παρθένον ἑαυτοῦ καλῶς ποιεῖ, καὶ ὁ μὴ γαμίζων κρεῖσσον ποιήσει. [SBLGNT]

---

235. Robert J. Matthews, "The Plain and Precious Parts: How Modern Scripture Helps Us Understand the New Testament," *Ensign* 5 (September 1975): 8–10.

King James Version

36 But if any man think that he behaveth himself uncomely toward his virgin, if she pass the flower of her age, and need so require, let him do what he will, he sinneth not: let them marry. 37 Nevertheless he that standeth steadfast in his heart, having no necessity, but hath power over his own will, and hath so decreed in his heart that he will keep his virgin, doeth well. 38 So then he that giveth her in marriage doeth well; but he that giveth her not in marriage doeth better.

New Rendition

36 If anyone thinks he is not treating his fiancée fairly, if she is past her prime, and he feels an obligation, let him do as he wants; he is not committing a sin. They should get married. 37 But one who stands firm in his heart, feeling no necessity, and complete freedom to choose, and has decided of his own volition to preserve his fiancée's virginity, does well. 38 So one who marries his fiancée does well, but one who does not get married does better.

Translation Notes and Comments

7:36 *if any man think that he behaveth himself uncomely toward his virgin / If anyone thinks he is not treating his fiancée fairly:* The concern in this verse was with engaged men who were either called or could be called on missions. Paul addressed the question as to whether they should postpone marriage. He set his advice on three conditions. This phrase contains the first.

The term "virgin," in this instance referred to the young man's fiancée. The JST makes this point very clear by stating that "his virgin" is the person "whom he hath espoused" (JST 7:36). Our Rendition carries this nuance.[236]

The verb ἀσχημονεω (*aschēmoneō*), "to behave unseemly, to treat unfairly,"[237] does not provide specifics as to why the young man would consider his actions inappropriate. The context suggests that it is likely that it centered on the time he would have to devote to the ministry and, thus, have to postpone the marriage. Given that the time of service appears not to have been set, keeping the girl indefinitely betrothed could be seen by her and others as shamefully unfair.[238]

---

236. Because the background to the epistle is unknown, scholars have postulated three additional options for this verse: The older tradition took the generative pronoun αὐτοῦ (*autou*), "of him," as referring to a father who had care and possession of his daughter. Another tack was that Paul was talking about some kind of "spiritual marriage." The last option was that the Apostle was referring to the Jewish practice of levirate marriage. For discussion and sources see Thiselton, *First Epistle*, 595–97. For Latter-day Saints, the JST settles the issue.

237. BDAG, 147.

238. Ogden and Skinner, *Verse by Verse*, 136–37.

if she pass the flower of her age / if she is past her prime: Here Paul lists
the second of his conditions. This phrase presents a number of translation difficulties. The first is with the phrase, ἐὰν ᾖ ὑπέρακμος (*ean ē hyper-*
akmos), literally, "if something be beyond a peak," and translated as "if
she pass the flower of her age" in the KJV. The problem is that the verb
ē has no clear subject and could refer either to the man or woman. The
adjective *hyperakmos*, "highest point, prime," is of no help. It is found only
here in the New Testament and, therefore, the text provides no check on
precisely how to interpret it. Further ambiguity arises because the adjective had only two endings, rather than the usual three, with both male
and female genders indicated the same way. It can be taken to mean "past
one's prime,"[239] or, "past the bloom of youth."[240] In that case, it applied
to the fiancée and indicated that she was already beyond marriageable
age. A number of interpreters, however, have suggested that the adjective
referred to being "at one's sexual peak" or having "strong passions."[241] In
that case, it referred to the young man connoting the idea that if his sexual
drives were too strong, he should marry.[242]

The JST is helpful here in two ways. First, it makes no change to the
translation in the KJV, suggesting Paul did have the woman in mind. Second, it does make one at the end of the verse which also strengthens this
position (see below). Our Rendition follows this interpretation.[243]

and need so require / and he feels an obligation: Here Paul lists the
third of his requirements. The text reads καὶ οὕτως ὀφείλει γίνεσθαι (*kai*
houtōs opheilei ginesthai), literally "and so ought to be" and is translated as
"if need so require" in the KJV. The verb *opheilei* meant to feel an obligation
toward someone or something.[244] The subject is unclear, but its impersonal nature suggests it did not point to either the young man or his fiancée.
Likely Paul was referring to the obligation that was pushing for marriage,
and our Rendition carries this nuance.

let him do what he will, he sinneth not: let them marry / let him do as
he wants; he is not committing a sin. They should get married: Instead

---

239. BDAG, 1032.

240. LSJ, 1,859, s.v. *hyperakmazō,* lists this as the primary idiomatic meaning.

241. BDAG, 1032.

242. See, for example, the RSV, NRSV, and REB.

243. For discussion see Thiselton, *First Epistle,* 594; Fee, *First Epistle,* 351–52. Besides
the KJV, the NKJV and NIV also translate the verse his way. Most scholars today, however,
see the phrase as pertaining to the man. See Gottlob Schrenk, "θέλημα," in *TDNT,* 3:52–62.

244. BDAG, 743.

of "let him do as he wants," the JST reads, "let him do what he hath promised" (JST 7:36), indicating the man should marry his fiancée. The inspired change suggests that the adjective *hyperakmos* referred to concerns about the woman getting past her prime and not about the young man's libido.

Paul, once again, was very clear that marriage carried no bane. It was not a less righteous action especially when his conditions were met. Paul made this clear in the one word sentence, γαμείτωσαν (*gameitōsan*), literally, "let them get married!" The connotation of the imperative is permissive which our Rendition catches with "they should get married."[245]

7:37 Nevertheless he that standeth stedfast in his heart / But one who stands firm in his heart: With this phrase Paul began another list, this one consisting of four stipulations in determining if a marriage should be postponed. This is the first. The noun καρδία (*kardia*), "heart," served as a metaphor for the disposition, as opposed to the mental state, of a person and, therefore, represented his wholehearted convictions.[246] Paul's use of the adjective ἑδραῖος (*hedraios*), "steadfast, firm,"[247] connoted security in one's belief and enhanced the metaphorical force of *kardia*.

having no necessity / feeling no necessity: Here Paul lists his second stipulation. The noun ἀνάγκη (*anankē*), as we have already seen (7:26), meant "necessity, pressure," but looked to external, not internal, forces and, therefore, connoted pressures put on one by others.

but hath power over his own will / and complete freedom to choose: Here Paul lists his third stipulation. The noun ἐξουσία (*exousia*) denoted "authority, power,"[248] and connoted a person's inherent right to determine as one willed, and in Paul's case, it carried the idea of complete freedom of choice with no external constraints.[249]

and hath so decreed in his heart that he will keep his virgin / and has decided of his own volition to preserve his fiancée's virginity: Here Paul states the last of his stipulations. The verb τηρέω (*tēreō*) meant "to keep" or "preserve."[250] As in the preceding verse we have translated παρθένος (*parthenos*) as "fiancée" to clarify the sense of the passage.

---

245. See Wallace, *Greek Grammar,* 488–89, who also refers to the form as an "Imperative of Toleration."

246. Louw-Nida, §26.3; Johannes Behm and Friedrich Baumgärtel, "καρδία," in *TDNT,* 3:605–13.

247. BDAG, 276.

248. BDAG, 352–53.

249. Louw-Nida, §§37.13; 76.12; 30.122; Werner Foerster, "ἐξουσία," in *TDNT,* 2:562–74.

250. BDAG, 1002.

doeth well / does well: The adverb *kalōs*, "well," denoted doing something to one's advantage.[251] Paul climaxed the sentence with the phrase *kalōs poiēsei*, "it is good," putting a positive spin on the decision not to marry because of the impending crisis.

In this verse, Paul emphasized the importance of the person's full, unwavering confidence in the rightness of his decision. He did not, however, recommend that the engagement be broken off. This fact suggests that he viewed missionary service as not taking an inordinate period of time.

7:38 So then he that giveth her in marriage doeth well; but he that giveth her not in marriage doeth better / So one who marries his fiancée does well, but one who does not get married does better: The JST changes this to read, "he that giveth himself in marriage doeth well; but he that giveth himself not in marriage doeth better" (JST 7:38). The change makes it clear that someone (a father or guardian?) is not giving the young woman away in marriage, but it is the young man who is giving himself.[252]

Paul made his position very clear by stating that the person who decided to marry does καλῶς (*kalōs*), "well," but to stay single was κρεῖσσον (*kreisson*), "better." This adverb denoted doing something that was more advantageous than doing something else.[253]

Analysis and Summary

We must keep in mind that Paul developed his counsel within the context of problems faced by the Saints living in Roman Corinth who asked him for answers. Some of the members were hostile to Paul and may have demanded he explain himself. His answers are, therefore, highly contextualized. Since we do not have the full context there are simply some areas that must be left open. On the whole, however, Paul's message comes through very clearly. What shaped his counsel was the necessary service to Christ that demanded the peculiar and particular circumstances in which the Church found itself, that is, the impending Apostasy.

In this section, Paul addressed those who were called to serve after they were engaged. Some questioned the rightness of a couple getting married under prevailing circumstances. The Apostle's counsel was very practical. Marriage might be best based on three conditions: First, if an individual

---

251. BDAG, 504–5.
252. This change plays against the old notion that in this section Paul was addressing father and daughter.
253. The lexical form is κρεῖττον (*kreittōn*). BDAG, 566.

felt that waiting would be a disservice to his fiancée; second, if waiting would put her beyond normal marriageable age and, thereby, make her less attractive to other suitors; and third, if he had promised her that they would marry within a short time. Paul was once again careful to state that if the young man decided not to serve the mission but marry instead, he did not sin. Paul was scrupulous not to attach any sense of shame to those who chose wedlock. They were not less righteous citizens by any means.[254] Nevertheless, having made himself clear on that point, but due to the impending crisis (the Apostasy), the Apostle could not push this case too far. It was Paul's counsel, as stated by an LDS scholar, that "it would be better for them [engaged men] to remain single until they had completed their missionary service so that they could more easily focus on the work, and hence do more good."[255]

For the Apostle, the key issue was whether the young man was making the decision to postpone marriage for the time being due to his own conviction or was yielding to external pressures. As a safeguard, in 7:37, Paul laid down four guidelines to assure that the choice was completely the young man's own. First, he had to have a personal and deeply held conviction that what he was doing was right. Second, he was to feel no external pressure from anyone in making his decision. Third, he was exercising his own right to make this decision. And fourth, he was determined to keep his fiancée chaste, that is, unmarried for the time being.[256]

Paul made his position very clear that there was no bad choice between marriage and mission. However, given the circumstances, he felt that postponing marriage was the better option. The reason was because there was a "greater good" that could be served by missionary service (JST 7:26).

The impending crisis directed Paul's counsel. It was a desperate time and desperate times call for desperate measures. Sometimes that means postponing marriage. For example, due to prevailing and extraordinarily harsh conditions, God counseled the prophet Jeremiah not to marry (Jer. 16:2). Paul could see the impending crisis coming and knew that the time for its arrival was shorter than he had previously believed. It could have been the schismatic environment in the Corinth branch that convinced the Apostle that conditions were moving very rapidly toward a full apostasy.

---

254. Thiselton, *First Epistle*, 598–601.
255. Brooks, "Paul's Inspired Teachings on Marriage," 85.
256. Thiselton, *First Epistle*, 589–601.

ON WIDOWS
(7:39–40)

Greek Text

39 Γυνὴ δέδεται ἐφ᾽ ὅσον χρόνον ζῇ ὁ ἀνὴρ αὐτῆς· ἐὰν δὲ κοιμηθῇ ὁ ἀνήρ, ἐλευ-
θέρα ἐστὶν ᾧ θέλει γαμηθῆναι, μόνον ἐν κυρίῳ· 40 μακαριωτέρα δέ ἐστιν ἐὰν
οὕτως μείνῃ, κατὰ τὴν ἐμὴν γνώμην, δοκῶ δὲ κἀγὼ πνεῦμα θεοῦ ἔχειν. [SBLGNT]

King James Version	New Rendition
39 The wife is bound by the law as long as her husband liveth; but if her husband be dead, she is at liberty to be married to whom she will; only in the Lord. 40 But she is happier if she so abide, after my judgment: and I think also that I have the Spirit of God.	39 A woman is bound in marriage as long as her husband is alive. But if her husband dies, she is free to marry whoever she wants, but only in the Lord. 40 However, in my opinion, she will be happier if she remains a widow, and I think that I have the Spirit of God.

Translation Notes and Comments

7:39 *The wife is bound by the law as long as her husband liveth; but if her husband be dead, she is at liberty to be married to whom she will; only in the Lord / A woman is bound in marriage as long as her husband is alive. But if her husband dies, she is free to marry whoever she wants, but only in the Lord:* Paul used the aorist passive subjunctive form of the verb κοιμάω (*koimaō*), "to sleep," here. It was the common euphemism for death.[257] He clearly acknowledges that death gave a woman freedom to marry whoever she wished, however, with one caveat, she was to marry, μόνον ἐν κυρίῳ (*monon en kyriō*), "only in the Lord." The last phrase, as most scholars agree, restricted her to marry within the faith.[258]

7:40 *But she is happier if she so abide, after my judgment: and I think also that I have the Spirit of God / However, in my opinion, she will be happier if she remains a widow, and I think that I have the Spirit of God:* Once again Paul was clear that his statement was κατὰ τὴν ἐμὴν γνώμην

---

257. BDAG, 551.
258. For example, Fee, *First Epistle*, 356; Meyer, *Exegetical Commentary*, 1:231; Fitzmyer, *First Corinthians*, 329; Robertson and Plummer, *Critical and Exegetical Commentary*, 161. For discussion, see Thiselton *First Epistle*, 604–5.

(*kata tēn emēn gnōmēn*), "in my opinion" (see 7:26). Due to the impending distress of the Apostasy, Paul consistently recommended that all stay as they were. He did not back away from this stand even in the case of widows. Though somewhat cautious, he did feel his counsel was inspired.

Analysis and Summary

Paul, following the Lord, was against divorce, but there was a question about remarriage after a spouse died. Likely following Old Testament precedence but making sure everyone knew it was his opinion, Paul stated that the widow was free to marry whomever she chose.[259] The Apostle made one stipulation, that she marry a fellow Christian. His advice does not contradict the position he expressed in 7:12–15, where he counseled against the breakup of mixed marriages. Those had been contracted before the spouse had converted, not after. Paul fully expected his readers to marry within the Church whether it was an original or later marriage.

Paul did, however, recommended that widows remain unmarried because he felt that they would find themselves happier if they did so. His statement in no way devalued his positive view of marriage so clearly expressed earlier. Marriage, including intimate husband/wife relationships, was a gift of God. So also was putting off marriage for divine service. Some were called to one and some to the other. Though he did not explain why he took the position he did, looming over everything was his knowledge of "the impending crisis," that is, the Apostasy. His very carefully stated view that single people were more able to give themselves fully to the service of the Lord provides a clue to his intent here. Because the Church was verging on a crisis and had only a short time to accomplish its mission, he wanted everyone who could to devote themselves in full measure to God's cause without distractions. He was careful not to overstep his bounds, however. Even though he felt he was inspired, he did not want to raise this teaching to that of Church doctrine. Even as an Apostle, he did not have that authority. Even today, the material in this section of Paul's writings has never become Church doctrine.

---

259. Remarriages were to be contracted only with other Israelites. See Deut. 7:3; Ezra 9:2, 12.

Chapter 8

On Eating Foods That Were Once Used as Sacrifices to Idols

INTRODUCTION

At this point in his epistle, Paul turned to yet another question posed by the Corinthian Saints: that of eating meats that had been offered in sacrifice to idols. Because chapters 8–10 discuss this topic, this introduction serves as background for all three chapters.

Paul's response here, as elsewhere, is contextualized. Without understanding the context, Paul's counsel causes tension. At one point he clearly counsels the most enlightened—those who know that an idol is nothing and, therefore, cannot pollute meat—not to eat it (8:8–10), but just a few paragraphs later, he gives them sweeping permission to eat it (10:25–27). Reading outside the context, the two positions seem to be in contradiction. However, such is not the case when viewed within their contexts.[1]

One context that can be gleaned from the past is that of the social setting of Paul's counsel. For the vast majority of people living in the Greco-Roman world, meat was an extravagance. The masses lived on breads (usually made from wheat) with a little fish as relish, olives, porridges, and a little wine.[2] Only the very wealthy could afford meat on a regular basis. On occasion, the rich would distribute meat to the poor as a benefice in the name of one

---

1. Peter S. Zaas, "Paul and the Halakhah: Dietary Laws for Gentiles in I Corinthians 8–10," in *Jewish Law Association Studies VII: The Paris Conference volume,* ed. S. M. Passamaneck and M. Finley (Atlanta: Scholars Press, 1994), 239.

2. Theissen, *Social Setting,* 126–27.

of the pagan gods or goddesses.[3] The poor were also invited, from time to time, to feast at a temple in honor of some pagan deity.[4]

In addition to their cultic functions, pagan temples were places of social gathering and merrymaking. Sometimes a social superior would entertain guests at their temple. "Preserved among the 'waste papers' of antiquity," one LDS scholar noted, "are invitations to private dinners, wedding feasts, and dining at pagan temples."[5] Further, guilds and burial societies occasionally hosted dinners for their members in their temple precincts. In short, portions of pagan temples were, in effect, like local restaurants with commodious areas for banquets and various celebrations.[6]

Being invited to a temple feast was no small matter, and the attraction of having a goodly portion of meat added to the draw. Such an invitation was hard to turn down. The more wealthy Christians likely felt that to do so would put a major damper on their lifestyle and social status and, therefore, resisted the idea.[7] Due to a more polemic feel in parts of this letter, it is likely that Paul addressed this topic in his previous letter to the Corinthian Saints (5:8) and now had to explain to his detractors why he took the stand he did.[8]

The propriety of participating in such a feast did cause some concern for an element within the Christian community. "All touched the daily life of the Corinthians," noted one LDS scholar, "and church members had to decide on the morality of eating at the table of a god. Animals sacrificed to the 'idol' were available for temple feasts with the surplus marketed for food."[9] Exacerbating the problem was that many temple feasts also involve heavy drinking and sexual immorality. In cautioning his readers not to participate in these events, Paul used the example of the Israelites who,

---

3. Anthony J. Blasi, *Early Christianity as a Social Movement* (New York: Peter Lang Publishing, 1988), 61.

4. Peter Garnsey, *Food and Society in Classical Antiquity* (Cambridge: Cambridge University Press, 1999), covers this subject in detail.

5. Anderson, *Understanding Paul,* 106; for example, see the material preserved in Arthor S. Hunt and Campbell C. Edgar, eds., *Selected Papyri, Non-literary Papyri, Private Affairs,* Loeb Classical Library (Cambridge: Harvard University Press, 1941), 1:401–3.

6. Ben Witherington III, "Why Not Idol Meat?: Is It What You Eat or Where You Eat It?" *Bible Review* 10 (June 1994): 40.

7. Witherington, "Why Not Idol Meat?" 42.

8. Fee, *First Epistle,* 357–58.

9. Anderson, *Understanding Paul,* 106.

having built the golden calf, "rose up to play," a euphemism for orgiastic dancing (Ex. 32:6).[10]

Though the general directive of the Church council issued some years before (see Acts 15:29) never surfaces here, it does sit importantly under what was happening. This directive, aimed at the Gentile element in the Church, included the command that they abstain from partaking of blood. In Corinth, that created two problems. The first concerned whether the meat had been butchered according to kosher laws, and the second was if it had been offered as a sacrifice in a pagan temple. Paul's response to the issue, "knowledge puffeth up, but charity edifieth" (8:1), suggests that for him the "arrogance of knowledge is a greater problem than the actual eating of nonkosher meat."[11]

The question Paul addressed arose because of differences between those who felt they had a superior spiritual depth of knowledge and those whom the Apostle identified as the "weak"—that is, the innocent, naïve, trusting, or credulous. We have already run into the attitude of the former (expressed in 10:23) in chapter 6. They insisted that, because of the Atonement of the Savior, nothing was prohibited to them (6:12). Further, they clearly understood that an idol was nothing and, therefore, neither contaminated nor infused numinous power into meat (8:6–8). Thus, there was nothing wrong with attending banquets or other feasts at the pagan temples. The disadvantage of those Paul describes as "weak," on the other hand, came from not being fully initiated into Church doctrine. They had not yet broken all ties with pagan tradition. Therefore, seeing someone whom they knew was a fellow Christian and a pillar in the Church participating in a pagan feast could lead them to conclude that pagan gods were real. Chapter 8 contains Paul's response to those who consider themselves knowledgeable and insisted on their right to eat idol meat when and where they pleased.

---

10. William Wilson, *Old Testament Word Studies* (Grand Rapids, Mich.: Kregel Publications, 1978), 313.

11. Holzapfel and Wayment, *Making Sense,* 353.

MEAT OFFERED TO IDOLS
(8:1–13)

Greek Text

1 Περὶ δὲ τῶν εἰδωλοθύτων, οἴδαμεν ὅτι πάντες γνῶσιν ἔχομεν. ἡ γνῶσις φυσιοῖ, ἡ δὲ ἀγάπη οἰκοδομεῖ. 2 εἴ τις δοκεῖ ἐγνωκέναι τι, οὔπω ἔγνω καθὼς δεῖ γνῶναι· 3 εἰ δέ τις ἀγαπᾷ τὸν θεόν, οὗτος ἔγνωσται ὑπ' αὐτοῦ. 4 Περὶ τῆς βρώσεως οὖν τῶν εἰδωλοθύτων οἴδαμεν ὅτι οὐδὲν εἴδωλον ἐν κόσμῳ, καὶ ὅτι οὐδεὶς θεὸς εἰ μὴ εἷς. 5 καὶ γὰρ εἴπερ εἰσὶν λεγόμενοι θεοὶ εἴτε ἐν οὐρανῷ εἴτε ἐπὶ γῆς, ὥσπερ εἰσὶν θεοὶ πολλοὶ καὶ κύριοι πολλοί, 6 ἀλλ' ἡμῖν εἷς θεὸς ὁ πατήρ, ἐξ οὗ τὰ πάντα καὶ ἡμεῖς εἰς αὐτόν, καὶ εἷς κύριος Ἰησοῦς Χριστός, δι' οὗ τὰ πάντα καὶ ἡμεῖς δι' αὐτοῦ. 7 Ἀλλ' οὐκ ἐν πᾶσιν ἡ γνῶσις· τινὲς δὲ τῇ συνηθείᾳ ἕως ἄρτι τοῦ εἰδώλου ὡς εἰδωλόθυτον ἐσθίουσιν, καὶ ἡ συνείδησις αὐτῶν ἀσθενὴς οὖσα μολύνεται. 8 βρῶμα δὲ ἡμᾶς οὐ παραστήσει τῷ θεῷ· οὔτε γὰρ ἐὰν φάγωμεν, περισσεύομεν, οὔτε ἐὰν μὴ φάγωμεν, ὑστερούμεθα. 9 βλέπετε δὲ μή πως ἡ ἐξουσία ὑμῶν αὕτη πρόσκομμα γένηται τοῖς ἀσθενέσιν. 10 ἐὰν γάρ τις ἴδῃ σὲ τὸν ἔχοντα γνῶσιν ἐν εἰδωλείῳ κατακείμενον, οὐχὶ ἡ συνείδησις αὐτοῦ ἀσθενοῦς ὄντος οἰκοδομηθήσεται εἰς τὸ τὰ εἰδωλόθυτα ἐσθίειν; 11 ἀπόλλυται γὰρ ὁ ἀσθενῶν ἐν τῇ σῇ γνώσει, ὁ ἀδελφὸς δι' ὃν Χριστὸς ἀπέθανεν. 12 οὕτως δὲ ἁμαρτάνοντες εἰς τοὺς ἀδελφοὺς καὶ τύπτοντες αὐτῶν τὴν συνείδησιν ἀσθενοῦσαν εἰς Χριστὸν ἁμαρτάνετε. 13 διόπερ εἰ βρῶμα σκανδαλίζει τὸν ἀδελφόν μου, οὐ μὴ φάγω κρέα εἰς τὸν αἰῶνα, ἵνα μὴ τὸν ἀδελφόν μου σκανδαλίσω. [SBLGNT]

King James Version

1 Now as touching things offered unto idols, we know that we all have knowledge. Knowledge puffeth up, but charity edifieth. 2 And if any man think that he knoweth any thing, he knoweth nothing yet as he ought to know. 3 But if any man love God, the same is known of him. 4 As concerning therefore the eating of those things that are offered in sacrifice unto idols, we know that an idol is nothing in the world, and that there is none other God but one. 5 For though there be that are called gods, whether in heaven or in earth, (as there be gods many, and lords many,) 6 But to us there is but one God, the Father, of whom are all things, and we in him; and one Lord Jesus Christ, by whom are all

New Rendition

1 Now concerning meat sacrificed to idols, we know that "We all have knowledge." Knowledge makes people conceited, but love builds them up. 2 If someone thinks he has come to understand something, he does not yet understand as well as he ought to. 3 But if someone loves God, that person is acknowledged by him. 4 Returning to the topic of eating food sacrificed to idols, we know that "there is no such thing as an idol in the entire universe," and "there is no God but one." 5 Indeed, even if there are those who are called gods, whether in heaven or on the earth—as in fact there are many gods and many lords— 6 Nevertheless, for us there is one God, the Father, from whom all things are and in him we live;

things, and we by him. 7 Howbeit there is not in every man that knowledge: for some with conscience of the idol unto this hour eat it as a thing offered unto an idol; and their conscience being weak is defiled. 8 But meat commendeth us not to God: for neither, if we eat, are we the better; neither, if we eat not, are we the worse. 9 But take heed lest by any means this liberty of yours become a stumblingblock to them that are weak. 10 For if any man see thee which hast knowledge sit at meat in the idol's temple, shall not the conscience of him which is weak be emboldened to eat those things which are offered to idols; 11 And through thy knowledge shall the weak brother perish, for whom Christ died? 12 But when ye sin so against the brethren, and wound their weak conscience, ye sin against Christ. 13 Wherefore, if meat make my brother to offend, I will eat no flesh while the world standeth, lest I make my brother to offend.

and one Lord, Jesus Christ, through whom all things are, and through whom we are. 7 But not everyone has this knowledge. And some having previously become accustomed to idols, still consider the food they eat as food offered to idols, and because their sense of right and wrong is weak, it is defiled. 8 Now food will not bring us closer to God. For if we eat it we are not any better off, and if we do not eat it, we are no worse off. 9 But be careful that your own liberty does not somehow become an obstacle for the weak. 10 For if anyone sees you, one who has knowledge, having a meal in an idol's temple, since that person's sense of right and wrong is weak, will he not be encouraged to eat food offered to idols? 11 So by your knowledge, a weak person is brought down to destruction, a brother or sister for whom Christ died. 12 But if you sin against your brothers and sisters and wound their weakened sense of right and wrong, you sin against Christ. 13 For this very reason, if some food causes my brother or sister to sin, I would never eat any kind of meat again, so that I would not cause a brother or sister to sin.

Translation Notes and Comments

8:1 *Now as touching / Now concerning:* Paul introduced his new topic with his usual περὶ δέ (*peri de*), "now concerning," or "now regarding."

things offered unto idols / meat sacrificed to idols: This English phrase is translated from a single Greek nominal adjective, εἰδωλόθυτα (*eidōlothyta*), literally "things sacrificed to idols." The word referred to the meat of animals sacrificed in pagan temples, "part of which was burned on the altar as the deities' portion . . . part was eaten at a solemn meal in the temple, and part was sold in the market . . . for home use."[12] Sometimes translated as "idol meat," the word was a pejorative term used by some

---

12. BDAG, 280; Louw-Nida, §5.15.

Christians. Pagans referred to their sacramental offering as ἱερεόθυτον (*hierothyton*), "holy meat," but from the perspective of some Christians, it was profane "meat consecrated to heathen deities" (REB 8:1). It is important to note that the term Paul used not only described meat sacrificed at a temple, but more particularly, the meat that was eaten there.[13]

we all have knowledge / "We all have knowledge": This is another case of a slogan quoted by Paul that was used by the Corinthian Saints, this time to justify the eating of the flesh of animals sacrificed in pagan temples.[14] The noun γνῶσις (*gnōsis*), "knowledge," in this instance pertained to practical matters.[15] It was used by these people to connote that they understood exactly how everything fit together and were, therefore, in a perfect position to judge and execute proper behavior. As one LDS scholar noted, "Paul's response implies that the issue of whether to eat meat that had been used in a sacrifice to a pagan deity was a result of a higher law–lower law mentality, which the apostle instantly recognized and rebuked."[16] He refused to let their claim to "higher knowledge" stand without understanding the limits that gospel living placed on it.

Knowledge puffeth up, but charity edifieth / Knowledge makes people conceited, but love builds them up: The verb φυσιόω (*physioō*), literally "to puff up," was derived from the noun φῦσα (*physa*), "bellows."[17] Here it has the abstract sense of "to make proud or conceited." For further discussion, see Translation Notes on 4:6. The noun ἀγάπη (*agapē*), "charity, love," is the Greek word Paul usually uses when he refers to Christlike love.

The verb οἰκοδομέω (*oikodomeō*) is made up of two words: οἶκος (*oikos*), "house," and δέμω (*demō*), "to build," and has the basic meaning of "to build, erect," as in constructing a building.[18] Here, however, Paul used it in the more abstract sense of "to strengthen, build up."[19]

In this verse Paul pulled no punches. His point was that practical knowledge was not enough. To decide how to act properly, a person's knowledge must be informed by love. Otherwise, the action could not only be inappropriate but also soul destroying. Love builds the self not by promoting self-importance but by ennobling one's spirit, making way for the care of others.

---

13. Zaas, "Paul and the Halakhah," 236; Fee, *First Epistle,* 359.

14. Fee, *First Epistle,* 363; Conzelmann, *1 Corinthians,* 140.

15. BDAG, 203–4.

16. Wayment, *Persecutor to Apostle,* 165.

17. LSJ, 1964.

18. BDAG, 696.

19. BDAG, 696.

8:2 *And if any man think that he knoweth any thing / If someone thinks he has come to understand something:* ἐγνωκέναι (*egnōkenai*) is a perfect infinitive of γινώσκω (*ginōskō*), "to know, learn, understand."[20] The perfect tense of the infinitive indicates the present result of a past action. Also, the pronoun τί (*ti*), "something, anything," does not strictly reflect a qualitative kind of knowledge, but rather refers to some piece of knowledge.[21] Hence, our Rendition translates the whole phrase as, "he has come to understand something."

he knoweth nothing yet as he ought to know / he does not yet understand as well as he ought to: In the phrase οὔπω ἔγνω (*oupō egnō*), "begun to know," the aorist tense of the verb γινώσκω (*ginōskō*) was used ingressively, that is, to express the beginning of an action.[22] Paul's point is that the person who thinks he has come to understand has not yet even begun the process real understanding necessitates. The phrase καθὼς δεῖ γνῶναι (*kathōs dei gnōnai*), literally "to the degree that it is necessary to understand," described exactly their problem.

Paul's words in this paragraph are fairly scathing, but given the arrogance of those objecting to his counsel, it is understandable. These smug, self-important people felt themselves superior to those whom they considered weak. Their attitude was contributing to the schisms in the branch.[23] They needed to be knocked down a peg or two in order to find humility and insight.

8:3 *But if any man love God, the same is known of him / But if someone loves God, that person is acknowledged by him:* For Paul, the key to gaining true knowledge was based on εἰ δέ τις ἀγαπᾷ τὸν θεόν (*ei de tis agapa ton theon*), "if one loves God." By his use of the perfect passive ἔγνωσται (*egnōstai*), "he is known," he revealed the result of this kind of knowledge.

The Apostle deliberately uses several different nuanced meanings of the verb γινώσκω (*ginōskō*), "to know," and the related noun γνῶσις, (*gnōsis*), "knowledge, understanding," in these first three verses. In 8:1 he uses *gnōsis* to mean practical "knowledge." In 8:2 he uses different tenses to express "come to understand" (perfect) and "not yet begun to understand" (ingressive aorist). Here he uses the perfect passive to indicate that if a person

---

20. BDAG, 199.

21. Barrett, *First Epistle,* 190. There is a textual variant here with some of the earliest texts omitting the *ti.* Due to the large number of early texts that do not, it is retained here.

22. Wallace, *Greek Grammar,* 558; Smyth, *Greek Grammar,* §1924.

23. Thiselton, *First Epistle,* 622.

loved God, he or she was then in a state where God continually recognized and acknowledged that person as his own.[24] Thus, love mastered knowledge, bringing not only the key to true understanding but also an abiding relationship with God.

8:4 *As concerning therefore the eating of those things that are offered in sacrifice unto idols / Returning to the topic of eating food sacrificed to idols:* Though this sentence began with the usual περὶ δέ (*peri de*), "now concerning," in this case, it did not mark a new subject but a return to a former one and thus is translated as "returning to the topic"[25] in our Rendition. The term βρῶσις (*brōsis*), "eating," nuanced the eating of sacrificial foods.[26]

The JST rearranges this verse to read, "As concerning therefore the eating of those things which are in the world offered in sacrifice unto idols, we know that an idol is nothing, and that there is none other God but one" (JST 8:4). By changing the position of the phrase "in the world," the inspired version does two things: first, it emphasizes the terrestrial nature of the sacrificial offerings made to idols, and second, it broadens beyond this world the reality of the nothingness of idols.

we know that an idol is nothing in the world / we know that "there is no such thing as an idol in the entire universe": This also seems to be a quote from the letter the Corinthian Saints sent to Paul. The plural pronoun "we" refers to those who wrote the question and showed that this view was held by quite a number of the Saints. The phrase οὐδὲν εἴδωλον ἐν κόσμῳ (*ouden eidōlon en kosmō*), literally "no idol in universe," as is often done with short sayings or maxims in Greek, lacks a linking verb, which our Rendition supplies as "there is." The noun κόσμος (*kosmos*) has the basic sense of "an orderly arrangement," but it was regularly used to describe "the sum total of everything here and now, the world, the (orderly) universe."[27] The word in this sense has been adopted into English as "cosmos." The phrase emphasizes the eternal nonexistence of the false gods represented by idols. Paul did not take exception to the idea.

there is none other God but one / "there is no God but one": This is yet another phrase Paul lifted from the Corinthian letter. In this case it is a variation on the *Shema* found in Deuteronomy 6:4, "Hear, O Israel: the Lord

---

24. The nuance of the verb here has very strong ties to the idea of being the elect of God. BDAG, 199–201.

25. Margaret M. Mitchell, "Concerning *peri de* in 1 Corinthians," *Novum Testamentum* 31 (1989): 233–34.

26. BDAG, 184–85.

27. BDAG, 561.

our God is one Lord." Again, Paul took no exception to the idea but rather acknowledged the truth of what the "strong" were saying. Where he disagreed was in their application, for both this and the previous quote were used by the "strong" as a justification for eating meat sacrificed in pagan temples. Their argument must have been something like, "We all have knowledge. We know that pagan gods do not exist, and that there is only one true God, therefore, there is nothing wrong with eating meat that has been sacrificed to these false gods."

8:5 *For though there be that are called gods, whether in heaven or in earth / Indeed, even if there are those who are called gods, whether in heaven or on the earth:* This statement is usually taken to refer to the false, pagan gods, which it certainly does in part, but the following phrase makes it clear that there are also real gods and lords.

(as there be gods many, and lords many) / as in fact there are many gods and many lords: Our Rendition takes the coordinating conjunction ὥσπερ (*hōsper*) as emphasizing the factual nature of the previous statement and, therefore, translates the word, "as in fact."[28] Paul made it clear that besides the pagan deities, which are called "gods" and "lords," there are also true "gods" and "lords."

8:6 *But to us there is but one God, the Father, of whom are all things, and we in him; and one Lord Jesus Christ, by whom are all things, and we by him / Nevertheless, for us there is one God, the Father, from whom all things are and in him we live; and one Lord, Jesus Christ, through whom all things are, and through whom we are:*[29] There are indeed other gods and other lords, but for us, the inhabitants of this earth, the spirit children of our Father and Mother in heaven, there is only one God whom we worship, our Father, and one Lord, our Savior and Redeemer, Jesus Christ.

In this verse, Paul's use of the prepositions skillfully distinguishes the role of the Father and the Son. Of the Father he said, ἐξ οὗ τὰ πάντα (*ex hou ta panta*), "from whom all things are," the preposition ἐξ (*ex*) with the genitive indicating source or origin and thus meaning both "derived from" and "dependent upon."[30] Thus, the Apostle showed that the Father is the source

---

28. Barrett, *First Epistle*, 191; and Blass and Debrunner, *Greek Grammar of the New Testament*, §454, take it this way as well.

29. The creedal nature of his verse has given opportunity for some scribes to turn it into a trinitarian statement by adding the phrase "and one Holy Spirit, in whom are all things, and we in him" in their copies. The added phrase was not in the original. Metzger, *Textual Commentary*, 491.

30. Wallace, *Greek Grammar*, 109.

from which all things originate. Paul described our relationship with him as being εἰς αὐτόν (*eis auton*), "in him," the accusative with *eis*, "in," suggesting a close, even intimate, association with him.[31] Of Jesus, Paul said, δι' οὗ τὰ πάντα (*di' hou ta panta*), "through whom all things are," thus showing that Jesus was not the originator but the organizer of all things. Of our relationship to him, Paul stated, ἡμεῖς δι' αὐτοῦ (*hēmeis di' autou*), "we are through him," that is, he was the agent through whom our spiritual rebirth as new creatures of God took place.[32]

8:7 ***Howbeit there is not in every man that knowledge / But not everyone has this knowledge:*** Paul's word order here, especially with the strong adversative ἀλλά (*alla*), "but," emphasized his point. Not all converts understood this doctrine.

for some with conscience of the idol unto this hour eat it as a thing offered unto an idol / And some having previously become accustomed to idols, still consider the food they eat as food offered to idols: The noun συνήθεια (*synētheia*), "custom," carries the nuance of "being accustomed" to something and, in this case, it was believing in and worshiping idols.[33] These Saints, though accepting the Father and Son as the Gods they worshiped, had not yet divested themselves of all belief in the reality of other gods. This lack of knowledge made them vulnerable to misinterpreting the actions of those who had that knowledge.

their conscience being weak is defiled / because their sense of right and wrong is weak, it is defiled: The noun συνείδησις (*syneidēsis*) is derived from the verb σύνοιδα (*synoida*), "to be aware of, to be conscious of."[34] It is the equivalent of the Latin *conscientia*, which English has adopted as "conscience." In our Rendition, we have translated it as "sense of right and wrong" to better express the idea of the Greek original. The very verb μολύνω (*molynō*), "to soil, pollute," suggested an extreme defilement in which one's innocence was completely destroyed.[35]

---

31. Wallace, *Greek Grammar*, 360.

32. Wallace, *Greek Grammar*, 368. The scriptures refer to Jesus as the Father (Mosiah 15:2; Ether 3:14) because he is the author of our eternal lives (Mosiah 5:7; 27:24–27; 2 John 2:12).

33. BDAG, 971. Some variants substitute συνειδήσει (*syneidēsei*), "consciousness." Because the word connotes a strong moral tone, it can also mean "conscience." BDAG, 967–68. However, it is likely that it arose because of assimilation with the word συνείδησις (*syneidēsis*) which follows in the same sentence. Metzger, *Textual Commentary*, 491.

34. BDAG, 967–68, 973.

35. Thiselton, *First Epistle*, 640.

The idea of right and wrong as used by Paul in this instance did not pertain to moral issues but to gospel principles. It is likely that the reason some of the Saints were in this condition was because they were new converts and had not fully understood *and* internalized the doctrine. Because of this, they could misinterpret the actions of those they considered strong in the gospel as actually giving credence to the reality and power of pagan gods. This would more especially be the case if their Christian benefactor invited them to a cultic feast at the temple. In such instances, real spiritual harm could be done by opening the door to a return to paganism with all its ills.[36]

8:8 *But meat commendeth us not to God / Now food will not bring us closer to God:* This verse presents some difficulties in interpretation. The problem centers on whether this is a catchphrase that Paul lifted from the letter the Corinthian Saints sent him or his own feelings.[37] Though we cannot be certain, our Rendition takes the view that it is a paraphrase of material that Paul had received, so it is not placed in quote marks.[38] The verb παρίστημι (*paristēmi*) means "to bring before" with the idea of coming closer.[39]

for neither, if we eat, are we the better; neither, if we eat not, are we the worse / For if we eat it we are not any better off, and if we do not eat it, we are no worse off: Those Corinthian Saints who claimed superior knowledge (the "strong") were insisting that eating idol meat was absolutely neutral so far as God was concerned. They were, they insisted, unquestionably in no danger of incurring any divine wrath come Judgment Day.[40]

8:9 *But take heed lest by any means this liberty of yours become a stumblingblock to them that are weak / But be careful that your own liberty does not somehow become an obstacle for the weak:* The verse contains Paul's rejoinder to the Corinthian Saints' position. Key to understanding the issue between Paul and the Corinthians is the noun ἐξουσία (*exousia*), "authority, power." Among other nuances, the word carried the idea of "the

---

36. Paul Douglas Gardner, *The Gifts of God and the Authentication of a Christian: An Exegetical Study of 1 Corinthians 8–11* (Lanham, Md.: University Press of America, 1994), 40–45; Fee, *First Epistle,* 379; Thiselton, *First Epistle,* 639–40.

37. Two important studies of this verse are Jerome Murphy-O'Connor, "Food and Spiritual Gifts in 1 Corinthians 8:8," *Catholic Biblical Quarterly* 41 (1979): 292–98; and Gardner, *Gifts of God,* 48–54.

38. Here we follow Bruce, *1 and 2 Corinthians,* 81; Barrett, *First Epistle,* 195; and Thiselton, *First Epistle,* 647–51.

39. Some authorities see the verb as meaning "to be brought before God in judgment." This forensic use, however, is in question. BDAG, 778.

40. *DNTC,* 2:348; Murphy-O'Connor, "Food and Spiritual Gifts," 292.

right to choose."[41] Both the KJV and Rendition translate the word as "liberty." There was no question as to the correctness of doctrine these Corinthians' held. The problem was in their conclusion that their understanding gave them the right to act as they did. It was their misunderstanding resulting in the misuse of their liberty that was at issue. Wrongly applied, their liberty could easily become a πρόσκομμα (*proskomma*), the noun meaning "that which causes one to stumble."[42] In short, their insistence on exercising their "right" could cause the "weak" to stumble off the path of righteousness and out of the kingdom.

8:10 *For if any man see thee which hast knowledge sit at meat in the idol's temple, shall not the conscience of him which is weak be emboldened to eat those things which are offered to idols / For if anyone sees you, one who has knowledge, having a meal in an idol's temple, since that person's sense of right and wrong is weak, will he not be encouraged to eat food offered to idols?:*[43] In this verse, Paul stated clearly the rub. His use of the conjunction γάρ (*gar*), "for," marked his statement as a point of clarification. His use of the future passive indicative οἰκοδομηθήσεται (*oikodomēthēsetai*), literally "he will be built up," pushed his point. The word is translated as "emboldened" in the KJV, but this totally misses the irony Paul used here.[44] The force of the word dealt with building something.[45] The "strong," apparently, were encouraging the "weak" to act on their superior knowledge and join them in pagan sacral meals so that they might "build" in them an emancipated faith that allowed the "weak" to also express their "right" (ἐξουσία, *exousia*) to eat idol meat. The problem was that the "weak" might miss the point and rather than being "built up" in knowledge could be "built up" to easily move back into idolatry.[46]

8:11 *And through thy knowledge shall the weak brother perish, for whom Christ died? / So by your knowledge, a weak person is brought down to destruction, a brother or sister for whom Christ died:* Again,

41. Thiselton, *First Epistle*, 649; italics added.

42. BDAG, 882.

43. Some manuscripts leave out the pronoun *se*, "you," thus broadening Paul's audience. Given the textual evidence, however, it seems more likely that the pronoun was in the original. Metzger, *Textual Commentary*, 491.

44. Fee, *First Epistle*, 386 and n. 57.

45. BDAG, 696–97.

46. Khiok-khing Yeo, *Rhetorical Interaction in 1 Corinthians 8 and 10: A Formal Analysis with Preliminary Suggestions for the Chinese Cross-Cultural Hermeneutic* (Leiden: Brill, 1955), 192; Thiselton, *First Epistle*, 651–52.

Paul's use of the conjunction γάρ (*gar*) is telling. In this instance it stressed the self-evident conclusion that the misuse of their "knowledge" was hurting other members of the Church.[47] The verb ἀπόλλυται (*apollytai*), "is ruined, destroyed," clearly expressed Paul's concern.[48] The end result of the misapplication of knowledge and the insistence on the right to act on it would not be building the individual but, rather, causing the destruction of a soul, thus rendering the suffering of Christ void for that person. As noted previously, the phrase ἀδελφός (*adelphos*), though masculine in form, can refer to either a brother or sister and is, thus, translated as "person" in our Rendition. Paul's use of the term should have engendered a feeling of care and warmth of the "strong" toward the "weak" and, thus, motivated them to act in love as the Savior had done.

8:12 *But when ye sin so against the brethren, and wound their weak conscience, ye sin against Christ / But if you sin against your brothers and sisters and wound their weakened sense of right and wrong, you sin against Christ:*[49] With these very strong words, the Apostle showed those who felt they were so superior just how much trouble acting on their knowledge could cause them. The use of οὕτως (*houtōs*), "thus, so," is emphatic, pointing back to the act described in the previous verse and, therefore, carrying the meaning of "in such a way as this" or "by this means."[50] The verb τύπτω (*typtō*), "strike, wound," meant to inflict blows upon another and looked to the actual damage that was inflicted.[51] The participle τύποντες (*typontes*) denotes the severity a wrong action could cause another. With the last phrase, the Apostle reached the climax of his whole argument: to sin against a Christian brother or sister was to sin against Christ himself, a sin with very grievous consequences.

8:13 *Wherefore, if meat make my brother to offend, I will eat no flesh while the world standeth, lest I make my brother to offend / For this very reason, if some food causes my brother or sister to sin, I would never eat any kind of meat again, so that I would not cause a brother or sister to sin:*

---

47. BDAG, 696.

48. Louw-Nida, §20.31.

49. A few manuscripts leave out the participle ἀσθενοῦσαν (*asthenousan*), "to weaken," perhaps "to prevent the reader from assuming that wounding a brother's conscience is allowable except when it is 'weak.'" Metzger, *Textual Commentary*, 491. However, the evidence suggests the word was in the original.

50. BDAG, 741–42; Fee, *First Epistle*, 388 n. 63; Robertson and Plummer, *Critical and Exegetical Commentary*, 172.

51. Gustav Stählin, "τύπτω," in *TDNT*, 8:260–69.

Paul's opening word—διόπερ (*dioper*), "therefore," an emphatic logical connective—tied the point he was about to make to his past sentence and carried the sense of "for this very reason," that is, to avoid sinning against Christ. The phrase οὐ μή (*ou mē*) with the subjunctive expressed strong negation, "by absolutely no means." With these two words, Paul made it absolutely clear where he stood on the issue. Not content therewith, however, Paul broadened his stand further by the use of the plural noun κρέα (*krea*), "meats." The plural was mostly used in the collective sense, that is, "kinds of meat."[52] Hence, it is translated "any kind of meat" in our Rendition. Before, Paul had used the word βρῶμα (*brōma*), which was a general term for "food."[53] So Paul is saying that not only would he not eat meat sacrificed to idols, but he would not eat any other kind of food, even meat *not* sacrificed to idols, if it were to cause spiritual harm to another brother or sister.

Analysis and Summary

As noted in the introduction, the issue around which chapters 8–10 turn was that of eating food offered to idols. Paul clearly stated his stand and, in the process, set the record straight. He acknowledged the correctness of the doctrine expressed by those who felt themselves superior in γνῶσις (*gnōsis*), "knowledge" (meaning, in this case, gospel knowledge), but disallowed their conclusions. He agreed completely with their teaching that "there is no such thing as an idol in the entire universe" and that "there is [only] one God" (8:4, 6, Rendition). He disagreed with their conclusion that this meant they could do whatever they wished, especially feasting in pagan temples. The Apostle's first task was, then, to give a correct definition of *gnōsis*. Authentic knowledge, he taught, was not based on the accumulation of facts, history, and doctrine, even though these were all helpful and valuable. The problem with them was that they could actually result in hurting one new in the faith. Milk before meat was Paul's axiom (3:1–2). Real knowledge, he insisted, was grounded in love and genuine care for what was best for the other (8:2–3). The importance of truth should never be downplayed. On the other hand, kindness and care should never be sacrificed upon truth's altar, especially if that were to destroy the faith of a

---

52. LSJ, 992. Note that the KJV is confusing in this case since it translates βρῶμα (*brōma*) as "meat," which in seventeenth-century English meant "food" in general, rather than the more restricted sense of "the flesh of animals" that it has in modern English.

53. BDAG, 184.

brother or sister (8:9). "In the Christian faith," one scholar noted, "'knowledge' or 'insight' is never an end in itself; it is only a means to a greater end, the building up of others."[54] The same is true with church attendance and ritual participation—when over emphasized, they can get in the way of service and following the simple aspects of the gospel.

The upside of knowledge informed by love was that it brought one into a special relationship with God. Indeed, one came to be acknowledged, even chosen, by him and thereby entered into the ranks of the elect of God (8:3).[55] Paul's position certainly paralleled that of his fellow Apostle John, who noted that "he that loveth not knoweth not God" (1 John 4:8). The loveless person may know a lot of facts, but these have not translated into a knowledge of God and his ways. "Beloved," admonished John, "let us love one another: for love is of God; and every one that loveth is born of God, and knoweth God" (1 John 4:7). With love came a familial relationship with the Father and, with that intimate association, the seat of real "knowledge." Out of this grew how to properly apply the doctrines in real life.

The "strong" Corinthian Saints knew that there were many false gods and lords. They also knew enough not to worship them. Paul agreed but also noted that there were other gods and lords besides the false ones that idols represented. Joseph Smith made it clear that Paul was not referring to pagan gods. "I have a witness of the Holy Ghost . . . ," the Prophet said, "that Paul had no allusion to the heathen gods in the text."[56] Latter-day Saint doctrine is clear that those who follow the Father can become as he is. In section 132 of the Doctrine and Covenants, the Lord speaks of those who are married for time and eternity in the holy temples and have been sealed by the Holy Spirit of promise: "Then shall they be gods, because they have no end; therefore shall they be from everlasting to everlasting, because they continue; then shall they be above all, because all things are subject unto them. Then shall they be gods, because they have all power, and the angels are subject unto them" (D&C 132:20). The Lord further explains that Abraham, Isaac, and Jacob "have entered into their exaltation, according to the promises, and sit upon thrones, and are not angels but are gods" (D&C 132:37). In the marvelous revelation in which Joseph Smith and Oliver Cowdery saw the three degrees of glory, they describe

---

54. Fee, *First Epistle*, 368–69.
55. BDAG, 199–201.
56. Smith, *History of the Church*, 6:475.

the inhabitants of the Celestial Kingdom, declaring, "Wherefore, as it is written, they are gods, even the sons of God" (D&C 76:58).[57]

The Corinthian "strong" knew that there was for them one God and one Lord. Paul agreed, noting that all things are *of* the Father, and all things are *by* Christ (8:6). President Harold B. Lee emphasized the importance of the prepositions Paul used: "I would have you note particularly the use of the preposition 'of,' in reference to the Father, and the preposition 'by,' in reference to our Lord, Jesus Christ. In this statement is clearly defined the role of each, the Lord to do the bidding of the Father, in the execution of the whole plan of salvation for all mankind (Abr. 4:1–31)."[58]

Paul's challenge was to make the "strong" see how their behavior could affect those with weak consciences (συνείδησις ἀσθενής, *syneidēsis asthenēs*), that is, those lacking a keen sense of right and wrong so far as Church doctrine was concerned. The Greek adjective *asthenēs,* translated "weak," designated that which had limited capacity.[59] It may be that those with weak consciences were those who had a limited capability of understanding the full ramifications and nuances of the gospel because of lack of education or other avenues of training. Therefore, they lacked critical thinking skills, which allowed them to easily misread what others did.[60] Further, these had believed in and were accustomed (τῇ συνηθείᾳ, *tē synētheia*) to worshiping idols (8:7), and they had not totally abandoned their belief in them. As a result, the actions of those who knew that an idol was nothing could prove a stumbling block to those yet weak in the faith (8:9). An insistence on the part of the "strong" that eating idol meat was their right, ἐξουσία (*exousia*), and also an authenticating mark of their superior knowledge, could have exacerbated the problem. They may have seen eating idol meat as the touchstone of their liberty provided by the gospel. They may have even encouraged the "weak" to join them in their

---

57. Joseph Smith expanded on this doctrine in the "King Follett Discourse" that he gave on April 7, 1844. "Discourse, 7 April 1844, as Reported by *Times and Seasons,*" 614, available online at Church Historian's Press, *The Joseph Smith Papers,* http://www .josephsmithpapers.org/paper-summary/discourse-7-april-1844-as-reported-by-times -and-seasons/3. For two excellent studies on the discourse and its impact on church doctrine, see Donald Q. Cannon, "The King Follett Discourse: Joseph Smith's Greatest Sermon in Historical Perspective," *BYU Studies* 18, no. 2 (1978): 179–92; and Van Hale, "The Doctrinal Impact of the King Follett Discourse," *BYU Studies* 18, no. 2 (1978): 209–25.

58. Harold B. Lee, *The Teachings of Harold B. Lee* (Salt Lake City: Deseret Book, 1996), 29–30.

59. BDAG, 142–43.

60. Willis, *Idol Meat,* 92–96; Theissen, *Social Setting,* 121–44.

pagan temple meals.[61] If this were the case, they were creating a stumbling block for the "weak" who, not knowing that idols did not exist, mistook the actions of the "strong" not as denying idols, but as authenticating them (8:9). Their action would then lead the "weak" back into idolatry with its attendant ills. In this way, the ability of the "weak" to distinguish between right and wrong would be destroyed and with it, their very souls (8:10–11).

The result of expressing such liberty would be an annulling of the power of the Atonement in the lives of the "weak." What the "strong" could not seem to grasp was the lesson housed in the Savior's Atonement. The Savior did it not by way of self-assertion or an expression of his "rights," but as an act of self-sacrifice and self-giving on behalf of the weak (in this case, everyone). Paul's point, and the real warning that stood behind his position, was that to sin against a brother or sister for whom Christ died was to sin against Christ himself (8:12).[62] Well did Paul understand this doctrine; it was taught to him forcefully by the Lord himself. When Paul first met the Savior in a blinding light on the road to Damascus, Jesus' question to him was, "Why persecutest thou me?" In response to Paul's question, "Who art thou?" the Savior replied, "I am Jesus whom thou persecutest," (Acts 9:4–5). Thus, to persecute one who was the Lord's disciple and child was to persecute the Lord himself. From that time on, Paul could never look into another Christian's eyes without seeing those of the Lord.[63] And for this Apostle, to hurt his Savior, even indirectly, was unconscionable.

One of the problems with Paul's counsel is that it appears to go against direct Church order. Church leadership, at the Jerusalem Council in AD 49 (Acts 15:6–29), had already determined that much of the Mosaic law did not pertain to Gentile converts, but there were certain restrictions that were necessary so that Jew and Gentile could both participate in their sacramental services. These prohibitions were clearly spelled out: "abstain from meats offered to idols, and from blood, and from things strangled, and from fornication" (Acts 15:29).[64] Since Paul was a member of the council that dictated these prohibitions, he clearly understood them. Because the Apostle advocated that Gentile converts were free to eat idol meat, albeit under

---

61. Gardner, *Gifts of God,* 54; Murphy-O'Connor, "Food and Spiritual Gifts," 296.

62. Thiselton, *First Epistle,* 653–54.

63. John A. T. Robinson, *The Body: A Study in Pauline Theology,* 2d ed. (Louisville, Ky.: Westminster John Knox Press, 1977), 58.

64. Including a prohibition against immorality in counsel dealing with food use may seem odd until one remembers that fornication was often associated with pagan feasts. David J. Williams, *Acts* (Peabody, Mass.: Hendrickson Publishers, 1990), 266.

certain conditions, some scholars have felt that Paul's stance was nothing short of rebellion.[65] The key in determining whether he rejected a Church decree is in understanding his intent.

An overriding concern for both Paul and the other members of the Jerusalem Council was πορνεία (*porneia*), that is, sexual immorality. The Gentile prohibitions of Acts 15 all look to one activity where immorality often occurred. That activity can be determined by ascertaining where all four prohibitions came together: that is, where meat was prepared by strangling the animal and not draining the blood, where priests offered its meat as sacrifice to the god, where there was a ritual feast in which the meat was eaten, and where sexual dalliance, *porneia,* often resulted. That activity was cultic feasts held in pagan temples. All this suggests that the prohibition of the council was not concerned with eating idol meat per se, but with the circumstances under which it was eaten.[66] If this is the case, then Paul's counsel aligned with the Gentile prohibitions.

Paul definitely felt that the Church's position recognized a difference in certain behavioral activities between Jewish and Gentile converts based on their varied cultures. Was that the case with eating meat? Under Jewish law, meat was rendered unfit for consumption if there was an explicit connection between it and idolatrous sacrifices. Otherwise, it was fine.[67] For Jewish members, then, eating meat was one activity where the situation governed the response. What Paul advocated was the same pattern for Gentiles. The Apostle's concern was with the brother whose knowledge of the gospel was shallow and, therefore, upon seeing someone he viewed as an authority participating in a pagan temple feast he might conclude that idolatry had something going for it. But if this condition did not exist, Paul saw no reason not to eat the meat. Thus, the issue was not the meat and whether it was kosher, but rather with the idolatry itself (see 10:8–9).

In sum, the restriction placed on Christians was they "should avoid a venue where sacrificial meat and immorality are *both* found—namely, pagan temples, where, indeed, all four of the items listed in Acts 15:20 and 29 were

---

65. This topic has generated a good deal of literature. Two good studies are John Brunt, *Paul's Attitude Toward and Treatment of Problems Involving Dietary Practices* (Atlanta: Emory University, 1978); and Wendell Willis, *Idol Meat in Corinth: The Pauline Argument in 1 Corinthians 8 and 10* (Chico, Calif.: Scholars Press, 1985). For extended study on the subject, see Fee, *First Epistle,* 357–63.

66. Witherington, "Why Not Idol Meat?" 42–43.

67. Zaas, "Dietary Laws," 238.

available. The issue is not where we might find these four elements separately, but where we might find them together."[68]

The concern, like that in 6:10, dealt with what was right vis-à-vis what was lawful. Paul readily agreed that the "strong" in knowledge had the *right* to eat wherever and whatever they pleased, especially since they understood that an idol was nothing. However, what they had as a *right* did not necessarily define what was *best* for them to do. The issue was not with the right to choose but with choosing the right. Paul stressed that "not everyone has this knowledge. And some having previously become accustomed to idols, still consider the food they eat as food offered to idols, and because their sense of right and wrong is weak, it is defiled" (8:7, Rendition). So here Paul was concerned about the "weak" when the context of eating meats within the precincts of a pagan temple, or in any other way, could be construed as validating idolatry. On the other hand, he took the side of the "strong" when it came to purchasing meat, which is then eaten at home.[69] As one LDS scholar noted, "It is apparent that [Paul] prefers to judge food concerns on a situational basis rather than make blanket regulations."[70]

Paul clearly taught that the spiritual life of each member counted more than one's rights; therefore, those with knowledge had to practice a self-abrogation of those rights for the sake of others (8:11–12). Right from the start, Paul stated the foundation on which his counsel stood: "Knowledge makes people conceited, but love builds them up" (8:1, Rendition). That was the sum of it. Neither God nor Jesus nor Paul would tolerate anything that smacked of validating idolatry, nor would they put up with anyone's grumbling about not being able to participate in pagan feasts.[71] If they had love—that powerful Christlike love—any Saint should clearly see how to apply doctrine correctly. Paul understood where true "knowledge" lay: "But if someone loves God, that person is acknowledged by him" (8:3, Rendition).

So the situation that governed whether one should eat meat boiled down to this: how visibly was the act connected to idolatry? If the connection was explicit, then, for a brother's sake, one should not eat it. If, however, the connection were oblique or nonexistent, then one should freely

---

68. Witheringnton, "Why Not Idol Meat?" 43.
69. Thiselton, *First Epistle,* 612.
70. Holzapfel and Wayment, *Making Sense,* 354.
71. Zaas, "Dietary Laws," 241.

eat it (10:25).[72] The final decision had to be made through that kind of love that would sacrifice one's right for what would be another's good.

Here we clearly see Paul's ethics. Everything he did was grounded in moral behavior that glorified God and brought souls under the power of the cross. Thus, though Paul's starting point may have been with legal principles growing out of the Gentile Prohibitions stated in Acts 15, he concluded with an ethical principle that found "alternative ways to influence the behavior of his audience than simply quoting sentences of law."[73] In this chapter we find a profound theological lesson. The Apostle to the Gentiles taught that both religious rights and freedoms must be bridled by self-discipline driven by Christlike love for the vulnerable or insecure, those for whom freedom might prove their ruin.

Paul was effective in defining his point by using the strategy of redefinition. He quoted freely from the letter he had received from the Corinthian Saints and, by this means, showed that he had gotten their message and understood the points they made. He then, very cleverly, used their own language but gave it a very definite yet proper twist to bring about the proper application.[74] What Paul did here was both astute and effective. He answered the Corinthians' questions, not by citing a specific doctrine, but by changing the focus to the application of Christian love.[75]

---

72. Thiselton, *First Epistle,* 609–11.

73. Zaas, "Dietary Laws," 243.

74. R. A. Horsley, "Consciousness and Freedom among the Corinthians: 1 Corinthians 8–10," *Catholic Biblical Quarterly* 40 (1978): 587, 574–89.

75. John C. Brunt, "Rejected, Ignored, or Misunderstood? The Fate of Paul's Approach to the Problem of Food Offered to Idols in Early Christianity," *New Testament Studies* 31 (1985): 115.

Chapter 9

The Rights of an Apostle

INTRODUCTION

This chapter continues the discussion Paul began in chapter 8. Though the major topic in that chapter concerned eating meats offered to idols, the real issue was the subordination of a person's rights or freedom of choice (ἐξουσία, *exousia*) for the good of the Christian community on both the individual and collective level. In this chapter, the Apostle's tone becomes sharper. He used one rhetorical question after another like blows intended to put down a foe.[1] And he did have foes. As a result, he had to spend a considerable amount of time defending his credentials as an Apostle because some seem to have felt there was something deficient about them. It may be that his refusal to exercise his resources as they viewed them (using skill in argument and rhetorical expertise to preach the word)[2] or make full use of his rights (financial support from Church members, including paying expenses for a wife) gave ammunition to his detractors to question his status. They seem to have felt that if he really were an Apostle, he would not allow himself to be restricted in any way.[3]

Paul defended his credentials with two points: first, his recognition that his status did, indeed, give him certain rights (9:1–14), and second, that as an Apostle, he would, indeed, voluntarily deny himself of those rights when necessity required it (9:15–27).

---

1. He uses sixteen in all, with four found in 9:1 alone.

2. One need only think of the very successful methods of the Greek Demosthenes (see *The Public Orations of Demosthenes,* trans. A. W. Pickard-Cambridge, 2 vols. [Oxford: Clarendon Press, 1912]), or the Roman Cicero (see Marcus Tullius Cicero, *Cicero: Selected Political Speeches,* trans. Michael Grant [Great Britain: Penguin Books, 1969]) to get a feel for the methods that could be employed.

3. Barrett, *First Epistle,* 200; Thiselton, *First Epistle,* 665–66.

"Paul gives himself as an example of self-restraint," stated one LDS scholar, "and the conversion of the Corinthians is the seal on his Apostleship. As an Apostle he has the right to be supported and lead a wife around with him (9:1–14), but this right he has not used (9:15–18); Paul has given up his liberty and has become all things to all men, in order that he may save souls. All he does is for the Gospel's sake, that he may share in its blessings (9:19–23)."[4] The Apostle's detractors did not see it that way. As another LDS scholar noted, for his enemies, Paul's lowly manual labor and artisan-class skills were evidence enough he was not equal in stature to the other apostles.[5] This scholar went on to state, "The issue was not whether Paul could ask for financial support from the members, but whether he chose to, and, therefore he argued that others who did not have either the ability or time to earn their own living should not be used to disparage Paul's practice of working to provide for himself."[6]

His defense of his credentials ran as follows: First, he agreed that he was as free (ἐλεύθερος, *eleutheros*) as any of the Apostles or members of the Corinthian branch to exercise the rights and freedoms being a Christian gave him (9:1–14). Second, he explained why he did not take advantage of those rights and was willing to limit his freedom (9:15–23). And finally, he set himself up as a model of how the gospel should be lived (9:24–27). His life forcefully taught these people the need to willingly lay aside rights for the sake of effectively preaching "Christ, and him crucified" (2:2).[7]

THE CORINTHIAN CONVERTS ARE THE SEAL OF PAUL'S APOSTLESHIP (9:1–2)

Greek Text

1 Οὐκ εἰμὶ ἐλεύθερος; οὐκ εἰμὶ ἀπόστολος; οὐχὶ Ἰησοῦν τὸν κύριον ἡμῶν ἑόρακα; οὐ τὸ ἔργον μου ὑμεῖς ἐστε ἐν κυρίῳ; 2 εἰ ἄλλοις οὐκ εἰμὶ ἀπόστολος, ἀλλά γε ὑμῖν εἰμι, ἡ γὰρ σφραγίς μου τῆς ἀποστολῆς ὑμεῖς ἐστε ἐν κυρίῳ. [SBLGNT]

---

4. Sperry, *Paul's Life*, 124.

5. Wayment, *Persecutor to Apostle*, 164. Generally, in the Greco-Roman world, working with one's hands was considered the work of slaves. In the Jewish world, however, working with one's hands was respectable. Richard Neitzel Holzapfel and others, *Jesus Christ and the World of the New Testament* (Salt Lake City: Deseret Book, 2006), 182.

6. Wayment, *Persecutor to Apostle*, 164.

7. Thiselton, *First Epistle*, 666–67.

King James Version

1 Am I not an apostle? am I not free? have I not seen Jesus Christ our Lord? are not ye my work in the Lord? 2 If I be not an apostle unto others, yet doubtless I am to you: for the seal of mine apostleship are ye in the Lord.

New Rendition

1 Am I not free? Am I not an apostle? Have I not seen Jesus our Lord? Are you not the evidence of my work in the Lord? 2 Even if I am not an apostle to others, to you at least I am, for you are the certification of my apostleship in the Lord.

Translation Notes and Comments

9:1 *Am I not an apostle? am I not free? / Am I not free? Am I not an apostle?:* The Textus Receptus and many later manuscripts reverse the order of the first two phrases, whereas all the early manuscripts have "Am I not free?" first, as found in our Rendition.[8] Because this order emphasizes Paul's main point for the entire chapter—his freedom in Christ—it is fitting that it should come first. He was never under any external coercion to do other than what he did. He always expressed his freedom to do as he chose. The Greek construction of these two questions invites a strong affirmative set of answers showing that no one should have had any doubt that he knew he was free and he knew that he was an Apostle. But of what did his freedom consist? Some have suggested it was freedom from the constraints of the Mosaic law. Though that is no doubt true, the context of this chapter suggests Paul had in mind a more personal freedom, which he later enumerated (9:3–5, 13–14), one that was grounded on his being an Apostle.

On Paul's apostleship, see Translation Notes on 1:1.

have I not seen Jesus Christ our Lord? / Have I not seen Jesus our Lord?: The Textus Receptus, on which the KJV is based, adds "Christ," whereas all the earliest and best manuscripts leave it out and, therefore, it is omitted in our Rendition.[9] Again, the grammatical construction here demands an emphatic affirmative. Paul's question pointed to the first essential qualification for apostleship, that of being an eyewitness to the world of the Resurrection of Christ (see D&C 27:12; 107:23). That Paul used the Savior's name but not his

---

8. Fitzmyer, *First Corinthians,* 356. The switch may have been done in later texts to lessen the weight of Apostolic authority—a possible indication that the Apostasy was moving forward.

9. The Christological controversies that raged during the fourth century may have caused some copyist during that era to insert the word "Christ" to emphasize that Jesus and Christ were one and the same. For a good discussion of the issues and their influence into the present era, see Richard A. Norris Jr., *The Christological Controversy* (Minneapolis: Fortress Press, 1980).

title suggests that he wanted to emphasize that it was Jesus of Nazareth whom he had seen and who now was resurrected and glorified.[10]

are not ye my work in the Lord? / Are you not the evidence of my work in the Lord?: The noun ἔργον (*ergon*), "deed, action," is here used in the sense of "manifestation" or "practical proof,"[11] hence it is translated as "the evidence of my work" in our Rendition. This is the second qualification of Paul's apostleship, namely preaching the gospel of Jesus Christ to the world through the power of the Spirit (compare 2:4). In the words of the Lord in this dispensation, the Twelve Apostles are "special witnesses of the name of Christ in all the world—thus differing from other officers in the church in the duties of their calling" (D&C 107:23). Whether Paul was in the quorum, he was still a "special witness of the name of Christ" whose assignment took in the entire Greco-Roman world.

9:2 If I be not an apostle unto others, yet doubtless I am to you / Even if I am not an apostle to others, to you at least I am: The phrase ἀλλά γε ὑμῖν εἰμι (*alla ge hymin eimi*), "to you at least I am," carries the idea that these people were duty bound to accept his authority.[12] Paul's rhetorical question (actually a statement) about the truth of his apostleship in the first verse should have left no doubt where he stood. The Apostle is not saying that other places reject his apostolic authority, but that it was not his preaching to these other people that brought the gospel or the Lord's power to establish the Church among them. Of course, those in the world, similar to today, would not recognize it. These Christians, however, must.

for the seal of mine apostleship are ye in the Lord / for you are the certification of my apostleship in the Lord: The noun σφραγίς (*sphragis*) referred to a seal that was used on official documents to certify their authenticity. The word denoted that which affirms or attests to the genuineness of something.[13] Here, Paul used it figuratively in sense of "certification,"[14] as in our Rendition.[15] These members, whether followers or detractors of Paul, were all "in the Lord" (that is, members of his kingdom) because of the Apostle's

---

10. The continuity of the identity of Jesus with the risen Lord is one of the themes that unifies the whole of the New Testament. See James D. G. Dunn, *Unity and Diversity in the New Testament* (Philadelphia: Westminster Press, 1977), 183–266.

11. BDAG, 390.

12. Conzelmann, *1 Corinthians*, 151 n. 2.

13. Louw-Nida, §37.9. This term is subtle evidence that the authority of the early church was associated with apostles, a position some doubt today, but the idea of apostolic authority is found here and there in the New Testament.

14. BDAG, 980; Louw-Nida, §73.9, but see also §§6.54, 62; 33.483.

15. Edwards, *Commentary*, 227.

authority. To doubt his authority would be to doubt the authenticity of their membership in the Church.

Analysis and Summary

There was no question in Paul's mind that he was an Apostle. The issue he addresses was not, therefore, one of Church authority but of Christology. He based his power not on being a member of the original Twelve but on the fact that he had been chosen and empowered by the Savior himself to carry out a specific mission (9:17).[16] His witness was, then, not only in his words but also in his way of life—a life that reflected the self-sacrifice modeled by the Lord.[17]

Paul concluded this portion of his defense by appealing to one fact that all should have agreed on: namely, that by his power, whether directly or indirectly, they had become one with Christ. The basis of his argument reached back to an event that happened just after the close of his first mission. He with his companion Barnabas went to Jerusalem to report on their success. He met with the Church authorities and, according to his own word, "when they saw that the gospel of the uncircumcision was committed unto me, as the gospel of the circumcision was unto Peter; (For he that wrought effectually in Peter to the apostleship of the circumcision, the same was mighty in me toward the Gentiles:) And when James, Cephas [that is, Peter], and John, who seemed to be pillars, perceived the grace that was given unto me, they gave to me and Barnabas the right hands of fellowship; that we should go unto the heathen, and they unto the circumcision" (Gal. 2:7–9). Thus, Paul became *the* Apostle to the Gentiles, and those members at Corinth were the certification or proof that he was fulfilling that charge.

PAUL DEFENDS HIS APOSTLESHIP (9:3–7)

Greek Text

3 Ἡ ἐμὴ ἀπολογία τοῖς ἐμὲ ἀνακρίνουσίν ἐστιν αὕτη. 4 μὴ οὐκ ἔχομεν ἐξουσίαν φαγεῖν καὶ πεῖν; 5 μὴ οὐκ ἔχομεν ἐξουσίαν ἀδελφὴν γυναῖκα περιάγειν, ὡς καὶ οἱ λοιποὶ ἀπόστολοι καὶ οἱ ἀδελφοὶ τοῦ κυρίου καὶ Κηφᾶς; 6 ἢ μόνος ἐγὼ καὶ Βαρναβᾶς οὐκ ἔχομεν ἐξουσίαν μὴ ἐργάζεσθαι; 7 τίς στρατεύεται ἰδίοις ὀψωνίοις ποτέ;

---

16. Thiselton, *First Epistle,* 668.
17. Thiselton, *First Epistle,* 668.

τίς φυτεύει ἀμπελῶνα καὶ τὸν καρπὸν αὐτοῦ οὐκ ἐσθίει; τίς ποιμαίνει ποίμνην καὶ ἐκ τοῦ γάλακτος τῆς ποίμνης οὐκ ἐσθίει; [SBLGNT]

King James Version

3 Mine answer to them that do examine me is this, 4 Have we not power to eat and to drink? 5 Have we not power to lead about a sister, a wife, as well as other apostles, and as the brethren of the Lord, and Cephas? 6 Or I only and Barnabas, have not we power to forbear working? 7 Who goeth a warfare any time at his own charges? who planteth a vineyard, and eateth not of the fruit thereof? or who feedeth a flock, and eateth not of the milk of the flock?

New Rendition

3 My defense to all those who question my apostleship is this: 4 Do we not have a right to be provided with food and drink? 5 Do we not have the right to travel together with our wives, even as the other apostles, and the Lord's brothers, and Cephas? 6 Or is it only I and Barnabas who do not have the right to not work? 7 Who serves in the army at his own expense? Who plants a vineyard and does not eat the grapes? Who shepherds a flock and does not drink some of the goat's milk?

Translation Notes and Comments

9:3 *Mine answer / My defense:* The noun ἀπολογία (*apologia*) was the legal term for a defense in a law court.[18] Paul's use of it suggests how seriously he saw his position. He and his apostolic calling were, so to speak, on trial.

to them that do examine me is this / to all those who question my apostleship is this: The verb Paul used here, ἀνακρίνω (*anakrinō*), was another legal technical term that meant to question in a judicial hearing.[19] There is some debate as to whether the pronoun αὕτη (*hautē*), "this, as follows," referred back to the Apostle's statement in 9:1–2 or ahead to what he would say in 9:4–27. If the pronoun referred back, Paul's defense was that he had seen Jesus and used the Lord's authority to establish the Corinthian branch of the Church.[20] If it pointed forward, Paul's defense sat in the apostolic rights that were his.[21] Our Rendition follows the latter as the better alternative because the emphatic position of *hautē* at the end of the sentence points to what immediately follows it as body of the defense. Had the pronoun's referent been what came before, its position would have been at

---

18. An excellent example would be Plato's *Apology*.

19. BDAG, 66.

20. See Robertson and Plummer, *Critical and Exegetical Commentary,* 179; Edwards, *Commentary,* 227.

21. Fee, *First Epistle,* 397; Barrett, *First Epistle,* 202; Collins, *First Corinthians,* 335.

the beginning of the sentence.[22] Either way, Paul's point comes across: he was an Apostle of the Lord and had acted accordingly.[23]

9:4 *Have we not power to eat and to drink? / Do we not have a right to be provided with food and drink?:* Paul switched from "I" to "we" here.[24] Verse 9:6 makes it clear that he had himself and Barnabas, his old mission companion, in mind. The noun ἐξουσία (*exousia*) had the basic meaning of "power, authority to do a thing."[25] Paul was using it here to describe the range of "rights" that Apostles had by virtue of their office. Among these were the right to φαγεῖν καὶ πεῖν (*phagein kai pein*), literally "to eat and to drink,"[26] but more broadly to receive help in the form of food, clothing, and shelter from Church members.[27]

9:5 *to lead about a sister, a wife / to travel together with our wives:* The phrase ἀδελφὴν γυναῖκα περιάγειν (*adelphēn gynaika periagein*) translates literally as "to travel together with a sister wife." One of the rights that the Apostles had was to bring their wives with them and have the members take care of them. The noun *adelphēn*, "sister," in apposition with *gynaika*, "woman" or "wife," indicated that the wife was a member of the Church.[28] It is omitted in our Rendition because the phrase is awkward in English. It does show, however, that the early Saints, like the Church today, did refer to one another as "brother" or "sister." Further, Paul's remarks clearly show that the early Apostles did not practice celibacy.

the brethren of the Lord, and Cephas / the Lord's brothers, and Cephas: The Gospel of Matthew names Christ's brothers as James, Joses (or Joseph), Judas (or Judah), and Simon (Matt. 13:55).[29] Paul referred to the Apostle

---

22. The SBLGNT also supports this view by starting a new paragraph with this sentence.

23. Thiselton, *First Epistle*, 675.

24. It was very common for ancient writers to use the first person plural form to refer to themselves and, therefore, there may be times when he is using "we" to refer to himself.

25. LSJ, 599.

26. Some have suggested Paul is looking back at eating idol meat. See Barrett, *First Epistle*, 202. The context of Paul's argument, however, suggests he was thinking in much broader terms.

27. Fee, *First Epistle*, 402.

28. Some ancient sources take the word γύνή (*gynē*) not as "wife" but as "woman" and interpret Paul as referring to "a sister in the faith." See Clement, *Strom.* 4:3; Jerome, *Jov.* 1:26; Tertullian, *Mon.* 8. These, however, were all influenced by their belief that the Apostles were, by and large, not married.

29. This verse also mentions at least three sisters. By the mid-second century, the idea of Mary's perpetual virginity gained footing among some Christians. They then insisted that the scriptural references to Jesus' brothers and sisters actually referred to his half brothers and sisters, the children of Joseph from a previous marriage. See *Prot. Jas.* 9:2; 19:1–20:3. Not long after, some clergyman insisted that the word ἀδελφοί (*adelphoi*),

James as "the Lord's brother" (Gal. 1:19). He has traditionally been identified as the author of the Epistle of James. The author of the Epistle of Jude is traditionally identified as the "Judas" mentioned by Matthew and is also said to be an Apostle and the Lord's half-brother. Cephas, of course, was the Aramaic name of Peter, the chief Apostle. All these men seem to have been engaged in Church service and missionary labors with their respective wives. There are no explicit statements that celibacy was considered as a Church doctrine by the earliest Saints.[30]

9:6 *Or I only and Barnabas, have not we power to forbear working? / Or is it only I and Barnabas who do not have the right to not work?*: The verb ἐργάζομαι (*ergazomai*), "to work" or "to do manual labor," also carried the idea of working for a living.[31] Among the rights Apostles had, by virtue of their office, was not having to work to support themselves and their families. The reason was so that they could devote full and complete service to the Lord and the Church. In his defense for not doing what others had, Paul referred to his former missionary companion, Barnabas (see Acts 4:36–7; 11:22–26). He may have mentioned his friend because he, like Paul, chose to pay his own way rather than depend on Church members to support him. Paul's wording about the "right" not to have to work is a semi-ironic reference to the issue of the "right to choose" already addressed in 8:8–11.

9:7 *Who goeth a warfare any time at his own charges? / Who serves in the army at his own expense?*: The phrase τίς στρατεύεται ἰδίοις ὀψωνίοις ποτέ (*tis strateuetai idiois opsōniois pote*), literally "who ever performs military service by means of his own expenses," uses a dative of means.[32]

"brothers," actually referred to close kinsmen, such as cousins. On this, see Thomas Aquinas, *Commentary on St. Paul's First Epistle to the Galatians* (Albany, N.Y.: Magi Books, 1966), 28–30, who sides with Jerome and Origin. For discussion, see Barrett, *First Epistle*, 203. and Richard J. Bauckham, "The Brothers and Sisters of Jesus: An Epiphanian Response to John P. Meier," *Catholic Biblical Quarterly* 56 (1994): 686–700. Against these views, Latter-day Saints would agree with Fee, *First Epistle*, 403–4, that these were Mary and Joseph's children.

30. Due to the influence of Middle- and Neo-Platonism on many church leaders during the second through fourth centuries, the view that matter was evil gained popularity and with it the idea that celibacy was a higher good. Accepting that as a tenet, these leaders reinterpreted the New Testament through that lens and began imposing their ideas upon it. For a discussion, see Everette Ferguson, *Backgrounds of Early Christianity* (Grand Rapids, Mich.: Wm. B. Eerdmans, 2003); and for a study of Middle Platonism, see John M. Dillon, *The Middle Platonists, 80 B.C. to A.D. 220* (New York: Cornell University Press, 1996).

31. BDAG, 389; NIV 1 Cor. 9:6; Thiselton, *First Epistle*, 683.

32. Wallace, *Greek Grammar*, 162–63.

The noun *opsōniois,* "expenses," had a broad range of meaning that ran from "food rations" through "allowance" to "pay for services," but most particularly "provisions."[33] Paul's point is clear: it would be ridiculous to expect a soldier to bring his own provisions to a battle.

who planteth a vineyard, and eateth not of the fruit thereof? / Who plants a vineyard and does not eat the grapes?: The noun καρπός (*karpos*), "fruit,"[34] is translated as "grapes" in our Rendition, being the sole product of a vineyard. Again, Paul makes a good point: it would not be reasonable for someone to plant a vineyard with no intent of eating the fruit thereof.

or who feedeth a flock, and eateth not of the milk of the flock? / Who shepherds a flock and does not drink some of the goat's milk?: The noun ποίμνη (*poimnē*) sometimes denoted a fold of sheep but more generally a flock of sheep and goats.[35] The verb ἐσθίω (*esthiō*) meant literally "to eat," but when used to refer to liquids, it carried the sense of "partake of" or "drink."[36] Though sheep could be milked, it was more commonly done with goats, and this is reflected in our Rendition. Paul's final analogy made the same point as the first two: no one puts effort into something without expecting to get something in return.

Analysis and Summary

One LDS authority noted that "in his epistle to the Corinthians, Paul mentions how Peter traveled about accompanied by his wife, and that both were supported by contributions of the Church. (I Cor. 9:5.) He may have visited Corinth as Paul lists the faction of Cephas (or Peter) there together with the Pauline and Apollos groups of saints. This may indicate that he became a symbol of the Jewish Christian party which opposed Paul upon so many occasions during the latter's missionary work in Asia Minor and Greece."[37]

Peter was not alone in having his wife with him as he traveled. Other Apostles seem to have been supported by the Church. Paul chose not to or, if he was indeed widowed, he no longer had a wife. That he emphasized ministering without charge may have been part of his effort to make

---

33. Moulton and Milligan, *Vocabulary,* 471–72.

34. BDAG, 509.

35. Joachim Jeremias, "ποίμνη, ποίμνιον," in *TDNT,* 6:499–502.

36. BDAG, 396.

37. Russel B. Swensen, *The New Testament: The Acts and the Epistles* (Salt Lake City: Deseret Sunday School Union Board, 1955), 34–35, 65–66.

a connection with that element of the Church that came from the lower classes. As they were menial laborers when they accepted the gospel, so, too, was he when he preached it.[38]

Paul's writings give us a very early witness that the Apostles with their wives, and likely other Church authorities, shared the responsibility of Church and missionary service. This is based on his statement that the "Lord's brothers" were doing so (9:5, Rendition; Matt. 13:55). How widely this practice was carried out is unknown, but it does not appear to have been uncommon. Otherwise, it would have weakened Paul's argument.

In his defense of the right for Apostles, including himself, to have Church support, Paul used three analogies: that of soldier, farmer, and shepherd. He did so not as mere illustrations but as a buttress for his argument that what was true in these varied fields was also true for Barnabas and him, and he recognized that fact.[39] His examples made it perfectly clear that he knew what his rights were and, therefore, Paul's choosing not to take advantage of these came not out of ignorance but out of his sincere desire to be neither a burden on Church members nor beholden to anyone. On the other hand, he had no problem if other general authorities wanted to exercise these rights. Even so, there were members of the Corinthian church that used this as evidence that he was not an Apostle.

THE PRIVILEGES OF THOSE WHO PREACH THE GOSPEL (9:8–12A)

Greek Text

8 Μὴ κατὰ ἄνθρωπον ταῦτα λαλῶ ἢ καὶ ὁ νόμος ταῦτα οὐ λέγει; 9 ἐν γὰρ τῷ Μωϋσέως νόμῳ γέγραπται· Οὐ κημώσεις βοῦν ἀλοῶντα. μὴ τῶν βοῶν μέλει τῷ θεῷ, 10 ἢ δι᾽ ἡμᾶς πάντως λέγει; δι᾽ ἡμᾶς γὰρ ἐγράφη, ὅτι ὀφείλει ἐπ᾽ ἐλπίδι ὁ ἀροτριῶν ἀροτριᾶν, καὶ ὁ ἀλοῶν ἐπ᾽ ἐλπίδι τοῦ μετέχειν. 11 εἰ ἡμεῖς ὑμῖν τὰ πνευματικὰ ἐσπείραμεν, μέγα εἰ ἡμεῖς ὑμῶν τὰ σαρκικὰ θερίσομεν; 12 εἰ ἄλλοι τῆς ὑμῶν ἐξουσίας μετέχουσιν, οὐ μᾶλλον ἡμεῖς; [SBLGNT]

---

38. Holzapfel and Wayment, *Making Sense*, 355.

39. Herbert M. Gale, *The Use of Analogy in the Letters of Paul* (Philadelphia: Westminster Press, 1964), 101. Both Paul and Barnabas are designated as Apostles in Acts 14:14.

King James Version

8 Say I these things as a man? or saith not the law the same also? 9 For it is written in the law of Moses, Thou shalt not muzzle the mouth of the ox that treadeth out the corn. Doth God take care for oxen? 10 Or saith he it altogether for our sakes? For our sakes, no doubt, this is written: that he that ploweth should plow in hope; and that he that thresheth in hope should be partaker of his hope. 11 If we have sown unto you spiritual things, is it a great thing if we shall reap your carnal things? 12a If others be partakers of this power over you, are not we rather?

New Rendition

8 I am not saying these things from a human perspective; does not the law also say the same thing? 9 For in the law of Moses it is written, "You shall not muzzle an ox that is threshing grain." Surely God is not concerned about oxen. 10 Isn't he certainly speaking for our benefit? It was indeed written for us, because the plowman should plow and the thresher should thresh in hope of sharing in the harvest. 11 If we have sown spiritual things among you, is it a big deal that we wish to reap material benefits from you? 12a If others share in this claim on you, don't we have a greater one?

Translation Notes and Comments

9:8 *Say I these things as a man? or saith not the law the same also? / I am not saying these things from a human perspective; does not the law also say the same thing?*: The words κατὰ ἄνθρωπον (*kata anthrōpon*) are translated literally as "according to a human being." Our Rendition gives the sense in modern English. The force of the negative particle μή (*mē*), "not," is designed to illicit a strong participatory agreement.

9:9 *For it is written in the law of Moses, Thou shalt not muzzle the mouth of the ox that treadeth out the corn / For in the law of Moses it is written, "You shall not muzzle an ox that is threshing grain"*: Paul turned to scripture for support for his position. He quoted Deuteronomy 25:4 from the Septuagint.[40] The prohibition forbade oxen from being muzzled while pulling the sledge around the threshing floor. Under divine decree, the working animal had a right to eat some of what it worked to produce. Paul used this example as an analogy for the way God intended work to be rewarded.

---

40. There is a minor textual variant in this verse with some manuscripts using the more literary κημώσεις (*kēmōseis*), "you muzzle" (see BDAG, 542, s.v. κημόω [*kēmoō*]) and others the more common φιμώσεις (*phimōseis*), "you muzzle" (see BDAG, 1060, s.v. φιμόω [*phimoō*]). Since the LXX uses the former, it is likely some copyists changed Paul's *phimōseis* to correspond to it. Metzger, *Textual Commentary*, 558.

Doth God take care for oxen?* / *Surely God is not concerned about oxen: On face value, Paul's comment seems to go against scripture. There is little doubt that God *is* concerned about the ox.[41] But, taking the scripture in its Old Testament context, Paul's exegesis was to the point. The laws in Deuteronomy 24–25 deal almost exclusively with how Israelites were to treat others. All, Gentiles included, deserved to be treated with dignity and justice. Therefore, it is a bit startling to see in the middle of these laws one sentence dealing with the ox. The prohibition, however, does fit the theme that God's people were to act with compassion toward the needy and defenseless, animals being the supreme example.[42]

9:10 ***Or saith he it altogether for our sakes? For our sakes, no doubt, this is written* / *Isn't he certainly speaking for our benefit? It was indeed written for us:*** The preposition δία (*dia*) with the accusative indicates cause, "for our sakes" or "for us."[43] By the use of that word, Paul moved the application of that scripture from the Old Testament to his own time period. The word shows that the Apostle took the verse in its higher context of dealing more with humankind than with animals. The Apostle accorded the scripture a proper place in showing how the Saints were to act generally and also how it was to be applied to the specific situation he was in.[44]

that he that ploweth should plow in hope; and that he that thresheth in hope should be partaker of his hope* / *because the plowman should plow and the thresher should thresh in hope of sharing in the harvest: The Greek here is very compact, a literal translation being, "Because in hope a plower ought to plow and the thresher in hope of having a share." In our Rendition, we have rearranged the word order and added a couple of explanatory words to make the sense of the passage clear. The passage proved difficult even for the early copyists, and there are a number of variant readings in the manuscript tradition where changes and additions were used to clarify the meaning, but none of the variants affect the theology.[45] The key phrase here is ἐπ' ἐλπίδι (*ep' elpidi*), "in hope" or "in confidence," which Paul repeated twice. The Apostle's words indicate what ought to be. Neither man nor animal should be reduced to mere machines that must carry out the drudgery of hard labor without hope of or confidence in

---

41. After all, God is even aware of the fall of a sparrow (Matt. 10:29–31; Luke 12:6–7).

42. Fee, *First Epistle*, 406–8; Hays, *Echoes of the Scriptures,* 165–66; Hays, *First Corinthians,* 151.

43. BDAG, 225.

44. Thiselton, *First Epistle,* 686–87.

45. Metzger, *Textual Commentary,* 558.

sharing in the reward such would bring. Rather, the worker should see how his efforts benefited himself and those for whom he worked, that is, both his employer and his family.[46]

9:11 *If we have sown unto you spiritual things, is it a great thing if we shall reap your carnal things? / If we have sown spiritual things among you, is it a big deal that we wish to reap material benefits from you?:* The phrase μέγα εἰ (*mega ei*) translates literally as "big thing if." The colloquial English phrase "big deal" catches the flavor of the idiom, and it is so translated in our Rendition.

Paul makes his point by drawing a comparison that highlights the hugely different scales between the supernal spiritual blessings the Corinthian Saints had reaped from the work of the Apostles and the few mundane items the Apostles asked for in return. Of what value were a few material objects when compared with the gifts and powers of the Holy Spirit? As Paul had shown, the laborer should get just compensation for his work. That being the case, no matter how much the Corinthians might give, it in no way compensated for the work the Apostles had done in bringing them the power of the Spirit.[47]

9:12a *If others be partakers of this power over you, are not we rather? / If others share in this claim on you, don't we have a greater one?:* The "others" referred to here could be Peter and other Apostles that Paul alluded to in 9:4. The "we" was likely Paul and Barnabas, both of whom refused assistance. Since these two brought the gospel to the Gentiles, and Paul more especially to the Corinthians, their "right" to material help was all the greater. Our Rendition takes the pronoun *hymōn,* "on you," as an objective genitive, showing that some leaders exercised claim on the Corinthian Saints. This fact separated them from Paul, who refused to exercise such authority.

Analysis and Summary

To give his argument clarity and force, Paul appealed to the scriptures. According to the Mosaic law, oxen threshing grain were not to be muzzled, thus allowing them to eat as they worked. Though the law evidenced God's concern for animals, the lesson behind it was that no labor should be performed either for self or for others without reward. One of the many problems with slavery was that it contradicted this order. Too many slaves worked without hope of sharing in the bounty of the harvest. To militate

---

46. Thiselton, *First Epistle,* 688.
47. Edwards, *Commentary,* 231; Gale, *Use of Analogy,* 101–5.

against this, the Deuteronomic law demanded that when a man was freed, the master was to "not let him go away empty." Indeed, the Lord commanded that "thou shalt furnish him liberally out of thy flock, and out of thy floor, and out of thy winepress: of that wherewith the Lord thy God hath blessed thee" (Deut. 15:12–15).[48]

Paul's phrase ἐπ' ἐλπίδι (*ep' elpidi*), "with hope," emphasized the idea that a person's work should be in the hope or confidence that benefit would come. The law was designed to protect this right. As one scholar noted, "Hope invites a forward expectation above and beyond the toils and trials of the present. It brings a perspective and a horizon which can transform the constraints of a present situation."[49]

In order to give real punch to the fact that he voluntarily relinquished rights or influence (ἐξουσία, *exousia*) that were clearly his, Paul had to define what those rights were, prove that he understood them, show that he qualified for and could have insisted on them, and that others had, indeed, done so. In short, it was crucial to Paul's case that he clearly establish the difference between accepting certain benefits and the authority or right to do so.[50]

Verse 9:5 suggests that other leaders took advantage of offers of assistance. Likely, Paul received offers as well. If so, his refusal could have been seen as a rebuff and caused hurt feelings and even anger among some very influential people.[51] Given the social conditions in Corinth, such offers may have been motivated to win over a leader to one side or the other, if not to obligate him directly. This may explain why Paul freely accepted assistance from the Saints at Philippi; there it was offered from the branch as a whole with no strings attached. That he refused offers from certain Corinthian Saints while other Apostles accepted them could have been a reason his detractors raged against him.[52] One important outcome of Paul's voluntary restraint on exercising his rights was that it safeguarded him against the potentially vulnerable position of becoming indebted to and likely dictated to by a patron. Paul was a servant of but one master and that was the Lord, Jesus Christ.

---

48. Rushdoony, *Institutes*, 250–51.

49. Thiselton, *First Epistle*, 688.

50. Thiselton, *First Epistle*, 689. As a Roman citizen who enjoyed special rights, Paul is particularly conscious of the importance of rights.

51. Peter Marshall, *Enmity in Corinth* (Tübingen: Mohr Press, 1987), 232.

52. J. K. Chow, *Patronage and Power* (Sheffield, Eng.: Sheffield Academic Press, 1992), 106–7; Marshall, *Enmity in Corinth*, 231–33.

PAUL HAS CHOSEN NOT TO AVAIL HIMSELF OF THESE PRIVILEGES (9:12B–14)

Greek Text

Ἀλλ' οὐκ ἐχρησάμεθα τῇ ἐξουσίᾳ ταύτῃ, ἀλλὰ πάντα στέγομεν ἵνα μή τινα ἐγκοπὴν δῶμεν τῷ εὐαγγελίῳ τοῦ Χριστοῦ. 13 οὐκ οἴδατε ὅτι οἱ τὰ ἱερὰ ἐργαζόμενοι τὰ ἐκ τοῦ ἱεροῦ ἐσθίουσιν, οἱ τῷ θυσιαστηρίῳ παρεδρεύοντες τῷ θυσιαστηρίῳ συμμερίζονται; 14 οὕτως καὶ ὁ κύριος διέταξεν τοῖς τὸ εὐαγγέλιον καταγγέλλουσιν ἐκ τοῦ εὐαγγελίου ζῆν. [SBLGNT]

King James Version

12b Nevertheless we have not used this power; but suffer all things, lest we should hinder the gospel of Christ. 13 Do ye not know that they which minister about holy things live of the things of the temple? and they which wait at the altar are partakers with the altar? 14 Even so hath the Lord ordained that they which preach the gospel should live of the gospel.

New Rendition

12b But we have not made use of this right. Instead we endure all things so that we will not cause any hindrance to the gospel of Christ. 13 Don't you understand that those who perform holy services eat from the offerings of the temple? Don't those who serve regularly at the altar receive a portion of that which is sacrificed at the altar? 14 Likewise the Lord has also arranged for those who preach the gospel to receive their living from the gospel.

Translation Notes and Comments

9:12b *Nevertheless we have not used this power; but suffer all things, lest we should hinder the gospel of Christ / But we have not made use of this right. Instead we endure all things so that we will not cause any hindrance to the gospel of Christ:* The aorist verb in the phrase οὐκ ἐχρησάμεθα (*ouk echrēsametha*), "have not made use of,"[53] referred back to Paul's practice of refusing help during his eighteen-month stay at Corinth. His use of the perfect tense of the verb in 9:15, however, emphasized that his stance had not changed and, therefore, he still felt the same way. Again the central point was on the legitimacy of the Apostle's ἐξουσία (*exousia*), "right," which he freely gave up. The verb στέγω (*stegō*), "suffer, endure" or "put up with,"[54]

---

53. BDAG, 1087–88.
54. BDAG, 942; Louw-Nida, §13:148.

identified the cost. He and Barnabas had to put up with a lot of opposition. His use of the noun ἐγκοπή (*engkopē*), "hindrance" or "impediment," explained his reason.[55] He and Barnabas did not want anything to hinder or impede their missionary efforts. Given the nature of Corinthian society where *quid pro quo* played a big role in relationships, a person could easily become obliged to another.[56] Whether such would have happened had Paul taken advantage of his rights from church members is unknown, but he clearly did not want to take the chance and have it slow down his efforts.

9:13 *Do ye not know that they which minister about holy things live of the things of the temple? and they which wait at the altar are partakers with the altar? / Don't you understand that those who perform holy services eat from the offerings of the temple? Don't those who serve regularly at the altar receive a portion of that which is sacrificed at the altar?:* After the brief note at the end of 9:12, Paul surprisingly returned to his argument about the legitimacy of Church authorities and missionaries receiving assistance. A reason he may have picked up his defense again was that he suddenly remembered an excellent instance that did not need an analogy (that is, the threshing ox). It came from both Old Testament practice and pagan rites and made a point against which no one could argue. This was that those who served in the temple had a right to a portion of the offerings (see, for example, Lev. 6:14–18).[57]

Again Paul asked the question οὐκ οἴδατε (*ouk oidate*), "Do ye not know?" to underscore a self-evident truth his readers should have known. The verb ἐργάζομαι (*ergazomai*), "labor" or "toil,"[58] in this case, identified those who were engaged in sacred tasks and who drew sustenance from them.[59] In short, the word suggested not merely eating from the altar but of making a living by performing sacred duties.

9:14 *Even so hath the Lord ordained that they which preach the gospel should live of the gospel / Likewise the Lord has also arranged for*

---

55. BDAG, 274;

56. Here the idea of reciprocal χάρις (*charis*) could be at play. For discussion, see the "Excursus on Grace" in the first chapter.

57. Fee, *First Epistle*, 411; Meyer, *Exegetical Commentary*, 2:263, who cites Lucan, *Asin* 5; Demosthenes, 1300.6; and Ambrosiaster, 101, as evidence that priests ate from the altars of the gods.

58. BDAG, 389.

59. Louw-Nida, §57.198. There is a slight manuscript variant in this verse with one manuscript having the definite article τά (*ta*), "the things," before ἐκ τοῦ ἱεροῦ (*ek tou hierou*), of the temple," thus, priests partake of "the things" donated or sacrificed for temple worship. The Rendition follows this variant.

those who preach the gospel to receive their living from the gospel: This
verse is Paul's moral corollary. The verb διατάσσω (*diatassō*), "to arrange
carefully,"[60] denoted the giving of "detailed instructions as to what must
be done."[61] Clearly, there was an established policy that governed the case
at hand. To make it clear what the Lord had arranged, Paul used the verb
ζάω (*zaō*), "to live,"[62] connoting the making of a living from gospel service.[63]

Analysis and Summary

As an Apostle, Paul had the right to make certain claims upon the Corinthian Saints. This, however, he refused to do. "Paul has given up his liberty," noted one LDS scholar, "and has become all things to all men, in
order that he may save souls. All he does is for the Gospel's sake, that he
may share in its blessings."[64] Paul's willingness to put up with all that was
necessary in order to not hinder the cause of the gospel was precisely
what the Corinthian "strong" were not willing to do (compare 8:8–9).[65]
Among both Gentiles and Jews, the Christian message continued to be
hindered by the "foolishness of the cross." Indeed, this doctrine was the
chief σκάνδαλον (*skandalon*), "offense" or "stumbling block," to the work.
Because of this concern, every effort had to be made to illuminate all false
stumbling blocks that would have exacerbated the problem. Thus, Paul
felt that certain rights which could act as *skandalon* had to be forfeited to
promote others accepting and living the gospel.[66]

After his brief digression in 9:12, Paul continued to legitimize the right
some had of receiving benefit from the Church. His proof text this time did
not involve an analogy as did the law of the ox. He referred to both pagan
and Jewish practices in which those who served at the temple received
their livelihood therefrom.[67]

Many Christian denominations take Paul's counsel as the basis for paying their ministers. There is tension in the New Testament on this subject.
During the early portion of his ministry, the Lord instructed those he sent
to preach the gospel to go without purse or scrip (Matt. 10:5–10; Mark 6:8;

---

60. BDAG, 237.
61. Louw-Nida, §33.325.
62. Louw-Nida, §23.88 notes that the word means to live while §41.2 notes that it also
describes a way of life or behavior.
63. BDAG, 425.
64. Sperry, *Paul's Life,* 124.
65. Martin, *Slavery as Salvation,* 119–20.
66. Thiselton, *First Epistle,* 691.
67. Fee, *First Epistle,* 412, n. 83; Barrett, *First Epistle,* 207; Thiselton, *First Epistle,* 692.

Luke 9:3; 10:4). In today's vernacular that would mean to travel "without wallet or suitcase."[68] Later on, as conditions changed, the Lord reversed his instructions, telling the missionaries to carry both wallet and suitcase (Luke 22:35–37). This change gives evidence for the need of continual revelation for guidance dictated by changing circumstances.[69] Even so, the Lord's instructions were to those who were missionaries, not those who were local leaders. The same is true with Paul. The people he was referring to in chapter 9 were those engaged in full-time missionary service. He does not address the issue of the local ministry.[70] As two LDS scholars noted, it is important to "remember that these instructions and promises are for the [general] leaders of the Church and other missionaries sent out by them, as they travel without purse or scrip (see JST Matthew 6:25; 3 Nephi 13:25). These instructions and promises are *not* intended as commandments or advice for the Saints generally in living their everyday lives. . . . On the contrary, the Lord expects his Saints to be wise stewards and to take appropriate 'thought for the morrow' and beyond." This scholar also noted that though early missionaries of the LDS Church did go out without purse or scrip, "that hardly amounts to a 'paid ministry' because the brethren received only their bare sustenance and accumulated nothing—having no purse to put it in."[71]

PAUL HAS FREELY TAUGHT THE GOSPEL (9:15–18)

Greek Text

15 Ἐγὼ δὲ οὐ κέχρημαι οὐδενὶ τούτων. οὐκ ἔγραψα δὲ ταῦτα ἵνα οὕτως γένηται ἐν ἐμοί, καλὸν γάρ μοι μᾶλλον ἀποθανεῖν ἤ—τὸ καύχημά μου οὐδεὶς κενώσει. 16 ἐὰν γὰρ εὐαγγελίζωμαι, οὐκ ἔστιν μοι καύχημα, ἀνάγκη γάρ μοι ἐπίκειται· οὐαὶ γάρ μοί ἐστιν ἐὰν μὴ εὐαγγελίσωμαι. 17 εἰ γὰρ ἑκὼν τοῦτο πράσσω, μισθὸν ἔχω· εἰ δὲ ἄκων, οἰκονομίαν πεπίστευμαι. 18 τίς οὖν μού ἐστιν ὁ μισθός; ἵνα εὐαγγελιζόμενος

---

68. Robinson and Garrett, *Commentary*, 3:57.

69. McConkie and Ostler, *Revelations of the Restoration*, 610.

70. There is no paid ministry in LDS wards or stakes. In local congregations, lay ministers preside. Only those serving on the general level receive a living allowance. See Brian L. Pitcher, "Callings," in *EM*, 1:248–50.

71. Robinson and Garrett, *Commentary*, 3:58.

ἀδάπανον θήσω τὸ εὐαγγέλιον, εἰς τὸ μὴ καταχρήσασθαι τῇ ἐξουσίᾳ μου ἐν τῷ εὐαγγελίῳ. [SBLGNT]

King James Version

15 But I have used none of these things: neither have I written these things, that it should be so done unto me: for it were better for me to die, than that any man should make my glorying void. 16 For though I preach the gospel, I have nothing to glory of: for necessity is laid upon me; yea, woe is unto me, if I preach not the gospel! 17 For if I do this thing willingly, I have a reward: but if against my will, a dispensation of the gospel is committed unto me. 18 What is my reward then? Verily that, when I preach the gospel, I may make the gospel of Christ without charge, that I abuse not my power in the gospel.

New Rendition

15 But I have not used any of these rights, nor am I writing these things to obtain them, for I would rather die than that—no one will deprive me of my reason for pride. 16 For if I preach the gospel, I have no reason for pride, for I am under obligation, and woe to me if I do not preach the gospel! 17 For if I do this willingly, I have a reward. But if unwillingly, I have been entrusted with a commission. 18 So what is my reward? To offer the gospel free of charge when I preach, without taking advantage of my authorized rights in the gospel.

Translation Notes and Comments

9:15 *But I have used none of these things / But I have not used any of these rights:* Paul's use of the emphatic personal pronoun ἐγώ (*egō*), "I," emphasized his individuality.[72] The word stressed that his decisions were in no way intended to dictate or even influence the actions of other leaders. The force of the perfect verb in the phrase οὐ κέχρημαι (*ou kechrēmai*), "I have not used," emphasized his unaltered but personal stance on this issue; he had not nor would he ever exercise these rights.

neither have I written these things, that it should be so done unto me / nor am I writing these things to obtain them: The verb ἔγραψα (*egrapsa*), "I write," as an epistolary aorist, has a present force and thus is translated that way in our Rendition.[73] The pronoun ταῦτα (*tauta*), "these things," referred to all the evidence the Apostle had mounted up to this point.[74]

for it were better for me to die, than that any man should make my glorying void / for I would rather die than that—no one will deprive me

---

72. Meyer, *Exegetical Commentary*, 1:264.

73. Wallace, *Greek Grammar*, 562–63, 753.

74. Robertson and Plummer, *Critical and Exegetical Commentary*, 188.

of my reason for pride: There are textual variants for this phrase. The KJV follows one and our Rendition the other. Paul breaks off his thought mid-sentence (a speech pattern called aposiopesis). Apparently not recognizing this, some copyists tried to smooth out the reading by replacing οὐδείς (*oudeis*), "no one," with ἵνα τις (*hina tis*), "in order that anyone." The best manuscripts support the aposiopesis, which our Rendition acknowledges with a dash.[75] It is likely that Paul's thought was broken at this point by a sudden and emotional inrush of feeling that intruded into his consciousness, a deep appreciation for his ground for glorying.[76]

Paul expressed his feelings very clearly. Rather than become obligated to anyone except the Lord, he would rather die. The noun καύχημα (*kauchēma*), "glory" or "pride," denoted that in which a person took pride to the point that he was willing to boast about it. In Paul's case, it was forfeiting his rights for a great cause—that cause being the glory of the cross (that is, the Lord's Atonement; see 1:18–31). Having been one who received freely of God's grace, Paul felt compelled to freely share it with others through preaching the gospel without price. In doing so, as one scholar noted, his ministry "becomes a living paradigm of the gospel itself."[77]

9:16 *For though I preach the gospel, I have nothing to glory of: for necessity is laid upon me; yea, woe is unto me, if I preach not the gospel! / For if I preach the gospel, I have no reason for pride, for I am under obligation, and woe to me if I do not preach the gospel!:* Paul's glorying was in keeping with the Lord's command, "Freely ye have received, freely give" (Matt. 10:8). To fulfill the spirit of this injunction, not only must the task be done, but also rights, wages, or rewards must be voluntarily renounced. Certainly, the Apostle insisted, he could not boast of his missionary efforts, for the Lord laid him under strict charge to do it. The noun ἀνάγκη (*anangkē*), "necessity" or "obligation," denoted the necessity that was inherent in an important task and, therefore, connoted "what had to be done."[78] The verb ἐπίκειμαι (*epikeimai*), "lie on," stressed the same idea, denoting the force of obligation a task demanded.[79] Paul's use of both words reveal his consciousness of the weight he carried due to the grace that God had bestowed upon

75. Metzger, *Textual Commentary*, 558–59.
76. Thiselton, *First Epistle*, 694.
77. Fee, *First Epistle*, 421.
78. BDAG, 61; Louw-Nida, §71.38.
79. BDAG, 373.

him, calling him from sin to service.[80] His word οὐαί (*ouai*), "woe," showed he recognized what would happen if he refused. This word, as a substantive, denoted "a state of intense hardship or distress."[81] For Paul, it connoted the terrible consequences that would follow if he did not carry out the Lord's will.[82] If he did not reciprocate the divine favor, it could be withdrawn from him at the expense of his eternal life.

9:17 *For if I do this thing willingly, I have a reward / For if I do this willingly, I have a reward:* This is the first of two contrasting conditional clauses. The pronoun τοῦτο (*touto*), translated as "this" in our Rendition, refers to preaching the gospel. Paul did this ἑκών (*hekōn*) "willingly." Ever since Christ's appearance to him on the road to Damascus, he had served the Lord with all his might, mind, and strength. In 9:18, he explains what his reward is.

but if against my will, a dispensation of the gospel is committed unto me / But if unwillingly, I have been entrusted with a commission: This is the second conditional clause, and in it Paul uses the contrasting adjective ἄκων (*akōn*). This word is derived from ἑκών (*hekōn*) but an alpha-privative is prefix to it thus replacing the ἑ- (*he-*) with ἀ- (*a-*). It is comparable to English "un-" as in "*un*-willing." In this case the condition is hypothetical. It could be more idiomatically rendered, "But even if I were *not* willing, the fact remains that I have been entrusted with a commission (to preach the gospel)." For Paul, preaching the gospel had been a challenging assignment that, perhaps, he would not have chosen on his own. Nevertheless, he would follow his Savior and say, "Not *my* will, but *thine*, be done" (Luke 22:42; italics added).

The noun οἰκονομία (*oikonomia*), translated as "a dispensation," in the KJV, in its root sense, referred to managing a household, but in a more abstract sense, it meant supervising things in general and particularly of fulfilling a commission or managing a stewardship.[83] In Paul's case, the word emphasized the responsibility God had placed upon him as steward

---

80. Paul's point would have resonated with his Gentile readers because they understood grace to have an obligatory or reciprocal aspect. Even if a gift or other favor could not be repaid, receiving it bound the recipient to the giver and demanded, at the least, loyalty. The result of not honoring the relationship was, indeed, "woe" for the giver could take back what was given.

81. BDAG, 734.

82. Louw-Nida, §22.9.

83. BDAG, 697–98; Louw-Nida, §§42.25; 46.1; Ogden and Skinner, *Verse by Verse*, 138.

over the Gentile branches of the Church (see 4:1).[84] The force of the perfect passive verb πεπίστευμαι (*pepisteumai*), "trust, entrust,"[85] carried the
idea of having been entrusted or commissioned with a task for which one
still carried responsibility. Paul's putting the verb in that tense showed that
he knew his obligation continued.[86] The phrase "of the gospel" is not found
in any Greek manuscript and is, therefore, left out of our Rendition.

**9:18 *What is my reward then? Verily that, when I preach the gospel,
I may make the gospel of Christ without charge / So what is my reward?
To offer the gospel free of charge when I preach:*** The phrase "of Christ" is
found only in later manuscripts. Because none of the earliest and best ones
have it, it is left out of our Rendition.

Paul's question, "What is my reward?" explains the reward he referred
to in 9:17. He was in a position to preach the gospel without charge. The
noun ἀδάπανος (*adapanos*), "free of charge," reflected the beneficial act,
kindness, or largess a patron gave to those under his patronage. Paul, who
rebuffed patronage, now became the patron to all he taught.

***that I abuse not my power in the gospel / without taking advantage
of my authorized rights in the gospel:*** With this statement, Paul ended
the argument where it began, with ἐξουσία (*exousia*), "power, influence,
authority," and, more especially, "rights." In our Rendition we have here
translated *exousia* as "authorized rights" to emphasize that Paul could legit-
imately claim those rights, but he was in a position, because of his skills and
divine blessings, to do what few could. He could forsake his authorized
"rights" and preach the gospel freely. For him, this was his reward and his
ground for boasting, and he did not want anyone to take that away from
him. The verb καταχράομαι (*katachraomai*) referred to taking full advantage of something. It is directly related to the previously used verb χράομαι
(*chraomai*) "to use, take advantage of," from which it differs little in meaning and is, therefore, translated as "taking advantage of" in our Rendition.[87]

---

84. By assignment, his area of responsibility was over the Gentile branches of the
Church. See Gal. 2:9.

85. Louw-Nida, §35.50.

86. Paul's readers could well identify his position with that of the Lord, who said,
"When ye shall have done all those things which are commanded you, say, We are unprof-
itable servants: we have done that which was our duty to do" (Luke 17:10; compare
Mosiah 2:20–25).

87. LSJ, 921. The verb has the intensive prefix "κατα-, *kata-*" added which usually gives
the idea of completion to the action of the verb. See Smyth, *Greek Grammar*, §1680, but
does not do so here. See BDAG, 530.

Analysis and Summary

Paul, it would appear, to the chagrin of certain Corinthians, had refused to take advantage of his rights (ἐξουσία, *exousia*). In this part of his epistle, he explained why. He did not want anything to take away his reason for glorying. That reason was being able to preach the gospel freely and thus eliminate one obstacle that might cause some to reject it. Nothing could get in the way of the message. Though Paul never used the term, there was a real danger that conditions were ripe for the introduction of priestcraft among the people. This condition is realized when "men preach and set themselves up for a light unto the world, that they might get gain and praise of the world; but they seek not for the welfare of Zion. . . . But the laborer in Zion shall labor for Zion; for if they labor for money they shall perish" (2 Ne. 26:29, 31).[88] Due to the status-hungry nature of the Corinthian Saints, perverting the gospel and turning its preaching into a profitable vocation could have been a real temptation. Paul's lifestyle militated against that.

Though Paul was willing to glory in his ability to preach about Christ freely, he was not willing to glory in his own missionary and administrative efforts (9:16). Indeed, he felt compelled to serve. As he stated elsewhere, he was "overpowered" (κατελήμφθην, *katelēmphthēn*, Philip. 3:12) and under compulsion (ἀνάγκη, *anankē*, 9:16) due to his commissioning from the Lord himself. Paul, like Jeremiah, was foreordained to lifelong service (Jer. 1:4–10; Gal. 1:15), and this ordination, once revealed by the Savior, pressed upon the Apostle. He well knew what the consequences of shirking his duty would be (9:16). Indeed, even today, those who God calls to service must respond. The Lord has clearly stated to those who "embark in the service of God, [that they must] serve him with all [their] heart, might, mind and strength, that [they] may stand blameless before God at the last day" (D&C 4:2). The Savior has warned that every leader must learn his duty "and to act in the office in which he is appointed, in all diligence. He that is slothful shall not be counted worthy to stand, and he that learns not his duty and shows himself not approved shall not be counted worthy to stand" (D&C 107:99–100).

President Wilford Woodruff noted that "each man claiming a standing among this people should do his duty to the trust committed to our charge. Our responsibility is great before God and man. Any people into whose hands is committed a dispensation of the Gospel has a great responsibility.

88. See Charles D. Tate Jr., "Priestcraft," in *EM,* 3:1133.

And Joseph Smith, Brigham Young, and the Twelve Apostles, would have been under condemnation and would have rendered themselves liable to the curse of God if they had not gone forth into the world and borne record of this work. Paul was placed in the same position and he sensed it."[89] Indeed, the ancient Apostle's choice of the word οὐαί (*ouai*), "woe" (9:16), to describe his concern emphasized the point. The word used alone denoted displeasure or pain, but with the copula ἐστίν (*estin*), "is" (as in this verse), it meant misfortune, trouble, even agony.[90] Thus, what motivated Paul, in part, was concern about the agony that threatened him if he did not fulfill his obligation to his Lord.

Paul preached the gospel, then, not because he was compelled to—he still had his freedom to choose—but because he felt duty-bound to do so since God had commissioned him. He felt no need either for boasting or for a reward. In short, there was no prize for doing one's duty.[91] He accepted the Lord's assignment as a sacred trust from which, no matter how much he might wish otherwise, he would not back away.[92] In this, he once again modeled his Savior's example (Matt. 26:39; Mark 14:36; Luke 22:42).

The condition is little different today. The Prophet Joseph Smith taught: "When the Twelve or any other witnesses stand before the congregations of the earth and they preach in the power and demonstration of the Spirit of God and the people are astonished and confounded at the doctrine and say, 'That man has preached a powerful discourse, a great sermon,' then let that man or those men take care that they do not ascribe the glory unto themselves, but be careful that they are humble and ascribe the praise and glory to God and the Lamb, for it is by the power of the Holy Priesthood and Holy Ghost [that] they have power thus to speak. What art thou, O man, but dust? And from whom dost thou receive thy power and blessings but from God?"[93]

When Paul gave up his right to Church assistance, he went beyond any call of duty. By doing menial labor, something he was not obligated to do, he had both grounds for boasting and merited a reward. Indeed, Paul did *this*—surrendered his rights—in order to receive that reward (9:17).

---

89. Wilford Woodruff, in *JD*, 23:80.

90. REB 1 Cor. 9:16; Thiselton, *First Epistle*, 696.

91. Bailey, *Mediterranean Eyes*, 250–51.

92. Thiselton, *First Epistle*, 696–97.

93. "History, 1838–1856, Volume C-1," 10 [addenda]; spelling, punctuation, and capitalization have been standardized.

What then was Paul's reward? He could do that which had not been imposed upon him; he could preach the gospel without pay. This was the center of his boasting. He was fortunate enough not to have to demand that to which he and other Apostles had a full right, being taken care of by the congregations. His pay was, as it were, to be in a position not to have to receive any pay. He could give freely. His toil as a leather worker, tent maker, or sail weaver in the agora (Acts 18:1–3) was his free gift so that others were not burdened with his care.[94] Further, his ability to work made him fully independent.

His independence had excellent results. The first was his absolute freedom that expressed itself in two ways: (1) he was free from all human constraints or influences, being beholden to no one but God and Christ; and (2) he was free to teach the truth fully and completely without worrying about offending anyone. The second result of his independence was his ability to preach the gospel "free of charge." The adjective ἀδάπανος (*adapanos*), "free of charge," described the beneficial act of a patron to those under his patronage. Paul's freedom had, then, turned the tables on those who likely offered him patronage. He would not accept their patronage in order to become their patron. Thus, Paul's freedom put him in a position not only of being able to be a blessing to the Saints but also to have power over them. Having forcefully made his point, Paul closed this portion of his argument.

Behind Paul's words there stands a very important lesson. He set the example in giving up his gospel rights in order to push the gospel forward. He did not ask all his readers to do so. There were those who simply had few if any rights, and so they were in no position to give them up. But there were some, "the strong," who could. Paul set the example he expected those in his position to follow.[95] They should be willing to relinquish their right, such as eating meat offered to idols or any other activity that would spiritually prove to be a stumbling block to a fellow Saint.[96] Love of the gospel, their brothers and sisters, and God must drive all that they did (see chapter 13).

---

94. Fee, *First Epistle*, 420; Collins, *First Corinthians*, 346.
95. Martin, *Slavery as Salvation*, 120–21.
96. Thiselton, *First Epistle*, 698.

PAUL HAS DONE EVERYTHING HE COULD TO WIN CONVERTS TO CHRIST (9:19–23)

Greek Text

19 Ἐλεύθερος γὰρ ὢν ἐκ πάντων πᾶσιν ἐμαυτὸν ἐδούλωσα, ἵνα τοὺς πλείονας κερδήσω· 20 καὶ ἐγενόμην τοῖς Ἰουδαίοις ὡς Ἰουδαῖος, ἵνα Ἰουδαίους κερδήσω· τοῖς ὑπὸ νόμον ὡς ὑπὸ νόμον, μὴ ὢν αὐτὸς ὑπὸ νόμον, ἵνα τοὺς ὑπὸ νόμον κερδήσω· 21 τοῖς ἀνόμοις ὡς ἄνομος, μὴ ὢν ἄνομος θεοῦ ἀλλ᾽ ἔννομος Χριστοῦ, ἵνα κερδάνω τοὺς ἀνόμους· 22 ἐγενόμην τοῖς ἀσθενέσιν ἀσθενής, ἵνα τοὺς ἀσθενεῖς κερδήσω· τοῖς πᾶσιν γέγονα πάντα, ἵνα πάντως τινὰς σώσω. 23 πάντα δὲ ποιῶ διὰ τὸ εὐαγγέλιον, ἵνα συγκοινωνὸς αὐτοῦ γένωμαι. [SBLGNT]

King James Version

19 For though I be free from all men, yet have I made myself servant unto all, that I might gain the more. 20 And unto the Jews I became as a Jew, that I might gain the Jews; to them that are under the law, as under the law, that I might gain them that are under the law; 21 To them that are without law, as without law, (being not without law to God, but under the law to Christ,) that I might gain them that are without law. 22 To the weak became I as weak, that I might gain the weak: I am made all things to all men, that I might by all means save some. 23 And this I do for the gospel's sake, that I might be partaker thereof with you.

New Rendition

19 For although I am free from all, I have made myself a slave to all, so that I can gain more converts. 20 To the Jews, I became like a Jew, so that I could gain converts among the Jews. To those under the Law, I became like one under the Law—although I was myself not under the Law—so that I could gain converts among those under the Law. 21 To those without the Law, I became like one without the Law, although I was not without the law of God but was rather subject to the law of Christ, so that I could gain converts from those without the Law. 22 To the weak, I became weak, so that I could gain converts among the weak. I became all things to all people so that I might at least save some from death. 23 I do all these things on account of the gospel, so that I might share in its blessings.

Translation Notes and Comments

9:19 *For though I be free from all men, yet have I made myself servant unto all, that I might gain the more / For although I am free from all, I have made myself a slave to all, so that I can gain more converts:* In the Greek text, the first word in this sentence is ἐλεύθερος (*eleutheros*), "free," the position giving emphasis to Paul's point. He was first and foremost a free man obligated to no mortal. He did not, however, let that stand in his way. His words πᾶσιν ἐμαυτὸν ἐδούλωσα (*pasin emauton edoulōsa*), "I made myself a slave to all," underscored his self-sacrificing act. It's noteworthy that Paul referred to himself as δοῦλος τοῦ Χριστοῦ Ἰησοῦ (*doulos tou Christou Iēsou*), "a slave of Christ Jesus," in both the epistle to the Romans (Rom. 1:1) and to the Philippians (Philip. 1:1). He willingly sacrificed not only his rights but also his freedom for a divine purpose—gaining "more converts." The word "converts" is not found in the Greek manuscripts, but our Rendition adds it for clarity. This same addition appears in 9:20, 21, and 22.

9:20 *And unto the Jews I became as a Jew, that I might gain the Jews / To the Jews, I became like a Jew, so that I could gain converts among the Jews:* His words show that he was not playacting, but genuine in what he did. Only in that way could he gain converts.

to them that are under the law, as under the law, that I might gain them that are under the law / To those under the Law, I became like one under the Law—although I was myself not under the Law—so that I could gain converts among those under the Law: In this verse and the next, when "law" refers to the law of Moses, our Rendition capitalizes it to distinguish it from "law" in a general sense. Paul's reference to τοῖς ὑπὸ νόμον (*tois hypo nomon*), "those under the law," likely expanded the definition of Judaism to include proselytes and God-fearers.[97] The phrase between the dashes is not found in the KJV, having been left out of the Greek manuscript on which it was based.[98] Since the earliest manuscripts include it, it is in our Rendition. Paul made it clear to his readers that he was well aware that he knew Jesus had fulfilled the law, thus freeing his disciples from its constraints. Nonetheless, understanding that participating in Jewish ceremonies and rites was not forbidden to any Christian, when among them the Apostle was scrupulous to honor their traditions as a means of bringing them to the Savior (for example, see Acts 21:18–26).[99]

9:21 *To them that are without law, as without law, (being not without law to God, but under the law to Christ,) that I might gain them that are without law / To those without the Law, I became like one without*

---

97. Findlay, "St. Paul's First Epistle," 854.

98. It is likely that a copyist's eyes passed inadvertently from the first ὑπὸ νόμον (*hypo nomon*) to a second one below. Metzger, *Textual Commentary*, 559.

99. Bruce, *1 and 2 Corinthians*, 86–87.

the Law, although I was not without the law of God but was rather sub-ject to the law of Christ, so that I could gain converts from those without the Law: Though the adjective ἄνομος (*anomos*), "lawless," could refer to "unrighteous or godless people,"[100] given the context, Paul certainly meant Gentiles who were not constrained by the requirements of the Mosaic law. Paul did make it clear to his readers that he did not sacrifice his Christian standards—being always under the "law of Christ."

9:22 *To the weak became I as weak, that I might gain the weak / To the weak, I became weak, so that I could gain converts among the weak:* It is likely that the adjective ἀσθενής (*asthenēs*), "weak," was a designation given by "the strong" in reference to those who were insecure in their understanding of the gospel and station in the Church. This contingent was likely made up of the poor of the branch who were dependent on slave masters, employers, or patrons for their sustenance. Paul's words that he became as "the weak," however, hardly meant he felt insecure in his station. Rather he took their side, not flaunting his power or authority. This may be one of the reasons he worked at a menial job and made his own living. Doing so allowed these lower-class people to relate to him and, thus, be more willing to listen to his message and emulate his example.[101]

I am made all things to all men, that I might by all means save some / I became all things to all people so that I might at least save some: The force of the perfect active verb γέγονα (*gegona*), "I became," stressed the perma-nent result of Paul's past decisions and actions.[102] He continually accom-modated himself "to people in all kinds of different situations."[103]

9:23 *And this I do for the gospel's sake, that I might be partaker thereof with you / I do all these things on account of the gospel, so that I might share in its blessings:* The phrase διὰ τὸ εὐαγγέλιον (*dia to euangelion*), "on account of the gospel," explained precisely why Paul did what he did. The nominal adjective συγκοινωνός (*syngkoinōnos*), "participant, partner," denoted a participant in some joint enterprise or relationship but placed stress on the joint nature of that participation with emphasis on that which

---

100. BDAG, 85–86; Louw-Nida, §33.57.

101. Thiselton, *First Epistle*, 706.

102. Robertson and Plummer, *Critical and Exegetical Commentary*, 192.

103. This is the translation in the NJB, but it moves too far from the actual Greek even though the sentiment is on target.

was held in common.[104] Paul did what he did so that he could have a share in the gospel with others. The genitive pronoun αὐτοῦ (*autou*), "in it/of it," referred to certain aspects of the gospel (see Analysis below).

Analysis and Summary

Verses 9:19–23 united this part of the epistle with chapter 8 and allowed Paul to tie his argument together. Here Paul summarized the point made in that chapter of the need to give up certain rights. He went further and explained why he was so willing to relinquish the right of assistance. At the heart of Paul's argument stands one very important idea, namely that being in oneness with "the other," as opposed to insisting on autonomy or self-affirmation, is the very heart of the gospel of Jesus Christ.[105]

Speaking of Paul's purposes, Elder McConkie stated:

> Paul here says he made himself all things to all men in an effort to get them to accept the gospel message; that is, he adapted himself to the conditions and circumstances of all classes of people, as a means of getting them to pay attention to his teachings and testimony. And then, lest any suppose this included the acceptance of their false doctrines or practices, or that it in any way involved a compromise between the gospel and false systems of worship, he hastened to add that he and all men must obey the gospel law to be saved.

> Our missionary approaches follow the same course today. To gain the interest of the learned, we reason and philosophize; to help the faith-endowed Maori to see the light, we certify of the healing power that is in Christ. There is one approach in finding investigators among the Jews, another among the Buddhists, and still another among the sects of Christendom, but the final teaching is always the same—accept Christ and the legal administrators who he hath sent in this day, and live the laws of the restored gospel.[106]

"Paul adapted to the circumstances of each situation he came across and incorporated aspects of each people's culture to teach them," noted one LDS scholar. "In a spirit of accommodation but not compromise, Paul

---

104. Louw-Nida, §§34.6; 57.10; BDAG, 952. The word could also be translated as "joint partaker." It is a rare compound. Though the roots are well known, it is difficult to pinpoint the nuances with certainty.

105. Thiselton, *First Epistle,* 698.

106. *DNTC,* 2:353.

worked hard to establish common ground with those he taught."[107] The Church does the same thing today. For example, LDS worship services are held on the holy day of the country in which the Saints find themselves. In Israel, sacrament meetings are held on Saturday, but in Muslim countries they are held on Friday. In the islands of the Pacific, LDS men wear skirts (*sulus*) to church. Thus, accommodations are made for the culture but no compromise is made so far as worship service is concerned.

In making his accommodations, Paul subtly but emphatically redefined what it meant for Christians to be "free." Theirs is a freedom that willingly submits to a voluntary slavery to the Lord such that they become spiritually free from sin and the second death. Their slavery is based on Christlike love and obedience that generates a *wholesome* relationship with others that opens the way to their salvation.[108]

It is of note that the once very Jewish Paul (Acts 22:3; Rom. 11:1) would state that he made himself a Jew in order to win the Jews. His words, however, betray the depth of his understanding about the nature of conversion to the Lord. He knew that the convert belonged to something much greater than any ethnic group or social strata. The convert was, as the Apostle insisted, a new creature whose loyalties to Christ transcended that of all cultural allegiances (2 Cor. 5:17; Gal. 6:15).[109] For Paul, this condition freed him from having to conform to fulfilled religious requirements, pagan rituals, or Corinthian social norms. Being free of the law of Moses, however, did not mean he could run wild with self-indulgence as some of the Corinthian Saints seemed to have interpreted the gospel message. No, the Apostle lived with a profound sense of his obligation both to his God and Savior as now defined by the "law of Christ."[110] As the Apostle to the Gentiles, even though many aspects of gentile society were contrary to his own cultural background and traditions, Paul seems to have understood the need for restraint, sensitivity, and that measure of accommodation that his assignment and station demanded. Thus, the Apostle was careful to observe conventions. In this way he defined and illustrated his radical, yet creative, call to freedom in the Lord.[111]

---

107. Ogden and Skinner, *Verse by Verse*, 138.
108. Thiselton, *First Epistle*, 701.
109. Hays, *First Corinthians*, 153.
110. Hays, *First Corinthians*, 154.
111. Thiselton, *First Epistle*, 705.

The single passion of Paul's life was the gospel and bringing others under its saving power.[112] He very clearly stated, "I do all these things on account of the gospel, so that I might share in its blessings" (9:23, Rendition). The context of the phrase suggests that Paul had in mind neither bringing gospel benefits to others nor of sharing in those benefits. On the contrary, he meant something far deeper as revealed in his choice of the nominal adjective συγκοινωνός (*synkoinōnos*). The word referred to one who participates with another in some relationship, enterprise, or matter of joint concern, thus the word designated "a partner or associate." The word differed from κοινωνός (*koinōnos*), "companion,"[113] in emphasizing, first, the joint nature of the participation and, second, that which the partners held in common.[114] The pronominal prefix συν- (*syn-*) here includes the various forms of Christian solidarity. What Paul was saying was that he did what he did on account of the *nature* of the gospel that he might be a co-sharer in that nature.[115] As one scholar noted, "To stand alongside the Jew, the Gentile, the socially dependent and vulnerable, or to live and act in solidarity with every kind of person in every kind of situation is to have a share in the nature of the gospel, i.e., to instantiate what the gospel is and how it operates."[116] Paul's life took the abstraction of the gospel and transformed it into concrete reality. His action made him *syngkoinōnos,* "a fellow-sharer" in the very essence of the gospel with all others who lived it.

In summary, Paul did all he did to disclose to all who would see that his everyday life reflected the very character of the gospel. His clear and continual proclamation was "Christ, and him crucified" (2:2). The Apostle believed that the gospel derived its character—not simply its benefits—from the example of the Lord himself. Paul's apostolic witness, as exemplified by his Lord, was housed in his insistence on the voluntary renunciation of his rights. Paul lived in such a way as to stand as an independent witness of Christ, whether in his everyday lifestyle or in his apostolic work. Continually he stood alongside those whom he sought to convert. "Paul's ultimate purpose [was] to be part of all that; to have a joint share in it."[117]

---

112. Fee, *First Epistle,* 421.

113. BDAG, 553.

114. Louw-Nida, §§34.6; 57.10; BDAG, 952.

115. Collins, *First Corinthians,* 356; Thiselton, *First Epistle,* 707; Friedrich Hauck, "κοινωνός, κοινωνέω, κοινωνία, συγκοινωνός, συγκοινωνέω," in *TDNT,* 3:797–809.

116. Thiselton, *First Epistle,* 707.

117. Thiselton, *First Epistle,* 708.

Do All You Can to Win the Prize of Salvation (9:24–27)

Greek Text

24 Οὐκ οἴδατε ὅτι οἱ ἐν σταδίῳ τρέχοντες πάντες μὲν τρέχουσιν, εἷς δὲ λαμβάνει τὸ βραβεῖον; οὕτως τρέχετε ἵνα καταλάβητε. 25 πᾶς δὲ ὁ ἀγωνιζόμενος πάντα ἐγκρατεύεται, ἐκεῖνοι μὲν οὖν ἵνα φθαρτὸν στέφανον λάβωσιν, ἡμεῖς δὲ ἄφθαρτον. 26 ἐγὼ τοίνυν οὕτως τρέχω ὡς οὐκ ἀδήλως, οὕτως πυκτεύω ὡς οὐκ ἀέρα δέρων· 27 ἀλλὰ ὑπωπιάζω μου τὸ σῶμα καὶ δουλαγωγῶ, μή πως ἄλλοις κηρύξας αὐτὸς ἀδόκιμος γένωμαι. [SBLGNT]

King James Version

24 Know ye not that they which run in a race run all, but one receiveth the prize? So run, that ye may obtain. 25 And every man that striveth for the mastery is temperate in all things. Now they do it to obtain a corruptible crown; but we an incorruptible. 26 I therefore so run, not as uncertainly; so fight I, not as one that beateth the air: 27 But I keep under my body, and bring it into subjection: lest that by any means, when I have preached to others, I myself should be a castaway.

New Rendition

24 Don't you understand that in a race, everyone runs, but only one receives the prize? Run in such a way that you will win the prize. 25 Everyone who competes in sports prepares himself through self-discipline, and they do this so that they can receive a perishable prize, but we will receive an imperishable one. 26 Accordingly I, for my part, do not run as one uncertain of his goal, nor do I box as one swinging at shadows. 27 Instead, I discipline my body and bring it under control, so that having preached to others, I myself do not somehow end up disqualified.

Translation Notes and Comments

9:24 Know ye not that they which run in a race run all, but one receiveth the prize? / Don't you understand that in a race, everyone runs, but only one receives the prize?: Once again, Paul used a favorite phrase, οὐκ οἴδατε (*ouk oidate*), "don't you understand," to provoke his readers into seeing what they had either taken too casually or had overlooked. The noun στάδιον (*stadion*), "arena, stadium," referred to the place where athletic contests where held. Taken literally, the phrase οἱ ἐν σταδίῳ τρέχοντες (*hoi en stadiō trechontes*) is "those running in the stadium." In this case, however, the emphasis was not on the place but on the activity and, therefore, our

Rendition translates the word as "in a race."[118] There is a minor JST change in this verse which reads, "all run, but only one receiveth the prize." The change simply emphasizes that in any given race there is only one winner.

Paul's statement that there is but one winner should not be pushed theologically to suggest some kind of exclusivity or elitism in the gospel.[119] His focus was not on how few won, but on the energy and self-denial athletes put into training knowing that only one runner would win. The Apostle's point was that the Saints, like athletes, must forfeit lesser goods to obtain greater gains. For Paul, the highest goal is the gospel of Christ and its attendant blessings. To fall short of gaining these blessings by being distracted by lesser things, such as standing on one's rights, would undermine the whole purpose of entering into the gospel race.[120]

So run, that ye may obtain / Run in such a way that you will win the prize: The Greek here is very compact: οὕτως τρέχετε ἵνα καταλάβητε (*houtōs trechete hina katalabēte*). That compactness made the expression simple and likely more memorable to Paul's audience. The adverb οὕτως (*houtōs*) describes the manner in which an action is carried out, "so" or "in such a way." The conjunction ἵνα (*hina*) introduces a result clause, "so that." The verb καταλαμβάνω (*katalambanō*), literally "seize, grasp," has here the sense of "win, attain." Translated literally then, we have "Run in such a way that you will win." Our Rendition has added "the prize" for clarity. Though in the gospel context all who finish the race are winners, the athlete is still the perfect example of the sacrifice the gospel demands in order to win salvation. Paul's admonition was that each Saint must run, as does the athlete, to win the prize of eternal life.

9:25 *And every man that striveth for the mastery is temperate in all things / Everyone who competes in sports prepares himself through self-discipline:* This sentence brings Paul to his point. The participle ἀγωνιζό-μενος (*agōnizomenos*) referred to one who entered an athletic contest.[121] The verb ἐγκρατεύομαι (*engkrateuomai*), "exercise self-control or self-discipline,"[122] denoted complete self-mastery, including control over desires and passions.[123] The word was a compound of κρατέω (*krateō*), "to

---

118. Louw-Nida, §7.55.

119. Gale, *Use of Analogy*, 109.

120. Thiselton, *First Epistle*, 709.

121. BDAG, 17.

122. BDAG, 274.

123. Louw-Nida, §88.83.

control," and the prepositional prefix ἐν- (*en-*), "in, within," and, therefore, denoted "to control within." The key to both physical and spiritual success is self-mastery—the willful subjugation of one's flesh to the desires and objectives to both one's spirit and God.

Now they do it to obtain a corruptible crown; but we an incorruptible / and they do this so that they can receive a perishable prize, but we will receive an imperishable one: The στέφανος (*stephanos*) was "a wreath made of foliage or designed to resemble foliage and worn by one of high status or held in high regard."[124] But here it was used figuratively for an "award or prize for exceptional service or conduct," notably that of winning a race.[125] Paul's emphasis was on the nature of the wreath. It was φθαρτός (*phthartos*), the word denoting "that which is subject to decay" and, therefore, "perishable."[126] Since the ancient *stephanos* was made of plant materials, it quickly wilted away. On the other hand, the prize for which the Saints ran Paul described as ἄφθαρτος (*aphthartos*), "imperishable," denoting that which is not subject to decay, change, or deterioration, thus, that which is incorruptible, immortal, and eternal.[127] Paul's admonition was that if athletes were willing to muster so much effort and to sacrifice in order to win a perishable reward, how much harder should the Saints work for one that was not?

9:26 *I therefore so run, not as uncertainly / Accordingly I, for my part, do not run as one uncertain of his goal:* At this point, Paul changed the subject from the athlete to himself. He used the emphatic ἐγώ (*egō*), "I," together with οὕτως (*houtos*), "in this manner" or "in this way," and enhanced the effect with τοίνυν (*toinyn*), "therefore, for," which is translated in our Rendition as "I, for my part." He did this to draw attention to his own case as an example that others should follow.[128] The adverb ἀδήλως (*adēlōs*), "uncertainly," was derived from the adjective ἄδηλος

---

124. BDAG, 943.

125. BDAG, 944. Crowns were worn to demonstrate excellence in the ancient world. The *corona civica* of oak leaves was given as the second highest military honor to a Roman soldier who killed an enemy on the battlefield and saved a fellow soldier's life (Pliny, *Natural History* 16.5). Crowns were given to the victors in the Olympic Games. For a discussion of the various kinds of crowns given as rewards in the different Greek games, see Olympic Museum and Studies Centre, "The Olympic Games in Ancient Greece," 2002, http://blogs.uprm.edu/huma3111/files/2013/05/The-Olympic-Games-in-Ancient-Greece.pdf, p. 11.

126. BDAG, 1053.

127. BDAG, 155–56.

128. Fee, *First Epistle*, 437.

(*adēlos*), which denoted something that was not clearly defined and was therefore indistinct.[129] Paul was not saying that the goal was unknown but that some runners did not keep their eye on it and, therefore, it became indistinct.[130] Paul, on the other hand, knew precisely what the goal was because he did not let distractions pull his eye away.[131]

so fight I, not as one that beateth the air / nor do I box as one swinging at shadows: The phrase ἀέρα δέρων (*aera derōn*), literally "beating the air," could have referred either to missing the intended target of one's blows in an actual fight or to shadowboxing.[132] Our Rendition takes the latter view because of the context of the epistle up to this point. It seems most likely that Paul's intent was to teach the Corinthian "strong," who value σοφία (*sophia*), "wisdom," over ἀγάπη (*agapē*), "love," that going through the motions of religion was no more effective than swinging at shadows.[133]

9:27 *But I keep under my body, and bring it into subjection / Instead, I discipline my body and bring it under control:* The verb ὑπωπιάζω (*hypōpiazō*), literally "to strike under the eye," denoted putting something under the strictest of disciplines.[134] The verb δουλαγωγέω (*doulagōgeō*), "to enslave" or "to subjugate," was used figuratively to mean "to prepare something for service."[135] Paul's use of these very unusual verbs again reached back to his athletic metaphor, emphasizing the necessity of self-restraint and discipline in order to be competitive in the games.[136] The Apostle's point was that he kept his body under strict discipline as the means of keeping it ever ready for service.

lest that by any means, when I have preached to others, I myself should be a castaway / so that having preached to others, I myself do not some-how end up disqualified: With this phrase, Paul explained his reason for

---

129. BDAG, 19.

130. Victor C. Pfitzner, *Paul and the Agon Motif: Traditional Athletic Imagery in the Pauline Epistles,* Novum Testamentum, suppl. vol. 16 (Leiden: E. J. Brill, 1967), 90.

131. Thiselton, *First Epistle,* 715.

132. Both Pfitzner, *Agon Motif,* 90–92, and Karl Ludwig Schmidt, "πυγμή, πυκτεύω," in *TDNT,* 6:915–17, give examples of each.

133. Thiselton, *First Epistle,* 715; David J. Williams, *Paul's Metaphors: Their Context and Character* (Peabody, Mass.: Hendrickson Publishers, 1999), 266–70.

134. BDAG, 1043.

135. BDAG, 259; Louw-Nida, §35.30. Some interpretations emphasize the more literal connotation of the word and see Paul advocating some form of asceticism in which the body is punished (NRSV, NJB) or beaten (NIV). However, this is pushing the literalism too far. See Fee, *First Epistle,* 439–40.

136. Fitzmyer, *First Corinthians,* 374.

his strict self-discipline. The verb κηρύσσω (*kēryssō*), "preach," referenced making an official and public announcement.[137] The adjective ἀδόκιμος (*adokimos*), "unqualified," denoted the inability to withstand a test or to prove less than what something promised.[138] Having preached for all to hear, Paul was determined that he would not fail the test. He would, indeed, win the prize. The old saying, "Do as I say, not as I do," would not fit Paul's theology. Saying and doing were, for him, concomitant.

Analysis and Summary

The Isthmian Games, sponsored by the city of Corinth, were second only in popularity to the Olympic Games in Ancient Greece. One was held during the time Paul labored there. Whether he attended is unknown, but given his Jewish background, which eschewed pagan festivals, it is unlikely that he did.[139] One LDS scholar noted, "This competition might have been the source for Paul's use of athletic imagery (foot races). The prize for the winner of the Isthmian games was a perishable crown of celery. The gospel race, however, which everyone could win, promises an everlasting crown of glory (see Mosiah 4:27)."[140] Given the popularity of the games, it is not surprising that Paul would appeal to such imagery to make his points.[141]

"[Paul] knew," wrote another LDS author, "that accepting Christ was but the beginning of the long race for eternal life. Over twenty years after his conversion he wrote: 'Everyone who competes in the games goes into strict training. They do it to get a crown of laurel that will not last; but we do it to get a crown that will last forever. Therefore, I do not run like a man running aimlessly; I do not fight like a man shadow boxing. No, I beat my body and make it my slave so that after I have preached to others, I myself will not be disqualified for the prize.' (1 Cor. 9:25–27, NIV.)"[142]

The use of sports analogies allowed Paul to continue his theme that a voluntary renunciation of rights was needed to achieve a greater good. The

---

137. BDAG, 543.

138. BDAG, 21; Thiselton, *First Epistle*, 717.

139. For a discussion, see Broneer, "Apostle Paul and the Isthmian Games," 1–31.

140. Ogden and Skinner, *Verse by Verse*, 138. For a discussion, see Murphy-O'Conner, *St. Paul's Corinth*, 16–17.

141. Ogden and Skinner, *Verse by Verse*, 138. For a discussion, see Murphy-O'Conner, *St. Paul's Corinth*, 16–17.

142. Rodney Turner, "Grace, Mysteries, and Exaltation," in *Studies in Scripture, Volume 6: Acts to Revelation*, ed. Robert L. Millet (Salt Lake City: Deseret Book, 1987), 107–24.

athlete was, indeed, an excellent example. Because he had his eye on the prize, he was willing to forego privileges and abstain from pleasures and even endure pain and exhaustion. Nothing would stop him from being at the peak of performance so that he could successfully compete for the prize. This condition, Paul insisted, was the model all Christians should follow. Sacrifice to win the prize was how the gospel game was played and won.

Paul's analogy does have a danger if pushed in the wrong direction. That danger is allowing his emphasis on *only* one person winning a race as proof for some kind of spiritual exclusivity or elitism. Such an attitude, unfortunately common among a segment of the Corinthian Saints (as will be shown), could promote a "holier than thou" attitude. The truth of the matter is that in the gospel race, all who cross the finish line are winners. "The Apostle Paul likened life to a race with a clearly defined goal," stated President Thomas S. Monson. "He urged the Saints at Corinth onward. . . . In our zeal, let us not overlook the sage counsel from Ecclesiastes [9:11]: 'The race is not to the swift, nor the battle to the strong.' Actually, the prize belongs to him who endures to the end."[143] As it states in the Book of Mormon, "See that all these things are done in wisdom and order; for it is not requisite that a man should run faster than he has strength. And again, it is expedient that he should be diligent, that thereby he might win the prize; therefore, all things must be done in order" (Mosiah 4:27). What the Lord expects of his Saints appears to be paced diligence. The only people who lose the gospel race are those who leave the track before they cross the finish line.

Paul's reference in 9:25 to the self-discipline (ἐγκρατεύομαι, *engkrateuomai*) that runners must exercise to compete successfully in a foot race hit the central issue in these verses—namely, self-mastery.[144] On more than one occasion, the Savior described the cost of discipleship. He said, "If any man will come after me, let him deny himself, and take up his cross daily, and follow me" (Luke 9:23; compare Matt. 16:24; Mark 8:34). In his discourse to the Nephites, he warned them against anger, adultery, and fornication. Then he said, "I give unto you a commandment, that ye suffer none of these things to enter into your heart; For it is better that ye should deny yourselves of these things, wherein ye will take up your cross, than

---

143. Thomas S. Monson, *Invitation to Exaltation* (Salt Lake City: Deseret Book, 1997), 10.
144. Pfitzner, *Agon Motif,* 23–35, 76–107.

that ye should be cast into hell" (3 Ne. 12:29–30). Self-denial is the key to spiritual success. As President Brigham Young explained:

> The spirits of the human family are pure and holy at the time they enter tabernacles; but the Lord has so ordered that the enemy has great power over our tabernacles, whose organization pertains to the earth. Through this plan arises our probationary warfare. ... [O]ur spirits are striving to bring our bodies into subjection, and to overcome the Devil and the evils in the world. This war and striving to overcome that evil power must continue until we triumph. To accomplish this, we must so yield obedience to the Divine influence as to learn the principles of eternal life—to learn to bring the whole man—all the passions, sympathies, and feelings in subjection to the spirit. Our spirits are warring against the flesh, and the flesh against our spirits; and all we have to do is to let the spirits that have come from our Father in heaven reign triumphant, and bring into subjection everything that tends to evil: then we are Christ's.[145]

The word ἐγκράτεια (*engkrateia*) meant, literally, "power within." Based on Paul's teachings in Galatians 5:22–23, it was a gift of the Spirit. Therefore, the idea that a person could have total self-control all by him- or herself is misleading. To overcome the flesh, God's assistance is necessary. His Spirit augments and strengthens one's determination to do all that the Father requires. Therefore, "the power within" is, at least in part, the Holy Spirit.[146]

Paul's use of the term ὁ ἀγωνιζόμενος (*ho agōnizomenos*) works well. In a limited sense, it referred, either literally or symbolically, to one engaged in an athletic contest. But it also connoted fighting or struggling toward a goal and, especially, the exertion it took to overcome all obstacles in order to achieve that goal. The word emphasized restraint from indulgence and overcoming passions.[147]

The reward one receives was a στέφανος (*stephanos*). Though the word is translated as "crown" in the KJV, it should not be confused with the διάδημα (*diadēma*), "royal head band" as worn by kings. The *stephanos* had nothing to do with rulership but was, rather, *the* sign of victory. This is the nuance it has in the Bible (1 Pet. 5:4; James 1:12; 2 Tim. 4:8; Rev. 2:10). Those who overcome the world wear the "crown of righteousness" and "the crown of life." Those who sacrifice all for the glory of the world, on

---

145. Brigham Young, in *JD,* 8:118.

146. Walter Grundmann, "ἐγκράτεια (ἀκρασία), ἐγκρατής (ἀκρατής), ἐγκρατεύομαι," in *TDNT,* 2:339–42.

147. Pfitzner, *Agon Motif,* 7–11.

the other hand, wear perishable crowns that wilt, harden, and eventually turn to dust, and as the crown fades, so does the glory and renown they spawned.

In sum, any who sincerely enter into a contest must exercise self-control (ἐγκρατεύομαι, *engkrateuomai*) in every aspect of their lives (taking πάντα, *panta,* as an accusative of respect). Paul's principle drive was "Everything for the sake of the gospel," exemplified in his voluntary renunciation of his rights in order to win "the crown of life."[148] Again turning to athletic imagery, Paul explained in 9:27 that he kept his body under strict discipline (ὑπωπιάζω, *hypōpiazō*) so that he was prepared for instant service (δουλαγωγέω, *doulagōgeō*). Paul concluded this section of his epistle by noting how ironic it would be if, after his continual admonitions to others, Judgment Day found him having failed the test (ἀδόκιμος, *adokimos*). Under no condition, he assured his readers, would he lose his reputation, his prize, and those souls he had won for the Lord.

---

148. Pfitzner, *Agon Motif,* 40.

Chapter 10

The Apostle's Concluding Argument

INTRODUCTION

In this section of his epistle, the Apostle again turned directly to the issue of eating meats once offered to idols. Over the ages, the interpretation of this chapter has been bedeviled mostly by hermeneutical issues that, frankly, barely touch on Paul's main points. Even so, one needs to be mentioned because it deals with the extent and makeup of the original passage.

Many commentators have noted the strong correlation between chapter 8 and this chapter. In both places Paul addresses the same issue. But in 10:1–22, though making the same point, he presents a very different line of reasoning. Because of this, some scholars have argued that this pericope has been inserted at this point and did not belong to the original writing. Some have further divided it into two sections consisting of 10:1–14 and 10:15–22, which they feel were later stitched together and then inserted.[1] A close examination of this block, however, shows that the first set of verses, dealing with the lesson to be learned from "our ancestors," actually forms the building block for Paul's main point that he expresses starting in 10:15. This verse opens his discussion on the Lord's Supper, which continues through 10:22. Thus, the organization suggests these passages were always a single unit. Further, this pericope contributes substantially to Paul's main point—that one must seek not his own good alone, but that of others (10:24, 33). Thus, all the pieces likely formed a complete unit that made up the original document.[2]

---

1. For an example, see Wayne A. Meeks, "'And Rose Up to Play,' Midrash and Paraenesis in 1 Corinthians 10:1–22," *Journal for the Study of the New Testament* 16 (1982): 64.

2. Fitzmyer, *First Corinthians*, 378–79.

The Apostle addressed a good part of this chapter directly to his detractors who, against his counsel, continued to attend cultic meals and, likely, brought others with them. He had already argued against this practice by appealing to the affect it might have on those "weak of conscience" (8:7–13). He now gives his antagonists an explanation and a clear and unmistakable warning. He uses Old Testament examples involving those whose actions went contrary to God's will and the consequences that followed (10:1–13). He then applies it to the Corinthian situation by showing his readers that the activities of some Christians were most incompatible with the lifestyle the Lord demanded of his people (10:14–22).[3]

Paul then readdressed more directly the problem at hand. This centered on eating the εἰδωλόθυτον (*eidōlothyton*), that is, meats offered to idols. He had already conceded that that an idol, being nothing, could not have any influence on meat and, therefore, eating it could not hurt an individual who understood this point. Paul stated clearly his underlying premise, "To us there is [only] one God, the Father, of whom are all things, and we in him; and one Lord Jesus Christ, by whom are all things, and we by him" (8:6). Though idols were nothing and, therefore, did nothing to the participants eating meats offered to them, such was not the case with devils. Therefore, Paul addressed this issue in 10:18–20. He was clear that the sacrifices made by pagan priests were not, as some Christians apparently insisted, actually—if unknowingly— to God. Rather, they were sacrifices to devils and Paul did not want any Christian to share in such a sacrament. It is important to note that the issue was not with the meat itself, but with the idolatrous rite during which it was consumed. Therefore, Paul could say in effect, just a few sentences later, whatever is sold in the market, don't question where it came from, just enjoy it (10:25). In sum, the issue was participating in pagan rituals, not eating temple foods.

Paul was careful in building his argument. He began by appealing to scripture, focusing on certain events that occurred during the Exodus. These dealt with the times when some of the children of Israel sinned against God and, thereby, lost their standing before him and suffered the consequences (10:1–5). He then made his point that the same could happen to the Christians if they commit the same sins. He assured them, however,

---

3. Fee, *First Epistle*, 441. Some have seen Paul's digression in chapters 9 and 10 (as well as Paul's change of tone in chapter 10) as evidence that these portions were part of earlier epistles later stitched together by a redactor. It is more likely that Paul was simply responding to information he had in hand and the change in tone was due to the need to be tough on those who insisted on participating in pagan rites. We find the case for unity—presented by such writers as Bailey, Fee, Mitchell, Thiselton, and Willis—to be more compelling. For summary, see Thiselton, *First Epistle*, 717–18.

that God would help them prevail (10:6–13). Next, he turned to the sin of participating in pagan temple rituals and contrasted this with the proper worship associated with the Lord's Supper. He ended the section with the clear warning for the Christians not to provoke God by continuing such a practice (10:14–24). He then addressed the subject of eating meats bought at the marketplace. On this he gave the same counsel he did in chapter 8, namely, don't ask questions, and just enjoy eating the meat (10:25–26). Finally, he addressed what to do when invited to a meal in the home of a pagan friend. His counsel was, again, enjoy the meal asking no questions. He does, however, provide a caveat: If someone indicates the meat has indeed been part of the pagan ritual, abstain for the sake of the weak Saint's conscience (10:27–31). He concludes by admonishing his readers to give no offense to anyone but to live in harmony with all (10:32–33).

THE EXAMPLE OF THE EXODUS (10:1–5)

Greek Text

1 Οὐ θέλω γὰρ ὑμᾶς ἀγνοεῖν, ἀδελφοί, ὅτι οἱ πατέρες ἡμῶν πάντες ὑπὸ τὴν νεφέλην ἦσαν καὶ πάντες διὰ τῆς θαλάσσης διῆλθον, 2 καὶ πάντες εἰς τὸν Μωϋσῆν ἐβαπτίσαντο ἐν τῇ νεφέλῃ καὶ ἐν τῇ θαλάσσῃ, 3 καὶ πάντες τὸ αὐτὸ πνευματικὸν βρῶμα ἔφαγον 4 καὶ πάντες τὸ αὐτὸ πνευματικὸν ἔπιον πόμα, ἔπινον γὰρ ἐκ πνευματικῆς ἀκολουθούσης πέτρας, ἡ πέτρα δὲ ἦν ὁ Χριστός· 5 ἀλλ᾽ οὐκ ἐν τοῖς πλείοσιν αὐτῶν ηὐδόκησεν ὁ θεός, κατεστρώθησαν γὰρ ἐν τῇ ἐρήμῳ. [SBLGNT]

King James Version

1 Moreover, brethren, I would not that ye should be ignorant, how that all our fathers were under the cloud, and all passed through the sea; 2 And were all baptized unto Moses in the cloud and in the sea; 3 And did all eat the same spiritual meat; 4 And did all drink the same spiritual drink: for they drank of that spiritual Rock that followed them: and that Rock was Christ. 5 But with many of them God was not well pleased: for they were overthrown in the wilderness.

New Rendition

1 Now I don't want you to be unaware, brothers and sisters, that our forefathers were all under the cloud and all passed through the sea. 2 And all of them were baptized unto Moses in the cloud and in the sea. 3 All of them ate the same spiritual food 4 and all of them drank the same spiritual drink, for they were all drinking from that spiritual rock which was following them, and that rock was Christ. 5 Nevertheless, God was not pleased with most of them, so they were struck down in the wilderness.

Translation Notes and Comments

10:1 *Moreover, brethren, I would not that ye should be ignorant / Now I don't want you to be unaware, brothers and sisters:* Paul's use of the particle γάρ (*gar*), "now," is important here, acting as a marker of clarification.[4] It ties this section to the point Paul had just made in 9:26–27. There he stressed the need to be self-disciplined and run the mortal race with the intent of crossing the finish line. That race was unique in that it was about endurance, not speed. All who crossed the finish line won. The Apostle now turned to the scriptures to explain why it was so important to stay on course for the duration of the race.

Though the verb ἀγνοέω (*agnoeō*), "to be ignorant," denoted being uninformed about something, it also meant to fail to recognize or understand its importance and thus is translated as "unaware" in our Rendition.[5]

our fathers / our forefathers: The Greek noun πατήρ (*patēr*) can refer to one's biological father, a more remote ancestor,[6] or "revered deceased persons with whom one shares beliefs or traditions."[7] It is in this third sense that Paul is using the word, since all who had accepted the gospel of Jesus Christ became the descendants of Israel. As Paul told the Galatians, "There is neither Jew nor Greek, there is neither bond nor free, there is neither male nor female: for ye are all one in Christ Jesus. And if ye be Christ's, then are ye Abraham's seed, and heirs according to the promise" (Gal. 3:28–29).[8]

were under the cloud, and all passed through the sea / were all under the cloud and all passed through the sea: For Paul's purpose, the operative word in this phrase is πάντες (*pantes*), "all." It allowed him to emphasize those saving events in which every Israelite participated.

---

4. BDAG, 189.

5. Louw-Nida, §§28.13; 32.7.

6. BDAG, 786.

7. BDAG, 787; *DNTC,* 2: 355. The phrase οἱ πατέρες ἡμῶν (*hoi pateres hēmōn*), "our fathers," denoted one's direct ancestors (for example, see Matt. 23:30, 32; Heb. 1:1; 8:9; Josephus, *A.J.* 14.297), but it could also refer to one's spiritual ancestors, that is, those who shared certain imitative virtues (for example, see Epictetus, *Diss.* 3.22.82). Adoption is a very important institution in Roman society. Emperors sometimes adopt their successors and in this way became their "fathers." Adoption is frequently mentioned in Roman law. Gentiles would have understood that one's father grants all benefits he possesses. For discussion see Hugh Lindsay, *Adoption in the Roman World* (Cambridge: Cambridge University Press, 2009).

8. See also Rom. 9:6–8; 2 Ne. 30:2; Abr. 2:9–11.

In developing his argument, Paul used examples that came from Exodus 13:21; 14:19–22, where a fiery cloud guided Israel by night and day and also served to keep Pharaoh's army at bay while the Israelites crossed the Red Sea. That Paul uses the phrases ὑπὸ τὴν νεφέλην (*hypo tēn nephlēn*), "under the cloud," and διὰ τῆς θαλάσσης (*dia tēs thalassēs*), "through the sea," without any explanation suggests that this story was well-known to his readers. Therefore, his use of the verb ἀγνοέω (*agnoeō*), "be unaware," in 10:1 pointed not to their lack of knowledge of the Old Testament but to its application in the present situation.[9]

10:2 *were all baptized unto Moses / And all of them were baptized unto Moses in the cloud and in the sea:* Paul used the aorist passive verb ἐβαπτίσθησαν (*ebaptisthēsan*), "were baptized,"[10] metaphorically. He moreover indicates that they were baptized εἰς τὸν Μωϋσῆν (*eis ton Mōysēn*), "unto Moses." This is the same terminology that Paul uses elsewhere in describing the Christian baptism, for example, εἰς Χριστὸν ἐβαπτίσθητε (*eis Christon ebaptisthēte*), "you were baptized unto Christ" (Gal. 3:27), and ἐβαπτίσθημεν εἰς Χριστὸν (*ebaptisthēmen eis Christon*), "we were baptized unto Christ" (Rom. 6:3). Thus, Israel shared with Moses the redemptive experience of God's saving grace in their behalf, not unlike what the Christian experiences with his or her personal baptism.[11]

---

9. Conzelmann, *1 Corinthians*, 165. This fact gives tacit evidence that at least some of the Gentile Christians were well acquainted with the Jewish scriptures and accepted them as the basis of their own belief.

10. There is a textual variant among the various manuscripts. Some have the aorist passive ἐβαπτίσθησαν (*ebaptisthēsan*), "they were baptized," while others have the aorist middle ἐβαπτίσαντο (*ebaptisanto*), "they had themselves baptized." This reading would have referred to the Jewish custom. See Metzger, *Textual Commentary*, 493. The SBLGNT chose the aorist middle, whereas Eberhard Nestle and others, eds., *Novum Testamentum Graece: Nestle-Aland*, 28th ed. (Stuttgart: German Bible Society, 2012), went with the aorist passive. Based on the available evidence and Pauline usage, the aorist passive seems to be the better reading, and that is what we have used in the Rendition.

11. This reading suggests that Paul understood that the ordinance of baptism reached back at least as far as Moses. This position undercuts the idea that it was an ordinance of rather recent origin. Joseph Smith saw in the imagery proof that the ordinances were the same through all dispensations. See "Baptism," *Times and Seasons* 3 (September 1, 1842): 904. See also 1 Ne. 20:1. The same typological aspects of the ordinance of baptism are still at play today. See Rudolf Schnackenburg, *Baptism in the Thought of St. Paul: A Study in Pauline Theology* (Oxford: Blackwell, 1964), 30–61; Thiselton, *First Epistle*, 724–25 n. 29. In baptism the participant is bound up with those in whose name and through whose power the ordinance is performed. For Israel, the binding was with Moses. Indeed, Jehovah had made Moses "a god" to Pharaoh, with Aaron acting as prophet (Ex. 7:1). Thus,

10:3 *And did all eat the same spiritual meat / All of them ate the same spiritual food:* The noun βρῶμα (*brōma*), "food," denoted anything that was eaten.[12] Paul's allusion was to Exodus 16:13, 15–35 and Numbers 11:31–34, where Jehovah provided both quail and manna to sustain Israel during their forty-year journey. The adjective πνευματικός (*pneumatikos*), "spiritual," did not denote a nonphysical substance but rather an item provided by the Lord through miraculous means.[13]

10:4 *And did all drink the same spiritual drink / and all of them drank the same spiritual drink:* Paul's reference here is to Exodus 17:6 and Numbers 20:7–13, where Moses brought forth water by striking a rock. On the use of the adjective "spiritual," see 10:3.

for they drank of that spiritual Rock that followed them / for they were all drinking from that spiritual rock which was following them: Paul used the present participle, ἀκολουθούσης (*akolouthousēs*), "following," to describe the rock from which Moses struck water. According to Jewish legend, the rock somehow followed Israel, thus accounting for Moses' striking the rock twice—first in Horeb (Ex. 17:6) and then later at Meribah (Num. 20:7).[14] It is more likely, however, that Moses was inspired to use the same method on two different occasions to take care of Israel's needs. That Paul describes the Rock as "spiritual" suggests he was not talking of a physical stone at all but a miraculous event.

that Rock was Christ / that rock was Christ: Paul likely alluded here to Deuteronomy 32:4, 15, 18, 30–31. The Apostle's use of the imperfect verb ἦν (*ēn*), "was," suggests he was identifying Jehovah and Jesus as one and the same. The Hebrews did refer to Jehovah in his capacity as helper and aid as צוּר (*ṣūr*), "Rock" (Deut. 32:4, 15, 18, 30–31; 2 Sam. 22:3; Ps. 18:3). Compare Moses 7:53, where Jehovah is referred to as "the Rock of Heaven," alluding to "his eternal strength and stability."[15] This is one of several passages in the New Testament that shows that Christ was Jehovah of the Old Testament.[16]

Moses became a type for Jehovah. By joining the images of cloud, sea, and baptism, Paul tied together those aspects of the saving and redemptive powers of the Lord in which *all* of God's children participate, whether in the mosaic or apostolic dispensation.

12. BDAG, 184.

13. Fitzmyer, *First Corinthians*, 382–83.

14. See *Targum Onqelos* (Aramaic translation of Num. 21:17); midrash *Sipre* on Num. 11:21; for analysis, see Ellis, *Paul's Use of the Old Testament*, 66–70; and Peter Enns, *The Evolution of Adam* (Grand Rapids, Mich.: Brazos Press, 2012), 115–16.

15. *DNTC*, 2:355.

16. Another is Christ's statement to the Pharisees where he said, "Before Abraham was, I am," (John 8:58). This is a clear allusion to the passage in Ex. 3:13–14, "And Moses said

10:5 *But with many of them God was not well pleased: for they were overthrown in the wilderness* / *Nevertheless, God was not pleased with most of them, so they were struck down in the wilderness:* The phrase τοῖς πλείοσιν αὐτῶν (*tois pleiosin autōn*) denotes "the majority of them."[17] Due to their rebellion, God's favor was withdrawn from most of the Israelites. To highlight Paul's point, the contrastive ἀλλά (*alla*), "but," is translated as "nevertheless" in our Rendition.

The particle γάρ (*gar*) is here used as a marker of inference and is translated "so."[18] Coupled with the aorist passive verb κατεστρώθησαν (*katestrōthēsan*), "to be killed," it shows the result of Israel's rebellion.[19] The verb, in its metaphorical sense, looked less to the act and more to its consequences. The people were, indeed, killed but the focus is on their bodies, which were spread over a wide area. Paul's phrase presents a graphic if hyperbolic image of the corpses of the rebellious strewn across the wilderness.[20]

Analysis and Summary

Paul speaks of the Savior as being the spiritual meat, drink, and rock of Israel. In each case, the Apostle was using a metaphor or type.[21] Though he could be prefiguring baptism and the sacrament, his images should not be pressed too far.[22] It is more likely that he was referring to the shared events of which all Israel partook and that the Lord stood behind.

---

unto God, Behold, when I come unto the children of Israel, and shall say unto them, The God of your fathers hath sent me unto you; and they shall say to me, What is his name? what shall I say unto them? And God said unto Moses, I AM THAT I AM: and he said, Thus shalt thou say unto the children of Israel, I AM hath sent me unto you." In the LXX "I AM" is εἰμί (*eimi*) just as it is in John 8:58. It is clear that the Pharisees understood what he was saying because "then took they up stones to cast at him" (John 8:59). See also Isa. 43:11; 45:21; Mosiah 3:5; 5:2, 15; D&C 29:1; 38:1; 39:1.

17. BDAG, 848.

18. BDAG, 190.

19. BDAG, 528.

20. Louw-Nida, §20.63. In Jdt 7:14; 14:4; and 2 Macc. 5:26, the word is used to describe the result of the death of the rebellious Israelites.

21. Over the years there has been a good deal of scholarly debate on the Christology that comes from this verse. Some take the words "the rock was Christ" to mean that the "rock" was the premortal Christ, and others think that it symbolized the work of Christ, that is, it typified him as sustainer and nourisher. For analysis and summary, see Thiselton, *First Epistle,* 727–30. Because the issue tends to detract from Paul's point, we have simply taken "Rock" as a figure for the Savior and made it a proper noun in this volume, feeling it is the best option.

22. Hays, *Echoes of the Scriptures,* 91.

Elder McConkie, commenting on Paul's imagery, noted that "Christ is the bread which came down from heaven, the Bread of Life, the spiritual manna, of which men must eat to gain salvation. (John 6:31–58.) He is the spiritual drink, the living water, the water of life, which if men drink they shall never thirst more. (John 4:6–15.) He is the rock-foundation upon which all must build to gain an inheritance in his Father's kingdom. To eat of the bread and drink of the waters of life is to keep the commandments of God, which includes (as the Corinthians are here being counseled) the forsaking of all that is carnal and evil."[23]

To make his point, Paul lists the experience *all* Israel shared with Moses (he uses the word πάντες [*pantes*], "all," five times in the first four verses). They *all* enjoyed Jehovah's redemptive act in bringing them out from bondage by the power of God; they *all* enjoyed the guidance and protection of the cloud; they *all* passed through the Red Sea; *all* enjoyed the manna, quail, and water that God provided; and *all* entered into the covenant with their God. This covenant is unique in that it was communal rather than individual in nature.

Paul used the Exodus story as a paradigm for what God was doing for the Corinthian Saints. The Lord was bringing those who would hear out of sin and bondage to a new life in Christ.[24] But what was the result of Jehovah's attempt at redeeming his people Israel? Most turned from him and not only lost divine protection but their very lives. As a result, Paul notes, their corpses were scattered over the desert (10:5).[25]

It is important to note that Paul's appeal to the Exodus story, as the seat for the lesson the Christians were to learn, ties both the Old and New Testament together and legitimizes the lessons and doctrines found in the First Covenant. His use of the holy word here shows he does not quote scripture only when engaged in polemics against his detractors or as proof texts for some doctrinal point. His use here shows a deep and profound respect for the Old Testament as essential to understanding and properly interpreting the gospel of Christ.[26]

Given that the law of Moses was a preparatory gospel holding the keys of repentance and baptism (D&C 84:26–27), the faithful Israelites would have had the knowledge and authority to practice these things. The

---

23. *DNTC*, 2:355.
24. Thiselton, *First Epistle*, 724.
25. Fee, *First Epistle*, 450 and n. 41.
26. Thiselton, *First Epistle*, 718–19.

Corinthian Saints would have understood this. Therefore, Paul's reference to the Hebrews being "baptized unto Moses" would have been very persuasive to his audience who would have seen an analogy to their own baptism as an escape from the lusts of the world and entrance into God's kingdom on earth.[27]

PAUL'S APPLICATION—A WARNING AGAINST IDOLATRY (10:6–13)

Greek Text

6 Ταῦτα δὲ τύποι ἡμῶν ἐγενήθησαν, εἰς τὸ μὴ εἶναι ἡμᾶς ἐπιθυμητὰς κακῶν, καθὼς κἀκεῖνοι ἐπεθύμησαν. 7 μηδὲ εἰδωλολάτραι γίνεσθε, καθώς τινες αὐτῶν· ὥσπερ γέγραπται· Ἐκάθισεν ὁ λαὸς φαγεῖν καὶ πεῖν, καὶ ἀνέστησαν παίζειν. 8 μηδὲ πορνεύωμεν, καθώς τινες αὐτῶν ἐπόρνευσαν, καὶ ἔπεσαν μιᾷ ἡμέρᾳ εἴκοσι τρεῖς χιλιάδες. 9 μηδὲ ἐκπειράζωμεν τὸν Χριστόν, καθώς τινες αὐτῶν ἐπείρασαν, καὶ ὑπὸ τῶν ὄφεων ἀπώλλυντο. 10 μηδὲ γογγύζετε, καθάπερ τινὲς αὐτῶν ἐγόγγυσαν, καὶ ἀπώλοντο ὑπὸ τοῦ ὀλοθρευτοῦ. 11 ταῦτα δὲ τυπικῶς συνέβαινεν ἐκείνοις, ἐγράφη δὲ πρὸς νουθεσίαν ἡμῶν, εἰς οὓς τὰ τέλη τῶν αἰώνων κατήντηκεν. 12 ὥστε ὁ δοκῶν ἑστάναι βλεπέτω μὴ πέσῃ, 13 πειρασμὸς ὑμᾶς οὐκ εἴληφεν εἰ μὴ ἀνθρώπινος· πιστὸς δὲ ὁ θεός, ὃς οὐκ ἐάσει ὑμᾶς πειρασθῆναι ὑπὲρ ὃ δύνασθε, ἀλλὰ ποιήσει σὺν τῷ πειρασμῷ καὶ τὴν ἔκβασιν τοῦ δύνασθαι ὑπενεγκεῖν. [SBLGNT]

King James Version

6 Now these things were our examples, to the intent we should not lust after evil things, as they also lusted. 7 Neither be ye idolaters, as were some of them; as it is written, The people sat down to eat and drink, and rose up to play. 8 Neither let us commit fornication, as some of them committed, and fell in one day three and twenty thousand. 9 Neither let us tempt Christ, as some of them also tempted, and were destroyed of serpents. 10 Neither murmur ye, as some of them also murmured, and were

New Rendition

6 These things happened as an example for us, so that we would not crave evil things like they did. 7 So do not worship idols like some of them did, as it is written, "The people sat down to eat and drink, and got up to play." 8 We should not engage in illicit sex like some of them did, and twenty-three thousand of them were destroyed in a single day. 9 And we should not put Christ to the test like some of them did, and they were killed by snakes. 10 Do not murmur like some of them did, and they

---

27. *DNTC* 2:355.

destroyed of the destroyer. 11 Now all these things happened unto them for ensamples: and they are written for our admonition, upon whom the ends of the world are come. 12 Wherefore let him that thinketh he standeth take heed lest he fall. 13 There hath no temptation taken you but such as is common to man: but God is faithful, who will not suffer you to be tempted above that ye are able; but will with the temptation also make a way to escape, that ye may be able to bear it.

were killed by the Destroyer. 11 These things happened to serve as a warning to them, and they were written down as an admonition for us, on whom the end of the age has come. 12 And so anyone who thinks he is standing firm, let him beware that he does not fall. 13 No temptation has come upon you except that which is common to all mankind. But God can be trusted—he will not let you be tempted beyond that which you are able to overcome, but with that temptation he will provide a means of escape so that you will be able to endure.

Translation Notes and Comments

10:6 *Now these things were our examples / Theses things happened as an example for us:* The neuter plural adjective ταῦτα (*tauta*), "these things," refers to the events Paul just listed. The noun τύπος (*typos*), "type" or "example," also denotes a "pattern" or "formative model" from which lessons are to be gleaned.[28]

to the intent we should not lust after evil things, as they also lusted / so that we would not crave evil things like they did: With this phrase, Paul begins his list of sins that caused the Israelites to lose divine favor. The noun ἐπιθυμητής (*epithymētēs*) denoted "one who desires," in a pejorative sense.[29] The KJV translation of the word with the very negative connotation of "lust" could express this nuance if broadened beyond its sexual aspect.[30] Since "crave" more precisely updates the idea, it is used in our Rendition.

The nominally used adjective κακῶν (*kakōn*), "evil things," denoted not only that which is bad or immoral but also that which is harmful and injurious to self and others.[31] Israel's expression of such wants through actions provoked God's wrath and brought condemnation upon those who did the harm. The lesson for the Christians should have been clear.

---

28. Louw-Nida, §58.58, 59; G. Schunack, "τύπος," in *Exegetical Dictionary of the New Testament,* ed. Gerhard Schneider and Horst Balz, trans. James W. Thompson, 3 vols. (Grand Rapids, Mich.: Eerdmans, 1990–93), 3:374.

29. BDAG, 372.

30. BDAG, 371–72; Louw-Nida, §25.13.

31. BDAG, 501; Louw-Nida, §88.106.

10:7 *Neither be ye idolaters, as were some of them / So do not worship idols like some of them did:* With this phrase, Paul lists the second of Israel's sins. They were εἰδωλολάτραι (*eidōlolatrai*), "idol worshipers," those who worship false gods.[32] The operative word here is "worship." Idolatry is not passive. It is giving homage to and putting trust in things other than the Lord. Among the Israelites, it acted as a no-confidence vote in, if not an act to humiliate, Jehovah. Further, some of the more extreme forms of idolatry included acts very repugnant to Jehovah such as human sacrifices and immoral practices.[33]

as it is written, The people sat down to eat and drink, and rose up to play / as it is written, "The people sat down to eat and drink, and got up to play": To make his point, Paul quotes from LXX Exodus 32:1–6, wherein Israel worshiped the golden calf. They sat down φαγεῖν καὶ πεῖν (*phagein kai pein*), "to eat and drink." The phrase carries the idea of participating in a cultic meal. Afterwards, they ἀνέστησαν παίζειν (*anestēsan paizein*), "rose up to play." It is difficult to translate the infinitive *paizein*, "to play," as used in the story. The verb παίζω (*paizō*) means, simply, "to play" or "amuse oneself,"[34] but the semantic range also includes "to sport, to jest, to joke, to dance and sing" and also "to play amorously."[35] The Hebrew verb it is the translation of, צָחַק (*siḥēq*), includes the idea not only of sporting and dancing but also of practicing sexual license.[36] The point of the story seems to be that the Israelites abandoned the ethical restraints and sober self-control that God demanded of his people and gave themselves over to the revelry and unbridled self-indulgence that idolatry not only allowed but fostered.[37] This was the means by which they worshiped the false god.

10:8 *Neither let us commit fornication, as some of them committed / We should not engage in illicit sex like some of them did:* Here Paul lists the third sin of which some Israelites were guilty. On πορνεία (*porneia*), "illicit sex," see Translation Notes on 5:1. While, in Paul's context, the word παίζω (*paizō*) probably connoted sexual license on a community level, *porneia* did so on an individual level.

and fell in one day three and twenty thousand / and twenty-three thousand of them were destroyed in a single day: Paul's reference is to

---

32. BDAG, 280.
33. For example, see Abr. 1:11–12.
34. BDAG, 750.
35. LSJ, 1109.
36. BDB, 850; TWOT, 1905.
37. Thiselton, *First Epistle*, 734–36.

Numbers 25:1–9, where twenty-four thousand Israelites died of plague for participating in the sensual rites of Baal-Peor. The number Paul used is mystifying since it is a thousand short of that given in the Old Testament. The Apostle may have misremembered, confusing it with Numbers 26:62 that records the number of Levites as twenty-three thousand. There is, however, no sure answer.[38]

10:9 *Neither let us tempt Christ, as some of them also tempted, and were destroyed of serpents / And we should not put Christ to the test like some of them did, and they were killed by snakes:* The manuscript tradition is varied here with some texts replacing the word Χριστός (*Christos*), "Christ," with either κύριος (*kyrios*), "Lord," or θεός (*theos*), "God." The KJV reading, however, is the more likely and is followed in our Rendition for two reasons: First, the greatest number of manuscripts support the reading of "Christ," and second, it is likely that various copyists, believing Jehovah and Jesus to be two separate beings, sought to correct the text by substituting either of the two alternatives.[39] It is notable that during what Latter-day Saints refer to as "the Apostasy" some copyists seem to have tried to change the text to conform to their notions of the nature of God. These variants provide evidence for an apostasy or rebellion against the gospel of Jesus Christ. Revelation 22:18, although directed specifically to the book of Revelation, certainly forewarned these copyists about adding or taking away from any of the biblical text.

In this verse, Paul lists the fourth sin of which the ancient Israelites were guilty—testing the Lord. Paul's warning comes from the story in Numbers 21:4–6, where the people continued to cast doubt on the ability of the Lord to save them. The imperfect passive verb Paul used, ἀπώλλυντο (*apōllynto*), meant to be destroyed or suffer destruction,[40] and it revealed God's response to Israel's faithlessness. He sent "fiery serpents among the people," causing many to die.

The active verb ἐκπειράζω (*ekpeirazō*), "to try" or "to test," means more than testing someone's nature or character by putting them through a trial. The prepositional prefix ἐκ- (*ek-*) pushes the idea to "trying thoroughly"

---

38. Fee, *First Epistle*, 456. Numbers in antiquity were never expected to be precise. For example, a myriad or ten thousand in ancient Greek often meant "too many to count." Most classicists believe that the majority of numbers reported in Greco-Roman texts are purposely exaggerated.

39. Metzger, *Textual Commentary*, 494.

40. BDAG, 115–16; Findlay, "St. Paul's First Epistle," 861, translates the word very graphically as "lay a-perishing."

or "to the upmost."[41] Such an act on the Israelites' part was nothing short of hubris considering Jehovah's display of power in bringing them out of Egypt. But these faithless people continually insisted that God prove himself to the point that they provoked him to wrath. Paul's use of the hortatory subjunctive case with the negative, connective particle μηδέ (*mēde*), "and not," could be translated as "let us not continue to test Christ," suggesting that the Corinthian Saints were already pushing their relationship with him.[42]

10:10 *Neither murmur ye, as some of them also murmured, and were destroyed of the destroyer / Do not murmur like some of them did, and they were killed by the Destroyer:* Here Paul lists that last of Israel's sins, which was, unfortunately, also common in the Corinthian branch. The verb γογγύζω (*gongyzō*), "murmur," carries the idea of griping, complaining, and whining.[43] The context of Israel's wilderness journey, however, suggests that Paul's use of the word did not describe petty bickering, but expressed a constant, unrelenting, querulous griping. Their complaining revealed the depth to which the Israelites saw themselves as being victimized by God. Their unrelenting murmuring actually evidenced a keen distrust in Jehovah, which raised his ire. That resulted in their destruction. The agent was ὁ ὀλοθρευτής (*ho olothreutēs*), "the destroyer."[44] The imagery comes from Exodus 12:23, where "the destroyer" passed over the Hebrew homes while striking those of the Egyptians. The word may have referred to a destroying angel who executed the divine sentence of punishment upon the recalcitrant Israelites (see 1 Chr. 21:15) or even to Satan.[45] Since the agent is vague, "destroyer" seems the best and, therefore, our Rendition follows the KJV but makes the word a proper noun.

10:11 *Now all these things happened unto them for ensamples / These things happened to serve as a warning to them:* The adjective πάντα (*panta*), "all," is found in some ancient manuscripts. Because it shows up in various positions and not in most of the best representatives, it is likely a gloss and, therefore, our Rendition does not use it.[46] The imperfect verb συνέβαινεν (*synebainen*), "happened," carries the idea of events occurring

---

41. Louw-Nida, §27.46; Findlay, "St. Paul's First Epistle," 860.
42. Thiselton, *First Epistle,* 740.
43. BDAG, 204.
44. BDAG, 703.
45. Louw-Nida, §20.36 with n. 5. The cognate ὄλεθρος (*olethros*) suggests a ruin or destruction that is quite violent and extensive.
46. Metzger, *Textual Commentary,* 494.

in order, one following the next. The adverb τυπικῶς (*typikōs*) means "as a type, example or warning."[47] Paul's phrase shows that God designed the successive events the Israelites went through to shape their faith in him and to teach them proper conduct as a covenant people. These experiences were *their* formative models from which they were to draw life's lessons.

they are written for our admonition / they were written down as an admonition for us: The lessons these events taught, however, were not only for the Hebrews but also for Gentiles and future generations. The noun νουθεσία (*nouthesia*) denotes counsel given to stop an improper course of action; thus, the word can be understood as an "admonition" or "warning."[48] Paul's point was that the Old Testament was not written merely as a history, but as a guide, warning, and admonition for later generations.

the ends of the world are come / the end of the age has come: The phrase τὰ τέλη τῶν αἰώνων κατήντηκεν (*ta telē tōn aiōnōn katēntēken*) presents some challenges in translating. Although *telē* is plural in form, it can have the singular sense of "end." The noun *aiōnōn,* also plural in form, likewise carries a singular sense, so that the phrase is best understood as "the end of the age."[49] Thus, Paul seems to be referring to the imminent apostasy as he does elsewhere in this and other epistles attributed to him.[50]

The JST changes this phrase to read, "And they were written for our admonition also, and for an admonition for those upon whom the end of the world shall come." The change suggests that the lessons and warnings coming out of the wilderness wanderings have universal application and should stand as a warning for those living not just in Paul's day but in the last days as well.

10:12 ***Wherefore let him that thinketh he standeth take heed lest he fall / And so anyone who thinks he is standing firm, let him beware that he does not fall:*** Here Paul makes his point. The sting is in his words ὁ δοκῶν ἑστάναι (*ho dokōn hestanai*), "he who thinks he stands." The perfect infinitive, *estanai,* means "to stand firm" or "to stand fast." The participial phrase *ho dokōn,* "he who thinks," denotes a sureness that amounts to cockiness.[51] It hints at an insolent pride. In this case, the pride-based sureness comes from the attitude of the Corinthian "strong" that God will not let them fall

---

47. BDAG, 1019.
48. BDAG, 679.
49. BDAG, 33.
50. See Translation Notes on 7:26.
51. Conzelmann, *1 Corinthians,* 168.

even when they place themselves in spiritual danger. The problem was that their "knowledge" was illusory and deceptive because it was based on a wrong understanding of the Atonement and its results.[52] Their problem was that they did not actually believe in God, but rather in their own understanding of him and his dealings with them.[53] Based on their false theology, they *knew* that they could not fall from grace no matter what they did. Such presumption and arrogance, Paul warned, would lead to a hard fall out of grace, the Lord not long abiding such pride. Paul's Gentiles should have understood that χάρις (*charis*), "grace," implied an obligation on the receiver's part. All Christians, whether Jew or Gentile, should have understood the covenant connection and the attendant obligation. To break covenant was to forfeit the gift of the Atonement and fall from grace.

10:13 *There hath no temptation taken you but such as is common to man / No temptation has come upon you except that which is common to all mankind:* The key word in translating this verse is the noun πειρασμός (*peirasmos*), "trial" or "temptation." Taking the word in context, "temptation" works best, but it is important to keep in mind the word's broader semantic range that includes both the concept of temptation *and* trial. For Paul, sin springs from an improper stand, attitude, or orientation. The Apostle had already shown that the sins of Israel he listed were based on ἐπιθυμία (*epithymia*), "craving," for that which was forbidden. The position of the Corinthian "strong" was dictated by those things that drew, beguiled, or seduced them.[54] Primary among these, as Paul could see, was a false superior "knowledge" that justified and fed the attitude and conduct that they craved and which they had to give up.

The perfect active verb εἴληφεν (*eilēphen*), from λαμβάνω (*lambanō*), has a wide semantic range, including "has taken hold of" and "has experienced."[55] But here the nuance that best fits is "to have been exploited by deception,"[56] much like the colloquial English "he was really taken in." By using the perfect tense, Paul is telling his readers that they, neither now nor any time in the past, have been exploited by undue pressure from temptation.[57] They are not, nor have they ever been, the prey of any sin. They not only have

---

52. Thiselton, *First Epistle,* 747.

53. Barth, *Resurrection of the Dead,* 17.

54. Thiselton, *First Epistle,* 747.

55. BDAG, 583–85.

56. Louw-Nida, §88.146.

57. The perfect portrays a past action, the consequences of which reach into the present. See Wallace, *Greek Grammar,* 572–73.

their agency but also the standards set by the Church. Further, their temptations are neither stronger nor more seductive than those which everyone else faces. The "strong" may have felt that because of their social status in Corinth they were unusually pressured to attend pagan feasts and festivals. Such demands may have caused them to feel that they made up a special class that, as one scholar noted, "influenced or educated people often claim for themselves."[58] Paul refused to let them see themselves as victims. They were not in a special class. Pressures on them were no greater than those on any of their Christian peers.

but God is faithful, who will not suffer you to be tempted above that ye are able / But God can be trusted—he will not let you be tempted beyond that which you are able to overcome: The word order, πιστὸς δὲ ὁ θεός (*pistos de ho theos*), "God is faithful," is emphatic, putting stress on the adjective "faithful." The Corinthian Saints can have complete trust in God because of his faithfulness in keeping covenants.[59] The verb ἐάω (*eaō*), "to allow, permit," shows that God will always act in the manner specified.[60] The verb δύναμαι (*dynamai*), "to be able," "to have strength," or "to have capacity," carries the idea of being able to carry a task to conclusion.[61] In this case, Paul assures the Corinthian "strong" that God will put a damper on any temptation such that they can resist it if they will.

but will with the temptation also make a way to escape, that ye may be able to bear it / but with that temptation he will provide a means of escape so that you will be able to endure: The preposition σύν (*syn*), "with," is important here. God's means of escape does not come *after* the temptation appears, but simultaneously *with it.* In other words, one does not endure the temptation only later to find escape and relief; both are there from the beginning. If a person does yield to temptation, it is because he or she has not taken advantage of the escape God has or will provide. The verb ὑποφέρω (*hypopherō*), "to bear up under," describes a major way God provides for his people to escape their trials: He gives them the strength to bear them.

---

58. Thiselton, *First Epistle,* 748.

59. In the LXX this construction appears only twice (Deut. 7:9; 34:4), both in connection with the covenant between Jehovah and his people. See Gardner, *Gifts of God,* 154.

60. Wallace, *Greek Grammar,* 586.

61. BDAG, 261–62.

Analysis and Summary

The noun "type" connotes, in modern English, a paradigm or model that can be construed as either an example or a warning.[62] That fits well with the Greek word τύπος (*typos*, "type") that Paul used. For him the word connoted an archetype (usually an Old Testament person or event) that served as a formative model or pattern that the Christian was either to follow or avoid.[63] When construed as an example, the lamb slain in many Jewish temple sacrifices (see Lev. 1–5) was a type, that is, a pattern of the Atonement of Christ. When construed as a warning, the rebellion of Korah (Num. 16; 26:9–11) served as an example for what happens when a people challenge God's authority. It was in this way that Paul used events in the Exodus story. These events played a role in both character and concept formation by acting as windows to show how God deals with his people. There is a mutual interlinking of past and present events, each sharing a commonality through the dealings of Jehovah with Israel now revealed in the actions and words of his mortal form, Jesus Christ. Paul used each paradigm to reveal what conditions were actually like and, thus, gave his readers a clear understanding of what had happened so that they could see parallels to their own condition and respond accordingly.[64]

Without hesitation, Paul applied the Exodus story to the situation in which the Corinthian Saints found themselves. In doing so, he acknowledged that the God of the Old Testament was the same as that of the New.[65] That being the case, the Corinthian Saints could expect a similar action in response to a similar sin.

---

62. For example, the KJV, NIV, and NRSV translate the word as "example," while the REB translates it as "warning." The word τύπος (*typos*) can be translated directly as "type," but because that word, along with "typology," is used today by scholars as a technical term associated with the field of hermeneutics, we have chosen other words (pattern, model, example, or warning) that we feel best fits with Paul's intended use. For references on the subject, see Patrick Fairbairn, *The Typology of Scripture* (Edinburgh: T. and T. Clark, 1947); Leonhard Goppelt, *Typos: The Typology Interpretation of the Old Testament in the New* (Grand Rapids, Mich.: Eerdmans, 1982); and Peter Martens, "Revisiting the Allegory/Typology Distinction: The Case of Origen," *Journal of Early Christian Studies* 16 (2008): 283–317.

63. BDAG, 1020.

64. Gardner, *Gifts of God,* 113; Thiselton, *First Epistle,* 732.

65. The early Church Fathers, fighting against Marcionism, were careful to show that, for Paul, the God of Moses and the God of the Christians were one and the same. For example, see Irenaeus, *Haer.* 4.27.1–4.

Illustrating this idea, one LDS scholar noted that Paul "drew numerous parallels between the life, ministry, and death of Jesus and the Exodus story. . . . Additionally, he emphasized that the children of Israel's experiences were preserved as an example for us . . . (1 Corinthians 10:1–11). . . . As the children of Israel made their escape from Egypt through the Red Sea, we escape the world symbolically through the waters of baptism." This scholar went on to say that, additionally, the Red Sea "could be analogous to the blood of the Lamb which washes us from our sins." He noted further that after the children of Israel's escape through the sea, they were "led in the wilderness by a pillar of fire and a cloud. These elements are not only symbolic of God's presence but for the modern Saint are representative of the promise of the Father: the baptism of fire and of the Holy Ghost received as a gift from God following baptism (see Matthew 3:11)." He concluded, "The Holy Ghost is given as a comforter and a testifier but also as a guide leading us toward truth, as it says in scripture: 'He will guide you into all truth' (John 16:13). Telestial existence into a terrestrial existence spiritually prepares us to enter into the celestial kingdom. While in the wilderness, the faithful are nourished with living water and with the bread of life, just as ancient Israel's thirst was relieved when Moses struck the rock and water gushed forth and just as the children of Israel received manna for bread from heaven (see John 4:6–14, 6:31–35)."[66]

Paul emphasized those events in which all Israel had a share. Among these were partaking of the same "meat" and "drink." Likewise, the Corinthian Saints had shared together the joy and benefits of the same baptism and the sacrament that renewed their covenant. This experience should have brought them into a unity of the faith, but due to factions, it did not. Paul, therefore, gave them a stiff warning. It was couched in Jehovah's actions toward wayward Israel. The Christians, through Christ, enjoyed the same sort of benefits the ancient Hebrews did. But these benefits did not secure a single Israelite from losing his or her blessings and perishing in the wilderness. Paul's moral corollary was that the Corinthian Saints must follow God's way or lose their blessings as well.[67]

This is a doctrinal point that must be stressed. For Paul, rebellion was a special and abhorrent kind of sin. It constituted a Christian returning to his precovenantal ways. The Apostle's reference in 10:6 to "evil things" (κακά,

66. Richard Neitzel Holzapfel, *The Exodus Story: Ancient and Modern Parallels* (Salt Lake City: Bookcraft, 1997), 40–41, 56–57.

67. Fee, *First Epistle*, 448; Witherington, *Conflict and Community*, 219.

kaka) meant more than eating idol meats, but looked to an inordinate desire (ἐπιθυμέω, *epithymeō*) for former activities and associations forbidden by gospel covenant. Some in Paul's audience seem to have felt that election allowed them total freedom to do as they pleased. The Apostle shows clearly that, though "all" of Israel became an elected people and shared in great blessings and promises, some—indeed, most—rebelled and stepped outside the protection of the covenant and thereby lost their divine status, as evidenced by their dying in the wilderness. That principle was still applicable in Paul's day (and in ours). The Corinthian Saints could not count on their election as a preventative against judgment. Indeed, yielding to the enticing of "evil things" would result in their rejection and spiritual death. The lesson was clear: God can guarantee a corporate reward, but a rebellious subgroup or individual therein can fall. As the Lord has said to his modern Saints, speaking of the Church, he was "pleased, speaking . . . collectively and not individually—For . . . the Lord cannot look upon sin with the least degree of allowance" (D&C 1:30–31).

Paul's warning was very clear: those who committed offences to the point that they incurred God's wrath would lose not only their station but also their spiritual life. Seen in this light, Paul alleviates the tension between election, predestination, and perseverance on the one hand and rebellion and divine judgment on the other. He did this by revealing that the divine guarantee applies *only* on the corporate level, not on the individual level.[68]

Paul's warning came in large part because of the "cravings" of the Corinthian "strong" to participate in temple sacral feasts. Such participation, however, amounted to nothing short of idolatry.[69] For the Apostle, there is a strong correlation between ἐπιθυμία (*epithymia*), "inordinate desire" or "craving," and the kind of sin that alienates a person from God. This kind of sin does not include acts that fail to conform to a moral code or to religious

---

68. B. J. Oropeza, *Paul and Apostasy: Eschatology, Perseverance, and Falling Away in the Corinthian Congregation* (Tübingen: Mohr Siebeck, 2000), 223–29. A modern example would be the promise that the gospel will remain on the earth and the Latter-day Church will never fall. See Milton R. Hunter, *The Gospel through the Ages* (Salt Lake City: Deseret Book, 1945), 93; Hoyt W. Brewster Jr., *Behold, I Come Quickly: The Last Days and Beyond* (Salt Lake City: Deseret Book, 1999), 71–72. That assurance does not, however, pertain to individuals who must "endure to the end" in order to receive eternal life (D&C 14:7; 50:5; 66:12).

69. G. D. Collier, "'That We Might Not Crave Evil': The Structure and Argument in 1 Cor 10:1–12," *Journal for the Study of the New Testament* 55 (1994): 55–75.

or social norms, though these can be serious. Rather, they reflect a distrust in God resulting in an ill reverence toward him. Such persons seek not to do God's will but to please their peers and betters, often hoping for one of two results: either being held in high esteem by them or gaining greater power over them. The whole intent is driven by a craving to be at the center of all that happens. That craving carries with it a willingness to use all the means necessary to get there.[70]

The specific problems that the Apostle saw as parallels between the Hebrews and the Corinthian "strong" were trying the Lord's patience, fornication, and murmuring. It is of note that two of these sins flowed from ἐπιθυμία (*epithymia*), "craving," or "lusting" for the forbidden, evidenced by their participating in both idolatry and immorality. But fostering these two sins led to another sin—that of presumption. The Corinthian "strong" felt that they were immune from the spiritual dangers concomitant with pagan feasts. Their presumptuous attitude did nothing less than put God's love, grace, and long suffering sorely to the test by insisting that he would preserve them when they knowingly entered into spiritually dangerous activities. Their actions reflected an overconfident stance in the superior "knowledge" (γνῶσις, *gnōsis,* see 8:1) that they mistakenly felt they had. The result was a false security that would all too soon prove fickle and turn to their hurt. Therefore, it had to be abandoned.[71]

But there was yet another sin undergirding these, both feeding and directing them. As two LDS scholars have clearly identified, Paul "seems to imply that the issue is actually pride: 'Wherefore, let him that thinketh he standeth take heed lest he fall' (10:12)."[72] Paul's warning here tacitly reflects the one he gave in 4:6–19: the dangerous results of being "puffed up" (φυσιόω, *physioō*) due to pride which characterized these people (see Translation Notes on 4:6).

It needs to be stressed that Paul's concern was not with eating meat that came from pagan temples. It was with participating in pagan cultic rites. Some of the Corinthian "strong," not wishing to appear unfriendly, overly scrupulous, or even bigoted, may readily have joined in certain cultic functions. They may have rationalized that since "we all know that God is one" (8:3–6), any religious service was but homage to the universal Father of

---

70. Wolfhart Pannenberg, *Systematic Theology,* trans. Geoffrey W. Bromiley, vol. 2 (Grand Rapids, Mich.: Eerdmans, 2013), 241–43.

71. Witherington, *Conflict and Community,* 220; Jürgen Moltmann, *Theology of Hope,* trans. James W. Leitch (London: SCM Press, 1967), 21.

72. Holzapfel and Wayment, *Making Sense,* 356.

all who manifested himself with many faces. After all, they may have reasoned, Paul himself taught that the Christians were not to withdraw from the world.[73]

For Paul, however, the source of these activities was derived from hell itself (see Translation Notes on 10:20–21) and God had no place in any of it. As a student of the Old Testament, Paul believed that idols had no real existence, but they did represent baleful, demonic powers that provided religious sanction for all kinds of misconduct and wishful indulgence. What the Apostle did was present his readers with a scriptural tradition that demanded covenantal loyalty to the one God. His position excelled Greco-Roman "religiosity" with its many forms, centering as it did on "Christ, and him crucified" (2:2).[74]

Paul nullified the possible excuse of the "strong" that they were in an unusually difficult position that other members did not face by assuring them that "no temptation has come upon you except that which is common to all mankind. But God can be trusted—he will not let you be tempted beyond that which you are able to overcome" (10:13, Rendition). Thus, the "strong" could not claim special privilege or play the "victim" game. He assured them that God, who has ever been faithful in his assistance to his children, will continue to be so. God never leaves his people to face impossible odds. Though he does not remove temptations, he does provide a means of overcoming them. Faithfulness on the part of the Saint is not to expect trials to be eliminated, but to take advantage of the escape God provides. As an example, it would be wise for a Saint not to place herself or himself in a position where her or his values could be compromised. Refusing to go to a bar or partaking of an alcoholic beverage precludes one from ever becoming an alcoholic. Further, keeping the Word of Wisdom (see D&C 89) guards against addiction to nicotine or other drugs. But in addition, God can and will militate against the power of temptation so that it is not beyond the believer's capacity to resist. This action of divine grace is part of the blessings of the Atonement.[75]

Addressing this subject, Elder Joseph B. Wirthlin stated:

> I suppose some of you, at one time or another, feel that you are "hitting the wall" [an analogy taken from running a marathon], feeling an almost compelling urge to quit, give up, or give in to temptation. You will meet challenges, adversities, and temptations that seem to be more than you

---

73. Thiselton, *First Epistle,* 737.

74. Thiselton, *First Epistle,* 737.

75. Thiselton, *First Epistle,* 749.

can bear. In times of sickness, death, financial need, and other hardships, you may wonder whether you have the strength, courage, or ability to continue.

You young people face the same temptations that have been common throughout history, plus many others that were unknown to earlier generations. However, be sure you understand that God will not allow you to be tempted beyond your ability to resist. (See 1 Cor. 10:13.) He does not give you challenges that you cannot surmount. He will not ask more than you can do, but may ask right up to your limits so you can prove yourselves. The Lord will never forsake or abandon anyone. You may abandon him, but he will not abandon you. You never need to feel that you are alone.[76]

Paul's understanding that temptations are part of the human experience acts in a twofold way. First, it rejects any special pleading that the Corinthian "strong" may try to use to excuse themselves. Paul stresses that their temptations are not so unusually potent or overpowering that they cannot be resisted. The Apostle gives three reasons for this: (1) All suffer temptation, some of which can be very trying and, therefore, are not unique to any one class or party; (2) God, when necessary, will extend his grace, empowering the individual to resist; and (3) God will prepare a way for their escape. Second, understanding the universality of temptations could comfort the Corinthian "weak," assuring them that their seeming weaknesses, self-doubt, and station is not a handicap. They can overcome because their temptations are no greater than those of others, and God will allow neither their station nor their disadvantages to limit his grace toward them.[77]

In sum, what Paul has done in these verses is return to the promise he made to the Saints in the introduction of the epistle. There he assured his readers that God "will also strengthen you until the end, so that you will be found blameless in the day of our Lord, Jesus Christ," and why? Because "God is faithful, who has called you to fellowship with his Son" (1:8–9, Rendition). The Father can be relied on. Though trials are to be endured, not side stepped, God is ever there. Even Paul had to put up with what he called "a thorn in the flesh," but God reassured him with the words, "My grace is sufficient for thee: for my strength is made perfect in weakness" (2 Cor. 12:7, 9). One of the major ways the Lord does this is by giving the Saint the ability to bear up under (ὑποφέρω, *hypopherō*) the stress. We see this power in his dealing with the people of Alma. Placed under the

---

76. Joseph B. Wirthlin, "Running Your Marathon," *Ensign* 19 (November 1989): 75.
77. Gardner, *Gifts of God,* 155.

unrelenting cruelty of Amulon and his cohorts, the Lord reassured Alma when he said, "I know of the covenant which ye have made unto me; and I will covenant with my people and deliver them out of bondage. And I will also ease the burdens which are put upon your shoulders, . . . even while you are in bondage . . . that ye may know of a surety that I, the Lord God, do visit my people in their afflictions" (Mosiah 24:13–14). He has promised his modern Saints that he knows "the weakness of man and how to succor them who are tempted" (D&C 62:1).

THE PROHIBITION AGAINST ATTENDING PAGAN TEMPLE FEASTS (10:14–22)

Greek Text

14 Διόπερ, ἀγαπητοί μου, φεύγετε ἀπὸ τῆς εἰδωλολατρίας. 15 ὡς φρονίμοις λέγω· κρίνατε ὑμεῖς ὅ φημι. 16 τὸ ποτήριον τῆς εὐλογίας ὃ εὐλογοῦμεν, οὐχὶ κοινωνία ἐστὶν τοῦ αἵματος τοῦ Χριστοῦ; τὸν ἄρτον ὃν κλῶμεν, οὐχὶ κοινωνία τοῦ σώματος τοῦ Χριστοῦ ἐστιν; 17 ὅτι εἷς ἄρτος, ἓν σῶμα οἱ πολλοί ἐσμεν, οἱ γὰρ πάντες ἐκ τοῦ ἑνὸς ἄρτου μετέχομεν. 18 βλέπετε τὸν Ἰσραὴλ κατὰ σάρκα· οὐχ οἱ ἐσθίοντες τὰς θυσίας κοινωνοὶ τοῦ θυσιαστηρίου εἰσίν; 19 τί οὖν φημι; ὅτι εἰδωλόθυτόν τί ἐστιν, ἢ ὅτι εἴδωλόν τί ἐστιν; 20 ἀλλ' ὅτι ἃ θύουσιν, δαιμονίοις καὶ οὐ θεῷ θύουσιν, οὐ θέλω δὲ ὑμᾶς κοινωνοὺς τῶν δαιμονίων γίνεσθαι. 21 οὐ δύνασθε ποτήριον κυρίου πίνειν καὶ ποτήριον δαιμονίων· οὐ δύνασθε τραπέζης κυρίου μετέχειν καὶ τραπέζης δαιμονίων. 22 ἢ παραζηλοῦμεν τὸν κύριον; μὴ ἰσχυρότεροι αὐτοῦ ἐσμεν; [SBLGNT]

King James Version

14 Wherefore, my dearly beloved, flee from idolatry. 15 I speak as to wise men; judge ye what I say. 16 The cup of blessing which we bless, is it not the communion of the blood of Christ? The bread which we break, is it not the communion of the body of Christ? 17 For we being many are one bread, and one body: for we are all partakers of that one bread. 18 Behold Israel after the flesh: are not they which eat of the

New Rendition

14 For this very reason, my dear friends, flee from the worship of idols. 15 I am speaking to you as sensible people. Carefully consider what I am saying. 16 The cup of blessing that we bless, isn't it a sharing in the blood of Christ? And the bread that we break, isn't it a sharing of the body of Christ? 17 Because there is one loaf of bread, we, who are many, are one body, for we all share in that one loaf of bread. 18 Consider the people of

sacrifices partakers of the altar? 19 What say I then? that the idol is any thing, or that which is offered in sacrifice to idols is any thing? 20 But I say, that the things which the Gentiles sacrifice, they sacrifice to devils, and not to God: and I would not that ye should have fellowship with devils. 21 Ye cannot drink the cup of the Lord, and the cup of devils: ye cannot be partakers of the Lord's table, and of the table of devils. 22 Do we provoke the Lord to jealousy? are we stronger than he?

Israel. Aren't those who eat the sacrifices partners with the altars? 19 What am I implying? That food offered to idols is anything or that an idol itself is anything? 20 No. I am saying that what they offer on the altar, "they offer to demons and not to God," and I don't want you to be partners with demons. 21 You cannot drink both the cup of the Lord and the cup of demons. You cannot participate in the Lord's supper and the supper of demons. 22 What! Shall we provoke the Lord to jealousy? We are certainly not stronger than him, are we?

Translation Notes and Comments

10:14 *Wherefore, my dearly beloved, flee from idolatry / For this very reason, my dear friends, flee from the worship of idols:* The conjunction διόπερ (*dioper*), "therefore, for this very reason," is important here, serving as a marker of result that Paul does not want his readers to miss. It shows that all can do as he now requests. Paul's use of the affectionate ἀγαπητοί (*agapētoi*), "dear friends," could have served to disarm his readers and make them more amenable to his plea. Though the verb φεύγω (*pheugō*) carries the nuance of "eluding or avoiding danger," the force of Paul's warning is best served by translating it as "flee," as in both the KJV and our Rendition.[78]

10:15 *I speak as to wise men; judge ye what I say / I am speaking to you as sensible people. Carefully consider what I am saying:* The phrase ὡς φρονίμοις (*hōs phronimois*), "as to wise [people]," is often translated as "people of discernment."[79] Paul's use of the term suggests a vote of confidence in these people, who he now asks to use their common sense in judging the case he has presented and the case he will next present. Paul is asking the people to carefully consider the points he has and will make.

10:16 *The cup of blessing which we bless / The cup of blessing that we bless:* Paul's reference to τὸ ποτήριον τῆς εὐλογίας (*to potērion tēs eulogias*), "the cup of blessing," is problematic in that the phrase is found nowhere else in the New Testament. While its roots are common, scholars are unsure what nuances it may have had in antiquity. The phrase most

---

78. BDAG, 1052.
79. Thiselton, *First Epistle*, 755.

probably referred to an aspect of the sacramental meal celebrated weekly by the early Christians as part of their *agapē* feasts. The term was likely related to some aspect of the Last Supper, a Seder meal celebrating Israel's exodus from Egypt, in which the Savior drew attention to a cup of wine, explaining that from that point on it symbolized first, the blood he shed for his people, and second, the renewal of the new covenant he had established (Matt. 26:27–28; Mark 14:23–24; Luke 22:20–21).[80] But in the full Christian context, the act represented more than the point of transition between old and new covenants. Paul's phrase emphasized the godward nature of the blessing and, therefore, his words can be understood to mean, "The cup over which the blessing is spoken," suggesting that a sacramental prayer was given over the wine.[81]

is it not the communion of the blood of Christ?/ isn't it a sharing in the blood of Christ?: The heart of the Apostle's question is in the noun κοινωνία (*koinōnia*). The word is related to κοινωνός (*koinōnos*), denoting a person who shares something in common with another, thus, "a companion" or "partner."[82] The word *koinōnia* referred to that kind of fellowship, but in a religious sense, it is sometimes translated as "communion" as in the KJV and is described as a sharing of a spiritual connection and communication that transcends words.[83] It connoted a covenant relationship designed to bring about a most intimate and close association between parties. Such an association was made possible only through the Atonement of Christ. Paul's phrase points not only to the horizontal relationships enjoyed by those in the community of the Saints but also to the vertical one in which

---

80. Because this section, along with 11:19–22, gives readers a view into Paul's understanding of the meaning of the sacrament, it has received a great deal of attention. On the LDS side, see *DNTC*, 1:718–24; 2:358–59; Janne M. Sjodahl and George Reynolds, *Commentary on the Book of Mormon*, 4 vols. (Salt Lake City: Deseret Book, 1959), 4:368–72. Among those who see Paul using the term "cup of blessing" as referring to the Seder meal, there is some debate as to whether the term alluded to the third or fourth cup of wine. For discussion, see I. Howard Marshall, *Last Supper and the Lord's Supper* (Grand Rapids, Mich.: Eerdmans, 1980), 57–75; Joachim Jeremias, *Eucharistic Words of Jesus*, 3d ed. (London: SCM Press, 1966), 15–88; for comments, see Fitzmyer, *First Corinthians*, 390; Robertson and Plummer, *Critical and Exegetical Commentary*, 211. For a summary, see Thiselton, *First Epistle*, 757–60.

81. Meyer, *Exegetical Commentary*, 1:295. For a discussion of the history of sacramental services in Christianity, see Richard Lloyd Anderson, "Religious Validity: The Sacrament Covenant in Third Nephi," in *By Study and Also by Faith*, ed. Stephen D. Ricks and John M. Lundquist, 2 vols. (Salt Lake City: Deseret Book, 1990), 2:21–30.

82. BDAG, 553.

83. *Dictionary of Synonyms*, 459, s.v. "intercourse."

each Saint is joined to Christ (that is, has fellowship with him), a joining made possible by accepting and sharing in the benefits of the blood he shed. Thus, the word is translated as "sharing in" in our Rendition.[84] In such a sharing, the participant not only remembers what the Lord has done but also accepts his example as the pattern of his or her own behavior. Indeed, that remembrance should dictate one's whole lifestyle and all activities associated therewith.[85]

The bread which we break, is it not the communion of the body of Christ? / And the bread that we break, isn't it a sharing of the body of Christ?: The noun ἄρτος (*artos*) means "bread, or a loaf of bread."[86] Though one would expect to see the nominative ὁ ἄρτος (*ho artos*) as subject of the verb ἐστίν (*estin*), Paul uses the accusative τὸν ἄρτον (*ton arton*), likely because it has been attracted to the case of the relative pronoun.[87] On κοινωνία (*koinōnia*), "communion, sharing," see above.

The single loaf of bread represents the ground of unity that the Saint, the Church, and the Savior all share.[88] Paul uses this element of the sacrament to symbolize the corporate unity so needed for the Corinthian Saints to be one in Christ. The sharing in unity is symbolized by the partaking of the single loaf. Again, the act looks to the Atonement of Christ, which makes unity possible. The result is *koinōnia,* "a sharing," through which the Saint, the Church, and the Savior become one. For Paul, to have communion with the body and blood of Christ was to appropriate to oneself the purpose of Christ's suffering, death, and Resurrection, that is, for glorification and exaltation (compare Philip. 1:5–9; 2 Cor. 8–9 with Philip. 3:10–11). Thus, renewal of covenant, among other things, means a willingness to suffer for Christ's cause when necessary. This suffering, however, was not suffering for suffering's sake, but for the reception of eternal reward in which the Saint was made one with the Father and the Son (see John 17:20–23).

10:17 *For we being many are one bread, and one body / Because there is one loaf of bread, we, who are many, are one body:* The translation in the KJV reduces the force of the phrase οἱ πολλοί ἐσμεν (*hoi polloi esmen*), "being many," to mere description, thus weakening the force of Paul's point.

---

84. BDAG, 552–53.

85. Thiselton, *First Epistle,* 761.

86. BDAG, 136.

87. Wallace, *Greek Grammar,* 338–39.

88. Elmer Prout, "One Loaf . . . One Body," *Restoration Quarterly* 25, no. 1 (1982): 78–81. The noun can also denote unleavened bread, such as that used at Passover.

The adjective "many" has the force of a subordinate concessive.[89] Thus, what the Apostle was saying is that although there are many Saints, yet they compose but one body, that is, the metaphorical body of Christ, which the one loaf represents. The Saints are, as it were, his eyes, his ears, his hands, his feet (see 12:12–23). Therefore, unity was critical in getting the body to do the work that it was intended to do. That unity must be between the Christians themselves *and* with the Lord.

for we are all partakers of that one bread / for we all share in that one loaf of bread: The key word in this phrase is the verb μετέχομεν (*metechomen*), "we share in."[90] Paul's emphasis here is not just that of the unity of the one body but of a spiritual sharing that enhances the solidarity of the community of the redeemed. That solidarity makes up the metaphorical unity of the body of Christ.[91] This oneness forbids any union with any other body or god, which sharing in a pagan rite would do.[92]

10:18 *Behold Israel after the flesh: are not they which eat of the sacrifices partakers of the altar? / Consider the people of Israel. Aren't those who eat the sacrifices partners with the altars?:* The verb βλέπω (*blepō*), "to see, behold," when used in a metaphorical sense means "to consider."[93] The unusual term Ἰσραὴλ κατὰ σάρκα (*Israēl kata sarka*), literally "Israel according to the flesh," likely refers to ancient Israel,[94] and we have translated it as "the people of Israel" in our Rendition. When they offered certain sacrifices to Jehovah, some of the meat was returned to them with which they made a sacred meal shared with family, friends, and even the poor (Deut. 12:6–7; Lev. 3:1–17; 7:11–36; 10:12–15; 1 Sam. 9:12–13). In receiving back part of the ritually blessed food, they became κοινωνοί (*koinōnoi*), "ritually associated with the altar and also with the Lord."[95]

---

89. Thiselton, *First Epistle,* 767.

90. BDAG, 642.

91. Fee, *First Epistle,* 469; Gundry, Sōma *in Biblical Theology,* 232–44.

92. Holzapfel and Wayment, *Making Sense,* 356, notes that the particular concern Paul has in mind is that of eating nonkosher meat. The problem could be easily overcome if the Saints would become "one bread, and one body."

93. Louw-Nida, §30.1.

94. Fitzmyer, *First Corinthians,* 392, notes that this phrase refers to "ethnic or historical-empirical Israel" whom Paul separates from true Israel (Rom. 9:6), that is, those—both Jew and Gentile convert—who are the people of God.

95. Gardner, *Gifts of God,* 165, and Thiselton, *First Epistle,* 771, both argue that Paul has picked up his earlier imagery of the Exodus (in 10:10–13) and has the golden calf incident in mind (10:7). He uses κατὰ σάρκα (*kata sarka*), "according to the flesh," in a pejorative way, that is, as a reminder to the Saints of the Hebrew's sin against Jehovah

10:19 *What say I then? that the idol is any thing, or that which is offered in sacrifice to idols is any thing? / What am I implying? That food offered to idols is anything or that an idol itself is anything?:* Paul's question refers not only to 10:18 but more particularly to 10:15, where he asked his readers to carefully consider the point he is making about the worshiping of idols.

Paul's rhetorical questions look back to his discussion of eating meats offered to idols in 8:1, 4, and 10. It functions to deflect any objections to the point he is about to make. Although he does not introduce his questions with the usual μή (*mē*), "not," the structure still demands the negative response, "No."

His point is, first, that an idol is nothing more than the components from which it was made. It was just metal or stone or wood. It had neither spiritual essence nor numinous powers. Second, the εἰδωλόθυτον (*eidōlothyton*) was only an animal that would eventually become portions of meat. Offering any substance to an idol did not change it. In this case, it was still just meat.[96]

10:20 *But I say, that the things which the Gentiles sacrifice, they sacrifice to devils, and not to God / I am saying that what they offer on the altar, "they offer to demons and not to God":* A number of manuscripts do not have the words τὰ ἔθνη (*ta ethnē*), "the Gentiles," in them. It is likely that the words in the KJV were inserted by a scribe who missed Paul's point and mistakenly ascribed the action to the Gentiles rather than the Israelites (10:18).[97] Many times in the Old Testament, the Israelites sacrificed to other gods.

The noun δαιμόνιον (*daimonion*), "demon," though originally referring to any heavenly or spiritual being, in New Testamant usage it took on the sense of a malevolent spirit (for example, see LXX Deut. 32:17; Ps. 91:6; Tob. 3:8;

---

when the people partook of the sacrifice placed on the altar before the golden calf (Ex. 32:5–6). Though this reasoning does fit the context, it seems too limited for Paul's more generic imagery.

96. Fitzmyer, *First Corinthians,* 393.

97. Metzger, *Textual Commentary,* 494. The passage is also problematic in that a neutral plural subject in Greek takes a singular ending not a plural, as found here. This passage provides evidence that, during the apostasy, scribes were not familiar with the Old Testament. Indeed, some early Christian sects, like the Marcionites, only read parts of the New Testament and rejected the Old Testament altogether. See F. L. Cross, *The Oxford Dictionary of the Christian Church* (Oxford: Oxford University Press, 1983), 870–71. Such a practice clearly shows how apostates took away scripture.

Matt. 9:34; 1 Tim. 4:1).[98] The Apostle clearly shows that he understood that evil forces stood behind pagan worship pushing to open doors to misconduct and ungodliness.[99]

LXX Deuteronomy 32:16–17 notes that Israel "provoked me [Jehovah] to anger with strange gods; with their abominations they bitterly angered me. They sacrificed to devils, and not to God." There is no doubt that Paul had this passage in mind when he wrote because he quotes the latter portion exactly with the exception of changing the tense of θύω (*thyō*), "to make a sacrifice," from the past to the present tense,[100] which is why it is enclosed in quotation marks in our Rendition. This simple change, however, is of utmost importance because it gives the passage the force of a timeless axiom. Though Paul was referring to the Israelites, he refigured the event in such a way that it had universal application and, thus, relevance to the circumstances in which the Corinthian Saints found themselves.[101]

What he understood was that, though an idol was no god and had no living reality at all, it still evidenced a yielding to influences by evil spirits.[102] There was, after all, a demonic component, a subtle inspiration, that stood behind the pagans' worship.[103] The Apostle's words imply that the idea of the Christian "strong"—that their superior knowledge allowed them to freely associate with Gentiles and feast on meat in pagan temple rites—was woefully wrong. What they were overlooking was the connection of that meat to the subjective convictions of idolaters. The pagans believed their rites were sacramental and bound them to some god and some god to them. In reality, they were sacrificing to demons and, thus, unwittingly opening themselves up to satanic influence[104] (compare LXX Ps. 106:28–29).

I would not that ye should have fellowship with devils / I don't want you to be partners with demons: The key word here is the noun κοινωνός

---

98. BDAG, 210.

99. Werner Foerster, "δαίμων, δαιμόνιον," in *TDNT,* 2:1–19.

100. The LXX has the aorist plural tense ἔθυσαν (*ethusan*) while Paul uses the present plural θύουσιν (*thyousin*).

101. Hays, *Echoes of the Scriptures,* 93; Conzelmann, *1 Corinthians,* 173 with nn. 34–35.

102. Fee, *First Epistle,* 471. According to the LSJ, 365–66, *daimōn* referred to the power of a god or goddess as well as to the divine being themselves, but the Jews accepted demons as a reality (see *The Jewish Encyclopedia; A Descriptive Record of the History, Religion, Literature, and Customs of the Jewish People from the Earliest Times to the Present Day,* ed. Isidore Singer [New York: Funk and Wagnalls, 1901–6], s.v. "demonology," available online at jewishencyclopedia.com/articles/5085-demonology) and Paul is likely reflecting tradition.

103. Bailey, *Mediterranean Eyes,* 282.

104. Fitzmyer, *First Corinthians,* 393.

(*koinōnos*), "associate, partner, companion, fellow," but as mentioned earlier (see Translation Notes on 10:16), the word connotes a most intimate and close association. Paul explains his reason for his counsel: he does not want the Saints to have any association, let alone an intimate one, with demons.

Here Paul brings into perspective his references to both Israelite history and the Lord's Supper. Those who participate in pagan rites become fellow sharers with demons just as ancient Israel became associates in Jehovah's covenant and Christians become associates in the effects of the Atonement of Christ. In each case, the unity revealed itself in a special and intimate fellowship that forbade any other association and loyalty.[105] Thus, no association with pagan gods could be allowed.

10:21 *Ye cannot drink the cup of the Lord, and the cup of devils / You cannot drink both the cup of the Lord and the cup of demons:* Paul uses the strongest of language here by intoning both a warning and a command. He contrasts the "cup of the Lord" with "the cup of devils." He is likely referring to the pagan practice of offering a cup of wine to the god Sarapis.[106] In the Christian sacrament, the cup looked to the vertical aspect of the rite, that between participant and Lord. A Christian, understanding that the sacrament produced a binding covenant relationship between him or her and God made possible through the blood the Lord shed, simply could not dishonor that relationship by raising a cup of wine in honor of a pagan god, such as Sarapis.[107]

ye cannot be partakers of the Lord's table, and of the table of devils / You cannot participate in the Lord's supper and the supper of demons: Paul, again using very strong language, repeats his warning and command. The noun τραπέζα (*trapeza*), "table," denoted "a structure or surface on which food or other things can be placed," but also, by metonymy, it referred to the food or meal itself.[108] It was also used for the table upon which the cultic meal was eaten in the temple of Sarapis, Isis, and other pagan deities.[109] It was not a reach, therefore, for Paul to draw a parallel between the sacramental meal of the Christians and pagan temple feasts.

---

105. Fee, *First Epistle,* 472.

106. P. Oxy. 110.1–3 can be found translated in G. H. R. Horsley and Stephen R. Llewelyn, eds., *New Documents Illustrating Early Christianity: A Review of the Greek Inscriptions and Papyri,* 10 vols. (North Ryde, Aus.: Ancient History Documentary Research Centre, Macquarie University; Grand Rapids, Mich.: Eerdmans, 1981–2002), 1:5; Fitzmyer, *First Corinthians,* 394.

107. Fee, *First Epistle,* 473.

108. BDAG, 1013.

109. BDAG, 1013.

The infinitive phrase τραπέζης μετεχειν (*trapezēs metexein*) was an idiom meaning literally "to share in a table," but it could also connote "belonging to a particular religious group as evidence by ceremonial eating."[110] Thus, the word is translated as "the Lord's Supper" in our Rendition.

The bread looks to the horizontal aspect of the sacramental ritual, the one loaf of which all partook, that signified their own fellowship and unity one with another, a unity made possible by the death and Resurrection of the Lord. The Apostle drew a parallel to that of pagan temple offerings, but his parallel was not between what was offered and eaten at the respective services but between the Lord and devils.[111] He wanted the Christians to understand that the pagan festival opened the door to becoming fellows not just with Gentiles but more specifically with demons, and Paul did not want the Christians to have anything to do with them. He insisted that a double fellowship between God and demons was not possible.[112]

10:22 *Do we provoke the Lord to jealousy? / What! Shall we provoke the Lord to jealousy?*: By using the plural pronoun "we," Paul identified himself with his readers, likely to gain their support. The coordinating conjunction ἤ (*ē*), "or" (untranslated in the KJV) could suggest that Paul had in mind an alternative to what he said in 10:21. That, however, is clearly not the case. Since in Greek rhetoric this conjunction can be translated in such a way as to reflect that rhetorical context, the exclamation "What!" gets at the idea.[113] The verb παραζλόω (*parazēloō*), "provoke to jealousy," denotes both aspects of the English word "jealousy": first, the deep "intolerance of a rival for the possession of a thing which one regards as peculiarly one's own," and second, the "intensly zealous efforts to keep or maintain what one possesses."[114] On the one hand, it describes God's protective zeal for those who keep covenant, and on the other, his divine wrath by forsaking him for other gods.[115] To provoke God to jealousy is to bring upon oneself his righteous indignation with its deadly spiritual consequences. Paul uses *parazēloō* in the same way as that found in LXX Deuteronomy 32:21 (compare Rom. 10:19). In the Old Testament, idolatry provoked God's anger against Israel (Ex. 32:5). The Apostle's question seems to be showing "the

---

110. BDAG, 642; Louw-Nida, §34.32.
111. Gardner, *Gifts of God*, 170.
112. Fee, *First Epistle*, 473.
113. BDAG, 432; see Moffett's translation of 10:22.
114. *Dictionary of Synonyms*, 295, s.v. "envious."
115. Albrecht Stumpff, "ζῆλος, ζηλόω, ζηλωτής, παραζηλόω," in *TDNT*, 2:877–88.

strong" that if they insist on partaking of both meals (the Lord's Supper and temple sacrifices) they will end up provoking the Lord similar to the way ancient Israel had. At issue was more than the consumption of meat during temple rites. Paul's point is that "the strong" were walking in dangerous territory and could provoke God to jealousy with dire results.[116]

are we stronger than he? / We are certainly not stronger than him, are we?: Again Paul identified with his readers by using the first person plural ἐσμέν (*esmen*), "we are." His use of μή (*mē*), "not," in this, his last rhetorical question, shows that he expects a "no" answer.[117] In essence, he is asking, "Are we so brazen as to think we can challenge him, outmatch him, or get around him?"[118] A reasonable person would answer, "Of course not." The moral, then, would be, "Then don't provoke God to anger."

Analysis and Summary

In 10:14, speaking of the sin of idolatry, Paul used the command "flee," φεύγετε (*pheugete*). He did not say to depart or even to leave. Rather, the Saints were to move with all speed away from that which would spiritually injure if not kill them and others. He explained his reason: Gentile sacrifices are to devils, "and I don't want you to be partners with demons" (10:20, Rendition). As noted in 10:9 and above, the noun κοινωνία (*koinōnia*), "to be partners with," or "associated with" connoted a sharing in a deep and intimate relationship that a community of people had with one another and their god, what- or whoever that was. Paul was emphatic when he said, "you cannot participate in the Lord's supper and the supper of demons" (10:21, Rendition). Paul's coupling *koinōnia* in 10:20 with μετέχω (*metechō*), "to participate in," in 10:21 emphasized the need for the Corinthian Saints to be true to their covenant with God alone. The sacrament was a pledge of loyalty to the one God and his Son, not to idols and the gods which they represented.

Paul knew, as did the Corinthian "strong," that an idol was nothing and meat offered to it was still just meat (10:19–20). The problem was that others did not see it that way, including some of the Corinthian "weak."

---

116. Fitzmyer, *First Corinthians*, 394; Fee, *First Epistle*, 473.

117. Smyth, *Greek Grammar*, §2689.

118. This idea was current at the time. In the Old Testament passage cited in Qoh 6:10b, the writer cautions his readers not to dispute with anyone stronger than they are. Job 9:32, 37:23; and Isa. 45:9 also carry the same idea. None of these, however, mention either divine wrath or idolatry and, therefore, it is unlikely Paul had them in mind.

The Apostle's use of the sacramental imagery acted as a foil against any Christian participating in pagan temple rites. Paul was using implications of the meaning of the sacrament to stress his point.[119] Both Christian and pagan worship included participation in the religious ordinances that were designed to bring the worshiper and the object of worship into closer association. What the Corinthian "strong" did not seem to see was the incompatibility of the two systems.[120] Paul understood that the Christian victory was centered in "Christ, and him crucified" (2:2). The sacramental meal symbolically united the Saints with the Lord and brought them under the power of that victory.

The question was, under what context did it do so? The Apostle's reference to "the cup of blessing" (10:16) is telling. It likely echoed some aspect of the Seder meal that celebrated, among other things, the covenantal relationship between Israel and Jehovah. During the Last Supper, the Lord transferred the participants' allegiance from the Mosaic covenant to the new covenant. Indeed, the bread and wine were tokens of ἡ καινὴ διαθήκη (*hē kainē diathēkē*), "the new covenant" (translated as "new testament" in the KJV at Luke 22:20 but as "new covenant" here in 11:25). Paul's context here is, therefore, one of covenant. Through this means the Saints shared in Christ's victory and gained the unity so necessary for salvation.

By participating in the covenantal meal, the Saints acknowledged that they remembered what the Lord had done so that they could have his Spirit with them (see 3 Ne. 18:3–11; 20:6–9; D&C 20:76–79). But receiving his Spirit was not an end in itself. Its purpose was to help the Saints translate the Lord's work into their own lives. Indeed, the covenant was a pledge to transform the Lord's example into actions of service that worked toward the salvation of others. It defined a way of life that centered on selfless giving. On the other hand, those who shared the table of demons manifested another kind of life, one centered on self-edification, self-fulfillment, self-enjoyment, or self-advancement.[121] The two lifestyles were simply incompatible. The Lord made it very clear that one cannot serve two masters, "for either he will hate the one, and love the other or else he will hold to one, and despise the other" (Matt. 6:24). Every disciple had to choose which master she or he would serve.

---

119. Fitzmyer, *First Corinthians,* 391.

120. See the study by Mark D. Ellison, "The Setting and Sacrament of the Christian Community," in *Go Ye into All the World,* 145–66.

121. Thiselton, *First Epistle,* 777.

Understanding what the Savior did through his victory on the cross should have weakened the appeal of false gods and the satanic influence behind them and liberated his people from them. The problem with some of the Corinthian Saints was that they were putting themselves in places and situations where these false gods were still considered potent.[122] Indeed, the pagan temples were pockets of power where these evil forces operated. There, these swayed, influenced, and promoted the ways of the natural man. Carnality, sensuality, and devilishness could be the results (compare Moses 6:49). It was imperative, therefore, that Christians stay clear of such places.[123]

When the Lord appeared to Paul, he asked him, "Why do you persecute me?" (Acts 9:1–4, Rendition). In doing so, he identified himself with the Christian community which, at the time, was feeling the brunt of Paul's efforts. The Apostle, in this chapter, reverses the imagery and identifies the Church with the body of Christ, a single body though composed of many organs (10:16–17; 12:14–22). The problem at Corinth was that factionalism was in the process of destroying the unity of that body and, in the process, the body itself. Paul had already taught that Christ could not be divided or apportioned out (1:13). Likewise, his Church could not be divided and still live.[124] But there was more to Paul's imagery than that. Κοινωνία (*koinōnia*), "fellowship," "association" or "sharing" in the "one body" denoted solidarity within the community that forbade any outside cultic associations.[125] To participate in these, therefore, was to destroy the unity and threaten the demise of the Church. On the personal level, those who participated in those rites set themselves outside the power of the blood of Christ which, according to Romans 3:25; 5:9, mediated to the Saint the blessings of the Atonement, namely, the justification and reconciliation necessary for salvation.[126] To be outside the power of Christ's blood was to be damned.

Paul's concern was with actual idolatry, but for the modern Saint, an idol can be anything that she or he places before God. The prohibition, therefore, still applies.

The point is that the center stage of "the new covenant" is the care for "the other" in which the Christian follows the example of the Lord who gave his body and his blood in service to others.[127] One way the believer

---

122. Bruce, *1 and 2 Corinthians*, 96.

123. Thiselton, *First Epistle*, 775–76.

124. Thiselton, *First Epistle*, 768–69.

125. Mitchell, *Paul and the Rhetoric of Reconciliation*, 254.

126. Marshall, *Lord's Supper*, 120–21; Barrett, *First Epistle*, 232.

127. Thiselton, *First Epistle*, 751.

transmits the covenant into action is to take care of those "for whom Christ died" (8:11), that is, those in the community of the Saints.[128] To "always remember him" (D&C 20:77, 79) includes remembering how he acted and responding appropriately. In that way, the participants' life and lifestyle are one with the Lord. To act otherwise is to break covenant and run the risk of provoking God's jealousy (10:22, compare Deut. 32:15–38). Nothing is to supersede God in the Christian lifestyle or value system. The imperative is to set a proper example. In the case of the Corinthian Saints, that would include, among other things, not attending pagan temple rites no matter what the social cost.

Even today the sacramental cup points to an exclusive covenant loyalty to the Savior. It is, therefore, incompatible with any practices or distractions (some of which could have devils standing behind them) that pull one away from him. The point is that demonic forces still haunt anything that weakens or severs one's loyalty to the Lord. From these the Saints must flee.[129]

Speaking of the importance of the sacrament, President Brigham Young taught:

> There are many passages of Scripture which refer to the administering of the sacrament. A saying, direct from the lips of Jesus, has not been understood by all those who have believed in his name. When he was about to take his departure from this world he called his disciples into an upper room and he took bread and brake it and blessed it and gave it to his disciples, and said, "Take, eat; this is my body." He then took the cup and blessed it and gave to his disciples, saying, "Drink ye all of it." If we were to stop here, I think it would be more difficult to understand than if we were to read the rest of his sayings on this subject. ["]This is my body which is given for you; this is my blood of the New Testament. This do in remembrance of me; I will not drink henceforth of this fruit of the vine, until that day when I drink it new with you in my Father's kingdom.["]
>
> We do this in remembrance of the death of our Savior; it is required of his disciples until he comes again, no matter how long that may be. No matter how many generations come and go, believers in him are required to eat bread and drink wine in remembrance of his death and sufferings until he comes again. Why are they required to do this? To witness unto the Father, to Jesus and to the angels that they are believers in and desire to follow him in the regeneration, keep his commandments, build up his kingdom, revere his name and serve him with an undivided heart,

---

128. Yeo, *Rhetorical Interaction*, 174.

129. Paul Tillich, *Systematic Theology*, 3 vols. (Chicago: Chicago University Press, 1951–63), 1:14–17, 42; 2:6–11.

that they may be worthy to eat and drink with him in his Father's kingdom. This is why the Latter-day Saints partake of the ordinance of the Lord's Supper.[130]

Paul brought his argument full circle in the warning he gave his readers in 10:22, "Shall we provoke the Lord to jealousy? We are certainly not stronger than him, are we?" (as in our Rendition). He began by showing how Israel provoked Jehovah to jealousy and ended with a warning for the Christians not to follow suit. In the process, he answered their questions with force, citing scriptural authority as well as his own. He undercut their insistence that they (1) had superior knowledge and, thus, knew that an idol was nothing and, therefore, had no effect on the meat offerings made to it; (2) had a right as well as a need to attend pagan feasts; and (3) were building up others, namely the "weak," as they invited them to attend these devotions. Paul slammed the door on this attitude. Christian behavior was not based on knowledge but on love. Their actions were driven not by charity but by pride. More importantly, their superior knowledge had clouded their thinking such that they would not see that the altar of the idol was incompatible with "the Lord's table" (10:21). In effect, Paul removed their blinders with his very clear examples, warnings, and demands. He made it very plain that they were coming very close to provoking God to jealousy and, in doing so, like ancient Israel, risking his wrath. Attendance at pagan temple celebrations was, therefore, absolutely forbidden under any circumstance.[131]

On Eating Meat from the Marketplace and as a Guest (10:23–33)

Greek Text

23 Πάντα ἔξεστιν· ἀλλ᾽ οὐ πάντα συμφέρει. πάντα ἔξεστιν· ἀλλ᾽ οὐ πάντα οἰκοδομεῖ. 24 μηδεὶς τὸ ἑαυτοῦ ζητείτω ἀλλὰ τὸ τοῦ ἑτέρου. 25 πᾶν τὸ ἐν μακέλλῳ πωλούμενον ἐσθίετε μηδὲν ἀνακρίνοντες διὰ τὴν συνείδησιν, 26 τοῦ κυρίου γὰρ ἡ γῆ καὶ τὸ πλήρωμα αὐτῆς. 27 εἴ τις καλεῖ ὑμᾶς τῶν ἀπίστων καὶ θέλετε πορεύεσθαι, πᾶν τὸ παρατιθέμενον ὑμῖν ἐσθίετε μηδὲν ἀνακρίνοντες διὰ τὴν συνείδησιν· 28 ἐὰν δέ τις ὑμῖν εἴπῃ· Τοῦτο ἱερόθυτόν ἐστιν, μὴ ἐσθίετε δι᾽ ἐκεῖνον τὸν μηνύσαντα καὶ τὴν συνείδησιν· 29 συνείδησιν δὲ λέγω οὐχὶ τὴν ἑαυτοῦ ἀλλὰ τὴν τοῦ ἑτέρου· ἱνατί

130. Brigham Young, in *JD,* 13:139–40.
131. Fee, *First Epistle,* 474.

γὰρ ἡ ἐλευθερία μου κρίνεται ὑπὸ ἄλλης συνειδήσεως; 30 εἰ ἐγὼ χάριτι μετέχω, τί βλασφημοῦμαι ὑπὲρ οὗ ἐγὼ εὐχαριστῶ; 31 Εἴτε οὖν ἐσθίετε εἴτε πίνετε εἴτε τι ποιεῖτε, πάντα εἰς δόξαν θεοῦ ποιεῖτε. 32 ἀπρόσκοποι καὶ Ἰουδαίοις γίνεσθε καὶ Ἕλλησιν καὶ τῇ ἐκκλησίᾳ τοῦ θεοῦ, 33 καθὼς κἀγὼ πάντα πᾶσιν ἀρέσκω, μὴ ζητῶν τὸ ἐμαυτοῦ σύμφορον ἀλλὰ τὸ τῶν πολλῶν, ἵνα σωθῶσιν. [SBLGNT]

King James Version

23 All things are lawful for me, but all things are not expedient: all things are lawful for me, but all things edify not. 24 Let no man seek his own, but every man another's wealth. 25 Whatsoever is sold in the shambles, that eat, asking no question for conscience sake: 26 For the earth is the Lord's, and the fulness thereof. 27 If any of them that believe not bid you to a feast, and ye be disposed to go; whatsoever is set before you, eat, asking no question for conscience sake. 28 But if any man say unto you, This is offered in sacrifice unto idols, eat not for his sake that shewed it, and for conscience sake: for the earth is the Lord's, and the fulness thereof: 29 Conscience, I say, not thine own, but of the other: for why is my liberty judged of another man's conscience? 30 For if I by grace be a partaker, why am I evil spoken of for that for which I give thanks? 31 Whether therefore ye eat, or drink, or whatsoever ye do, do all to the glory of God. 32 Give none offence, neither to the Jews, nor to the Gentiles, nor to the church of God: 33 Even as I please all men in all things, not seeking mine own profit, but the profit of many, that they may be saved.

New Rendition

23 "Everything is permissible," but not everything is beneficial. "Everything is permissible," but not everything is useful. 24 Don't seek to benefit yourself, but to benefit others. 25 Eat whatever is sold in the meat market without asking questions of conscience, 26 for the earth is the Lord's and everything that is in it. 27 If any unbeliever invites you to dinner, and you want to go, eat whatever is set before you without questions of conscience. 28 But if someone says to you, "This is from a sacrifice," then don't eat it because of the one who informed you and because of conscience. 29 I don't mean your own conscience, but because of the other person's conscience. For why should my freedom of choice be condemned by another's conscience? 30 If I eat with gratitude, why should I be condemned for food that I have given thanks for? 31 Therefore, whatever you eat or drink or do, do them all for the glory of God. 32 Do not give offence to either Jews or Gentiles or the Church of God, 33 just like I try to please everyone in everything, not seeking my own benefit, but the benefit of the many, so that they might be saved.

Translation Notes and Comments

10:23 *All things are lawful for me, but all things are not expedient: all things are lawful for me, but all things edify not / "Everything is permissible," but not everything is beneficial. "Everything is permissible," but not*

everything is useful: Here Paul quotes then refutes a slogan that the Corinthian Saints were using to justify some of their sinful behavior. The dative pronoun μοί (*moi*), translated "for me" in the KJV, is not found in the major manuscripts and is, therefore, left out of our Rendition.[132]

The JST changes both phrases. "All things are lawful for me" is changed to "all things are not lawful for me." In doing so, it gives a corrected nuance to the KJV translation that suggests Paul was speaking of himself.

The slogan "All things are permissible" (πάντα ἔξεστιν, *panta exestin*), evidenced a misunderstanding of the Atonement on the part of some of the Corinthian Saints. The Apostle had already addressed this philosophy in 6:12 and in other epistles he wrote or that are attributed to him. Indeed, his statement here is almost verbatim to what he said there. For discussion, see Translation Notes on that verse. Paul was addressing a false belief that degenerated into an insistence on an autonomy that yielded to license and self-gratification.[133]

Paul's purpose here appears to have been to straighten out their thinking by showing that just because Christ has freed them from the constraints of the old covenant, their newly found freedom does not mean anything they do is proper. Indeed, to be proper, any action must meet one of two criteria. In describing the first criterion, Paul used the verb συμφέρω (*sympherō*), connoting the idea of something being of advantage to, benefiting, or assisting another to be better off, thus, "to be profitable" or "expedient."[134] In describing the second criterion, the Apostle used the verb οἰκοδομέω (*oikodomeō*), meaning "to help improve ability to function in living responsibly and effectively," and, therefore, "to strengthen" or "build up."[135] These two qualifiers harnessed ἔξεστιν (*exestin*), "to be permissible," and brought it into Christian service by negating the universality of "freedom."[136] Together they show that, for Paul, the only proper actions for a Christian are those that "benefit" and "build up" the Saints either individually or as a community.[137]

---

132. Metzger, *Textual Commentary,* 494–95.

133. Thiselton, *First Epistle,* 781.

134. Louw-Nida, §65.44. The word means, literally, "to bring together" but carries the idea of doing so for advantage or profit. See also Konrad Weiss, "συμφέρω, σύμφορος," in *TDNT,* 9:69–78.

135. BDAG, 696; Otto Michel, "οἰκοδομέω," in *TDNT,* 5:136–44.

136. Thiselton, *First Epistle,* 781.

137. Fitzmyer, *First Corinthians,* 399; Fee, *First Epistle,* 479.

10:24 *Let no man seek his own, but every man another's wealth / Don't seek to benefit yourself, but to benefit others:* The Greek here is very condensed, μηδεὶς τὸ ἑαυτοῦ ζητείτω ἀλλὰ τὸ τοῦ ἑτέρου (*mēdeis to heautou zēteitō alla to tou heterou*), literally "Let no one seek his own [thing], but the other's [thing]." Some late variants insert the pronoun ἕκαστος (*ekastos*), translated "every man" (as in the KJV), but because there is no early textual evidence for this, our Rendition leaves it out. Also, the word "wealth" is absent in all Greek texts. Paul uses the vague definite accusative neuter article τό (*to*), "the," leaving the object unstated but inferring the noun "thing." The article does, however, carry a positive nuance, suggesting something that is good for another.[138] The JST changes the word "wealth" to "good," thus bringing the verse in line with the idea conveyed in the Greek text. In our Rendition, we have changed from third person singular to second person singular to bring it more in line with modern English usage.

10:25 *Whatsoever is sold in the shambles, that eat, asking no question for conscience sake / Eat whatever is sold in the meat market without asking questions of conscience:* Paul used the unusual term μάκελλον (*makellon*) (this is its only occurrence in the New Testament), a word that denoted "market for provisions" but is understood to mean a "meat market."[139]

In this verse, then, Paul used the example of eating meat one has purchased at the market. Given Paul's statement, the question arises if sacrificial and nonsacrificial meats were distinguishable at such places. It seems possible that sacrificial meats, probably fetching a higher price, were separated out. Because meat was generally scarce, however, it is very likely that those portions not burned in the actual sacrifice would have shown up at the market.[140] Still, Paul's words suggest that there was, at least occasionally, nonsacrificial meat available.

That being the case, what does the Christian do? Because much of the meat did come from temple sacrifices, the Jews, in order not to violate kosher laws, had to ask if the meat was εἰδωλόθυτον (*eidōlothyton*), that is, an idol offering.[141] The question was if the Christian had to follow suit. Paul's answer was based on what he called "conscience." As noted earlier (see Translation

138. Findlay, "St. Paul's First Epistle," 867.

139. BDAG, 611; Moulton and Milligan, *Vocabulary*, 386, lists it as parallel to the Hebrew *miklah*, "enclosure." Compare Deissmann, *Light from the Ancient East,* 276 and n. 4.

140. David W. J. Gill, "The Meat Market at Corinth," in *Tyndale Bulletin* 43, no. 2 (1992): 323–37; Murphy-O'Connor, *St. Paul's Corinth,* 33.

141. Fee, *First Epistle,* 481.

Notes on 8:7), the noun συνείδησις (*syneidēsis*) was derived from the verb σύνοιδα (*synoida*), "to be aware of, to be conscious of."[142] In our Rendition, we have translated the word as "questions of conscience." Paul used the word not in connection with moral issues but those involving gospel principles. Some of the Saints did not understand some of these and, therefore, had little foundation for proper application. As a result, their conscience was, at times, unduly and unnecessarily tried. This was such an instance.

The Apostle used the verb ἀνακρίνω (*anakrinō*), which meant basically "to examine by questioning."[143] His counsel—μηδὲν ἀνακρίνοντες (*mēden anakrinontes*), literally, "asking no question"—meant to not question where the meat came from. Such over concern, though important to Jews, was not required of Christians.

10:26 *For the earth is the Lord's, and the fulness thereof / for the earth is the Lord's and everything that is in it:* In this verse the conjunction γάρ (*gar*), "for," plays a critical role because it acts as a marker of cause or reason for Paul's point.[144] The principle he is teaching is found in LXX Psalm 24:1, "The earth is the Lord's and the fulness thereof." According to the Psalmist, this also includes "the world, and all that dwell in it." Paul's use of this scripture did three things: First, it focused his readers' attention not on themselves but on the Lord, who had claim on all things and that included the care of the Saint. Second, it served to remind all believers that God owns all and, therefore, just because something has passed through a pagan ritual, the act in no way lessened God's claim to it. And finally, it showed that every good thing comes from God and need not be questioned but, rather, accepted with gratitude.[145]

The problem was that some of the Saints were so focused on their own scruples and preoccupations that they were forgetting the Lord and the freedom he brought them through the cross.[146] Properly understood, this principle gave the Christians a liberty outside of the Mosaic law the Jews did not know. In short, the Saints were to feel free to purchase meat at the market and not to worry their conscience about it.

10:27 *If any of them that believe not bid you to a feast, and ye be disposed to go; whatsoever is set before you, eat, asking no question for conscience sake / If any unbeliever invites you to dinner, and you want to*

---

142. BDAG 967–68, 973.
143. BDAG, 66.
144. BDAG, 189.
145. Thiselton, *First Epistle*, 785–86; Collins, *First Corinthians*, 387.
146. Gardner, *Gifts of God*, 175; Fitzmyer, *First Corinthians*, 400.

go, eat whatever is set before you without questions of conscience: Paul's focus in this example is what to do if one accepts an invitation to dine in the home of a nonmember. The phrase τις . . . τῶν ἀπίστων (*tis . . . tōn apistōn*), "some non-believer," nuances the idea not just of accepting an invitation to a dinner from a nonmember but of serving as a reminder that the Christian has agreed to enter into a pagan home where almost everything would be touched by the socioreligious culture of the hosts. The environment would be very pagan.[147] If members decided to go, Paul's counsel is that they should enjoy the food. It shows that he sees this situation very differently from that of attending a pagan feast at a temple.

The Apostle's use of the plural phrase καλεῖ ὑμᾶς (*kalei hymas*), "invites you," contains the nuance of more than one member being invited at the same time and, therefore, could be rendered "some of you."[148] The plural reveals that he was talking to the branch at large and not just to those "who have knowledge." His counsel, therefore, had a wider range of application.

The JST changes the verse to read "and ye be disposed to eat," and in doing so, brings the focus not on the decision of going but of eating once these people have arrived. In this context, if they decide to accept the meal, Paul's counsel is not to question where the meat came from διὰ τὴν συνείδησιν (*dia tēn syneidēsin*), "with concern about its moral rightness or wrongness," for there is none.

10:28 *But if any man say unto you, This is offered in sacrifice unto idols, eat not for his sake that shewed it, and for conscience sake / But if someone says to you, "This is from a sacrifice," then don't eat it because of the one who informed you and because of conscience:* In this verse, Paul gives his caveat. If someone, likely another Christian guest, points out the meat ἱερόθυτόν ἐστιν (*hierothyton estin*), "has been offered in sacrifice to an idol," then do not eat it. Paul's use of the preposition διά (*dia*) (with accusative), "because of, for the sake of," provides his twofold reason for abstaining. The first is for the sake of the individual who voiced the concern. His feelings must be taken into consideration. The second is συνείδησις (*syneidēsis*), that keen sense of right and wrong noted above.

for the earth is the Lord's, and the fulness thereof / —: This phrase is not found in the early manuscripts. It appears to be a later addition by a copyist who determined that this verse should be parallel with 10:26. Because of the lack of early evidence, it is left out of our Rendition.[149]

147. Thiselton, *First Epistle*, 786.

148. Robertson and Plummer, *Critical and Exegetical Commentary*, 221–22.

149. Metzger, *Textual Commentary*, 495.

10:29 *Conscience, I say, not thine own, but of the other / I don't mean your own conscience, but because of the other person's conscience:* The disturbed conscience, as Paul makes clear, is that of a fellow Christian, not the Apostle's addressees. Those who take Paul's counsel seriously should not be concerned about the matter at all.[150] It is the overly scrupulous and ill-informed whose conscience would be pricked at such a setting. Even so, Paul's counsel is, "Don't eat the meat," for sake of the other man's conscience.

for why is my liberty judged of another man's conscience?/ For why should my freedom of choice be condemned by another's conscience?:[151] It appears that Paul is here asking a rhetorical question in the first person that could be posed by "the strong" to counter his counsel.[152] The interrogative adverb he uses, ἱνατί (*hinati*), is a shortened form of ἱνατί γένηται (*hinati genētai*), "for what reason does it happen (that)?"[153] The word puts force to the question of why another person's overly scrupulous conscience should determine another's actions. The passive of the verb κρίνομαι (*krinomai*), "to be judged," here means "to be condemned."[154]

10:30 *For if I by grace be a partaker, why am I evil spoken of for that for which I give thanks? / If I eat with gratitude, why should I be condemned for food that I have given thanks for?:* Paul seems to be continuing his rhetorical question. The noun χάρις (*charis*), "grace, thanks" here refers to the prayer of thanksgiving the Saints offered before a meal.[155] That the person felt free to give thanks to God for the food suggests his conscience was clear. The use of the passive verb βλασφημέομαι (*blasphēmeomai*), "to suffer defamation of character,"[156] shows why the person would be incensed at a negative response for his doing so. His expression of the freedom Christ has given him to eat what he pleases becomes the source of his defamation

---

150. Robertson and Plummer, *Critical and Exegetical Commentary*, 221–22.

151. The translation of 29b and 30 presents all kinds of difficulties. Fee, *First Epistle*, 486, calls it "a notorious crux," while Barrett, *First Epistle*, 242, describes it as "notoriously difficult." The work of Duane F. Watson, "1 Corinthians 10:23–11:1 in the Light of Greco-Roman Rhetoric: The Role of Rhetorical Questions," *Journal of Biblical Literature* 108 (1989): 302–3, however, has presented evidence that answers nearly all the problems and, therefore, is followed in the Commentary. For discussion, see Thiselton, *First Epistle*, 788–92.

152. C. A. Pierce, *Conscience in the New Testament* (London: SCM Press, 1955), 78; Bailey, *Mediterranean Eyes*, 291.

153. Fitzmyer, *First Corinthians*, 402.

154. BDAG, 567.

155. Louw-Nida, §33.350 with n. 64.

156. BDAG, 178.

by others. The point of that defamation would be the accusation of inconsistency between what he professes to believe and what he practices.[157]

10:31 *Whether therefore ye eat, or drink, or whatsoever ye do, do all to the glory of God / Therefore, whatever you eat or drink or do, do them all for the glory of God:* This sentence provides the essence of Paul's counsel. Whatever his reader decides to do, it should be motivated for one purpose, "to the glory of God." The noun δόξα (*doxa*), "glory," though often denoting the splendor associated with God, here means to promulgate the praise that one should give him.[158]

10:32 *Give none offence, neither to the Jews, nor to the Gentiles, nor to the church of God / Do not give offence to either Jews or Gentiles or the Church of God:* The adjective ἀπρόσκοπος (*aproskopos*), "without causing offenses," denoted the state of being faultless on multiple levels due to inoffensive behaviors. The word connoted avoiding any action that could prove to be a stumbling block to others. In short, it meant to be blameless in every way.[159] Paul references three groups for whom the Christian should have concern: two outside the covenant and one inside the covenant. The three groups provide the range of people for whom the Christian should have concern and be willing to shape his or her conduct. The outcome of such a willingness to be inoffensive would act to give the Church appeal to all classes of people.[160]

It is of note that the term τῇ ἐκκλησίᾳ τοῦ θεοῦ (*hē eklēsia tou theou*), "The Church of God," is used here for the first time in Christian literature to set the Saints off from the rest of the world. The significance of this context suggests a rising consciousness on the part of the Christians that "the people of God" are a distinct class of beings.[161]

10:33 *Even as I please all men in all things, not seeking mine own profit, but the profit of many / just like I try to please everyone in everything, not seeking my own benefit, but the benefit of the many:* Paul here sets himself up as an example of one to be followed. Though the verb ἀρέσκω (*areskō*), "to please," can denote acting in a fawning or subservient manner, Paul uses it to mean "to accommodate" or "to find favor with." His

---

157. Thiselton, *First Epistle,* 790.

158. The full semantic range of the word can be found in Carey C. Newman, *Paul's Glory-Christology: Tradition and Rhetoric* (Leiden: Brill, 1992), 157–63.

159. BDAG, 126; Gustav Stählin, "προσκόπτω, πρόσκομμα, προσκοπή, ἀπρόσκοπος," in *TDNT,* 6:745–58.

160. Fitzmyer, *First Corinthians,* 403.

161. Fitzmyer, *First Corinthians,* 403.

counsel was simply not to give deference to one party over another but to treat all equally.[162] The word had a very positive nuance. In ancient Greek documents it was used to commend those who pleased the Greco-Roman populace through their generous service.[163]

The neuter noun σύμφορον (*symphoron*) referred to a "benefit" or "advantage."[164] Paul was never interested in his own *symphoron*. His whole mission was to make the lives of others better than they had ever been. He invited his fellow Saints to do the same.

that they may be saved / so that they might be saved: Here Paul gives the basis of all he does and the ground on which he bases all his decisions and actions. The passive verb σώζομαι (*sōzomai*), though having a range of positive meanings from temporal deliverance to being spared from the wrath of God at the Second Coming, suggests all the blessings bestowed on faithful humankind by God through the work of Christ.[165] The Apostle had but one goal—the salvation of others (1:18)—and wanted others to adopt it.

Analysis and Summary

Paul had not only closed but also locked the door on the matter of attending pagan temple feasts. There were, however, a few items tangentially associated with pagan worship that were not absolute. Though matters of indifference, they still needed to be addressed. The Apostle, therefore, had to speak to the issue of ἐξουσία (*exouosia*), that is, "rights" or "freedoms" dealing with these matters. These he took up in the remainder of this chapter.[166]

In 10:25–29, the Apostle returned to the issue of the εἰδωλόθυτον (*eidōlothyton*), which was to respond when presented with a choice of eating or not eating sacrificial meats. The first deals with purchasing meat from a butcher's shop.[167] His counsel was simply don't ask where the meat came from, just enjoy eating it.

His second example deals with a situation in which some of the branch members were invited to a private dinner in a nonmember's home. The

---

162. BDAG, 129.

163. For example, see Demosthenes, *Ep.* 3.27.

164. BDAG, 960.

165. Werner Foerster and Georg Fohrer, "σῴζω, σωτηρία," in *TDNT*, 7:965–1003; BDAG, 983.

166. Fee, *First Epistle*, 474.

167. Louw-Nida, §57.207, 208. His word, μάκελλον (*makellon*), denotes a particular area of an agora, the business center of a town.

Apostle's counsel was to eat what was placed before them unless another Christian guest identified a certain dish as being leftovers from a sacrificial offering.[168] Then, the Apostle stated, "Don't eat it" (10:28, Rendition).

The decision to eat or not, Paul notes, must be based on συνείδησις (*syneidēsis*), "conscience." The word here does not reference the consciousness of one who has a genuine understanding of the inherent moral goodness or badness of a given action. In this case it pointed to the conscience of a person who either misunderstood or did not understand a gospel principle. This condition resulted in an overly fussy attention to details that were really of no consequence. Paul's counsel was, therefore, based not on matters of true conscience but on what was best for the welfare of another Saint.[169]

It is in such situations that the Christian can express what it really means to have "liberty" or "freedom" (*exousia*) in Christ. In essence, as one scholar has pointed out, Paul is saying, "If it genuinely does not matter whether I eat or not, why choose the path that raises unnecessary difficulties? What is the point of 'freedom' if I cannot choose to not cause problems?"[170] In sum, Paul was saying that while Christ had indeed made believers "free" in such matters, a Christian's top priority should be for the well-being of others.[171]

Paul had already laid down, in chapter 8, the principles that dictated his counsel. There he mentioned idol meat, idols themselves, knowledge, temple attendance, and "the weak." Since none of those terms appear here, this section does not reiterate what he had said earlier. Rather, Paul addressed different if related concerns designed, it seems likely, to reach a much broader audience.[172] Indeed, his focus seems to have been on the "strong," the "weak," and everyone in between.

It is important to note, however, that Paul spoke to a deeper issue that transcends the mere eating of market-sold meat. The real problem was confusion on the part of certain Corinthian Saints between nonessentials and absolutes. Some determined that attending pagan temple rituals was nonessential, but they were wrong. As Paul argued, such an act was idolatry plain and simple and, therefore, was absolutely forbidden to a Christian.

---

168. Sperry, *Paul's Life,* 124–25.

169. Watson, "1 Corinthians 10:23–11:1 in the Light of Greco-Roman Rhetoric," 305.

170. Thiselton, *First Epistle,* 790; italics in original removed.

171. Collins, *First Corinthians,* 388; Watson, "1 Corinthians 10:23–11:1 in the Light of Greco-Roman Rhetoric," 318.

172. Fee, *First Epistle,* 476–77.

These same people were also confused as to the basis of proper Christian behavior. As one scholar noted, "For them it was a question of knowledge and rights (*gnōsis* and *exousia*). For Paul it was a question of love and freedom (*agapē* and *eleutheria*). Knowledge and rights lead to pride; they are ultimately non-Christian because the bottom line is selfishness—freedom to do as I please when I please. Love and freedom lead to edification; they are ultimately Christian because the bottom line is the benefit of someone else—that they may be saved (v. 33)."[173] Therefore, Paul returns to the theme of "building up" others (οἰκοδομή, *oikodome*) that he developed earlier (see 3:9; 8:1, 10) and which he will further develop (14:3–5, 12, 17, 26).

It must be kept in mind that the Apostle uses the two examples of eating meat only as illustrations that allow him to address the greater issue of "freedoms and rights" when it comes to nonessentials. He set for himself two tasks. First, he ensconced the fact that, when it comes to nonessentials, the Christian is truly free to do as he or she wishes. Paul's writings show that these include such things as practicing circumcision (7:19; Acts 16:3), observing Jewish holy days (Rom. 14:5; Col. 2:16), participating in Jewish temple rites (Acts 21:26), and, as noted here, eating certain foods. Paul is forthright in standing up for the freedom of choice each Saint has in such matters (10:29–30). Such freedom, however, is not the soul of the Christian life, and this creates the need for his second task: he had to show that caring for the physical and spiritual welfare of others is the true soul of Christianity. Each Saint's freedom, therefore, must be bound by both love and care. The binding agent included three conditions: that which "benefited" others (συμφέρω, *symphero*) (10:23), "edified" them (οἰκοδομέω, *oikodomeō*) (10:23–24, 32–33), *and* brought glory to God (δόξα, *doxa*) (10:31). That balance is all important.[174] Paul summarized his counsel very nicely with his words in 10:24, "Don't seek to benefit yourself, but to benefit others." Paul's point is that "walking the borderline of any principle is not living the principle."[175]

Because Paul was working through these two tasks simultaneously, his argument does not flow smoothly as evidenced by certain jumps in logic (for example, what he says in 10:25 does not fit with his intent in 10:24). Even so, he does make his points. In this pericope (10:24–11:1) there are seven imperatives and three explanatory comments, one a quote from the

173. Fee, *First Epistle*, 477–78.
174. Fee, *First Epistle*, 478–79.
175. Anderson, *Understanding Paul*, 106.

Old Testament. The seven imperatives are as follows: "Let no one seek his own advantage (v. 24); eat what is sold in the market (v. 25); eat what is set before you as a guest (v. 27); do not eat meat declared sacrificial (v. 28); do all for the glory of God (v. 31); avoid giving offense to any one (v. 32); and be imitators of me, as I am of Christ (11:1)."[176] The explanatory comments justify the imperatives. They are: seek the other person's good (10:24, 33), and all things belong to the Lord (10:28).

What appears to be a bit disjointed, however, does have good continuity when one realizes the Apostle is using a chiastic format:

A (23–24) The criterion: the good of others;

  B (25–27) Personal freedom with regard to food;

    C (28–29a) The criterion illustrated: freedom curtailed for the sake of another;

  B′ (29b–30) Personal freedom defended;

A′ (31–33f) The criterion generalized: that all may be saved.[177]

Verse 10:24 actually acts as a summary, in the form of an axiom, for the point Paul has been making in the last three chapters. The simple phrase "Don't seek to benefit yourself, but to benefit others" focuses on the mode of life the Christians should live (compare 10:33 and 11:1).[178]

The rhetorical question Paul proposes in 10:30, "If I eat with gratitude, why should I be condemned for food that I have given thanks for?" is a good one and could easily be raised by "the strong." The question asks, in essence, "Why should another person's overly scrupulous conscience dictate what I do when I know their concern is a nonissue?"

Paul's counsel is that when another, weak in the faith, points out a problem, one must act or not act for "conscience sake . . . not thine *own*, but of the other" (10:28–29). Paul's point is that "the Saints should act with consideration of the sensibilities of others."[179]

It must be emphasized that Paul is dealing with what he considers to be a nonissue. In the two examples he used, he showed that it would be proper for his readers to do something so different that it would set them apart from all others, both Jew and Gentile. There was a caveat, however. The

---

176. Fitzmyer, *First Corinthians*, 398.

177. Fee, *First Epistle*, 478.

178. This principle is also restated and emphasized in 13:5; Rom. 14:7; 15:2; Gal. 6:2; Philip. 2:1–7.

179. Holzapfel and Wayment, *Making Sense*, 357.

act was not to be done if all it was doing was strictly catering to the overly scrupulous and misplaced conscience of "the weak." It should be done only if it served the spiritual welfare of the other. Such an act of personal grace and consideration is the essence and full expression of true gospel freedom. As the Lord based his actions out of concern for the salvation of others, so, too, should the Saint (10:29–33; compare 8:13; Rom. 14:21–23).[180]

In essence, what Paul was trying to get the Corinthian Saints to realize is that it was up to each one of them to determine how they would use the freedom Christ had given them. He counsels, however, that the proper way is to do that which, as one scholar noted, does the least harm and "show[s] love and respect for the other." In doing so, Paul points out that the Saint is not compromising his or her freedom "by entering into the bondage of the other's scruples. Quite the reverse: you are using your freedom to help the other and to serve the gospel. To do otherwise would return you into bondage to your own personal desires and preferences."[181]

In sum, the ground of choice is twofold: what brings glory to God and salvation to the soul. As President Howard W. Hunter noted:

> If such little things as eating and drinking are to be done to the glory of God, how much more important it must be that all of our thoughts, the words we speak, or acts, conduct, dealings with neighbors, business transactions, and all of our everyday affairs, be in harmony with our religious beliefs. In the words of Paul, "whatsoever ye do, do all to the glory of God" (1 Cor. 10:31). Can we therefore eliminate religion from our weekday affairs and relegate it to the Sabbath day only? Surely not, if we follow Paul's admonition.
>
> Religion can be part of our daily work, our business, our buying and selling, building, transportation, manufacturing, our trade or profession, or of anything we do. We can serve God by honesty and fair dealing in our business transactions in the same way we do in Sunday worship. The true principles of Christianity cannot be separate and apart from business and our everyday affairs.[182]

Certainly Paul's writings show that the life of a Christian should be consistently true to the teachings and practices that demonstrate love for mankind and God the Father as commanded by the Master at all times and in all places.

---

180. Thiselton, *First Epistle,* 793.
181. Thiselton, *First Epistle,* 792.
182. Howard W. Hunter, in CR, October 1961, 107–9.

Chapter 11

On Proper Modes of Worship

INTRODUCTION

At this point Paul moves on to the next topic, which looks not at Christians attending pagan cultic celebrations, but at Christians in their own worship services. He addresses three items where abuse had surfaced: first, concerning a woman's praying and preaching in church with an unveiled head (11:2–16); second, concerning the mishandling of the poor during sacrament services (11:17–34); and third, concerning the speaking in tongues in the Church (chapters 12–14). His counsel once again reveals his ability to judge matters within the context of bedrock theological principles and doctrinal matters.[1]

Just how Paul became aware of the issue of people speaking in tongues is clearly indicated by his statement, "Now concerning spiritual gifts" (12:1), which suggests that he was responding to a letter he had received. That, however, is not clear in the cases of unveiled women participating in worship services and the poor being abused at Church. That he praises them for holding "fast to the traditions just as I have passed them on to you" (11:2, Rendition), suggests, however, that he had been assured by some means of their belief that they were following his will. A letter seems the most likely informant.[2] Whatever the case, the subject matter does fit comfortably into Paul's development of and counsel concerning the issues the Corinthian Saints faced.

The major challenge in interpreting this chapter is that Paul's response assumes an understanding of the issues he was addressing and, therefore, leaves some elements unexplained. Translators and interpreters are left

---

1. Fitzmyer, *First Corinthians,* 405.
2. Fee, *First Epistle,* 491.

to wonder about the exact cultural issue he was addressing as well as the exact meaning of certain terms he used that are critical in understanding his argument.[3] We will proceed in this chapter with a note of caution, knowing how little we really understand about early Christian worship services.[4] For example, we don't know how often they met, how big their congregations were, the role played by the local leadership, to what extent they understood a hierarchy of authority, and so on. We do recognize that at some of the services, the Saints enjoyed a full meal together and that the sacrament was administered. We also understand that in Jerusalem, the Saints continued to worship at the temple and, at least for a time, held their worship services on Saturday. Thus, there seems to have been from what little evidence we have at this early date, a fair amount of fluidity in practices and procedures.

Furthermore, during this era of Roman history, there was a great deal of flux in the status of and expectations placed on women. As a result, it is hard to know what was influencing the Christian women to behave as they did and what precisely Paul's concerns were.[5]

In sum, many of the modern works written on chapters 11–14 are often far more certain about conditions than they should be.[6] In reality, the two critical questions, "What exactly is going on and why?" can be answered only approximately.[7] Insight from the Restoration suggests why this is the case. The fluidity of the modern Church's development during the early years of its existence suggests the same was likely to be true during the days of the Lord's Apostles. Paul was writing only twenty-five years after Jesus had established his Church. Based on our own experience, we can extrapolate how much flux was going on during the first few decades of the meridian Church's existence. Knowing how dynamic that period was should serve as a warning of the danger of being too dogmatic about what was going on in Paul's day. Having stated that, however, although

---

3. Some terms that need more exact definitions in Paul's context are "head" (11:3–5), "uncovered" (11:5, 13), "glory" (11:7), "because of the angels" (11:10), and "such custom" (11:16).

4. Richard Lloyd Anderson, "The Restoration of the Sacrament (Part 1: Loss and Christian Reformations)," *Ensign* 22 (January 1992): 40.

5. Thiselton, *First Epistle*, 801.

6. These include those produced as a result of the resurgence of the feminist movement beginning in the 1960s. Unfortunately, many of these have only served to muddy the waters. For a list of more than eighty articles dealing with the issues in 11:2–16 produced by the various theological and philosophical schools over the years, see Thiselton, *First Epistle*, 806–9.

7. Fee, *First Epistle*, 492 and n. 5.

we are left to wonder about some particulars and have to deal with some approximations, the major issues confronting Paul and the Saints can be comprehended, the Apostle's biggest concerns grasped, and his counsel understood.

COVERING THE HEAD IN WORSHIP (11:1–16)

Greek Text

1 μιμηταί μου γίνεσθε, καθὼς κἀγὼ Χριστοῦ. 2 Ἐπαινῶ δὲ ὑμᾶς ὅτι πάντα μου μέμνησθε καὶ καθὼς παρέδωκα ὑμῖν τὰς παραδόσεις κατέχετε. 3 θέλω δὲ ὑμᾶς εἰδέναι ὅτι παντὸς ἀνδρὸς ἡ κεφαλὴ ὁ Χριστός ἐστιν, κεφαλὴ δὲ γυναικὸς ὁ ἀνήρ, κεφαλὴ δὲ τοῦ Χριστοῦ ὁ θεός. 4 πᾶς ἀνὴρ προσευχόμενος ἢ προφητεύων κατὰ κεφαλῆς ἔχων καταισχύνει τὴν κεφαλὴν αὐτοῦ· 5 πᾶσα δὲ γυνὴ προσευχομένη ἢ προφητεύουσα ἀκατακαλύπτῳ τῇ κεφαλῇ καταισχύνει τὴν κεφαλὴν αὐτῆς, ἓν γάρ ἐστιν καὶ τὸ αὐτὸ τῇ ἐξυρημένῃ. 6 εἰ γὰρ οὐ κατακαλύπτεται γυνή, καὶ κειράσθω· εἰ δὲ αἰσχρὸν γυναικὶ τὸ κείρασθαι ἢ ξυρᾶσθαι, κατακαλυπτέσθω. 7 ἀνὴρ μὲν γὰρ οὐκ ὀφείλει κατακαλύπτεσθαι τὴν κεφαλήν, εἰκὼν καὶ δόξα θεοῦ ὑπάρχων· ἡ γυνὴ δὲ δόξα ἀνδρός ἐστιν. 8 οὐ γάρ ἐστιν ἀνὴρ ἐκ γυναικός, ἀλλὰ γυνὴ ἐξ ἀνδρός· 9 καὶ γὰρ οὐκ ἐκτίσθη ἀνὴρ διὰ τὴν γυναῖκα, ἀλλὰ γυνὴ διὰ τὸν ἄνδρα. 10 διὰ τοῦτο ὀφείλει ἡ γυνὴ ἐξουσίαν ἔχειν ἐπὶ τῆς κεφαλῆς διὰ τοὺς ἀγγέλους. 11 πλὴν οὔτε γυνὴ χωρὶς ἀνδρὸς οὔτε ἀνὴρ χωρὶς γυναικὸς ἐν κυρίῳ· 12 ὥσπερ γὰρ ἡ γυνὴ ἐκ τοῦ ἀνδρός, οὕτως καὶ ὁ ἀνὴρ διὰ τῆς γυναικός· τὰ δὲ πάντα ἐκ τοῦ θεοῦ. 13 ἐν ὑμῖν αὐτοῖς κρίνατε· πρέπον ἐστὶν γυναῖκα ἀκατακάλυπτον τῷ θεῷ προσεύχεσθαι; 14 οὐδὲ ἡ φύσις αὐτὴ διδάσκει ὑμᾶς ὅτι ἀνὴρ μὲν ἐὰν κομᾷ, ἀτιμία αὐτῷ ἐστιν, 15 γυνὴ δὲ ἐὰν κομᾷ, δόξα αὐτῇ ἐστιν; ὅτι ἡ κόμη ἀντὶ περιβολαίου δέδοται. 16 εἰ δέ τις δοκεῖ φιλόνεικος εἶναι, ἡμεῖς τοιαύτην συνήθειαν οὐκ ἔχομεν, οὐδὲ αἱ ἐκκλησίαι τοῦ θεοῦ. [SBLGNT]

King James Version

1 Be ye followers of me, even as I also am of Christ. 2 Now I praise you, brethren, that ye remember me in all things, and keep the ordinances, as I delivered them to you. 3 But I would have you know, that the head of every man is Christ; and the head of the woman is the man; and the head of Christ is God. 4 Every man praying or prophesying,

New Rendition

1 Follow my example as I myself follow Christ's example. 2 Now I commend you because you remember me in everything and hold fast to the traditions just as I have passed them on to you. 3 But I want you to understand that the head of every man is Christ, and the head of every woman is the man, and the head of Christ is God. 4 Any man who prays

having his head covered, dishonoureth his head. 5 But every woman that prayeth or prophesieth with her head uncovered dishonoureth her head: for that is even all one as if she were shaven. 6 For if the woman be not covered, let her also be shorn: but if it be a shame for a woman to be shorn or shaven, let her be covered. 7 For a man indeed ought not to cover his head, forasmuch as he is the image and glory of God: but the woman is the glory of the man. 8 For the man is not of the woman; but the woman of the man. 9 Neither was the man created for the woman; but the woman for the man. 10 For this cause ought the woman to have power on her head because of the angels. 11 Nevertheless neither is the man without the woman, neither the woman without the man, in the Lord. 12 For as the woman is of the man, even so is the man also by the woman; but all things of God. 13 Judge in yourselves: is it comely that a woman pray unto God uncovered? 14 Doth not even nature itself teach you, that, if a man have long hair, it is a shame unto him? 15 But if a woman have long hair, it is a glory to her: for her hair is given her for a covering. 16 But if any man seem to be contentious, we have no such custom, neither the churches of God.

or prophesies with his head covered dishonors his head. 5 But any woman who prays or prophesies with her head uncovered dishonors her head, for it is the same thing as having her head shaved. 6 For if a woman does not cover her head, then she should get her hair cut off. Now if it is disgraceful for a woman to have her hair cut off or her head shaved, then she should keep her head covered. 7 For a man should not cover his head, since he is the image and glory of God, but the woman is the glory of the man. 8 For man did not come from woman, but woman from man, 9 neither was man created for the sake of woman, but woman for man. 10 For this reason a woman ought to have control over her head because of the angels. 11 Nevertheless, neither is woman independent of man nor man independent of woman in the Lord. 12 For just as woman came from man, so also man comes through woman. But all things come from God. 13 Judge for yourselves, is it proper for a woman to pray to God with her head uncovered? 14 Doesn't nature itself teach you that if a man has long hair, it is a disgrace to him, 15 but if a woman has long hair, it is her glory? Because long hair is given her for a covering. 16 Now if anyone is disposed to argue about this, we have no such custom, neither do any of the churches of God.

Translation Notes and Comments

11:1 *Be ye followers of me, even as I also am of Christ / Follow my example as I myself follow Christ's example:* This verse should probably go with the previous chapter because it makes a very strong conclusion of the point Paul made there. In that section, he noted his desire to be all things to all people in order to bring them to Christ (10:32–33). This sentence marks his request for his readers to do the same. He sincerely wanted them to be μίμηται (*mimētai*), which is very literally, "imitators" of him, the word denoting one who follows another as a model or example of proper behavior.[8]

11:2 *Now I praise you, brethren, that ye remember me in all things / Now I commend you because you remember me in everything:* The word "brethren," ἀδελφοί (*adelphoi*), found in the KJV, is a later addition. The earliest manuscripts do not have it and, therefore, it is left out of our Rendition.[9]

The verb ἐπαίνω (*epainō*), "praise, commend," expresses admiration for something done well.[10] Paul commends his readers for doing two things: First, they remembered him "in all things." The plural passive verb μέμνησθε (*memnēsthe*), "remember," denotes not only calling someone to mind but also responding to that memory in an appropriate manner. In this context, it likely refers to prayers the Saints offered in the Apostle's behalf.[11] For the second item, see the next paragraph.

and keep the ordinances, as I delivered them to you / and hold fast to the traditions just as I have passed them on to you: The second item Paul praises them for is holding fast to Church traditions. Since Paul has been castigating many of his readers, it seems a bit odd that he would here commend them. Paul could be reaching out to his audience by softening his approach in an attempt to win them to his position. Though he had reached out to them before,[12] it seems unlikely, however, that he is doing so here. Some early and medieval commentators felt that his words were ironic, if not sarcastic.[13] Again, that is unlikely. What is more likely comes from understanding Paul's intent here. The noun παράδοσις (*paradosis*), translated as "ordinance" in the KJV, denotes both content and instructions that were passed down over time through authority. Hence, though the Church was still young, the best translation of the word, in this context, would be "traditions" to give it the necessary weight of authority.[14] The verb κατέχω

---

8. BDAG, 652.

9. Metzger, *Textual Commentary*, 495.

10. BDAG, 357.

11. Louw-Nida, §29.16.

12. Fee, *First Epistle*, 500.

13. Thomas Aquinas, *Super Ep. Pauli*, 344, §584; Peter Lumbard, in J.-P. Migne, ed., *Patrologiae Cursus Completus: Series Latina*, 221 vols. (Paris: Garnier, 1844–64), 91:1629; Ambrosiaster, *Commentarius in epistulas Paulinas (ad Corinthios)*, part 2 of *Corpus Scriptorum Ecclesiasticorum Latinorum* vol. 81, ed. H. J. Vogels (Vindobonae: Hoelder-Pichler-Tempsky, 1968), 252. Compare Moffatt, *First Epistle*, 149.

14. BDAG, 763. Among the Greek-speaking Jews, the word referred to the teachings of the rabbis. It therefore carried the idea of authority and, with Paul, it was a tacit reminder

(*katechō*) denotes "adhering firmly to convictions and traditions."[15] In their letter to Paul, it would seem that the Corinthian Saints expressed a willingness to follow what had become a tradition in many of the branches of the Church, and this was what Paul was commending them for. The particular tradition in focus was allowing women to participate in worship services. In their letter to him, however, they raised concerns about a new development and wanted his direction.[16]

11:3 But I would have you know, that the head of every man is Christ; and the head of the woman is the man; and the head of Christ is God / But I want you to understand that the head of every man is Christ, and the head of every woman is the man, and the head of Christ is God: Paul's introduction, θέλω δὲ ὑμᾶς εἰδέναι (*thelo de hymas eidenai*), "But I want you to understand," ties what he is about to say to what he has already said. Though he commends them for what they have accepted, they need to clearly understand a point that they have missed. Therefore, the coordinating conjunction δέ (*de*) is translated adversatively as "but."[17] In sum, they have accepted the tradition found in other branches of the Church that women have the right to prophetic speech, "but" (*de*) they have missed an important principle that has contributed to the present problem.[18]

With this sentence, Paul lays down the foundation on which he will build his argument. In doing so, he uses a wordplay on the noun κεφαλή (*kephalē*), "head," taking it in both its literal and metaphorical senses. Literally, it denotes that part of the body in which the brain is encased and that houses the organs of sight, sound, smell, and taste. As a metaphor, however, it has a whole range of meanings. For instance, it can stand for the whole person or for someone of higher or superior rank, such as a ruler or leader.[19] *Kephalē* can denote one who has preeminence. In addition, it can refer to a source, such as the "head" of a river or the progenitor of a family. Because of the semantic range of the word, precisely translating Paul's

---

that his instructions originated with the Divine. Friedrich Büchsel, "παράδοσις," in *TDNT*, 2:172–73.

15. BDAG, 533.

16. Hays, *First Corinthians*, 181–84, makes a very good case for this position.

17. See Fee, *First Epistle*, 493, who follows the NRSV, NJB, and REB.

18. Jerome Murphy-O'Connor, "Sex and Logic in 1 Corinthians 11:2–16," *Catholic Biblical Quarterly* 42 (1980): 483.

19. BDAG, 541–42. In Roman times, an honorable means of execution and a right of citizens was to be executed by decapitation, derived from *capitalis* in Latin meaning "of the head" instead of being tortured, beaten, and crucified.

intent presents some difficulties.[20] To keep the ambiguity, our Rendition follows the KJV and translates *kephalē* simply as "head." Nonetheless, we have chosen to explore its possible meanings.

Paul's initial use of the word *kephalē* is metaphorical. From the context he most likely used the word to indicate the preeminent or foremost nature of the subject in each case.[21] The word "preeminence" denotes that which has the highest eminence or rank due to superlativeness and uniqueness. The word does not connote, as does the word "supremacy," the idea of unequalled superiority such that there are no equals, nor does it connote domination or autocratic power, as does the word "ascendancy." Rather, it points to that which is distinctive above all others and, thereby, commands respect and difference, like a citizen of the Roman Empire which Paul was.[22] It does not necessarily refer to a leader or ruler, but designates anyone holding the position of prominence or superiority in a particular situation. One who is preeminent in one instance, therefore, may not be in another.

God has preeminence over Christ who has preeminence over all men. Men, in turn, have preeminence over women in Paul's metaphor.[23] There is an order in the Church, that is, a hierarchy, that determines how some practices are done and by whom.[24]

In Christ's Church, women, especially Jewish women, enjoyed freedom and place in Church worship as never before. Though Jewish women attended worship services in the synagogue, they were forbidden to pray, read scripture aloud, and preach.[25] It would appear that some of the more progressive Christian women, on the other hand, began pushing the boundaries of decorum and respect. Paul pushed back, insisting that tradition dictated that certain Jewish religious norms were yet to be observed during Christian worship services.

---

20. As Thiselton, *First Epistle*, 812, notes, "The history of claims about the meaning of κεφαλή is immense and daunting." See his study on pp. 812–22. See also Fitzmyer, *First Corinthians*, 409–11, for a shorter but solid analysis.

21. Thiselton, *First Epistle*, 821.

22. *Dictionary of Synonyms*, 803, s.v. "supreme."

23. Some translations translate the noun *anēr*, "man" or "husband," in the second clause as "husband" (for example, see NRSV), but the issue here seems to be with gender relations that transcend the narrow confines of the family circle and, therefore, our Rendition translates the word as "man," following the majority of translations (see REB, NIV, NJB).

24. This is true in the Church today. See D&C 20:68; 28:13; 58:55; 107:84.

25. Here Paul is definitely following Jewish tradition. In certain Hellenistic cult rites, women participated freely, and this may have influenced the attitude of some of the Christian women. Tomson, *Paul and the Jewish Law*, 133–34.

11:4 *Every man praying or prophesying, having his head covered, dishonoureth his head / Any man who prays or prophesies with his head covered dishonors his head:* The present active participle προφητεύων (*prophēteuōn*), "prophesying," though never losing the nuance of foretelling, centers more on inspired speech that included teaching, preaching, and testimony bearing.[26] (We will return to this topic in more detail in chapter 14.) Paul's phrase κατὰ κεφαλῆς ἔχων (*kata kephalēs exōn*), literally "down from the head having [something]," is vague. It does not mention specifically any kind of head covering. As a result, some have argued that the Apostle was referring to long hair.[27] Though this idea cannot be firmly discounted, the context—especially given 11:5 that clearly refers to some kind of head covering for women—suggests he had such in mind.[28]

The verb καταισχύνει (*kataischynei*), "dishonor," denoted acts that bring shame, humiliation, or disgrace upon oneself or another person or persons.[29] In Corinth (as well as in much of the Roman world, as noted in the introduction to this book) the society was highly attuned to shame and honor. That led to a continual competition and defensiveness concerning one's dignity and status. The degree of shame or honor that a person had attached to himself or herself became the litmus test of his or her value, not only in society's eyes but in his or her own.[30]

Again, Paul employed the noun κεφαλή (*kephalē*) in a metaphorical sense. Thus, his reference to a man dishonoring his "head" could refer to the man who, taking on the practice of Jewish, Greek, and Roman men in having his head covered in worship service, dishonored his head, that is, brought shame upon himself as a Christian who yielded to non-Christian

---

26. Louw-Nida, §33.459; BDAG, 890.

27. R. A. Horsley, *I Corinthians* (Nashville: Abingdon Press, 1998), 154; Murphy-O'Connor, "Sex and Logic," 484–85.

28. See Fitzmyer, *First Corinthians,* 412. For further study, see Hays, *First Corinthians,* 184; Richard E. Oster Jr., "Use, Misuse, and Neglect of Archaeological Evidence in Some Modern Works on 1 Corinthians (1 Corinthians 7:1–5; 8:10; 11:2–16; 12:14–26)," *Zeitschrift für die neutestamentliche Wissenschaft* 83 (1992): 68. A number of male statues and busts dating from the first century show men with part of their toga draped over their heads. For example, see Franklin P. Johnson, *Corinth: Results of Excavations,* vol. 9 (Cambridge: Harvard University Press, 1931), 70–72 §134. Some scholars have suggested that Paul was not referring to an actual practice, but making up a hypothetical situation as a means of contrast. See Fitzmyer, *First Corinthians,* 413; Fee, *First Corinthians,* 505; Robertson and Plummer, *Critical and Exegetical Commentary,* 229. Given the context, however, a literal practice seems the better choice.

29. BDAG, 517; Louw-Nida, §25.194.

30. Moxnes, "Honor, Shame and the Outside World," 208.

practices.[31] A dishonorable practice such as this would be extremely significant in this honor/shame culture.

On the other hand, since a man's status also reflected on those to whom he was responsible (including his family, employer, patron, or even god), the man's act of covering his head could also be seen as demeaning Christ. In that case, his dishonorable act would come from his concealing that he is the "image and glory of God" (11:7; compare Gen. 1:26; Moses 2:26; Abr. 4:26), as if he were ashamed of the fact.[32] Since Paul clearly states that the head of the man was Christ, it is likely that Paul was referring to dishonoring the Savior. The man's dress would certainly contribute to discord, thus distracting his fellows and drawing their attention away from the Lord, who should at all times have the preeminence.[33]

11:5 *But every woman that prayeth or prophesieth with her head uncovered dishonoureth her head / But any woman who prays or prophesies with her head uncovered dishonors her head:* The coordinating conjunction, δέ (*de*), is translated here adversatively as "but" to stress the contrast between the point Paul has just made with the one he now makes. Paul's statement shows clearly that women participated actively in worship services in multiple roles, including bearing witness, teaching, and praying, and that these roles had been in the Church long enough to be considered "traditions" (παραδόσεις, *paradoseis*, 11:2).

The issue, then, was not that these women were participating in worship service but in how certain ones elected to do so. Paul's phrase ἀκατακαλύπτῳ τῇ κεφαλῇ (*akatakalyptō tē kephalē*), "with her head uncovered," defines the issue. His words do not specify the nature of the covering the woman ceased to wear.[34] It could have been a small or nearly transparent veil, a heavy veil, a hood, a scarf, or even part of her outer dress draped over her head.

---

31. Thiselton, *First Epistle*, 827–28.

32. Bailey, *Mediterranean Eyes*, 305.

33. Hays, *First Corinthians*, 184; Bruce, *1 and 2 Corinthians*, 104.

34. Elisabeth Schüssler Fiorenza, *In Memory of Her: A Feminist Theological Reconstruction of Christian Origins* (New York: Crossroads Publishing/Herder and Herder, 1994), 227–30, puts forth the thesis that Paul was referring to a practice wherein the women loosened their hair. She states that these women were using their "loose and unbounded hair" as a symbol of their prophetic-charismatic power (a sign of their ecstatic endowment), imitating the maenads in the cult of Dionysus or Cybele, the Pythia at Delphia. But her thesis has been discounted by Christopher Forbes, *Prophecy and Inspired Speech in Early Christianity and Its Hellenistic Environments* (Tübingen: Mohr, 1995), 103–217, and, therefore, has not been developed here.

for that is even all one as if she were shaven / for it is the same thing as having her head shaved: A shaved head had a number of connotations in the ancient world. It was associated with slavery and with the sexual abuse that was often heaped upon slaves. It was also the hallmark of a prostitute.[35] Members of God's kingdom on earth should be identified with none of these.

Conversely, in both Jewish and Roman rituals shaving the head allowed a person to marry someone of a higher rank.[36] Nonetheless, the freedom embodied in the ritual of shaving never lost its association with sexual license.

Moreover, Paul believed that God's creation of the two genders in different ways (11:8–9) demanded that distinctions be maintained during worship services.[37] In this light, the perception of shame could have come from self-advertising dress and sexless, genderless costume. Removing a woman's hair altogether would have had the same de-feminizing effect as her worshiping without a head covering. It was therefore, for Paul, a small step between praying with an uncovered head and having shorn locks (thus, his words, ἓν γάρ ἐστιν [*hen gar estin*], "it is the same thing"); both resulted in a loss of femininity.[38]

11:6 *For if the woman be not covered, let her also be shorn / For if a woman does not cover her head, then she should get her hair cut off:* The imperative κειράσθω (*keirasthō*), "to be shorn," carries a causative force and can be translated as, "Let her have her hair cut off."[39] This verse largely repeats the point Paul had already made, and he was likely restating it for effect. It also allowed him to stress the point he makes with his next phrase.

---

35. Thiselton, *First Epistle*, 829.

36. In ancient Rome, slaves often had sexual relationships with their masters. The Roman poet Horace was notorious for mentioning this practice. See, for example, *Sat.* 1.2.116–18. Among the Israelites, women captured in war became slaves but could marry an Israelite man after shaving their heads and, thus, renouncing their past. See Deut. 21:10–14. Among the Romans, manumitted slaves (men and women) were shaved as part of a Roman *Pileus* ritual that granted freedom. That freedom, in the first century, likely held connotations of newly discovered sexual freedom or license. See Diodorus Siculus, *Exc. Leg.* 22; Plaut., *Amphit.* 1.1.306; *Persius.* 5.82. The authors are very appreciative for the insights and assistance of Brent Schmidt for this section. Brent Schmidt to Richard Draper, August 18, 2014, email attachment.

37. Collins, *First Corinthians*, 400–402; J. M. Gundry-Volf, "Gender and Creation in 1 Cor 11:2–16: A Study in Paul's Theological Methods," in Peter Stuhlmacher and others, ed., *Evangelium, Schriftauslegung, Kirche: Festschrift für Peter Stuhlmacher zum 65 Geburstag* (Göttingen: Vandenhoeck Ruprecht, 1997), 151–71.

38. C. R. Hallpike, "Social Hair," *Man*, n.s., 4 (1969): 256–64.

39. BDAG, 538; Fitzmyer, *First Corinthians*, 414.

Paul appealed to social convention and public norms to make his point. His statement was couched in such a way as to elicit a strong negative reaction from his readers who would insist that such a thing would bring shame upon these women.

but if it be a shame for a woman to be shorn or shaven, let her be covered / Now if it is disgraceful for a woman to have her hair cut off or her head shaved, then she should keep her head covered: The middle/passive present infinitive ξυρᾶσθαι (*xyrasthai*) means to have one's head shaved. Paul's intent seems to show that these women should not just go halfway with a shorn head, but all the way with shaved ones.[40] In this way, they became like bald men. With force, Paul's words balance the great shame of short or no hair with that of worshiping with an uncovered head. Women were to maintain their dignity, gender, and station as well as show respect to their "head" by wearing a covering.

11:7 *For a man indeed ought not to cover his head, forasmuch as he is the image and glory of God / For a man should not cover his head, since he is the image and glory of God:* In this and the next verse, Paul does two things: he explains why he takes the position he does on head coverings and, in the process, explains why he thinks men have preeminence over women. He appeals to LXX Genesis 1:26 but makes some modifications. There it states that God desired to "make human being after [his] image and likeness," (ἄνθρωπον κατ᾽ εἰκόνα ἡμετέραν καὶ καθ᾽ ὁμοίωσιν, *anthrōpon kat' eikona hēmeteran kai kath' homoiōsin*), but Paul replaced ἄνθρωπος (*anthrōpos*) "human being" with ἀνήρ (*anēr*), "male." He also adds δόξα (*doxa*), "glory," to εἰκόνα (*eikōna*), "image," and ὁμοίωσις (*homoiōsis*), "likeness."

The idea of "likeness" is important because it carries the idea of not only being in the image of something but also of sharing in its character and attributes. The Fall, though it introduced corruption into the world, did not entirely efface the "image" of God upon Adam. He still carried godlike qualities, that is, a "likeness," and could enhance these to return to the Father. Paul's point seems to be that the male, having come into existence first, had the direct and primary responsibility of bringing glory to the Father by living in imitation of God (compare Moses 1:39).[41]

---

40. Fitzmyer, *First Corinthians,* 414. For the disgrace associated with female shaved heads, see Aristophanes, *Thesm.* 831 for the Greeks and *T. Job* 23:7; 24:7–10 for the Jews.

41. Gerhard Kittel, Gerhard von Rad, and Hermann Kleinknecht, "εἰκών," in *TDNT,* 2:381–97.

By adding δόξα (*doxa*), "glory," to the Genesis text, Paul emphasized the key role the man was to play—he was to bring glory, that is, honor to God. At the same time the Apostle maintained his readers' focus on the differences between the function of the two genders. The themes of honor and dishonor are the opposite poles around which he builds his argument. In this case, *doxa* denotes the honor and respect one garners from family, friends, peers, or associates who themselves are people of honor.[42] The man was not to cover his head, for to do so was to suggest he was ashamed of his likeness to God. One so ashamed would not be willing to give glory (bring honor) to his God.

but the woman is the glory of the man: Again, the focus is on the noun δόξα (*doxa*), "glory." The issue is who gives glory to whom and how. As the man is to honor God, so the woman is to honor the man. It is important to note that *doxa* does not carry any connotation of involuntary submission, or even obedience. It does, in this case, carry the idea of respect.[43] For instance in LXX Proverbs 11:16 it states that "a gracious wife brings glory to her husband." It is not, therefore, a case of man *or* woman, but a case of man *and* woman. It is she who brings the man glory. Without her, he would be hard pressed to receive any.

11:8 For the man is not of the woman; but the woman of the man / For man did not come from woman, but woman from man: Paul appeals to LXX Genesis 2:7, 22–23. He puts stress on the preposition ἐκ (*ek*), "out of" or "from," which acts here as a marker for source or origin.[44] According to the creation account, God created Adam first and later took one of his ribs and made it into a woman (Gen. 2:7, 22–23). The LXX is very specific on this point, noting that she is "woman," ὅτι ἐκ τοῦ ἀνδρὸς αὐτῆς ἐλήμφθη αὕτη (*hoti ek tou andros autēs elēmphthē hautē*), "because she was taken from her man."[45] The man received preeminence because he was there first and was the source of her origin.

---

42. Louw-Nida, §§33.357; 87.4. In its use here, δόξα (*doxa*), "glory" does not refer to an aspect of God's divine nature that expresses itself, in part, through astonishingly powerful light (for example, see JS–H 1:16; Acts 26:13). For a study on this aspect, see Richard D. Draper, "Light, Truth, and Grace: Three Themes of Salvation (D&C 93)," in *Sperry Symposium Classics: The Doctrine and Covenants*, ed. Craig K. Manscill (Provo, Utah: Religious Studies Center, Brigham Young University, 2004), 234–47.

43. BDAG, 256–58.

44. BDAG, 295–98.

45. The Hebrew text reads כִּי מֵאִישׁ לֻקֳחָה־זֹּאת (*kî mē'îš luqŏḥāh zō't*) "because she (literally 'this one') was taken from man."

11:9 *Neither was the man created for the woman; but the woman for the man / neither was man created for the sake of woman, but woman for man:* Continuing his reference to Genesis 2 but looking at verses 18 and 20, Paul moves to his next point. Here he puts his emphasis on the preposition διά (*dia*), "through." The preposition with the accusative has a causal force meaning "owing to" or "for the sake of."[46] According to the LXX Genesis account, the woman was created αὐτῷ βοηθὸν αὐτόν (*autō boēthon kat' auton*), "[as] a helper perfectly suited for him." In short, she was created for his sake, because "it is not good that the man should be alone" (Gen. 2:18; compare D&C 132:15–20). A nuance in this verse is that women lift, build, and inspire men. Women do not exist to selflessly serve men (or be slaves to them) but to complement them so that all God's children may be exalted (D&C 132).

11:10 *For this cause ought the woman to have power on her head / For this reason a woman ought to have control over her head:* In this verse, Paul concludes his biblical and theological argument. He marks this with the resumptive phrase, διὰ τοῦτο (*dia touto*), "for this reason." Paul's use of the word ὀφείλει (*opheilei*), "ought to," is both telling and important. It carries no sense of external compulsion but of social or spiritual obligation. There is no hint of imposed constraint but one of moral duty.[47] It denotes "the woman's positive obligation, which corresponds to the negative obligation of the man."[48]

Determining exactly what Paul meant in this verse is difficult on at least two levels. First, not all sources agree on the exact phrase. Some early Christian writers have the noun κάλυμμα (*kalymma*), "covering," referring to a veil or some other head covering,[49] while the majority have the noun ἐξουσία (*exousia*), "authority."[50] Secondly, the latter noun can denote either a sign or symbol of authority or one of subjugation.[51] Almost always in the New Testament, the word means to have the right, freedom, and power to act, control, or do something.[52] Taking that as the case here, the

---

46. BDAG, 223–26.

47. Friedrich Hauck, "ὀφείλω," in *TDNT,* 5:559–64.

48. Fitzmyer, *First Corinthians,* 416.

49. If that is what Paul meant, he could be obliquely referring to temple ritual.

50. This is not a modern problem. Some ancient manuscripts and patristic witnesses include an explanatory gloss that defines the word with *kalymma,* "a veil." See Metzger, *Textual Commentary,* 495.

51. Fitzmyer, *First Corinthians,* 417.

52. BDAG, 352–53.

word connotes that, in covering her head, the woman "actively exercises control over it" with the result that she need not be exposed to indignity.[53] The head covering, acting as a symbol of the power she has received from the Lord and of the right she has to worship, certifies her place not only to worship but to participate actively in that worship. On the other hand, as one authority stated, "If she unveils [her head], every one has control over it and can gaze at her so as to put her out of countenance."[54]

because of the angels: It is not clear what Paul meant by the term "angels." Speculation ranges far and wide. Among proposals are: (1) fallen angels, sometimes referred to as "watchers," who lust after mortal women;[55] (2) the animals called "seraphim" who stand in the presence of God;[56] (3) mortal priesthood leaders;[57] (4) holy angels who participate in the worship service and are pleased with order in the Church,[58] and (5) guardian angels responsible for the safety of the Saints.[59]

Based on long-standing Jewish tradition with corroboration coming out of Qumran (all contemporary with Paul),[60] the best understanding is that these are heavenly beings who are conscious of and participate in earthly proceedings.[61] They expect the order of earth to match that of heaven. It is likely that Paul had these personalities in mind when he noted that the

---

53. Fitzmyer, *First Corinthians*, 417.

54. Robertson and Plummer, *Critical and Exegetical Commentary*, 232; see also David R. Hall, "A Problem of Authority," *Expository Times* 102 (1990–91): 39–42.

55. For example, Tertullian, *On the Veiling of Virgins*, 7.

56. This is based on Isa. 6:2.

57. Based on Rev. 2:1, 8, 12, 18; 3:1, 7, 14. For example, see Ambrose in Migne, *Patrologia Latina*, 17.240C.

58. For example, see Augustine, *On the Trinity*, 12.7.10.

59. This is based on Matt. 18:10. See Theodoret in J.-P. Migne, ed., *Patrologiae Cursus Completus: Series Graeca*, 162 vols. (Paris: Garnier, 1857–86), 82.312D–313A.

60. 1 QM 7:4–6; 1 QS 2:3–11 refer to angels being among God's people.

61. Joseph Smith instructed the Saints on the nature and ministry of angels (see "History, 1838–1856, Volume C-1 Addenda," 69), and reported a number of instances when angels minister to the Saints (see "History, 1838–1856, Volume A-1 [23 December 1805–30 August 1834]," 25, 51, Church History Library, available online at Church Historian's Press, *The Joseph Smith Papers*, http://www.josephsmithpapers.org/paper-summary/history-1838-1856-volume-a-1-23-december-1805-30-august-1834/31; "History, 1838–1856, Volume B-1 [1 September 1834–2 November 1838]," 696–99, Church History Library, available online at Church Historian's Press, *The Joseph Smith Papers*, http://www.josephsmithpapers.org/paper-summary/history-1838-1856-volume-b-1-1-september-1834-2-november-1838/150; "History, 1838–1856, Volume C-1 Addenda," 13); and taught that angels "minister to embodied spirits" ("History, 1838–1856, Volume C-1," 1229).

law of God was "ordained by angels in the hand of a mediator" (Gal. 3:19).[62] These beings act as guardians of this law and assure the order and peace it was designed to bring. On that basis, because of the angels, respect, reverence, and willing submission on the part of each Christian supersedes individual autonomy. In God's Church, there should be no push for individual "rights" or "freedoms" when it comes to assisting and raising others to Christ. Saints are to combine with angels for this cause.[63] Thus, Christian women and men should be willing to follow Church norms in behalf of others by avoiding offenses and distractions.

11:11 *Nevertheless neither is the man without the woman, neither the woman without the man / Nevertheless, neither is woman independent of man nor man independent of woman:* The preposition χωρίς (*chōris*), "without," expresses a state of being "separate from, apart from," or "independent of" something else.[64] There is more than one way to nuance Paul's phrase but important among them is the idea that women and men are essential to each other—one is as nothing without the other.[65]

in the Lord: Since Paul has already referred to the order of creation and to those societal conventions that exist both within and without the Church, the phrase ἐν κυρίῳ (*en kyriō*), "in the Lord," likely refers to the order that Christ had established in his kingdom, both in heaven and on earth. Paul could, therefore, be looking to Church proceedings and protocols that had eternal ramifications.[66]

11:12 *For as the woman is of the man, even so is the man also by the woman / For just as woman came from man, so also man comes through woman:* To make his point, Paul contrasts the prepositions ἐκ (*ek*), "from," here a marker showing source or origin,[67] with that of διά (*dia*), "through," here a marker of instrumentality.[68] According to Genesis, woman came into edenic existence from man, but according to everyday life, man comes into mortal existence when he is born through the woman.

62. On the New Testament's view of the angels' role in ordering the affairs of church and nations, see George B. Caird, *Principalities and Powers: A Study in Pauline Theology* (Eugene, Ore.: Wipf and Stock Publishers, 2003), 17–18.

63. For a full discussion, see Fitzmyer, *First Corinthians,* 417–19; Thiselton, *First Epistle,* 839–41.

64. BDAG, 1095, which translates the idea contained here as "Neither is woman anything apart from man, nor man from woman."

65. On this, compare the translations of the verse in the NIV, NRSV, and NJB.

66. Gundry-Volf, "Gender and Creation," 163; Thiselton, *First Epistle,* 842.

67. BDAG, 295–8.

68. BDAG, 223–6.

Paul uses both the creation account and the experience of human birth to show how God's order has been set up. In these two kinds of creation, the mutual interdependence of men and women is realized and the reciprocity that each ideally brings to the other is achieved. Since the creation account suggests some kind of priority of men over women in terms of God's action, the everyday experience of birth shows man's dependence on woman by her action. His birth, therefore, stresses her indispensability and value. There is, thus, mutual dependency. Seen in this light, it seems that woman was not created nor does she exist in some subordinate position for man's expectations or purposes.[69] The theology Paul presents here is vital. Differences in physiology, temperament, duties, assignment, and the other's expectations are the necessary basis for true mutuality, reciprocity, and relationships. Mutual respect of each gender for the other, coupled with submission to each one's "head," constitutes the order of the kingdom.

but all things of God / But all things come from God: As is his wont, Paul again puts God center stage. Though woman came from man and men through women, all come from God. Paul's use of the preposition ἐκ (*ek*), "from," puts emphasis on God as the ultimate source of both men and women, and, for that matter, everything else he has created. It is his eternal plan.

11:13 *Judge in yourselves: is it comely that a woman pray unto God uncovered? / Judge for yourselves, is it proper for a woman to pray to God with her head uncovered?:* Paul now summarizes his argument. In doing so, he asks two rhetorical questions. This is the first. Its thrust is found in his use of the impersonal participle πρέπον (*prepon*), "it is proper." It denotes an act that is fitting or proper for its circumstance.[70] Thus, the question's appeal is to propriety, looking at both church protocols and social conventions and, in addition, to the force of the reasoning he has carefully presented. The key phrase here is τῷ θεῷ (*tō theō*), "to God." Using it, Paul points his readers to the most sacred of Christian activities—prayer—and asks if this is the time or place for women to address the issue of their equality with men.[71]

11:14 *Doth not even nature itself teach you, that, if a man have long hair, it is a shame unto him? / Doesn't nature itself teach you that if a man has long hair, it is a disgrace to him:* The appeal in Paul's second rhetorical question is to φύσις (*physis*), "nature." Greeks had often made arguments

---

69. Fee, *First Epistle*, 523.
70. BDAG, 861.
71. Fitzmyer, *First Corinthians*, 420.

about what is man-made law (*nomos*) and what is universally given (*physis*).[72] Paul insists his position rests upon the latter. In this case, the word means "the natural and established order of things."[73] Paul couches his question such that it requires a "yes" answer (indicated by οὐδέ [*oude*], "does not"). The issue is over καμάω (*kamaō*), the wearing of hair long. The reference is not to beards, which distinguishes men from women, but to tresses, which do not.

To what part of "nature" Paul is appealing is unclear. An appeal to social custom does not work well, for though Roman males wore their hair close-cropped, Greek males were much less consistent.[74] Whatever the basis of his appeal, he is clear about the result; it is a disgrace. Paul chose the noun ἀτιμία (*atimia*) to make his point. The word denotes living in a "state of dishonor or disrespect."[75] This condition stood exactly opposite that of δόξα (*doxa*), "honor, respect, glory," and therefore carried the idea of shame.

11:15 *But if a woman have long hair, it is a glory to her / but if a woman has long hair, it is her glory?:* Paul's question again focuses on gender differentiation as expressed in the nature of clothing and hair.[76] Long hair for women was very appealing to most people and expressed the principle of modesty; indeed, it is her glory. Here the noun δόξα (*doxa*) carries the idea of "favorable reputation,"[77] where for the male, it is his shame.

for her hair is given her for a covering / Because long hair is given her for a covering: The pronoun αὐτῇ (*autē*), "her," is missing in several early manuscripts,[78] but it is found in other equally ancient manuscripts.[79] On the whole, although editors of SBLGNT, which we generally follow, chose to omit it, the evidence seems to best support retaining it, and so it is retained in our Rendition as in the KJV. The perfect passive voice of the verb δέδοται (*dedotai*), "is given," does not identify the giver. It is likely, however, since Paul has already made an appeal to the ordering of all things by the will of God, that he has the Divine in mind. Paul describes the purpose of a woman's long hair: it is to act as a replacement (ἀντί, *anti*) for

---

72. In the modern era the same idea can be seen in the "nature vs. nurture" debates.

73. BDAG, 1069–70.

74. According to Thucydides, *Hist.* 1.5–8, the Athenians wore their hair short while the Spartans wore it long.

75. BDAG, 149.

76. Thiselton, *First Epistle*, 846.

77. BDAG, 256–8.

78. Notably 𝔓[46], D, E, F, G, and Ψ.

79. Such as ℵ, A, and B. See Metzger, *Textual Commentary*, 495–96.

a περιβολαίου (*peribolaiou*), literally "a wraparound mantle."[80] The perfect tense of the verb suggests that her long hair is a permanent endowment by God. It is also a symbol of the principle of modesty in the law of chastity. The nuance of the whole verse points to the folly of those who are trying to go against God's established order in the Church.[81]

11:16 *But if any man seem to be contentious, we have no such custom, neither the churches of God / Now if anyone is disposed to argue about this, we have no such custom, neither do any of the churches of God:* Paul here makes his last appeal. The indefinite pronoun τις (*tis*), "anyone," can refer to either a masculine or feminine subject. Thus, Paul is referring to all, male or female, who might yet disagree with him. The verb δοκεῖ (*dokei*), usually "seem" or "think,"[82] here carries the idea of "being disposed to."[83]

Paul describes the attitude of these people with the very interesting adjective φιλόνεικος (*philoneikos*), "quarrelsome, contentious."[84] The compound adjective is made up of two words, φίλος (*philos*), "loving," and νεῖκος (*neikos*), "strife," and is related to νίκος (*nikos*), "victory."[85] It expresses the idea that one's willingness to argue is not for the purpose of discovering truth but expressly for the sake of winning.[86] To counter this bent, Paul makes a very strong appeal to that of Church discipline. None of the other established branches have such a practice. Thus, behind his words stands the force of broad-based apostolic authority. For Paul, that is where the argument stops once and for all.[87]

Analysis and Summary

By way of background, in the Greco-Roman world, due to a woman's potential of bringing great shame to her family through improper behavior and especially sexual misconduct, "women were controlled, enclosed, and guarded."[88] That dictated not only how they were to act in public but also

---

80. Louw-Nida, §6.172.

81. Fitzmyer, *First Corinthians*, 421.

82. BDAG, 254–55.

83. BDAG, 254; Louw-Nida, §25.7. Thus, the translation in the NRSV; Meyer, *Exegetical Commentary*, 1:330–31.

84. BDAG, 1058.

85. Greek Word Study Tool, http://www.perseus.tufts.edu/hopper/morph?l=neikos &la=greek#lexcon.

86. Wire, *Corinthian Women*, 15.

87. Fiorenza, *In Memory of Her*, 229.

88. Osiek and Blach, *Families in the New Testament Times*, 40–41.

what they wore. Further, in this society few, either man or woman, would have raised the question of equality. "No ancient Mediterranean man," noted one scholar, "would have ever have thought that a woman could be his equal; only a man of similar education and social status could be. Only a man could be equal to a man, a woman to a woman."[89] The social boundaries were not to be crossed without censure. Therefore, many in society were sensitive to the breaking of social strictures in attitude, decorum, or dress. To step outside of these was considered shameful, a condition no family or social group wanted its members to be in.

Within the Christian circle, from the time of the Savior's ministry, women had a remarkable participatory role. That Christian women could participate directly in worship service shows how far Christianity had moved from Judaism. For example, during the formal worship at the synagogue, though wives likely sat with their husbands, other than saying "amen" to prayers, blessings, and invocations, they played no direct role.[90] They did not pray aloud, read or comment on scripture, give talks, or teach. Thus, Christianity, having women do all of these, gave them not only a greater participatory role unknown within Jewish culture but also more responsibility with its accompanying recognition of their importance. It also brought with it the possibility to push religious opportunities beyond their bounds. This epistle suggests some women did so by discarding their head coverings during worship service.

In Roman and Hellenistic culture, the veil or hood was important because it gave a clear indication that the wearer was a person of status and respectability.[91] There was a direct correlation between proper dress and personal success, enjoyment of public honor, and esteem by women within the general society.[92] Most importantly, their apparel acted as a defense, showing that the woman was neither potentially nor actually available for sexual

---

89. Osiek and Blach, *Families in the New Testament Times*, 40–41.

90. Monique Susskind Goldberg, *The Meḥitzah in the Synagogue*, trans. Diana Villa (Jerusalem: Schechter Institution of Jewish Studies, 2004), 14–16. Tomson, *Paul and the Jewish Law*, 134, notes that women at this time may have been seated separately in some cases but such seating became standardized only during the middle ages. Further, inscriptions exist that mention women as "leaders," "elders," and "mothers of the synagogue," but it is very unlikely, especially in light of the Tannaim (*t. Meg.* 3:11), that women actually served in liturgical capacities.

91. Martin, *Corinthian Body*, 229–49, discusses this social practice in detail.

92. Mary R. Lefkowitz and Maureen B. Fant, *Women's Life in Greece and Rome: A Source Book in Translation* (Baltimore: Johns Hopkins University Press; London: Duckworth, 1982), 104–10, 157–71.

advances.[93] According to the poet Ovid (43 BC–AD 18), who was viewed as scandalous by many contemporaries because he advocated sexual license, men should hunt women. In his poem *Ars Amatoria, or the Art of Love,* women who were "available" went out to places like the theater for the express purpose to see and be seen.[94]

But there was more going on that likely concerned Paul far more than such social mores. In the Christian circle, as with the man's attire, the woman's dress could give a very distracting signal in public worship. It was especially important that it not have any sexual overtones. For a woman to go with head uncovered made a bold statement that pushed beyond Jewish protocols and, at its core, was self-advertising. The act was dishonoring, at least in part, because it took the attention of the worshiper away from where it belonged, that is, on the Lord.

This act betrayed even more about these women. It suggested an attitude among them, based on a false understanding of the gospel that "anything goes." It may be, as Ovid suggests, that they were drawing attention to themselves; they came "to be seen as well." Such an attitude allowed them to push propriety and, in doing so, challenge the boundaries between males and females. In short, their actions obscured gender differences. They were confusing equality with sameness. These women were ascribing to themselves prerogatives that belonged to the men of the congregation and, in that way, were dishonoring those who were at the head.[95]

We must emphasize, as noted by Elder Bruce R. McConkie in the forepart of this chapter, that the Apostle Paul "approves or disapproves of certain local customs and traditions—not that the local customs were of themselves either good or bad, but that their practice either added to or diminished from the proper reverence for and adherence to the great basic concepts being set forth."[96]

Because the issues Paul addresses here, unlike those in most of this letter, are based so heavily on customs and attitudes of his day rather than on more universal norms, this portion of his epistle has little application for today. This point becomes especially evident when one understands

---

93. Rousselle, "Body Politics in Ancient Rome," 315.

94. Ovid, *Ars Amatoria,* book 1, part 4. The translation comes from A. S. Kline, Poetry in Translation, http://poetryintranslation.com/PITBR/Latin/ArtofLoveBk1.htm.

95. Fitzmyer, *First Corinthians,* 413. Among the Jews, women did not officiate in meetings. Opposition to such a practice was also known among the Romans. Tomson, *Paul and the Jewish Law,* 134, 137.

96. *DNTC,* 2:360.

precisely the matter Paul is addressing in this pericope. Otherwise, as the breadth of scholarship shows, one can easily get sidetracked or read into it issues that are not there.[97] Paul's concern is with "any woman who prays or prophesies with her head uncovered."[98] This point is clearly made in 11:5–6, 10, 13, 15.

The Greek adjective ἀκατακάλυπτος (*akatakalyptos*) means "uncovered" or "unveiled."[99] Some have argued, based on Paul's statement in chapter 14 that women should be silent in church, that his counsel here does not pertain to worship service.[100] The context clearly shows, however, that that is exactly the circumstance he is referring to. He states plainly that what some of the women were doing—participating in worship services with unveiled heads—was certainly not in any of the "the churches of God" (11:16), that is, in their assemblies.[101]

It is clear from 11:5 that the issue is not about women participating in worship services. There is no objection to their offering prayers, teaching, or bearing testimony. Indeed, they have the right to speak under inspiration. The force of Paul's verb προφητεύω (*prophēteuō*), which—unlike the English

---

97. Such as how men and women should comport themselves in prayer and proclamation (Wire, *Women Prophets*, 116–34); how men and women should wear their hair (Fiorenza, *In Memory of Her*, 227); that Christian men were preaching and prophesying with uncovered heads (Bruce W. Winter, *After Paul Left Corinth: The Influence of Secular Ethics and Social Change* [Grand Rapids, Mich.: Eerdmans, 2001], 121); or male homosexual styles of hair dressing, the latter being a wholly gratuitous interjection into the material and a notable distraction to the message of the epistle (see Martin, *Corinthian Body*, 296 n. 19).

98. There are three schools of thought on this issue. The traditional view takes the stand that Paul is talking about a head covering or veil. Some object to this idea because in 11:15, Paul describes the hair as a *peribolaion,* a garment that covers much of the body such as a robe, cloak, or shawl (BDAG, 800) and they do not feel scarf or veil works. Basing its contention on this, the second school of thought sees the issue as women cutting their hair, but this falls apart on Paul's insistence in 11:5–6 that a woman may as well be shaved or shorn if they insist on worshiping with an uncovered head. The last school of thought bases its argument on the use of the adjective *akatakalyptō,* "uncovered," in the LXX where it refers to "loosened hair" or letting hair down in public, thus, bringing shame on the person. The problem here rests first on 11:7 which refers to a man not covering his head and second on 11:15 which notes that a woman's long hair is her *peribalaion,* "covering." The traditional version seems the strongest. Paul's reference in 11:15 to the hair as a covering negate his insistence that a woman's head be covered during prayer and preaching. See Fee, *First Epistle,* 496.

99. BDAG, 35; Louw-Nida, §79.116–17.

100. This issue is discussed in full in the Analysis of 14:33b–35.

101. Fitzmyer, *First Corinthians,* 406.

word "prophesy," that only touches on prognostication—stresses the idea of proclaiming that which cannot be known by natural means and, thus, can only be had from God. Therefore, at its heart, the word denotes speaking the mind and counsel of God. This ability is a gift of the Spirit (12:10; 13:8; 14:1–3; Rom. 12:6) and is as readily available to women as to men.

"Paul's statements concerning the role of women," notes an LDS scholar, "are partly informed by social context, and it is important to note that in his summary of gender roles he draws an analogy that is based on the natural world and his own conclusions, rather than on scripture or the word of the Lord as he has done in other instances."[102] That being said, it should be noted that, though nowhere in this section does he directly quote scripture, he does make tacit references to it, especially Genesis 2.

Though the explicit issue Paul was addressing was about women who were participating in worship services with their heads uncovered, he was also concerned with and generally advocated rigid and conservative gender roles.[103] It must be emphasized that the matter Paul addresses is not whether women can pray, teach, and bear witness during worship service. Paul does not object to women doing so, but he reminds his readers that women show grave dishonor when they do so with their heads uncovered. The implication is that women normally veiled their faces or covered their heads during worship services through this period of Church history. Some, however, had taken the liberty of following the practice of men in not doing so. Though not all Gentile males wore head coverings during cultic exercises,[104] Jewish men always did. Paul here shows the Church has broken with Jewish tradition and started a new one, which he defends.

The head covering served a very important function in that society by protecting vulnerable women from undue and unwanted attention and avoiding the licentious Roman practices of women wanting to "see and be seen." Certainly the covering was not to be discarded as some sign of freedom, and especially not of defiance, of the culture and of Church norms.[105]

It is more likely, however, that it was not just infringements on either local or general culture that were driving Paul's concerns. This is because, though much of present scholarship seeks insights into understanding what was

---

102. Holzapfel and Wayment, *Making Sense,* 357–58.

103. Holzapfel and Wayment, *Making Sense,* 357–58.

104. Oster, "Use, Misuse and Neglect," 68, notes that males did wear head coverings during worship in many areas of the Roman Empire.

105. Martin, *Corinthian Body,* 233–48.

going on through a study of social and cultural issues, as we look at Paul's argument, his appeal rests less on societal and cultural issues and more on the application of gospel principles that promote modesty and proper decorum.[106] The point is that, while looking at the culture of the time can often be helpful, it becomes dangerous when we start assigning reasons for an apostolic decree that is different from what the author gives. Paul bases his argument on church discipline and doctrinal understanding. Specifically, he looks to the order of creation and the witness of nature as well as angels and church practice. All of these transcend social culture. Therefore, he may not have been overly concerned that by not wearing a head covering these women could be mistaken for prostitutes.[107] Women covering their heads, he clearly states, was part of official church practice for long enough that it had become a broad-based tradition (παράδοσις, *paradosis*) (11:2, 16). The point is that the local situation in Corinth cannot explain Paul's concerns, but going against church policy can.

The Apostle sets forth, in a surprisingly sober tone, five reasons why a woman should neither pray nor prophesy with an uncovered head. They are, as one scholar outlined:

1. Biblically, the order of creation found in the Genesis story reveals that woman has been created "for man," to be his companion and helper; hence, as "the glory of the man," she should cover her head (vv. 7–12).

2. Theologically, the ordered headship of God, Christ, man, and woman calls for it (v. 3).

3. Sociologically, convention, based on "nature" itself, considers a woman's uncovered head in such a situation as shameful and a disgrace (vv. 6, 13–15).

4. As a matter of ecclesiastical discipline, "the churches of God" have no such custom as uncovering heads of women at prayer in a cultic assembly (v. 16).

5. "Because of the angels" (v. 10).[108]

Sensing that not all will welcome his arguments, Paul ends this discussion by noting that "if anyone is disposed to argue about this," he or she

---

106. Robert Charles Sproul, *Knowing Scripture* (Nottingham: Inter-Varsity Press, 1977), 110.

107. David W. J. Gill, "The Importance of Roman Portraiture for Head-coverings in 1 Corinthians 11:1–16," *Tyndale Bulletin* 41, no. 2 (1990): 245–60. The author, using marble portraiture, suggests that it was acceptable for noble women to go out without head coverings and the practice did not invite unwanted attention.

108. Fitzmyer, *First Corinthians,* 407.

should consider the broad practice of the Church and accept that as the final authority (11:16, Rendition).

Paul insists on proper subordination and submission. He states that there is a hierarchy of relationships: God and Christ, Christ and man, man and woman, woman and child.[109] To emphasize his point, Paul employs a play on the word κεφαλή (*kephalē*), "head." As in English, the term can refer to both a part of the body and to a person who has high status or superior rank,[110] but in this situation, it better refers to preeminence.

At issue are actions that can bring honor or shame to an individual, his or her family, the Church, or to Christ and God. Paul focuses his concern on δόξα (*doxa*), "glory." The word denotes "a sign of honor," but its semantic range includes "that which makes impressive or weighty the person or thing that is glorious."[111] According to the creation account, a man is to exhibit the character and attributes of God as reflected in the commandments in both his life and role as guide, provider, and protector of the family (see Moses 5:5, 14–15, 58–59). In addition, he is to teach his children to do the same (see Moses 5:10–12; 6:4–5, 57–58; D&C 68:25). In this way he honors God, making him and his ways weighty and impressive and, thus, brings him glory.

Paul's statement that a man is the "glory of God" (11:7) is instructive. It means that his very existence is a means by which God can receive praise and honor.[112] In the Apostle's view this is because, by creating a man in his own image, God placed his own glory upon him. The reception of that glory gave a man additional value. Due to that value, a man can return glory to God.

---

109. In the modern world, the idea of superiority of man over woman has met with strong resistance, as it should. However, reinterpreting Paul through that lens distorts understanding him and what he has to say. To see the extent that culture has influenced people's view of Paul on this issue, see Linda Mercadante, *From Hierarchy to Equality: A Comparison of Past and Present Interpretations of 1 Cor 11:2–16 in Relation to the Changing Status of Women in Society* (Vancouver, B.C.: G-M-H Books, 1980).

110. BDAG, 541–42.

111. Thiselton, *First Epistle*, 835–36.

112. Moses 1:39 originally read, "This is my work *to* my glory, to the immortality and eternal life of man" instead of "This is my work *and* my glory . . . ." "History of Joseph Smith," *Times and Seasons* 4 (January 16, 1843): 73, and the 1851 edition of the Pearl of Great Price; italics added to highlight the changes. The Father certainly does things to bring himself glory through the acts of his children. For discussion, see Hyrum L. Andres, *Doctrinal Commentary on the Pearl of Great Price* (Salt Lake City: Deseret Book, 1967), 490–91.

Yet man, by himself, as Paul teaches, was incomplete and therefore lacked the ability to bring full glory to the Father. He needed a companion—one who was like him but different from him; one who corresponded to him as he did to God and who could bring him glory as he brought God glory. Thus, "the woman is the glory of the man" as a man is the "glory of God" (11:7). When men honor women, these women receive additional value. The more honor he gives her, the greater is her value. The greater her value, the more glory she can bestow upon him through her honoring him. In sum, Paul seems to be saying that as with God and a man, so it is with a man and a woman. He finds his glory through her creation and the honor she brings to him.[113]

Genesis is clear that the woman completes and complements the man and brings to him an incomparably richer life. Paul, therefore, does not hint of feminine inferiority. Further, as humankind, woman and man together manifest the fullness of divine attributes as expressions of God's creative being. Even so, this does not bring precise symmetry, for she is different from man. As Adam noted, she is "bone of my bone, and flesh of my flesh," but she was also "woman, because she was taken out of man" (Gen. 2:23). Her genesis was different from his. Thus, her glory comes in a different way. It comes by distinguishing herself from man in her own unique role to which the Creator assigned her, not in imitating man. And in this she finds greatness and glory, not inferiority.[114]

Elder McConkie noted that "women are not one whit behind men in spiritual things; perhaps, on the whole, they are ahead of them. . . . And women, here and now, are as much entitled to revelation, visions, and the gifts of the Spirit as are men."[115]

As President N. Eldon Tanner stated: "From the beginning God has made it clear that woman is very special, and he has also very clearly defined her position, her duties, and her destiny in the divine plan. Paul said that man is the image and glory of God, and that woman is the glory of the man; also that the man is not without the woman, neither the woman without the man in the Lord. (See 1 Cor. 11:7, 11.) You will note that significantly God is mentioned in connection with this great partnership, and we must never forget that one of woman's greatest privileges, blessings, and

---

113. Fee, *First Epistle*, 514–17.
114. Thiselton, *First Epistle*, 835.
115. *DNTC*, 2:361.

opportunities is to be a co-partner with God in bringing his spirit children into the world."[116] In any case, her presence gives glory to her "head,"
whether it be her priesthood leaders or husband.

In the gospel, the ideal relationships between the "head" and those
under him or her is that of "distinctiveness, reciprocity, and oneness."[117]
The Apostle's idea seems to be that of complimentary, not competing roles.
That the Greek Fathers employed the term περιχώρησις (*perichōrēsis*),
"rotation,"[118] implying a dance, to describe the relationship Paul is here
unfolding shows their understanding.[119] In this activity, one leads and one
follows. One willingly, perhaps even eagerly, submits to the direction of
the other. The result is harmony and beauty.

Because the idea of submission is definitely part of Paul's system, his
view must be thoroughly understood in order to get the Apostle's point.
In the vocabulary the Apostle chooses, there is no hint of coercion, compulsion, intimidation, or duress. There is, however, order and hierarchy.
God is at the head and Christ is subject to him; in turn, man is subject to
Christ; and finally, woman is subject to man (children are subject to the
woman but, because Paul does not address that issue here, it is saved for
another discussion).

It must be kept in mind that, with the exception of 11:11, Paul is talking
here about Church order, not family or civil order. As Elder Dallin H. Oaks
has stated:

> The authority of the priesthood functions in the family and in the
> Church, according to the principles the Lord has established. . . . There
> are many similarities and some differences in the way priesthood author-
> ity functions in the family and in the Church. If we fail to recognize and
> honor the differences, we encounter difficulties. . . . One important differ-
> ence between its function in the Church and in the family is the fact that
> all priesthood authority *in the Church* functions under the direction of the
> one who holds the appropriate priesthood keys. In contrast, the authority
> that presides *in the family*—whether father or single-parent mother—func-
> tions in family matters without the need to get authorization from anyone
> holding priesthood keys. . . . A most important difference in the func-
> tioning of priesthood authority in the family and in the Church results
> from the fact that the government of the family is patriarchal, whereas

---

116. N. Eldon Tanner, "Thou Mayest Choose for Thyself," *Ensign* 3 (July 1973): 7.
117. Thiselton, *First Epistle*, 804.
118. LSJ, 1394.
119. Thiselton, *First Epistle*, 804.

the government of the Church is hierarchical. The concept of partnership functions differently in the family than in the Church. . . . The family proclamation gives this beautiful explanation of the relationship between a husband and a wife: While they have separate responsibilities, "in these sacred responsibilities, fathers and mothers are obligated to *help one another as equal partners.*"[120]

For Paul, submission is not imposed from the top down. It is, rather, voluntarily given from the bottom up; otherwise, it would not serve God's purpose. It is he who set the order and has revealed the way by which it works. Charity is the key. The Lord explained that when one is filled with love toward others and when virtue garnishes one's thoughts unceasingly, certain blessings flow. Among these are confidence in the presence of the Lord, the Holy Ghost becoming one's constant companion, and—most importantly for this discussion—"thy dominion shall be an everlasting dominion, and without compulsory means it shall flow unto thee forever" (D&C 121:45–46). Two-way love makes it possible for submission without compulsion. This state is achieved when each individual fully and voluntarily honors, respects, and follows those whom God has put at the head.

The basis of Paul's understanding of submission becomes clear as we look at the relationship between the Father and the Son. As an LDS scholar noted, "When one uses Christ as the personification of submission, a deeper definition unfolds. True submission requires restraint when one-upmanship is possible; the complete absence of pride when recognition is meted out; strength to stay the Spirit-directed course when letting go may be expected and even rewarded."[121] What Paul is commending is a voluntary renunciation of genuine "rights" (ἐξουσία, *exousia*; see Philip. 2:6–11). There is to be no affirmation of self at the expense of the other. The subordination is to be both voluntary and desired, expressing, as it does, a shared love. "This shared love controls the use of freedom," as one scholar noted, "and thereby each brings 'glory' to the other by assuming distinctive roles for a common purpose."[122] It is on this basis that the relationship between husband and wife, or a man and a woman in general, parallels that between God and Christ.[123]

---

120. Dallin H. Oaks, "Priesthood Authority in the Family and the Church," *Ensign* 35 (November 2005): 26; italics in original.

121. Camille Fronk, "Submit Yourselves . . . As unto the Lord," in *Go Ye into All the World,* 101.

122. Thiselton, *First Epistle,* 804.

123. Morna Dorothy Hooker, *From Adam to Christ: Essays on Paul* (Cambridge: Cambridge University Press, 1990), 113.

540 Paul's First Epistle to the Corinthians

It is in this light that we should read Joseph F. Smith's counsel that:

We have got to learn to stand or fall for ourselves, male and female. It is true that we are taught in the principles of the Gospel that man is the head of the woman, and Christ is the head of the man; and according to the order that is established in the kingdom of God, it is the duty of the man to follow Christ, and it is the duty of the woman to follow the man in Christ, not out of [that is, away from] him.

But has not a woman the same volition that the man has? Can she not follow or disobey the man as he can follow or disobey Christ? Certainly she can, she is responsible for her acts, and must answer for them. She is endowed with intelligence and judgment, and will stand upon her own merits as much so as the man. . . . The man is responsible for the woman only so far as she is influenced by, or is obedient to, his counsels. Christ is responsible for the man so far as the man walks in obedience to the laws and commandments he has given, but no further, and so far will his atoning blood redeem and cleanse from sin; so far as they obey them will the principles of eternal life revealed in the Gospel have effect upon the souls of men, so also with women.[124]

That a woman is subject to the man should not be taken to imply that she is somehow inferior. Elder James E. Faust stated clearly that "nowhere does the doctrine of this Church declare that men are superior to women. Paul said to the Corinthians, 'Nevertheless neither is the man without the woman, neither the woman without the man, in the Lord' (1 Cor. 11:11). Each brings his or her own separate and unique strengths to the family and the Church. Women are not just cooks, stewards of our homes, or servants. They are much more. They are the enrichment of humanity."[125] Elder Charles W. Penrose also noted, "we shall find that through all eternity the sexes go together, and that the female portion of God's children have a part and a lot in this matter as well as the male."[126]

Paul rejects the status-questioning stance of some by insisting on a strict male-female hierarchy. He insists on gender distinctiveness, which goes as much for men (11:4, 7a) as it does for women (11:5, 6, 7b). Freedom in Christ was constrained by care, concern, and respect for the other (as Paul will show more fully in chapters 12 and 13). There was to be no competitiveness between men and women over the issue of authority in the new order.

---

124. Joseph F. Smith, in *JD*, 16:247.
125. James E. Faust, "The Highest Place of Honor," *Ensign* 18 (May 1988): 36.
126. Charles W. Penrose, in *JD*, 21:50.

Each had a place, which promoted "a reciprocity of relationship," allowing for "different inputs to the relation of mutuality" that Paul insisted was to be recognized and maintained.[127]

In sum, the Apostle believes in basic gender equality (see 7:2–4; Gal. 3:28) but also in traditional gender differences. What he is objecting to, then, is the symbolic disregard for gender differences in dress and decorum during worship services.[128]

So far as the issue stands today, Elder McConkie clearly stated: "In the eternal sense it is wholly immaterial whether a woman wears a hat or is bareheaded when she prays. ... In other words, gospel principles are eternal, and it is wise to adhere to the passing customs which signify adherence to that course which adds to rather than detracts from the great and important revealed truths."[129]

For Latter-day Saints, Paul's witness that "neither is woman independent of man nor man independent of woman in the Lord" (11:11, Rendition) is very important because it looks to the concept of eternal marriage. Concerning this subject, Elder Orson Pratt stated:

> What! Can I, can you, can the inhabitants of the earth really not be in the Lord, and yet not be united together in the holy covenant of marriage, the male with the female? So Paul says [in 11:11]. It is a very curious kind of saying, however, in the case of this generation, who have lost the knowledge of God though the apostasy of their fathers. ... They have all the time supposed that they could enter into a fulness of the glory of the celestial world without being united in the bonds of eternal union. But it is not so; it was not so in the beginning. The very first marriage that was ever known in this creation, was not a marriage between the children of mortality, but was a marriage consummated by divine authority, by divine power. It was a marriage between two immortal beings. No other marriage could be so important, so essentially necessary, to the inhabitants of this creation, as the first one celebrated in the beginning. ... The Latter-day Saints have a different form of marriage from these sectarians. We have a marriage in our church, between the male and female, which reaches forward to the endless ages of eternity; we do not consider a marriage of very great importance, unless it takes hold of eternity.[130]

---

127. Thiselton, *First Epistle*, 822.
128. Meeks, *First Urban Christians*, 161.
129. *DNTC*, 2:361.
130. Orson Pratt, in *JD*, 21:291.

Using Genesis 1 as his text, Elder Hugh B. Brown declared:

Thus it is seen that God instituted marriage in the very beginning. He made man, male and female, in his own image and likeness (Gen. 1:26–27) and designed that they should be united together in sacred bonds of marriage and declared that one is not perfect without the other (1 Cor. 11:11).

Marriage, the family, and the home are among the most important subjects of our whole theological doctrine, and as the family is the basic and fundamental unit of the Church and of society, its preservation and its righteous needs should take precedence over all other interests.

A family may be defined as a group of people of various ages, united by agreement and covenant, living together in the most intimate relationship. In such a society children learn that certain things are right and others are wrong. They grow from stage to stage of confidence, skill, affection, understanding, and responsibility. In other words, they build character. A family is a project in group living in which the thing to do and the thing not to do are absorbed through precept, example, and practice."[131]

Elder McConkie noted that "as eternal life grows out of the continuation of the family unit in eternity, and as a family unit consists of a husband and wife, so—'in the Lord'—it takes a man and a woman together to gain the glorious state of exaltation. Such is the whole object and end of the gospel."[132] Elder Russell M. Nelson stated that "marriage is not only an exalting principle of the gospel; it is a divine commandment."[133] Elder Erastus Snow summarized the point, stating that "man was created, male and female, and two principles are blended in one; and the man is not without the woman nor the woman without the man in the Lord; and there is no Lord, there is no God in which the two principles are not blended, nor can be; and we may never hope to attain unto the eternal power and the Godhead upon any other principle."[134]

In addition to gender roles and submission, there was another issue that influenced Paul's counsel. It was respect for others in public worship. This included not only one's dress and decorum during meetings but also one's behavior toward others.[135] Paul addresses this subject next in his epistle.

131. Hugh B. Brown, in CR, October 1966, 101.
132. *DNTC*, 2:361.
133. Russell M. Nelson, "Celestial Marriage," *Ensign* 38 (November 2008): 93.
134. Erastus Snow, in *JD*, 19:272.
135. Murphy-O'Connor, "Sex and Logic," 483.

ABUSES AT THE LORD'S SUPPER (11:17–22)

Greek Text

17 Τοῦτο δὲ παραγγέλλων οὐκ ἐπαινῶ ὅτι οὐκ εἰς τὸ κρεῖσσον ἀλλὰ εἰς τὸ ἧσσον συνέρχεσθε. 18 πρῶτον μὲν γὰρ συνερχομένων ὑμῶν ἐν ἐκκλησίᾳ ἀκούω σχίσματα ἐν ὑμῖν ὑπάρχειν, καὶ μέρος τι πιστεύω. 19 δεῖ γὰρ καὶ αἱρέσεις ἐν ὑμῖν εἶναι, ἵνα καὶ οἱ δόκιμοι φανεροὶ γένωνται ἐν ὑμῖν. 20 συνερχομένων οὖν ὑμῶν ἐπὶ τὸ αὐτὸ οὐκ ἔστιν κυριακὸν δεῖπνον φαγεῖν, 21 ἕκαστος γὰρ τὸ ἴδιον δεῖπνον προλαμβάνει ἐν τῷ φαγεῖν, καὶ ὃς μὲν πεινᾷ, ὃς δὲ μεθύει. 22 μὴ γὰρ οἰκίας οὐκ ἔχετε εἰς τὸ ἐσθίειν καὶ πίνειν; ἢ τῆς ἐκκλησίας τοῦ θεοῦ καταφρονεῖτε, καὶ καταισχύνετε τοὺς μὴ ἔχοντας; τί εἴπω ὑμῖν; ἐπαινέσω ὑμᾶς; ἐν τούτῳ οὐκ ἐπαινῶ. [SBLGNT]

King James Version

17 Now in this that I declare unto you I praise you not, that ye come together not for the better, but for the worse. 18 For first of all, when ye come together in the church, I hear that there be divisions among you; and I partly believe it. 19 For there must be also heresies among you, that they which are approved may be made manifest among you. 20 When ye come together therefore into one place, this is not to eat the Lord's supper. 21 For in eating every one taketh before other his own supper: and one is hungry, and another is drunken. 22 What? have ye not houses to eat and to drink in? or despise ye the church of God, and shame them that have not? What shall I say to you? shall I praise you in this? I praise you not.

New Rendition

17 Now in giving the following instruction, I do not commend you, because you hold your meetings in such a way that they are not beneficial, but rather the opposite. 18 For in the first place, when you meet together as a church, I hear that there are dissensions among you, and, in part, I believe it. 19 For there must indeed be factions among you so that it becomes evident which of you is genuine. 20 Consequently, although you meet together in the same place, it is not really to partake of the Lord's Supper, 21 because when it is time to eat, each goes ahead with his own meal, and some go hungry and others get drunk! 22 Don't you have homes to eat and drink in? Or are you showing contempt for the church of God and humiliating those who do not have anything? What should I say to you? I will certainly not commend you in this action!

Translation Notes and Comments

11:17 *Now in this that I declare unto you / Now in giving the following instruction:* In this new section, Paul turns to another serious error the Corinthian Saints have fallen into. Because the Greek phrase here is very

compact—τοῦτο δὲ παραγγέλλων (*touto de parangellōn*), literally "this
now instructing"—it requires some additional words to clarify the sense
in English. The pronoun *touto*, "this," as employed here, refers to what is
about to follow.[136] The participle *parangellōn* carries the direct meaning of
"command," but it also denotes "instruction" or "direction."[137] The word,
however, never loses the force of something that is not to be ignored by
the listener.

I praise you not / I do not commend you: The verb ἐπαινέω (*epaineō*)
expresses the idea of "approve, applaud, commend, or praise."[138] The force
of the Greek in Paul's construction stresses grave displeasure.

*ye come together not for the better, but for the worse / you hold your
meetings in such a way that they are not beneficial, but rather the opposite:* The Greek here is again quite condensed. The phrase οὐκ εἰς τὸ
κρεῖσσον ἀλλὰ εἰς τὸ ἧσσον συνέρχεσθε (*ouk eis to kreisson alla eis to hēsson
synerchesthe*) translates literally as, "not for the better but for the worse you
gather together." The verb συνέρχομαι (*synerchomai*), "come together,"[139]
connotes a church assembly, and the context suggests it refers to a sacrament meeting.[140] To make this phrase flow in English, our Rendition uses
a free translation that best catches the sense of the Greek rather than the
overly literal translation of the KJV.

Dissension, lack of unity, and uncharitable behavior of the Corinthian
Saints resulted in meetings where the Spirit was not present and in which
the peaceable gospel of Jesus Christ could not be properly taught or
understood. As a result the meetings seem to have been doing more harm
than good.

11:18 *For first of all, when ye come together in the church, I hear that
there be divisions among you / For in the first place, when you meet
together as a church, I hear that there are dissensions among you:* With
the adverb πρῶτον (*proton*), "first," Paul signals this as the beginning of a
list of items he has against some of the Saints. However, he never finishes
the list; thus, there is no "second" anywhere in this pericope. His use of the
verb ἀκούω (*akouō*), "I hear," suggests he is responding to oral reports that
he has received rather than to a letter. The phrase ἐν ἐκκλησίᾳ (*en ekklēsia*),

136. Louw-Nida, §92.29 with n. 7. Thus, the translation in the NRSV, NIV, and (by
implication) the NJB.
137. BDAG, 760.
138. BDAG, 357.
139. LSJ, 603; BDAG, 969–70; Thiselton, *First Epistle*, 856.
140. Fitzmyer, *First Corinthians*, 426.

"as a church" (as translated in our Rendition), does not refer to a building but to the assemblage of the Saints for sacrament service likely at someone's home.[141] The noun σχίσματα (*schismata*), "divisions, dissentions," defines the problem.[142] The word denotes the condition that results when parties with conflicting aims or objectives take a stand.[143] Paul's use of the word here does not seem to be in reference to what he discussed in 1:10. There it referred to certain Saints' allegiance to this or that strong personality and the theology or philosophy which that person espoused. Here it seems to focus on the bad manners and ill treatment of some Church members toward others. The results worked against the unity and caring that such meetings were supposed to produce.[144]

and I partly believe it / and, in part, I believe it: Paul's words show both caution and force. He upholds the report of his informants, but he tacitly admits they may be overly biased and, therefore, he is not going to be either rash or overly hasty in accepting the information.[145] It may be that his information came from those "of the house of Chloe" (1:11), and, if so, they were likely trusted slaves. Since slaves would have been the group who would take the most abuse at meetings, they had reason to complain. Taking their word as the full truth, however, may have antagonized those whom Paul was addressing and, therefore—in order not to alienate them— he probably used a softer tone.[146]

11:19 ***For there must be also heresies among you / For there must indeed be factions among you:*** With use of the connective γάρ (*gar*), "for," Paul signals that he is going to explain what he means. This verse is, therefore, an aside in which Paul gives his reason for believing the reposts. He knew that dissensions had already arisen because there were factions that were operating during this time. The impersonal verb δεῖ (*dei*), "is necessary, must be," is very telling. It carries the sense of what seems to be inevitable.[147]

---

141. Murphy-O'Connor, *St. Paul's Corinth*, 178–85. Though some manuscripts read ἐν τῇ ἐκκλησίᾳ (*en tē ekklēsia*), "in the church," including the one from which the KJV is translated, that is a late reading. The phrase ἐν ἐκκλησίᾳ (*en ekklēsia*) should not be taken as a locative, but as denoting substance, "in an assembly." BDAG, 326–30; see also Robertson and Plummer, *Critical and Exegetical Commentary*, 239; Thiselton, *First Epistle*, 857.

142. Louw-Nida, §39.13.

143. BDAG, 981.

144. Fitzmyer, *First Corinthians*, 433.

145. Thiselton, *First Epistle*, 858.

146. Fee, *First Epistle*, 537 with n. 31.

147. Louw-Nida, §71.34.

The noun αἱρέσεις (*haireseis*), "factions," is related to the verb αἱρέω (*haireō*) which means "to take something" and often carries the nuance of taking something out of context. The noun denotes any group that has distinctive tenets, but it could appear in a more restricted negative sense pointing to a dissenting faction,[148] which is how Paul uses it here. In later Christian literature it designated a heretical sect,[149] but it connotes a group that holds self-initiated and uncompromising opinions that its members will not yield. For this reason, it is important that members of the Church accept and strive to live the gospel because those who take parts of it out of context easily fall into apostasy. Later, some will reject anything as true except their own dogma and will recognize no authority but their own. Paul knew that if these dissentions were left unchecked, the result would be apostasy. Of course, he would not be a bit surprised (indicated by καί [*kai*], used here as an additive marker and translated as "indeed" in our Rendition[150]) given what he knows about the upcoming apostasy (see Matt. 7:15; 24:11, 24; and Paul's own witness in Acts 20:29–31). Even so, he put all his efforts into trying at least to impede it.

that they which are approved may be made manifest among you / so that it becomes evident which of you is genuine: Paul here explains why the Lord allows "divisions" to take place. They are necessary (δεῖ, *dei*) to reveal the δόκιμοι (*dokimoi*), "the approved" or "genuine."[151] The nominal adjective denotes that which is proved to be what it claims by passing the necessary test.[152] Paul's words show that he understands that the dissensions and quarrelling that are taking place at the meetings actually work to God's ends. They serve to reveal those who are truly disciples of Christ. The "genuine" will not participate in dissension but will either try to avoid it or act to ameliorate the situation.

11:20 *When ye come together therefore into one place, this is not to eat the Lord's supper / Consequently, although you meet together in the same place, it is not really to partake of the Lord's Supper:* With the use of the resumptive οὖν (*oun*), "therefore, consequently," coupled with the repetition of the phrase, "when you meet together," Paul signals that he is picking up his argument from 11:18. The participle συνερχομένων (*synerchomenōn*),

---

148. BDAG, 27–28.
149. BDAG, 28.
150. BDAG, 495–96.
151. BDAG, 256.
152. Louw-Nida, §§30.115; 73.4.

"coming together," can be taken temporally, "when you meet together," or concessively, "although you meet together."[153] The context suggests the latter is the better translation and is used in our Rendition. The phrase ἐπὶ τὸ αὐτό (*epi to auto*), "in the same place," not only denotes meeting in one place but can also carry the sense "for the same purpose." In this case it would be to partake of the Lord's Supper and enjoy the fellowship it was to provide. This connotation would make any quarreling at sacrament services all the more damning.[154]

From the sources it is clear that the meetings consisted mainly of communal meals made to echo the Lord's last supper.[155] It is safe to say that scripture citations, analysis, and admonitions were part of the service. The focus, however, was on partaking of the sacrament. The phrase κυριακὸν δεῖπνον (*kyriakon deipnon*), "the Lord's Supper," is the only designation Paul uses for this ordinance.[156] The adjective *kyriakon* means, literally, "belonging to the Lord," but this does not carry the weight of the nuance. The idea is that it is a meal eaten "in honor of the Lord" or, even better, one "consecrated to the Lord."[157]

Based on what he has heard, the Apostle now reports on what the divisions have caused. Though the Saints have joined together in one place, they are not united as a people. There are those who show respect for some while dishonoring others. Their actions reveal that they have lost sight of the purpose of these meetings—to partake of the Lord's Supper. Instead they have substituted it for a place for the wealthy to preen for one another.

11:21 *For in eating every one taketh before other his own supper / because when it is time to eat, each goes ahead with his own meal:* Paul ties 11:18 and 20 together at this point, explaining, first, the nature of the divisions that are causing the disunity and, second, why the meals have lost their sacred meaning. Though Paul does not give an exact picture of what is going on, his words do give us some indication. He begins his sentence with the word ἕκαστος (*hekastos*), "each one," and in doing so emphasizes the individuality that is splitting the branches. The phrase ἴδιον δεῖπνον (*idion deipnon*), "his own meal," suggests that the food for the common

---

153. Fitzmyer, *First Corinthians,* 433.

154. Fitzmyer, *First Corinthians,* 433.

155. See Translation Notes on 10:16–17.

156. Though Paul does refer to "the Lord's table" in 10:21, he is using the image to contrast the sacrament with the "table of god" used in cultic meals. As a result, the phrase was not regularly used to refer to the sacrament.

157. Fee, *First Epistle,* 540.

meal was not provided by the host but that each family supplied its own. Paul's use of the verb προλαμβάνω (*prolambanō*), "to take beforehand, go ahead with,"[158] suggests that some ate without waiting for others. This seems borne out by Paul's admonition in 11:33 that they should "wait for" (ἐκδέχομαι, *ekdechomai*) one another before commencing the meal. The word *prolambanō* was beginning to take on the nuance of consuming or devouring a meal such that there was nothing left.[159] In this context, it places emphasis on the selfish greed of certain guests who were not willing to wait for fear they would have to share.[160]

and one is hungry, and another is drunken / and some go hungry and others get drunk: Paul appeals to a strong example to highlight the problem. Some of the members, who likely were slaves or poor freedmen and had to work late, came without dinner and were given no share in meals of other members. They would, however, be accorded the bread and wine, which being part of the service, could not be denied them.[161] Paul contrasts their state with that of the others who had imbibed to such an excess that they were drunk. Such a condition would have been frowned upon in a culture influenced by Jewish norms and certainly not appropriate for a sacred meal in any setting. Because of that, it is likely that Paul is not making a comment on drunkenness, per se, but using the idea for the sake of contrast. He points out the extremes by taking aspects of the two parts of the meal—the lack of bread and the overindulgence of wine. The one extreme is receiving little or nothing to eat while the other extreme is drinking wine to excess. His point with the latter is likely to show that there was abundance and none needed to go hungry or thirsty.[162]

11:22 *What? have ye not houses to eat and to drink in? / Don't you have homes to eat and drink in?:* Paul here asks the first of two questions. The construction of the first question, with μὴ γάρ (*mē gar*), anticipates a negative response, and the question could more literally be translated, "Surely

---

158. BDAG, 872.

159. Though it became the meaning in later Greek, the word likely carried this nuance even as early as Paul's day. See Moulton and Milligan, *Vocabulary,* 542; Bruce W. Winter, "The Lord's Supper at Corinth: An Alternative Reconstruction," *Reformed Theological Review* 37 (1978): 73–82.

160. Thiselton, *First Epistle,* 863.

161. Some have suggested that, at this time, the meal was separate from the sacramental service proper (see Conzelmann, *1 Corinthians,* 195 and n. 23), but nothing in the text suggests this. See Theissen, *Social Setting,* 153–54; Fee, *First Epistle,* 541 and n. 52.

162. Fee, *First Epistle,* 543.

it's not the case that you do not have houses to eat and drink in."[163] The articular infinitive phrase εἰς τὸ ἐσθίειν (*eis to esthiein*), "to eat in," connotes that one of the purposes of a person's house is for eating or drinking.[164] What Paul is saying is that if the purpose behind the gathering of these people was simply to eat or, perhaps, have a party, then they should do it at their own houses.

or despise ye the church of God, and shame them that have not? / Or are you showing contempt for the church of God and humiliating those who do not have anything?: The way Paul couches his second question attributes a very negative reason for his readers' attendance at meetings. The genitive construction in the phrase τῆς ἐκκλησίας τοῦ θεοῦ (*tēs ekklēsias tou theou*), "the church of God," stresses the idea that the Church is not a social institution organized by and for people, but an assembly that belongs to God. That includes not only the Church as a whole but also each individual within it.

Paul uses two very strong words in his castigation of the Saints. The first word, καταφρονέω (*kataphroneō*), "despise, hold in contempt," carries the idea of viewing something or someone as having little or no value.[165] In this case, Paul is trying to help the offending party see that his actions suggest that he values but little the Church as a whole. The second word, καταισχύνω (*kataischynō*), "shame, humiliate," denotes not only dishonoring someone but deliberately putting him to shame and, thus, humiliating him.[166] Paul refers to those whom these people scorn as τοὺς μὴ ἔχοντας (*tous mē echontas*), "those who have not." These "have-nots" were those who had no property. That group would probably have been largely composed of the slave class or those who had been recently manumitted.[167] Paul reaches out to his readers to help them understand that since the Church belongs to God, so, too, does each member. To show contempt for any in the assembly is, in reality, to show contempt for God since all are his.[168]

What shall I say to you? shall I praise you in this? I praise you not / What should I say to you? I will certainly not commend you in this action: Here Paul concludes this portion of his instructions. As noted above, the verb ἐπαινέω (*epaineō*) expresses the idea of "approve, applaud, commend

---

163. Smyth, *Greek Grammar,* §2651.
164. Thiselton, *First Epistle,* 864.
165. BDAG, 529.
166. BDAG, 517.
167. Findlay, "St. Paul's First Epistle," 2:879; Winter, "Lord's Supper," 73–82.
168. Thiselton, *First Epistle,* 864.

or praise."[169] In the Corinthian Saints' case, Paul cannot do this. The neuter phrase ἐν τούτῳ (*en toutō*), "in this thing," points to the specific act that has raised his ire, and so for clarity, our Rendition has added "action." Their actions have not only destroyed the purpose of the sacramental service, but worse, they have prostituted it by turning it into an occasion, not for honoring and remembering the Lord, but for preening and self-glory through the humiliation of others—incredibly, God's own children.

Analysis and Summary

Paul had already addressed the problem of divisions among the Saints (see 1:10–16), but here his tone takes on an additional edge and urgency. Before, he was concerned with divisions created by parties; here he is concerned with something much deeper and far more threatening to both the physical and spiritual life of the Church. Whether they realize it or not, certain Christians, by their actions, are despising the Church of God and humiliating the people who have nothing (11:22). Paul's strong language is warranted. "The unity of the church is something more than physical juxtaposition in a determined space," one authority has written. "Their behavior, in addition to humiliating the 'have-nots,' shows that they hold the true community in contempt."[170] All were invited to "the Lord's Supper," but by the time the "have-nots" got off work, the idle rich had already consumed both food and drink, some even overindulging (11:21). The sacramental service, designed to show unity and love and to sustain oneness and remember the Savior's sacrifice, had become nothing more than a corrupt social gathering in which the rich gloated over and humiliated the poor. The worst part, however, was that the offenders did not even care. Such a lack of feeling could spread like cancer and, if not remedied, would eventually contribute to the death of "the Church of God."[171]

In this pericope, Paul is likely not responding to a question posed in a letter but rather, based on 11:18, to an oral report. The situation it described required immediate and strong action. Paul is clear that unlike their acceptance of certain Church traditions (παραδόσεις, *paradoseis*), likely accepting women as participants in church meetings, these Saints had strayed outside of church protocol. Paul addresses the issue of comportment during actual

---

169. BDAG, 357.
170. Murphy-O'Connor, *1 Corinthians,* 111.
171. Bailey, *Mediterranean Eyes,* 318–19.

church meetings (shown by his use of the verb συνέρχομαι [*synerchomai*], denoting people coming together for a common purpose).[172]

Unfortunately, how sacramental services proceeded in the ancient Church has not been preserved.[173] It does seem clear, as noted above, that they were a communal meal designed to echo the Lord's last supper.[174] That echo included admonitions and instructions. As one LDS scholar noted,

> Early Christian worship involved organization and participation. Standardized ceremonies today tend to create a passive Christian audience, but attending the Early Church was anything but a "spectator sport." Paul insisted that there be worship, not chaos. The difference came from priesthood leadership. In Paul's writings, we glimpse the common elements of meetings in several branches of the Church: "Quench not the spirit; despise not prophesyings" (1 Thes. 5:19–20). Where he had never been, Paul could mention prophecy, teaching, and exhortation (Rom. 12:6–8). An early Christian might speak by revelation, knowledge, prophecy, or teachings (1 Cor. 14:6). "Teaching" can also be translated as "doctrine." Meetings also included psalms, the praise of God in poetry, sometimes set to music (1 Cor. 14:26); the use of psalms is emphasized in letters to Ephesus (5:19) and Colossae (2:16). And at Corinth Paul adds speaking in tongues and the interpretation of tongues (1 Cor. 14:26), listed as general gifts of the Spirit (1 Cor. 12:10).[175]

A meal, in the Mediterranean world, was designed for fellowship and reconciliation and served as a solemn and binding act between participants. This sentiment would have served as the basis of the sacramental service. Part of the service was to remember—the word "re-member" connoting the idea of becoming a member again. Thus, an important part of the service was for reuniting the participants.[176]

The meeting had two other major purposes: the commemoration and celebration of God's grace-filled act to save humankind in giving the gift of his Son and the acknowledgment of the Atonement, which the Savior so graciously effected for all.

---

172. BDAG, 969. Paul's use of the word five times in this pericope (11:17, 18, 20, 33, 34) shows he is looking at church assemblies.

173. Justin Martyr, *1 Apol.* 1.67, gives a good account of the proceedings in his day, but this order took place a hundred years after Paul's time and, by then, the *agapē* feast was no longer in practice.

174. See Translation Notes on 10:16–17.

175. Anderson, *Understanding Paul*, 109.

176. Ellison, "Setting and Sacrament," 151–54.

But there was another aspect that was important. The meeting served as messianic anticipation. Echoing the Passover, as it did, the feast looked to the time when earth would rest under the Messiah's blessed reign.[177]

Understanding the purposes and intent of the meeting goes a long way in seeing the issue Paul is addressing. Christians met in houses (the noun ἐκκλησία, *ekklēsia*, "church," did not refer to a building but to an assembly[178]). The early Saints did not build chapels. It is true that, later in church history, some houses were renovated as strictly meeting places (*domus ekklesiae*)—for example, the house of Peter in Capernaum and the house-church at Dura-Europos[179]—but this was not the practice during Paul's period. One reason may have been that the Church was young and poor and, therefore, could not sustain a building program. Taking as a model our own Church history, however, the Lord's insistence that the Saints build houses of worship in Kirtland, Ohio, and Nauvoo, Illinois, when the Church was new and the people were poor, suggests that this was not the reason.[180] Another likely reason was that, not being officially recognized by the Romans as a legitimate entity, the Christians could not establish separate, legal and permanent places of worship. Houses, however, worked well and also offered protection from spying eyes. Homes also lent themselves to the sacramental meal, having the kitchen and other accessories needed. In Paul's day, it appears, therefore, that the wealthy Saints opened their houses for worship service.[181]

There were both advantages and disadvantages in such a system. Certainly, when properly executed, the setting lent itself to close familiarity, understanding, and caring. It could also, again when properly executed, generate feelings of equality among social groups wherein all felt they were the household or the family of God. Certainly we see this in the use of familial imagery that Paul used. As one LDS scholar noted: "Paul taught that the Saints were brothers and sisters (ἀδελφοί, *adelphoi*), 'children of God' who had 'received the Spirit of adoption'; Jesus' Father was their father; they were 'heirs of God, and joint-heirs with Christ' (Romans 8:14–17; see 2 Corinthians 6:18; Galatians 4:5–7; Philippians 2:15; Hebrews

---

177. Ellison, "Setting and Sacrament," 155–56; for evidence that the setting looked back to the Passover, see Thiselton, *First Epistle*, 871–74.

178. Louw-Nida, §11.78.

179. Ellison, "Setting and Sacrament," 147–49.

180. At those places, effort was put into the building of temples, but since these edifices were also designed to function as meeting houses, the argument seems sound.

181. Ellison, "Setting and Sacrament," 145–47.

12:5–9). Among the Christians, an elderly man was to be treated 'as a father; . . . the younger men as brethren; the elder women as mothers; the younger as sisters, with all purity' (1 Timothy 5:1–2). Philemon was to accept and forgive a servant who had run away, for as a fellow believer, the servant was now 'a brother beloved' (Philemon 1:16)."[182]

However, the separateness of the various assemblies could contribute to a lack of communication and correlation. Further, false teachers could arise and gather to themselves adherents. As a result, false doctrines and heresies could more easily spread. This would especially be the case if a house owner only allowed those of a certain status or belief into his "church," ἐκκλησια (*ekklēsia*). Even in mixed congregations, such as the ones Paul addressed, those with higher status could easily honor and only care for the elite while ignoring those of lesser social status. Indeed, it may have been due to abuses that the sacrament, in the second century, was separated from a communal meal. By the fourth century, common meals and sacramental services in households were forbidden.[183]

Taking Paul's statements as a whole, it becomes apparent that, in at least some of the *ekklēsia* during the first century, the practice was not working as designed. The problem was likely exacerbated due to the nature of the homes in which they were meeting. Common features in a Greco-Roman villa included a vestibule, a central atrium or court yard, and a formal dining area called a *triclinium*. The *triclinium* could hold no more than about a dozen guests while the court yard and vestibule could hold considerably more. This layout, if not carefully watched, could allow grades among attendees with only the most favored in the *triclinium*, forcing others to find a place as best they could.[184] Those Saints not of the upper class could well ask just who was hosting the meal. Was it the Lord's Supper or that of the home owner and his circle of friends and associates?[185]

The heart of the problem was two-fold: first, disrupting the order of the community and, second, pulling attention away from the Lord "by self-affirming insistence on individual or group 'freedoms,' and 'rights.'"[186] Those who held positions of honor or prestige were very willing to take advantage of their station during the worship service. That allowed them to

---

182. Ellison, "Setting and Sacrament," 152.

183. Everett Ferguson, "Agape Meal," in *ABD*, 1:90–91.

184. Theissen, *Social Setting*, 145–74; Murphy-O'Connor, *St. Paul's Corinth*, 153–61.

185. Thiselton, *First Epistle*, 862.

186. Thiselton, *First Epistle*, 850.

ignore, if not dismiss, those whom they saw as lesser individuals during the celebration of the sacrament. Had the proper spirit prevailed, the wealthy should have welcomed the more needy members and willingly fed them. Unfortunately, they, like most Gentiles during this time, treated them as social inferiors. The result was that the meals focused more on those who belonged to the inner group rather than on the Lord.[187] Under such conditions, among those who were left out, feelings of resentment, bitterness, and even anger were apparently generated.

Paul was not willing to dismiss reports that abuses and σχίσματα (*schismata*), "divisions," existed in the branches (11:18). Though a bit cautious about accepting these reports whole cloth, he knew there were problems. He was concerned that these *schismata* betrayed the existence of αἱρέσεις (*haireseis*) (11:19), that is, dissenting groups that pulled people away from the truth. Though he understood full well that these would prove deadly to the spiritual and physical life of the Church, he was resigned to them based on the Savior's teachings (Matt. 24:4–5, 24; compare JS-M 1:5–11). His earlier epistle to the Thessalonians portrayed his clear understanding that an apostasy was coming (see 2 Thes. 2:1–7; he would later confirm that understanding, as seen in Acts 20:28–31). His words show that he saw the divisiveness at Corinth not just in a sociological or ecclesiastical framework but in a theological one that bespoke of the Church's coming end.[188]

The implications of Paul's statement that there must be heresies working in the Corinthian branch are important. A number of early Christian non-canonical texts (called "agrapha") contain the statement by Jesus that there would be quite a number of men who would come in his name dressed outwardly in sheep skins, but were inwardly plundering wolves. One tells its readers that "even the Lord, the Savior himself, said that there will be heresies and divisions" (authors' translation).[189] On this, one LDS scholar notes, "A good case could be made that with these verses [that is, 11:18–19] Paul is applying the formula of Jesus to the Corinthians; that is, when he

---

187. Winter, "Lord's Supper," 73–82.

188. Fee, *First Epistle*, 539.

189. Didascalia Apostolorum, 6.5, but the phrase is found in three other Greek sources as well. These are: Justin Martyr, *Dial.* 35; Clementine Homilies 16. 21; Didymus' De Trinitate 3. 22. See Alfred Resch, *Agrapha: Aussercanonische Schriftfragmente* (Leipzig: Hinrichs, 1906), 100–101. Joachim Jeremias, *Unknown Sayings of Jesus* (Eugene, Ore.: Wipf and Stock Publishers, 2008), 76–77, notes that the saying did, very likely, originate with Jesus.

heard that there were divisions among them, he knew from the domini-
cal saying that heresies would soon follow. And again, if the agraphon is
genuine, it argues for Paul's thorough knowledge of the traditional sayings
of Jesus."[190] If that is the case, the Master's teachings, which would eventually be codified in the Gospels, were already circulating among the various
branches of the Church by the mid-first century AD.

What suggested that the reports were correct, Paul states, was that some
of the Saints were not waiting for others to begin the service (11:21). Rather
than eating the meal so that the food would be shared, as was the design
and intent of this sacred occasion, some selfishly went ahead with their
supper. With his use of the adjective ἴδιον (*idion*), "his own [meal]," the
Apostle stresses the point.[191]

Paul notes, however, that as bad as their selfish acts were, God was
working out his own designs (11:19). The condition they created was allowing those who were truly God's own—the tried and proven (οἱ δόκιμοι,
hoi dokimoi), that is, those who had passed the examination—to become
apparent. Though the situation in Corinth could be seen as the "more fortunate" acting as they too often do toward the "less fortunate," as one scholar
noted, "at the Lord's Table such activities must be seen against the larger
divine drama. Such 'divisions' have the net effect of revealing those who are
genuinely Christ's. And the 'proof,' lies not in a correct belief system, but in
behavior that reflects the gospel."[192]

In 11:22, Paul forces his readers to consider their reason for assembling.
He does this through two rhetorical questions. First, he asks them if they
are acting thus because they have no houses in which to eat and drink. His
implication is that they are using the Church merely to satisfy their appetites. Since lacking accommodations is not the reason, he poses a second
question, asking them if the reason is so that they can heap indignity on
the poor (τοὺς μὴ ἔχοντας, *tous mē echontas*, literally, "the have-nots") as a
means of making themselves feel superior.[193] This question suggests, to his
readers' shame, a "yes" answer. Because this was likely the cause of their
actions, Paul declares, in stinging rebuke, "I praise you not!" (11:22).

---

190. Stephen E. Robinson, "The Noncanonical Sayings of Jesus," *BYU Studies* 36, no. 2
(1996): 74–91. See also Ogden and Skinner, *Verse by Verse,* 139–40.

191. Fitzmyer, *First Corinthians,* 434.

192. Fee, *First Epistle,* 539. See also Holzapfel and Wayment, *Making Sense,* 358.

193. Findlay, "St. Paul's First Epistle," 879.

The Institution of the Lord's Supper (11:23–26)

Greek Text

23 Ἐγὼ γὰρ παρέλαβον ἀπὸ τοῦ κυρίου, ὃ καὶ παρέδωκα ὑμῖν, ὅτι ὁ κύριος Ἰησοῦς ἐν τῇ νυκτὶ ᾗ παρεδίδετο ἔλαβεν ἄρτον 24 καὶ εὐχαριστήσας ἔκλασεν καὶ εἶπεν· Τοῦτό μού ἐστιν τὸ σῶμα τὸ ὑπὲρ ὑμῶν· τοῦτο ποιεῖτε εἰς τὴν ἐμὴν ἀνάμνησιν. 25 ὡσαύτως καὶ τὸ ποτήριον μετὰ τὸ δειπνῆσαι, λέγων· Τοῦτο τὸ ποτήριον ἡ καινὴ διαθήκη ἐστὶν ἐν τῷ ἐμῷ αἵματι· τοῦτο ποιεῖτε, ὁσάκις ἐὰν πίνητε, εἰς τὴν ἐμὴν ἀνάμνησιν. 26 ὁσάκις γὰρ ἐὰν ἐσθίητε τὸν ἄρτον τοῦτον καὶ τὸ ποτήριον πίνητε, τὸν θάνατον τοῦ κυρίου καταγγέλλετε, ἄχρι οὗ ἔλθῃ. [SBLGNT]

King James Version

23 For I have received of the Lord that which also I delivered unto you, That the Lord Jesus the same night in which he was betrayed took bread: 24 And when he had given thanks, he brake it, and said, Take, eat: this is my body, which is broken for you: this do in remembrance of me. 25 After the same manner also he took the cup, when he had supped, saying, This cup is the new testament in my blood: this do ye, as oft as ye drink it, in remembrance of me. 26 For as often as ye eat this bread, and drink this cup, ye do shew the Lord's death till he come.

New Rendition

23 For I received from the Lord what I have passed on to you, that the Lord Jesus, on the night he was handed over, took bread, 24 gave thanks and broke it, and said, "This is my body which is for you. Do this in remembrance of me." 25 Likewise, after the meal he took the cup and said, "This cup is the new covenant in my blood. Do this, as often as you drink it, in remembrance of me." 26 For as often as you eat this bread and drink this cup you proclaim the Lord's death until he comes.

Translation Notes and Comments

11:23 *For I have received of the Lord that which also I delivered unto you / For I received from the Lord what I have passed on to you:* Paul's use of the technical terms παρέλαβον (*parelabon*), "I received," and παρέδωκα (*paredōka*), "I passed on," is telling. The first term carries the idea of not only taking something into close association with oneself but also of receiving jurisdiction over it.[194] The second term denotes conveying to another person something one has strong interest in for the purpose of care and

---

194. BDAG, 767–68.

preservation.[195] Thus, Paul not only received the tradition, he also had jurisdiction over it and, therefore, the full right to pass it on. Further, his intent in doing so was for safekeeping. The actions and attitudes of some, however, greatly threatened his intentions.

The Apostle's words show that he is appealing to a long-standing tradition. The sacramental service was nothing new. The roots of this ordinance reach back without a break to the beginning of the apostolic ministry. And it is this ordinance that Paul has precisely passed on to the Corinthian Church. The source for his knowledge of the ordinance is ἀπὸ τοῦ κυρίου (*apo tou kyriou*), "from the Lord" (11:23). Though it is possible that Paul received his knowledge directly through revelation, it is more likely that the Spirit had, at some point, confirmed the accuracy and correctness of the tradition as it had come down to him. By beginning his sentence with ἐγώ (*egō*), "I," Paul puts stress on his personal witness to the truthfulness of what he is saying in this and the next few verses.[196]

That the Lord Jesus the same night in which he was betrayed took bread / that the Lord Jesus, on the night he was handed over, took bread: With the phrase ὁ κύριος Ἰησοῦς (*ho kyrios Iēsous*), "the Lord Jesus," Paul affirms that the sacramental ordinance was begun by no less than the divine Jesus. What the Apostle meant by using the imperfect passive verb παραδίδετο (*paradideto*) is somewhat ambiguous. Though translated as "was betrayed" in the KJV, the word denotes primarily the act of handing or giving something over to something else. Only in a tertiary sense does it mean to be betrayed.[197] The passage, therefore, probably does not refer to the act of Judas Iscariot.[198] It is the synoptic tradition (of which Paul is very aware) that most likely explains Paul's intent. There the emphasis is on the death of Jesus—he asked his disciples to remember his body and blood that he was about to give for them (Matt. 26:26–29; Mark 14:22–25; Luke 22:19–20). On that basis, it would seem that Paul was revealing his understanding of the dynamics of what was happening at that time. He would express his understanding more clearly in Romans 8:32, where he stated that it was God who "handed over" (παρέδωκεν, *paredōken*) Jesus to death for our trespasses that we might live (compare LXX Isa. 53:6).

---

195. BDAG, 761–63.

196. Fitzmyer, *First Corinthians,* 435–36. As far as Paul being aware of the synoptic tradition, see Tomson, *Paul and the Jewish Law,* 53.

197. BDAG, 761–63.

198. Hays, *First Corinthians,* 198; Fee, *First Epistle,* 549.

This interpretation fits well with the theme that Paul is developing in this whole section—concern for the "weak" or the "have-nots" whom the "strong" were humiliating.[199] It was to ransom these, as well as the "strong," that God handed over Christ. The "strong," however, were missing the point of the sacrament and seem to be using it as a celebration of Christ's victory over death. They overlooked the fact that they were renewing ἡ καινὴ διαθήκη (*hē kainē diathēkē*), "the new covenant" (Luke 22:20), in which they were to remember all for whom Jesus gave his body and shed his blood. They missed the point that the service was a covenant of fellowship in which all—poor and rich—have been made one by the self-giving act of Jesus and that they, in turn, were to share with others in imitation of that act.

11:24 *And when he had given thanks, he brake it, and said, Take, eat / gave thanks and broke it, and said:* The words λάβετε φάγετε (*labete phagete*), "take, eat," are not found in the earliest manuscripts and are clearly a gloss from Matthew 26:26. For that reason they are not included in our Rendition.[200] The aorist participle εὐχαριστήσας (*eucharistēsas*), "having given thanks," expresses an appreciation for what one has received; in this case, the thanks go to God.[201] The verb εὐχαριστέω (*eucharisteō*) is the basis for the English "Eucharist" used by many Christian religions to refer to the sacrament.

this is my body, which is broken for you / This is my body which is for you: Though supported by some ancient texts, the word "broken" is most likely an addition and is, therefore, not translated in our Rendition.[202] Even without it, the force of the preposition in the phrase τὸ ὑπὲρ ὑμῶν (*to hyper hymōn*), "which is for you," is still strong. It denotes an activity or event that is done in someone else's best interest.[203] It recalls the "suffering servant" of Isaiah 53:12 who bore "the sin of many." Paul associates the preposition ὑπέρ (*hyper*) with the Atonement, it being "for us" or "for our sins" (15:3; Rom. 5:6, 8). The phrase not only stresses Jesus' selfless act of giving his life for others but also invites them to share in "his body," such that they directly share in the meaning and benefits of the Atonement.[204]

---

199. Hays, *First Corinthians,*198. See Eriksson, *Traditions as Rhetorical Proof,* 4, whose study puts this pericope in its proper context.

200. Metzger, *Textual Commentary,* 496.

201. BDAG, 415.

202. Metzger, *Textual Commentary,* 496.

203. BDAG, 1030–31.

204. Fee, *First Epistle,* 551.

The phrase τοῦτό μού ἐστιν τὸ σῶμα (*touto mou estin to soma*), "this is my body," contrary to some religious traditions, is not to be taken literally. Jesus is saying that the bread *represents* or *signifies* what he is about to do for his people, that is, give his life for them.[205]

this do in remembrance of me / Do this in remembrance of me: The noun ἀνάμνησις (*anamnēsis*), "remembrance," has a number of different nuances.[206] At the word's heart, however, it connotes more than the simple remembrance of someone who has passed away. The ordinance is done, not merely in memory *of* Jesus, but in recalling *him*—remembering his nature, life, and ministry. But there is more. The word also connotes not simply keeping him in mind but translating his life and service into our own. On the other hand, "failure to remember is not absent-mindedness," as one scholar noted, "but unfaithfulness to the covenant and disobedience."[207]

11:25 ***After the same manner also he took the cup, when he had supped, saying, This cup is the new testament in my blood / Likewise, after the meal he took the cup and said, "This cup is the new covenant in my blood":*** The words "he took" are not in the Greek but for clarity's sake, are added in the KJV as well as our Rendition.[208] The sacramental emblems represent the new covenant. The phrase ἡ καινὴ διαθήκη (*hē kainē diathēkē*) is translated as "new testament" in the KJV, but it is better translated as "new covenant," as in our Rendition. The adjective καινός (*kainos*) means "new" in the sense of something that was previously unknown.[209] The noun διαθήκη (*diathēkē*) in Koine Greek had two senses. First, it was the legal term for a "last will and testament."[210] Second, in the LXX, it was regularly used as the translation of the Hebrew בְּרִית (*bĕrīt*), "covenant." It is the latter meaning

---

205. Fee, *First Epistle,* 550. This phrase has generated a good deal of debate because it is used as the basis of the idea of transubstantiation, that is, that the bread and wine become literally the flesh and blood of Jesus. Given that the setting was a Passover meal, the *Haggadah* itself uses the term bread symbolically, stating that the *karpas* (the "bitter herbs" dipped in salt water and eaten to represent the bitterness of the Hebrew's bondage in Egypt) "is the bread of affliction which our forefathers ate in the land of Egypt." Cecil Roth, *The Haggadah* (London: Soncino Press, 1934), 8 and n. 9. The herbs are certainly not the bread, but represent it, thus, suggesting that Jesus' phrase is also symbolic. For discussion, see Thiselton, *First Epistle,* 875–77.

206. BDAG, 68.

207. Thiselton, *First Epistle,* 879.

208. The phrase "he took" best represents the sense of the Greek text. Due to the complex inflectional grammar of Greek, it can leave out words and phrases that English cannot.

209. BDAG, 496–97.

210. BDAG, 228.

that is in force here. At this point, the Savior established "the new and everlasting covenant" of the gospel of Jesus Christ, which enables God's children to obtain exaltation.[211]

The theological implications in the phrase ἐν τῷ ἐμῷ αἵματι (*en tō emō haimati*), "in my blood," must not be overlooked. For Paul, the covenant consisted of the continuity of God's promise to Israel (Rom. 9:4; 11:27; compare LXX Isa. 49:21) being fulfilled in Paul's day through the free gift of grace expressed in the Atonement of the Savior (Gal. 3:15, 17; 4:24)—an Atonement made possible only through the blood of Christ. The emphasis in 11:25, and in the covenant renewal made when partaking of the sacrament, looks to the Lord's death, not to his resurrection.[212] He established the "the new covenant *in my blood*," that is, in giving up his life. It was this act through which full redemption is assured to all who believe.[213]

this do ye, as oft as ye drink it, in remembrance of me / Do this, as often as you drink it, in remembrance of me: On "remember," see 11:24. That covenant would and, indeed, could be instituted only by an atonement. But the purpose of the sacrament is to remember not only the covenant but, more particularly, the one who made that covenant possible.

11:26 *For as often as ye eat this bread, and drink this cup, ye do shew the Lord's death till he come / For as often as you eat this bread and drink this cup you proclaim the Lord's death until he comes:* The causal conjunction γάρ (*gar*), "for," is important here because it signals that Paul is presenting his reason for reviewing the genesis of the sacramental ordinance. He is not doing it because "they have forgotten the words, nor because they have abandoned the Supper," as one scholar noted. "Rather, it is because their version of the Supper gives the lie to its original intent."[214]

Here Paul shares his understanding of what the ordinance is really all about. The heart of his insight is in his use of the verb καταγγέλλω (*katangellō*), "show, proclaim." The word denotes making something known *in public,* but it also includes the notion of disseminating what is known far and wide. In the Christian context it means an open witnessing of Christ and

211. See D&C 22:1–2; 131:2; 132:4, 6, 19, and 26. The translators of the KJV, being Protestant, may have wanted to downplay covenants influenced by their dislike for rituals in general.

212. Brigham Young, in *JD*, 13:139–40.

213. Thiselton, *First Epistle,* 885.

214. Fee, *First Epistle,* 556.

the preaching of his word.[215] Thus, the verb carries the force of a very open but personal proclamation—a sincere bearing of testimony—to all who will hear. What each Saint does in participating in the sacrament is to personally and publicly witness the truthfulness of Christ and his Atonement. That witness is then made full when he or she translates it into a disciplined life full of selfless giving that reflects the Lord's own.

With the words ἄχρι οὗ ἔλθῃ (*achri hou elthē*), "until he comes," Paul gives the ordinance a continual and an eschatological emphasis. It was not designed to be a one-time only event. It is to be repeated continually until the Lord comes and judgment is met. The ordinance itself looks back to the Lord's *death,* but that is not the full story. He did not stay dead. There is, therefore, an aspect of the ordinance that anticipates the future when the *living* Messiah shall return.[216] At that time, the purpose of the Atonement will be realized and the ordinance will cease.[217]

Analysis and Summary

Because 11:23 and 24, which relate the institution of the sacrament, have a number of non-Pauline idioms, it is likely that he is closely paraphrasing or even quoting material that has come down to him.[218] That would mean that he was relating a long-established tradition known to his readers and was using it as an authoritative proof text. That the story became part of the synoptic gospels supports its historical nature.[219] It is of note that Paul closely follows the account given in Luke 22:19–20. Though the JST makes a number of changes to the accounts given in Matthew 26:26–29 and especially Mark 14:22–25, it does not do so to Luke's brief account, suggesting these verses are accurate as far as they go.

Paul's purpose is to stress the importance of this ordinance. Concerning this, President David O. McKay observed:

---

215. BDAG, 515. In extra-biblical texts the word often signifies the public glorification of the gods during sacred festivals. Julius Schniewind, "καταγγέλλω, προκαταγγέλλω, καταγγελεύς," in *TDNT*, 1:70–72.

216. Fee, *First Epistle,* 557.

217. Jeremias, *Eucharistic Words,* 253, insists the phrase is not merely a temporal expression but connotes a final or purpose clause giving it the meaning of "until (the goal is reached, that) he comes." Fitzmyer, *First Corinthians,* 445, agrees, citing the force of the Hebrew עַד (*'ad*), "till, until," in Isa. 62:1, 6–7; Job 14:14; Ps. 123:2.

218. For a good study, see Jeremias, *Eucharistic Words,* 104.

219. Eriksson, *Traditions as Rhetorical Proof,* 100.

No more sacred ordinance is administered in the Church of Christ than the administration of the sacrament. It was initiated just after Jesus and the Twelve had partaken of the last supper; and the Saints in the early days followed that custom. That is, they ate before they administered the sacrament (1 Cor. 11:20–22), but that custom was later discontinued by instructions from Paul to the Saints to eat their meal at home so that when they met for worship they might meet as a body of brethren and sisters on the same level to partake of the sacrament in remembrance of the life and the death, particularly the death, of their Lord (1 Cor. 11:33–34).[220]

Though the exact nature of early Christian services is unknown, some items seem clear. As one LDS scholar noted:

> The type of church services conducted in the early church was very simple, informal but fervent. Paul had trouble in Corinth with too much ecstatic speaking and disorder. He did his best to introduce more of the order and sobriety of the synagogue, and yet not to stifle the spirit. Pliny and the Christian writers of the second and third centuries, Justin Martyr and Tertullian, also describe the services. During the New Testament period it is apparent that the meetings on a Sunday were held in a private dwelling, usually the home of one of the more wealthy members. They met together before daybreak because they had to work on Sunday; there were no legal weekly holidays then. There were hymns, prayers, and preaching of a very informal sort. In the evening a love feast, a communal meal, was followed by the Lord's Supper.[221]

It is likely that the early Christians followed the same pattern as the meetings described in the Book of Mormon where they "were conducted by the church after the manner of the workings of the Spirit, and by the power of the Holy Ghost; for as the power of the Holy Ghost led them whether to preach, or exhort, or to pray, or to supplicate, or to sing, even so it was done" (Moro. 6:9). Today, to more efficiently conduct the Lord's business, the meetings are much more formal.

For the Latter-day Saints, as Elder Francis M. Lyman has noted,

> it seems to be very important that this sacred ordinance of the Gospel should be attended to frequently, that by partaking of it we may witness to the Lord that we are willing to take upon us His name, that we have not forgotten Him, that we do keep His commandments, and are still willing

---

220. David O. McKay, in CR, April 1946, 112.

221. Russel B. Swensen, *New Testament Literature* (Salt Lake City: LDS Department of Education, 1940), 32.

to keep them, and to walk according to His counsel. Hence it is important that all Saints, not only presiding officers, but all Saints who have named the name of Jesus Christ and entered into covenant with God, should meet together often and partake of the sacrament and renew their covenants, in order that they may have the Spirit of the Lord.[222]

President Joseph F. Smith affirmed the importance of partaking of the sacrament regularly:

The ordinance has a tendency to draw our minds from the things of the world and to place them upon things that are spiritual, divine, and heavenly; and that are in accordance with the nature, desires, and attributes of man. It is a great privilege to have one day in seven set apart for the worship of the living God. Men differ in their opinions as to what day it ought to be. That is a matter, however, of very little importance. We meet together as servants and handmaidens of the Lord Jesus Christ, and we participate in the emblems of his broken body and shed blood. We think, we reflect, speak and cogitate upon things that are calculated to elevate our minds, to impart comfort to our spirits, and to bring peace, joy and happiness, whether reflecting upon things of the past, present or future."[223]

Taking his text from 11:26, President Brigham Young stated:

We do this in remembrance of the death of our Savior; it is required of his disciples until he comes again, no matter how long that may be. No matter how many generations come and go, believers in him are required to eat bread and drink wine in remembrance of his death and sufferings until he comes again. Why are they required to do this? To witness unto the Father, to Jesus and to the angels that they are believers in and desire to follow him in the regeneration, keep his commandments, build up his kingdom, revere his name and serve him with an undivided heart, that they may be worthy to eat and drink with him in his Father's kingdom. This is why the Latter-day Saints partake of the ordinance of the Lord's Supper."[224]

---

222. Francis M. Lyman, in *JD,* 25:61.
223. Joseph F. Smith, in *JD,* 12:346–37.
224. Brigham Young, in *JD,* 13:139–40.

Partaking of the Lord's Supper Unworthily (11:27–34)

Greek Text

27 Ὥστε ὃς ἂν ἐσθίῃ τὸν ἄρτον ἢ πίνῃ τὸ ποτήριον τοῦ κυρίου ἀναξίως, ἔνοχος ἔσται τοῦ σώματος καὶ τοῦ αἵματος τοῦ κυρίου. 28 δοκιμαζέτω δὲ ἄνθρωπος ἑαυτόν, καὶ οὕτως ἐκ τοῦ ἄρτου ἐσθιέτω καὶ ἐκ τοῦ ποτηρίου πινέτω· 29 ὁ γὰρ ἐσθίων καὶ πίνων κρίμα ἑαυτῷ ἐσθίει καὶ πίνει μὴ διακρίνων τὸ σῶμα. 30 διὰ τοῦτο ἐν ὑμῖν πολλοὶ ἀσθενεῖς καὶ ἄρρωστοι καὶ κοιμῶνται ἱκανοί. 31 εἰ δὲ ἑαυτοὺς διεκρίνομεν, οὐκ ἂν ἐκρινόμεθα· 32 κρινόμενοι δὲ ὑπὸ κυρίου παιδευόμεθα, ἵνα μὴ σὺν τῷ κόσμῳ κατακριθῶμεν. 33 Ὥστε, ἀδελφοί μου, συνερχόμενοι εἰς τὸ φαγεῖν ἀλλήλους ἐκδέχεσθε. 34 εἴ τις πεινᾷ, ἐν οἴκῳ ἐσθιέτω, ἵνα μὴ εἰς κρίμα συνέρχησθε. Τὰ δὲ λοιπὰ ὡς ἂν ἔλθω διατάξομαι. [SBLGNT]

King James Version

27 Wherefore whosoever shall eat this bread, and drink this cup of the Lord, unworthily, shall be guilty of the body and blood of the Lord. 28 But let a man examine himself, and so let him eat of that bread, and drink of that cup. 29 For he that eateth and drinketh unworthily, eateth and drinketh damnation to himself, not discerning the Lord's body. 30 For this cause many are weak and sickly among you, and many sleep. 31 For if we would judge ourselves, we should not be judged. 32 But when we are judged, we are chastened of the Lord, that we should not be condemned with the world. 33 Wherefore, my brethren, when ye come together to eat, tarry one for another. 34 And if any man hunger, let him eat at home; that ye come not together unto condemnation. And the rest will I set in order when I come.

New Rendition

27 Consequently, whoever eats the bread or drinks the cup of the Lord unworthily, will be guilty of sin against the body and blood of the Lord. 28 So each person should examine himself, and in this way partake of the bread and drink the cup. 29 For whoever eats and drinks without due regard for the body, eats and drinks condemnation against himself. 30 For this reason, many of you are weak and sick, and quite a few are even dead. 31 But if we would regularly examine ourselves, we would not be judged. 32 But when we are judged, we are chastened by the Lord, so that we might not be condemned with the rest of the world. 33 And so, my brothers and sisters, when you come together to eat, wait for each other. 34 If someone is hungry, let him eat at home so that when you meet together it will not be to your condemnation. Now as for the other things, I will give detailed instructions when I come.

Translation Notes and Comments

11:27 *Wherefore whosoever shall eat this bread, and drink this cup of the Lord, unworthily / Consequently, whoever eats the bread or drinks the cup of the Lord unworthily:* The conjunction ὥστε (*hōste*) acts as a marker for logical consequences and can be translated as "therefore" or "accordingly," but the English word that best captures its force in this context is "consequently,"[225] as in our Rendition. In English, the word "unworthily" connotes the idea of evilly or sinfully;[226] however, the Greek adverb ἀναξίως (*anaxiōs*), "unworthily," carries the idea of doing something in a careless or improper manner.[227] Therefore, in this instance, it seems to mean not coming to the worship service to honor and remember the Lord but exclusively to meet friends and have dinner. Paul's point is that the Corinthian Saints' conduct is not matching the seriousness and solemnity of the occasion.[228]

   shall be guilty of the body and blood of the Lord / will be guilty of sin against the body and blood of the Lord: The adjective ἔνοχος (*enochos*), "guilty," denotes being blameworthy for having done something wrong and, therefore, "liable" or "answerable" for the sin.[229] Here it points to the person against whom the deed is being committed, namely, the Lord.[230] Therefore, the guilt does not derive from some sacrilege against the elements of the sacrament, but from disrespecting the Savior and his atoning act. Thus, Paul is warning these Saints that they are going to be answerable for claiming identification with Christ through sharing in the Lord's Supper and what it proclaims but without real intent. They will be answerable because, in reality, they are using the meeting for status enhancement and social enjoyment.[231] As with all that Paul does, his focus is on "Christ, and him crucified" (2:2).

---

225. BDAG, 1107; Louw-Nida, §89.52; Thiselton, *First Epistle,* 888; Fitzmyer, *First Corinthians,* 445.

226. *Roget's International Thesaurus,* 6th ed. (New York: Harper-Collins Publishers, 2001), s.v. "unworthily," §654.16. The English word does not carry such negative connotations but describes an act "inappropriate to one's condition or station." *Collegiate Dictionary,* 1374.

227. BDAG, 69; Louw-Nida, §66.7.

228. Fee, *First Epistle,* 560 with n. 10; Hays, *First Corinthians,* 200; Bailey, *Mediterranean Eyes,* 322.

229. BDAG, 338–39.

230. Louw-Nida, §88.312.

231. Edwards, *Commentary,* 298.

**11:28 *But let a man examine himself, and so let him eat of that bread,
and drink of that cup / So each person should examine himself, and in
this way partake of the bread and drink the cup:*** The third person singular imperative δοκιμαζέτω (*dokimazetō*), "let him/her examine," points
to what the Saints should be doing before they partake of the sacrament.
The word denotes more than introspective examination. As noted in the
analysis of 11:19 above, the noun δοκιμάζω (*dokimazō*) describes those
who are found genuine through testing.[232] What Paul is demanding is that
each Saint carefully examine just how genuine his or her understanding
and motives are. The adverb οὕτως (*houtōs*) means "in this way"[233] and
indicates that a person should eat the bread and drink the wine only after
careful self-examination and deciding that their understanding, conduct,
and motives are genuine.[234]

**11:29 *For he that eateth and drinketh unworthily, eateth and drinketh
damnation to himself, not discerning the Lord's body / For whoever eats
and drinks without due regard for the body, eats and drinks condemnation against himself:*** Neither the words ἀνάξιος (*anaxios*), "unworthily,"
nor τοῦ κυρίου (*tou kyriou*), "the Lord's" are found in the best manuscripts.
Both are unnecessary scribal additions (for the text is clear without them,
based on 11:27)[235] and, therefore, remain untranslated in our Rendition. The
present participle διακρίνων (*diakrinōn*), "discerning," means to evaluate
something carefully in order to make a distinction.[236] In our Rendition we
have translated the participial phrase μὴ διακρίνων τὸ σῶμα (*mē diakrinōn
to sōma*, literally "not discerning the body") as "without due regard for the
body." Not discerning or giving proper respect for the Lord's body reveals
that the person is overlooking what the meeting was all about—a remembering of "Christ, and him crucified" (2:2). In the process they made the
sacred mundane, concentrating on the meal rather than on the Lord. To
discern the body entailed having an awareness of the uniqueness of Christ
who gave himself for others out of sheer grace and who asks the same of his
followers. Thus, the Saints were to take stock of themselves, ensuring that
they were properly focused on the reason and importance of the ordinance

---

232. Louw-Nida, §27.45.

233. BDAG, 741–42, thus the NJB and NRSV read "and only then eat."

234. Thiselton, *First Epistle*, 891.

235. Metzger, *Textual Commentary*, 496. It may be that later scribes sought to emphasize the sacredness of the ordinance and wanted to harmonize this passage with instructions coming from other places in the New Testament.

236. BDAG, 231.

and the commitment it entailed. If this were done, the unconscionable act of humiliating another Saint would be clearly seen and avoided.[237]

The noun κρίμα (*krima*), "condemnation," denotes the condition of one judged guilty of a sin and, thus, liable to punishment.[238] Its translation as "damnation" in the KJV looks to the final result.[239] Paul, however, based on 11:27, was not looking so far into the future but focused more on what the Atonement demanded of the Saints in the present—treating others well and even sacrificing for the good of all those in the household of faith.[240] That the JST changes "damnation" to "condemnation" aligns well with Paul's thought.

11:30 *For this cause many are weak and sickly among you, and many sleep / For this reason, many of you are weak and sick, and quite a few are even dead:* The prepositional phrase διὰ τοῦτο (*dia touto*) gives the reason or cause of something. In this case it looks to the result of the misuse of the sacramental service. Paul's words show that the κρίμα (*krima*), "condemnation," mentioned in 11:29 is already in effect as evidenced by weakness, sickness, and even death among the Corinthian Saints. The adjective ἀσθενής (*asthenēs*), "weak," can describe ailments reaching from mere physical limitation to debilitating illnesses.[241] The adjective ἄρρωστος (*arrōstos*), "sick," denotes a condition of powerlessness and is the general term used for any *physical* sickness or infirmity.[242] The verb κοιμάομαι (*koimaomai*), literally "to sleep," is a euphemism for death. Though some have suggested that Paul is referring to spiritual weakness and death,[243] the force of the passage, especially given the physical nuance of the adjective *arrōstos*, argues otherwise. Paul's understanding of what was happening could be based on his Jewish background in which sickness and death were sometimes attributed to sinful conduct.[244]

---

237. Fitzmyer, *First Corinthians,* 446; Thiselton, *First Epistle,* 893; Barrett, *First Epistle,* 274–75.

238. Louw-Nida, §56.30.

239. Christ gave a similar admonition to his Nephite leaders when he appeared to them after his resurrection: "For whoso eateth and drinketh my flesh and blood unworthily," he warned, "eateth and drinketh damnation to his soul" (3 Ne. 18:29).

240. Fitzmyer, *First Corinthians,* 447.

241. BDAG, 142–43.

242. BDAG, 135.

243. Robertson and Plummer, *Critical and Exegetical Commentary,* 253; Holzapfel and Wayment, *Making Sense,* 358–59.

244. Note the implications in John 9:1–3; see also Ex. 4:11; Deut. 32:39; Sir. 27:27–29; 38:9–10; 2 Macc. 4:38; 9:5–6.

11:31 *For if we would judge ourselves, we should not be judged / But if we would regularly examine ourselves, we would not be judged:* Again, Paul switches from the third person plural to the first person plural. In doing so, it is likely he is again reaching out to his readers. The verb διακρίνω (*diakrinō*), "judge, examine," as noted above, has at its root the idea of separating one thing from another in order to make a distinction or determination.[245] In this context, the best English word to catch Paul's meaning is "self-examination," as in our Rendition. The passive of the verb κρίνομαι (*krinomai*), "to be judged," often implies being condemned.[246] Paul uses a contrary-to-fact condition here with εἰ (*ei*), "if," plus the imperfect in the protasis and the particle ἄν (*an*), plus imperfect in the apodosis.[247] The use of the imperfect tense expresses action that is ongoing. Thus, the full sense of the conditional sentence is, "If we were continually examining ourselves (but at this point we are not), then we would not continue to be judged (but at this point we are still being judged)." Paul's point is that if the Saints would repent (something that up to this point they have *not* done) and continually take stock of themselves and make what adjustments were necessary, they would ever avoid any kind of condemnation.

11:32 *But when we are judged, we are chastened of the Lord, / But when we are judged, we are chastened by the Lord:* The present passive participle κρινόμενοι (*krinomenoi*), "being judged," looks to the current state of some of the Saints. Paul lets his readers know that some of them are presently under divine judgment. The force of the present passive verb παιδεύομαι (*paideuomai*), "to be chastened," carries the idea of being corrected by divine discipline.[248] God's purpose is not to bring punishment but repentance. Thus, the judgment spoken of here is for this world only. This judgment acts as divine discipline. It is being used by a loving God to correct his children and bring them back to the proper course.[249]

that we should not be condemned with the world / so that we might not be condemned with the rest of the world: Here Paul explains the purpose of God's discipline. The passive verb κατακρίνομαι (*katakrinomai*), "to be condemned," denotes the passing of a judicial sentence on a convicted party.[250] In this case, it is "the world" that stands under censure. The

---

245. BDAG, 231.
246. Friedrich Büchsel and Volkmar Herntrich, "κρίνω," in *TDNT*, 3:921–41.
247. Smyth, *Greek Grammar*, §2302–3.
248. BDAG, 749.
249. Fee, *First Epistle*, 566.
250. BDAG, 519.

noun κόσμος (*kosmos*), "world," carries a negative connotation, pointing to those on the earth who oppose God (see 1:27–28; 6:2; 2 Cor. 1:12; 5:19; Rom. 3:6; and particularly JS–M 1:4).[251] God disciplines his children to bring them back to him so that they might avoid the inevitable judgment upon a guilty world.

11:33 *Wherefore, my brethren, when ye come together to eat, tarry one for another / And so, my brothers and sisters, when you come together to eat, wait for each other:* On "brothers and sisters," see Translation Notes at 1:10. By using the subordinating conjunction ὥστε (*hōste*), "therefore" or "and so," Paul indicates that he is now going to make his point. In this case, it is how to avoid the Lord's disciplining hand. The present participle συνερχόμενοι (*synerchomenoi*), "coming together," points to the purpose of the meeting.[252] It is not for a regular dinner with friends but the sharing of a common meal *as a church* in which the participants partake of the sacrament. Using the imperative ἐκδέχεσθε (*ekdechesthe*), "wait," the Apostle shows how to avoid judgment. The word denotes remaining in a state until an expected event occurs.[253] In this case, it is waiting for each other (ἀλλήλους, *allēlous*, that is, rich, poor, bond, or free) before beginning the sacramental service. By not going ahead with the meal, the members would show that they respected all and wanted all to have a share in the proceedings and be renewed spiritually and physically.[254] In this way, they would promote the fellowship the Lord designed to produce repentance and avoid judgment.

11:34 *And if any man hunger, let him eat at home; that ye come not together unto condemnation / If someone is hungry, let him eat at home so that when you meet together it will not be to your condemnation:* Paul's point is that filling one's stomach is not the purpose of the meeting. That should be done at home (the expression ἐν οἴκῳ [*en oikō*], "at home," used here, stands in contrast to ἐν ἐκκλησίᾳ (*en ekklēsia*), "in the Church," used in 11:18). Eating at home would show that the person did, indeed, understand the purpose of the meeting and, thereby, would avoid any condemnation coming upon himself or herself.[255]

---

251. Fitzmyer, *First Corinthians*, 448.

252. BDAG, 969.

253. Louw-Nida, §13.28.

254. Bailey, *Mediterranean Eyes*, 323.

255. The Savior faced a similar situation during his ministry. Due to his miraculous feeding of the five thousand, many chose to follow him. When, however, he refused to continue to feed them physically and demanded that they look to their spiritual needs, many turned from him. See John 6:1–66.

And the rest will I set in order when I come / Now as for the other things, I will give detailed instructions when I come: The phrase suggests that Paul addressed only his major concerns about the worship service. His use of the future verb διατάξομαι (*diataxomai*), "to set in order" or "give detailed instructions,"[256] hints that the other matters needed more specifics than he wanted to give in a general letter. He determined to wait to address these until he could do so in person. Since identifying just what these other issues were would require the greatest of speculation, they are not addressed here.[257]

Analysis and Summary

In 11:29, Paul uses a wordplay on the words containing the root κριν- (*krin-*), that is, words dealing with making judgments. That he does this can best be seen by paraphrasing his words so that they read: "If we were discerning (*diakrinō*) ourselves, we would not be coming under judgment (*ekkrinō*); but, when we are being judged (*krinō*), it is to correct us by discipline so that we will not be condemned (*katakrinō*) with the world."[258] The wordplay, looking as it does toward divine displeasure and its results, puts emphasis on the seriousness of the sacrament and the need to properly partake of it.

Underscoring this idea, one LDS scholar noted, "for Paul, the 'cup of blessing' and the broken bread are visible signs of 'communion' with Christ (1 Cor. 10:16). The term (*koinōnia*) means a 'common sharing' and is usually translated 'fellowship.' In the letters one has 'fellowship' with heaven and with the Church if one's life is in order. There is a 'fellowship' or 'communion of the Holy Ghost' (2 Cor. 13:14), but it comes only 'to them that obey' God (Acts 5:32). Paul states this general principle (2 Cor. 6:14): 'And what communion hath light with darkness?' Thus, the sacrament of the Lord's Supper was a symbol of visible relationship to God through Christ, accompanied by self-examination of the worthiness of one's life."[259]

The sacramental elements symbolize Christ's Atonement in which the participant shares by renewing his or her covenant when partaking of the emblems. When lifestyle and deportment make empty the purpose and seriousness of the ordinance, the participant will be held liable for dishonoring the Lord.[260]

---

256. BDAG, 237–38.
257. Robertson and Plummer, *Critical and Exegetical Commentary*, 255.
258. Fee, *First Epistle*, 566 n. 40.
259. Anderson, *Understanding Paul*, 108.
260. Thiselton, *First Epistle*, 890.

Paul's warning in 11:30 should cause serious reflection. Those who partake of the sacrament with no intent in carrying out its responsibilities commit grievous sin. The sacrament—which God designed, at least in part, as a healing balm for the wounded soul—could prove toxic to one who hypocritically partook. Such an idea is in keeping with Paul's beliefs. He clearly saw a double sided effect of spiritual things. For example, in his second epistle to these same people, he testified, concerning the teaching of his fellow Apostles, that to some members it was a "savour of life unto life," but for others, it was the "savour of death unto death" (2 Cor. 2:16).[261] The sacrament is the same.

Elder Francis M. Lyman testified,

> It is not pleasing in the sight of the Lord, for us to partake of the sacrament if there be hard feelings in our hearts, if there be jealousness, if there be enmity or strife, if we are not in fellowship with one another, if we are not in fellowship with the Church, if we are not keeping the commandments of the Lord, if we are not living in peace, if we are not obedient to the counsels of heaven; I say that it is not pleasing in the sight of the Lord to partake of the sacrament under such circumstances. This is an ordinance that should be partaken of properly, understandingly, thoughtfully, and with faith that we will receive an increased portion of the Holy Spirit.[262]

When not done according to rule, states Elder McConkie, the act is "not sealed by the Holy Spirit of Promise" and has no "efficacy, virtue, and force for this life and for the life to come. (D&C 76:53; 132:7.)"[263]

The Savior made it very clear how he felt about the ordinance when he commanded his Nephite church leaders, saying: "Ye shall not suffer any one knowingly to partake of my flesh and blood unworthily, when ye shall minister it; For whoso eateth and drinketh my flesh and blood unworthily eateth and drinketh damnation to his soul; therefore if ye know that a man is unworthy to eat and drink of my flesh and blood ye shall forbid him" (3 Ne. 18:28–29; compare Morm. 9:29; D&C 46:4).

It should be noted, as Elder McConkie makes clear, that "this penalty applies only to those who partake of the sacrament in total and complete unworthiness and rebellion. It is only this class of damned souls upon whose hands, in the full sense of the word, the blood of Christ is found."[264]

---

261. Thiselton, *First Epistle*, 896.
262. Francis M. Lyman, in *JD*, 25:61. Compare President John Taylor's counsel in *JD*, 21:250–51.
263. *DNTC*, 2:365.
264. *DNTC*, 2:365.

Even so, the fullness of the Spirit can come only to those who humbly and sincerely approach the sacrament. "The participation in the sacrament should, therefore, be preceded by self-examination," counseled Elder Janne M. Sjodahl. "This does not mean, however, that a Church member who, on a searching self-examination, finds many weaknesses and imperfections in himself, must absent himself from the Lord's Table. The great question is, whether we are willing to resist temptations, overcome weaknesses, and exercise faith for the increase of spiritual strength. That truth is beautifully expressed in the consecrating prayer, in which we ask that we may witness before our eternal Father, that we are willing to take upon us the name of His Son, and keep His commandments."[265]

As one LDS scholar noted, "Parallel processes should occur while one is taking the sacred symbols—as one thinks on the Lord, he evaluates himself in relation to the Lord. . . . Such self-judgment in preparation for the sacrament implies the same attitude while partaking of it. The worldly Corinthians would be condemned with the world unless they truly repented through remembering Christ in the sacrament. So Paul's reasoning suggests a double purpose for partaking of the sacrament—remembrance, and resolve to live a righteous life."[266]

As we properly partake of the sacrament, we confirm who and whose we are.[267] The title "Christian" takes on a fuller meaning in showing our identification with the Lord and the character we should possess. Partaking worthily means that each person approaches the Lord's Table sincerely, contritely, and with a determination of doing better. Covenant renewal looks to performing service in imitation of the Lord's own. That imitation opens the way for his spirit to be with each devoted person always (see D&C 20:77).

To summarize Paul's point, real remembrance looks to the past and what the Redeemer did for each of us individually but with the intent to both make his sacrifice effective in the present and give direction to the future. Paul's desire was to evoke in each of his readers a total recommitment to Christ that makes the Atonement real in the present and, in that way, capable of releasing a power that will shape the future.[268] That shaping comes in taking care of, sharing with, and loving God's children.

---

265. [J. M. S.], "The Lord's Supper," *Millennial Star* 78 (January 20, 1916): 35.
266. Anderson, "Restoration of the Sacrament," 40–41.
267. Fee, *First Epistle*, 566.
268. Murphy-O'Connor, *1 Corinthians*, 112.

Chapter 12

The Importance and Use of Gifts of the Spirit

INTRODUCTION

Having completed his instructions concerning certain abuses taking place during worship service, Paul turned to the next item on his agenda, that of spiritual gifts. Based on the amount of space he devoted to this topic (it continues through chapter 14), of all the subjects the Apostle had covered thus far, this one seems to be of greatest concern. It is in this section where the difference between him and many of his readers comes into the clearest focus, specifically in understanding what constitutes true spirituality.[1]

"Good analysts," writes one LDS scholar, "have called 1 Corinthians 12 the 'Constitution of the Church,' for nothing in the New Testament better describes God's plan for Church structure and operation."[2] On this topic, Paul pays a good deal of attention to the relationship of the Saints to one another but more especially to the ἐκκλησία (ekklēsia), "church," as a well-organized and spirit-guided body. He begins, however, noting the necessity of having the Spirit operate on the individual level. He focuses on its power to give witness to the reality of the Lord (12:3).[3]

Paul's focus on spirituality likely came in response to the letter that has driven much of his discussion thus far. His argument does not reveal the precise questions the Saints asked but, based especially on statements he makes in chapter 14, their concern seems to be on the use, and likely misuse, of the gift of tongues in Church meetings. There is, however, an

---

1. Fee, *First Epistle*, 570.
2. Anderson, *Understanding Paul*, 112.
3. Fitzmyer, *First Corinthians*, 454.

underlying concern that he also addresses. That concern again expressed itself in competitiveness, but in this case, it was among some of the Saints over spiritual gifts. There seems to have been a general misconception that some gifts were superior to others. The moral corollary was that these "higher gifts" proved that their recipients were on a higher spiritual level than other Saints and, therefore, had a much deeper spirituality. The mistaken belief was nothing short of an insistence that God favored some of the Saints more than others. This attitude is but one more expression of the competitive drive that dominated the lives of so many of the Saints, a drive that was destroying the unity of the Church.

The temptation to glory in one's gift—especially one that was rather showy, namely glossolalia, "speaking tongues"—was more insidious and damaging to the unity of the Church than either the social or financial segregation already noted.[4] For those who were not "in," the idea was most discouraging. It was one thing to be looked down upon by society, but quite another, the implication went, to be looked down upon by God.[5] The temptation among these downcast members was either to leave the Church or pull it in a different direction.

Thus, the issues Paul addresses in this section (chapters 12–14) tie back to the concerns he had already addressed in chapters 8–11 and, ultimately, to those in chapters 1–4. As such, this section is a polemic against factionalism, a concern he voiced clearly in 1:10.[6] Here the issue is not social or financial status but spiritual. Paul, in chapters 12–14, set out to correct this grievous misunderstanding.[7] What Paul had to get his readers to understand was the true meaning of spirituality. He did so by redefining spirituality and, thereby, teaching them what it really was.

Addressing the question of spiritual gifts allowed the Apostle to give his readers a general overview of their nature, importance, and use. In doing so, he also gave them proper perspective. "By inviting all Saints to

---

4. Thiselton, *First Epistle,* 900.

5. Paul's intent was ever to be as inclusive as possible. That he wrote in Greek, not Aramaic or Hebrew, is telling. It suggested that for him, the native language of the Corinthians was perfectly suited to express the "mysteries of God," and, therefore, there was no such thing as a sacred language. By doing so, he also tacitly jettisoned the idea that there was a sacred culture. Bailey, *Mediterranean Eyes,* 331. The Apostle does, however, insist that there is a sacred people.

6. Mitchell, *Paul and the Rhetoric of Reconciliation,* 159.

7. Fitzmyer, *First Corinthians,* 454.

anxiously pursue such gifts [12:31]," noted one LDS scholar, "Paul rejected the theology of 'spiritual elitism' as God's method of allocating spiritual gifts. Instead, Paul sought to educate the Saints about the need for each to petition God for the various gifts promised to all worthy Saints."[8] He continued, noting that "Paul's masterful sermon on spiritual gifts seems as much a personal reflection as it does a doctrinal discourse. Indeed, from the very beginning of his personal ministry until his martyrdom in Rome, Paul was showered with extraordinary gifts from God. Moreover, the gifts he enumerated were exemplified during his ministry as a special witness of Christ."[9]

"The Church would be lifeless without the inspiration of God's spirit," noted another LDS scholar. "Thus, 1 Corinthians 12 begins by surveying the power of the Holy Ghost within the Church."[10] Here "Paul enumerated several of the chief gifts and outlined the principles associated with their use in Christ's church."[11] After noting the importance of the Spirit in order to know that Jesus is the Messiah (12:1–3), the Apostle stressed the need for the *diversity* of spiritual gifts among the members, but he also noted each one was but a manifestation of the power of the Holy Ghost (12:4–11). To illustrate his point, he used the analogy of the body which, though being made up of many parts, functions as a whole (12:12–26). To seal his point, he concluded by listing the various officers and their associated gifts (12:27–31).

THE TESTIMONY OF JESUS (12:1–3)

Greek Text

1 Περὶ δὲ τῶν πνευματικῶν, ἀδελφοί, οὐ θέλω ὑμᾶς ἀγνοεῖν. 2 οἴδατε ὅτι ὅτε ἔθνη ἦτε πρὸς τὰ εἴδωλα τὰ ἄφωνα ὡς ἂν ἤγεσθε ἀπαγόμενοι. 3 διὸ γνωρίζω ὑμῖν ὅτι οὐδεὶς ἐν πνεύματι θεοῦ λαλῶν λέγει· Ἀνάθεμα Ἰησοῦς, καὶ οὐδεὶς δύναται εἰπεῖν· Κύριος Ἰησοῦς εἰ μὴ ἐν πνεύματι ἁγίῳ. [SBLGNT]

---

8. Freeman, "Paul's Earnest Pursuit," 35.
9. Freeman, "Paul's Earnest Pursuit," 36.
10. Anderson, *Understanding Paul,* 112.
11. Freeman, "Paul's Earnest Pursuit," 34.

King James Version

1 Now concerning spiritual gifts, brethren, I would not have you ignorant. 2 Ye know that ye were Gentiles, carried away unto these dumb idols, even as ye were led. 3 Wherefore I give you to understand, that no man speaking by the Spirit of God calleth Jesus accursed: and that no man can say that Jesus is the Lord, but by the Holy Ghost.

New Rendition

1 Now concerning spiritual matters, brothers and sisters, I do not want you to be uninformed. 2 You know that when you were nonmembers that you were constantly enticed being led astray to idols that could not speak. 3 So I want you to understand that no one speaking by the Spirit of God says, "Jesus is cursed," and no one can say, "Jesus is the Lord," except by the Holy Spirit.

Translation Notes and Comments

12:1 *Now concerning spiritual gifts, brethren, I would not have you ignorant / Now concerning spiritual matters, brothers and sisters, I do not want you to be uninformed:* For ἀδελφοί (*adelphoi*), "brothers and sisters," see Translation Notes on 1:10. The Greek phrase τῶν πνευματικῶν (*tōn pneumatikōn*) can be either a masculine or neuter genitive plural nominal adjective functioning as a substantive adjective. However, what it refers to is unclear. If it is interpreted as a masculine plural, then it is substantively referring to "spiritual persons."[12] If it is translated as a neuter, then it is referring to "spiritual matters."[13] Fortunately, 12:4 clarifies the issue. The Apostle refers to χαρίσματα (*charismata*), a neuter plural noun, which specifically denotes gifts of the Spirit, that is, those powers that God freely and graciously bestows upon the faithful.[14] The JST changes this phrase to read "spiritual *things*," thus, following the sense of the Greek. For these reasons, our Rendition translates the phrase as "spiritual matters."

The phrase οὐ θέλω ὑμᾶς ἀγνοεῖν (*ou thelō hymas agnoein*), "I do not want you to be uninformed," is formulaic and shows that Paul is now introducing another important topic. The infinitive ἀγνοεῖν (*agnoein*), "to be ignorant," denotes failing to recognize or understand the importance of something; it also means "to be uninformed." Though translated as "unaware" at 10:1, the context here suggests "uninformed" better catches the nuance of the

---

12. For example, see Bruce, *1 and 2 Corinthians*, 116, and John D. Ekem, "'Spiritual Gifts,' or 'Spiritual Persons'? 1 Corinthians 12:1a Revisited," *Neotestamentica* 28 (1980): 54–74.

13. Giving weight to this view is 14:1, where Paul uses the neuter form τὰ πνευματικά (*ta pneumatika*), "spiritual things."

14. BDAG, 1081.

Greek.[15] The phrase tells Paul's readers that he is going to explain something "not quite obvious and highly important."[16]

12:2 *Ye know that ye were Gentiles / You know that when you were nonmembers:* The KJV does not translate the subordinate conjunction ὅτε (*hote*), "when," while our Rendition does. The Greek noun ἔθνους (*ethnous*) referred to a nation or people.[17] In the LXX, when used in the plural, τὰ ἔθνη (*ta ethnē*), as in this verse, corresponded to the Hebrew גּוֹיִם (*gōyyīm*), which designated a non-Israelite. At this time, the Christians seem to have used it to designate those who were not members of the Church.[18]

carried away unto these dumb idols, even as ye were led / that you were constantly enticed being led astray to idols that could not speak: The Greek phrase from which this clause is translated presents some grammatical difficulties, but the sense is clear. The conjunction ὡς (*hōs*) takes up the preceding ὅτι (*hoti*) and is translated "that."[19] The imperfect passive verb ἤγεσθε (*ēgesthe*) means "to be led away," and even "arrested," but the moral overtone that is at play here, plus the suggestion of being charmed or seduced to do an action, is best picked up by the word "enticed."[20] Further, the imperfect tense together with the particle ἄν (*an*) emphasizes the repetitive nature of the action,[21] therefore, it is translated as "constantly enticed" in our Rendition. The verb ἀπάγω (*apagō*) means "to lead away" but emphasizes the idea of deceiving someone.[22] Here it is a present passive participle used circumstantially, "being led astray," as in our Rendition. The thrust of the whole phrase stresses the repetitive nature of the action, that is, these people were being led astray over and over again to dumb idols.[23]

Before their conversion, the pagan Christians had been worshiping idols. To stress the absurdity of such devotion—an absurdity that they could not see until their conversion—Paul uses the phrase τὰ εἴδωλα τὰ ἄφωνα (*ta*

---

15. Both the NIV and NET translate the word this way.

16. Findlay, "St. Paul's First Epistle," 885.

17. BDAG, 276.

18. BDAG, 276. The term did act to separate Greeks (and others) from Jews and, thereby, could be divisive. Indeed, from a conservative Jewish standpoint, a Gentile, even as a God-fearer or proselyte, was never fully accented into the community. Paul's words show that was not the case with Christians. Nonmembers could easily become members with no taint. See Bailey, *Mediterranean Eyes,* 331–33.

19. BDAG, 16.

20. BDAG, 16.

21. BDAG, 16.

22. Louw-Nida, §88.152.

23. BDAG, 16. For a discussion of the whole problem, see Thiselton, *First Epistle,* 911–12.

eidōla ta aphōna), "idols that cannot speak." The adjective *aphōna*, "mute, dumb, unable to speak," carries the force of something that is lifeless and, thus, unable to respond. The Apostle had indicated already what should have been obvious to all, that an idol is nothing (8:4). Their inability to speak proves this fact. But if that were not enough, another obvious fact is that they are deaf and blind as well.

Pagans, however, were ignoring these traits and had so for millennia, or had they? Paul does not say that pagans were led astray *by* mute idols, but rather that they were led astray *to* them. What force could have been so seductive that it held whole populations for centuries? Ironically, it was because idols were deaf and blind and dumb. As one LDS scholar noted, their "appeal was precisely that they could *not* see or hear [or speak] but ever remained perfectly compliant to the wishes and purposes of their owners."[24] Idol worship gave the illusion of propriety, correctness, even morality, to anything its practitioners wanted to do. The rites were sometimes, however, associated with ritual prostitution and even human sacrifices.[25]

12:3 *Wherefore I give you to understand, that no man speaking by the Spirit of God calleth Jesus accursed / So I want you to understand that no one speaking by the Spirit of God says, "Jesus is cursed":* The verb γνωρίζω (*gnōrizō*) means "to make known" or "to impart information."[26] The preposition ἐν (*en*), "in," with the dative πνεύματι (*pneumati*), "spirit," is translated here in an instrumental sense as "by," showing that the action is under the influence of the Holy Spirit. Under that power, Paul states, no one can say "ἀνάθεμα Ἰησοῦς" (*anathema Iēsous*), literally, "Jesus cursed." The noun *anathēma* designates something devoted exclusively to a god but, in this context, it denotes something so abhorrent that it is "cut off from God" (see also Gal. 1:8–9; Rom. 9:3).[27] Because the Greek quote has no verb, the phrase can be translated as "Jesus is cursed" or "Jesus be cursed." To decide which, it is necessary to put the verse in its historical context.[28]

---

24. Hugh Nibley in an unpublished introduction to *Victoriosa Loquacitas,* but quoted in *Of All Things!: Classic Quotations from Hugh Nibley,* comp. Gary P. Gillum (Salt Lake City: Signature Books, 1981), 191.

25. Joseph P. Healey, "Fertility Cults," in *ABD,* 2:791–93. For a more full discussion, see Theodor H. Gaster, *Thespis: Ritual, Myth, and Drama in the Ancient Near East* (New York: Henry Schuman, 1961).

26. BDAG, 203.

27. BDAG, 63. For the translation as "cursed," see Louw-Nida, §33.474.

28. For a discussion of all the ways this phrase can be understood, see Thiselton, *First Epistle,* 918–23.

Paul is likely quoting a slogan used by Jews to thwart the Christians.[29] This assertion is based on two terms that Paul uses in this verse. The first is the phrase τὰ ἔθνη (*ta ethnē*), literally, "the nations," used by Greek-speaking Jews to identify the Gentiles (see 12:2 above). The second is the word *anathēma*, "accursed," a popular and largely Jewish curse.[30] Taking as a text Deuteronomy 21:22–23, Jews could easily insist that Jesus was accursed of God. Thus, the phrase *anathema Iēsous* would be confessional and translates as "Jesus is cursed."[31] Understood in this way, it parallels the countering Christian confession Paul notes in the next phrase below.

no man can say that Jesus is the Lord, but by the Holy Ghost / no one can say, "Jesus is the Lord," except by the Holy Spirit: The verb λέγω (*legō*), "to say" or "to speak,"[32] denotes the enumeration or narration of an idea. It connotes the thought or understanding the speaker has about the subject.[33] Therefore, in this context, to "say" something is to understand it as true and to openly bear witness to that truth.

The noun κύριος (*kyrios*), "lord," is properly an adjective signifying "to have power or authority," but it is consistently used as a noun in the New Testament. When applied to humans, it denotes any person of authority.[34] When applied to supernatural beings, it denoted one who was a god. The Christians, following the Greek-speaking Jews, used it as a title for Jehovah.[35] The Savior assumed this title apparently in the Jewish context (Matt. 7:21, 22; 9:38; 22:41–45; Mark 5:19; Luke 19:31; John 13:13) to tie himself to the Old Testament.[36]

---

29. Some commentators suggest that Paul made up the phrase himself to put more force behind the contrast with "Jesus is Lord." For discussion, see Fitzmyer, *First Corinthians*, 455. This seems rather unlikely, however, given the context in which Paul uses it.

30. *TDNT*, 1:354. Some scholars have argued that the phrase came from Ophite Gnostic Christians who separated the physical and, therefore, inferior Jesus from the spiritual and, therefore, exalted Christ. This view is based on Origen, *Cels*, 6.28 and *Contena* frag. 47 as well as Irenaeus, *Adv. Haer.* 1.24.4. Given that these sources are much later than Paul's period and it is unlikely such heretics were living in Roman Corinth at the time, it is unlikely the slogan came from them.

31. W. C. van Unnik, "Jesus: Anathema or Kyrios (1 Cor. 12:3)," in *Christ and Spirit in the New Testament: Studies in Honour of Charles Francis Digby Moule*, ed. Barnabas Lindars and Stephen S. Smalley (Cambridge: Cambridge University Press, 1973), 120.

32. BDAG, 286–87.

33. A. Debrunner, H. Kleinknecht, O. Procksch, and G. Kittel, "λέγω, λόγος, ῥῆμα, λαλέω," in *TDNT*, 4:69–136.

34. BDAG, 578.

35. BDAG, 576–77.

36. Gottfried Quell and Werner Foerster, "κύριος," in *TDNT*, 3:1039–95; Louw-Nida, §12.9.

Thus, one who says, "Jesus is Lord," witnesses to his status as the living vindicated King (Rev. 19:16) who has triumphed over the hostile and fallen world. It reflects a heart-felt stance oriented toward performance and self-involvement in the Lord's mission and ministry for his people.[37]

Analysis and Summary

Paul's objective in this pericope is twofold: first, to establish a general criterion for the working of the Holy Spirit in the Church (12:3) and second, to show the wide and varied manifestations of its gifts (12:4–11).[38]

"Paul's discussion at this point," noted one LDS scholar, "is part of the answer to a larger question faced by the early Church: How does the gospel of Jesus Christ really work when applied to every nation, kindred, tongue, and people? How can one mix the great cultural extremes of Jew and Gentile or the economic and social extremes of bond and free and have the unity required by Christ? Paul's answer is simple yet profound."[39]

Paul begins by explaining the role of the Spirit in its epistemological aspect (12:1–3). Without its directing power, the gentile Corinthians had been seduced over and over to follow this or that dumb idol. With the Spirit, however, they can now say that "Jesus is Lord."[40]

Their witness was a result of "being born again," that is of becoming "quickened in the inner man" (Moses 6:65), a process that requires "bapti[sm] with fire, and with the Holy Ghost. This is the record of the Father, and the Son, from henceforth and forever" (Moses 6:66). Concerning this record, President Harold B. Lee stated, "I feel certain, [this] is what Paul [referred to when he] wrote to the Corinthians [that] no man can say . . . Jesus is the Lord, but by the Holy Ghost. (1 Corinthians 12:3.) . . . Without it man cannot know the Father and the Son."[41]

Paul undercuts the idea of a greater holiness and, therefore, a superior divine favor somehow evidenced by certain spiritual manifestations. A specific gift, he clarifies, determines neither the depth of spirituality nor the amount of divine favor a person has. Instead, he shows that all who "know"

---

37. Thiselton, *First Epistle,* 923–25.

38. Findlay, "St. Paul's First Epistle," 885.

39. Rex C. Reeve Jr., "The Holy Ghost Brings Testimony, Unity, and Spiritual Gifts," in *Apostle Paul, His Life and His Testimony,* 168.

40. Fitzmyer, *First Corinthians,* 455.

41. Harold B. Lee, *Stand Ye in Holy Places* (Salt Lake City: Deseret Book, 1975), 54.

that "Jesus is Lord," are spiritual, in fact, deeply spiritual, because such knowledge comes only to those who enjoy that endowment. By redefining what constitutes spirituality, the Apostle brings equality and parity back into the Church.[42]

"We preach ... Christ Jesus the Lord" (κύριος, *kyrios*), Paul proclaims (2 Cor. 4:5). That he uses the term *kyrios* as *the* title for the Savior (12:3; he uses it some 220 times) shows his understanding of exactly who and what Jesus was and is, namely, the divine Son of God who is also the Messiah and Redeemer. What "we preach" expressed the belief that Jesus, the one who lived and died, was also the Lord over the Church by virtue of his Resurrection from the dead.[43] But behind Paul's preachment stands a commitment to give service to him as the supreme authority in one's life. Paul's stance on this is reflected in Romans 10:9, where he states that "if you confess with your lips and believe in your heart that Jesus is Lord and that God raised him from the dead, you will be saved" (authors' translation). His statement strongly parallels Deuteronomy 30:14, where it states, "The word is ... on your lips and in your heart, *that you may do it*" (authors' translation with italics added). The verb translated "confess" (ὁμολογέω, *homologeō*) carried a legal nuance denoting the admission of guilt to an accusation. On the positive side, it meant bearing witness to an inner conviction.[44] The point of the scripture is that true confession expresses itself in action. There is little doubt that Paul sees this audible witness of faith as *the* requirement necessary to participate in salvation. That can be so because the action signifies a commitment and personal devotion to the Master so strong that it translates itself into a truly Christian lifestyle.[45]

The title *kyrios* also expresses the recognition by the Saint that he or she belongs to Christ as his purchased slave (δοῦλος, *doulos*, 6:20; 7:23). In this context, the title "Lord" carries the idea of "Master," and emphasizes that the Christian is under the Lord's authority and must do his bidding (compare Luke 6:46; Matt. 7:21). That bidding dictates his or her lifestyle and ethics. The title also carries the idea that the one holding it is responsible

---

42. Mitchell, *Paul and the Rhetoric of Reconciliation*, 241, 248, 256, 258–83; Eriksson, *Traditions as Rhetorical Proof*, 217.

43. Vernon H. Neufeld, *The Earliest Christian Confessions* (Leiden: Brill, 1963), 43–49.

44. Otto Michel, "ὁμολογέω, ἐξομολογέω, ἀνθομολογέομαι, ὁμολογία, ὁμολογουμένως," in *TDNT*, 5:199–220.

45. Eriksson, *Traditions as Rhetorical Proof*, 111–14, 217–22.

for the care and keeping of his people and stands as a warning against any who might in any way deign to humiliate, abuse, or hurt them.[46]

But when does this witness of the Spirit come? Some members of the LDS community have felt it can occur only after a person has been baptized and received the gift of the Holy Ghost. Responding to this idea, Elder Charles W. Penrose stated that "under the Judaic regime, it was an adage that 'cursed is everyone that hangeth on a tree' [Deut. 21:22–23]. Paul desired to show the wrong of applying that to Jesus of Nazareth, and so declared that no one would say that when under the influence of the Spirit of God; and that it required that influence to say, as of knowledge, that Jesus is the Lord. But the question asked is, 'can anyone *know* that Jesus is the Son of God before that person has received the Holy Ghost *by the laying on of hands?*' This it will be seen, is adding somewhat to the saying of the Apostle."[47] In other words, the Spirit can witness the reality of Christ to a person who is not baptized.

Paul's point agrees with that of Elder McConkie, who noted that "revelation is the sole and only sure source of knowledge about God and Christ and gospel truths. A knowledge of these things does not and cannot come by reason, research, or rationalization. God stands revealed, or he remains forever unknown."[48] That revealed knowledge is, or should be, a uniting force in the Church as we publicly share and declare it to each other.

"To achieve the unity in the Church that Christ requires," noted one LDS scholar, "each member must view himself first and foremost as a true follower of Jesus Christ. Members must also recognize that every other member, regardless of background and circumstance in life, is [also] a true follower of Christ. Whether they be Jew, Gentile, bond, free, male, female, black, or white, all are united in Christ. If members see themselves or others primarily as Jew or Gentile, or bond or free, or male or female, the Spirit is offended and unity is destroyed."[49]

---

46. Werner Kramer, *Christ, Lord, Son of God*, trans. B. Hardy (Norwich, Eng.: SCM-Canterbury Press, 1966), 181. When it came to the relationship between slaves and masters, the latter could grant freedom if the slave were loyal and hardworking. Likewise, today those who are loyal in keeping covenants will become free from both the bondage of spiritual and temporal death.

47. Charles W. Penrose, "Ancient Scripture and the Living Spirit," *Millennial Star* 72 (February 10, 1910): 89–91.

48. *DNTC*, 2:367.

49. Reeve, "Holy Ghost," 169.

Spiritual Gifts
(12:4–11)

Greek Text

4 Διαιρέσεις δὲ χαρισμάτων εἰσίν, τὸ δὲ αὐτὸ πνεῦμα· 5 καὶ διαιρέσεις διακονιῶν εἰσιν, καὶ ὁ αὐτὸς κύριος· 6 καὶ διαιρέσεις ἐνεργημάτων εἰσίν, ὁ δὲ αὐτὸς θεός, ὁ ἐνεργῶν τὰ πάντα ἐν πᾶσιν. 7 ἑκάστῳ δὲ δίδοται ἡ φανέρωσις τοῦ πνεύματος πρὸς τὸ συμφέρον. 8 ᾧ μὲν γὰρ διὰ τοῦ πνεύματος δίδοται λόγος σοφίας, ἄλλῳ δὲ λόγος γνώσεως κατὰ τὸ αὐτὸ πνεῦμα, 9 ἑτέρῳ πίστις ἐν τῷ αὐτῷ πνεύματι, ἄλλῳ χαρίσματα ἰαμάτων ἐν τῷ ἑνὶ πνεύματι, 10 ἄλλῳ ἐνεργήματα δυνάμεων, ἄλλῳ προφητεία, ἄλλῳ διακρίσεις πνευμάτων, ἑτέρῳ γένη γλωσσῶν, ἄλλῳ ἑρμηνεία γλωσσῶν· 11 πάντα δὲ ταῦτα ἐνεργεῖ τὸ ἓν καὶ τὸ αὐτὸ πνεῦμα, διαιροῦν ἰδίᾳ ἑκάστῳ καθὼς βούλεται. [SBLGNT]

King James Version

4 Now there are diversities of gifts, but the same Spirit. 5 And there are differences of administrations, but the same Lord. 6 And there are diversities of operations, but it is the same God which worketh all in all. 7 But the manifestation of the Spirit is given to every man to profit withal. 8 For to one is given by the Spirit the word of wisdom; to another the word of knowledge by the same Spirit; 9 To another faith by the same Spirit; to another the gifts of healing by the same Spirit; 10 To another the working of miracles; to another prophecy; to another discerning of spirits; to another divers kinds of tongues; to another the interpretation of tongues: 11 But all these worketh that one and the selfsame Spirit, dividing to every man severally as he will.

New Rendition

4 Now there are a variety of spiritual gifts, but the same Spirit. 5 There are a variety of ways of serving, but the same Lord. 6 There are a variety of activities, but the same God, who produces all of them in everyone. 7 Each person is given a manifestation of the Spirit for the common good. 8 For to one the gift of speaking wisely is given through the Spirit, to another the gift of speaking knowledgeably in accordance with the same Spirit. 9 To another faith by the same Spirit, to another the gifts of healing by the very same Spirit, 10 to another the performing of miracles, to another prophecy, to another the ability to distinguish between spirits, to another various kinds of tongues, to another the ability to translate languages. 11 But one and the same Spirit produces all these things, who, in accordance with his own will, allocates them privately to each individual.

Translation Notes and Comments

12:4 *Now there are diversities of gifts, but the same Spirit / Now there are a variety of spiritual gifts, but the same Spirit:* The noun διαίρεσις (*diairesis*) is found only three times in the New Testament—in this verse and the two following—making it a bit tricky to define precisely. The reason is that when there are only a few examples of a word, it forces translators to infer its meaning according to context. Here the word *diairesis* can be used to describe various appointments or kinds of divisions as well as reference the distribution or variety of related items.[50] In this case, it refers to the broad and varied gifts activated by the Spirit. The stress behind the word is that God allots the gifts freely and, therefore, they and their distribution are not to be questioned or undervalued. On the noun χάρισμα (*charisma*), "gifts," see Translation Notes on 1:7; 7:7. The word denotes any and all things freely given by God. Paul's use of the word shifts the focus away from the status claims of some of the Saints, who believe that they possess greater spirituality, toward the more humbling realities of God's allotments of varied but equally important gifts to all his people.[51]

12:5 *And there are differences of administrations, but the same Lord / There are a variety of ways of serving, but the same Lord:* On the noun διαίρεσις (*diairesis*), "diversity, variety," see 12:4. The noun διακονία (*diakonia*) means "service,"[52] but in the context here, it refers to the act of providing service, whether in a formal calling or office within the Church or as moved upon by the Spirit. As no one gift can be deemed the most important, no one kind of service can either. All aspects of God's work must be done—leading, teaching, or ministering—if that work is to move smoothly forward. And every aspect is commissioned by the same Lord, giving equal purpose and importance to each one.[53]

12:6 *And there are diversities of operations, but it is the same God which worketh all in all / There are a variety of activities, but the same God, who produces all of them in everyone:* On the noun διαιρέσεις (*diaireseis*),

---

50. Louw-Nida, §§58.39; 57.91. Various attempts have been made to categorize the gifts by placing them in some kind of order, but such is neither needed nor helpful in understanding Paul's intent. See Fee, *First Epistle*, 590–91.

51. Thiselton, *First Epistle*, 929–30. Fee, *First Epistle*, 583, 586 n. 13, places stress on the diversity of the gifts while Conzelmann, *1 Corinthians*, 207, stresses the allocation of those gifts through the Holy Spirit.

52. BDAG, 230.

53. Hinckley, *Teachings of Gordon B. Hinckley*, 63.

"diversities, varieties," see 12:4. The noun ἐνέργημα (*energēma*) denotes an "activity as expression of capability,"[54] and therefore refers to work that is effectively carried out. Paul's phrase διαιρέσεις ἐνεργημάτων (*diaireseis energēmatōn*), then, connotes an actualization of power, that is, an "empowerment" or "energizing" that transforms testimony into effective work.[55] Paul uses the plural form to indicate the wide range of productive activities of those who are called of God. The Apostle uses the present participle with the related verb ἐνεργέω (*energeō*). The word can be translated two ways: intransitively, it would mean "to be at work" or "to operate"; transitively, it would mean "to produce effects" or "bring about results."[56] In our Rendition we have translated it as "activities" to highlight the common root of the noun and the verb. Since the participle is coupled with the accusative plural τὰ πάντα (*ta panta*), "all things," the phrase carries the idea that God brings about all things by "energizing" his people to do his will.[57]

12:7 *But the manifestation of the Spirit is given to every man to profit withal / Each person is given a manifestation of the Spirit for the common good:* The nominal adjective ἕκαστος (*hekastos*), "each one," though masculine, is used generically and therefore includes women, thus the translation in our Rendition as "each person." The verb δίδοται (*didotai*), "is given," is a divine passive and, therefore, presupposes God as agent.[58] The verb connotes God's sovereignty in choosing upon whom to bestow each gift and of what sort.[59] The noun φανέρωσις (*phanerōsis*), "manifestation," denotes an open or public disclosure.[60] The nuance of the word is that these spiritual gifts are not to be concealed but openly used to bless the lives of others. The genitive noun τοῦ πνεύματος (*tou pneumatos*), "of the spirit," can be translated either subjectively, and thereby denote the gifts that the Spirit manifests, or objectively, and thereby denote "the operation of the Spirit in public."[61] The context suggests the latter since *phanerōsis* denotes a public

---

54. BDAG, 335.

55. Collins, *First Corinthians*, 261.

56. To better express the idea found in the Greek text, Bailey, *Mediterranean Eyes*, 326, 334–35 coins the word "energizings," to show how God makes possible the expression of the spiritual gifts by energizing the recipient.

57. Bailey, *Mediterranean Eyes*, 334–35; Thiselton, *First Epistle*, 933.

58. Louw-Nida, §57.71.

59. This idea is reflected in 15:38, where God gives to each thing its own "body" (*sōma*) as he chooses.

60. BDAG, 1048–49,

61. Fitzmyer, *First Corinthians*, 465–66; Thiselton, *First Epistle*, 936; Robertson and Plummer, *Critical and Exegetical Commentary*, 264.

manifestation. The nominalized neuter singular participle τὸ συμφέρον (*to sympheron*), "to profit withal, for the common good," referred to a person's contribution to the welfare of the public.[62]

Paul's point is that although there are a diversity of public manifestations of the Spirit, a single power stands behind each of them. The Apostle constructs the sentence such that it puts contrasting emphasis on the first and last words. The gifts are given "to each person," but "for the common good" of the community at large. This action militates against self-aggrandizement, self-fulfillment, or even self-affirmation.[63] No gift has more or less worth than another for two reasons: First, they are all derived from God and, therefore, have divine status, and second, they are all needed to promote "the common good."

12:8 *For to one is given by the Spirit the word of wisdom / For to one the gift of speaking wisely is given through the Spirit:* On the phrase λόγος σοφίας (*logos sophias*), "the word of wisdom," see Translation Notes on 1:17. The Greek noun λόγος (*logos*), very inadequately translated as "word," has a remarkably broad variety of meanings.[64] Paul uses it here, with *sophia*, to refer to the act of speaking wisely and knowledgeably. The noun *sophia* in this instance denotes a comprehension that transcends the mortal plane and reflects the heavenly.[65] The genitive phrase can be understood in two ways: subjectively, it would refer to clear and effective expressions derived from God's wisdom; objectively, it would denote clear and effective expressions about God's wisdom. Since the context states that it is a gift empowered by inspiration and used to benefit the Church as a whole (12:7), our Rendition takes it as subjective. Thus, the phase connotes the ability to comprehend and effectively declare the divine mind.[66] Elder Orson Pratt declared that "when a person receives, by the power of the Holy Ghost, the word or gift of wisdom, he receives revelation."[67] According to the Book of Mormon, this gift includes teaching the word of wisdom (Moro. 10:9). Through it, people are made aware of God's purpose both in the public and

---

62. BDAG, 960; Bailey, *Mediterranean Eyes,* 336.

63. Thiselton, *First Epistle,* 936.

64. Louw-Nida, §33.99; BDAG, 598–601.

65. James D. G. Dunn, *Jesus and the Spirit: A Study of the Religious and Charismatic Experience of Jesus and the First Christians as Reflected in the New Testament* (London: SCM Press, 1975), 220; See James A. Davis, *Wisdom and Spirit* (Lanham, Md.: University Press of America, 1984), 71–149, for an extended study on the wisdom tradition.

66. Fitzmyer, *First Corinthians,* 466.

67. Orson Pratt, in *JD,* 16:288.

private arenas.[68] Thus, the word connotes a declaration of what the Lord is presently revealing.[69]

Paul's words make a distinction between pretentious, status-seeking human wisdom so prevalent in Corinth (1:17–22; 2:1–5; 3:19) and the Spirit-driven divine wisdom that some of the Saints were expressing (1:24–31; 2:6–13).

to another the word of knowledge by the same Spirit / to another the gift of speaking knowledgeably in accordance with the same Spirit: In the phrase λόγος γνώσεως (*logos gnōseōs*), "word of knowledge," *logos* once again refers to the ability to speak wisely and knowledgably. The noun *gnōseōs* denotes the comprehension of a body of knowledge. In this verse, "wisdom" and "knowledge" are closely related, but the latter carries the idea of understanding both the content and meaning of the scriptures[70] and, therefore, suggests the declaration of what God *has* revealed. The Book of Mormon again ties the idea to teaching God's word (Moro. 10:10). Nevertheless, Paul's use of the noun gives it another nuance that should be considered. In 14:6 he places it between ἀποκάλυψις (*apokalypsis*), "revelation," and προφητεία (*prophēteia*), "prophecy," and in 13:2 beside μυστήριον (*mysterion*), "mystery." In doing so, he gives the word an extraordinarily recondite quality that ties it to the mystery cults and, thereby, to temple worship.[71] The noun clearly suggests insight into the real nature of the cosmos and the forces that drive it.[72]

12:9 *To another faith by the same Spirit /to another faith by the same Spirit:* The adjective ἕτερος (*heteros*), "another," can denote "another" of two or more and, therefore, designates a different person than the one mentioned previously.[73] Paul's use of the word πίστις (*pistis*), "faith," cannot refer to the general faith that one must have in order to be saved in Christ, since that is presumably found among all believers (A of F 1). Rather, the faith spoken of here is likely what the Book of Mormon calls

---

68. Thiselton, *First Epistle,* 939.

69. Anderson, *Understanding Paul,* 114, is correct in suggesting it means teaching.

70. BDAG, 203. See also Orson Pratt, in *JD,* 16:288, who addressed the difference between the word of wisdom and the word of knowledge, noting that the latter is the acquisition of understanding and the former its proper application.

71. BDAG, 203; Louw-Nida, §28.17, 19. There were a number of these cults in the Greco-Roman world whose temple secrets could be known only by initiates. See Walter Burkert, *Ancient Mystery Cults* (Cambridge, Mass.: Harvard University Press, 1989).

72. Dunn, *Jesus and the Spirit,* 218; Fitzmyer, *First Corinthians,* 466.

73. BDAG, 399; Thiselton, *First Epistle,* 944.

"exceedingly great faith" (Moro. 10:11). That kind of faith denotes a true understanding of the Savior, his character and attributes, that compels one to act in accordance to the Lord's will and direction.[74] That enhanced faith is a specific gift given to a specific person. But there is even more to it. According to the "Lectures on Faith," faith "is the principle of power."[75] Its use in the present context connotes a special endowment of power given to a specific individual for the benefit of others. This faith-power ranges from healing people to moving mountains.[76] As the author of Hebrews noted, it was people filled with this kind of faith who "subdued kingdoms, wrought righteousness, obtained promises, stopped the mouths of lions, Quenched the violence of fire, escaped the edge of the sword, out of weakness were made strong, waxed valiant in fight, turned to flight the armies of the aliens. Women received their dead raised to life again: and others were tortured, not accepting deliverance; that they might obtain a better resurrection" (Heb. 11:33–35).

to another the gifts of healing by the same Spirit / to another the gifts of healing by the very same Spirit: There is a minor but somewhat significant variant in the manuscript tradition for this phrase. There is good textual support for the word ἑνί (*heni*), "one," instead of αὐτῷ (*autō*) "same."[77] However, the numeral *hen* can also be translated "one and the same,"[78] and thus in Rendition, we have "by the very same Spirit." The plural phrase χαρίσματα ἰαμάτων (*charismata iamatōn*), "gifts of healings," points to more than one kind of healing. It includes, besides physical diseases, mental and spiritual ailments as well.[79]

12:10 *To another the working of miracles / to another the performing of miracles:* The noun ἐνέργημα (*energēma*), denotes an activity that reveals capabilities, thus, "action, operation, deed."[80] The noun δύναμις (*dynamis*), means literally "power" or "might," but is here used, as it often is in the

---

74. "Bible Dictionary," in the LDS Edition of the King James Version of the Bible (1979), 669, s.v. "faith." Other possible translations of πιστίς (*pistis*) include confidence, hope, a strong belief or trust. All of these fit well with Restoration ideas.

75. "Lecture 1," in Dahl and Tate, *Lectures on Faith in Historical Perspective*, 33.

76. "Lecture 1," in Dahl and Tate, *Lectures on Faith in Historical Perspective*, 32–34.

77. It is likely that a scribe changed the word ἵνα (*hina*) for "stylistic reasons to avoid the monotony of three successive instances of the phrase 'the same spirit.'" Metzger, *Textual Commentary*, 497.

78. BDAG, 291–93.

79. Louw-Nida, §§13.66; 23.136–41.

80. Louw-Nida, §42:11; BDAG, 335.

New Testament, to describe a "deed of power," that is, "a miracle."[81] Our Rendition follows the KJV in translating the word that way.[82]

to another prophecy / to another prophecy: The noun *prophēteia*, "prophecy," is derived from the preposition πρό (*pro*), "before, in front of," and φημί (*phēmi*), "to speak, to declare," and denotes the ability and authority to speak for someone else.[83] In this case, due to the inspiration of the Spirit, it connotes the authoritative speaking of the mind and will of God. This can refer to declaring the active word of God (all that God is now revealing) or to revealing the intent of the scriptures (that is, "all that God has revealed"; compare A of F 9). The Book of Mormon states that this gift includes "prophesy[ing] concerning all things" (Moro. 10:13). In this instance, it refers to the "dynamic, effective, and hortatory preaching of the gospel as a gift of the Spirit."[84] Given Paul's understanding of the necessity of his own mission to preach the gospel and bring the repentant to Christ (9:16), the central message of prophecy would likely have been the need for repentance and the joy of forgiveness through Christ the Lord.[85]

to another discerning of spirits / to another the ability to distinguish between spirits: The noun translated "discerning" in the KJV, διάκρισις (*diakrisis*), means "the ability to distinguish and evaluate."[86] The plural noun πνεύματα (*pneumata*), "spirits," must not be confused with πνευματικά (*pneumatika*), "spiritual matters," referred to in 12:1. The latter denotes all the gifts of the Spirit while the former looks primarily at the range of noncorporeal beings, including human, divine, and demonic. But it also includes forces derived from and propagated by each of these.[87] The phrase διακρίσεις πνευμάτων (*diakriseis pneumatōn*), literally "discernings of spirits," refers

---

81. BDAG, 263–64. The plural form of δύναμις (*dynamis*), as found here, is used to describe the miracles of Jesus (Matt. 7:22; 11:20, 21, 23; 13:54, 58; Mark 6:2; Luke 10:13; 19:37).

82. Fee, *First Epistle*, 594–95; Fitzmyer, *First Corinthians*, 467; Dunn, *Jesus and the Spirit*, 209–10.

83. BDAG, 889–90.

84. Fitzmyer, *First Corinthians*, 467. The word tied the prophet or prophetesses' speech directly to God. In Lucian, *Alex.* 40, 60, it is described as ἡ δὲ προφητείη δίης φρενός ἐστιν ἀπορρώξ (*hē de prophēteiē diēs phrenos estin aporrōx*), "a portion broken off of the divine mind," suggesting the degree to which the gift expressed the will of God. See also LSJ, 1539. For an excursus on the subject, see Thiselton, *First Epistle*, 956–64.

85. David E. Aune, *Prophecy in Early Christianity and the Ancient Mediterranean World* (Grand Rapids, Mich.: Eerdmans, 1983), 256–58. See also David Hill, *New Testament Prophecy* (Louisville, Ky.: Westminster John Knox Press, 1979), 110–40, for a full discussion.

86. BDAG, 231.

87. BDAG, 832–36.

to various but inspired abilities that distinguish and evaluate those spiritual forces that impact both Saint and Church and identify the source.[88] The Book of Mormon defines it as "the beholding of angels and ministering spirits" (Moro. 10:14). Because of the various sources of *pneumata,* John warned his readers to "believe not every spirit, but try the spirits whether they are of God: because many false prophets are gone out into the world" (1 John 4:1). Paul's words show that some of the Saints did, indeed, have the ability to discern various cases (thus, the plural) whether the spiritual manifestation was from heaven, earth, or hell.[89]

Joseph Smith felt that the reasons some Christians had been led astray was because they did not know how to "try the spirits": "They have not a key to unlock, no rule wherewith to measure, and no criterion whereby they can test it. . . . No man can do this without the Priesthood, and having a knowledge of the laws by which Spirits are governed; for as 'no man knows the things of God but by the Spirit of God,' so no man knows the spirit of the devil and his power and influence but by possessing intelligence which is more than human, and having unfolded through the medium of the Priesthood the mysterious operations of his devices."[90]

According to the scriptures, "unto the bishop of the church, and unto such as God shall appoint . . . are to have it given unto them to discern all those gifts lest there shall be any among you professing and yet be not of God" (D&C 46:27).

to another divers kinds of tongues / to another various kinds of tongues: Paul uses the phrase γένη γλωσσῶν (*genē glōssōn*), literally "kinds of tongues," as a figurative expression for "language or speech."[91] The phrase denotes any kind of vocal utterance that is unusual and not understood by others. Thus, it can refer to anything from satanically ecstatic babblings to speaking the words of angels (13:1). In LDS parlance it usually, but not always, describes a spiritual endowment that manifests itself in the remarkable ability of Latter-day Saint missionaries around the world to quickly learn and speak the native language of the people they serve.[92]

---

88. Fitzmyer, *First Corinthians,* 468.

89. Robertson and Plummer, *Critical and Exegetical Commentary,* 267.

90. "History, 1838–1856, Volume C-1," 1305.

91. BDAG, 194–95.

92. Some Saints have exercised speaking in tongues, including Brigham Young, second president of the Church. On the subject, see H. George Bickerstaff, "Gifts of the Spirit," in *EM,* 2:544–56; Robert W. Blair, "Vocabulary, Latter-day Saint," in *EM,* 4:1538; and Leonard J. Arrington, "Young, Brigham," in *EM,* 4:1602.

This gift comes with limitations. The Prophet Joseph Smith declared: "Speak not in the gift of tongues without understanding it or without interpretation. The devil can speak in tongues."[93] He counseled further, "You may speak in tongues for your own comfort, but I lay this down for a rule that if anything is taught by the gift of tongues[,] it is not to be received for doctrine."[94] President Brigham Young stated: "The gift of tongues is not . . . empowered to dictate . . . [to] the church. All gifts and endowments given of the Lord to members of His church are not given to control the church; but they are under the control and guidance of the priesthood, and are judged of by it."[95]

to another the interpretation of tongues / to another the ability to translate languages: The noun ἑρμηνεία (*hermēneia*) in one sense describes the ability to translate or interpret what is said in tongues.[96] Those Christians coming out of a pagan background would have known that myths attributed this power to the gods, with Hermes being the agent who delivered it and assisted the individual with its use.[97] Thus, the gift connoted divine inspiration. Paul's use of the word presupposes two conditions: first, what others say under the influence of the Spirit is not mere babblings but can be interpreted into the language of the hearers, and second, what is said is a community affair.[98] In another and more broad sense, the gift denotes the interpretation not of what another says in tongues but in understanding foreign languages.[99] The Book of Mormon describes the gift as "the interpretation of languages and of divers kinds of tongues" (Moro. 10:16). Hence our Rendition uses "ability to translate languages." In sum, this gift, like all others, is not to be used exclusively for personal edification but for that of the community as a whole and largely in missionary work.[100]

12:11 *But all these worketh that one and the selfsame Spirit, dividing to every man severally as he will / But one and the same Spirit produces all these things, who, in accordance with his own will, allocates them privately to each individual:* The phrase πάντα δὲ ταῦτα (*panta de tauta*), "but all these," placed at the first of the sentence, holds emphatic position and thereby signals

---

93. "History, 1838–1856, Volume C-1," 13 [addenda]; spelling and punctuation standardized.
94. "History, 1838–1856, Volume C-1 Addenda," 42.
95. Brigham Young, in *JD*, 11:136.
96. Louw-Nida, §33.145.
97. Hornblower, *Oxford Classical Dictionary*, 690–91.
98. Fitzmyer, *First Corinthians*, 471.
99. BDAG, 393.
100. Blair, "Vocabulary, Latter-day Saint," 4:1537–38.

that Paul is now summing up what he has said in 12:4–10.[101] He repeats, for emphasis, his point that all the gifts come from one divine source (12:6), but here his focus is on the work of the Holy Ghost. The verb βούλομαι (*boulomai*), "will," expresses the will or intention of an agent to execute a course of action to bring about a desired result.[102] In this context, it connotes the actual implementation of that intention. It is the Holy Spirit who, working under God's will, empowers, and thus implements, the individual's facility to use the divinely bestowed gift. These gifts are, therefore, neither native abilities nor skills that one develops.[103] They are additional endowments that come by necessity of standing, calling, office, and God's will. The verb διαιρέω (*diaireō*) means to "distribute, divide," or "allocate" (see 12:4) and carries the idea of the power an agent has to determine who gets what. The adverb ἰδίᾳ (*idia*), which the KJV wrongly translates as "severally," means "by oneself" or "privately,"[104] as is found in our Rendition, and denotes that each gift is intended for and of restricted use by the recipient. The whole verse stresses that whatever spiritual manifestation the Holy Ghost apportions out to each Saint, it is not a personal achievement, but a benefaction empowered by divine operation for the benefit of all.[105] Therefore, no one has "bragging rights" for any one gift.

Analysis and Summary

This pericope deals with both diversity and unity, with unity being the major thrust. The diversity consists of the various manifestations of the Spirit found among the Corinthian Saints. The unity consists in the one power that lies behind and allocates the manifold expressions of those manifestations. They are all governed by "the same Spirit … the same Lord … the same God" (12:4–6). In short, it is the Godhead that is the one and only source of the diversity of gifts, and, therefore, multiplicity does not negate unity. Paul's use of the human body (12:12–24) as an analogy for the way the Godhead designed the Church to work is brilliant. By putting stress where he does, the Apostle overcomes the divisiveness that has grown out of the various valuations some of the Saints have assigned to spiritual gifts, with tongues seeming to be of the highest status.[106] By stressing the unity that stands behind χαρίσματα (*charismata*)—those "spiritual gifts" that God

---

101. Fee, *First Epistle,* 599.

102. BDAG, 182; Louw-Nida, §24.3; 30.56.

103. Bailey, *Mediterranean Eyes,* 339.

104. BDAG, 467.

105. Barrett, *First Epistle,* 286; Fitzmyer, *First Corinthians,* 471.

106. Martin, *Corinthian Body,* 87.

freely pours upon all the Saints—Paul undercuts the position of the elitist group. He shows that their belief that they have somehow achieved a higher degree of spirituality is mistaken.[107]

Since Paul's major concern in the whole of this epistle is with factionalism, on the surface it might seem strange that he would dwell on the varied spiritual gifts experienced by the Saints. "At first glance" noted one LDS scholar, "one might think that every person's experiencing a different spiritual gift would emphasize differences and further divide the Saints. Nevertheless, the opposite is true: spiritual gifts are given by the Lord to perfect and unite the Saints in true service one to another. Paul's words combined with the other scriptures clearly teach the uniting power of spiritual gifts."[108]

Another scholar pointed out that it appears that many of the Saints "took a low and half superstitious view of the Holy Spirit's influence, seeing in such charisms as the 'tongues'—phenomena analogous to, though far surpassing, pagan manifestations . . . —the proper evidence of His working, while they underrated endowments of a less striking but more vital and serviceable nature."[109]

The problem with the Corinthian Saints was that they believed that the showy gifts revealed a higher degree of spirituality. On this subject the Prophet Joseph Smith observed,

> There are several gifts mentioned here, yet which of them all could be known, by an observer, at the imposition of hands? The word of wisdom, and the word of knowledge, are as much gifts as any other, yet if a person possessed both of these gifts, or received them by the imposition of hands, who would know it? Another might receive the gift of faith, and they would be as ignorant of it. . . . There are only two gifts that could be made visible—the gift of tongues and the gift of prophecy. These are things that are <the> most talked about, and yet if a person spoke in an unknown tongue, according to Paul's testimony, he would be a barbarian to those present. They would say that it was gibberish; and if he prophesied they would call it nonsense. The gift of tongues is the smallest gift perhaps of the whole, and yet it is—one that is the most sought after.[110]

He then concluded, "The greatest, the best, and the most useful gifts would be known nothing about by an observer."[111]

---

107. Thiselton, *First Epistle*, 929.

108. Reeve, "Holy Ghost," 170.

109. Findlay, "St. Paul's First Epistle," 884–85.

110. "History, 1838–1856, Volume C-1 Addenda," 68.

111. "History, 1838-1856, Volume C-1 Addenda," 68.

As Latter-day Saints, "we believe in the gift of tongues, prophecy, revelation, visions, healings, interpretation of tongues, and so forth" (A of F 7).[112] Their reception is predicated upon the faith, obedience, and the personal righteousness of the individual.[113] In speaking of spiritual gifts in these last days, the Lord has been very clear. His counsel and teachings are recorded in D&C 46:8–29. There he admonished the Saints to seek after the "best gifts," but he also put a restriction on those who asked for them. They must do so, but not "for a sign that they may consume it upon their lusts" (D&C 46:9). "Behold, . . . signs follow those that believe," the Lord said. "Yea, signs come by faith, not by the will of men, nor as they please, but by the will of God. Yea, signs come by faith, unto mighty works" (D&C 63:9–11). Indeed, the Holy Ghost "maketh manifest unto the children of men, according to their faith" (Jarom 1:4).

The Lord stresses that the Saints are to remember that the reason gifts are given is to "benefit . . . those who love me and keep all my commandments, and him that seeketh so to do" (D&C 46:9). He assures them that every member "is given a gift by the Spirit of God. To some is given one, and to some is given another, that all may be profited thereby" (D&C 46:11–12). Indeed, "all these gifts come from God, for the benefit of the children of God" (D&C 46:26). As President Brigham Young noted, "The gifts of the Gospel are given to strengthen the faith of the believer."[114] Elder McConkie writes, "Their purpose is to enlighten, encourage, and edify the faithful so that they will inherit peace in this life and be guided toward eternal life in the world to come."[115] Indeed, "if the saints are to be saved, they must accept, understand, and experience the gifts of the Spirit."[116]

The list of gifts recorded in D&C 46:10–26 follows that in 1 Corinthians but with an exception. The Lord adds that some will know that "Jesus Christ is the Son of God, and that he was crucified for the sins of the world. To others it is given to believe on their words, that they also might have eternal life if they continue faithful" (D&C 46:13–14). The Lord also explains why the Saints should seek after the "best gifts"—because they act as a guard against deception (D&C 46:8).

---

112. For a full analysis of LDS understanding of spiritual gifts, see Talmage, *Articles of Faith,* 217–35; Bruce R. McConkie, *A New Witness for the Articles of Faith* (Salt Lake City: Deseret Book, 1985), 367–77; Dallin H. Oaks, "Spiritual Gifts," *Ensign* 16 (September 1986): 68–70.

113. McConkie, *New Witness,* 367.

114. Brigham Young, in *JD,* 10:324.

115. *DNTC,* 2:368.

116. *DNTC,* 2:366.

In addition to the Doctrine and Covenants, the Book of Mormon also addresses the importance of spiritual gifts and provides a second witness to Paul's teachings. There, the prophet Moroni, speaking to those living in the last days, exhorts them to "deny not the gifts of God, for they are many; and they come from the same God. And there are different ways that these gifts are administered; but it is the same God who worketh all in all; and they are given by the manifestations of the Spirit of God unto men, to profit them.... And I would exhort you, my beloved brethren, that ye remember that every good gift cometh of Christ" (Moro. 10:8, 18). His list, found in Moroni 10:9–16, like that in D&C 46, follows that found in 1 Corinthians 12.

Moroni does add an admonition, asking his readers to "remember that he [God] is the same yesterday, today, and forever, and that all these gifts of which I have spoken, which are spiritual, never will be done away, even as long as the world shall stand, only according to the unbelief of the children of men" (Moro. 10:19). His witness follows that found in Mark 16:17 where the Lord assured his disciples that the gifts of the Spirit "shall follow them that believe." Addressing this subject, the prophet Mormon assured his latter-day readers that "God has not ceased to be a God of miracles" (Morm. 9:15). Looking to the reality of the performance of past miracles, he asked any skeptics, "If there were miracles wrought then [in the days of the Apostles], why has God ceased to be a God of miracles and yet be an unchangeable Being? And behold, I say unto you he changeth not; if so he would cease to be God; and he ceaseth not to be God, and is a God of miracles" (Morm. 9:19).

Though all three sources address the need and purpose of spiritual gifts, Paul differs from the other two witnesses in that he adds "a powerful statement suggesting a comparative value of some of the gifts."[117]

It needs to be noted that Paul's list is in no way comprehensive. As Elder McConkie has written, "In the fullest sense, they [the spiritual gifts] are infinite in number and endless in their manifestations."[118] Even so, notes another LDS writer, the Apostle's "short list of spiritual powers stretches wide with possibilities. The Holy Ghost comes to each Church member, but with different results in each member's life. Such a reality makes meeting together all the more significant because all the gifts of the Saints come together when the Saints come together, teaching 'one another the doctrine of the kingdom' (D&C 88:77)."[119]

---

117. Holzapfel and Wayment, *Making Sense,* 359.
118. McConkie, *Mormon Doctrine,* 315.
119. Anderson, *Understanding Paul,* 114.

596   *Paul's First Epistle to the Corinthians*

"Paul's first spiritual gift," states this same writer, "stands independent of his list, perhaps because it is the essential gift for each Church member— no one 'can say that Jesus is the Lord, but by the Holy Ghost' (1 Cor. 12:3). Christ promised the Holy Ghost would come and 'testify' of him (John 15:26). This reward of faith either brings one into the true Church or holds him there, for a lifetime of purposeful sacrifice cannot rest on guesswork. Paul no doubt assumed that one saying that Christ was the Lord would do so with knowledge, but Joseph Smith did not like a verbal loophole here; he thought it should read, 'no man can know, etc.'"[120]

With the exception of faith, which undergirds all other gifts of the spirit, Paul lists them in pairs: Word of wisdom/word of knowledge; Healing/the working of miracles; prophesying/discerning of Spirits; Speak in tongues/ interpretation of tongues. Paul lists the gift of faith right after listing the gifts that allow one to explain the gospel.[121] Joseph Smith understood the connec- tion, teaching that "every word that proceedeth from the mouth of Jehovah has such an influence over the human mind[,] the logical mind[,] that it is convincing without other testimony. Faith cometh by hearing."[122]

This pericope again illustrates Paul's pattern of returning the focus of the discourse back to God and Christ. Paul's witness parallels that of the prophet Moroni, who admonished his readers to "remember that every good gift cometh of Christ" (Moro. 10:18). The Apostle's words that "ye are the body of Christ" (12:27) and that "God hath set some in the church" (12:28) testify that everything happens because of the Father and Son. In this chapter, however, he goes a step further and actually reveals the coor- dinated and interdependent workings of the Father, Son, and Holy Ghost. The Apostle shows that through his grace, God dispenses his various gifts to his faithful children (12:6). He is, therefore, the source of all things.[123] He does this, however, through the Son, who is the mediator between God and humankind (12:5; compare 1 Tim. 2:5). But it is the Holy Ghost who activates the gift, for he is the empowering agent (12:8).[124]

The Savior has invited Latter-day Saints to actively and appropriately seek those "best gifts" known of old (D&C 46:8). This makes Mormon- ism notable among many other Christian religions. As an LDS author has

---

120. Anderson, *Understanding Paul*, 113.

120. Anderson, *Understanding Paul*, 113.

121. Anderson, *Understanding Paul*, 114.

122. Ehat and Cook, *Words of Joseph Smith*, 237.

123. Paul describes him as the author, authorizer, and destiny of all things. See 6:13–14; 8:6; 12:4–6; Rom. 12:1–2; 13:1–4; 1 Thes. 4:3.

124. Thiselton, *First Epistle*, 935.

stated, "Scholars have remarked about the abundance of gifts in what is termed 'the apostolic age' as well as the gradual cessation of those gifts, reflecting the loss of authority on earth."[125] Speaking of this phenomenon, a biblical scholar noted, "Concerning these [spiritual gifts], our whole information must be derived from Scripture, because they appear to have vanished with the disappearance of the Apostles themselves, and there is no authentic account of their existence in the Church in any writings of a later date than the books of the New Testament."[126] John Wesley lamented the loss of these gifts sometime after the third century and left little hope for their return.[127] "The latter-day return of the Lord's gospel to the earth included the revival of spiritual gifts, which for centuries had remained dormant," noted the LDS scholar. He went on to say, "Indeed, the characterization of the latter days as the dispensation of the fulness of times hinges in great part upon the reemergence of the full array of spiritual gifts among mankind."[128]

ONE BODY WITH MANY PARTS (12:12–26)

Greek Text

12 Καθάπερ γὰρ τὸ σῶμα ἕν ἐστιν καὶ μέλη πολλὰ ἔχει, πάντα δὲ τὰ μέλη τοῦ σώματος πολλὰ ὄντα ἕν ἐστιν σῶμα, οὕτως καὶ ὁ Χριστός· 13 καὶ γὰρ ἐν ἑνὶ πνεύματι ἡμεῖς πάντες εἰς ἓν σῶμα ἐβαπτίσθημεν, εἴτε Ἰουδαῖοι εἴτε Ἕλληνες, εἴτε δοῦλοι εἴτε ἐλεύθεροι, καὶ πάντες ἓν πνεῦμα ἐποτίσθημεν. 14 Καὶ γὰρ τὸ σῶμα οὐκ ἔστιν ἓν μέλος ἀλλὰ πολλά. 15 ἐὰν εἴπῃ ὁ πούς· Ὅτι οὐκ εἰμὶ χείρ, οὐκ εἰμὶ ἐκ τοῦ σώματος, οὐ παρὰ τοῦτο οὐκ ἔστιν ἐκ τοῦ σώματος; 16 καὶ ἐὰν εἴπῃ τὸ οὖς· Ὅτι οὐκ εἰμὶ ὀφθαλμός, οὐκ εἰμὶ ἐκ τοῦ σώματος, οὐ παρὰ τοῦτο οὐκ ἔστιν ἐκ τοῦ σώματος· 17 εἰ ὅλον τὸ σῶμα ὀφθαλμός, ποῦ ἡ ἀκοή; εἰ ὅλον ἀκοή, ποῦ ἡ ὄσφρησις; 18 νυνὶ δὲ ὁ θεὸς ἔθετο τὰ μέλη, ἓν ἕκαστον αὐτῶν, ἐν τῷ σώματι καθὼς ἠθέλησεν. 19 εἰ δὲ ἦν τὰ πάντα ἓν μέλος, ποῦ τὸ σῶμα; 20 νῦν δὲ πολλὰ μὲν μέλη, ἓν δὲ σῶμα. 21 οὐ δύναται δὲ ὁ ὀφθαλμὸς εἰπεῖν τῇ χειρί· Χρείαν σου οὐκ ἔχω, ἢ πάλιν ἡ κεφαλὴ τοῖς ποσίν· Χρείαν ὑμῶν οὐκ ἔχω· 22 ἀλλὰ πολλῷ μᾶλλον τὰ δοκοῦντα μέλη τοῦ σώματος ἀσθενέστερα

---

125. Freeman, "Paul's Earnest Pursuit," 44.

126. William J. Conybeare and J. S. Howson, *The Life and Epistles of St. Paul* (Hartford, Conn.: S. S. Scranton, 1900), 372.

127. *John Wesley's Works*, 7:26, 27, as quoted in Talmage, *Articles of Faith*, 495–96.

128. Freeman, "Paul's Earnest Pursuit," 44.

ὑπάρχειν ἀναγκαῖά ἐστιν, 23 καὶ ἃ δοκοῦμεν ἀτιμότερα εἶναι τοῦ σώματος, τούτοις τιμὴν περισσοτέραν περιτίθεμεν, καὶ τὰ ἀσχήμονα ἡμῶν εὐσχημοσύνην περισσοτέραν ἔχει, 24 τὰ δὲ εὐσχήμονα ἡμῶν οὐ χρείαν ἔχει. ἀλλὰ ὁ θεὸς συνεκέρασεν τὸ σῶμα, τῷ ὑστεροῦντι περισσοτέραν δοὺς τιμήν, 25 ἵνα μὴ ᾖ σχίσμα ἐν τῷ σώματι, ἀλλὰ τὸ αὐτὸ ὑπὲρ ἀλλήλων μεριμνῶσι τὰ μέλη. 26 καὶ εἴτε πάσχει ἓν μέλος, συμπάσχει πάντα τὰ μέλη· εἴτε δοξάζεται μέλος, συγχαίρει πάντα τὰ μέλη. [SBLGNT]

King James Version

12 For as the body is one, and hath many members, and all the members of that one body, being many, are one body: so also is Christ. 13 For by one Spirit are we all baptized into one body, whether we be Jews or Gentiles, whether we be bond or free; and have been all made to drink into one Spirit. 14 For the body is not one member, but many. 15 If the foot shall say, Because I am not the hand, I am not of the body; is it therefore not of the body? 16 And if the ear shall say, Because I am not the eye, I am not of the body; is it therefore not of the body? 17 If the whole body were an eye, where were the hearing? If the whole were hearing, where were the smelling? 18 But now hath God set the members every one of them in the body, as it hath pleased him. 19 And if they were all one member, where were the body? 20 But now are they many members, yet but one body. 21 And the eye cannot say unto the hand, I have no need of thee: nor again the head to the feet, I have no need of you. 22 Nay, much more those members of the body, which seem to be more feeble, are necessary: 23 And those members of the body, which we think to be less honourable, upon these we bestow more abundant honour; and our uncomely parts have more abundant comeliness. 24 For our comely parts have no need: but God hath

New Rendition

12 For just as the body is one and yet has many parts, and all the parts of the body, although they are many, are a single body, so too is Christ. 13 For in one Spirit we were all baptized into one body, whether Jews or Gentiles, whether slaves or free, and we all have been given to drink of the very same Spirit. 14 Now the body is not just a single part, but many. 15 If the foot were to say, "Because I am not a hand, I am not part of the body," is it then, because of that, not part of the body? 16 And if the ear were to say, "I am not an eye, I am not part of the body," is it then, because of that, not part of the body? 17 If the entire body were an eye, how would it hear? If the entire body were an ear, how would it smell? 18 But in fact God has assembled each of the parts of the body just as he wanted. 19 But if they were all a single part, where would the body be? 20 So now there are many parts, but one body. 21 And the eye cannot say to the hand, "I don't need you." Furthermore, the head cannot say to the feet, "I don't need you." 22 On the contrary, even more so, those parts of the body that seem to be less important are essential, 23 and as for those parts of the body we think are insignificant, we bestow upon them even more respect, and those parts of our body that should not be displayed are treated with greater respect.

tempered the body together, having given more abundant honour to that part which lacked: 25 That there should be no schism in the body; but that the members should have the same care one for another. 26 And whether one member suffer, all the members suffer with it; or one member be honoured, all the members rejoice with it.

24 Now the parts of our body that are respectable do not need this. But God has assembled the body together into a harmonious whole, giving much greater honor to the inferior part, 25 so there will be no divisiveness in the body; instead the individual parts of the body will be equally concerned about each other. 26 If one part of the body suffers, then all parts suffer together. If one part of the body is honored, then all parts rejoice together.

Translation Notes and Comments

12:12 *For as the body is one, and hath many members, and all the members of that one body, being many, are one body / For just as the body is one and yet has many parts, and all the parts of the body, although they are many, are a single body:* Once again, the conjunction γάρ (*gar*), "for," signals that Paul will now offer further explanation to the point he has made. The subordinate conjunction καθάπερ (*kathaper*) introduces an analogy or comparison and is translated as "just as" in our Rendition.[129] Paul's explanation takes the form of an analogy in which the Church is likened unto the human body.[130] In King James English, the noun "member" often referred to body parts. The Greek noun μέλος (*melos*) refers to any part of the body, whether organ or limb, but can also be used figuratively, thus, referring to a member of a group.[131]

Paul has already applied this imagery to the Church in 10:17, but he returns to it here as the basis on which he will expand on his point that

---

129. BDAG, 488.

130. The use of the human body as a symbol for some aspect of society was quite common before and during Paul's era. For example, see Livy, *Hist.* 2.32; Josephus, *J.W.* 4.406; Seneca, *Ep.* 95.52. For a study of the origin and development of the metaphorical use of the term σῶμα (*soma*), "body," see Fitzmyer, *First Corinthians,* 475–76. The archeological museum at Corinth has on display many terra-cotta models of various bodily organs found at the temple at Asclepius, the god of healing. These were likely used for inducing the power of the god to heal certain diseases. See G. G. Garner, "The Temple of Asklepius at Corinth and Paul's Teachings," *Buried History* 18 (1982): 52–58, who sees this as the source of Paul's analogy, and Collins, *First Corinthians,* 462, who believes it was more likely that the figures contributed in making the Saints more aware of the disparate nature of the human body.

131. BDAG, 628.

though a body is a single unit, it is made up of various organs and limbs, all of which contribute to the whole. He uses this analogy to negate the view held by many of his readers that uniformity in spiritual matters was of chief value and the touchstone of deep spirituality. Paul emphasizes the value of diversity and proves that it does not counter unity; indeed, it is necessary for the kind of unity Paul seeks.[132]

so also is Christ / so too is Christ: Paul here is likely using metonymy in which he shortens the phrase "body of Christ" (10:16; 12:27), referring to the Church, to just "Christ."[133] He already told the Corinthian Saints that their bodies were the μέλη Χριστοῦ (*melē Christou*), "members of Christ" (6:15), meaning that they belonged to his Church. The Church is "Christ" and the members his *melē*, "parts," in that they are the agents through whom his word, will, and saving work are ministered.[134]

12:13 *For by one Spirit are we all baptized into one body, whether we be Jews or Gentiles, whether we be bond or free / For in one Spirit we were all baptized into one body, whether Jews or Gentiles, whether slaves or free:* With this verse, Paul begins his elaboration and elucidation of his point that the Christians are parts of a whole. His opening words, καὶ γάρ (*kai gar*), can be understood as "for in fact" and used to show how, in a somatic sense, all Christians make up "Christ." The Apostle uses the term σῶμα (*soma*), "body," figuratively to illustrate the degree to which the Spirit unifies members of the Church.[135] That role is defined by the preposition ἐν (*en*), denoting either something "under the control or influence of" something else or "in close association with it."[136] Grammar allows the preposition to be understood in two ways: either agentive, denoting the agent of an action, or locative, denoting wherein an action takes place. Since the Spirit is not the agent who does the baptizing, our Rendition takes the preposition as locative, that is, identifying the element in which every Christian has been immersed.[137] Our Rendition captures this nuance by translating the phrase ἐν ἑνὶ πνεύματι (*en heni pneumati*) as "in one Spirit" rather than "by one Spirit" as in the KJV.

---

132. Fee, *First Epistle*, 601–2.

133. Fee, *First Epistle*, 603.

134. Jerome Murphy-O'Connor, "Christ and Ministry," *Pacifica* 4 (1991): 126.

135. The metaphor apparently worked well enough that he will use it again Rom. 12:4–5.

136. BDAG, 327–28. This preposition has so many varied uses that only context can decide its exact nuance. Here the context suggests "under the influence of" rather then "by."

137. Fee, *First Epistle*, 605–6; Conzelmann, *1 Corinthians*, 212 and n. 17. There is much debate on how this preposition should be interpreted because it has theological implications. For the study, see Thiselton, *First Epistle*, 997.

With the use of the adjective *heni*, "one," Paul emphasizes that the whole community shares in a single divine power. As the human spirit endows the whole body, with all its various organs, with the ability to function as a united whole, so too does the Holy Spirit in the community of the Church. To emphasize this point, Paul alludes to the baptismal ordinance comprising first water immersion and then, through the confirmation process, spirit immersion.[138]

have been all made to drink into one Spirit / we all have been given to drink of the very same Spirit: This phrase explains the point Paul made above.[139] The aorist passive verb ἐποτίσθημεν (*epotisthēmen*), "be given to drink," tacitly acknowledges that God's action stands behind what the Christian does, that is, that God has made it possible for all these people to "drink" from the same spirit.[140] The idea is that they have become immersed in or, to use nonmetaphorical words, imbued with God's spirit. The idea is that each Saint has or should have been filled with that uniting spirit which flows through the Church as a whole (see 3:16).

12:14 For the body is not one member, but many / Now the body is not just a single part, but many: This sentence is a literary clause that Paul uses for two purposes: first, to emphasize the point he has just made— that the Spirit that is given through baptism and confirmation unites all into the one "body of Christ"—and, second, as a springboard for the point he makes next.

12:15 If the foot shall say, Because I am not the hand, I am not of the body; is it therefore not of the body? / If the foot were to say, "Because I am not a hand, I am not part of the body," is it then, because of that, not part of the body?:[141] To express precisely his point that every organ and limb of the body is necessary, Paul uses the aorist subjunctive verb εἴπῃ (*eipē*), "were to say," in the protasis of this conditional sentence. In doing so he emphasizes the unfulfillable and, therefore, ridiculous nature of the

---

138. Fitzmyer, *First Corinthians*, 478.

139. Thiselton, *First Epistle*, 1000.

140. BDAG, 857.

141. Due to the nature of Greek grammar, there is a question of whether this sentence is interrogative. See Fitzmyer, *First Corinthians*, 479; and BDAG, 758. Since it makes no difference to Paul's point, it is acknowledged only in this footnote. Nestle and others, *Novum Testamentum Graece: Nestle-Aland*, 28th ed., Greek text has a (Greek) question mark (;) in both this and the following verse. The SBLGNT has a question mark in 12:15 and a colon in 12:16. Because the rhetorical question best fits Paul's style, as illustrated by the very next verse in which there are two more rhetorical questions, it is treated as a question in the Rendition.

hypothesis he is proposing. The phrase παρὰ τοῦτο (*para touto*), "because of that," as found in our Rendition, expresses cause and looks to what certain members think about their condition, not to their position in the body.

In Near Eastern culture, nothing is so unclean as the feet (and by extension, the shoes). The same is true, but not to the same degree, of the left hand. The English adjective "sinister" comes from the Latin adjective referring to the left hand. The right hand, however, has honor.[142] The imagery here likely points at those Saints who feel themselves, for some reason, inferior.[143] These would likely be those of the slave class. But as each organ or limb of the body has its particular and important function, it does not matter how it metaphorically feels. Its feelings do not abstract it from the body. Paul's point is that the subjective feeling that one does not belong, no matter how sincere and strong, in no way negates the objective fact of that belonging. All belong—period, and that is the end of the argument.[144]

12:16 *And if the ear shall say, Because I am not the eye, I am not of the body; is it therefore not of the body? / And if the ear were to say, "I am not an eye, I am not part of the body," is it then, because of that, not part of the body?:* The grammatical points made for 12:15 are relevant for this verse and, therefore, do not need repeating. That is not the case, however, with the imagery. Though the ear, in ancient culture, had status, it fell below that of the eye. Paul's point, therefore, seems directed at those who had some status but felt it was inferior to that of others. These would likely be free men and women who did not have the status or dignity of the wealthy.[145]

12:17 *If the whole body were an eye, where were the hearing? If the whole were hearing, where were the smelling? / If the entire body were an eye, how would it hear? If the entire body were an ear, how would it smell?:* The Greek here is very compact with no verbs used at all. A literal translation into English would be, "If the whole body [is] eye, where [is] the hearing? If whole [is] hearing, where [is] the sense of smell?" Our Rendition has somewhat expanded on the text to give the sense of the passage in flowing English. In this verse, Paul simply pushes the point he has made before, but with a different emphasis. No one organ can be seen as best or

---

142. To show the sole of the foot to anyone in that area of the world to this day is an insult. Also, the words "foot" and "shoe" in certain contexts are, in that culture, "four letter-words," the use of which demands an apology on the part of the speaker.

143. Bailey, *Mediterranean Eyes*, 341.

144. Thiselton, *First Epistle*, 1002.

145. Bailey, *Mediterranean Eyes*, 342.

even as the more desirable. All are necessary. So, too, is each member of the Church.[146]

12:18 *But now hath God set the members every one of them in the body, as it hath pleased him / But in fact God has assembled each of the parts of the body just as he wanted:* The phrase νυνὶ δέ (*nyni de*), "but in fact," is adversative and means, "but now in this situation."[147] It shows that Paul is replying to his own rhetorical question. The aorist middle verb ἔθετο (*etheto*), "set, assembled," means to bring about an arrangement and, thus, to assemble something.[148] Paul's point is that the diversity set in the body is by God's deliberate and exacting design.[149] In other words, each organ or limb is where it is by divine appointment. The phrase recalls what the Apostle said in 12:7–11: the Spirit bestows godly gifts upon each person "in accordance with his own will" (12:11, Rendition) To consider one gift (or person) above another is nothing short of blasphemy because it challenges God's order and intent as to what is best for his people. The corollary is that a person's place in the kingdom is by divine design and, therefore, of importance. No one should feel inferior or unneeded and, on the other hand, none should feel superior and arrogant.[150]

12:19 *And if they were all one member, where were the body? / But if they were all a single part, where would the body be?:* The adverbial interrogative ποῦ (*pou*) means "where, in what place."[151] The phrase has no verb and reads literally, "Where the body?" The connotation is that the body would be nowhere, that is, it would not exist.[152] If all the body were one organ or limb, that thing could not even be considered a body. Paul uses the imagery to put emphasis on the inconceivable nature of his initial proposition.

12:20 *But now are they many members, yet but one body / So now there are many parts, but one body:* The phrase νῦν δέ (*nyn de*), "but now, so

---

146. Fee, *First Epistle*, 610–11.

147. Fee, *First Epistle*, 611, n. 12.

148. BDAG, 1003–5. Though the verb is a second aorist middle indicative, it still retains its active force and means to put, place, or set something in order. Since God's organization of the body (and by inference, the Church) was by pre-appointed divine plan, the idea of the parts being placed or arranged is better than "set," as in the KJV. Robertson and Plummer, *Critical and Exegetical Commentary*, 274.

149. Thiselton, *First Epistle*, 1004.

150. Deluz, *Companion*, 179–80; Fee, *First Epistle*, 611.

151. BDAG, 857–58.

152. Bailey, *Mediterranean Eyes*, 345–46.

now," expresses the reality of the situation.[153] The one undisputed fact is that God has indeed created the body but with many members, and all work together as a single unit. The same is true of his Church.

12:21 *And the eye cannot say unto the hand, I have no need of thee: nor again the head to the feet, I have no need of you / And the eye cannot say to the hand, "I don't need you." Furthermore, the head cannot say to the feet, "I don't need you":* With this verse, Paul makes explicit what had been implicit before. No one organ is superior to another organ. Before, he was targeting his remarks to those who felt inferior. Now, his words focus on those who feel themselves superior either by status or spiritual gift. His words, again, are designed to undercut any notion that any one gift or person in the kingdom has more value than another. No single gift, experience, person, or office—or even multiples of these—makes up the essence of the Church. What does is the whole working together (in love, as we shall see in the next chapter) to promote the Lordship of Christ (12:3) and the common good of the community at large (12:7).[154]

12:22 *Nay, much more those members of the body, which seem to be more feeble, are necessary / On the contrary, even more so, those parts of the body that seem to be less important are essential:* The adversative conjunction ἀλλά (*alla*) carries the full force of "no!" or "on the contrary," as a means of contrasting what has been said with what is being said.[155] In this verse, the force is stressed even more by the addition of the phrase πολλῷ μᾶλλον (*pollō mallon*), literally "by much more" or "even more so" as in our Rendition. The adjective ἀσθενής (*asthenēs*) has a wide range of meanings that include being physically weak or ill, morally lax, and helpless.[156] Here it looks to those in the Church who, either by temperament, social station, or role, have less perceived power or status than others.[157] It is, thus, translated as "less important" in our Rendition. The adjective ἀναγκαῖος (*anangkaios*), "necessary, indispensable," denotes that which cannot be done without.[158] Since Paul is countering the feelings of the Church's self-appointed elite that they somehow make up the *essence* of the Church, the translation of the word as "essential" seems best and is used in our

---

153. Barrett, *First Epistle*, 290; Godet, *Commentary*, 2:214, translates the phrase as meaning "actual fact."

154. Thiselton, *First Epistle*, 1005–6.

155. BDAG, 44–45.

156. Louw-Nida, §§22.3; 23.145; 79.69; 88.117.

157. Thiselton, *First Epistle*, 1007. The participle δοκοῦντα (*dokounta*), "seeming," picks up the idea of misperception.

158. BDAG, 60.

Rendition. The verb δοκέω (*dokeō*) expresses "to appear to one's understanding, to seem."[159] Its use here as a neuter plural participle modifying μέλη (*melē*), "parts," is best translated by a relative clause, "that seem," as in our Rendition. The phrase is most telling. It emphasizes that the fact that certain parts of the body only *seem* to be nonessential. The perception of some members is actually wrong, for they have been taken in by deceptive appearances. All organs are important if the body is to be whole and well. So, too, are all the members for the same reason.[160]

12:23 *And those members of the body, which we think to be less honourable, upon these we bestow more abundant honour / and as for those parts of the body we think are insignificant, we bestow upon them even more respect:* Once again the Apostle plays on the verb δοκέω (*dokeō*), "to seem" or "to think." Appearances may not tell the truth. To emphasize this point, Paul contrasts the noun τιμή (*timē*), "honor, respect," with that of the comparative adjective ἀτιμότερος (*atimoteros*), "less honorable, without respect." The verb περιτίθημι (*peritithēmi*) means, literally, to put something around something else and, by extension, "to bestow."[161] The comparative adjective περισσότερος (*perissoteros*), literally "more abundantly," expresses "being beyond a standard of abundance, greater, more, even more."[162] Paul does not identify what body parts he is referring to, but he may have been alluding to hands, arms, and legs, which are, indeed, often covered. Further, they are often adorned and, sometimes, elaborately so.[163]

and our uncomely parts have more abundant comeliness / and those parts of our body that should not be displayed are treated with greater respect: The coordinating conjunction καί (*kai*), "and," connects this phrase to the one before, showing the result of "bestowing honor." The adjective ἀσχήμονα (*aschēmona*), "shameful, unpresentable, indecent," denotes that which is not displayed or discussed in polite society because it is indecent, unpresentable, or unmentionable.[164] By extension, that included items delicate in nature or requiring particular modesty.[165] Paul placed the word opposite the noun εὐσχημοσύνη (*euschēmosynē*), "comeliness, respect,"

---

159. BDAG, 255.

160. Fee, *First Epistle*, 613.

161. BDAG, 807; Martin, *Corinthian Body*, 94–95.

162. BDAG, 806.

163. Fitzmyer, *First Corinthians*, 480–81.

164. BDAG, 147.

165. BDAG, 147; Louw-Nida, §79.16 translates it as "ugly." The related noun ἀσχημοσύνη (*aschēmosynē*) denoted indecent behavior or shameful deeds that defied social standards and resulted in embarrassment, shame, or disgrace. Louw-Nida, §88.149.

that denotes what is proper for display and, when pertaining to clothing, connotes that which is attractive, well suited for the occasion, and, more especially, modest.[166] In this light, *aschēmona* referred to those parts of the body that needed to be treated with special modesty, that is, the genitalia.[167] The Apostle uses the pains people take to put something around, περιτίθημι (*peritithēmi*), this area—that is, to clothe it—to show just how important it is. Again he uses the comparative adjective περισσότερος (*perissoteros*), "much more, greater," to stress the extreme care or respect people gave to this part of the body.

This phrase could be translated as "our unpresentable parts receive greater presentability," meaning they are to be treated with greater modesty,[168] or "our unseemly parts [require] more than ordinary seemliness."[169]

In sum, the Apostle's statement highlights the careful use of clothing, in most societies, to cover the private and sacred parts of the body. Though these are the well-springs of human life, they are carefully protected from public display.[170] Paul's point seems to be if people give such careful attention to such parts of the body, the Saints should do the same with every member of the community.[171]

12:24 *For our comely parts have no need / Now the parts of our body that are respectable do not need this:* The neuter plural nominal adjective εὐσχήμονα (*euschēmona*), literally "things appropriate for display,"[172] refers to those graceful limbs that need no covering. Paul's point is that necessity and propriety determine how we treat various organs and limbs of the body. Some, like the arms or face, simply do not need the attention that more private parts do. In making this statement, the Apostle could be seen as suggesting that, according to station, members should be treated differently. He corrects such a misconception in the following clause.

but God hath tempered the body together / But God has assembled the body together into a harmonious whole: Paul here reiterates the point he

---

166. BDAG, 414; Louw-Nida, §79.13.

167. BDAG, 147; Louw-Nida, §§66.4, 79.13, 88.50.

168. BDAG, 414.

169. Louw-Nida, §79.13.

170. Fitzmyer, *First Corinthians*, 481.

171. Since Paul is using a rather broad analogy, he may not have specific individuals or stations in mind, and therefore, it is best not to try to identify them. Ernest Best, *One Body in Christ: A Study in the Relationship of the Church to Christ in the Epistle of the Apostle Paul* (London: SPCK, 1955), 103.

172. BDAG, 414. Fitzmyer, *First Corinthians*, 481; Louw-Nida, §§79.15; 87.33.

made in 12:18: it was God who determined how the body was assembled. Where in the former verse he used the verb τίθεμαι (*tithemai*), "to set, fix, arrange," in this verse he uses the verb συγκεράννυμι (*syngkerannymi*), "to blend, to unite, compose." The force of the verb, however, is in what it connotes: the deliberate bringing together of various parts to form a harmonious whole.[173] Paul's appeal is again to divine design. God set every part of the body—and by analogy, every member of the Church—in its place, making a harmonious whole. Therefore, all being necessary for that harmony, all have value.

having given more abundant honour to that part which lacked / giving much greater honor to the inferior part: Again the focus is on God's action. It is he who περισσοτέραν δοὺς τιμήν (*perissoteran dous timēn*), "giving much greater honor," to τῷ ὑστεροῦντι (*tō hysterounti*), "the inferior part." The term includes members of two kinds, the "feeble" and the "less honorable" (12:22, 23). Both of these are greatly lacking and, therefore, stand in particular need. It is unclear just how God bestows upon these "much greater honor," but it is likely by giving them status as his sons and daughters with positions in his earthly kingdom and making them heirs with his Son to all that he has (Eph. 2:19; Rom. 8:17). Be that as it may, in the next clause (12:25), the Apostle clearly expresses his intended application of this analogy to the circumstances found in the Church.[174]

12:25 *That there should be no schism in the body / so there will be no divisiveness in the body:* The ἵνα (*hina*) clause, "so that, so there," with the subjective verb ᾖ (*ē*), "will be," forcefully expresses purpose and emphasizes precisely why God composed the body the way he did. On the word σχίσμα (*schisma*), "schism, divisiveness," see Translation Notes on 1:10. God's purpose in giving even the most lacking among the Saints station and honor was to prevent divisions in the body. In short, all were of equal rank and of equal importance. Because of this, if properly implemented and lived, those forces that would tear the body apart would be eliminated, thus assuring the working of the whole in harmony.

but that the members should have the same care one for another / instead the individual parts of the body will be equally concerned about each other: The first clause (above) addresses the negative aspect of why God composed the body the way he did. Here Paul gives the positive

---

173. BDAG, 951–52.
174. Fee, *First Epistle*, 614.

purpose. The verb μεριμνάω (*merimnaō*), "to care for, be concerned about,"[175] expresses that purpose. The adjectival phrase τὸ αὐτό (*to auto*), "the same," connotes being as concerned for another as one is for one's self. The idea is translated as "equally" in our Rendition. Paul's point is that the Christian should not center his or her concerns on status and prestige but on caring for others.

12:26 *And whether one member suffer, all the members suffer with it; or one member be honoured, all the members rejoice with it* / *If one part of the body suffers, then all parts suffer together. If one part of the body is honored, then all parts rejoice together:* The only translation difficulty in this sentence is understanding the passive verb δοξάζεται (*doxazetai*). The root word, δόξα (*doxa*), can denote such things as splendor, renown, and fame.[176] In the passive, the verb can mean "to deem weighty or impressive."[177] Here it is best understood as "the recognition of status and enhancement."[178] Our Rendition follows the KJV in translating the word as "honored."

With this verse, Paul rounds off his application of the analogy by emphasizing the positive side of why God set up the Church the way he did—that all the Saints should care for each other, a care expressed in the mutual sharing of both joys and sorrows. The forepart of Paul's point is easy to understand. If, for example, a person has a bad headache, it is hard to concentrate on anything else. The latter part is a bit harder. Likely, Paul has in mind that when a musician is praised for her "ear" or a skilled craftsman for his "hands," it's the whole person who is complimented.[179] Whatever the case, this verse does illustrate how the proper Christian mindset would express itself in generating sympathy, empathy, or joy for all within the community. It emphasizes that all experiences, both joyful and sorrowful, would be mutual and reciprocal in nature (compare Rom. 12:15).[180]

---

175. BDAG, 632.

176. BDAG, 256–58.

177. For the range of semantic meanings, see Louw-Nida, §§1.15; 12.49; 14.49; 25.205; 33.357; 76.13; 79.18; 87.4, 23. The nuance of deeming something mighty or impressive comes from Old Testament coloring. Thiselton, *First Epistle*, 1012.

178. See Translation Notes on 2:7; 10:31; and 11:7 to see how *doxa* was translated there.

179. Fee, *First Epistle*, 615, but see also Barrett, *First Epistle*, 291–92, who feels that this is the point where Paul leaves his analogy.

180. Fitzmyer, *First Corinthians*, 481.

Analysis and Summary

In this pericope, Paul continues to push his point for the need of diversity in unity. To make his point more easily understood, he compares the Church to a human body. His development here is quite Aristotelian following classical models and, therefore, it would carry considerable weight with the Apostle's educated Gentile readers. Such development gives evidence that Paul was adept at teaching and writing to Gentiles.

He develops his argument in four parts. In the first part, he shows that the Church is like a body that is a single entity but composed of various limbs and organs (μέλη, *melē*) (12:12–14). In the second part, he emphasizes the importance of diversity (12:15–20). In the third part, he emphasizes the need for unity (12:21–26), and in the fourth part, he defines his use of the term "Christ," showing he is referring to the Church (12:27–30).[181]

The body is a perfect example of unity in diversity. The body cannot be a fully functioning organism if it is but one organ. The point is that church members do not all have to have the same talents and abilities, social status, financial state, or spiritual endowments in order to be necessary in getting the whole unit to function as God designed. Everyone is necessary to bring about his purposes. As President John Taylor observed, "When the Church is organized in all its various departments with the President at the head, the Twelve in their place, the High Priests, Seventies and Elders in theirs, together with the Bishops and lesser Priesthood, the local aids and governments each acting in their appointed sphere and calling, and all operated upon and influenced by the Holy Spirit, then the whole becomes as the body of a man, sound and complete in all its members, and everything moves harmoniously and pleasantly along."[182]

The Prophet Joseph Smith taught that "the cause of God is one, common cause, in which all the Saints are alike interested; . . . The advancement of the cause of God and the building up of Zion is as much one man's business as another. The only difference is, that one is called to fulfill one duty, and another, another duty; 'but if one member suffers, all the members suffer with it, and if one member in honored all the rest rejoice with it [12:26]. . . .' Party feelings, separate interests, exclusive designs should be lost sight off in the one common cause, in the interest of the whole."[183]

---

181. Fitzmyer, *First Corinthians*, 474; Fee, *First Epistle*, 600–601.
182. John Taylor, in *JD*, 19:54.
183. "History, 1838–1856, Volume C-1," 1327.

As President Howard W. Hunter has said,

> Within this Church there is a constant need for unity, for if we are not one,
> we are not his. (See D&C 38:27.) We are truly dependent on each other,
> "and the eye cannot say unto the hand, I have no need of thee: nor again
> the head to the feet, I have no need of you." (1 Cor. 12:21.) Nor can the
> North Americans say to the Asians, nor the Europeans to the islanders of
> the sea, "I have no need of thee." No, in this church we have need of every
> member, and we pray, as did Paul when he wrote to the church in Corinth,
> "that there should be no schism in the body; but that the members should
> have the same care one for another."[184]

Wrote one LDS scholar, unity makes "jealousy impossible. The unity of
the Church should exclude pride and contempt among its members, for by
analogy parts of the human body which seem somewhat feeble are nevertheless indispensable [12:22]."[185] Paul's point is that, because God has set
the order of his Church, no one can be considered as dishonorable or nonessential to the work. On the extreme end, even those who fall to human
weakness or are overtaken by physical ailments or suffer from spiritual
problems cannot be counted out, for they give others the chance to serve.[186]

"To me, what [Paul] is saying," noted another LDS scholar, "is that each of
us as a member of Christ's body is incomplete—as incomplete as any given
organ of our body is incomplete: 'If the whole body were an eye, where were
the hearing? If the whole were hearing, where were the smelling?' (1 Corinthians 12:17), and so on. Truly, none of us can be saved as individuals. We are
saved as Zion, because you and I complement each other. What I cannot do,
you can do. What you cannot do, I (or someone else) can."[187]

The point must be emphasized that all members must fulfill their calling
if the Church is to function fully. If not, to a greater or lesser degree, all suffer. As President John Taylor taught,

> A teacher who keeps the commandments of God and fulfills his duties is
> more honorable than the Apostle who does not. You hurt any part of the
> body, for instance, cut your finger, and the entire body feels it immedi-
> ately. Touch the head and every part of the body senses it. And so it is with
> every particle of the body—it is a perfect system; and so is the Church of
> God, and each of the organs, members in particular, thus the organized

184. Howard W. Hunter, "That We May Be One," *Ensign* 6 (May 1976): 105–6.
185. Sperry, *Life and Letters,* 126.
186. Thiselton, *First Epistle,* 1007–8.
187. John S. Robertson, "A Complete Look at Perfect," *BYU Speeches,* July 13, 1999,
https://speeches.byu.edu/talks/john-s-robertson_complete-look-perfect/.

body walks in the path that God marks out, and seeks to accomplish all things that he designs for us to do. Hence there is a mutual sympathy, affection and regard, and a brotherhood and fellowship among the Saints of God who are living their religion, all through the organization of the Priesthood, from the head to the foot.[188]

As Paul understood, within the community of Christ there is, strictly speaking, no private suffering (12:26). Everyone shares in the life of the whole. A wrong done to one member, therefore, is a wrong done to all, and since the Savior identifies himself with the community of the Saints, it is done to him.[189] But, much suffering could be avoided if members would remember Paul's point in 12:15–18. Saints must not compare themselves with others. Among other problems, it leads to discouragement, jealousy (compare 1:10–12; 3:1–4), and blindness to the blessing of what one has. Often this results in unnecessary feelings of inferiority that lead to loss of joy in service and the hope of eternal life. Too much time is spent grumbling because one person sees himself as the foot having to bear all the weight or another wishes she were the eye that oversees all or yet another wants to be the mouth that directs everything. It must never be forgotten that God knows each one of his children and how to maximize their potential in the one body that is Christ.

And how do all become a part of that body? Paul stated it was by being immersed in the same water and the same spirit (12:3). As Elder Orson Pratt explained, "They [the church members in Paul's day] were not baptized into half a dozen or a hundred different bodies, or denominations of people, called Christians; but they were all baptized into the same body by the same spirit, and all made partakers of the gifts of that spirit, enjoying the blessings and powers of the same. The members constituting the body of Christ are diversified: and being filled with the Holy Ghost it operates in various ways."[190]

For Paul, the *sine qua non* of Christian life is the operation of the Holy Spirit in the lives of the members of the Church and in the Church itself. It is having the Spirit that is the distinguishing factor between member and nonbeliever (2:10–14). It is having the Spirit that makes one a child of God (Rom. 8:14–17) and unites all into the one body of the Church in Christ. As a result, divisions such as "bond or free," "Jew or Gentile," or even "male or female" (Gal. 3:28) are meaningless.[191]

---

188. John Taylor, in *JD*, 18:202.

189. Lionel Spencer Thornton, *The Common Life in the Body of Christ*, 4th ed. (London: Darce Press, 1963), 36.

190. Orson Pratt, in *JD*, 14:292.

191. Fee, *First Epistle*, 603–4.

Paul's doctrine centers on an equality of status brought about through a correct understanding of the Atonement and what it means to be "in Christ" and share in the various gifts of the Spirit so graciously given by the Father. In 12:21, we see his delineation of an attitude of self-sufficiency in which certain people feel they have no need for others.[192] Feelings of superiority, self-sufficiency, autonomy, even of a right to do as one wishes are precisely the sin Paul finds so contrary to the attitude true Christians should have in a Church that exists for the mutual benefit of all.

As Paul understood, a major power of having the Spirit operate in the Church is that it binds all members together and, thereby, prevents factions (12:12). The same is true today. President John Taylor asked, "Why do we [as Latter-day Saints] feel alike?" and then answered, "Because we have all partaken of one spirit, which proceeds from our Heavenly Father, it is the Holy Ghost. How does it affect us? It affects our spirits. And although we do not understand, sometimes, one another's speech, and are ignorant of the ideas entertained by one another; and although the habits, customs, and manners are diverse and various among the different nations from which we have come, we still are one in sentiment, one in faith and in confidence, and one in assurance."[193]

In these verses, Paul teaches his readers how Church members should apply the Atonement in the real world. By toppling the notion current in his day that some parts of the body were more honorable than others, Paul shows that the scheme of a body hierarchy is wrong, being based only on a superficial worldly philosophy.[194] Paul's position validates the idea of status reversals found in the scriptures. It is best stated by the Savior, who observed that the "greatest among you shall be your servant" (Matt. 23:11) and that the man who desires to "be first, the same shall be last of all" (Mark 9:35). The Lord taught firmly that the "first shall be last; and the last shall be first" (Matt. 19:30, compare Matt. 20:16). Status in the Lord's kingdom is not based on educational opportunity, social privilege, or economic advantage but on sacrifice for the kingdom expressed primarily as sincere service to others. Gospel life is such that, though many are called, few will prove themselves chosen (Matt. 19:29; 20:16). Joseph Smith clearly explained the reason why: "We have learned by sad experience that it is the nature and disposition of almost all men, as soon as they get a little authority, as they

---

192. Thiselton, *First Epistle,* 1006.

193. John Taylor, in *JD,* 11:24.

194. Martin, *Corinthian Body,* 94–95. Note Paul's status reversals between 1:26–29 and 1:30–31, between 2:1–5 and 2:6–11, and most importantly, between 1:18–22 and 1:23–25.

suppose, they will immediately begin to exercise unrighteous dominion. Hence many are called, but few are chosen" (D&C 121:39–40). An official explanation of what this scripture means appeared in print in 1961:

> It is the doctrine that those who hold this power and authority will be chosen for an inheritance of eternal life if they exercise their priesthood upon principles of righteousness; if they walk in the light; if they keep the commandments; if they put first in their lives the things of God's kingdom and let temporal concerns take a secondary place; if they serve in the kingdom with an eye single to the glory of God. It is the doctrine that even though men have the rights of the priesthood conferred upon them, they shall not reap its eternal blessings if they use it for unrighteous purposes; if they commit sin; if the things of this world take pre-eminence in their lives over the things of the Spirit. It is a fearful thing to contemplate this priesthood truth: *Behold, many are called to the priesthood, and few are chosen for eternal life.*[195]

This statement makes it clear that the road to eternal life does not depend on any high calling or station, but on how well each individual fulfills the one he or she has. As each does what she or he is assigned, unity prevails and God's work moves forward. That is the theme Paul is emphasizing.

This pericope is, therefore, a strong polemic against factionalism. Some postmodern commentators have insisted that Paul's words promote the idea "that within certain boundaries everyone 'does one's own thing.'"[196] That is absolutely *not* the case. The precise, coordinated, and proper function of all the organs in the body contributes to its overall capacity, ability, and wellness. They do not do their "own thing," but their assigned thing. If each did not do its indispensable part, the organism would cease to function and likely die. Paul's analogy is, then, an assurance of the absolute necessity of those in his audience who were either devalued by others or felt inferior to them in either status or gifts. All were indeed a part of the body; and more, they played an indispensable role in giving that body the strength, ability, and coherent unity it needed to carry out its divinely appointed destiny.[197]

---

195. "What Is the Doctrine of the Priesthood?" *Improvement Era* 64 (February 1961): 115; italics in original. Hoyt W. Brewster Jr., *Doctrine and Covenants Encyclopedia* (Salt Lake City: Bookcraft, 1988), 141.

196. Thiselton, *First Epistle*, 1002. See Arnold Bittlinger, *Gifts and Graces: A Commentary on 1 Corinthians 12–14* (London: Hodder and Stoughton, 1968), 58; Mitchell, *Paul and the Rhetoric of Reconciliation*, 68–83; and Martin, *Corinthian Body*, 38–63, 94–103.

197. Thiselton, *First Epistle*, 1002.

The Order of Officers and Gifts in the Church (12:27–31)

Greek Text

27 Ὑμεῖς δέ ἐστε σῶμα Χριστοῦ καὶ μέλη ἐκ μέρους. 28 καὶ οὓς μὲν ἔθετο ὁ θεὸς ἐν τῇ ἐκκλησίᾳ πρῶτον ἀποστόλους, δεύτερον προφήτας, τρίτον διδασκάλους, ἔπειτα δυνάμεις, ἔπειτα χαρίσματα ἰαμάτων, ἀντιλήμψεις, κυβερνήσεις, γένη γλωσσῶν. 29 μὴ πάντες ἀπόστολοι; μὴ πάντες προφῆται; μὴ πάντες διδάσκαλοι; μὴ πάντες δυνάμεις; 30 μὴ πάντες χαρίσματα ἔχουσιν ἰαμάτων; μὴ πάντες γλώσσαις λαλοῦσιν; μὴ πάντες διερμηνεύουσιν; 31 ζηλοῦτε δὲ τὰ χαρίσματα τὰ μείζονα. καὶ ἔτι καθ᾽ ὑπερβολὴν ὁδὸν ὑμῖν δείκνυμι. [SBLGNT]

King James Version

27 Now ye are the body of Christ, and members in particular. 28 And God hath set some in the church, first apostles, secondarily prophets, thirdly teachers, after that miracles, then gifts of healings, helps, governments, diversities of tongues. 29 Are all apostles? are all prophets? are all teachers? are all workers of miracles? 30 Have all the gifts of healing? do all speak with tongues? do all interpret? 31 But covet earnestly the best gifts: and yet shew I unto you a more excellent way.

New Rendition

27 Now you yourselves are the body of Christ, and each one of you are a part of it. 28 God has appointed in the church first apostles, second prophets, third teachers, then miracles, then gifts of healing, helpful deeds, leadership skills, the ability to speak other languages. 29 Certainly all are not apostles, nor are all prophets, nor are all teachers, nor are all able to perform miracles. 30 Certainly all do not have the gift of healing, nor are all able to speak other languages, nor are all able to interpret. 31 You should earnestly strive for the greatest spiritual gifts. And now I will show you a far better way.

Translation Notes and Comments

12:27 *Now ye are the body of Christ, and members in particular / Now you yourselves are the body of Christ, and each one of you are a part of it:* With this verse, Paul "ties all the preceding pieces together."[198] The phrase ἐκ μέρους (*ek merous*), translated as "in particular" in the KJV, means "separately" or "part by part" and stresses the individuality of each Christian as part of the Church.[199] The idea is that each person, individually, is an indispensable part of the body.

---

198. Fee, *First Epistle*, 617.
199. Thiselton, *First Epistle*, 1013.

12:28 *And God hath set some in the church, first apostles, secondarily prophets, thirdly teachers / God has appointed in the church first apostles, second prophets, third teachers:* This verse presents a couple of translation challenges. The first is Paul's intent in listing certain offices as "first," "second," or "third." Did he mean to give them rank or was he simply using the numbers to help him give order to a list? Since the Apostle has been arguing that each part of the body, meaning each member of the Church, is critical and of equal worth to all the others, it seems unlikely he was creating a hierarchy of individuals. Unity in diversity (his theme) also means unity in equality. That, however, is not the case so far as offices are concerned. It could be said that, in God's eyes, all officers have the same rank but not all offices. There are simply some offices that hold more power and have heavier responsibility than others. When an individual holds a certain office, he or she has both the power and responsibility that go with it but, once released, that is no longer the case. The power is in the office, not in the individual member. Offices can, therefore, be ranked even if individual members cannot.[200]

With the phrase ἔθετο ὁ θεός (*etheto ho theos*), "God has appointed," Paul blunts any objections to his point and settles all arguments, for God is in charge. For the term "apostle," see Translation Notes on 1:1. There is no doubt that the office of Apostle has first rank in Church order (4:9; 15:8–9; Rom. 11:13; 15:15–16; Eph. 3:5; 4:11–14). Their special calling is to bear witness of Christ to the entire world (Matt. 28:19–20; D&C 107:23).

Though Paul has used the term "prophecy" before (12:10), this is the first time he has mentioned "prophets." The noun προφήτης (*prophētēs*) specifically designates individuals who have the power to proclaim or expound "divine matters or concerns that could not ordinarily be known except by special revelation."[201] The root combines the prefix προ (*pro*), "for" or "in behalf of," with the verb φημί (*phēmi*), "to speak," or, in a religious sense, "to utter" and together the two words connote the power to speak for another with authority and that includes for the gods.[202] Their purview includes prophesying as well as admonition and instruction with emphasis falling on the latter two.[203] The primary requirement for one so called,

---

200. Bruce, *1 and 2 Corinthians*, 122–23; Robertson and Plummer, *Critical and Exegetical Commentary*, 279.

201. BDAG, 890–91.

202. Helmut Krämer, Rolf Rendtorff, Rudolf Meyer, and Gerhard Friedrich, "προφήτης, προφῆτις, προφητεύω, προφητεία, προφητικός, ψευδοπροφήτης," in *TDNT*, 6:781–861.

203. Ralph A. Britsch and Todd A. Britsch, "Prophet: Prophets," in *EM*, 3:1164.

however, is to have a testimony of Christ (Rev. 19:10).[204] Being true to that spiritual witness enables a person to act as a prophet by understanding and proclaiming the will of God (D&C 52:9).

The noun διδάσκαλος (*didaskalos*) denotes a teacher. In this instance, it refers to a person who, under divine authority and inspiration, can declare the things of God. Though both prophets and teachers are inspired, they differ from another. Prophets are empowered to proclaim doctrine, give judgments, and make challenges as well as give support, comfort, encouragement and direction to those under their authority. Teachers, on the other hand, are empowered to transmit, interpret, explain, and give expositions on the meaning and implication of texts, doctrines, and teachings. Their authority includes bearing witness of Christ. They, however, do not have the authority to proclaim new doctrine.[205]

after that miracles, then gifts of healings, helps, governments, diversities of tongues / then miracles, then gifts of healing, helpful deeds, leadership skills, the ability to speak other languages: The second major translation challenge in this verse is Paul's use of adjectival titles for offices in the forepart of this list (above) and abstract nouns to describe various spiritual activities in this part. It is likely that the reason he did so was to separate these gifts and powers from the offices they support. The varieties of gifts he lists here certainly are those that various members contribute to the Church. His use of the adverb ἔπειτα (*epeita*), "after, then," emphasizes that these powers and gifts, though important and praiseworthy, do not eclipse the authority, dignity, and function of the offices but rather support them (compare Heb. 2:3–4). Bearing witness of the Lord, the primary duty of the three offices, stands paramount to all other expressions of the Spirit.

The plural noun δυνάμεις (*dynameis*), "miracles," in light of 12:10 should be understood as the power to do mighty deeds, that is, those things described as marvelous works and wonders (compare Isa. 29:14; 2 Ne. 27:26; D&C 18:44; 76:114). With the use of the word χαρίσματα (*charismata*), "gifts," Paul signals that what follows are specifically "gifts of the Spirit." The plural noun ἰάματα (*hiamata*), "healings," denotes the power to heal various afflictions, including those that are physical, mental, and spiritual. The meaning of the plural noun ἀντιλήμψεις (*antilēmpseis*), "helps," is vague because it is rarely found in the New Testament. It can refer to the giving of

204. See Joseph Smith's definition, "History, 1838–1856, Volume B-1," 794.
205. Thiselton, *First Epistle*, 1017.

help generally[206] or, more specifically, of giving administrative assistance. This could include scribal and secretarial work.[207] In this context, however, it seems to refer to giving assistance and support particularly to those in need. Since, however, the broad term "helpful deeds" covers all of these, it is used in our Rendition.[208] The plural noun κυβερνήσεις (*kybernēseis*), "governments, leadership skills," denotes various gifts of administration, including the ability to guide and direct Church members as well as oversee Church functions.[209] The plural phrase γένη γλωσσῶν (*genē glōssōn*), "diversity of tongues, ability to speak in other tongues," means just that (see 12:10). The emphasis of the plural, however, is on the number of languages that this gift allows its recipients to speak.

12:29 *Are all apostles? are all prophets? are all teachers? are all workers of miracles? / Certainly all are not apostles, nor are all prophets, nor are all teachers, nor are all able to perform miracles:* With this and the next verse, Paul pushes the thesis of this pericope, namely, that of unity in diversity. The Lord set up the Church with various offices and officers, and he bestowed various gifts and powers. The Apostle's use of a series of rhetorical questions in this and the next verse helps him emphasize his point. He so constructed his questions that they demand a "no" answer and, thereby, substantiate his thesis that everyone is needed in the Church.[210]

12:30 *Have all the gifts of healing? do all speak with tongues? do all interpret? / Certainly all do not have the gift of healing, nor are all able to speak other languages, nor are all able to interpret:* In this verse, Paul continues to use rhetorical questions to push his point that all the Saints, with their gifts, talents, and abilities, are needed in the Church. Each of these rhetorical questions begin with μή (*mē*), which indicates an expected

---

206. BDAG, 89. The word is found only here in the New Testament, making it hard to define.

207. Moulton and Milligan, *Vocabulary,* 47–48; LSJ, 144. Robertson and Plummer, *Critical and Exegetical Commentary,* 290; Thiselton, *First Epistle,* 1019–20.

208. This is based on the noun's use in LXX Ps. 22:20; Sir. 11:12; 2 Macc. 8:19; 3 Macc. 5:50. See also Fee, *First Epistle,* 621, and Fitzmyer, *First Corinthians,* 483. Note that the versification in LXX differs from the KJV.

209. Louw-Nida, §36.3; BDAG, 573. This word shows up only here in the New Testament but is found in LXX Prov. 1:15; 11:14; 24:6. The related verb κυβερβάω (*kybernaō*) refers to the task of piloting a ship and thus suggests that the noun κυβέρνησις (*kybernēsis*) used metaphorically connotes "guiding." Note that the versification in LXX differs from the KJV.

210. Paul's mode of argument is very similar to that found in *1 Clem.* 37.3–4, where the Church Father uses titles drawn from the military services to make his point.

answer of "No!" Since such a construction is awkward in English (for example, "All do not have the gift of healing, do they?"), in our Rendition these have been converted to statements. To the list of gifts he has already mentioned, he adds διερμηνεύω (*diermēneuō*), "to translate; interpret, make understandable."[211] Again, Paul puts the gifts dealing with tongues last, likely to limit their importance among the gifts.

12:31 *But covet earnestly the best gifts / You should earnestly strive for the greatest spiritual gifts:* Paul uses this sentence as a bridge leading to the identification of the "greatest gifts" that he will turn to in the next pericope. Paul does not identify here the "greatest gifts," but by placing tongues and the interpretation of tongues last, he does suggest these do not rank as "best gifts." The verb ζηλόω (*zēloō*), "covet earnestly, earnestly strive for," denotes the positive intensity that drives one to acquire a specific object or achieve a given objective.[212] The form of the verb allows it to be interpreted in two ways. If taken as an indicative, Paul is making an observation that these people were, at that very time, striving for the best gifts.[213] As an imperative, the Apostle was giving them a command to do something they were not. Though the indicative interpretation cannot be ruled out, our Rendition follows most translations and takes the verb as an imperative.[214] The adjective μείζων (*meizōn*) is a comparative and, therefore, can refer to things that are "better" or "greater" than others.[215] However, in contexts such as this one, the word usually denotes the superlative "best" or "greatest."[216] It would appear that Paul has in mind those gifts that he considered superior to all the others.[217] The phrase τὰ χαρίσματα τὰ μείζονα (*ta charismata ta meizona*), "the greater gifts," identifies what the objective of the Saints striving should be: gaining these gifts. Prayer and habitual preparation would define such striving.[218]

---

211. BDAG, 244.

212. BDAG, 427.

213. J. F. M. Smit, "Two Puzzles: 1 Corinthinas 12.31 and 13.3, a Rhetorical Solution," *New Testament Studies* 39, no. 2 (1993): 255, shows that this verse concludes Paul's point and sets up his argument presented in chapter 13.

214. For example, see the NIV, NJB, NRSV. For additional support, see Smit, "Two Puzzles," 247; Robertson and Plummer, *Critical and Exegetical Commentary,* 282.

215. Louw-Nida, §87.28.

216. For example, see 2 Pet. 1:4. There is general support for this point. See Thiselton, *First Epistle,* 1025; Smit, "Two Puzzles," 247.

217. BDAG, 623–24.

218. Robertson and Plummer, *Critical and Exegetical Commentary,* 282; Barrett, *First Epistle,* 296. It should be noted that Paul's comment, under this circumstance, is ironic.

and yet shew I unto you a more excellent way / And now I will show you a far better way: The verb δείκνυμι (*deiknymi*), "to show" or "point out,"[219] though in the present tense, has a future connotation and is thus translated as "will show" in our Rendition. The noun ὑπερβολή (*hyperbole*) denotes anything that exceeds something else to an extraordinary or extreme degree.[220] Thus, our Rendition translates the prepositional phrase καθ' ὑπερβολήν (*kath' hyperbolēn*) as "far better." The noun ὁδός (*hodos*), "road, way," is used here metaphorically to mean "teaching" or "direction."[221] The prepositional phrase *kath' hyperbolēn* acts in an adjectival capacity to modify the verb δείκνυμι (*deiknymi*) and, as such, tells Paul's readers that he is going to show them a far better way that will take them on the most direct route to their goal of accessing the greatest of all the gifts.[222]

Analysis and Summary

It is of note that the first three offices that Paul lists (12:28)—apostle, prophet, teacher—are all concerned primarily with bearing witness of the Lord and promoting his ministry. All other powers and assistants, as Paul shows, must stand behind these.[223] "The overall point is that Christ's Church must be governed by inspired officials," notes one LDS scholar.[224]

Paul made sure his readers understood that God is the one who set in order the Church, with apostles at the head (12:28). On the nature and function of the apostolic office, see Translation Notes on 1:1; 12:28. These men, as the title of their office denotes, constituted the traveling council, that is, those who were "sent out" to see that Church order was kept everywhere. "The Church of Christ is not perfect without Apostles," noted Elder George Q. Cannon. "Apostles were as necessary as Teachers; they were as necessary as Evangelists; they were as necessary as Pastors. But the wicked would not allow Apostles to live, for Apostles were men who had revelation, Apostles were inspired of God; they became, as it were, the oracles

---

These people are striving for that which is, in reality, a gift and is therefore beyond their control. Fitzmyer, *First Corinthians,* 484. This being the case, it makes the next phrase even more telling and corrective.

219. BDAG, 214–15.
220. Louw-Nida, §78.33. Paul uses the same word in Gal. 1:13; 2 Cor. 1:8; 4:17; Rom. 7:13.
221. BDAG, 691–92.
222. Barth, *Resurrection of the Dead,* 79; Conzelmann, *1 Corinthians,* 216.
223. Barrett, *First Epistle,* 295.
224. Anderson, *Understanding Paul,* 116.

of Jehovah to the inhabitants of the earth."[225] The disappearance of the apostolic office is one of the major signs that an apostasy took place, and its reappearance in the last days is a major sign that the gospel has been restored.[226]

The second office Paul lists is that of prophet. "A prophet is not so great as an Apostle," explained President Wilford Woodruff. "Christ has set, in his Church, first, Apostles; they hold the keys of the kingdom of God."[227] Even so, prophets do hold authority and can declare godly matters. This office, unlike that of apostle, is neither restricted to the general level of the Church nor to the male gender. "By scriptural definition, a prophet is anyone who has a testimony of Jesus Christ and is moved by the Holy Ghost (Rev. 19:10)."[228] On this subject President Brigham Young stated, "Many persons think if they see a prophet they see one possessing all the keys of the kingdom of God on the earth. This is not so; many persons have prophesied without having any Priesthood on them at all. It is no particular revelation or gift for a person to prophesy."[229] As noted above, what stands behind the word is the authority that the prophet or prophetess has to speak and administer in the name of the Lord. Thus, local units of the Church were and are run by prophets and prophetesses.[230]

The last office Paul lists is that of teacher, but in doing so, declared Elder M. Russell Ballard, he "placed the priority of teachers in the Church next only to the Apostles and the prophets."[231] President David O. McKay said, "No greater responsibility can rest upon any man [or woman], than to be a

---

225. Cannon, George Q. in *JD*, 22:265.

226. Not long before his death, the Savior warned his Apostles that they would not be accepted for very long, even by members of the Church. Indeed, there would be those who would come in his name deceiving many and they shall "deliver you up to be afflicted, and shall kill you; and ye shall be hated of all nations for my name's sake" (Matt. 24:4, 9; JS–M 1:6–7).

227. Wilford Woodruff, in *JD*, 13:165.

228. Britsch and Britsch, "Prophet: Prophets," in *EM*, 3:1165. Joseph Smith taught that every man "who has the testimony of Jesus" is a prophet based on Rev. 19:10, "for the testimony of Jesus is the spirit of prophecy." "History, 1838–1856, Volume B-1," 794. He went on to say, "No man is a minister of Jesus Christ without being a Prophet—No man can be the minister of Jesus Christ, except he has the testimony of Jesus and this is the Spirit of Prophesy." "History, 1838–1856, Volume C-1," 12 [addenda].

229. Brigham Young, in *JD*, 13:144.

230. Wilford Woodruff, in *JD*, 13:165; Britsch and Britsch, "Prophet: Prophets," in *EM*, 3:1165.

231. M. Russel Ballard, "Teaching—No Greater Call," *Ensign* 13 (May 1983): 69.

teacher of God's children."[232] Like that of apostle and prophet, their major duty is to bear testimony of Christ and to declare his gospel.

In this modern day, after giving instructions to the officers in the various Melchizedek priesthood quorums, the Lord states that "the above offices I have given unto you, and the keys thereof, for helps and for governments, for the . . . ministry and the perfecting of my saints" (D&C 124:125–43). In this context, the powers do not support the offices but, rather, are housed by them for the assistance of others.

Paul's list of powers in 12:28 is a bit more extensive than the one noted above found in the Doctrine and Covenants. He mentions the ability to do impressive deeds, healings, charitable acts, govern, and finally, speak in various tongues (12:28). It is of note that Paul lists "tongues" last, likely because it was a major source of contention among the Corinthian branches, and he did not want it to have any more cachet than that of the other gifts.

In 12:29–30, Paul emphasizes that the Lord set up the Church such that no one person exercises all the gifts or fills all the roles. This fact includes every unit from the smallest branch to the general level of the Church. Though it is true that the current prophet holds all the keys of the priesthood,[233] he does not fill all the offices or exercise all the gifts. That limitation assures each Saint that his or her gifts and talents are sorely needed in the kingdom. The questions Paul asks in these verses point to the fact that no one holds all the offices or has all the gifts of the Spirit and, therefore, the Church needs everyone.[234]

Paul admonished his readers to "earnestly strive for the greatest spiritual gifts" (12:31, Rendition). His counsel put the burden on his readers. "Like the acquisition of anything worthwhile," noted President Henry D. Moyle, "it takes effort to attain the spiritual. Faith, dedication, and devotion must be ours to bring ourselves closer and closer to our Heavenly Father. We enjoy our communion with God here and now in mortality. We do not need to wait for immortality to enjoy the fruits of our spiritual labors. We learn to appreciate the Spirit of God more and more as we draw nearer to the Lord in the keeping of his commandments. The harder we knock, the wider is the door is opened."[235] He also noted that "Paul enumerates many gifts of the Spirit. The greatest gift, however, is not the performing

---

232. David O. Mckay, in CR, October 1916, 57.

233. Alan K. Parrish, "Keys of the Priesthood," in *EM*, 2:780–81.

234. Thiselton, *First Epistle*, 1023.

235. Henry D. Moyle, in CR, April 1963, 44–48.

of miracles or talking in tongues, or prophesying, etc.; but the inception of an individual testimony is the greatest of all gifts of the Spirit. And that is a gift which comes from God through the Holy Ghost and can be received by any man, woman, or child in the world who desires to know the truth. It is at once the greatest and certainly the most universal of all gifts born of the Spirit. It is indeed the Comforter promised to all who, through faith in God and repentance, seek with a contrite heart a remission of sins in the waters of baptism."[236]

Elder Dallin H. Oaks noted that "most of us have more things expected of us than we can possibly do. As breadwinners, as parents, as Church workers and members, we face many choices on what we will do with our time and other resources." His counsel was to "forego some good things in order to choose others that are better or best because they develop faith in the Lord Jesus Christ and strengthen our families."[237]

When Paul promises his readers, in 12:31, that he will show them "a far better way" (Rendition), he helps them understand how the diverse gifts and endowments of the Spirit he listed in 12:4–11 "can find a 'way' that goes beyond them and thus serves the 'one body' of the Christian Church, 'the body of Christ,' in a surpassing way."[238]

---

236. Henry D. Moyle, in CR, April 1957, 31–34.
237. Dallin H. Oaks, "Good, Better, Best" *Ensign* 37 (November 2007): 104, 107.
238. Fitzmyer, *First Corinthians*, 485.

Chapter 13

A More Excellent Way

INTRODUCTION

With acute insight, one LDS scholar stated that "First Corinthians 13 is the most moving chapter of the New Testament outside of Jesus' teachings, a fact that suggests its real source."[1] He further noted that its power comes, in part, like that of the Sermon on the Mount because "it treats the disease, not the symptoms."[2] Paul's intent, as he so precisely stated in 12:31, was to show his readers "a more excellent way," and in this chapter he does so. To identify that way, he chose a single word: ἀγάπη (*agapē*), "love." The KJV translates it with the English word "charity."

This chapter, as another scholar noted, contains "a rhetorical encomium of love, intended as an exhortation for Corinthian Christians."[3] Indeed, Paul used a very deliberate style carefully and beautifully designed to persuade. This encomium also established the ground on which all Christian morality sits.[4] It acts as a climax to what Paul has been teaching about πνευματικά (*pneumatika*), "spiritual gifts," and their importance and place

---

1. Anderson, *Understanding Paul,* 117. There were literary parallels. For example, Wis. 7:22–23 with its further development in 7:24–8:1, where twenty-one attributes of σοφία (*sophia,* "wisdom") are listed. Both Plato, *Symp.* 197c–e, and Maximus of Tyre, *Diss.* 20.2, list the qualities of *eros* (romantic love), and *1 Esd.* 4:34–40 does the same for ἀλήθεια (*alētheia*), "truth." However, for sheer inspiration and beauty, none of these touches Paul's inspired words.

2. Anderson, *Understanding Paul,* 117. Lowell L. Bennion, *Legacies of Jesus* (Salt Lake City: Deseret Book, 1990), 34, called it "a stirring eulogy on love."

3. Fitzmyer, *First Corinthians,* 487; see also Mitchell, *Paul and the Rhetoric of Reconciliation,* 273.

4. Ceslaus Spicq, *Agape in the New Testament,* 3 vols. (Eugene, Ore.: Wipf and Stock Publishers, 2006), 2:141. The second volume of this work, with the exception of 1 Peter, is devoted to the study of love in the Pauline corpus.

in the gospel. It also sums up what he has been saying in much of the epistle about how Christians live their lives "in Christ."[5] In this beautiful exhortation, he asks his readers to consider their attitudes and behavior as illumined by love and to assess whether this power is the basis of their social interactions.[6]

Paul shows love to be the greatest of all the gifts of God and the basis on which all the others operate. In this, he is supported by the Book of Mormon prophet Moroni who also addressed the importance of love (Moro. 7:44–47; 10:20–22). In the Pauline epistles, however, as LDS scholars have noted, charity is "not included as a gift in the way as it is in Moroni, but rather is the principle upon which the [other] gifts are based."[7] The reason that the Apostle sets love above all the other spiritual endowments is because it belongs to an altogether different class. The only other members are hope and faith.[8] Love transcends all other endowments of the Spirit and is the supernal gift from God.

Agapē, for Paul, is not an ethereal concept but is a concrete reality fully expressed in the teachings and actions of the Master. It is neither a sweet sentiment nor even some motivational power behind certain actions. For him, it is action; nothing less will do.[9] Where inaction resides, love does not. As such *agapē* is neither a human virtue inherent within the soul nor a talent developed by discipline and hard work. It is *the* touch of the divine. It is, as Paul knew, "shed abroad in our hearts by the Holy Ghost which is given unto us" (Rom. 5:5). As Latter-day Saints understand, it comes only to those "who are true followers of his [God's] Son, Jesus Christ" and who ask for it "with all the energy of heart" (Moro. 7:48). Even then, it must be maintained "by diligence unto prayer" (Moro. 8:26).

Love's essence was expressed by the Savior when he said, "If ye love me, keep my commandments" (John 14:15). Therefore, the depth of this kind

---

5. Fitzmyer, *First Corinthians,* 488. Because this pericope can be easily dropped without breaking the flow of Paul's thought between 12:31a and 14:1, some scholars have felt it is an insertion. Others feel it is a major digression. For discussion, see Thiselton, *First Epistle,* 1027–28. Given that the whole chapter is *the* answer to the major problems facing the Corinthian Saints, it is highly unlikely it is either of these but rather an organic and indispensable part of the Apostle's message. See Spicq, *Agape,* 2:139; Craig, "First Epistle," 10:165.

6. Mitchell, *Paul and the Rhetoric of Reconciliation,* 274.

7. Holzapfel and Wayment, *Making Sense,* 360.

8. Fee, *First Epistle,* 628.

9. Fee, *First Epistle,* 628.

of love can be measured. Clearly, for Paul, "love is the fulfilling of the law" (Rom. 13:10). This is because, if one loves God—truly loves him—such a person will not commit immoral acts, take human life, spoil a reputation, take neither credit nor property, or covet what another has (Rom. 13:9). Indeed, under its power such things would be unthinkable. Love propels one to take care of others and see to their welfare.

Elder McConkie testified that "above all the attributes of godliness and perfection, charity is the one most devoutly to be desired. Charity is more than love, far more; it is everlasting love, perfect love, the pure love of Christ which endureth forever. It is love so centered in righteousness that the possessor has no aim or desire except for the eternal welfare of his own soul and for the souls of those around him" (compare 2 Ne. 26:30; Moro. 7:47; 8:25–26).[10]

Finally, its possession and use are demanded of all those who will have eternal life, for "except ye have charity ye can in nowise be saved in the kingdom of God" (Moro. 10:21). In sum, Paul shows us that love alone counts, triumphs, and endures.[11] For further development, see "Excursus on Love/Charity" below in this chapter.

Clement of Rome, writing some forty years after Paul penned his letter to the Corinthians, asked them to remember Paul's words and cited a verse from chapter 13. But the church father went on to list an additional eight elements about love not included by Paul. Since, in the same section, Clement also asked the Corinthians to "remember the words of the Lord Jesus which he spoke when he was teaching gentleness and longsuffering,"[12] scholars have wondered if both Paul and Clement were quoting from portions of one of the Lord's lost sermons.[13]

The subject of this chapter, *agapē*, plays a critical, essential, and central role in Paul's overall exhortation. Paul carefully, even ingeniously, organized his epistle to highlight its importance. He chose the chiastic form as

---

10. *DNTC*, 2:378.

11. Karl Barth, *Church Dogmatics*, 14 vols. (Peabody, Mass.: Hendrickson Publishers, 2010), 4/2 §68.825.

12. *1 Clem.* 13:1–2; Anderson, *Understanding Paul*, 119; *DNTC*, 2:379.

13. John, the Apostle, assured his readers that "there are also many other things which Jesus did" (John 21:25) that were never included in his record, and Mormon said much the same thing, "Now there cannot be written in this book even a hundredths part of the things which Jesus did truly teach unto the people" (3 Ne. 26:6). A discourse on love could have been among these unpublished teachings.

his means. In this construction, the central element has the emphasis. Paul used not one, but three levels of chiasmus, each one enhancing more his point. The largest level runs from chapter 11 through 14 and can be constructed as follows.[14]

A Men and women in worship service: On proper dress (11:2–16)

    B An order of worship: The sacrament (11:17–34)

        C Spiritual gifts and the metaphor of the body (12:1–31)

            D The discourse on love (13:1–13)

        C' Spiritual gifts and the building up of the body (14:1–25)

    B' An order of worship: Prophets and speaking in tongues (14:26–33a)

A' Men and women in worship: On proper decorum (14:33b–36)[15]

The second level runs from chapter 12 through 14 and can be constructed thus:

A Gifts of the Spirit (12:1–31)

    B Love and the gifts of the Spirit (13:1–3)

        C Love defined (13:4–7)

    B' Love and gifts of the Spirit (13:8–13)

A' Gifts of the Spirit (14:1–25)[16]

The third level is the pericope itself and can be constructed as follows:

A Continue in zeal for spiritual gifts but follow "a more excellent way" (12:31)

    B Love and other spiritual gifts (13:1–3)

        C Love positively defined (13:4a)

            D Love negatively defined (13:4b–6)

        C' Love positively defined (13:7)

    B' Love and spiritual gifts (13:8–13)

A' Continue in zeal to follow after spiritual gifts (14:1)[17]

---

14. For alternate constructions, see Fee, *First Epistle,* 654–55.

15. Bailey, *Mediterranean Eyes,* 352.

16. The quote is from Bailey, *Mediterranean Eyes,* 353. The numbers in the original have been replaced by letters to emphasize the chiastic structure of this section.

17. Bailey, *Mediterranean Eyes,* 353.

Paul's care in placing the subject of love at the center of all three levels emphasizes how much he desired his readers to get his point. It also shows that he understood fully the problems that afflicted the Corinthian house churches and how they could be solved.

To win the Saints to his side, he carefully and brilliantly set forth the manifold gifts of the Spirit that contributed so positively to the spiritual and temporal life of the Church in chapter 12. He made it clear that all spiritual gifts were derived from the one Godhead and were both honorable and necessary. But he also made sure that his readers understood that some gifts are more desirable than others. Indeed, there were greater gifts that he identifies in this chapter. But if selfish emulation were the motivation for the use of any gift,[18] its true purpose and blessing would be unrealized. Indeed, all the gifts would be good for nothing (οὐδείς, *oudeis,* 13:2). The Apostle, therefore, shows them the "way" (ὁδόν, *hodon,* 12:31b) to make sure the gifts are properly used and their benefits fully realized.[19]

By contrasting the various χαρίσματα (*charismata*), "spiritual gifts," including tongues, with ἀγάπη (*agapē*), "love," the Apostle highlighted for his readers the relative temporal nature of one against the eternal nature of the other and, in that way, emphasized the importance of the latter. In doing so, he in no way made the *charismata* any less valuable—the truth is, he heightened their value for mortality—but he was able to show, as a scholar noted, that "love is both for now and forever."[20] Thus, in this pericope, 13:1–3 show that without love, all other gifts—including faith, knowledge, prophecy, and tongues—are profitless. Verses 13:4–8a lists sixteen characteristics of love, seven affirmatives and nine opposites. Verses 13:8b–12 explains why all other gifts will end. And finally, in 13:13 he identifies faith, hope, and charity as the only gifts eternal in nature and again repeats that love is the greatest.

---

18. Paul's use of the verb *zēloō,* "jealously" or "envy," in 12:31a suggests that some of the Christians were motivated to use their gifts due to an ambitious or envious rivalry.

19. Findlay, "St. Paul's First Epistle," 896.

20. Fee, *First Epistle,* 628.

THE NECESSITY OF LOVE
(13:1–3)

Greek Text

1 Ἐὰν ταῖς γλώσσαις τῶν ἀνθρώπων λαλῶ καὶ τῶν ἀγγέλων, ἀγάπην δὲ μὴ ἔχω, γέγονα χαλκὸς ἠχῶν ἢ κύμβαλον ἀλαλάζον. 2 καὶ ἐὰν ἔχω προφητείαν καὶ εἰδῶ τὰ μυστήρια πάντα καὶ πᾶσαν τὴν γνῶσιν, καὶ ἐὰν ἔχω πᾶσαν τὴν πίστιν ὥστε ὄρη μεθιστάναι, ἀγάπην δὲ μὴ ἔχω, οὐθέν εἰμι. 3 καὶ ἐὰν ψωμίσω πάντα τὰ ὑπάρχοντά μου, καὶ ἐὰν παραδῶ τὸ σῶμά μου, ἵνα καυθήσομαι, ἀγάπην δὲ μὴ ἔχω, οὐδὲν ὠφελοῦμαι. [SBLGNT]

King James Version

1 Though I speak with the tongues of men and of angels, and have not charity, I am become as sounding brass, or a tinkling cymbal. 2 And though I have the gift of prophecy, and understand all mysteries, and all knowledge; and though I have all faith, so that I could remove mountains, and have not charity, I am nothing. 3 And though I bestow all my goods to feed the poor, and though I give my body to be burned, and have not charity, it profiteth me nothing.

New Rendition

1 If I were to speak in the tongues of men or even of angels, but did not have love, I would have become like a noisy gong or a clashing cymbal. 2 And if I should have prophetic powers and understand all mysteries and all knowledge, and if I should have complete faith so that I could move mountains, but did not have love, I am nothing! 3 And if I should give away all my possessions, and if I should give over my body that I be burned, but did not have love, I would gain no benefit.

Translation Notes and Comments

13:1 *Though I speak with the tongues of men and of angels, and have not charity / If I were to speak in the tongues of men or even of angels, but did not have love:* Verses 13:1–3 contain a series of contrary to fact conditional sentences. The grammatical sense of these is caught by the word "if" in our Rendition. By using these contrary to fact conditions,[21] Paul contrasts love above all the other gifts of the Spirit and elevates it to the highest position.

The verb λαλέω (*laleō*), "to speak," denotes any kind of human sound from whispering to yelling.[22] Paul, likely, used the implied pronoun "I" not in a personal sense but as referring to anyone. The phrase "tongues of men or even of angels" denotes all possible languages, both human and

---

21. Wallace, *Greek Grammar,* 471; 696–98.
22. Most often it denotes any kind of informal speech. BDAG, 582–83.

divine.[23] Paul excludes, then, any possibility of there being any others. When unaccompanied by love, all become nothing more than senseless noise.[24] His contrasting this gift first emphasizes its lack of importance not only to the gift of love but to all others.[25] Since the gift of tongues was a major point of interest but, unfortunately, also of contention among the Saints, it is not surprising that he did not want it to seem superior to love. On ἀγάπη (*agapē*), "charity/love," see "Excursus on Love/Charity" below.

I am become as sounding brass, or a tinkling cymbal / I would have become like a noisy gong or a clashing cymbal: The noun χαλκός (*chalkos*) refers to anything made out of copper, including instruments of bronze that are alloys composed of copper and a little zinc or tin. The verb ἠχέω (*ēcheō*) denotes a ringing, clashing, or clanging sound. To pick up this nuance, the participial phrase χαλκὸς ἠχῶν (*chalkos ēchōn*), "sounding brass" in the KJV, is translated as "a noisy gong" in our Rendition.[26] Since, however, this phrase is found nowhere in Greek literature in connection with a musical instrument, it is probable that Paul was referring to the bronze echoing vases that acted as acoustic amplifiers in theaters to enhance a speaker's voice.[27]

The verb ἀλαλάζον (*alalazon*), an onomatopoeic expression that literally means "to wail loudly," emphasizes the shrillness of the tone.[28] As an adjective with the word κύμβαλον (*kymbalon*), "cymbal," it connotes a very unpleasant sound and is, therefore, translated as "clashing" in our Rendition.[29] Paul's insistence that any supposedly inspired speaking when unmotivated by love was only a most unpleasant noise would have been shocking to his readers. It is likely, however, that he designed it to be so.[30]

Both bronze devices were, for Paul, an excellent metaphor for what he saw as the empty but noisy cacophony of the sophists and others who constantly harangued the people but who had nothing of real consequence to say except to promote themselves.[31] The truth was that, because these

---

23. R. P. Martin, *Worship in the Early Church*, rev. ed. (Grand Rapids, Mich.: Eerdmans, 1974), 43, along with others, argues that the two genitives infer "eloquence and ecstatic speech," but the context suggests Paul means human and divine languages.

24. Findlay, "St. Paul's First Epistle," 896.

25. Fitzmyer, *First Corinthians*, 491–92.

26. Louw-Nida, §14.80.

27. BDAG, 1076, gives both possibilities. See William Harris, "'Sounding Brass' and Hellenistic Technology," *Biblical Archaeology Review* 8 (January/February 1982): 38–41.

28. BDAG, 41; Louw-Nida, §25.139.

29. Louw-Nida, §14:82.

30. Thiselton, *First Epistle*, 1035–36.

31. Harris, "'Sounding Brass,'" 41. Paul was not the only one. Plato, *Prot.* 329a, described the oratory of certain sophists as a gong that reverberated long after it was struck.

philosophers and teachers had no love for them, they were using people to their own ends, including gaining tuition fees and more clients. Paul's point was that without love—that abiding concern for others—eloquence in speech—no matter its source—brings no mutually beneficial result. It is love and love alone that gives any tongue relevance and eternal quality.

13:2 *And though I have the gift of prophecy / And if I should have prophetic powers:* On "prophecy," see Translation Notes and the associated Analysis on 12:10. The context of the noun προφητεία (*prophēteia*), "prophecy," here refers to the full range of prophetic powers, including vaticination, revelation, and exhortation. The next two phrases ("all mysteries" and "all knowledge") show both the depth and breadth on which the power of prophecy draws.[32]

understand all mysteries / understand all mysteries: On "mysteries," see Translation Notes and the associated Analysis on 2:7. The emphasis in this phrase comes from the adjective πάντα (*panta*), "all." Paul is exaggerating for effect. The phrase shows that Paul is referring to the entire depth and breadth of the hidden and most sacred things of God.

all knowledge / all knowledge: On "knowledge," see Translation Notes and the associated Analysis on 12:8. Again, Paul exaggerates his point with the use of the adjective πάντα (*panta*), "all." The phrase connotes a full breadth of understanding of sacred things. For some of the Jewish Saints, it would have taken on an even wider nuance being a reference to the omniscience of Jehovah.[33]

though I have all faith, so that I could remove mountains / if I should have complete faith so that I could move mountains: For "faith," see Translation Notes and the associated Analysis on 12:9. As in the phrases above, the operative word here is the adjective πάντα (*panta*), "all." It gives a limited breadth but profound depth to the superlative gift of faith. That connotation is highlighted in Paul's use of the same imagery the Savior used about faith being able to remove a mountain (see Matt. 17:20; Mark 11:22–23).[34] The illustration defines faith, as used in this context, as an overwhelming operative power.[35] The Apostle, however, exaggerates the Savior's point.

---

32. Findlay, "St. Paul's First Epistle," 897.

33. The Dead Sea scrolls use the phase in 1QH[a], 19:8; 1QS, 11:18; 4Q418, 69.2.11.

34. The metaphor connoted either doing an extremely difficult task or an improbable occurrence. See Morna D. Hooker, *The Gospel According to Saint Mark*, Black's New Testament Commentary (Peabody: Hendrickson Publishers, 1991), 269; and R. T. France, *The Gospel According to Matthew* (Grand Rapids, Mich.: Eerdmans, 1985), 266.

35. His use of this example suggests he was "acquainted with the teaching" of the Master. Fee, *First Epistle*, 632, n. 32.

By using a resultant present infinitive, μεθιστάναι (*methistanai*), "to move," connoting a continuous action, the image he creates is that of removing one mountain after another.[36]

have not charity, I am nothing / did not have love, I am nothing: Paul's choice of words here is telling. They look to the value of the person who holds and expresses an unquestionable power of faith. The neuter singular adjective οὐδέν (*ouden*) denotes that which is worthless, pointless, or valueless.[37] The exaggeration stresses the absolute worthlessness of a loveless individual even when, hypothetically, he or she evidences complete and full faith.

13:3 ***And though I bestow all my goods to feed the poor / And if I should give away all my possessions:*** The KJV phrase "to feed the poor" is an extrapolation from the verb ψωμίζω (*psōmizō*), "to distribute, to dole out, or to give away." Since the words are not found in any Greek manuscripts, they are left out of our Rendition.[38] The verb *psōmizō* suggests the idea of doling out one's property bit by bit until there is nothing left.[39]

and though I give my body to be burned / And if I should give over my body that I be burned: The verb παραδίδωμι (*paradidōmi*) means "to hand over" with the idea of putting that which is surrendered into the full disposal of another.[40] In this case, it connotes the deliberate giving up of oneself for destruction. A number of early manuscripts have the present subjunctive καυχήσωμαι (*kauchēsōmai*), "I might glory," rather than the future indicative καυθήσομαι (*kauthēsomai*), "I might be burned." Much ink has been spilled arguing which is the better reading, with the ancient manuscript evidence being about evenly distributed.[41] Paul could be cautioning against those who push gospel prohibitions or requirements too far and, because these acts are not motivated by charity, bring little or no good. In our Rendition, we have taken "be burned" as the better reading because giving up one's life logically fits in with the other positive virtues that Paul is enumerating, whereas boasting is something Paul counsels against (for example, see 1:29; 3:21).[42] During Paul's time period, the idea of martyrdom

---

36. Wallace, *Greek Grammar,* 592–94; Findlay, "St. Paul's First Epistle," 897.

37. BDAG, 735.

38. Louw-Nida, §23.5 notes that one nuance of the word is feeding the hungry.

39. BDAG, 1100.

40. BDAG, 761–63.

41. Metzger, *Textual Commentary,* 497–98.

42. For arguments in support of καυθήσομαι (*kauthēsomai*), "to be burned," see J. K. Elliot, "In Favor of καυθήσομαι in 1 Corinthians 13:3," *Zeitschrift für die neutestamentliche Wissenschaft* 62 (1971): 297–98; Chrys C. Caragounis, "'To Boast' or 'To Be Burned'? The

by fire was unknown, although in older Jewish writings there were two examples.[43] The imagery here is most shocking and Paul, likely, intended it that way as a means of forcing his readers to recognize the worthlessness of even the most supreme acts of sacrifice when not properly motivated.[44]

have not charity, it profiteth me nothing / did not have love, I would gain no benefit: The passive of the verb ὠφελέω (*ōpheleō*) means "to receive help, be benefitted."[45] Paul shows his readers that the great sacrifice of giving one's life in a most torturous way gains no benefit whatsoever to the martyr if it is unmotivated by love. What nullifies the worth of such a sacrifice is that it is not motivated out of care or concern of others but to bring attention, perhaps even status, to the self.[46]

Analysis and Summary

Putting the first three verses in perspective, Elder McConkie has stated:

> These verses must be interpreted in the context of Paul's whole presentation on charity and spiritual gifts. They are a form of reasoning and argumentation designed to dramatize the pre-eminent position of charity among the attributes of godliness, and standing alone they are not to be taken literally. It is not possible, for instance, to have faith without first having charity, but by speaking as though faith to move mountains is as nothing compared to charity, the point is driven home that there is nothing so transcendent as having the pure love of Christ in one's soul. In principle, it is as though, in order to emphasize the importance of the family unit, a man should say: 'Though I gain exaltation itself, and have not my wife by my side, I shall have nothing'—a thing which is impossible, for exaltation consists in the continuation of the family unit in eternity.[47]

Crux of 1 Corinthians 13:3," *Svensk Exegetisk Årsbok* 60 (1995): 115–27; and J. H. Petzer, "Contextual Evidence in Favor of καυθήσομαι in 1 Corinthians 13:3," *New Testament Studies* 35 (1989): 229–53. For those supporting καυχήσομαι (*kauchēsomai*), "to glory," see Fee, *First Epistle*, 629 n. 19, 632–35; Thiselton, *First Epistle*, 1042–44; and Bailey, *Mediterranean Eyes*, 363–64.

43. Dan. 3:16–28; 4 Macc. 9:17–25. There was another way in which one's body could be burned that was more common during this time—by selling oneself into slavery in order to help others. This could entail submitting to very painful branding. See Thiselton, *First Epistle*, 1043. Branding of slaves, however, was not universally practiced except as a punishment for misconduct and, therefore, it is doubtful Paul had this in mind. See Jane F. Gardner, "Slavery and Roman Law," in *The Cambridge World History of Slavery*, 3 vols. (Cambridge: Cambridge University Press, 2011), 1:429.

44. Petzer, "Contextual Evidence," 233, 244–45.

45. BDAG, 1107–8.

46. Thiselton, *First Epistle*, 1049.

47. *DNTC*, 2:380.

Paul promised his readers in the previous chapter that he would show them "a more excellent way" (12:31), which he does in this chapter in 13:4–7. First, however, he must prove its necessity. He does this in the first three verses of this chapter by using five parallel hypotheses respecting tongues, prophecy, mystery, knowledge, and the devotion of goods or persons to God. He explains that the use of any of these impressive gifts and sacrifices, when unmotivated by love, is worthless.[48]

Paul's first thrust is against those who insisted that the gift of tongues is the highest expression and endorsement of superior spirituality (13:1). Indeed, from their point of view, the gift evidenced that they had spiritually arrived because they could speak by divine power both the languages of men and of angels.[49] With cutting irony, Paul compares the gift, if unmotivated by love, to incomprehensible and highly annoying clanging, gonging, and wailing. Paul's Corinthian audience would have easily responded to the imagery of bronze or brass instruments since vessels made by Corinthian coppersmiths were prized throughout the Mediterranean basin, resulting in a brisk trade.[50]

It must be emphasized that Paul is not attacking any of the spiritual gifts as either unimportant or unnecessary. He is emphasizing their valueless character on an eternal scale when exercised without proper motivation. The case is more particular with tongues, which has relevance only to mortality. His point is that when unmotivated by love, this gift is little more than senseless, irritating noise.

President Brigham Young recognized the importance of speaking with assisted divine power that filled the speaker with affection. He stated that "if men who are called to speak before a congregation rise full of the Holy Spirit and power of God, their countenances are sermons to the people. But if their affections, feelings, and desires are like the fool's eyes, to the ends of the earth, looking for this, that, and the other, and the kingdom of God is far from them, and not in all their affections, they may rise here and talk what they please, and it is but like sounding brass or a tinkling cymbal— mere empty, unmeaning sounds to the ears of the people."[51]

Paul's second thrust is against those who are overly taken with knowledge, both human and divine (13:2). His focus is on a profound prophetic

---

48. Findlay, "St. Paul's First Epistle," 896.

49. Fee, *First Epistle,* 630.

50. Herodotus, *Hist,* 4.180–200; Jerome Murphy-O'Connor, "Corinthian Bronze," *Revue biblique* 90 (1983): 80–93; Murphy-O'Conner, *St. Paul's Corinth,* 218.

51. Brigham Young, in *JD,* 8:142.

ability grounded (impossibly for mortals) on possessing an understanding of all mysteries and all knowledge. His metaphor combines the intellect of the philosopher with the inspiration of the seer.[52] In sum, he makes the possessor nearly omniscient. He shows that these gifts when expressed without love make the gifts worthless for they will not last into eternity.

His next thrust seems to be against those who put emphasis on "mighty deeds" (2 Cor. 12:12) generated by faith (13:2 in light of verses 12:9, 28). Certainly, moving mountains—if any of them had ever done so—would have evidenced tremendous spiritual power that none could question. It would also confirm the supreme height of their spirituality.[53] And yet Paul insists that not only is the deed worth nothing, so is the Saint who did the miracle. Again, the reason is that it was done neither to benefit others nor to serve God, but to bring glory to oneself.

He finalizes this portion of his message with two examples of self-sacrifice exaggerated to such an extent that they would catch his readers' attention (13:3). The first is that of parceling out *all* of one's property for the good of others. The end result could mean living homeless and in poverty. The second is that of giving one's life through the horrible method of immolation. In creating these images, Paul was deliberately using the power of shock to force upon his readers a reappraisal of their beliefs—compelling them to see, as it were, with new eyes so that they could come to a new understanding.[54]

Up to this point, Paul has carefully established that love is "a more excellent way" (12:31). He has shown that the benefit and worth of any of God's gifts can be gained only if they are motivated by love. The Greek noun Paul uses is ἀγάπη (*agapē*). The KJV translates the noun as "charity," but, as an LDS scholar noted, "the charity of which Paul speaks is more than simple love. It is the 'pure love of Christ' which God bestows 'upon all who are true followers of his Son, Jesus Christ'"[55] (Moro. 7:47–48). The Lord's

---

52. Findlay, "St. Paul's First Epistle," 897.

53. The idea is not hyperbole. The scriptures record two instances when this actually happened. See Moses 7:13; Ether 12:30. There are hints that there may have been others. See Jacob 4:6.

54. Petzer, "Contextual Evidence," 244–45; Anthony C. Thiselton, *New Horizons in Hermeneutics* (Grand Rapids, Mich.: Zondervan, 1997), 117–20, explores the use of the rhetorical device of "defamiliarization." This technique forces a rethinking and a new and deeper understanding of familiar and ordinary ideas by breaking the rules of usual descriptive presentations through the use of exaggerated and often shocking images. The end result forces the audience to better appreciate the point being made. Paul's purpose is to assist his readers in really understanding the importance of love.

55. Sperry, *Life and Letters*, 127.

definition of "charity" can be found in D&C 88:125, where he states that
this virtue consists of "the bond of perfectness and peace." The words echo
those of Paul to the Colossians, "And above all these things put on charity,
which is the bond of perfectness" (Col. 3:14). The Greek noun σύνδεσμος
(*syndesmos*), "bond," denotes that which "brings various entities into a unified relationship." The word, therefore, describes a "uniting force."[56] What
love unites and binds Paul describes with the noun τελειότης (*teleiotēs*),
"completeness, perfection."[57] Taking these two passages together, we see
that love is a kind of bond, one that binds all that is good together in perfect
harmony and peace. It is not surprising, then, that the Master has commanded his Saints to both seek and obtain it (16:14; D&C 121:45; 124:116;
2 Ne. 33:7–9; Alma 7:24; 1 Tim. 4:12; 2 Tim. 2:22; Titus 2:2; 2 Pet. 1:7).
These scriptures make it easy to see its necessity in order to be saved in
God's kingdom (Moro. 10:20–21).

All along, Paul has corroborated the theological "rights" of the "strong"
to exercise their freedom (ἐξουσία, *exousia*) and knowledge (γνῶσις,
gnōsis). He has also continually insisted that their knowledge and freedom
must be bounded by love, a love that, when fully practiced, showed respect
for and understanding of the "weak." Such love protected the weak by
allowing them to fall neither into error nor into poverty. Indeed, it would
protect and even enhance both their self-respect and status as children
of God. The result would be a leveling of differences between social rank,
wealth, and prestige. It would also smooth out the differences between
genders and parties, bringing the unity that Paul so greatly desired and that
the Corinthian Saints so desperately needed.[58]

Joseph Smith nicely summarized Paul's intent. After reading 13:2, the
Prophet said, "Though a man should become mighty, do great things, over-
turn mountains, perform mighty works, and should then turn from his high
station to do evil, to eat and drink with the drunken, all his former deeds
would not save him, but he would go to destruction! As you increase in
innocence and virtue, as you increase in goodness, let your hearts expand,
let them be enlarged towards others; you must be long-suffering, and bear
with the faults and errors of mankind."[59]

---

56. BDAG, 966.
57. BDAG, 996.
58. Thiselton, *First Epistle*, 821.
59. "History, 1838–1856, Volume C-1 Addenda," 41; spelling and punctuation
standardized.

CHARACTERISTICS AND ACTIONS OF LOVE (13:4–8A)

Greek Text

4 Ἡ ἀγάπη μακροθυμεῖ, χρηστεύεται ἡ ἀγάπη, οὐ ζηλοῖ ἡ ἀγάπη, οὐ περπερεύεται, οὐ φυσιοῦται, 5 οὐκ ἀσχημονεῖ, οὐ ζητεῖ τὰ ἑαυτῆς, οὐ παροξύνεται, οὐ λογίζεται τὸ κακόν, 6 οὐ χαίρει ἐπὶ τῇ ἀδικίᾳ, συγχαίρει δὲ τῇ ἀληθείᾳ· 7 πάντα στέγει, πάντα πιστεύει, πάντα ἐλπίζει, πάντα ὑπομένει. 8 Ἡ ἀγάπη οὐδέποτε πίπτει. [SBLGNT]

King James Version

4 Charity suffereth long, and is kind; charity envieth not; charity vaunteth not itself, is not puffed up, 5 Doth not behave itself unseemly, seeketh not her own, is not easily provoked, thinketh no evil; 6 Rejoiceth not in iniquity, but rejoiceth in the truth; 7 Beareth all things, believeth all things, hopeth all things, endureth all things. 8a Charity never faileth:

New Rendition

4 Love is patient, love is kind, love is not jealous, does not brag, is not conceited. 5 Does not behave rudely, is not self-serving, is not easily angered, does not hold a grudge. 6 It does not delight in wickedness, but delights in truth. 7 It bears all things, believes all things, hopes all things, endures all things. 8a Love never fails.

Translation Notes and Comments

Throughout this section, Paul uses verbs, not adjectives, as he defines love. His focus is, therefore, not on the nature of love (that is, its timeless qualities) but on its actions (that is, how it manifests itself in life).[60] Since it is difficult to make an exact translation of this grammatical form from Greek into English, our Rendition follows the KJV in using adjectives in some verses since they adequately carry Paul's meaning.

13:4 *Charity suffereth long / Love is patient:* The verb μακρωθυμέω (*makrōthymeō*) has two denotations. One is "to bear up under provocation without complaint" while the other is "to remain tranquil while waiting."[61] The two combine to expresses love's ability to wait patiently for the proper time or circumstance before taking any kind of direct action (compare James 5:7–8, where the same verb is used).[62]

is kind / love is kind: The verb χρηστεύομαι (*chrēsteuomai*), "to be kind," is found only here in the New Testament, making it hard to define precisely

---

60. Craig, "First Epistle," 172.
61. BDAG, 612.
62. Anderson, *Understanding Paul*, 120.

because it lacks multiple contexts through which precision is gained. It carries a range of meanings, including being loving and merciful, in addition to being kind.[63] The weight of the verb is on providing something beneficial to another as a kindness.[64] Since the verb connotes acts that are warm, thoughtful, caring, and generous,[65] our Rendition stays with the KJV in translating it as "is kind."

charity envieth not / love is not jealous: On the verb ζηλόω (*zēloō*), "be jealous," see Translation Notes on 12:31. The verb here carries the very negative connotation of being filled with envy, resentment, even anger over another's good fortune because of pride.[66] The force of the word is in the depth of the feeling. In the LXX it is used to translate the Hebrew קַנֵּא (*qinnē'*), which refers to very intense emotions, especially those of jealousy and envy.[67] The action of not being jealous or envious would certainly separate the true Christian from his false counterpart in the status seeking and social climbing environment of Corinth where any success of another was looked upon, at best, begrudgingly and, at worst, with burning envy.[68]

charity vaunteth not itself / does not brag: The verb περπερεύομαι (*perpereuomai*), "to brag," carries the idea of heaping praise upon oneself.[69] The noun refers to one who constantly boasts about his or her accomplishments.[70] Paul's point is that love never "plays the braggart."[71]

is not puffed up / is not conceited: For the verb φυσιόομαι (*physioomai*), "become puffed up, conceited," see Translation Notes on 4:6 with associated Analysis. The verb points to an inflated ego manifesting itself in arrogant behavior and feelings of self-importance.[72] It is self-conceit at its worst and stands opposite of self-respect. For that reason the verb is translated as "conceited" in our Rendition. The vice that promotes this ungodly behavior is pride. That Paul denounces this wickedness three times in this epistle

---

63. BDAG, 1089.

64. Louw-Nida, §88.67. In *1 Clem.* 14:3, the verb is used to indicate a very dynamic action motivated by the will to do another good and is translated as "showing kindness." See also Anderson, *Understanding Paul,* 120.

65. Spicq, *Agape,* 2:151; Anderson, *Understanding Paul,* 121.

66. BDAG, 427.

67. BDB, 888–89; E. Reuter, "qn', qin'â; qannā'; qannô'" in *TDOT,* 13:47–58.

68. Thiselton, *First Epistle,* 1048.

69. BDAG, 808.

70. Barrett, *First Epistle,* 303; Spicq, *Agape,* 2:153.

71. Moulton and Milligan, *Vocabulary,* 510; Robertson and Plummer, *Critical and Exegetical Commentary,* 293; Anderson, *Understanding Paul,* 120.

72. BDAG, 1069.

(4:6, 18–19; 5:2) shows that it is one of his major concerns.[73] He, therefore, stresses that love avoids, at all cost, ostentatious and conceited behavior.

13:5 *Doth not behave itself unseemly / Does not behave rudely:* The verb ἀσχημονέω (*aschēmoneō*), "to behave disgracefully, dishonorably, indecently,"[74] is also found in 7:36 and points to actions that go well beyond propriety. Paul used the adjectival form, ἀσχήμων (*aschēmōn*), in 12:23 to allude to those parts of the body that were not presentable in public. In all three cases where the idea appears, it stands in contrast to that which is courteous, proper, and in good taste. It is, therefore, the opposite of good manners.[75] Since the English verb "rude" describes a person who has a comparatively low state of mind and culture and more especially a dearth of sensitivity toward the feelings of those around him or her, the adverbial form is used in our Rendition.[76] One who loves, on the other hand, does that which is proper, in good taste, and makes others feel comfortable.

seeketh not her own / is not self-serving: The KJV phrase accurately captures the structure of the Greek it translates, οὐ ζητεῖ τὰ ἑαυτῆς (*ou zētei ta heautēs*), but does not exactly convey its meaning in modern English. The phrase means that love "does not seek its own interests" and conveys the idea that it is not self-promoting or insistent on getting its own way.[77] Our Rendition, therefore, translates the idea as "not self-serving."

is not easily provoked / is not easily angered: The basic sense of the verb παροξύνω (*paroxynō*) means "to urge, spur on, stimulate" but especially "to irritate" or "provoke to anger," and in the passive, it means "to be irritated, angered."[78] The adjective ὀξύς (*oxys*), from which the verb παροξύνω (*paroxynō*) is derived, has the sense of "sharp, keen,"[79] and when applied to emotions, it denotes very sharp or keen feelings. On the light side, it refers to being touchy or overly sensitive; in the middle, it means being piqued or irritated; on the heavy side, it refers to anger that expresses itself in sharp disagreement and contention.[80] The context here points to the offense taken when one's self-regard has been pricked or punctured. Paul's point

---

73. Craig, "First Epistle," 175.

74. BDAG, 147; LSJ, 267; Anderson, *Understanding Paul,* 122.

75. Thiselton, *First Epistle,* 1049.

76. *Dictionary of Synonyms,* 704, s.v. "rude."

77. Thiselton, *First Epistle,* 1050.

78. LSJ, 1342–43; BDAG, 780.

79. LSJ, 1236.

80. BDAG, 780; Heinrich Seessemann, "παροξύνω, παροξυσμός," in *TDNT,* 5:857; Anderson, *Understanding Paul,* 123.

is that love does not become upset, irritated, embittered, or angry over injuries whether perceived or real.[81]

thinketh no evil / does not hold a grudge: The verb λογίζομαι (*logizomai*) means to reckon or calculate. In a commercial sense, it means to keep track of credits and debits. When associated with mental activity, it has two aspects: The first denotes pondering and deep thought. The second looks to careful consideration, particularly in the keeping of mental records for the purpose of some future action.[82] Paul associates it with the neuter singular adjective κακόν (*kakon*), used nominally to mean "evil, wrong," referring specifically to actions that are harmful or injurious to an individual.[83] Paul is saying that love does not keep track of injuries received and, therefore, never seeks vengeance.[84] In our Rendition, we have translated it as "does not hold a grudge." In this it follows the Lord's admonition in LXX Zechariah 8:17 that prohibits God's people from plotting evil against their neighbors.

13:6 *Rejoiceth not in iniquity / It does not delight in wickedness:* The verb χαίρω (*chairō*), denotes a state of wellbeing and can be translated as "rejoice,"[85] but it also carries the nuance of taking pleasure or delight in something. The noun ἀδικία (*adikia*) looks more specifically at "an act that violates standards of right conduct" and more broadly denotes all wrongdoing.[86] Since the noun is set against ἀλήθεια (*alētheia*), "truth," in the connected phrase (see below), it connotes deliberate lies and deceits that hurt others.[87] An example, coming from earlier in the epistle, would be the selfish and deceitful actions of certain members in taking others to gentile courts to unjustly get their property (6:1–2).[88] That deed is, admittedly, the worst example. The more usual sin would be gloating or delighting in some heavy loss by another member of the Church.[89]

rejoiceth in the truth / delights in truth: The verb συγχαίρω (*syngchairō*), "rejoice, delight," has the same root as the verb χαίρω (*chairō*) in the

---

81. Robertson and Plummer, *Critical and Exegetical Commentary*, 294; Thiselton, *First Epistle*, 1052.

82. Louw-Nida, §§30.9; 29.4.

83. BDAG, 501.

84. Fitzmyer, *First Corinthians*, 496; Anderson, *Understanding Paul*, 123.

85. BDAG, 1075.

86. Louw-Nida, §88.21; BDAG, 20.

87. In 3 Ezra 4:33–39, ἀλήθεια (*alētheia*) and ἀδικία (*adikia*) are set against each other to highlight how bad certain deeds can be.

88. Thiselton, *First Epistle*, 1054.

89. Fitzmyer, *First Corinthians*, 496.

preceding phrase. The prefix συν- (*syn*), however, intensifies the quality and adds the idea of participation since it means to do something *with* another person. Here it connotes taking great delight *with* another in some truth.[90] The noun ἀλήθεια (*alētheia*), "truth," denotes the reality on which appearance sits. For Paul and other Christians, truth is gospel doctrine.[91] It is grounded on the Atonement of the Savior and is expressed in his teachings. Paul's point is that love applauds, rejoices, or delights with others in finding and sharing truth.[92] Because love has no agenda, it does not fear truth and, therefore, boldly seeks it wherever it can be found with the intent of delightedly sharing it.[93]

13:7 Beareth all things / It bears all things: The difficulty in translating this verse is how to convey the force of Paul's fourfold use of the nominal neuter plural adjective πάντα (*panta*), "all things." The word conveys the idea of completeness and wholeness.[94] It connotes the absence of all limits.[95] It does not, therefore, define what might otherwise be seen as the inclusive limits of love. Rather it forces an expansion that reveals its full limitlessness and all-encompassing nature.

The verb στέγω (*stegō*) has two definitions that work here: The first means to keep something confidential, that is, to pass over it in silence. The other definition is to bear up under difficulties with emphasis on endurance.[96] The idea the verb conveys is keeping quiet about what is displeasing about another person. This quality is grounded in love's continually enduring nature that makes allowances for another's weakness.[97]

believeth all things / believes all things: The verb πιστεύω (*pisteuō*), "believe," means "to give credit to" or "to entrust." It suggests more than mere credence but shows a willingness on the part of the lover to take another's word rather than being unduly suspicious.[98] It suggests such strong faith in the other that one is completely willing to rely on him or her.[99]

90. Anderson, *Understanding Paul*, 123.

91. Gottfried Quell, Gerhard Kittel, and Rudolf Bultmann, "ἀλήθεια," in *TDNT*, 1:232–47; BDAG, 42–43.

92. Spicq, *Agape*, 2:158; BDAG, 953.

93. Nygren, *Agape and Eros*, 77–78.

94. BDAG, 782–84.

95. Louw-Nida, §§59.23; 78.44.

96. BDAG, 942; Anderson, *Understanding Paul*, 123.

97. Fitzmyer, *First Corinthians*, 496.

98. Spicq, *Agape*, 1:159.

99. Rudolf Bultmann and Artur Weiser, "πιστεύω, πίστις, πιστός, πιστόω, ἄπιστος, ἀπιστέω, ἀπιστία, ὀλιγόπιστος, ὀλιγοπιστία," in *TDNT*, 6:174–228.

hopeth all things / hopes all things: The verb ἐλπίζω (*elpizō*), "hope," denotes "favorable and confident expectations." It looks to the future with complete assurance of promised blessings, especially those promised in the gospel message.[100] In Paul's context, it is the ability to see a good outcome in the potential of other people and, therefore, provide a willingness to stay with them.

endureth all things / endures all things: The verb ὑπομένω (*hypomenō*), "to stand one's ground, hold out, endure" denotes something staying in place longer than is expected, especially as it pertains to maintaining a belief or course of action in face of opposition.[101]

13:8 ***Charity never faileth / Love never fails:*** The verb πίπτω (*piptō*), here translated "fail," has a wide range of semantic nuances, including falling down, losing station or position, being ruined or destroyed, and failing in one's faith.[102] The context here suggests something becoming invalid, falling apart, or collapsing.[103] The phrase, therefore, does not mean that love never ends,[104] albeit Paul brings in that quality in 13:13. Since the English verb "fail" means the abandonment or omission of something that is expected or required of a person, it is used in our Rendition.[105] Paul's point is that love will never become invalid or unnecessary. It will never fall apart when needed. It continually and consistently meets all that is required of it and always will. In sum, "it stands when all else falls."[106]

Analysis and Summary

Paul's list of the qualities of ἀγάπη (*agapē*), "love," likely stung some of his readers. His clear and pointed exposition, however, was greatly needed in those house churches where self-interest and impropriety marked even the most sacred of moments. His sting would have rested hardest on those whose actions were motivated by self-interest. This would include those who insisted on having things their way; who came early to sacrament service in order to get the best seats; who refused to share their bounty; who interrupted the services by speaking in tongues; who, in an effort to show spiritual superiority,

---

100. Rudolf Bultmann and Karl Heinrich Rengstorf, "ἐλπίς, ἐλπίζω," in *TDNT,* 2:517–33.
101. BDAG, 1039; Louw-Nida, §25.174.
102. See Louw-Nida, §2:197–98.
103. BDAG, 815.
104. Fitzmyer, *First Corinthians,* 497. The authors take this point of view with all due respect to the RSV, NRSV, NEB, and Ogden and Skinner, *Verse by Verse,* 143.
105. *Dictionary of Synonyms,* 319, "failure."
106. Fitzmyer, *First Corinthians,* 497.

paraded their gifts and blessings; or who, in an effort to raise their own self-importance, treated those whom they felt were inferior rudely and with great disrespect. That sting, however, would not have missed those who were the objects of rudeness, but who also allowed themselves to feel irritated, piqued, or angered by ill treatment. Among this group, it would have hit particularly hard those who were nursing their wounds and planning to pay the offending party back in their own coin.[107] Paul shows that if any of these people truly loved, they would have been incapable of self-serving, abusive, or unforgiving actions. They would have, rather, put others before themselves.[108] Indeed, love nips the problem in the bud on the one hand by never giving offense and on the other by not keeping track of any personal hurt.

Speaking of the power of love, Elder Neal A. Maxwell said:

> The men and women of Christ magnify their callings without magnifying themselves. Whereas the natural man says "Worship me" and "Give me thine power," the men and women of Christ seek to exercise power by long-suffering and unfeigned love. (See Moses 1:12; 4:3; D&C 121:41.)
>
> Whereas the natural man vents his anger, the men and women of Christ are "not easily provoked." (1 Cor. 13:5.) Whereas the natural man is filled with greed, the men and women of Christ "seeketh not [their] own." (1 Cor. 13:5.)
>
> Whereas the natural man seldom denies himself worldly pleasures, the men and women of Christ seek to bridle all their passions. (See Alma 38:12.)
>
> Whereas the natural man covets praise and riches, the men and women of Christ know such things are but the "drop." (D&C 117:8.) Human history's happiest irony will be that the covenant-keeping, unselfish individuals will finally receive "all that [the] Father hath"! (D&C 84:38.)[109]

As noted above, 13:6–7 reveals the limitlessness and all-encompassing nature of love. Though the translation does not follow the actual syntax of the Greek to the degree our Rendition does, the idea conveyed in the Revised English Bible gets at the force of Paul's thought. It states, "There is nothing love cannot face; there is no limit to its faith, its hopes, its endurance." Or, as given in another translation, "It bears everything, believes everything, hopes everything, endures everything."[110]

The Apostle is not, however, saying that love is content with absolutely everything just the way it is. He is not opening the door to "servile mediocrity"

---

107. Bruce, *1 and 2 Corinthians*, 127; compare Bailey, *Mediterranean Eyes*, 374.

108. Thiselton, *First Epistle*, 1051.

109. Neal A. Maxwell, "Put Off the Natural Man, and Come Off Conquerer," *Ensign* 30 (November 1990): 160.

110. Collins, *First Corinthians*, 478.

as some modern antagonists insist.[111] We must remember it was the Corinthians who coined the phrase "all things are lawful" (see Translation Notes on 6:12 and related Analysis). Paul, however, insists on differentiation and discrimination, more especially in worship and prophecy. In no way is ἀγάπη (*agapē*) docile or conformist. It seeks for neither the quiet life nor settles for mediocre performance. Therefore, as one scholar noted, it "never tires of support, never loses faith, never exhausts hope, never gives up."[112] Because it lacks any self-interest, it pushes for creativity, innovation, transformation, and reaching for the ideal.[113] We must never confuse ἀγάπη (*agapē*) with sentimentality, which takes the easy way out by refusing firm action, refusing to do the distasteful, or not looking at the long-term good. In the process, it leaves the loved one uncorrected in his or her sin, thus reinforcing the very flaw that true love would never tolerate.[114] Indeed, *agapē* has its tough side. Nonetheless, though love expects growth, it also allows for time.

God does not generally grant the gift of a fullness of love all at once. With keen insight, one LDS scholar noted:

> The concept of love is not dramatic sacrifice but steady relationship. It is not a giant gift on a special occasion but the continued support of personal caring. . . . The tragedy of many unloving people is that they only imagine they love. In truth they want to love but do not pay the price to move from wishful thinking to reality. As a good teacher, Paul confronts the Saints with their inconsistencies. The impatient jerk on a child, the harsh word to someone trying to assist, or the cold shoulder to a spouse all reveal a smallness of soul. Paul sketches gross egotism, but it is subtly disguised in appearing to care but being too busy, or in blaming others for not caring. . . . Parents in tune with their divine calling know that eternal potential is wrapped up with their helpless and uncoordinated infant. Parents of resistant teenagers are wise if they remember that the potential is still there, and gospel brothers and sisters with this vision will do the same. The future is unlocked by pure love, which "believes" and "hopes all things. . . ."

For Paul, knowledge must be supplemented and revised, but love never fails (1 Cor. 13:8). The gospel experience of unselfish love is closer

---

111. Among those critics who see Paul's words as, firstly, permitting all that is weak, low, or botched into the circle of acceptance and, secondly, excluding the reach for the higher and the better are the following: Friedrich Nietzsche, *Works—XVI: The Antichrist and Twilight of the Gods* (Brooklyn: Gordon Press, 1974), aphorisms 5–7, 18; and Michel Foucault, *Discipline and Punish* (New York: Pantheon Press, 1977), 190–94. Their viewpoint draws largely from not understanding the force of Paul's Greek.

112. Thiselton, *First Epistle*, 1057.

113. Thiselton, *First Epistle*, 1057.

114. Leon Morris, *Testaments of Love* (Grand Rapids, Mich.: Eerdmans, 1981), 25.

to eternity than anything else. It may be counterfeited by immorality and cheapened in superficial society. But genuine love is a taste of eternity.[115]

THE PERMANENCE OF LOVE (13:8B–13)

Greek Text

Εἴτε δὲ προφητεῖαι, καταργηθήσονται· εἴτε γλῶσσαι, παύσονται· εἴτε γνῶσις, καταργηθήσεται. 9 ἐκ μέρους γὰρ γινώσκομεν καὶ ἐκ μέρους προφητεύομεν· 10 ὅταν δὲ ἔλθῃ τὸ τέλειον, τὸ ἐκ μέρους καταργηθήσεται. 11 ὅτε ἤμην νήπιος, ἐλά-λουν ὡς νήπιος, ἐφρόνουν ὡς νήπιος, ἐλογιζόμην ὡς νήπιος· ὅτε γέγονα ἀνήρ, κατήργηκα τὰ τοῦ νηπίου. 12 βλέπομεν γὰρ ἄρτι δι᾽ ἐσόπτρου ἐν αἰνίγματι, τότε δὲ πρόσωπον πρὸς πρόσωπον· ἄρτι γινώσκω ἐκ μέρους, τότε δὲ ἐπιγνώσομαι καθὼς καὶ ἐπεγνώσθην. 13 νυνὶ δὲ μένει πίστις, ἐλπίς, ἀγάπη· τὰ τρία ταῦτα, μείζων δὲ τούτων ἡ ἀγάπη. [SBLGNT]

King James Version

8b but whether there be prophecies, they shall fail; whether there be tongues, they shall cease; whether there be knowledge, it shall vanish away. 9 For we know in part, and we prophesy in part. 10 But when that which is perfect is come, then that which is in part shall be done away. 11 When I was a child, I spake as a child, I understood as a child, I thought as a child: but when I became a man, I put away childish things. 12 For now we see through a glass, darkly; but then face to face: now I know in part; but then shall I know even as also I am known. 13 And now abideth faith, hope, charity, these three; but the greatest of these is charity.

New Rendition

8b If there are prophecies, they will pass away; if there is speaking in tongues, it will cease; if there is knowledge, it will pass away. 9 For we now understand imperfectly, and we prophesy imperfectly. 10 But when perfection comes, that which is imperfect will pass away. 11 When I was a child, I spoke like a child, I thought like a child, I reasoned like a child. When I became a man, I set aside childish things. 12 Because now we see indirectly in a mirror, but then face to face. Now I understand imperfectly, but then I will understand completely even as I have been completely understood. 13 And now these three things endure, faith, hope, and love, but the greatest of them is love.

---

115. Anderson, *Understanding Paul*, 119, 124.

Translation Notes and Comments

13:8b *but whether there be prophecies, they shall fail / If there are prophecies, they will pass away:* This and the next two phrases are introduced by the conjunction εἴτε (*eite*), "whether" or "if."[116] The conjunction emphasizes Paul's understanding that, contrary to never-failing love, certain gifts will become obsolete and therefore no longer used and therefore set aside. In this phrase the Apostle looks specifically at προφητεῖαι (*prophēteiai*), "prophecies," the plural here denoting the various kinds of prophesying that fall under "Spirit-inspired dynamic and effective preaching" (12:10) that includes both vaticination and exhortation.[117] The verb καταργέω (*katargeō*) means "to cause something to cease to exist."[118] Paul uses the future passive form indicating that, for the present, the gift is necessary but, in the future, it will not be.

whether there be tongues, they shall cease / if there is speaking in tongues, it will cease: The verb παύω (*pauō*) in the passive denotes the cessation of an action.[119] Again, Paul uses the future tense to indicate that it is the future that will find no use for tongues.

whether there be knowledge, it shall vanish away / if there is knowledge, it will pass away: Here the word γνῶσις (*gnōsis*), "knowledge," represents the God-given gift of understanding the things of the divine.[120] Paul again uses the future passive of the verb καταργέω (*katargeō*), "cease to exist, pass away," to indicate that even this inspired and powerful kind of knowledge will not be needed in the future.[121]

13:9 *For we know in part, and we prophesy in part / For we now understand imperfectly, and we prophesy imperfectly:* This verse explains why the superb gifts of prophecy, tongues, and knowledge will eventually cease. The phrase ἐκ μέρους (*ek merous*), "in part, partially, incompletely, imperfectly,"[122] being placed at the first of the clause, holds emphatic position. It acts, therefore, to emphasize Paul's point that the best that humans can do, even when given spiritual assistance, is to know things of the past, the present, or the future only imperfectly.

---

116. Louw-Nida, §§89.65; 90.26.

117. Fitzmyer, *First Corinthians*, 497.

118. BDAG, 525–6.

119. BDAG, 790.

120. Louw-Nida, §28.1, 19.

121. In classical literature, the verb denotes leaving something unemployed or idle. LSJ, 908.

122. BDAG, 633–34.

13:10 *But when that which is perfect is come, then that which is in part shall be done away / But when perfection comes, that which is imperfect will pass away:* The operative word in this phrase is the substantive adjective τέλειος (*teleios*). It denotes that which meets the highest of standards, but also that which is fully developed, whole, finished, full grown, mature, and complete. By extension, then, it can mean perfect. This calls to mind Christ's admonition in the Sermon on the Mount, "Be ye therefore perfect, even as your Father which is in heaven is perfect" (Matt. 5:48). The phrase ὅταν δὲ ἔλθῃ (*hotan de elthē*), "but when [something] comes," means whenever some event finally takes place. Its use by Paul suggests that the coming perfection he is looking for is likely a ways off. At that point, only that which is perfect and complete will survive and that which is ἐκ μέρους (*ek merous*), "imperfect, incomplete," καταργηθήσεται (*katargēthēsetai*), "shall pass away."

The problems with the temporal expressions of the gifts of the Spirit, as great and necessary as they are in the present, are twofold: first, many (like healings and tongues) are peculiar to mortality only and, therefore, have no eternal use; second, many (like knowledge and wisdom) are only fractions of what can be realized. Every gift in its temporal fashion ever remains incomplete both in quality and quantity and, thus, must either yield to that which is whole, full, or perfect or become completed and amplified to that level.[123]

13:11 *When I was a child, I spake as a child, I understood as a child, I thought as a child / When I was a child, I spoke like a child, I thought like a child, I reasoned like a child:* Paul's use of the noun νήπιος (*nēpios*), "child," stands in contrast to his use of the word in 3:1. There its connotation was pejorative and referred to that which was infantile or childish. Here its use stands in contrast to τέλειος (*teleios*), "mature," and therefore carries the value-neutral and more literal sense of "child."[124] In this phrase, Paul uses three verbs in the imperfect active tense. The force of the tense is that of continual past action.[125] The first verb ἐλάλουν (*elaloun*),[126] "spoke," denotes that as a child, each soul always speaks as a child. He or she is incapable of anything else. The second, ἐφρόνουν (*ephronoun*), "to think,

---

123. Findlay, "St. Paul's First Epistle," 900; Gerhard Delling, "τέλειος," in *TDNT*, 8:67–78.

124. Though the noun can refer to any person from infancy through adolescence, the context suggests an older child. BDAG, 671.

125. Thiselton, *First Epistle*, 1066.

126. It is often used to designate informal conversations. BDAG, 582.

understand," has a rather wide range of meanings. Though it can refer to simple mental processes, the context here focuses more on giving "carefuly consideration to something . . . to develop an attitude based on careful thought."[127] In either case, the context underscores the idea of limited ability. The child can plan and form opinions only on a continually limited basis. The last verb, ἐλογιζόμην (*elogizomēn*), means "to calculate, evaluate," or "to reason."[128] Again, the context suggests the continually limited ability of a child, in this case, to evaluate or reason.

> *but when I became a man, I put away childish things / When I became a man, I set aside childish things:* The two perfect active verbs in this phrase, γέγονα (*gegona*), "became," and κατήργηκα (*katērgēka*), "put away, set aside," stand in contrast to the three imperfect verbs used in the first phrase. The perfect tense shows the finality of an event. Once an individual becomes a man or woman, there is no going back, and once childlike things are put away, they are put away forever. On the meaning of the verb κατεργέω (*katergeō*), see Translation Notes on 13:8b above. Here, the word stresses the fact that the mature turn their backs on the things of childhood.[129]

> **13:12** *For now we see through a glass, darkly; but then face to face / Because now we see indirectly in a mirror, but then face to face:* With the use of the introductory γάρ (*gar*), "for," Paul signals that he is now going to explain what he has said in 13:9–11. He uses an analogy to show why the partial must give way to the whole, the immature to the mature. To do so he effectively sets up a contrast using ἄρτι (*arti*), "now," which stresses the present moment, with τότε (*tote*), "then," which looks to the future. He enhances the contrast by using the conjunction δέ (*de*), "but." The preposition διά (*dia*) denotes something done by use of an instrument and here means "through the means of" or "via."[130] In this case the instrument is a ἔσοπτρον (*esoptron*), "a mirror."[131] Anciently most mirrors were made of

---

127. BDAG, 1065–66.

128. BDAG, 597–98.

129. Reginald St. John Parry, *The First Epistle of Paul the Apostle to the Corinthians: With Introduction and Notes: Cambridge Greek Text,* 2d ed. (Cambridge: Cambridge University Press, 1926), 195.

130. BDAG, 223–26.

131. Because the word is used rarely in the New Testament, the translation as "mirror" is based on the use of the word *eisoptron* used in late antiquity to refer to a looking-glass. See Greek Word Study Tool, http://www.perseus.tufts.edu/hopper/morph?l=e%29so%2Fptrou&la=greek&can=e%29so%2Fptrouo&prior=di%27&d=Perseus:text:1999.01.01 55:book=I%20Corinthians:chapter=13:verse=12&i=1#lexicon.

polished bronze.[132] Mirrors made in Corinth were highly valued because of the fine workmanship used in their making.[133] Paul, however, notes that there is a problem with the reflection. He describes what one sees as ἐν αἰνίγματι (*en ainigmati*), literally "in a riddle." The expression, however, also could mean "in an indirect way."[134] Paul is *not,* therefore, referring to the quality of the mirror. Poorly made mirrors would, indeed, give a distorted, dimmed, or unclear image, but that is not his point. His point is that no matter how high the quality of the mirror, it does not reproduce the real thing, but only an indirect nonreality of it.[135] For that reason, our Rendition translates the phrase as "indirectly in a mirror."

In contrast, when the τέλειον (*teleion*), "perfection, maturity," comes, it will allow one to see him- or herself (and anything else, for that matter), not as an indirect reflection, but fully and completely revealed, that is, "face to face."

now I know in part; but then shall I know even as also I am known /
Now I understand imperfectly, but then I will understand completely even
as I have been completely understood: The verb γινώσκω (*ginōskō*) means "to know" to a certain level about something or someone. Because it also denotes "grasping the meaning of" something, it is translated as "understand" in our Rendition.[136] The verb carries a nuance of limitation. Paul contrasts the word with the verb ἐπιγινώσκω (*epiginōskō*), to know with a high "degree of thoroughness or competence."[137] Paul looks at the temporal experience noting the impossibility of knowing anything fully, and that includes oneself. However, when the τέλειον (*teleion*) comes, the Saints will understand all things, more especially themselves, even as God understands.[138]

---

132. Adding zinc to copper made the product, bronze, very durable.

133. Henry S. Robinson, *Corinth: A Brief History of the City and a Guide to the Excavations* (Athens: American School of Classical Studies at Athens, 1972), 5. By the first century, glass mirrors began to be introduced, but because these were generally inferior in giving an accurate reflection, metal mirrors remained popular for quite some time. See J. D. Douglas, *The Illustrated Bible Dictionary,* part 2 (Nottingham: Inter-Varsity Press, 1980), 1011–12.

134. BDAG, 27.

135. Fee, *First Epistle,* 647–48; Fitzmyer, *First Corinthians,* 499–500; Thiselton, *First Epistle,* 1068–70.

136. BDAG, 199–201.

137. Louw-Nida, §28.2. The word can be a synonym for γινώσκω (*ginōskō*), but it often carries the nuance of knowing fully and deeply. See Rudolf Bultmann, "γινώσκω, γνῶσις, ἐπιγινώσκω, ἐπίγνωσις," in *TDNT,* 1:689–714.

138. Fitzmyer, *First Corinthians,* 500–501.

13:13 *And now abideth faith, hope, charity, these three; but the greatest of these is charity / And now these three things endure, faith, hope, and love, but the greatest of them is love:* With this sentence, Paul brings his argument to a close. As simple as the sentence looks, it does present a series of translation problems. The first is how to take the phrase νυνὶ δὲ (*nyni de*), "and now." It can be translated with either temporal or logical force. Logically it means "but, as it is." Understanding the phrase this way allows one to see Paul's words as saying essentially, "The fact is, these three gifts remain forever." Temporally the phrase means "at this present time," and looks to the immediate moment. Understanding the phrase is this way, Paul is saying, "These three virtues abide in the present." The present active verb μένει (*menei*) does not help with the difficulty since it means not only "to continue to exist" or "to remain," but also "to await" or "wait for" something to happen. Note that these two disparate definitions give the verb both a present and future color. Though a temporal understanding suggests some kind of present situation, it does not negate a future one as well. Therefore, it seems best to take a middle course here, seeing faith, hope, and love as remaining active both in present and also in the future.[139] That would mean that faith, hope, and love are not just for eternity. They exist in the present and can, therefore, be directing forces of the lives of the Saints under everyday circumstances.[140]

The second problem is how to account for the sudden appearance of "hope" (13:7, 13) in a discussion that has barely mentioned faith (13:2) and has focused only on love. The phrase "faith, hope, and love" appears to have been an aphorism widely known by the early Christians.[141] They understood these as interrelated in defining the whole of the Christian experience in the present state: Faith in the Lord, expressed as obedience to his will,[142] is essential to salvation while hope supplies the energy that keeps faith strong and active.[143] Love of the Lord and his children dictates the direction that faith takes. This

---

139. Fitzmyer, *First Corinthians,* 502.

140. Spicq, *Agape,* 2:169.

141. For example, see in the New Testament, Rom. 5:1–5; Gal. 5:5–6; Eph. 4:2–5; Col. 1:4–5; 1 Thes. 1:3; 5:8; Heb. 6:10–12, 18–19; 7:19. In other Christian writing, see Barnabas 1:4; 11:8; Polycarp, *Phil.* 3:2–3. Archibald McBride Hunter, *Paul and His Predecessors* (London: Westminster Press, 1961), 33–35.

142. In Rom. 1:5, Paul refers to the ὑπακοὴν πίστεως (*hypakoēn pisteōs*), "obedience of faith," that carries the idea of "the obedience that is faith" because faith always expresses itself as something a person does. Such obedience will be necessary forever. Bailey, *Mediterranean Eyes,* 382.

143. Draper, *Fulness of Joy,* 60.

is how the passage is often understood and the idea works. It is more likely, however, that love is the force of the enduring nature energizing the other two gifts. Paul singles out love, however, as μείζων (*meizōn*). The word is a comparative, "greater," but was often used, as probably here, as a superlative meaning, "greatest."[144] Love is the greatest, in part, because of its power to give the other two eternal virtues their necessary bounds, limitations, and direction. It is this supernal force that assures that "God doth not walk in crooked paths, neither doth he turn to the right hand nor to the left, neither doth he vary from that which he hath said, therefore his paths are straight, and his course is one eternal round" (D&C 3:2).

Analysis and Summary

Paul's discussion should not be seen as demeaning spiritual gifts but in recognizing that most are but partial and temporal. Since the ultimate object of every endowment is to assist both the recipient and benefactor in becoming more godlike, when these souls come into eternal life, the major purpose of the gifts will have been realized. They will, therefore, pass away because the fragmentary must always give way to the complete, the partial subsumed into the whole.[145] Since love (along with hope and faith) requires no transformation or metamorphosis into some higher form, it can ever remain as it is. Even knowledge, wisdom, and prophecy do not possess this characteristic and, therefore, must give way to omniscience.[146]

In 13:11, Paul's analogy to speaking, thinking, and reasoning as a child does more than simply allude to "the experience of spiritual gifts, but to how they are expressed (λαλεῖν, *lalein*), what opinions are held about them (φρονεῖν, *phronein*), and how they are valued or evaluated (λογίζεσθαι, *logizesthai*)."[147] The child's world is self-centered with drives for gratification in the immediate. It is motivated by dreams and wishes.[148] On the other hand, the mature are able to sacrifice immediate gratification for a greater good. They can think long term and engage in strategies designed to bring about a pleasant and comfortable future even if it means self-sacrifice in the present. They are motivated by eternal realities. More especially,

144. Wallace, *Greek Grammar,* 299–300.
145. Fitzmyer, *First Corinthians,* 497–98.
146. Barth, *Church Dogmatics,* 4/2 §68.837–38.
147. Thiselton, *First Epistle,* 1067; italics and bold in original not reproduced.
148. Gunther Bornkamm, *Early Christian Experience,* trans. P. L. Hammer (London: SCM Press, 1969), 185.

the spiritually mature include and are influenced by the needs of others, and this sets their priorities. Paul's words, as noted above, would have stung many in the Corinthian branches. They had either forgotten or never understood the "present versus the future" and "the temporal versus the eternal" dimensions that stood behind Paul's preaching. They were hindered by perceptions and spatial categories that consisted only of "above" and "below" and of social relations that consisted of "them" versus "us."[149] Paul's words dictate a complete change of perception that reaches beyond the narrow and limited understanding of childhood to that of the spiritually mature (τέλειος, *teleios*) who saw special categories as "across" and social relations in terms of "them *and* us."

In 13:12 Paul uses an analogy to make his point more clear. In 13:8 he noted that love, unlike the other χαρίσματα (*charismata*), "spiritual gifts," will never end. It is precisely because the other spiritual gifts have an ending point that makes love of a different order. That does not make the other gifts inferior or unimportant. What it makes them is relative. Throughout 13:9–12, Paul's stress is strictly on the temporal, "present age" nature of the *charismata*. They shall "pass away" (13:8, Rendition) because they are only ἐκ μέρους (*ek merous*) "in part" (13:9, KJV). Their place is strictly in the here and now (13:10–12). Therefore, an insistence by any one of the Corinthian Saints that one or another gift (especially tongues) somehow marks him or her as more highly spiritual simply is not true. The marks of true spirituality are possessing and expressing love. Only there does anyone find the "more excellent way" (12:31) that leads to a fullness of life in both the present and eternal worlds.[150]

For the present, all gifts are necessary and appreciated. The Lord promised his disciples that "these signs shall follow them that believe" (Mark 16:17). Elder Orson Pratt, arguing against those who insisted that the gifts of the Spirit do not belong in the present era, stated that by reading all of 13:8–12, a person can "find out the time when these miracles, such as prophecy, healing the sick, speaking with tongues, etc., were to cease." He went on to say,

> It is clearly foretold that when there will be no more need of prophecy, healing, speaking in tongues, etc., the day of perfection will have arrived; in other words, when the Church of God shall have overcome and be perfected, when the Church of God shall need no more Prophets, when

149. Hays, *First Corinthians*, 229.
150. Fee, *First Epistle*, 649.

it shall have no more sick, (for if all its members become immortal, there will be no sick to be healed, hence healing will be done away, when the Church of God all speak one language—the pure language, the language spoken by angels, restored to the earth by the Lord), there will be no need of speaking with tongues. But until that day of perfection comes, all these gifts will be necessary.[151]

He also taught,

There is a language in the spirit world that can communicate more to the mind in one minute than could be learned here in a hundred years of intense study and reasoning. There is an eternity of knowledge. There are worlds, as it were, without number; . . . they all have their way of communication one with another; therefore, when the Apostle says, that tongues shall cease, he had reference to the imperfect tongues upon the earth; knowledge will not cease, but knowledge in part will be done away, not knowledge in full. . . . We shall be able by the power of the Holy Ghost to obtain a language by which the angels speak, and by which a higher order of beings speak, and by these means attain to a greater degree of knowledge, that will produce a greater amount of happiness.[152]

After quoting 13:9–10, 12, Elder LeGrand Richards stated, "To me, that says there will be a complete restoration of all that we knew before we came here into mortality when we lived in the spirit world."[153]

Paul understood that there comes a time when one must move beyond childhood. In this context, he was not talking of being infantile or childish, but of moving from a state of lesser to greater ability. There is, however, nothing wrong with being childlike in some aspects. On this topic, President Henry B. Eyring stated:

For some that will not be easy to understand or to accept. Most of us want to be strong. We may well see being like a child as being weak. Most parents have wanted their children at times to be less childish. Even the Apostle Paul used these words as he was about to urge us to incorporate charity, the pure love of Christ, into our lives: "When I was a child, I spake as a child, I understood as a child, I thought as a child: but when I became a man, I put away childish things." (1 Cor. 13:11.)

But King Benjamin, who understood as well as any mortal what it meant to be a man of strength and courage, makes it clear that to be like

151. Orson Pratt, in *JD*, 16:137; compare Orson Pratt, in *JD*, 16:295.
152. Orson Pratt, in *JD*, 3:103.
153. LeGrand Richards, "Call of the Prophets," *Ensign* 11 (May 1981): 32.

a child is not to be childish. It is to be like the Savior, who prayed to His Father for strength to be able to do His will and then did it. Our natures must be changed to become as a child to gain the strength we must have to be safe in the times of moral peril.[154]

Everyone needs the power of the Spirit in order to direct their lives. Elder Delbert L. Stapley made it clear that "in the confusion of today's beliefs, philosophies, sophistries, changing standards of personal behavior, and the bold voice of unorthodox extremists, man's need for spiritual guidance to choose the right and forsake the wrong is of paramount importance to his assurance of hope for peace and happiness. Without the light of the spirit, people see through a glass, darkly (1 Cor. 13:12). Their judgments and decisions are so often faulty. They bog down in confusion, frustration, and utter bewilderment."[155]

Speaking of our time in mortality when we see things indirectly as we do in a mirror, President Brigham Young stated that sometimes "we cannot behold objects clearly with the natural eye. We have not faith sufficient to have revelation, to have the visions of eternity opened unto us so clearly that we may see things as they are, consequently, we have to live by faith and not by sight. We have to live by the principles of the Gospel, which is faith in the heart and obedience to its requirements. It is our joy and salvation that we have this privilege."[156] The motivating force, of course, is love for the Lord. It was he who said, "If ye love me, keep my commandments" (John 14:15).

Speaking of the greatness of love, Elder Vaughn J. Featherstone noted that "if Paul is correct and I believe he is, then charity is greater than faith. That is quite a declaration when we consider what can be accomplished by faith. . . . How is it, then, that charity could be greater than faith? In the thirteenth chapter of 1 Corinthians, Paul describes what those with faith may accomplish and still not possess charity. . . . Charity is the very essence of the gospel of Jesus Christ. It is the very conduct and total being of the Savior. . . . And ultimately, if we are possessors of charity, we will be possessed by Him who is the author of charity."[157]

Two statements from modern Apostles act to summarize this chapter. Elder Dallin H. Oaks stated,

---

154. Henry B. Eyring, "As a Child," *Ensign* 36 (May 2006): 15.
155. Delbert L. Stapley, in CR, October 1966, 111–14.
156. Brigham Young, in *JD,* 3:191.
157. Featherstone, *Incomparable Christ,* 97–98, 104.

We are challenged to move through a process of conversion toward that status and condition called eternal life. This is achieved not just by doing what is right, but by doing it for the right reason—for the pure love of Christ. The Apostle Paul illustrated this in his famous teaching about the importance of charity (1 Cor. 13). The reason charity never fails and the reason charity is greater than even the most significant acts of goodness he cited is that charity, "the pure love of Christ" (Moro. 7:47), is not an *act* but a *condition* or state of being. Charity is attained through a succession of acts that result in a conversion. Charity is something one becomes. Thus, as Moroni declared, "except men shall *have* charity they cannot inherit" the place prepared for them in the mansions of the Father (Ether 12:34).[158]

And Elder Featherstone, after noting the Lords statement, "A new commandment I give unto you, That ye love one another; as I have loved you, that ye also love one another" (John 13:34), stated,

Only those who are true possessors of charity can measure up to the full stature of this new commandment. This is the commandment that lifts us to the more noble and virtuous life. We cannot nor ever will love one another as He has loved us until we exercise in our own lives the full dimensions of charity. Those who practice charity may not always receive the promised benefits and ultimate successes. Ours is a different time schedule, but by and by we will all learn and know that "charity never faileth" (1 Cor. 13:8). The pure love of Christ will eventually triumph over all the evils, including power, pride, boasting, worldly acclaim, cruelty, wars, perversion, sadness, and heartache. . . . One day charity, the pure love of Christ, will triumph over all the world.[159]

---

158. Dallin H. Oaks, "The Challenge to Become," *Ensign* 30 (November 2000): 34.
159. Featherstone, *Incomparable Christ*, 78–79.

EXCURSUS ON LOVE/CHARITY

Of all the gifts of the Spirit, three make up a category all their own: faith, hope, and love. They are the only members of this category because they alone, of all the gifts of the Spirit, are eternal in nature. Of the three, Paul identified the greatest as love. To understand why, it is necessary to see love in its greater theological context.

The prophet Lehi taught his children that "Adam fell that men might be; and men are, that they might have joy" (2 Ne. 2:25). The prophet's insight is stated so succinctly that it is easy to dismiss or pass over with little awareness of its depth and theological importance. Here, in just fourteen words, Lehi answers the age old question, "What is the purpose of life?" To appreciate the pertinence of his answer, expansion is necessary. Adam made a decision to fall, and he made it consciously and deliberately. His objective was to bring humankind into being. If Adam had not made that choice, there would have been no humans on this planet—ever (2 Ne. 2:19–26).

The noun "human," as used in this excursus, refers to "mortals." The word-stem comes from the Latin *mors,* meaning "death." The Book of Mormon did not use the word "mortals," it used the word "men," but given the context, it seems to have mortals in mind—people who would occupy this world for a brief time and then die.

But was death to be the end of existence? If so, why bother bringing humans into being at all? The answer is that only the physical part of "men" was mortal (and even that will not be the case after the resurrection), while the spiritual part was eternal. So, Lehi's view swept beyond mortality to find the meaning and purpose of existence as a whole. In so doing, he identified the grand objective of the Divine. God's purpose for his children is more than experiencing a mere flash of mortality but, both in mortality and beyond, to bring them joy—a fullness of joy.[160] In that one little word, Lehi summed up the purpose of life.

Joseph Smith, the translator of Lehi's words, paraphrased the prophet's insight this way: "Happiness is the object and design of our existence; and will be the end thereof, if we pursue the path that leads to it."[161] The

---

160. To Moses, God stated that his work and glory was "to bring to pass the immortality and eternal life of man" (Moses 1:39). Lehi revealed what was beyond that. Modern scripture testifies that the faithful will "enter into the joy of his Lord, and shall inherit eternal life" (D&C 51:19). Indeed, the Lord crowns "the faithful with joy" (D&C 52:43).

161. Smith, *History of the Church,* 5:134.

Lord seems very interested in whether we are happy, and investigating his teachings clearly shows us that he has laid down a great plan to bring us to that state.

The critical point that we must understand for our discussion here is that love is the vehicle by which God brings his children into salvation and, thereby, into a fullness of joy.[162] The scriptures unite in their testimony concerning the importance of love in God's work. Within Judeo-Christian tradition the primary object of love is God (Deut. 6:4–5; Mark 12:29–30). It is something he demands of his children because he loves them (Deut. 7:8, 13; 33:3; Hosea 3:1; 11:1, 8–9; 14:4; Isa. 43:4). As Paul understood, God is the originator of love, whose "love has been poured into our hearts through the Holy Spirit which has been given to us" (Rom. 5:5, authors' translation). Jesus, however, is its channel. The Savior poured out his love for us when we were yet sinners (Rom. 5:8; 8:31–39; 2 Cor. 13:11, 14; see also 1 John 4:10). In doing so, he taught us an important principle: a Christian cannot wait for his neighbors to become perfect before serving them. Paul understood that faith itself works its way by love which is *the* fruit of the Spirit (Gal. 5:22). Love is what gives Christian existence its force and power. Once justified and sanctified by the Lord, each Saint becomes the channel the Savior uses to spread his love to others.

So what is love and how does it work to bring a fullness of joy? Before investigating this subject, it is important to define precisely what we mean by "love." Unfortunately, the overuse and misapplication of the noun has resulted in a blurring of its meaning and force. To appreciate Paul's insights, we must let his words speak for themselves and teach us. Only then can we fully understand love's depth, power, and purpose.[163]

Ancient Greek was rich in words for love and, therefore, can provide modern inquirers with a way to precisely understand certain nuances that might otherwise pass beyond them. The various words do not define love as a whole, but rather reveal certain aspects. Think of love as a box with a top, bottom, back, front, and sides. Each aspect of the box can be examined independent of the others, but only when all the aspects are brought together and understood can one really know the box. So it is with love.

---

162. For a study, see Draper, *Fulness of Joy,* 2–4, 53–62.
163. Morris, *Testaments of Love,* 3.

Of the many Greek words for love,[164] three have the greatest bearing on assisting the reader in understanding the message Paul was conveying.[165] These words are στοργή (*storgē*), φιλία (*philia*), and ἀγάπη (*agapē*) with their cognate verbs στέργω (*stergō*), φιλέω (*phileō*), and ἀγαπάω (*agapaō*).

The noun στοργή (*storgē*) is best translated as affection or friendship.[166] In the New Testament, it is found only in its negative cognate adjective

---

164. Among those not covered in the text are εὔνοια (*eunoia*), ἐπιθυμία (*epithymia*), and ἔρως (*erōs*), but see the note below.

165. Two words deserve a note because each expresses a dimension of love and is used by the New Testament writers. However, since none of them is translated as "love" in the KJV, and also because they contribute only a small degree to an understanding of love, they are developed only here. The first word is the Greek ἐπιθυμία (*epithymia*). It denoted an intense desire and was often associated with strong passion. The Greeks used it to describe both positive and negative passionate feelings. The New Testament follows suit. On the negative side, John warns against the "lust of the flesh" (1 John 2:16), and Paul cautions the Saint not to give into "evil concupiscence [passions]" (Col. 3:5). On the positive side, the Savior used it to explain the deep yearning the Old Testament prophets had to see the day of his earthly ministry (Matt. 13:17) and to describe how much he ached to celebrate the Passover with his friends (Luke 22:15). See Morris, *Testaments of Love*, 119–20; and Friedrich Büchsel, "θυμός," in *TDNT*, 3:167–71. The last word, εὔνοια (*eunoia*), meant "to be well-disposed" toward another or to be on "friendly" terms. It carried the idea of close attachment. It had no negative aspect. Its meaning is expressed in the Savior's demand that his disciples have good will toward an adversary (Matt. 5:25) and in Paul's admonition that the household servants show kindness toward their masters (Eph. 6:5–7). See J. Behm, "εὐνοέω, εὔνοια," in *TDNT*, 4:971–73, where the word is covered under νοῦς (*nous*), and Sqicq, *Agape*, 1:39, where he treats the related term εὐδοκέω (*eudokeō*).

One other word deserves at least a note even though it appears nowhere in the New Testament (though it does occur in LXX Prov. 7:18; 30:16; note that the versification in LXX differs from the KJV). That word is ἔρως (*erōs*). The Greeks used the noun to express a wide set of emotions ranging from a crude infatuation to an exalted and pure passion. No other word for love carried the breadth that this one did. Most often, however, it described a real, genuine love that included the physical dimension. Indeed, those feelings expressed in proper intimacy can only be described as *erōs* and, therefore, the physical dimension cannot be dissociated from it. See Morris, *Testaments of Love*, 120–21. It must be emphasized that it did not denote an inferior love that stood in contrast to a pure, "Christian" kind of love. *Erōs* was both real and necessary in God's work, but it, like στοργή (*storgē*), did not describe the special characteristics of God's love and the love the Savior commended.

166. The word is found in LXX 3 Macc. 5:32; 4 Macc. 14:13, 14, 17; but it is not in the New Testament itself. Φιλία (*philia*), more directly than στοργή (*storgē*), denoted that love associated with friendship, especially that between persons of the same gender, but without sexual connotation. Since the word does not appear in the Bible except in the compound φιλαδελφία (*philadelphia*), brotherly love, we do not explore it here.

ἄστοργος (*astorgos*), which denoted the feelings of one who was heartless, who had no affection even for those whom a good person naturally loves. The Apostle Paul condemned certain persons because they were, among other things, "without natural affection" (*astorgos,* Rom. 1:31; 2 Tim. 3:3). *Storgē* stands at the other end of the spiritual spectrum, defining that strong feeling that binds people into a defined group such as a club or fraternity. Its most pure and strongest expression, however, is found in the binding love of a family.[167] Indeed, its force promotes family love: a mother and father's love for their children and the children's love for their parents and one another. Paul's condemnation of those without "natural affection" shows us that *storgē* is a natural love that can arise easily and fully. However, it can also be destroyed when people become "lovers of their own selves, covetous, boasters, proud, blasphemers, disobedient to parents, unthankful, unholy" (2 Tim. 3:2). *Storgē* is necessary to tame and transform passion and erotic love and places both in the service of God and the family. Without it, these powers can become unbridled and hurtful. *Storgē* promotes unselfishness, care, obedience, and safety. Therefore, its power safeguards and binds the family together by defining the correct relationship between its members, providing boundaries over which all refuse to step.

Children need a safe haven, a place to retreat to from the fear and tension of a less than kind world. *Storgē* is the assurance that the home will be the place of security, protection, acceptance, and care. The word teaches us that family members, both parents and children, are meant to be friends— dear and best friends.

Righteousness promotes *storgē,* and in so doing, it keeps the family— and society—strong and well protected. When society becomes unrighteous and selfish, *storgē* disappears and the family unit suffers. Therefore, the Savior warned, concerning the last days, that "because iniquity shall abound, the love of many shall wax cold" (Matt. 24:12).[168] He understood

---

However, for a good discussion on the association and importance of these words to understand love, see C. S. Lewis, *The Four Loves* (New York: Harcourt Brace Jovanovich, 1960), 53–83.

167. Compare this with William Barclay, *The Letters to Timothy, Titus, and Philemon* (Philadelphia: Westminster Press, 1960), 216, where he insists that the Greek word "*storgē* is the word used especially of *family love,* the love of child for parent and parent for child. If there is no human affection, the family cannot exist."

168. The Greek word translated "love" here is ἀγάπη (*agapē*) the favorite form of the word in the New Testament. However, as is shown below, it has a strong tie to στοργή (*storgē*).

that for many the home would cease to be a haven and become a hell. Society would fail because family affection would disappear.[169]

The importance of *storgē* cannot be over stressed. The word connotes a necessary, relaxed love promoting happiness, unity, and tolerance. But therein we find a danger. Family members can become too relaxed around one another and demand too much acceptance. Some justify unwarranted acts because, at home, they can be themselves without having to put on any phony airs. But one really can become too comfortable and, thus, discourteous and even obnoxious toward those he or she is supposed to love the most. C. S. Lewis warns: "Affection is an affair of old clothes, and ease, of the unguarded moment, of liberties which would be ill-bred if we took them with strangers. But old clothes are one thing; to wear the same shirt till it stank would be another."[170] Affection does not uncouple love from respect and courtesy even at home. *Storgē* never gives license to the children of disrespect: thoughtlessness, negligence, rudeness, and abuse in any form. In truth, it is given to guard against them and should be promoted by all.[171]

It should be noted that the Gospel writers never use the word στοργή (*storgē*) to express the Father's love for his Son.[172] The term they chose was "beloved" (ἀγαπητός, *agapētos*; for examples, see Matt. 3:17; 17:5; Mark 9:7).[173] This suggests that the early Christians assumed the importance and necessity of *storgē* but did not see in it that distinctive element of love in which the Father honored the Son and the Son the Father. It simply did not hold

---

169. In this regard, see D&C 45:26–27.

170. Lewis, *Four Loves*, 67.

171. We have here extended the meaning more than first century Christian documents actually allow. Nonetheless, the spirit of what we have stressed is correct and shows why στοργή (*storgē*) must be promoted and practiced.

172. The word is not found in the New Testament. We only see it in its negative aspect, ἄστοργος (*astorgos*), meaning "unloving." In Rom. 1:31 and 2 Tim. 3:3, it is translated as "without natural affection."

173. By using the term the way they did, the writers of the Gospels expressed an important element in the relationship between the Father and the Son. The word suggests that God does not reach down to his Son as a mortal father to his little one with a rush of warm, protecting, and benevolent feeling. The Father's words suggest a relationship of near equality, showing the Father's intent to honor the Son. Of note also is that the first time the word "love" appears in the New Testament, at the Savior's baptism, it marks the proclamation of the divinity of the Savior and of his standing as God's beloved. "On the banks of the Jordan he named Jesus his son, and his *agapētos*, his beloved. Clearly, *agapē* exists in God; it is the force uniting the two divine Persons unchangeably, from all eternity." Spicq, *Agape*, 1:39, 49.

the unique dimension that the gospel proclaimed.[174] They did use another word, φιλία (*philia*).

Philia has a wide range of meanings, but it is best understood as friendship and, therefore, touches some of the same field as στοργή (*storgē*). It often describes pure affection between persons of the same gender, but is not exclusive to that.[175] It connotes all that makes life gratifying and even rich. People could live in a world without friends, but their existence would be small and impoverished. It is true that modern man makes less of friendship than his more ancient counterpart; Cicero wrote a book about its necessity and delight while Aristotle classified friendship as one of the cardinal virtues.[176] C. S. Lewis, in this light, noted it was "the least *natural* of loves; the least instinctive, organic, biological, gregarious and necessary." He expounded his idea by saying that "without Eros none of us would have been begotten and without Affection none of us would have been reared; but we can live and breed without Friendship. The species, biologically considered, has no need of it." Going on, he says, "Friendship is unnecessary, like philosophy, like art. . . . It has no survival value; rather it is one of those things which give value to survival."[177]

Friendship is built on something that friends have in common—like taste, interest, or bias—but which others do not share. While ἔρως (*erōs*) is a private love between two people, φιλία (*philia*) is a more, though not a complete, public love and can exist between quite a number of people. Unlike *erōs,* it spawns no jealously. It may begin with simple interest, but, developed over time, it can turn into esteem so great that often "each member of the circle feels, in his secret heart, humbled before all the rest. Sometimes he wonders what he is doing there among his betters."[178]

---

174. Morris, *Testaments of Love*, 116–17.

175. Denis de Rougemont, *Love Declared* (New York: Pantheon Books, 1963), 6, especially n. 3, investigates the breadth of the word as used by ancient philosophers. Though the basic meaning is that of affection between two persons, the philosophers saw four types: that which best described true friendship (φυλοσική, *phylosikē*), that associated with parent and child relationships and what united those with common blood (φυσική, *physikē*), that between host and guest expressed in hospitality (ξενική, *xenikē*), and an amorous love expressed between persons of the same or opposite gender (ἐροτική, *erotikē*). See also Morris, *Testaments of Love*, 117–18.

176. Cicero, *De Amicitia*; Aristotle, *Magna Moralia*; see especially *Ethica Nicomachea* 1166.31, which notes that a friend is but another self. See for discussion Brent J. Schmidt, *Utopian Communities of the Ancient World: Idealistic Experiments of Pythagoras, the Essenes, Pachomius and Proclus* (Lewiston, N.Y.: Edwin Mellen, 2010), 50, 65 n. 94.

177. Lewis, *Four Loves*, 88, 103.

178. Lewis, *Four Loves*, 104.

The great benefit of friendship is that it brings out the best in each participant. Each member finds strength in and reinforcement from the others. However, there is also a downside. Lewis notes that "friendship (as the ancients saw) can be a school of virtue; but also (as they did not see) a school of vice. It is ambivalent. It makes good men better and bad men worse."[179] As the social circle can strengthen virtues, it can reinforce vices. The group can rationalize a stand to the point that it refuses to accept any law or rule except that which is within the association, because that is what defines the self-identity of the circle of friends.[180] Thus, it can become a hot house where narrow-mindedness, intolerance, bigotry, and lawlessness flourish. This can grow into pride with its extreme exclusiveness, forbidding entrance to all outsiders with a fierceness and absoluteness beyond that of any scribbled "No Girls Allowed" sign.

However, the scriptures do not view the word in any negative way. Indeed, John used the verb form to describe the relationship between the Father and the Son, saying, "The Father loveth [φιλεῖ, *philei*] the Son, and sheweth him all things that himself doeth" (John 5:20). He further translates the Savior as using it to describe the Father's feelings for all the disciples and the disciples' feelings for the Savior: "The Father himself loveth [φιλεῖ, *philei*] you, because ye have loved [πεφιλήκατε, *pephilēkate*] me, and have believed that I came out from God" (John 16:27). In this regard, the Savior said to his disciples, "I call you not servants; for the servant knoweth not what his lord doeth: but I have called you friends [φίλους, *philous*, "confidants"]; for all things that I have heard of my Father I have made known unto you" (John 15:15). Friendship, especially that which is contained within the family, defines the scriptural sense of the term. Though we have approached the scriptural ideal of love here, we have not fully arrived.[181]

This brings us to the last word in our study. Of the choices available in the very rich Greek language to express its particular view of love, the New Testament prefers one noun above all others. That noun is ἀγάπη (*agapē*). What is of note is that this noun was rarely used in prebiblical

---

179. Lewis, *Four Loves*, 115.

180. Morris, *Testaments of Love*, 118–19.

181. Actually, the gospel writers show little distinction between the meaning of φιλέω (*phileo*) and ἀγαπάω (*agapaō*). Both express the ideal love commended by the Savior. For a comprehensive study, see Roy F. Butler, *The Meaning of* Agapao *and* Phileo *in the Greek New Testament* (Lawrence, Kan.: Coronado Press, 1977).

Greek literature before the Christians adopted it.[182] The Septuagint uses
the word twenty times, showing that it had some use in Jewish circles and,
therefore, would have been known to the early Christians through that
source. Still, its use, even among the Jews, was rare.[183] The reason the early
Christians may have chosen this relatively obscure word to express their
idea about love was because its very scarcity allowed them to put their own
spin on it.[184] Unlike the other terms for love, it did not carry a lot of semantic baggage. Indeed, the force of the word was rather insipid and weak
before the Saints took it as their own and breathed a pure and powerful fire
into it.[185] They used it to describe exactly their new understanding of love
as revealed by the Master.[186]

The word stood apart from ἔρως (*erōs*). Though this word often denoted
a pure if passionate but nonetheless authentic love, it was sometimes, like
the modern word, misused. In such cases, a more accurate word would
have been ἐπιθυμία (*epithymia*), a longing for that which is forbidden—
lust.[187] *Erōs*, though giving and concerned, nevertheless seeks its own satisfaction. It drives to capture and possess the object it loves. Therefore, its
characteristics include cunning, seductive, and winning ways. Its Greek
embodiment, Cupid, is depicted with a bow and arrow, the instruments of

---

182. Gottfried Quell and Ethelbert Stauffer, "ἀγαπάω, ἀγάπη, ἀγαπητός," in *TDNT*,
1:21–55. The verb form of the word, ἀγαπάω (*agapaō*), however, was very common. It
was the use of the noun that was unusual.

183. It occurs in Aristeas, 229; Philo, *Deus* 69; *T. Reu.* 6.9; *T. Gad* 4.2, 6, 7; 5.2; *T. Ash.*
2.4; *T. Jos.* 17.3; *T. Benj.* 3.5; 8.1, 2; *Sib. Or.* 2.65, 6.25; *Pss. Sol.* 18.4.

184. Of course the linguistics do not prove the point. The Christian idea of love is best
defined in books where the word ἀγάπη (*agapē*) is not found. The meaning is derived
from the way the Christians defined love, not from the word they chose to express it. In
fact, just the opposite is true, for their definition would have prevailed with whatever
word they used. However, their choice of a more obscure word, unladen with the trap-
pings of heavy use, better allowed them to put their own twist on it. On this, see Morris,
Testaments of Love, 125–27; and especially James Barr, *The Semantics of Biblical Language*
(Oxford: Oxford University Press, 1961), 215–43, who stresses that it was the conceptual
use of the word, not the word itself, that was distinctive. Therefore, the reader must keep
in mind the range of meaning that the word has and allow context to dictate the proper
denotation or connotation.

185. In general, secular Greek defined the verb ἀγαπάω (*agapaō*) as much more color-
less—either ἐράω (*eraō*) or φιλέω (*phileō*) and some scholars believe that in that context
it carries the feeling of "prefer." For discussion, see Gottfried Quell and Ethelbert Stauffer,
"ἀγαπάω, ἀγάπη, ἀγαπητός," in *TDNT*, 1:21–55.

186. Nygren, *Agape and Eros*, 48.

187. The noun reflects the whole range of desires and passions almost always with a
negative connotation. See Friedrich Büchsel, "ἐπιθυμία, ἐπιθυμέω," in *TDNT*, 3:168–71.

the clever hunter. *Erōs*, therefore, cannot shed the suggestion of self-love that is ever attached to it. Paul chose to use the noun *agapē* and, in so doing, disengaged this aspect of love from anything that was sensual, carnal, or erotic. *Agapē*, then, stands in direct contrast to *erōs*. It "seeketh not her own" (13:5). It will have nothing to do with anything driven by ego or self-interest. Its touch brings to the recipient a new center, a transformation from concern for self to a concern for others and doing the will of the Master.[188] The result is a total disinterest in what would be personal advantage. Though advantage may come, that possibility in no way influences love's action. The Savior did not come to please himself but to please God through assistance to others (Rom. 15:3). The disciple should do the same (10:24). Such action is the truest sign of pure love.[189] *Agapē* is often used to describe the love that should exist among close family members. In healthy familial relationships, one always wants the best for them. Sometimes this love is expressed in a church setting among "brothers and sisters" who may need a hug, a word of encouragement, a sincere compliment, or an occasional word of rebuke. It continually seeks for the other's well-being. *Agapē* is found obliquely in the scriptures where God disciplines his children or allows them to pass through trials for their own spiritual good. More directly it is found when he gives them gifts such as talents. Its greatest expression, however, is in the Atonement.

God created his children, as noted above, with the desire to bring them to a fullness of joy. Prompted by the same spirit, the Apostle John wrote to the early Saints, in part, so that their "joy [might] be full" (1 John 1:4). To assist him to that end, he spent a major portion of his epistle dealing with love, *agapē*, and its importance. He admonished his readers with the kind words, "Beloved, let us love one another: for love is of God; and every one that loveth is born of God, and knoweth God" (1 John 4:7). His words testify that one comes to really know God by possessing love.

John revealed clearly the process by which one can gain such knowledge and come to possess an even greater degree of love. "Whoso keepeth his word," the Apostle testified, "in him verily is the love of God perfected: hereby know we that we are in him" (1 John 2:5). The verb translated "perfected" (τελειόω, *teleioō*) denotes something that is "whole" or "complete."[190] It is through commandment keeping—especially the "new commandment"

---

188. Nygren, *Agape and Eros*, 130–31; Deluz, *Companion*, 190–91.
189. Spicq, *Agape*, 2:155–56.
190. BDAG, 996.

that Jesus gave to his Saints to love one another (John 13:34)—that we come to fully love. "If we love one another," John promised, "God dwelleth in us, and his love is perfected in us" (1 John 4:12). These words reveal that there are stages in acquiring this love. The first step is coming to Christ in love. This love leads to the next step, keeping his commandments (John 14:15). When that happens, the next step occurs; we are endowed with greater spirituality, for "he that dwelleth in love dwelleth in God, and God in him" (1 John 4:16). This brings about the final step, a more full love that comes only to those "who are true followers of his [God's] Son, Jesus Christ" and who ask for it "with all the energy of heart" (Moro. 7:48). Even then, it must be maintained "by diligence unto prayer" (Moro. 8:26). Thus, "herein is our love made perfect" (1 John 4:17), and we come to a fullness of joy.

Two themes dominate the distinctive theological meaning of ἀγάπη (*agapē*) for Paul. First, it represented the power behind the restored gospel that was breaking into the New Testament era (and, by extension, that of the Restoration). As such, it was, as one scholar noted, "the only vital force which has a future."[191] Indeed, it is *the* fervent virtue of the future celestial realm where respect, regard, and the welfare of others dominate all that transpires. Second, it denotes an attitude or stance taken by the Christian which manifests itself most purely not just in willful acts of kindness and consideration but more so in self-sacrifice for the good of others.[192] In short, it is a personal manifestation of the pure love of Christ.

So what did the early Christians want to tell the world about love as they understood it? The word *agapē* expressed a love freely given without respect of worth or merit. Ἀγάπη (*agapē*) denotes a love even for those who would be otherwise unappealing, even repellent. Its reach is very broad. Not only does it include those who have nothing to give in return but also those who would spurn and abuse it.[193] This aspect can best be seen and appreciated as we look at the work of the Father and the Son. It was through love that God extended his grace to old and new Israel.[194] Beyond that, God's love spread even further, to that portion of the world which did not even know him and worshiped in his place dumb idols of gold, silver, wood, and stone. As noted, he gave his Son to a world that was anything

---

191. Ethelbert Stauffer, "ἀγαπάω, ἀγάπη, ἀγαπητός," in *TDNT*, 1:51.

192. Thiselton, *First Epistle*, 1035.

193. Morris, *Testaments of Love*, 128.

194. Morris, *Testaments of Love*, 128.

but worthy of him. God's statement to Enoch is telling: "I can stretch forth mine hands and hold all the creations which I have made; and mine eye can pierce them also, and among all the workmanship of mine hands there has not been so great wickedness as among thy brethren" (Moses 7:36). These people had rejected both him and his word. However, that rejection—that extreme wickedness—did not repulse God's love. Even in the face of it, he sent his Son, even his Word (John 1:1; 3:16), to atone for their rebellion and all humankind's sins. *Agapē* was the motivational force that moved the Son to pay the debt—to suffer death and hell, not just for the righteous but also for all those in this wicked, cruel, and evil world. In the work of the Father and the Son, we can clearly see that love "never faileth" (13:8), that is, it never falls apart, it never quits, it never gives up. Well did the Apostle John declare, "God is love" (1 John 4:16).

Chapter 14

"Covet Prophecy, and Forbid Not the Speaking in Tongues"

INTRODUCTION

Returning to the subject of πνευματικά (*pneumatika*), "spiritual gifts," begun in chapter 12, Paul concludes his discussion here. Even though he has left the subject of ἀγάπη (*agapē*), "love," that divine force continues to stand as the foundation for all that goes on in this chapter. Love is, as Paul has made clear, the greatest of all the gifts (13:13) and "a more excellent way" (12:31). It alone dictates the proper use of all other spiritual gifts and forms the basis for an estimation of their relative quality and use as instruments in promoting edification (12:3–5, 26). It is the animating principle and ultimate aim that should govern all that goes on in a Christian's life.[1] Thus, Paul's exhortation to his readers to "seek after love" (14:1, authors' translation) must be remembered while reading this chapter.

Many of the Corinthian Saints needed a corrective due to an apparent unbridled display of tongues during their worship services. In chapter 12, Paul set all gifts of the Spirit in their broad theological context so that specifics could be understood. He argued for a need of diversity in the manifestation of spiritual powers, with *glossolalia* being but one of a dozen such gifts. All are bestowed by God "for the common good" (12:7–11).

It is little wonder that *glossolalia* (speaking in tongues) was prized among the gifts. Though it was certainly showy, it also served a very practical purpose. There were dozens of spoken languages in the Roman Empire because of the many slaves that were taken from their homes to live in distant places. The Romans typically sold slaves far from their homeland so

---

1. Findlay, "St. Paul's First Epistle," 902.

that they would be isolated not only from their former traditions but more importantly from others who shared the same language, partly to impede any move to revolt. Though most Corinthians and visiting Roman elite would have spoken Greek, many slaves—Berbers, Celts, Germanic tribesmen, Arabs, Africans, and so on—would not. Since these people likely composed part of the Christian congregations, they would need translation assistance unless the gift of tongues was present. In many ways, this gift demonstrates that God is no respecter of persons but reaches out even to the slave class.

In chapter 13, in light of the "common good," Paul argued that no one, including himself, "no matter how 'spiritual'" they thought they were, were worth anything unless they possessed and were motivated by love.[2] It is, indeed, the litmus test for proper use of the gifts of God and also the authentication of a Christian.[3] Through his emphasis on love, the Apostle showed that this supernal gift is more valuable in Christian living than any of the others and, thereby, serves notice on where the disciples should put their effort. In chapter 14, he puts his whole argument together, insisting that the single objective of their zealous drive to higher spirituality should be the acquisition of love (14:1). Only this will result in the achievement of two paramount conditions. Both are expressed by the same Greek word, οἰκοδομέω (*oikodomeō*), "building up" the Church and "edifying" the Saints (14:3–5, 12, 17, 26).

Already Paul has shown that "knowledge makes people conceited" but love "builds them up" (8:1, Rendition). The term "building up" has both a negative and positive connotation. "On one side," noted a scholar, "it excludes a self-sufficient, indulgent, religious individualism and egoism which can lead to the disintegration of the community; on the other side, it entails helping the other person since thereby the whole community is built up as a cohesive and mutually supportive whole."[4]

Paul develops the theme of building up and edifying the Church through two approaches: First, he insists on *intelligibility* during the Christian meetings (14:2–28), and second, he gives specific guidelines pertaining to a meeting's order and an individual's decorum therein (14:29–40).[5]

Paul feels there are two gifts that deserve special attention: prophecy and speaking in tongues. Here, by comparing and contrasting them, he

---

2. Fee, *First Epistle,* 652.
3. Thiselton, *First Epistle,* 1074.
4. Thiselton, *First Epistle,* 1076.
5. Fee, *First Epistle,* 652.

emphasizes their place in the service of the Church. The gift of tongues, "in their more dramatic manifestations," noted Elder Bruce R. McConkie, "consist[s] in speaking or interpreting, by the power of the Spirit, a tongue which is completely unknown to the speaker or interpreter. Sometimes it is the pure Adamic language which is involved."[6] Less dramatically, the gift expressed itself in all of the attendees being able to understand the message in their own tongues, as on the day of Pentecost (Acts 2:7–12). The gift of prophecy denotes inspired speech and particularly testimony bearing.[7] Between the gifts of tongues and prophecy, Paul shows a definite preference for the latter. By contrasting them "in antithetical parallelism" he emphasizes his point: "He that speaketh in an unknown tongue speaketh . . . unto God" (14:2); but "he that prophesieth speaketh unto men" (14:3); "he that speaketh in an unknown tongue edifieth himself; but he that prophesieth edifieth the church" (14:4).[8] There is a way the gift of tongues could be edifying. "The gift of tongues is not profitable without the gift of interpretation," noted an LDS scholar.[9]

In chapter 12, perhaps Paul lessened the importance of both tongues and their interpretation by placing them last among the twelve gifts he listed. Likely the reason was that some Corinthian Saints were giving this gift undue importance, vaunting it as the sign of the highest level of spirituality. An unfortunate result was that it affected the social intercourse of and heightened the tension in the larger Christian community. Nonetheless, the Apostle does not suggest that speaking in tongues per se is a problem.[10] The actual problem lay in seeing it for more than it was. Though it did, indeed, help with missionary work and communication in the branches, its reach was still limited. That was not true of prophecy. The dynamic of Spirit-inspired preaching was to the soul—the very seat of persuasion—and it profited all who heard and felt it. The best boast the gift of tongues could give was that it was a sign for unbelievers (14:22).[11]

---

6. *DNTC*, 2:383.

7. See Translation Notes on 12:10 with the associated Analysis.

8. For a study, see T. W. Gillespie, *The First Theologians: A Study in Early Christian Prophecy* (Grand Rapids, Mich.: Eerdmans, 1994), 202–17.

9. Sperry, *Life and Letters*, 127.

10. See Stendahl, *Paul among Jews and Gentiles*, 113–21, where he maintains that *glossolalia* was an "ecstatic" form of religious experience that was proper to Christianity. The gift was widely experienced among the Christian branches but was later restrained by the institutional church.

11. Fitzmyer, *First Corinthians*, 508–9.

Even so, tongues and their interpretation are important to the work even today. During the dedication of the Kirtland Temple, Joseph Smith prayed, "Let the gift of tongues be poured out upon thy people, even cloven tongues as of fire, and the interpretation thereof" (D&C 109:36). A number of early Saints enjoyed the gift, Brigham Young among them, but the primary use of this gift is for missionary work.[12]

It is of note that Paul himself spoke in tongues while in Corinth (14:18). That being the case, as an LDS scholar wrote, "Perhaps the Saints' fondness for this particular gift was in emulation of Paul rather than simple fascination."[13] Even if that were so, many of the Saints seem to have missed a major point—the gift of tongues in no way evidenced superior spirituality. To make that point, another LDS scholar observed, "Paul is obviously trying to extend Corinthian horizons on other spiritual gifts that they should seek. . . . Paul is clearly saying that Church leaders must direct the use of gifts in each branch of the Church. Modern revelation relists the spiritual gifts and makes Paul's point of supervision more directly: 'And unto the bishop of the church, and unto such as God shall appoint and ordain to watch over the church and to be elders unto the church, are to have it given unto them to discern all those gifts lest there shall be any among you professing and yet be not of God. And it shall come to pass that he that asketh in Spirit shall receive in Spirit'" (D&C 46:26–28).[14] Paul also teaches that the God of love endows his people with spiritual gifts. These, however, must be exercised with all propriety and order so unity and harmony may prevail in the Church (see Mosiah 4:27; D&C 20:68; 28:13; 58:55; 107:84).

The central point of Paul's discussion should not be missed since it deals neither with tongues nor prophecy. The issue is building up the kingdom of God on earth. That can only happen if the doctrinal teachings and witnessing during Church service is intelligible to all. The power of the gift of prophecy does that better than any other gift and, therefore, should be the ruling endowment during Church services (14:39).[15]

This chapter can be divided into two major sections with six subsections. The first section centers on the gifts of tongues and prophecy. It can be broken down as follows: The first subsection contains a contrast of the speaking in tongues with prophecy and delineation of their respective values for

---

12. Bickerstaff, "Gifts of the Spirit," in *EM,* 2:544–46.
13. Holzapfel and Wayment, *Making Sense,* 361.
14. Anderson, *Understanding Paul,* 112.
15. Fee, *First Epistle,* 652.

edification (14:2–5); the second has three didactic arguments that focus on the ambiguity and dubious merits of tongues (14:6–11); the third is an admonition to do that which edifies the Church (14:12–13); the fourth shows the valueless nature of tongues during worship service (14:14–17); the fifth expresses the need for a speaker to be understood by all (14:18–21); the sixth insists on the use of tongues and prophecy as signs and their effects (14:22–25). The second and longest section focuses on due order during Church services so necessary to produce harmony and peace focusing especially on the women's decorum during Church service (14:26–38). Verses 14:39–40 serve as a conclusion.

THE IMPORTANCE OF DIVINE INSPIRATION AND TONGUES (14:1–12)

Greek Text

1 Διώκετε τὴν ἀγάπην, ζηλοῦτε δὲ τὰ πνευματικά, μᾶλλον δὲ ἵνα προφητεύητε. 2 ὁ γὰρ λαλῶν γλώσσῃ οὐκ ἀνθρώποις λαλεῖ ἀλλὰ θεῷ, οὐδεὶς γὰρ ἀκούει, πνεύματι δὲ λαλεῖ μυστήρια· 3 ὁ δὲ προφητεύων ἀνθρώποις λαλεῖ οἰκοδομὴν καὶ παράκλησιν καὶ παραμυθίαν. 4 ὁ λαλῶν γλώσσῃ ἑαυτὸν οἰκοδομεῖ· ὁ δὲ προφητεύων ἐκκλησίαν οἰκοδομεῖ. 5 θέλω δὲ πάντας ὑμᾶς λαλεῖν γλώσσαις, μᾶλλον δὲ ἵνα προφητεύητε· μείζων δὲ ὁ προφητεύων ἢ ὁ λαλῶν γλώσσαις, ἐκτὸς εἰ μὴ διερμηνεύῃ, ἵνα ἡ ἐκκλησία οἰκοδομὴν λάβῃ.

6 Νῦν δέ, ἀδελφοί, ἐὰν ἔλθω πρὸς ὑμᾶς γλώσσαις λαλῶν, τί ὑμᾶς ὠφελήσω, ἐὰν μὴ ὑμῖν λαλήσω ἢ ἐν ἀποκαλύψει ἢ ἐν γνώσει ἢ ἐν προφητείᾳ ἢ ἐν διδαχῇ; 7 ὅμως τὰ ἄψυχα φωνὴν διδόντα, εἴτε αὐλὸς εἴτε κιθάρα, ἐὰν διαστολὴν τοῖς φθόγγοις μὴ δῷ, πῶς γνωσθήσεται τὸ αὐλούμενον ἢ τὸ κιθαριζόμενον; 8 καὶ γὰρ ἐὰν ἄδηλον φωνὴν σάλπιγξ δῷ, τίς παρασκευάσεται εἰς πόλεμον; 9 οὕτως καὶ ὑμεῖς διὰ τῆς γλώσσης ἐὰν μὴ εὔσημον λόγον δῶτε, πῶς γνωσθήσεται τὸ λαλούμενον; ἔσεσθε γὰρ εἰς ἀέρα λαλοῦντες. 10 τοσαῦτα εἰ τύχοι γένη φωνῶν εἰσιν ἐν κόσμῳ, καὶ οὐδὲν ἄφωνον· 11 ἐὰν οὖν μὴ εἰδῶ τὴν δύναμιν τῆς φωνῆς, ἔσομαι τῷ λαλοῦντι βάρβαρος καὶ ὁ λαλῶν ἐν ἐμοὶ βάρβαρος. 12 οὕτως καὶ ὑμεῖς, ἐπεὶ ζηλωταί ἐστε πνευμάτων, πρὸς τὴν οἰκοδομὴν τῆς ἐκκλησίας ζητεῖτε ἵνα περισσεύητε.
[SBLGNT]

King James Version

1 Follow after charity, and desire spiritual gifts, but rather that ye may prophesy. 2 For he that speaketh in an

New Rendition

1 Seek after love and strive for spiritual gifts, and especially that you might speak with divine inspiration. 2 Because

unknown tongue speaketh not unto men, but unto God: for no man understandeth him; howbeit in the spirit he speaketh mysteries. 3 But he that prophesieth speaketh unto men to edification, and exhortation, and comfort. 4 He that speaketh in an unknown tongue edifieth himself; but he that prophesieth edifieth the church. 5 I would that ye all spake with tongues, but rather that ye prophesied: for greater is he that prophesieth than he that speaketh with tongues, except he interpret, that the church may receive edifying. 6 Now, brethren, if I come unto you speaking with tongues, what shall I profit you, except I shall speak to you either by revelation, or by knowledge, or by prophesying, or by doctrine? 7 And even things without life giving sound, whether pipe or harp, except they give a distinction in the sounds, how shall it be known what is piped or harped? 8 For if the trumpet give an uncertain sound, who shall prepare himself to the battle? 9 So likewise ye, except ye utter by the tongue words easy to be understood, how shall it be known what is spoken? for ye shall speak into the air. 10 There are, it may be, so many kinds of voices in the world, and none of them is without signification. 11 Therefore if I know not the meaning of the voice, I shall be unto him that speaketh a barbarian, and he that speaketh shall be a barbarian unto me. 12 Even so ye, forasmuch as ye are zealous of spiritual gifts, seek that ye may excel to the edifying of the church.

one who speaks in another language is not speaking to other people but to God, for no one understands him; he is speaking mysteries by the Spirit. 3 However, one who speaks by divine inspiration is speaking to people for their edification, encouragement, and consolation. 4 One who speaks in another language edifies himself, but one who speaks by divine inspiration edifies the entire church. 5 I wish all of you could speak in other languages, but I would much rather have you speak by divine inspiration. One who speaks by divine inspiration is greater than one who speaks in other languages, unless he also interprets, so that the whole church can receive edification. 6 Now, brothers and sisters, if I come to you speaking in other languages, how will I help you, unless I speak to you by revelation or knowledge or divine inspiration or doctrine? 7 In the same way, lifeless things that produce sound, such as a flute or harp, if they do not produce distinct notes, how will anyone recognize what is played on the flute or harp? 8 For indeed, if a trumpet produces an indistinct sound, who will prepare themselves for battle? 9 So it is also with you, unless you speak intelligibly with your tongue, how will what you have said be understood? For you will just be speaking into the air. 10 There are indeed all sorts of languages in the world, and none of them are devoid of meaning. 11 So if I do not understand the meaning of the language, I will be a foreigner to the speaker and the speaker a foreigner to me. 12 So you also, since you are eager for spiritual gifts, should seek for an abundance of them for the edification of the church.

Translation Notes and Comments

14:1 *Follow after charity / Seek after love:* The verb διώκω (*diōkō*) has the basic sense of "to move rapidly and decisively toward an objective."[16] The force of the present tense of the imperative used here suggests the continuation of an act already begun.[17] The force of Paul's choice of words shows the intensity with which he wants his readers to pursue love. Here Paul exalts love in the interest of all the other πνεύματα (*pneumata*). His insistence on pursuing that gift, however, in no way demeans any of the others but sets them in their place and discloses what should motivate them.[18]

desire spiritual gifts / strive for spiritual gifts: The word translated "spiritual gifts," πνευματικά, (*pneumatika*), literally "spiritual things," is the same word Paul used in 12:1 when talking about divine gifts and, therefore, shows he has these in mind here. Thus, he is encouraging the Corinthian Saints to strive to acquire those spiritual gifts that God gives to those who are obedient. The verb ζηλόω (*zēloō*) denotes a positive and intense interest in something and suggests an eagerness to have or achieve it.[19] For that reason, its translation as "desire" in the KJV is too weak; "strive for" as in our Rendition, is better.[20] Though the verb *zēloō* is strong, it falls somewhat behind διώκω (*diōkō*) in force. Paul's use of both shows that he wants the greatest effort put into gaining love but he also wants these people to put energy in making themselves worthy of these spiritual gifts. There is good reason since these are divine gifts. The Saints cannot go after them directly but rather must put themselves in a position to receive them since they come through continual personal righteousness.

but rather that ye may prophesy / and especially that you might speak with divine inspiration: The comparative adverb μᾶλλον (*mallon*), "rather" or "especially," designates something that is of a greater or higher degree.[21] The coordinating conjunction, δέ (*de*), "but," should be translated as "and" in this instance, showing that Paul is encouraging "a person to seek

---

16. BDAG, 254.

17. Wallace, *Greek Grammar,* 519–20. On the objective of ἀγάπη (*agapē*), "love," see Translation Notes on 13:1 with the associated Analysis.

18. Findlay, "St. Paul's First Epistle," 902.

19. BDAG, 427. Louw-Nida, §25.76, notes that it carries the idea of deep commitment drawn from a strong desire for something and, therefore, "to be earnest" or "to set one's heart on [something]."

20. On the noun πνευματιξακά (*pneumatika*), "spiritual gifts," see the Introduction above as well as Translation Notes on 12:1 with the associated Analysis.

21. BDAG, 613–14.

spiritual gifts, *particularly* the gift of prophecy."[22] On the verb προφητεύω (*prophēteuō*), from which the English word "prophesy" is derived, see the Translation Notes on 12:10 with the associated Analysis. The basic force of the Greek is that a prophet or prophetess is an "interpreter of the gods."[23] In the broadest context, it denotes speech that is inspired, intelligible, articulate, and communicative.[24] In the specific context of the New Testament, it means to "expound, interpret, preach, under the influence of the Holy Spirit."[25]

The term "prophet" had a much broader sense than it does for Latter-day Saints today. Anciently it described anyone who spoke with divine inspiration. It was not exclusively used to refer to members of the First Presidency and Quorum of the Twelve Apostles. Hence, in our Rendition, we often use "speak with divine inspiration" for the verb προφητεύω (*prophēteuō*), and "one who speaks with divine inspiration" for the noun προφήτης (*prophētēs*).

14:2 *he that speaketh in an unknown tongue / one who speaks in another language:* The JST changes "unknown" to "another,"[26] which suggests the language spoken under divine influence is likely one that is of this earth but known neither to the one who speaks it nor to those who hear it.[27] The Greek text does not have the words "an unknown," but simply γλώσσῃ (*glōssē*) in the dative case, "with [a] tongue." But like the English word, the *glōssē* can designate a language. Thus, following the JST, our Rendition translates this as "another language," when found in the singular as it is here and in 14:4, 13, 14, 19, 26, and 27.[28] When found in the plural, it is translated "other languages," as in 14:5, 6, 18, 22, 23, and 28. The idea the word carries, and that must be kept in mind, still means speech that is incomprehensible to a listener.

speaketh not unto men, but unto God: for no man understandeth him / is not speaking to other people but to God, for no one understands him: Paul's

---

22. Holzapfel and Wayment, *Making Sense,* 361.

23. In classical Greek, a prophet or prophetess interpreted oracles where in Jewish culture they spoke of Jehovah. See LSJ, 1539; Helmut Krämer, Rolf Rendtorff, Rudolf Meyer, and Gerhard Friedrich, "προφήτης, προφῆτις, προφητεύω, προφητεία, προφητικός, ψευδοπροφήτης," in *TDNT,* 6:781–864.

24. Thiselton, *First Epistle,* 1084.

25. LSJ, 1540; Gillespie, *First Theologians,* 141–44.

26. The same change is made in the JST in 14:4, 13, 14, 19, and 27.

27. This contradicts the idea of some that Paul is not referring to known tongues. For example, see Fitzmyer, *First Corinthians,* 510; R. H. Gundry, "'Ecstatic Utterance' (NEB)?" *Journal of Theological Studies* 17 (1966): 299–307; C. G. Williams, *Tongues of the Spirit: A Study of Pentecostal Glossolalia and Related Phenomena* (Cardiff: University of Wales Press, 1981), 26.

28. The NIV (in footnote *a* to 14:2) notes, "Or *another language*" (italics in original).

statement clearly indicates he feels the act is authentic. He tacitly acknowledges a deeply spiritual connection between the Saint and the Father from
which all other humans are excluded. This idea is brought out by his use of
the subordinate conjunction γάρ (*gar*), "for or because," which explains the
reason why this is the case—the communication is exclusively between God
and the speaker.[29] The verb ἀκούω (*akouō*) means literally "to hear," but it
carries the nuance that what is heard is also understood.[30]

**howbeit in the spirit he speaketh mysteries / he is speaking mysteries
by the spirit:** The noun μυστήριον (*mysterion*), "mystery," in this context,
does not have its usual meaning of spiritual knowledge that can only come
from God and which mere mortal intellect cannot grasp without divine
help. Rather, it expresses ideas that are hidden from the audience and
known only to the recipient and the Divine.[31] The dative noun πνεύματι
(*pneumati*), "by spirit," does not indicate the agent but rather the means
by which the person speaks. The grammar shows that the moving force
here is not specifically the Holy Ghost. Rather, the action is accomplished
through the means of a spiritual gift.[32]

**14:3 *But he that prophesieth speaketh unto men to edification, and
exhortation, and comfort / However, one who speaks by divine inspiration is speaking to people for their edification, encouragement, and consolation:*** On "prophesy," see Translation Notes on 12:10. The phrase ὁ δὲ
προφητεύων (*ho de prophēteuōn*), "he who prophesies," can be taken either
as habituation (pointing to a person who does the act of prophesying) or
to the temporal condition in which the act is performed (pointing to *when*
the act occurs).[33] Our Rendition, taking the latter view, follows the majority of translations because the context suggests that Paul has reference to

---

29. BDAG, 189–90.

30. Louw-Nida, §32.1; BDAG, 37–38, allows for "to learn something," but, though sufficiently forceful and accurate, it is too specific for the context.

31. Fee, *First Epistle*, 656. Some commentators view πνεύματι (*pneumati*), "by the spirit,"
as referring to the human spirit. For example, see Edwards, *Commentary*, 357; Robertson
and Plummer, *Critical and Exegetical Commentary*, 306. They do this based on the clear
reference to the human spirit in 14:14 and 32. Semantic and contextual considerations,
however, do not support this view for 14:2. See, in addition to Fee, Conzelmann, *1 Corinthians*, 234. For a more full discussion of μυστήριον, see Translation Notes on 1:26–27.

32. This is not to say that Paul did not understand that the Godhead had distinct personalities and duties, but, in this case, he is noting that it is *by* spiritual power that the
person is endowed with this ability. Wallace, *Greek Grammar*, 164–66. It is likely he is
referring to the "light of Christ." See D&C 80:45–47; 88:6–13.

33. The NRSV, NJB, and NIV, with most others, translate it as habituation ("he who prophesies") while the REB and MSG translates it as condition ("when a person prophesies . . .").

speaking by divine inspiration whenever and wherever that occurs and not to a person with an already prepared sermon. The idea is, then, that spirit-prompted testimony bearing is what brings edification to others.[34] Peter's speech on the day of Pentecost (Acts 2:14–47) and to the household of Cornelius (Acts 10:34–44) are good examples.

The purpose of this witness is threefold. The first purpose is to "edify." The noun οἰκοδομή (*oikodome*), literally, "building, construction," metaphorically means "edifying, edification, building up."[35] In this case it is "the qualitative building-up of the Christian community" (as in 8:1; 10:23).[36] Since the English word "edify" means "to instruct and improve especially in moral and religious knowledge," it is used in our Rendition.[37] The second purpose is for "exhortation." The noun παράλκησις (*paraklesis*) means "comfort" or "consolation," but it carries the idea of "the act of emboldening another in belief and course of action," and, therefore, "exhortation" works well.[38] The final purpose is to bring "comfort." The noun παραμυθία (*paramythia*) looks to the consolation or comfort one brings to another in distress, depression, or grief.[39]

Since love was the subject of chapter 13, it is of note that Paul does not list it as one of the objectives for prophesying. Perhaps the reason is that he feels it is obvious that love stands behind the three reasons he does articulate.

14:4 *He that speaketh in an unknown tongue edifieth himself; but he that prophesieth edifieth the church / One who speaks in another language edifies himself, but one who speaks by divine inspiration edifies the entire church:* In this verse, Paul sharpens the contrast between these two gifts. The central issue for Paul is οἰκοδομέω (*oikodomeo*), that is, to "build up" the Church and its people. Since no one can understand what is being spoken in "tongues," there may be amazement and even titillation, but no promoting of fellowship and unity. Though it is true that the individual can

---

34. Fee, *First Epistle*, 660. A spontaneous spiritual outpouring of testimony supersedes the prepared, perhaps clever, self-promoting speeches so common among the sophist when it comes to edifying the hearers.

35. BDAG, 696–97.

36. Fitzmyer, *First Corinthians*, 511. Paul had spent eighteen months living in the bustling city of Corinth where, it can be assumed, significant construction was going on. That being the case, his audience would have been attuned to οἰκοδομή (*oikodome*), the building up of structures, as a metaphor for building up both people and the Church. That condition also allowed the Apostle to use the metaphor of the master builder and of the need for proper foundation in 3:10–17. Bailey, *Mediterranean Eyes*, 391.

37. *Merriam-Webster's Collegiate Dictionary*, 396.

38. BDAG, 766.

39. BDAG, 769.

be edified by this divine gift, when improperly used, the gift could easily promote the excessive individualism that Paul is fighting.[40]

14:5 *I would that ye all spake with tongues, but rather that ye prophesied / I wish all of you could speak in other languages, but I would much rather have you speak by divine inspiration:* This passage does present a translation difficulty, which is how to understand the verb θέλω (*thelō*), "I would" or "I wish." Does it express conciliation or concession? Is Paul grudgingly giving into the practice, or is he expressing a wish for its broader use but one that he does not believe will happen? Our Rendition takes the second view because the conjunction ἵνα (*hina*), "in order that," in the second phrase, complements the verb *thelō* showing that Paul really does want them to speak in tongues.[41] With his use of the conjunction δέ (*de*), "but," the Apostle creates a contrast. The adverb μᾶλλον (*mallon*), "much rather," expresses a high degree or preference.[42] Paul's point is that, as much as he wishes all could speak in tongues, he much prefers that they all speak through the power of inspiration.[43]

for greater is he that prophesieth than he that speaketh with tongues, except he interpret, that the church may receive edifying / One who speaks by divine inspiration is greater than one who speaks in other languages, unless he also interprets, so that the whole church can receive edification: In this phrase, Paul gives his reason for preferring inspired speaking. The comparative adjective μείζων (*meizōn*), "greater," in this context, does not denote something that is more important or better than something else, but rather something that is "more prominent or outstanding because of certain advantage."[44] In this case, it is the possession of the gift of inspired speaking that is the most advantageous and, therefore, should be the most sought after.

Paul's point has nothing to do with a person's spiritual or public standing but with the importance of the gift she or he exercises for the "building up" of the Christian community.[45] With the phrase ἐκτὸς εἰ μὴ (*ektos ei mē*),

---

40. Fitzmyer, *First Corinthians,* 511. Gordon D. Fee, *God's Empowering Presence* (rpt., Grand Rapids, Mich.: Baker Book, 2009), 219, believes that there is no self-centeredness in the act, while Thiselton, *First Epistle,* 1095, believes the private act is edifying, but the public act touches on self-centeredness and self-affirmation.

41. Wallace, *Greek Grammar,* 476; Robertson and Plummer, *Critical and Exegetical Commentary,* 307.

42. BDAG, 613–14.

43. Bailey, *Mediterranean Eyes,* 389.

44. BDAG, 623–24.

45. Thiselton, *First Epistle,* 1098.

"unless," Paul inserts a caveat. If the person speaking in tongues, διερμηνεύῃ (*diermēneuē*), "interprets," what he or she says, then it can edify. The verb means both to "translate" from one language to another and "to explain" something so as to make it clearer.[46] When a person does this, he or she is equal to the one who "prophesies," for both now edify the congregation.

14:6 *Now, brethren, if I come unto you speaking with tongues, what shall I profit you, except I shall speak to you either by revelation, or by knowledge, or by prophesying, or by doctrine? / Now, brothers and sisters, if I come to you speaking in other languages, how will I help you, unless I speak to you by revelation or knowledge or divine inspiration or doctrine?:* On ἀδελφοί (*adelphoi*), "brothers and sisters," see Translation Notes on 1:10. In this verse, Paul continues to make his point. His argument centers on the verb ὠφελέω (*ōpheleō*), "to provide assistance."[47] The word denotes helping or assisting others to their profit. Paul lists four activities that are profitable to the Saints. The first is ἀποκάλυψις (*apokalypsis*), "revelation," here meaning the immediate disclosure of the word and will of God that would otherwise remain ever hidden.[48] The second is γνῶσις (*gnōsis*), "knowledge." Its position between *apokalysis* and προφητεία (*prophēteia*) invests the word with "the significance of extraordinary mystical knowledge" which ties it closely to the mysteries of godliness.[49] The third is *prophēteia*, "inspired speaking." For details, see 14:1 above. The final one is διδαχή (*didachē*), "doctrine." The word connotes a deep, authoritative instruction.[50]

One note is important here before pressing on. In the last four clauses, the second couple matches the first. Revelation is paired with prophecy and teaching with doctrine. It is the prophet who provides God's ongoing will to the people (*apokalypsis*) while it is the task of the teacher to keep before the people what God has already revealed (*didachē*).[51]

14:7 *And even things without life giving sound, whether pipe or harp, except they give a distinction in the sounds, how shall it be known what is piped or harped? / In the same way, lifeless things that produce sound, such as a flute or harp, if they do not produce distinct notes, how will anyone recognize what is played on the flute or harp?:* With this verse, Paul

46. BDAG, 244.
47. BDAG, 1107–8.
48. Albrecht Oepke, "ἀποκαλύπτω, ἀποκάλυψις," in *TDNT*, 3:563–92.
49. BDAG. 203.
50. BDAG, 241; Karl Heinrich Rengstorf, "διδαχή," in *TDNT*, 2:163–65.
51. Findlay, "St. Paul's First Epistle," 903.

continues to give evidence for his argument. The adverb ὅμως (*homōs*) usually means "nevertheless," but here it is equivalent to ὁμοίως (*homoiōs*), "similarly, in the same way,"[52] and is used by Paul to connect his former point with this one. The noun αὐλός (*aulos*) refers to a flute,[53] while κιθάρα (*kithara*) can denote either a harp or lyre though it usually points to the former.[54] The noun διαστολή (*diastolē*) refers to a "difference" or "distinction" between things. When pertaining to musical instruments, it denotes playing so that each musical note can be clearly distinguished.[55] The noun φθόγγος (*phthongos*), denoting as it does a measured harmonious sound, stresses this idea.[56] The verb γινώσκω (*ginōskō*) means "to understand, comprehend," or "grasp the significance" of something, but also to identify what one already knows.[57] In this case, it means "to recognize" what is being played. The problem Paul alludes to, as one scholar noted, "is not that notes are produced badly or inappropriately, but that untuned strings or overblown wind produces mere noise" causing the piece to lose its distinctness with the result that it is unrecognizable.[58] In contrast to the point Paul has made above, mostly concerning the revelation of new things, he looks here at recognizing what is already known, the repetition of the doctrine by reinforcing it. When it is clouded in an unknown language, no matter how clearly articulated, it is but noise.

14:8 *For if the trumpet give an uncertain sound, who shall prepare himself to the battle? / For indeed, if a trumpet produces an indistinct sound, who will prepare themselves for battle?:* Paul continues to push his point with yet another example. This time he turns to warfare. The noun σάλπιγξ (*salpingx*), "trumpet," in this context refers to what is called today a "bugle," which is used to sound instructions during battle.[59] The conditional clause introduced by ἐάν (*ean*), "if," and ending with the subjunctive verb δῷ (*dō*), "to give," shows that no one expects the trumpeter, at the verge of battle, to

---

52. BDAG, 710; Fee, *First Epistle,* 663, n. 20; Findlay, "St. Paul's First Epistle," 904, renders the phrase, "So also in your case."

53. BDAG, 151.

54. BDAG, 544; Louw-Nida, §6.83.

55. BDAG, 237.

56. BDAG, 1054; Findlay, "St. Paul's First Epistle," 904.

57. BDAG, 199–201.

58. Thiselton, *First Epistle,* 1103.

59. Louw-Nida, §6.89. According to Ogden and Skinner, *Verse by Verse,* 143, "Paul's audience anciently would have been familiar with the use of the trumpet to signal warnings, such as impending battles or other important events (Numbers 10:9: Joshua 6:4, 9). The trumpet (a ram's horn) was also used by the Jews to announce the arrival of the Sabbath."

play indistinct sounds.[60] The force of the clause is rendered "should give" in our Rendition.

Again, the issue is with clarity. The adjective ἄδηλος (*adēlos*) means "unclear" or "indistinct."[61] The issue is not that the sound is faint or of poor quality, but that, without clear differentiation between the notes, the sound is, again, nothing more than noise.[62] The verb παρασκευάζομαι (*paraskeuazomai*), in the middle voices, denotes preparing oneself to act.[63] In war, an unclear order will find soldiers unprepared, which could lead to disaster. Paul's point is that, no matter how clear or loud the sound may be, if it is unrecognizable, it will not bring the needed results.

14:9 *So likewise ye, except ye utter by the tongue words easy to be understood, how shall it be known what is spoken? / So it is also with you, unless you speak intelligibly with your tongue, how will what you have said be understood?:* With the use of the adverb οὕτως (*houtōs*) "in this manner," or "so,"[64] Paul connects his examples to the present problem. He keys on the adjective εὔσημος (*eusēmos*), "clear, distinct," which, when connected to the noun λόγος (*logos*), "word," denotes clear, intelligible speech."[65] Paul's question makes his point: no understanding will come unless one speaks intelligibly.

for ye shall speak into the air / For you will just be speaking into the air: The conjunction γάρ (*gar*), "for," explains the effect of intelligible speech. The noun ἀήρ (*aēr*), means "air,"[66] but the modern idiom "talking to the wind" carries the idea of the uselessness of the exercise.[67]

14:10 *There are, it may be, so many kinds of voices in the world, and none of them is without signification / There are indeed all sorts of languages in the world, and none of them are devoid of meaning:* Still pushing his point, Paul uses yet another example. The noun φωνή (*phōne*) denotes "sound" or "voice," but in the phrase γένη φωνῶν (*genē phōnōn*), it refers to various human languages.[68] The adjective ἄφωνος (*aphōnos*) denotes that which is "silent" or

---

60. Wallace, *Greek Grammar*, 698; Smyth, *Greek Grammar*, §2336.
61. BDAG, 19.
62. Thiselton, *First Epistle*, 1104.
63. BDAG, 771.
64. BDAG, 741–42.
65. BDAG, 413.
66. Louw-Nida, §1.6.
67. Fee, *First Epistle*, 664.
68. BDAG, 1071–72; Louw-Nida, §33.1. There is a reason why he does not use γλῶσσα (*glōssa*) here. The concept carried by that noun would include divine language. Conzelmann, *1 Corinthians*, 256.

"mute."[69] When associated with language, it means that which is incapable of "conveying meaning as a language normally does."[70] In the phrase οὐδὲν ἄφωνον (*ouden aphōnon*), the noun οὐδέν (*ouden*), "not one, none" refers back to the previously mentioned languages, that is, none [of the languages] are without meaning. Paul is saying that all human languages are capable of clearly expressing ideas.

14:11 *Therefore if I know not the meaning of the voice, I shall be unto him that speaketh a barbarian, and he that speaketh shall be a barbarian unto me / So if I do not understand the meaning of the language, I will be a foreigner to the speaker and the speaker a foreigner to me:* The adjective βάρβαρος (*barbaros*) refers to the use of a language foreign to the hearer and, therefore, carries the force of "alien speech."[71] Since the word was also applied to anyone who did not speak Greek, it came to designate a "foreigner." Paul wants his readers to focus on the negative effect that speaking in an unknown tongue had on others. It makes them feel like outsiders and thereby estranged from fellowship.[72] What exacerbates the problem is the potential that they could be missing out on precious and important divine information. That possibility could result in even greater frustration and alienation on their part.[73]

14:12 *Even so ye, forasmuch as ye are zealous of spiritual gifts, seek that ye may excel to the edifying of the church / So you also, since you are eager for spiritual gifts, should seek for an abundance of them for the edification of the church:* Paul now proceeds to his point. The phrase οὕτως καὶ ὑμεῖς (*houtōs kai hymeis*), literally "so also you," stresses the applicability of the example to his audience.[74] The noun ζηλωτής (*zēlōtēs*) describes "one who is earnestly committed to a side or cause, enthusiast."[75] The English word "zealot" is derived from the Greek. And what are they zealous to possess? Paul says it is πνευμάτων (*pneumatōn*), literally "spirits," which, at first blush,

---

69. Louw-Nida, §33.106, 135.

70. BDAG, 159.

71. BDAG, 166.

72. Fitzmyer, *First Corinthians*, 514–15. Often the nuance of the word was to someone who was not as educated or cultured as another. Hans Windisch, "βάρβαρος," in *TDNT*, 1:546–53.

73. Findlay, "St. Paul's First Epistle," 905.

74. Fee, *First Epistle*, 665, renders the idea as: "So it is with you."

75. BDAG, 427. The cognate verb ζηλόω (*zēloō*) has both a positive sense, "to be positively and intensely interested in something, strive, desire, exert oneself earnestly, be dedicated," and a negative sense, "to have intense negative feelings over another's achievements or success, be filled with jealousy or envy."

seems strange. The noun πνεῦμα (*pneuma*), however, has a broad range of meaning in Greek. Its root sense is "air in movement, blowing, breathing,"[76] but its derived meanings have a broad range: wind, breath, spirit (that non-physical part of a living human being), the Spirit of God, the Holy Ghost, and also evil spirits.[77] So which of these possible meanings is Paul referring to? In 12:1, Paul described the various spiritual gifts available to the Saints. He used the adjective πνευματικά (*pneumatika*), literally "spiritual things," derived from the noun *pneuma*. Paul's Jewish background would have influenced him to understand the word as "spiritual gifts." At the end of that same chapter (12:31), Paul admonished the Saints ζηλοῦτε δὲ τὰ χαρίσματα τὰ μείζονα (*zēloute de ta charismata ta meizona*), "You should earnestly strive for the greater spiritual gifts." Note that he uses the verb ζηλόω (*zēloō*), "to earnestly seek," from which the above mentioned noun *zēlōtēs* is derived. The parallel with *zēlōtēs pneumatōn* is obvious. The noun *charismata*, translated here "spiritual gifts," describes a gift that is freely given,[78] and it refers back to the *pneumatika* at the beginning of the chapter. Clearly *pneumatōn* in 14:12 must also refer to spiritual gifts, and is so translated in our Rendition.

So far, however, the Corinthians' eagerness for spiritual gifts has focused primarily on speaking in tongues. Paul wants the Corinthian Saints to seek after additional gifts of the spirit so that they will περισσεύητε (*perisseuēte*), "have an abundance" of them, with the aim of building up the Church, as he also stated in 14:5 above.

Analysis and Summary

Having shown his readers "the more excellent way," Paul returns to the topic of spiritual gifts. The text suggests that the reason he brings up the subject again is because certain manifestations of the Spirit have gotten out of hand. Therefore, he no longer speaks of these gifts in general but narrows his focus to just three, all having to do with inspired speaking: tongues, their interpretation, and prophecy.[79] His discourse is an invitation to his readers to join with him in the prophetic call (see Gal. 1:15–16). Like Moses (Num. 11:29), he does not see the gift of inspired speaking as something peculiar to any office. It should be, rather, a general gift that permeates the

---

76. BDAG, 832. It is derived from the verb πνέω (*pneō*), "to blow," like the wind, and "to breathe," BDAG, 837–38.

77. BDAG, 832–36.

78. BDAG, 1081.

79. Gillespie, *First Theologians,* 129–30; Conzelmann, *1 Corinthians,* 233.

whole of the Christian assemblage.[80] As he admonished them earlier (4:16), he wanted them to be his imitators (μίμηταί μου γίνεσθε, *mimētai mou ginesthe*), and that included sharing in prophetic power. His concern is for the welfare of others, especially for their edification (οἰκοδομή, *oikodomē*) during worship service.[81]

Even though the gift of prophecy is shared broadly, it is still among the highest a person can receive in mortality. Indeed, for the here and now, "prophecy is greater than charity," as Elder McConkie stated, "because in order to prophesy a man must first have the pure love of Christ in his soul (which is charity), and then he must attune himself to the Holy Spirit so as to receive the spirit of revelation and prophecy. Chiefly the gift of prophecy is to know by revelation from the Holy Ghost of the divine Sonship of our Lord."[82] He went on to say that "prophecy is revelation; it is testimony; it is Spirit speaking to spirit; it is knowing by revelation that Jesus is the Lord; that salvation is in Christ, that he has redeemed us by his blood. Prophecy is walking in paths of truth and righteousness; it is living and doing the will of Him whose we are; and in its final and perfect form—known as, 'the more sure word of prophecy'—it consists in 'a man's knowing that he is sealed up unto eternal life, by revelation and the spirit of prophecy, through the power of the Holy Priesthood.'"[83]

Paul does, however, spend a lot of time in chapter 14 on the gift of tongues. "In his discourse on spiritual gifts," notes an LDS scholar, "Paul referred to the gift of tongues in approximately one-third of the verses.[84] This gift is one of the so-called charismatic gifts and was subject to much misuse, owing to its strange and wonderful elements."[85]

The Apostle's thrust, as expressed in 14:3, is on his preference of prophecy over tongues for specific reasons. Inspired speaking, as noted by one scholar, accomplishes three tasks: First, it acts to further build up the Christian life (οἰκοδομή, *oikodomē*); second, it stimulates the Christian will (παράκλησις, *paraklēsis*); and third, it strengthens the Christian spirit (παραμυθία,

---

80. K. O. Sandnes, *Paul—One of the Prophets? A Contribution to the Apostle's Self-Understanding* (Tübingen: Mohr, 1991), 123–26.

81. Gillespie, *First Theologians,* 142–44.

82. *DNTC,* 2:384.

83. *DNTC,* 2:386.

84. In the eighty-four verses that comprise chapters 12–15, approximately twenty-three, about 30 percent, examine the gift of tongues.

85. Freeman, "Paul's Earnest Pursuit," 42–43.

paramythia).[86] As the Apostle shows in 14:6, this gift can benefit the people in four ways: (1) by disclosing the mind and will of God (ἀποκάλυψις, *apokalypsis*), (2) by teaching the breadth and depth of what God has revealed (γνῶσις, *gnōsis*), (3) by inspired witnessing (προφητεία, *prophēteia*), and (4) by keeping the Church anchored to correct instruction (διδαχή, *didachē*). Each of these, as Paul can see, will contribute to Christian meetings bringing a deeper understanding of and commitment to the faith in Christ. It is of note that both of the above lists provide services that the gift of tongues cannot.[87]

In 14:6, Paul lists four categories of such speaking: disclosure of the word and will of God (*apokalypsis*); a pronouncement of the mysteries of the kingdom (*gnōsis*); dynamic, effective, and hortatory preaching (*prophēteia*); and finally, an effective explanation of doctrine (*didachē*). He insists that a person cannot be edified by what he does not understand and, therefore, speaking in tongues is of little worth in building up the Church. There is, however, an exception. If the person translates what he has said in the unknown tongue, edification can take place (14:5).

To drive home the importance and usefulness of inspired speech over speaking in tongues, Paul uses three examples: first, the need for a performer to play each note of his or her musical instrument clearly and distinctly so that the melody may be recognized (14:7); second, the need for a bugler to clearly sound instructions so that soldiers are properly prepared for battle (14:8); and third, the need for two individuals to speak the same language if they are to view each other as something other than unwelcome foreigners (14:11).

Using a musical instrument for his example allows Paul to make a striking point—no matter how clear or how carefully the notes are played, if the timing, rhythm, tone, and pitch are off, the piece cannot be recognized. The same is true of language. Though the sounds may convey profound thoughts to those who speak that tongue, to those who do not, it is just so much frustrating noise. Because such expression will have no edifying effect, it is no better than speaking into the air (14:9). To have the effect Paul desires, speech must be articulate, ordered, and conform to usage. At Corinth, *glossolalia* did none of those things.[88]

His example of the reaction of two individuals who do not know one another's language really helped him push his point. As a multinational city, though Latin would have been prominent, many other languages would

---

86. Findlay, "St. Paul's First Epistle," 902.
87. Bailey, *Mediterranean Eyes,* 392.
88. Findlay, "St. Paul's First Epistle," 905.

have been spoken, especially among the slave class.[89] Because people were not well versed in all these languages, problems resulting from miscommunication were, likely, a daily challenge. Further, people tend to live in enclaves where the same language and culture are shared and where others are often shut out. As a result, the Corinthian Saints would have been well aware of the divisive power that language had. Paul played on this to show that such could (and probably was) happening in the Church.[90] The result was feelings of mutual discomfort and, on the part of some, being deliberately excluded (14:10–11).[91] Paul here illustrates that there is a built-in wrongness with anything that would cause such a feeling to exist in the Church. Speaking in tongues does that and thereby sets up, even if unconsciously, artificial barriers that cause some to feel unwelcome and, therefore, unwanted. Such should not happen in a community composed of brothers and sisters.[92] The issue is whether worship is a case of "God and me" or of "God and us." Paul argues for the latter.[93]

Paul is particularly concerned when prayers are not understood by all. In 14:14, he states the result of such prayers as ἄκαρπος (*akarpos*), "fruitless," that is, "unproductive." For that reason, Paul insists that in public prayers, both mind and spirit must be engaged. Paul's desire is for a combination of both. In this he echoes the Lord's promise to Oliver Cowdery that "I will tell you in your mind and in your heart [here a synonym for spirit], by the Holy Ghost, which shall come upon you and which shall dwell in your heart" (D&C 8:2).

Like Paul, Joseph Smith was concerned with the excessive display of tongues during the early period of the Restoration. Concerning the gift, he made the following points: Do not be overly curious about this gift or indulge in it; in meetings, do not speak in tongues unless there is an interpreter; the primary use of this gift is to teach nonbelievers in their own language; the devil can mimic the gift of tongues; and anything revealed through tongues will not be accepted as doctrine unless confirmed by another source.[94] His ready

---

89. Most of the preserved stone inscriptions from Paul's day are in Latin. Murphy-O'Connor, *St. Paul's Corinth*, 8.

90. Bailey, *Mediterranean Eyes*, 393.

91. Meyer, *Exegetical Commentary*, 2:10, notes that it makes others feel "useless."

92. Freeman, "Paul's Earnest Pursuit," 43; Ogden and Skinner, *Verse by Verse*, 143; Sperry, *Life and Letters*, 127; Thiselton, *First Epistle*, 1106.

93. Thiselton, *First Epistle*, 1116–17.

94. Joseph Smith addressed this issue four different times. See "History, 1838–1856, Volume C-1," 13 [addenda]; "History, 1838–1856, Volume C-1," 1266; "History, 1838–1856, Volume C-1 Addenda," 42; and "History, 1838–1856, Volume C-1 Addenda," 68.

willingness to profess tongues as an authentic gift while cautioning against its overuse directly parallels the counsel of Paul.[95]

So far as the gift of prophecy is concerned, neither Paul nor Joseph Smith gives such precautions. The reason is because of what inspired speaking can do. For Paul, it is οἰκοδομή (*oikodomē*), the "edification" of others that is the object of any kind of church related activity. The Greek word means "to build up," and it focuses on the ability of inspired speech to lift others and bring to them grace and its enabling power.[96]

With 14:12, Paul brings his argument full circle. In 14:1, he admonished his readers to "strive (ζηλοῦτε, *zēloute*) for spiritual gifts," more especially for prophecy. In 14:12, he admonishes them to "seek (ζητεῖτε, *zēteite*) for" an abundance of these gifts, the force of the imperative stressing the serious effort they should put into obtaining them.[97] His earnest appeal came from his conviction that these gifts—properly used when channeled by love—would be a uniting force among these divisive branches.[98]

Verse 14:12 also highlights the difference between Paul's humility and his detractors' pride shown in their boast of deep spirituality. The display of the gift of tongues was, apparently, too often a childish and thoughtless exhibition of self-centeredness. Paul in no way intimates that the display of this gift is childish, but its use to show off is. Such self-advertising evidences a lack of appreciation for oneself and of concern for others.[99]

The Apostle shows them that their premise is wrong. Speaking in tongues is not a sign of a great spiritual endowment. They have been striving for the wrong thing and should, rather, reach for true higher spiritual powers. Those powers are anchored in having the Spirit and its fruits in their lives. That Spirit is derived from Christ and is meant to testify of his works. True spirituality is manifest by doing what the Lord did: serving and edifying others, neither of which tongues do. Paul explains to these Christians that, like their Lord, they should be zealous in building up all within the community of the Saints. Thus, they are to forget about parading their gift and to communicate intelligibly and sincerely during public worship services.[100]

It is of note that Paul never questions the genuineness of the gift of tongues. It is the public parading of the gift that concerns him. The question

---

95. Ogden and Skinner, *Verse by Verse*, 143.
96. Louw-Nida, §74.15.
97. BDAG, 428.
98. Bailey, *Mediterranean Eyes*, 394.
99. Thiselton, *First Epistle*, 1119.
100. Thiselton, *First Epistle*, 1107.

he does not address is how a person who uses the gift for self-benefit can be open to spiritual influence. The answer may reside in the long-suffering of the Lord. These people were members of a society where prestige, honor, and station meant everything. Being baptized did not immediately change long-held attitudes and actions. The Lord's patience coupled with the powers of the Atonement, at least for the present, allowed the Spirit to flow and the gifts to be enjoyed. The history of Christianity reveals, however, the gradual demise of these gifts, suggesting that the necessary change did not come and, therefore, the Lord's grace was withdrawn.

One final point on tongues seems in order. Though speaking in tongues should not be gainsaid, nowhere in the New Testament is it shown to be a normal or necessary condition of Christian life. It is not, therefore, a necessary element in the spiritual development of either the individual Saint or the corporate Church.[101] Its primary function is to assist in missionary work and little else.[102] Among the branches of the Church in the very cosmopolitan city of Corinth, however, the gift could facilitate oneness among the members as each was able to better understand the gospel in his or her own tongue. The gift was certainly an expression of divine charity for all members.

THE IMPORTANCE OF THE GIFT OF PROPHECY (14:13–25)

Greek Text

13 Διὸ ὁ λαλῶν γλώσσῃ προσευχέσθω ἵνα διερμηνεύῃ. 14 ἐὰν γὰρ προσεύχωμαι γλώσσῃ, τὸ πνεῦμά μου προσεύχεται, ὁ δὲ νοῦς μου ἄκαρπός ἐστιν. 15 τί οὖν ἐστιν; προσεύξομαι τῷ πνεύματι, προσεύξομαι δὲ καὶ τῷ νοΐ· ψαλῶ τῷ πνεύματι, ψαλῶ δὲ καὶ τῷ νοΐ. 16 ἐπεὶ ἐὰν εὐλογῇς πνεύματι, ὁ ἀναπληρῶν τὸν τόπον τοῦ ἰδιώτου πῶς ἐρεῖ τὸ Ἀμήν ἐπὶ τῇ σῇ εὐχαριστίᾳ; ἐπειδὴ τί λέγεις οὐκ οἶδεν· 17 σὺ μὲν γὰρ καλῶς εὐχαριστεῖς, ἀλλ᾽ ὁ ἕτερος οὐκ οἰκοδομεῖται. 18 εὐχαριστῶ τῷ θεῷ, πάντων ὑμῶν μᾶλλον γλώσσαις λαλῶ· 19 ἀλλὰ ἐν ἐκκλησίᾳ θέλω πέντε λόγους τῷ νοΐ μου λαλῆσαι, ἵνα καὶ ἄλλους κατηχήσω, ἢ μυρίους λόγους ἐν γλώσσῃ.

20 Ἀδελφοί, μὴ παιδία γίνεσθε ταῖς φρεσίν, ἀλλὰ τῇ κακίᾳ νηπιάζετε, ταῖς δὲ φρεσὶν τέλειοι γίνεσθε. 21 ἐν τῷ νόμῳ γέγραπται ὅτι Ἐν ἑτερογλώσσοις καὶ ἐν χείλεσιν ἑτέρων λαλήσω τῷ λαῷ τούτῳ, καὶ οὐδ᾽ οὕτως εἰσακούσονταί μου, λέγει

---

101. F. W. Beare, "Speaking in Tongues: A Critical Survey of the New Testament Evidence," *Journal of Biblical Studies* 83 (1964): 229–46.

102. "History, 1838–1856, Volume C-1 Addenda," 8.

κύριος. 22 ὥστε αἱ γλῶσσαι εἰς σημεῖόν εἰσιν οὐ τοῖς πιστεύουσιν ἀλλὰ τοῖς ἀπίστοις, ἡ δὲ προφητεία οὐ τοῖς ἀπίστοις ἀλλὰ τοῖς πιστεύουσιν. 23 ἐὰν οὖν συνέλθῃ ἡ ἐκκλησία ὅλη ἐπὶ τὸ αὐτὸ καὶ πάντες λαλῶσιν γλώσσαις, εἰσέλθωσιν δὲ ἰδιῶται ἢ ἄπιστοι, οὐκ ἐροῦσιν ὅτι μαίνεσθε; 24 ἐὰν δὲ πάντες προφητεύωσιν, εἰσέλθῃ δέ τις ἄπιστος ἢ ἰδιώτης, ἐλέγχεται ὑπὸ πάντων, ἀνακρίνεται ὑπὸ πάντων, 25 τὰ κρυπτὰ τῆς καρδίας αὐτοῦ φανερὰ γίνεται, καὶ οὕτως πεσὼν ἐπὶ πρόσωπον προσκυνήσει τῷ θεῷ, ἀπαγγέλλων ὅτι Ὄντως ὁ θεὸς ἐν ὑμῖν ἐστιν. [SBLGNT]

King James Version

13 Wherefore let him that speaketh in an unknown tongue pray that he may interpret. 14 For if I pray in an unknown tongue, my spirit prayeth, but my understanding is unfruitful. 15 What is it then? I will pray with the spirit, and I will pray with the understanding also: I will sing with the spirit, and I will sing with the understanding also. 16 Else when thou shalt bless with the spirit, how shall he that occupieth the room of the unlearned say Amen at thy giving of thanks, seeing he understandeth not what thou sayest? 17 For thou verily givest thanks well, but the other is not edified. 18 I thank my God, I speak with tongues more than ye all: 19 Yet in the church I had rather speak five words with my understanding, that by my voice I might teach others also, than ten thousand words in an unknown tongue. 20 Brethren, be not children in understanding: howbeit in malice be ye children, but in understanding be men. 21 In the law it is written, With men of other tongues and other lips will I speak unto this people; and yet for all that will they not hear me, saith the Lord. 22 Wherefore tongues are for a sign, not to them that believe, but to them that believe not: but prophesying serveth not for them that believe not, but for them which believe. 23 If

New Rendition

13 Therefore, anyone who speaks in another language should pray that he may also interpret. 14 For if I pray in another language, my spirit prays, but my mind is unproductive. 15 So what should I do? I will pray with my spirit, but I will also pray with my mind. I will sing praises with my spirit, but I will also sing praises with my mind. 16 Otherwise, if you say a blessing with the spirit, how can an investigator say "Amen" on the blessing, since he does not know what you are saying? 17 Indeed you may be giving thanks well enough, but the other is not edified. 18 I thank God I speak in tongues more than all of you. 19 But in a meeting, I would rather speak five words with my mind, so that I might instruct others, than speak ten thousand words in another language. 20 Brothers and sisters, do not be children in your thinking, instead be as a child in regard to evil, but be mature in your thinking. 21 In the Law it is written, "By people with a foreign language and by the lips of strangers I will speak to this people, but even then they will not listen to me, says the Lord." 22 And so speaking in other languages is not a sign for those who believe, but for those who do not believe. Speaking by divine inspiration, on the other hand, is not for unbelievers,

therefore the whole church be come together into one place, and all speak with tongues, and there come in those that are unlearned, or unbelievers, will they not say that ye are mad? 24 But if all prophesy, and there come in one that believeth not, or one unlearned, he is convinced of all, he is judged of all: 25 And thus are the secrets of his heart made manifest; and so falling down on his face he will worship God, and report that God is in you of a truth.

but for believers. 23 So if the whole church meets together and everyone is speaking in other languages, and investigators or unbelievers come in, won't they say you are out of your mind? 24 On the other hand, if all are speaking by divine inspiration, and some unbeliever or investigator comes in, he will be convinced by all and examined by all. 25 The hidden things of his heart will be disclosed, and he will fall upon his face and will worship God, exclaiming that "Truly God is among you!"

Translation Notes and Comments

14:13 *Wherefore let him that speaketh in an unknown tongue pray that he may interpret / Therefore, anyone who speaks in another language should pray that he may also interpret:* The conjunction διό (*dio*), "thus, therefore," strongly ties Paul's admonition to what he has said. The purpose of Church meetings is for edification and, to see that that happens, the one who has and expresses the gift of tongues should also pray for the gift of interpretation (διερμηνεύω, *diermēneuō*, see 14:5).[103] The present imperative προσευχέσθω (*proseuchesthō*) is best translated into idiomatic English as "should pray," as in our Rendition.[104] Because of the syntax of this phrase, some commentators argue that, following the form of 14:27, an indefinite subject should be supplied, which would mean that the one who speaks in a foreign tongue is someone other than the one who interprets it.[105] However, since Greek grammar dictates that the subject of both the subordinate and main verbs is the same, our Rendition follows this rule.

14:14 *For if I pray in an unknown tongue, my spirit prayeth, but my understanding is unfruitful / For if I pray in another language, my spirit prays, but my mind is unproductive:* In this verse, Paul accomplishes two tasks. First, he explains why the person who speaks in tongues should also interpret, and second he opens a new set of arguments against the superiority of the gift of tongues. His use of the first person singular, "I," is rhetorical, referring to anyone who does this act. He sets up here a contrast

---

103. Fitzmyer, *First Corinthians*, 515.
104. Thiselton, *First Epistle*, 1108.
105. Fitzmyer, *First Corinthians*, 515.

between "spirit" and "mind." The noun πνεῦμα (*pneuma*), "spirit," denotes that portion of the soul which gives life to and animates the body.[106] It also defines a person's inward faculty where the will resides and to that which acts emotionally to the surroundings. Finally, it is the core that the Spirit can influence.[107] On the other hand, the noun νοῦς (*nous*), "mind," denotes "the faculty of intellectual perception." It can therefore refer to both intellect and understanding as well as to attitudes and opinions.[108] It stands in contrast to "the flesh" (Rom. 7:23–25) and is the center of the new nature that rebirth in Christ brings.[109] Even so, in Paul, it is distinct from the spirit, and thus the spirit can be engaged in activity while the mind is not. The result Paul expresses with the adjective ἄκαρπος (*akarpos*). The word refers to activities that are unfruitful and, therefore, useless.[110] Since the English word "unproductive" denotes that which does not yield results, benefits, or profits, it is used in our Rendition.

The point is this: when the spirit exalts in praise to God in an unknown tongue, the mind, of both he who prays and they who listen, is bypassed, and therefore the act is unproductive. That is not to say that the one praying somehow misses out, for that is certainly not the case. But his prayer, as wonderful as it may be, does not benefit others because it does not produce in them the fruit of faith in Christ. Therefore, a prayer in tongues is *akarpos,* having little value because there is no edification for the Church (14:12).[111] This verse shows that in public prayer a greater blessing to the speaker comes largely from profit to the hearer.[112]

14:15 *What is it then? / So what should I do?:* The Greek phrase here is τί οὖν ἐστιν (*ti oun estin*), literally "what then is it," with an unstated, but understood, "I should do?," which our Rendition supplies for clarity. The Greek phrase (as in 14:26; Rom. 3:9; 6:15) signals to Paul's readers that he is concluding his counsel to a specific event reported to him, namely, that of speaking or praying in tongues.

I will pray with the spirit, and I will pray with the understanding also / I will pray with my spirit, but I will also pray with my mind: On "spirit"

---

106. Here the noun "soul" is defined as in D&C 88:15, "the spirit and the body are the soul of man." Louw-Nida, §26.9 defines this aspect of the word as "inner being."

107. Fitzmyer, *First Corinthians,* 516.

108. BDAG, 680.

109. Johannes Behm, "νοῦς," in *TDNT,* 4:951–60.

110. BDAG, 35.

111. Ernest Käsemann, *Perspectives on Paul* (Philadelphia: Fortress Press, 1971), 122–37.

112. Findlay, "St. Paul's First Epistle," 907.

and "mind," see 14:14. Again, Paul's use of the first person singular "I" is rhetorical, looking to anyone who does these things. The inference here is that people should indeed pray, but not in some foreign tongue. The pronoun "my" is derived from the definite article which can take the place of an emphatic possessive.[113] It is of note that the Apostle does not set the mind and spirit opposite each other. It is not a case of "either . . . or" but of "both . . . and."[114] Paul is emphasizing that true worship must involve both a person's spiritual and intellectual faculties. Praying in faith entails a sincere, strenuous, even stern effort in which both the spirit and mind lift to God in praise, adoration, thanksgiving, or supplication.

I will sing with the spirit, and I will sing with the understanding also / I will sing praises with my spirit, but I will also sing praises with my mind: The verb ψάλλω (*psallō*) denotes singing praises either *a cappella* or with accompaniment.[115] Because the context here is public worship, the singing would likely be Old Testament psalms or newly fashioned works of praise and supplication in behalf of the Christian community. Again, Paul shows the need for a combined spiritual and intellectual effort in bringing praises and requests to the Father.

14:16 *Else when thou shalt bless with the spirit, how shall he that occupieth the room of the unlearned say Amen at thy giving of thanks / Otherwise, if you say a blessing with the spirit, how can an investigator say "Amen" on the blessing:* The verb εὐλογέω (*eulogeō*) refers to the calling down of a blessing on a person or, in this context, a congregation.[116] Though sometimes referring to the sacrament, Paul most often uses the noun εὐχαριστία (*eucharistia*), "giving of thanks," as a synonym for "blessing."[117] The phrase εὐλογῆς πνεύματι (*eulogēs pneumati*), "bless with the spirit" infers the calling down of a blessing in prayer that leaves out the mind, perhaps, because it is spoken in tongues. Such a prayer, as Paul has already stated, will not communicate to others. As a result, they will not be able to give "the Amen" at the prayer's close. The particle ἀμήν (*amēn*), used in both Jewish and Christian worship services, denotes strong affirmation to what was said, meaning as it does, "let it be so."[118]

---

113. Smyth, *Greek Grammar,* §1121, and Wallace, *Greek Grammar,* 215–16.
114. Thiselton, *First Epistle,* 1111.
115. BDAG, 1096.
116. BDAG, 407–8.
117. BDAG, 416.
118. BDAG, 53–54. It is even so today. As Elder McConkie states in *DNTC,* 2:385, "It is proper practice for the congregation to say Amen at the conclusion of a gospel sermon,

The Greek phrase ὁ ἀναπληρῶν τὸν τόπον τοῦ ἰδιώτου (*ho anaplērōn ton topon tou idiōtou*), literally "the one occupying the place of the unin-structed," presents some translation difficulties as is illustrated by the variety of ways it has been rendered.[119] The verb ἀναπληρόω (*anaplēroō*) has the root sense of "to complete the quantity of something," that is "to make complete."[120] Used together with the noun τόπος (*topos*), "place," it expresses "to take or fill someone's place."[121] The noun ἰδιώτης (*idiōtēs*) designates a "layperson, amateur, outsider."[122] In pagan religious asso-ciations, the term was used for "nonmembers" that could nevertheless participate in the sacrifices.[123] In 14:23 and 24, they are contrasted with the ἄπιστοι (*apistoi*), "unbelievers." The *idiōtai,* therefore, are neither unbelievers nor full-fledged members, but are prospective members or catechumens[124]—what Latter-day Saints might call "investigators," hence the use of that word in our Rendition.

seeing he understandeth not what thou sayest? / since he does not know what you are saying?: With these words, Paul makes his point: when one enjoins God only through use of the spirit, likely because he or she is speaking in tongues, no one else can know or understand what is being said. Only when the νοῦς (*nous*), "mind," is involved can there be commu-nication with others and, thereby, edification. Thus, both spirit and mind must be engaged in public worship.

14:17 *For thou verily givest thanks well, but the other is not edified / Indeed you may be giving thanks well enough, but the other is not edified:* Again the concern is that what they are doing is not οἰκοδομέω (*oikodomeō*), "edifying." The adverb καλῶς (*kalōs*), "well," describes an act that is done

---

thus signifying acceptance of and concurrence in what has been said." In the case of praising the Lord, the utterance shows that the hearers are willing if not anxious to join that praise (LXX Neh. 5:13; 8:6; 1 Chr. 16:36). The affirmation is also found in the Dead Sea scrolls 1Qs 1:20; 2:10, 18. In curses and blessings it was repeated twice. It can also be found in Paul's other writings at Gal. 1:5; Rom. 1:25; 9:5; 11:36; 15:33; 16:24, 27.

119. The NRSV renders it "anyone in the position of an outsider"; the NIV, "in the posi-tion of an inquirer" or "among the inquirers"; and the NET, "someone without the gift" or "one who fills the place of the unlearned." For discussion, see Thiselton, *First Epistle,* 1114–15.

120. BDAG, 70; Fitzmyer, *First Corinthians,* 517.

121. BDAG, 70.

122. BDAG, 468.

123. BDAG, 468.

124. BDAG, 468. Robertson and Plummer, *Critical and Exegetical Commentary,* 313, argue that the term ἰδιῶται (*idiōtai*) referred to those who are "without gifts" because they did not yet have the power of the Spirit.

in a proper and beneficial manner, but it also introduces a deferential tone, which is expressed in English by "may be" as in our Rendition.[125] In this verse, Paul does not suggest that the prayer was improperly done. He makes it clear that the issue is not whether the expression of gratitude was done in a proper manner, but whether it was beneficial to others. Did it "build up" the members (see 8:1, Rendition)? If not, the act, no matter how well, proper, or exact in execution, was not in keeping with the purpose of the worship service. Paul here uses a strictly utilitarian standard as the basis of estimating Christian devotion. That which is abstractly beautiful and appealing must be subordinated to that which is practical and edifying.[126]

14:18 *I thank my God, I speak with tongues more than ye all / I thank God I speak in tongues more than all of you:* This is a good example of the vernacular use of parataxis in place of subordination.[127] One would expect the conjunction ὅτι (*hoti*), "that" to follow εὐχαριστῶ τῷ θεῷ (*eucharistō tō theō*), "I thank God." Instead, the two independent phrases are set side by side. This is common in English, which allows our Rendition to follow the Greek. The phrase *eucharistō tō theō*, "I thank God," is very forceful and is meant to drive Paul's point. The adverb μᾶλλον (*mallon*), "more than," suggests that Paul is not saying that he speaks more languages than anyone else, but that he is more gifted in tongues than any of the others.[128] His statement does two things: not only does it show that he is not disparaging the gift but also that he has been highly endowed with it.[129] By saying this, Paul undercuts any argument from his detractors that he feels the gift to be unimportant. On the other hand, it is possible, as one LDS scholar noted that, at least for some of the Saints, the "fondness for this particular gift was in emulation of Paul rather than simple fascination."[130]

---

125. BDAG, 505–6.

126. Findlay, "St. Paul's First Epistle," 908. Paul applies the same test to a different matter in vv. 23, 33.

127. Blass and Debrunner, *Greek Grammar*, §471; Smyth, *Greek Grammar*, §2170.

128. This follows the translation in the REB. The central issue is not on tongues, but the "giftedness" that Paul enjoys. The Apostle was well versed in Greek, Hebrew, and Aramaic, and likely got by with Latin because of his Roman citizenship. The history reported in Acts 21:37–22:2 suggests that Paul was very fluid in these languages. The question is if Paul is referring to quantity (that is, he speaks in tongues more often than anyone else) or quality (that is, he speaks more intently or fully than others). See Meyer, *Exegetical Commentary*, 2:16; Barrett, *First Epistle*, 321. For discussion, see Hays, *First Corinthians*, 237. It is likely that Paul is speaking qualitatively, saying in effect, "I am more gifted in tongues than any of you." Thiselton, *First Epistle*, 1117.

129. Freeman, "Paul's Earnest Pursuit," 43.

130. Holzapfel and Wayment, *Making Sense*, 361.

14:19 *Yet in the church I had rather speak five words with my understanding, that by my voice I might teach others also, than ten thousand words in an unknown tongue / But in a meeting, I would rather speak five words with my mind, so that I might instruct others, than speak ten thousand words in another language:* Having admitted to the abundance of the gift of tongues he enjoys, Paul here immediately deprecates it.[131] The phrase ἐν ἐκκλησίᾳ (*en ekklēsia*), literally "in the assembly," confines Paul's remarks, however, to church meetings. They do not apply to a private setting. Again, he emphasizes the importance of νοῦς (*nous*), "mind" or "understanding," because it is here that the purpose of the meeting can be realized. That purpose is summed up in the verb κατηχέω (*katēcheō*), which refers to sharing information that one has received and, thus, means "to teach" or "to instruct."[132] Paul has already shown the importance of teachers by ranking them with "apostles" and "prophets" (12:28). The gifts of wisdom and knowledge are two of the "greatest spiritual gifts" that Paul has already mentioned (12:31; see also 12:8; 14:6). The adjective μυρίοι (*myrioi*), "ten thousand," is often used hyperbolically and should not always be taken literally.[133] The case is the same with the phrase πέντε λόγους (*pente logous*), "five words." Paul uses it as a rounded number to mean "several."[134] Paul's point is that a few words delivered rationally and intelligently will be persuasive and uplifting, while thousands of words spoken in some unknown tongue will not.[135] Though the plural adjective ἄλλους (*allous*), "others," could apply just to the investigators, it likely refers to the whole congregation.[136]

14:20 *Brethren, be not children in understanding: howbeit in malice be ye children / Brothers and sisters, do not be children in your thinking, instead be as a child in regard to evil:* On ἀδελφοί (*adelphoi*), "brothers and sisters," see Translation Notes on 1:10. The noun παιδίον (*paidion*), "child," spans a range of meaning from infant to preteen.[137] Here the focus is on the very young. The noun φρήν (*phrēn*) denotes both thinking and understanding,[138] two areas in which children lack both ability and sophistication. The breadth of meaning

---

131. Bruce, *1 and 2 Corinthians,* 132.
132. BDAG, 534.
133. BDAG, 661.
134. Conzelmann, *1 Corinthians,* 240.
135. Fitzmyer, *First Corinthians,* 518.
136. BDAG, 46–47.
137. BDAG, 749.
138. BDAG, 1065.

for the noun κακία (*kakia*), "malice, evil," is wide and includes everything from outright wickedness and depravity to trouble and misfortune.[139] Its basic nuance, however, is the desire to do harm.[140] Paul pleads with his readers to retain the innocence of a child, but not its tendency to self-centered and immature thought.[141]

but in understanding be men / but be mature in your thinking: As noted above, the noun *phrēn* denotes thinking and understanding. The range of the word encompasses both the mental activity of considering, pondering, or determining something coupled with the grasping of its meaning and significance. The adjective τέλειος (*teleios*), "mature," refers to anything that meets the highest of standards and also to that which is complete, fully finished, or mature.[142] Thus, Paul admonishes his adult readers to be ταῖς φρέσιν τέλειοι (*tais phresin teleioi*), "mature in thoughts."

14:21 *In the law it is written, With men of other tongues and other lips will I speak unto this people; and yet for all that will they not hear me, saith the Lord / In the Law it is written, "By people with a foreign language and by the lips of strangers I will speak to this people, but even then they will not listen to me, says the Lord":* Paul quotes from Isaiah 28:11–12. Though the phase ὁ νόμος (*ho nomos*), "the Law," usually refers to the Pentateuch, the Apostle's coupling Isaiah to the phrase suggests he is referring to the whole Old Testament.[143] The quote makes Paul's purpose clear. He has determined that it is likely that some of his readers will not be persuaded by his arguments. He, therefore, buttresses them with the authority of scripture. It is of note, however, that his quote conforms neither to the LXX nor the MT.[144] As it stands, however, it brings his point home.

Isaiah's prophecy was struck against the kingdoms of both Judah and Ephraim because they would not heed Jehovah's prophets. Isaiah's warning was that the Assyrians would become masters of both areas and, by force of arms, the Israelites would listen to Jehovah's words albeit spoken

---

139. BDAG, 500.

140. Louw-Nida, §88.105, 199.

141. Deluz, *Companion*, 203.

142. BDAG, 995–96.

143. Ogden and Skinner, *Verse by Verse*, 143–44. Though Paul uses the phrase ἐν τῷ νόμῳ (*en tō nomō*), "in the Law," which he quotes not from Moses but Isaiah, he shows that he is referring to the whole Old Testament as it existed in his day.

144. Whether Paul's memory was faulty or he was reconstructing the passage to make his point or he had a different Greek copy of the prophecy cannot be ascertained. For discussion, see Thiselton, *First Epistle*, 1120.

in a foreign tongue. Even so, the prophet noted, these people would be so hardened that, even under such harsh conditions, they would still not respond.

Paul uses the passage as a warning. Though the adjective ἑτερόγλωσσος (*heteroglōssos*) denotes "a foreign language,"[145] Paul is using it here in reference to speaking in tongues. The emphasis in this verse is not on the incomprehensibility of what is spoken, but on the hardness of the people evidenced by their unwillingness to listen. With full transparency, and no little irony, the Apostle applies the prophecy to his Corinthian detractors.[146] It is in this context that his boast regarding his gift of tongues outstripping that of any of the Corinthian Saints should be taken (14:18). Even with such a show of power as he has evidenced, he insinuates, they will not listen to him. The inference is that they will, therefore, come under God's judgment.[147]

14:22 *Wherefore tongues are for a sign, not to them that believe, but to them that believe not / And so speaking in other languages is not a sign for those who believe, but for those who do not believe:* By introducing this sentence with ὥστε (*hōste*), "therefore, and so," Paul signals his readers that he is drawing his total argument to a close.[148] Paul's statement is problematic in that he does not explain what he means by the use of the word σημεῖον (*sēmeion*), "sign."[149] How is the act of speaking in tongues a "sign" for nonbelievers? The answer lies in what the Apostle means by his use of the term. The prepositional phrase εἰς σημεῖον (*eis sēmeion*) means that the gift of tongues "serves as a sign," that is, an outward indicator or signal of either confirmation or warning.[150] The word, therefore, has both a positive and negative connotation. It is clear that Paul is asking his readers to make an evaluation of the relative *effects* of the gifts of tongues and prophecy. Essentially, he is asking what signal each conveys.[151] The *sēmeion* of tongues could serve as a warning to investigators because it confirms that the Spirit is working among the Saints. In that case, its effect would

---

145. BDAG, 398.

146. Hardheadedness is not an attribute unique to the Corinthian Saints. Joseph Smith complained that "there has been great difficulty in getting anything into the heads of this generation. It has been like splitting hemlock knots with a corn-dodger [a pancake] for a wedge, and a pumpkin for a beetle [mallet]. Even the Saints are slow to understand." *History*, 6:184.

147. Fitzmyer, *First Corinthians*, 520.

148. Louw-Nida, §89.52.

149. Scholars have been troubled by this passage for millennia. For example, see Chrysostom, *I Cor. Hom.* 36:2; Hays, *First Corinthians*, 239–40; Fee, *First Epistle*, 681–83; Bailey, *Mediterranean Eyes*, 402–3. For discussion, see Thiselton, *First Epistle*, 1122–26.

150. BDAG, 920–21.

151. Thiselton, *First Epistle*, 1123.

portend judgment if an investigator did not respond with faith in Christ. Since the Saint already believes, she or he needs no such warning.[152]

but prophesying serveth not for them that believe not, but for them which believe / Speaking by divine inspiration, on the other hand, is not for unbelievers, but for believers: Again, Paul is asking his readers to look at the effect of the "sign." The *sēmeion* of prophecy could serve as a confirmation for the believers. Its effect would be a harbinger of blessing, approval, and acceptance by God. The resistant unbeliever, however, would not be touched by the Spirit and, therefore, is unresponsive to the divine word.[153]

14:23 *If therefore the whole church be come together into one place, and all speak with tongues, and there come in those that are unlearned, or unbelievers, will they not say that ye are mad? / So if the whole church meets together and everyone is speaking in other languages, and unbelievers or investigators come in, won't they say you are out of your mind?:* With this verse, Paul creates an extreme but plausible scenario. The setting is the mutual reaction of either of two types of people who attend a meeting with ἡ ἐκκλησία ὅλη (*hē ekklēsia holē*), "the whole assembly." The first type is the ἰδιώτης (*idiōtēs*), "investigator" (see 14:16), and the second is the ἄπιστος (*apistos*), "unbeliever." The latter word denotes a person who is resistant to any commitment to a particular ideology, theology, person, or group.[154] Hypothetically, when they enter, the entire congregation is gibbering in various unknown tongues. The reaction of both, Paul states, would be the same; they will think the whole congregation is mad. The verb μαίνομαι (*mainomai*), "to be out of one's mind," generally means to be insane.[155] Looking at the nuance of the word in the LXX and other Jewish writings, however, shows that it also connotes a state of being emotionally out of control.[156] Therefore, the English word "raving" (making wild, irrational, and incoherent utterances, driven by insanity) works well.[157]

---

152. Barrett, *First Epistle*, 323; *TDNT*, 7:200–61; W. A. Grundem, "I Corinthians 14:20–25: Prophecy and Tongues as Signs of God's Attitude," *Westminster Theological Journal* 41 (1979): 381–96.

153. Ogden and Skinner, *Verse by Verse*, 144, notes that "Paul seems to believe that the gift of tongues can be of some benefit to unbelievers, perhaps because it is dramatic, whereas prophecy is for believers because it communicates the mind and will of God." See also Holzapfel and Wayment, *Making Sense*, 361.

154. BDAG, 103–4.

155. Louw-Nida, §30.24.

156. See Acts 26:24, 25; Wis. 14:28; 4 Macc. 7:5; 8:5; 10:13; Josephus, *J.W.*, 1.352.

157. *Merriam-Webster's Collegiate Dictionary*, 1033. Some scholars argue that μαίνομαι (*mainomai*) does not carry the same pejorative inference that the English word "insanity" does. See, for example, Hays, *First Corinthians*, 238; and Christopher Forbes, "Early

14:24 *But if all prophesy, and there come in one that believeth not, or one unlearned / On the other hand, if all are speaking by divine inspiration, and some unbeliever or investigator comes in:* Continuing his argument, Paul looks at a contrasting but plausible scenario. He emphasizes the contrast with the phrase ἐὰν δέ (*ean de*), "but if," translated as "on the other hand, if" in our Rendition.[158] In this case, he picks up the effect that an ordered meeting filled with inspired teaching and testifying would have on these same two types of people.

he is convinced of all, he is judged of all / he will be convinced by all and examined by all: This phrase ἐλέγχεται ὑπὸ πάντων, ἀνακρίνεται ὑπὸ πάντων (*elengchetai hypo pantōn, anakrinetai hypo pantōn*) presents some translation challenges as is illustrated by the variations found in other versions of the Bible.[159] The verb ἐλέγχω (*elengchō*), found here in the passive, means "to be convinced after careful examination"[160] while ἀνακρίνω (*anakrinō*) has the basic meaning of "to engage in careful study" of a thing or person.[161] Where the problem lies is in the translation of the prepositional phrase ὑπο πάντων (*hypo pantōn*), which occurs twice. The preposition ὑπο (*hypo*) followed by the genitive case can designate "agency or cause" and should be translated as "by." A passive verb identifies either the personal agent of the action or the thing by which the action was done.[162] Since the genitive plural adjective πάντων (*pantōn*) has the same case ending for all genders, it is ambiguous as to whether the phrase refers to "all people" or "all things." We have preserved that ambiguity in our Rendition by simply translating the phrase "by all" in both cases. The most likely interpretation (but not the only one) seems to be that when an investigator or unbeliever attends a church meeting and the members are speaking under the influence of the Holy Ghost, these nonmembers are convinced of the truth *by*

Christian Inspired Speech and Hellenistic Popular Religion," *Novum Testamentum* 28 (1986): 257–70, who argue the nuance looks to being whipped into frenzy rather than being insane. Because the connotation of insanity cannot be dismissed, the Rendition does not follow this argument.

158. The phrase is an unreal but general truth as covered in Smyth, *Greek Grammar,* §2336.

159. The NRSV gives, "is reproved by all and called to account by all"; the NIV, "they are convicted of sin and are brought under judgment by all"; and the NET, "he will be convicted by all, he will be called to account by all."

160. BDAG, 315.

161. BDAG, 66.

162. BDAG, 1035–36. For inanimate objects, the preposition διά (*dia*) with the genitive is the normal way to express instrumentality or cause. See also BDAG, 224.

what is being said, and they will be examined *by* those members who are present to determine if their conversion is real.

14:25 ***And thus are the secrets of his heart made manifest; and so falling down on his face he will worship God / The hidden things of his heart will be disclosed, and he will fall upon his face and will worship God:*** The phrase καὶ οὕτως, (*kai outōs*), "and thus," is not found in the early manuscripts and is, therefore, left out of our Rendition. In this verse, Paul identifies the result upon both an investigator and nonbeliever when confronted by the power of prophetic speaking. The phrase τὰ κρύπτα (*ta krypta*), "secrets, hidden things," connotes deep but unexpressed desires, hopes, and dreams.[163] The noun καρδία (*kardia*), "heart," metaphorically denotes the "center and source of the whole of inner life [with] its thinking, feeling, and volition." It is also the center on which the Spirit of God acts.[164] In short, it represents the very being of the individual.[165] The adjective φανερός (*phaneros*), describes something that is open, clear, plain, or evident.[166] The verb προσκυνέω (*proskyneō*), "worship," denotes a gesture of complete surrender and submission to a higher authority.[167] The phrase πεσὼν ἐπὶ πρόσωπον προσκυνήσει (*pesōn epi prosōpon proskynēsei*), "having fallen upon his face, he will worship," denotes the highest form of self-surrender and self-giving.[168] Paul points out the results upon both a nonbeliever and an investigator when touched and convinced (ἐλέγχω, *elengchō*) by the Spirit. In both, the deepest and often hidden feelings of the inner-self are disclosed to themselves and to those around them.[169] The result will cause them to fully, completely, and sincerely give themselves to the Lord.

report that God is in you of a truth / exclaiming that "Truly God is among you!": The verb ἀπαγγέλλω (*apangellō*) denotes, first, the giving of a public declaration and confession about something and, second, the

---

163. BDAG, 570–71; Albrecht Oepke and Rudolf Meyer, "κρύπτω, ἀποκρύπτω, κρυπτός, κρυφαῖος, κρυφῇ, κρύπτη, ἀπόκρυφος," in *TDNT*, 3:957–1000.

164. BDAG, 508–9.

165. The metaphorical use of "heart" in modern culture, with its emphasis on romantic feelings and notions, clouds its ancient nuance. In the LXX καρδία (*kardia*) translates the Hebrew לֵב (*lēb*), which looks to the subconscious seat that determines one's "inclinations, resolutions, and determinations." In short, it summarizes the whole of the "inner man." BDB, 524–25. See also Friedrich Baumgärtel and Johannes Behm, "καρδία," in *TDNT*, 3:605–13.

166. BDAG, 1047–48; Louw-Nida, §§24.20; 28.28.

167. BDAG, 882–83.

168. Louw-Nida, §§17.21; 53.56; Thiselton, *First Epistle*, 1129–30.

169. Gerd Theissen, *Psychological Aspects of Pauline Theology*, trans. John Galvin (Endinburgh: T. and T. Clark, 1987), 88, but for context see 59–95.

source from which that declaration comes.[170] The word shows that a person's testimony is Spirit-driven. The preposition ἐν (*en*) expresses position, "in" or "among."[171] Here it is clear that it does not mean that God is *inside* these people, but that he is *in their midst* or *among* them. The Prophet Joseph Smith stated, "The idea that the Father and the Son dwell in a man's heart is an old sectarian notion, and is false."[172]

It must be noted, however, that when it comes to the "Spirit of God," the case is different. The term can refer to either the spiritual influence of the Father or to the Holy Ghost, both of which can dwell in the heart.[173] Joseph Smith stated, "the Holy Ghost has not a body of flesh and bones, but is a personage of Spirit. Were it not so, the Holy Ghost could not dwell in us" (D&C 130:22).

The convert's response to the divine outpouring of spirit, as formulated by Paul, is a partial quote from LXX Isaiah 45:14—ἐν σοὶ ὁ θεός ἐστιν (*en soi ho theos estin*), "God is with you"—albeit, Paul changes the plural pronoun to a singular to make his point.[174] The adverb ὄντως (*ontos*), "truly," emphasizes the profound revelation the person has received. The English phrases "in all reality" or "in absolute truth" give the sense. Paul's point is that, because of the experience, the convert willingly confesses what the Spirit has revealed: God is in all reality with the Christians.[175]

Analysis and Summary

With 14:13, Paul launches into the second part of his discussion dealing with the superiority of inspired speaking over the speaking in unknown tongues. Paul makes an important point in 14:15–16 when he stresses the need for both "mind" and "spirit" to be engaged in the process. In English parlance, the spirit is the seat of emotion and can be equated with the "heart." Thus, speaking of the process of revelation, the Lord says, "I will tell you in your mind and in your heart, by the Holy Ghost, which shall come upon you and

---

170. BDAG, 95; Louw-Nida, §33.198.

171. BDAG, 326–30.

172. Smith, *History of the Church*, 5:323.

173. Rodney Turner, "Glory of God," in *EM*, 2:551; Joseph Fielding McConkie, "Holy Ghost," in *EM*, 2:649; and C. Kent Dunford, "Light of Christ," in *EM*, 2:835.

174. In the LXX, the phrase describes the confession of Egypt, Ethiopia, and Seba and points to the cause of their bringing tribute to Jerusalem. Compare 1 Kgs. 18:36; Dan. 2:46–47; Zech. 8:23. The Hebrew is simply אֵל בָּךְ (*bāk 'ēl*) "God (is) in/among you."

175. Thiselton, *First Epistle*, 1130.

which shall dwell in your heart" (D&C 8:2). Such revelations are, as Joseph Smith taught, adapted to the circumstances, capacity, and language of the person or persons who receive them and are experienced independent of the body.[176]

Some LDS scholars have noted that "the Lord works with both systems—the mind—our intellect—and the heart, our feelings. . . . Revelation is neither emotion devoid of sense nor intellect without feeling, but a combination of both faculties working together in harmony. Because the Holy Ghost is a revelator, his presence will enlighten the mind; no truly spiritual exercise can ever be 'mindless.' The Holy Ghost, however, dwells not in our mind, but in our *heart*—we will feel his influence rather than deduce it. While the Holy Ghost speaks *to* our minds, he speaks *from* our hearts, and those who will not trust their hearts are at a disadvantage in following the Spirit."[177]

In this regard, a statement by the Prophet Joseph Smith is instructive. He said that "a person may profit by noticing the first intimation of the spirit of revelation, for instance, when you feel pure intelligence flowing into you, it may give you sudden strokes of ideas."[178] His insight stands in sharp contrast to the belief in "divine dictation" that some Christian religions profess.[179] This idea, noted another LDS scholar, "maintains that when the Lord chooses to speak through someone, all of his or her bodily functions are suspended. The recipient of the revelation becomes a dummy in the lap of the divine ventriloquist, voicing only those words that are given it. This, it is reasoned, must be the case so that the culture, understanding, and temperament of the revelation's recipient do not influence its expression. Thus, it is argued revelation is both inerrant and infallible. Here [in D&C 8:2] we learn that the Lord gave us as his children both minds and hearts, with the intent that they be used to converse with him."[180] Though Paul would say "mind and spirit," both phrases sustain the same position.

176. He mentioned this idea on three different occassions. See Smith, *History of the Church*, 5:135; "History, 1838–1856, Volume C-1 Addenda," 13; "Discourse, 7 April 1844, as Reported by *Times and Seasons*," 615.

177. Robinson and Garrett, *Commentary*, 1:62–63; italics in original.

178. "History, 1838–1856, Volume C-1," 9 [addenda]; spelling and grammar have been standardized.

179. Millard J. Erickson, *Christian Theology* (Grand Rapids, Mich.: Baker Book House, 1983), 206–7. For a good overview, see Jason Dulle, "The Nature of Inspiration," http://www.onenesspentecostal.com/inspiration.htm.

180. McConkie and Ostler, *Revelations of the Restoration*, 85–86.

In 14:22–25, to further bolster his point, Paul paints a hypothetical picture of the reaction of a nonmember attending a general meeting of the Saints in which he or she finds all gibbering in various unknown tongues.[181] Paul states that this person would likely conclude that the whole assemblage was raving mad and even socially depraved. On the other hand, if she or he attended a meeting filled with order and inspired speaking and testimony bearing—that is, prophecy—they would not only be edified (14:25) but moved toward conversion. By having his readers focus on the *effect* that an abundant outpouring of the gift of tongues or of prophecy would have on an observer, Paul ably shows the superiority of the latter gift.

The prophetic power, even to this day, is central to the work of the Church. That power is kindled by the Holy Ghost. It is that influence that "showeth all things, and teacheth the peaceable things of the kingdom" (D&C 39:6). Indeed, the Holy Ghost "is the spirit of revelation" (D&C 8:3). To the faithful the Lord has promised, "You shall receive the Holy Ghost, which giveth utterance, that you may stand as a witness of the things of which you shall both hear and see" (D&C 14:8). It then becomes the responsibility of the Saint to "declare whatsoever thing ye declare in my name, in solemnity of heart, in the spirit of meekness, in all things. And I give unto you this promise, that inasmuch as ye do this the Holy Ghost shall be shed forth in bearing record unto all things whatsoever ye shall say" (D&C 100:7–8). It is not surprising then, that the leaders of the Church are commanded "to conduct the meetings as they are led by the Holy Ghost, according to the commandments and revelations of God" (D&C 20:45; compare D&C 46:2).

Paul testified that, touched by the spiritual power that stands behind proper teaching and witnessing (προφητεία, *prophēteia*), the attendee receives a profound and new grasp of truth. He or she becomes convinced of one thing: that God is unmistakably with these people. That conviction is so strong that it erupts in a spontaneous outburst of testimony, "Truly God is among you!" (14:25).[182] In so doing the prophetic gift acts as a σημεῖον (*sēmeion*), "sign," that is, a divine witness to truth, for it touches and "builds up" (οἰκοδομέω, *oikodomeō*) everyone (14:22).[183] Further, this spirit-driven conviction stands in contrast to the confusion the gift of tongues brings.

---

181. Paul uses an unreal conditional in this potential clause. See Smyth, *Greek Grammar*, §2336. Conzelmann, *1 Corinthians*, 243 and n. 5, points out that Paul is exaggerating for effect and such an event likely never actually happened.

182. Barrett, *First Epistle*, 327.

183. Fitzmyer, *First Corinthians*, 522.

That being the case, the insistence by some of Paul's detractors that speaking in tongues is the sure evidence of superior spirituality is grossly mistaken.[184] Paul tells them, therefore, that the gift of inspired speech should be highly respected and sought for by all (14:39). Further, it should hold sway over tongues in all meetings.[185]

In summary, Paul's writings in this section betray his strong desire for the Saints to use both mind and spirit while speaking in church service. Speaking in tongues, because it was used by some as a sign of precedence over others and preference by God, needed to be fully understood. Because of its misuse, it had become divisive, sending the signal that some simply did not belong.[186] The practice was, therefore, damaging on two fronts: First, it made some of the believers feel out of place, foreign, and unwanted; second, it deprived nonbelievers of hearing spirit-filled preaching and converting testimony.[187] To speak clearly, intelligibly, and under inspiration shows love for "the other" (ὁ ἕτερος, *ho eteros*, 14:17). The power of that love excludes the need to be competitive and the urge to show off.

ORDERLY WORSHIP (14:26–33A)

Greek Text

26 Τί οὖν ἐστιν, ἀδελφοί; ὅταν συνέρχησθε, ἕκαστος ψαλμὸν ἔχει, διδαχὴν ἔχει, ἀποκάλυψιν ἔχει, γλῶσσαν ἔχει, ἑρμηνείαν ἔχει· πάντα πρὸς οἰκοδομὴν γινέσθω. 27 εἴτε γλώσσῃ τις λαλεῖ, κατὰ δύο ἢ τὸ πλεῖστον τρεῖς, καὶ ἀνὰ μέρος, καὶ εἷς διερμηνευέτω· 28 ἐὰν δὲ μὴ ᾖ διερμηνευτής, σιγάτω ἐν ἐκκλησίᾳ, ἑαυτῷ δὲ λαλείτω καὶ τῷ θεῷ. 29 προφῆται δὲ δύο ἢ τρεῖς λαλείτωσαν, καὶ οἱ ἄλλοι διακρινέτωσαν· 30 ἐὰν δὲ ἄλλῳ ἀποκαλυφθῇ καθημένῳ, ὁ πρῶτος σιγάτω. 31 δύνασθε γὰρ καθ᾽ ἕνα πάντες προφητεύειν, ἵνα πάντες μανθάνωσιν καὶ πάντες παρακαλῶνται 32 (καὶ πνεύματα προφητῶν προφήταις ὑποτάσσεται, 33 οὐ γάρ ἐστιν ἀκαταστασίας ὁ θεὸς ἀλλὰ εἰρήνης), [SBLGNT]

---

184. Thiselton, *First Epistle*, 1130.
185. Bailey, *Mediterranean Eyes*, 399.
186. In LXX Isa. 28:11–12, unintelligible speech served as a sign of not belonging and also of God's judgment.
187. Thiselton, *First Epistle*, 1118–19.

King James Version

26 How is it then, brethren? when ye come together, every one of you hath a psalm, hath a doctrine, hath a tongue, hath a revelation, hath an interpretation. Let all things be done unto edifying. 27 If any man speak in an unknown tongue, let it be by two, or at the most by three, and that by course; and let one interpret. 28 But if there be no interpreter, let him keep silence in the church; and let him speak to himself, and to God. 29 Let the prophets speak two or three, and let the other judge. 30 If any thing be revealed to another that sitteth by, let the first hold his peace. 31 For ye may all prophesy one by one, that all may learn, and all may be comforted. 32 And the spirits of the prophets are subject to the prophets. 33a For God is not the author of confusion, but of peace,

New Rendition

26 So what should you do, brothers and sisters? When you meet together, each contributes a hymn, or a lesson, or a revelation, or a speaking in another language or an interpretation. All of these things should be edifying. 27 If someone speaks in another language, then two, or at most three, should speak, one at a time, and someone should interpret. 28 But if there is no interpreter, he should keep silent in the church meeting and speak to himself and to God. 29 Two or three who are divinely inspired should speak, and the others should carefully evaluate what they say. 30 If someone who is sitting down receives a revelation, then the first person should stop speaking. 31 For you can all speak by divine inspiration one after the other, so that all can learn and all can be encouraged. 32 The spirits of prophets are subject to prophets, 33a for God is a God of peace, not disorder.

Translation Notes and Comments

14:26 *How is it then, brethren / So what should you do, brothers and sisters:* On ἀδελφοί (*adelphoi*), "brothers and sisters," see Translation Notes on 1:10. As in 14:15, the opening Greek phrase here is τί οὖν ἐστιν (*ti oun estin*), literally "what then is it," with an unstated but understood "that you should do?" Our Rendition again takes this into account.

when ye come together, every one of you hath a psalm, hath a doctrine, hath a tongue, hath a revelation, hath an interpretation. / When you meet together, each contributes a hymn, or a lesson, or a revelation, or a speaking in another language or an interpretation: The phrase ὅταν συνέρχησθε (*hotan synerchēsthe*), "when you come together," gives the setting for Paul's counsel. It is confined to public meetings. The Apostle describes yet another imaginary meeting into which the Saints bring their various talents and gifts. He lists five in all. The adjective ἕκαστος (*ekastos*), "everyone, each," should not be taken to mean that all the Saints come with all these gifts. Rather, it refers to one member having one gift and another member another gift.

The noun ψαλμός (*psalmos*) refers to a hymn of praise,[188] but it connotes the talent of singing.[189] The noun διδαχή (*didachē*) denotes a teaching or lesson but, by nuance, connotes that which has the weight and authority of doctrine.[190] The noun ἀποκάλυψις (*apokalypsis*) refers to a revelation of a type that makes known what was unknown before.[191] It therefore reveals what God hides from the world but makes known to the Saints. The singular noun γλῶσσα (*glōssa*), "tongue," as already noted, refers to the gift of speaking in tongues.[192] The noun ἑρμηνεία (*hermēneia*) denotes the act of interpreting tongues.[193] Once again, Paul places the speaking in another tongue and its interpretation last. By doing so, he acknowledges they are legitimate gifts but also reduces their overall importance. The problem Paul is either trying to fix or avoid is that the abundance and expression of so many gifts, if not controlled and organized, could lead to chaos.

Let all things be done unto edifying / All of these things should be edifying: On οἰκοδομή (*oikodomē*), "edification," see Translation Notes on 14:3. Here it expresses the ideal objective of any activity done in the church and the spiritually strengthening effects such activities should have. Every aspect of a church meeting should be for the building up of the community of believers and the uniting of the faith.

14:27 *If any man speak in an unknown tongue, let it be by two, or at the most by three, and that by course; and let one interpret / If someone speaks in another language, then two, or at most three, should speak, one at a time, and someone should interpret:* In this verse, Paul begins his instruction on how to set Church worship services in order. He puts three limitations on the use of tongues. First, the number that speaks is restricted to not more than three, likely to make sure the service has plenty of time for the other spirit-driven activities that he has mentioned.[194] Second, the speakers are to speak singly, the phrase ἀνὰ μέρος (*ana meros*), meaning "in

188. BDAG, 1096.

189. Fitzmyer, *First Corinthians,* 525.

190. Louw-Nida, §33.224, 236.

191. BDAG, 112. Though it can also carry the idea of secrets pertaining to God's work in the last days, that is not the case here.

192. BDAG, 201–2.

193. BDAG, 393.

194. Thiselton, *First Epistle,* 1138–39.

turn" or "one by one."[195] Finally, there must be an interpreter. The numeral εἷς (*heis*), "one," that Paul used refers to the person who does the translating and is, therefore, translated as "someone" in our Rendition. The context does not prohibit one of the speakers to also act as translator though that gift could fall on any in the congregation.[196]

14:28 *But if there be no interpreter, let him keep silence in the church; and let him speak to himself, and to God / But if there is no interpreter, he should keep silent in the church meeting and speak to himself and to God:* With this verse, Paul puts the fourth condition on speaking in another language in Church—the gift of interpretation must also be present. If it is not, speaking in tongues is of no value so far as the congregation is concerned (see 14:9). Such is not the case with the bearer of the gift, however. Though Paul insists that they should be silent in Church, that does not mean Paul wants to prohibit communion between the individual and God from taking place. The context, however, suggests that such communion should be done privately, not during the service, so as not to interfere with the person enjoying the spirit of the meeting.[197] Because of the complicated syntax of the sentence (the imperative σιγάτω, *sigatō,* "let him be silent," immediately following the protasis as it does), the imperative could apply to either the interpreter or the speaker. Though we cannot be fully certain, the context suggests that Paul is referring to the one who speaks in tongues.[198]

14:29 *Let the prophets speak two or three, and let the other judge / Two or three who are divinely inspired should speak, and the others should carefully evaluate what they say:* In this verse, Paul also puts certain restrictions on the use of inspired speaking. First, their number, too, should be limited to no more than three at a time. This follows his counsel on speaking in tongues, but there is a difference. He notes in 14:31 that during the meetings, all who have the spirit of prophecy should be allowed to speak. Thus, the counsel here is that two or three should speak and then there should be a break allowing the next step to take place.[199] Second, the

---

195. Findlay, "St. Paul's First Epistle," 912.

196. Fee, *First Epistle,* 692, n. 18.

197. Robertson and Plummer, *Critical and Exegetical Commentary,* 321; Bruce, *1 and 2 Corinthians,* 134.

198. Edwards, *Commentary,* 379; Fitzmyer, *First Corinthians,* 525–26. Because the syntax does allow for the speaker to also be the interpreter, the prohibition would be in effect only if the person could not translate his or her word into a known tongue. For discussion, see Thiselton, *First Epistle,* 1139.

199. Fee, *First Epistle,* 693.

speakers' words are to be carefully evaluated. The verb διακρίνω (*diakrinō*), "judge, evaluate," carries, first, the idea of separating or sifting items for the purpose of evaluation and, second, of putting special care into the process.[200] Therefore, it is translated as "carefully evaluate" in our Rendition. But who is to do the judging? The plural adjective ἄλλοι (*alloi*), "others," does not specify. It could refer only to those who are also inspired by the Spirit. On the other hand, since others could have the gift of "discerning of spirits" (12:10), it may refer to them (compare 1 Thes. 5:20–21). Whoever they are, it is their responsibility to assay the speakers' discourses for their correctness and exactness. The purpose of this action is to distinguish between inspired declarations, which cohere with both established doctrines and practices, and self-generated proclamations reflecting only the speaker's opinions or position.[201]

14:30 *If any thing be revealed to another that sitteth by, let the first hold his peace / If someone who is sitting down receives a revelation, then the first person should stop speaking:* In this verse, Paul focuses on what should happen if, during the course of a meeting, an attendee (either male or female) should receive divine inspiration (ἀποκάλυψις, *apokalypsis*). The verb κάθημαι (*kathēmai*) denotes one in a sitting position.[202] In Jewish synagogues, both audiences and teachers sat. However, when a person was reading from the scriptures, praying, or uttering prophetic speech, he stood.[203] If that were the practice during these early Christian worship services, anyone in the audience could indicate his or her need to speak by standing. When that happened, the speaker was to yield the floor. In this way, input from multiple people could bring a more full disclosure of the topic under study. This could yield to an even greater understanding as others added their insights and feelings. The end result would be a more fruitful and productive meeting.[204]

The person speaking must ever keep in mind that he or she is subject to the spirit of the prophets (14:32). In 2 Peter 1:20, the writer emphasized this same theme, stating, "That no prophecy of the scripture is of any private interpretation." The JST changes this verse, as noted by the italicized words, to read, "No prophecy of the scriptures is *given* of any

---

200. BDAG, 231.

201. Thiselton, *First Epistle,* 1140.

202. BDAG, 491.

203. Edwards, *Commentary,* 379; Fee, *First Epistle,* 665 n. 35.

204. For discussion, see Hans-George Gadamer, *Truth and Method,* trans. William Glen-Doepel, 2d English ed. (London: Sheed and Ward, 1989), 369–79.

private *will of man.*" The change emphasizes that God is in control. True prophecy is expressed only when men and women speak as moved upon by the Holy Ghost (2 Pet. 1:21). When this is indicated during a meeting, the first speaker must yield the floor and be still.

The verb Paul used, σιγάω (*sigaō*), "to be silent," is important inferring as it does a deep respect for the spirit of inspiration coupled with a willingness to allow it to dominate the meeting. He has applied it to one who speaks in tongues (14:28) and now to one who prophesies. He will do so again in 14:34 to certain women.[205]

14:31 *For ye may all prophesy one by one, that all may learn, and all may be comforted / For you can all speak by divine inspiration one after the other, so that all can learn and all can be encouraged:* In this verse, Paul explains the reason order is necessary. The phrase καθ' ἕνα (*kath' hena*) is distributive and therefore means "one by one" or "in turn."[206] Such an action precludes people not hearing what others say or missing a turn. Paul uses the adjective πάντες (*pantes*), "all," three times. The first time is restrictive, referring only to "all" who have the gift of prophecy. In the other two instances it is general and refers to "all" in the congregation. The verb μανθάνω (*manthanō*) means "to learn" with the idea of appropriating knowledge to oneself.[207] In the Christian context, it denotes an application of gospel knowledge such that a person's behavior is so modified that he or she no longer walks after the manner of the world.[208] The verb παρακαλέω (*parakaleō*) means "to instill someone with courage or cheer."[209] The Apostle's words indicate that while not everyone shares in the gift of prophecy, everyone can still be built up or edified (οἰκοδομέω, *oikodomeō*) through those who do. Paul's point is that church order is necessary so that learning, encouraging, and comforting are not restricted.

14:32 *the spirits of the prophets are subject to the prophets / the spirits of prophets are subject to prophets:* This phrase, because of its concise wording, is a bit challenging to translate, although the general sense is clear:

---

205. Bailey, *Mediterranean Eyes*, 407.

206. The phrase is parallel to *ana meros* in 14:27.

207. BDAG, 615.

208. K. H. Rengstorf, "μανθάνω," in *TDNT*, 4:390–413.

209. BDAG, 764–65. As is often the case, it is nearly impossible to translate some Greek words with a single English equivalent because none exists. That is the case with παρακαλέω (*parakaleō*). The NIV solves the problem by translating it with two words, "instructed and encouraged," but it also carries the nuance of "exhort and warn." See Thiselton, *First Epistle*, 1143–44.

those things that are spoken by divine inspiration can only be understood by divine inspiration. Just what Paul meant by the plural noun πνεύματα (*pneumata*), "spirits," is unclear. The verb ὑποτάσσω (*hypotassō*) means to be placed in a position of submission.[210] The text is unclear as to who is subject to whom. The JST change in 2 Peter 1:20–21 may shed light on this. There the phrase reads, "No prophecy of the scriptures is given of any private will of man . . . but holy men of God spake as they were moved by the Holy Ghost." This passage shows that men do not determine the actions of the Holy Ghost. It acts as it will. The agents who are to oversee that what the Spirit dictates is done are those who also possess this discerning gift. There are three possibilities as to who or what these agents are. First, it could be the prophet's own spirit that acts as an internal editor, making sure his words conform to the will of God.[211] Second, it could be that the agent is the word of prophecy as found in the scriptures.[212] Third, it could refer to each branch leader who possesses the spirit of discernment as well as that of prophecy.[213] In 1 Thessalonians 5:19–21, which Paul wrote some years before this letter, he said, "Quench not the Spirit. Despise not prophesyings. Prove all things; hold fast that which is good." In the verse here, he is insisting that the Corinthians branches follow this admonition.

To those among Paul's detractors who might insist that no one should restrain the Spirit by putting some kind of order in place, the Apostle insists that all spiritual utterances remain ever subject to God's purposes and, in this case, that means the edification of the whole branch.[214] In turn, that means there must be order.

14:33 *For God is not the author of confusion, but of peace / for God is a God of peace, not disorder:* The conjunction γάρ (*gar*), "for," in this case, is causative, showing why the spirits of the prophets are subject to the prophets. The noun "author" is not in the Greek text and, therefore is not found in our Rendition. The noun ἀκαταστασία (*akatastasia*), "confusion, disorder," denotes an "opposition to established authority."[215] It, therefore, describes very well the condition in which the Corinthian Church found itself.[216] The noun εἰρήνη (*eirēnē*), "peace," on the other hand, describes

---

210. BDAG, 1042.
211. Thiselton, *First Epistle*, 1144.
212. Holzapfel and Wayment, *Making Sense*, 362.
213. This assumes the same situation as in the modern Church. See D&C 46:27; 101:95.
214. Findlay, "St. Paul's First Epistle," 913.
215. The word also denoted pandemonium and civil strife. BDAG, 35.
216. Mitchell, *Paul and the Rhetoric of Reconciliation*, 173.

"a state of concord" were tranquility and harmony prevail.[217] *Akatastasia* goes against all that God is and does both in heaven and on earth. In modern times God has stated, "Behold, mine house is a house of order, saith the Lord God, and not a house of confusion" (D&C 132:8). That fact stood in the ancient Church as well.

Analysis and Summary

Paul concluded his long discussion on the proper use of tongues, interpretation of tongues, and prophecy by insisting that inspired speaking (προφητεία, *prophēteia*), no matter what form it takes, must take priority over tongues and their interpretation. He now turns to the need for due order in using any of the gifts in a church setting. "Paul's conclusion to this section . . . appears to reflect his understanding of how an ideal meeting should be conducted."[218]

He uses the example of a meeting in which the Spirit manifests itself in five ways: in singing, teaching, revelation, speaking in an unknown tongue, and its interpretation (14:26). Proper use of all of these gifts, he insists, should be but for one thing: the building up and edification (οικοδομή, *oikodomē*) of the community. Properly executed order would assure that the correct use of all these gifts would be met and the necessary unity and peace prevail.

In his directive, Paul begins with what he considers to be the least useful and the most troubling of the gifts, that of speaking in an "another language" (γλῶσσα, *glōssa*). He then turns to "inspired speech" (προφητεία, *prophēteia*), a gift he considers of high value. He instructs those possessing each of these gifts. Paul's statement in 14:26–27 about limiting the use of tongues in Church, suggests he would like to completely avoid speaking in tongues during church service, but he realizes, given the present condition, that would be impossible.[219]

Certifying Paul's point, Joseph Smith taught, "The gift of tongues was necessary in the Church. . . . The gift of tongues by the power of the Holy Ghost, in the Church, is for the benefit of the servants of God to preach to unbelievers, as on the days of Pentecost. When devout men from every nation shall assemble to hear the things of God, let the Elders preach to

---

217. The term is often used in the Hellenistic world to describe a utopian state of happiness or what we might call Zion. It also is an ideal found in Hellenistic treaties. BDAG, 287–88.

218. Holzapfel and Wayment, *Making Sense,* 362.

219. Fitzmyer, *First Corinthians,* 526.

them in their own mother tongue, whether it is German, French, Spanish or Irish, or any other, and let those interpret who understand the language spoken, in their own mother tongue, and this is what the Apostle meant in First Corinthians 14:27."[220] Such a gift would prove a real blessing to missionaries who worked with slaves brought in from the far reaches of the Roman Empire and, therefore, who spoke various languages.

It is of note that, in his whole discussion on how a meeting should be run, the Apostle mentions neither priesthood leadership nor the sacrament. The latter is not too surprising since he has addressed that earlier, but not addressing what role the priesthood leaders should play in all this is a bit striking. It may be that it was among these that the trouble brewed and, therefore, they were his target audience. It seems more likely, however, that he sought to first take care of the spontaneity that was disrupting the meetings and creating chaos. Only after everyone was on the same page could he then focus his counsel on the presiding officers.[221]

The freewheeling nature of the meetings, which the text reveals, suggests that the Church in general was not yet ordered. Their meetings during this period seem to have followed the pattern described in the Book of Mormon for "their meetings were conducted by the church after the manner of the workings of the Spirit, and by the power of the Holy Ghost; for as the power of the Holy Ghost led them whether to preach, or to exhort, or to pray, or to supplicate, or to sing, even so it was done" (Moro. 6:9).

Though the modern Church is well ordered, what Paul describes conforms quite well to those early LDS church meetings called the School of the Prophets. As the name indicates, those who attended either had or were being trained to have the prophetic spirit. Giving instructions for the school's organization, the Lord commanded, "Appoint among yourselves a teacher, and let not all be spokesmen at once; but let one speak at a time and let all listen unto his sayings, that when all have spoken that all may be edified of all, and that every man may have an equal privilege" (D&C 88:122). The Lord also noted that "he that receiveth the word by the Spirit of truth receiveth it as it is preached by the Spirit of truth[.] Wherefore, he that preacheth and he that receiveth, understand one another, and both are edified and rejoice together" (D&C 50:21–22).

---

220. "History, 1838–1856, Volume C-1," 1266. Spelling and grammar have been standardized.

221. Fitzmyer, *First Corinthians*, 524.

In 14:26–33, the Apostle insists that unchecked spontaneity, no matter how spiritually driven, cannot set the agenda for the meeting. "God is not the author of confusion," he testified, "but of peace" (14:33). Left unchecked, unbridled displays could lead to chaos and anarchy. On the other hand, by ordering worship procedures, more care could be given to edifying others and building up the Church. Yielding to the self-constraint that order imposes evidences love and concern for others, especially the timid and vulnerable. Since these meetings must be, at their heart, "spiritual" (meaning that the agency and power of the Holy Spirit are present), then God's coherent and rational processes must prevail.[222]

"We, all of us, believe that our God is a God of order, that all things that are conducted by him are conducted in the most perfect order, according to law," stated Elder Orson Pratt. Going on, he noted that 14:33 shows that "everything pertaining to the salvation of men, which is acceptable in the sight of heaven, must be in accordance with strict law. In other words, that the Lord designed a work among the human family according to those laws that were ordained by him from before the foundation of the world."[223]

Even those exercising the gift of prophecy must put it into service through order. "Who may prophesy?" asks Elder McConkie, and he answers, "God who is no respecter of persons and who loves all his children, speaks to every person who will heed his voice. Prophecy is for all: men, women, and children, every member of the true Church."[224] Thus, though there is but one Prophet who heads the Church, the spirit of prophecy does not belong to him alone. "To learn to communicate with others by the gifts of that Holy Spirit makes it possible for one to be a prophet or prophetess of God," noted an LDS scholar. Going on he said, "Latter-day Saints believe that through divine revelation every child of Christ may, and should, become a prophet or a prophetess to his or her own divinely appointed stewardship (Num. 11:29), holding fast to that which is good and rejecting that which is evil (1 Thes. 5:19–21)."[225]

Revelation is restricted, however, to each person's own sphere of stewardship. Only the president of the Church can receive revelation for the whole Church, but stake presidents can have such for their stakes and

---

222. Thiselton, *First Epistle*, 1075.

223. Orson Pratt, in *JD*, 14:271. On this subject, see also Joseph Fielding McConkie, "Chosen Vessels and the Order of the Priesthood," in Dahl and Tate, *Lectures on Faith in Historical Perspective*, 186.

224. *DNTC*, 2:387.

225. Chauncey C. Riddle, "Revelation," in *EM*, 3:1227.

bishops for their wards. Thus, the channel of communication is from the top down. "I will inform you that it is contrary to the economy of God for any member of the Church, or any one, to receive instruction for those in authority, higher than themselves," taught Joseph Smith, "therefore you will see the impropriety of giving heed to them; but if any have a vision or a visitation from a heavenly messenger, it must be for his own benefit and instruction, for the fundamental principles, government, and doctrine of the Church are invested in the keys of the kingdom."[226]

Individuals are expected to be guided by revelation in their own lives and stewardships. God is a God of order. He recognizes the right of each person to receive revelation directly from him and from and through those in authority over her or him.

Paul's concern in 14:31–32 seems to be with whether those, while exercising the gift of prophecy, have the critical self-awareness, self-control, and concern for others that allows them to yield to others. When this power is exercised in a Church meeting, Paul insists, the spirits of the prophets must yield to the prophets (14:32). Nothing that is said is exempt from scrutiny, clarification, or expansion. God reveals his will line upon line, and following church order is one way of allowing this to happen. That means that prophecy is not without its checks and balances. Because God is dealing with human beings, such is necessary. Thus, even today checks are in place, and these reach to the highest levels of the Church. All decisions by the First Presidency of the Church and Quorum of the Twelve Apostles must be unanimous (see D&C 107:27, 29). Speaking of the reason for this, President Boyd K. Packer stated: "These procedures protect the work from the individual weaknesses apparent in all of us."[227]

Even so, the Church holds the position that though apostolic and prophetic revelation is inspired, it is not infallible. Leaders, on the other hand, are not immune from the foibles of humanity and, as Elder McConkie has

---

226. Joseph Smith and Frederick G. Williams to John S. Carter, April 13, 1833, in "Letterbook 1," 30, Church History Library, available online at Church Historian's Press, *The Joseph Smith Papers,* http://www.josephsmithpapers.org/paper-summary/letterbook-1/42. Spelling and grammar have been standardized. For the official position of the Church on this subject, see the statement by the First Presidency, "A Warning Voice," *Improvement Era* 16 (September 1913): 1148.

227. Boyd K. Packer, "I Say unto You, Be One," devotional address, Brigham Young Univeristy, Provo, Utah, February 12, 1991, available at https://speeches.byu.edu/talks/boyd-k-packer_say-unto-one/. In the talk from which this quote comes, President Packer explains how unanimity in the Quorums of the First and Twelve is reached.

noted, have "their opinions and prejudices and are left to work out their own problems without inspiration in many instances."[228] Elder Dallin H. Oaks explained: "Revelations from God . . . are not constant. We believe in continuing revelation, not continuous revelation. We are often left to work out problems without the dictation or specific direction of the Spirit."[229] When light does come, therefore, the current prophet can clarify, correct, enlarge, or change any previous teachings or practice.

In the meantime, each member is responsible to determine for himself or herself by personal inspiration if the leaders are correct. President Brigham Young taught, "The greatest fear I have is that the people of this Church will accept what we say as the will of the Lord without first praying about it and getting the witness within their own hearts that what we say is the word of the Lord."[230] Members are instructed to rely on the Holy Ghost to make judgments about what the Brethren say or write. President Harold B. Lee stated that if a church authority "says something that contradicts what is found in the standard works (I think that is why we call them 'standard'—it is the standard measure of all that men teach), you may know by that same token that it is false; regardless of the position of the man who says it."[231] President Joseph Fielding Smith confirmed this position, writing that "you cannot accept the books written by the authorities of the Church as standards in doctrine, only in so far as they accord with the revealed word in the standard works. Every man who writes is responsible, not the Church, for what he writes." He went on to say that if someone "writes something which is out of harmony with the revelations, then every member of the Church is duty bound to reject it. If he writes that which is in perfect harmony with the revealed word of the Lord, then it should be accepted."[232]

Once a teaching or principle becomes the doctrine of the Church by "common consent," it becomes part of the standard works, and then takes precedence over any other revelation.[233] Members of the Church are bound only

---

228. McConkie, *Mormon Doctrine*, 608.

229. Dallin H. Oaks, "Teaching and Learning by the Spirit," *Ensign* 27 (March 1997): 14.

230. *Discourses of Brigham Young*, comp. John A. Widtsoe (Salt Lake City: Deseret Book, 1941), 135. President Harold B. Lee stressed this point. See Lee, *Stand Ye in Holy Places*, 162–63; Lee, "Place of the Living Prophet."

231. Lee, "Place of the Living Prophet."

232. Joseph Fielding Smith, quoted in McConkie, *Doctrines of Salvation*, 3:203–4.

233. Robert E. Quinn, "Common Consent," in *EM*, 1:297.

by doctrine found in the standard works. As Elder B. H. Roberts noted, "The Church has confined the sources of doctrine by which it is willing to be bound before the world to the things that God has revealed, and which the Church has officially accepted, and those alone. These would include the Bible, the Book of Mormon, the Doctrine and Covenants, the Pearl of Great Price."[234] Therefore, for the modern Church, Paul's teaching that "the spirits of the prophets are subject to the prophets" means that both leaders and members—all of whom have access to the spirit of prophecy—are bound to follow the standard works and the current revelations from God.

COUNSEL TO DISRUPTIVE WOMEN (14:33B–35)

Greek Text

ὡς ἐν πάσαις ταῖς ἐκκλησίαις τῶν ἁγίων. 34 Αἱ γυναῖκες ἐν ταῖς ἐκκλησίαις σιγάτωσαν, οὐ γὰρ ἐπιτρέπεται αὐταῖς λαλεῖν· ἀλλὰ ὑποτασσέσθωσαν, καθὼς καὶ ὁ νόμος λέγει. 35 εἰ δέ τι μαθεῖν θέλουσιν, ἐν οἴκῳ τοὺς ἰδίους ἄνδρας ἐπερωτάτωσαν, αἰσχρὸν γάρ ἐστιν γυναικὶ λαλεῖν ἐν ἐκκλησίᾳ. [SBLGNT]

King James Version

33b as in all the churches of the saints. 34 Let your women keep silence in the churches: for it is not permitted unto them to speak; but they are commanded to be under obedience, as also saith the law. 35 And if they will learn any thing, let them ask their husbands at home: for it is a shame for women to speak in the church.

New Rendition

33b As in all the churches of the saints, 34 women should keep silent in church meetings, for they are not permitted to speak, but should be subordinate, as the law also says. 35 If they want to find out about something, they can ask their own husbands at home, because it is shameful for a woman to speak in a church meeting.

Translation Notes and Comments

14:33b *as in all churches of the saints / As is in all the churches of the saints:* Though these words are the concluding phrase of 14:33 in the KJV, they are better understood as the introductory phrase for Paul's new discussion

---

234. B. H. Roberts, *Deseret News,* July 23, 1921, sec. 4, p. 7.

beginning in 14:34 that refers to the conduct of women.[235] The noun ἐκκλησία (*ekklēsia*) normally denotes an assemblage of people, but when coupled with the phrase τῶν ἁγίων (*tōn hagiōn*), "of [all] the saints," the phrase connotes the Church as a whole.[236] It is Paul's assurance to the Corinthians that the practice he is promoting is universal among the Christian congregations. It is also his appeal to the Corinthian branches to fall in line.

14:34 *Let your women keep silence in the churches: for it is not permitted unto them to speak / women should keep silent in church meetings, for they are not permitted to speak:* With this verse, Paul addresses yet another case of misconduct that has disrupted meetings of worship.[237] A few ancient manuscripts move 14:34–35 to the end of the chapter so that they follow 14:40. The move seems to be an attempt by some scribe to find a more appropriate location for Paul's comments concerning women. It is not followed in our Rendition.[238] The Textus Receptus and several other manuscripts have ὑμῶν (*hymōn*) "your" after γυναῖκες (*gynaikes*) "women," but the best and oldest manuscripts do not have it.[239] Thus our Rendition omits it. The noun γυνή (*gynē*) can mean "woman" in general or "wife." Here, it is clearly referring to certain women in the Corinthian branch.

The meaning of the imperative verb σιγάτωσαν (*sigatōsan*) can range from the more stern "keep silent" to the gentler "be quiet."[240] The verb ἐπιτρέπω (*epitrepō*) means "to allow" or "to permit."[241] The verb λαλέω (*laleō*) denotes

---

235. Its position has created a lot of debate. For summary, see Fitzmyer, *First Corinthians,* 699–705.

236. BDAG, 303–4. The phrase ταῖς ἐκκλησίαις τῶν ἁγίων (*tais ekklēsiais tōn hagiōn*), "the churches of the saints," appears only here in the New Testament and, therefore, its meaning is unsure. However, taking this comment in light of 16:19, Paul seems to be referring specifically to meetings held in the various house-churches scattered across the Roman Empire.

237. Verses 14:33–36 have contributed much to the debate on the role of women in Christian churches. Thiselton, *First Epistle,* 1146–62 covers all the issues in great detail and provides a very extensive bibliography.

238. Metzger, *Textual Commentary,* 499–500. The idea that these verses are an interpolation that made its way into the text has found adherents on both sides. The best studies are Philip Payne, "Fuldensis, Sigla for Variants in Vaticanus, and 1 Corinthians 14:34–35," *New Testament Studies* 41 (1995): 240–62, who argues that these verses are an interpolation later inserted into the text, and Curt Niccum, "The Voice of the Manuscripts on the Silence of Women: The External Evidence from 1 Corinthians 14:34–35," *New Testament Studies* 43 (April 1997): 242–55, who very convincingly argues that it belongs to the original text.

239. Metzger, *Textual Commentary,* 500.

240. BDAG, 922; Louw-Nida, §33.121.

241. BDAG, 384–85.

any kind of utterance, though in archaic Greek it referred to informal communication, including small talk and chatting. By Paul's day its meaning had merged quite closely with that of λέγω (*legō*), "to speak" or "to write," in formal or precise ways.[242]

One of the major problems with this verse is that it seems to contradict what Paul said in 11:5 where he shows no hesitation with women teaching, preaching, or bearing testimony during church services as long as they follow proper decorum. The JST reduces the tension by changing the word "speak" to "rule." In doing so, Joseph Smith reveals the real issue. Certain women were pushing for authority that did not belong to them. Paul was sustaining the right that men had to preside over Church meetings. When referring to the right of leaders to "rule" in the Church, Paul always uses the verb προΐστημι (*proistēmi*) "to exercise a position of leadership, rule, direct."[243] In LDS parlance that would translate to "preside." For example, in Paul's instructions to Timothy concerning the qualifications for a bishop, he notes that a bishop should be a man who "ruleth well [that is, presides over, προϊστάμενον, *proistamenon*] his own house. . . . For if a man know not how to rule [that is, preside over, προστῆναι, *prostēnai*] his own house, how shall he take care of the church of God?" (1 Tim. 3:4–5). So also in 1 Timothy 5:17, "Let the elders that rule well [preside, προεστῶτες, *proestōtes*] be counted worthy of double honour."

**but they are commanded to be under obedience, as also saith the law /
but should be subordinate, as the law also says:** The translation in the KJV is too strong, for the word "commanded" is not in the Greek text. It is also struck from the JST. It is, therefore, not used in our Rendition. The word Paul uses is the passive imperative ὑποτασσέσθωσαν (*hypostassesthōsan*), "let them subordinate themselves."[244] The force of the passive voice with the imperative construction is important. It makes the imperative an entreaty.[245] Thus, these women are not commanded to obedience but

---

242. BDAG, 582–83, but compare with λέγω (*legō*), 588–90. See Barrett, *First Epistle,* 332. Of note is that Norber Baumert and others, *Woman and Man in Paul: Overcoming a Misunderstanding* (Collegeville, Minn.: Liturgical Press, 1996), 197, translate the word as "speak her mind in public," but that may be a bit too strong.

243. BDAG, 870.

244. BDAG, 1042.

245. Wallace, *Greek Grammar,* 487–88. That this softer use of the imperative is correct is born out in that some ancient texts have the infinitive form of ὑποτάσσω (*hypotassō*) rather than the imperative. In that case the thrust of the sentence would be that the women must be allowed to subordinate themselves. The evidence is stronger for the traditional reading, however. See Fitzmyer, *First Corinthians,* 531.

requested to willingly yield themselves to the law and church practice. Though the phase ὁ νόμος (*ho nomos*), "the law," is a clear reference to the Mosaic law (as in 9:8, 9, 20–22; 14:21),[246] there is nothing in the Pentateuch that addresses this issue directly. Therefore, Paul seems to be appealing to a general condition rather than specific statements in the law. If that is the case, there are at least two strands that work. One is that throughout the Old Testament, priests are the chief administers and officiators in all religious functions suggesting that women do not preside at religious functions and in meetings. The other is that God is a God of order as seen in the creation and every ritual he has instituted. Order demands everyone play her or his part and everything be in its position so that nothing or no one oversteps established bounds.

14:35 *And if they will learn any thing, let them ask their husbands at home / If they want to find out about something, they can ask their own husbands at home:* The neuter adjective τι (*ti*), "anything, something," is indefinite[247] and indicates that women should ask any and all questions at home. However, Paul may have specific questions in mind, namely those dealing with a woman's relationship to the priesthood (see Analysis below). The verb μανθάνω (*manthanō*) denotes gaining knowledge or skill by instruction and, thus, "to learn, find out," or "ascertain" information from another.[248] The verb ἐπερωτάω (*eperōtaō*) means "to ask" or "enquire" about something.[249] The phrase τοὺς ἰδίους ἄνδρας (*tous idious andras*), literally "their own men," most likely refers to the women's husbands, although some commentators argue that it refers to all adult males in the women's individual families. The request would, in that case, exclude daughters, widows, and female slaves.[250] Because that seems unlikely, our Rendition follows the former interpretation.

for it is a shame for women to speak in the church / it is shameful for a woman to speak in a church meeting: For λαλέω (*laleō*), "speak," see 14:34. The adjective αἰσχρός (*aischros*) has the basic meaning is "ugly" or "deformed," and in its metaphorical use, it never loses this tone. Thus, its nuance refers to that which is base or morally deformed. In its lightest sense it means "that which fails to meet expected moral or cultural

246. Some have suggested Paul has Roman law in mind, but the context of the whole epistle is against this view.
247. BDAG, 1007–9.
248. BDAG, 615.
249. BDAG, 362.
250. Wire, *Women Prophets,* 56; Fitzmyer, *First Corinthians,* 532.

standards."[251] The word certainly reflects the degree of disgust with which Paul viewed the action of these women. Thus, the English words "disgraceful" or "shameful" work well.

But what were they doing that was so shameful? Again, the JST suggests an answer. After noting that women should ask their questions to the men at home, the text states that this is because it is not proper for "women to rule in the church." It would appear that these women were not making simple enquiries on points of procedure or doctrine. Rather, they were pushing an agenda.[252] Their questions likely focused on who had the right to preside at church meetings. Paul felt such discussions should be had at home.

The "shame" these women were bringing upon themselves was multilevel. The first was breaking Jewish custom in which women were not to participate directly in worship services.[253] The second was breaking Gentile custom, which looked down upon women being too pushy and visible in public.[254] The third was breaking Church protocols and practice by seeking authority that did not belong to them.

Analysis and Summary

In 14:34–36, Paul addresses yet another problem that was causing disruptions during worship services in Corinth. In this case, it was women going beyond propriety while at meetings. Since the action of these women seems to have been challenging proper authority and, thereby disrupting not only the proper order in meetings but also their purpose ("all things be done unto edifying," 14:26), it is not surprising that Paul addresses it here. His counsel is also connected with what he has said, first, about others being silent during meetings and thereby showing respect (14:28, 30) and, second, about the importance of learning in church (14:31).

It would be nice to know if Paul were issuing a universal directive or giving a necessary corrective to a unique problem. Based on his counsel in 1 Timothy 2:9–15 (a woman should learn in silence and not "usurp authority

---

251. BDAG, 29.

252. Ben Witherington III, *Women in the Earliest Church* (Cambridge: Cambridge University Press, 1988), 104, translates it as "abusive speech."

253. Fitzmyer, *First Corinthians,* 532, cites Jewish practice that does not allow women to even approach the podium.

254. Juvenal's satire, "The Ways of Women" (*Sat.* 6.434–56); Aristophane's Comedy *Ecclesiazusae,* and Plutarch (*Conj. Preac.* 31 §142d) are full of negative criticism directed toward women acting out in public.

over the man"), it would appear that the problem of women not being reverent in church was not unique to the Corinthian branches.[255] Just how far
it extended, though, cannot be ascertained. It should not be overlooked, as
one scholar has insightfully noted, that "what an individual says to correct
an error cannot be taken as a full or definitive statement of his views on a
particular subject."[256] For example, Paul's statement in this chapter should
not negate what he said in chapter 11. Here he is correcting a specific problem—women speaking out in meetings—there he was confirming a general
right—women and men speaking through inspiration in Church.

The background in which this issue was being played out can be helpful.
Among the Greeks, it was not customary to allow women to participate
in public deliberations. For example, Plutarch wrote, "A woman ought to
take care of her home and be quiet; for she should either converse with
her husband or through him."[257] That, however, was not the case in certain
pagan religious practices, especially those honoring Aphrodite (the chief
goddess of Corinth), Demeter, and Dionysius. An ecstatic endowment
and outpouring of utterance assured women respect and prophetic rank
as sibyls. Likewise, in Jewish tradition, though women did not preside at
the altar or in the temple, they were admitted to the lower offices at the
entrance to the tabernacle, God's house of revelation (Ex. 38:8). Those who
particularly expressed the gift of prophecy (for example, Miriam, Huldah,
and Noadiah) obtained respect and status almost equivalent to that of men.[258]

With the restoration of the gospel in Paul's day, women were again
allowed to teach, preach, and testify in Church. Unfortunately, as with
other church related matters, the Corinthian Saints were pushing the
envelope and that included certain women.

Decorum was all important in the shame-honor society that existed in
the Roman world where people of class were expected to adhere to family,

---

255. Compare 1 Pet. 3:1–5. In *1 Clem.* 1.3; 21.6–7, Clement, Bishop at Rome, writing
to the Corinthians a few decades after Paul, mentions the need for women to remain
"the rule of obedience" (τῷ κανόνι τῆς ὑποταγῆς, *tō kanoni tēs hypotagēs*) and to show
forbearance or courtesy (ἐπιεικής, *epieikēs*) through their silence. According to Chrysostom (fourth century), the problem still existed. He stated emphatically that the women
make "a great noise among them, much clamor and talking, and nowhere so much as in
this place [the catherdral]." Chrysostom, "Homily IX [I Timothy ii. 11–15]," in *Nicene and
Post-Nicene Fathers* (New York: Christian Literature Company, 1889), 13:435.

256. Witherington, *Women in the Earliest Church*, 25.

257. Plutarch, *Mor.*, 142d. See also Frederick W. Danker, *Benefactor: Epigraphic Study
of a Graeco-Roman and New Testament Semantic Field* (St. Louis: Clayton Press, 1982),
164, with reference to *Inscriptiones Graecae* 1873–76.

258. Albrecht Oepke, "γυνή," in *TDNT*, 1:776–89.

societal, and civil standards. That expectation was heightened when it came to adherence to the law. The action of these women seems to have trespassed upon all these.

Using the structure of the epistle contributes to an understanding of the issue. This section begins with 11:2 and concludes with 14:40. A broad chiastic structure, as presented by one scholar, can be outlined as follows:

A Men and women *leading* in worship (11:2–16)

   B Disorder in worship—Holy Communion: *Sacrament* (11:17–34)

      C The spiritual gifts—In theory (12:1–31)

         D Love (13:1–13)

      C' The spiritual gifts—In practice (14:1–15)

   B' Disorder in Worship—Preaching: *Word* (14:16–33a)

A' Women and men in *worshiping* (14:33b–40).[259]

This structure shows that in both chapters 11 and 14, Paul was concerned about the place of men and women in worship. Certain practices needed addressing because of the disorder it was causing in sacramental meetings. The care of his construction in this section shows how important it was for Paul to clearly and forcefully communicate with his readers.

As noted in chapter 11, Paul affirmed the right of men and women to prophesy in church. He now returns to that subject. Peter had already established the right to this gift for both genders (Acts 2:17–18), and Paul never questions that. That right to express one's spiritual gift, however, did not come without restrictions. Paul had already insisted that there were two conditions that demanded silence in Church. The first condition was if no interpreter was present. In that case, those who might wish to speak in tongues must be silent (14:28). The second condition was if a member (male or female) was speaking, even by inspiration, he or she must yield the floor and, while another spoke, remain silent (14:30). Here he addresses a third condition. In this case, it was directed at certain women.

So the question is, what was the condition that Paul addressed? The structure yields a number of possibilities. Taking Paul's counsel in chapter 11 and 14, one could be certain that women worshipers were not teaching, bearing testimony, or praying but, rather, were disrespectfully chatting in Church, paying little or no attention to those addressing the congregation,

---

259. Bailey, *Mediterranean Eyes*, 15. The numbers in the original have been replaced by letters to emphasize the chiastic structure of this section.

whether men or women.[260] Paul uses the verb λαλέω (*laleō*), "to speak," to describe what these ladies were doing. One nuance of the word is to make small talk or chat.[261] Thus, Paul was not commanding women with the spirit of prophecy to be still, but rude women who would not listen but made small talk or probably chatted about trivial things.[262] The problem with this view is that Paul never uses the word *laleo* with this nuance anywhere else in his writings. His use suggests more ordered and deliberate speaking.[263]

Another possibility is that the sentiment actually reflects an attitude among certain men. Certainly some Jewish converts likely wanted all women to hold their tongues during worship services. Thus, these verses are a paraphrase of an inappropriate attitude by some men that was reported to Paul. He clearly did not hold this view.[264] Seeing these verses in that light squares with his view on the properness of women praying and prophesying in Church; it also aligns with his insistence that, within the gospel framework, all are equal. Indeed, "there is neither Jew nor Greek, there is neither bond nor free, there is neither male nor female: for ye are all one in Christ Jesus" (Gal. 3:28). The caveat is, of course, that each of these groups was contributing to the harmony that should prevail during the services, which certainly was not happening in Corinth. The problem with this view is that, unlike other instances where Paul was responding to slogans coming out of Corinth, there is no clear indication that he is doing so here.

Yet another possibility, and the most prominent, is that Paul is trying to save women from shaming themselves. Paul's use of the adjective αἰσχρός (*aischros*), "shameful, disgraceful," shows that some people were deeply offended by these women's actions. Once again the JST provides insight into why this was the case. It changes the word "speak" to "rule" in 14:34–35, thus stating that it is a shame for women to rule in church. Thus, "the issue is not participation but control" noted an LDS scholar, and "Paul seems to be reminding the sisters to be subject to priesthood leadership, as the priesthood is subject to God. . . . There must be order in the Church on earth, as

---

260. Bailey, *Mediterranean Eyes,* 15–16, 412–17.

261. BDAG, 582–83.

262. Three centuries later, John Chrysostom, Archbishop of Constantinople, had to rebuke women in his congregation for not paying attention to the sermons, chatting noisily, and contributing to the general confusion. See *Hom. 1 Tim. 2:11–15.*

263. Fitzmyer, *First Corinthians,* 532–33.

264. An excellent articulation of this view is found in D. W. Odell-Scott, "Let the Women Speak in Church: An Egalitarian Interpretation of 1 Corinthians 14:33b–36," *Biblical Theology Bulletin* 13 (1983): 90–93.

there is order in heaven (compare 14:40). Women may teach, counsel, testify, and exhort, but God did not intend for them to usurp the authority he designated for priesthood leaders. . . . Yet that is also true for all Church members, male and female, who are asked to follow priesthood leaders."[265]

Elder Bruce R. McConkie wrote: "May women speak in Church? Yes, in the sense of teaching, counseling, testifying, exhorting, and the like; no, in the sense of assuming rule over the Church as such, and in attempting to give direction as to how God's affairs on earth shall be regulated: 'A woman has no right to found or organize a church; God never sent them to do it.' Paul is here telling the sisters they are subject to the priesthood, that it is not their province to rule and reign, that the bishop's wife is not the bishop."[266]

Paul buttresses his admonition with an appeal to the law of Moses when he states that women "should be subordinate [ὑποτάσσω, *hypotassō*], as the law also says" (14:34, Rendition). Some commentators maintain that Paul is saying these women should be subordinate to the men in the previous phrase. They then appeal to LXX Genesis 3:16, often called "the subordination of Eve," where Elohim tells Eve that Adam shall "rule over you."[267] There are a number of problems with this view, but a major one is that the context does not suggest Paul is concerned about a women's submission to the men in her life, for that has little to do with her being quiet in Church.

There is a narrative, however, that does fit; this comes out of God's dealings with his children, including creating this earth for them.[268] In this narrative, the emphasis is on bringing order out of chaos. This thread runs throughout all the scriptures. Everywhere boundaries and markers determine what is in place and what is not. The conflict between Paul and his detractors is where to draw the line between proper and improper behavior and between the expression of authority and submission in the Church.

---

265. Ogden and Skinner, *Verse by Verse*, 144. See *DNTC*, 2:387; Sperry, *Life and Letters*, 127–28.

266. *DNTC*, 2:387–88. Elder McConkie's quoted material can be found at "History, 1838–1856, Volume C-1," 1310.

267. Josephus, *Ag. Ap.* 2.24, shows that the view that women were somehow inferior to and, therefore, necessarily under the rule of men was clearly Jewish. Some commentators, then, see Paul's use of the term "the law" as referring merely to Jewish tradition that did not allow women to preach in synagogue. For example, see Norbert Baumert and others, *Woman and Man in Paul: Overcoming a Misunderstanding* (Collegeville, Minn.: Liturgical Press, 1996), 197. The proper use of the term ὁ νόμος (*ho nomos*), however, precludes such a narrow view and relativization. Fitzmyer, *First Corinthians*, 532.

268. Bruce, *1 and 2 Corinthians*, 136.

Some of Paul's detractors apparently felt that spiritual outpourings should trump everything else in a charismatic gospel community. Order would stifle it. The Apostle, however, appeals to order, insisting that it is God's way, "for God is a God of peace, not disorder," (14:32, Rendition). To make his case the Apostle appeals to scripture, unifying definitions, and general church practices.[269] In doing so, he substantiates the need for order in all God does, and that includes the position of men and women in his kingdom.

Whatever the case, Paul's words certainly reveal the high state of contention that existed in the Corinthian branches. Paul's counsel should not be taken as intending to limit feminine emancipation, for that is a modern issue and not in his purview. Rather, he takes the position that, due to their newly found freedom in Christ, certain women have gone too far. This feeling reflects the view not only of the men but also of other women. His remarks then should not be taken to suggest that all the women in the branches were pushing the limits. Rather, they were directed at some contentious and chatty souls, and that included both men and women (11:16). He asked the women, both married and unmarried, to think of the good of the community and to subordinate themselves thereto. This is an important point. The Greek imperative is a third person middle/passive, ὑποτασσέσθωσαν (*hypotassesthōsan*), and thus stresses self-imposed subordination. It is an internal act, not an external command. That subordination would then apply only indirectly to men but directly to the edifying and building up of fellow Saints.[270] Love would allow that to take place.

Conclusion (14:36–40)

Greek Text

36 ἢ ἀφ' ὑμῶν ὁ λόγος τοῦ θεοῦ ἐξῆλθεν, ἢ εἰς ὑμᾶς μόνους κατήντησεν; 37 Εἴ τις δοκεῖ προφήτης εἶναι ἢ πνευματικός, ἐπιγινωσκέτω ἃ γράφω ὑμῖν ὅτι κυρίου ἐστίν· 38 εἰ δέ τις ἀγνοεῖ, ἀγνοεῖται. 39 ὥστε, ἀδελφοί μου, ζηλοῦτε τὸ προφητεύειν, καὶ τὸ λαλεῖν μὴ κωλύετε γλώσσαις· 40 πάντα δὲ εὐσχημόνως καὶ κατὰ τάξιν γινέσθω. [SBLGNT]

---

269. Wire, *Corinthian Women*, 13–38, though pushing a feminist agenda, shows how Paul integrates various differentiations to appeal to order. On the whole argument, see Thiselton, *First Epistle*, 1153–55.

270. Baumert, *Woman and Man*, 195–98.

King James Version

36 What? came the word of God out from you? or came it unto you only? 37 If any man think himself to be a prophet, or spiritual, let him acknowledge that the things that I write unto you are the commandments of the Lord. 38 But if any man be ignorant, let him be ignorant. 39 Wherefore, brethren, covet to prophesy, and forbid not to speak with tongues. 40 Let all things be done decently and in order.

New Rendition

36 Did the word of God originate with you, or are you the only ones to whom it has come? 37 If anyone thinks he is divinely inspired or a spiritual person, he should recognize that what I write to you is a commandment of the Lord. 38 But if anyone disregards it, he should be disregarded. 39 And so, my brothers and sisters, be eager to speak with divine inspiration, and don't prevent anyone from speaking in other languages. 40 Let all things be done correctly and in an orderly manner.

Translation Notes and Comments

14:36 *What? came the word of God out from you? or came it unto you only? / Did the word of God originate with you, or are you the only ones to whom it has come?*: Here the phrase ὁ λόγος τοῦ θεοῦ (*ho logos tou theou*), "the word of God," refers to the teachings and doctrines given by the Savior and perpetuated by the Church.[271] Though the verb ἐξέρχομαι (*exerchomai*) denotes moving out or away from something, it also carries the nuance of being its source or origin, and our Rendition takes this nuance.[272] In these rhetorical questions, Paul twice uses the plural pronoun "you," and in doing so provides a clue to who his intended audience is. In the first instance (ὑμῶν, *hymōn*), the pronoun could be either feminine or masculine, but in the second (ὑμᾶς, *hymas*), it is modified by a masculine adjective showing that Paul's questions are not posed just to the women. As in English, a masculine noun can also include a feminine element. Therefore, in this verse, Paul is no longer directing his remarks solely to the sisters. He seems to be looking at all those who are causing the dissension.

Paul's questions were a way of forcing his readers to consider what their actions implied. His focus is specifically on the alternative voices in the community, both men and women, who have been pushing their own agenda. His questions force this segment of his readership to consider whether they are guilty of inventing their own gospel. His question identifies first the

---

271. Louw-Nida, §33.260. Compare *euangelizō* at §33.215 and *euanglion* at §33.217.
272. BDAG, 347–48.

hubris of their thinking that somehow they had the authority to declare Church doctrine and practice, and second, that they could flaunt Church-wide practices and reinterpret the doctrine as if it applied only to them.[273] The questions should have been very sobering.

14:37 *If any man think himself to be a prophet, or spiritual, let him acknowledge that the things that I write unto you are the commandments of the Lord / If anyone thinks he is divinely inspired or a spiritual person, he should recognize that what I write to you is a commandment of the Lord:* With this verse, Paul gives a test of authenticity by which the Corin-thian Saints can judge if one who claims unique spirituality is correct. The verb δοκέω (*dokeō*) means "to think" or "believe" something to be true but carries a degree of uncertainty and, therefore, can also be translated as "suppose."[274] The verb ἐπιγινώσκω (*epiginōskō*), "know, acknowledge, recognize," stands in contrast to *dokeō* in connoting a sureness of what is known.[275] Most ancient manuscripts include the noun ἐντολή (*entolē*), "commandment," at the end of this verse. However, a few omit it, and the SBLGNT chose to follow these. Nevertheless, in our Rendition we have chosen to include it because of its ancient support. The *entolē* denotes any "mandate or ordinance," but in Christian circles it also referred to both the commandments of God and the precepts of the Lord.

Paul contrasts what a possible detractor might "suppose" (*dokeō*) abut Paul's teachings with that of the Apostle's sureness about what he has writ-ten. Paul even gives his words the status of an *entolē*, "commandment." In doing so, he offsets any claim others may have to superior authority. Paul insists that anyone who is truly spiritual will acknowledge the divin-ity behind what he has written. The verse also tacitly appeals to Paul's own authority that allows him to speak for deity.[276]

14:38 *But if any man be ignorant, let him be ignorant / But if anyone disregards it, he should be disregarded:* The verb ἀγνοέω (*agnoeō*) means both to not understand something or be uniformed about it. The word also means to disregard a matter.[277] The manuscript tradition for this verse is varied. Some manuscripts have ἀγνοείτω (*agnoeitō*), "let him be disre-garded," while others read ἀγνοεῖται (*agnoeitai*), "he is disregarded." The

---

273. Witherington, *Women in the Earliest Church*, 98.
274. BDAG, 254–55; Louw-Nida, §31.29.
275. BDAG, 369; Louw-Nida, §28.2.
276. Fitzmyer, *First Corinthians*, 536–37.
277. BDAG, 12–13.

KJV and our Rendition follow the first reading as more logical and as the more likely original.[278] Paul is simply instructing the Corinthian Saints to pay no attention to anyone who claims that what Paul has written to them is not inspired.

14:39 *Wherefore, brethren, covet to prophesy, and forbid not to speak with tongues /And so, my brothers and sisters, be eager to speak with divine inspiration, and don't prevent anyone from speaking in other languages:* With the conjunction, ὥστε (*hōste*), "wherefore, and so," Paul signals his readers that this is his conclusion on the subject. On ἀδελφοί (*adelphoi*), "brothers and sisters," see Translation Notes on 1:10. The verb ζηλόω (*zēloō*), "covet, seek after, be eager," denotes striving earnestly for something and carries the connotation of the deep concern one should have to obtain it.[279] The English idiom "to set one's heart on something" carries the idea.[280] The imperative κωλύετε (*kōlyete*) means to "hinder, prevent," or "forbid" something from taking place.[281] Coupled with μή (*mē*), "not," it is a command to see that something is not forbidden or hindered in any way. Paul's use of the phrase shows that he does not want the gift of tongues stifled. He, however, much prefers that the Saints seek for the gift of prophecy.

14:40 *Let all things be done decently and in order / Let all things be done correctly and in an orderly manner:* With this sentence Paul summarizes all he has said in chapter 14. The adverb εὐσχημόνως (*euschēmonōs*) refers to that which is done properly and correctly.[282] The phrase κατὰ τάξιν (*kata taxin*), "according to order," implies doing things in a proper sequence.[283] Thus, to assure harmony and edification throughout the Church, all things should be done correctly and in order.

Analysis and Summary

The two rhetorical questions Paul asks in 14:36 expose the heart of the Corinthian problem. It was one of arrogance. Paul is asking them if they really think that they somehow have some special divine authority that allows them to reject both Paul's teachings and the general practices of the Church. In 14:33, he noted that peace prevails ἐν πάσαις ταῖς ἐκκλησίαις

---

278. Metzger, *Textual Commentary*, 500.
279. BDAG, 427; Louw-Nida, §25.46.
280. Louw-Nida, §25.76.
281. BDAG, 580.
282. BDAG, 414.
283. Louw-Nida, §61.3.

(*en pasais tais ekklēsiais*), "in all the congregations." The operative words are "in all," for it shows he is appealing to general Church protocols. Here he contrasts that situation with what is happening in Corinth, asking if the Gospel came εἰς ὑμᾶς μόνους (*eis hymas monous*), "to only you," since they are setting their own standards. In essence he is asking, "Are you the starting point of the gospel? Or are you its only destination?"[284] Thus, this summary statement, couched as a question, directs all the guilty parties in Corinth, both men and women, to conform.[285]

In 14:39–40, Paul succinctly brings his whole argument to a close: the gift of speaking by inspiration should be sought for with zeal (ζηλόω, *zēloō*), but the gift of speaking in other languages should not be suppressed, only controlled. Every meeting should be conducted so that both proper form and sequence are followed. The result would bring edification to all who attended, both those of high and low rank as well as members and nonmembers. Such harmony and orderliness among the Saints would go a long way in commending respect from those outside the Church (see 1 Thes. 4:12a).

The undergirding issue of this whole chapter focuses on what it means to be spiritual. The context shows the criteria are threefold: (1) the reception and variety of the gifts of the spirit, (2) the use of those gifts to edify, and (3) a display of the unifying power of these gifts reflected through Church order and discipline.[286] It is in these that true spirituality manifests itself. But, as criterion 3 shows, the Spirit always yields to Church order and law. The witness of both Isaiah 2:3 and Micah 4:2 shows that from Zion (or wherever the Church's headquarters is), "the law shall go forth." Therefore, as Paul so forcefully expresses himself in 14:36, the Corinthian Saints were not the original source of authority, and their "wisdom" did not set the standard of Church priority.[287] Both came from priesthood authority and general Church practice. Therefore, they were to conform to those practices found in all the Churches of the Saints of God.[288] The result would yield true spirituality.

---

284. Robertson and Plummer, *Critical and Exegetical Commentary,* 326.

285. Had Paul used the feminine plural pronoun μόνας (*monas*) rather than the masculine plural pronoun μόνους (*monous*), he would have been speaking only to the women. However, since the masculine form can include a group of both men and women, the use here suggests he is talking to both. See Smyth, *Greek Grammar,* §1015.

286. Fee, *First Epistle,* 709, lists two while Thiselton, *First Epistle,* 1162, lists all three.

287. Bruce, *1 and 2 Corinthians,* 136.

288. Sperry, *Life and Letters,* 128.

Chapter 15

The Doctrine of the Resurrection

INTRODUCTION

In this chapter Paul addresses his final doctrinal concerns that are the result of problems that have arisen within the Corinthian branches. He learned that certain Corinthian Saints were teaching that there was no corporeal resurrection and had apparently formed an antiresurrection party that was gaining ground. Whether Paul's response addressed yet another concern in the letter from Chloe or was a tangent arising from it or something else cannot be known.[1] One thing is sure—this heresy was the greatest threat yet to the Christian message and to the existence of the Church as a whole. Thus, the issue he addresses here is the most important in the entire letter. As is his pattern, he first places the issue in its broader theological and doctrinal context. With no formal transition from what he has said in the former chapter, he signals his readers he is now going to treat a new subject with the use of the emphatic verb γνωρίζω (gnōrizō), "I make known to you" (15:1). The verb emphasizes his absolute certainty about the topic he now turns to, one he has formerly taught them in detail.[2]

In this chapter, Paul deals with "the creation of an immortal soul; it consists in uniting or reuniting of body and spirit in immortality," noted Elder Bruce R. McConkie.[3] "Human hopes never exploded with more power than in Paul's doctrinal climax," noted an LDS scholar. He went on to say, "This chapter's brilliant beginning, middle sequences, and final completeness become vivid realities as one perceives its blending of prophecy and

---

1. Holzapfel and Wayment, *Making Sense*, 365.
2. Fitzmyer, *First Corinthians*, 539–40.
3. McConkie, *Mormon Doctrine*, 451–54. For full discussion, see Joseph Fielding Smith, quoted in McConkie, *Doctrines of Salvation*, 2:258–301.

clear knowledge of the apostles. These truths can be ignored or ridiculed but not refuted, for here they come from an eyewitness who soberly reports personal knowledge and that of the Twelve. The fiery dawn of immortality glows in the triumphant words of the apostle."[4]

This chapter is both the crown and close of the whole epistle but, more importantly, it holds the key to the epistle's real intent. Though resurrection is this chapter's overriding theme, behind it and giving it force and meaning is Paul's understanding of the grace of God. It is the doctrine of the Resurrection that provides the insight necessary to understanding what grace really is and how it actually works. Grace is an expression of the Father's love for his children shown by his free gift to them of immortal life through the Resurrection. That gift, however, came about through another of God's supernal gifts, that of his Son (John 3:16). The Son himself, through his own act of grace, opened the door to its power. This was accomplished through the Lord's death, carried out by the instrument of the cross.

Grace operates because it is "God who gives life to the dead" (Rom. 4:17, authors' translation). Indeed, the Resurrection is a pure act of grace because the dead contribute nothing to it. They neither earn nor merit it. Grace truly is a free gift and that gift is life—an immortal life given through the power of a universal Resurrection (Alma 11:42; 40:22–23; Moses 7:62). It was Christ's death and the grace it released that made this possible.[5] In sum, the Resurrection reveals what grace truly is. Often thought of in terms of favor, kindness, and good will, grace expresses itself as an enabling and empowering divine action, released through love and freely given, that makes quality of life possible.[6] Admittedly, not all will share in the same quality of immortal life (15:39–42; D&C 76:31–119), nonetheless, everyone will participate, to a greater or lesser degree, in the transformative powers of the Resurrection.

The whole of the chapter centers on two issues. The first Paul expresses with the question, "How say some among you that there is no resurrection of the dead?" (15:12). Just who these Saints were Paul does not say nor does he explain why they came to this conclusion. At stake, however, is the reality and nature of postmortal existence and, just behind it, the nature and

---

4. Anderson, *Understanding Paul*, 125.
5. Thiselton, *First Epistle*, 1169.
6. Draper, "Light, Truth, and Grace," 243–451; Draper, *Fulness of Joy*, 27–28, 85, 153–54.

work of God. Therefore, it is of little wonder that, as one theologian noted, Paul "refers to the doctrine of the resurrection as the Gospel."[7]

That being the case, some have wondered why Paul did not address the issue much earlier in this letter. The answer, however, seems clear from the organization of the epistle itself. The Apostle could not introduce the theology of the Resurrection until he had clearly established the doctrine of the cross as the seat and test of Christian identity.[8] He also had to put in place the importance of divine grace and the role it played in the life of the Church, especially in the bequeathal of the gifts of the Spirit, more especially love.

Once that was done, the Apostle could address the issues raised by the antiresurrection party. To what degree people in the Roman world believed in life after death is unknown, but large segments of the population did not—among the philosophers, it was especially the Epicureans, and among the Jews, the Sadducees. These were influential enough that the idea would not have been foreign to members of the Church.[9] Some may have accounted for the Resurrection as an event that took place at conversion, when the spirit was raised, as it were, above the mortal, physical plain to new spiritual heights. Thus, they could have concluded, that a corporeal resurrection was not a reality.[10]

The second issue Paul expressed with the questions, "How are the dead raised up? and with what body do they come?" (15:35). Those who asked these questions were concerned about the nature of the resurrected body. The more educated may have been influenced by a general philosophical suspicion that the flesh was the seat of evil and must be shunted off. Their concern with resurrection τῶν νεκρῶν (*tōn nekrōn*), "of the dead," was likely based on the macabre image of raising decaying corpses.[11]

In sum, the information necessary to determine exactly what the parameters of this issue were does not exist. Indeed, there may have even been more than one issue. Further, there may have been even more than one group. It seems that most of the Saints did accept the Resurrection of the

---

7. John Calvin, *First Epistle of Paul to the Corinthians,* trans. John W. Fraser (Edinburgh: Oliver & Boyd and St. Andrews, 1960), 312.

8. Thiselton, *First Epistle,* 1171.

9. Walter Schmithals, *Gnosticism in Corinth: An Investigation of the Letters to the Corinthians,* trans. John E. Seely (Nashville: Abingdon Press, 1971), 156; Ramsay MacMullen, *Paganism in the Roman Empire* (New Haven: Yale University Press, 1981), 49–61.

10. Chrysostom, *Cor.,* 37.1.

11. Martin, *Corinthian Body,* 130, 132, 135–36.

Savior. Even so, to support the reality of the corporeal resurrection, Paul cites as witnesses the leading Apostle, the Twelve as a whole, five hundred men—most of whom were still alive—and, finally, himself (15:5–8). He assures his readers of these witnesses' integrity (15:15).[12]

The problem with the members of the antiresurrection party was that they simply could not see the implications and importance of this doctrine.[13] In 15:34, Paul identifies the reason: "Some" he says, "have not the knowledge of God: I speak this to your shame." This statement is the lantern that sheds light on the source of the problem. A correct understanding of the Resurrection was dependent on a correct understanding of God. The basis for a belief in the reality of the Resurrection did not rely on some innate human capacity. Rather, it derived from an understanding of the creative and quickening powers of an almighty God, a God who created and made alive the appropriate body for beings both on earth (15:39) and in heaven (15:42–44), and then empowered them such that they could reach full potential.[14]

It was so critical that the Corinthian Saints understand this doctrine that Paul devoted a large section of his epistle to teach and reinforce it. Paul's carefully constructed discussion on the Resurrection falls into four major stages.

In the first stage he presents the two doctrines on which he will build the rest of his argument, which consists of (1) an introduction in which he reaffirms what he has already taught them concerning the death and Resurrection of the Lord and lists witnesses to the event, and (2) an introduction of the concept of grace (15:1–11).

In the second stage he shows the dire consequences if there were no Resurrection, specifically, that all the Saints believed in was false and they, with their dead, were headed toward spiritual ruin (15:12–19).

In the third stage he confirms the Resurrection of the Lord but only as the "firstfruit" (ἀπαρχή, *aparchē*) thereof. He shows that more "fruits" were to follow (15:20–34).

In the fourth stage he tackles the logical conceivability of the Resurrection, showing that God will determine what kind of body resurrected souls will have. It will, Paul assures his readers, neither be earthly nor suffer from corruption. Instead, it will be "a spiritual body," that is, it would have physical substance and bear the image of the heavenly type.

---

12. Anderson, *Understanding Paul*, 125.
13. For an extensive discussion see Thiselton, *First Epistle*, 1172–76.
14. Thiselton, *First Epistle*, 1178.

In the last stage, he bears his testimony that God gives "us the victory through our Lord Jesus Christ" (15:35–57). He concludes the chapter and his entire theological discussion (chapter 16 deals with temporal matters) with a peroration, identifying what they should do to take full advantage of the gift God has given them (15:58).

CHRIST'S RESURRECTION (15:1–11)

Greek Text

1 Γνωρίζω δὲ ὑμῖν, ἀδελφοί, τὸ εὐαγγέλιον ὃ εὐηγγελισάμην ὑμῖν, ὃ καὶ παρελά-βετε, ἐν ᾧ καὶ ἑστήκατε, 2 δι᾽ οὗ καὶ σῴζεσθε, τίνι λόγῳ εὐηγγελισάμην ὑμῖν, εἰ κατέχετε, ἐκτὸς εἰ μὴ εἰκῇ ἐπιστεύσατε.

3 Παρέδωκα γὰρ ὑμῖν ἐν πρώτοις, ὃ καὶ παρέλαβον, ὅτι Χριστὸς ἀπέθανεν ὑπὲρ τῶν ἁμαρτιῶν ἡμῶν κατὰ τὰς γραφάς, 4 καὶ ὅτι ἐτάφη, καὶ ὅτι ἐγήγερται τῇ ἡμέρᾳ τῇ τρίτῃ κατὰ τὰς γραφάς, 5 καὶ ὅτι ὤφθη Κηφᾷ, εἶτα τοῖς δώδεκα· 6 ἔπειτα ὤφθη ἐπάνω πεντακοσίοις ἀδελφοῖς ἐφάπαξ, ἐξ ὧν οἱ πλείονες μένουσιν ἕως ἄρτι, τινὲς δὲ ἐκοιμήθησαν· 7 ἔπειτα ὤφθη Ἰακώβῳ, εἶτα τοῖς ἀποστόλοις πᾶσιν· 8 ἔσχατον δὲ πάντων ὡσπερεὶ τῷ ἐκτρώματι ὤφθη κἀμοί. 9 ἐγὼ γάρ εἰμι ὁ ἐλάχιστος τῶν ἀποστόλων, ὃς οὐκ εἰμὶ ἱκανὸς καλεῖσθαι ἀπόστολος, διότι ἐδίωξα τὴν ἐκκλησίαν τοῦ θεοῦ· 10 χάριτι δὲ θεοῦ εἰμι ὅ εἰμι, καὶ ἡ χάρις αὐτοῦ ἡ εἰς ἐμὲ οὐ κενὴ ἐγενήθη, ἀλλὰ περισσότερον αὐτῶν πάντων ἐκοπίασα, οὐκ ἐγὼ δὲ ἀλλὰ ἡ χάρις τοῦ θεοῦ ἡ σὺν ἐμοί. 11 εἴτε οὖν ἐγὼ εἴτε ἐκεῖνοι, οὕτως κηρύσσομεν καὶ οὕτως ἐπιστεύσατε. [SBLGNT]

King James Version

1 Moreover, brethren, I declare unto you the gospel which I preached unto you, which also ye have received, and wherein ye stand; 2 By which also ye are saved, if ye keep in memory what I preached unto you, unless ye have believed in vain. 3 For I delivered unto you first of all that which I also received, how that Christ died for our sins according to the scriptures; 4 And that he was buried, and that he rose again the third day according to the scriptures: 5 And that he was seen of Cephas, then of the twelve: 6 After that,

New Rendition

1 Now I am reminding you, brothers and sisters, of the gospel which I preached to you, which you also accepted, on which you also stand firm, 2 and by which you are also saved, if you hold fast to the message that I preached to you. Otherwise, you have believed in vain. 3 For I passed on to you those things of greatest importance, which I also received, namely that Christ died for our sins according to the scriptures, 4 that he was buried, that he was raised up on the third day according to the scriptures, 5 that he appeared

he was seen of above five hundred brethren at once; of whom the greater part remain unto this present, but some are fallen asleep. 7 After that, he was seen of James; then of all the apostles. 8 And last of all he was seen of me also, as of one born out of due time. 9 For I am the least of the apostles, that am not meet to be called an apostle, because I persecuted the church of God. 10 But by the grace of God I am what I am: and his grace which was bestowed upon me was not in vain; but I laboured more abundantly than they all: yet not I, but the grace of God which was with me. 11 Therefore whether it were I or they, so we preach, and so ye believed.

to Cephas, then to the twelve. 6 Then he appeared to more than five hundred brothers and sisters at one time, most of whom are still alive, although some have fallen asleep. 7 Then he appeared to James, then to all the apostles. 8 Last of all he appeared also to me, as to one untimely born. 9 For I am the least of the apostles, unworthy to be called an apostle because I persecuted the church of God. 10 Nevertheless, by the grace of God I am what I am, and his grace toward me has not been in vain. On the contrary, I have worked harder than all of them, yet not I, but the grace of God which is with me. 11 And so, whether I or they, this is the way we preach and this is the way you came to believe.

Translation Notes and Comments

15:1 *Moreover, brethren, I declare unto you the gospel which I preached unto you / Now I am reminding you, brothers and sisters, of the gospel which I preached to you:* On ἀδελφοί (*adelphoi*), "brothers and sisters," see Translation Notes on 1:10. The verb γνωρίζω (*gnōrizō*) means "to make known."[15] However, since Paul is referring to things that he has already taught the Corinthian Saints but now must re-teach them, it carries the idea of restoring or reacquainting them with knowledge that was once theirs. The noun εὐαγγέλιον (*euangelion*), "gospel," denotes "good news" and, in the Christian context, witnesses specifically that salvation is found only in the Lord on the basis of his expiatory death and Resurrection.[16] The word tacitly includes the transforming and saving grace of God that he bestows upon those who respond to his call as found in the Old Testament scriptures.[17] The verb εὐαγγελίζω (*euangellizō*), "to preach," refers specifically to declaring publicly the gospel message.[18]

15. BDAG, 203.
16. Gerhard Friedrich, "εὐαγγέλιον," in *TDNT*, 2:721–36.
17. Thiselton, *First Epistle*, 1184–85.
18. BDAG, 402–3.

wherein ye stand / on which you also stand firm: The verb ἑστήκατε (*hestēkate*), though perfect in form, is present in meaning, and here has the sense of "stand firm" in one's beliefs,[19] as found in our Rendition. The implication is that both Paul and his readers have already agreed on the basic premises of the gospel. All should, therefore, agree that what he says is valid doctrine.[20]

15:2 *By which also ye are saved, if ye keep in memory what I preached unto you / and by which you are also saved, if you hold fast to the message that I preached to you:* The verb σώζω (*sōzō*), "to save," carries the nuance of both delivering and protecting from danger. In the gospel context, it refers to being delivered from death, both spiritual and physical, and protected from the powers of hell.[21] In Paul's context here, however, it refers more specifically to receiving eternal life.[22] The form of the verb Paul uses is a present passive and indicates that the Saints are presently in the condition of salvation, but they have to maintain it. In other words, salvation is conditional. That condition Paul expressed with the verb κατέχω (*katechō*), "to hold fast." The KJV translation of the word as "keep in memory" is not precise enough. The Greek verb means "to adhere to firmly" and connotes the determined effort a Saint must put into following the way of the Lord.[23]

The syntax of the last clause is a bit tricky. The issue is how to understand the phrase τίνι λόγῳ (*tini logō*), which consists of the dative case of the pronoun τίς (*tis*) and the noun λόγος (*logos*). The first challenge is deciding which of the many possible meanings of *logos* is the correct one—word, statement, speech, matter, thing, account, reckoning, reason, ground, motive, etc. Some translators, taking their cue from its translation in Acts 10:29, render the whole clause as "for what reason (*logos*) I preached unto you," showing that the reason Paul preached the gospel was for their salvation. The Vulgate supports this understanding, using *qua ratione*, "for which reason." Another possibility is "by which word/message (τίνι λόγῳ) I preached the

---

19. BDAG, 482–83.

20. Fitzmyer, *First Corinthians,* 544.

21. Those who will be saved from death and hell include all who inherit either celestial or terrestrial glory. See Larry E. Dahl, "Degress of Glory," in *EM,* 1:367. Spiritual death here refers to what John the Revelator called "the second death" (Rev. 20:14). Only those who remain filthy after suffering and resisting the purifying fires of hell will know this fate (Alma 12:16–18; Hel. 14:16–19; D&C 76:36–37).

22. In LDS parlance, that would mean exaltation. See Margaret McConkie Pope, "Exaltation," in *EM,* 2:479.

23. BDAG, 532–33.

gospel (εὐηγγελισάμην, *euēngelisamen*) to you," which is rather awkward. Many translators, like those of the KJV, have ignored the grammatical problem of the dative case. Instead, they have rendered the passage rather freely as "what I preached to you."[24] We have followed this course in our Rendition as well, taking the phrase as modifying εὐαγγελισάμην (*euangelisamen*), "I preached," and translating the word as "the message." It is thus the message (*logos*) to which the Saints must hold true.[25]

unless ye have believed in vain / Otherwise, you have believed in vain: The adverb εἰκῇ (*eikē*) has a number of possible senses: here including "without purpose, at random, in vain" or "without careful thought, thoughtlessly."[26] Most translations render this "in vain," and the Vulgate supports that with the translation *frusta*, "without effect, in vain." We have followed this in our Rendition, although "without careful thought" is a possible but less likely translation. Paul's point is that unless the Corinthian Saints continue to strictly adhere to the principles of the gospel as he taught them, their belief will not lead them to eternal life.

15:3 *For I delivered unto you first of all* / *For I passed on to you those things of greatest importance:* Here Paul defines what he meant by τίνι λόγῳ (*tini logo*), "the message," in the previous verse. The verb παραδίδωμι (*paradidōmi*), literally "to give over," is here used in the sense of passing on to another what one has learned from oral or written tradition.[27] The gender of the dative plural adjective πρώτοις (*prōtois*), "the first," is ambiguous and presents some difficulty in translation. If the gender is construed as masculine, it could be translated as "among (you) first," meaning that the Corinthian Saints were the first to whom Paul preached the gospel. On the other hand, if the gender is construed as neuter, it could be translated as "among the first things," that is, "the most important things."[28] The KJV takes the first view. Since, however, Paul already preached in a number of locations before coming to Corinth, this view seems unlikely. Therefore, our Rendition takes the second view and translates the phrase as "things of greatest importance."[29] That being the case, Paul is stressing that he declared to

---

24. So the NIV, NET, NRSV, etc.

25. For discussion, see Barrett, *First Epistle,* 336; Thiselton, *First Epistle,* 1185; Fitzmyer, *First Corinthians,* 545.

26. BDAG, 281.

27. BDAG, 761–63.

28. BDAG, 892–93.

29. Robertson and Plummer, *Critical and Exegetical Commentary,* 332; Fee, *First Epistle,* 722 and n. 5.

them the most important of the doctrines of the kingdom. These were the very heart of the Christian traditions that the Church had adhered to from the beginning and on which the Apostle was making his stand.[30]

that which I also received, how that Christ died for our sins / which I also received, namely that Christ died for our sins: With this verse, Paul begins what might be termed the primitive Church's "articles of faith." This statement of belief was composed of four elements, each of which Paul introduces with the conjunction ὅτι (*hoti*), "that," which serves as the equivalent of quotation marks,[31] showing that Paul is quoting established Church doctrine. He lists the first article of faith in this verse.

The key word in this clause is the verb παραλαμβάνω (*paralambanō*), "to receive." It denotes acquiring information from another and implies "the type of information passed on by tradition."[32] There is, however, another nuance that is important. The word connotes receiving something by way of assignment or task.[33] Taking both meanings together, Paul seems to be saying that he not only received the information but was also charged with its accurate distribution. What he was charged to accurately distribute, as seen from the rest of this chapter, was the vicarious nature of the Savior's work.[34] The charge was the doctrine that Christ died ὑπὲρ τῶν ἁμαρτιῶν ἡμῶν (*hyper tōn hamartiōn hēmōn*), "for our sins." The preposition ὑπὲρ (*hyper*) is a "marker indicating that an activity or event is in some entity's interest" and, therefore, means "in behalf of" or "because of."[35] In this case, it was because of our sins that the Savior had to die.

according to the scriptures / according to the scriptures : The preposition κατά (*kata*), "according to," denotes the standard by which something is judged.[36] The noun γραφαί (*graphai*), "scriptures," though generally indicating any writing, here connotes specifically the holy writings of the Jews and Christians.[37] Though Paul appeals to the standard of the scriptures, he does not identify which particular passages he had in mind. They

---

30. Fitzmyer, *First Corinthians,* 545.

31. Thiselton, *First Epistle,* 1189.

32. Louw-Nida, §27.13.

33. Louw-Nida, §37.99.

34. The use of the conjunction ὅτι (*hoti*), "that," stresses the content of what was preached. Wallace, *Greek Grammar,* 678.

35. BDAG, 1030–31.

36. Wallace, *Greek Grammar,* 377.

37. BDAG, 206. Based on LXX 1 Chr. 15:15 and 2 Chr. 30:5, the Greek phrase referred to the whole Old Testament.

must, however, have been familiar to his audience, likely through their use by the missionaries. Speculations run high as to which they were, but none are very convincing.[38] Paul's appeal to them, however, was to emphasize that the Savior's death and Resurrection were ever part of the divine plan.[39]

15:4 *that he was buried / that he was buried:* Paul mentions the second article of faith here. The verb θάπτω (*thaptō*) indicated the burial of a dead body.[40] The Savior's death was a central doctrine (see Rom. 6:4) necessary to counter the propaganda perpetrated by the Jewish rulers that the Lord did not really die but was resuscitated and then appeared to his followers (Matt. 28:11–17).[41]

he rose again the third day / he was raised up on the third day: This is the third "article of faith." The force of the perfect passive verb ἐγήγερται (*egēgertai*), literally "he has been raised," does three things. First, it stresses the abiding result of the event.[42] Christ was raised on the third day *and* he yet lives.[43] Second, through the use of the "divine passive," the verb tacitly ascribes the action to God (as in 15:14, 16–17, 20). Third, the word implies more than mere resuscitation, as in the case of Lazarus (John 12:1), but of exaltation (see Philip. 2:9).[44] This "article of faith" points to when the Resurrection took place: τῇ ἡμέρᾳ τῇ τρίτῃ (*tē hēmera tē tritē*), "on the third day." Because the Jews counted inclusively, any portion of a day was calculated as a full day. Thus, Jesus need be in the tomb for only one full day (Saturday,

---

38. Likely candidates are LXX Isa. 53:5–12 (based on 1 Pet. 2:22–25) and Ps. 22; Deut. 18:15, 18; Lam. 1:12, 18. For discussion, see Barrett, *First Epistle*, 338–39; Fee, *First Epistle*, 724; David M. Stanley, *Christ's Resurrection in Pauline Soteriology* (Rome: Pontifical Biblical Institute, 1961), 108–27.

39. Fitzmyer, *First Corinthians*, 546.

40. BDAG, 444. In this connection, see LXX Gen. 35:19; Deut. 10:6; Judg. 8:32 where ἀπέθνεν . . . καὶ ἐτάφη (*apethanen . . . kai etaphē*), death and burial, are tied together.

41. Because the belief statement does not mention the empty tomb, some have claimed this idea was a later addition. See R. J. Sider, "St. Paul's Understanding of the Nature and Significance of the Resurrection in I Corinthians xv 1–19," *Novum Testamentum* 19 (April 1977): 124–41; C. F. D. Moule, "St. Paul and Dualism: The Pauline Conception of Resurrection," *New Testament Studies* 12 (1965–66): 106–23. What the detractors overlook is the stereotyped four-part formula Paul used that follows a well-established tradition. See Bailey, *Mediterranean Eyes*, 426–28; Fitzmyer, *First Corinthians*, 547. The formula itself assumes that the body of the resurrected Lord would no longer be in the tomb.

42. Wallace, *Greek Grammar*, 577; Findlay, "St. Paul's First Epistle," 2:919.

43. Moule, *Idiom Book*, 15.

44. BDAG, 271–22; Louw-Nida, §23.94; compare Acts 2:32–33; 5:30–31 where the activities of raising and exalting are mentioned together.

Mark 16:1) to be credited with being in the tomb for three.[45] The record does not say when he was actually resurrected. When the women reached the tomb at sunup on Sunday, he was already gone.

according to the scriptures / according to the scriptures: Again, as shown by his repeated use of preposition κατὰ (*kata*), "according to," Paul appeals to the standard of the scriptures for authentication of the doctrine. For him and the early Christians, the "scriptures" referred only to the Old Testament, since most of the writings that comprise the New Testament had not yet been written. He does not, however, as mentioned above, state which passages of scripture he is referring to, which leads to the problem as to whether he has in mind the Resurrection or the three-day interment. That the Savior cited Old Testament scriptures to indicate he would be in the tomb for three days (Matt. 12:39–41; 16:4; Luke 11:29–30) suggests that Paul could have had reference to this event.[46] It seems more likely based on his reference in 15:3 that he actually has in mind the broad themes of sacrifice, expiation, vicarious work, and God's saving mission as found throughout the Old Testament.[47]

15:5 *And that he was seen of Cephas / that he appeared to Cephas:* This is the fourth "article of faith." The verb ὁράω (*horaō*), "to see," can carry the nuance of an eye witness. Its aorist passive form, ὤφθη (*ōphthē*), means "to be seen, to appear."[48] The Jews felt the passive form had significance. They insisted that the Bible did not say "the prophet saw God," but that "God was seen by the prophet." The implication is that a person on his own could not see, that is, perceive or understand the nature of God unless it was revealed to him from that divine source.[49] Paul's use of this form suggests

---

45. Tertullian, *Adv. Marc.* 4.43.1. Not understanding the Savior's work in the spirit world (see D&C 138), some commentators have wondered if the Resurrection was on Friday since the Lord told the thief, "To day shalt thou be with me in paradise" (Luke 23:43). Also, because John's gospel seems to suggest there were only two days between the Crucifixion and Resurrection, many puzzle over the "three-day gap." For example, see N. T. Wright, "Jesus' Resurrection and Christian Origins," *Gregorianum* 83 (2002): 627.

46. Some see Hosea 6:2 and Jonah 2:1 as the reference, but neither of these has any direct bearing on the New Testament events.

47. Hays, *First Corinthians,* 256; Barrett, *First Epistle,* 340; Bruce M. Metzger, "A Suggestion concerning the Meaning of 1 Corinthians XV.4b," *Journal of Theological Studies* 8 (1957): 118–23.

48. BDAG, 719–20. The use of the aorist passive is unusual and seems to preserve a Hebraism found in the LXX at Gen. 12:7; 17:1; 18:1; 26:2, 24; 31:13; 35:9; 48:3; Ex. 3:2; 6:3; 16:10; Lev. 9:23; Num. 14:10; 16:19; 17:7; 20:6; Judg. 13:3; 1 Kgs. 3:5.

49. It is significant that in nearly every New Testament use of passive ὤφθη (*ōphthē*), "appeared," it is the subject of the verb (in this case, God) who initiates the visible

the Christians were adopting this view.[50] The noun *Kēphas,* "Cephas," is the Greek rendering of כֵּיפָא (*kēypā'*), Aramaic for "the rock," which was the leading Apostle's nickname.[51] Luke 24:34 also speaks of Jesus appearing to Peter before the other ten.[52]

then of the twelve / then to the twelve: The cardinal number δώδεκα (*dōdeka*), "twelve," is an adjective acting as a noun and refers to the Twelve Apostles (see Luke 6:13).[53] Some variants have ἕνδεκα (*hendeka*), "eleven,"[54] but this change may have been motivated by a tradition that did not allow for the perpetuation of this ecclesiastical office.

15:6 ***After that, he was seen of above five hundred brethren at once / Then he appeared to more than five hundred brothers and sisters at one time:*** As in 15:5, the passive verb ὤφθη (*ōphthē*) means "to appear." Its use rules out any notion, as some claim, that the participants experienced only an internal witness of the Savior's presence, but not an actual personal presence.[55] The masculine plural noun ἀδελφοί (*adelphoi*), literally "brothers," can also include females. Based on the Lord's appearance to the Nephites (3 Ne. 11:8–10), it seems unlikely that he would have appeared only to men.[56]

---

manifestations. In no instance does the object of the verb (in the dative case) do so. Wallace, *Greek Grammar,* 165 and n. 72.

50. See Philo, *Abr.* 17 §8.

51. BDAG, 544. The English transliteration of the Apostle's nickname "Peter" comes from the Greek πέτρος (*petros*), which is the masculine form of πέτρα (*petra*), "rock," a designation the Savior gave the fisherman the first time they met (John 1:42). Identifying the importance of this title, the JST notes that the word has reference to a "seer stone," thus, the nickname foreshadowed Simon's eventual Church leadership as its Seer. See also Matt. 16:18; compare D&C 10:69; 33:13.

52. Findlay, "St. Paul's First Epistle," 2:920.

53. Paul's list suggests he included Matthias but, by Paul's day, the term had become a formal title of those who were the personal witnesses to the Lord's ministry and Resurrection. Thiselton, *First Epistle,* 1204–5.

54. Fitzmyer, *First Corinthians,* 550.

55. For example, Eduard Lohse, "πεντηκοστή," in *TDNT,* 6:51 n. 51; S. M. Gilmour, "The Christophany to More than Five Hundred Brethren," *Journal of Biblical Studies* 80 (1961): 248–52. These argue that Paul is referring to the event at Pentecost, but that was not a Chistophany; for other explanations, see Peter J. Kearney, "He Appeared to 500 Brothers (1 Cor. xv 6)," *Novum Testamentum* 22 (1980): 264–84. For an example of those believing that Paul was referring to an actual corporeal appearance of the Lord, see Jerome Murphy-O'Connor, "Traditions and Redactions in 1 Corinthians 15:3–7," *Catholic Biblical Quarterly* 43 (1981): 582–89; Fitzmyer, *First Corinthians,* 550; Holzapfel and Wayment, *Making Sense,* 362; *DNTC,* 1:860.

56. Findlay, "St. Paul's First Epistle," 2:920, notes that Jesus' summons recorded in Matt. 28:7, 10 and Mark 16:7 implies a larger audience than just the eleven.

The adverb ἐφάπαξ (*ephapax*), "at once, at one time," denotes events that happened simultaneously. In this case, it was the Lord's appearance at a single gathering of the Saints.[57] Moreover, it also counters the idea of some that this was a visionary experience without any physical component. The crowd is simply too large for all to have been swept up in some ecstasy of the moment. Although a few people's faith may be based on confused perceptions of an event, that would not be the case with such a large cross-section of the Saints.[58]

of whom the greater part remain unto this present / most of whom are still alive: The verb μένω (*menō*), "remain," emphasizes that though some of the Saints who saw the resurrected Christ had died, the majority were yet alive. In our Rendition we have translated the clause somewhat freely to better get the sense across in modern English. Paul's point is that the witnesses of Christ's Resurrection are not a few.[59]

but some are fallen asleep / although some have fallen asleep: The verb κοιμάομαι (*koimaomai*), literally "to fall asleep," was used euphemistically to denote death.[60] The story of Lazarus in John 11:11–14 provides an example of taking the euphemism literally.

15:7 *After that, he was seen of James / Then he appeared to James:* Again, as in 15:5 and 6, the passive force of the verb ὤφθη (*ōphthē*), "to appear," is at play, stressing the reality of a personal appearance and eliminating the possibility of some purely inner experience. The noun Ἰακώβῳ (*Iakōbos*), the Old Testament name translated "Jacob," is rendered as "James" in nearly all English Biblical translations of the New Testament.[61] In reference to James, Paul is not referring to either of the two original Apostles (Matt. 10:2; Mark 3:17–18; Luke 6:14; Acts 1:13) even though this James is referred

---

57. BDAG, 417.

58. Meyer, *Exegetical Commentary*, 2:45; Thiselton, *First Epistle*, 1205.

59. J. Peter Hansen, "Paul the Apostle: Champion of the Doctrine of the Resurrection," in *Go Ye into All the World*, 20.

60. Thiselton, *First Epistle*, 1206–7.

61. A notable exception is the HNV, which transliterates the Hebrew *Ya'aqōb* as *Ya'acov*. The unfortunate transliteration of the Greek Ἰάκωβος (*Iakōbos*) into "James" came about through a series of steps. First, it was transliterated into Latin as *Jacobus* and then, through the dissimilation of the bilabial *b* into the bilabial *m*, it became *Jacomus*. When it was transliterated into Old French, the "c" dropped out and the word became *Gemmes*. Old English picked up the word and changed it to "James." See Douglas Harper, "James," *Online Etymological Dictionary*, http://www.etymonline.com/index.php?term=James (accessed February 7, 2014). By coincidence, it was King James I who sponsored the translation of the KJV.

to as an Apostle in Galatians 1:19.[62] He is, rather, referring to the Lord's younger brother who was a bishop at Jerusalem when Paul first visited the Christians there. Early Christian tradition maintains that it was Christ's appearance to James that converted him.[63] James's experience parallels rather closely the conversion of Paul himself. The event, in a revolutionary way, produced a strong conversion in both Apostles.[64]

all the apostles / all the apostles: The word ἀποστόλοις (*apostolois*), "apostles," in this instance does not refer to the original members of the Twelve, whom Paul has already mentioned. It refers to those who—like James, the brother of Christ; Jude; Barnabas; and perhaps others we do not know of— were ordained to the holy office of Apostle. It could, possibly, be taken in its more generic sense indicating an empowered messenger or envoy. Even so, there is always a limit or boundary implied in the use of the term.[65] Only those charged with and set apart for bearing special witness of the Lord bear the title. Paul's use of the adjective πᾶσιν (*pasin*), "all," sets up a contrast between all these earlier witness and himself, who he lists as "last of all."[66]

15:8 *last of all he was seen of me also, as of one born out of due time / Last of all he appeared also to me, as to one untimely born:* The phrase ἔσχατον δὲ πάντων (*eschaton de pantōn*), "and last of all," should not be taken to mean that Paul saw himself as the last person who ever saw the risen Lord. He is rather saying that, on his list, he is the last witness he will mention.[67] Again, Paul uses the thrust of the passive voice of the verb ὤφθη (*ōphthē*), "appeared," to stress the reality of his experience. His testimony here does two things: it makes him another eyewitness to the Resurrection and it also, tacitly, affirms his apostolic authority as a special witness of the Lord (as he did in 9:1–2).[68] The noun ἔκτρωμα (*ektrōma*) refers to a birth that has occurred before the normal period of gestation, such as a premature

---

62. Paul's words clearly show he regarded this James as an Apostle. F. F. Bruce, *Men and Movements in the Primitive Church* (Exeter, U.K.: Paternoster, 1979), 89.

63. Bruce, *Men and Movements,* 86–119; see also the study by Walter Schmithals, *Paul and James,* trans. Dorothea M. Barton (London: SCM Press, 1965). A pseudepigraphical account of this visit can be found in *Gos. Heb.* §7. Jerome, *vir. ill,* 2, also tells the story of such a meeting.

64. Bruce, *Men and Movements,* 87; compare Robertson and Plummer, *Critical and Exegetical Commentary,* 338.

65. BDAG, 122; Thiselton, *First Epistle,* 1208.

66. Murphy-O'Connor, "Tradition and Redactions," 587–88.

67. Fitzmyer, *First Corinthians,* 552.

68. Fitzmyer, *First Corinthians,* 551.

birth, a miscarriage, or an abortion.[69] The phrase suggests Paul's view of his conversion—sudden, disruptive, and painful—compared to that of the other Apostles—gradual, steady, and moving normally toward maturation.[70] The meaning of Paul's metaphor probably comes out of LXX Numbers 12:12 and Job 3:16, referring to a premature baby that could die but who, through the grace of another, is kept alive.[71] Given his deep feelings about being saved from spiritual death strictly through the intervention of the Savior, it is not surprising Paul would feel this way.

15:9 *For I am the least of the apostles, that am not meet to be called an apostle / For I am the least of the apostles, unworthy to be called an apostle:* With the use of personal pronoun ἐγώ (*egō*), "I," Paul stresses how deeply he feels the weight of insignificance.[72] The superlative adjective ἐλάχιστος (*elachistos*), "least," denotes something that, in both value and status, is of the lowest worth.[73] Paul likely had only the idea of status in mind since all know very well of his high value as a missionary. The adjective ἱκανός (*hikanos*), "meet, worthy," denotes that which meets a standard and, by connotation, that which is "good enough" or "worthy."[74] With the negative, it means "insufficient" and even "unfit" for a task.[75]

Though Paul previously set himself as equal to Peter and James, in this verse he places himself below any of those commissioned disciples of the Lord, not just the Twelve. He goes so far as to say that he is not good enough to even bear the title. In saying this, he is neither reflecting the view of his detractors nor comparing himself with his fellow missionaries. He is, rather, looking at himself in comparison with the magnitude of the witness that he bears. He feels an acute awareness that he is insufficient for his

---

69. BDAG, 311; Johannes Schneider, "ἔκτρωμα," in *TDNT*, 2:465–67. Johannes Munck, "Paulus Tanquam Abortivus, 1 Corinthians 15:8," in *New Testament Essays: Studies in Memory of T. W. Manson*, ed. A. J. B. Higgins (Manchester: Manchester University Press, 1959), 183, argues that the term applies to "a prematurely born dead fetus" and, by the term's use in the LXX, denotes the full extent of human wretchedness.

70. Findlay, "St. Paul's First Epistle," 2:921.

71. Fitzmyer, *First Corinthians*, 551–52. Matthew W. Mitchell, "Reexamining the 'Aborted Apostle': An Exploration of Paul's Self-description in 1 Corinthians 15.8," *Journal for the Study of the New Testament* 25 (June 2003): 469–85, argues that the word should be taken as "abortion," referring to a fetus that is cast aside. Paul would then be referring to the feelings and reactions toward him from his detractors.

72. Wallace, *Greek Grammar*, 320–22 and n. 11.

73. Louw-Nida, §§65.57; 87.66; BDAG, 314; Wallace, *Greek Grammar*, 301–2.

74. BDAG, 472; Findlay, "St. Paul's First Epistle," 2:921.

75. Thiselton, *First Epistle*, 1211.

calling and, therefore, accepts it as a gift coming solely out of divine grace.[76] In the same self-effacing way, he will later state that he is the least of those who bear the title of Saint (see Eph. 3:8; but compare 1 Tim. 1:15). With the phrase, he is attempting to get the Saints to see past their feelings for him to the high value of the gospel message he brought to them.[77]

because I persecuted the church of God / because I persecuted the church of God: The verb διώκω (*diōkō*) means "to persecute" or "harass." Behind it stands the idea of moving "rapidly and decisively toward an objective,"[78] and, therefore, the word emphasizes, in this case, the energy Paul put into his former persecution of the Saints. Luke's statement that Paul was "breathing out threatenings and slaughter against the disciples of the Lord" catches the energy Paul put into that work (Acts 9:1).[79] It is little wonder Paul felt this shameful deed disqualified him from bearing the title of Apostle.

15:10 *But by the grace of God I am what I am / Nevertheless, by the grace of God I am what I am:* The particle δέ (*de*), "but," can mark strong contrast.[80] To catch this nuance, our Rendition translates it as "nevertheless." Thus, it carries the idea that, in spite of Paul's past, the Father's favor is upon him and God has placed him in his high position. Though one would expect Paul to use the masculine relative pronoun ὅς (*hos*), "what" in this clause (for he is clearly referring to himself), he uses the neuter form ὅ (*ho*), "what." In doing so, he takes the spotlight from him and places it on his office, that of Apostle.[81] However, he takes no credit for his status. He holds the position solely due to "the grace of God."[82] Even so, none should challenge what he is—a rightfully commissioned emissary of the Lord. His words express both delight and humility in what God has made him. For χάρις (*charis*), "grace," see Translation Notes on 1:3.

and his grace which was bestowed upon me was not in vain; but I laboured more abundantly than they all / and his grace toward me has not been in vain. On the contrary, I have worked harder than all of them:

---

76. Thiselton, *First Epistle*, 1211.

77. Fitzmyer, *First Corinthians*, 552–53.

78. BDAG, 254.

79. The story of Paul's persecution of the Church can be found in Acts 8:3; 9:1, 4, 21; 22:4, 7, 19; 26:10–11, 14; Gal. 1:13; Philip. 3:6.

80. BDAG, 213.

81. Wallace, *Greek Grammar*, 338.

82. The noun χάρις (*charis*), "grace," here does not have the definite article. Nonetheless, based on Apollonius' Corollary, it is understood that the definite article "the" should be supplied. Wallace, *Greek Grammar*, 250–52.

In this clause, Paul looks at the effect of God's grace upon him. The preposition εἰς (*eis*), "to, towards," in this instance looks to the result of the Lord's action.[83] The translation of the word as "bestowed upon" in the KJV is an extrapolation and is not found in the Greek. The adjective κενός (*kenos*) looks to activities that bring about no result, thus "empty, worthless, vain."[84] In Paul's case, he made sure the divine forgiveness and empowerment he received was put to good use. The force of the disjunctive ἀλλά (*alla*), "on the contrary,"[85] emphasizes this idea. Paul uses two words that capture why God's bestowal of grace upon him was not in vain. The first word is the comparative adverb περισσότερον (*perissoteron*) which denotes that which is "extraordinary in amount."[86] The second word is the verb κοπιάω (*kopiaō*), "to work," but the word carries the nuance of an effort that taxes completely.[87] Thus, God's grace was not wasted on Paul because of the extraordinary amount of hard work he put into his calling (see 2 Cor. 11:5, 23–27, where he details his labors). Paul's confidence was, however, not grounded in his great success but in his faithful obedience.[88]

yet not I, but the grace of God which was with me / yet not I, but the grace of God which is with me: On χάρις (*charis*), "grace," see Translation Notes on 1:3. The preposition σύν (*syn*), "with," denotes assistance or aid given to another.[89] The word shows that God's grace had come to Paul's

---

83. BDAG, 288–91; emphasizing the idea of ineffectiveness, Robertson and Plummer, *Critical and Exegetical Commentary*, 341; and Conzelmann, *1 Corinthians*, 260, translate the word as "fruitless." This interpretation stresses the result of Paul's detractor's misbelief.

84. BDAG, 539; some variants replace κενή (*kenē*), "vain, fruitless," with πτωχή (*ptōchē*), "poor." The move was likely motivated by theological reasons, the scribe not willing to conceive God's grace as ever being fruitless or empty in content or effect. Some place ἡ (*hē*), "the" or "this one, this thing" before εἰς ἐμέ (*eis eme*), "towards me." With or without the article, the basic sense is unchanged. The article adds a sense of emphasis or clarification to the prepositional phrase.

85. BDAG, 44–45.

86. BDAG, 805. The phrase αὐτῶν πάντων (*autōn pantōn*) suggests he worked harder than the rest combined. Findlay, "St. Paul's First Epistle," 2:921.

87. Louw-Nida, §§23.78; 42.47; BDAG, 558; Findlay, "St. Paul's First Epistle," 921.

88. Bailey, *Mediterranean Eyes*, 427.

89. BDAG, 961–62. Some ancient texts add the definite article ἡ (*hē*), "the" (referencing "the grace" in the previous clause), before σὺν ἐμοί (*syn emoi*), "with me." See Metzger, *Textual Commentary*, 501. Whether or not it is retained makes little difference to the translation of the text. That Paul did not use the prepositions ἐν (*en*), "in," or εἰς (*eis*), "into," is telling. God's grace was not "in him," meaning Paul, forcing him into dependent action, but "with him," enabling him to do what he desires. Paul's words reveal the

aid. With these words, the Apostle affirms that he does not consider himself to be better than others because of his extraordinary ability to do hard labor. Rather, he wants his readers to understand that it was the empowering grace of God that enabled him to do it.[90]

15:11 *Therefore whether it were I or they, so we preach, and so ye believed / And so, whether I or they, this is the way we preach and this is the way you came to believe:* With the conjunction οὖν (*oun*), "therefore, and so," Paul signals he is wrapping up his argument and making his point. The verb κηρύσσω (*kēryssō*), "preach," denotes an official public announcement.[91] There is nothing hidden or oblique about what he has or is teaching, and it stands as doctrine. The adverb οὕτως (*houtōs*), "in this manner, thus, so" describes the way both Paul and the other Apostles preach the gospel, namely by emphasizing Christ and his Atonement. With the phrase εἴτε . . . ἐγὼ εἴτε ἐκεῖνοι (*eite . . . egō eite ekeinoi*), "whether I or they," Paul shows that all those whom he identifies as "apostles" have taught the same thing. Paul's use of the ingressive plural aorist ἐπιστεύσατε (*episteusate*), "came to believe," is important.[92] It shows that, at least initially, these people believed what had been preached and, thereby, became Christians. That doctrine yet remained intact and, therefore, they should not put it aside.

Analysis and Summary

Paul introduces this section by reminding, or perhaps even chiding, his readers about what he and others have already taught them. Paul's introductory argument in these verses is based on the central teachings of the nascent Church that salvation is found only in and through Christ Jesus. The Apostle stresses that this was the message from the beginning which he, as founder of the Corinthian branches (3:10; 4:15) and other missionaries taught (1:12). He insists that he teaches only the core doctrine which is both traditionally and scripturally based and which all should respect (15:3–4). He then lists those elements of the doctrine that fall to history. In chronological order, they are "Christ died for our sins, . . . he was buried, . . . he was raised up on the third day, . . . he appeared to Cephas [that is,

---

correctness of synergy. Both he and God work together, each committing his unique resources to meet mutually important aims. Fitzmyer, *First Corinthians,* 553.

90. Fitzmyer, *First Corinthians,* 553.

91. BDAG, 543–44.

92. Wallace, *Greek Grammar,* 558–59. Paul's use puts stress on these Saints' initial entrance into a state of belief. It does not imply they remained there.

Peter], then to the Twelve [and then] to more than five hundred brothers and sisters." After that, he appeared to James, then other Apostles, and lastly, to Paul (15:3–8, Rendition).[93] Though he admits that he is the least and last of those who hold this apostolic office, he nonetheless appeals to it as a reason that his teaching should hold force.[94] "Paul's teachings are identical with the teachings of the other apostles," noted President Howard W. Hunter. "We are assured, therefore, that the resurrection of Jesus Christ was regarded as one of the foundation doctrines of the early church and was taught to all converts 'first of all.'"[95]

Without citing a particular scripture, Paul assures his readers that the doctrines he proclaims and that they have believed are found there (15:3–4). The specific ones known to the earliest Saints could have been initially pointed out by the Lord himself. On the very day of his Resurrection, he appeared to two of his disciples "and beginning at Moses and all the prophets, he expounded unto them in all the scriptures the things concerning himself." These two witnesses expressed their reaction to these insights, declaring, "Did not our heart burn within us, while he talked with us by the way, and while he opened to us the scriptures," specifically that the Messiah had to suffer these things, "to enter into his glory" (Luke 24:26–27, 32). Those verses and perhaps chapters that the Lord disclosed could have formed the basis and proof texts the Church used.[96] Two key points that

---

93. Some biblical commentators feel the first four elements constituted the earliest κέρυγμα (*kerygma*) (that is, the original apostolic proclamation) about Jesus that defined their message. The use of the conjunction ὅτι (*hoti*), "that," which Paul uses four times in this section, can introduce an actual quote. Paul's multiple use of this word allowed him to stress each element as a point of doctrine. Bailey, *Mediterranean Eyes,* 428. See also Murphy-O'Connor, "Traditions and Redactions," 583–84; Fitzmyer, *First Corinthians,* 541. There is some debate as to whether or not Paul's words translate a Semitic original, likely Aramaic, arising from Jerusalem or if they were reflecting an origin the Greek-speaking portion of the Christians. On this, see Jeremias, *Eucharistic Words,* 101–5, who argues for the former position while Hans Conzelmann, "On the Analysis of the Confessional Formula in 1 Corinthians 15:3–5," *Interpretation* 20 (1966): 15–25, urges caution.

94. Fitzmyer, *First Corinthians,* 542–43.

95. Howard W. Hunter, in CR, April 1963, 106.

96. Charles Harold Dodd, *According to the Scriptures* (London: Nisbet, 1952), 127, using both New Testament and early Christian writings, analyzes how the early Christians used the Old Testament to elucidate their beliefs. Thiselton, *First Epistle,* 1190 n. 104, concludes that it was not so much the use of single scriptures but citing "extended portions of textual units as a whole, especially from Isaiah, Jeremiah, Psalms, and some of the prophetic books" that they used as evidence and to provide understanding. The prophets of the Book of Mormon turned to the writings of Moses and Isaiah to do the same thing.

can be found weaving their way through the whole tapestry of the Old Testament are (1) the saving work of Jehovah that finds its fulfillment in the ministry, teachings, and atonement of the Savior, and (2) that forgiveness and cleansing come by vicarious expiation and atonement, the first act paying the necessary penalty so that the person again becomes clean, and the second act restoring the bond and unity that sin destroyed.[97]

The prophets of the Book of Mormon appealed to the writings of Moses to prove the coming and work of Christ, "For this end hath the law of Moses been given; and all things which have been given of God from the beginning of the world, unto man, are the typifying of him" (2 Ne. 11:4). Though Moses gave Israel the law "to keep them in remembrance of God and their duty towards him," it was filled with "types of things to come," specifically, intimations and shadows of the work and death of the Messiah (Mosiah 13:30–31). This allowed those with eyes to see to "look forward to the coming of Christ, considering that the law of Moses was a type of his coming" (Alma 25:15). They understood that the whole meaning of the law, indeed, "every whit [pointed] to that great and last sacrifice; and that great and last sacrifice will be the Son of God, yea, infinite and eternal" (Alma 34:14).[98]

Paul tacitly "indicates the source of his knowledge of the resurrection," stated President Hunter. "The story of the crucifixion has been related in scripture from the visible facts of what was seen and what was actually heard during those dark hours, but the account of the resurrection was a proclamation or a declaration of what had happened when the crucified Lord took up his body from the dead and arose from the tomb. Paul indicates in these opening words that his knowledge came to him by revelation from God, not from man."[99]

The foundation for Paul's argument is Church tradition—the central doctrine that Christ overcame sin and death through the cross and Resurrection. The Apostle had already traced the tradition directly to the Lord himself (11:23), and that echo remains here. When he wrote to the Galatians (Gal. 1:1, 11–12), he insisted that what he preached was not of human origin, coming as it did δι' ἀποκαλύψεως Ἰησοῦ Χριστοῦ (*di' apokalypseōs Iēsou Christou*), "by the revelation of Jesus Christ." His words should not be taken to contradict his insistence here on tradition. To the Galatian Saints

---

97. Compare Barrett, *First Epistle*, 338–39.

98. An excellent study of Old Testament types based on the book of Leviticus is Andrew Jukes, *The Law of the Offerings* (Grand Rapids, Mich.: Kregel Publications, 1966).

99. Howard W. Hunter, in CR, April 1969, 136.

he was identifying the content of the gospel and not its formulation. The phrase τίνι λόγῳ (*tini logo*), "the message" (15:2, Rendition), refers to its formulation, that is, just how the doctrine is expressed. These words, coming down through tradition, codify the most important (ἐν πρώτοις, *en prōtois*) doctrines of the kingdom (15:3).[100]

The phrase in 15:3 that "Christ died for our sins" was the first element in the primitive Christian's "articles of faith" (compare Gal. 1:4; 1 Thes. 5:10; Rom. 4:25; 5:6, 8; 2 Cor. 5:15),[101] which Paul and the other missionaries proclaimed. Paul's words show that the nascent Church viewed the Savior's death as a vicarious act. When the Apostle writes to the Corinthian Saints again, he will emphasize this idea: "For he [God] made him, who knew no sin, to be sin, for our sake, so we might become God's righteousness through him" (2 Cor. 5:21, authors' translation).[102] He restated the idea in Romans 4:25 and tied it to the Resurrection, stating that Jesus "was handed over [to death] for our sins and was raised for our justification" (authors' translation). Thus, Paul not only affirmed the salvific nature of the Redeemer's death but also the end result of both aspects of the Atonement—death and Resurrection. That result was justification—that is, becoming sin free—a necessary step in returning to God's presence.[103] Paul's words in 15:3 that Christ died ὑπὲρ τῶν ἁμαρτιῶν ἡμῶν (*hyper tōn hamartiōn hēmōn*), "for our sins," must be seen to include the notion of expiation.[104] This is because the phrase περὶ ἁμαρτίας (*peri hamartias*) in the LXX denotes, among other things, a sin offering (Lev. 5:11; 7:37). Paul's usage of these terms reinforces the doctrine that the Savior's death was a propitiation or expiation for sin, ἱλαστήριον (*hilastērion*) in Romans 3:25 and ἱλασμος (*hilasmos*) in 1 John 2:2; 4:10.

---

100. Fitzmyer, *First Corinthians*, 545–46.

101. The formula holds true for the modern Church as well. See D&C 18:11–12; 2 Ne. 2:8–10.

102. The plan was all worked out before humankind was placed on the planet. Joseph Smith noted that before "man had cut himself off from an immediate intercourse with his Maker [through sin] without a Mediator, it appears that the great and glorious plan of His redemption was previously meditated; the sacrifice prepared; the atonement wrought out in the mind and purpose of God, even in the person of the Son, through whom man was now to look for acceptance, and through whose merits he was now taught that he alone could find redemption." "The Elders of the Church in Kirtland, to their Brethren Abroad," *Evening and Morning Star* 2, no. 18 (March 1834): 286. Compare Alma 13:3.

103. Fitzmyer, *First Corinthians*, 546. Nothing unclean can dwell in God's presence. See Moses 6:57. For a more complete discussion on justification, see the BYU New Testament Commentary on Romans.

104. Edwards, *Commentary*, 392–93.

The Greek nouns *hilasmos* and *hilastērion,* which are related to the verb ἱλάσκομαι (*hilaskomai*), "to propitiate, conciliate, expiate, wipe out," nuance the ideas found in the English words "propitiation" and "expiation." Both reference the process by which sins are covered and remitted. Expiation looks at undoing both the wrong and its effects by suffering a penalty, doing penitence, and making reparations or giving redress.[105] Simply put, expiation is paying the necessary price. It points to what must be done *by* the offending party. Propitiation, on the other hand, points to the act that quiets the aroused anger or malevolence of the person with power or superiority by pacifying or averting his anger and winning his favor.[106] Thus, it looks to what must be done *for* the offended party.

In the New Testament, Christ is the propitiation. President John Taylor noted that

> through the great atonement, the expiatory sacrifice of the Son of God, it is made possible that man can be redeemed, restored, resurrected and exalted to the elevated position designed for him in the creation as a Son of God: that eternal justice and law required the penalty to be paid by man himself, or by the atonement of the Son of God: that Jesus offered Himself as the great expiatory sacrifice; that this offering being in accordance with the demands of requirements of the law, was accepted by the great Lawgiver; that it was prefigured by sacrifices, and ultimately fulfilled by Himself according to the eternal covenant.[107]

The Doctrine and Covenants explains that Christ does this by being a sinner's advocate. The result is given by the Greek καταλλαγή (*katallagē*). The noun is translated as "atonement" in KJV Romans 5:11 and as "reconciling" in Romans 11:15 and as "reconciliation" in 2 Corinthians 5:18–19. It expresses a reestablishment of proper and friendly relationships between estranged parties. In God's case, it is the Savior who reconciles the repentant soul to God and, thus, restores him or her to divine favor. It is of note that no one has to live perfectly for Christ to reconcile him or her to God. A willingness to obey the commandments (evidenced by striving to do God's will) triggers the blessing. That blessing is having the Lord's empowering Spirit with the Saint continually (Moro. 4:3; D&C 20:77). It needs to be stressed that reconciliation is brought about by the rendering of satisfaction for evil that has been

---

105. BDAG, 473–74.
106. BDAG, 588.
107. John Taylor, *The Mediation and Atonement* (Salt Lake City: Deseret Book, 1882), 170–71; see also Larry E. Dahl, "Lectures on Faith," in *EM*, 2:820.

done by doing acts that are good and meritorious. When the term is applied on a personal level, the Saint *expiates* a sin by doing penance for it, but he or she *atones* for it by living a good and moral life.[108]

Christ died for the entire world (2 Cor. 5:14–15; Alma 34:8; 3 Ne. 11:14) and in so doing made reconciliation possible to all by satisfying the demands of justice (2 Ne. 9:26; Alma 42:15). By this gift, the Savior opened the door to mercy and grace, both expressions of the love he and the Father have for all of God's children.[109] As a result, none are excluded from God's grace and mercy unless they exclude themselves. The irony and wonder of this process is that it is God who is the offended party, and yet he is the one who supplies the priceless gift (the Son) that makes propitiation possible (John 3:16; Rom. 8:32), resulting in an atonement, that is, a restored relationship.

Let us stress that the Atonement is made possible through the ἀπολύ-τρωσις (*apolytrōsis*) of Jesus. The noun denotes both deliverance and redemption (1:30; Rom. 3:24; 8:23; Eph. 1:7, 14; 4:30; Col. 1:14; Heb. 9:15). The word, in its theological sense, describes the Lord's act of purchasing a person from the slave market of sin. For the release to be executed, the Savior had to pay the necessary ransom (Matt. 20:28; Mark 10:45; 1 Tim. 2:6). That ransom expressed itself in acts of both propitiation and expiation. It redeems the Saint not only from the consequences of transgression, but from the transgression itself (Heb. 9:15) for God remembers it no more (Isa. 43:25; D&C 58:42). It brings a freedom not only from the effects of sin but also from bad desires and actions.[110] It delivers the repentant soul from the presence and power of sin through justification and sanctification (D&C 20:31) and the body from corruption through the Resurrection.[111]

President John Taylor taught that "in some mysterious, incomprehensible way, Jesus assumed the responsibility which naturally would have devolved upon Adam; but which could only be accomplished through the mediation of Himself, and by taking upon Himself their sorrows, assuming their responsibilities, and bearing their transgressions or sins. In a manner to us incomprehensible and inexplicable, he bore the weight of the sins of the whole world."[112]

---

108. Friedrich Büchsel, "καταλλαγή," in *TDNT*, 1:258; Louw-Nida, §40.1.

109. Johannes Herrmann, "ἱλάσκομαι, ἱλασμός," in *TDNT*, 3:301–10.

110. Louw-Nida, §37.128.

111. Friedrich Büchsel, "ἀπολύτρωσις," in *TDNT*, 4:351–56; Jeffrey R. Holland, "Atonement of Jesus Christ," in *EM*, 1:82–86.

112. Taylor, *Mediation and Atonement*, 148–49.

Returning to chapter 15, the phrase "he was buried" in 15:4 expresses the second element in the early Christian expression of faith. Its inclusion is important because it both affirms the reality of the Savior's suffering and death and, in addition, undergirds the reality of his Resurrection. It also undercuts any docetic notions that the suffering of the Lord was merely apparent, that is, that he just seemed to suffer and die but really did not.[113] It also countered the insistence by some of the Church's detractors that the Savior's body was never buried but stolen (Matt. 28:13).[114]

Also, in that verse, we find the third "article of faith" that Christ was "raised the third day." Paul expressed the historical reality of the event through the force of the perfect passive verb ἐγήγερται (*egēgertai*), literally "he has been raised," coupled with the explanatory frame of reference, τῇ ἡμέρᾳ τῇ τρίτῃ (*tē hēmera tē tritē*), "on the third day." The verb, being a divine passive, stresses the idea that God was behind this action and, therefore, the event was miraculous in nature.[115] That being the case, it need have neither logical nor scientific explanation. Paul again appeals to the authority of the scriptures to substantiate that the whole event was foreknown *and* foretold.

The fourth element in the early Church's "articles of faith" is found in 15:5, that Jesus was "seen of Cephas," that is, Peter. Luke 24:34 also preserves the tradition of an independent appearance to the chief Apostle. Such makes sense given Peter's position as both the senior Apostle and head of the Church.

Though Paul may have been able to mention more appearances of the Lord, he lists enough to defuse any idea that only a scattered few witnessed the event. Indeed, the Apostle presents "a formidable gallery of witnesses

---

113. Docetism, the belief that Christ only appeared to be mortal and physical and to have suffered and died, was ascribed to Cerinthus (c. AD 120–30), but it seems to have had proponents as early as the writings of Paul and John. See Ignatius, *Smyrm.* 2.1. It continued for centuries. See Ireneaus, *Haer.* 3.18.3; and Tertullian, *Res.*, 48; *Adv. Marc.* 5.9.

114. The idea was also refuted by Origin, *Cels.* 2.56. Even so, being adopted by the Gnostics and others, it never died. It resurfaced with force in the late eighteenth century. For an example, see David F. Strauss, *The Life of Jesus, Critically Examined* (Philadelphia: Fortress Press, 1972).

115. Though the idea counters that in John 6:39, 40, 54, where Jesus is the cause of the Resurrection, the vast majority of texts ascribe the action and power to the Father. See M. E. Dahl, *The Resurrection of the Body* (London: SCM Press, 1962), 96–100; Barrett, *First Epistle,* 341. The problem is resolved by realizing that it was God who gave Jesus the power of life over death, but that that power ultimately belongs to God.

waiting to testify they that have seen [the Lord] alive."[116] It is of note that Paul lists Peter as the first witness with himself as the last. In doing so, he ties both of them together.[117] The appearance to more than five hundred Saints at one time—most of whom were still alive and could, therefore, verify the experience—was a tremendous witness to the reality of the Resurrection. Unfortunately, the scriptures do not record this incident and Paul does not elaborate. We do have the record of the Lord's appearance to another group of Saints, those in America. During that meeting, he had all the participants touch his wounds as witnesses that it was truly him and that he lived as a corporeal being (3 Ne. 11:12–17). One wonders if this same situation could have happened at the meeting with the five hundred.

Of all these appearances, the most personal to Paul is, of course, the Lord's appearance to him. "Thus Paul adds his personal witness," noted President Hunter, "referring to his experience on the way to Damascus when he was suddenly changed from a persecutor to one of the greatest exponents. He refers to himself as 'one born out of due time.' ... His dramatic change and conversion is used in his argument as the final point to prove the actual resurrection of Jesus. Paul was anxious that the saints would not only believe, but should never have the least doubt as to this basic fact upon which eternal life hinges."[118]

Paul's description of himself in 15:8 as a prematurely born babe (ἔκτρωμα, *ektrōma*), either dead or nearly so, emphasizes his understanding of how the grace of God operates in behalf of his children. As he travelled toward Damascus, the Apostle was "yet breathing out threatenings and slaughter against the disciples of the Lord" (Acts 9:1). Spiritually he was dead and, therefore, in no position or condition to contribute anything to his salvation. But that did not prevent Christ from reaching out to him. In doing so, the Savior brought vitality to one whose spiritual life was humanly beyond hope. Thus, the nature of Paul's conversion acts as a perfect type of the Resurrection, an act in which God's sovereign grace alone gives life to *all* the dead,[119] even those who yet physically live.

---

116. Hays, *First Corinthians,* 257. See also Fee, *First Epistle,* 729–30.

117. Given that Paul and Peter had had their differences (see Gal. 2:11–14) and that there were parties in Corinth that pitted Paul against Peter, it was a nice touch for Paul to show that he and Peter stood together on the doctrine of the Resurrection. Bailey, *Mediterranean Eyes,* 423.

118. Howard W. Hunter, in CR, April 1969, 137.

119. Thiselton, *First Epistle,* 1210.

Though in 15:5–8, Paul listed many proofs that the Lord's Resurrection was an objective historical event, he did not have to prove it. His words show that those who initially joined the Church understood and accepted that incident as fact. In short, Christ's Resurrection was not the issue. The problem arose because some misinterpreted its implications and denied its consequences, that is, what it said about their own eternal destiny.[120]

Verse 15:10 contains the very heart of Paul's argument as he witnesses to the power of divine grace. This argument rests on his understanding of the free and independent nature of that grace as it springs from the love of God and becomes operative in the lives of the Saints. This empowering force is the center of Paul's apostolic vocation and also at the seat of any Christian's call to the work. It is fully expressed in the universal nature of the Resurrection. Paul stresses that it is God's empowering grace alone that has enabled and does enable the Apostle to do the exhausting toil required by his calling. It is of note that God does not take the toil away. Rather, he extends his grace, making it possible for the Saint to accomplish it.[121]

A rather dramatic example of this is seen in God's assistance to the people of Alma. Having been put under harsh task masters, these people felt the full weight of persecution and heavy toil. However, because of their righteousness, the Lord came to their aid promising, "I will also ease the burdens which are put upon your shoulders, that even you cannot feel them" (Mosiah 24:14). The burdens remained, but the weight did not. "And now it came to pass that the burdens which were laid upon Alma and his brethren were made light; yea, the Lord did strengthen them that they could bear up their burdens with ease" (Mosiah 24:15). That grace continued until their eventual escape from bondage.

In 15:11, Paul stresses that the doctrine of the Resurrection (identified in 15:12), was taught by every single missionary. Further, it was responding to that doctrine, that is, by acting in faith, that these Corinthians initially became Saints. Paul again appeals to their faith in the truthfulness of the Resurrection to hear him out. His affirmation, as he ends this section of his epistle, sets the ground for the argument he will develop as he responds to the most pressing questions and objections concerning the doctrine posed by the antiresurrection party.[122]

---

120. Conzelmann, "On the Analysis," 23; Fitzmyer, *First Corinthians,* 544.

121. Thiselton, *First Epistle,* 1212.

122. Fitzmyer, *First Corinthians,* 553–54.

THE DIRE CONSEQUENCES OF DENYING THE RESURRECTION OF THE DEAD (15:12–19)

Greek Text

12 Εἰ δὲ Χριστὸς κηρύσσεται ὅτι ἐκ νεκρῶν ἐγήγερται, πῶς λέγουσιν ἐν ὑμῖν τινες ὅτι ἀνάστασις νεκρῶν οὐκ ἔστιν; 13 εἰ δὲ ἀνάστασις νεκρῶν οὐκ ἔστιν, οὐδὲ Χριστὸς ἐγήγερται· 14 εἰ δὲ Χριστὸς οὐκ ἐγήγερται, κενὸν ἄρα τὸ κήρυγμα ἡμῶν, κενὴ καὶ ἡ πίστις ὑμῶν, 15 εὑρισκόμεθα δὲ καὶ ψευδομάρτυρες τοῦ θεοῦ, ὅτι ἐμαρτυρήσαμεν κατὰ τοῦ θεοῦ ὅτι ἤγειρεν τὸν Χριστόν, ὃν οὐκ ἤγειρεν εἴπερ ἄρα νεκροὶ οὐκ ἐγείρονται. 16 εἰ γὰρ νεκροὶ οὐκ ἐγείρονται, οὐδὲ Χριστὸς ἐγήγερται· 17 εἰ δὲ Χριστὸς οὐκ ἐγήγερται, ματαία ἡ πίστις ὑμῶν, ἔτι ἐστὲ ἐν ταῖς ἁμαρτίαις ὑμῶν. 18 ἄρα καὶ οἱ κοιμηθέντες ἐν Χριστῷ ἀπώλοντο. 19 εἰ ἐν τῇ ζωῇ ταύτῃ ἐν Χριστῷ ἠλπικότες ἐσμὲν μόνον, ἐλεεινότεροι πάντων ἀνθρώπων ἐσμέν. [SBLGNT]

King James Version

12 Now if Christ be preached that he rose from the dead, how say some among you that there is no resurrection of the dead? 13 But if there be no resurrection of the dead, then is Christ not risen: 14 And if Christ be not risen, then is our preaching vain, and your faith is also vain. 15 Yea, and we are found false witnesses of God; because we have testified of God that he raised up Christ: whom he raised not up, if so be that the dead rise not. 16 For if the dead rise not, then is not Christ raised: 17 And if Christ be not raised, your faith is vain; ye are yet in your sins. 18 Then they also which are fallen asleep in Christ are perished. 19 If in this life only we have hope in Christ, we are of all men most miserable.

New Rendition

12 Now if it is being preached that Christ has been raised from the dead, how is it that some of you say that there is no resurrection of the dead? 13 If there is no resurrection of the dead, then neither has Christ been raised. 14 But if Christ has not been raised, then our preaching is in vain, and your faith also is in vain, 15 and we are found to be false witnesses of God, because we have testified against God that he raised Christ, whom he did not raise if indeed the dead are not raised. 16 For if the dead are not raised, neither has Christ been raised. 17 And if Christ has not been raised, your faith is useless, you are still in your sins. 18 So also those who have fallen asleep in Christ have perished. 19 If only in this life we have hope in Christ, we are of all people most to be pitied.

Translation Notes and Comments

15:12 *Now if Christ be preached that he rose from the dead, how say some among you that there is no resurrection of the dead / Now if it is being preached that Christ has been raised from the dead, how is it that some* *of you say that there is no resurrection of the dead:* The verb κηρύσσω (*kēryssō*), "to preach," denotes an authoritative declaration. With the use of the word, Paul makes it clear that what they have heard is Church doctrine.[123] The tense of the perfect passive verb ἐγήγερται (*egēgertai*), "has been raised up," is very important here. The force of the tense is that Christ was raised to life and continues to live. Paul's addition of the phrase ἐκ νεκρῶν (*ek nekrōn*), "from the dead," only makes the point more explicit.[124] Introducing his question with the adverb πῶς (*pōs*), "how," betrays the Apostle's complete astonishment, even indignation, that there was any possibility that anyone could deny the idea of a universal resurrection.[125]

15:13 *But if there be no resurrection of the dead, then is Christ not risen / If there is no resurrection of the dead, then neither has Christ been raised:* The connective δέ (*de*) is adversative, "but," used by Paul to continue his contrast.[126] He appeals to logic. Any denial of the resurrection logically excludes also the Resurrection of the Lord.[127]

15:14 *And if Christ be not risen, then is our preaching vain, and your faith is also vain / But if Christ has not been raised, then our preaching is in vain, and your faith also is in vain:* The connective δέ (*de*), "but," Paul uses again in its adversative mode. It serves to emphasize the logical flow of the argument he is making concerning the consequences of what these Saints believe. The conjunction ἄρα (*ara*), "then, therefore," accentuates the force of Paul's point.

Paul again uses the adjective κενός (*kenos*), "empty, void," denoting that which is without substance and, therefore, incapable of producing anything of worth.[128] Paul shows that worthlessness hits two areas. The first is the κήρυγμα (*kerygma*). The noun denotes an official declaration but, in this context, looks not at the declaration itself, but more specifically at its content.[129] Paul's point is that if there is no resurrection then the whole gospel message is worth nothing.[130] The second area that would prove

---

123. Gerhard Friedrich, "κηρύσσω," in *TDNT*, 3:697–714.

124. An influential segment of the philosophical community among the Greeks believed there was no afterlife. For example, see Plato, *Sym.* 179c; Herodotus, *Hist.* 3.62; Aeschylus, *Eum.* 647–48; Sophocles, *Elec.* 137–42.

125. Fitzmyer, *First Corinthians,* 562.

126. BDAG, 213.

127. Findlay, "St. Paul's First Epistle," 923.

128. BDAG, 539; Findlay, "St. Paul's First Epistle," 923–24.

129. Louw-Nida, §33.258.

130. BDAG, 543; Findlay, "St. Paul's First Epistle," 917.

worthless is πίστις ὑμῶν (*pistis hymōn*), "your faith."[131] The phrase points to
the very doctrine and core of what they believe.[132] Because their belief can
yield no positive results, it is also worthless.

**15:15 *Yea, and we are found false witnesses of God; because we have tes-
tified of God that he raised up Christ: whom he raised not up, if so be that
the dead rise not / and we are found to be false witnesses of God, because
we have testified against God that he raised Christ, whom he did not raise
if indeed the dead are not raised:*** Paul continues to show the disastrous
consequences in believing there is no resurrection. The present passive
verb εὑρισκόμεθα (*heuriskometha*), "we are found," denotes something
that is discovered or revealed.[133] A ψευδόμαρτυς (*pseudomartys*) is a "false
witness." The nuance of the word points to a person who lies. What makes
this sin so awful is the person's false claim to be an eyewitness to the event.[134]
This makes him very culpable and his condemnation all the more proper
and necessary. Thus, if there were no resurrection, the Apostles would not
only be false witnesses but also the blackest of liars.[135] In short, Paul and
the other missionaries would have foisted upon the Saints a hoax of unparalleled proportions.[136] Showing the depth of such culpability, Paul states
they would have ἐμαρτυρήσαμεν κατὰ τοῦ θεοῦ (*emartyrēsamen kata tou
theou*), "witnessed against God." The preposition κατά (*kata*) here means
"against" in the sense of being not only opposed but also hostile to another.[137]
Such a stand was blasphemy and, therefore, liable to the death penalty
(Lev. 24:16).

Paul makes another point here that must not be overlooked: it is God,
he affirms, who is the efficient causality of the Lord's Resurrection (6:14;
also Rom. 4:24; 8:11). The Apostle's words are designed such that his readers are not allowed to forget who is ultimately responsible for all that goes
on in the salvation process.

**15:16 *For if the dead rise not, then is not Christ raised / For if the dead
are not raised, neither has Christ been raised:*** Paul here repeats what he
has already said in 15:13 for the purpose of emphasis.

---

131. Some variants read ἡμῶν (*hēmōn*), our, rather than ὑμῶν (*hymōn*), *your,* but the
context suggest, "your faith" is correct. See Metzger, *Textual Commentary,* 501.

132. Louw-Nida, §31.4, 102, 104.

133. BDAG, 411–12.

134. Louw-Nida, §33.273.

135. Findlay, "St. Paul's First Epistle," 924.

136. Fitzmyer, *First Corinthians,* 563.

137. LSJ, 883; Thiselton, *First Epistle,* 1219.

15:17 *And if Christ be not raised, your faith is vain; ye are yet in your sins / And if Christ has not been raised, your faith is useless, you are still in your sins:* Paul continues to trace the downward spiral of devastating consequences if the Savior were not resurrected. He notes two more consequences. He returns to the effect on their faith. Where, in 15:14, he stated it was κενός (*kenos*), "vain, worthless," here he states it would be μάταιος (*mataios*), "useless," because it is "fruitless," unable to produce what it promises.[138] The real horror of there being no resurrection, however, is that they are yet in their sins. Though Paul stresses "Christ, and him crucified" (2:2) (whereby he paid the necessary ransom), he also teaches that the Savior's death alone did not produce all that was necessary. The full force of the atoning, liberating, and redemptive act was dependent on the Resurrection as well.[139]

15:18 *Then they also which are fallen asleep in Christ are perished / So also those who have fallen asleep in Christ have perished:* With the phrase ἄρα καί (*ara kai*), "so also," Paul signals his reader that he is continuing his list of the devastating effects if there were no resurrection. As noted above, the verb κοιμάομαι (*koimaomai*), "to sleep, fall asleep," is a euphemism for death. The imagery works well on two levels. First, it suggests that death is not an unconscious period in which the soul sleeps a dreamless sleep, but a period of activity promising a new hope (see 7:39; John 11:11; Acts 7:60; 13:36; Alma 40:7, 11–14; D&C 138). This nuance is highlighted particularly as Paul places the word opposite ἐγείρω (*egeirō*), "to wake up, awaken" (15:34; see also Matt. 10:8; 11:5; 16:21; 27:52; John 5:21). The latter carries the idea of awakening to a new dawn full of renewed vigor, opportunity, and quality of life.[140] So those Saints who had died ἐν Χριστῷ (*en Christō*) "in Christ," that is, true to their faith in Christ ἀπώλοντο (*apōlonto*) "have perished."

15:19 *If in this life only we have hope in Christ, we are of all men most miserable / If only in this life we have hope in Christ, we are of all people most to be pitied:*[141] This verse also presents a translation challenge, which is where to place the adverb μόνον (*monon*), "only." Because Paul placed it at the end of the clause, an emphatic position, there is some question as

---

138. BDAG, 621.

139. Thiselton, *First Epistle*, 1220.

140. Thiselton, *First Epistle*, 1220.

141. The adverb μόνον (*monon*), "only," comes at the end of the clause and could modify the whole. In that case it would mean that hope in Christ is in this world with nothing beyond, that is, hope is good *only* here and, therefore, ultimately of no use at all. See Barrett, *First Epistle*, 349–50.

to what it modifies. Given the options, however, the best solution seems to be to construe it with the phrase ἐν τῇ ζωῇ ταύτῃ (*en tē zōē tautē*), "in this life."[142] The adjective ἐλεεινότεροι (*eleeinoteroi*) denotes one deserving of pity because of his or her pathetic and miserable condition.[143] Although comparative in form, it is best translated as a superlative, because the tendency in Koine Greek was to use the comparative form for both.[144] For the Christians, this pitiable condition would be that their religion is only one dimensional, good only to benefit them in this life with no hope of anything after. To stress his point, Paul uses the term with a genitive of comparison, πάντων ἀνθρώπων (*pantōn anthrōpōn*), "of all humankind." Thus, Paul is saying that the loss of all he has mentioned—the gospel in its entirety (15:11–18)—would be the cause of such pity.[145] The sentence suggests the deep commiseration that deception of this magnitude should bring upon the Saints.[146]

Analysis and Summary

It is unlikely that Paul mentions all the concerns and objections of the antiresurrection party and, thus, just what they were is unknown. Given developments later in church history, however, there are four broad possibilities: (1) a belief that followed some teachings of the Epicureans and the Jewish Sadducees that there was no postmortal existence;[147] (2) a belief that the Resurrection was an "inner" or "spiritual" awakening that had occurred, and was occurring at the time; (3) a belief that denied, or at best questioned, a corporeal Resurrection and the immortal nature of the soul (ψύχη, *psychē*); and (4) a belief that combined some or all of these elements in some way.[148]

Given Paul's acquaintance with Greek and Roman ideas, he likely knew that many of the Corinthians held vague notions about the existence of the

---

142. For discussion, see Fitzmyer, *First Corinthians,* 565.

143. BDAG, 315.

144. BDF, *A Greek Grammar of the NT,* §60.

145. Fee, *First Epistle,* 744–45.

146. Findlay, "St. Paul's First Epistle," 925.

147. On the position of the Epicureans, see Hornblower, *Oxford Classical Dictionary,* 23–24; on that of the Sadducees, see Gary G. Porton, "Sadducees," in *ABD,* 5:892–94.

148. Martinus C. De Boer, *The Defeat of Death: Apocalyptic Eschatology in 1 Corinthians 15 and Romans 5* (Sheffield, Eng.: JSOT Press, 1988), 96–105; Jack H. Wilson, "The Corinthians Who Say There Is No Resurrection of the Dead," *Zeitschrift für die Neutestamentliche Wissenschaft* 59 (1968): 90–107.

Elysium or Isle of the Blessed where the soul (*psychē*) enjoyed some form of immortal life and that his detractors were likely feeding off these.[149] He, however, through personal experience, knew full well the concrete nature of the afterlife with the joy that awaited the righteous who endured to the end (2 Cor. 12:1–4).[150]

Paul's method of attack was to assume for the sake of argument his antagonists' views on the Resurrection and then show the consequences of their belief. In that way they could see that, when pointed out, they very likely did not want to accept them.[151]

In 15:14, Paul clearly articulates the various unimaginable consequences if Christ were not resurrected. His words reveal his understanding that the reality of this event is the linchpin of Christian belief. As Joseph Smith observed, "If the resurrection from the dead is not an important point, or item in our faith, we must confess that we know nothing about it: for if there is no resurrection from the dead, then Christ has not risen; and if Christ has not risen he was not the Son of God; and if he was not the Son of God there is not nor cannot be a Son of God."[152]

Remove that linchpin and a multitude of dependent derivatives instantly collapse. Among these are: "(i) the content and currency of the gospel; (ii) the authenticity of Christian faith; (iii) the truthfulness of testimony to the acts of God (v. 15); (iv) liberation from the destructive and damaging power of sin (v. 17); and (v) the irretrievable loss of believers who have died (v. 18)."[153] In sum, the result of disbelief is not only a discrediting of the veracity of the Apostles but also of the entire theology.[154]

The end result, as Paul notes (15:19), would place the Christians in a position more to be pitied than any among humankind. As one scholar noted, Paul is saying that "if our hope in Christ is limited only to what we may share with him in this life, with no prospect of a share in his glorious and resurrected life, then we are to be pitied indeed."[155] And why? Because

---

149. Hornblower, *Oxford Classical Dictionary*, 23.

150. Fitzmyer, *First Corinthians*, 565.

151. Duane F. Watson, "Paul's Rhetorical Strategy in 1 Corinthians 15," in *Rhetoric and the New Testament,* ed. S. E. Porter and T. H. Olbricht (Sheffield: Sheffield Academic Press, 1993), 239.

152. "The Elders of the Church in Kirtland, to their Brethren Abroad," *Evening and Morning Star* 2, no. 18 (March 1834): 288.

153. Thiselton, *First Epistle*, 1218.

154. Findlay, "St. Paul's First Epistle," 917, 922; Anderson, *Understanding Paul*, 125–26; compare Ogden and Skinner, *Verse by Verse,* 145; Wayment, *From Persecutor to Apostle*, 162.

155. Fitzmyer, *First Corinthians*, 565.

everything the Christian believes in falls apart. It is because the promises and expectations are so high that their lack of realization places the Christians in this position. As President Harold B. Lee explained, "If one were to doubt in a life after death or in a resurrection from the dead, as such a belief would imply, than man would be of all men most miserable (1 Cor. 15:19), because he lacks faith in that which would follow after his life here upon this earth."[156]

GOD RAISED UP CHRIST AS THE FIRSTFRUITS (15:20–28)

Greek Text

20 Νυνὶ δὲ Χριστὸς ἐγήγερται ἐκ νεκρῶν, ἀπαρχὴ τῶν κεκοιμημένων. 21 ἐπειδὴ γὰρ δι' ἀνθρώπου θάνατος, καὶ δι' ἀνθρώπου ἀνάστασις νεκρῶν· 22 ὥσπερ γὰρ ἐν τῷ Ἀδὰμ πάντες ἀποθνῄσκουσιν, οὕτως καὶ ἐν τῷ Χριστῷ πάντες ζῳοποιηθή-σονται. 23 ἕκαστος δὲ ἐν τῷ ἰδίῳ τάγματι· ἀπαρχὴ Χριστός, ἔπειτα οἱ τοῦ Χριστοῦ ἐν τῇ παρουσίᾳ αὐτοῦ· 24 εἶτα τὸ τέλος, ὅταν παραδιδῷ τὴν βασιλείαν τῷ θεῷ καὶ πατρί, ὅταν καταργήσῃ πᾶσαν ἀρχὴν καὶ πᾶσαν ἐξουσίαν καὶ δύναμιν, 25 δεῖ γὰρ αὐτὸν βασιλεύειν ἄχρι οὗ θῇ πάντας τοὺς ἐχθροὺς ὑπὸ τοὺς πόδας αὐτοῦ. 26 ἔσχα-τος ἐχθρὸς καταργεῖται ὁ θάνατος, 27 πάντα γὰρ ὑπέταξεν ὑπὸ τοὺς πόδας αὐτοῦ. ὅταν δὲ εἴπῃ ὅτι πάντα ὑποτέτακται, δῆλον ὅτι ἐκτὸς τοῦ ὑποτάξαντος αὐτῷ τὰ πάντα. 28 ὅταν δὲ ὑποταγῇ αὐτῷ τὰ πάντα, τότε αὐτὸς ὁ υἱὸς ὑποταγήσεται τῷ ὑποτάξαντι αὐτῷ τὰ πάντα, ἵνα ᾖ ὁ θεὸς πάντα ἐν πᾶσιν. [SBLGNT]

King James Version

20 But now is Christ risen from the dead, and become the firstfruits of them that slept. 21 For since by man came death, by man came also the resurrection of the dead. 22 For as in Adam all die, even so in Christ shall all be made alive. 23 But every man in his own order: Christ the firstfruits;

New Rendition

20 But in reality Christ has been raised from the dead, the first of those who have fallen asleep. 21 For since death came through a man, the resurrection of the dead also came through a man. 22 For just as in Adam all die, so also in Christ will all be made alive. 23 But each in his own turn; first Christ, then

---

156. Harold B. Lee, in CR, April 1944, 85. President Kimball took another tack on the verse, noting that "we could paraphrase it to say: 'If in this life only our marriages are firm, our marital bliss real, and our family life happy, we are of all men most miserable.'" Spencer W. Kimball, in CR, October 1964, 27.

afterward they that are Christ's at his coming. 24 Then cometh the end, when he shall have delivered up the kingdom to God, even the Father; when he shall have put down all rule and all authority and power. 25 For he must reign, till he hath put all enemies under his feet. 26 The last enemy that shall be destroyed is death. 27 For he hath put all things under his feet. But when he saith all things are put under him, it is manifest that he is excepted, which did put all things under him. 28 And when all things shall be subdued unto him, then shall the Son also himself be subject unto him that put all things under him, that God may be all in all.

those who belong to Christ at his coming. 24 Then the end comes, when he hands over the kingdom to God, even the Father, after he has eliminated every other dominion and every other authority and power. 25 For Christ must rule until God has put all enemies under Christ's feet. 26 The last enemy, death, will be eliminated, 27 for "he has put all things in subjugation under his feet." And when it says "all things are put in subjugation," it is clear that it does not include God, who put all things in subjugation to Christ. 28 And when all things are put in subjugation to God, the Son himself will be subject to God, who put all things in subjugation to Christ, so that God might be all things in all things.

Translation Notes and Comments

15:20 *But now is Christ risen from the dead, and become the firstfruits of them that slept / But in reality Christ has been raised from the dead, the first of those who have fallen asleep:* The emphatic adverb νυνί (*nyni*) denotes not only a logical or temporal "now" but can also introduce "a real situation after an unreal clause or sentence" and can, therefore, be translated as "in reality," as in our Rendition.[157] Again, Paul uses the perfect passive verb ἐγήγερται (*egēgertai*), "has been raised," to stress that not only was Christ raised from the dead, but he still lives (see 15:4).[158] The noun ἀπαρχή (*aparchē*) was originally a technical term describing the first portion of agricultural produce or domestic animals that had to be sacrificed as the "firstfruits" before the rest could be used.[159] These were also seen as harbingers of much more to come. Over time this nuance weakened so that the word lost the force of "firstfruits" and became almost equal to πρῶτος (*prōtos*), "first," and thus its translation in our Rendition.[160] Nonetheless, it never fully lost the hint of a promise of an abundant harvest.[161]

---

157. BDAG, 682.

158. As Barrett, *First Epistle*, 341, notes the significance of the force of this tense cannot be overemphasized. See also De Boer, *Defeat of Death*, 105–9.

159. BDAG, 98.

160. BDAG, 98; Gerhard Delling, "ἀπαρχή," in *TDNT*, 1:484–86.

161. Thiselton, *First Epistle*, 1223; Findlay, "St. Paul's First Epistle," 925.

The Christological implications of the phrase ἐγήγερται ἐκ νεκρῶν (*egēgartai ek nekrōn*), "has been raised from the dead," are arresting. It shows that Jesus shared a common mortality with both Adam and all humankind in that he, as with all others, had to be raised up. All mortals, including the Lord, share therefore an aspect of the same nature and thus the same death.

15:21 *For since by man came death, by man came also the resurrection of the dead / For since death came through a man, the resurrection of the dead also came through a man:* In this verse, Paul draws an analogy between what one scholar called "two uniquely representative men," Adam and Jesus.[162] The noun ἄνθρωπος (*anthrōpos*), "man," in this context, points to the mortality that both the primal man and the Savior share but which only one of them overcame (see Mosiah 3:7; 13:34; 15:1–8; Alma 11:39–40; 34:10, 14). Paul's point is that as one man's action affected the whole race in bringing death, so, too, another man's actions affected the whole race by bringing life.

15:22 *For as in Adam all die, even so in Christ shall all be made alive / For just as in Adam all die, so also in Christ will all be made alive:* A key word in this verse is the adjective πάντες (*pantes*), "all." Though the form here is masculine, the word allows for the inclusion of both genders. Adam's transgression brought death upon all. No one has or will escape its power. To the same degree, Christ's sacrifice brings immortal life to all. No one has or will escape its power either (Rom. 5:12–19; 2 Ne. 9:22; Mosiah 16:8; Alma 11:41–42; Morm. 7:5; D&C 29:26). As will be shown below, however, just because a person becomes immortal does not mean that he or she will share in the same quality of immortal life as others.

15:23 *But every man in his own order / But each in his own turn:* The noun τάγμα (*tagma*) is derived from the verb τάσσω (*tassō*) "to bring about an order of things by arranging,"[163] thus the root sense of the noun *tagma* is an ordered arrangement of people or things.[164] *Tagma* could also be used in the sense of "rank" or "status."[165] In a broader sense, it described "a stage in a sequence, order or turn,"[166] and that is how it is being used here. Hence ἐν τῷ ἰδίῳ τάγματι (*en tō idiō tagmati*) could be translated "each according to his rank or status." Paul's point is that there is a sequential order to the Resurrection that is determined by one's standing.

---

162. Bruce, *1 and 2 Corinthians*, 145.

163. BDAG, 991.

164. BDAG, 987–88.

165. LSJ, 1752.

166. BDAG, 988.

Christ the firstfruits; afterward they that are Christ's at his coming / first Christ, then those who belong to Christ at his coming: As noted above, ἀπαρχή (*aparchē*), "firstfruits," here has the sense of "first" and is so translated in our Rendition. Christ is the first to be resurrected. The adverb ἔπειτα (*epeita*), "afterwards, then," "indicates a firmly marked sequence."[167] It connotes that the sequence will not be varied. Only after the Lord's Resurrection will come οἱ τοῦ Χριστοῦ (*hoi tou Christou*), literally "they of Christ." Since, however, the genitive phrase is one of possession, it is translated "who belong to Christ" in our Rendition.[168] These are they who will be resurrected and raised up to meet Christ at his second coming. There are various designations for this event in the scriptures, including "the first resurrection" (Rev. 20:6; D&C 63:18; 76:64), "the resurrection of the just" (D&C 76:17, 50, 65), and "the resurrection of life" (John 5:29). The noun παρουσία (*parousia*), "coming," is replete with meaning. It denotes foremost the expectation of the personal presence of the one who is coming. No envoy or ambassador is expected. When associated with the Second Coming, it nuances the dynamic quality in Christ who personally brings all things to its completion.[169] Paul refers to only two of the four groups that will be resurrected, probably because he is focusing only on the Resurrection of the just. Why he does not specifically mention the Resurrection of the unjust is unknown.[170] For further study, see the "Excursus on the Order of the Resurrection of the Dead" below in this chapter.

15:24 *Then cometh the end, when he shall have delivered up the kingdom to God, even the Father / Then the end comes, when he hands over the kingdom to God, even the Father:* The JST changes "Then" to "Afterward" and in so doing stresses the sequence of these future events. The phrase τὸ τέλος (*to telos*), literally "the end," refers to the last part of a process and, in eschatology, to the final act in the cosmic drama.[171] In this case, it is the end of the Lord's rule. The Greek temporal adverb ὅταν (*hotan*), "when," leaves the timing of these events unspecified and open-ended. It shows that the end will not come until the two conditions Paul specifies have been completed. This phrase mentions only the first that will bring an end to the cosmic drama. It is the Lord's handing "over [his] kingdom" to the Father. The

---

167. Thiselton, *First Epistle,* 1229; BDAG, 361.

168. See Wallace, *Greek Grammar,* 81–82.

169. Jürgen Moltmann, *The Coming of God: Christian Eschatology* (London: SCM Press, 1996), 23–29.

170. Bailey, *Mediterranean Eyes,* 444. Barrett, *First Epistle,* 972, notes that because Paul knew of another Resurrection, his silence here must simply be accepted.

171. BDAG, 998–99.

verb παραδίδωμι (*paradidōmi*) conveys the idea of transferring something to another in which a person has had a relatively strong interest.[172] In this case, it is the Lord's millennial kingdom (D&C 76:106–7).

when he shall have put down all rule and all authority and power / after he has eliminated every other dominion and every other authority and power: The second act in bringing to a close the divine drama is putting down everything that opposes God. The verb καταργέω (*katargeō*), "put down, eliminate," is very strong. The prefix κατα- (*kata-*) intensifies its usual meaning. It stresses the notion of rendering something inoperative, generally by causing it to cease to exist. The verb, therefore, carries the idea of complete annihilation. This destructive force is leveled at three corporate areas that have, from time immemorial, opposed God. The first is ἀρχή (*archē*), "rule, dominion." The noun denotes any given sphere of influence and authority outside that of God's sphere. It, therefore, includes both natural and supernatural areas of control.[173] In short, not only is the realm of the natural man to be destroyed but also that of demonic powers. The second area is ἐξουσία (*exousia*), "authority." The noun overlaps in meaning with some of the elements of *archē*, especially in the area of influence and power. It emphasizes, however, the authority that dominates and subjugates those in the area of control.[174] The final area is δύναμις (*dynamis*), "power." The noun again shares much in common with the other two, especially that of governing. The emphasis here, however, is on the ability to carry out any deeds that are necessary to maintain domination and control.[175] The three terms taken together are abstract ideas connoting governing agents and powers. These words carry a supraterrestrial nuance behind them that points to coercive influences both earthly and demonic. With their annihilation, all powers that oppose the sovereignty of the Father and the Son will cease to exist.[176]

The two verbs in the whole sentence (παραδίδωμι, *paradidōmi*, "to hand over," and καταργέω, *katargeō*, "to put down" or "eliminate") denote two distinct but complementary actions.[177] Only when both are completed will the end come.

---

172. BDAG, 761–62.

173. Louw-Nida, §§12.44; 37.55, 56.

174. BDAG, 352–53; Louw-Nida, §§37.13, 35, 37; 76.12; also the realm of supernatural might, §12.44.

175. Louw-Nida, §§74.1; 76.1, 7; also supernatural might, §12:44.

176. Fitzmyer, *First Corinthians*, 572–73.

177. Findlay, "St. Paul's First Epistle," 927.

15:25 *For he must reign, till he hath put all enemies under his feet / For Christ must rule until God has put all enemies under Christ's feet:* The Greek text is unclear as to whom the pronouns in this phrase refer. For clarity, our Rendition has replaced the third person singular pronouns "he," "him," and "his" with "Christ," "God," and "Christ's."

Paul here alludes to LXX Psalm 110:1 but rephrases it for his own purpose.[178] In its original context, it refers to Jehovah placing all enemies under the feet of the Davidic king. It was, therefore, an easy step for Paul, who understood Christ as that king, to apply the scripture to him.

A difficulty in translating this verse is that the subject of the verb βασιλεύω (*basileuō*), "to reign," is vague. It could refer to either the Father or the Son.[179] It seems, however, more likely that the subject is Christ for three reasons: First, Paul only alludes to but does not quote the passage in Psalms, thus weakening the idea that it is God who reigns; second, it more naturally follows the Greek grammar; and third, it is God who put all enemies under the Savior's feet by giving him the power and authority to rule. The Lord then executes that power and *then* presents the kingdom to his Father.[180] The unstated object of the subjunctive aorist θῇ (*thē*), "has put," based on Paul's reference to LXX Psalm 8:7, is God. Paul never lets his readers forget that the source of all power, though often acting behind the scenes, is the Father.

The verb δεῖ (*dei*), "must," is important because it nuances the necessity of the Savior's reign until he has fulfilled all that God requires of him. Also important is the verb τίθημι (*tithēmi*), "to put," here carrying the nuance of completing an arrangement.[181] The prepositional phrase ἄχρι οὗ (*achri hou*), functioning as a temporal conjunction, takes the subjunctive to express "until," and "indicates a future contingency from the perspective of the time of the main verb."[182] Taken together they reveal the arrangement between Father and Son that determines the length of the Son's reign. The phrase ὑπὸ τοὺς πόδας αὐτοῦ (*hypo tous podas autou*), "under his feet," explains the arrangement. The imagery is very strong as a Near Eastern metaphor. In the Greco-Roman world, victor's placing their

---

178. The LXX reads ἕως ἂν θῶ τοὺς ἐχθρούς σου ὑποπόδιον τῶν ποδῶν σου (*heōs an thō tous echthrous sou hypopodion tōn podōn sou*), "until I make your enemies a footstool for your feet." Paul adapts this by changing the pronoun "I" (referring to God) and the first "your" to "all" and the second to "his" (referring to Christ).

179. Barrett, *First Epistle,* 358; Conzelmann, *1 Corinthians,* 272–73.

180. Fee, *First Epistle,* 755–76; Thiselton, *First Epistle,* 1234.

181. BDAG, 1003–4; Louw-Nida, §13.9.

182. Wallace, *Greek Grammar,* 479.

foot on an enemy's neck was the sign of total subjugation.[183] In Paul's writings, it denotes the full range of the divinely assigned conquest given to the Messiah. That conquest includes everything. Further, it implies not only an enemy's total surrender but also the impossibility of it ever being able to rise again.[184]

15:26 *The last enemy that shall be destroyed is death / The last enemy, death, will be eliminated:* Again, Paul uses the very verb καταργεῖται (*katargeitai*), "to eliminate." Though translated as a future tense, it is actually a present tense. However, the present tense can be used instead of the future in statements that are considered immediate, likely, or certain, which is the case here.[185]

This act will be the culmination of Christ's work. It will fulfill God's plan of salvation for his children. Its breadth shall include even those "who shall not be redeemed from the devil until the last resurrection, until the Lord, even Christ the Lamb, shall have finished his work" (D&C 76:85).[186] Death will, therefore, be forever abolished for all.

15:27 *For he hath put all things under his feet / for "he has put all things in subjugation under his feet":* To give scriptural force to his point, Paul quotes from LXX Psalm 8:7 (8:6 in the KJV). The verb ὑποτάσσω (*hypotasso*), "put under, subjugate," means to cause something or someone to be subjected to something or someone else. The word nuances the firm control that one exercises over events, forces, and people.[187] The verb's implied subject is God. The genitive pronoun αὐτοῦ (*autou*), "his," refers to Christ. The force of the scripture is, then, that the Father has put all things—including death—under the control of the Son.

when he saith all things are put under him, it is manifest that he is excepted, which did put all things under him / And when it says "all things are put in subjugation," it is clear that it does not include God, who put all things in subjugation to Christ: The Greek text is unclear as to whom the pronouns in this phrase refer. For clarity, our Rendition has replaced the third person singular pronouns "he" and "him," with "God" and "Christ." The JST

---

183. Images from the time of the Assyrian conquests to those of Rome have been depicted in art and coin. For examples, see "Feet on the Necks," *Ancient Bible History,* http://ancientbiblehistory.com/blog/feet-on-the-necks/.

184. Bailey, *Mediterranean Eyes,* 446–47. The act was also a way of illustrating the Roman states' power over both individuals and subjected peoples expressed by the Latin term *imperium.*

185. Grammatically, it is the "present of anticipation." Smyth, *Greek Grammar,* §1879.

186. See also Alma 11:41–42; D&C 43:18; 88:100–101.

187. BDAG, 1042; Louw-Nida, §37.31.

is very helpful. It reads, "For he saith, When it is manifest that he hath put all things under his feet, and that all things are put under, he is excepted of the Father who did put all things under him." The change shows that when both the manifestation and actual subjugation of all things are assured, then God will exempt the Savior from any domination or subjugation.

Paul here clarifies the scripture he has just quoted. The adjective δῆλος (*dēlos*) means "clear, plain, evident."[188] The preposition ἐκτός (*ektos*), "except," is a marker of exception.[189] Paul's point is that when the scripture speaks of πάντα (*panta*), "all things," being in subjugation to Christ, that does not include God. Indeed, God is *the* subjecting Subject and supreme power over all others, including the Savior.[190] Paul is not, however, looking at the cessation of the Savior's work, but at its culmination.[191]

15:28 *And when all things shall be subdued unto him, then shall the Son also himself be subject unto him that put all things under him / And when all things are put in subjugation to God, the Son himself will be subject to God, who put all things in subjugation to Christ:* As in the previous verse, for clarity, our Rendition replaces the third person singular pronouns with "God" and "Christ." This verse restates for emphasis the point that Paul has already made. In it, Paul uses the pronoun αὐτός (*autos*), "himself," to emphasize that *even Jesus* will be subject to God.[192] There will be no exceptions. The Apostle also wants it clear that the Savior's power to subjugate came directly from and under the Father's authority.

that God may be all in all / so that God might be all things in all things: With this last phrase, Paul explains why the subjugation of all things, even the Son, is necessary. The phrase πάντα ἐν πᾶσιν (*panta en pasin*) puts together two neuter adjectives both translated as "all things" in our Rendition. The phrase shows that, after the work of the Son is complete, everything will be subordinate to the Father and subject unto him. Thus, he will be "in all things." Further, no type of mediation—neither of the Son nor his kingdom—will be necessary any longer. God will rule all things personally and directly.[193] In that way, he will "be all things" in that he will be all that is necessary or needed.

---

188. BDAG, 222.
189. BDAG, 311.
190. Thiselton, *First Epistle,* 1236.
191. Findlay, "St. Paul's First Epistle," 928.
192. The pronoun emphasizes identity so that no mistake can be made as to whom the subject is. Wallace, *Greek Grammar,* 349.
193. Fitzmyer, *First Corinthians,* 575.

Analysis and Summary

Having forcefully refuted the erroneous beliefs of "some" of the Corinthian Saints by exposing the unacceptable consequences of their position, Paul reverses his argument (15:20). Now he emphasizes the wonderful results because there was a Resurrection.[194] The series he lists accents the tie between this doctrine and that of the gospel as a whole.

Paul described the Savior as ἀπαρχή (*aparchē*), "first" or "firstfruits." The word is important because it shows that God never intended Jesus to be the only person resurrected. "He had power over death," witnessed President N. Eldon Tanner, "and willingly gave his life and was literally resurrected so that man might be saved and resurrected from the dead and enjoy eternal life."[195] Because of the number of connotations of the word *aparchē*, Paul used it as the pivot of his argument.[196] The first connation is temporal, showing that Christ is the "first one" raised from the dead. The second is representative, showing he represents all those who would follow. It also suggests that they will share in the same quality and character.[197] "By the power of his divine Sonship," noted President Hinckley, "he rose from the grave, becoming 'the firstfruits of them that slept' (1 Cor. 15:20), assuring for all a resurrection from the dead and inviting each of us to partake of eternal life according to our obedience to his laws and commandments."[198] President J. Reuben Clark testified that "we all shall be resurrected, even as was he, and come forth, even as he came forth, in the image in which we live."[199]

The third connotation points to the order of the events. Where there is a first, there must be either a second or a last. The Apostle already noted that all things must be done "in an orderly manner" (κατὰ τάξιν, *kata taxin*, 14:40). So, too, the Resurrection will proceed in God's way according to his time table.[200]

---

194. Thiselton, *First Epistle,* 1223.

195. N. Eldon Tanner, in CR, April 1964, 60.

196. De Boer, *Defeat of Death,* 109, argues convincingly that the idea behind the word was pivotal in Paul's argument showing as it does that God never intended Jesus to be the only fruit of the Resurrection.

197. Jooste Hollemann, *Resurrection and Parousia: A Tradition-Historical Study of Pauline Eschatology in 1 Corinthians 15* (Leiden: Brill, 1996), 19–25, 31–33.

198. Gordon B. Hinkley, "Five Million Members—a Milestone and Not a Summit," *Ensign* 12 (May 1982): 44.

199. J. Reuben Clark Jr., in CR, October 1954, 40.

200. Edwards, *Commentary,* 409.

In 15:22, Paul made the source of death clear. It was the result of a deliberate action taken by Adam. According to President Hugh B. Brown, "Through the Fall, Adam and Eve and all their posterity became subject to bodily disintegration and death and also to banishment from the presence of God, which is in the nature of spiritual death, and this despite the fact that the cause was individual transgression."[201]

In this same verse, Paul also makes it clear that because of the actions of one man, all will be made alive. As Elder Charles W. Penrose stated, "Jesus came in the meridian of time as 'the Lamb of God, which taketh away the sin of the world,' to bring mankind up from the effects of the transgression of our first parents. Hence he is called 'the Second Adam,' and we are told that as in the first Adam all die, even so in Christ, the second Adam, shall all be made alive again."[202] "All mortals have been saved from the permanence of death through the Resurrection of Jesus Christ," noted Elder Oaks.[203]

"It is because of our Redeemer's life and sacrifice that we are here," testified President Hinckley, "It is because of His sacrificial atonement that we and all of the sons and daughters of God will partake of the salvation of the Lord. . . . It is because of the sacrificial redemption wrought by the Savior of the world that the great plan of the eternal gospel is made available to us under which those who die in the Lord shall not taste of death but shall have the opportunity of going on to a celestial and eternal glory."[204] That is not to say all will. According to President Faust, "The members of The Church of Jesus Christ of Latter-day Saints believe in universal salvation as well as individual salvation. We believe that through the Resurrection and Atonement there will be a resurrection of both the just and the unjust."[205]

"Through the restoration of the gospel through the Prophet Joseph Smith," Elder LeGrand Richards pointed out, "the Lord corrects another false teaching, one of the doctrines of men. . . . The Christian world teaches that children are born into this world with the sin of Adam and Eve resting upon them, thus denying the atonement of Jesus Christ."[206] Such a notion is repugnant to Latter-day Saints. According to the Book of Mormon, little children "are whole, for they are not capable of committing sin; wherefore

---

201. Hugh B. Brown, in CR, April 1962, 108.
202. Charles W. Penrose, in *JD*, 21:82.
203. Dallin H. Oaks, " Have You Been Saved?" *Ensign* 28 (May 1998): 55.
204. Gordon B. Hinckley, "Our Mission of Saving," *Ensign* 21 (November 1991): 54.
205. James E. Faust, "The Resurrection," *Ensign* 15 (May 1985): 32.
206. LeGrand Richards, in CR, April 1969, 89.

the curse of Adam is taken away from them in [Christ], that it hath no power over them." Indeed, "little children are alive in Christ, even from the foundation of the world" (Moro. 8:8, 12; compare D&C 29:47), and "God having redeemed man from the fall, men became again, in their infant state, innocent before God" (D&C 93:38).

Again, it is important to remember that *aparchē*, "first" or "firstfruits," connotes an orderly manner. After these, those who are not of the first-fruits will be resurrected. For details, see "Excursus on the Order of the Resurrection of the Dead" below.

In 15:24, Paul explains that "the end" will not come until the Savior has accomplished two final tasks. The first is to hand over (παραδίδωμι, *paradidōmi*) his kingdom to the Father. The second is to annihilate (καταργέω, *katargeō*) all opposing forces. In 15:25, Paul adapts Psalm 110:1 to bolster the point he is making. This scripture, though speaking about God's subjugating all the enemies for the future Davidic king, was seen by the early Christians as a reference to all things—especially death—being overcome by Christ through the Resurrection (see Acts 2:33–34; Rom. 8:34; Mark 12:36; Luke 20:42–44; 22:69; Col. 3:1; Heb. 1:13). In 15:26, Paul notes that death will be the last enemy overcome. Once it has been vanquished nothing remains that can oppose God.

Joseph Smith taught that "salvation is nothing more nor less than to triumph over all our enemies and put them under our feet. And when we have power to put all enemies under our feet in this world, and a knowledge to triumph over all evil spirits in the world to come, then we are saved, as in the case of Jesus, who was to reign until He had put all enemies under His feet, and the last enemy was death."[207]

As Paul notes in 15:25–28, God granted full sovereignty over the earth to the Son during its telestial and terrestrial periods. He did this for a definite purpose. It was so that the Son would have full power to assist him in bringing "to pass the immortality and eternal life" of all those who would follow his commandments (Moses 1:38–39; Rom. 8:17; 2 Ne. 2:15; Alma 42:26; D&C 29:43).[208] Even when the Savior had been raised by the Father unto life, his work was not yet finished. He had to see through to the very end the full extent of his vicarious, victorious, and atoning work. That meant he had to not only overcome mortal corruption and sin through the Resur-

---

207. Smith, *History of the Church*, 5:387.
208. Robertson and Plummer, *Critical and Exegetical Commentary*, 355.

rection but also annihilate the very vast structural and corporate evil that had dominated the world since it turned from the love and ways of God.[209] Therefore, he had to destroy all dominions, authorities, and powers that undergirded and supported it.

In 15:27, Paul picks up another scripture used by the Christians to support the doctrine of the Resurrection. This is LXX Psalm 8:7, "he has put all things in subjugation under his feet." Paul's commentary shows that it is God who placed all things, including death, in subjugation to Christ. Paul's commentary counters a primary position of the antiresurrection party. In doing so, it sheds light on their misinterpretation of the scriptures. It appears that they believed that the phrase "For he hath put all things under his feet" included the flesh. From that they extrapolated that there would be no corporeal resurrection. Paul counters the argument by insisting that there was no exception to Christ's powers of subjugation and that included physical death. Paul was thus arguing that, as an LDS scholar noted, "the conquering of death did not include ridding Christ's spirit of its mortal tabernacle."[210]

Paul ends this section of his epistle explaining why God needed to put all things in subjugation (ὑποτάσσω, *hypotassō*) to the Savior. It was so that the Father could be "all things in all things" (15:28, Rendition). It was through the subjugation of all rule, authority, and power that the Savior allowed this to happen. He prepared the way by first subjugating *himself* to both physical and spiritual death. By doing that, he "ascended up on high, as also he descended below all things, in that he comprehended all things, that he might be in all and through all things, the light of truth" (D&C 88:6). The Son experienced both the heights of exaltation and the depths of hell. With his condescension to become mortal, with all that that entailed, as well as his yielding to all the forces of an ignoble death (1 Ne. 11:16–33) and placing himself in the powers of spiritual death, he gained total comprehension of the full range of mortal and postmortal experience.

It also made it possible for the spiritual aspect of his divine nature, that is, "the light of truth" (also known as the "light of Christ"), to permeate all things everywhere.[211] Thus, he is "in all . . . and is through all things," both animate and inanimate (D&C 88:41). As an LDS scholar pointed out, "The

---

209. Thiselton, *First Epistle*, 1231.
210. Holzapfel and Wayment, *Making Sense*, 364.
211. For discussion, see Dunford, "Light of Christ," in *EM*, 2:835.

Lord's omnipresence is spatial as well as experiential."[212] The omnipresent and omnipotent powers derived though the "light of truth" allow him to subjugate all things.[213] When he has fully done so, he will present his finished work to the Father. In that way, as the Prophet Joseph Smith explained, God will "obtain kingdom upon kingdom, and it will exalt him in glory. He will then take a higher exaltation and [Jesus] will take his place, and thereby become exalted. [Therefore] Jesus treads in the tracks of his Father and inherits what God did before; and God is thus glorified and exalted in the salvation and exaltation of all his children."[214]

This entire pericope reaffirms the unlimited and universal dominion which God assigned to Christ. It also reasserts most impressively that only through the Lord's absolute victory can God's kingdom be finally and fully consummated.[215] The solemn conclusion is very well expressed in Paul's note that "then shall the Son also himself be subject unto" the Father. The loyal purpose of the Son in his self-subjugation is to put his Father in the position to personally rule once more.[216]

The end result will be dramatic. From the time of the Fall, *all* interaction between humankind and the Father had to be done through a mediator. Paul knew full well, as he explained to Timothy, that there is "one mediator between God and men, the man Christ Jesus" (1 Tim. 2:5; see also Gal. 3:19–20; Heb. 8:6; 9:15; 12:24). In a sense, Christ's Church, that is his kingdom on earth, also acts as a mediator because it holds the keys and authority through which the natural man is put off and the new person becomes a child of Christ and is reunited once more with the Divine.[217] The Lord assured his disciples that "if a man love me, he will keep my words: and my

---

212. Robinson and Garrett, *Commentary*, 3:100.

213. This "light"—being the power that creates, comprehends, and superintends suns, moons, worlds, and people (see D&C 88:7–13), and which is in and through all things— gives the Lord control over these as well (Moses 7:36; 1 Ne. 1:14; 7:12; D&C 38:2; 45:75; 61:1; 88:41; 93:17).

214. The quote used here is from an amalgamation of sources and is reproduced in Donald Q. Cannon and Larry E. Dahl, *The Prophet Joseph Smith's King Follett Discourse: A Six-Column Comparison of Original Notes and Amalgamations* (Provo, Utah: Religious Studies Center, Brigham Young University, 2001), 32–33.

215. Findlay, "St. Paul's First Epistle," 928.

216. Findlay, "St. Paul's First Epistle," 930.

217. See Eph. 4:11–14; 2 Ne. 31:5–21; Mosiah 5:7; 27:25; D&C 5:16; Moses 6:59. The title of the presiding authority is "prophet," the Hebrew word denoting one who intercedes between contending parties as well as one authorized as a spokesperson for Jehovah. BDB, 611.

Father will love him, and we will come unto him, and make our abode with him" (John 14:23). Because of the work of Christ, the mediation between Father and his creation—and more especially his children—will no longer be necessary. Indeed, the righteous inhabitants of the earth will be "begotten sons and daughters unto God" (D&C 76:24). The preposition "unto" is arresting. All were born *of* God at one time but, due to the misuse of agency, most have lost association with him. The Savior's work will allow the relationship to be restored through a spiritual birth and, thus, the righteous will be reborn *unto* God.

The Savior's work will allow a reversal of current conditions in two ways. First, God will now be directly "in all things." That is to say, his Holy Spirit, also referred to as "light" in the scriptures, will directly infuse itself into all this created order. His "light" will proceed forth from his presence "to fill the immensity of space." Indeed, the "light which is in all things, which giveth life to all things, which is the law by which all things are governed, even the power of God who sitteth upon his throne, who is in the bosom of eternity, who is the midst of all things" will be his alone (D&C 88:12–13). Second, he will, once again, "be all things" (15:28) to his children, for "God himself shall be with them, and be their God. And [he] shall wipe away all tears from their eyes; and there shall be no more death, neither sorrow, nor crying, neither shall there be any more pain: for the former things are passed away" (Rev. 21:3–4).

EXCURSUS ON THE ORDER OF THE RESURRECTION OF THE DEAD

Paul testifies that "in Christ shall all be made alive" (15:22), and that means everyone. He also said, ἐν τῷ ἰδίῳ τάγματι (*en tō idiō tagmati*), "each in his [or her] own turn" (15:23, Rendition). Thus, the Resurrection of the dead will proceed in an orderly manner. Jesus spoke of two Resurrections, "the resurrection of life; and . . . the resurrection of damnation" (John 5:26–29).

The first began with the Resurrection of the Lord and those who came forth at that time (Matt. 27:52; 3 Ne. 23:9–10). As the Millennium begins, "the face of the Lord will be unveiled," noted Elder Pratt, "and those who are alive will be quickened, and they will be caught up; and the Saints who are in their graves, will come forth and be caught up, together with those who are quickened, and they will be taken into the heavens into the midst of those celestial beings who will make their appearance at that time. These are the ones who are the firstfruits, that is, the firstfruits at the time of his coming" (compare D&C 88:97–98).[218] These are they who will inherit a fullness of joy and glory in the celestial kingdom. They include those who believed on the name of Christ and entered into covenants with him and strove to keep them. They are the ones who received the Holy Ghost by the laying on of hands and who endured to the end in faith. Further, they were sealed by the Holy Spirit of Promise and became members of the Church of the Firstborn and were ordained kings and queens, priests and priestesses (see D&C 76:50–57) and entered into the eternal state of marriage (D&C 131:2–3).

After these, the Resurrection of the just will continue: the first will be "those who are Christ's at his coming; who have received their part in that prison which is prepared for them, that they might receive the gospel, and be judged according to men in the flesh" (D&C 88:99). Their inheritance will be that of the terrestrial kingdom. They include Latter-day Saints who reneged on their covenant to defend the truth and did not endure to the end in faith. It also includes those who were presented with but rejected the gospel in this life but accepted it in the spirit world. It also includes honorable men who were deceived by the philosophies and sophistries of the world. Finally, it includes those of the heathen nations who knew not the law (D&C 76:71–79).

---

218. Orson Pratt, in *JD*, 16:328.

After this, the Resurrection of the unjust will take place. This will include "the spirits of men who are to be judged, and are found under condemnation; And these are the rest of the dead; and they live not again until the thousand years are ended, neither again, until the end of the earth." And finally, there are those who wait in hell "until that great and last day, even the end." These are they who "remain filthy still" (D&C 88:100–102). This Resurrection, then, has two components as well. The first group includes those who refused under all circumstances to receive the gospel but sponsored factions and discord. They include murderers (D&C 42:18), and "sorcerers, and adulterers, and whoremongers, and whosoever loves and makes a lie." These will "suffer the wrath of God on the earth" and the "vengeance of eternal fire." Indeed, they "are cast down to hell and suffer the wrath of Almighty God" (D&C 76:103–6). Nonetheless, they will come forth, once cleansed by the fires of hell, to their reward of the telestial kingdom.

The second group will be composed of those who are "filthy still" (2 Ne. 9:16; Morm. 9:14). These are they who knew by revelation God's laws and deliberately broke them, seeking to become a law unto themselves. They willed to abide in sin and did so (D&C 88:35). They knew God's power and partook thereof but, yielding to the powers of Satan, they denied the truth and defied God's power. In a hell-inspired fury, they "denied the Only Begotten Son of the Father, having crucified him unto themselves and put him to an open shame" (D&C 76:35). They are "sons of perdition" and "vessels of wrath, doomed to suffer the wrath of God, with the devil and his angels in eternity" (D&C 76:32–33).

Even so, they, with everyone else, will be "taken home to that God who gave them life" (Alma 40:11; see also 2 Ne. 2:10; 9:38; Alma 42:23). Before they appear before him, however, these souls are in "darkness, and a state of awful, fearful looking for the fiery indignation of the wrath of God upon them" (Alma 40:14). Indeed, "they are consigned to an awful view of their own guilt and abominations, which doth cause them to shrink from the presence of the Lord into a state of misery and endless torment, from whence they can no more return; therefore they have drunk damnation to their own souls" (Mosiah 3:25).

The torment of all those who come forth in the Resurrection of the unjust is truly tragic in the full sense of the word because it is so unnecessary. Christ died for all. Of the experience, he has testified, "how sore you know not, how exquisite you know not, yea, how hard to bear you know not." Indeed, this "suffering caused myself, even God, the greatest of all, to tremble because of pain, and to bleed at every pore, and to suffer both body and spirit—and would that I might not drink the bitter cup, and shrink—Nevertheless, glory be to the Father, and I partook and finished my preparations unto the children of men" (D&C 19:15, 18–19). The Savior proclaimed, "I, God, have suffered these things for all, that they might not suffer if they would repent" (D&C 19:16).

Those who are part of the Resurrection of the unjust will suffer such pains because, when they initially had the chance, they refused to repent. They will awake in the next world to a "lively sense of [their] own guilt, which doth cause [them] to shrink from the presence of the Lord, and doth fill [their] breast[s] with guilt, and pain, and anguish, which is like an unquenchable fire" (Mosiah 2:38; compare Morm. 9:5) These pains are described as a lake of fire and brimstone whose flames can never be quenched (2 Ne. 9:16; 28:23; Jacob 3:11; 6:10; Mosiah 3:27; Alma 12:17; 14:14). The suffering has its purpose, to drive these sinners into the forgiving arms of Christ. And though they can never obtain the heights of the righteous, nevertheless, their sins will be forgiven, their pain turned to joy, and they shall receive a glory "which surpasses all understanding" (D&C 76:89). Another positive result is that they will know that they would be "more miserable to dwell with a holy and just God, under a consciousness of [their] filthiness before him" than "to dwell with the damned souls in hell" (Morm. 9:4) and, therefore, they will be most content to be forever out of his presence.

The greatest tragedy of all is what the sons of perdition allow to happen to them. These will have also experienced the cleansing powers of hell, but resisted them. With his suffering, the Savior delivered all who will accept his Atonement "from that awful monster the devil, and death, and hell, and that lake of fire and brimstone, which is endless torment" (2 Ne. 9:19). These hardened beings, however, even under the most torturous of conditions and knowing those conditions would continue, hate the Savior to such a degree that they will refuse his forgiveness, his love, and his Atonement. These "who are filthy shall be filthy still; . . . and they shall go away into everlasting fire, prepared for them; and their torment is as a lake of fire and brimstone, whose flame ascendeth up forever and ever and has no end" (2 Ne. 9:16; compare Mosiah 26:27). After their Resurrection, the full force of the "second death" will be upon them and, along with Satan and his angels, they shall be cast away (Rev. 20:12–15; 21:8; Jacob 3:11; Alma 12:16–18; Hel. 14:16–19; D&C 76:36–37). This is not another physical death because their bodies will be immortal. Instead it is a spiritual death in which they die as pertaining to righteousness and are forever sealed by Satan as his own to live in misery forever (2 Ne. 1:13; Alma 12:16, 32; 34:35; 40:26).

With the Resurrection of the filthy still, physical death will be eliminated once and for all for those who have sojourned on this earth. Then the Lord will have "subdued all enemies under his feet, and shall have perfected his work," and at that time, "he shall deliver up the kingdom, and present it unto the Father, spotless" (D&C 76:106–7).

Four items are of note: first, physical death will be overcome for everyone—none shall remain in the grave; second, the first spiritual death will be overcome for everyone because, no matter their state of righteousness or wickedness, all will return to the presence of God; third, the quality of one's afterlife depends on what he or she has chosen they want to become in mortality; and finally, with the exception of the sons of perdition, all will be raised to a kingdom of glory. For a discussion, see "Excursus on the Three Degrees of Glory" below in this chapter.

One final point is worth mentioning. The redemption of all people will come, in the end, on the merits of Christ alone. For all those who—either willingly or by the force of hell fire—accept him, he pleads their case *the same,* "saying: I have overcome and have trodden the wine-press alone, even the wine-press of the fierceness of the wrath of Almighty God" (D&C 76:107). He has entreated all of us, saying, "Listen to him who is the advocate with the Father, who is pleading your cause before him—Saying: Father, behold the sufferings and death of him who did no sin, in whom thou wast well pleased; behold the blood of thy Son which was shed, the blood of him whom thou gavest that thyself might be glorified; Wherefore, Father, spare these my brethren that believe on my name, that they may come unto me and have everlasting life" (D&C 45:3–5). Notice that Jesus never brings up the merits of those for whom he pleads. There is good reason, "For all have sinned, and come short of the glory of God" (Rom. 3:23). His pleadings with the Father must, therefore, center on his own merits. They will have force largely because the Father "put all things in subjugation under [the Savior's] feet" (15:27, Rendition)—that includes both sin and death—which the Savior overcomes for all. Therefore, the Father will forgive and grant the degree of glory that each person has prepared himself or herself to receive (D&C 88:21–24).

PAUL'S ARGUMENTS FOR THE RESURRECTION OF THE DEAD (15:29–34)

Greek Text

29 Ἐπεὶ τί ποιήσουσιν οἱ βαπτιζόμενοι ὑπὲρ τῶν νεκρῶν; εἰ ὅλως νεκροὶ οὐκ ἐγείρονται, τί καὶ βαπτίζονται ὑπὲρ αὐτῶν; 30 τί καὶ ἡμεῖς κινδυνεύομεν πᾶσαν ὥραν; 31 καθ' ἡμέραν ἀποθνῄσκω, νὴ τὴν ὑμετέραν καύχησιν, ἣν ἔχω ἐν Χριστῷ Ἰησοῦ τῷ κυρίῳ ἡμῶν. 32 εἰ κατὰ ἄνθρωπον ἐθηριομάχησα ἐν Ἐφέσῳ, τί μοι τὸ ὄφελος; εἰ νεκροὶ οὐκ ἐγείρονται, Φάγωμεν καὶ πίωμεν, αὔριον γὰρ ἀποθνῄσκομεν. 33 μὴ πλανᾶσθε· φθείρουσιν ἤθη χρηστὰ ὁμιλίαι κακαί. 34 ἐκνήψατε δικαίως καὶ μὴ ἁμαρτάνετε, ἀγνωσίαν γὰρ θεοῦ τινες ἔχουσιν· πρὸς ἐντροπὴν ὑμῖν λαλῶ.
[SBLGNT]

King James Version

29 Else what shall they do which are baptized for the dead, if the dead rise not at all? why are they then baptized for the dead? 30 And why stand we in jeopardy every hour? 31 I protest by your rejoicing which I have in Christ Jesus our Lord, I die daily. 32 If after the manner of men I have fought with beasts at Ephesus, what advantageth it me, if the dead rise not? let us eat and drink; for to morrow we die. 33 Be not deceived: evil communications corrupt good manners. 34 Awake to righteousness, and sin not; for some have not the knowledge of God: I speak this to your shame.

New Rendition

29 Otherwise, what are those who are baptized on behalf of the dead doing? If in fact the dead are not raised, why indeed are they being baptized on their behalf? 30 Why are we also constantly in danger? 31 I face death every day, as surely as my pride in you, brethren, which I have in Christ Jesus our Lord. 32 If, for merely human reasons, I fought wild beasts in Ephesus, what good is it to me? If the dead are not raised, "Let us eat and drink, for tomorrow we die." 33 Do not be deceived, "Bad company corrupts good morals." 34 Come to your senses as you should and stop sinning. Some, you see, have no knowledge of God. I am saying this to your shame!

Translation Notes and Comments

15:29 *Else what shall they do which are baptized for the dead, if the dead rise not at all? why are they then baptized for the dead? / Otherwise, what are those who are baptized on behalf of the dead doing? If in fact the dead*

are not raised, why indeed are they being baptized on their behalf?: In this verse, Paul continues his argument to show the validity of the Resurrection. The conjunction ἐπεί (*epei*), "else, otherwise," marks a cause or reason for an event or practice.[219] The nominal present passive participle οἱ βαπτιζόμενοι (*hoi baptizomenoi*) refers to "those being baptized." It is followed by the prepositional phrase ὑπέρ τῶν νεκρῶν (*hyper tōn nekrōn*). The preposition ὑπέρ (*hyper*) has the root sense of "over" or "above."[220] Here, however, being governed by the genitive case, it means "for" or "in behalf of" and denotes doing something for the sake of someone else.[221] Paul is clear that this is for τῶν νεκρῶν (*tōn nekrōn*) "the dead."[222] For further discussion, see "Excursus on the Ancient Practice of Vicarious Baptism in Behalf of the Dead" below in this chapter.

15:30 ***And why stand we in jeopardy every hour? / Why are we also constantly in danger?:*** Just who Paul is referring to by the plural pronoun ἡμεῖς (*hēmeis*), "we," is unknown, but it definitely includes the Twelve about whom the Savior prophesied peril (Matt. 24:9; JS–M 1:7). Though the verb κινδυνεύω (*kindyneuō*) means to have one's life in danger, more importantly, it connotes running a risk in behalf of others.[223] The phrase πᾶσαν ὥραν (*passan hōran*), "every hour," denotes the ceaseless proximate nature of the danger, and is thus translated as "constantly" in our Rendition.

15:31 ***I protest by your rejoicing which I have in Christ Jesus our Lord, I die daily / I face death every day, as surely as my pride in you, brethren, which I have in Christ Jesus our Lord:*** Though Paul's meaning is clear, his words are hard to translate exactly into English. The JST reads, "I protest unto you the resurrection of the dead; and this is my rejoicing which I

---

219. BDAG, 360.

220. Thus, some have argued that baptisms of the living were performed over the graves of the dead. This literal locative sense of the word, however, is not found in either the New Testament or LXX. See BDAG, 1030; see also Joel R. White, "'Baptized on Account of the Dead': The Meaning of 1 Corinthians 15:29 in Its Context," *Journal of Biblical Literature* 116, no. 3 (1997): 491–92.

221. BDAG, 1030–31. In Greek papyri, the phrase ὑπερ αὐτοῦ (*hyper autou*), used as a legal technical term, explains that the writer of the papyrus is "the representative of" an illiterate person, that is, he is acting as proxy for him or her. A number of both Catholic and Protestant scholars have supported the view that Paul was referring to vicarious work of the dead. For examples, see Sperry, *Paul's Life and Letters*, 134–36.

222. BDAG, 1030–31.

223. BDAG, 544; Robertson and Plummer, *Critical and Exegetical Commentary*, 360–61, note that, though the word is active, it carries a passive force, thus showing that the Apostles were continually putting their lives at risk.

have in Christ Jesus our Lord daily, though I die." The word "protest" in this instance means "to make a solemn declaration or affirmation as to a fact."[224] and refers to the reality of the Resurrection. Paul here affirms that he rejoices in the doctrine and is willing to give his life as witness to it.

The phrase καθ᾽ ἡμέραν (*kath' hēmeran*), "every day," denotes the daily nature and thereby the unrelenting force of the danger the missionaries are in.[225] The verb ἀποθνῄσκω (*apothnēskō*) means both "to die" and "to face death."[226] Obviously Paul does not literally "die daily" but rather faces the threat of it, as in our Rendition. The noun καύχησις (*kauchēsis*), "pride, boasting," points to a reason for one's boast in something or someone.[227] Though translated in our Rendition as "pride," the word does not carry the sense of haughtiness and self-conceitedness that φυσίωσις (*physiōsis*), "swell-headedness, pride, conceit,"[228] does. Rather, it shows the pleasure and delight one has for another. The particle νή (*nē*), "as surely as," affirms an oath and is usually translated as "by." So the phrase here is literally "by my pride" or "by my boasting in you." The possessive adjective ὑμετέραν (*hymeteran*), "your," is an objective genitive rather than a subjective genitive, and therefore does not refer to the Corinthians' pride, but rather of Paul's pride in them, as in our Rendition.

In sum, to further emphasize his point, Paul identifies what the ministry costs him, notably the daily threat of death.[229] To explain why he is so willing to face death on a daily basis, he swears an oath by (*nē*) that which is most dear to him, namely, his pride—even to the point of boasting—in their commitment to Christ. Though the boast is his, it is neither self-serving nor self-exalting because, as the last phrase shows, it is grounded in his Savior.[230]

15:32 *If after the manner of men I have fought with beasts at Ephesus / If, for merely human reasons, I fought wild beasts in Ephesus:* The prepositional phrase κατὰ ἄνθρωπον (*kata anthrōpon*), literally "according to a human being," that is, from a merely human point of view stands in contrast as opposed to God's point of view. The verb θηριομαχέω (*thēriomacheō*)

224. *Merriam-Webster's Collegiate Dictionary*, 999.
225. Thiselton, *First Epistle*, 1250.
226. BDAG, 111.
227. BDAG, 537; Louw-Nida, §25.204.
228. BDAG, 1070.
229. In a later epistle to them, he will actually list some of these. See 2 Cor. 1:8–10; 11:23.
230. Fee, *First Epistle*, 769–70. Bailey, *Mediterranean Eyes*, 452; Thiselton, *First Epistle*, 1251. Hays, *First Corinthians*, 268, notes that Paul is alluding to the many times he has put his life at risk to preach the gospel and that this risk remains ever present.

means "to be forced to fight with animals as a punishment,"[231] but it is very unlikely that Paul actually did this. A Roman citizen could not be sentenced *ad bestias*.[232] More likely, he is using the words figuratively to describe his Ephesian adversaries' opposition to and contention against him, which was very beast-like.[233]

what advantageth it me, if the dead rise not? / what good is it to me? If the dead are not raised: The noun ὄφελος (*ophelos*) denotes an advantage that comes to one from doing or possessing something. Paul is asking what advantage all the pain, suffering, and fear for his very life that preaching the gospel has cost him if there is no resurrection.[234] Tacitly he is asking why he would even put up with such distress if he did not know the truth of the Resurrection.

let us eat and drink; for to morrow we die / "Let us eat and drink, for tomorrow we die": Paul quotes from LXX Isaiah 22:1, but the idea was not unique to the Bible. The Roman historian Plutarch noted that those who lived only for the present, passing their time in eating and drinking, lead a dissolute and empty existence.[235] Paul uses the phrase to highlight what his attitude and that of others should be if there were no hope of the Resurrection.[236]

15:33 *Be not deceived: evil communications corrupt good manners / Do not be deceived, "Bad company corrupts good morals":* This is a quote from the Greek playwright Menander,[237] but Plato and Euripides likely also used it. Thus, it became a well-known axiom by Paul's time.[238] The phrase μὴ πλανᾶσθε (*mē planasthe*), "do not be deceived," cautions against being led astray by others.[239] Paul had already admonished his readers to this end (6:9) and would do so again (Gal. 6:7; compare Matt. 24:4;

---

231. Louw-Nida, §39.28.

232. BDAG, 455.

233. Though some commentators take Paul literally, most feel he is using a metaphor. For discussion, see Abraham Johannes Malherbe, "The Beasts at Ephesus," *Journal of Biblical Literature* 87 (March 1968): 71–80; Thiselton, *First Epistle*, 1251–52.

234. Fitzmyer, *First Corinthians*, 583.

235. Plutarch, *Mor.* 1098c; 1100d; 1125d. See also Fee, *First Epistle*, 583.

236. Eriksson, *Traditions as Rhetorical Proof*, 266.

237. Menander, *Thais*, frag. 218.

238. Jerome, Letter LXX, To Magnus an Orator of Rome, gives credit to Menander, while others have given credit to Euripides, whom Menander admired and imitated. E. W. Bullinger, *Figures of Speech Used in the Bible* (Grand Rapids, Mich.: Eerdmans, 1985), 801.

239. Fitzmyer, *First Corinthians*, 583.

Luke 21:8; James 1:16). The noun ὁμιλίαι (*homiliai*), "communication, company," here used in the plural, denotes "a close association of persons," particularly those with whom one chooses to be involved.[240] It connotes any group of associates, but when modified by the adjective κακαί (*kakai*), "corrupt, bad," it refers to a clique or gang and, more especially, to a group that deliberately excludes others.[241] The word implies a reciprocal relationship in which all associates participate and, thereby—when the influence is bad—it really corrupts a person.[242] The noun ἤθη (*ēthē*), in the plural, "manners, morals," denotes wide-spread custom or usage,[243] while the adjective χρηστά (*chrēsta*), "good," denotes that which meets a high standard of moral quality.[244] Together they refer to good character and high moral behavior expressed in a Christian lifestyle.[245] The verb φθείρω (*phtheirō*), "corrupt," points to that which causes harm by corruption or ruin and, in a moral sense, makes one depraved.[246] Paul is, once again, warning his readers to watch who their associates are. In this case, he is pointing to the antiresurrection party, whose beliefs threaten to corrupt the very framework of the gospel. He hints at the idea that, for those who listen to these detractors, they open the doors to a life of depravity.

15:34 *Awake to righteousness, and sin not / Come to your senses as you should and stop sinning:* The verb ἐκνήφω (*eknēpho*) means literally "to become sober," but here Paul uses the imperative figuratively to mean "come to your senses."[247] A bit of a sting still remains because there is a hint that these people have been exhibiting the same low level of reasoning power as a drunk. The adverb δικαίως (*dikaiōs*) denotes doing what is proper or right.[248] Modifying ἐκνήφω (*eknēpho*), "awake," it connotes doing what is proper or correct and is translated "as you should" in our Rendition. The verb ἁμαρτάνω (*hamartanō*), "to sin" denotes committing a wrong, often with the nuance of doing so against God's moral law.[249] Both imperatives are continuous presents and, therefore, denote continuing in

240. BDAG, 705.

241. Thiselton, *First Epistle*, 1254.

242. BDAG, 705; Louw-Nida, §34.1.

243. BDAG, 435.

244. BDAG, 1090.

245. Barrett, *First Epistle*, 367; Thiselton, *First Epistle*, 1254.

246. BDAG, 1054; Louw-Nida, §88.266.

247. BDAG, 307.

248. Louw-Nida, §§66.5; 88.12.

249. BDAG, 49–50; Louw-Nida, §88.289.

an action. Paul's admonition is, therefore, twofold: first they are to wake up to their dangerous condition, that is, come to their senses and stay that way, and second, they are to stop doing wrong and do right.[250] In other words, they are to leave sin alone.[251]

for some have not the knowledge of God / Some, you see, have no knowledge of God: The pronoun τινες (*tines*), "some," refers to certain individuals who are at the seat of the Church's problems in Corinth; these are the agitators who push their own agenda. The noun ἀγνωσία (*agnōsia*), "ignorance," connotes a lack of spiritual discernment and an almost deliberate failure to understand what is presented.[252] The conjunction γάρ (*gar*), "for," is important here. It functions as a marker of clarification, allowing Paul to make very clear the source of the problems the Corinthian branch is facing. To stress that point, our Rendition translates it as "you see."[253] It is because these individuals lack a correct understanding of God and his ways that they can hold the position they do.

I speak this to your shame / I am saying this to your shame!: Paul repeats a sentiment he has already expressed in 6:5. The noun ἐντροπή (*entropē*), "shame," in the very honor-bound society of ancient Corinth, carried a very sharp sting.[254] It implied a humiliating disgrace that boarded on a deep contemptibility. These people had brought this stain upon themselves through their willingness to follow those who did not have a correct understanding of God and whose ideas Paul brands as foolishness (15:36).

Analysis and Summary

Debate over whether some of these passages should be taken literally or figuratively—like Paul's life being in danger daily and baptism for the dead—has raged from the beginning of the second century into the present. But the solution, largely overlooked, is found in the function of these verses. Paul is not simply countering the notion of those who reject the idea of a corporeal Resurrection but the implication that the witness of Paul and the other missionaries is a lie. He is particularly upset by the implication that vicarious work for the dead is, therefore, a useless exercise. Since the heart of Christianity—the reality of its history, doctrine, ordinances, and

---

250. Thiselton, *First Epistle,* 1255–56.
251. As the phrase is translated in the NJB.
252. BDAG, 14; Louw-Nida, §32.7.
253. BDAG, 189.
254. BDAG, 341; Louw-Nida, §25.195.

message—all center on the reality of the Resurrection, to deny that reality is to deny the truth of the gospel message.[255]

Verse 15:29 serves as a rejoinder in which Paul looks to the practice of vicarious baptism for the dead. His point is that the practice makes no sense at all if there is no resurrection. The third-person plural "they" suggests that the practice was not being done at that time in Corinth. That Paul briefly mentions it shows, however, that it was well-known to them.[256] "Paul was not writing to them about a new doctrine," noted Elder Pratt, "but about one which they understood and practiced, and he tried to prove to them the nature of the resurrection and that such a principle as the resurrection was true, from the very fact that they were practicing baptism for those who were dead, in order that they might receive a more glorious resurrection."[257] Elder Pratt also said that "it was a strong argument that Paul brought forward, and one that the Corinthians well understood. . . . [He used it] to show that the dead would have a resurrection, and that baptism or immersion in water, a being buried in and the coming forth out of the water, was a simile of the resurrection from the dead."[258]

President Hunter observed that Paul's "is a challenging question. Why are you performing vicarious baptisms for those who are dead if there is no resurrection? History bears out the facts of the practice of baptizing for those who had died without the benefit of this ordinance. . . . There would be no sense in such ordinances except there be a resurrection. Nothing matters if there is not a resurrection; everything would end in the darkness of death. Paul then quotes Isaiah: '. . . let us eat, and drink; for to morrow we die' (1 Cor. 15:32). Only a person of atheistic beliefs could sink to such depths of irreverence, but the reality of a resurrection gives hope; it is uplifting, a joy to the righteous."[259]

To further push his point, Paul mentions the dangers he was in "daily" (καθ᾽ ἡμέραν, *kath' hēmeran*) but which the hope of the Resurrection gives him boldness to face (15:30–31). "If there is no resurrection," pointed out an LDS scholar, "there is no purpose or sense to the sufferings or persecutions endured by the Apostles and saints in this life."[260]

---

255. Holzapfel and Wayment, *Making Sense,* 363.

256. Holzapfel and Wayment, *Making Sense,* 364. Zech. 9:11 may be a foreshadowing of the practice.

257. Orson Pratt, in *JD,* 16:297.

258. Orson Pratt, in *JD,* 15:51–52.

259. Howard W. Hunter, in CR, April 1969, 135–39.

260. Sperry, *Paul's Life and Letters,* 129.

In 15:33–34, Paul reaches the theological center not only of the whole chapter but of the entire epistle. Here we find the hinge of his argument. It swings on one word, ἀγνωσία (*agnōsia*), "ignorance." As noted above, the Corinthian "strong" had prided themselves in having a superior spirituality (πνευματικός, *pneumatikos*) and knowledge (γνῶσις, *gnōsis*). Here Paul attacks that attitude by using a wordplay with *agnosia*. The noun connotes the darkened state in which all the Saints lived before finding Christianity,[261] but he hints that some never left it. Therefore, rather than having superior spirituality and knowledge, these people were no better than the heathens.[262] Paul knows that knowing God and comprehending his purpose and power holds the key to meeting all the objections concerning the Resurrection.[263] Further, he understands that acceptance of this doctrine promotes a high moral lifestyle, a way of life some of the Saints desperately needed to follow.

The key to the unity so lacking among the Corinthian Saints and the answer to nearly all the questions they asked and arguments they raised was a true knowledge of God. If they had only known his character, attributes, sovereignty, power, grace, purposes, and methods the whole mess would never have occurred. The antiresurrection party did not seem to understand that God is the one who has the power to organize, orchestrate, give life—both mortal and immortal, both physical and spiritual—and bring exaltation. That Paul calls shame upon them shows the enormity of their position and undercuts their notions of superiority in either spirituality or knowledge.

The Savior had made it abundantly clear that "this is life eternal, that they might know thee the only true God, and Jesus Christ, whom thou hast sent" (John 17:3).[264] For both the Savior and Paul, the linchpin of the gospel is an accurate knowledge of God. The verb γινώσκω (*ginōskō*), "to know," often indicates a relationship between the person and object and suggests that the thing known has value or importance to the knower. Therefore, the verb does not connote knowing *about* something, but actually having

---

261. This has been determined by lexicographical work on ἀγνωσίαν ἔχειν (*agnōsian echein*). See Edwards, *Commentary*, 430.

262. Thiselton, *First Epistle*, 1256.

263. Barth, *Resurrection of the Dead*, 17–18, 113, 127, 179, 189–97.

264. The verb γινώσκω (*ginōskō*), "to know," is in the subjunctive mood here and, "in this respect answers the question *What?*" namely, what constitutes eternal life. Wallace, *Greek Grammar*, 475.

a relationship with it.[265] In this instance, it is the person who, in order to have eternal life, must have a personal relationship with God that he or she highly values. The road to this relationship and true knowledge begins with faith in Christ, the Greek word πίστις (*pistis*) implies not just believing in him but doing his will, a will that reflects that of the Father as well. "If any man will do his [God's] will, he shall know of the doctrine," pointed out the Savior, "whether it be of God, or whether I speak of myself" (John 7:17).

To have that faith in him, three things are necessary. The "Lectures on Faith" lists these requirements: "First, the idea that he actually exists; Secondly, a *correct* idea of his character, perfections, and attributes; Thirdly, an actual knowledge that the course of life which one is pursuing is according to His will."[266] Some of the Corinthian Saints lacked this *correct* idea and, thereby, introduced heresy among the branches. As a result, their lives did not conform to Christian standards and the Spirit could not confirm that their lives conformed to God's will. The product was a misplaced faith that leads neither to life nor a Christian lifestyle. It became necessary, then, for Paul to teach these people about God as he addresses the logical conceivability of the Resurrection and the nature of the resurrected body.

265. Rudolf Bultmann, "γινώσκω, γνῶσις, ἐπιγινώσκω, ἐπίγνωσις," in *TDNT,* 1:689–714.
266. "Lecture 3," in Dahl and Tate, *Lectures on Faith in Historical Perspective,* 65.

Excursus on the Ancient Practice of Vicarious Baptism in Behalf of the Dead

One of the more misunderstood practices of the LDS Church by those not of the faith is the ordinance of baptisms for the dead. While most Christian denominations do not practice this, Latter-day Saints see the ordinance as one that is solidly based on scripture and logically consistent with the love and mercy of God. On August 15, 1840, Joseph Smith spoke at the funeral of Seymour Brunson and read large portions of 1 Corinthians 15.[267] During the discourse he introduced the doctrine of baptism for the dead. It is of note that he did this in the context of a funeral speech and that he positioned the practice of baptism for the dead in the context of an entire scriptural chapter concerning the Resurrection. The Prophet made the point that at that time some of the Saints in Corinth were very aware of the practice of baptizing for the dead and that, therefore, they would have found Paul's reasoning very persuasive.

It is of note, however, that the LDS doctrine grows out of but one sentence in the New Testament, 1 Corinthians 15:29, and even that reference is in passing. Paul made his reference in the context of showing how either belief or unbelief in the Resurrection affects how people live their lives.[268] For effect, he used a rhetorical question, "Otherwise, what are those who are baptized on behalf of the dead doing?" (Rendition). The question draws attention to a practice that anticipates a corporeal Resurrection. This brief mention of the practice, unfortunately, tells us nothing about how or where the ordinance was done. It does, however, tell us "why," that is, in anticipation of the Resurrection. Paul's mention does confirm that the practice was so well-known that it needed no elaboration. As an LDS scholar observed:

> There is some evidence, in addition to the statement in 1 Corinthians 15:29, that proxy baptism for the dead was practiced among and by early Christians. Indeed, in the iconography, in the typology, and in the baptismal instruction of the early church fathers one may discern at least two different sorts of initiation: one through water baptism, and the other through certain initiatory oblations and anointings and baptism for the dead. . . .
>
> That men and women are privileged to "go through" each and all of the patterns and ordinances for and in behalf of their deceased families and

---

267. Ehat and Cook, *Words of Joseph Smith,* 49.
268. Thiselton, *First Epistle,* 1240.

others is unusual in contemporary religious practice. But, again, the proxy and representational ideas are not at the periphery of early Jewish and Christian practice; they are at the core.[269]

Because of its implications on theology and particularly soteriology, it is not surprising that the verse has generated a large amount of scholarly research, interpretations, and debate, especially outside of the Church. The concept of baptism for the dead simply does not align with mainstream Christian theology. But they cannot just ignore it. Their problem is, in part, that Paul refers to a practice that is mentioned nowhere else in the Bible and, therefore, cannot be elucidated. And further, he does not explicitly condemn it, suggesting it was among the accepted Christian practices.

Such a practice does go against certain aspects of Christian dogma but the rub is that it does not make sense for Paul to use a practice that he would consider heretical in order to support sound doctrine. The problem has forced some theologians and scholars to insist that this practice must really refer to something besides proxy baptisms. This insistence has resulted in a plethora of different interpretations passed down from various authorities. Among these are such notables as Martin Luther and John Calvin. Both of these sought to interpret this verse so as not to interfere with established theology. Their work has laid the foundation upon which others have built.[270] Some of the alternate explanations force an interpretation on the Greek phrase "βαπτιζόμενοι ὑπὲρ τῶν νεκρῶν" (*baptizomenoi hyper tōn nekrōn*) differently than its clear meaning. The phrase reads literally "those baptized on behalf of the dead people." Some, however, say that "the dead" refers to people who are on their deathbed, or, more figuratively, to those suffering in mortal sins. Others suggest that baptism refers symbolically to martyrdom or, more mundanely, to mere bodily washings.

---

269. Truman G. Madsen, "The Temple and the Restoration," in *Temple in Antiquity: Ancient Records and Modern Perspectives,* ed. Truman G. Madsen (Salt Lake City: Deseret Book, 2010), 12. See also Roger James Adams, "Iconography of Early Christian Initiation," Church Educational System Special Projects, unpublished manuscript, 1977, n.p.; Hugh Nibley, *Mormonism and Early Christianity,* vol. 4 of The Collected Works of Hugh Nibley (Salt Lake City: Deseret Book; Provo, Utah: F.A.R.M.S., 1987), 100–167; Bernard Foschini, "'Those Who Are Baptized for the Dead': 1 Cor 15:29," *Catholic Biblical Quarterly* 12 (1950): 260–76, 379–88; 13 (1951): 46–78, 172–98, 276–83.

270. For an extensive analysis of various interpretations, see Thiselton, *First Epistle,* 1242–49. Fee, *First Epistle,* 762, notes that there are at least forty different attempts to find a solution.

Others suggest alterative meaning to the preposition ὑπέρ (*hyper*), "in behalf of," such as "out of concern for." And the list goes on.[271]

Many scholars, however, agree that those who "are baptized for the dead" were actually performing vicarious work in their behalf.[272] As one non-LDS scholar noted, "This reading [that the verse refers to vicarious baptisms] is such a plain understanding of the Greek text that no one would ever have imagined the various alternatives were it not for the difficulties involved."[273] Another scholar noted, "The explanation of vicarious or proxy baptism remains the most plausible, even though its meaning is not fully clear."[274] Admittedly, that some kind of work for the dead was going on among the early Saints tells the reader nothing about precisely who was doing it and how it was done, but it does tell us why—in anticipation of a corporeal Resurrection.[275]

Going outside the New Testament to try to find references to vicarious baptisms for the dead also yields little useful information. One early Christian writer, Tertullian, mentions that the Marcionites practiced vicarious baptisms. That is not much help since they were a heretical sect.[276] Other early Christian writings seem to hint at dead spirits receiving some type of baptism, but the connections are vague at best with one exception.[277] One source points strongly to an early Christian belief in vicarious baptisms. It is *The Shepherd of Hermas*. In that work we find this statement: "These Apostles, and the teachers who had proclaimed the name of the Son of God, after they had fallen asleep in [the] power and faith of the Son of God preached likewise to the dead; and they gave them the seal of the preaching. They accordingly went down with them into the water and came out again. But although they went down while they were alive and came up alive, those who had fallen asleep before them went down dead, but came out again living; for it was through these that they were made alive, and learned the name of the Son of God."[278] While of course there may be various ways to

271. Thiselton, *First Epistle*, 1240–42; White, "Baptized on Account of the Dead," 488.

272. See Fitzmyer, *First Corinthians*, 578–80; Fee, *First Epistle*, 766.

273. Fee, *First Epistle*, 764.

274. Fitzmyer, *First Corinthians*, 580.

275. Fee, *First Epistle*, 767.

276. David L. Paulsen and Brock M. Mason, "Baptism for the Dead in Early Christianity," *Journal of the Book of Mormon and Other Restoration Scripture* 19, no. 2 (2010): 32.

277. See Paulsen, "Baptism for the Dead," 33–42, for examples and analysis of the sources.

278. *Herm. Sim.* 3.9.16, as quoted in Nibley, *Mormonism and Early Christianity*, 121–22.

interpret the figurative language, it does appear that the author was alluding to certain people (those who went down and came up alive) performing baptisms for others (those who before went down dead, but came out living).[279] While the text does not conclusively state that there were some who believed it right to perform vicarious baptisms for the dead in the early Church, it remains a distinct possibility. In a detailed and well-documented study of the evidence for posthumous work for the dead among early Christians, Jeffrey A. Trumbower notes that for orthodox Christianity, "belief in salvation for the faithful has usually meant non-salvation for others."[280] However there are notable exceptions to this general principle among early Christians, and "the principle itself was slow to develop and not universally accepted in the Christian movement's first four hundred years."[281]

Thankfully, Latter-day Saints are not dependent on scanty ancient evidence for information and justification for the practice of vicarious baptisms for the dead but on revelation from God.[282] For Latter-day Saints, the doctrine and principle behind the necessity of proxy baptisms resolves a thorny issue of Christianity. It provides the key for solving the soteriological problem of evil. This problem stems from three apparently true statements that are seemingly irreconcilable: First, that God loves all His children and desires the salvation of all (John 3:16–17; 2 Ne. 26:33); second, salvation can only come through Christ Jesus (Acts 4:12; 2 Ne. 31:21); third, there are billions of people who have lived without any knowledge of Jesus Christ and hence were unable to learn of and, therefore, have a chance to follow him.[283] The third point is even more pressing for Latter-day Saints because they believe that salvation is partly dependent on taking part in ordinances administered by those who possess proper priesthood authority, which was restored only in 1830 after nearly two thousand years of apostasy. Since the third point is fairly indisputable, it appears that either billions of people are damned for all eternity through no choice of their own or that one does not need to have faith in Jesus Christ to be saved. Neither option is consistent with scripture. However, the principle behind

---

279. Nibley, *Mormonism and Early Christianity*, 122; Paulsen, "Baptism for the Dead," 39.

280. Jeffrey A. Trumbower, *Rescue for the Dead: The Posthumous Salvation of Non-Christians in Early Christianity* (Oxford: Oxford University Press, 2001), 3.

281. Trumbower, *Rescue for the Dead*, 3.

282. Paulsen, "Baptism for the Dead," 23.

283. Paulsen, "Baptism for the Dead," 22.

vicarious baptisms for the dead shows how those who died without knowledge of Christ can be saved.

The key point that solves this soteriological problem is that there is a way whereby those who have died can learn of the gospel. That position is not without scriptural support. In 1 Peter 4:6, it states that "for this cause was the gospel preached also to them that are dead, that they might be judged according to men in the flesh, but live according to God in the spirit." This book makes another reference to the missionary work among departed spirits, stating that Christ "went and preached unto the spirits in prison" (1 Pet. 3:19). While these scriptures also have copious amounts of scholarship that debate their meaning, there are those who insist that these verses show that there is a system in place whereby God provides for the salvation of the dead.[284] As Origen stated, "We declare that even while in his physical body he [Jesus] persuaded not just a few people, but so many that they plotted against him because of the number of those who were persuaded. And also as a disembodied soul he met together with other disembodied souls and converted to his gospel those among them who were willing, or those whom he saw, for reasons only he himself knew, to be better adapted to such a course."[285] Although this belief was prevalent and accepted among early Christianity, later Christian authors, especially during the Protestant reformation, chose to reject it with the result that today it is not present among most Christian denominations.[286]

Through modern-day revelation, the Latter-day Saints have gained a clear understanding of how salvation of the dead works. As early as 1836 Joseph Smith learned that "all who have died without a knowledge of this gospel, who would have received it if they had been permitted to tarry, shall be heirs of the celestial kingdom of God" (D&C 137:7). This verse shows that God does not automatically damn those who did not have access to the gospel, but he has somehow provided a way for them to hear and accept or reject it, namely by having the Savior bring the message

---

284. See Nibley, *Mormonism and Early Christianity*, 101–21. Also David L. Paulsen, Roger D. Cook, and Kendel J. Christensen, "The Harrowing of Hell: Salvation for the Dead in Early Christianity," *Journal of the Book of Mormon and Other Restoration Scripture* 19, no. 1 (2010): 56–77.

285. Origen, *Against Celsus* 2.43, in Migne, *Patrologia Graeca*, 11:864–65, translation by author. Also quoted in Nibley, *Mormonism and Early Christianity*, 120; English translation in *Ante-Nicene Fathers*, 4:448.

286. Paulsen, "Harrowing of Hell," 68–70.

to them (1 Pet. 3:19) so that they might "be judged" (1 Pet. 4:6). A modern revelation through President Joseph F. Smith gives further light on Christ's visit to the dead. It states that the Savior selected righteous spirits and authorized them to "carry the light of the gospel to them that were in darkness, even to all the spirits of men" (D&C 138:30). Those spirits who choose to repent and obey God's laws will be redeemed and receive part in the resurrection of the just (D&C 138:58).

The caveat, nonetheless, remains that baptism is still necessary (John 3:5; 3 Ne. 11:33–34). Therefore, in order for the dead to receive their salvation, the living must do vicarious baptisms for them (D&C 128:18; 138:33–34). This baptism does not automatically ensure the salvation of these souls. They must still accept the Lord as their Savior, repent, and follow his will.[287] Vicarious baptism does allow them the choice to accept or reject the opportunity it provides. While it is not exactly clear how vicarious baptisms work, it is analogous to the vicarious work the Savior has done for all.[288] In some way not fully understood, he suffered for all so that they need not suffer provided they have faith in him. If God has authorized Christ's suffering to be sufficient to pay the price of sin for humankind, God can authorize that vicarious baptisms are sufficient for those who are unable to be baptized while they were alive. As it was with Paul, the practice in these last days not only presages the Resurrection but also shows how all can come forth to the immortal glory for which they have prepared themselves.

---

287. Anderson, *Understanding Paul*, 410.
288. Howard W. Hunter, "Elijah the Prophet," *Ensign* 1 (December 1971): 70–72.

THE LOGICAL CONCEIVABILITY OF THE RESURRECTION AND THE NATURE OF THE RESURRECTED BODY (15:35–50)

Greek Text

35 Ἀλλὰ ἐρεῖ τις· Πῶς ἐγείρονται οἱ νεκροί, ποίῳ δὲ σώματι ἔρχονται; 36 ἄφρων, σὺ ὃ σπείρεις, οὐ ζῳοποιεῖται ἐὰν μὴ ἀποθάνῃ· 37 καὶ ὃ σπείρεις, οὐ τὸ σῶμα τὸ γενησόμενον σπείρεις ἀλλὰ γυμνὸν κόκκον εἰ τύχοι σίτου ἤ τινος τῶν λοιπῶν· 38 ὁ δὲ θεὸς δίδωσιν αὐτῷ σῶμα καθὼς ἠθέλησεν, καὶ ἑκάστῳ τῶν σπερμάτων ἴδιον σῶμα. 39 οὐ πᾶσα σὰρξ ἡ αὐτὴ σάρξ, ἀλλὰ ἄλλη μὲν ἀνθρώπων, ἄλλη δὲ σὰρξ κτηνῶν, ἄλλη δὲ σὰρξ πτηνῶν, ἄλλη δὲ ἰχθύων. 40 καὶ σώματα ἐπουράνια, καὶ σώματα ἐπίγεια· ἀλλὰ ἑτέρα μὲν ἡ τῶν ἐπουρανίων δόξα, ἑτέρα δὲ ἡ τῶν ἐπιγείων. 41 ἄλλη δόξα ἡλίου, καὶ ἄλλη δόξα σελήνης, καὶ ἄλλη δόξα ἀστέρων, ἀστὴρ γὰρ ἀστέρος διαφέρει ἐν δόξῃ.

42 Οὕτως καὶ ἡ ἀνάστασις τῶν νεκρῶν. σπείρεται ἐν φθορᾷ, ἐγείρεται ἐν ἀφθαρσίᾳ· 43 σπείρεται ἐν ἀτιμίᾳ, ἐγείρεται ἐν δόξῃ· σπείρεται ἐν ἀσθενείᾳ, ἐγείρεται ἐν δυνάμει· 44 σπείρεται σῶμα ψυχικόν, ἐγείρεται σῶμα πνευματικόν. Εἰ ἔστιν σῶμα ψυχικόν, ἔστιν καὶ πνευματικόν. 45 οὕτως καὶ γέγραπται· Ἐγένετο ὁ πρῶτος ἄνθρωπος Ἀδὰμ εἰς ψυχὴν ζῶσαν· ὁ ἔσχατος Ἀδὰμ εἰς πνεῦμα ζῳοποιοῦν. 46 ἀλλ᾽ οὐ πρῶτον τὸ πνευματικὸν ἀλλὰ τὸ ψυχικόν, ἔπειτα τὸ πνευματικόν. 47 ὁ πρῶτος ἄνθρωπος ἐκ γῆς χοϊκός, ὁ δεύτερος ἄνθρωπος ἐξ οὐρανοῦ. 48 οἷος ὁ χοϊκός, τοιοῦτοι καὶ οἱ χοϊκοί, καὶ οἷος ὁ ἐπουράνιος, τοιοῦτοι καὶ οἱ ἐπουράνιοι· 49 καὶ καθὼς ἐφορέσαμεν τὴν εἰκόνα τοῦ χοϊκοῦ, φορέσομεν καὶ τὴν εἰκόνα τοῦ ἐπουρανίου.

50 Τοῦτο δέ φημι, ἀδελφοί, ὅτι σὰρξ καὶ αἷμα βασιλείαν θεοῦ κληρονομῆσαι οὐ δύναται, οὐδὲ ἡ φθορὰ τὴν ἀφθαρσίαν κληρονομεῖ. [SBLGNT]

King James Version

35 But some man will say, How are the dead raised up? and with what body do they come? 36 Thou fool, that which thou sowest is not quickened, except it die: 37 And that which thou sowest, thou sowest not that body that shall be, but bare grain, it may chance of wheat, or of some other grain: 38 But God giveth it a body as it hath pleased him, and to every seed his own body. 39 All flesh is not the same flesh: but there is one kind

New Rendition

35 But someone will say, "How is it possible that the dead are raised? With what kind of a body do they come forth?" 36 How foolish! What you sow does not come to life unless it dies. 37 And what you are sowing is not the body which will be produced, but a bare seed, perhaps of wheat or something else. 38 But God gives it a body just as he intended, and each kind of seed has its own body. 39 Not all physical bodies are the same,

of flesh of men, another flesh of beasts, another of fishes, and another of birds. 40 There are also celestial bodies, and bodies terrestrial: but the glory of the celestial is one, and the glory of the terrestrial is another. 41 There is one glory of the sun, and another glory of the moon, and another glory of the stars: for one star differeth from another star in glory. 42 So also is the resurrection of the dead. It is sown in corruption; it is raised in incorruption: 43 It is sown in dishonour; it is raised in glory: it is sown in weakness; it is raised in power: 44 It is sown a natural body; it is raised a spiritual body. There is a natural body, and there is a spiritual body. 45 And so it is written, The first man Adam was made a living soul; the last Adam was made a quickening spirit. 46 Howbeit that was not first which is spiritual, but that which is natural; and afterward that which is spiritual. 47 The first man is of the earth, earthy: the second man is the Lord from heaven. 48 As is the earthy, such are they also that are earthy: and as is the heavenly, such are they also that are heavenly. 49 And as we have borne the image of the earthy, we shall also bear the image of the heavenly. 50 Now this I say, brethren, that flesh and blood cannot inherit the kingdom of God; neither doth corruption inherit incorruption.

rather, humans have one kind of physical body, animals another, birds another, and fish yet another. 40 There are also heavenly bodies and earthly bodies. Now the glory of heavenly bodies is one kind, but the glory of earthly bodies is a different kind. 41 One is the glory of the sun, another the glory of the moon, and another the glory of the stars, for one star differs in glory from another star. 42 So too is the resurrection of the dead. It is sown as something perishable, it is raised as something imperishable. 43 It is sown in dishonor, it is raised in glory. It is sown in weakness, it is raised in strength. 44 It is sown as a natural body, it is raised as a spiritual body. If there is a natural body, there is also a spiritual body. 45 Thus it is also written, "The first man, Adam, became a living soul," The last "Adam" became a life-giving spirit. 46 And the spiritual was not the first, but the natural, then the spiritual. 47 The first man is from the earth, made of dust. The second man is from heaven. 48 Like the earthly man, so also are those who are earthly, and like the heavenly man, so also are those who are heavenly. 49 And just as we have borne the likeness of the earthly man, we will also bear the likeness of the heavenly man. 50 Now this is what I mean, brothers and sisters, that flesh and blood cannot inherit the kingdom of God, neither can the perishable inherit that which is imperishable.

Translation Notes and Comments

15:35 *But some man will say, How are the dead raised up? and with what body do they come? / But someone will say, "How is it possible that the dead are raised? With what kind of a body do they come forth?":* The interrogative adverb πῶς (*pōs*), "how," carries the force of "how is it possible."[289] It is generally used in such a way that a person "can question an assumption and then reject it."[290] Thus, the first question asks how can such a thing as the Resurrection be? In the second question, the noun σῶμα (*sōma*) can designate the body of a human being, an animal, or a plant.[291] The pronoun ποῖος (*poios*) asks the question, "what kind of,"[292] and the verb ἔρχομαι (*erchomai*) means "to come" or "to appear" and refers to what will arise from the grave. Paul carefully poses their questions about the Resurrection so that he can now give a clear answer to them.

15:36 *Thou fool, that which thou sowest is not quickened, except it die / How foolish! What you sow does not come to life unless it dies:* The adjective ἄφρων (*aphrōn*) refers to both ignorance and foolishness with emphasis on the latter. Though it could be translated as in the KJV, that weakens the force of Paul's exclamation. The Apostle is not addressing moral obliquity but the basic stupidity of the question.[293] With the use of the word σπείρω (*speirō*), "to sow," Paul picks up the imagery of the field. The Savior had already used the analogy (John 12:24) to show that if his disciples are willing to "die" for his cause (that is, surrender themselves to him), they will bear the rich harvest of eternal life. Paul, however, is not emphasizing the necessity of death but rather the transforming power that happens under the soil that brings forth a living, vibrant plant. This idea he applies to the Resurrection that will bring a great empowerment to the body.[294]

15:37 *And that which thou sowest, thou sowest not that body that shall be, but bare grain, it may chance of wheat, or of some other grain / And what you are sowing is not the body which will be produced, but a bare seed, perhaps of wheat or something else:*[295] To stress his point, Paul uses the rather rare articular future participle γενησόμενον (*genēsomenon*), "which will be produced." This form carries a very active and dynamic force showing something coming into being from a point of origin.[296] The

---

289. Thiselton, *First Epistle,* 1261.
290. Watson, "Paul's Rhetorical Strategy," 245 n. 50.
291. BDAG, 983–84.
292. BDAG, 843; the force of the dative here looks at the thing possessed. In this case, it asks what kind of body the resurrected will possess. Wallace, *Greek Grammar,* 151.
293. Findlay, "St. Paul's First Epistle," 934. Some commentators construe the pronoun σύ (*su*), "you," with the adjective, but this leaves the next phrase without a subject.
294. Barrett, *First Epistle,* 370.
295. The JST reads, "And that which thou sowest, thou sowest not that body which shall be, but grain, it may be of wheat, or some other." The change is negligible and does not affect the passage.
296. BDAG, 196–99.

noun κόκκον (*kokkon*) denotes the seed of any plant. By using the adjective γυμνόν (*gymnon*), "naked, bare," Paul stresses the idea of the simpleness and plainness of the seed that is sown compared with the complexity and bounty of the plant that comes forth.

15:38 *But God giveth it a body as it hath pleased him / But God gives it a body just as he intended:* In this verse, Paul gives the only answer to his detractor's question that he really can. The whole issue comes down to one fact: God, the creator, determines the nature of the body. Every living thing has the exact physical body that God planned and engineered for it. The present active verb δίδωσιν (*didōsin*), "to give," points to God's current active force in creation. The aorist verb ἠθέλησεν (*ethelēsen*), "to will" or "desire," does not denote what pleases him (the nuance in the KJV) but what is in accordance with his past decrees. Thus, it is translated as "intended" in our Rendition.[297]

and to every seed his own body / and each kind of seed has its own body: The noun σπέρμα (*sperma*) designates the source from which any living thing is propagated, thus it can refer not only the seed of a plant, but to the semen of any animal.[298] The nominal adjective ἑκάστῳ (*hekastō*), "every, each," is in the dative case, which expresses the possessor.[299] To catch this nuance, our Rendition supplies the verb "has." Paul is explaining how the "seed" of each type of living organism, whether plant or animal, will develop into a physical body that matches the organism that produced the seed.

15:39 *All flesh is not the same flesh / Not all physical bodies are the same:* Rather than using σῶμα (*sōma*) for "body," Paul now uses σάρξ (*sarx*) which, in its basic sense, describes the material that covers the bones of a human or animal body.[300] But it can also designate the physical body as a functioning entity.[301] It is in the latter sense that Paul is using it here, and so our Rendition translates it as "physical body." This sentence has no verb but, in Greek, the copula "to be" is often omitted, especially in the third person present singular ἐστί (*esti*), "is," and plural εἰσί (*eisi*), "are,"[302] and must be supplied in an English translation. It is the same case with the sentences in 15:40–41. Paul shifts his analogy from garden to barnyard and, in so doing, comes closer to the point he wishes to make.

297. Findlay, "St. Paul's First Epistle," 934.
298. BDAG, 937.
299. Smyth, *Greek Grammar,* §§1474–1480; Wallace, *Greek Grammar,* 149–51.
300. BDAG, 914.
301. BDAG, 915.
302. Smyth, *Greek Grammar,* §§944–45.

but there is one kind of flesh of men, another flesh of beasts, another of fishes, and another of birds / humans have one kind of physical body, animals another, birds another, and fish yet another: The noun σάρξ (*sarx*), "flesh," again helps Paul emphasize his point that, though all these bodies are physical, they are not all the same. The adjective ἄλλος (*allos*) has the basic meaning of "another," but here Paul uses it in the extended sense of "another kind" or "a different kind."[303] This nuance is reflected in our Rendition. Paul's point is that each species has a unique physical body that God fashioned for it and one that exactly fits its needs.[304]

15:40 *There are also celestial bodies, and bodies terrestrial / There are also heavenly bodies and earthly bodies:* Paul changes his emphasis from σάρξ (*sarx*), "flesh," back to σῶμα (*sōma*), "body." Just as there are differences in the physical bodies of mortal humans and animals, there are also differences between mortal bodies and resurrected bodies. The immortal, resurrected body Paul designates as ἐπουράνιος (*epouranios*), "heavenly." The Greek adjective describes something that is "associated with a locale for transcendent things and beings," that is, what is either heavenly or actually in heaven.[305] Mortal bodies he designates as ἐπίγειος (*epigeios*), "earthly." This adjective describes something that "is characteristic of the earth" and stands opposite that which is heavenly.[306] The KJV uses the adjectives "celestial" and "terrestrial," which are borrowed from Latin *caelestialis,* "heavenly," and *terrestrialis,* "earthly."

The JST adds a third type of body, "bodies telestial." The word "telestial" is not found in any dictionary. It does appear in section 76 of the Doctrine and Covenants, a revelation given in February 1832. It appears to be a neologism, perhaps combining the root "teles-" from the Greek noun τέλος (*telos*), "end," with the Latin adjectival ending "-(t)ialis," which is found in the words "celestial" and "terrestrial." Besides the JST and section 76, the only other scriptural passages where it is found is in D&C 88:21, 24, and 31.

but the glory of the celestial is one, and the glory of the terrestrial is another / Now the glory of heavenly bodies is one kind, but the glory of earthly bodies is a different kind: In the New Testament and the LXX,

---

303. BDAG, 46–47; the genitive here is attributive rather than possessive and, therefore, refers not to the flesh that belongs to a man or a beast, but rather indicates what they are composed of, thus, "beastly flesh" and "manly flesh." Wallace, *Greek Grammar,* 82, n. 31.

304. Findlay, "St. Paul's First Epistle," 935.

305. BDAG, 388.

306. BDAG, 368.

the noun δόξα (*doxa*), here translated "glory," has a very broad range of meanings.[307] Generally, it denotes "the condition of being bright or shining." In that nuance it refers to such diverse things as polished metals and stars.[308] It also denotes the magnificence of transcendent beings like God and angels.[309] More metaphorically, it refers to the honor or respect that someone derives from having a well-earned reputation.[310] But there is an even higher nuance, one that goes beyond respect to magnificent splendor based on outstanding and transcendent qualities.[311]

Paul's point is that, as there are different types of bodies so, too, there are different types of glories. He refers to just two, but the JST adds a third, the "telestial," in keeping with the addition first met in the beginning of this verse. Again, Paul contrasts resurrected bodies with mortal ones, insisting that they have entirely different kinds of glory or splendor.

15:41 *There is one glory of the sun, and another glory of the moon, and another glory of the stars: for one star differeth from another star in glory / One is the glory of the sun, another the glory of the moon, and another the glory of the stars, for one star differs in glory from another star:* Again, Paul plays on the idea of δόξα (*doxa*), "glory," but this time he applies it to astral bodies. In doing so, he suggests, as one scholar pointed out, that there is a "broad principle of dynamic diversified life in the resurrection mode of existence."[312] It is also likely that Paul has in mind three distinct sets of physical bodies that correspond to these glories. He himself had been caught up to what he calls "the third heaven" (2 Cor. 12:2). Therefore, Joseph Smith's adding a third kind of glory in 15:40 fits with Paul's model.[313]

Paul's terminology "glory of the sun" also calls to mind Matthew's account of the transfiguration of Christ where his face "did shine as the sun" (Matt. 17:2).

---

307. For the full semantic range, see Louw-Nida, §§1.15; 12.49; 14.49; 25.205; 33.357; 76.13; 79.18; 87.4, 23.

308. BDAG, 256–58.

309. BDAG, 257.

310. Louw-Nida, §12.49.

311. BDAG, 256–58; Gerhard Kittel and Gerhard von Rad, "δόξα," in *TDNT*, 2:233–53; Thiselton, *First Epistle*, 1273.

312. Thiselton, *First Epistle*, 1271.

313. Paul's own tripartite cosmological model may be seen in Philip. 2:9–11, which, relevantly, uses the identical words ἐπουρανίων (*epouraniōn*) "heavenly" and ἐπιγείων (*epigeiōn*) "earthly," while including a third, καταχθονίων (*katachthoniōn*), "under the earth, subterranean" (BDAG, 530), which corresponds rather nicely with Paul's tripartite division of heavenly glories in this verse. The JST seems to synthesize these two Pauline passages.

15:42 *So also is the resurrection of the dead. It is sown in corruption; it is raised in incorruption / So too is the resurrection of the dead. It is sown as something perishable, it is raised as something imperishable:* Paul continues his explanation of the difference between a mortal and an immortal body. The adverb οὕτως (*houtōs*), "so too," means "likewise" or "in the same way." The word presupposes and takes into consideration all that Paul has said in 15:37–41. Paul does an excellent job in developing the contrast between the two. The clauses in this verse and the next one have no stated subject and, therefore, "it" is supplied. Taking the entire section through 15:44 together, it is clear that Paul is not referring to the Resurrection but to bodies, both mortal and immortal. Paul uses the present passive verb σπείρομαι (*speiromai*), "to be sown," to describe what happens to the body with death.[314] Like a seed, it is buried, but like a seed, the intent is not to have it stay dead but rather to produce something alive and marvelous. The mortal body, which is ἐν φθορᾷ (*en phthora*), "in a perishable state,"[315] is buried/sown, but it will be resurrected ἐν ἀφθαρσίᾳ (*en aphtharsia*), "in an imperishable state."[316] For this reason, it will last forever. Further, as God did with mortal bodies so too he will do with immortal ones, providing for each person the exact kind of body that he or she needs for habitation and work in the next world that they have prepared themselves for.[317]

15:43 *It is sown in dishonour; it is raised in glory / It is sown in dishonor, it is raised in glory:* The noun ἀτιμία (*atimia*), "dishonor," denotes being in a position that has no honor or respect. In contrast, the noun δόξα (*doxa*) denotes a state that goes even beyond that of high respect to great honor and high esteem due to outstanding and transcendent qualities.[318] Because Paul places *atimia* opposite *doxa,* it suggests that, compared to what it will be, the earthly body is in a most lowly and humble state.

it is sown in weakness; it is raised in power / It is sown in weakness, it is raised in strength: The noun ἀσθενία (*asthenia*), "weakness," means just

314. BDAG, 936. Among other less popular views, quite a number of commentators see the sowing as referring to the whole of mortal existence because the body is in a state of corruption before it reaches the grave. For discussion, see Fitzmyer, *First Corinthians,* 594–95. That Paul uses the word in contrast to ἐγείρομαι (*egeiromai*), "to arise," as well as in the context of this section as a whole, suggests, however, he is referring specifically to death and burial.

315. BDAG, 1054–55.

316. BDAG, 155.

317. Findlay, "St. Paul's First Epistle," 936.

318. BDAG, 256–58; Gerhard Kittel and Gerhard von Rad, "δόξα," in *TDNT,* 2:233–53; Thiselton, *First Epistle,* 1273.

that, a highly limited ability to carry out a task.[319] It expresses Paul's acute awareness of the mortal body's limitations, that is, of its frailty, vulnerability, and constraints.[320] The noun δύναμις (*dynamis*), "power, strength," on the other hand, denotes an exceptional ability to complete a task.[321] It expresses not mere competency but an expansive capacity and full capability to do whatever is required.[322] In sum, the weakness of the human body disallows the soul from performing fully all that God intends while the resurrected body is completely capable of doing so.

15:44 *It is sown a natural body; it is raised a spiritual body / It is sown as a natural body, it is raised as a spiritual body:* Before the Resurrection, the body is sown σῶμα ψυχικόν (*sōma psychikon*), "a natural body," but with the Resurrection it is raised σῶμα πνευματικόν (*sōma pneumatikon*), "a spiritual body." The phrases show these two types of bodies are very different, but how? Earlier in this same epistle, Paul used these same two adjectives to describe a human being. He explains that ψυχικός ἄνθρωπος (*psychikos anthrōpos*), "a natural human being," is one who receives the spirit of the world (2:12) but does not receive the things of the spirit of God (2:14). On the other hand, a πνευματικὸς ἄνθρωπος (*pneumatikos anthrōpos*), "spiritual human being," is one who receives the things of the Spirit of God (2:14) and, through the power of that Spirit, is able to discern all things (2:15). Thus a spiritual body is a body that is filled with the Spirit of God, whereas a natural body is one that lacks that communion with the Spirit.[323]

In both instances it is of note that there is a σῶμα (*soma*), "body," at play. The noun, when applied to people, most often refers to the body as a whole.[324] By synecdoche, it can also refer to the "complete person" (Matt. 5:29; 6:22; Rom. 12:1; James 3:6; Rev. 18:13). The body, however, is not the complete person because he or she can exist without it (see 2 Cor. 12:2–3; Alma 40:11–14; D&C 138:11–24). Nonetheless, it is an essential component of the soul and, therefore, a person is not redeemed until both the eternal spirit and transformed body are permanently united in the Resurrection (D&C 88:14–16).[325]

---

319. BDAG, 142.

320. For example, see 1:18, 24: 2:4, 5; 4:9–10; 2 Cor. 11:30; 12:5; Thiselton, *First Epistle*, 1274.

321. BDAG, 262–63.

322. Louw-Nida, §§12.44; 74.1; 76.1; Thiselton, *First Epistle*, 1275.

323. BDAG, 1100; 837.

324. Louw-Nida, §§8.1; 9.8.

325. Eduard Schweizer and Friedrich Baumgärtel, "σῶμα, σωματικός, σύσσωμος," in *TDNT*, 7:1024–94.

There is a natural body, and there is a spiritual body / If there is a natural body, there is also a spiritual body: The KJV does not reflect the conditional nature of the Greek as does our Rendition. The conditional conjunction εἰ (*ei*), "if," indicates "the assumption of truth for the sake of argument."[326] Paul uses it to emphasize that if there is one kind of body then it is a matter of fact that there is another kind. One body is bound by earthly and worldly constraints while the other is not. Rather, it responds to the influences and powers of Deity.

15:45 *And so it is written, The first man Adam was made a living soul; the last Adam was made a quickening spirit / Thus it is also written, "The first man, Adam, became a living soul," The last "Adam" became a life-giving spirit:* In this clause, Paul paraphrases the last part of LXX Genesis 2:7, adding the adjective πρῶτος (*prōtos*), "first." In the LXX, the Hebrew הָאָדָם (*ha-'adam*), "the man," is replaced with τὸν ἄνθρωπον (*ton anthrōpon*), "the man." The majority of New Testament manuscripts read, "the man, Adam," although some leave out ἄνθρωπος (*anthrōpos*), "man."[327] In the Hebrew text, because *ha-'adam* has the definite article, it indicates that it is *not* a proper name and should thus be translated "the man/human being." The preposition εἰς (*eis*), "into," is not translated because it simply reflects the Septuagintal equivalent of the Hebrew לְ (*lĕ*), "to."

In this verse, Paul contrasts the difference between the first Adam and the last "Adam." It is of note in this instance that Christ is not the "second" Adam but the ἔσχατος (*exchatos*), "last" one. In Paul's model, Christ, like the first man, Adam, is representative of the whole race. As such, he is then the consummation and end of all that humans were meant to be.[328] The contrast is seen in the words Paul uses to describe the nature of each. The first Adam ἐγένετο (*egeneto*), "became," ψυχὴν ζῶσαν (*psychēn zōsan*), "a living soul." The last "Adam" became πνεῦμα ζωοποιοῦν (*pneuma zōopoioun*), "a life-giving spirit."[329] Paul's point is that the first Adam was given life, but the last "Adam" gives it. The contrast could not be more striking. One was dependent and receiving, the other independent and giving.[330]

---

326. Wallace, *Greek Grammar,* 451, 690.

327. For discussion see Christopher D. Stanley, *Paul and the Language of Scripture: Citation Techniques in the Pauline Epistle and in Contemporary Literature,* rev. ed. (Cambridge: Cambridge University Press, 1992), 208–9.

328. Findlay, "St. Paul's First Epistle," 938.

329. BDAG, 431–32; Louw-Nida, §23.92.

330. Bailey, *Mediterranean Eyes,* 466.

There is some overlap in the semantic domains of ψυχή (*psychē*) and πνεῦμα (*pneuma*) and their Hebrew equivalents, וֶפֶשׁ (*nepeš*) and רוּחַ (*rûaḥ*), respectively. The Greek noun *psychē* describes the "life, life-principle, [or] soul" of both animals and human beings as well as the "seat and center of the inner-human life," including "desires . . . feelings and emotions."[331] The Hebrew *nepeš* can refer to "throat," "neck," "breath," "a living being," "soul," "personality," and "life."[332] The Greek *pneuma* has the root sense of "air in movement, blowing, breathing," but in a more abstract sense, "that which animates or gives life to the body, . . . (life-)spirit" as well as "a part of human personality, spirit."[333] The Hebrew *rûaḥ* denotes a breeze, breath, wind, spirit, mind, intellect and spirit being.[334] A similar overlap in meaning exists in the English words "soul" and "spirit." Paul is using both of these terms, soul/*psyche* and spirit/*pneuma,* to describe the noncorporal element of a human being that is the essence of a person's identity and that animates and gives life to the inert matter of the physical body. The term "soul," as used here, should not be taken in the same sense as that in D&C 88:15, "the spirit and the body are the soul of man."

Paul's depiction of the Savior as a πνεῦμα ζωοποιοῦν (*pneuma zōopoioun*), "life-giving spirit," describes not only that noncorporeal being but also the essential portion of his being—his spirit—that is the most sensitive and responsive to the will of his Father. It also refers to Christ's divine power and influence termed "the light of Christ." It centers in him but is not confined to the limits of his body. Rather, it proceeds forth from him "to fill the immensity of space" and is the "light which is in all things, which giveth life to all things" (D&C 88:12–13). Since it is the life and light of the world (John 8:12; 3 Ne. 15:9), the Savior is constantly a life-giving spirit.[335]

Paul is also using the image of "Adam" in an allegorical sense to represent humankind before and after spiritual regeneration. He does this to contrast the two natures and emphasize again the great change that occurs upon resurrection. He explains this point in 15:47–48 (see below). The most important point of this verse, however, is not the contrast between the *psychē* and the *pneuma,* but between the need to receive life and the power to give it.

---

331. BDAG, 1098–99.
332. HAL, 712–13.
333. BDAG, 832–33.
334. HAL, 1198–200.
335. Dunford, "Light of Christ," in *EM,* 2:835.

15:46 *Howbeit that was not first which is spiritual, but that which is natural; and afterward that which is spiritual / And the spiritual was not the first, but the natural, then the spiritual:* The JST changes this verse to read, "Howbeit, that which is natural first, and not that which is spiritual; but afterwards, that which is spiritual." The change makes Paul's thought more clear, namely his point is that the spiritual aspect came after the natural aspect. He elaborates on this idea in the next two verses.

15:47 *The first man is of the earth, earthy / The first man is from the earth, made of dust:* The Apostle describes the first man as ἐκ γῆς (*ek gēs*), literally "from the earth," and χοϊκός (*choikos*), "earthly, made of earth/dust," referring to Genesis 2:7.[336] Paul's imagery, however, looks more to "Adam's" nature than his composition. The phrase emphasizes Adam's (and everyone else's) fragility, weakness, and—more especially—his impermanence. Adam, and others, will return to the dust from which they are made (Gen. 3:19).[337]

the second man is the Lord from heaven / The second man is from heaven: The textual variant for this clause is worth noting. The translation in the KJV came from a late manuscript. In that textual family, the noun κύριος (*kyrios*), "Lord" was added to the original. This appears to be a later scribal alteration supplied only for dogmatic reasons to counter the heretic Marcion.[338] It is neither necessary nor used in our Rendition.

The second "Adam," unlike the first, is ἐξ οὐρανοῦ (*ex ouranou*). The preposition ἐκ (*ek*), "from," in this context is a marker of origin pointing to the material that composes the "second man."[339] Therefore, the noun οὐρανός (*ouranos*), "heaven," does not refer to the dwelling place of God and angels but to the composition of those who dwell there, that is, they have a heavenly makeup.[340] That gives the "second man" a nature that is strong, powerful, and—most importantly—permanent.

---

336. Paul's statement is a paraphrase of the LXX. It appears that in order to make his point, Paul coined the word χοϊκός (*choikos*) because it is found in no Greek sources before his use. Eduard Schweizer, "χοϊκός," in *TDNT,* 9:472–79.

337. Thiselton, *First Epistle,* 1286.

338. Metzger, *Textual Commentary,* 501–2; Fitzmyer, *First Corinthians,* 599. Marcion developed a di-theistic approach to the Godhead based on his idea that there were two gods, a higher transcendent one and a lower world creator one. The scribal addition was designed to show that Jesus, the creator God, was also transcendent. For a discussion, see E. C. Blackman, *Marcion and His Influence* (Eugene, Ore.: Wipf and Stock Publishers, 2004).

339. BDAG, 295–98.

340. BDAG, 737–39.

15:48 *As is the earthy, such are they also that are earthy: and as is the heavenly, such are they also that are heavenly / Like the earthly man, so also are those who are earthly, and like the heavenly man, so also are those who are heavenly:* Based on 15:47, Paul's point here is clear—inheriting the same nature as the first man, all are fragile, weak, and impermanent. Conversely, through the Resurrection, inheriting the nature of the second man, the Saints will be strong, powerful, and permanent. How can this be done? Paul answered that question much earlier, testifying that "God hath both raised up the Lord, and will also raise up us by his own power" (6:14).

15:49 *And as we have borne the image of the earthy, we shall also bear the image of the heavenly / And just as we have borne the likeness of the earthly man, we will also bear the likeness of the heavenly man:* Paul pushes his point. As with 15:44, he uses logic to bolster his position. As the Christians have inherited a physical (ψυχικόν, *psychikon*) body from the first Adam, they will also inherit a spiritual (πνευματικόν, *pneumatikon*) body from the last Adam. The textual tradition varies on the mood of the verb φορέω (*phoreō*), literally "to wear."[341] Some have the future indicative φορέσομεν (*phoresomen*), "we shall wear the image," where others have the aorist subjective, "let us wear the image." Though uncertainty remains, our Rendition follows the SBLGNT and accepts the mood as indicative because the context seems to be didactic.[342]

Whatever the mood of the verb φορέω (*phoreō*), its meaning is clear. It denotes the habitual wearing, bearing, or carrying of something.[343] In this case, it is an εἰκών (*eikon*), "image," the noun denoting a living likeness to something. Given the context here, Paul is stressing that, to the degree that the Saints have inherited the image of earthy things, so, too, they shall the heavenly. The Corinthian Saints who are worried about the nature of the resurrected body should understand that as they inherited certain mortal characteristics from Adam, they will inherit immortal ones through Christ.[344]

15:50 *Now this I say, brethren, that flesh and blood cannot inherit the kingdom of God / Now this is what I mean, brothers and sisters, that flesh and blood cannot inherit the kingdom of God:* With this verse, Paul pushes the idea of the need for the Resurrection. Though the verb φημί

---

341. Louw-Nida, §49.11.
342. Metzger, *Textual Commentary,* 502.
343. BDAG, 1064.
344. Fitzmyer, *First Corinthians,* 599.

(*phēmi*) can mean simply "to say," it can have the sense of "I mean." It is used in this way to signal a clarification of a point that has been made.[345] The phrase σάρξ καὶ αἵμα (*sarx kai haima*), "flesh and blood," refers to the mortal body with all its frailty and weakness (compare Gal. 1:16; Matt. 16:17). Given its use elsewhere in the literature, it connotes no taint of sin, but rather an inability to be self-sustaining.[346] The phrase emphasizes the radical incompatibility between the earthly nature of the body and what it must become. It connotes the utter need for a severe transformation in order for the body to be prepared to enter the heavenly realm.[347]

neither doth corruption inherit incorruption / neither can the perishable inherit that which is imperishable: To stress his point, Paul supplies another difference between the mortal and immortal condition. He describes the mortal condition as φθορά (*phthora*), "corruption." The noun denotes, as noted in 15:42, that which has no permanence and is therefore perishable. The emphasis is on its destructible nature.[348] He describes the immortal condition, again as noted in 15:42, as ἀφθαρσία (*aphtharsia*). The noun denotes that which is not subject to decay or destruction and thus imperishable.[349] The two conditions sit opposite each other such that having one negates possessing the other.

Analysis and Summary

With 15:35, Paul begins another round of argument. It addresses the issue with which the antiresurrection party had the most trouble, the nature of the resurrected body. In essence they are saying, "We cannot conceive of such a thing. No one should be expected to believe what is inconceivable and illogical."[350] Their objection may have been influenced by beliefs held by certain Jews that the body will come out of the grave exactly as it went in with all the frailties and deformities it had in life.[351] It is also possible they rejected the idea that

---

345. BDAG, 1053.
346. Fitzmyer, *First Corinthians,* 603.
347. The phrase relates back to Jewish tradition. See LXX Sir. 14:18; 17:31; Philo, *Her.* 12§57. Robertson and Plummer, *Critical and Exegetical Commentary,* 376; Collins, *First Corinthians,* 573–74.
348. BDAG, 1054–55.
349. BDAG, 155.
350. See Robertson and Plummer, *Critical and Exegetical Commentary,* 368.
351. 2 *Bar.* 49:2; 50:1–2. For discussion of this view, see R. H. Charles, *Apocrypha and Pseudepigrapha of the Old Testament,* vol. 2: *Pseudepigrapha* (Oxford: Clarendon Press, 1913), 2:508, notes on 50–52.

the body would come out of the grave zombie-like, that is, as an animated rotting corpse.[352]

Through 15:36–39, the Apostle exposes as a fallacy the argument that a corporeal Resurrection is illogical and unintelligible. He does this with two refutations. With the first, he stresses that the body that goes into the grave is not the same one that comes out of the grave any more than a bulb is the tulip or an apple seed the whole tree (15:35–37). He does insist, however, that identity somehow remains. With the second, he emphasizes that the heart of the problem is the false understanding of God that is held by the members of the antiresurrection party. Paul's witness is that God, as creation itself testifies, is totally capable of creating the exact type of body for whatever conditions call for (15:38). Paul's point is that each person is given, with his new body, a new life. Both of these are gifts bestowed according to the will or intent (θέλω, *thelō*) of God.[353]

In 15:40–41, Paul uses yet another example to illustrate the vast differences between mortal and resurrected bodies. He uses the word δόξα (*doxa*), "glory." The word became associated with magnificence and carried the idea of greatness. From there it was an easy step to denote that which was bright, radiant, and shining.[354] Since the English word "splendor" catches the idea of both brilliance or luster and grandeur or magnificence, it nicely catches the range of Paul's meaning.[355] Paul's point in using the word is there is a stark contrast between the splendor one finds on the earth and that in the sky. What thing on earth can compete with the splendor of the sun? Nonetheless, earthly objects and persons of rank do, indeed, have their own splendor. Still, there can be great differences even between these. The source of all this glory, however, is God. It is he who gave bodies not only to animals and man but also to suns and planets. Paul's point is that if he can do all of that, why should anyone be concerned about his ability to fashion a body fit for resurrected souls.[356]

But there is another nuance of the word that needs mentioning. At its root, *doxa* denotes the respect, honor, or esteem held by an individual who has exhibited great concern for others.[357] Thus, in the Old Testament, it is not Jehovah's brute force, overwhelming power, and majesty that

---

352. Thiselton, *First Epistle*, 1217.
353. Compare Gen. 1:11; Conzelmann, *1 Corinthians*, 281.
354. BDAG, 256–58; Gerhard Kittel and Gerhard von Rad, "δόξα," in *TDNT*, 2:233–53.
355. Thiselton, *First Epistle*, 1269–70.
356. Robertson and Plummer, *Critical and Exegetical Commentary*, 371.
357. BDAG, 257–58.

constitutes his glory, but the selfless and gracious love that he bestows upon his people.[358] One of the highest expressions of that love is the Resurrection.

In 15:40, Joseph Smith added an additional component of the Resurrection. Not only are there celestial and terrestrial bodies, but there are also telestial bodies. The Prophet explained that "Paul ascended into the third heavens [2 Cor. 12:2], and he could understand the three principal rounds of Jacob's ladder—the telestial, the terrestrial, and the celestial glories or kingdoms."[359] In adding the idea of a third kingdom to Paul's writings, what Joseph Smith did was make the verse parallel with sun, moon, and stars and thereby link this scripture to a profound vision that he and Sidney Rigdon had experienced (for discussion, see "Excursus on the Three Degrees of Glory" below). When viewing Paul's writings in light of this vision, they seemed incomplete and so Joseph Smith was inspired to add what was needed.

That being said, the Greek text suggests that what Paul was willing to share was much more limited than what the Prophet did. That is not surprising since the Lord's technique is to "give unto the faithful line upon line, precept upon precept; and I will try you and prove you herewith" (D&C 98:12; compare D&C 128:21; Isa. 28:10).[360] Given the bitter doctrinal disputes the Corinthian letters reveal, these people were not ready for such meat (3:2) and therefore Paul could only hint at some ideas. To those living in the last days, however, the Lord has promised that he would reveal truths that have been "hid from before the foundation of the world."[361] One of those gems is, likely, found in Joseph Smith's vision of the three degrees of glory (see D&C 76).[362] Paul could have known these things based on a vision in which he learned by experience that there were three heavens (2 Cor. 12:2).

---

358. Thiselton, *First Epistle*, 1270.

359. Smith, *History of the Church*, 5:402.

360. Joseph Smith, in *History of the Church*, 5:387, taught, "The Lord deals with his children as a tender parent with a child, communicating light and intelligence and the knowledge of his ways as they can bear it." In much the same vain he taught, "It is not wisdom that we should have all knowledge at once presented before us: but that we should have a little at the time: that we can comprehend it." "History, 1838–1856, Volume C-1," 8 [addenda].

361. Smith, *History of the Church*, 5:424; compare 54:530. The Prophet taught that "God hath not revealed anything to Joseph, but what He will make known unto the Twelve, and even the least saint may know all things as fast as he is able to bear them."

362. The ideas presented in D&C 76 were so novel that a number of the Saints were disturbed, some to the point that they even left the Church. See Brigham Young, in *JD*, 16:42.

What Paul stresses in these verses, however, is that there are different types of physical bodies. One is earthly and mortal (terrestrial) while the other is heavenly and spiritual (celestial). The former we now possess and the latter we eventually will. But a subpoint is that "not all mankind will come forth in the same type of resurrected body, and their glory will differ as do the 'sun' and 'moon' and 'stars.'"[363]

In a series of parallel couplets, Paul contrasts mortal and immortal bodies (15:42–44). The earthly body is perishable, without honor, weak, and worldly while the heavenly is imperishable, radiant, powerful, and spiritual.[364] He does not distinguish between what glories the resurrected bodies will have but lists their common properties. It is important to note, however, that they all have a σῶμα (*soma*), "body." Paul at times identifies the earthbound and weak part of the human as σάρξ (*sarx*), "flesh" (15:39).[365] At the Resurrection, however, the *soma* is more than reconstituted *sarx,* for that is left behind. God, through the power of the Resurrection, will completely renovate the physical body such that it will be able to dwell in a new, completely different, and glorious mode of existence.

That Paul describes the Lord as πνεῦμα ζῳοποιοῦν (*pneuma zōopoioun*), "a life-giving spirit" (15:45, Rendition), does not preclude his having a corporeal body. Indeed, he describes Adam as a ψυχὴν ζῶσαν (*psychēn zōsan*), "a living soul," but there is no question he had a body at the time (see Gen. 2:7).

The central objection to the Resurrection held by some of Paul's detractors was that they believed more in a bodily resuscitation than in a resurrection. They did not understand that "the soul shall be restored to the body, and the body to the soul; yea, and every limb and joint shall be restored to its body; yea, even a hair of the head shall not be lost; but all things shall be restored to their proper and perfect frame" (Alma 40:23; compare Alma 11:42–44). Paul understood that God would "change our lowly body to be like [Christ's] glorious body" (Philip. 3:21, authors' translation). "Those who attain to the blessing of the first or celestial resurrection," taught President Young, "will be pure and holy, and perfect in body. Every man and woman that reaches to this unspeakable attainment will be as beautiful as

---

363. Holzapfel and Wayment, *Making Sense,* 365.

364. The physical bodies of the sons of perdition, however, do not share these qualities because they are all dependent on and generated by the δόξα (*doxa*), "glory," that one attained in mortality. Since the sons of perdition obtained no glory, their bodies will also be bereft of those qualities generated by it.

365. Though there are times he uses it as a synonym for σῶμα (*soma*). See 6:16, quoting Gen. 2:24; 2 Cor. 4:10–11.

the angels that surround the throne of God; . . . those of the first resurrection will be free from sin and from the consequences and power of sin."[366]

Of this Paul needed to convince the Saints. Each person is resurrected with the body to which she or he is entitled. According to modern revelation: "They who are not sanctified through the law which I have given unto you, even the law of Christ, must inherit another kingdom [than the celestial], even that of a terrestrial kingdom, or that of a telestial kingdom. For he who is not able to abide the law of a celestial kingdom cannot abide a celestial glory. And he who cannot abide the law of a terrestrial kingdom cannot abide a terrestrial glory. And he who cannot abide the law of a telestial kingdom cannot abide a telestial glory; therefore he is not meet for a kingdom of glory. Therefore he must abide a kingdom which is not a kingdom of glory" (D&C 88:21–24). Thus, the rewards in the Resurrection will range from those totally capable of receiving a fullness of glory to those who will be able to abide none. "Even as there is a difference between the flesh of men and beasts and fish and birds," noted Elder McConkie, "so there is a difference between celestial, terrestrial, and telestial bodies."[367] Each one, however, will be capable of doing what is required in its realm. Those, however, in the lower kingdoms will not have the same capabilities as those in the higher.

In 15:44, Paul refers to the resurrected body as a σῶμα πνευματικόν (*sōma pneumatikon*), "spiritual body." It is of note he did not call it a σῶμα τοῦ πνεύματος (*sōma tou pneumatos*), "a body of spirit," that is, one having no corporeal element. The Book of Mormon teaches that "this mortal body is raised to an immortal body, that is from death, even from the first death unto life, that they can die no more; their spirits uniting with their bodies, never to be divided; thus the whole becoming spiritual and immortal, that they can no more see corruption" (Alma 11:45). A spiritual body, noted Elder McConkie, is one that is "immortal, resurrected, or incorruptible . . . a body of flesh and bones, one in which body and spirit are inseparably connected, one not subject to physical pain, disease, or death."[368]

In 15:45, Paul continues to stress the vast differences between mortal and resurrected bodies. In doing so, he contrasts the first Adam with the last, that is, Jesus. The Apostle focuses on their respective differences so far as life is concerned. The first Adam had to receive it while the last "Adam"

---

366. Brigham Young, in *JD*, 10:24.
367. *DNTC*, 2:398.
368. *DNTC*, 2:402.

gives it. There was a reason the Savior could do so. In speaking of the mission of the Lord, John testified, "In him was life; and the life was the light of men" (John 1:4) and, therefore, "as many as received him, to them gave he power to become the sons [and daughters] of God" (John 1:12; compare John 10:10). To do this, the Father endowed the Son with life independent of his own. Jesus testified that "as the Father hath life in himself; so hath he given to the Son to have life in himself" (John 5:26). The Spirit holds within itself life-power or vitality that is independent of all other things.[369] Speaking of Jesus, President Young taught, "He had the issues of life and death in his power; ... Jesus had this power in and of himself; the Father bequeathed it to him; it was his legacy. ... He had the streams and issues of life within him and when he said 'LIVE' to individuals, they lived."[370]

Paul is not so much addressing here the composition of the divine body, but the mode of its existence, that is, one subjected fully to the Spirit of God. Still, he does not negate a physical component of that body which highly contributes to the quality of the soul's state of existence. Indeed, the physical portion is necessary if the person is to experience a fullness of joy (D&C 93:33; compare D&C 138:17). Paul understands that the body is sown a σῶμα ψυχικός (*sōma psychikos*), "a physical body," but raised a σῶμα πνευματικός (*sōma pneumaticos*), "a spiritual body." In Paul's thought, the former was that deep, inner, and mortal portion of the person that belonged to the natural world and existed apart from God (2:13).[371] The latter also referred to the deep, inner, but immortal portion of a person that lived in harmony with God.

The difficulty Paul was addressing was that the Corinthian "strong" felt they were already of the latter type because they possessed what they considered superior knowledge and certain gifts of the Spirit. Paul, in scolding them, revealed they were deluding themselves. They certainly had risen neither to the level of the *pneumatikos* nor even the *psychikos*. They were but σάρκινος (*sarkinos*) "of the flesh," because of their jealousies and the promotion of strife and division (3:1–3).[372]

It is important to note that in none of these three divisions—*sarkinos, psychikos,* and *pneumatikos*—is there any hint in either the minds of Paul or

---

369. Findlay, "St. Paul's First Epistle," 938.

370. Brigham Young, in *JD,* 13:141.

371. Judith L. Kovacs, *1 Corinthians: Interpreted by Early Christian Commentators* (Grand Rapids, Mich.: Eerdmans, 2005), 271 n. 21.

372. Bailey, *Mediterranean Eyes,* 464.

the Saints of some kind of disembodied spirit. The tension between mortal and immortal life is not between physical and spirit bodies but between the natural and spiritual ones. Paul affirms that a *psychikos* is a living mortal human being and that includes his physical body, but one bound by natural conditions. He also affirms that a *pneumatikos* is a living immortal human being including a corporeal body but one expanded by heavenly conditions.[373]

The point is that a *spiritual* body stands in contrast to a body *of spirit*. The latter is a body made solely of spirit matter while the former is a physical one dominated by the Spirit and reconstituted in such a way as to possess power and glory.[374] For Paul, based on 3:1, *pneumatikos,* "spiritual," points to a life controlled and directed by God and endowed by the power of the Holy Spirit, which the physical body, properly trained, does not impede.

It needs to be stressed that the resurrected body is, however, much more than physical but not less than that. It transcends earthly and mortal limitations. The Resurrection purifies and expands all its capabilities, powers, and endowments. Joseph Smith observed that "the nearer man approaches perfection: the more conspicuous [that is, clearer] are his views, and the greater his enjoyments, until he has overcome the evils of his life and lost every desire of sin." He went on to note that "this is a station to which no man ever arrived in a moment."[375] But what must not be overlooked is that a righteous man or woman never loses desire. Instead they increase in it, but it is holy, pure, and completely under their control and can, therefore, be enjoyed eternally in its fullness.[376]

Paul further showed why a resurrected body was necessary by noting that "flesh and blood cannot inherit the kingdom of God" (15:50). The belief of those who use this scripture, as well as the one that states "It is sown a natural body; it is raised a spiritual body" (15:44), to prove that there is no physical resurrection actually corresponds very closely to the

---

373. Bailey, *Mediterranean Eyes,* 465.

374. Fee, *First Epistle,* 786.

375. "The Elders of the Church in Kirtland, to their Brethren Abroad," *Evening and Morning Star* 2, no. 18 (March 1834): 283.

376. Alma 38:12 speaks of bridling passions. Such an instrument does not destroy or even diminish the power of a steed, but places it under control. As Truman G. Madsen, *Four Essays on Love* (Provo, Utah: Communications Workshop, 1972), 36, noted, "We are given our bodies and our emotions not to destroy but to ride. They magnify our feelings and increase enjoyments." When fully bridled, he went on, we can, like straddling a powerful steed, "ride [them] free, bareback like the wind."

Corinthian heresy.[377] The metaphor "flesh and blood," however, refers to mortality. Jesus noted that Peter received his witness not from "flesh and blood" (Matt. 16:17), and Paul noted that, after his conversion, he did not confer "with flesh and blood" but went to Arabia, likely for contemplation and study (Gal. 1:16). Joseph Smith taught that "when our flesh is quickened by the Spirit, there will be no blood in this tabernacle,"[378] and that though "flesh and blood cannot go [where God is] . . . flesh and bones, quickened by the Spirit of God, can."[379]

Paul does agree with his detractors on one point, the mortal body "cannot inherit the kingdom of God" (15:50). That does not mean, however, that there is no physical component to a resurrected body. As one LDS scholar noted, "the use of the word *spiritual* in reference to the resurrected body should be interpreted not as a noncorporeal existence but rather as a way to contrast what is mundane and earthly with what is glorious."[380] Jesus' appearance to the ten and later eleven Apostles clearly demonstrates that a spiritual body has a physical component (Luke 24:36–42; John 20:26–27). As Elder Penrose observed, "Now, Jesus appeared in the same body that was placed in the tomb, and yet it was not the same, there was a change in it. What change was it? We read that Jesus Christ shed his blood 'for the remission of sins: not for ours only, but for the sins of the whole world.' Jesus was raised up from the dead by the power of God. . . . Blood is corruptible, the blood-quickened body is subject to the law of death. But Christ's body when it was raised from the dead was 'quickened by the spirit.' There was a great deal of difference not only in this respect but in others."[381]

Those who claim that Jesus was an "evidential" exception to the idea that resurrected beings have no physical bodies but are spirit, must dismiss Paul's witness that Christ is the example, *sine qua non*, of the Resurrection (15:47, 49).[382] Speaking of the Saints, D&C 88:27–28 states that "notwithstanding they die, they also shall rise again, a spiritual body. They who are of a celestial spirit shall receive the same body which was a natural body; even ye shall receive your bodies, and your glory shall be that glory by which your bodies are quickened."

377. Anderson, *Understanding Paul,* 129.
378. Smith, *History of the Church,* 6:366.
379. Smith, *History of the Church,* 6:52.
380. Holzapfel and Wayment, *Making Sense,* 366.
381. Charles W. Penrose, *J.D.* 21: 228.
382. Anderson, *Understanding Paul,* 129.

President Hunter taught, "The resurrection will again unite the spirit with the body, and the body becomes a spiritual body, one of flesh and bones but quickened by the spirit instead of blood. Thus, our bodies after the resurrection, quickened by the spirit, shall become immortal and never die. This is the meaning of the statements of Paul that 'there is a natural body, and there is a spiritual body' and 'that flesh and blood cannot inherit the kingdom of God.' The natural body is flesh and blood, but quickened by the spirit instead of blood, it can and will enter the kingdom."[383]

Paul's instruction in 15:49–50 seems to show that he fully understood that nothing mortals possess can go as it is into the heavenly realm. Not only must the lowest and bestial be shunted off, but the best and most noble purified and enlarged. Everything must move from φθορά (*phthora*), "corruption" to ἀφθαρσία (*aphtharsia*), "incorruption," from that which can be destroyed to that which never can. It is not so much that the body, with its appetites and passions, is too rank, but that it is too weak.[384] It is the power of the Resurrection that makes not only the body but also its passions and appetites pure, strong, powerful, and eternal.

---

383. Howard W. Hunter, in CR, April 1969, 135–39.

384. C. S. Lewis, *The Great Divorce* (New York: Macmillan Publishing, 1946), 104–5.

Excursus on the Three Degrees of Glory

Paul's comment that the Resurrection consists of at least those who "are Christ's at his coming" and those who later come forth (15:23; compare Rev. 20:6–13) opens the door to more "glories" than one in the Resurrection. His knowledge likely came from an experience he had had more than a decade before when he was "caught up to the third heaven" (2 Cor. 12:2).[385] He was also privileged to be "caught up into paradise, and [to hear] unspeakable words, which it is not lawful for a man to utter" (2 Cor. 12:4). His experiences certainly vouch for multiple "glories" in the afterlife and contradict the widely held belief that it consists of only heaven and hell. The Lord himself had taught that "in my Father's house are many mansions" (John 14:2) and spoke of those who "shall come forth; they that have done good, unto the resurrection of life; and they that have done evil, unto the resurrection of damnation" (John 5:29). This verse was the trigger for a remarkable vision had by Joseph Smith and Sidney Rigdon.

According to their account,

> while we were doing the work of translation, which the Lord had appointed unto us, we came to the twenty-ninth verse of the fifth chapter of John, which was given unto us as follows— Speaking of the resurrection of the dead, concerning those who shall hear the voice of the Son of Man: And shall come forth; they who have done good, in the resurrection of the just; and they who have done evil, in the resurrection of the unjust. Now this caused us to marvel, for it was given unto us of the Spirit. And while we meditated upon these things, the Lord touched the eyes of our understandings, and they were opened, and the glory of the Lord shone round about. And we beheld the glory of the Son, on the right hand of the Father, and received of his fulness; And saw the holy angels, and them who are sanctified before his throne, worshiping God, and the Lamb, who worship him forever and ever. (D&C 76:15–21)

The contents of this vision can be found in D&C 76.[386] As a result of this remarkable revelation, Latter-day Saints have a rather detailed understanding of the afterlife.

---

385. Though Paul speaks obliquely in this passage, "I knew a man," the reference is to himself. See Holzapfel and Wayment, *Making Sense,* 377.

386. "History, 1838–1856, Volume A-1," 184–85.

The idea of three heavens in the eternal world, though not widely preached, was known to some early Christians. Irenaeus, bishop of Lyon, was a student of Polycarp, bishop of Smyrna.[387] The latter had known John the Beloved. Through Polycarp a number of teachings held by "the elders, the disciples of the apostles," were transmitted to the third generation of Christians. One of these was the belief in three very different rewards in the afterlife as well as the punishment of hell. According to this source, the most righteous live in heaven, the second most in paradise, and the third in the Holy City. To give scriptural force to this idea, Irenaeus alluded to the Lord's parable of the seeds (Matt. 13:1–8) noting that the distinction in the eternal worlds is based upon whether a person brought forth a hundred-fold, sixty-fold, or thirty-fold.[388] Though this view differs from the more full understanding that Latter-day Saints have, it is still quite remarkable that the idea of multiple rewards was taught anciently.[389]

That this knowledge has come forth as part of the "fullness of times" (D&C 112:30) is not surprising. The Lord stated that during this period, he "will gather together in one all things, both which are in heaven, and which are on earth" (D&C 27:13). The Lord further promised that "nothing shall be withheld, whether there be one God or many gods, they shall be manifest. . . . Also, if there be bounds set to the heavens or to the seas, or to the dry land, or to the sun, moon, or stars. . . . [All] according to that which was ordained in the midst of the Council of the Eternal God" (D&C 121:28, 30, 32). Indeed, the Lord insists that he is "merciful and gracious unto those who fear me, and delight to honor those who serve me in righteousness and in truth unto the end. . . . To them will I reveal all mysteries, yea, all the hidden mysteries of my kingdom from days of old, and for ages to come, will I make known unto them the good pleasure of my will concerning all things pertaining to my kingdom" (D&C 76:5, 7).

Out of Joseph Smith and Sidney Rigdon's remarkable vision came an understanding of the final end of the devil and his angels and all those who are overcome by them (D&C 76:25–38). "They shall go away into everlasting punishment, which is endless punishment, which is eternal punishment, to reign with the devil and his angels in eternity, where their worm dieth not, and the fire is not quenched, which is their torment—And the end thereof, neither the place thereof, nor their torment, no man knows;

---

387. Polycarp lived between AD 70 and 155 and Irenaeus between 130 and 200.
388. Irenaeus, *Haer.* 5.36.1–2; English translation in *Ante-Nicene Fathers,* 1:567.
389. Anderson, *Understanding Paul,* 127.

Neither was it revealed, neither is, neither will be revealed unto man, except to them who are made partakers thereof; Nevertheless, I, the Lord, show it by vision unto many, but straightway shut it up again; Wherefore, the end, the width, the height, the depth, and the misery thereof, they understand not, neither any man except those who are ordained unto this condemnation" (D&C 76:44–48).

These are the only ones on whom the second death will have full effect, "for all the rest shall be brought forth by the resurrection of the dead, through the triumph and the glory of the Lamb, who was slain, who was in the bosom of the Father before the worlds were made" (D&C 76:39). Speaking on this subject, President George Albert Smith observed, "While we should struggle to obtain the greater blessings, we should never disparage those who may fall short of attaining the highest glory. ... But in these various glories will be found all denominations and all honorable men—every one in accordance with those things which he has done in this life."[390]

"We read in the Bible," noted President Young, "that there is one glory of the sun, another glory of the moon, and another glory of the stars. In the Book of Doctrine and Covenants, these glories are called telestial, terrestrial, and celestial, which is the highest. These are worlds, different departments, or mansions, in our Father's house."[391] Elaborating on this ideal, President Marion G. Romney observed that "there will be many gradations among immortal souls. As 'one star differeth from another star in glory so also is the resurrection of the dead' (1 Cor. 15:41–42). That's Paul's doctrine. Immortality connotes life without end. Eternal life, on the other hand, connotes quality of life—exaltation, the highest type of immortality, the kind of life enjoyed by God himself."[392] Speaking on this subject, Elder Orson Pratt taught,

All who are placed within the power of redemption will be redeemed—not redeemed to the same degree of salvation, but some will inherit one kingdom, and some another; some receiving the highest or celestial glory, being crowned with crowns of glory in the presence of God forever, shining forth like the sun in its meridian strength; while others, though celestial, will be subject to them, inheriting a less degree of celestial glory. Others will inherit a terrestrial glory, or the glory of the moon. Others will inherit a glory still less than this, which may be termed a telestial

390. George Albert Smith, in *JD,* 15:99.
391. Brigham Young, in *JD,* 1:312.
392. Marion G. Romney, "The Worth of Souls," *Ensign* 8 (November 1978): 14.

glory, like that of the stars—a glory small indeed! They are all redeemed, according to their repentance, faithfulness, and works of righteousness, into these various degrees of glory.[393]

Joseph Smith was very positive about the future of those faithful Saints who had died during his day. He observed, "We have seen them walk worthily in our midst, and seen them sink asleep in the arms of Jesus; and those who have died in the faith are now in the celestial kingdom of God. And hence is the glory of the sun."[394]

Elder McConkie observed that those who inherit terrestrial glory, compared to the moon, bask, as it were, in reflected glory, "for there are restrictions and limitations placed on them. They 'receive the presence of the Son, but not of the fulness of the Father' (D. & C. 76:77), and to all eternity they remain unmarried and without exaltation. (D. & C. 132:17.)"[395] Concerning those who inherit telestial glory, their splendor is compared to that of the stars. They receive the ministration of neither the Father nor the Son, but the Holy Ghost. Just like the stars, their range of glory is considerable. Still, it is far less than that of either the celestial or terrestrial spheres (D&C 76:81–112). Even so, it "surpasses all [mortal] understanding" (D&C 76:89).

393. Orson Pratt, in *JD,* 7:89.

394. This is again an amalgamation. The pieces can be found in Cannon, *King Follett Discourse.*

395. *DNTC,* 2:400.

The Nature of the Resurrected Body (15:51–58)

Greek Text

51 ἰδοὺ μυστήριον ὑμῖν λέγω· πάντες οὐ κοιμηθησόμεθα πάντες δὲ ἀλλαγησόμεθα, 52 ἐν ἀτόμῳ, ἐν ῥιπῇ ὀφθαλμοῦ, ἐν τῇ ἐσχάτῃ σάλπιγγι· σαλπίσει γάρ, καὶ οἱ
νεκροὶ ἐγερθήσονται ἄφθαρτοι, καὶ ἡμεῖς ἀλλαγησόμεθα. 53 δεῖ γὰρ τὸ φθαρτὸν
τοῦτο ἐνδύσασθαι ἀφθαρσίαν καὶ τὸ θνητὸν τοῦτο ἐνδύσασθαι ἀθανασίαν. 54 ὅταν
δὲ τὸ φθαρτὸν τοῦτο ἐνδύσηται ἀφθαρσίαν καὶ τὸ θνητὸν τοῦτο ἐνδύσηται ἀθανασίαν, τότε γενήσεται ὁ λόγος ὁ γεγραμμένος· Κατεπόθη ὁ θάνατος εἰς νῖκος.
55 ποῦ σου, θάνατε, τὸ νῖκος; ποῦ σου, θάνατε, τὸ κέντρον; 56 τὸ δὲ κέντρον τοῦ
θανάτου ἡ ἁμαρτία, ἡ δὲ δύναμις τῆς ἁμαρτίας ὁ νόμος· 57 τῷ δὲ θεῷ χάρις τῷ
διδόντι ἡμῖν τὸ νῖκος διὰ τοῦ κυρίου ἡμῶν Ἰησοῦ Χριστοῦ.

58 Ὥστε, ἀδελφοί μου ἀγαπητοί, ἑδραῖοι γίνεσθε, ἀμετακίνητοι, περισσεύοντες ἐν τῷ ἔργῳ τοῦ κυρίου πάντοτε, εἰδότες ὅτι ὁ κόπος ὑμῶν οὐκ ἔστιν κενὸς ἐν
κυρίῳ. [SBLGNT]

King James Version

51 Behold, I shew you a mystery; We shall not all sleep, but we shall all be changed, 52 In a moment, in the twinkling of an eye, at the last trump: for the trumpet shall sound, and the dead shall be raised incorruptible, and we shall be changed. 53 For this corruptible must put on incorruption, and this mortal must put on immortality. 54 So when this corruptible shall have put on incorruption, and this mortal shall have put on immortality, then shall be brought to pass the saying that is written, Death is swallowed up in victory. 55 O death, where is thy sting? O grave, where is thy victory? 56 The sting of death is sin; and the strength of sin is the law. 57 But thanks be to God, which giveth us the victory through our Lord Jesus Christ. 58 Therefore, my beloved brethren,

New Rendition

51 Look, I am telling you a mystery. Not all of us will fall asleep, but we will all be changed 52 in a moment, in the blink of an eye, at the last trumpet. For the trumpet will sound, and the dead will be raised imperishable, and we will be changed. 53 For this perishable body must put on imperishability, and this mortal body must put on immortality. 54 And when this perishable body puts on imperishability, and this mortal body puts on immortality, then the saying will be fulfilled which is written, "Death is swallowed up in victory. 55 Where, O Death is your victory? Where, O Death, is your sting?" 56 The sting of death is sin, and the power of sin is the law. 57 Thank God who gives us the victory through our Lord Jesus Christ. 58 And so my beloved brothers

be ye steadfast, unmoveable, always abounding in the work of the Lord, forasmuch as ye know that your labour is not in vain in the Lord.	and sisters, be firm, immovable, always doing your best in the work of the Lord, since you know that in the Lord your labor is not in vain.

Translation Notes and Comments

15:51 *Behold, I shew you a mystery / Look, I am telling you a mystery:*
The verb λέγω (*legō*), "to tell," does not mean to show something, but rather to express it either orally or in writing.[396] For the second time, Paul refers to part of his teachings as a μυστήριον (*mysterion*), "a mystery" (see Translation Notes on 2:7). The noun describes spiritual knowledge of such high degree that it is impossible for mere mortal intellect, without divine help, to conceive.[397] The word suggests that Paul is sharing information he received through inspiration or revelation. Given the deeply spiritual and informative visions he had had (see 2 Cor. 12:1–4), it is little wonder he understood the gospel so well.

We shall not all sleep, but we shall all be changed / Not all of us will fall asleep, but we will all be changed: There are four variant readings of this passage in ancient manuscripts, three of which undoubtedly arose to compensate for the fact that Paul and those to whom he wrote had died.[398] The version that has the best support and best explains the other three is the one used in translating both the KJV and Rendition.[399]

The verb κοιμάομαι (*koimaomai*), "to sleep," as noted above, was a euphemism for death.[400] The verb ἀλλάσσω (*allassō*), "to change," means to transition or transform from one thing into another. It also carries an eschatological nuance pointing to the transformation of the human body from mundane to empyreal at the time of the Resurrection.[401] Paul's use of a first person plural verb conjugation, translated as "we," presents a problem. Taking the passage at face value, it appears that Paul believed that the

---

396. BDAG. 588–90.

397. BDAG, 661–62.

398. Both Fee, *First Epistle,* 796 n. 3, and Conzelmann, *1 Corinthians,* 288–89 and n. 1, address these in detail. In sum, it appears that a copyist determined to correct the problem by taking the "not" from the first clause and put it with the second so that the text reads, "We shall all die, but we shall not all be changed."

399. It is also of note that a few variants replace "sleep" with "resurrection." This was likely to offset the influence of gnostic thinking. For discussion, see Metzger, *Textual Commentary,* 502.

400. Louw-Nida, §23.104.

401. BDAG, 45–46.

Second Coming, though not imminent, would occur in his lifetime. He had already suggested that idea in his epistle to the Thessalonian Saints, stating that "we which are alive and remain shall be caught up" at that time of Christ's coming (1 Thes. 4:15–17). Thus, it appears that he did believe the Second Coming was not too far off.[402]

There is, however, another way to take the passage and that is to see the "we" in a generic frame of reference referring to those in the Church during any period of time reaching from Paul's day into the future. That he could be saying "Not all of us Saints shall be asleep" whenever the Parousia happens seems very likely.[403]

That issue is not, however, at the center of Paul's argument here. His point—which he had already stated in 6:14 (and would again state later in Philip. 3:20–21)—is that if a person has died at the time of the Second Coming, he or she will be resurrected and, thus, their bodies transformed.

15:52 *In a moment, in the twinkling of an eye / in a moment, in the blink of an eye:* The adjective ἄτομος (*atomos*), "in a moment," denotes something so small it cannot be divided. In connection with time, it could be expressed with the English idiom "in a flash."[404] The noun ῥιπῇ (*rhipē*) means to jerk or blink and denotes any kind of sudden movement.[405] Both images emphasize the suddenness by which the body will be transformed at the time of the Resurrection.[406] The imagery negates any concerns the

---

402. The issue is debated as to whether or not Paul expected an immanent Parousia. Speaking of the ancient Apostles, Brigham Young noted that "there can be no doubt but they were mistaken with regard to the time of the winding up scene, thinking it was much nearer than it really was." *JD*, 12:65. When Paul wrote another epistle to Corinthians some time later, however, it appears that he felt he and others would not live to see the Parousia (see 2 Cor. 5:1–5). For a discussion of this matter, see the Translation Notes in the 2 Corinthians volume in this series. For an example of opposing scholarly views on the subject, see Barrett, *First Epistle,* 381; and A. C. Perriman, "Paul and the Parousia: 1 Corinthians 15:50–57 and 2 Corinthians 5:1–5," *New Testament Studies* 36 (October 1989): 512–21.

403. This view has been sustained by a number of writers who have accepted the very careful work of Johannes P. Louw, "An Examination of Attempts to Detect Developments in St. Paul's Theology," *Journal of Theological Studies* 42 (1941): 129–42, including D. E. H. Whiteley, *The Theology of St. Paul* (Minneapolis: Fortress Press, 1964), 241–58; and Thiselton, *First Epistle,* 1293–94. Author L. Moore, *The Parousia in the New Testament* (Leiden: Brill, 1966), 47, makes a very good point: had the Christians really believed that the Parousia was in their lifetime, one would be hard pressed to explain why their disappointment did not destroy the movement.

404. BDAG, 149.
405. BDAG, 906.
406. Bailey, *Mediterranean Eyes,* 472.

Saints might have had about whether the change would be a slow and per-haps painful process. It will not.[407]

at the last trump / at the last trumpet: The JST reads "at the sound of the last trump." The change simply clarifies that it is not the trump but its sounding that signals souls to come forth. The σάλπιγξ (*salpinx*), "trum-pet," was not a musical instrument but a metal horn or, particularly among the Jews, a ram's horn that was used to summon people or call instructions during battle.[408] The imagery of the blowing horn was common in Jewish apocalyptic writing as the means by which events were signaled to begin.[409] The "last trump" signals the end of the telestial era (D&C 88:110). Where the first two images looked to the suddenness of the event, this one, based on Matthew 24:31 (compare 1 Thes. 4:16), looks to its solemn finality.[410]

for the trumpet shall sound, and the dead shall be raised incorruptible, and we shall be changed / For the trumpet will sound, and the dead will be raised imperishable, and we will be changed: With this verse, Paul brings the Corinthians Saints into the picture assuring them that they will have part in the future event. The key point here, and one that answers the antiresur-rection party's key question, "with what kind of body," is that the dead are raised ἄφθαρτος (*aphthartos*), "imperishable." Of all the changes that will happen to the human body, this is perhaps the most noteworthy. (For *aph-thartos,* see Translation Notes on 15:42.)

15:53 *For this corruptible must put on incorruption, and this mortal must put on immortality / For this perishable body must put on imperish-ability, and this mortal body must put on immortality:* To stress his point, Paul repeats here what he has said before but he emphasizes the reality of what will take place with the use of the verb δεῖ (*dei*), "must." The word not only shows what must necessarily be done but also implies what is inevitable.[411] The subject of this sentence is τὸ φθαρτὸν τοῦτο (*to phtharton touto*), literally "this perishable thing." Though Paul does not explicitly say he means the σῶμα (*sōma*), "body," he definitely has that in mind. For the sake of clarifying Paul's thought, the noun is supplied in our Rendition.[412]

---

407. Findlay, "St. Paul's First Epistle," 941.

408. BDAG, 911.

409. Examples can be found in Zech. 9:14; Isa. 27:13; Joel 2:1, 15; 2 Esd. 6:23; Matt. 24:31; 1 Thes. 4:16; Rev. 8:2, 13; 11:15. In LDS scripture, the same imagery appears in Mosiah 26:25; Morm. 9:13; D&C 29:13; 88:92; 109:75.

410. Findlay, "St. Paul's First Epistle," 941.

411. Louw-Nida, §71.34.

412. Thiselton, *First Epistle,* 1297.

15:54 *So when this corruptible shall have put on incorruption, and this mortal shall have put on immortality, then shall be brought to pass the saying that is written, Death is swallowed up in victory / And when this perishable body puts on imperishability, and this mortal body puts on immortality, then the saying will be fulfilled which is written, "Death is swallowed up in victory":*[413] As in 15:53, though Paul does not use the noun σῶμα (*sōma*), "body," it is implied so strongly that it is added in our Rendition. It appears that, in order to strengthen his point, Paul paraphrases MT Isaiah 25:8.[414] The Hebrew verb found in Paul's reference—בִּלַּע (*billaʾ*), literally "to swallow"—figuratively means to engulf or overwhelm something, but connotes its total destruction.[415] It is God's transformation of the human body from mortal to immortal that destroys death once and for all and brings to the Divine total victory.

15:55 *O death, where is thy sting? O grave, where is thy victory? / Where, O Death, is your victory? Where, O Death, is your sting?:* Textual variants for this verse have the two phrases reversed. Our Rendition follows the format in the better manuscripts. Paul here paraphrases LXX Hosea 13:14, and in the second line drops ᾅδης (*hadēs,* a word Paul never uses), "Hades," and replaces it with a repeated θάνατος (*thanatos*), "death."[416] The whole, in translation, reads: "I [Jehovah] will deliver them out of the hand of Hades, and I will redeem them from death: Where is thy punishment, O death? O Hades, where is thy sting?" (authors' translation). These phrases, taken in their Old Testament context, tell of Jehovah's promise to the righteous in Ephraim that, even though the wicked will bring death and destruction upon all, Jehovah will eventually save his people from both death and hell.[417]

---

413. There is a significant manuscript variant in this verse in which a number of words have been left out. It is generally believed that this took place due to the copyist's eyes dropping to an identical word in a line below. The change does not affect Paul's point, so the problem is mentioned only here. See Metzger, *Textual Commentary*, 502–3.

414. He seems to be paraphrasing because he gets the sense but does not use exactly the same words. Paul's idea is fully developed in the Isaiah Apocalypse 24:1–17 that looks at the consummation of Jehovah's work in which he will be totally victorious and royally banquet his people. In 15:54–55, Paul could also be combining Isa. 25:8 and Hosea 13:14 in a very carefully thought out use of proof texting. See Stanley, *Paul and the Language of Scripture,* 205–15.

415. BDB, 118; Findlay, "St. Paul's First Epistle," 942, states that the word connotes the "final and unqualified overthrow of the King of Terrors."

416. Metzger, *Textual Commentary*, 503.

417. C. F. Keil and F. Delitzsch, *Commentary on the Old Testament*, 10 vols. (1857–78; rpt., Grand Rapids, Mich.: Eerdmans, 1977), 10:159–60.

The noun κέντρον (*kentron*) refers to the bite of a venomous serpent or an insect's sting. It also denotes the sharp iron goad used for both driving animals and torturing people.[418] In Paul's paraphrase, δίκη (*dike*), "punishment," is replaced by νίκη (*nike*), "victory." The change is instructive. In the LXX, Jehovah curtails death's judicial ability to impose and execute a penalty. In Paul's version, the result of Christ's work is much broader; death's ability to have any kind of mastery over the soul is taken away. Thus, death's fearsome reign is but temporary. Though mortals may die, it is but a necessary stage in the transition into a better life and, therefore, nothing to be feared.[419]

15:56 *The sting of death is sin; and the strength of sin is the law / The sting of death is sin, and the power of sin is the law:* This verse is but an aside made by Paul with no elaboration. The brevity of his statement suggests that he expects the Corinthian Saints to fully understand his reference. Though Paul develops the theology hinted at here more fully in Romans 6–9, he likely preached it while at Corinth. For a full treatment, the reader should consult the volume in this series dealing with Romans. For now, we need only say that, from Paul's perspective, death still carries a sting for the unrepentant because, for them, it never loses its judicial ability to impose and execute punishment (Rom. 5:10–21), and thus, the terror of the second death abides.

Unfortunately, in this, the law plays a part. It indirectly gives sin power over a person. As Paul will tell the Romans, "Where there is no law, there is no sin" (Rom. 4:15, authors' translation), and therefore no punishment and that means no second death. On the other hand, where there is law, there is sin and further death. This is because the law reveals the will of God and, thereby, puts a person in a position to rebel against it (Rom. 6:7–13). As a result, the sinner becomes "a stench (ὀσμή, *osmē*) from death unto death" (2 Cor. 2:16, authors' translation). Thus, the law indirectly empowers sin, the sting of death.

15:57 *But thanks be to God, which giveth us the victory through our Lord Jesus Christ / Thank God who gives us the victory through our Lord Jesus Christ:* As is usual with Paul, he brings his entire argument back to God and Christ. On χάρις (*charis*) translated as "thanks" here, see "Excursus on Grace" in chapter 1. The present tense of the participial phrase θεῷ ... τῷ διδόντι (*theō ... tō didonti*), "God ... who gives," is important. It reminds

---

418. BDAG, 539–40; Acts 26:14; Euripides, *Bacch.* 795.
419. Fitzmyer, *First Corinthians,* 607.

Paul's readers that God is the author of the victory over death and hell. He did it "through Christ." The Savior's victory in their behalf has already taken place and that will continue to be the case. He did this by satisfying the demands of the law (Rom. 8:4; compare 2 Ne. 2:7, 10; 9:26) and by so doing opened the way for a new and higher relationship with the Father "apart from the law" (Rom. 3:21, authors' translation).[420] His words should have also brought a dose of humility to his readers, for the victory was not won by any of them. It came singly and fully "through our Lord Jesus Christ." It was a pure act of grace. Now what they must do is avail themselves of it. They can do this by first, accepting the corrected understanding that Paul has now given them of the breadth of the power of the Father and the Son and second, by following their ways. In doing so, all the problems they face—from in-house fighting to attending pagan feasts and supporting immoral behaviors—will all disappear.[421]

15:58 *Therefore, my beloved brethren, be ye steadfast, unmoveable, always abounding in the work of the Lord / And so my beloved brothers and sisters, be firm, immovable, always doing your best in the work of the Lord:* With the use of the conjunction ὥστε (*hōste*), "therefore, and so," Paul signals his readers that he is now drawing a conclusion based on all that he has said in chapter 15. It consists of three admonitions that will, as they are carried out, allow his readers to partake of the victory the Father and Son have won for them. The first is to be ἑδραῖος (*hedraios*), "steadfast, firm,"[422] that is, true to their testimony. The second is to be ἀμετακίνητος (*ametakinētos*), "immoveable,"[423] that is, unyielding in their righteousness. The third is περισσεύοντες ἐν τῷ ἔργῳ (*perisseuontes en tō ergo*), "abounding in the work" of the Lord. The verb περισσεύω (*perisseuō*) means to be outstanding in something through doing one's best. This is a means by which one can achieve excellence.[424] In this case, that excellence is assisting in the Lord's work (ἔργον, *ergon*[425]), that is, to bring souls unto him and the Father (compare Moses 1:39).

forasmuch as ye know that your labour is not in vain in the Lord / since you know that in the Lord your labor is not in vain: The force of the participle εἴδοτες (*eidotes*, perfect in form, but present in meaning), "since you

---

420. Thiselton, *First Epistle,* 1302.
421. Bailey, *Mediterranean Eyes,* 475.
422. BDAG, 276.
423. BDAG, 53.
424. BDAG, 805.
425. BDAG, 390–91.

know," is important because it anticipates and answers the question, "Why should we do as you ask?"[426] The verb οἶδα (*oida*), "to know," carries the idea of grasping the importance and meaning of an experience, in this case the truthfulness of the gospel.[427] The noun κόπος (*kopos*) means to do hard labor,[428] while the noun κενός (*kenos*) refers to that which is "empty or vain," but carries the idea of not being worth one's while.[429] Thus, the answer to their implied question is based on the assurance upon which their testimonies rest. Paul is saying that since they really do know the power that is in the Savior, they also know their labors will be worth all the effort they put into them.

Analysis and Summary

To both bolster his position and assure the Saints that he knows what he is talking about, Paul affirms that what he is telling them is a "mystery" (15:51). Since the word connotes a revelation from God, it appears that Paul is referencing a revelation he has had. It informed him that, at the time of the Second Coming, the righteous dead will be instantly transformed from mortal to immortal.[430] In the Millennium, when the living approach death, the same will also happen to them. What he knew seems to be reflected in the modern scripture that states, "He that liveth when the Lord shall come, and hath kept the faith, blessed is he; nevertheless, it is appointed to him to die at the age of man. Wherefore, children shall grow up until they become old; old men shall die; but they shall not sleep in the dust, but they shall be changed in the twinkling of an eye" (D&C 63:50–51). In the Book of Mormon we read,

> Even this mortal shall put on immortality, and this corruption shall put on incorruption, and shall be brought to stand before the bar of God,

---

426. Though the tense here is perfect, it is used as a present but carries a causal nuance caught by the addition of the word "since" in the Rendition and "forasmuch" in the KJV. See Wallace, *Greek Grammar,* 631 and n. 47.

427. BDAG, 693–94.

428. BDAG, 558–59.

429. BDAG, 539.

430. Holzapfel and Wayment, *Making Sense,* 366. Wayment, *From Persecutor to Apostle,* 170–71, states that after his terrifying ordeal in Ephesus where he apparently could have died, he never again uses the pronoun "we" when speaking of what will happen to the Saints when the Lord comes again. Apparently, he realized that he had no assurance that he would live to see the end. Other commentators, however, have argued that Paul did not believe this to be the case. See footnote 693 in this chapter.

to be judged of him according to their works whether they be good or whether they be evil—If they be good, to the resurrection of endless life and happiness; and if they be evil, to the resurrection of endless damnation, being delivered up to the devil, who hath subjected them, which is damnation—Having gone according to their own carnal wills and desires; having never called upon the Lord while the arms of mercy were extended towards them; for the arms of mercy were extended towards them, and they would not; they being warned of their iniquities and yet they would not depart from them; and they were commanded to repent and yet they would not repent. (Mosiah 16:10–12)

The Lord made it clear that "they that die not in me, wo unto them, for their death is bitter" (D&C 42:47). On the other hand, he said, "Those that die in me shall not taste of death, for it shall be sweet unto them" (D&C 42:46). Using the force of the vocative mood ("O death"), Paul presses home his point about the powerlessness of death with a taunt such as those addressed to a captured and now powerless enemy.[431] He exclaims, "Where, O Death, is your victory? Where, O Death, is your sting?" (15:55, Rendition). As President Kimball pointed out, "There is no victory in the grave, for death is replaced with life. Immortality is a free gift for all men through the atoning ransom paid by the Son of God."[432] The threatened sting holds no fear for the repentant precisely because Christ himself absorbed the sting.[433] "That the Savior conquered death, after having taken upon himself mortality," taught President Brown, "gives us the divine assurance that our spirits also transcend death and that our loved ones who have gone before still live."[434]

Deep sin is not just the deliberate turning away from God. It is also the attempt to turn everything toward oneself. It manifests itself in those who seek to be a law unto themselves. It disallows any sanctification by law, mercy, judgment, or justice (D&C 88:35). The price of such rebellion is death.[435] Paul could, therefore, declare "the sting of death is sin" (15:56). Explaining this, Elder Russell M. Nelson stated: "If physical death should strike before moral wrongs have been made right, opportunity for repentance will have been forfeited. Thus, 'the [real] sting of death is sin.' Even

---

431. Thiselton, *First Epistle,* 1301.

432. Spencer W. Kimball, "An Eternal Hope in Christ," Ensign 8 (November 1978): 72.

433. Thiselton, *First Epistle,* 1300.

434. Hugh B. Brown, in CR, April 1967, 48–51. In CR, April 1962, 106–10, President Brown stated that it was Paul's comprehension that Christ was but the first fruits of the Resurrection (15:20) that led him to make this joyful exaltation.

435. Robertson and Plummer, *Critical and Exegetical Commentary,* 378–79.

the Savior cannot save us in our sins. He will redeem us from our sins, but only upon condition of our repentance. We are responsible for our own spiritual survival or death."[436]

This point is indeed the case. Though law acts as a moral indicator pointing out both sin and its gravity, it also acts as a principle of rule sustained by cause and effect that applies to everyone. It, thereby, ties everyone to the consequences of their past actions from which they have no power, on their own, to escape (Alma 42:12, 14). This is what arms death with its lethal sting. It can claim the creature and impose the horrible penalty of eternal death (Alma 42:9–11). The Atonement not only frees the individual from his or her past deeds but also their consequences (Alma 42:15; 2 Ne. 9:10–12). The Atonement, then, allows the individual to live free and fearless so far as the future is concerned.[437] Therefore, Paul could admonish his readers to "thank God who gives us the victory through our Lord Jesus Christ" (15:57, Rendition).

It is of note that the death Jesus suffered was not the stingless death he promised others, but the horrifying godforsaken kind that justice required. One that caused even a God to "tremble because of pain" and "suffer both body and spirit" (D&C 19:18).

Paul understood that to enjoy the benefits of Christ's victory in their behalf, the Saints must do something. He could have ended this section by admonishing them to wait in patient endurance for the end by placing full confidence in the assurance of their reward to come—a reward guaranteed through the victory of Christ. But he does not. Rather, he admonishes them to let the future promise energize them to be proactive and labor hard in the present. Theirs was not to be a movement that quietly waited for the end. There was to be nothing passive about it.[438] Because of what was coming—the eminent Apostasy and the future Resurrection—all efforts needed to be directed toward the "now." The kingdom of God on earth had to be protected and its stay lengthened. Therefore, the Saints had to be ever steadfast in adhering to righteousness, unmovable in their witness, and excel in their good works (15:58).

436. Russell M. Nelson, "Doors of Death," *Ensign* 22 (May 1992): 73.
437. John S. Welch, "Law: Overview," in *EM*, 2:807–8; Thiselton, *First Epistle*, 1303.
438. Bailey, *Mediterranean Eyes*, 477.

Chapter 16

Matters of Christian Business

INTRODUCTION

Having discussed the primary doctrinal issues he wanted to, Paul now turns to more temporal matters before finishing his epistle. His main concern is making a collection to assist the needy in the Holy Land. A hard famine, having hit a large area of the Roman Empire during the late fifth and early sixth decades of the first century, caused great hardship among many. In the spirit of true Christian giving, Paul worked with the members in his area of labor to secure funds to help relieve the suffering.

This section teaches that the ideals of Christianity looked not only to rewards coming in the world hereafter, but also to the necessity of helping to relieve the suffering of those yet bound in mortality. Though the gospel of Jesus Christ sets its sights to the lofty realm of the Spirit, it has a definite practical side that demands that the Saints be engaged in the challenges of the here and now. Indeed, the family of believers was to pull its temporal resources together for the benefit of all (Gal. 2:10). The ideal was to have "no poor among them" (Acts 4:34; Moses 7:18).

At the base of this ideal there was a kind of reciprocity. As the Jerusalem Church had used its means to bring spiritual blessings to the Gentiles, so now the Gentiles could use their means to bring temporal blessings to the Jewish Saints (Rom. 15:27). The result very likely strengthened the bond between those at the Church's center and those of the surrounding areas.[1] It also brought the Saints together in another way. From Old Testament times onward, almsgiving was an important form of righteousness (צְדָקָה, ṣĕdāqāh) that Jehovah demanded of his people. The word nuanced the moral act at the center of being a covenant people. Due to that covenant,

---

1. Fitzmyer, *First Corinthians*, 611–12.

they were responsible for taking care of their own.[2] Almsgiving, therefore, bound all the Saints together under one law, one power, one Savior, one Father, and into one family.

In addition to concerns dealing with the collection of money to assist the Christian poor (16:1–4), this section also contains Paul's travel plans, including sensitive issues dealing with the ministry of Timothy and Apollos (16:5–12); his concluding admonitions (16:13–18); his final farewells (16:19–20); and his peroration (16:21–24), which brings the epistle to a climatic, tender, solemn, and spiritual close.

A Collection to Aid Christians at Jerusalem (16:1–4)

Greek Text

1 Περὶ δὲ τῆς λογείας τῆς εἰς τοὺς ἁγίους, ὥσπερ διέταξα ταῖς ἐκκλησίαις τῆς Γαλατίας, οὕτως καὶ ὑμεῖς ποιήσατε. 2 κατὰ μίαν σαββάτου ἕκαστος ὑμῶν παρ’ ἑαυτῷ τιθέτω θησαυρίζων ὅ τι ἐὰν εὐοδῶται, ἵνα μὴ ὅταν ἔλθω τότε λογεῖαι γίνωνται. 3 ὅταν δὲ παραγένωμαι, οὓς ἐὰν δοκιμάσητε δι’ ἐπιστολῶν, τούτους πέμψω ἀπενεγκεῖν τὴν χάριν ὑμῶν εἰς Ἰερουσαλήμ· 4 ἐὰν δὲ ἄξιον ᾖ τοῦ κἀμὲ πορεύεσθαι, σὺν ἐμοὶ πορεύσονται. [SBLGNT]

King James Version

1 Now concerning the collection for the saints, as I have given order to the churches of Galatia, even so do ye. 2 Upon the first day of the week let every one of you lay by him in store, as God hath prospered him, that there be no gatherings when I come. 3 And when I come, whomsoever ye shall approve by your letters, them will I send to bring your liberality unto Jerusalem. 4 And if it be meet that I go also, they shall go with me.

New Rendition

1 Now concerning the contributions for the saints, you should do just as I instructed the churches of Galatia. 2 On the first day of the week, each of you should put aside some money at home in proportion to what you have earned, so that a collection will not have to be made after I come. 3 Then when I arrive, I will send whoever you have approved accompanied by letters of introduction to carry the donations to Jerusalem. 4 And if it seems advisable for me to go also, they will go with me.

---

2. Fitzmyer, *First Corinthians*, 612; BDB, 842.

Translation Notes and Comments

16:1 *Now concerning the collection for the saints / Now concerning the contributions for the saints:* Paul again follows his formula by introducing the new topic with περὶ δέ (*peri de*), "now concerning." The noun λογεία (*logeia*) denotes both a collection of taxes and voluntary contributions.[3] In this case, it looks to freewill offerings dedicated to the welfare of others. In ancient Israel, new converts to Judaism, along with sympathizers, made donations as means of almsgiving.[4] These righteous deeds served both to expiate sins and manifest solidarity and unity with the people of Jehovah.[5] Paul may have seen in the request for assistance such a unifying power.[6]

as I have given order to the churches of Galatia, even so do ye / you should do just as I instructed the churches of Galatia: The verb διατάσσω (*diatassō*) means to "give detailed instructions as to what must be done," and therefore "to set in order" or "to instruct."[7] Paul's reference to ἐκκλησίαις (*ekklēsiai*), "churches," a plural noun, suggests he has distinct congregations in mind and that, therefore, the gospel was spreading.

The province of Galatia (now central Turkey) included the principle cities of Derby, Lystra, and Iconium. Paul evangelized these cites during his first missionary journey and visited them during his second. Paul's words reveal that he had arranged for the Saints in this area to collect offerings for the needy in and around Jerusalem, and he wanted the Corinthian Saints to follow their example.

16:2 *Upon the first day of the week / On the first day of the week:* The Greek reads κατὰ μίαν σαββάτου (*kata mian sabbatou*), literally "upon each first day of the week." The noun σάββατον (*sabbaton*) referred to a period of seven days—that is, a week—but also to the last day of the week in the Hebrew calendar, that is, Saturday. That day was set aside as a holy day used for rest and worship.[8] The Christians, however, used the term to

---

3. LSJ, 1055; BDAG, 597.

4. These sympathizers are referred to in modern literature as "God-fearers" and in the New Testament as those "who feared God." These were Gentile men and women who were not proselytes but who were drawn to and followed the moral law of the Jews. See Sperry, *Paul's Life,* 75. Among these were Cornelius (Acts 10:1–2) and Justus (Acts 18:7). Paul and Silas made inroads among these in Thessalonica (Acts 17:1–4).

5. Sir. 3:30; Tob. 4:7–11.

6. Fitzmyer, *First Corinthians,* 613.

7. BDAG, 237–38.

8. Using the seventh day as a day of rest was customary among neither the Greeks nor the Romans. The Romans used an eight-day cycle while the Greeks had a ten-day cycle.

denote the first day of the week, that is, Sunday.[9] Its association with the Resurrection of the Lord gave it a special and sacred nuance (see Mark 16:2; Luke 24:1). This is the first clear reference to the Christians' use of Sunday as their day of worship.

let every one of you lay by him in store, as God hath prospered him / each of you should put aside some money at home in proportion to what you have earned: The Greek here is somewhat difficult to translate, reading literally "let each one of you put aside with himself, saving whatever has prospered." The phrase παρ᾽ ἑαυτῷ (*par' heautō*) in this context is best understood as "at home."[10] The verb εὐδόομαι (*euodoomai*) means literally "to be led along a good road," but is here used in the sense of "to have things turn out well," that is, "to prosper" or "succeed,"[11] and is translated as "what you have earned" in our Rendition. The present participle θησαυρίζων (*thēsaurizōn*), "saving," is purposive and shows why the Saints should "put aside" the offering, namely as a savings until Paul arrives.[12]

that there be no gatherings when I come / so that a collection will not have to be made after I come: Paul's words suggest two points. First, he does not want a last-minute drive to raise welfare funds. Because these are to be freewill offerings (λογεία, *logeia*), the Saints should get in the habit of setting something aside on a weekly basis. No additional pressure or begging is to be used, which might happen when Paul arrived. Second, since the task was to be done *before* his arrival, it implied that the collection was not a fundraising event in his behalf. Indeed, it is important that all understand that no portion of these offerings is for his benefit. His motives and priorities (noted in 9:15) dictated that he must move along and that meant taking as little interest in temporal affairs as possible.[13]

16:3 *And when I come, whomsoever ye shall approve by your letters, them will I send to bring your liberality unto Jerusalem / Then when I arrive, I will send whoever you have approved accompanied by letters of introduction to carry the donations to Jerusalem:* Paul's use of the indefinite

---

Josephus, a near contemporary of Paul, however, claims that during his time, most of the Greco-Roman world had adopted the Jewish practice. See *Ag. Ap.* 2.39 §282.

9. BDAG, 909–10. Some later manuscripts read σαββάτων (*sabbatōn*), "Sabbaths," but the singular is well supported by the earliest ones and used in the Rendition. See Fitzmyer, *First Corinthians,* 614.

10. BDAG, 756–58. Because there was often no close place to keep funds safe, people often buried coins in fields. For example, see Matt. 13:44.

11. BDAG, 410.

12. Wallace, *Greek Grammar,* 635–37.

13. Hays, *First Corinthians,* 285; Fitzmyer, *First Corinthians,* 615.

construction ὅταν δὲ παραγένωμαι (*hotan de paragenōmai*), "when I arrive," stresses his full intention to visit Corinth—not "if I come" but "whenever I should arrive," the latter translation catching the force of the second aorist middle subjunctive of the verb παραγίνομαι (*paraginomai*).

Since ancient manuscripts did not consistently use punctuation, placement of these marks is often a matter of conjecture, but of importance, because the placement could change the meaning of a sentence. This sentence is a case in point. The translation depends on whether one places a comma before or after the phrase δι᾽ ἐπιστολῶν (*di' epistolōn*), "through letters." By placing the comma after the phrase yields "whomsoever you approve by letters, I will send." Placing it before yields "whomsoever you approve, with letters I will send." The KJV assumes the comma comes after, as do the editors of the SBLGNT.[14] On the other hand, the Nestle-Aland and United Bible Society version place it before. In our Rendition, we have followed the latter because the verb πέμπω (*pempō*), "to send," is regularly syntactically associated with ἐπιστολαί (*epistolai*), "letters," in Greek papyri.[15] The *epistlolai* are, therefore, letters of introduction and explanation produced by Paul in behalf of those carrying the offerings to the leaders in Jerusalem.[16]

Paul refers to the offerings with the noun χάρις (*charis*), "grace," which could denote simply "a gift" or "donation," but given the theological implications of the word, it connotes a very generous or bountiful offering, one that reveals the munificence of those making it (compare 2 Cor. 8:4, 6–7, 19).[17] To assure the purity of his motives, Paul insists that the transmission of the funds not be made by him but only by those whom the Corinthian Church leaders appoint. The verb δοκιμάζω (*dokimazō*), "to approve," denotes more than simple trust. It is approval granted only to those who have proven themselves to be true at all costs.[18] Since it is likely that the offering would have been converted into gold for ease of traveling, Paul—along with the church members—would have been very concerned for its safety. Therefore, those given the assignment had to be men of the highest integrity. Paul trusted the Corinthian leadership to know who these men were.[19]

---

14. See also Findlay, "St. Paul's First Epistle," 2:946.

15. Thiselton, *First Epistle,* 1324.

16. Translated thus in the NJB, NIV, and REB. See Raymond F. Collins, *Models of Theological Reflections* (Lanham, Md.: University Press of America, 1984), 41, who notes that the plural ἐπιστολῶν (*epistolōn*), "letters," is properly used because each member of the delegation would have needed to supply one.

17. Barrett, *First Epistle,* 387.

18. BDAG, 255–56; Thiselton, *First Epistle,* 1324.

19. Murphy-O'Connor, *Paul,* 345–46.

16:4 *And if it be meet that I go also, they shall go with me / And if it seems advisable for me to go also, they will go with me:* The adjective ἄξιος (*axios*), "fit, right" or "proper," denotes that which is fitting or appropriate for a given occasion.[20] Just what the present subjunctive verb *ē*, "it be, it seems," modifies is unclear. It could be construed with the noun χάρις (*charis*) in the previous verse, thus suggesting that if the result of the collection warrants it (that is, if it was fitting or proper), Paul would travel with it.[21] The verb could, however, refer to conditions in Jerusalem that could also necessitate he travel with the couriers. He may have deliberately left his intent vague to allow for options to make themselves apparent as the time approached.[22] Certainly, he did not need to go and, given the dangers of sea travel at the time, he may have initially determined to not go, but feeling a grave sense of responsibility and of concern for those in Jerusalem, he did not want to rule out the possibility.[23] By the time he wrote 2 Corinthians, conditions had so manifested themselves that he had decided to brave the dangers and go (2 Cor. 1:15–16; Rom. 15:25–26).

Analysis and Summary

This pericope refers to the practice of almsgiving or making freewill offerings for the benefit of the poor and distressed among God's people. It was established as a principal doctrine and practice of the Church during the Jerusalem Council in AD 49. It connoted a tangible recognition of the mutual caring and sharing that befell those of all economic classes and ethnicities that made up the Church as a whole (Gal. 2:10).[24] Therefore, the collection of these offerings was, for Paul, far more than a mundane task imposed upon him. The offerings were meant to maintain the Church, not just in some mechanical or routine way but in the sense of nourishing and sustaining its members. It was, more importantly, a matter and tangible means of passing on the grace (χάρις, *charis*) that God and Christ had bestowed upon these later Saints through the efforts and sacrifices of the earliest ones. Through the donations of their means—a token of time and, therefore, of life—these later Christians reciprocated and, thereby, strengthened the overall "fellowship" (κοινωνία, *koinōnia*) by serving (διακονέω, *diakoneō*) in similitude of

---

20. BDAG, 93–94.
21. Parry, *First Epistle*, 246.
22. Fee, *First Epistle*, 816.
23. Murphy-O'Connor, *Paul*, 343.
24. Thiselton, *First Epistle*, 1319.

the Savior's own way. The end result was a double blessing (εὐλογία, *eulogia*) as one gave and the other received and both were lifted by God.

In 16:1–4, Paul gives a concrete example of how the Saints can fulfill his admonition to "always [do] your best in the work of the Lord" (15:58, Rendition). The verb περισσεύω (*perisseuō*), "to abound more and more" or "to overflow," indicates a growth in ability, means, and power.[25] In 2 Corinthians 9:8 Paul will articulate this idea again, stating that God gives to the Saints abundance so that they can "abound in every good work" (authors' translation). A nuance behind the word is that of doing one's best, that is, of putting effort into one's service to the Lord and to one's fellow Saints. Such effort opens the doors to assistance from the Father. The Apostle's point is that it is God who bestows grace, expressed in divinely inspired motives as well as the bequeathing of spiritual gifts and increased abilities and powers. He does so in part to allow the Saints to reciprocate that grace to others with the result that all abound more and more. The Savior, as expressed in his life and ministry, is the embodiment of this process.[26] He went "from grace to grace" as he gave grace for grace until he abounded in a fullness of grace, truth, and glory (D&C 93:12–16). This enabled him to do all that the Father required. He could then empower others to do the same (see D&C 93:19–20). Thus, in 1 Thessalonians 3:12–13, Paul could pray that "the Lord cause you increase and abound in love for each other and for all people, ... so that your hearts may be strengthened in holiness to be blameless before our God and Father" (authors' translation). Giving grace is thus a key to gaining holiness. The point is that seemingly mundane service cannot be separated from spiritual service and, therefore, both lend purity to the soul.

The Apostles instituted a welfare program very early in their ministry that seems to have incorporated elements of the law of consecration. Members shared what they had and divided their goods among all according to their need (Acts 2:45; 4:31–35). Contributions came in from areas outside Jerusalem, including Syrian Antioch and Cyprus (Acts 4:34–37; 11:27–29).[27] That contributions came in from so far away argues against the idea of some that Paul's work in this area was primarily meant to unify the Greek and Jewish segments of the Church.[28] The work had already been going on for

---

25. BDAG, 805; Louw-Nida, §§57.24; 78.31, 32; Thiselton, *First Epistle*, 1319.

26. David F. Ford, "The Economy of God," in Frances Margaret Young and David F. Ford, *Meaning and Truth in 2 Corinthians* (London: SPCK, 1987), 177–78.

27. Barnabas was a native of Cyprus but seems to have been living in Antioch at this time.

28. Anderson, *Understanding Paul*, 139.

some time, and most (if not all) of the unity it generated was already felt. The Apostles called seven men to manage the program, thus allowing the leaders to concentrate their work on more spiritual Church matters and missionary work (Acts 6:1–6).

Not long after Paul's own conversion, he, with Barnabas, was sent from Antioch with "relief unto the brethren which dwelt in Judaea" (Acts 11:29). As a result, Paul was well acquainted with the inner workings of the welfare system.

During the proceedings of the Jerusalem Council in AD 49, Paul and Barnabas were officially assigned to oversee the missionary work to the Gentiles while the other Apostles, at least for a time, continued to work among the Jews. One of their assignments was to "remember the poor" (Gal. 2:10), and that meant sending funds to the officers of the general Church in Jerusalem. Because of an acute famine that hit the Near East during the reign of the emperor Claudius, needs in the mid to late 50s were particularly great.

Paul was given the responsibility to collect contributions and either bring them or see that they were brought to Jerusalem from his area of ministry. In this epistle, he notes that collections were being raised not only in Corinth but also in the regions of Galatia and Macedonia (16:1–5). As evidenced in both Romans and Acts, Paul fulfilled his responsibility, meeting with James, the leader of the Jerusalem branch of the Church, and giving him "alms . . . and offerings" from the Saints abroad (Acts 24:17).[29]

Paul instructed the Saints to lay aside their gifts, λογεία (*logeia*), each Sunday. His admonition suggests that already the Christians viewed Sunday as a special day of worship. During Paul's time, the σάββατον (*sabbaton*), or "first day of the week" (John 20:1, 19; Acts 20:7), was referred to as ἡ κυριακὴ ἡμέρα (*hē kyriakē hēmera*), "the Lord's day" (Rev. 1:10). As such it looked back to the Easter event and became its memorial.[30]

To what degree the practice of Sunday worship was universal is unknown. For decades, many Christians continued to worship on Saturday. It would seem, however, that the first day of the week was widely accepted as being special due to its association with the Resurrection of the Lord and was used for sacramental services. Jewish polemics against the Christians during the later first and second centuries motivated the Christians to separate

---

29. Anderson, *Understanding Paul,* 139–40.

30. Over time, it came to designate the day in which the risen Lord was honored. See Joseph A. Fitzmyer, "κύριος, κυριακός," in Schneider and Balz, *Exegetical Dictionary of the New Testament,* 2:331.

themselves from the Jews, and a major way of doing so was to replace Saturday with Sunday as the holy day. This change, however, seems to have taken well into the second century before most congregations united in making it *the* day of worship. Eventually, it did attain the full weight of tradition and force of the fourth commandment.[31] It would seem that during Paul's time, the day of worship had not become an issue.

Referring to this practice, President Brigham Young observed, "Here we are commanded to assemble ourselves together on the first day of the week, as the ancient disciples did and to offer up our sacraments before the Lord, confessing our faults one to another. ... Persons professing to be Saints should assemble themselves together on the Lord's day, except those who may be necessarily detained at home to keep the house, take care of the children, or to perform some work of necessity and mercy; the rest should assemble in the place appointed for worship and the offering up of our sacraments."[32]

PAUL'S PLANS TO VISIT CORINTH (16:5–12)

Greek Text

5 Ἐλεύσομαι δὲ πρὸς ὑμᾶς ὅταν Μακεδονίαν διέλθω, Μακεδονίαν γὰρ διέρχομαι, 6 πρὸς ὑμᾶς δὲ τυχὸν παραμενῶ ἢ καὶ παραχειμάσω, ἵνα ὑμεῖς με προπέμψητε οὗ ἐὰν πορεύωμαι. 7 οὐ θέλω γὰρ ὑμᾶς ἄρτι ἐν παρόδῳ ἰδεῖν, ἐλπίζω γὰρ χρόνον τινὰ ἐπιμεῖναι πρὸς ὑμᾶς, ἐὰν ὁ κύριος ἐπιτρέψῃ. 8 ἐπιμενῶ δὲ ἐν Ἐφέσῳ ἕως τῆς πεντηκοστῆς· 9 θύρα γάρ μοι ἀνέῳγεν μεγάλη καὶ ἐνεργής, καὶ ἀντικείμενοι πολλοί.

10 Ἐὰν δὲ ἔλθῃ Τιμόθεος, βλέπετε ἵνα ἀφόβως γένηται πρὸς ὑμᾶς, τὸ γὰρ ἔργον κυρίου ἐργάζεται ὡς κἀγώ· 11 μή τις οὖν αὐτὸν ἐξουθενήσῃ. προπέμψατε δὲ αὐτὸν ἐν εἰρήνῃ, ἵνα ἔλθῃ πρός με, ἐκδέχομαι γὰρ αὐτὸν μετὰ τῶν ἀδελφῶν.

12 Περὶ δὲ Ἀπολλῶ τοῦ ἀδελφοῦ, πολλὰ παρεκάλεσα αὐτὸν ἵνα ἔλθῃ πρὸς ὑμᾶς μετὰ τῶν ἀδελφῶν· καὶ πάντως οὐκ ἦν θέλημα ἵνα νῦν ἔλθῃ, ἐλεύσεται δὲ ὅταν εὐκαιρήσῃ. [SBLGNT]

---

31. J. C. Laansma, "Lord's Day," in *Dictionary of the Later New Testament and Its Developments,* ed. Ralph P. Martin and Peter H. Davids (Downers Grove: InterVarsity Press, 1998), 679–86. For discussion, see Thiselton, *First Epistle,* 1321–22.

32. Brigham Young, in *JD,* 10:283–84.

King James Version

5 Now I will come unto you, when I shall pass through Macedonia: for I do pass through Macedonia. 6 And it may be that I will abide, yea, and winter with you, that ye may bring me on my journey whithersoever I go. 7 For I will not see you now by the way; but I trust to tarry a while with you, if the Lord permit. 8 But I will tarry at Ephesus until Pentecost. 9 For a great door and effectual is opened unto me, and there are many adversaries. 10 Now if Timotheus come, see that he may be with you without fear: for he worketh the work of the Lord, as I also do. 11 Let no man therefore despise him: but conduct him forth in peace, that he may come unto me: for I look for him with the brethren. 12 As touching our brother Apollos, I greatly desired him to come unto you with the brethren: but his will was not at all to come at this time; but he will come when he shall have convenient time.

New Rendition

5 But I will come to you after I travel through Macedonia—for I am going to travel through Macedonia—6 and, if possible, I will stay with you or even spend the winter, so that you can send me on my way wherever I go next. 7 For I do not want to just see you in passing, but I hope to spend some time with you, if the Lord should permit it. 8 But I will remain in Ephesus until Pentecost, 9 for a great and effective door has opened for me, although there are many who oppose me. 10 Now when Timothy comes, see that he has nothing to fear when he is with you, for he is doing the Lord's work just as I do. 11 Therefore, no one should despise him. Rather send him on his way in peace so he can come to me, because I am waiting for him with the brethren. 12 Now as for brother Apollos, I strongly urged him to come to you with the brethren, but he was not at all willing to come now, but he will come when he has the opportunity.

Translation Notes and Comments

16:5 *Now I will come unto you, when I shall pass through Macedonia: for I do pass through Macedonia / But I will come to you after I travel through Macedonia—for I am going to travel through Macedonia:* The future active verb ἐλεύσομαι (*eleusomai*), "I will come," gives force to Paul's assurance to the Corinthian Saints that he would be coming as soon as possible. His route, however, would not be direct; he had to first pass through Macedonia, Greece's northern neighbor. The Apostle had set up congregations in Thessalonica, Philippi, and perhaps Berea. When referring to his intended course, Paul uses the same verb twice: διέρχομαι (*dierchomai*), "to pass through." The word carries the force not only of moving through an area but also of having "imminent purpose" or "firm intention" for doing so.[33] The

---

33. BDAG, 244; Findlay, "St. Paul's First Epistle," 2:946–47; Barrett, *First Epistle,* 819. Though the verb is in the present tense it has full future force. Wallace, *Greek Grammar,* 535–36.

Apostle's use of that term suggests he felt compelled to make the swing to the north.

16:6 *And it may be that I will abide, yea, and winter with you / and, if possible, I will stay with you or even spend the winter:* The Apostle begins this clause with πρὸς ὑμᾶς (*pros hymas*), "with you."[34] By placing it in the first position, Paul makes it emphatic and, thus, emphasizes that his stay in Corinth is no less important to him just because he is taking the time to visit Macedonia.[35] His use of the adverb τυχόν (*tychon*), "may be, if possible,"[36] reveals his yet unsettled plans for his visit. He is not even sure how long he will remain with them, but he prepares them for a possibility of a stay of three or four months—the verb παραχειμάζω (*paracheimazō*), meaning "to spend the winter."[37] Dangers of sea travel during the winter months were high, thus, he appears to have determined to do some productive pastoral work while waiting for better travel conditions.[38]

that ye may bring me on my journey whithersoever I go / so that you can send me on my way wherever I go next: Here Paul identifies part of his reason for coming to Corinth. The verb προπέμπω (*propempō*) means to assist someone in making a journey "with food, money, by arranging for companions, means of travel, etc."[39] Paul's choice of word shows his full confidence that his relationship with at least some of the Saints in Corinth is sufficiently strong and trusting that they will fully support him on the next phase of his mission, no matter what that may be.[40] With the phrase οὗ ἐὰν πορεύομαι (*hou ean poreuomai*), "to wherever I go next," Paul leaves open all possibilities for the future. His is a mission driven by both spiritual direction and member need. He will, therefore, let nothing dictate otherwise.[41]

16:7 *For I will not see you now by the way; but I trust to tarry a while with you, if the Lord permit / For I do not want to just see you in passing, but I hope to spend some time with you, if the Lord should permit it:* The phrase

---

34. The syntax here indicates the preposition *pros,* usually meaning "to" or "toward," refers to a state rather than to a motion. Thus, Paul will be "with" them rather than moving "toward" them. Wallace, *Greek Grammar,* 358–59.

35. Fitzmyer, *First Corinthians,* 618.

36. Technically, the word is the neuter accusative second aorist participle of the verb τυγχάνω (*tyngchanō*), but here it is used in an adverbial capacity.

37. BDAG, 773.

38. Conzelmann, *1 Corinthians,* 297; compare Acts 27:9–12.

39. BDAG, 873.

40. Findlay, "St. Paul's First Epistle," 2:946–47; Barrett, *First Epistle,* 389.

41. Thiselton, *First Epistle,* 1329.

ἄρτι ἐν παρόδῳ (*arti en parodō*), "just in passing," carries the idea of a fleeting visit, but Paul is clear that such is not his intent. His purpose, as he had already made very clear, is to give directives and settle other matters (11:34), which would necessitate a longer stay. The phrase ἐὰν ὁ κύριος ἐπιτρέψῃ (*ean ho kyrios epitrepsē*), literally "if the Deity allows,"[42] is most telling. Paul places his ministry totally "in the hands of the Lord" in full faith and trust.[43]

16:8 But I will tarry at Ephesus until Pentecost / But I will remain in Ephesus until Pentecost: The future tense of the verb ἐπιμενῶ (*epimeno*), "will remain,"[44] reveals that Paul is writing from Ephesus. The noun πεντηκοστή (*pentēcostē*), "Pentecost," usually refers to the Jewish holy day that was celebrated fifty days after the Passover and known as "the feast of weeks" (Deut. 16:10; compare Ex. 23:16; Lev. 23:16).[45] Though Paul may have had the actual feast in mind, he could also be referring to the more general idea of spring when travel conditions once more became good.[46] Whichever the case, Paul's words did give the Corinthian Saints an approximate time of his arrival.

16:9 For a great door and effectual is opened unto me / for a great and effective door has opened for me: Paul explains why he does not plan to leave Ephesus immediately. An opportunity has presented itself which the Apostle describes as a θύρα . . . μεγάλη καὶ ἐνεργής (*thyra . . . megalē kai energēs*), "a great and effective door." He uses the noun *thyra*, "door," as a "metaphor for opportunity."[47] The adjective μέγας (*megas*), "great," denotes something that goes well beyond the usual standard.[48] Here, in keeping with the metaphor, it connotes the unusually wide breadth of the opening.[49] The adjective ἐνεργής (*energēs*), "effective," means that which is "effective in causing something to happen."[50] An open door allows one to move from one area to another. An effective door facilitates that process. Through the metaphor, Paul explains that an excellent opportunity has developed and, by taking advantage of it, his influence will be greatly enhanced.[51] His desire is not to leave until he has taken full advantage of it.

---

42. Fitzmyer, *First Corinthians*, 619.
43. Thiselton, *First Epistle*, 1329.
44. BDAG, 375–76.
45. *ABD*, 5:222–23.
46. Collins, *First Corinthians*, 593; Acts 27:9–12.
47. Thiselton, *First Epistle*, 1330.
48. BDAG, 623–24.
49. Findlay, "St. Paul's First Epistle," 2:947.
50. Louw-Nida, §13.124.
51. Findlay, "St. Paul's First Epistle," 2:947.

Paul does not identify how the "great and effective door" was opened to him. He had been laboring in Ephesus for quite sometime, but something had recently happened that presented new opportunities for missionary work. It may have been associated with the "wild beasts" he successfully overcame (15:32, Rendition), but unfortunately, he does not supply any details.

and there are many adversaries / although there are many who oppose me: The conjunction καί (*kai*) is used here in a contrasting sense[52] and is thus translated as "although" in our Rendition. Paul is realistic. He knows that opposition is also very strong. The verb ἀντίκειμαι (*antikeimai*) denotes an opposition to or adversarial role toward something. The participial form that is used here denotes those who play such a role. Paul describes them as πολλοί (*polloi*), "many," thus, revealing their strength in numbers and suggesting the power behind them.[53] As Lehi noted, "It must needs be, that there is an opposition in all things" (2 Ne. 2:11). Therefore, as wide as the door of opportunity was, it was matched by the power of those who have organized against Paul. Still, the Apostle was undaunted.

16:10 *Now if Timotheus come, see that he may be with you without fear / Now when Timothy comes, see that he has nothing to fear when he is with you:* The KJV translates the Greek proper name "Timothy" with the nominative subject Latin ending *eus.* In the phrase ἐὰν δὲ ἔλθῃ (*ean de elthē*), the conjunction ἐάν (*ean*), which normally functions as a conditional particle, "if," here closely approaches the sense of ὅταν (*hotan*), "whenever, when."[54] Thus the phrase should be translated "when Timothy comes," not "if [Timothy] comes," because Paul has indicated that he has already given Timothy his assignment and the young man is on his way (4:17).[55] The adverb ἀφόβως (*aphobōs*), "fearlessly," betrays Paul's concern that some of the Corinthian members may mistreat his emissary. Paul's use of the imperative βλέπετε (*blepete*), "see to it that,"[56] reveals his anxiety and his determination to have his friends see that Timothy lives "fearlessly" while among them.

for he worketh the work of the Lord, as I also do / for he is doing the Lord's work just as I do: With this phrase, Paul explains why Timothy should be treated with special respect. The verb ἐργάζομαι (*ergazomai*),

52. BDAG, 494–96.
53. Thiselton, *First Epistle,* 1330.
54. BDAG, 268.
55. Fee, *First Epistle,* 821; Conzelmann, *1 Corinthians,* 297.
56. Thiselton, *First Epistle,* 1331.

"to work,"[57] is used here as a progressive present, showing that the young man is continuing in the work of the Lord.[58] The phrase ὡς καγώ (*hōs kagō*), "even as I [do]," gives apostolic authority to Timothy's assignment and further stresses the members' need to honor him.

16:11 *Let no man therefore despise him / Therefore, no one should despise him:* Paul's chief concern for why Timothy would not be treated well is revealed by his use of the verb ἐξουθενέω (*exoutheneō*), "to despise." The word denotes a show, by one's attitude or manner, that "an entity has no merit or worth" and, by extension, to despise or show disdain for another resulting in their rejection.[59] Paul's use of the imperative emphasizes that no one should see Timothy as having little or no worth. Just what the problem was, the Apostle does not identify. It could have been that Timothy was rather young, was only half Jewish, did not belong to the social class the Corinthian Saints respected, or some other reason that history has lost.

but conduct him forth in peace, that he may come unto me / Rather send him on his way in peace so he can come to me: Paul asks his supporters to assist Timothy in two ways. The first way is denoted by the imperative προπέμψατε (*propempsate*) meaning, as noted above, to assist one on a journey by providing whatever is necessary (see 16:6). The second way he denotes with the noun εἰρήνη (*eirēnē*), normally meaning "peace," but here connoting a state free from worry and anxiety.[60] The Apostle's words suggest that Timothy will not have means of his own to carry out his mission and then report back to Paul. He, therefore, will need the Saints' assistance.

for I look for him with the brethren / because I am waiting for him with the brethren: The syntax of this clause is unclear. The verb ἐκδέχομαι (*ekdechomai*), "to wait," can mean that Paul is waiting with certain brethren for Timothy's arrival or that he is waiting for Timothy and the brethren to arrive.[61] In the next verse, however, he also refers to "the brethren" and, in that case, it is clear they are fellow travelers with Timothy. It is also ambiguous as to which "brethren" Paul refers. They could be close friends or just traveling companions. They were for sure members of the Church and likely made up a delegation assigned to this investigation.[62]

---

57. BDAG, 389.

58. Wallace, *Greek Grammar,* 518–19.

59. BDAG, 352.

60. Louw-Nida, §25:248.

61. Though the REB retains the ambiguity, the NRSV takes the first view while the NJB takes the second.

62. Fitzmyer, *First Corinthians,* 622.

16:12 *As touching our brother Apollos, I greatly desired him to come unto you with the brethren / Now as for brother Apollos, I strongly urged him to come to you with the brethren:* Apollos had a strong following in Corinth and it is likely that, for this reason, Paul preferred to have him check out conditions there. This position is reinforced by the force of the verb, παρακαλέω (*parakaleō*), that Paul used. It means "to make a strong request" and, therefore, "to implore" or "entreat."[63] Its use suggests that some of the members may have requested that Paul ask him to come, and he wanted to make sure that they understood that he had put effort in to honoring their request. The Apostle's mention of "the brothers" points to the assignment of a delegation, not just one person, to carry out the assignment.[64]

but his will was not at all to come at this time; but he will come when he shall have convenient time / but he was not at all willing to come now, but he will come when he has the opportunity: The phrase οὐκ ἦν θέλημα (*ouk ēn thelēma*), literally "it was not the will," does not state explicitly whose will it was not to come, but the context suggests it was Apollos' and it is translated that way in both the KJV and the Rendition. Just why the missionary was unwilling to come at that time is unknown. Though some scholars have speculated that it was due to God's will, nothing in the text suggests that is the case.[65] By using the verb εὐκαιρέω (*eukaireō*), meaning "to experience a favorable time or occasion,"[66] Paul reassures his readers that Apollos' refusal was only temporary. Therefore, it would seem that the Apostle's fellow missionary simply felt that conditions were not right at that time for his return.

Analysis and Summary

It is difficult to determine with certainty how many visits Paul made to Corinth.[67] Luke mentions only two (Acts 18:1 for the first one and Acts 20:1–2 for the second), while Paul's writings suggest three. However, two of Paul's passages are ambiguous: 2 Corinthians 12:14, "Behold, the third time I am ready to come to you," could be interpreted to mean that Paul has prepared to visit the people three times but never yet made it, or that he is preparing to visit them for the third time, having done so twice before.

---

63. BDAG, 764–65.

64. Fitzmyer, *First Corinthians,* 622.

65. For example, Barrett, *First Epistle,* 391; Bruce, *1 and 2 Corinthians,* 160, hold the view that it was in response to God's will while Fee, *First Epistle,* 824; Robertson and Plummer, *Critical and Exegetical Commentary,* 392, do not.

66. BDAG, 406–7.

67. Murphy-O'Connor, *Paul,* 291–351, has one of the best studies on this subject.

Also 2 Corinthians 13:2, "as if I were present, the second time," could be understood to mean that he had expressed his wish two times or he had come to them twice. Verse 1 of that chapter is, however, very helpful, "This is the third time I am coming to you." It indicates that Paul is planning on a third visit as soon as he can make arrangements. Thus, Luke's account does not mention this hurried visit.[68]

Conditions that warranted this swift visit were likely generated after Paul had written 1 Corinthians and Timothy, with his delegation, had arrived. There are a couple of clues in 1 Corinthians that may explain what happened. First, the Apostle mentions that he sent Timothy, a young emissary, to bear witness of Paul's integrity and Christian lifestyle (4:17). Second, Paul was very concerned about how the young man would be treated (16:10) and made it very clear that if things did not go well, he would personally come to set things straight (4:18–19). Apparently, as Timothy later reported to Paul, things did not go well, so Paul made good on his threat with the quick visit.[69] He apparently did not stay a long time, thus not realizing his goal at that time for an extended visit (16:6).

By repetition, Paul emphasized his need to visit the Saints in Macedonia (16:5). It appears that he sensed or learned that they were in spiritual danger and, therefore, he felt the need for a personal visit. The problem most likely had arisen due to the work of the "Judaizers" who had arrived in the area. These were Jews who were only partly converted to Christianity. They believed and forcefully taught that the Mosaic law had not been fulfilled and, therefore, it had to be practiced with all its rites and ordinances. They accepted Jesus as the Messiah and saw his role as showing how the law was to be properly interpreted and adopted to life. Salvation, they insisted, came only through obedience to the law.[70] Because they did not appreciate the greatness of Christ nor understand his mission, Paul knew that their beliefs were heresy and that it would lead people away from the truth. Therefore, he felt it was paramount that these people be stopped and that only a personal visit would do that.

In the meantime, Paul had no intentions of letting events in Corinth go unchecked. He put pressure on (παρακαλέω, *parakaleō*) his fellow

---

68. Sperry, *Paul's Life*, 115–16.

69. Murphy-O'Connor, *Paul*, 292–94.

70. For a study, see Translation Notes and the accompanying Analysis of Acts 15:1 in this series.

missionary, Apollos, to head a delegation to oversee matters there. For reasons unknown, the missionary refused to go until he felt the time more suitable (16:12). It is likely that he felt disgust toward some of the Corinthian Saints for using, and probably abusing, his teachings to promote their personal agenda and pitting him against Paul. He, too, would have been well aware of the αἱρέσεις (*haireseis*), "parties, factions" (see 11:19, Rendition), and, like Paul, disapproved of them. His refusal to come could therefore have been his means of emphasizing his contempt and irritation for their actions.[71] Paul was careful to point out that the decision was Apollos's alone, thus, undermining any suggestion from his detractors that the Apostle was somehow responsible for it.

Paul then turned to his concerns for Timothy. The young man's mission was twofold: to disabuse the Saints of the notion promoted by some that the Apostle was neither living nor teaching what he should (4:17) and to report conditions back to Paul (16:10–11).

The Apostle was deeply concerned about how some of the Saints might treat this young man. Since he was Paul's delegate, the Apostle's detractors would likely be hostile to the missionary. These status-conscious souls could regard the young man as of little account—revealed by Paul's use of the word ἐξουθενέω (*exoutheneō*), "to despise." On his part, it is likely that Timothy was not a backward soul. He had accompanied Paul on a number of occasions (1 Thes. 1:1; 2 Cor. 1:1; Philip. 1:1) and, with others, had previously acted as the Apostle's delegate (Acts 19:22; Philip. 2:19–22). Thus, he had earned Paul's deepest trust and respect. His courage and defense of Paul could easily rub some of the Saints the wrong way.[72] To bolster his representative's position, Paul reminded his readers that Timothy was "doing the Lord's work just as I do" (16:10, Rendition). To see that Timothy was accorded proper respect while visiting the Saints, Paul laid three charges upon them: (1) to see that Timothy could accomplish his mission free from anxiety and worry, (2) to neither despise nor undervalue him, and (3) to give him all that was necessary in support and provisions so that he could accomplish his assignment and return to Paul (16:10–11).[73]

71. Fitzmyer, *First Corinthians*, 623.

72. C. R. Hutson, "Was Timothy Timid: On the Rhetoric of Fearlessness (1 Corinthians 16:10–11) and Cowardice (2 Timothy 1:7)," *Biblical Review* 42 (1997): 58–73.

73. Thiselton, *First Epistle*, 1331–32.

FINAL ADMONITION
(16:13–16)

Greek Text

13 Γρηγορεῖτε, στήκετε ἐν τῇ πίστει, ἀνδρίζεσθε, κραταιοῦσθε. 14 πάντα ὑμῶν ἐν ἀγάπῃ γινέσθω.

15 Παρακαλῶ δὲ ὑμᾶς, ἀδελφοί· οἴδατε τὴν οἰκίαν Στεφανᾶ, ὅτι ἐστὶν ἀπαρχὴ τῆς Ἀχαΐας καὶ εἰς διακονίαν τοῖς ἁγίοις ἔταξαν ἑαυτούς· 16 ἵνα καὶ ὑμεῖς ὑποτάσσησθε τοῖς τοιούτοις καὶ παντὶ τῷ συνεργοῦντι καὶ κοπιῶντι. [SBLGNT]

King James Version

13 Watch ye, stand fast in the faith, quit you like men, be strong. 14 Let all your things be done with charity. 15 I beseech you, brethren, (ye know the house of Stephanas, that it is the firstfruits of Achaia, and that they have addicted themselves to the ministry of the saints,) 16 That ye submit yourselves unto such, and to every one that helpeth with us, and laboureth.

New Rendition

13 Keep alert, stand firm in the faith, be courageous and strong. 14 Let all you do be done with love. 15 You are aware that the household of Stephanas were the first converts in Achaia and they have devoted themselves to serving the saints, so I urge you, brothers and sisters, 16 to also subject yourselves to men such as them as well as to every other who joins in and labors with them.

Translation Notes and Comments

16:13 *Watch ye / Keep alert:* In this verse, there are four imperatives. The first, γρηγορεῖτε (*grēgoreite*), means to be in a state of continual readiness, but the word also carries the nuance of remaining fully alive.[74] Jesus used the term in an eschatological context (Mark 13:35, 37; compare Rev. 3:1–3), but it applies to any Christian living in any age. The Saints must be ever watchful for anything that would pull them from the Christian lifestyle and, thereby, diminish or destroy their spiritual lives. The plea here is to general alertness. In the next three admonitions he becomes a bit more specific.[75]

  stand fast in the faith / stand firm in the faith: The second imperative, στήκετε (*stēkete*), means to stand, but it carries the metaphorical force of being "firmly committed in conviction or belief."[76] Paul's addition of the phrase ἐν τῇ πίστει (*en tē pistei*), "in your faith," shows exactly where

---

74. BDAG, 207–8.
75. Fitzmyer, *First Corinthians*, 624.
76. BDAG, 944–45.

that commitment must lie; it is in and *only* in the gospel, the center of which is "Christ, and him crucified" (2:2).[77] The ways and philosophies of men are to be eschewed.

quit you like men / be courageous: The third imperative, ἀνδρίζεσθε (*andrizesthe*), literally "to act like men," means to be courageous.[78] It carries the idea of taking a valiant and immovable stance when it comes to righteousness. The force of the verb ἀνδρίζομαι (*andrizomai*) is that of exhibiting courage in the face of danger, of not backing down from one's ideals—especially when challenged.[79] Behind it is the idea that contrasts the mature with the immature, the man with the child. Men are to "put away childish things" (13:11).[80]

be strong / and strong: The final imperative, κραταιοῦσθε (*krataiousthe*), means to become strong, but, in a psychological sense, it means to remain firm to one's convictions.[81] It is, therefore, similar in meaning to *andrizomai* (as discussed above).[82] It differs, however, in two important ways. First, the former is more active while the latter is more passive. One must be willing to go into battle but must maintain strength whether a battle is called for or not. Second, the former is static while the latter is dynamic. One is to have courage at all times, but to also grow in strength.

16:14 *Let all your things be done with charity / Let all you do be done with love:* This verse adds an additional imperative. Here Paul has his readers look back at his counsel in chapter 13. He emphasizes the breadth that love's influence must have with the nominal adjective πάντα (*panta*), "all things" (13:7). Love is to be the foundation, motivation, influence, and driving force behind all that the Christian does.

16:15 *I beseech you, brethren, (ye know the house of Stephanas, that it is the firstfruits of Achaia . . .) / You are aware that the household of Stephanas were the first converts in Achaia . . . so I urge you, brothers and sisters:* The Greek text for this verse is unusual because it begins with a strong appeal—παρακαλῶ δὲ ὑμᾶς, ἀδελφοί (*parakalō de hymas,*

---

77. Fee, *First Epistle,* 827 and n. 11.

78. BDAG, 76.

79. Louw-Nida, §25.165.

80. Thiselton, *First Epistle,* 1336.

81. BDAG, 564.

82. The combination of the two imperatives parallels a combination of verbs, "courage and manliness" found in LXX 2 Sam. 10:12; Ps. 27:14; 31:35. In Hebrew the phrase is *hazaq weamas.* The three scriptures are a recommendation to take "a courageous and valiant stance or mode of action." Fitzmyer, *First Corinthians,* 624.

adelphoi), "I beseech you brethren," which is then interrupted with a parenthetical phrase that continues for the rest of the verse. For clarity's sake, our Rendition puts the parenthetical phrase first and then follows it with the admonition. Paul uses the aside to put the admonition he will give in the next verse into perspective. It forces his readers to recall those individuals whom he is going to recommend for imitation.

The verb παρακαλέω (*parakaleō*) means to urge or exhort someone to an action.[83] Those to whom he directs his request are the ἀδελφοί (*adelphoi*), here—as is often the case in Paul's writings—the word refers to both male and females, and is translated as "brothers and sisters" in our Rendition.[84] Paul, however, does not identify what action he wants his readers to take until after the parenthetical aside.

The Apostle had already mentioned that he had baptized Stephanas and those of his household (1:16).[85] Here he notes they were ἀπαρχὴ τῆς Ἀχαΐας (*aparchē tēs Achaias*), literally "the firstfruits of Achaia," that is, those who first joined the Church in the Roman province of Achaia. The phrase does not necessarily mean that they were the very first people baptized. At Athens, the principle city in Achaia, he did convert some individuals. Among these were a woman named Damaris and a prominent civic leader named Dionysus (Acts 17:34).[86] These appear to be the actual first converts. The term *aparchē*, therefore, should be understood in its primary meaning as that which foreshadows "more to come."[87] What makes the conversion of Stephanas stand out was that he brought his entire household into the Church with him. Paul saw that as the promise of a greater inflowing of converts that did, indeed, come to be.

and that they have addicted themselves to the ministry of the saints / and they have devoted themselves to serving the saints: The verb τάσσω (*tassō*) means to arrange, order, put in place.[88] Here with the reflexive pronoun ἑαυτούς (*heautous*), "themselves," it conveys the idea of "to devote

---

83. BDAG, 764–65.

84. For an explanation, see Translation Notes on 1:10.

85. The noun *oikia*, "house," usually referred to all those associated with a wealthy man's estate, including relatives and even servants. See Otto Michel, "οἰκία," in *TDNT*, 5:131–34.

86. Dionysus was a member of the council of the Areopagus. This council functioned as a court dealing with religious and civil matters, including cases of homicide. See *ABD*, 1:370–71.

87. Thiselton, *First Epistle*, 1338; Collins *First Corinthians*, 604.

88. BDAG, 991.

oneself."[89] The force of the word is that of self-appointment.[90] The house of Stephanas had done so with great personal investment εἰς δικονίαν τοῖς ἁγίοις (*eis dikonian tois hagiois*), "in service to the Saints."[91] Paul, therefore, holds up the household as the model of those who have devoted themselves, that is, "set themselves aside" for the work of the ministry.[92] The Lord has clearly stated that "it is not meet that I should command in all things; for he that is compelled in all things, the same is a slothful and not a wise servant; wherefore he receiveth no reward. Verily I say, men should be anxiously engaged in a good cause, and do many things of their own free will, and bring to pass much righteousness; For the power is in them, wherein they are agents unto themselves. And inasmuch as men do good they shall in nowise lose their reward" (D&C 58:26–28). The house of Stephanas had proved itself a model of living this principle.

16:16 *That ye submit yourselves unto such, and to every one that helpeth with us, and laboureth / to also subject yourselves to men such as them as well as to every other who joins in and labors with them:* The force of the plural passive subjunctive verb ὑποτάσσησθε (*hypotassēsthe*) identifies what Paul wants them to do. It denotes being willing to place oneself in a subordinate relationship to another.

But the context here gives it the force of "submission in the sense of voluntary yielding in love."[93] No coercion is to be exercised. This self-submission should be τοῖς τοιούτοις καὶ παντὶ τῷ συνεργοῦντι καὶ κοπιοῦντι (*tois toioutois kai panti tō synergounti kai kopiounti*), "to men such as them as well as to all those who serve and labor," where "men such as them" refers to the household of Stephanas. The verb συνεργέω (*synergeō*) means to serve or assist but carries the nuance of doing so in conjunction with others.[94] The verb κοπιάω (*kopiaō*) denotes to perform labor that is exceptionally hard or difficult.[95] It may be that aspect of the service that especially commends itself to the admiration and self-submission that Paul requests.

---

89. Louw-Nida, §68.69.

90. Collins, *First Corinthians,* 605. Robertson and Plummer, *Critical and Exegetical Commentary,* 395, see the word as denoting a "self-imposed duty."

91. The noun *diakonia* is one of the few that takes the dative case after it. It denotes an element of personal interest on the part of the subject. Wallace, *Greek Grammar,* 173–74.

92. Thiselton, *First Epistle,* 1339.

93. BDAG, 1042.

94. BDAG, 969.

95. BDAG, 558.

Analysis and Summary

As noted in the Analysis on 1:1–3, Paul followed Roman epistolary conventions in the opening of his epistles, but gave them a decidedly Christian twist. He followed the same practice in his closings.[96] Often letters of this period ended with some kind of admonition or wish in behalf of the receivers, such as "prosper," "be strong," and so on.[97] Paul follows suit with his list of five imperatives. It is Paul's style to give terse and short admonitions at the end of his epistles (for example, see Rom. 16:17–19; Philip. 4:8–9; 1 Thes. 5:12–22).

The four virtues Paul commands in 16:13 are directed against the vices of "heedlessness, fickleness, childishness, and moral enervation."[98] Each is conveyed with the use of a present imperative. Their force must not be overlooked. "He does *not* say *wake up, stand up on your feet*, but *stay watchful* [γρηγορεῖτε, *grēgoreite*] or *keep alert*; *stand firm* [στήκετε, *stēkete*]." The Saints are to have already gained these virtues and must keep them alive and active.[99] And they are to grow in strength.

Identifying Paul's words with the modern Church, Bishop Joseph L. Wirthlin stated, "The strong people will be the Saints of God, who have lived his word, and kept his commandments."[100] And identifying a ramification of Paul's idea, Elder Robert D. Hales noted that by "standing obedient and strong on the doctrine of our God, we stand in holy places, for His doctrine is sacred and will not change in the social and political winds of our day."[101]

Spiritual maturity is the issue here. Paul has already shown that childishness expresses itself in self-centeredness and short-term gratification. It is a world in which love is weak, narcissistic, inward, and self-serving. The Apostle's plea is for the Corinthian Saints to become mature through the development of the greatest of the gifts of the Spirit, ἀγάπη (*agapē*), "the pure love of Christ" (Moro. 7:47). "Whatever the Corinthian Christians do," notes one scholar, "the motivation and attitude should be that of love, [that is] a concern for the good of 'the other' which embodies respect and seeks to build them up in the long term"[102] (compare 8:7–13; 13:1–13). Elder Hales admonished the Saints, "'Let all your [decisions] be done with charity.' (1 Cor. 16:14.)

---

96. Thiselton, *First Epistle,* 1333.
97. Deissmann, *Light from the Ancient East,* 180 n. 4.
98. Findlay, "St. Paul's First Epistle," 2:949.
99. Thiselton, *First Epistle,* 1336; italics in original; bolding changed to italics.
100. Joseph L. Wirthlin, in CR, April 1951, 71.
101. Robert D. Hales, "Stand Strong in Holy Places," *Ensign* 43 (May 2013): 51.
102. Thiselton, *First Epistle,* 1337; bold and italics have been removed.

Beware of fear and greed. Be aware of your true motives. We make poor and irrational decisions if our decision is motivated by greediness: greed for monetary gain; greed that results in a conflict of interest; desire for power, titles, and recognition of men."[103] Love guards against such greed.

MESSAGES AND GREETINGS (16:17–20)

Greek Text

17χαίρω δὲ ἐπὶ τῇ παρουσίᾳ Στεφανᾶ καὶ Φορτουνάτου καὶ Ἀχαϊκοῦ, ὅτι τὸ ὑμέτερον ὑστέρημα οὗτοι ἀνεπλήρωσαν, 18 ἀνέπαυσαν γὰρ τὸ ἐμὸν πνεῦμα καὶ τὸ ὑμῶν. ἐπιγινώσκετε οὖν τοὺς τοιούτους.

19 Ἀσπάζονται ὑμᾶς αἱ ἐκκλησίαι τῆς Ἀσίας. ἀσπάζεται ὑμᾶς ἐν κυρίῳ πολλὰ Ἀκύλας καὶ Πρίσκα σὺν τῇ κατ᾽ οἶκον αὐτῶν ἐκκλησίᾳ. 20 ἀσπάζονται ὑμᾶς οἱ ἀδελφοὶ πάντες. ἀσπάσασθε ἀλλήλους ἐν φιλήματι ἁγίῳ. [SBLGNT]

King James Version

17 I am glad of the coming of Stephanas and Fortunatus and Achaicus: for that which was lacking on your part they have supplied. 18 For they have refreshed my spirit and yours: therefore acknowledge ye them that are such. 19 The churches of Asia salute you. Aquila and Priscilla salute you much in the Lord, with the church that is in their house. 20 All the brethren greet you. Greet ye one another with an holy kiss.

New Rendition

17 I am glad at the arrival of Stephanas, Fortunatus, and Achaicus, because they made up for your absence, 18 for they revived both my spirit and yours. You should give recognition to such people. 19 The churches in the province of Asia send you greetings. Aquila and Prisca send you warm greetings in the Lord as well as the church that meets at their house. 20 All the brothers and sisters here send their greetings to you. Greet each other with a holy kiss.

Translation Notes and Comments

16:17 *I am glad of the coming of Stephanas and Fortunatus and Achaicus: for that which was lacking on your part they have supplied / I am glad at the arrival of Stephanas, Fortunatus, and Achaicus, because they made up for your absence:* Paul expresses delight in the coming of these three

103. Robert D. Hales, "Making Righteous Choices at the Crossroads of Life," *Ensign* 18 (November 1988): 11.

acquaintances from Corinth. His delight is emphasized in his use of the verb χαίρω (*chairō*), "to rejoice" or "be glad."[104] The noun παρουσία (*parousia*) can refer to being present at a place or to the first stage in presence, that is a coming or arrival.[105] The noun ὑστέρημα (*hysterēma*), "lack, absence," connotes a need brought on by the absence of something.[106] Paul's use of the word suggests that, in spite of all the indignation some of these people were causing him, the Apostle greatly missed all the Saints. The verb ἀναπληρόω (*anaplēroō*) means "to fill" or "replace" and to make up for something's lack.[107] Paul's use of the word suggests that the coming of these brothers help assuage his longing for his brothers and sisters in Corinth.

16:18 *For they have refreshed my spirit and yours / for they revived both my spirit and yours:* Paul identifies how richly blessed he feels with their coming by using the verb ἀναπαύω (*anapauō*), "to refresh" or "to revive."[108] His reference to his πνεῦμα (*pneuma*), "spirit," is vague but should most likely be taken in the psychological sense of referring to the seat of insight and feeling.[109] In modern English, the Apostle's idea could be expressed with the phrase "they have raised my spirits."[110] What Paul meant by the phrase καὶ τὸ ὑμῶν (*kai to hymon*), "and yours," is vague. Just how did their coming raise the spirits of the Corinthian Saints? It is most likely that their bringing additional information to Paul caused those at Corinth, who supported Paul, comfort in knowing that these men carried additional information and assurances.[111]

therefore acknowledge ye them that are such / You should give recognition to such people: The verb ἐπιγινώσκω (*epiginōskō*) means to recognize another as having value.[112] Paul's use of the imperative form, ἐπιγινώσκετε (*epiginōskete*), stresses his desire that the Saints value and emulate people exhibiting the quality of life these men have shown.

16:19 *The churches of Asia salute you / The churches in the province of Asia send you greetings:* Paul's use of the plural noun ἐκκλησίαι (*ekklēsiai*)

---

104. BDAG, 1074–75.

105. BDAG, 780–81.

106. BDAG, 1044; Louw-Nida, §§57.38; 85.29.

107. BDAG, 70. Robertson and Plummer, *Critical and Exegetical Commentary*, 396, argue successfully that there are two ways of understanding what Paul meant. These are "my want of you" or "your want of me." Given the context, it is the former that seems the best choice.

108. BDAG, 69.

109. BDAG, 832–36.

110. Thiselton, *First Epistle*, 1340–41.

111. Thiselton, *First Epistle*, 1341 n. 138; Fitzmyer, *First Corinthians*, 626.

112. BDAG, 369.

denotes particular communities or congregations of Saints. The verb ἀσπάζομαι (*aspazomai*) means "to greet [another] warmly."[113] Asia was the most western province in Asia Minor (now Turkey). The city of Ephesus, from which Paul was sending the letter, was one of Asia's chief cities. The gospel had spread quite widely in the whole area.[114]

Aquila and Priscilla salute you much in the Lord, with the church that is in their house / Aquila and Prisca send you warm greetings in the Lord as well as the church that meets at their house: While the Textus Receptus has Πρίσκιλλα (*Priskilla,* the diminutive form of the name), the earliest and best manuscripts have Πρίσκα (*Priska*),[115] and so our Rendition follows suit. The couple had once lived in Corinth and ran a business there. In Ephesus, they had become church leaders and held services in their home.

16:20 *All the brethren greet you / All the brothers and sisters here send their greetings to you:* On ἀδελφοί (*adelphoi*) being translated as "brothers and sisters" see Translation Notes on 1:10. The force of the adjective πάντες (*pantes*), "all," is important for Paul's purpose. As noted above, one of his interests is in raising the consciousness of the Corinthian Saints that they belong to a larger community of believers. The adjective emphasized that there were quite a number of the Asian Saints who felt warmth toward and concern for their fellow Christians in Corinth. It also acted against potential complaints from any of these that they had been omitted.[116]

Greet ye one another with an holy kiss / Greet each other with a holy kiss: The noun φίλημα (*philēma*) refers to a "kiss."[117] Paul qualifies the word with the adjective ἅγιος (*hagios*), "holy," thus guaranteeing its use not only as a sign of affection but also of solemnity. It also assured all that the act did not nuance any impropriety. The gesture was a show of respect and honor and often used by disciples to honor their teachers.[118] The JST changes this

---

113. BDAG, 144. The word was regularly used in the close of Greco-Roman epistles. Moulton and Milligan, *Vocabulary,* 85.

114. By the end of the first century, when Pliny the Younger was the governor of Bithynia in northwest Asia Minor, there were so many Christian converts that the Roman government had to take a position. Pliny's letter (10.96–97) to the emperor Trajan (AD 112) asked what to do about the Christians there.

115. Metzger, *Textual Commentary,* 503. 𝔓46 has Πρεισκας (*Preiskas*), which at that time would have been pronounced the same as Πρισκας (*Priskas*).

116. Jerome Murphy-O'Connor, *Paul the Letter-Writer: His World, His Opinions, His Skills* (Collegeville, Penn.: Literature Press, Michael Glazier Book, 1994), 105.

117. BDAG, 1057, takes the more liberal translation "kiss of esteem."

118. Gustav Stählin, "φιλέω, καταφιλέω, φίλημα," in *TDNT,* 9:138–41. The hypocrisy of Judas' kiss of the Lord is clearly evident.

word to "salutation," thus making Paul's request conform more to western and modern practices.[119]

Analysis and Summary

Stephanas, as noted above, was one of the pioneers of the faith in Greece. It appears he had become a local Christian leader and was greatly admired by Paul. Other than being a faithful Saint, nothing is known of Fortunatus and Achaicus. Both names are, however, Roman (as opposed to "Stephanas," which is Greek), which suggests they were of the freedman class, likely descendents of people who had once been slaves but who, either they themselves or their descendents, had gained freedom.[120] The name Achaicus means "the Achaian," the region on the extreme north of the Peloponnesus. Since that name would make little sense for one living in that province, he was likely a descendent of a person from Achaia who had lived in Italy and received the nickname. Eventually, his descendants returned to Greece.[121]

Aquila and Priscilla were longtime friends and missionary companions of Paul, and he had labored in their shop while he stayed in Corinth (Acts 18:2–3).[122] They apparently had relocated their business to Ephesus and used their home as one of the house churches in the area (Acts 18:18–26).[123] At some point, in serious peril to themselves, they had defended the Apostle (Rom. 16:3–4). Paul is careful to note that the salutation was not just from them, but from all who were associated in that congregation, plus many more. The Apostle's reason for noting the wide circle that sent their best wishes could have been motivated in part by the hope that Corinthian Saints would sense a bond and unity with the larger community of Christians and better identify with them and the traditions of the gospel they followed.[124]

---

119. Ogden and Skinner, *Verse by Verse,* 148, notes that the kiss was, among the ancient Jews, a form of salutation. Holzapfel and Wayment, *Making Sense,* 366, notes that it was more of an eastern Mediterranean custom, the West preferring the handshake. See also William Klassen, "The Sacred Kiss in the New Testament: An Example of Social Boundary Lines," *New Testament Studies* 39, no. 1 (1993): 122–35.

120. Meeks, *First Urban Christians,* 53–56; Louw-Nida, §87.86. Freedmen had a synagogue in Jerusalem with which Paul was associated (Acts 6:9).

121. Meeks, *First Urban Christians,* 56; Collins, *First Corinthians,* 603.

122. For a more full treatment, see Translation Notes in this commentary series for Acts 18.

123. Barrett, *First Epistle,* 396, notes that they seem to have been people of considerable means.

124. Fitzmyer, *First Corinthians,* 627.

The Final Peroration
(16:21–24)

Greek Text

21 Ὁ ἀσπασμὸς τῇ ἐμῇ χειρὶ Παύλου. 22 εἴ τις οὐ φιλεῖ τὸν κύριον, ἤτω ἀνάθεμα. Μαράνα θά. 23 ἡ χάρις τοῦ κυρίου Ἰησοῦ μεθ' ὑμῶν. 24 ἡ ἀγάπη μου μετὰ πάντων ὑμῶν ἐν Χριστῷ Ἰησοῦ. [SBLGNT]

King James Version

21 The salutation of me Paul with mine own hand. 22 If any man love not the Lord Jesus Christ, let him be Anathema Maran-atha. 23 The grace of our Lord Jesus Christ be with you. 24 My love be with you all in Christ Jesus. Amen.

New Rendition

21 I, Paul, write this greeting with my own hand. 22 If anyone does not love the Lord, let him be accursed. Come, O Lord! 23 The grace of our Lord Jesus be with you. 24 My love is with all of you in Christ Jesus.

Translation Notes and Comments

16:21 *The salutation of me Paul with mine own hand / I, Paul, write this greeting with my own hand:* The handwritten ἀσπασμός (*aspasmos*), "greeting," at the end of a letter had not yet become common in Paul's day.[125] As was the custom in the Greco-Roman world, Paul had dictated his words to a trained secretary.[126] Now the Apostle felt it necessary to append his own distinctive signature. The reason seems to have been at least twofold: first, to add a personal touch showing a special sincerity and affection, and second, to assure the letter was not a counterfeit.[127] From what Paul indicated when he wrote his letters to the Thessalonian branch, forged letters containing false doctrine were circulating at the time (2 Thes. 2:2). His signature, written in what appears to be unusually large letters (Gal. 6:11), added an important authentication.

    16:22 *If any man love not the Lord Jesus Christ, let him be Anathema Maran-atha / If anyone does not love the Lord, let him be accursed. Come, O Lord!:* It is of note that Paul ends his epistle with a rather strong command. It is directed at anyone who does not love the Lord. Paul does not use his usual ἀγαπάω (*agapaō*), "to love," here but rather φιλέω (*phileō*),

---

125. Thiselton, *First Epistle*, 1347, albeit this personal touch was beginning to show up. See Murphy-O'Connor, *Paul the Letter-Writer,* 36, 110–13; Barrett, *First Epistle*, 398.

126. Murphy-O'Connor, *Paul the Letter-Writer,* 7.

127. Barrett, *First Epistle*, 398; Thiselton, *First Epistle,* 1347.

"to have affection for." Since he so seldom uses this verb, he is likely quoting or paraphrasing a stereotypical formula well-known to his readers. The loveless are to be "accursed." The noun, ἀνάθεμα (*anathema*), originally denoted an object devoted solely to the use of God and, to assure this happened, it was usually destroyed. Over time, the idea of destruction became dominant and the word came to connote the necessary response to an act that was so egregious that it fell under divine censure and warranted severe action.[128] That action could range from ostracization to excommunication and even execution. That Paul personally wrote this command suggests how strongly he felt about what action should be taken toward those who did not love the Lord. What promoted him to give such a command was likely that these people were the ones who, because they served themselves and not the Lord, were and would continue to cause the Church grievous trouble. They would also, most probably, agitate against the admonitions Paul had written in this letter.[129]

The final word in the sentence has not been rendered correctly in the transliteration preserved in the KJV. It represents the Aramaic of either מָרַנָא תָא (*māranā' tā'*), "Our/O Lord, come!" or מָרַן אֲתָה (*māran 'ătāh*), "the Lord has come." The first, as supported in a modern Greek text,[130] seems to be the more likely reading and is followed in our Rendition. The phase was likely a popular salutation among the Christians. The whole phrase "may also be interpreted to mean that when someone is declared 'anathema,' Christians may yearn, 'Come, Lord,' so that vengeance may be carried out."[131]

16:23 *The grace of our Lord Jesus Christ be with you / The grace of our Lord Jesus be with you:* Paul's desire again turns to a bright thread that runs through the tapestry of the whole epistle, the χάρις (*charis*), "grace of the Lord." Never does the Apostle allow his reader to forget the central place the Messiah and his Atonement and its resultant power plays in their salvation.

16:24 *My love be with you all in Christ Jesus. Amen / My love is with all of you in Christ Jesus:* Paul returns to his usual word for "love," ἀγάπη (*agapē*). The power of this sentence is in the adjective πάντων (*pantōn*), "all." His love is all inclusive. It is bigger than any quarrel or dispute, greater than any detraction and malediction. It is all encompassing.

128. Johannes Behm, "ἀνάθεμα, ἀνάθημα, κατάθεμα," in *TDNT*, 1:354–55.
129. Fitzmyer, *First Corinthians*, 629.
130. The SBL Greek text has μαράνα θά (*marana tha*).
131. Holzapfel and Wayment, *Making Sense*, 367.

Most of the better manuscripts do not have the benedictory ἀμήν (*amēn*), "amen," and therefore it is left out of our Rendition. It was likely added later for liturgical reasons.[132]

A note needs to be made concerning the subscription found in the KJV, "The first (epistle) to the Corinthians was written from Philippi by Stephanas, and Fortunatus, and Achaicus, and Timotheus." This was added to a manuscript of late production and copied into even later ones. It is inaccurate and should, therefore, be ignored.[133] The earliest and best manuscripts have simply πρὸς Κορινθίους ᾱ (*pros Korinthious I*) "to Corinthians 1."[134]

Analysis and Summary

The final portion of the letter was so important for Paul that although he dictated the bulk of the letter, he chose to personally write his name to guarantee the authenticity of the letter. There is a clear reason why but to see it one must expound the whole closing together for only in that way can each of the separate elements be fully appreciated.[135] As one does so, it becomes apparent that it reinforces his basic aims and strategy and acts as a perfect conclusion for the letter. The key to understanding his intent is knowing that we are dealing with enthymemes. These are "incomplete syllogisms; their conclusions rest upon premises which are often embedded in a tradition and usually presupposed rather than declared."[136]

The tradition and presupposition here is that the readers understand the *shema* "Hear, O Israel: The Lord our God is one Lord: And thou shalt love the Lord thy God with all thine heart, and with all thy soul, and with all thy might" (Deut. 6:4–5). The Old Testament text goes on to lay out the blessings for doing so and the curses for not (Deut. 6:12–25; see also Deut. 11:26–28; Josh. 8:33–34). The verb that Paul uses, φιλέω (*phileō*), "to love," connotes the force that stands behind covenantal loyalty. The concern of the Old Testament prophets was not simply with the absence of love on the part of some, but with its rejection, which led to covenant

---

132. Metzger, *Textual Commentary*, 504.

133. The earliest is D², a sixth-century document. It next is in 075 and 1739, both tenth-century documents. See Fitzmyer, *First Corinthians*, 631.

134. Metzger, *Textual Commentary*, 504.

135. Eriksson, *Traditions as Rhetorical Proof*, 279–98, has done an excellent study on these final verses, castigating those commentaries which have swiftly passed over them and showing their importance to the work as a whole.

136. Thiselton, *First Epistle*, 1350.

breaking and active opposition to Jehovah.[137] Their particular fear was that the loveless would lead others to do the same (for example, see Deut. 11:13–17; 13:6–9).[138] This background provides the setting and reason for Paul's curse.

Already the Lord had taught, "No man can serve two masters: for either he will hate the one, and love the other; or else he will hold to the one, and despise the other. Ye cannot serve God and mammon" (Matt. 6:24). It is for this reason that Paul can say, "Though we, or an angel from heaven, preach any other gospel unto you than that which we have preached unto you, let him be accursed. As we said before, so say I now again, If any man preach any other gospel unto you than that ye have received, let him be accursed" (Gal. 1:8–9). The reason for the cursing, expressed in excommunication, is because preaching "any other gospel" would take the people away from God. Paul will have none of this. Any person doing so, therefore, must be anathematized. The imposition of the curse ἀνάθεμα (*anathema*), "anathema," followed by the wish "Come, O Lord" suggests that the Messiah, at the time of the final Judgment, would both sanction and reinforce it.[139]

But the curse must not be seen as the major element in the close. That theme is reconciliation. The Apostle's cry is for unity and oneness. These virtues are best evidenced in the last sentence of the epistle, "My love (ἀγάπη, *agapē*) is with you all in Christ Jesus." This epistle's closing is unique among Paul's letters in its stress on the importance of and need for love. Paul refers to it three times (16:14, 22, 24). That it is the predominant virtue mentioned evidences how necessary it was for the Corinthian Saints to express and feel love. In none of his other epistles does Paul assure his readers of his love with the sincerity, urgency, and solemnity that he does here.[140] There were at least three reasons for this. First, the Apostle had a special sincerity and affection for these people. Second, he had been very hard on some of them, pulling a few punches. It was necessary for them to understand that his reproofs were given in love. Third, it was their feeling of that love that would allow them to accept those reproofs and make the necessary changes. Paul's use of the adjective πάντων (*pantōn*), "all," shows that none were excluded from his love. Indeed, Paul brings

---

137. Edwards, *Commentary*, 474; Thiselton, *First Epistle*, 1351.

138. Note the Lord's warning, "It is impossible but that offences will come: but woe unto him, through whom they come! It were better for him that a millstone were hanged about his neck, and he cast into the sea" (Luke 17:1–2).

139. Thiselton, *First Epistle*, 1351.

140. Collins, *First Corinthians*, 601.

everyone under the umbrella of all embracing *agapē* as it flows from the Messiah Jesus through him to them.[141]

In summary, "Paul pleads for diligence in living gospel principles, especially love, unity, kindness toward leaders, and assisting the Lord's work to move forward."[142] In 16:15–16, Paul requests a self-submission (ὑποτάσσω, *hypotassō*) based on mutual and reciprocal respect. Those who have unselfishly assigned themselves (τάσσω, *tassō*) to the service of the Saints—especially through doing demanding and exhausting labor (κοπίαω, *kopiaō*)—deserve the honor, respect, submission, and devotion that such calls for. This mutual respect should also go to the συνεργοῦντι (*synergounti*), "co-worker," who shares in the common work. It is of note that Paul's commendation for honor and respect does not rest on social status or even ecclesiastical rank but on the quality of service. By focusing on this, he unties one's status from any temporal moorings and anchors it to dedication to the Lord and his ministry. By this means, all service becomes mutual and complementary as engaged in by the ἀδελθοί (*adelphoi*), that is, all the "brothers and sisters." This is the way in which love, so necessary in Paul's spiritual world, expresses itself. As Paul noted, love "is not self-serving" (13:5, Rendition) but yields itself in service to others.[143] Elder B. H. Roberts repeated a phrase which beautifully captures Paul's thought, "In essentials, unity; in nonessentials, liberty; and in all things, charity."[144]

In his closing, Paul fulfills the purposes of a discourse, which this is. First, it summarizes very succinctly what has been said, and second, it closes with an emotional appeal.[145] But to be complete, a peroration had to do one more task; it had to end on a high note. For the Christian, nothing could be higher than an apostolic appeal for the Lord to come. That coming promised the Saints joy, vindication, and reward. The plea shifts attention from station and status—and even deep spirituality with its attendant gifts—to a covenantal theme centered on the love of the Lord, his people, and the redemption that will come through him.[146] Thus, the final two verses emphasize Paul's mutual themes of χάρις (*charis*), "grace," and ἀγάπη (*agapē*), "love." Indeed, grace has been a bright silver thread that has run through the tapestry of the whole epistle. It is from the grace of God

---

141. Mitchell, *Paul and the Rhetoric of Reconciliation*, 179.

142. Ogden and Skinner, *Verse by Verse*, 148.

143. Thiselton, *First Epistle*, 1339.

144. B. H. Roberts, in CR, October 1912, 30.

145. Quintilian, *Inst.* 6.1.1; Eriksson, *Traditions as Rhetorical Proof*, 287.

146. Eriksson, *Traditions as Rhetorical Proof*, 297–98.

that Christlike love flows, a love that is the golden thread that has bound the fabric of the whole piece together.

Such love is more than a transient feeling but an enduring attitude of concern and care that pushes one to do whatever is necessary for the spiritual and eternal well being of the other. Paul knows that love personally and expresses it with both sincerity and solemnity. In spite of all the problems certain members of the Church have caused him, his love for them has not lessened. He loves them all—not only the weak but also the strong, not only his friends but also his detractors.

He has preached nothing but "Christ, and him crucified" (2:2), but he has explored all the ramifications of this doctrine. In doing so, he has exposed and highlighted the underlying, overreaching, final, and most beautiful of its aspects–that of self-sacrificing love. Paul, being filled with that supernal virtue, loves the Corinthian Saints ἐν Χριστῷ ᾿Ιησοῦ (*en Christō Iēsou*), "in Christ Jesus" (16:24), the source of all such love.

Selected Bibliography

Aland, Kurt and Barbara. *The Text of the New Testament: An Introduction to the Critical Editions and to the Theory and Practice of Modern Textual Criticism.* Trans. Erroll F. Rhodes. Grand Rapids, Mich.: Eerdmans; Leiden, Neth.: E. J. Brill, 1995.

Anderson, Richard Lloyd. *Guide to Acts and the Apostles' Letters.* 3d ed. Provo, Utah: Brigham Young University, 1999.

———. "Religious Validity: The Sacrament Covenant in Third Nephi." In *By Study and Also by Faith,* ed. Stephen D. Ricks and John M. Lundquist, 2:21–45. 2 vols. Salt Lake City: Deseret Book, 1990.

———. "The Restoration of the Sacrament (Part 1: Loss and Christian Reformations)." *Ensign* 22 (January 1992): 40–46.

———. *Understanding Paul.* Salt Lake City: Deseret Book, 1983.

Andrus, Hyrum L. *Joseph Smith—a Modern Witness for Christ.* Provo, Utah: Brigham Young University, BYU Extension Publications, 1963.

Aune, David E. *Prophecy in Early Christianity and the Ancient Mediterranean World.* Grand Rapids, Mich.: Eerdmans, 1983.

Bailey, Derrick S. *Homosexuality in the Western Christian Tradition.* New York: Longmans, 1955.

———. *The Man-Woman Relation in Christian Thought.* London: Longmans, 1959.

Bailey, Kenneth E. *Paul through Mediterranean Eyes: Cultural Studies in 1 Corinthians.* Downers Grove, Ill.: Intervarsity Press, 2011.

Barr, James. *The Semantics of Biblical Language.* Oxford: Oxford University Press, 1961.

Barrett, C. K. *A Commentary on the First Epistle to the Corinthians.* 2d ed. London: Black, 1968.

———. *Essays on Paul.* Louisville, Ky.: Westminster John Knox Press, 1982.

———. *The First Epistle to the Corinthians.* Peabody, Mass.: Hendrickson Publishers, 1993.

Barth, Karl. *Church Dogmatics.* 14 vols. Peabody, Mass.: Hendrickson Publishers, 2010.

———. *The Resurrection of the Dead.* Trans. Henry J. Stenning. London: Hodder and Stoughton 1933.

Bauckham, Richard J. "The Brothers and Sisters of Jesus: An Epiphanian Response to John P. Meier." *Catholic Biblical Quarterly* 56 (1994): 686–700.

Bauer, Walter. *A Greek-English Lexicon of the New Testament and Other Early Christian Literature.* Trans. William F. Arndt and F. Wilbur Gingrich. 2d ed. rev. and ed. F. Wilbur Gingrich and Frederick W. Danker from Bauer's 5th ed., 1958. Chicago: University of Chicago Press, 1979. Cited as BAGD.

Bauer, Walter. *A Greek-English Lexicon of the New Testament and Other Early Christian Literature.* Ed. F. W. Danker. 3d English ed. Chicago: University of Chicago Press, 2000. Cited as BDAG.

Beare, F. W. "Speaking in Tongues: A Critical Survey of the New Testament Evidence." *Journal of Biblical Studies* 83 (1964): 229–46.

Bennion, Lowell L. *Legacies of Jesus.* Salt Lake City: Deseret Book, 1990.

———. *Teachings of the New Testament.* Salt Lake City: Deseret Book, 1956.

Benson, Ezra Taft. *A Witness and a Warning.* Salt Lake City: Deseret Book, 1988.

Best, Ernest. *One Body in Christ: A Study in the Relationship of the Church to Christ in the Epistle of the Apostle Paul.* London: SPCK, 1955.

Black, Matthew. *The Scrolls and Christian Origins: Studies in the Jewish Background of the New Testament.* New York: Charles Scribner's Sons, 1961.

Blasi, Anthony J. *Early Christianity as a Social Movement.* New York: Peter Lang, 1988.

Blass, Friedrich, and Albert Debrunner. *Greek Grammar of the New Testament.* Trans. Robert W. Funk. Chicago: University of Chicago Press, 1961.

Boecker, H. J. *Law and the Administration of Justice in the Old Testament and Ancient Near East.* London: SPCK, 1980.

Boswell, John. *Christianity, Social Tolerance, and Homosexuality.* Chicago: University Chicago Press, 1980.

Botterweck, G. Johannes, and Helmer Ringgren, eds. *Theological Dictionary of the Old Testament.* Trans. John T. Willis. 15 vols. Grand Rapids, Mich.: Eerdmans, 1976–2004. Cited as *TDOT.*

Bound, J. F. "Who Are the 'Virgins' Discussed in 1 Corinthians 7:25–38." *Evangelical Journal* 2 (1984): 3–15.

Bradley, K. R. *Slaves and Masters in the Roman World: A Study in Social Control.* Oxford: Oxford University Press, 1987.

Brewster, Hoyt W., Jr. *Behold, I Come Quickly: The Last Days and Beyond.* Salt Lake City: Deseret Book, 1999.

———. *Doctrine and Covenants Encyclopedia.* Salt Lake City: Bookcraft, 1988.

Broneer, Oscar. "The Apostle Paul and the Isthmian Games." *Biblical Archaeologist* 25, no. 1 (1962): 2–31.

Brooks, Kent R. "Paul's Inspired Teachings on Marriage." In *Go Ye into All the World: Messages of the New Testament Apostle,* 75–97. Salt Lake City: Deseret Book, 2002.

Brown, Frances, Samuel R. Driver, and Charles A. Briggs. *A Hebrew and English Lexicon of the Old Testament.* 1952. Rpt., Oxford: Clarendon Press, 1987. Cited as BDB.

Bruce, F. F. *1 and 2 Corinthians.* London: Oliphants, 1971.

———. *Men and Movements in the Primitive Church.* Exeter: Paternoster, 1979.

———. *Paul: Apostle of the Free Spirit.* Exeter: Paternoster, 1977.

Brunt, John C. *Paul's Attitude toward and Treatment of Problems Involving Dietary Practices.* Atlanta: Emory University, 1978.

———. "Rejected, Ignored, or Misunderstood? The Fate of Paul's Approach to the Problem of Food Offered to Idols in Early Christianity." *New Testament Studies* 31 (1985): 113–24.

Bullmore, Michael A. *St. Paul's Theology of Rhetorical Style: An Examination of 1 Cor. 2:1–5 in Light of First-Century Greco-Roman Rhetorical Culture.* San Francisco: International Scholars Publication, 1995.

Burkert, Walter. *Ancient Mystery Cults.* Cambridge, Mass.: Harvard University Press, 1989.

Burton, A. Theodore. *God's Greatest Gift.* Salt Lake City: Deseret Book, 1976.

Bushman, Richard Lyman. *Joseph Smith: Rough Stone Rolling.* New York: Alfred A. Knopf, 2005.

Butler, Roy F. *The Meaning of* Agapao *and* Phileo *in the Greek New Testament.* Lawrence, Kan.: Coronado Press, 1977.

Bybee, Ariel E. "From Vestal Virgin to Bride of Christ: Elements of a Roman Cult in Early Christian Asceticism." *Studia Antiqua* 1 (Fall 2001): 3–19.

Byrne, Brendan. "Sinning against One's Own Body: Paul's Understanding of Sexual Relationships in 1 Cor. 6:18." *Catholic Biblical Quarterly* 45 (October 1983): 608–16.

Caird, George B. *The Language and Imagery in the Bible.* London: Duckworth Publishing, 1988.

———. *Principalities and Powers: A Study in Pauline Theology.* Eugene, Ore.: Wipf and Stock Publishers, 2003.

Cannon, Donald Q. "The King Follett Discourse: Joseph Smith's Greatest Sermon in Historical Perspective." *BYU Studies* 18, no. 1 (1978): 179–94.

Cantarella, Eva. *Pandora's Daughters: The Role and Status of Women in Greek and Roman Antiquity.* Baltimore: Johns Hopkins University Press, 1987.

Caragounis, Chrys C. "'To Boast' or 'To Be Burned'? The Crux of 1 Corinthians 13:3." *Svensk Exegetisk Årsbok* 60 (1995): 115–27.

Chow, J. K. *Patronage and Power.* Sheffield, Eng.: Sheffield Academic Press, 1992.

Clarke, Andrew D. *Secular and Christian Leadership in Corinth: A Socio-historical and Exegetical Study of 1 Corinthians 1–6.* 2d ed. Waynesboro, Ga.: Paternoster, 2006.

Clements, R. E. *Isaiah 1–39.* Grand Rapids, Mich.: Eerdmans, 1980.

Collier, G. D. "'That We Might Not Crave Evil': The Structure and Argument in 1 Cor 10:1–12." *Journal for the Study of the New Testament* 55 (1994): 55–75.

Collins, Raymond F. *First Corinthians.* Collegeville, Minn.: Glazier/Liturgical Press, 1999.

Colson, F. N. "Μετεσχημάτισμα in I Cor iv 6." *Journal of New Theological Studies* 17 (July 1916): 380–83.

Conzelmann, Hans. *1 Corinthians: A Commentary on the First Epistle to the Corinthians.* Minneapolis: Fortress Press, 1975.

Craig, C. T. "The First Epistle to the Corinthians." In *Interpreter's Bible,* 10:3–262. 12 vols. New York: Abingdon Press, 1953.

Cullmann, Oscar. *Christ and Time: The Primitive Christian Concept of Time and History.* 2d ed., rev. Louisville, Ky.: Westminster Press, 1964.

Dahl, Larry E., and Charles D. Tate Jr. *The Lectures on Faith in Historical Perspective.* Provo, Utah: Religious Studies Center, Brigham Young University, 1990.

Dahl, Nils A. "Paul and the Church at Corinth according to 1 Corinthians 1:10–4:21." In *Christian History and Interpretation: Studies Presented to John Knox,* ed. W. R. Farmer, C. F. D. Moule, and R. R. Niebuhr, 313–36. Cambridge: University Press, 1967.

———. *Studies in Paul.* Minneapolis: Augsburg Press, 1977.

Danby, Herbert. *The Mishnah.* Oxford: Oxford University Press, 1977.

Danker, Frederick William, ed. *A Greek-English Lexicon of the New Testament and Other Early Christian Literature.* 3d ed. Chicago: University of Chicago Press, 2000. Cited as BDAG.

Davies, Margaret. "New Testament Ethics and Ours: Homosexuality and Sexuality in Romans 1:26–27." *Biblical Interpretation* 3, no. 3 (1995): 315–31.

Davies, Rupert E. *Studies in 1 Corinthians.* London: Epworth Press, 1962.

Davis, James A. *Wisdom and Spirit.* Lanham, Md.: University Press of America, 1984.

De Boer, Martinus C. *The Defeat of Death: Apocalyptic Eschatology in 1 Corinthians 15 and Romans 5.* Sheffield, Eng.: JSOT Press, 1988.

Deissmann, Adolf. *Light from the Ancient East.* Trans Lionel R. M. Strachan. Rev. ed. London: Hodder and Stoughton, 1927.

Deluz, Gaston. *A Companion to I Corinthians.* London: Darton, Longman and Todd, 1963.

Deming, Will. *Paul on Marriage and Celibacy: The Hellenistic Background of 1 Corinthians 7.* Cambridge: Cambridge University Press, 1995.

Dillenberger, John. "Grace and Works in Martin Luther and Joseph Smith." In *Reflections on Mormonism: Judaeo-Christian Parallels,* ed. Truman G. Madsen, 175–86. Provo, Utah: Religious Studies Center, 1978.

Dillon, Matthew, and Lynda Garland. *Ancient Rome: From the Early Republic to the Assassination of Julius Caesar.* Florence, Ky.: Rutledge Press, 2005.

Discourses of Brigham Young. Comp. John A. Widtsoe. Salt Lake City: Deseret Book, 1941.

Douglas, J. D. *The Illustrated Bible Dictionary,* part 2. Nottingham: Inter-Varsity Press, 1980.

Draper, Richard D. *A Fulness of Joy.* American Fork, Utah: Covenant Communications, 2002.

———. "Light, Truth, and Grace: Three Themes of Salvation (D&C 93)." In *Sperry Symposium Classics: The Doctrine and Covenants,* ed. Craig K. Manscill, 234–47. Provo, Utah: Religious Studies Center, Brigham Young University, 2004.

———. "New Light on Paul's Teachings." *Ensign* 39 (September 1999): 22.

Draper, Richard D., and Michael Rhodes, *The Revelation of John the Apostle.* Provo, Utah: BYU Studies, 2013. Ebook.

Dugan, David. L. *The Sayings of Jesus in the Church of Paul.* Oxford: Blackwell Press, 1971.

Dunn, James D. G. *Baptism in the Holy Spirit: A Re-examination of the New Testament Teaching on the Gift of the Spirit in Relation to Pentecostalism Today.* London: SCM, 1970.

———. *Jesus and the Spirit: A Study of the Religious and Charismatic Experience of Jesus and the First Christians as Reflected in the New Testament.* London: SCM Press, 1975.

———. *Jesus Remembered.* Vol. 1 of Christianity in the Making. Grand Rapids, Mich.: Eerdmans Publishing, 2003.

———. *Unity and Diversity in the New Testament.* Philadelphia: Westminster Press, 1977.

Dyer, Alvin R. *Who Am I?* 4th ed. Salt Lake City: Deseret Book, 1973.

Edwards, Thomas C. *A Commentary on the First Epistle to the Corinthians.* 2d ed. London: Hodder and Stoughton, 1885.

Ehat, Andrew F., and Lyndon W. Cook, comps. and eds. *The Words of Joseph Smith: The Contemporary Accounts of the Nauvoo Discourses of the Prophet Joseph.* Religious Studies Monograph Series, no. 6. Provo, Utah: Religious Studies Center, Brigham Young University, 1980.

Ehrman, Bart D. *The New Testament: A Historical Introduction to the Early Christian Writings.* Oxford: Oxford University Press, 1997.

Ekem, John D. "'Spiritual Gifts' or 'Spiritual Persons'? 1 Corinthians 12:1a Revisited." *Neotestamentica* 28 (1980): 54–74.

Ellingworth, Paul, and Howard A. Hatton. *A Handbook on Paul's First Letter to the Corinthians.* 2d ed. UBS Handbook Series Helps for Translators. New York: United Bible Society, 1995.

Elliot, J. K. "In Favor of καυθήσομαι in 1 Corinthians 13:3." *Zeitschrift für die neutestamentliche Wissenschaft* 62 (1971): 297–98.

Ellis, E. Earle. *Paul's Use of the Old Testament.* Reprint. Grand Rapids, Mich.: Baker Book, 1981.

Ellison, Mark D. "The Setting and Sacrament of the Christian Community." In *Go Ye into All the World: The Message of the New Testament Apostles,* 145–66. Salt Lake City: Deseret Book, 2002.

Engels, Donald W. *Roman Corinth: An Alternative Model for the Classical City.* Chicago: University of Chicago Press, 1990.

Epstein, Louise M. *Marriage Law in the Bible and in the Talmud.* Cambridge, Mass.: Harvard University Press, 1942.

Eriksson, Anders. *Traditions as Rhetorical Proof: Pauline Argumentation in 1 Corinthians.* Stockholm: Almqvist and Wiksell, 1988.

Evans, Owen E. "New Wine in Old Skins: XIII. The Saints," *Expository Times* 86 (1975): 196–200.

Fairbairn, Patrick. *The Typology of Scripture.* Edinburgh: T. and T. Clark, 1947.

Featherstone, Vaughn J. *The Incomparable Christ: Our Master and Model.* Salt Lake City: Deseret Book, 1995.

Fee, Gordon D. *First Epistle of the Corinthians.* The New International Commentary on the New Testament. Grand Rapids, Mich.: Eerdmans, 1987.

Findlay, G. G. "St. Paul's First Epistle to the Corinthians." In *The Expositor's Greek Testament,* ed. W. Robertson Nicoll, 2:727–953. [1901]. Reprint, Grand Rapids, Mich.: Wm B. Eerdmans, 1980.

Finney, Mark T. *Honour and Conflict in the Ancient World: 1 Corinthians in Its Greco-Roman Social Setting.* New York: Bloomsbury T and T Clark, 2012.

Fiore, Benjamin. "'Covert Allusion' in 1 Corinthians 1–4." *Catholic Biblical Quarterly* 47 (1985): 85–102.

Fiorenza, Elisabeth Schüssler. *In Memory of Her: A Feminist Theological Reconstruction of Christian Origins.* New York: Crossroads Publishing/Herder and Herder, 1994.

Fischer, James A. "1 Corinthians 7:8–24—Marriage and Divorce." *Biblical Research* 23 (1978): 26–30.

Fitzmyer, Joseph A. *First Corinthians: A New Translation with Introduction and Commentary.* New Haven, Conn.: Yale University Press, 2008.

Flory, Marleen B. "Family and *Familia:* Kinship and Community in Slavery." In *American Journal of Ancient History* 3 (1978): 78–95.

Forbes, Christopher. *Prophecy and Inspired Speech in Early Christianity and Its Hellenistic Environments.* Tübingen: Mohr, 1995.

Ford, J. Massingberd. "Levirate Marriage in St. Paul (I Cor. vii)." *New Testament Studies* 10 (April 1964): 361–65.

———. "St. Paul the Philogamist (I Cor. vii in Early Patristic Exegesis)." *New Testament Studies* 11 (July 1965): 326–48.

———. "You Are God's 'Sukkah' (I Cor. III. 10–17)." *New Testament Studies* 21 (October 1974): 139–42.

Foschini, Bernard. "'Those Who Are Baptized for the Dead': 1 Cor 15:29." *Catholic Biblical Quarterly* 12 (1950): 260–76, 379–88; 13 (1951): 46–78, 172–98, 276–83.

Freedman, David Noel, ed. *The Anchor Bible Dictionary.* 6 vols. New York: Doubleday, 1992. Cited as *ABD.*

Freeman, Robert C. "Paul's Earnest Pursuit of Spiritual Gifts." In *The Apostle Paul, His Life and His Testimony: The 23d Annual Sidney B. Sperry Symposium,* 34–46. Salt Lake City: Deseret Book 1994.

Frid, B. "The Enigmatic ἀλλά in 1 Cor. 2:9." *New Testament Studies* 31 (1985): 603–11.

Fronk, Camille. "Submit Yourselves . . . As unto the Lord." In *Go Ye into All the World: Messages of the New Testament Apostles,* 98–113. 31st Annual Sidney B. Sperry Symposium. Salt Lake City: Deseret Book, 2002.

Fuller, Reginald H. "First Corinthians 6:1–11: An Exegetical Paper." *Ex Auditu* 2 (1986): 96–104.

Gale, Herbert M. *The Use of Analogy in the Letters of Paul.* Philadelphia: Westminster Press, 1964.

Gardner, Paul Douglas. *The Gifts of God and the Authentication of a Christian: An Exegetical Study of 1 Corinthians 8–11.* Lanham, Md.: University Press of America, 1994.

Garland, David E. (2003). *1 Corinthians.* Baker Exegetical Commentary on the New Testament. Grand Rapids, Mich.: Baker Academic, 2003.

Garner, G. G. "The Temple of Asklepius at Corinth and Paul's Teachings." *Buried History* 18 (1982): 52–58.

Garnsey, Peter. *Social Status and Legal Privilege in the Roman Empire.* Oxford: Oxford University Press, 1970.

Gaster, Theodor H. *Thespis: Ritual, Myth, and Drama in the Ancient Near East.* New York: Henry Schuman, 1961.

Gill, David W. J. "Corinth: A Roman Colony in Achaea." *Biblische Zeitschrift* 37 (1993): 259–64.

———. "Erastus the Aedile." *Tyndale Bulletin* 40, no. 2 (1989): 146–51.

———. "The Importance of Roman Portraiture for Head-coverings in 1 Corinthians 11:1–16." *Tyndale Bulletin* 41, no. 2 (1990): 245–60.

———. "The Meat Market at Corinth." *Tyndale Bulletin* 43, no. 2 (1992): 323–37.

Gilmour, S. M. "The Christophany to More than Five Hundred Brethren." *Journal of Biblical Studies* 80 (1961): 248–52.

Go Ye into All the World: Messages of the New Testament Apostle. Salt Lake City: Deseret Book, 2002.

Godet, Frédéric Louis. *Commentary on St. Paul's First Epistle to the Corinthians.* 2 vols. 1893; rpt., Grand Rapids, Mich.: Kregel Publications, 1979.

Gooch, P. W. "'Conscience' in I Cor 8 and 10." *New Testament Studies* 33 (1987): 244–54.

Goppelt, Leonhard. *Typos: The Typology Interpretation of the Old Testament in the New.* Grand Rapids, Mich.: Eerdmans, 1982.

Gundry-Volf, J. M. "Gender and Creation in 1 Cor 11:2–16: A Study in Paul's Theological Methods." In *Evangelium, Schriftauslegung, Kirche, Festschrift für Peter Stuhlmacher zum 65. Geburstag,* ed. Peter Stuhlmacher, Jostein Ådna, Scott J. Hafemann, and Otfried Hofius, 151–71. Göttingen: Vandenhoeck Ruprecht, 1997.

Gundry, R. H. Sōma *in Biblical Theology with Emphasis on Pauline Anthropology.* Cambridge: Cambridge University Press, 1976.

Hagner, Donald A. *Matthew 14–28.* Vol. 33B of Word Biblical Commentary. Dallas: Word Books, 1995.

Hale, Van. "The Doctrinal Impact of the King Follett Discourse." *BYU Studies* 18, no. 1 (1978): 209–26.

Hall, David R. "A Problem of Authority." *Expository Times* 102 (1990–91): 39–42

Hallpike, C. R. "Social Hair." In *Man*, n.s., 4 (June 1969): 256–64.

Hatch, Edwin. *The Influence of Greek Ideas on Christianity.* Gloucester, Mass.: Peter Smith, 1970.

Hatch, Gary Layne. "Paul among the Rhetoricians: A Model for Proclaiming Christ." In *The Apostle Paul, His Life and His Testimony: The 23d Annual Sidney B. Sperry Symposium,* 65–79. Salt Lake City: Deseret Book, 1994.

Hays, Richard B. *Echoes of the Scriptures in the Letters of Paul.* New Haven, Conn.: Yale University Press, 1989.

———. *First Corinthians.* Interpretation: A Bible Commentary for Teaching and Preaching. Louisville, Ky.: John Knox Press, 1997.

Héring, J. *The First Epistle of St. Paul to the Corinthians.* London: Epworth Press, 1962.

Hill, David. *New Testament Prophecy.* Louisville, Ky.: Westminster John Knox Press, 1979.

Hinckley, Gordon B. *Teachings of Gordon B. Hinckley.* Salt Lake City: Deseret Book, 1997.

———. "What Are People Asking about Us?" *Ensign* 18 (November 1998): 70–72.

Hock, Ronald F. *The Social Context of Paul's Ministry: Tentmaking and Apostleship.* Philadelphia: Fortress Press, 1980.

———. "The Workshop as a Social Setting for Paul's Missionary Preaching." *Catholic Biblical Quarterly* 41 (1979): 438–50.

Hodgson, Robert. "Paul the Apostle and First Century Tribulation Lists." *Zeitschrift für die neutestameltliche Wissenschaft* 74 (1983): 59–80.

Hollemann, Jooste. *Resurrection and Parousia: A Tradition-Historical Study of Pauline Eschatology in 1 Corinthians 15.* Leiden: Brill, 1996.

Holzapfel, Richard Neitzel. "From Temple and Synagogue to House-Church." In *The Life and Teachings of the New Testament Apostles: From the Day of Pentecost through the Apocalypse,* ed. Richard Neitzel Holzapfel and Thomas A. Wayment. Salt Lake City: Deseret Book, 2010.

Holzapfel, Richard Neitzel, and David Rolph Seely. *My Father's House: Temple Worship and Symbolism in the New Testament.* Salt Lake City: Bookcraft, 1995.

Holzapfel, Richard Neitzel, and others. *Jesus Christ and the World of the New Testament.* Salt Lake City: Deseret Book, 2006.

Holzapfel, Richard Neitzel, and Thomas A. Wayment. *Making Sense of the New Testament: Timely Insights and Timeless Messages.* Salt Lake City: Deseret Book, 2010.

Hooker, Morna Dorothy. *From Adam to Christ: Essays on Paul.* Cambridge: Cambridge University Press, 1990.

———. "Hard Sayings: 1 Cor. 3:2." *Theology* 69 (1966): 19–22.

Hornblower, Simon, and Antony Spawforth, ed. *The Oxford Classical Dictionary.* 3d rev. ed. Oxford: Oxford University Press, 2003.

Horsley, G. H. R., and Stephen R. Llewelyn, eds. *New Documents Illustrating Early Christianity: A Review of the Greek Inscriptions and Papyri.* 10 vols. North Ryde, Aus.: Ancient History Documentary Research Centre, Macquarie University; Grand Rapids, Mich.: Eerdmans, 1981–2002.

Horsley, R. A. "Consciousness and Freedom among the Corinthians: 1 Corinthians 8–10." *Catholic Biblical Quarterly* 40 (1978): 574–89.

———. *I Corinthians.* Nashville: Abingdon Press, 1998.

Hoyle, R. B. *The Holy Spirit in St. Paul.* London: Hodder and Stoughton, 1927.

Hunter, Howard W. "The Reality of the Resurrection." *Improvement Era* 72 (June 1969): 106–8.

Hunter, Milton R. *The Gospel through the Ages.* Salt Lake City: Deseret Book, 1945.

Hurd, J. C. *The Origin of I Corinthians.* London: SPCK, 1965.

Hutson, C. R. "Was Timothy Timid: On the Rhetoric of Fearlessness (1 Corinthians 16:10–11) and Cowardice (2 Timothy 1:7)." *Biblical Review,* 42 (1997): 58–73.

Jeremias, Joachim. *Eucharistic Words of Jesus.* 3d ed. London: SCM Press, 1966.

———. *Unknown Sayings of Jesus.* Eugene, Ore.: Wipf and Stock Publishers, 2008.

Johnson, Franklin P. *Corinth: Results of Excavations.* Vol. 9. Cambridge: Harvard University Press, 1931.

Jones, Howard. *The Epicurean Tradition.* New York: Routledge Press, 1989.

Judge, E. A. *The Social Pattern of the Christian Groups in the First Century.* London: Tyndale Press, 1960.

Kearney, Peter J. "He Appeared to 500 Brothers (1 Cor. xv 6)." *Novum Testamentum* 22 (1980): 264–84.

Kennedy, George A. *The Art of Rhetoric in the Roman World.* Princeton: Princeton University Press, 1972.

Kent, J. H. *Corinth: Results of Excavations Conducted by the American School of Classical Studies at Athens,* vol. 8, part 3, *The Inscriptions, 1926–1950.* Princeton: American School of Classical Studies at Athens, 1966.

Kierkegaard, Søren. *The Present Age* and *Of the Difference between a Genius and an Apostle.* Trans. Alexander Dru. London: Fantana Library, 1962.

Kimball, Spencer W. *The Miracle of Forgiveness.* Salt Lake City: Bookcraft, 1969.

———. *The Teachings of Spencer W. Kimball.* Ed. Edward L. Kimball. Salt Lake City: Bookcraft, 1982.

Kittel, Gerhard, and Gerhard Friedrich, eds. *Theological Dictionary of the New Testament.* Trans. Geoffrey W. Bromiley. 10 vols. Grand Rapids, Mich.: Eerdmans, 1964. Cited as *TDNT.*

Koehler, L., W. Baumgartner, and J. J. Stamm. *The Hebrew and Aramaic Lexicon of the Old Testament.* Trans. and ed. M. E. J. Richardson. 5 vols. Leiden: E. J. Brill, 1994–2000. Cited as *HAL.*

Kovacs, Judith L. *1 Corinthians: Interpreted by Early Christian Commentators.* Grand Rapids, Mich.: Eerdmans, 2005.

Kramer, Werner. *Christ, Lord, Son of God.* Trans. B. Hardy. Norwich, Eng.: SCM-Canterbury Press, 1966.

Kubo, Sakae. "I Corinthians vii. 16: Optimistic or Pessimistic?" *New Testament Studies* 24 (July 1978): 539–44.

Kuyper, L. J. "Exegetical Study on 1 Corinthians 7:14." *Reformed Review* 31 (1977): 62–64.

Lassen, Eva M. "The Use of the Father Image in Imperial Propaganda in 1 Cor 4:14–21." *Tyndale Bulletin* 42, no. 1 (May 1991): 127–39.

Lee, Harold B. *Stand Ye in Holy Places.* Salt Lake City: Deseret Book, 1975.

———. "Time to Prepare to Meet God." CR, October 1970, 113–18.

Lefkowitz, Mary R., and Maureen B. Fant. *Women's Life in Greece and Rome: A Source Book in Translation.* Baltimore: Johns Hopkins University Press; London: Duckworth, 1982.

Lewis, C. S. *The Four Loves.* New York: Harcourt Brace Jovanovich, 1960.

———. *Mere Christianity: An Anniversary Edition of the Three Books, The Case for Christianity, Christian Behavior, and Beyond Personality.* New York: Macmillan, 1981.

Lightfoot, J. B. *Notes on the Epistles of St Paul from Unpublished Commentaries.* London: Macmillan, 1895.

Lindsay, Hugh. *Adoption in the Roman World.* Cambridge: Cambridge University Press, 2009.

Liu, Youlin. *Temple Purity in 1–2 Corinthians.* Tübingen: Mohr Siebeck, 2013.

Long, A. A. "The Socratic Tradition: Diogenes, Crates, and Hellenistic Ethics." In *The Cynics: The Cynic Movement in Antiquity and Its Legacy,* ed. Robert Bracht Branham and Marie-Odile Goulet-Cazé, 28–46. Berkeley: University of California Press, 2000.

Louw, Johannes P., and Eugene A. Nida. *Greek-English Lexicon of the New Testament Based on Semantic Domains.* 2 vols. New York: United Bible Societies, 1988.

Ludlow, Daniel H., ed. *Encyclopedia of Mormonism.* 4 vols. New York: Macmillan, 1992. Cited as *EM.*

Ludlow, Victor L. *Isaiah: Prophet, Seer, and Poet.* Salt Lake City: Deseret Book, 1982.

MacMullen, Ramsay. *Paganism in the Roman Empire.* New Haven: Yale University Press, 1981.

———. *Roman Social Relations, 50 BC to AD 284.* New Haven: Yale University Press, 1974.

Madsen, Truman G. "The Meaning of Christ—The Truth, the Way, the Life: An Analysis of B. H. Roberts' Unpublished Master Work." *BYU Studies* 15, no. 3 (1975): 259–93.

———. "The Temple and the Restoration." In *Temple in Antiquity: Ancient Records and Modern Perspectives,* ed. Truman G. Madsen, 1–18. Salt Lake City: Deseret Book, 2010.

Malick, David E. "The Condemnation of Homosexuality in Romans 1:26–27." *Bibliotheca Sacra* (July–September 1993): 327–40.

Marcovich, Miroslav. "From Ishtar to Aphrodite." *Journal of Aesthetic Education* 30, no. 2, Special Issue: Distinguished Humanities Lectures II (Summer 1996): 43–59.

Marshall, I. Howard. *Last Supper and the Lord's Supper.* Grand Rapids, Mich.: Eerdmans, 1980.

Marshall, Peter. *Enmity in Corinth.* Tübingen: Mohr Press, 1987.

Martens, Peter. "Revisiting the Allegory/Typology Distinction: The Case of Origen." *Journal of Early Christian Studies* 16 (2008): 283–317.

Martin, Dale B. *The Corinthian Body.* New Haven, Conn.: Yale University Press, 1995.

———. *Slavery as Salvation: The Metaphor of Slavery in Pauline Christianity.* New Haven, Conn.: Yale University Press, 1990.

Martin, R. P. *Worship in the Early Church.* Rev. ed. Grand Rapids, Mich.: Eerdmans, 1974.

Matthews, Robert J. *The Parables of Jesus.* Provo, Utah: Brigham Young University Press, 1969.

———. "The Plain and Precious Parts: How Modern Scripture Helps Us Understand the New Testament." *Ensign* 5 (September 1975): 8–10.

Maxwell, Neal A. *All These Things Shall Give Thee Experience.* Salt Lake City: Deseret Book, 1976.

———. *But for a Small Moment.* Salt Lake City: Bookcraft, 1986.

————. *One More Strain of Praise.* Salt Lake City: Deseret Book, 2002.

————. *A Wonderful Flood of Light.* Salt Lake City: Bookcraft, 1990.

McConkie, Bruce R. *Doctrinal New Testament Commentary.* 3 vols. Salt Lake City: Bookcraft, 1965–73. Cited as *DNTC.*

————, ed. *Doctrines of Salvation: Sermons and Writings of Joseph Fielding Smith.* 1954–56; rpt., three volumes in one, Salt Lake City: Bookcraft, 1999.

————. *The Millennial Messiah: The Second Coming of the Son of Man.* Salt Lake City: Deseret Book, 1982.

————. *Mormon Doctrine.* 2d ed. Salt Lake City: Bookcraft, 1979.

————. *The Mortal Messiah.* 4 vols. Salt Lake City: Deseret Book, 1979.

————. *A New Witness for the Articles of Faith.* Salt Lake City: Deseret Book, 1985.

————. "Upon This Rock," *Ensign* 11 (May 1981): 75–77.

McConkie, Joseph Fielding, and Craig J. Ostler. *Revelations of the Restoration.* Salt Lake City: Deseret Book, 2000.

Meeks, Wayne A. "'And Rose Up to Play,' Midrash and Paraenesis in 1 Corinthians 10:1–22." *Journal for the Study of the New Testament* 16 (1982): 64–78.

————. *The First Urban Christians: The Social World of the Apostle Paul.* New Haven, Conn.: Yale University Press, 1983.

Meggitt, Justin J. *Paul, Poverty and Survival.* Edinburgh: T and T Clark, 1998.

Mercadante, Linda. *From Hierarchy to Equality: A Comparison of Past and Present Intepretations of 1 Cor 11:2–16 in Relation to the Changing Status of Women in Society.* Vancouver, B.C.: G-M-H Books, 1980.

Merriam Webster's Dictionary of Synonyms. Springfield, Mass.: Merriam-Webster, 1984.

Metzger, Bruce M. *A Textual Commentary on the Greek New Testament.* 2d ed. New York: United Bible Society, 1994.

Meyer, Heinrich A. W. *Critical and Exegetical Commentary on the New Testament.* Trans. and ed. William P. Dickson and Frederick Combie. 2 vols. Edinburgh: T and T Clark, 1892.

Migne, J.-P., ed. *Patrologiae Cursus Completus: Series Graeca.* 162 vols. Paris: Garnier, 1857–86.

————, ed. *Patrologiae Cursus Completus: Series Latina.* 221 vols. Paris: Garnier, 1844–64.

Miller, James E. "The Practices of Romans 1:26: Homosexual or Heterosexual?" *Novum Testamentum* 37 (January 1995): 1–11.

Millet, Robert L. *Getting at the Truth.* Salt Lake City: Deseret Book, 2004.

————. *Grace Works.* Salt Lake City: Deseret Book, 2003.

————. "The Perils of Grace." *BYU Studies Quarterly* 53, no. 2 (2014): 7–19.

Mitchell, Alan C. "Rich and Poor in the Courts of Corinth: Litigiousness and Status in 1 Cor. 6:1–11." *New Testament Studies* 39 (1993): 562–86.

Mitchell, Margaret M. "Concerning *peri de* in 1 Corinthians." *Novum Testamentum* 31 (1989): 229–56.

————. *Paul and the Rhetoric of Reconciliation: An Exegetical Investigation of the Language and Composition of 1 Corinthians.* Louisville: Westminster/John Knox Press, 1992.

Mitchell, Matthew W. "Reexamining the 'Aborted Apostle': An Exploration of Paul's Self-description in 1 Corinthians 15.8." *Journal for the Study of the New Testament* 25 (June 2003): 469–85.

Moffett, James. *The First Epistle of Paul to the Corinthians.* London: Hodder and Stoughton, 1983.

Moiser, Jeremy. "A Reassessment of Paul's View of Marriage with Reference to 1 Corinthians 7." *Journal of the Study of the New Testament* 18 (1983): 103–22.

Moltmann, Jürgen. *Theology of Hope.* Trans. James W. Leitch. London: SCM Press, 1967.

Monson, Thomas S. *Be Your Best Self.* Salt Lake City: Deseret Book, 1979.

———. *Invitation to Exaltation.* Salt Lake City: Deseret Book, 1997.

———. *Pathway to Perfection.* Salt Lake City: Deseret Book, 1973.

Moo, Douglas J. *The Epistle to the Romans.* In *The New International Commentary on the New Testament.* Grand Rapids, Mich.: Eerdmanns, 1996.

———. *We Still Don't Get It: Evangelicals and Biblical Translation Fifty Years after James Barr.* Grand Rapids, Mich.: Zondervan, 2014.

Moores, John D. *Wrestling with Rationality in Paul.* Cambridge: Cambridge University Press, 1995.

Morris, Leon. *Testaments of Love.* Grand Rapids, Mich.: Eerdmans, 1981.

Moule, C. F. D. *Idiom Book of New Testament Greek.* 2d ed. Cambridge: Cambridge University Press, 1956.

———. "St. Paul and Dualism: The Pauline Conception of Resurrection." *New Testament Studies* 12 (1965–66): 106–23.

Moulton, James H., and George Milligan. *The Vocabulary of the Greek Testament: Illustrations from the Papyri and Other Non-literary Sources.* 1930. Rpt., Grand Rapids, Mich.: Eerdmans, 1985.

Moxnes, Halvor. "Honor, Shame, and the Outside World in Paul's Letter to the Romans." In *The Social World of Formative Christianity and Judaism: Essays in Tribute to Howard Clarke Kee,* ed. Jacob Neusner and Peder Borgan, 207–18. Philadelphia: Fortress Press, 1988.

Munck, Johannes. *Paul and Salvation of Humankind.* London: John Knox Press, 1959.

Murphy-O'Connor, Jerome. "Christ and Ministry." *Pacifica* 4 (1991): 121–36.

———. "Corinthian Bronze." *Revue biblique* 90 (1983): 80–93.

———. "Corinthian Slogans in 1 Cor. 6:12–20." *Catholic Biblical Quarterly* 40 (1978): 391–96.

———. *1 Corinthians.* Wilmington, Del.: Michael Glazier Books, 1979.

———. "Food and Spiritual Gifts in 1 Corinthians 8:8." *Catholic Biblical Quarterly* 41 (1979): 292–98.

———. *Paul: A Critical Life.* Oxford: Oxford University Press, 1998.

———. *Paul the Letter-Writer: His World, His Opinions, His Skills.* Collegeville, Penn.: Literature Press, Michael Glazier Book, 1994.

———. "Sex and Logic in 1 Corinthians 11:2–16." *Catholic Biblical Quarterly* 42 (1980): 482–500.

———. *St. Paul's Corinth: Texts and Archaeology.* Wilmington, Del.: Michael Glazier Books, 1983.

———. "Traditions and Redactions in 1 Corinthians 15:3–7." *Catholic Biblical Quarterly* 43 (1981): 582–89.

———. "Works without Faith in 1 Corinthians VII:14." *Revue biblique* 84 (1977): 349–69.

Nestle, Eberhard, and others, eds. *Novum Testamentum Graece: Nestle-Aland.* 28th ed. Stuttgart: German Bible Society, 2012.

Neufeld, Vernon H. *The Earliest Christian Confessions.* Leiden: Brill, 1963.

Newman, Carey C. *Paul's Glory-Christology: Tradition and Rhetoric.* Leiden: Brill, 1992.

Nibley, Hugh. *The Ancient State: The Rulers and the Ruled.* Ed. Donald W. Parry and Stephen D. Ricks. Vol. 10 of The Collected Works of Hugh Nibley. Salt Lake City: Deseret Book; Provo, Utah: Foundation for Ancient Research and Mormon Studies, 1991.

———. *An Approach to the Book of Mormon.* Salt Lake City: Deseret Book, 1964.

———. *Mormonism and Early Christianity.* Vol. 4 of The Collected Works of Hugh Nibley. Salt Lake City: Deseret Book; Provo, Utah: Foundation for Ancient Research and Mormon Studies, 1987.

———. *Of All Things!: Classic Quotations from Hugh Nibley.* Comp. Gary P. Gillum. Salt Lake City: Signature Books, 1981.

———. *Old Testament and Related Studies.* Ed. John W Welch, Gary P Gillum, and Don E Norton. Vol. 1 of The Collected Works of Hugh Nibley. Salt Lake City: Deseret Book; Provo, Utah: Foundation for Ancient Research and Mormon Studies, 1986.

———. *Temple and Cosmos: Beyond This Ignorant Present.* Ed. Don E. Norton. Vol. 12 of The Collected Works of Hugh Nibley. Salt Lake City: Deseret Book; Provo, Utah: Foundation for Ancient Research and Mormon Studies, 1992.

Nygren, Anders. *Agape and Eros.* Two volumes in one. London: SPCK, 1953.

Oaks, Dallin H. "Spiritual Gifts." *Ensign* 16 (September 1986): 68–70.

Odell-Scott, D. W. "Let the Women Speak in Church: An Egalitarian Interpretation of 1 Corinthians 14:33b–36." *Biblical Theology Bulletin* 13 (1983): 90–93.

Ogden, D. Kelly, and Andrew C. Skinner. *Verse by Verse: Acts through Revelation.* Salt Lake City: Deseret Book, 2006.

Omanson, Roger L. "Acknowledging Paul's Quotations." *Bible Translator* 43 (April 1992): 201–13.

Oropeza, B. J. *Paul and Apostasy: Eschatology, Perseverance, and Falling Away in the Corinthian Congregation.* Tübingen: Mohr Siebeck, 2000.

Orr, William F., and James A. Walther. *1 Corinthians.* Garden City, N.Y.: Doubleday, 1976.

Osiek, Carolyn, and David L. Blach. *Families in the New Testament Times: Household and House Churches.* Louisville, Ky.: Westminster John Knox Press, 1997.

Oster, Richard E., Jr. "Use, Misuse and Neglect of Archaeological Evidence in Some Modern Works on 1 Corinthians (1 Corithians 7:1–5; 8:10; 11:2–16; 12:14–26)." *Zeitschrift für die neutestamentliche Wissenschaft* 83 (1992): 52–73.

Pannenberg, Wolfhart. *Systematic Theology.* Trans. Geoffrey W. Bromiley. Vol. 2. Grand Rapids, Mich.: Eerdmans, 2013.

Parry Jay A., and Donald W. Parry. "The Temple in Heaven: Its Description and Significance." In *Temples of the Ancient World: Ritual and Symbolism,* ed. Donald W. Parry. Salt Lake City: Deseret Book; Provo, Utah: Foundation for Ancient Research and Mormon Studies, 1994.

Parry, Donald W., and Stephen D. Ricks, eds. *The Temple in Time and Eternity.* Provo, Utah: Foundation for Ancient Research and Mormon Studies at Brigham Young University, 1999.

Parry, Reginald St. John. *The First Epistle of Paul the Apostle to the Corinthians: With Introduction and Notes: Cambridge Greek Text.* 2d ed. Cambridge: Cambridge University Press, 1926.

Paulsen, David L., and Brock M. Mason. "Baptism for the Dead in Early Christianity." *Journal of the Book of Mormon and Other Restoration Scripture* 19, no. 2 (2010): 22–49.

Paulsen, David L., Roger D. Cook, and Kendel J. Christensen. "The Harrowing of Hell: Salvation for the Dead in Early Christianity." *Journal of the Book of Mormon and Other Restoration Scripture* 19, no. 1 (2010): 56–77.

Perriman, A. C. "Paul and the Parousia: 1 Corinthians 15:50–57 and 2 Corinthians 5:1–5." *New Testament Studies* 36 (October 1989): 512–21.

Petersen, Mark E. "Signs of the True Church." *Ensign* 9 (May 1979): 21–22.

Petzer, J. H. "Contextual Evidence in Favor of καυθήσομαι in 1 Corinthians 13:3." *New Testament Studies* 35 (1989): 229–53.

Pfitzner, Victor C. *Paul and the Agon Motif: Traditional Athletic Imagery in the Pauline Epistles.* Novum Testamentum, suppl. vol. 16. Leiden: E. J. Brill, 1967.

Pickett, Raymond. *The Cross in Corinth: The Social Significance of the Death of Jesus.* Sheffield, Eng.: Sheffield Academic Press, 1997.

Pierce, C. A. *Conscience in the New Testament.* London: SCM Press, 1955.

Pogoloff, Stephen M. *Logos and Sophia: The Rhetorical Situation of I Corinthians.* Atlanta: Scholars Press, 1992.

Porter, Stanley E. "The Theoretical Justification for Application of Rhetorical Categories to Pauline Epistolary Literature." In *Rhetoric and the New Testament: Essays from the 1992 Heidelberg Conference,* ed. S. E. Porter and T. H. Olbricht, 100–22. Sheffield, Eng.: Sheffield Academic Press, 1993.

Pratt, Orson. *Divine Authenticity of the Book of Mormon.* Liverpool: Printed by R. James, 1850–51.

Prout, Elmer. "One Loaf . . . One Body." *Restoration Quarterly* 25, no. 1 (1982): 78–81.

Ramsarin, R. A. "More than an Opinion: Paul's Rhetorical Maxim in First Corinthians 7:25–26." *Catholic Biblical Quarterly* 57 (1995): 532–41.

Reeve, Rex C., Jr. "The Holy Ghost Brings Testimony, Unity, and Spiritual Gifts." In *The Apostle Paul, His Life and His Testimony: The 23d Annual Sidney B. Sperry Symposium,* 166–77. Salt Lake City: Deseret Book 1994.

Richardson, Peter. "Judgment in Sexual Matters in 1 Corinthians 6:1–11." *Novum Testamentum* 25 (1983): 37–58.

Robertson, Archibald T., and Alfred Plummer. *A Critical and Exegetical Commentary on the First Epistle of Paul to the Corinthians.* 2d ed. Edinburgh: T and T Clark, 1958.

Robertson, John S. "A Complete Look at Perfect." Address given at Brigham Young University, Provo, Utah, July 13, 1999. Transcript available at https://speeches.byu.edu/talks/john-s-robertson_complete-look-perfect/.

Robinson, John A. T. *The Body: A Study in Pauline Theology.* 2d ed. Louisville, Ky.: Westminster John Knox Press, 1977.

Robinson, Stephen E. "The Noncanonical Sayings of Jesus." *BYU Studies* 36, no. 2 (1996): 74–91.

Robinson, Stephen E., and H. Dean Garrett. *A Commentary on the Doctrine and Covenants.* 4 vols. Salt Lake City: Deseret Book, 2000.

Rosner, B. S. "Moses Appointing Judges: An Antecedent to 1 Cor. 1–6?" *Zeitschrift für die neutestamentliche Wissenschaft* 82 (1990): 275–78.

Roth, Cecil. *The Haggadah.* London: Soncino Press, 1934.

Rousselle, Aline. "Body Politics in Ancient Rome." In *A History of Women in the West: From Ancient Goddess to Christian Saint,* ed. Pauline Schmitt Pantel, 296–337. Cambridge: Harvard University Press, 1992.

Rushdoony, Rousas John. *Institutes of Biblical Law.* Phillipsburg, New Jersey: P and R Publishing, 1980.

Sandnes, K. O. *Paul—One of the Prophets? A Contribution to the Apostle's Self-Understanding.* Tübingen: Mohr, 1991.

Savage, Timothy B. *Power through Weakness: Paul's Understanding of the Christian Ministry in 2 Corinthians.* Cambridge: Cambridge University Press, 2004.

Schmidt, Brent J. *Relational Grace: The Reciprocal and Binding Covenant of* Charis. Provo, Utah: BYU Studies, 2015.

Schnackenburg, Rudolf. *Baptism in the Thought of St. Paul: A Study in Pauline Theology.* Oxford: Blackwell, 1964.

Schneider, Gerhard, and Horst Balz, eds. *Exegetical Dictionary of the New Testament.* Trans. James W. Thompson. 3 vols. Grand Rapids, Mich.: Eerdmans, 1990–93.

Scroggs, Robin. *The New Testament and Homosexuality.* Philadelphia: Fortress Press, 1983.

Seete, Henry B. *The Holy Spirit in the New Testament.* London: Macmillan, 1909, 1921.

Senft, C. *La Première Épitre de Saint Paul aux Corinthiens.* Commentaire du Nouveau Testament. 2d ed. Geneva: Labor et Fides, 1990.

Sevenster, J. N. *Paul and Seneca.* Leiden: Brill, 1961.

Sharp, Daniel B. "Vicarious Baptism for the Dead: 1 Corinthians 15:29." *Studies in the Bible and Antiquity* 6 (2014): 36–66.

Sider, R. J. "St. Paul's Understanding of the Nature and Significance of the Resurrection in I Corinthians xv 1–19." *Novum Testamentum* 19 (April 1977): 124–41.

Sjodahl, Janne M., and George Reynolds. *Commentary on the Book of Mormon.* 4 vols. Salt Lake City: Deseret Book, 1959.

Smit, J. F. M. "Two Puzzles: 1 Corinthinas 12.31 and 13.3 a Rhetorical Solution," *New Testament Studies* 39, no. 2 (1993): 246–64.

Smith, Hyrum M., and Janne M. Sjodahl. *Doctrine and Covenants Commentary.* Rev. ed. Salt Lake City: Deseret Book, 1978.

Smith, Joseph, Jr. *History of The Church of Jesus Christ of Latter-day Saints.* Ed. B. H. Roberts. 2d ed., rev. 7 vols. Salt Lake City: Deseret Book, 1973.

Smyth, Herbert Weir. *Greek Grammar.* Cambridge: Mass.: Harvard University Press, 1956.

South, James T. *Disciplinary Practices in Pauline Texts.* Lewiston, N.Y.: Mellen Biblical Press, 1992.

Sperry, Sidney B. *Paul's Life and Letters.* Salt Lake City: Bookcraft, 1955.

Spicq, Ceslaus. *Agape in the New Testament.* 3 vols. Eugene, Ore.: Wipf and Stock Publishers, 2006.

Sproul, Robert Charles. *Knowing Scripture.* Nottingham: InterVarsity Press, 1977.

Stanley, Christopher D. *Paul and the Language of Scripture: Citation Techniques in the Pauline Epistle and in Contemporary Literature.* Rev. ed. Cambridge: Cambridge University Press, 1992.

Stanley, David M. *Christ's Resurrection in Pauline Soteriology.* Rome: Pontifical Biblical Institute, 1961.

Stendahl, Krister. *Paul among the Jews and Gentiles.* Philadelphia: Fortress Press, 1976.

Stowers, Stanley K. "Paul on the Use and Abuse of Wisdom." In *Greeks, Romans, and Christians: Essays in Honor of Abraham J. Malherbe,* ed. David Balch, 253–86. Minneapolis: Fortress Press, 1991.

Swensen, Russel B. *The New Testament: The Acts and the Epistles.* Salt Lake City: Deseret Sunday School Union Board, 1955.

———. *New Testament Literature.* Salt Lake City: LDS Department of Education, 1940.

Talmage, James E. *The Articles of Faith.* Salt Lake City: The Church of Jesus Christ of Latter-day Saints, 1962.

———. *The Great Apostasy.* Salt Lake City: The Church of Jesus Christ of Latter-day Saints, 1968.

Taylor, Robert D. "Toward a Biblical Theology of Litigation: A Law Professor Looks at 1 Cor. 6:1–11." *Ex Auditu* 2 (1986): 105–16.

The First Presidency and Council of the Twelve Apostles of The Church of Jesus Christ of Latter-day Saints, "The Family: A Proclamation to the World," *Ensign* 25 (November 1995): 102, available online at https://www.lds.org/ensign/1995/11/the-family-a-proclamation-to-the-world?lang=eng.

Theissen, Gerd. *The Social Setting of Pauline Christianity: Essays on Corinth.* Trans. John H. Schütz. Philadelphia: Fortress Press, 1982.

Thiselton, Anthony C. *The First Epistle to the Corinthians: A Commentary on the Greek Text.* Grand Rapids, Mich.: William B. Eerdmans Publishing; Carlisle, U.K.: Paternoster Press, 2000.

———. "The Logical Role of the Liar Paradox in Titus 1:12, 13: A Dissent from the Commentaries." *Biblical Interpretation* 2 (1994): 207–23.

———. "Luther and Barth on 1 Cor. 15: Six Theses for Theology in Relation to Recent Interpretation." In *The Bible, the Reformation, and the Church: Essays in Honour of*

James Atkinson, ed. W. P. Stephens, 275–78. Sheffield, Eng.: Sheffield Academic Press, 1995.

Thornton, Lionel Spencer. *The Common Life in the Body of Christ.* 4th ed. London: Darce Press, 1963.

Tillich, Paul. *Systematic Theology.* 3 vols. Chicago: Chicago University Press, 1951–63.

Tomson, Peter J. *Paul and the Jewish Law: Halakha in the Letters of the Apostle to the Gentiles.* Minneapolis: Fortress Press, 1990.

Trumbower, Jeffrey A. *Rescue for the Dead: The Posthumous Salvation of Non-Christians in Early Christianity.* Oxford and New York: Oxford University Press, 2001.

Turner, Rodney "Grace, Mysteries, and Exaltation." In *Studies in Scripture, Volume 6: Acts to Revelation,* ed. Robert L. Millet, 107–24. Salt Lake City: Deseret Book, 1987.

Unnik, W. C. van. "Jesus: Anathema or Kyrios (1 Cor. 12:3)." In *Christ and Spirit in the New Testament: Studies in Honour of Charles Francis Digby Moule,* ed. Barnabas Lindars and Stephen S. Smalley, 113–26. Cambridge: Cambridge University Press, 1973.

Wallace, Daniel B. *Greek Grammar beyond the Basics: An Exegetical Syntax of the New Testament.* Grand Rapids, Mich.: Zondervan, 1996.

Ward, R. B. "Musonius and Paul on Marriage." *New Testament Studies* 36 (1990): 281–89.

Watson, Duane F. "1 Corinthians 10:23–11:1 in the Light of Greco-Roman Rhetoric: The Role of Rhetorical Questions." *Journal of Biblical Literature* 108 (1989): 301–18.

———. "Paul's Rhetorical Strategy in 1 Corinthians 15." In *Rhetoric and the New Testament,* ed. S. E. Porter and T. H. Olbricht. Sheffield: Sheffield Academic Press, 1993.

Wayment, Thomas A. *From Persecutor to Apostle: A Biography of Paul.* Salt Lake City: Deseret Book, 2006.

Wayment, Thomas A., and John Gee. "Did Paul Address His Wife in Philippi?" In *Studies in the Bible and Antiquity* 4 (2012): 71–93.

Welch, John W. *Illuminating the Sermon at the Temple and Sermon on the Mount: An Approach to 3 Nephi 11–18 and Matthew 5–7.* Provo, Utah: Foundation of Ancient Research and Mormon Studies, 1999.

White, Joel R. "'Baptized on Account of the Dead': The Meaning of 1 Corinthians 15:29 in Its Context." *Journal of Biblical Literature* 116, no. 3 (1997): 487–99.

Williams, David J. *Paul's Metaphors: Their Context and Character.* Peabody, Mass.: Hendrickson Publishers, 1999.

Willis, Wendell. *Idol Meat in Corinth: The Pauline Argument in 1 Corinthians 8 and 10.* Chico, Calif.: Scholars Press, 1985.

Wilson, Jack H. "The Corinthians Who Say There Is No Resurrection of the Dead." *Zeitschrift für die Neutestamentliche Wissenschaft* 59 (1968): 90–107.

Wimbush, Vincent L. *Paul, the Worldly Ascetic: Response to the World and Self-Understanding according to 1 Corinthians 7.* Macon, Ga.: Mercer Press, 1987.

Winter, Bruce W. *After Paul Left Corinth: The Influence of Secular Ethics and Social Change.* Grand Rapids, Mich.: Eerdmans, 2001.

———. "Civil Litigation in Secular Corinth and the Church: Forensic Background to 1 Cor. 6:1–8." *New Testament Studies* 37 (1991): 559–72.

———. "Gallio's Ruling on the Legal Status of Earliest Christianity (Acts 18:14–15)." *Tyndale Bulletin* 50 (1999): 213–24.

———. "The Lord's Supper at Corinth: An Alternative Reconstruction." *Reformed Theological Review* 37 (1978): 73–82.

———. "A Secular and Christian Response to Corinthian Famines." *Tyndell Bulletin* 48 (1997): 57–65.

———. *Seek the Welfare of the City: Christians as Benefactors and Citizens.* Grand Rapids, Mich.: Eerdmans; Carlisle, U.K.: Paternoster, 1994.

Wire, Antoinette Clark. *The Corinthian Women Prophets.* Minneapolis: Fortress Press, 1990.

Wirthlin, Joseph B. "Running Your Marathon," *Ensign* 19 (November 1989): 75.

Wiseman, James. "Corinth and Rome I: 228 B.C.–A.D. 267." In *Aufstieg und Niedergang der römischen Welt,* part 2, *Principat,* vol. 7, *Politische Geschichte (Provinzen und Randvölker: Griechischer Balkanraum; Kleinasien),* 1:438–548. Berlin: de Gruyter, 1979.

Witherington, Ben, III. *Conflict and Community in Corinth.* Grand Rapids, Mich.: Eerdmans; Carlisle: Paternoster, 1995.

———. "Why Not Idol Meat?: Is It What You Eat or Where You Eat It?" *Bible Review* 10 (June 1994): 38–43, 54–55.

Woodger, Mary Jane. "The 'I's' of Corinth: Modern Problems not New." In *Go Ye into All the World: Messages of the New Testament Apostles,* 41–56. Salt Lake City: Deseret Book, 2002.

Yeo, Khiok-khng. *Rhetorical Interaction in 1 Corinthians 8 and 10: A Formal Analysis with Preliminary Suggestions for the Chinese Cross-Cultural Hermeneutic.* Leiden: Brill, 1995.

Zaas, Peter S. "Paul and the Halakhah: Dietary Laws for Gentiles in I Corinthians 8–10." In *Jewish Law Association Studies VII: The Paris Conference volume,* ed. S. M. Passamaneck and M. Finley, 233–46. Atlanta: Scholars Press, 1994.

Scripture Index

This index is ordered by book under Old Testament, New Testament, Book of Mormon, Pearl of Great Price, Other Ancient Sources, and Doctrine and Covenants.

New Testament

1 Corinthians

Numbers in **bold italics** indicate the main discussion of the scriptural passage.

Subject Index

Q

R